Veda and Torah

Transcending the Textuality of Scripture

Barbara A. Holdrege

State University of New York Press

Published by
State University of New York Press, Albany

Printed in the United States of America

For information, address the State University of New York Press, State University Plaza, Albany, N.Y., 12246

Production by Christine Lynch
Marketing by Nancy Farrell

Library of Congress Cataloging-in-Publication Data

Holdrege, Barbara A.
Veda and Torah : transcending the textuality of scripture / by Barbara A. Holdrege.
p. cm.
Includes bibliographical references.
ISBN 0–7914–1639–9. — ISBN 0–7914–1640–2 (pbk.)
1. Judaism—Relations—Hinduism. 2. Hinduism—Relations—Judaism. 3. Bible. O.T. Pentateuch—Comparative studies. 4. Vedas—Comparative studies. 5. Creation—Comparative studies. I. Title.
BM536.H5H64 1996
291.8'2—dc20 92–42599
CIP

10 9 8 7 6 5 4 3 2 1

To my teacher

CONTENTS

Preface ix

Introduction 1

PART 1 THE WORD IN CREATION

1 Veda and Creation 29

Veda and Creation in Vedic Texts 30
Veda and Creation in Post-Vedic Mythology 70
Veda and Creation in the Darśanas 113

2 Torah and Creation 131

Torah and Creation in Pre-Rabbinic Texts 132
Torah and Creation in Rabbinic Texts 140
Torah and Creation in Kabbalistic Texts 196

Comparative Analysis 1 Veda and Torah in Creation 213

PART 2 FROM WORD TO TEXT

3 Veda and Cognition 227

Veda and Cognition in Vedic Texts 229
Veda and Cognition in Post-Vedic Mythology 243

4 Torah and Revelation 253

Torah and Revelation in Rabbinic Texts 255
Torah and Revelation in Kabbalistic Texts 315

Comparative Analysis 2 Cognition of Veda and Revelation of Torah 325

PART 3 TEXT IN PRACTICE

5 Veda in Practice 343

Recitative Transmission of the Vedic Saṃhitās 344
Theurgic Conceptions of Vedic Sacrifice and Recitation 347

Interpretation of the Vedas 351
Appropriation of the Veda 354

6 Torah in Practice 359

Written Transmission of the Sefer Torah 359
Interpretation of the Torah 361
Theurgic Conceptions of Torah Study and Practice 374
Appropriation of the Torah 382

Comparative Analysis 3 Veda and Torah in Practice 385

Conclusion 395

Notes 421

Abbreviations 561

Note on Translation and Transliteration 567

Selected Bibliography 569

Index 651

PREFACE

As a comparative historian of religions specializing in Hindu and Jewish traditions, I find myself in a peculiar position. First, I must confront the critiques of scholars who would condemn the comparative study of religion to a premature demise. Second, I must contend with the prevalent view that the religious traditions that are the focus of my inquiries not only have little in common but may even be antithetical. And yet every time I meet with the question, "What can you possibly hope to compare?" I am surprised that the question is even asked.

Although I am of course aware of the significant differences that distinguish "Hinduisms" and "Judaisms," I am equally struck by certain fundamental affinities shared by brahmanical "Hinduism" and rabbinic "Judaism" in particular: as elite "textual communities" that have codified the norms of orthodoxy in the form of scriptural canons; as ethnocultural systems concerned with issues of family, ethnic and cultural integrity, blood lineages, and the intergenerational transmission of traditions; and as religions of orthopraxy characterized by hereditary priesthoods and sacrificial traditions, comprehensive legal systems delineated in the Dharma-Śāstras and halakhic texts, elaborate regulations concerning purity and impurity, and dietary laws. Indeed, I would suggest that the comparative study of these traditions is of significance precisely because it provides the basis for developing an alternative model of "religious tradition" founded on categories other than the Christian-based categories of interpretation that have tended to dominate our scholarly inquiries.

As an entry point into the unique *Gestalt* of these traditions, as well as their structural affinities, the present study examines the status, authority, and function of scripture as a constitutive category of the brahmanical and rabbinic traditions, with some consideration also of kabbalistic traditions that have built upon rabbinic conceptions of scripture. The study is concerned in particular with the manner in which Veda and Torah, as the authoritative scriptures of these "textual communities," assume the role of multivalent symbols that encompass and at the same time transcend the textuality of scripture. Each is represented in certain strands of its respective tradition as a multileveled cosmological principle identified with the primordial Word, and while this Word might have found expression on the earthly plane as a concrete corpus of texts, it is not held to be bound by this textual referent. Veda and Torah each assume dual functions: on the one hand, as a circumscribed textual corpus, and, on the other, as an open-ended symbol that can be extended to include any normative text, teaching, or practice that has successfully assimilated itself to the paradigmatic Word. Each is ultimately ascribed the status of an encompassing symbol that provides transcendent legitimation for the entire normative tradition as a whole.

The present study thus has implications for our understanding of scripture as a relational category in the history of religions. In this context I hope to challenge scholars of religion to move beyond the tendency to define scripture solely in terms of textual categories, for in certain religious traditions scripture functions not simply as a text but as a transcendent—and hence supratextual—source of authority. It is important to emphasize, however, that I do not propose that the particular parallels in the conceptions of scripture developed by the brahmanical and rabbinic traditions are "universally" applicable to all scriptural traditions. Rather, my study suggests that there are certain basic features that are shared by these specific traditions that may account for the parallel ways in which they construct the category of scripture.

I thus attempt in this study the formidable task of addressing three types of audiences: specialists in Indian religion and culture, scholars of Judaica, and comparativists and other scholars who may be interested in the more general theoretical and methodological issues raised by the study. Because I have chosen to compare religious traditions that are rarely juxtaposed, I am faced with the problem of addressing two groups of specialists who, while fully conversant with the texts and practices of *either* Hindu *or* Jewish traditions, may have relatively little knowledge of the other tradition that is the focus of this comparative enterprise. At the same time, in the course of navigating the depths of two religious traditions, I also address at various junctures a broader range of issues that may be of concern to scholars outside the fields of Indology and Judaica: problems and methods in the comparative study of religion; scripture and canonical authority; language, text, and hermeneutics; oral and written cultures; and categories of tradition-identity and paradigms of "religious tradition."

Portions of this book have been published elsewhere in other forms: "The Bride of Israel: The Ontological Status of Scripture in the Rabbinic and Kabbalistic Traditions," in *Rethinking Scripture:*

Essays from a Comparative Perspective, ed. Miriam Levering (Albany: State University of New York Press, 1989), pp. 180–261; "Veda and Torah: The Word Embodied in Scripture," in *Between Jerusalem and Benares: Comparative Studies in Judaism and Hinduism*, ed. Hananya Goodman (Albany: State University of New York Press, 1994), pp. 103–179; "Comparative Religion with a Difference," in *The Notion of "Religion" in Comparative Research: Selected Proceedings of the XVIth Congress of the International Association for the History of Religions, Rome, 3rd–8th September, 1990*, ed. Ugo Bianchi, Storia delle Religioni, 8 (Rome: "L'Erma" di Bretschneider, 1994), pp. 803–812. "Veda in the Brāhmaṇas: Cosmogonic Paradigms and the Delimitation of Canon," in *Authority, Anxiety, and Canon: Essays in Vedic Interpretation*, ed. Laurie L. Patton, SUNY Series in Hindu Studies (Albany: State University of New York Press, 1994), pp. 35–66.

The seeds of this study of Veda and Torah were first sown many years ago when I was studying religion as an undergraduate at Vassar College. Since that time my study of this topic has manifested in a variety of forms—from my senior thesis at Vassar, to my doctoral dissertation at Harvard University, to its final fruition in the present book written at the University of California, Santa Barbara. I would like to take this opportunity to express my gratitude to the many people who have contributed to this study in the various stages of its development.

As an undergraduate at Vassar I initially pursued two separate tracks of study—biblical studies and South Asian studies—which eventually converged in an interest in the status and function of scripture in Jewish and brahmanical traditions. During this period, after a year of study in India, I became aware of the works of Maharishi Mahesh Yogi, to whom I am especially grateful for bringing to my attention certain brahmanical conceptions of Veda as the eternal knowledge that is the source and blueprint of creation. These conceptions resonated with certain notions of biblical revelation that I had encountered in my studies of the Bible. At the suggestion of my friend Vernon Katz I began to focus more specifically on Jewish traditions concerning the status and role of the Torah in creation and revelation, and in this context I was inspired in particular by Gershom Scholem's seminal article, "The Meaning of the Torah in Jewish Mysticism." Having become convinced of the possible fruits of comparative study of these scriptural traditions, I embarked on a preliminary inquiry into traditional representations of Veda and Torah, respectively, as cosmological principles inherent in the structure of reality. Among my mentors at Vassar, special mention should be made of Patrick Sullivan and Robert Fortna.

In the next phase of my study, during my doctoral research at Harvard, I was fortunate to have the opportunity to work with Wilfred Cantwell Smith and William A. Graham, whose reflections on scripture as a general religious category provided the theoretical framework on which my own work builds. I am also especially indebted to John Carman, whose insights and suggestions at various points of my research proved invaluable in the refinement of my arguments. Special thanks are also due to my other mentors during my doctoral studies at Harvard, from whose guidance I profited greatly in diverse ways: Frank Moore Cross, Diana Eck, David Eckel, Michael Fishbane, Judah Goldin, Daniel H. H. Ingalls, Louis Jacobs, Helmut Koester, James Kugel, Marc Saperstein, Krister Stendahl, and Gary Tubb.

In the third and final phase of my study, in which I completely reworked my doctoral dissertation and transformed it into the present book, I am grateful to my colleagues in the Department of Religious Studies at the University of California, Santa Barbara, for providing an environment of lively intellectual exchange that has deepened my appreciation of the complex methodological issues involved in comparative study. Ninian Smart and Gerald Larson in particular offered helpful criticism and suggestions on various aspects of my research. I would also like to thank C. Mackenzie Brown, Thomas Coburn, Ruth Katz, Paul Morris, and Brian K. Smith, whose perceptive comments on the penultimate draft helped substantially to improve the book. Other scholars whose insights contributed in significant ways to my research include Apostolos Athanassakis, Puruṣottama Bilimoria, Moshe Idel, Nathan Katz, Paul Muller-Ortega, Jacob Neusner, Sheldon Pollock, and Elliot Wolfson. I am also indebted to my graduate research assistants—Tracy Pintchman, Bradley Hawkins, Stephen Berkwitz, and Kathryn McClymond—for their help at critical points in the preparation of the book. I would like to extend my thanks more generally to the University of California, Santa Barbara, for fellowships and grants in support of my work. I am also grateful to the staff of the University of California libraries and of the Harvard Widener Library, who provided substantial assistance in my library research.

I owe special thanks to the State University of New York Press, and in particular to the director, Bill Eastman, and my production editor, Christine Lynch, for their patient efforts in seeing the book through the final stages of production.

I thank my family for their encouragement and support throughout the course of my research and writing. Among the numerous friends who have sustained me through this process, I wish to mention in particular my dear friend Judy Booth, who has championed my study of Veda and Torah in its various manifestations since its inception. Finally, I thank my husband, Eric Dahl, without whose constant inspiration and support I could not have brought this work to fruition.

Santa Barbara, California

INTRODUCTION

The differences between the Hindu and Jewish traditions have often been emphasized, so much so that these traditions have generally been characterized as representing opposite ends of the spectrum of world religions. Indeed, "Hinduism" and "Judaism" have been thought to have so little in common that few scholars have attempted substantive comparative analyses of these traditions. "Polytheistic," iconocentric "Hinduism," with its panoply of deities enshrined in images, is generally held to be antithetical to "monotheistic," iconoclastic "Judaism," with its emphasis on the unity and transcendence of God and abhorrence of image-making practices. These traditions have been characterized as further set apart by their cyclical vs. historical views of existence. However, such characterizations represent gross oversimplifications that fail to take into account the rich diversity of perspectives within the traditions themselves.

The categories "Hinduism" and "Judaism" are themselves problematic in this regard, for, like the category "religion," they represent abstract theoretical constructs that attempt to impose unity on a myriad of different religious systems. The complex amalgam termed "Hinduism" encompasses a variety of "Hinduisms." Beginning in the Vedic period and throughout Indian history the orthodox brahmanical tradition has been continually challenged by competing traditions and movements—local village traditions, ascetic groups, devotional (*bhakti*) sects, tantric movements, and, more recently, modern reform movements. While the centripetal force of brahmanical power structures has sought to absorb and domesticate competing currents, the centrifugal force of these countervailing centers of power has persisted, giving rise to that uneasy conglomerate of heterogeneous tendencies which Western scholars term "Hinduism." Similarly, "Judaism" represents a composite category within which are subsumed a variety of "Judaisms." Following the biblical period, a diversity of competing movements flourished in the Second Temple period, including the Sadducees, Pharisees, Zealots, Essenes, and various Hellenistic traditions. After the destruction of the Second Temple in 70 C.E., the Pharisaic trend prevailed in the form of rabbinic orthodoxy, which itself encompassed a variety of different schools. The medieval period saw the emergence of a number of contending currents, including the newly burgeoning kabbalistic and philosophical traditions. The modern period has similarly given birth to a variety of new "Judaisms"—Reform, Conservative, Orthodox, Zionist, and so on.[1]

Within this array of "Hinduisms" and "Judaisms," the present study focuses on those traditions for which scripture is a constitutive category: the brahmanical Sanskritic tradition and the rabbinic tradition, with some attention also to kabbalistic traditions that have absorbed and reinterpreted rabbinic conceptions of scripture. Both the brahmanical and rabbinic traditions constitute elite "textual communities"[2] that have sought to shape and articulate the central norms of their respective traditions through codifying symbol systems and practices in the form of scriptural canons of which they are the custodians. In the process of delineating the normative tradition and its standards of orthodoxy, these textual communities have accommodated, domesticated, and at times muted the multiplicity of voices representative of the competing trends in any particular period. Canonical authority is thus constitutive of both the brahmanical and rabbinic traditions. The authority of the brahmin priests and the rabbinic sages themselves is to a large extent derived from their privileged role as the preservers and transmitters of the scriptural canon. In each canon a certain corpus of texts has been set apart as having special sacrosanct and authoritative status: the Veda in the brahmanical tradition and the Torah in the rabbinic tradition. In the brahmanical tradition acceptance of the authority of the Veda has been the primary criterion for distinguishing orthodox from heterodox systems since at least the period of the early Dharma-Sūtras and Dharma-Śāstras (ca. 3d or 2d c. B.C.E.).[3] Acceptance of the authority of the Torah has constituted one of the few dogmas of the rabbinic tradition since as early as the Mishnah (ca. 220 C.E.).[4] The authoritative status of Veda and Torah is, moreover, connected to their roles as symbols, in which each functions simultaneously as a bounded textual category and as a potentially boundless, encompassing symbol that is paradigmatic for its respective tradition.[5]

A comparative study of the categories of Veda and Torah is of particular significance because of the ways in which these categories, as the paradigmatic symbols of the brahmanical and rabbinic traditions, reflect the more basic affinities between these religious traditions. Indeed, contrary to the stereotypical characterizations that emphasize the oppositions between "Hinduism" and "Judaism," and despite the fact that there is little evidence of historical contact between these traditions, I would suggest that brahmanical "Hinduism" and rabbinic "Judaism" represent two species of the same genus and provide a model of "religious tradition" that is distinctly different from the prevailing Christian-based model that has tended to dominate the academic study of religion. The paradigm of "religious tradition" that has developed out of a Christian context gives precedence to such categories as belief, doctrine, and theology and delineates notions of tradition-identity that are rooted in the missionary character of "Christianities." The brahmanical and rabbinic traditions, on the other hand, provide an alternative paradigm of "religious tradition," in which priority is given to issues of practice, observance, and law, and notions of tradition-identity are delineated primarily in terms of ethnic and cultural categories that reflect the predominantly nonmissionary character of these traditions.[6] These religions of orthopraxy have developed elaborate legal systems, sacrificial traditions, purity codes, and dietary laws that serve to inscribe and perpetuate the sociocultural taxonomies of their respective communities.[7]

The manner in which the brahmanical and rabbinic traditions construct categories of language and canon reflects the more fundamental categories of tradition-identity shared by these ethnic-based traditions. Each tradition defines itself in relation to a particular sacred language (Sanskrit, Hebrew) and to a particular corpus of sacred texts (Veda, Torah) that is held to be linguistically, ethnically, and culturally tied to a particular people (Aryans, Jews). The mechanisms through which the categories of Veda and Torah are circumscribed and subsequently expanded in the brahmanical and rabbinic traditions serve as a means of circumscribing the ethnic-cultural identity of their respective communities in relation to other peoples, of delineating and legitimating the hierarchical differentiation of functions within each community, of accommodating competing currents within the tradition, and of authorizing certain ritual and sociocultural practices.

From Text to Symbol

Veda and Torah are generally classified as types of "scripture," and thus any inquiry into the multivalent significations of these terms must begin with a consideration of the category of scripture as conceptualized by Western scholars during the last two centuries. The study of scripture since the nineteenth century has been almost exclusively the domain of biblical and orientalist scholars, who have used the tools of critical analysis in order to determine the cultural, historical, and literary influences that have given rise to individual texts. These historical and literary studies have primarily focused on the *content* of particular religious texts and on questions of *Entstehungsgeschichte,* or the "history of origins"—the history of causes and conditions that have produced specific texts. More recently, with the newly emerging interest in canon, scholars have begun to focus also on the *form* of particular scriptural traditions.[8]

In recent years historians of religions such as Wilfred Cantwell Smith and William A. Graham have emphasized the need for more inquiries into the *concept* of scripture as a general religious category to supplement the study of particular texts and canons.[9] What does it mean for a text to be regarded as "scripture" or for religious communities to "scripturalize"? Scripture as a concept in the history of religions is primarily a relational category, which refers not simply to a text but to a text in its relationship to a religious community for whom it is sacred and authoritative. Graham remarks that

> neither form nor content can serve to distinguish or identify scripture as a general phenomenon or category. . . . [F]rom the historian's perspective, the sacrality or holiness of a book is not an a priori attribute of a text but one that is realized historically in the life of communities who respond to it as something sacred or holy. A text becomes 'scripture' in active, subjective relationship to persons, and as part of a cumulative communal tradition. No text, written or oral or both, is sacred or authoritative in isolation from a community. . . . A book is only 'scripture' insofar as a group of persons perceive it to be sacred or holy, powerful and portentous, possessed of an exalted authority, and in some fashion transcendent of, and hence distinct from, all other speech and writing.[10]

The study of scripture as a relational category is thus concerned not only with questions of *Entstehungsgeschichte,* or history of origins, but also with *Wirkungsgeschichte,* the "history of effects," which encompasses the ongoing roles that a sacred text has assumed in the cumulative tradition of a religious community both as a normative source of authority and as a prodigious living force.[11]

One of the purposes of the present inquiry is to call into question the very category of scripture as it has generally been conceptualized by Western scholars. Graham's recent studies of the oral aspects of scripture in the history of religions have challenged scholars to stretch the boundaries of the concept beyond the limitations posed by the term "scripture" itself (which literally means "a writing") and its common equivalents such as "sacred writings" and "holy writ."[12] My study of Veda and Torah suggests that it is not sufficient simply to expand the concept to encompass the oral-aural dimensions of sacred texts. Rather, the category of scripture needs to be further exploded and the very notion of textuality implicit in the concept reexamined. For in certain traditional representations of Veda and Torah, scripture is depicted not simply as a textual phenomenon but as a cosmological principle that is inherent in the very structure of reality. The functional status of scripture within a particular religious community is to a certain extent shaped and informed by the community's conceptions of its cosmological status, and yet relatively little attention has been given to this important dimension of scripture.

The purpose of the present study is fourfold. First, I attempt to demonstrate that scripture, as represented in the symbol systems associated with Veda and Torah, is not a unidimensional textual phenomenon but is rather a multileveled cosmic reality that encompasses gross and subtle, mundane and supramundane dimensions. Second, I seek to demonstrate that these representations of Veda and Torah are not merely lifeless concepts embedded in the traditional texts but have functioned as living, activating symbols that reflect and inform practices with respect to the modes of transmission, study, and appropriation of these two scriptures. Third, I suggest that such traditional representations of scripture constitute a significant area of investigation that can help to illumine our understanding not only of the status, authority, and function of scripture within the brahmanical tradition and the rabbinic and kabbalistic traditions but also of scripture as a general religious category. In this context I hope to challenge historians of religions to move beyond the tendency to delimit scripture to the black and white text of "holy writ" and to embrace a broader conception that can also account for such representations of scripture as a supratextual cosmological principle. The significance of these formulations lies not in their truth claims about the nature of reality—for such truth claims are beyond the province of the history of religions—but rather in their contributions to our understanding of the authority and role of scripture as a relational category in the history of religions. Finally, I suggest that, while we might expect to find representations of scripture as a cosmological principle in other religious traditions, the specific parallels in the manner in which the categories of Veda and Torah are constructed are not generalizable to all scriptural traditions but rather reflect the more fundamental affinities shared by the brahmanical and rabbinic traditions as representatives of a distinctive paradigm of "religious tradition." In other words, the model of scripture exemplified by Veda and Torah is rooted in a specific model of "religious tradition" that is different from the paradigms of "religious tradition" that underlie Christian conceptions of the New Testament, Theravāda Buddhist notions of the Pali canon, or Islamic conceptions of the Qur'ān. Thus, this comparative study not only challenges us to rethink the category of scripture, it also challenges us to rethink the monolithic conception of "religious tradition" that presently dominates our scholarly inquiries.[13]

In discussing the category of canon in the history of religions, Jonathan Z. Smith has suggested that "canon is best seen as one form of a basic cultural process of limitation and of overcoming that limitation through ingenuity."[14] He further suggests that the task of overcoming the limitation posed by a closed canon is accomplished through the exegetical enterprise, in which the task of the interpreter is "continually to extend the domain of the closed canon over everything that is known or everything that exists *without* altering the canon in the process."[15] In order to test the applicability of this model of canon to the cases of Veda and Torah, two types of questions need to be addressed. First, if indeed Veda and Torah do constitute closed canons, what are the criteria and mechanisms by which each canon has been delimited? Second, what strategies have been used to overcome this limitation? Are they primarily exegetical in nature?

Both Veda and Torah would appear to conform to at least one aspect of Smith's model in that each functions within its respective tradition as an encompassing, paradigmatic symbol that is simultaneously delimited and potentially unlimited. At the center of each canon is a fixed corpus of texts, whether oral or written, that has been meticulously preserved in strictly unaltered form: the Vedic Saṃhitās and the Sefer Torah. At the same time the domains of both Veda and Torah have been extended through a variety of strategies so that each functions as an open-ended, permeable category within which can be subsumed potentially all texts, teachings, and practices authorized by the religious elite. In the case of Torah these strategies, in accordance with Smith's model, have been to a large extent exegetical, involving endless reinterpretations, applications, and extensions of the content of the core text. In the case of Veda, on the other hand, the mechanisms for expanding the canon generally involve an extension of status with little reference to the content of the Saṃhitās. Irrespective of whether the content of the Saṃhitās is known or understood, their status as transcendent knowledge is acknowledged by orthodox exponents, and it is this status that subsequent texts and teachings seek to acquire through various modes of assimilation.

Veda The term "Veda," derived from the root *vid*, "to know," means "knowledge." The term is used in the brahmanical tradition to designate a corpus of texts or teachings in at least four different senses. (1) The term Veda is used in its narrow sense to designate the four Saṃhitās, Ṛg-Veda, Yajur-Veda, Sāma-Veda, and Atharva-Veda, which constitute collections of verses (*ṛc*s), sacrificial formulae (*yajus*es), chants (*sāman*s), and incantations and imprecations (*atharvāṅgiras*es or *atharvan*s), respectively.[16] The versified portions of the Saṃhitās are termed *mantra*s.[17] (2) The term is subsequently extended to include not only the four Saṃhitās but also the Brāhmaṇas, sacrificial manuals attached to the Saṃhitās; the Āraṇyakas, "forest books" that reflect on the inner meaning of the sacrificial rituals; and the Upaniṣads, the latest speculative portions of the Vedas.[18] (3) In post-Vedic speculations the term is at times extended even further to include the Itihāsas or epics (the Mahābhārata and the Rāmāyaṇa of Vālmīki) and Purāṇas, which are respectively designated as the "fifth Veda."[19] (4) Finally, Veda becomes an encompassing symbol within which can be subsumed potentially all brahmanical texts, teachings, and practices.

In order to understand the mechanisms through which this expansion of the purview of the term Veda occurred, we need to examine more closely the distinction that is made in the brahmanical tradition between two categories of sacred texts: *śruti*, "that which was heard," and *smṛti*, "that which was remembered." The core *śruti* texts are the four types of *mantra*s—*ṛc*s, *yajus*es, *sāman*s, and *atharvāṅgiras*es or *atharvan*s—that are collected in the Saṃhitās.[20] The domain of *śruti* was subsequently extended to include not only the Saṃhitās but also the Brāhmaṇas, Āraṇyakas, and Upaniṣads. Although the canon of *śruti* is technically closed, the category of Upaniṣads has remained somewhat permeable, with new Upaniṣads being added to the traditionally accepted 108

Upaniṣads up to as late as the medieval period.[21] While the domain of *śruti* is thus in principle circumscribed, *smṛti* is a dynamic, open-ended category, which includes the Dharma-Śāstras, Itihāsas, and Purāṇas, as well as a variety of other texts that have been incorporated within this ever-expanding category in accordance with the needs of different periods and groups.[22] The primary criterion for distinguishing between *śruti* and *smṛti* texts is generally characterized by both Indian and Western scholars as an ontological distinction between "revelation" and "tradition."[23] *Śruti* texts—Saṃhitās, Brāhmaṇas, Āraṇyakas, and Upaniṣads—are traditionally understood to have been directly cognized—"seen" and "heard"—by inspired "seers" (*ṛṣis*) at the beginning of each cycle of creation.[24] The formal schools of Vedic exegesis, Pūrva-Mīmāṃsā and Vedānta, maintain that the *śruti* or Vedic texts are eternal (*nitya*), infinite, and *apauruṣeya*, not derived from any personal—human or divine—agent, while the Nyāya, Vaiśeṣika, and Yoga schools of Indian philosophy view the Vedic texts as the work of God.[25] All other sacred texts are relegated to a secondary status as *smṛti*, for they are held to have been composed by personal authors and are therefore designated as "that which was remembered" rather than "that which was heard." On the basis of this criterion the Itihāsas and Purāṇas are classified as *smṛti* texts, even though they may assimilate themselves to *śruti* by claiming the status of the "fifth Veda."

According to the above definitions, the term Veda refers strictly speaking only to *śruti* texts and not to *smṛti* texts. However, Sheldon Pollock has recently brought to light an essential mechanism whereby the domain of the Veda was extended to include not only *śruti* but also *smṛti*. He locates this mechanism in the definition of the terms *śruti* and *smṛti* themselves, which he argues have been incorrectly construed as representing a dichotomy between "revelation" and "tradition." He maintains rather that, according to the etymology derived from the Pūrva-Mīmāṃsā school that is still prevalent among certain traditional brahmanical teachers, *śruti* refers to the extant Vedic texts that can be "heard" in recitation, whereas *smṛti* is an open-ended category that encompasses any teachings or practices pertaining to *dharma* that have been "remembered" from lost Vedic texts. Understood in this way, Veda becomes a limitlessly expanding symbol that includes not only *śruti* but also *smṛti*. The meaning of the term Veda is extended beyond the circumscribed boundaries of the *śruti* texts—Saṃhitās, Brāhmaṇas, Āraṇyakas, and Upaniṣads—and through a process of "vedacization" comes to include within its purview not only the Itihāsas and Purāṇas but potentially all śāstric teachings—enshrined in practices as well as texts—that are promulgated by brahmanical authorities.[26]

While the original etymology of the term *śruti* may be debated, and may indeed be interpreted by certain strands of the brahmanical tradition to mean "that which is heard" in ongoing recitations of the Vedic texts, it is also clear that the related term *śruta* was used as early as the Ṛg-Veda to refer to the cognitions of the *ṛṣis*[27] and that the term *śruti* itself still retains this association among contemporary Indian thinkers: Veda as *śruti* is "that which was heard" by the ancient *ṛṣis* as part of a primordial cognition in the beginning of creation. Moreover, Veda is that which was seen by the *ṛṣis*, who as "seers" are traditionally designated as those who "see the truth" (*satya-darśin*). The notion that *śruti* is the direct cognition by enlightened seers of eternal knowledge in the form of speech has been emphasized by the contemporary scholar and teacher Maharishi Mahesh Yogi, who defines *śruti* as "vibrancy of intelligence in the form of sound generated by the self-referral dynamics of consciousness—those specific sounds that . . . have been heard by the seers in their own self-referral consciousness." The contemporary philosopher Aurobindo Ghose similarly describes *śruti* as "a rhythm not composed by the intellect but heard, a divine Word that came vibrating out of the Infinite to the inner audience of the man who had previously made himself fit for the impersonal knowledge."[28]

The transcendent status attributed to the Veda is itself constitutive of the Veda's legitimating authority as the encompassing symbol of the brahmanical tradition. The core *śruti* texts, the Vedic *mantras*, are represented in the mythological speculations of Vedic and post-Vedic texts as having a transhistorical dimension, in which they constitute that eternal, suprasensible knowledge which exists perpetually on the subtle level of creation as the source and "blueprint" of the universe.[29] The *ṛṣis* are portrayed as having the ability to station their awareness on that subtle level where they could "see" and "hear" the impulses of knowledge reverberating forth from the Transcendent as the fundamental rhythms of creation. They subsequently "recorded" on the gross level of speech that which they cognized on the subtle level, and in this way the *mantras* assumed a concrete form on earth as recited texts. The Vedic *mantras* are thus granted the status of transcendent knowledge. Any subsequent text or śāstric discourse can participate in that status only by assimilating itself to the Vedic *mantras* through a variety of strategies, including (1) claiming to form part of *śruti*, the original cognitions of the *ṛṣis*, in the case of the Brāhmaṇas, Āraṇyakas, and Upaniṣads; (2) claiming the status of the "fifth Veda," in the case of the Itihāsas and Purāṇas; (3) establishing a genealogy that directly links the text's teachings to the Veda or to some form of divine revelation, in the case of the Manu-Smṛti; (4) claiming that the text's teachings derive from lost Vedic texts, a claim that could apply to potentially all *smṛti* texts; or (5) otherwise conforming to the model of the Veda.[30]

Brian K. Smith has emphasized that such strategies, including a variety of other modes of assimilation, have been used not only by exponents of the brahmanical hierarchy but also by nonbrahmanical Hindu groups in order to invest their sacred texts with the transcendent authority of the Veda.[31] He goes so far as to claim that "the Veda functions as a touchstone for Hindu orthodoxy" and that Vedic authority is constitutive of "Hinduism" itself, including not only the brahmanical tradition but also devotional sects and tantric movements: "Hinduism is the religion of those humans who create, perpetuate, and transform traditions with legitimizing reference to the authority of the Veda."[32] Jan Gonda similarly defines Hinduism as "a complex of social-religious phenomena, which are based on that authority of the ancient corpora, called Veda."[33]

The paradigmatic function of the Veda is evidenced in the way in which certain devotional sects have sought to imitate the Veda by elevating their own vernacular texts to a quasi-*śruti* status. For example, the Tamil hymns of the *Tiruvāymoḷi* by the poet Nammāḷvār (ca. 9th c. C.E.), a low-caste exponent of the Vaiṣṇava Āḷvārs, are said to represent the four Vedic Saṃhitās and are designated as the "Dravidian Veda" or "Tamil Veda."[34] The *Rāmcaritmānas* of the poet Tulsīdās (ca. 16th c. C.E.), a Hindi version of the Rāmāyaṇa popular throughout North India, has been granted a similar status as the "fifth Veda" or "Hindi Veda" that is said to represent the concentrated essence of all the Hindu scriptures.[35]

While some devotional sects have thus sought to legitimate their texts through assimilating them to the Veda, the claim that all Hindu groups—nonbrahmanical as well as brahmanical—accept the authority of the Veda does not hold true in the case of certain *bhakti* and tantric movements. For example, the *vacana* poets of the Vīraśaiva sect, which originated in the Kannada-speaking region of South India in the tenth century C.E., were leaders of a protest movement that rejected the Vedic texts and rituals because of their association with the caste system and other brahmanical institutions.[36] Certain left-handed tantric sects such as the Kashmir Śaivas have not only rejected Vedic authority, they have treated the Veda as a symbol to be subverted by actively adhering to teachings and practices that directly transgress orthodox brahmanical traditions.[37]

Whether the Veda is revered or rejected, appropriated or subverted, it remains a symbol invested with authoritative power that must be contended with by all those who wish to position themselves in relation to the brahmanical hierarchy. As J. C. Heesterman emphasizes, "The crux of the matter is that the Vedas hold the key to ultimate legitimation. Therefore, even if the Vedas are in no way related to the ways of human life and society, one is still forced to come to terms with them."[38] Heesterman's remark points to an observation often made by Indologists: the authoritative power of the Veda does not lie in the content of the Vedic Saṃhitās themselves, for their content is primarily concerned with sacrificial rituals and is not directly relevant to the teachings and practices of post-Vedic Hinduism. Smith remarks:

> The great paradox of Hinduism . . . is that although the religion is inextricably tied to the legitimizing authority of the Veda, in post-Vedic times the subject matter of the Veda was and is largely unknown by those who define themselves in relation to it. Its contents (almost entirely concerning the meaning and performance of sacrificial rituals that Hindus do not perform) are at best reworked (being, for example, reconstituted into ritual formulas or mantras for use in Hindu ceremonies), and [in] many cases appear to be totally irrelevant for Hindu doctrine and practice.[39]

Louis Renou has observed that "even in the most orthodox domains, the reverence to the Vedas has come to be a simple 'raising of the hat', in passing, to an idol by which one no longer intends to be encumbered later on." He further remarks that "the term [Veda] tends to serve as a symbol."[40]

The critical point to be emphasized here is that the Veda serves as a symbol precisely because it transcends the confines of textuality that limit the term to a circumscribed body of texts and comes to represent the totality of knowledge, thus reclaiming its original etymology as "knowledge." Pollock remarks:

> As "Knowledge" *tout court*, as the *śāstra* par excellence, and as the "omniscient" text (Manu-Smṛti 2.7) and the "infinite" text (Taittirīya [Brāhmaṇa] 3.10.11.4, et al.), Veda is the general rubric under which every sort of partial knowledge—that is, the various individual *śāstras*—is ultimately subsumed.[41]

The legitimating authority of the Veda is thus inextricably linked to its symbolic function as knowledge—not the ordinary knowledge derived through the powers of human reasoning but that transcendent, infinite knowledge which is held to be the essence of ultimate reality and the source and foundation of creation.[42] This knowledge is said to have been cognized by the *ṛṣis* and preserved by them in the form of oral texts, but, as we shall see, certain brahmanical texts insist that the Veda, the limitless Word, cannot be limited to its finite expressions in the texts preserved by human beings on earth. Moreover, the power of the Veda as embodied in the recited texts is held to lie not in the discursive meaning of the texts but rather in the sounds through which the primordial impulses of knowledge are expressed. In this view the content of the Vedic Saṃhitās will always be of secondary value, as Indologists have observed, because the primary concern of the brahmanical exponents of the Vedic recitative tradition is to preserve the purity of the Vedic sounds irrespective of whether their semantic content is understood.[43]

Torah The term "Torah," according to the general consensus of most modern scholars, is connected with the hiphil conjugation of the root *yrh*, "to point out, direct, teach," and thus means "teaching" or "instruction."[44] In rabbinic literature the term is used to refer to a corpus of teachings or texts in at least four different senses. (1) The term is used in its narrow sense to refer to the Pentateuch, the Five Books of Moses or Sefer Torah (Book of the Torah), as distinct from the other two sections of the Hebrew Bible, Nevi'im (Prophets) and Ketuvim (Writings). (2) The term is subsequently extended to refer to the Hebrew Bible, the Tanakh, as a whole. (3) The meaning of the term is expanded further to include not only the Pentateuch, Nevi'im, and Ketuvim, which constitute the Written Torah (*tôrāh še bi-ḵṯāḇ*), but also the Mishnah, Talmud, and Midrash, which contain the halakhic and aggadic teachings that constitute the Oral Torah (*tôrāh še bᵉ-'al peh*).[45] (4) Finally, Torah becomes an encompassing symbol that includes potentially all of the laws, teachings, and practices of the normative rabbinic tradition.

This progressive expansion of the term Torah is reflected in the ways in which the categories of Written Torah and Oral Torah are defined and distinguished. The Written Torah is a fixed, bounded text, whether understood in its narrow sense as the Pentateuch or in its broader sense as the entire Hebrew Bible. The Oral Torah, on the other hand, is a fluid, open-ended category, which in its broadest sense includes not only the teachings contained in the Mishnah, Talmud, and Midrash, but also all the laws and teachings that are introduced by the rabbinic sages in each generation as part of the oral tradition. The distinction between Written Torah and Oral Torah is traditionally held to derive from the original revelation at Mount Sinai, in which God gave to Moses two Torahs: a written text, consisting of the Pentateuch, Nevi'im, and Ketuvim, and an oral tradition of interpretation that was destined to be preserved in the Mishnah, Talmud, and Midrash, as well as in the teachings of subsequent generations of rabbis.[46]

The legitimating authority of the Torah is linked in particular to the Pentateuch, which is ascribed a special status as divine revelation in that its every word is traditionally believed to have been directly dictated by God to Moses, who acted as a scribe and recorded the words of God verbatim in the Sefer Torah. The authority of all subsequent texts and teachings is legitimated by establishing a connection between those texts or teachings and the Sefer Torah, either through (1) granting them a subsidiary status as part of the Written Torah, in the case of the books of the Nevi'im and Ketuvim; (2) allotting them a designated place as part of the Oral Torah, in the case of the teachings of the Mishnah, Talmud, and Midrash; (3) linking them to the revelation at Mount Sinai as part of the open-ended category of Oral Torah; or (4) otherwise aligning them with the model of the Sefer Torah.

In discussing the documentary history of the term Torah, Jacob Neusner has delineated various strategies adopted by rabbinic texts to assimilate their teachings to the Torah. In the process the Torah was transformed from a limited, bounded text—the Sefer Torah—into a limitless, encompassing symbol, "the single critical symbol of the Judaism of the dual Torah," that represents the entire system of rabbinic Judaism.

> [The] documentary history [of this symbol] traces the story of how "the Torah" lost its capital letter and definite article

> and ultimately became "torah." What for nearly a millennium had been a particular scroll or book came to serve as a symbol of an entire system. When a rabbi spoke of torah, he no longer meant only a particular object, a scroll and its contents. Now he used the word to encompass a distinctive and well-defined world view and way of life. . . . In the Judaism of the dual Torah as it emerged from its formative age, everything was contained in that one thing, "Torah." It connotes a broad range of clearly distinct categories of noun and verb, concrete fact and abstract relationship alike. . . . As symbolic abstraction, the word encompasses things and persons, actions and statuses, points of social differentiation and legal and normative standing, as well as "revealed truth." . . . Every detail of the religious system at hand exhibits essentially the same point of insistence, captured in the simple notion of the Torah as the generative symbol, the total, exhaustive expression of the system as a whole.[47]

The critical question is why the Torah, and not something else, was singled out to serve as the generative symbol of rabbinic Judaism. For the answer we must return to the original referent of the term: the Sefer Torah. The Sefer Torah was granted an especially sacrosanct and authoritative status as "revealed truth," and therefore any text, teaching, practice, or person that wished to attain normative standing within the rabbinic tradition could do so only through becoming incorporated in the ever-expanding domain of Torah. While the Torah as a circumscribed written text constitutes a bounded category, in its status as revealed truth it becomes an endlessly expanding symbol that extends beyond the boundaries of the text and is capable of absorbing a host of candidates whose linkage to the revelation, however tenuous, has been established.

The encompassing nature of the Torah as a symbol is linked in particular to its identification with the Word of God, for while the Sefer Torah might be held to be the most perfect, concentrated expression of the Word of God on earth, the Word itself is not limited to that expression. The divine Word through which God manifested himself at the time of revelation is also represented as the creative power through which God manifested himself at the time of creation. In its identification with the Word of God the Torah is thus at times portrayed as existing prior to the revelation, since the beginning of creation, as the instrument through which God brought forth the universe. In certain representations of the Torah found in seminal form in rabbinic texts and subsequently elaborated in medieval kabbalistic texts, the Torah is personified as that primordial wisdom which had existed in heaven from "the beginning" as a living aspect of God and the immediate source of creation. At the time of the revelation at Mount Sinai the primordial Torah is said to have descended from its supernal abode and to have become embodied on earth in the concrete form of the Sefer Torah. It assumed the finite form of the Book of the Torah, but the book itself is understood in this context as simply the outer body in which the primordial reality of wisdom ever resides as its innermost soul. In this perspective the Sefer Torah itself becomes a symbol with transcendent significations in that it continually points beyond its own textuality to the divine reality enshrined within.

In rabbinic texts such speculations are not systematically developed as part of any consistent cosmology, and therefore it is difficult to assess whether such notions reflect a genuine interest in cosmological speculation or whether they are simply literary metaphors adopted in homiletical praise of the Torah.[48] It is also difficult to determine to what extent a particular view represents a consensus of opinion, or to what extent it represents the opinion of specific individuals or schools of rabbinic thought. Rabbinic texts do not present a single homogeneous perspective but rather a multiplicity of voices representing a variety of different schools with distinctive viewpoints and approaches. For example, Abraham Heschel has suggested that there were at least two contending schools among the second-century Tannaim with fundamentally different conceptions of the Torah's status: the school of R. Akiba, which emphasized the transcendent significance of every word and letter of the Torah, and the school of R. Ishmael, which maintained the more pragmatic stance that the Torah speaks in the language of human beings.[49] R. Akiba appears to be representative of certain more mystically oriented circles within the early rabbinic tradition that were concerned not only with more traditional matters of halakhah and aggadah but also with the "secrets of the Torah" (*sit̲rê tôrāh, rāzê tôrāh*), in particular with the mysteries of creation (*ma'ăśēh b^e^rē'šît̲*, literally, "works of creation") described in Genesis 1 and the mysteries of the throne-chariot (*ma'ăśēh merkāb̲āh*, literally, "works of the chariot") depicted in Ezekiel 1. Although the Mishnah placed certain restrictions on speculation and public discourse about *ma'ăśēh b^e^rē'šît̲* and *ma'ăśēh merkāb̲āh*,[50] it is clear from rabbinic texts that such speculation did indeed take place in certain circles.[51]

In contrast to the rather fragmentary nature of the rabbinic material, in which aggadic speculations about the Torah are interspersed throughout the texts, in medieval kabbalistic texts such speculations are generally presented as part of a grand cosmological scheme. The conceptions found in seminal form in rabbinic texts are fully elaborated and cosmologized by certain kabbalists, going beyond metaphorical personification to clear hypostatization.[52] Although there is clearly a difference in perspective and emphases with respect to the representations of Torah found in rabbinic and kabbalistic texts, there are also sufficient threads of continuity to warrant juxtaposing these two different approaches.[53]

The Word Embodied in Scripture

The cosmological status ascribed to Veda and Torah can be fully understood only on the basis of their respective traditions' theories of language, in which scripture represents the embodiment of the Word. This Word cannot be delimited to the written word, as the term "scripture" itself and its common equivalents—for example, "sacred writings" or "holy writ"—might suggest. Nor is it sufficient simply to expand the meaning of scripture to encompass its oral-aural dimensions as spoken word. The Word embodied in Veda and Torah also has a cosmological dimension, in which on one level it is represented as a cosmic reality that is a living aspect of the divine, while on another level it is depicted as the subtle plan of creation containing the elements of the divine language through which the creator brings forth the manifold forms of the universe.

The concept of the Word, as expressed in the theories of language developed by the brahmanical tradition and the rabbinic and kabbalistic traditions, encompasses not only the gross level of vocalized speech but also the subtler levels of nonvocalized speech as expressed in the entire range of development of thought. The Word is conceived as encompassing both unspoken thought and spoken utterance and thus has two aspects: a *cognitive dimension,* which is the unspoken thought or idea in the mind that constitutes the conceptual content of the word; and a *phonic dimension,* which encompasses both the internally perceived sound of mental discourse and the vocalized speech through which thought finds expression in externally audible sound. When translated onto the cosmic level, as described in certain strands of the traditions, the distinction between unspoken thought and vocalized speech is understood as a distinction between knowledge and speech. The unspoken thought in the cosmic mind is knowledge or wisdom,[54] which is the cognitive *content* of the Word. The Word is spoken by means of speech, which is the vehicle for the *expression* of the Word. Knowledge and speech—both of these aspects of the Word are necessary in order for the process of manifestation to be complete. On the one hand, without speech the content of the Word, which is knowledge, would remain hidden, undisclosed; on the other hand, without knowledge speech would have no content to express. Knowledge and speech, or unspoken thought and vocalized speech, are represented as two phases in the single continuum of the Word.

In certain representations of Veda and Torah, as will be discussed in the following analysis, scripture is depicted as a multileveled cosmic reality, its different levels corresponding to the different levels of creation and to the different levels of the Word, in which the principles of knowledge and speech both come into play: (1) *scripture as the totality of the Word,* which is the essence of the ultimate reality, particularly as it manifests itself in creation; (2) *scripture as knowledge,* which is identified with the creator principle[55] as the immediate source of creation; (3) *scripture as divine language,* its constituent sounds or letters representing the archetypal plan or "blueprint"[56] from which the creator structures the forms of creation; (4) *scripture as concrete text,* represented by the oral texts of the Vedic Saṃhitās, on the one hand, or the Written Torah together with an oral tradition of interpretation, on the other.

In the case of both Veda and Torah, the structure of relations that connects these symbolic complexes is twofold: spatial and temporal. The spatial relation is at times represented as a hierarchy of levels corresponding to the levels of creation on a continuum from subtle to gross, each symbolic complex representing a discrete level of the hierarchy. These symbolic complexes are also at times connected in a temporal set of relations in which each complex is correlated with a particular stage of manifestation in the process of creation.

Although there are significant structural similarities in the symbol systems associated with Veda and Torah,[57] we shall see that there are also significant differences between these scriptural traditions, particularly with respect to the theories of language that underlie their conceptions and practices. My study highlights in particular three fundamental points of divergence. (1) With respect to the *oral and written channels of language,* the brahmanical tradition gives precedence to the oral channel, while the rabbinic and kabbalistic traditions assign special status to the written register. (2) These diverging emphases on the oral vs. written channels of language result in a corresponding divergence in *modes of perception,* what Walter Ong has termed the "ratio of the senses," in which brahmanical conceptions of language and scripture give primary emphasis to the auditory channel, while rabbinic and kabbalistic conceptions tend to emphasize the visual channel. (3) With respect to the *cognitive and phonic dimensions of the word,* the brahmanical tradition gives priority to the phonic dimension and the rabbinic and kabbalistic traditions to the cognitive dimension. These divergent emphases are particularly evident, as we shall see, in the traditions and practices that have evolved concerning the proper methods of transmission and study of the Vedic Saṃhitās and the Sefer Torah. With respect to the Vedic Saṃhitās, the phonic dimension of the words and hence their phonological accuracy is emphasized, and study is through memorization and recitation as a means of maintaining the purity of every sound and syllable of the oral texts. With respect to the Sefer Torah, on the other hand, the cognitive dimension of the words and hence their semantic significance is emphasized, and study is through interpretation as a means of drawing out the manifold meanings of every word and letter of the written text.

The brahmanical tradition's focus on oral transmission as the most appropriate vehicle for the Vedic *mantras* has its counterpart in an emphasis on the auditory mode of perception, just as the rabbinic and kabbalistic traditions' focus on written transmission of the Sefer Torah results in a corresponding emphasis on the visual channel. Thus, although the process of Vedic cognition and the revelation at Mount Sinai are both described in terms of auditory and visual phenomena, the Veda is characterized above all as *śruti,* "that which was heard" by the Vedic *ṛṣis,* while the visionary dimensions of the Sinai experience tend to be given priority. This distinction is further reflected in these traditions' conceptions of their sacred language, in which Sanskrit is represented as a sound system composed of phones (*varṇas*) and not of visible symbols inscribed on parchment, while Hebrew is represented as an alphabet composed of letters (*'ôṯiyyôṯ*) in which the graphic forms of the letters are considered part of the primordial manifestation of the divine language. Finally, while the Veda as the Word is depicted as subtle reverberations of sound that are "heard" on earth in the oral recitations of the brahmin priests, the Torah as the Word of God is often associated with visual images of light and fire and is represented as assuming a concrete, visible form on earth as the scroll of the Torah.

The brahmanical emphasis on the oral-aural over the written-visual dimensions of language and of Veda is further linked to the essentially aniconic orientation of the Vedic tradition, in which *śrauta* rituals are traditionally performed in a temporary sacrificial enclosure, constructed for the purpose of the particular sacrifice, without iconic representations of deities.[58] It is only with the advent of popular *bhakti* traditions in post-Vedic "Hinduism" that we find a shift to iconic forms of worship, with the introduction of temples and *pūjā* ceremonies centered on offerings to images of the gods. In the post-Vedic period the gods become "incarnated" in images, and certain sacred texts, such as the epics and Purāṇas, become embodied in written form and are themselves at times revered as visible icons of the divine.[59] It is important to emphasize, however, that this represents a departure from the Vedic model, which gives priority to the oral-aural over the written-visual. The converse is true of rabbinic and kabbalistic conceptions of language and of Torah. While the rabbinic tradition is generally characterized as "aniconic" in that it eschews the use of images and other visual representations of the divine, we shall see that certain rabbinic conceptions, which are further developed in kabbalistic texts, point to an almost iconic veneration of the Sefer Torah as the visible presence of the Word of God. As we embark on this comparative study, then, we must temporarily hold in abeyance the opposition "iconic 'Hinduism' vs. aniconic 'Judaism'" as inappropriate and misleading for certain strands of the brahmanical and Jewish traditions that we will be investigating.[60]

The Problematics of Cross-Cultural Analysis

The critiques that certain scholars of religion have made in recent years of the comparative study of religion resonate with the critiques that poststructuralists have made of structuralist, idealist, and essentialist trends of scholarship and to a certain extent call into question the validity of the entire comparative enterprise. And yet, as Jonathan Z. Smith has emphasized, the process of comparison is itself a constitutive aspect of human thought and an essential part of our scholarly methods.

> The process of comparison is a fundamental characteristic of human intelligence. Whether revealed in the logical grouping of classes, in poetic similies, in mimesis, or other like activities—comparison, the bringing together of two or

> more objects for the purpose of noting either similarity or dissimilarity, is the omnipresent substructure of human thought. Without it, we could not speak, perceive, learn, or reason. . . . That comparison has, at times, led us astray there can be no doubt; that comparison remains *the* method of scholarship is likewise beyond question.[61]

After surveying and critiquing four basic modes of comparison—ethnographic, encyclopedic, morphological, and evolutionary—together with their more recent variants, Smith concludes that none of the proposed methods is adequate. Yet he suggests that the comparative enterprise should not thereby be abandoned, for questions of comparison are critical to the scholar of religion's task.

> We must conclude this exercise in our own academic history in a most unsatisfactory manner. Each of the modes of comparison has been found problematic. Each new proposal has been found to be a variant of an older mode. . . . We know better how to evaluate comparisons, but we have gained little over our predecessors in either the method for making comparisons or the reasons for its practice. . . . So we are left with the question [posed by Wittgenstein], "How am I to apply what the one thing shows me to the case of two things?" The possibility of the study of religion depends on its answer.[62]

Among the various modes of comparative analysis surveyed by Smith, the morphological approach in particular, especially as represented in the structural phenomenological studies of scholars such as Gerardus van der Leeuw[63] and Mircea Eliade,[64] has come under attack from a number of different perspectives. Three types of problems, which are closely interconnected, can be isolated. (1) *Insufficient attention to differences.* Such studies tend to be concerned with the common features and structural similarities among religious phenomena drawn from various religious traditions and consequently do not pay sufficient attention to the differences that give each tradition its unique character and integrity.[65] (2) *Insufficient attention to the diachronic dimension.* In their search for similarities and continuities, such studies are concerned primarily with synchronic structures and thus tend to disregard the diachronic dimension of religious phenomena. Religious phenomena are abstracted from history and treated as static, timeless structures, and hence the dynamic, changing nature of religious manifestations is ignored.[66] (3) *Insufficient attention to context.* Such studies thus fail to give adequate attention to the distinctive contours of each specific religious manifestation as shaped by the particular context—textual, historical, cultural, social, and/or religious—from which it emerges.

I have developed a method of comparative historical analysis that, while specifically appropriate to the religious traditions that are the focus of my inquiries, also attempts to redress some of these more general problems and to rescue cross-cultural study from the clutches of ahistorical universalism by giving proper attention to differences as well as to similarities and to diachronic transformations as well as to structural continuities. This method, the fruits of which are delineated in the present study, involves three principal phases of analysis: (1) history of interpretations, (2) comparative analysis, and (3) cultural interpretation.

Phase 1: History of Interpretations The first phase of my analysis is tradition specific and involves analyzing the network of symbols associated with Veda and Torah separately, within the context of each individual tradition. I call this phase "history of interpretations" in that my analyses are undertaken within a diachronic framework and involve tracing the history of certain representations of Veda and Torah, respectively, through the core texts of each tradition's formative development. The history with which I am concerned in this phase is not *Entstehungsgeschichte,* a history of origins and cause-effect relations, but rather *Wirkungsgeschichte,* a history of effects, understood as the tradition of successive interpretations of particular symbolic complexes associated with Veda and Torah in the core texts.

This method of analysis is not arbitrary but rather derives from the very nature of the traditions with which this comparative study is concerned. Both the brahmanical and rabbinic traditions, as discussed above, constitute "textual communities" that have self-consciously defined the parameters of their respective "traditions" through compiling a set of discrete documents as a textual repository of normative values and practices and investing these documents with the authoritative status of a canon. Any sustained study of the brahmanical and rabbinic traditions thus must inevitably have its basis in texts, and, in the case of the present analysis, the principal criterion for inclusion of particular texts is that they are considered authoritative in the traditions themselves. The texts on which this study is based are thus drawn primarily from the brahmanical canon of *śruti* and *smṛti* texts and the rabbinic canon of Written Torah and Oral Torah, although the Judaic phase of the analysis also considers certain pre-rabbinic and kabbalistic sources that are germane to the inquiry.

Two other factors necessitate reliance on normative texts as the primary source of our knowledge of the brahmanical and rabbinic traditions. First, these traditions are attested principally by textual evidence, and the texts that constitute the evidence are for the most part self-referential in that they form part of the canons of the traditions themselves. Our knowledge of the formative periods of the brahmanical and rabbinic traditions is thus limited primarily to the testimonies of the texts authorized by the brahmanical and rabbinic elite, with almost no independent sources of corroboration. Second, in the case of both brahmanical and rabbinic sources we are dealing with texts that were in most cases compiled by an anonymous, corporate authorship over long periods—sometimes hundreds of years—and that contain layers of accretions that may derive from different sociohistorical milieus. This fact precludes our ability to place such texts firmly within strictly delimited historical contexts, and any such attempts constitute at best speculative reconstructions that are reliant almost exclusively on the testimonies of the texts themselves.

The consequence of these two factors is that the most we can hope to arrive at is a history of interpretations of textual representations, not an interpretation of historical verities. We can trace, for example, certain symbolic complexes that are used in the various strata of brahmanical texts to represent the status and authority of the Veda, and we can map the epistemological shifts in the discursive framework that dominates each textual stratum, but we cannot thereby definitively determine the actual sociohistorical conditions that generated these complexes and epistemological shifts. We may at times, on the basis of the accumulated findings of Indological scholarship, suggest possible explanations for transformations in the dominant discourse—for example, from the discourse of sacrifice in the Brāhmaṇas to the discourse of knowledge in the Upaniṣads—but it is important to emphasize that such "explanations" remain to a large extent on the level of scholarly speculation.

A useful model for the history of interpretations phase of my analysis is stratigraphy in geology. Stratigraphy involves examining and classifying the properties of individual strata and cross-correlating the different strata in order to discern regular patterns and recurrences of species as well as evolutionary changes in species from stratum to stratum. Similarly, this phase of my study is concerned with examining the symbolic complexes found in the core strata of texts in each tradition and cross-correlating the various strata in order to discern structural continuities as well as diachronic transformations from layer to layer. This phase involves a dialectical movement between diachronic and synchronic analyses in a five-step process.

(1a) Excavation of Symbols in the Core Strata of the Traditions

With respect to the brahmanical material, this step entails unearthing the symbolic formulations of Veda in the core strata of the brahmanical tradition, beginning with the oldest layers of Vedic literature—Saṃhitās, Brāhmaṇas, Āraṇyakas, and Upaniṣads—through the more recent layers of post-Vedic literature—Manu-Smṛti, Mahābhārata, Harivaṃśa, and selected Purāṇas—to the philosophical speculations of the Darśanas, with particular emphasis on Pūrva-Mīmāṃsā and Advaita Vedānta. The Judaic portion of the analysis similarly involves excavating the symbolic configurations in which Torah is embedded in the earliest layers of pre-rabbinic speculation—wisdom literature of the Hebrew Bible, wisdom literature of the Apocrypha, and the Alexandrian Jewish philosophers Aristobulus and Philo—through the various strata of rabbinic literature—Mishnah, Tannaitic Midrashim, classical Amoraic Midrashim, Babylonian Talmud, and selected post-Talmudic Midrashim—to the speculations of medieval kabbalistic texts, with particular emphasis on the Zohar and the theosophical Kabbalah of thirteenth-century Spain.

(1b) Synchronic Analysis of Each Stratum

This second step involves a synchronic analysis of the symbols emerging from each discrete stratum of literature separately, layer by layer.

(1c) Cross-Correlation of Strata I: Structural Continuities

In the next two steps (1c and 1d) the analysis moves from synchronic to diachronic and involves the cross-correlation of layers in order to discern the continuities, transformations, and interjections that are brought into relief when the successive strata are viewed in relation to one another as a history of interpretations.

The first step in the process of cross-correlation is primarily concerned with delineating structural continuities. It involves separating out the discrete symbolic complexes in the organic network of symbols associated with Veda and Torah, respectively, and articulating a conceptual framework that can serve to elucidate the structure of relations among the various complexes. For example, having analyzed the network of symbols associated with the Veda in the strata of brahmanical literature, one begins to discern certain distinct clusters of symbols recurring at each layer. Four major symbolic complexes can in the end be distinguished, in which the Veda is variously represented as (1) the Word (*brahman*/Śabdabrahman), which is an aspect of Brahman, the ultimate reality; (2) knowledge, which is embodied in the creator principle; (3) the blueprint of creation containing the impulses of divine speech; and (4) a concrete corpus of oral texts. The excavation and analysis of the various strata of rabbinic and kabbalistic texts yield four types of symbolic complexes that persist through the different layers, in which the Torah is represented as (1) the Word (*dāḇār*) of God or Name (*šēm*) of God; (2) primordial wisdom, Ḥoḵmāh, which serves as the architect of creation; (3) the blueprint of creation containing the elements of the divine language; and (4) a concrete corpus of written texts together with an oral tradition of interpretation.

Another persistent trend of speculation concerns the mechanisms through which the primordial Word—Veda or Torah—came to be embodied in a particular corpus of texts, as described in brahmanical representations of the process of Vedic cognition, on the one hand, and rabbinic and kabbalistic accounts of the revelation of the Torah at Mount Sinai, on the other.

(1d) Cross-Correlation of Strata II: Diachronic Transformations

The second step in the process of cross-correlation focuses on diachronic transformations from layer to layer. This step is particularly concerned with analyzing documentary contexts and the ways in which the various symbolic complexes are reshaped and reformulated in different textual environments in accordance with the epistemological framework of each stratum or genre of texts. The analysis also attempts to illuminate the ways in which these differences in textual perspective may reflect competing or shifting sectional interests based on changing sociohistorical factors.

(1e) Analysis of Practices

The final step in this phase of the analysis involves re-embedding these scriptural conceptions in their larger cultural matrices through an analysis of practices concerning the modes of transmission, study, and appropriation of the Vedic Saṃhitās and the Sefer Torah, respectively.

Phase 2: Comparative Analysis Having examined the concepts and practices associated with Veda and Torah within the context of their respective traditions, I turn to the comparative phase of the analysis, which focuses on three types of material: first, representations of Veda and Torah, respectively, as multileveled cosmological principles identified with different levels of the Word; second, accounts of the mechanisms of cognition of Veda and revelation of Torah; and third, practices associated with the Vedic Saṃhitās and the Sefer Torah. In each phase of the comparative analysis I am concerned not only with delineating the structural similarities between these symbol systems and practices, but also with highlighting the essential differences that give each scriptural tradition its distinctive character.

Phase 3: Cultural Interpretation In the last phase of the analysis I turn to cultural interpretation in an attempt to understand the significance of these similarities and differences in scriptural conceptions and practices in light of the unique *Gestalt* of the religious traditions in which they are embedded. First, I consider the extent to which the parallels in the manner in which these traditions construct the category of scripture may be rooted in the more basic structural correlations between the brahmanical and rabbinic traditions. Second, I critically evaluate the extent to which my findings corroborate or contradict certain fundamental distinctions between oral and written cultures that have been delineated by anthropologists, literary historians, psychologists, and linguists.

This three-phase method of comparative historical analysis seeks to redress the three types of problems outlined earlier in that (1) it preserves the integrity of the individual religious traditions through first analyzing the symbol systems associated with Veda and Torah separately, within the context of their respective religious traditions, before attempting to delineate their structural similarities as well as their differences; (2) it incorporates synchronic analyses within a diachronic framework that can serve to illuminate transformations as well as structural continuities; and (3) it is concerned with the ways in which symbolic complexes are reshaped in different documentary contexts, which may in turn reflect distinctive sociohistorical milieus.

The following study presents the fruits of this method of comparative historical analysis. Each of the three parts of the study includes two chapters, which treat Veda and Torah separately, along with a concluding comparative section. Part 1, which constitutes the major portion of the study, is concerned with cosmogonic and cosmological conceptions of the role of the Word in creation, focusing in particular on representations of Veda (chapter 1) and Torah (chapter 2) as the source and blueprint of the universe. Part 2 examines the phenomenology of cognition of Veda (chapter 3) and revelation of Torah (chapter 4), with particular attention to the modes of reception through which the Word becomes embodied in concrete texts. Part 3 focuses on the functional status of the texts in practices, particularly with respect to the methods of transmission, study, and appropriation of the Vedic Saṃhitās (chapter 5) and the Sefer Torah (chapter 6). While the first two parts provide a history of interpretations of certain symbolic complexes associated with Veda and Torah, the third part, which focuses on practices rather than symbol systems, is organized in accordance with the different modes of practice, highlighting persistent trends without attempting to delineate the history of each.

I acknowledge that I have set for myself a daunting task in this comparative study: to address two different groups of specialists—scholars of Indology and Judaica—who have not generally been in conversation with one another, as well as to appeal to a wider range of scholars who may be interested in the broader theoretical issues concerning scripture, text, language, sources of religious authority, and tradition-identity that are raised by the study. The chapters in the history of interpretations phase of my analysis, which treat Veda (chapters 1, 3, 5) and Torah (chapters 2, 4, 6) separately, contain a detailed analysis of relevant sources, and although the extensive documentation may at times prove dense and wearisome to the nonspecialist, it is necessary in order to provide a nuanced, contextualized treatment that will hopefully shed new light on materials familiar to specialists of Indology and Judaica. For the sake of nonspecialists—including Judaica readers of the Veda chapters and Indological readers of the Torah chapters—I have included in chapters 1 and 2 introductory sections on each genre of texts as well as explications of technical terms. The comparative sections (comparative analyses 1, 2, and 3) will be more readily accessible to the general reader, but it should be emphasized that the arguments in these sections depend in each case upon the sustained expositions of the preceding two chapters.

Part 1

The Word in Creation

CHAPTER 1

Veda and Creation

> The *ṛcs* are limited (*parimita*), the *sāmans* are limited, and the *yajuses* are limited, but of the Word (*brahman*) there is no end.
>
> —Taittirīya Saṃhitā VII.3.1.4

In the cosmogonic and cosmological speculations of Vedic and post-Vedic mythology the corpus of Vedic *mantras* that has been preserved by the brahmanical lineages is represented as only a limited manifestation of the unlimited, eternal reality of Veda. Among the network of symbols associated with Veda, four complexes persist through the various strata of literature: (1) the Veda is described as the Word (*brahman*), which is the essence of Brahman, the ultimate reality, and is at times designated more specifically as Śabda-brahman (literally, "word-Brahman"), Brahman embodied in the Word; (2) the Veda as the totality of knowledge is also at times identified with the creator principle as the immediate source of creation; (3) the Veda*s* (plural) are represented as the archetypal plan or blueprint containing the primordial expressions of the divine speech that the creator utters in order to manifest the phenomenal creation; (4) the Vedas in their mundane, transmitted form are the *mantra* collections, or Saṃhitās, of the Ṛg-Veda, Yajur-Veda, Sāma-Veda, and Atharva-Veda that are recited by human beings on earth as part of the Vedic sacrificial rites. The following analysis will be primarily concerned with the first three conceptions, since it is these conceptions that point to the cosmological status of the Veda.

Some attention will be given at the end of this chapter to the various philosophical positions adopted by the six Darśanas with respect to the origin, ontology, and authority of the Vedas. While the cosmogonic and cosmological speculations of Vedic and post-Vedic mythology tend to limit their discussion of the textual manifestation of the Veda to the *mantras* or Saṃhitās, the philosophical discussions of the Darśanas focus on the Veda in the broader sense of the term, as encompassing not only the Saṃhitās but also the Brāhmaṇas, Āraṇyakas, and Upaniṣads.

The seminal speculations concerning the Veda found in the oldest texts of Vedic literature, the Saṃhitās (ca. 1500–800 B.C.E.), are reinterpreted and elaborated in later Vedic and post-Vedic texts, each genre of texts recasting the inherited paradigm from its own distinctive epistemological perspective and assimilating Veda to those aspects of reality that are of central importance to that perspective. Thus, while the various modes of representing Veda—as constitutive of Brahman, an aspect of the creator principle, or the blueprint of creation—may be found in each layer of texts, certain modes are at times given priority in accordance with the programmatic concerns of the texts. For example, the Brāhmaṇas (ca. 900–650 B.C.E.), which form part of the *karma-kāṇḍa*, the section of the Vedas pertaining to action (*karman*), focus on the sacrificial rituals that are to be performed in order to regenerate and maintain the relative creation. In accordance with this sacrificial perspective, the Brāhmaṇas elevate the creator Prajāpati, who is celebrated as the source of the sacrifice, the sacrificer, and the sacrifice itself, to the status of the supreme god, and in their discussions of the Veda they are above all concerned to establish the relationship of the Veda to Prajāpati and his consort Vāc, speech. On the other hand, the metaphysical speculations of the Upaniṣads (ca. 800–200 B.C.E.), which form part of the *jñāna-kāṇḍa*, the portion of the Vedas pertaining to knowledge (*jñāna*), reflect the sectional interests of certain forest-dwelling sages and ascetic groups that began to define themselves over against the priestly sacrificial tradition from the eighth century B.C.E. onward. Upaniṣadic speculations focus primarily on the ultimate reality—generally termed Brahman or Ātman (Self)—that is the source not only of creation but of the creator principle himself, and thus the relationship of the Veda to Brahman-Ātman becomes a paramount concern in the Upaniṣads. In post-Vedic texts that reflect the influence of sectarian devotionalism (*bhakti*), such as the Mahābhārata (ca. 400 B.C.E.–400 C.E.) and certain Purāṇas (ca. 300–1000 C.E. and after), Brahman generally assumes a personalized aspect through becoming identified with either Viṣṇu or Śiva, and the Veda is correspondingly represented as an aspect of Viṣṇu or Śiva.

VEDA AND CREATION IN VEDIC TEXTS

The dual mechanisms by means of which the Veda is identified with the limitless Word or knowledge and at the same time is delimited to a bounded corpus of texts—the Vedic *mantras*—are already evident in the Vedic texts themselves. In the Saṃhitās, Brāhmaṇas, Āraṇyakas, and Upaniṣads the terms "Veda," "Vedas," and their equivalents are used both in an abstract sense to refer to "knowledge" or "Word," and in a concrete sense to refer to a circumscribed body of texts.

In the Ṛg-Veda Saṃhitā we find numerous reflections by the *ṛṣis* themselves on the nature and origin of the Vedic hymns.[1] However, the term "Veda" used in a substantive sense occurs rarely, where it generally refers to "knowledge." Although we find isolated references throughout the Ṛg-Veda to the *ṛcs* (verses), *yajuses* (sacrificial formulae), and *sāmans* (chants), the most important reference for our purposes is Ṛg-Veda X.90.9, in which the three terms appear together as a triad, implying an emerging conception of the "threefold Veda" that was to become central in later Vedic texts.[2]

The triad *ṛcs*, *yajuses*, and *sāmans* commonly occurs in Vedic texts from the Atharva-Veda Saṃhitā onward, where it is sometimes juxtaposed with the term "Veda" or "Vedas."[3] The terms "Ṛg-Veda," "Yajur-Veda," and "Sāma-Veda" first appear in the Brāhmaṇas and thereafter are frequently used in the Āraṇyakas and Upaniṣads.[4] One of the most common designations for the Vedas in these texts is *trayī vidyā*, "threefold knowledge."[5] The expression *traya veda*, "threefold Veda," appears less frequently.[6] This prevalent emphasis in the Vedic texts on the "threefold knowledge" of the Ṛg-Veda, Yajur-Veda, and Sāma-Veda suggests that it took some time before the Atharva-Veda was accorded an equivalent status as the fourth Veda. The oldest name of the Atharva-Veda is *atharvāṅgirases*,[7] which occurs in the Atharva-Veda itself.[8] In another early reference from the Taittirīya Saṃhitā the term *aṅgirases* is used by itself to refer to the fourth of the Vedas mentioned after the *ṛcs*, *yajuses*, and *sāmans*.[9] In their discussions of the Veda the Brāhmaṇas, Āraṇyakas, and Upaniṣads tend to focus almost exclusively on the threefold Veda, *ṛcs*, *yajuses*, and *sāmans*, with the *atharvāṅgirases* or *atharvans* rarely mentioned along with the other three *mantra* collections.[10] Even when the formal designations Ṛg-Veda, Yajur-Veda, and Sāma-Veda are used for the other three Vedas, the expressions *atharvāṅgirases* or *atharvans* are used to refer to "the fourth" of the Vedas.[11] The term "Atharva-Veda" does not occur until the Sūtra period.[12]

We thus find that the Vedic texts themselves quite frequently refer to the textual status of the Veda as the *mantras* of the Ṛg-Veda, Yajur-Veda, and Sāma-Veda, with only occasional references to the *mantras* of the Atharva-Veda. However, when we examine the texts more closely we find that this textual definition of Veda as a concrete, finite corpus of *mantras* constitutes only one dimension of the term's meaning. Certain passages in the Vedic texts point to a conception of different levels of the Veda. Thus, while at times the Veda is explicitly identified with the *mantra* collections—"The *ṛcs* are the Veda. . . . The *yajuses* are the Veda. . . . The *atharvans* are the Veda. . . . The *sāmans* are the Veda."[13]—at other times the "Veda" (singular) is distinguished from the "Vedas" (plural). For example, the Aitareya and Śāṅkhāyana Āraṇyakas speak of the "person of the Veda" (*veda-puruṣa*) as distinct from the "Vedas": "That which we have called the person of the Veda is that by which one knows the Vedas, Ṛg-Veda, Yajur-Veda, and Sāma-Veda."[14] Moreover, in a passage in the Chāndogya Upaniṣad the *ṛcs*, *yajuses*, and *sāmans* are clearly distinguished from the Ṛg-Veda, Yajur-Veda, and Sāma-Veda, respectively. The passage, in its discussion of the sun as the honey extracted from the four Vedas, describes the *ṛcs*, *yajuses*, and *sāmans* as the bees that brood upon the flowers of the Ṛg-Veda, Yajur-Veda, and Sāma-Veda, respectively, in order to extract their essences.[15] Although the passage does not elaborate on what is meant by this distinction, it nevertheless appears that a clear differentiation is intended, particularly since the flower that the *atharvāṅgirases* brood upon as bees is the Itihāsa-Purāṇa, an entirely different set of texts.[16]

Passages such as those cited above remind us of the need to avoid the tendency to collapse the distinctions between various terms—for example, Veda, Vedas, *ṛcs*, Ṛg-Veda—into a single monolithic definition of Veda as a circumscribed body of texts. As we shall see in the following analysis, the textual dimension of Veda is represented in the Vedic texts themselves as only one aspect of the reality of Veda. The Vedic texts also emphasize the Veda's primordial status as that eternal, infinite Word or knowledge which is inherent in the fabric of reality and which is expressed as the impulses of divine speech from which the phenomenal creation is manifested.

Saṃhitās

During the Saṃhitā period (ca. 1500–800 B.C.E.) Aryan religious life became increasingly dominated by the fire sacrifice (*yajña*). In the period of the Ṛg-Veda Saṃhitā (ca. 1500–1200 B.C.E.), the oldest and most important text of Vedic literature, the sacrificial tradition had already attained a fairly high level of development. A simplified form of the fire sacrifice and a hereditary priesthood, with an incipient division of functions among various types of priests, are evident even in this early period.[17] The Ṛg-Veda itself contains a large number of hymns that were clearly intended to serve as sacrificial litanies. Even those hymns that arose independently of the sacrificial ritual later came to be used in liturgical contexts. However, it is not until the period of the liturgical Saṃhitās, the Sāma-Veda and Yajur-Veda Saṃhitās (ca. 900 B.C.E.), that we find the developed system of *śrauta* sacrifices that utilizes three fires—*gārhapatya*, *āhavanīya*, and *dakṣiṇa*—and four principal categories of priests—*hotṛ*, *udgātṛ*, *adhvaryu*, and *brahman*.

Along with the division of ritual functions among the four classes of priest came a demarcation of the respective roles of the different types of *mantras* in the sacrificial ritual: the *hotṛ* priest was assigned the responsibility of reciting the *ṛc*s of the Ṛg-Veda Saṃhitā, which consist primarily of praises of and invocations to the gods; the *udgātṛ* priest was responsible for chanting the *sāman*s of the Sāma-Veda Saṃhitā, which consist almost entirely of verses from the Ṛg-Veda set to fixed melodies; the *adhvaryu* priest was allotted the role of performing the sacrificial actions while muttering the *yajus*es of the Yajur-Veda Saṃhitās, which comprise sacrificial formulae that accompany the ritual manipulations; and the *brahman* priest was entrusted with the supervision of the entire sacrificial ritual in order to counteract by means of expiatory formulas (*prāyaścittas*) any mistakes made by the other priests. The *brahman* priest was originally associated not with any particular Veda but rather with the totality of the threefold Veda, *trayī vidyā*.[18] When the Atharva-Veda Saṃhitā (ca. 1100–800 B.C.E.), which contains popular religious elements in the form of incantations and imprecations as well as a number of speculative hymns, was eventually granted the status of the fourth Veda alongside the *trayī vidyā*, it also assumed a role in the sacrificial rituals as the Veda of the *brahman* priest.

The preeminent position granted to the sacrifice in the Vedic conception of reality is already evident in the Ṛg-Veda Saṃhitā, which represents the sacrifice as an inherent part of the cosmic order. *Ṛta*, the cosmic ordering principle, is described as governing not only the course of nature and the moral conduct of human beings but also the correct performance of the sacrifice (*yajña*). Moreover, the sacrifice is represented in several Ṛg-Vedic hymns as the means through which the creation is brought forth in the beginning. By the end of the Saṃhitā period the sacrifice had been elevated to the status of a separate order of reality (*adhiyajña*), which was correlated with the other orders of reality—the human order (*adhyātma*), natural order (*adhibhūta*), and divine order (*adhidaiva*)—and which was viewed as essential to the harmonious functioning of all levels of the cosmos.

The Vedic *mantras*, as the sound offerings of the sacrifice, are granted a special status in the Saṃhitās as a constitutive part of the cosmic order that emerges from the body of the creator principle in the beginning of creation. The *mantras* are celebrated as manifestations of the power of *brahman*, the Word, which is elevated in the Atharva-Veda Saṃhitā to the status of a cosmic principle. As expressions of the Word the *mantras* are also linked to Vāc, speech, which is hypostatized in the Ṛg-Veda as a feminine principle that finds its most potent expression on the human plane in the speech of the *ṛṣis*, whose hymns are recited in the sacrificial rituals.

The conception of Veda that is found in the Ṛg-Veda Saṃhitā is dynamic and reflexive, for the hymns are still in the process of emerging as the *ṛṣis*, the "seers" of the hymns, speak. The Ṛg-Vedic hymns do not refer to the Saṃhitās, in the sense of fixed collections, but rather to the *mantras* themselves, and in particular the *ṛcs*. The hymns are self-referential in that they are concerned with describing the mechanisms through which the *ṛṣis* received their divinely inspired cognitions and gave them vocalized expression in recited hymns.[19] Although the hymns make occasional reference to the *yajus*es (sacrificial formulae) and *sāman*s (chants), the triad *ṛcs*, *yajus*es, and *sāman*s only appears once in the Ṛg-Veda.[20] The notion of the threefold Veda as an objectified body of *mantra* collections occurs more frequently from the Atharva-Veda Saṃhitā onward, with occasional references to the *atharvāṅgiras*es.

Veda, the Creator, and Creation Brahmanical conceptions of the status and role of the Veda in creation, as reflected in the formulations of both Vedic and post-Vedic texts, have their foundation in the cosmogonic and cosmological speculations of the Ṛg-Veda. One of the preoccupations of the *ṛṣis*, as represented in the hymns, is to discern with their "mind's eye" the subtle realms of the gods and to fathom the mysteries of creation.[21] The speculations of the *ṛṣis* are not presented in the form of a single continuous creation narrative but rather appear in a number of discrete hymns, attributed to different *ṛṣis*, that each treat a certain piece of the cosmogonic puzzle without attempting to explain how the different pieces fit together.[22] In order to understand the Ṛg-Vedic conception of the role of the Veda in creation we first need to examine briefly the range of cosmogonic speculations found in the hymns, and in particular in the creation hymns of the tenth Maṇḍala (book), which is generally held to be the latest portion of the Ṛg-Veda.

The creation hymns of the Ṛg-Veda present in seminal form certain symbolic structures and patterns that are further developed in the cosmogonies of the Brāhmaṇas, Āraṇyakas, and Upaniṣads from different perspectives, becoming interwoven into a single creation narrative in the Manu-Smṛti and finally gaining their most detailed elaboration in epic and Purāṇic accounts. Among these symbolic structures we can distinguish a number of creative principles or agents and a variety of means through which the universe is brought forth.

Creative Principles

- the unmanifest Absolute, which is the ultimate source of creation (That One [Tad Ekam]—ṚV X.129; the Unborn [Aja]—ṚV X.82)
- the personal creator god, who is the fashioner of the three worlds—earth, midregions, and heaven (Prajāpati—ṚV X.121; Viśvakarman—ṚV X.81 and X.82)
- the waters (*ap, ambhas, salila*), which represent the feminine principle that serves as the primordial matrix of creation (ṚV X.129; X.121; X.82) and which are at times associated with Vāc, the goddess of speech (ṚV X.125; X.71)
- the cosmic embryo or egg (*garbha*), which contains the totality of creation in yet undifferentiated form (ṚV X.121; X.82)
- Puruṣa, the cosmic Man out of whose body the different parts of the universe are formed (ṚV X.90; X.130)

Creative Means

- desire (ṚV X.129; X.81)
- *tapas*[23] (ṚV X.129; X.190)
- procreation
- sacrifice (*yajña*) (ṚV X.90; X.81; X.82; X.130)
- speech (*vāc*) (ṚV X.125; X.71), which is at times linked to the Vedic *mantra*s

In order to understand the structure of relations among these various constituent elements of creation, we must distinguish first of all between different stages in the process of creation. F. B. J. Kuiper, in his attempt to reconstruct the Vedic cosmogonic myth, has suggested that this myth comprises two different stages. (1) In the first stage the primordial world was "an undivided unity, a *rudis indigestaque moles*," which consisted of the primordial waters and the undifferentiated totality of the cosmos—frequently represented by the image of the cosmic egg—floating on the surface of the waters. (2) In the second stage heaven and earth were separated out of the originally undifferentiated unity, either through an autonomous process of division or through the demiurgic act of a god.[24] Although the details of Kuiper's thesis need not concern us here, my own research confirms that this basic two-stage pattern of creation is fundamental to both Vedic and post-Vedic cosmogonies. These two stages are most clearly evident in the Brāhmaṇas and later texts, but the seeds of this two-phase paradigm can already be discerned as early as the Ṛg-Veda.

The account in Ṛg-Veda X.129, the Nāsadīya hymn, corresponds to the first stage, in that it describes the mechanisms of emergence from a state of unmanifest, undifferentiated unity in which Tad Ekam, "That One," alone exists, and along with it the primordial waters, stretching endlessly in the darkness. The hymn describes the very beginnings of the process through which That One, that single, primordial unity, begins to reverberate within itself and gives rise to duality. However, the hymn does not elaborate on how heaven and earth manifest from the unmanifest.

The creation of heaven and earth represents a later stage in the cosmogonic process, the second in our two-stage pattern. This second stage, in which the primordial unity differentiates in order to give rise to the three worlds—earth (*pṛthivī, bhūmi*), midregions (*antarikṣa*), and heaven (*div*)—and all beings, is described in other hymns of the Ṛg-Veda as the demiurgic act of a personal creator god. In Ṛg-Veda X.121 the creator and supporter of heaven and earth and the vivifier and lord of all beings is called Prajāpati ("lord of created beings") and Hiraṇyagarbha ("golden embryo or egg"), while in Ṛg-Veda X.81 and X.82 he is called Viśvakarman ("maker of all"). Ṛg-Veda X.81 is of particular significance in that it portrays the creator Viśvakarman as the lord of speech (*vācas-pati*) and the primordial *ṛṣi* and *hotṛ* priest who takes his place upon the seat of sacrifice and offers up (root *yaj*) heaven and earth in sacrifice.[25] Ṛg-Veda X.82 similarly alludes to the primeval sacrifice and points to the role of the *ṛṣis*, the seers of the Vedic *mantras*, in the cosmogonic process.[26]

Ṛg-Veda X.90, the famous Puruṣa-Sūkta, in contrast to such conceptions of a personal creator god, presents a more monistic perspective, in which the one, all-pervading principle that is the source and basis of the cosmos is Puruṣa, the cosmic Man, the unified ground of all existence. Like Ṛg-Veda X.81 and X.82, the Puruṣa-Sūkta describes the primordial sacrifice (*yajña*) as the means through which creation is brought forth, although in this hymn Puruṣa assumes the role not of the sacrificer but of the sacrificial victim. In verses 1–5 Puruṣa is described as both immanent and transcendent. Possessing a thousand heads, a thousand eyes, and a thousand feet, Puruṣa pervades (root *vṛ*) the earth on every side, and yet he extends beyond (root *sthā* + *ati*) it a measure of ten fingers. One quarter of him is manifested here on earth as all beings, while the other three quarters are the immortal (*amṛta*) in heaven. The differentiation of the totality of Puruṣa is described in verses 6–16 as occurring through a sacrifice in which the different parts of his cosmic body are offered up to form the different aspects of the universe. Although the Vedic *mantra*s are depicted as one of the original products of the primeval sacrifice, they are not explicitly allotted a role in the process of creation. However, as in Ṛg-Veda X.82, the *ṛṣis* are portrayed as assuming a cosmogonic role as those who, along with the gods and Sādhyas, perform the archetypal sacrifice through which the universe is brought forth.[27]

Verses 6–10 of the Puruṣa-Sūkta establish a reciprocal relationship between the sacrificial and natural orders. On the one hand, certain elements of the natural order—in particular, the seasons—are used as ritual materials in the primeval sacrifice. On the other hand, the sacrifice gives rise to different aspects of the natural order—in particular, various types of animals, including horses, cattle, goats, and sheep, which are the primary offerings used in animal sacrifices. This reciprocity is also reflected within the elements of the sacrifice itself. The *ṛc*s, *sāman*s, and *yajus*es, as well as the meters (*chandas*es) in which the Vedic *mantra*s are composed, are described as emerging from the primordial sacrifice of Puruṣa, and they in turn provide the sound offerings that are essential to the sacrificial ritual.

> From that sacrifice (*yajña*), in which all was offered, the *ṛc*s and *sāman*s were born; the meters (*chandas*es) were born from it; from it the *yajus* was born.[28]

Verses 11–14 go on to establish a series of correlations between the different parts of the cosmic body of Puruṣa and the different aspects of the human, natural, and divine orders.

> When they divided Puruṣa, into how many parts did they apportion him? What was his mouth? What were his arms? What were his thighs and feet declared to be?
>
> His mouth became the brahmin; [from] his arms the *kṣatriya* was made; his thighs became the *vaiśya*; from his feet the *śūdra* was born.
>
> The moon was born from his mind; from his eye Sūrya, the sun, was born; from his mouth came Indra and Agni, fire; from his breath Vāyu, wind, was born.
>
> From his navel arose the midregions; from his head the heaven originated; from his feet came the earth; from his ear the cardinal directions. Thus they fashioned the worlds.

The hymn thus establishes connections among the various orders of reality, in which the sacrificial order, by means of which the cosmic body of Puruṣa is divided, is represented as giving rise to different components of the human, natural, and divine orders. The human order in this schema includes not only the different parts of the human body, which is a microcosmic replica of the cosmic body of Puruṣa, but also the social order with its division into four classes (*varṇas*)—brahmins (priests), *kṣatriyas* (royalty and warriors), *vaiśyas* (merchants, agriculturalists, and artisans), and *śūdras* (servants and manual laborers). The natural order as described in the hymn encompasses the three worlds, elements such as fire, wind, and sun, and various types of animals. The divine order includes the presiding deities of these elements, Agni, Vāyu, and Sūrya, along with other gods such as Indra. In later Vedic texts, as we shall see, these various components are brought together in a more systematic tripartite classificatory schema, in which the homologies in verse 13 between the faculties of speech (mouth), breath, and eye and the elements fire, wind, and sun, together with their presiding deities, are extended to include direct correlations with the three Vedas, Ṛg, Yajur, and Sāma; the three worlds, earth, midregions, and heaven; and the three higher *varṇas*, brahmins, *kṣatriyas*, and *vaiśyas*.[29]

Ṛg-Veda X.130 provides an alternative image of the primeval sacrifice, in which Puruṣa is portrayed not as the sacrificial victim but rather as one of the primary performers who "weaves" the sacrifice along with the gods. The hymn also grants the Vedic *mantras* a significant role in the creative process. The gods, as the weavers, are each associated with a particular Vedic meter. Moreover, the gods are said to use the *sāmans* as shuttles that weave back and forth in order to produce the concrete fabric of creation from the original outstretched threads.[30]

The cosmogonic speculations of the Atharva-Veda and later Saṃhitās build and elaborate upon Ṛg-Vedic conceptions of the cosmic origin and status of the Veda. Prajāpati is singled out as the paramount creator god in the Atharva-Veda Saṃhitā, Vājasaneyi Saṃhitā (White Yajur-Veda), and Taittirīya Saṃhitā (Black Yajur-Veda), and thus the primordial Veda becomes associated in particular with Prajāpati. In the Taittirīya Saṃhitā, Prajāpati—who assumes a role tantamount to that of Puruṣa in the Puruṣa-Sūkta—is identified with the sacrifice[31] and is celebrated as its creator.[32] He is depicted as the primordial *ṛṣi* who "sees" (root *dṛś*) certain *ṛcs*, ritual formulae, meters, and sacrificial rites[33] and then, assuming the role of the first priest, performs the various sacrifices in order to bring forth beings.[34]

Taittirīya Saṃhitā VII.1.1.4–6 describes Prajāpati as bringing forth from different parts of his body certain aspects of the Vedas that are used in the sacrificial ritual: lauds (*stomas*), chants (*sāmans*), and Vedic meters. The *stomas*, *sāmans*, and meters are further correlated with specific gods, social classes, and animals that emerge from the corresponding parts of Prajāpati's body.

> Prajāpati desired, "May I reproduce." From his mouth he measured out the *trivṛt* (nine-versed) *stoma.* Subsequently the deity Agni was brought forth, the *gāyatrī* meter, the *rathantara sāman,* among human beings the brahmin, among animals the goat. Therefore they are foremost, for they were brought forth from the mouth. From his chest and arms he measured out the *pañcadaśa* (fifteen-versed) *stoma.* Subsequently the deity Indra was brought forth, the *triṣṭubh* meter, the *bṛhat sāman,* among human beings the *kṣatriya,* among animals the sheep. Therefore they are strong, for they were brought forth from strength. From his middle he measured out the *saptadaśa* (seventeen-versed) *stoma.* Subsequently the deities the Viśvadevas were brought forth, the *jagatī* meter, the *vairūpa sāman,* among human beings the *vaiśya,* among animals the cows. Therefore they are to be eaten, for they were brought forth from the receptacle of food. Therefore they are more abundant than the others, for they were brought forth after the

> most abundant of the deities. From his feet he measured out the *ekaviṃśa* (twenty-one-versed) *stoma*. Subsequently the *anuṣṭubh* meter was brought forth, the *vairāja sāman*, among human beings the *śūdra*, among animals the horse. Therefore these two, the horse and the *śūdra*, are dependent on others. Therefore the *śūdra* is not fit for the sacrifice, for he was not brought forth after any deities. Therefore they support themselves by their feet, for they were brought forth from the feet.[35]

In this passage a number of the components that are depicted in the Puruṣa-Sūkta as emerging from the sacrifice of Puruṣa—*sāmans*, Vedic meters, gods, *varṇas*, and animals—are incorporated in a fourfold taxonomy that directly correlates these various components and ranks them hierarchically. Two aspects of these correspondences are of particular significance. First, the connections established in this passage between certain *stomas*, meters, and *sāmans* are fairly consistently replicated in later Vedic and post-Vedic texts, becoming further correlated in the Purāṇas with the four Vedas—*ṛcs*, *yajuses*, *sāmans*, and *atharvans*—that emerge from the four mouths of the creator Brahmā.[36] Second, this fourfold set of correspondences is at times incorporated in later Vedic texts in a threefold taxonomy that eliminates the bottom stratum in the hierarchy and focuses on the correlations between certain triads: the meters *gāyatrī*, *triṣṭubh*, and *jagatī*; the *varṇas* brahmin, *kṣatriya*, and *vaiśya*; and the gods Agni, Indra, and Viśvadevas. This taxonomy, which homologizes the Vedic meters and *varṇas*, together with the alternative classificatory schema mentioned earlier, which connects the three Vedas and the *varṇas*, provides a transcendent source of legitimation for the social hierarchy through assimilating it to the primordial Veda.[37]

Veda and Brahman In the Atharva-Veda Saṃhitā the Veda is linked not only to the creator Prajāpati but also to that ultimate reality which is the source and foundation of the creator principle: Brahman. The conception of Brahman as a cosmic principle is not developed in the Ṛg-Veda. However, as we have seen, we do find antecedents of the notion of Brahman in the conception of a unitary ground of existence that is the ultimate source of the cosmos: Tad Ekam in Ṛg-Veda X.129 and Puruṣa in Ṛg-Veda X.90.

In the Ṛg-Veda and later Saṃhitās the term *brahman* itself is used, depending on the context, at times to refer to Veda, in the general sense of "Word," and at other times to refer more specifically to the Vedic *mantras*. The following passage from the Taittirīya Saṃhitā, for example, uses the term *brahman* to refer to that limitless totality of the Word, Veda, of which the Vedic *mantras*—*ṛcs*, *sāmans*, and *yajuses*—are but a limited manifestation.

> The *ṛcs* are limited (*parimita*), the *sāmans* are limited, and the *yajuses* are limited, but of the Word (*brahman*) there is no end.[38]

The term *brahman* is also used in the Saṃhitās to signify the power inherent in the Word or in the Vedic *mantras*. In the Atharva-Veda the meaning of the term is extended to encompass that cosmic power or principle which underlies and gives rise to the universe.[39]

It is in the Atharva-Veda that we first find the notion that the Vedic *mantras* form different parts of the cosmic body of Brahman. The antecedent of this conception is found in the Puruṣa-Sūkta's description of the *mantras* emerging from the sacrifice of the body of Puruṣa, but Puruṣa is not identified with Brahman in this hymn. Atharva-Veda X.7 celebrates Skambha (literally, "support") as Brahman, the all-pervading reality that is the foundation of the entire cosmos. Skambha is depicted as embracing the infinity of space, encompassing within his body all the worlds, natural phenomena, and gods, and also as embracing the infinity of time, incorporating within himself all divisions of time, past, present, and future. Skambha is described as distinct from and superior to the creator Prajāpati, serving as the foundation on which Prajāpati establishes the worlds.[40]

The term *brahman* is used a number of times in the hymn in at least two different senses: first, to refer to the highest Brahman, which is a cosmic principle identified with Skambha, of whom the earth is the basis, the midregions his belly, and the heavens his head;[41] and, second, to refer to the Vedic *mantras*, which as a limited manifestation of the totality of Veda are depicted in one verse as forming only a portion of the cosmic body of Skambha—his mouth.[42] In verse 14 the *ṛcs*, *yajuses*, and *sāmans* are explicitly described as residing within Skambha, while in verse 20 they are depicted, along with the *atharvāṅgirases*, as forming various parts of Skambha's body.

> Declare who, pray, is that Skambha from whom they cut off the *ṛcs*, from whom they scraped off the *yajus*, of whom the *sāmans* are the hairs, the *atharvāṅgirases* the mouth?

In Atharva-Veda IX.6.1–2 the Vedic *mantras* are similarly described as constituting different parts of the body of Brahman, with the *ṛcs* forming the spine, the *sāmans* the hairs, and the *yajuses* the heart.

Veda and Vāc In their identification with *brahman* the Vedic *mantras* are understood as expressions of the Word and therefore as manifestations of Vāc, speech. The conception of Vāc in the Ṛg-Veda Saṃhitā is already quite complex and multidimensional, encompassing both a divine dimension, in its hypostatization as the goddess Vāc, and an earthly dimension, in its diversified expressions in human language.[43] Ṛg-Veda I.164.45 emphasizes that this mundane dimension constitutes only one quarter of the total reality of Vāc.

> Vāc is measured in four quarters. Those *brāhmaṇas* whose thoughts are inspired know them. Three [quarters], hidden in secret, do not issue forth. The fourth [quarter] of Vāc is what human beings speak.[44]

In both her hidden and revealed, divine and earthly, dimensions Vāc is ascribed special creative powers. Ṛg-Veda X.125, a hymn of self-praise by and to the goddess Vāc, celebrates the "Queen" whose abode (*yoni*, literally "womb") is in the waters (*ap*), from which she spreads forth to pervade heaven and earth and all beings.[45] Vāc is described as both immanent, abiding in many places and entering into many forms,[46] and transcendent, extending beyond heaven and earth in her greatness.[47] Although the Vedic *mantras* are not explicitly mentioned, the goddess Vāc is ascribed the role of investing the *ṛṣis* with the power of *brahman*: "Him whom I love I make powerful, a possessor of the power of *brahman*, a *ṛṣi*, a sage."[48]

Ṛg-Veda X.71, the other hymn in the Ṛg-Veda that is devoted entirely to Vāc, links Vāc directly to the speech of the *ṛṣis* that gives vocalized expression to the Vedic *mantras*. Those who follow the "track of Vāc" will find her "entered into the *ṛṣis*," for it is the *ṛṣis* who have located the hidden source of speech. Having "distributed her in many places," the *ṛṣis* celebrate Vāc by giving her manifest expression in their own speech.[49] Vāc reveals her hidden nature to those who love her,[50] and it is the seers of the Vedic *mantras* who are celebrated throughout the Ṛg-Veda as especially beloved of Vāc, upon whom she bestows her creative powers. For it is the *ṛṣis* alone who are said to have directly apprehended the impulses of knowledge emanating forth from the Transcendent as the subtle expressions of speech. The *ṛṣis* then spoke forth on the gross level that which they cognized on the subtle level, and in this way they preserved the Vedic *mantras* through their own speech, initiating an unbroken line of oral transmission through which the Vedas would be passed down to subsequent generations.[51]

Brāhmaṇas

The speculations of the Saṃhitās concerning the origin and cosmological status of the Veda are reinterpreted in the Brāhmaṇas (ca. 900–650 B.C.E.), sacrificial manuals attached to the Saṃhitās, in light of an elaborate discourse of sacrifice. In their discussions of the textual manifestation of the Veda the Brāhmaṇas tend to focus almost exclusively on the three *mantra* collections, *ṛcs*, *yajuses*, and *sāmans*, that are essential to the performance of Vedic sacrifices. Although the Brāhmaṇas were accorded canonical status retroactively as part of the *karma-kāṇḍa*, the section of the Vedas concerned with action (*karman*), the Brāhmaṇas do not deem themselves to be part of the Veda. Nevertheless, they do establish the mechanisms whereby the purview of Veda could be subsequently expanded by emphasizing that, while on one level the Veda is delimited to a bounded corpus of texts—the Vedic *mantras*—on another level its domain is unlimited, for it constitutes the unbounded, primordial Word.

The Brāhmaṇas contain detailed prescriptions for the *śrauta* sacrifices, providing the rules (*vidhis*) for the performance of each ceremony as well as expositions (*arthavāda*) of the purpose and meaning of the sacrificial acts and *mantras*.[52] These sacrificial manuals are concerned with the correct performance of Vedic rituals in order to accomplish a twofold purpose: on an individual level, to attain for the patron of the sacrifice (*yajamāna*) certain worldly ends in this life and to construct for him a divine self (*daivātman*) in order to convey him to the world of heaven (*svarga loka*); and on a cosmic level, to regenerate and maintain the cosmic order. While the sacrificial perspective and cosmological orientation of the Brāhmaṇas are fairly consistently articulated throughout the various texts, certain differences are also evident in that each Brāhmaṇa emphasizes those aspects of the sacrificial ritual that are associated with the corresponding Saṃhitā and its priest. Thus, the Brāhmaṇas of the Ṛg-Veda, the Aitareya Brāhmaṇa and the Kauṣītaki Brāhmaṇa, focus primarily on the duties of the *hotṛ* priest; the Brāhmaṇas of the Yajur-Veda, the Taittirīya Brāhmaṇa of the Black Yajur-Veda and the Śatapatha Brāhmaṇa of the White Yajur-Veda, are concerned with the duties of the *adhvaryu* priest; and the Brāhmaṇas of the Sāma-Veda, the Pañcaviṃśa or Tāṇḍya Brāhmaṇa, its supplement the Ṣaḍviṃśa Brāhmaṇa, and the Jaiminīya Brāhmaṇa, focus on the duties of the *udgātṛ* priest.[53]

The generative epistemological framework for the cosmogonic and cosmological speculations of the Brāhmaṇas is thus the discourse of sacrifice. The sacrificial discourse of the Brāhmaṇas is founded upon the speculations of the Puruṣa-Sūkta and in this context evidences three principal concerns: to establish the identity of Puruṣa with Prajāpati, who, as in the later Saṃhitās, is celebrated as the supreme god and creator in the Brāhmaṇas; to establish the cosmic import of the sacrifice as the counterpart of the Puruṣa Prajāpati; and to delineate the role of the sacrificial order in regenerating the cosmic order through enlivening the connections (*bandhus*) between the human, natural, and divine orders. The Veda, both as a cosmological principle embedded in the cosmic order and as the recited texts that form an integral part of the sacrificial order, is granted a pivotal role in this sacrificial discourse.

In the Brāhmaṇas Prajāpati is explicitly identified with Puruṣa[54] and is celebrated as the primary participant in the primeval sacrifice from which the different parts of the universe are formed. Like Puruṣa in the Puruṣa-Sūkta, Prajāpati is described in the Brāhmaṇas as both immanent and transcendent, pervading the entire universe[55] and yet at the same time extending beyond it.[56] He encompasses both the human and the divine realms[57] and is both mortal (*martya*) and immortal (*amṛta*),[58] expressed (*nirukta*) and unexpressed (*anirukta*),[59] limited (*parimita*) and unlimited (*aparimita*).[60] In his role as the unitary source and foundation of creation Prajāpati is at times identified in the Brāhmaṇas with Brahman.[61]

Prajāpati is primarily portrayed in the Brāhmaṇas in his role as creator, and as such he is identified not only with Puruṣa but also with the other creative principles celebrated in the creation hymns of the Ṛg-Veda, such as Viśvakarman[62] and Hiraṇyagarbha.[63] In the Brāhmaṇas the various characteristics and functions ascribed to these creative principles are assumed by Prajāpati, who provides the integrating frame for the creation narrative into which are incorporated the various elements found in disjunctive form in Ṛg-Vedic hymns. Nearly all of the accounts of creation in the Brāhmaṇas begin with the statement, "In the beginning Prajāpati alone was here."[64] In the Brāhmaṇas it is Prajāpati who is the creator, ruler, and preserver of heaven and earth; the father of the gods, demons, and human beings; and the lord of all creatures. It is Prajāpati who desires to bring forth creation and who performs *tapas* in order to accomplish his desire. It is Prajāpati who implants his seed in the waters and who both generates and is born from the cosmic egg. It is Prajāpati who harnesses the power of Vāc and unites with her as his consort.[65]

Prajāpati is above all celebrated in the Brāhmaṇas, as in the Taittirīya Saṃhitā, as the creator of the sacrifice,[66] the first performer of the sacrifice,[67] and the sacrifice itself.[68] The Śatapatha Brāhmaṇa declares:

> Having given his self (*ātman*) to the gods, he [Prajāpati] then brought forth that counterpart (*pratimā*) of himself which is the sacrifice (*yajña*). Therefore they say, "The sacrifice is Prajāpati," for he brought it forth as a counterpart of himself.[69]

As Brian K. Smith has emphasized, the initial generative act of Prajāpati, as described in the creation accounts of the Brāhmaṇas, generally results in a chaotic creation rather than an ordered cosmos. It is only by creating the counterpart of himself, the sacrifice, that Prajāpati obtained the "instrument of cosmic healing and construction" that was necessary in order to structure an ordered cosmos as well as to revitalize his own disintegrated being.[70] The sacrifice is at times described not only as the instrument of reparation but also as the instrument of creation by means of which Prajāpati sets in motion the entire universe[71] and brings forth all beings.[72] Thus, every time human beings—and the brahmin priests in particular—reenact the primeval sacrifice on earth, they participate in the creative process of constructing an orderly cosmos.

> Prajāpati indeed is that sacrifice (*yajña*) which is being performed here and from which these beings were produced, and in the same manner are they produced thereafter even to the present day.[73]

The creative and renovative power of the sacrificial order (*adhiyajña*) is to a large extent attributed to its ability to activate the connections (*bandhus*) among the other orders of reality: the human order (*adhyātma*), the natural order (*adhibhūta*), and the divine order (*adhidaiva*). Smith notes that this principle of "hierarchical resemblance" among the various orders and levels of reality, which he considers to be "the central principle of Vedism,"[74] encompasses two types of connections.

> Vedic connections are of two sorts: what we might call vertical and horizontal correspondences. The former connects an immanent form and its transcendent correlative. . . . This type of connection operates between the elements of the same species located on different and hierarchically ranked cosmological levels. Horizontal connections link resembling components of two different species located within the same cosmological plane which share a similar hierarchical position within their respective classes.[75]

Smith goes on to discuss how the notion of the sacrifice as a counterpart of Prajāpati exemplifies the vertical type of connection.

> The construction of a sacrifice, an ideally continuous and complete entity made out of the joining of discrete parts (rites, performers, implements, offerings, etc.), is a reconstruction of the universe itself in the sense that one supposedly reproduces—in a different form—the other. They are not identical but resembling forms of unity, sharing the same essence but manifesting themselves differently. The sacrifice is composed of the counterparts to the cosmic prototypes (each element of the ritual being vertically connected to transcendent correlatives), and the sacrifice as a whole is the counterpart to the prototype that is Prajāpati, the universe. The sacrifice operates with "images," whereas Prajāpati's body or self is comprised of the "originals," but both participate in the same ontological essence.[76]

The Veda is represented in the Brāhmaṇas as participating in the "ontological essence" of both the prototype, Prajāpati, and the counterpart, the sacrifice. The Vedic *mantras* form an integral part of the sacrificial rituals performed by human beings, and their recitation is considered essential to the world-ordering and maintaining function of these rituals.[77] However, the mundane texts recited and studied by human beings on earth are viewed as constituting only a limited manifestation of that infinite (*ananta*) knowledge which is Veda.[78] Just as the sacrifice is held to be the gross counterpart of the cosmic prototype, Prajāpati, so the sound offerings of the sacrifice, the Vedic *mantras*, are represented as the gross manifestations of the cosmic reality of Veda, which is itself constitutive of Prajāpati. The Veda as a cosmic reality is correlated with the creator Prajāpati as well as with his consort Vāc, speech, and is represented as having both unlimited and limited, unexpressed and expressed dimensions even on the cosmic plane. The unlimited Veda is described as becoming delimited through the speech-acts of the creator. As the circumscribed expressions of Prajāpati's speech the Vedic *mantras* are allotted a cosmogonic role as the primordial utterances through which the creator brings forth the phenomenal creation and are represented as the subtle blueprint containing the sound correlatives of the concrete realm of forms.

Veda, Prajāpati, and Vāc The Veda as *brahman*, the Word,[79] is described in the Brāhmaṇas as participating in the essence of both Prajāpati and his consort Vāc. The Veda is at times identified with Prajāpati: "In the beginning Prajāpati was the Veda."[80] The Veda is represented as constitutive of Prajāpati's being, with the Vedic *mantras*, meters, and various components of the sacrifice forming different parts of his body or self (*ātman*).[81] At the same time the Veda is said to be derived from Prajāpati (*Prājāpatyo vedaḥ*),[82] for it is Prajāpati who brings forth the Veda in the beginning of creation.[83] These two notions—the Veda as constitutive of Prajāpati and the Veda as derived from Prajāpati—are brought together in the Jaiminīya Brāhmaṇa, which, in a variant of Taittirīya Saṃhitā VII.1.1.4–6, cited earlier, describes Prajāpati as bringing forth certain *stomas*, *sāmans*, and meters from various parts of his body.[84] The Veda is more specifically represented as the expression of Prajāpati's speech.[85]

In its role as divine speech the Veda becomes associated with Prajāpati's consort Vāc. Vāc as *brahman*[86] is correlated both with the unexpressed, undifferentiated Word, Veda, and with its expressed, differentiated manifestations as the Vedic *mantras*. The *ṛcs*, *yajuses*, and *sāmans* are said to be the threefold form of Vāc.[87] From Vāc, who is designated as the "Mother of the Vedas,"[88] the Vedic *mantras* flow out in the beginning of creation as her "thousandfold progeny."[89] The Taittirīya Brāhmaṇa proclaims:

> Vāc is the imperishable one (*akṣara*), the first-born of the cosmic order (*ṛta*), the Mother of the Vedas (*vedānām mātā*), the navel of immortality (*amṛta*).[90]

As the progeny of Vāc the Vedas partake of their Mother's infinite, immortal nature and are themselves said to be infinite (*ananta*),[91] immortal (*amṛta*),[92] and imperishable (*akṣita*).[93]

Through correlating the Veda with Prajāpati and Vāc, the Brāhmaṇas are concerned to establish the Veda's primordial status as an inherent part of the two creative principles that are responsible for generating and structuring the cosmic order: the principle of knowledge or mind, and the principle of speech. Prajāpati, as the cosmic intelligence underlying the universe, is the abode of knowledge and is associated in particular with the principle of mind (*manas*),[94] while his consort Vāc represents the principle of speech. Prajāpati is at times identified with the mind,[95] and it is by virtue of his identity with the mind that he is said to know everything.[96] Prajāpati is described as entering into union with Vāc by means of his mind.[97] *Manas* and *vāc* are consistently paired throughout the Brāhmaṇas as male and female consorts, the human faculties of mind and speech constituting "yoke-fellows" (*yuj*s)[98] that represent the microcosmic counterparts of Prajāpati and Vāc, who in their identification with mind and speech are also at times designated as Sarasvat and Sarasvatī.[99] Mind and speech are depicted in the Brāhmaṇas as mutually dependent upon one another. On the one hand, the mind upholds speech, for it is the mind that provides the cognitive content that speech expresses.[100] On the other hand, speech upholds the mind, for it is speech that gives vocalized expression to the cognitive content of the mind.[101] In the Brāhmaṇas the mind is given precedence over speech on both the human and cosmic planes, for while the mind is unexpressed (*anirukta*) and more unlimited (*aparimita*), speech is expressed (*nirukta*) and more limited (*parimita*).[102] On the human plane the mind precedes speech,[103] and on the cosmic plane Prajāpati precedes Vāc. Prajāpati, as the lord of thought (*cit-pati*) and the lord of speech (*vāk-pati* or *vācas-pati*),[104] brings forth Vāc and then unites with her in order to generate the gods and manifest creation.[105]

The Veda is described as emerging in this cosmogonic process as the manifestation of both Prajāpati and Vāc, both mind and speech. Śatapatha Brāhmaṇa VII.5.2.52 describes speech as the instrument by means of which the Veda, the threefold knowledge (*trayī vidyā*), is "dug out" from the silent depths of the ocean of mind and given vocalized expression as the Vedic *mantras*.

> Mind (*manas*) is the ocean (*samudra*). From the mind-ocean with speech (*vāc*) for a shovel the gods dug out (root *khan* + *nir*) the threefold knowledge (*trayī vidyā*). . . . Mind is the ocean, speech is the sharp shovel, the threefold knowledge is the offering (*nirvapaṇa*, literally, "pouring out").

A passage in the Pañcaviṃśa Brāhmaṇa depicts Prajāpati meditating silently (*tūṣṇīm*) in his mind and then using speech as the vehicle to bring forth (root *jan* + *pra*) that which is hidden (*antarhita*) in his mind. That which is hidden in Prajāpati's mind becomes the *bṛhat sāman*, and that which is expressed through his speech becomes the *rathantara sāman*.[106] Elsewhere in the Pañcaviṃśa Brāhmaṇa, as well as in other Brāhmaṇas, the *bṛhat* is identified with the mind and the *rathantara* with speech.[107] The *bṛhat* and *rathantara* are further equated with the *sāman* and *ṛc*, respectively,[108] which are themselves at times identified with mind and speech and portrayed as male and female consorts.[109] The following set of correspondences thus emerges.

Prajāpati	mind	*bṛhat*	*sāman*
Vāc	speech	*rathantara*	*ṛc*

In this schema the *sāman* is correlated with the unexpressed principle of mind, Prajāpati, while the *ṛc* is correlated with the expressed principle of speech, Vāc. However, Vāc is also said to have an unexpressed (*anirukta*) as well as an expressed (*nirukta*) dimension.[110] Moreover, the process through which unexpressed speech becomes expressed as vocalized utterances is itself represented in a number of passages as the means through which the creation manifests. In this context the cosmogonic process is described as a two-stage process in which an unmanifest state of undifferentiated unity gives rise to a manifest state of differentiation through a series of discrete speech-acts.

In my reconstruction of the two-phase process of creation, based on several accounts in the Brāhmaṇas, Prajāpati and Vāc both participate in each stage. The division between the first and second stages of the cosmogonic process is demarcated in certain accounts by the measure of time, generally the period of a year. (1) In the first stage the creator Prajāpati has a desire to reproduce and unites with his consort Vāc. The Vāc with which Prajāpati unites at this stage is the unexpressed, transcendent level of speech that is generally identified with the primordial waters.[111] Prajāpati implants his seed in the waters of Vāc and the seed becomes an egg, which represents the totality of the universe in yet undifferentiated form. (2) In the second stage a child, representing the "second self" of Prajāpati, is born and speaks. This speech, which represents the second phase of Vāc, is the expressed, vocalized speech by means of which the creator introduces distinctions in the originally distinctionless totality of creation represented by the egg, dividing it into the three worlds and manifesting various types of beings.[112] The Veda as the undifferentiated Word, *brahman,* is at times correlated with the first stage, while the differentiated Vedic *mantras* are connected with the second stage.

One of the most important passages that conforms to this basic pattern is Śatapatha Brāhmaṇa X.6.5.4–5, which also forms part of the Bṛhadāraṇyaka Upaniṣad.[113] In the first phase of creation the creator,[114] desiring to have a "second self" (*dvitīya ātman*), enters into union with Vāc by means of his mind (*manas*). The seed becomes the year, which is consistently identified with Prajāpati in the Brāhmaṇas.[115] In the second phase, which is distinguished from the first phase by the period of a year, a child, representing the "second self" of the creator, is born and cries out, producing speech (*vāc*). This speech represents the second phase of Vāc, and it is from this expressed level of speech that the *ṛcs*, *yajus*es, *sāman*s, meters, sacrifices, human beings, and animals are brought forth. It is significant that the Vedic *mantra*s are represented as the first products of the creator's speech, for in other passages, as will be discussed below, the words that the creator speaks in order to bring forth the phenomena of creation are explicitly identified with the words of the Vedas.

Another variation on this basic pattern of creation is described in Śatapatha Brāhmaṇa XI.1.6.1–3. In the first phase of creation the waters alone exist, with no mention of the male creative principle. From the waters a golden egg (*hiraṇmaya āṇḍa*) is produced. In the second phase, which is again separated from the first phase by the period of a year, the Puruṣa Prajāpati is born from the egg, and after another year he speaks (root *hṛ* + *vi-ā*). This expressed level of speech serves as the means by which Prajāpati separates out the earth, midregions, and heaven from the originally undivided totality represented by the egg.

> He uttered (root *hṛ* + *vi-ā*) "*bhūḥ*"—that became this earth; "*bhuvaḥ*"—that became the midregions; "*svaḥ*"—that became yonder heaven.[116]

Although no mention is made of the Vedas in this creation account, the three *vyāhṛtis*, or utterances—*bhūḥ, bhuvaḥ*, and *svaḥ*—are consistently represented throughout the Brāhmaṇas as the essences of the three Vedas—Ṛg-Veda, Yajur-Veda, and Sāma-Veda—as will be discussed further below.

A third variant of this two-stage cosmogonic process appears in Pañcaviṃśa Brāhmaṇa XX.14.2–3 and Jaiminīya Brāhmaṇa II.244 and distinguishes in particular between two different levels of Vāc.

> Prajāpati alone was here. Vāc alone was his own; Vāc was second to him. He reflected, "Let me send forth this Vāc. She will spread forth, pervading everything here." He sent forth Vāc. She spread forth, pervading everything here. She extended upward as a continuous stream of water (*ap*). [Uttering the sound] "*a*," he split off a third of it—that became the earth. . . . [Uttering the sound] "*ka*" he split off a [second] third—that became the midregions. . . . [Uttering the sound] "*ho*" he cast [the last] third upward—that became the heaven.[117]

In the first phase, as described in this passage, Vāc is one and undivided as the all-pervading waters. In the second phase she becomes divided, the one Vāc becoming threefold and expressed as three distinct sounds—*a, ka,* and *ho*—through the speech utterances of Prajāpati. The text goes on to describe how Prajāpati uses different parts of his mouth to articulate these three sounds, which are "manifestly speech" (*pratyakṣam vāc*).[118] As in Śatapatha Brāhmaṇa XI.1.6.1–3, discussed above, it is by means of three primordial utterances that Prajāpati brings forth the three worlds. The Pañcaviṃśa Brāhmaṇa account concludes: "Prajāpati divided this Vāc, which was one syllable (*ekākṣara*), into three parts. These became the worlds."[119]

Another variant of the two-phase process of creation is given in Śatapatha Brāhmaṇa VI.1.1.8–10, which, like the Pañcaviṃśa Brāhmaṇa and Jaiminīya Brāhmaṇa accounts, distinguishes between two levels of Vāc—as the undifferentiated waters and as the differentiated expressions of vocalized speech. This passage is of particular significance in that it describes the Veda emerging as part of this process in two stages of manifestation.

> This Puruṣa Prajāpati desired, "May I become many, may I reproduce." He exerted himself; he practiced *tapas*. Having exerted himself and practiced *tapas*, he brought forth first of all *brahman*, the threefold knowledge (*trayī vidyā*). It became a foundation (*pratiṣṭhā*) for him. Therefore they say, "*brahman* is the foundation of everything here." Therefore, having studied [the Veda] one is established on a foundation, for this *brahman* is his foundation. Resting on this foundation, he [Prajāpati] practiced *tapas*. He brought forth the waters out of Vāc, [who was] the world. Vāc alone was his; she was sent forth. She pervaded everything here, and because she pervaded (root *āp*) whatever was here, therefore [she is called] water (*ap*); because she covered (root *vṛ*), therefore [she is called] water (*vār*). He desired, "May I reproduce from these waters." He entered the waters together with this threefold knowledge. Thence arose an egg (*āṇḍa*). He came into contact (root *mṛś* + *abhi*) with it. "May it exist, may it exist, may it multiply," thus he spoke (root *brū*). Thence was first brought forth *brahman*, the threefold knowledge. Therefore they say, "*brahman* is the first-born of this all." For even before that Puruṣa, *brahman* was brought forth: it was brought forth as his mouth.

This passage points to two distinct stages of creation in which the Veda, along with Prajāpati and Vāc, participates. In the first stage the Veda as *brahman*, the Word, is brought forth to serve as the foundation not only of the entire creation but of the creator himself. After bringing forth the waters from his consort Vāc, Prajāpati together with the threefold Veda enters the waters—an apparent reference to the process of procreation—from which an egg (*āṇḍa*) is produced. In the second stage, having come into contact with the egg,[120] Prajāpati then speaks (root *brū*) three times—once again three primordial utterances are emphasized—and brings forth the second manifestation of the threefold Veda, which manifests as his mouth.[121]

The first stage in this two-phase process appears to be an unmanifest phase in which the process of differentiation has not yet begun. The Vāc with which Prajāpati unites in this stage is the primordial waters that represent the unexpressed, transcendent level of speech, and the Veda upon which Prajāpati rests as his foundation constitutes the totality of the Word, *brahman*, which although threefold has apparently not yet differentiated into three distinct Vedas. It is only in the second stage of creation that Vāc becomes expressed as vocalized speech, and corresponding to this more expressed level of speech is a more expressed level of Veda—the threefold Vedic *mantras*, which as the mouth of the creator are intimately associated with his speech. We thus find two levels of Veda corresponding to the two stages of creation: in the first stage the Veda is *brahman*, the Word, which serves as the foundation of the creator and of his creation; while in the second stage the Veda differentiates into the three Vedas, which are connected with the creator's speech.

This passage recalls a number of features that are also found in Atharva-Veda X.7, discussed earlier.[122] We saw that, on the one hand, Brahman is identified with Skambha as the "support" of the entire universe and the foundation upon which the creator Prajāpati establishes the worlds. On the other hand, *brahman* in its more limited manifestation as the Vedic *mantras* is described as forming only a portion of the cosmic body of Skambha—in particular, his mouth. In the passage from the Śatapatha Brāhmaṇa the first manifestation of *brahman* is not given such a glorified position as the cosmic Brahman of the Atharva-Veda, for this *brahman* is described as being brought forth by the creator himself, and only then does it serve as his foundation.[123] Nevertheless, we can discern a pattern emerging with respect to the twofold manifestation of the Veda that continues to appear in a variety of forms in later Vedic and post-Vedic cosmogonies.

The progression from the first stage of creation to the second stage is thus represented as a move from an unmanifest state of undifferentiated unity to a manifest state of differentiation: the primordial waters of Vāc, which represent the unexpressed level of speech, begin to flow out in streams of expressed, vocalized speech that issue forth as discrete utterances; the one Veda divides into the three Vedas; the undivided totality of creation represented by the egg differentiates into the three worlds. The essential elements of these two stages of creation can be schematized as follows.

	Male Principle	*Female Principle*	*Veda*	*Creation*
STAGE 1	creator Prajāpati →	waters of Vāc	Veda as *brahman*	undivided egg
STAGE 2	"second self" of Prajāpati →	vocalized speech →	three Vedas →	three worlds

Vedas as the Source and Basis of Creation In the cosmogonic paradigms discussed above the mechanism through which the unlimited Word becomes delimited as discrete speech utterances is represented as the means through which distinctions are introduced in the primordial unity. Vocalized speech serves as the differentiating principle by means of which the manifold forms of the phenomenal creation are projected into manifestation.

The original utterances by means of which Prajāpati brings forth the three worlds are generally identified in the Brāhmaṇas with the three *vyāhṛtis*, the essences of the three Vedas.[124] For example, Śatapatha Brāhmaṇa XI.1.6.3, cited earlier, declares,

> He uttered (root *hṛ* + *vi-ā*) "*bhūḥ*"—that became this earth; "*bhuvaḥ*"—that became the midregions; "*svaḥ*"—that became yonder heaven.

Another passage in the Śatapatha Brāhmaṇa describes how Prajāpati's utterance of the three *vyāhṛtis* generates, respectively, not only the three worlds but also the three powers that are the essence of the three higher *varṇas*—*brahman* (→ brahmins), *kṣatra* (→ *kṣatriyas*), and *viś* (→ *vaiśyas*)—as well as the self (*ātman*), human beings, and animals.[125]

In a number of passages in the Brāhmaṇas the words that Prajāpati speaks in order to manifest the forms of creation are explicitly identified with the words of the Vedic *mantras*. The Brāhmaṇas, like the Taittirīya Saṃhitā, portray Prajāpati as the primordial *ṛṣi* who originally "sees" (root *dṛś*) specific *ṛcs* and *sāmans*[126] as well as the sacrificial rituals in which the *mantras* are used.[127] He then performs the various sacrifices, assuming the functions of the different priests: as the *hotṛ* priest he recites the *ṛcs*, as the *udgātṛ* priest he chants the *sāmans*, and as the *adhvaryu* priest he utters the *yajuses*.[128]

The Aitareya Brāhmaṇa, in accordance with its perspective as a Ṛg-Veda Brāhmaṇa, emphasizes Prajāpati's role as the *hotṛ* priest.[129] For example, Aitareya Brāhmaṇa II.33 depicts the *hotṛ* Prajāpati as bringing forth all beings through a series of twelve utterances, which are identified with the twelve lines of the *nivid* ("proclamation"), a prose formulary that is inserted at specified points in the recitation of certain Ṛg-Vedic hymns of praise (*śastras*).[130]

> In the beginning Prajāpati alone was here. He desired, "May I reproduce and become many." He practiced *tapas*.

> He restrained (root *yam*) speech (*vāc*). After a year he uttered (root *hṛ* + *vi-ā*) twelve times. The *nivid* has twelve lines (*padas*). He uttered this, indeed, the *nivid*. Through that all beings were brought forth.

As in several passages discussed earlier, it is only in the second stage of creation, demarcated from the first by the period of a year, that Prajāpati utters vocalized speech in order to manifest diverse phenomena. In the first stage speech is restrained, indicating that although Vāc exists, it is not yet expressed.

The Pañcaviṃśa and Jaiminīya Brāhmaṇas, as the Brāhmaṇas of the Sāma-Veda, give precedence to the role of Prajāpati as the *udgātṛ* priest[131] who in the primeval sacrifice chants *sāmans* and *stotras* in order to bring forth creation. In Pañcaviṃśa Brāhmaṇa VI.9.15, and the corresponding variant in Jaiminīya Brāhmaṇa I.94, Prajāpati is depicted as chanting the words of a *sāman* (Sāma-Veda II.180 = Ṛg-Veda IX.62.1) in order to generate not only the gods, human beings, ancestors, and other beings, but also various aspects of the sacrificial order, including the Soma libations, *stotras* chanted by the *udgātṛ*, and *śastras* recited by the *hotṛ*.

> [Saying] "*ete*" ("these") Prajāpati brought forth the gods; [saying] "*asṛgram*" ("have been poured out") he brought forth human beings; [saying] "*indavaḥ*" ("Soma drops") he brought forth the ancestors; [saying] "*tiraḥ pavitram*" ("through the filter") he brought forth the [Soma] libations; [saying] "*āśavaḥ*" ("swift") he brought forth the *stotra*; [saying] "*viśvāni*" ("all") he brought forth the *śastra*; [saying] "*abhi saubhagā*" ("for the sake of blessings") he brought forth the other beings.[132]

In Pañcaviṃśa Brāhmaṇa VII.5.1 Prajāpati is described as producing beings by means of the *āmahīyava sāman*,[133] while in Jaiminīya Brāhmaṇa I.104 he generates beings through chanting the words of the *bahiṣpavamāna stotra*.[134]

Prajāpati's recitation of the Vedic *mantras*, like the sacrificial rituals in which the *mantras* are used, is portrayed not only as an instrument of creation but also as an instrument of rectification by means of which he establishes an ordered cosmos. For example, in the Pañcaviṃśa and Jaiminīya Brāhmaṇas Prajāpati is portrayed as chanting certain *sāmans* in order to subdue and domesticate his unruly creatures and to provide them with rain and food.[135]

The Vedic *mantras*, as the expressions of the divine speech of Prajāpati, are depicted in the Brāhmaṇas as part of the very fabric of reality and as reflective of the structures of the cosmos. The realm of concrete phenomena is held to have been brought forth through the sound impulses contained in the Vedic *mantras*, and thus the Vedic words are viewed as the subtle correlatives of the forms of creation. In this context the three Vedas—Ṛg-Veda, Yajur-Veda, and Sāma-Veda—are incorporated into the Brāhmaṇas' cosmological system of "hierarchical resemblance" as part of an elaborate set of correspondences that, building upon the speculations of the Puruṣa-Sūkta, correlate the various orders of reality—sacrificial order, human order, natural order, and divine order.

At the basis of this system of correspondences are the three *vyāhṛtis*—*bhūḥ*, *bhuvaḥ*, and *svaḥ*—which constitute the seed syllables of creation corresponding to the three worlds[136] and which are identified, respectively, with the Ṛg-Veda, Yajur-Veda, and Sāma-Veda, representing their essences (*śukras*, *rasas*).[137] With these three primordial utterances, as discussed above, Prajāpati brings forth not only the three worlds but also other aspects of creation.[138] A number of passages in the Brāhmaṇas establish correlations between the three *vyāhṛtis, bhūḥ, bhuvaḥ*, and *svaḥ*; the three Vedas, Ṛg, Yajur, and Sāma; the three worlds, earth, midregions, and heaven; and the three elements fire, wind, and sun, together with their presiding deities, Agni, Vāyu, and Sūrya/Āditya.[139] This system of homologies is at times extended to include certain human faculties, as will be discussed below.

A passage in the Jaiminīya Upaniṣad Brāhmaṇa describes Prajāpati as uttering the three *vyāhṛtis* in order to extract the essences of the three Vedas, from which in turn the three worlds and the three elements along with their deities are produced.

> Prajāpati indeed conquered this [universe] by means of the threefold Veda (*traya veda*). . . . He reflected, "If the other gods sacrifice thus by means of this Veda they will certainly conquer this conquest that is mine. Well then let me extract the essence (*rasa*) of the threefold Veda." [Saying] "*bhūḥ*," he extracted the essence of the Ṛg-Veda. That became this earth. The essence of it that streamed forth became Agni, fire, the essence of the essence. [Saying] "*bhuvaḥ*," he extracted the essence of the Yajur-Veda. That became the midregions. The essence of it that streamed forth became Vāyu, wind, the essence of the essence. [Saying] "*svaḥ*," he

> extracted the essence of the Sāma-Veda. That became yonder heaven. The essence of it that streamed forth became Āditya, the sun, the essence of the essence. Now of one syllable (*akṣara*) alone he was not able to extract the essence: Om, of this alone. That became this Vāc.[140]

While in the above passage the three *vyāhṛtis* are depicted as the primal utterances that represent the essences of the three Vedas from which the three worlds are manifested, in other passages—in a typical Vedic paradox of mutual creation—the three utterances are described as being drawn forth as the essences of the three Vedas after the three worlds have already been produced. The Śatapatha Brāhmaṇa's account is representative.

> In the beginning Prajāpati alone was here. He desired, "May I be, may I reproduce." He exerted himself; he practiced *tapas*. From him who had exerted himself and practiced *tapas* the three worlds—earth, midregions, and heaven—were brought forth. He infused heat into these three worlds. From those heated [worlds] three lights were produced: Agni, fire; he who purifies here [Vāyu, wind]; and Sūrya, the sun. He infused heat into these three lights. From those heated [lights] the three Vedas were produced: the Ṛg-Veda from Agni, the Yajur-Veda from Vāyu, and the Sāma-Veda from Sūrya. He infused heat into these three Vedas. From those heated [Vedas] three essences (*śukras*) were produced: *bhūḥ* from the Ṛg-Veda, *bhuvaḥ* from the Yajur-Veda, and *svaḥ* from the Sāma-Veda.[141]

The Aitareya Brāhmaṇa, in a parallel passage outlining the same progressive series of correspondences, goes on to describe how from the three *vyāhṛtis*—*bhūḥ, bhuvaḥ,* and *svaḥ*—three sounds (*varṇas*) are in turn produced—*a, u,* and *m*—which Prajāpati subsequently combines to form the syllable Om.[142] Om is generally described in the Brāhmaṇas as the most concentrated essence of the Veda, which cannot be further pressed out[143] and which represents truth (*satya*).[144] In post-Vedic cosmogonies, as we shall see, Om is represented as the fundamental, encompassing sound from which the three sounds *a, u, m,* the three *vyāhṛtis*, the three Vedas, and the three worlds progressively unfold.[145]

In the accounts of the Brāhmaṇas, it is only after Prajāpati draws forth the three Vedas and their essences, the *vyāhṛtis*, that he brings forth the sacrifice, establishing a further set of correlations between the three Vedas, the three *vyāhṛtis*, and various aspects of the sacrificial order: the three priests—*hotṛ, adhvaryu,* and *udgātṛ*—and the three sacrificial fires—*gārhapatya, āgnīdhrīya* or *dakṣiṇa,* and *āhavanīya*.[146] The sacrificial order is pivotal to the Brāhmaṇas' classificatory schema, for the regenerative power of the sacrifice is held to be the essential means of enlivening the connections (*bandhus*) between the human, natural, and divine orders. These connections are not thought to be arbitrary but are rather considered to be actual intrinsic relations that exist between the different orders of reality. In the Brāhmaṇas' tripartite taxonomy the three constituent sounds of the syllable Om, the three *vyāhṛtis,* and the three Vedas constitute an essential part of the cosmic order as the expressions of divine speech, which are incorporated in the sacrificial order as particularly potent words of power that are recited as part of the sacrificial rituals. The natural order in this schema is represented by the three worlds—earth, midregions, and heaven—and by the three elements—fire, wind, and sun—while the divine order is represented by the presiding deities of these elements—Agni, Vāyu, and Sūrya/Āditya. A final link is established between the macrocosm and the microcosm by correlating these different parts of the natural and divine orders with certain human faculties. The standard schema generally correlates the *ṛc, yajus,* and *sāman* with speech, breath, and the eye, respectively,[147] although alternative classifications are also presented. While the *ṛc* is consistently identified with speech, the *sāman* is at times identified with the mind, as discussed earlier, as well as with the breath (*prāṇa*). The *yajus* is also sometimes connected with the mind.[148]

Primordial Utterances/ Sacrificial Order			*Natural Order*		*Divine Order*	*Human Order*
a	*bhūḥ*	Ṛg-Veda	earth	fire	Agni	speech
u	*bhuvaḥ*	Yajur-Veda	midregions	wind	Vāyu	breath/mind
m	*svaḥ*	Sāma-Veda	heaven	sun	Sūrya/Āditya	eye/mind/breath

This tripartite taxonomy establishes a series of correlations between, on the one hand, the realm of sound, represented by the primordial utterances, and, on the other hand, the realm of form, represented by the human, natural, and divine orders. Implicit in this schema, as well as in the more general Vedic conception of the creative power of the divine speech, is the notion that an intrinsic relation exists between the Vedic word and the object that it signifies, between the name (*nāma*) and the form (*rūpa*) that it designates. In this conception *bhūḥ* is not simply a conventional designation, it is the natural name of the earth, and thus it represents the subtle correlative that contains the "reality" of the earth within its structure. The primordial utterances *bhūḥ*, *bhuvaḥ*, and *svaḥ* are like potent seeds containing the entire tree of creation about to sprout. These three seed syllables represent the concentrated essences of the divine speech, which are in turn elaborated in the three Vedas.

The Vedas in this perspective contain the primordial sounds from which the phenomenal creation is structured. Taittirīya Brāhmaṇa III.12.9.1–2 describes the *ṛcs*, *yajuses*, and *sāmans* as the sources of form (*mūrti*), motion (*gati*), and light (*tejas*), respectively, and then declares, "All this (*sarvam idam*) indeed was brought forth through *brahman* [Veda]." A passage in the Śatapatha Brāhmaṇa depicts the three Vedas as containing the entire universe in potential form.

> He [Prajāpati] then surveyed all existing things. He beheld all existing things in the threefold knowledge (*trayī vidyā*), for in that is the self (*ātman*) of all meters, of all *stomas*, of all breaths, and of all the gods. This indeed exists, for it is immortal, and that which is immortal exists, and this [also contains] that which is mortal. Prajāpati reflected, "Truly all existing things are in the threefold knowledge. Well then let me construct for myself a self (*ātman*) that is the threefold knowledge."[149]

The passage goes on to describe how, through putting the threefold Veda into his own self, Prajāpati becomes the soul animating the body of the universe, encompassing all existing things.[150]

While the three Vedas together correspond to the creation in its entirety, each Veda separately, in its correlation with one of the three worlds, represents the plan for that particular world. It is perhaps in this sense that the Śatapatha Brāhmaṇa establishes a direct identity between the three Vedas and the three worlds, declaring that the *ṛcs* are the earth, the *yajuses* are the midregions, and the *sāmans* are the heavens,[151] for the sounds of each Veda are held to reveal the underlying structure of the corresponding world.

The role of the Veda in the process of creation is thus twofold: the Veda, as the undifferentiated Word, *brahman*, serves as the foundation of creation, while the three Vedas, as the differentiated impulses of knowledge contained in the primordial expressions of divine speech, constitute the sound correlatives of the three worlds.

Form of Veda	*Level of Creation*
Veda as *brahman*, undifferentiated Word	undifferentiated totality of egg
Ṛg-Veda	earth
Yajur-Veda	midregions
Sāma-Veda	heaven

In the cosmogonic and cosmological speculations of the Brāhmaṇas the Veda thus assumes a multidimensional role as (1) the foundation of the creator Prajāpati and his creation; (2) the constitutive elements of the body and self of the creator principle; (3) the primordial impulses of the creator's speech, from which the three worlds and their manifold forms are structured; and (4) the oral texts recited by brahmin priests as part of the sacrificial order. The sacrificial order is represented in the Brāhmaṇas as subsuming all of these levels, for, as we have seen, the sacrifice is held to be the counterpart of Prajāpati and the means through which, in the beginning, he brings the process of creation to fruition. Prajāpati is portrayed as bringing forth the sacrifice and assuming the functions of the various priests, reciting the *ṛc*s, chanting the *sāman*s, and performing the sacrificial actions with the aid of the *yajus*es. In this perspective the brahmin priests—*hotṛ, udgātṛ, adhvaryu*, and *brahman*—represent the earthly counterparts of the primordial sacrificer Prajāpati, their recitations, chants, and actions mirroring the cosmogonic process through which the Vedic *mantra*s first emerged from the speech of the creator and manifested the realm of forms.[152]

The preeminent position allotted in the social order to the brahmin priests, as the custodians of the Vedas and the officiants of the sacrifice, thus receives cosmic sanction, for the fulfillment of their respective functions is considered critical to the ritual reconstruction and maintenance of the cosmic order. The discourse of sacrifice serves to perpetuate the social hierarchy by ensuring the priestly officiants of the sacrifice the highest status at the top. The hierarchical *varṇa* system is itself represented in the Brāhmaṇas as an inherent part of the tripartite system of correspondences among the various orders of reality. The three higher *varṇas*, brahmins, *kṣatriyas*, and *vaiśyas*, are correlated with the three *vyāhṛtis* and the three worlds and thereby indirectly with the three Vedas.[153]

brahmins	*bhūḥ*	earth	Ṛg-Veda
kṣatriyas	*bhuvaḥ*	midregions	Yajur-Veda
vaiśyas	*svaḥ*	heaven	Sāma-Veda

In addition to this schema, the Brāhmaṇas establish a second tripartite taxonomy in which the brahmins, *kṣatriyas*, and *vaiśyas* are connected with the Vedic meters *gāyatrī, triṣṭubh,* and *jagatī*, respectively.[154] The structure of the *varṇa* system thus gains transcendent legitimation through being homologized to the structure of the Veda, which is itself considered to reflect the structure of the cosmic order. Moreover, this tripartite classification system is hierarchical, with the brahmins, the Ṛg-Veda, and the *gāyatrī* meter ranked at the top of their respective triads.[155] In this context the brahmins who study and teach the Vedas are granted the status of human gods (*manuṣya-devas*), with the offering of sacrificial fees (*dakṣiṇās*) that gratifies these human gods viewed as parallel to the offering of oblations that gratifies the gods on high.[156]

The Brāhmaṇas emphasize the benefits that the sacrifice brings not only to the two kinds of gods, the brahmin priests and their divine prototypes, but also to the *yajamāna*, the patron of the sacrifice. For when both kinds of gods are gratified, they are said to grant the *yajamāna* well-being and convey him to the world of heaven (*svarga loka*).[157] Through the performance of the sacrifice a divine self (*daivātman*) is ritually constructed for the *yajamāna*. This self, which is fashioned through the ritual recitation and chanting of the Vedic *mantras*, is said to become, like the self of the primordial sacrificer Prajāpati, composed of the *ṛcs*, *yajuses*, and *sāmans*. His self having been ritually constituted by and of the Veda, the *yajamāna* ascends upward and becomes immortal (*amṛta*).[158]

> Having become composed of the *ṛc*, the *yajus*, and the *sāman*, of the Veda, of *brahman*, of the immortal (*amṛta*), he who knows thus and who, knowing thus, sacrifices with this sacrificial rite attains to divinity.[159]

The Brāhmaṇas thus present a variety of cosmogonic paradigms for delimiting the Vedic canon and investing it with transcendent authority. The creator himself is represented as circumscribing the potentially limitless domain of Vāc through his own speech-acts, in which he uses certain discrete utterances to manifest the phenomenal creation. These primordial utterances—in particular the three *vyāhṛtis* and their more elaborated expression in the Ṛg-Veda, Yajur-Veda, and Sāma-Veda—are represented as the sound correlatives of the realm of form, reflecting the structures of the human, natural, and divine orders. It is this circumscribed set of utterances that is granted the status of the blueprint of creation, and thus the Vedic canon would appear to be closed. The primordial *mantras* that constitute this blueprint are fixed and are to be preserved with scrupulous precision by the earthly counterparts of Prajāpati, the brahmin priests. At the same time the Brāhmaṇas provide a strategy for extending the purview of Veda beyond this bounded domain. For while the primordial Word might have found its consummate expression in the *ṛcs*, *yajuses*, and *sāmans*, it is not considered to be limited to that expression. Beyond its bounded, differentiated manifestation as the Vedic *mantras*, the Veda is celebrated as the unbounded, undifferentiated Word. While the domain of the threefold Veda is closed, the domain of the infinite Veda remains open. The mechanisms are thus established whereby later brahmanical texts may claim a place within the limitless purview of Veda by assimilating themselves to the core texts that retain their authoritative status at the center: the Vedic *mantras*.

Upaniṣads

In the Upaniṣads (ca. 800–200 B.C.E.)[160] the epistemological framework shifts from the discourse of sacrifice to the discourse of knowledge. This shift is articulated retrospectively by the brahmanical tradition as a distinction between the priestly sacrificial tradition of the *karma-kāṇḍa*, the section of the Vedas pertaining to action (*karman*), and the metaphysical speculations of the *jñāna-kāṇḍa*, the section of the Vedas pertaining to knowledge (*jñāna*). While the priestly exponents of the Brāhmaṇas are concerned with the correct performance of sacrificial rituals as a means of maintaining and controlling the relative phenomenal creation, the Upaniṣadic sages are concerned with the attainment of knowledge—in the sense of both intellectual understanding and direct experience—of ultimate reality as a means of achieving liberation (*mokṣa*) from the bondage of the relative world of *saṃsāra* and its endless cycles of birth and death.[161] The divergent textual perspectives of the Brāhmaṇas and Upaniṣads reflect the contending sectional interests of two types of groups that began to define themselves over against one another from the eighth century B.C.E. onward: the brahmanical priestly tradition, on the one hand, and various forest-dwelling sages and ascetic groups (*yatis* and *śramaṇas*), both brahmanical and non-brahmanical, on the other. By expanding the Vedic canon retroactively to include the Upaniṣads, the exponents of the brahmanical tradition accommodated and sanctioned certain currents of ascetic teachings as part of the "orthodox" tradition and thereby sought to mitigate the challenge posed by the rise of ascetic groups, especially the heterodox Jain and Buddhist movements.[162]

Cosmogonic and cosmological speculations assume a significant place in the sacrificial discourse of the Brāhmaṇas, as we have seen, for the emergence and structure of the phenomenal creation are viewed as intrinsically connected with the sacrificial order. In the Upaniṣads, on the other hand, cosmogonic and cosmological matters are important insofar as they contribute to the texts' ontological and epistemological concerns regarding the nature of ultimate reality. Thus, while the cosmogonic speculations of the Brāhmaṇas center on the creator Prajāpati, the primordial sacrificer, the Upaniṣads recast the narrative in light of the ultimate reality—variously termed Brahman, Ātman (Self), *sat* (existence), or *asat* (nonexistence)—that is the source not only of creation but of the creator himself. Most of the accounts of creation in the Upaniṣads begin from the level of this ultimate reality with one of the following statements: "In the beginning Brahman was here"; "In the beginning Ātman alone was here"; "In the beginning *sat* alone was here"; "In the beginning *asat* alone was here."[163] Moreover, in Upaniṣadic reformulations of the creation narrative, much of the concrete mythological language and imagery used in the accounts of the Saṃhitās and Brāhmaṇas is stripped away and replaced with more abstract metaphysical terminology and categories.

The most common Upaniṣadic designations for the ultimate reality are Brahman and Ātman. In certain Upaniṣads Brahman and Ātman are at times identified, and the two terms are used interchangeably to refer to the universal ground of all existence. In its identification with the ultimate reality, Brahman-Ātman is described as both transcendent and immanent, formless and formed. On the one hand, Brahman-Ātman is declared to be transcendent, beyond the phenomenal creation, and completely unmanifest, formless, distinctionless, and nonchanging in its essential, absolute nature. On the other hand, Brahman-Ātman is represented as that immanent, all-pervading reality which dwells in all aspects of the manifest, ever-changing relative world. The Bṛhadāraṇyaka Upaniṣad distinguishes between these two aspects of Brahman:

> There are indeed two forms of Brahman: the formed (*mūrta*) and the formless (*amūrta*), the mortal (*martya*) and the immortal (*amṛta*), the nonmoving (*sthita*) and the moving (*yat*), the actual (*sat*) and that which is beyond (*tyad*).[164]

In post-Vedic texts, as we shall see, the transcendent and immanent aspects of Brahman are termed, respectively, Nirguṇa Brahman, Brahman without attributes, and Saguṇa Brahman, Brahman with attributes.

The way in which the monistic perspective of the Upaniṣads is superimposed on earlier cosmogonic conceptions can be clearly seen in the Upaniṣadic treatment of Puruṣa and Prajāpati. As we saw earlier, in the Ṛg-Veda Prajāpati (ṚV X.121) is celebrated as a personal creator god, whereas Puruṣa (ṚV X.90) is represented from a more monistic perspective as the unitary world ground that constitutes the source and basis of creation. In the Brāhmaṇas Puruṣa becomes identified with and absorbed into the figure of Prajāpati, who assumes the paramount role as the supreme god and creator, the father of the gods, demons, and human beings. In the Upaniṣads, on the other hand, the ultimate reality of Brahman-Ātman is given precedence over the creator principle, and the figures of Puruṣa and Prajāpati are either identified with that reality or subordinated to it. Moreover, in contrast to the perspective of the Brāhmaṇas, Puruṣa is a more dominant figure than Prajāpati in the Upaniṣads. When the two are explicitly brought into relation Prajāpati is generally relegated to a secondary status as an aspect of Puruṣa.

In the Upaniṣads Puruṣa's identity as the unified ground of all existence, as celebrated in the Puruṣa-Sūkta, is reaffirmed. In this role Puruṣa is often explicitly identified with Brahman-Ātman, although at times he appears to be distinguished from the ultimate reality.[165] While in certain passages Puruṣa is associated with that transcendent aspect of Brahman-Ātman which is formless, nonchanging, and without parts,[166] he is more often depicted as that immanent, all-pervading aspect of Brahman-Ātman which dwells within the ever-changing forms of the relative creation. In this context Puruṣa is sometimes identified with the inner Self (*antarātman*) that is hidden in the heart of all things.[167]

Although Puruṣa is at times described as a creator principle who engages in the demiurgic act of creation,[168] it is generally in his manifestation as Prajāpati that Puruṣa assumes this role. Prajāpati is identified in the Upaniṣads with that aspect of Puruṣa which brings forth the universe and then enters into his creation as the animating principle of intelligence that endows embodied beings with consciousness.[169] As the immanent principle in creation, Prajāpati is sometimes identified with the indwelling Self, Ātman,[170] and with that aspect of Brahman-Ātman which is associated with time and has parts.[171] However, he more often assumes a subordinate role as the creator god who himself has his source in the supreme reality of Brahman-Ātman. The Bṛhadāraṇyaka Upaniṣad proclaims, "Brahman brought forth Prajāpati, Prajāpati the gods."[172]

In addition to Puruṣa and Prajāpati, the Upaniṣads at times mention a third principle, Brahmā, who is similarly depicted as an intermediary between Brahman-Ātman and creation. On one level Brahmā is depicted as distinct from Brahman-Ātman, for it is Brahman that creates Brahmā and delivers to him the Vedas.[173] However, on another level, like Puruṣa and Prajāpati, he is described as participating in the reality of Brahman-Ātman.[174] In the Upaniṣads Brahmā's role as the demiurge is alluded to but not elaborated,[175] and he appears to be distinguished from Prajāpati in certain contexts.[176] In post-Vedic literature, as we shall see, the figures of Brahmā and Prajāpati become fused, and Brahmā becomes the primary designation for the creator principle.

In their speculations concerning the Veda, the Upaniṣads, in contrast to the Brāhmaṇas, evidence little concern with the earthly manifestation of the Vedic *mantras* as recited texts that form a part of the sacrificial order. Knowledge of the mundane Vedic texts is relegated to a subsidiary position as a lower form of knowledge (*aparā vidyā*) than that higher knowledge (*parā vidyā*) by means of which the ultimate reality, Brahman-Ātman, is apprehended.[177] However, the Veda in its supramundane status as infinite, eternal knowledge forms part of the higher knowledge not only epistemologically but also ontologically, for it is represented as constituting the very fabric of Brahman-Ātman itself. Although the Veda is also at times connected to other principles, such as Puruṣa, Prajāpati,

Brahmā, and Vāc, these principles are themselves assimilated to Brahman-Ātman in certain contexts, and thus Brahman-Ātman remains the governing principle in relationship to which all other categories are defined.

Veda and Brahman-Ātman In the Saṃhitās the Vedic *mantras* are depicted as emerging from the cosmic body of Puruṣa (ṚV X.90.9) or Prajāpati (TS VII.1.1.4–6) or as forming parts of the body of Skambha/Brahman (AV X.7.20; AV IX.6.1–2). In the Brāhmaṇas the Vedic *mantras* emerge from, and form the constituent elements of, the body of the Puruṣa Prajāpati. In the Upaniṣads the relationship of the Vedas to the cosmic body is reinterpreted in light of the Upaniṣadic conception of Brahman-Ātman, and the Vedic *mantras* are represented as forming different parts of the body of Brahman-Ātman.

Taittirīya Upaniṣad II.3 describes the Ātman consisting of mind (*mano-maya*) as having the form of a person (Puruṣa), of which the Yajur-Veda constitutes the head, the Ṛg-Veda the right side, the Sāma-Veda the left side, and the *atharvāṅgiras*es the foundation. In the Kauṣītaki Upaniṣad the cosmic body that is constituted by the Vedic *mantras* is that of Brahman, the Imperishable.

> He whose belly is the *yajus,* whose head is the *sāman,* whose form is the *ṛc,* yonder Imperishable (*avyaya*) is to be known as Brahman, the great seer (*ṛṣi*), consisting of the Word (*brahma-maya*).[178]

This passage points to two levels on which the Veda participates in the reality of Brahman: (1) the Veda as *brahman,* the Word, constitutes the very fabric of which the cosmic principle of Brahman is made; while (2) the Vedic *mantras*—*ṛc*s, *yajus*es, and *sāmans*—each form a different part of the cosmic body. The Veda as the Word is the undifferentiated totality of knowledge, while the Vedic *mantras* are threefold knowledge (*trayī vidyā*), the differentiated expressions of knowledge.

The Śvetāśvatara Upaniṣad appears to distinguish between these two levels of the Veda when it declares:

> That which is hidden in the secret knowledge hidden in the Vedas—Brahmā knows that as the abode of the Word (*brahma-yoni*). Those gods and *ṛṣ*is of old who knew that

> came to be of Its nature (*tan-maya*) and indeed have become immortal (*amṛta*).[179]

That which is hidden in the Vedic *mantras* is the abode (*yoni*, literally, "womb") of the Veda, the Word. Veda as the Word is subtler, more hidden, than the Vedic *mantras* that are its differentiated manifestations. Its hidden abode is that imperishable Brahman in which it abides and the nature of which it partakes.

Veda as *brahman*, the Word, represents the totality of knowledge by means of which the Vedic *mantras* themselves are made greater.[180] The Taittirīya Upaniṣad eulogizes the eternal effulgence of Veda.

> I am the mover of the tree. My fame is like the peak of a mountain. Exalted, pure, like the excellent nectar in the sun, I am a shining treasure, wise, immortal (*amṛta*), imperishable (*akṣita*).[181]

The Vedic *mantras* issue forth as "breathings" from that imperishable totality of Veda which is an aspect of Brahman. A passage in the Bṛhadāraṇyaka Upaniṣad, which appears with slight variations in the Maitri Upaniṣad, describes how from "this great Being (*bhūta*)," which, "infinite, unbounded, is just a mass of knowledge (*vijñāna-ghana*),"[182] were breathed forth not only the Ṛg-Veda, Yajur-Veda, Sāma-Veda, and *atharvāṅgiras*es, but also the Upaniṣads, Itihāsa, Purāṇa and other sacred texts.[183]

Veda and the Creator In the Upaniṣads the Veda as the undifferentiated Word is thus described as participating in the reality of Brahman-Ātman, while the Vedic *mantras* constitute the more differentiated expressions of that reality. The Vedic *mantras* are also linked in the Upaniṣads to the creator principle, who is variously designated as Puruṣa, Prajāpati, or Brahmā. As discussed earlier, these three principles are at times relegated to a subordinate position to the ultimate reality, Brahman-Ātman, while at other times they are identified with it.

The Kauṣītaki Upaniṣad describes the Vedic *mantras* as forming the foundation and support of Brahmā in that they are the main constituents of which his throne and couch are composed.[184] Other passages depict the Vedas as constitutive of certain aspects of the creator principle himself. Muṇḍaka Upaniṣad II.1.1–10 describes the *ṛcs*, *sāmans*, and *yajus*es as emerging from Puruṣa along with the various parts of the sacrificial, human, natural, and divine orders. The manifest (*vivṛta*) Vedas are identified in particular with his speech[185]—an association that we encountered in earlier texts and will explore further below. Although the passage recalls the language of the Puruṣa-Sūkta, the concrete imagery of the sacrifice is stripped away and the creation narrative is recast in light of the Upaniṣadic monistic perspective by establishing the identity of Puruṣa with Brahman-Ātman.[186]

Taittirīya Upaniṣad II.3, discussed earlier, correlates Puruṣa more specifically with the Ātman consisting of mind and identifies the four Vedas with different parts of Puruṣa's body. The Chāndogya Upaniṣad goes even further and asserts that Puruṣa *is* the *ṛc*, the *sāman*, and the *yajus*.[187] The Praśna Upaniṣad, however, introduces a qualification: although the *mantras* constitute one of the sixteen parts of Puruṣa, Puruṣa in his essential nature is beyond all parts.[188]

Vedas as the Expressions of Divine Speech As in the Brāhmaṇas, in the Upaniṣads the Vedic *mantras* are associated in particular with the speech of the creator principle. As mentioned above, the Muṇḍaka Upaniṣad identifies the manifest Vedas with the speech of Puruṣa (= Brahman-Ātman).[189] Vāc, speech, is the uniting-point (*ekāyana*) of all the Vedas, as the ocean is the uniting-point of all waters.[190] Vāc, by means of which the four Vedas and other sacred texts are made known, is ultimately identified in the Upaniṣads with Brahman.[191]

The Upaniṣads, like the Brāhmaṇas, emphasize the creative power of speech as the vehicle through which the creator brings forth creation. For example, a passage in the Maitri Upaniṣad describes how in the beginning the world was unuttered (*avyāhṛta*) until Prajāpati, having practiced *tapas*, uttered (root *hṛ* + *anu-vi-ā*) it in the words *bhūḥ, bhuvaḥ, svaḥ*.[192] Although the passage invokes the imagery of the Brāhmaṇas, in accordance with the Upaniṣadic metaphysical perspective it interjects a new element into the creation narrative by identifying Prajāpati with the Self (Ātman) of all. The Vedas are not explicitly mentioned in this passage, although they are represented metonymically by the three *vyāhṛtis, bhūḥ, bhuvaḥ,* and *svaḥ,* an identification that had already been well established by this period and is developed elsewhere in the Upaniṣads, as will be discussed below.

A passage in the Bṛhadāraṇyaka Upaniṣad depicts the Vedic *mantras* as the first manifestation of that speech by means of which the creator brings forth the entire universe.[193] Another passage in the Bṛhadāraṇyaka Upaniṣad describes speech as the differentiating principle through which the creator—here identified with the Imperishable—introduces distinctions in the originally distinctionless totality.

> Verily, at the command (*praśāsana*) of that Imperishable (*akṣara*), O Gārgī, sun and moon stand apart. At the command of that Imperishable, O Gārgī, heaven and earth stand apart. At the command of that Imperishable, O Gārgī, moments, hours, days, nights, fortnights, months, seasons, and years stand apart. At the command of that Imperishable, O Gārgī, some rivers flow to the east from the snowy mountains, others to the west, in whatever direction each flows.[194]

The creator simply speaks—simply utters the names—and the corresponding forms "stand apart," differentiated out from their originally undifferentiated state of unity.[195]

Vedas as the Basis of Creation The Vedic *mantras*, as the primordial impulses of speech that underlie the forms of creation, constitute an inherent part of the cosmic order. The Upaniṣads develop further the system of correlations established in the Brāhmaṇas between the realm of sound, represented by the three Vedas and their concentrated essences in the three *vyāhṛtis* and the three constituent sounds of Om, and the realm of form, represented by the human, natural and divine orders.[196]

In accordance with the earlier view of the Brāhmaṇas, several passages depict the intrinsic connections (*bandhus*) between these orders of reality as manifesting through the demiurgic activity of Prajāpati.[197] However, in other passages the Upaniṣadic monistic perspective is superimposed on the inherited paradigm by identifying the various components of each order as different manifestations of Brahman-Ātman. Thus, while the Brāhmaṇas, in their emphasis on the relative phenomenal creation, are concerned with establishing correspondences between specific aspects of the macrocosm and the microcosm, the Upaniṣads, in their focus on the ultimate reality, are above all concerned to establish a more fundamental identity among all aspects of the universe as simply different expressions of the unitary ground of existence, Brahman-Ātman. For example, a passage in the Maitri Upaniṣad describes the constituent elements of Om, *a*, *u*, and *m*, as the sound-form (*svana-vati*) of Ātman; the Ṛg-Veda, Yajur-Veda, and Sāma-Veda as its knowledge-form (*vijñāna-vati*); the earth, midregions, and heaven as its world-form (*loka-vati*); and fire (Agni), wind (Vāyu), and sun (Āditya) as its light-form (*bhās-vati*).[198] The Taittirīya Upaniṣad, in addition to the three *vyāhṛtis* and their corresponding triads, includes a fourth utterance, *mahaḥ*, which is identified with Brahman-Ātman and which constitutes the "transcendent fourth" that transforms the triadic structure into a "3 + 1" structure that becomes paradigmatic in post-Vedic texts. In this schema the transcendent fourth that corresponds to *mahaḥ* in the triad of *ṛcs*, *yajuses*, and *sāmans* is *brahman*, the Word, which represents the undifferentiated totality of Veda that is beyond the Vedic *mantras*.[199]

Another way in which the brahmanical system of correspondences is assimilated to Brahman-Ātman in the Upaniṣads is through identifying the syllable Om with *brahman*, the Word that represents the most concentrated essence of the three *vyāhṛtis* and the three Vedas,[200] and with the cosmic principle of Brahman.[201] A passage in the Maitri Upaniṣad distinguishes two forms of Brahman—Word (*śabda*) and non-Word (*aśabda*)—and identifies Om with Śabdabrahman, Brahman embodied in the Word.[202] As we shall see, the term Śabdabrahman is used in post-Vedic texts to refer to the Veda, which corresponds to Om as the undifferentiated Word that constitutes an aspect of Brahman's nature.

In surveying the Upaniṣadic treatment of the notion of Veda, we thus find that at nearly every point the Upaniṣads have appropriated the cosmogonic and cosmological conceptions found in the Saṃhitās and Brāhmaṇas and have reformulated them in accordance with their monistic perspective. Many of the earlier structures and patterns are retained, but they are reinterpreted in relation to the ultimate reality of Brahman-Ātman.

VEDA AND CREATION IN POST-VEDIC MYTHOLOGY

The period between 200 B.C.E. and 200 C.E. marks the transition from the Vedic period to the post-Vedic period in which a new brahmanical synthesis—that "federation of cultures popularly known as Hinduism"[203]—emerged, which attempted to bring together and reconcile the diverse strands of Indian thought and practice. Three major streams—the *karman* (action) stream, the *jñāna* (knowledge) stream, and the *bhakti* (devotion) stream—converge in this brahmanical synthesis, which finds textual expression during this period and subsequent centuries in three types of texts that are pivotal to our discussion of post-Vedic mythology: the Dharma-Śāstras, the Itihāsas or epics—the Mahābhārata, including the Bhagavad-Gītā, and the Rāmāyaṇa of Vālmīki—and the Purāṇas.

(1) The Karman Stream. The *karman* or action stream has its beginnings in the *karma-kāṇḍa* of the Vedas, which includes not only the earliest sacrificial traditions found in the Saṃhitās and Brāhmaṇas but also the Kalpa-Sūtras (ca. 600–200 B.C.E.), which form one of the six Vedāṅgas, or subsidiary "limbs of the Veda." The Kalpa-Sūtras comprise three types of texts: the Śrauta-Sūtras, which give detailed instructions for the performance of the *śrauta* sacrifices, based on the Saṃhitās and Brāhmaṇas as well as on actual practice; the Gṛhya-Sūtras, which describe the domestic rites that regulate the various aspects of family life; and the Dharma-Sūtras, which prescribe the ritual and social duties of *varṇāśrama-dharma* that are to be performed by members of the four social classes (*varṇas*) at different stages of their lives (*āśramas*). In the post-Vedic period from 200 B.C.E. onward the ritual and social obligations delineated in the Dharma-Sūtras were further crystallized and expanded in the form of elaborate law codes, the Dharma-Śāstras. Large sections of traditional Dharma-Śāstra material were also incorporated in the Itihāsas and Purāṇas.

(2) The Jñāna Stream. The second major stream that flows into the post-Vedic brahmanical synthesis is the *jñāna* or knowledge stream, which has one of its sources in the *jñāna-kāṇḍa* of the Vedas. In addition to the metaphysical speculations of the Upaniṣadic sages, which received official sanction from the brahmanical authorities through incorporation in the Vedic canon, the *jñāna* stream was also fed by competing currents derived from non-brahmanical ascetic groups (*śramaṇas*), including Jain and Buddhist movements, which gained momentum from the fifth century B.C.E. onward. Certain cosmological conceptions found in the oldest Upaniṣads, such as the Chāndogya Upaniṣad (ca. 800–600 B.C.E.), together with the various psychological analyses of yogic experiences found in the Kaṭha and Śvetāśvatara Upaniṣads (both ca. 400–200 B.C.E.) and in early Jain and Buddhist meditation traditions, formed the basis of the more systematic Proto-Sāṃkhya speculations that began to develop in the period between 200 B.C.E. and 200 C.E. The speculations of this "fluid, pluralistic *sāṃkhya-cum-yoga* pre-philosophical Proto-Sāṃkhya," as Gerald Larson has

termed it,[204] are found in particular in the cosmological portions of the Mānava Dharma-Śāstra or Manu-Smṛti (ca. 200 B.C.E.–200 C.E.), in the Mokṣadharma and Bhagavad-Gītā of the Mahābhārata (both ca. 200 B.C.E.–200 C.E.), and in the early Purāṇas (ca. 300 C.E. and after). These speculations, as will be discussed below, had not yet been crystallized into a fixed philosophical system during this period but rather represented "a methodology of reasoning that results in spiritual knowledge (*vidyā, jñāna, viveka*) that leads to liberation from the cycle of frustration and rebirth."[205]

(3) The Bhakti Stream. The origins of the third stream, the *bhakti* (devotion) stream, are more obscure. Although certain proto-*bhakti* currents may be found in Vedic as well as pre-Aryan traditions, it is only in the period between 200 B.C.E. and 200 C.E. that we see the emergence of popular devotional movements. The *bhakti* stream, the underground currents of which may have been gathering force for centuries, suddenly bursts forth in certain areas of the Indian subcontinent in the last centuries before the Common Era, finding expression, on the one hand, in the rise of devotional sects centering on the gods Viṣṇu and Śiva and, on the other hand, in the upsurge of multiform popular cults at the village level. The first great textual monument to *bhakti* is the Mahābhārata, which focuses primarily on devotion to the god Viṣṇu. The various sectarian and popular devotional traditions are further crystallized in the Purāṇas.

The Dharma-Śāstras, Itihāsas, and Purāṇas represent products of the brahmanical synthesis that began to emerge between 200 B.C.E. and 200 C.E., and thus all these texts, to varying degrees, reflect the influence of the *karman, jñāna,* and *bhakti* streams from which this synthesis was formed. The *karman* stream of course prevails in the Dharma-Śāstras, although the Proto-Sāṃkhya currents of the *jñāna* stream are evident in the cosmological speculations of the Manu-Smṛti. All three streams intermingle in the Mahābhārata and the Purāṇas, which have been rightfully deemed the "encyclopedias of Hinduism" because of their all-encompassing, syncretistic character.

In the Manu-Smṛti, Mahābhārata, and Purāṇas, the symbolic complexes associated with Veda in Vedic texts are appropriated, expanded, and reinterpreted in accordance with the specific confluence of currents that gives each text its distinctive character. As we shall see, each of these texts, which are classified as *smṛti,* uses a variety of strategies to establish a connection between its own teachings and the transcendent authority of *śruti,* the Veda.

(1) Veda and Brahman. The relationship of the Veda to the cos-

mic principle of Brahman, which is emphasized especially in the Atharva-Veda Saṃhitā and in the Upaniṣads, is further elaborated in the Mahābhārata and Purāṇas. However, in accordance with the sectarian emphases of these texts, Brahman assumes a personalized aspect through becoming identified with the particular deity that is upheld as the ultimate reality. The Mahābhārata generally identifies the supreme Godhead Viṣṇu with Brahman, although the epic also contains Śaiva sections in which Śiva is allotted this status. Vaiṣṇava Purāṇas such as the Viṣṇu and Bhāgavata Purāṇas revere Viṣṇu as Brahman, while Śaiva Purāṇas such as the Liṅga and Śiva Purāṇas glorify Śiva as Brahman. The Veda as Śabdabrahman, Brahman embodied in the Word, is correspondingly depicted in these texts as an aspect of Viṣṇu or Śiva.

(2) Veda and the Creator. In post-Vedic mythology, as in Vedic texts, the Veda and its differentiated expressions are associated not only with Brahman, the ultimate reality, but also with the creator, the demiurge principle, who is responsible for giving shape to the manifest forms and phenomena of the material creation. The primary designation for the creator god in post-Vedic cosmogonies is Brahmā, who is explicitly identified with both Puruṣa and Prajāpati.[206] As in the Upaniṣads, in post-Vedic accounts the creator principle is generally relegated to a subsidiary role as a manifestation of the supreme reality of Brahman, which is identified in these texts with either Viṣṇu or Śiva.

(3) Vedas as the Expressions of Divine Speech: The Blueprint of Creation. As in Vedic texts, in post-Vedic cosmogonies the Vedic *mantras* are often depicted as emerging from the creator at the beginning of creation as the expressions of his speech. When the creator wishes to call the forms of creation into being, he simply recites the Vedic *mantras*, which are represented as the archetypal plan or blueprint from which the demiurge structures the manifold phenomena of the universe.

(4) Vedas as Concrete Texts. In post-Vedic mythology the textual manifestation of the Veda, as oral texts recited as part of the sacrificial rites, is generally extended beyond the conception of the threefold Veda emphasized in Vedic texts to the notion of the fourfold Veda: Ṛg, Yajur, Sāma, *and* Atharva. Athough the tripartite taxonomy established in Vedic texts is maintained and expanded, it is also supplemented by a quadripartite taxonomy that can accommodate the fourth Veda.

Post-Vedic conceptions of Veda are embedded in two new types of speculation that are introduced into the brahmanical cosmogonic myth cycle in the accounts of the Manu-Smṛti, Mahābhārata, and Purāṇas: Proto-Sāṃkhya speculations involving the enumeration of the elementary principles or *tattvas* that are constitutive of creation; and speculations concerning the cyclical nature of time, in which time is divided into a series of units that endlessly repeat themselves.

With respect to the *tattvas*, in the normative system of Sāṃkhya philosophy expressed in the *Sāṃkhya-Kārikā* of Īśvarakṛṣṇa (ca. 350–450 C.E.), twenty-five elementary principles or *tattvas* are enumerated: Puruṣa (pure consciousness), Prakṛti (primordial matter), intellect (*buddhi* or *mahat*), ego (*ahaṃkāra*), mind (*manas*), the five sense capacities (*buddhīndriyas*—hearing, touching, seeing, tasting, smelling), the five action capacities (*karmendriyas*—speaking, grasping, walking/motion, excreting, procreating), the five subtle elements (*tanmātras*—sound, contact, form, taste, smell), and the five gross elements (*mahābhūtas*—space/ether, wind/air, fire, water, earth).[207] In the normative Kārikā-Sāṃkhya system the *tattvas* are construed as ontological and psychophysiological categories, but they are not generally interpreted in a cosmogonic context. In the fluid Proto-Sāṃkhya speculations that are found in the Manu-Smṛti, Mahābhārata, and early Purāṇas, the list of twenty-five *tattvas* has not yet become standardized, and thus the technical terms as well as the number and function of the enumerated items may vary not only from text to text but also in different accounts within the same text. Moreover, in contrast to the later Kārikā-Sāṃkhya system, in these Proto-Sāṃkhya speculations the *tattvas* are mythologized and cosmologized by incorporating them into a cosmogonic framework and correlating each of the principles with particular deities. In addition, in contradistinction to the dualist perspective of the normative Kārikā-Sāṃkhya system, in the Proto-Sāṃkhya speculations of the Mahābhārata and Purāṇas a monistic or theistic perspective is often adopted that posits one supreme, all-encompassing principle at the apex of the *tattva* system.

The second type of speculation that is introduced in post-Vedic cosmogonies concerns the cyclical nature of time. In post-Vedic mythology the cosmogonic process is not represented as an event that happened once and for all at the beginning of time, for there is no beginning of time nor beginning of creation. Creation, like time, is cyclical and occurs in endlessly repeating cycles of creation and dissolution. The basic units of time that compose these cycles are *yugas*, *manvantaras*, and *kalpas*. A cycle of four *yugas* or ages—Kṛta or Sat (1,728,000 years), Tretā (1,296,000 years), Dvāpara (864,000 years), and Kali (432,000 years)—is termed a *mahāyuga*, which comprises a total of 4,320,000 years. One thousand *mahāyugas* (= 4,320,000,000 years) constitute a *kalpa*, a single day of the creator Brahmā. Every *kalpa*, or day of Brahmā, is also subdivided into 14 *manvantaras*, or intervals of Manu, each comprising 71 and a fraction *mahāyugas*.

The distinction between *yugas*, *manvantaras*, and *kalpas* is fundamental to the cosmogonic accounts found in the Manu-Smṛti, Mahābhārata, and Purāṇas. In the Manu-Smṛti and Mahābhārata these conceptions are still somewhat fluid and have not yet crystallized into a fixed system. By the time of the Purāṇas, however, a fairly standardized conception of time is evident, in which the cycles of time described in the earlier texts—that is, *yugas*, *manvantaras*, and *kalpas*—are subsumed within a more encompassing perspective that distinguishes between cycles of primary creation (*sarga*) and secondary creation (*pratisarga* or *visarga*). The *sarga* or primary creation takes place only at the beginning of each new lifetime of Brahmā, whereas a *pratisarga* or secondary creation occurs at the beginning of each new *kalpa* or day of Brahmā. At the end of each day Brahmā sleeps for a night and a minor dissolution occurs, after which Brahmā awakens and initiates a new *pratisarga*. At the end of Brahmā's lifetime, which consists of one hundred years of Brahmā days and nights, a major dissolution (*mahāpralaya*) takes place, after which the entire cycle begins again with a *sarga*. Purāṇic cosmogonies regularly incorporate certain Proto-Sāṃkhya speculations concerning the *tattvas* within this cyclical conception of time, with the *tattvas* ascribed a special role as the fundamental categories that emerge at the beginning of each new *sarga* and that remain intact during the minor dissolutions and creations of the *pratisargas*.

The cyclical conceptions of time that are delineated in post-Vedic cosmogonies have important implications for the notion of the eternality of the Veda, which appears in incipient form in Vedic texts. In our analysis of Vedic texts we noted several passages in the Brāhmaṇas and Upaniṣads that spoke of the immortal, imperishable status of the Veda,[208] but the nature and basis of this status is not elaborated. In post-Vedic cosmogonies, particularly in the Mahābhārata and Purāṇas, the eternality of the Veda is described on at least two different levels: the Veda, as the undifferentiated totality of knowledge, is considered to be eternal and to constitute the nonchanging essence of the imperishable Brahman itself; while the Vedas, as the differentiated expressions of Veda, are also said to exist eternally, becoming unmanifest at the time of dissolution and then manifesting again at the beginning of each new cycle as the immediate source and blueprint of creation.

Manu-Smṛti

The Dharma-Śāstras (ca. 200 B.C.E.–600 C.E.) are extensive law codes that, building on the teachings of the earlier Dharma-Sūtras, extend the scope of *dharma* to include not only religious law but also administrative, civil, and criminal law. In the Dharma-Śāstras the science of *dharma* becomes threefold: (1) *ācāra*—the rules of conduct that delineate *varṇāśrama-dharma*, the duties of the four social classes (*varṇas*) and stages of life (*āśramas*); (2) *prāyaścitta*—a system of sins and corresponding penances; and (3) *vyavahāra*—regulations concerning the administration of justice. By far the most celebrated of the Dharma-Śāstras is the Mānava Dharma-Śāstra or Manu-Smṛti (ca. 200 B.C.E.–200 C.E.), which constitutes the authoritative law code for all Hindus. It is also the most important for our purposes, in that it is the only Dharma-Śāstra that contains an extensive account of creation, including speculations concerning the cosmic status and role of the Veda. The cosmological portions of the Manu-Smṛti probably derive from the first centuries of the Common Era.

Like the other texts we have considered thus far, the Manu-Smṛti has a generative epistemological framework in the light of which it recasts the creation narrative: the discourse of *dharma*. The twelve books that delineate the science of *dharma* are framed by mythological material that connects Manu's teachings to the source (Book I) and goal (Book XII) of all existence: Brahman. Moreover, Manu's teachings on *dharma* are granted the status of *smṛti* and are linked to the transcendent authority of *śruti*, the Veda,[209] in three ways. First, the text claims that "whatever duty (*dharma*) has been proclaimed for anyone by Manu has been fully declared in the Veda," for Manu himself was omniscient (*sarva-jñāna-maya*) and thus by implication had direct access to the eternal knowledge of Veda.[210] Second, the text elevates Manu to the status of the supreme *ṛṣi*, who emerged from the Self-existent (Svayambhū) in the beginning of creation as the progenitor of the human race and himself brought forth the ten great *ṛṣis* who served as the lords of created beings.[211] Third, the text grants Manu's teachings the status of divine revelation: just as the *ṛṣis* obtained their cognitions of the Vedas through the practice of *tapas*, so the creator brought forth the *smṛti* teachings through *tapas* and taught them directly to Manu, who in turn taught them to the *ṛṣis*.[212]

Having established its own authority in relation to the Veda, the Manu-Smṛti declares that any tradition or philosophy that is not based on the Veda is worthless and untrue (*anṛta*) and produces no reward after death.[213] The Veda is represented in the Manu-Smṛti as the authoritative basis of all orthodox teachings, for it is held to be that eternal knowledge which is brought forth by the creator in the beginning of each cycle of creation and which serves as the divine architect's cosmic blueprint.

The Creation Narrative In Vedic texts we do not find one single creation narrative but rather numerous creation accounts interspersed throughout the texts that focus on specific aspects of the cosmogonic process. While Vedic accounts thus provide glimpses of certain isolated dimensions of the creative process, a comprehensive vision of the interconnections among all the various elements and phases of creation is not given. One of the principal innovations of the cosmogonic narrative in Book I of the Manu-Smṛti is its attempt to provide a synthetic overview that interweaves all of the fundamental components of creation, with the exception of the sacrifice, into a single—albeit complexly constructed—account.

The account in Manu-Smṛti I.5–13 provides a good starting point for our analysis, since it presents the basic pattern of creation upon which later post-Vedic cosmogonies elaborate.

> This existed in the form of darkness, indiscernible, without any distinguishing marks, inaccessible to reason, unknowable, as if entirely immersed in sleep. Then the self-existent Lord, [remaining] unmanifest (*avyakta*) [while] causing this—the gross elements (*mahābhūtas*) and the rest—to manifest, appeared (root *as* + *prādur*) with effective power, dispersing the darkness. He who can be grasped [only] by that which is beyond the senses, who is subtle, unmanifest, eternal, beyond thought, who contains all beings, shone forth (root *bhā* + *ud*) of his own accord. He, having meditated, desiring to bring forth various kinds of beings from his own body, first brought forth the waters (*ap*) and deposited his seed in them. That [seed] became a golden egg (*haima aṇḍa*), refulgent as the sun. In that he himself was born as Brahmā, the progenitor of all the worlds. The waters are called *nārāḥ*, [for] the waters are indeed the off-

> spring of Nara. Since they were his primordial resting place (*ayana*), he is therefore known as Nārāyaṇa. From that which is the [first] cause, unmanifest, eternal, whose nature is [both] existent (*sat*) and nonexistent (*asat*), was brought forth that Puruṣa who is known in the world as Brahmā. The Lord, having resided in that egg for a whole year, himself divided the egg into two halves by his own meditation. From these two halves he formed heaven and earth, the atmosphere in the middle, the eight cardinal directions, and the eternal abode of the waters.

The rest of the narrative continues with a rather confusing account of the emergence of certain *tattvas*—mind (*manas*), ego (*ahaṃkāra*), the five sense capacities, and the gross elements (*mahābhūtas*)—[214] as well as of the creation of various classes of animate and inanimate beings[215] and of the four social classes (*varṇas*).[216] The creation narrative also incorporates the post-Vedic cyclical conception of time, giving a description of the divisions of time and cycles of creation.[217]

The first part of the Manu-Smṛti's account of creation contains a number of elements that are also found in certain Vedic cosmogonies discussed earlier. In particular, we can discern the basic structure of the two-stage process of creation.[218] (1) In the first stage the unmanifest, which is the ultimate source of creation, "shines forth" and appears as the self-existent Nārāyaṇa. Having brought forth the waters, Nārāyaṇa implants his seed in them and the seed becomes a golden egg. (2) In the second stage Nārāyaṇa himself enters the egg and is born from it as the Puruṣa Brahmā, who is elsewhere called Prajāpati.[219] After the period of a year the creator Brahmā proceeds to divide the egg into the three worlds—earth, midregions, and heaven.

The synthetic nature of the Manu-Smṛti's account, which attempts to accommodate the perspectives of both the Brāhmaṇas and the Upaniṣads, can be seen in the way in which it assigns the unmanifest ultimate reality—corresponding to Brahman-Ātman in the Upaniṣads—to the first stage of creation and relegates the creator principle—who appears in both stages in the Brāhmaṇas' accounts—to the second stage as a manifestation of the ultimate reality. Moreover, in the first stage it distinguishes between the unmanifest aspect of the ultimate reality and its manifest aspect, which it terms Nārāyaṇa. In epic and Purāṇic cosmogonies, as will be discussed below, these two aspects become identified with Nirguṇa Brahman and Saguṇa Brahman, respectively.

Veda and the Creator The Manu-Smṛti does not discuss the relationship of the Veda to Brahman except in its manifestation as Brahmā. Although the creator Brahmā is not explicitly identified with the Veda in the Manu-Smṛti, he is directly linked to the Vedic *mantras* in a number of passages. It is Brahmā who draws forth the Vedas in the second stage of creation and who employs them as a blueprint from which he fashions the manifold forms of the universe.

In a brief recapitulation of the tripartite system of correspondences delineated in Vedic texts, the Manu-Smṛti describes Brahmā as drawing forth the Ṛg-, Yajur-, and Sāma-Vedas, respectively, from Agni, fire; Vāyu, wind; and Ravi, the sun.[220] He in turn extracts from the three Vedas their essences in the form of the three constituent sounds of Om and the three *vyāhṛtis*. To this familiar sequence of primordial utterances the Manu-Smṛti adds one additional element, which is also emphasized in other post-Vedic accounts: the three-lined *gāyatrī mantra*, also called *sāvitrī*.[221]

> Prajāpati [Brahmā] milked out from the three Vedas the sounds *a*, *u*, and *m*, and [the *vyāhṛtis*] *bhūḥ, bhuvaḥ, svaḥ*. Moreover, the supreme Prajāpati milked out from each of the three Vedas one of the [three] lines of the *ṛc* [called] *sāvitrī*, which begins with the word *tat*. . . . The three imperishable *mahāvyāhṛtis* preceded by the syllable Om and the three-lined *sāvitrī* are to be known as the mouth of *brahman* [Veda].[222]

Vedas as the Eternal Blueprint of Creation The Manu-Smṛti emphasizes the eternality of the Veda, which is crucial to its cosmogonic role as the blueprint of creation as well as to its authoritative status as the ultimate source of *dharma* teachings. In the midst of the endless cycles of creation and dissolution the "threefold eternal (*sanātana*) Veda" is said to exist perpetually.[223]

> The Veda is the eternal (*sanātana*) eye of the ancestors, gods, and human beings. The Veda-Śāstra is beyond human power (*aśakya*) and beyond measure (*aprameya*); this is an established fact.[224]

While all other traditions that are not based on the Veda arise and pass away, the Veda remains eternally.[225]

The Manu-Smṛti maintains that in each new cycle of creation each class of beings is allotted the same function that it had assumed in the previous cycle.[226] The eternal Vedas, unaffected by the ebb and flow of time, are drawn forth by the creator Brahmā at the beginning of each new cycle and serve as the archetypal plan that he employs in order to assign each being its respective name, nature, and function.

> In the beginning he [Brahmā] formed from the words (*śabdas*) of the Vedas alone the particular names, activities, and conditions of all [beings].[227]

In another passage the Manu-Smṛti describes the Vedas as not only the blueprint but also the source of creation. Moreover, in accordance with the Manu-Smṛti's preoccupation with *varṇāśrama-dharma*, the Vedas are represented as the source not only of the three worlds and all beings but also of the social order, as represented by the system of four classes (*varṇas*) and four stages of life (*āśramas*).

> The four classes (*varṇas*), the three worlds, the four stages of life (*āśramas*), the past, the present, and the future are all severally brought about through the Veda. Sound, touch, form, taste, and, fifthly, smell are produced from the Veda alone, together with their products, qualities, and activities. The eternal (*sanātana*) Veda-Śāstra sustains all beings. Therefore I regard it as the supreme means of fulfillment for these beings.[228]

Mahābhārata and Harivaṃśa

The brahmanical synthesis that emerged in the post-Vedic period found textual testimony not only in the Dharma-Śāstras but also in the two great Sanskrit epics, the Mahābhārata and the Rāmāyaṇa of Vālmīki, which are traditionally designated as "Itihāsas" in enumerations of the brahmanical canon. The Mahābhārata is of particular significance for the present analysis because it contains extensive cosmogonic material, including numerous speculations concerning the cosmological status of the Veda. The Harivaṃśa, the appendix (*khila*) to the Mahābhārata, which contains material closely allied with Purāṇic mythology, also includes a number of passages that are germane to our discussion.[229]

The composition of the Mahābhārata appears to have taken place over an eight-hundred-year period, between 400 B.C.E. and

400 C.E. This voluminous text, which is traditionally said to consist of 100,000 verses,[230] is an encyclopedia of lore and teaching in which numerous streams converge. V. S. Sukthankar rightfully refers to it as the "Encyclopaedia Brahmanica."[231] The core narrative derives from the *kṣatriya* or warrior class in Indian society and recounts the story of the great war fought at Kurukṣetra between the Pāṇḍavas and the Kauravas. This central narrative is embedded in a densely textured, multilayered textual repository that includes ancient bardic poetry, myths and legends, fables and parables, and didactic material.[232] In addition to the *kṣatriya* material, which contributes the basic heroic narrative and certain didactic teachings relevant to warriors, the other main streams that intermingle in the epic are those discussed earlier: (1) the *karman* stream, which delineates orthodox brahmanical teachings concerning the ritual and social duties of *varṇāśrama-dharma*; (2) the *jñāna* stream, which comprises certain Proto-Sāṃkhya speculations regarding the importance of knowledge as a means to attain proper understanding and experience of the basic constituents of reality and thereby to achieve *mokṣa*, liberation from the cycle of rebirth; and (3) the *bhakti* stream, which tends to engulf the other two streams in its recasting of the epic as essentially a *bhakti* text in which the claims of devotion to Viṣṇu at times take precedence over the claims of *dharma* and *jñāna*. Devotion to Śiva is also granted a subsidiary place in the epic through the interpolation of certain sections on Śaiva mythology and teachings.[233]

The cosmogonic and cosmological speculations of the Mahābhārata are located primarily in the Mokṣadharma section of the Śānti-Parvan (XII.168–353) and in the Bhagavad-Gītā (VI.23–40), both of which date from the period between 200 B.C.E. and 200 C.E. Both texts interweave traditional Vedic mythological and metaphysical conceptions with Proto-Sāṃkhya speculations concerning the *tattvas* and then superimpose a theistic veneer over the entire scheme by interpreting Viṣṇu as that supreme reality who is identical with the Upaniṣadic Brahman-Ātman and who is celebrated as the twenty-fifth (or twenty-sixth) of the *tattvas*. This Vaiṣṇava devotionalism constitutes the dominant epistemological framework in the Mahābhārata's speculations concerning the origin and status of the Veda. The epic appropriates earlier Vedic conceptions concerning the multidimensional nature of the Veda—as constitutive of Brahman, an aspect of the creator principle, and the expressions of divine speech at the basis of creation—and infuses them with new valences that accord with the text's overarching Vaiṣṇava perspective. More specifically, the Veda becomes assimilated to Viṣṇu both in his supreme reality as Brahman and in his secondary manifestation as the creator Brahmā. The identification of Viṣṇu with Brahman and with the eternal reality of Veda represents one of the essential mechanisms through which popular devotional elements were absorbed into the brahmanical synthesis and granted legitimacy as part of the normative tradition.

A second mechanism that served to authorize the Mahābhārata's place in the brahmanical canon is the epic's direct claim to Vedic status as the "fifth Veda."[234] It designates itself more specifically as the "Veda of Kṛṣṇa" (Kārṣṇa Veda), that is, the Veda of Kṛṣṇa Dvaipāyana Vyāsa.[235] Vyāsa is represented in the epic as a partial incarnation or portion (*aṃśa*) of Viṣṇu-Nārāyaṇa[236] and as the "great *ṛṣi*" (*maharṣi, mahān-ṛṣi*)[237] or "supreme *ṛṣi*" (*paramarṣi*)[238] who "saw" (root *dṛś*) the verses of the Mahābhārata just as the primordial *ṛṣis* saw the Vedic *mantras* in the beginning of creation.[239] Moreover, Vyāsa is called the "great repository (*nidhāna*) of Veda"[240] and the "foremost of the scholars of the Veda"[241] and is designated as Veda-Vyāsa, "the divider of the Veda,"[242] for he is said to have divided (root *as* + *vi*) the one Veda into four distinct Saṃhitās, or collections. Having arranged the Vedic Saṃhitās, he composed the Mahābhārata and then taught the four Saṃhitās, together with the Mahābhārata as the fifth Veda, to his five main disciples.[243]

The Mahābhārata declares itself to be a "holy Upaniṣad"[244] that is commensurate with the four Vedas as "a supreme means of purification equal to the Vedas."[245] However, the epic also distinguishes itself from the Vedas in that, unlike the Vedic *mantras*, which are to be recited and heard only by male members of the three higher *varṇas*, the teachings of the Mahābhārata are intended as a means of purification for all people, including *śūdras* and women.[246] Moreover, the epic departs from the Vedic paradigm in that the text was committed to writing and has been transmitted in both written and oral form, whereas the Vedic Saṃhitās have traditionally been transmitted only through oral recitation and are not to be written down.[247] A well-known passage that appears in some versions of the Mahābhārata maintains that the writing down of the epic received the divine sanction of the creator Brahmā, who recommended to Vyāsa that the god Gaṇeśa serve as his scribe.[248] Bruce M. Sullivan comments on the way in which this account inverts the Vedic model.

> Vyāsa's repeated references to the Vedic texts in his description of his own composition emphasize the epic's claim to be another *Veda,* the fifth *Veda,* and an all-inclusive text in which all topics are presented. It is remarkable, however, that in the creation of the MBh's written text, Vyāsa and Gaṇeśa invert the Vedic paradigm. Whereas the *Vedas* were regarded as divinely created, with the Vedic seers merely transmitting the divinely created verses, the seer Vyāsa created the MBh and the god Gaṇeśa helped to transmit the text more effectively by committing it to writing. In another departure from the Vedic paradigm, the *Vedas* were always transmitted orally, while the MBh was in written form as well as being transmitted orally. Thus, Vyāsa's role as the seer of the fifth *Veda* reveals certain differences from the relationship between the Vedic seers and the four *Vedas.*[249]

In contrast to the oral Vedic tradition, which requires brahmin reciters for its transmission, the commitment of the epic to writing opened the possibility, at least in principle, for the general populace to have direct access to the text without the mediation of brahmin priests. C. Mackenzie Brown, in discussing the Mahābhārata's account of the way in which the text was committed to writing, observes, "The story as a whole strongly suggests that one of the primary reasons for the commitment to writing is to benefit all people. While paying its respects to the high Vedic tradition, the epic makes clear that, unlike the Vedas, it is not the exclusive prerogative of the priestly class."[250]

The epic insists that even a brahmin's knowledge is incomplete unless he has knowledge of its teachings: "A brahmin who knows the four Vedas with their subsidiary limbs (*aṅgas*) and Upaniṣads but who does not know this epic is not really learned."[251] "With both Itihāsa and Purāṇa one should complement the Veda. The Veda is afraid of one with little knowledge."[252] The epic at times even claims superiority over the Vedas. It recounts a story in which the divine *ṛṣis* themselves are witness to the preeminent status of the Mahābhārata, which "outweighs" that of the four Vedas.

> Once the divine *ṛṣis,* who had assembled together, placed on a balance the four Vedas on one scale and the Bhārata on the other scale, and both in size and in weight it measured more. Therefore, because of its great size (*mahattva*)

and its weightiness (*bhāravattva*), it is called the Mahābhārata.[253]

While the Mahābhārata's conception of its own scriptural status thus diverges from the Vedic model in significant ways, the Veda nevertheless remains paradigmatic. Indeed, it is the Veda's supramundane status as the eternal, infinite Word that allows the epic to deem itself the "fifth Veda," for if the Veda were limited to its mundane textual manifestation as a finite corpus of *mantras*, its domain would be closed.

The Creation Narrative The role of the Veda as a cosmological principle is delineated primarily in the creation accounts of the Mahābhārata and Harivaṃśa, which provide a bridge between Vedic and Purāṇic narratives. The cosmogonic speculations of these texts build upon Vedic conceptions, while at the same time introducing new types of speculation that are still in a formative, fluid stage in the epic but that attain a more crystallized, standardized form in Purāṇic cosmogonies. In contrast to the Manu-Smṛti, the Mahābhārata and Harivaṃśa do not attempt to provide a single, definitive account of creation but rather include numerous creation narratives, which are often tentative and inconsistent in their formulations.[254] We thus encounter a bewildering array of cosmogonic notions that are at times uncomfortably spliced together and at other times simply juxtaposed with no attempt to reconcile them. Among the various strands that have contributed to this complex amalgamation in the Mahābhārata, four are of particular importance: Vedic mythological conceptions concerning the role of certain creative principles such as the creator god, the waters, and the cosmic egg; Upaniṣadic metaphysical speculations regarding Brahman-Ātman; Proto-Sāṃkhya speculations concerning the *tattvas*; and Pāñcarātra conceptions regarding the emanations (*vyūhas*) of Viṣṇu.

In spite of the inconsistencies among the different creation accounts, it is possible to reconstruct the basic cosmogonic sequence on the basis of the most commonly recurring patterns among the multiple variants. We can distinguish two main phases in this sequence corresponding to the paradigmatic two-stage process of creation: the first stage is linked to Viṣṇu as the ultimate source and foundation of creation, while the second stage is connected to the creator Brahmā as the demiurge who brings forth the three worlds and all beings.

(1) Viṣṇu as the Ultimate Source and Foundation of Creation

The first phase of creation is generally associated with Viṣṇu, who emerges in the later, speculative portions of the Mahābhārata as a composite deity who combines the names and qualities of earlier gods drawn from both priestly and popular traditions—the Vedic Viṣṇu, Nārāyaṇa, Vāsudeva, Kṛṣṇa, and Hari. Viṣṇu, under one or another of his appellations, is identified in the epic with the Upaniṣadic Brahman-Ātman, and as such he is described as both *nirguṇa*, without attributes, and *saguṇa*, with attributes. Viṣṇu in his identification with Nirguṇa Brahman transcends the relative phenomenal world and is completely unmanifest, formless, and nonchanging. He also at times assumes a manifest form as Saguṇa Brahman, by means of which he carries out his role as the creator, maintainer, and destroyer of the ever-changing universe. Drawing on the imagery of the Puruṣa-Sūkta of the Ṛg-Veda, the epic celebrates Viṣṇu as the Puruṣa who has a thousand heads, a thousand eyes, and a thousand feet and who pervades the universe on every side. The different aspects of the universe form the different parts of Viṣṇu's body, while in his essential nature he constitutes the innermost soul, the supreme Self (Paramātman), that dwells within and animates this cosmos-body.

At the time of dissolution Viṣṇu withdraws the entire universe into himself and retires to his unmanifest state as Nirguṇa Brahman. When the time for a new cycle of creation dawns, he awakens and becomes *saguṇa*, assuming a manifest form as the Puruṣa Viṣṇu-Nārāyaṇa, who initiates the process of creation. At this point one of two alternative scenarios is generally interjected into the creation narrative. The creation account is given either a Pāñcarātra inflection, through describing the emergence of the four emanations (*vyūhas*) of Viṣṇu, or a Proto-Sāṃkhya cast, through depicting the unfoldment of the *tattvas*.[255] In the latter scenario the *tattvas* are described as progressively emerging, either in accordance with the standard enumeration of twenty-five (Puruṣa = Viṣṇu; Prakṛti, primordial matter; and the twenty-three evolutes of Prakṛti),[256] or variant enumerations ranging from sixteen to twenty-four. A number of passages describe the *tattvas* as combining in order to form a body, into which Viṣṇu-Nārāyaṇa himself enters—a theme that is developed in Purāṇic cosmogonies in terms of the conception of the cosmic egg.

(2) Brahmā as the Creator of the Three Worlds and All Beings

Viṣṇu-Nārāyaṇa is thus celebrated in the Mahābhārata as the ultimate source from which Prakṛti, the material cause of creation, and its evolutes emerge. However, the cosmogonic process also requires an instrumental cause, a demiurge principle, who can give shape and form to the evolutes of matter. This role is generally assumed in the epic by the creator Brahmā, who is explicitly identified with Prajāpati as the lord of created beings. It is Brahmā who is responsible for bringing forth the three worlds—earth, midregions, and heaven—and all animate and inanimate beings—gods, *ṛṣis*, other celestial beings, human beings, animals, plants, and inanimate objects. As in the Upaniṣads, in the Mahābhārata the creator principle is relegated to a subsidiary role in the process of creation, for he himself has his source in a higher reality. Brahmā is described as the son of Viṣṇu, himself representing a manifestation of the supreme Godhead and in particular that form which Viṣṇu assumes in order to generate the worlds and various beings. Moreover, the epic emphasizes that whatever creative power Brahmā possesses is not his own but has been invested in him by the grace of Viṣṇu.[257] The birth of Brahmā is generally associated in the epic with two mythological motifs: the cosmic egg, a motif already familiar from Vedic accounts, and the lotus, a motif that becomes prevalent in the post-Vedic period in epic and Purāṇic cosmogonies. Thus, Brahmā is at times described as Hiraṇyagarbha ("golden egg or embryo"),[258] who is born from and resides in the cosmic egg. Alternatively, he is depicted as being born from a lotus that emerges from the navel of Viṣṇu-Nārāyaṇa[259] as he reclines on the cosmic waters.[260]

In the Mahābhārata, then, two of the creative principles that are fundamental to the cosmogonic speculations of Vedic texts as well as to the Manu-Smṛti—Brahman and the creator principle—are reinterpreted from a Vaiṣṇava theistic perspective, with Brahman becoming identified with Viṣṇu and the creator god becoming relegated to a secondary status as the manifestation and servant of the supreme deity. The seeds of this transformation are already present in the creation narrative of the Manu-Smṛti, in which Nārāyaṇa plays a central role, but it is not until the Mahābhārata that we have a full-fledged recasting of the cosmogonic myth cycle from a Vaiṣṇava sectarian viewpoint.

It should be noted in this context that in the Śaiva sections of the Mahābhārata the essential elements of the creation narrative generally remain intact. However, in these sections the role of the ultimate reality is assumed not by Viṣṇu but by Śiva, who becomes identified with Brahman-Ātman and is celebrated as the creator, maintainer, and destroyer of the universe from whom Brahmā and Viṣṇu arise.

Veda and Brahman In discussing the authority of the Veda the Mahābhārata declares that there are two forms of Brahman: Śabdabrahman and the supreme Brahman. One who knows Śabdabrahman attains the supreme (*para*) Brahman.[261] The Veda as Śabdabrahman represents that aspect of Brahman which manifests as the Word.[262] Although Brahman is at times represented in the Mahābhārata in impersonal terms, the conception of Brahman is more often personalized, as we have seen, through becoming identified with Viṣṇu—or, in the case of the Śaiva sections of the epic, Śiva. The Veda as an aspect of Brahman is correspondingly depicted in relation to either Viṣṇu or Śiva.

The relationship of the Veda to Viṣṇu is represented in the epic primarily in three ways: the Veda as knowledge is intrinsic to the essential nature of Viṣṇu; the Vedic *mantra*s are constitutive of Viṣṇu and of his body in particular; and at the same time the *mantra*s have their source and abode in Viṣṇu. Several passages suggest that knowledge is an inherent part of Viṣṇu's nature. Even during the time of dissolution when the entire universe has been absorbed, knowledge (*vidyā*) alone remains with Viṣṇu in his unmanifest state as Nirguṇa Brahman, and it is by means of this knowledge that he brings forth the universe in each new cycle of creation.[263]

Viṣṇu is directly identified with the Veda, and the Vedic *mantras* in particular, in a number of passages in the epic.[264] He is said to be the embodiment of the *ṛc*s, *yajus*es, *sāman*s, and *atharvan*s.

> Those people who are knowers of the Veda regard me as the Ṛg-Veda consisting of twenty-one branches (*śākhā*s) and as the Sāma-Veda consisting of a thousand branches. . . . I am known to the *adhvaryu* priest as the six and fifty and eight and seven and thirty branches of the Yajur-Veda. Brahmins versed in the *atharvan*s consider me to be the Atharva-Veda. . . .[265]

The Vedas and the Vedic *ṛṣi*s and sacrifices, along with other aspects of the universe, are depicted as forming various parts of Viṣṇu's body.[266] In one passage the Vedic meters (*chandas*es) are more specifically associated with his bodily hair.[267] The epic elsewhere describes Viṣṇu as assuming the form of a sacrificial boar (*yajña-varāha*), his body constituted by speech (*vāṅ-maya*) and the Vedas (*veda-sammita*), in order to rescue the earth from the cosmic waters in which it was submerged.[268]

While on one level the Vedic *mantras* are represented as constitutive of Viṣṇu, on another level he is described as the source of the *mantras*. He is the abode (*ālaya*) and receptacle (*nidhi*) of the Vedas,[269] from which the *mantras* go forth in the beginning of each cycle of creation and to which they return at the time of dissolution.[270] He is represented as the ultimate source not only of the four Vedas and their various branches (*śākhās*) but also of the methods of pronunciation (*śikṣā*) and recitation (*krama*) by means of which the *mantras* are accurately preserved.[271]

In the Śaiva sections of the Mahābhārata the Veda as an aspect of Brahman becomes associated with Śiva. We find conceptions similar to those found in the Vaiṣṇava passages, with particular emphasis on the Vedic *mantras* as constitutive of Śiva. For example, Śiva is deemed to be not only the lord of the Vedas but the Vedas themselves.[272] The *ṛcs*, *yajuses*, *sāmans*, and *atharvans* are described as forming different parts of Śiva's body, recalling Vedic conceptions.

> You [Śiva] have the *atharvans* for your head, the *sāmans* for your mouth, the thousand *ṛcs* for your countless eyes, the *yajuses* for your feet and arms.[273]

Veda and the Creator The creator Brahmā is represented in the Mahābhārata as that form which Viṣṇu assumes in order to bring forth the three worlds and various types of beings, and thus, like that supreme reality of which he is a manifestation, Brahmā is associated with the Veda in a number of passages.

As the embodiment of knowledge, who is the guru of the worlds and of the gods,[274] Brahmā's very substance is Veda (*veda-maya*).[275] He is also described as "the one with the four Vedas (*catur-veda*), the four forms (*catur-mūrti*), the four faces/mouths (*catur-mukha*)."[276] In the Purāṇas, as we shall see, the four Vedas become directly linked with the four mouths of Brahmā, with one Veda emerging from each mouth.[277] Although the epic does not use this image, it does depict Brahmā as bringing forth the Vedas in the beginning of each new cycle of creation. However, the epic is careful to emphasize at times that it is Viṣṇu who is the ultimate source of the Vedas and who assigns Brahmā his role as the intermediate instrument by means of which the Vedic *mantras* are manifested and promulgated.[278]

One passage clearly illustrates the subordinate position of Brahmā to Viṣṇu in relation to the Vedas. The passage recounts how while Brahmā is engaged in bringing forth the four Vedas, two demons, Madhu and Kaiṭabha, steal the Vedas from him. Brahmā, grief-stricken, laments:

> The Vedas are my principal eye, the Vedas are my principal strength, the Vedas are my principal abode, and the Vedas are my highest *brahman*. . . . Deprived of the Vedas, the worlds produced by me are darkness. Without the Vedas how shall I proceed when undertaking to bring forth the worlds?[279]

Brahmā then sings a hymn praising Viṣṇu-Nārāyaṇa as the ultimate source of creation, from which he himself has arisen, and beseeching him to restore to him his eyes, the Vedas, without which he is blind. Viṣṇu resolves to rescue the Vedas from the demons. Assuming "a radiant horse's head, which was the abode (*ālaya*) of the Vedas,"[280] and adopting a voice regulated by the rules of pronunciation (*śikṣā*), he begins to recite Vedic *mantras*. The demons are thereby induced to leave the stolen Vedas behind in the nether regions and to run toward the spot whence the sounds are coming. In the meantime Viṣṇu recovers the stolen Vedas from the nether regions and returns them to Brahmā. Brahmā then resumes the process of creation with the aid of Viṣṇu and the Vedas, bringing forth the worlds and animate and inanimate beings.[281]

This passage emphasizes the subordination of Brahmā to Viṣṇu at every point. Moreover, it makes clear that although Brahmā may be the immediate source through which the Vedas are manifested, their ultimate source is Viṣṇu, for even when the Vedas brought forth by the demiurge are stolen, Viṣṇu as the abode of the Vedas is himself capable of manifesting an alternative set of *mantras* that are not in any way dependent on Brahmā. And when Brahmā re-embarks on the process of creation by means of the Vedas, he does so only through the aid of Viṣṇu.

Vedas as the Expressions of Divine Speech In Vedic cosmogonies the Veda is associated not only with the creator Prajāpati but also with his consort Vāc, the goddess of speech. In post-Vedic accounts the role of Prajāpati is assumed by Brahmā, and correspondingly the role of Prajāpati's consort Vāc is assumed by Brahmā's consort, Sarasvatī or Gāyatrī/Sāvitrī, who is identified with the goddess of speech. In the Mahābhārata and Harivaṃśa, Sarasvatī and Gāyatrī/Sāvitrī generally retain their distinctive identities as two separate goddesses, with Sarasvatī portrayed as the daughter of Brahmā and Gāyatrī/Sāvitrī as his wife. In the Purāṇas, as we shall see, the two goddesses become identified, as do the roles of daughter and wife: Sarasvatī/Gāyatrī/Sāvitrī is depicted as issuing forth as the female half or daughter of Brahmā, with whom he subsequently unites as his wife. Both Sarasvatī and Gāyatrī/Sāvitrī are associated in the Mahābhārata and Harivaṃśa with Vāc, and, like Vāc in Vedic cosmogonies, both are celebrated as the "Mother of the Vedas."[282]

Sarasvatī, although retaining her earlier Vedic role as a river goddess associated with the waters, is at the same time represented in the epic as Vāc, the goddess of speech.[283] Sarasvatī is said to consist of speech (*vāg-bhūta*) and to be adorned with all the Sanskrit vowels (*svaras*) and consonants (*vyañjanas*).[284] In the system of correspondences that is established between the microcosm and the macrocosm she is correlated with the tongue, which is the abode of speech in both the human body and the cosmic body of Viṣṇu.[285] It is as speech that Sarasvatī fulfills her role as the Mother of the Vedas, for speech provides the vehicle by means of which the Vedic *mantras* issue forth in the beginning of each cycle of creation from the creator—whether in his supreme reality as Viṣṇu or in his relative manifestation as Brahmā. In accordance with the Vaiṣṇava emphasis of the epic, the Vedas are particularly associated with the speech of Viṣṇu, the lord of speech (*vācas pati*),[286] who is the ultimate source and abode of the Vedic *mantras*. Viṣṇu is portrayed as bringing forth speech, Sarasvatī, along with her progeny, the Vedas, at the beginning of creation[287] and as reciting the *mantras* in contexts outside of the creative process as well.[288] The Vedas are also at times depicted as emerging from the demiurge Brahmā as the expressions of his speech.

> In the beginning knowledge (*vidyā*), without beginning or end, divine speech (Vāc), consisting of the Vedas (*vedamayī*), from which all manifestations are derived, was sent forth by Svayambhū [Brahmā].[289]

The passage goes on to describe how by means of the primordial impulses of speech contained in the Vedic *mantras* Brahmā manifests the diverse phenomena of creation.[290] Sarasvatī, as the goddess of speech whose progeny are the Vedas, is thus directly involved in the process of creation. She is also represented in the epic as assuming a role in the process of Vedic cognition. A number of passages describe Sarasvatī as entering into the *ṛṣis* in order to grant them the ability to cognize the subtle mechanics of creation along with the Vedic *mantras* that play an essential role in the cosmogonic process.[291]

Gāyatrī, or Sāvitrī, is depicted in the Mahābhārata and Harivaṃśa as a goddess who, in her association with Vāc, speech, assumes a localized manifestation as the *gāyatrī* meter, "the most excellent of meters,"[292] and more specifically the *gāyatrī mantra*, or *sāvitrī*, which is composed in the *gāyatrī* meter and consists of three lines (*padas*) of eight syllables each (taken from Ṛg-Veda III.62.10) preceded by the invocation "*Om bhūr bhuvaḥ svaḥ.*"

> *Om bhūr bhuvaḥ svaḥ* |
> *tat savitur vareṇyam bhargo devasya dhīmahi* |
> *dhiyo yo naḥ pracodayāt* ||[293]

The *gāyatrī mantra* is recited daily by orthodox brahmins and is considered to represent the concentrated essence of the Vedas.

Like Sarasvatī, Gāyatrī/Sāvitrī, in her role both as a goddess and as the *gāyatrī mantra*, is celebrated in the epic as the Mother of the Vedas.[294] The Harivaṃśa contains a number of passages that elaborate on the mechanics through which the Vedas emerge from their Mother Gāyatrī/Sāvitrī. One passage describes the process through which the creator Brahmā unites with his consort Gāyatrī in order to bring forth the fourfold Veda.

> Brahmā, his mind absorbed in meditation, . . . having penetrated directly into the heart of Gāyatrī, [entered] between her eyes. From her womb was born a being who was fourfold, having the form of Puruṣa and consisting of the effulgence of the Word (*brahman*), unmanifest, eternal, nonchanging, imperishable, devoid of sense capacities or qualities, filled with the attribute of light, pure as the rays of the moon, shining, and embodied in sounds (*varṇa-saṃsthita*). The deity brought forth the Ṛg-Veda together with the Yajur-Veda from his eyes, the Sāma-Veda from the tip of his tongue, and the Atharva-Veda from his forehead. These Vedas, as soon as born, in truth (*tattvatas*) find (root *vid*) an abode. In this way they attain their "Veda-ness" (*vedatva*), for they find (root *vid*) that abode. These Vedas then bring forth, through their own mind-born nature, the primordial, eternal *brahman*, Puruṣa appearing in divine form.[295]

This passage describes how from the womb of Gāyatrī is born Puruṣa "consisting of the effulgence of the Word (*brahman*)" and composed of the *varṇa*-sounds of Sanskrit. This Puruṣa, who recalls the "person of the Veda" (*veda-puruṣa*) mentioned in Vedic texts,[296] is fourfold and from the different parts of his body brings forth the four Vedas, which in turn give rise to Puruṣa identified with *brahman*. The progression is from Gāyatrī—the goddess who manifests as the *gāyatrī* meter and the three-lined *gāyatrī mantra*—to the Word composed of Sanskrit *varṇas*, to the Vedic *mantras*, which represent special configurations of the *varṇas*.

A second passage in the Harivaṃśa gives a more detailed description of the sequential process by means of which the Vedas emerge from Gāyatrī. The creator is portrayed as desiring to divide himself in order to bring forth the universe when suddenly the means for this division manifests itself: differentiation through sound.

> "'Divide yourself'—thus have I been commanded. . . . But how is the self to be divided? Concerning this I have great doubt." While he was thus reflecting, the sound (*svara*) Om issued forth from him, and it resounded through the earth, midregions, and vault of heaven. While the Lord was thus repeating this, the essence of mind, the utterance *vaṣaṭ* issued from the heart of the god of gods. The auspicious *mahāvyāhṛtis* in the form of *bhūḥ, bhuvaḥ, svaḥ*, constituting the great tradition (*smṛti*), came forth from the earth, midregions, and vault of heaven. Then the goddess [Gāyatrī], the most excellent of meters, possessing twenty-four syllables, arose. Calling to mind the line [beginning with the word] *tat*, the Lord formed the divine *sāvitrī*. The divine Lord then formed all the four Vedas—Ṛg, Sāma, Atharva, and Yajur—together with their *mantras* and rituals.[297]

In this passage the process through which the creator divides himself is a progressive process of differentiation of sound: from the monosyllabic Om to the disyllabic *vaṣaṭ*, to the three *vyāhṛtis*—*bhūḥ, bhuvaḥ, svaḥ*—to the twenty-four syllable *gāyatrī* meter, particularly as expressed in the *gāyatrī mantra*, to the four Vedas. In Purāṇic cosmogonies, as we shall see, this process of unfoldment of primordial utterances is further delineated in terms of a sequence of stages that generally includes the elements enumerated in this passage and in the preceding passage: (1) Om; (2) the three *vyāhṛtis*;

(3) the Sanskrit *varṇas*; (4) the *gāyatrī mantra,* or *sāvitrī*; and (5) the four Vedas.[298] The *sāvitrī* includes and expands on the first two stages, for in traditional recitation of the *sāvitrī* the invocation "*Om bhūr bhuvaḥ svaḥ*" precedes the three-lined *mantra* proper.

Vedas as the Blueprint of Creation Several passages in the epic point to the cosmogonic role of the Vedas as the means by which Brahmā brings forth the phenomenal world.[299] For example, in the passage discussed earlier in which the demons steal the four Vedas from Brahmā, he laments, "Deprived of the Vedas, the worlds produced by me are darkness. Without the Vedas how shall I proceed when undertaking to bring forth the worlds?"[300] It is only after Viṣṇu recovers the Vedas from the demons and returns them to Brahmā that "recapacitated by the Vedas Brahmā then formed all the worlds with their inanimate and animate beings."[301]

The Vedas assist Brahmā in the process of creation by providing an eternal blueprint that contains the prototypes of all phenomena. As in the Manu-Smṛti, the notion of the Vedas as the plan of creation is linked to the epic's cyclical view of creation, in which each cycle follows a set, eternally repeated pattern in which the same classes of beings, each with its inherent name, nature, and function, are brought forth. It is the demiurge Brahmā to whom Viṣṇu assigns the role of the "ordainer (*dhātṛ*) of all beings," for it is Brahmā who manifests these various classes of beings anew in each cycle and reassigns to them their designated names and allotted duties.[302] The names, forms, and functions of all beings are said to be eternally preserved in the Vedic *mantras*, which reappear at the beginning of each new cycle as the blueprint that the architect Brahmā consults in order to fulfill his function as demiurge.

> In the beginning the Lord forms from the words (*śabdas*) of the Vedas alone the names of the *ṛṣis*, the creations in the Vedas, the various forms of beings, and the course of actions.[303]

The Eternality of the Veda In the epic, as in the Manu-Smṛti, the notion that the Vedas constitute the blueprint of creation is closely linked to the conception of the eternality of the Veda. The epic frequently refers to the Veda as the "eternal *śruti*" or "eternal Veda(s)."[304] The Vedas are the expressions of Veda, that primordial knowledge (*vidyā*) which is without beginning or end (*anādi-nidhana*).[305]

The Veda, as the nonchanging, eternal knowledge that is the foundation and source of creation, is represented as remaining intact in its original structure throughout the never-ending cycles of creation and dissolution. Even when the entire cosmic process ceases to be at the time of the dissolution, the Veda and its differentiated expressions in the Vedic *mantras* remain latent within Viṣṇu in his unmanifest state as Nirguṇa Brahman. When the cycle of creation begins anew, the Veda once again emerges from Viṣṇu and differentiates into the impulses of knowledge contained in speech that constitute the Vedic *mantras*. These eternal *mantras* are said to be cognized by the *ṛṣis* at the beginning of each new cycle and preserved through their speech in the form of recited texts that are subsequently passed down in an unbroken line of oral transmission. Even though in its mundane status as recited texts the Veda becomes subject to the vicissitudes of time and human consciousness, the epic emphasizes that in its supramundane status the Veda remains eternally nonchanging and imperishable.[306]

Purāṇas

The Purāṇas, like the Mahābhārata and Harivaṃśa, are products of the brahmanical synthesis that sought to preserve the authority of the Vedic tradition and the *varṇāśrama-dharma* system while at the same time absorbing and domesticating the competing claims of sectarian devotionalism and popular village cults. These encyclopedic works, the majority of which were composed during the first millennium C.E., include extensive mythological material that combines traditional Vedic speculations with post-Vedic philosopical and theistic conceptions. They also incorporate didactic sections on *varṇāśrama-dharma* alongside descriptions of popular devotional practices that could be performed not only by male members of the three higher *varṇas* but also by *śūdras* and women, such as the presentation of offerings to the image of a deity (*pūjā*),[307] pilgrimages to holy places (*tīrthas*), giving of gifts (*dāna*), and vows (*vratas*). The influence of certain tantric traditions and practices is also evident in the later Purāṇas, especially those that are Śākta or Śaiva in orientation. The heterogeneous material in the Purāṇas, as characterized by R. C. Hazra, includes

> extensive glorifications of one or more of the sectarian deities like Brahmā, Viṣṇu, and Śiva . . . numerous chapters on new myths, and legends, and multifarious topics

> concerning religion and society, for instance, duties of the different castes and orders of life, sacraments, customs in general, eatables and non-eatables, duties of women, funeral rites and ceremonies, impurity on birth and death, sins, penances and expiations, purification of things, names and description of hells, results of good and bad deeds (*karma-vipāka*), pacification of unfavourable planets, donations of various types, dedication of wells, tanks, and gardens, worship, devotional vows (*vratas*), places of pilgrimage, consecration of temples and images of gods, initiation, and various mystic rites and practices.[308]

The Purāṇas, according to the classical Hindu definition, are distinguished by five characteristics (*pañca-lakṣaṇa*): descriptions of creation (*sarga*) and re-creation (*pratisarga*) of the universe after its periodic dissolutions; genealogies of gods, sages, and kings (*vaṃśa*); accounts of the ages of Manu (*manvantara*); and histories of the royal dynasties (*vaṃśānucarita*).[309] Although the extant Purāṇas obviously contain much more than this definition suggests, and some give only minimal attention to these five topics,[310] it is nevertheless noteworthy that the traditional definition places such emphasis on cosmogonic concerns, genealogies, and histories. The Purāṇas are themselves considered to be "ancient (*purāṇa*) histories" that assume the role of exemplary narratives in which not only the protagonists—gods, kings, and sages—become paradigmatic, but also certain periods of history. Moreover, the "history" recounted in the Purāṇas is not linear but cyclical, forming part of the endlessly repeating cycles of *yugas* and *manvantaras* that are themselves part of the endlessly repeating cycles of primary (*sarga*) and secondary (*pratisarga*) creation. Cosmogonic concerns are thus given a prominent place in most of the major Purāṇas, since the creative process represents the generative matrix that brings forth the prototypes and patterns that will be continually activated and replicated in subsequent periods. The Vedas are allotted a central role in this process as the eternal blueprint in which the prototypes and patterns are encoded.

The Purāṇas, like the Mahābhārata, make use of a variety of strategies to assimilate themselves to the eternal Veda. They claim the status of the "fifth Veda" for both the Itihāsas and Purāṇas[311] and at times refer to themselves as the "Purāṇa-Veda."[312] Like the epic, the Purāṇas declare themselves to be equal to the Vedas[313] and a necessary complement to them. The Vāyu Purāṇa contains two *ślokas*, variants of which are also found in the Mahābhārata, that emphasize that knowledge of the Vedas is not sufficient but must be supplemented by knowledge of the Purāṇas.

> A brahmin who knows the four Vedas with their subsidiary limbs (*aṅgas*) and Upaniṣads but who does not know the Purāṇa is not really learned. With both Itihāsa and Purāṇa one should complement the Veda. The Veda is afraid of one with little knowledge.[314]

The Purāṇas further emulate the paradigmatic Veda by providing an account of their origins that establishes their own primordial status alongside that of the Vedas. For example, the Bhāgavata Purāṇa describes the four Vedas as issuing forth, respectively, from the four mouths of the creator Brahmā at the beginning of creation, followed by the Itihāsas and Purāṇas as the fifth Veda, which emerge from all four mouths together.[315] A tradition that is found in a number of Purāṇas goes even further and insists that originally there was one primordial Purāṇa that emerged from Brahmā as the first of all the *śāstras*, even prior to the Vedas. The Matsya Purāṇa ascribes to this Purāṇa the status of the eternal Word that is generally reserved for the Veda alone.

> Of all the *śāstras* the Purāṇa was first recalled (*smṛti*) by Brahmā—eternal (*nitya*), consisting of the Word (*śabdamaya*), holy, having the extent of a hundred crores [of *ślokas*]. Afterward the Vedas issued forth from his mouths and also Mīmāṃsā and the science of Nyāya together with the eightfold means of valid knowledge (*pramāṇa*).[316]

This tradition is reiterated in a second passage in the Matsya Purāṇa, which further maintains that it is Viṣṇu who originally transmits the Vedas, Purāṇas, and other *śāstras* to Brahmā, who in turn conveys them to the gods and *ṛṣis*. The passage then continues with an explanation of how the original, eternal Purāṇa, which was "the source (*pravṛtti*) of all the *śāstras*," came to assume its present earthly form as eighteen Purāṇas. Vyāsa, acclaimed as the partial incarnation of Viṣṇu who divides the one Veda into four Saṃhitās in every Dvāpara Yuga,[317] is also credited with condensing the original Purāṇa of one hundred crores (one billion) of *ślokas* into an abridged edition of four lakhs (400,000) of *ślokas*, which he subsequently divided into eighteen Purāṇas. Although it thus assumed a modified earthly form, the original Purāṇa of one hundred crores of *ślokas* continues to exist in the world of the gods (*deva-loka*).[318] Variants of this account are found in the Padma, Nārada, and Liṅga Purāṇas.[319]

According to an alternative tradition found in the Brahmāṇḍa, Vāyu, and Viṣṇu Purāṇas, Vyāsa compiled the Purāṇa Saṃhitā from tales, episodes, verses, and accounts of the *kalpas*.[320] When Vyāsa taught the four Vedic Saṃhitās to four of his disciples, respectively, he taught this Purāṇa Saṃhitā to his fifth disciple, Sūta Lomaharṣaṇa (or Romaharṣaṇa). Lomaharṣaṇa in turn taught it to his disciples, three of whom compiled their own Saṃhitās. These three Saṃhitās, together with that of Lomaharṣaṇa, constitute the original (*mūla* or *pūrva*) Saṃhitās from which the eighteen Purāṇas were derived.[321]

The Purāṇas thus seek to emulate and at times surpass the Vedas in their claims to a primordial status that, as the first of the *śāstras* brought forth by Brahmā in each new cycle of creation, is anterior even to the Vedas. They also reflect the Vedic paradigm in their accounts of Vyāsa's role in compiling, dividing, and disseminating the Purāṇa Saṃhitā as the "fifth Veda" alongside the four Vedic Saṃhitās. Moreover, the Purāṇas declare themselves to be the repositories of efficacious *mantras*, comparable in power to the Vedic *mantras*, and regularly proclaim the fruits of hearing (*phala-śruti*) the recitation of a particular Purāṇa or sections thereof.

Although the Purāṇas thus seek to align themselves with the Veda through various means, at the same time they depart from the *śruti* model in significant ways. For example, unlike recitations of the Vedas, Purāṇic recitations may be heard by *śūdras* and women as well as by male members of the three higher *varṇas*.[322] In addition, the Purāṇas emphasize not only the power of *mantra* but the power of sacred narrative as well. In contrast to recitation of the Vedic Saṃhitās, which focuses almost exclusively on *śabda*, on verbatim reproduction of the Vedic sounds, in Purāṇic recitations both *śabda* and *artha*, sound and meaning, are important, for the content of the texts is intended to convey important teachings to the general populace. Thomas Coburn has emphasized the contrast between the "sacramental" function of *śruti* texts, the sounds of which must be accurately reproduced irrespective of whether their discursive meaning is understood, and the "didactic" function of *smṛti* texts such as the epics and Purāṇas, which as salvific stories are intended to convey meaning to an audience and therefore give precedence to "dynamic recreation" through multiple retellings over "literal preservation" of a fixed oral text.[323] C. Mackenzie Brown has also noted the significance of this shift in emphasis from sound to meaning for post-Vedic conceptualizations of scripture.

> The Puranic synthesis of sound and meaning . . . involved a number of new conceptualizations regarding the nature of scripture. Earlier, the "*artha* tradition" was subservient to the "*śabda* tradition," the narrative history facilitating and ensuring the success of the mantra. In the Purāṇas, the narrative or story literature has become the primary holy word, reincorporating the old mantric tradition under new terms. The saving story itself has taken on the character of mantric efficacy though not the mantric immutability. The shift to an emphasis on meaning and the greater flexibility in the epic-Puranic traditions were crucial factors in the evolution of written scripture.[324]

As Brown indicates, this shift in emphasis from sound to meaning in the Purāṇic tradition was accompanied by a shift in modes of scriptural transmission. Like the Mahābhārata, the Purāṇas depart from the Vedic paradigm of exclusively oral transmission by emphasizing the importance of written transmission as well. They declare the fruits not only of hearing a Purāṇa recited but also of writing or copying the text itself and then giving the book away as a gift.[325] The giving of gifts, including presumably the giving of books, is open to *śūdras* and women, and thus this Purāṇic practice, like that of Purāṇic recitation, served to establish the Purāṇas as the scriptures of the general populace, accessible to all social classes. As Brown points out, it made possible "a significant reversal of roles: when scripture was purely oral, it was given by the Brahmans to others; in its written form, it can now be given by others to Brahmans."[326] This emphasis on the written form of the Purāṇas led to the development of the Purāṇic "cult of the book," in which the Purāṇic text itself, in its visible manifestation as a concrete book as well as in its audible manifestation as recited sounds, came to be viewed as an incarnation of the divine that was to be worshiped accordingly.[327]

In their representations of their own scriptural status, the Purāṇas thus appropriate the Vedic model when describing their primordial origins, but they diverge from it when discussing their earthly status as popular devotional texts that are to be taught in both oral and written form to people at all levels of the social hierarchy. The "Purāṇa-Vedas," like the epics, are socially inclusive scriptures that are intended to inspire and edify the general populace with their sacred narratives. However, they do not thereby supersede the original Veda altogether, for the Veda still remains the model on the supramundane level. When we turn to an analysis of Purāṇic cosmogonic and cosmological speculations, we find that despite Purāṇic claims to be the first of all the *śāstras*, the Veda is nevertheless accorded a special status as that eternal knowledge which constitutes the essence of the supreme deity—whether Viṣṇu or Śiva or Devī—who is identified with Brahman and who assumes a secondary manifestation as the creator Brahmā. Moreover, the Vedic *mantras* alone are granted the status of the archetypal plan that the creator employs to fashion the phenomena of creation.

The Creation Narrative Purāṇic cosmogonies, like the creation accounts of the Mahābhārata, are composite narratives that interweave material from a variety of sources, including Vedic mythological conceptions, Sāṃkhya speculations concerning the *tattvas*, and conceptions of Brahman-Ātman drawn from the Upaniṣads as well as, in later Purāṇas such as the Bhāgavata Purāṇa, Advaita Vedānta philosophy. The dualistic perspective of Sāṃkhya is generally subsumed within a monistic framework with a theistic cast: the deity that is deemed by a particular Purāṇa to be the ultimate reality is identified with Brahman and is described as encompassing and transcending both Puruṣa and Prakṛti.

The Purāṇas make a number of contributions to the brahmanical cosmogonic myth cycle. First, they tend to standardize the list of twenty-five *tattvas*, with a relatively consistent enumeration of the elementary principles given in the various Purāṇic accounts.[328] Second, they also standardize the concept of time, distinguishing between cycles of primary creation (*sarga*) and secondary creation (*pratisarga*). *Sarga* is characterized by the emergence of the *tattvas* as the *prākṛta* creations of Prakṛti, while *pratisarga* is characterized by the *vaikṛta* creations of the creator Brahmā. Finally, the Purāṇas recast the creation narrative from a variety of sectarian perspectives. Although the major Purāṇas generally agree in their descriptions of the basic structure and components of the *sarga* and *pratisarga*, including the enumeration of the *prākṛta* and *vaikṛta* creations, they diverge on the basis of the particular sectarian biases with which they modify certain details of the narrative. The principal point of divergence concerns the identity of that eternal, unmanifest Brahman which is the ultimate source of the universe.

For example, Vaiṣṇava Purāṇas proclaim that Viṣṇu is the supreme Brahman that gives impetus to the entire process of creation. Śaiva Purāṇas, on the other hand, identify Śiva with Brahman as the ultimate reality that is the source of Viṣṇu-Nārāyaṇa and of the entire cosmos.

The following analysis will focus primarily on the cosmogonic and cosmological speculations found in seven major Purāṇas: the Viṣṇu Purāṇa (ca. 300–500 C.E.) and the Bhāgavata Purāṇa (ca. 800–900 C.E.), which are Vaiṣṇava in orientation; the Liṅga Purāṇa (ca. 800–1000 C.E.) and the Śiva Purāṇa (ca. 800–1000 C.E.), which are Śaiva works; the Matsya Purāṇa (ca. 200–400 C.E.) and the Kūrma Purāṇa (ca. 550–800 C.E.), which are cross-sectarian, containing both Vaiṣṇava and Śaiva material; and the Mārkaṇḍeya Purāṇa (ca. 300–500 C.E.), which is nonsectarian.[329] Although the multiple cosmogonic accounts in these Purāṇas present the process of creation from a variety of perspectives, they are relatively consistent in their descriptions of the essential components of the *sarga* and *pratisarga*, as summarized below.[330]

(1) Sarga: Brahman and the Prākṛta Creations of Prakṛti

At the end of one hundred years of Brahmā, the entire universe—all the gods, demons, *ṛṣis*, other celestial beings, human beings, animals, plants, and inanimate objects, as well as the *tattvas*, and Brahmā himself—is dissolved in the *mahāpralaya* (also termed *prākṛtika pralaya*). The entire universe remains in potential form within Nirguṇa Brahman, the unmanifest absolute reality—generally identified with either Viṣṇu or Śiva, depending on the sectarian perspective—for a hundred more years of Brahmā, after which the whole process of creation begins anew. Brahman, while remaining unmanifest in its essential nature, becomes *saguṇa* and assumes a manifest form as Īśvara, the supreme Lord, who provides the spur for the *sarga* to begin by entering into and agitating Puruṣa and Prakṛti.[331] Īśvara is at times described as implanting his seed in Prakṛti, primordial matter, who is generally identified with the female principle as the material matrix from which creation evolves.[332] When the equilibrium of the three *guṇas*, the three constituents of Prakṛti, is broken, Prakṛti acts as the material cause from which the *tattvas*—termed *prākṛta* creations—evolve. The *tattvas* then combine to form the golden egg of creation.

(2) Pratisarga: Brahmā and the Vaikṛta Creations

Having entered the egg and infused it with life, Puruṣa is born from the egg in the *pratisarga* as either Brahmā (according to most Purāṇic accounts) or Viṣṇu-Nārāyaṇa in his second manifestation (according to the Bhāgavata Purāṇa). In accounts of subsequent *pratisargas* Brahmā is at times described as emerging from a lotus that issues forth from the navel of Viṣṇu-Nārāyaṇa while he is reclining on the primordial waters. The demiurge Brahmā is the instrumental cause who fashions the three worlds—earth, midregions, and heaven—and all animate and inanimate beings from the *tattvas*, evolutes of primordial matter, derived from the *sarga*. The *pratisarga*, with its *vaikṛta* creations derived from Brahmā, occurs at the beginning of each new day (*kalpa*) of Brahmā. At the end of each *kalpa* Brahmā sleeps, and a minor dissolution (*naimittika pralaya*) occurs in which the three lower worlds and all lower beings are absorbed within the body of Brahmā, while the *tattvas*, higher worlds, gods, and *ṛṣis* remain unaffected. When Brahmā awakens at the beginning of the next *kalpa*, the *pratisarga* again commences.

The primary and secondary cycles of creation described in Purāṇic cosmogonies correspond, respectively, to the two stages of creation outlined earlier from the Manu-Smṛti.[333] (1) The *sarga* corresponds to the first stage, in which the unmanifest (Nirguṇa Brahman) assumes a manifest form as Nārāyaṇa (Saguṇa Brahman), who deposits his seed in the womb of the female principle, represented in mythological terms as the waters or in metaphysical terms as Prakṛti. The seed bears fruit, emerging as the golden egg of creation. (2) The *pratisarga* corresponds to the second stage of creation, in which Nārāyaṇa himself enters the egg and is born

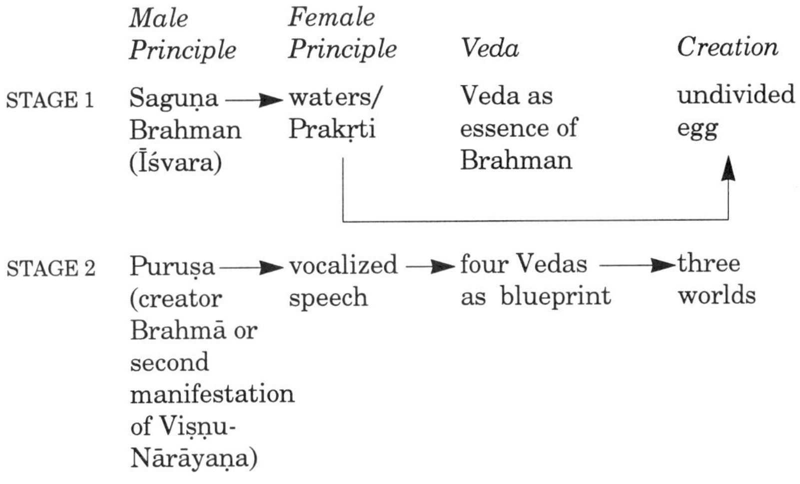
Male Principle
Female Principle
Veda
Creation
STAGE 1
Saguṇa Brahman (Īśvara)
waters/ Prakṛti
Veda as essence of Brahman
undivided egg
STAGE 2
Puruṣa (creator Brahmā or second manifestation of Viṣṇu-Nārāyaṇa)
vocalized speech
four Vedas as blueprint
three worlds

from it as Puruṣa, identified in the Manu-Smṛti and most Purāṇic accounts as the creator Brahmā. With the infusion of the life principle into the cosmic egg, the primordial undivided unity begins to differentiate, giving rise to the three worlds and the various classes of beings. In accordance with Vedic accounts, in Purāṇic cosmogonies it is only after the creator is born from the egg that he speaks, and among the primordial utterances that emerge from him are Om, the three *vyāhṛtis*, and the four Vedas.[334]

As in Vedic texts, different levels of Veda correspond to these two stages: in the first stage the Veda is that totality of knowledge which is the essence of Brahman; while in the second stage the Veda manifests as the Vedic *mantras*, which constitute the blueprint containing the words spoken by the creator Brahmā in order to bring the forms of creation into being. (See the figure on page 101.)[335]

Veda and Brahman In the Purāṇas, as in earlier brahmanical texts, the Veda is represented as an aspect of Brahman, with Brahman assuming a personalized form as either Viṣṇu or Śiva. The Purāṇas emphasize that the nature of Viṣṇu or Śiva, as the ultimate reality identified with Brahman, is knowledge, and the Veda constitutes both the inner essence and the outer form of this reality.

The Viṣṇu Purāṇa celebrates Viṣṇu as the supreme Brahman, whose essence is knowledge, who is knowledge incarnate (*jñāna-mūrti*),[336] and who is one with the Vedas,[337] his form being composed of the *ṛcs*, *yajuses*, and *sāmans*.

> He is composed of the *ṛcs*, of the *sāmans*, of the *yajuses*, and he is the Self (Ātman). He whose Self is the essence of the *ṛcs*, *yajuses*, and *sāmans*, he is the Self of embodied beings. Consisting of the Veda (*veda-maya*), he is divided; he forms the Veda with its branches (*śākhās*) into many divisions. Creator of the *śākhās*, he is the *śākhās* in their totality, the infinite Lord, whose very nature is knowledge (*jñāna-svarūpa*).[338]

This passage points to at least two levels on which the Veda participates in the nature of Viṣṇu/Brahman. (1) As the undifferentiated totality of knowledge, the Veda constitutes the very essence of Viṣṇu/Brahman, whose nature is knowledge and who thus consists of the Veda (*veda-maya*). (2) While Viṣṇu/Brahman's inner essence is Veda, knowledge, his outer form is composed of the Vedic *mantras*—*ṛcs*, *yajuses*, and *sāmans*. As Veda he is undivided, encompassing the totality of knowledge, while as the Vedas he is divided into parts composed of the Vedic *mantras* and their numerous branches (*śākhās*).[339]

Another passage in the Viṣṇu Purāṇa describes the Vedas and their supplements, the Vedāṅgas and Upavedas, together with the Itihāsas, Dharma-Śāstras, and other sacred texts, as the body of Viṣṇu in the form of sound/word (*śabda-mūrti*).[340] The Veda as such is Śabdabrahman, Brahman embodied in the Word. Elsewhere the Viṣṇu Purāṇa describes the threefold Veda—*ṛcs*, *yajuses*, and *sāmans*—as the body (*aṅga*) of Viṣṇu and as identical with his supreme energy (*śakti*) that abides within the sun and is responsible for the preservation of the universe.[341]

Viṣṇu-Nārāyaṇa is extolled as the embodiment of knowledge, whose form is constituted by the Vedas, not only in Vaiṣṇava Purāṇas such as the Viṣṇu Purāṇa and Bhāgavata Purāṇa, but also in nonsectarian Purāṇas such as the Mārkaṇḍeya Purāṇa and in cross-sectarian Purāṇas such as the Matsya and Kūrma Purāṇas that contain both Vaiṣṇava and Śaiva material. For example, the Matsya Purāṇa, in its account of creation, eulogizes Viṣṇu-Nārāyaṇa, who is identified with Brahman, as the secret essence of the Vedas (*vedānām rahasya*)[342] whose very substance is Veda (*veda-maya*).[343]

Like the epic, the Purāṇas particularly extol Viṣṇu-Nārāyaṇa as the incarnation of Veda when he assumes the form of a boar (*varāha*) at the beginning of the Vārāha Kalpa in order to rescue the earth that lies submerged beneath the waters. The Kūrma Purāṇa celebrates Viṣṇu-Nārāyaṇa in his boar form as "the secret essence of the Veda (*veda-rahasya*), the abode of Veda (*veda-yoni*), the awakened, pure, the embodiment of knowledge (*jñāna-rūpin*)."[344] A number of the Purāṇas, including the Matsya, Viṣṇu, and Bhāgavata Purāṇas, contain extensive eulogies of the boar Viṣṇu-Nārāyaṇa as Veda incarnate, whose nature is knowledge,[345] whose form is composed of the Vedas and of the various elements of the sacrifice,[346] and who emits a sound like the chanting of the Sāma-Veda.[347] The Kūrma and Liṅga Purāṇas proclaim this radiant boar Nārāyaṇa, consisting of speech (*vāṅ-maya*), to be Brahman.[348] In the nonsectarian Mārkaṇḍeya Purāṇa it is the creator Brahmā, not Viṣṇu, who is Nārāyaṇa and who assumes the form of a boar, "a divine form consisting of the Vedas and sacrifices (*veda-yajña-maya*)," in order to rescue the earth.[349]

In Śaiva Purāṇas such as the Śiva Purāṇa, it is Śiva who is extolled as the supreme Brahman whose Self is knowledge (*jñān-ātman*) and who is composed of the three Vedas (*trayī-maya*).[350]

Moreover, Śiva in his *saguṇa* form is described in the Śiva Purāṇa as Śabdabrahman, Brahman embodied in the Word, his body constituted by the forty-eight *varṇa*-sounds of Sanskrit and the three Vedas—Ṛg, Yajur, and Sāma.[351] The Śaiva sections of the Kūrma Purāṇa similarly celebrate Śiva as the eternal Brahman whose Self is knowledge (*jñānātman, vidyātman*)[352] and who as the secret essence of the Veda (*veda-rahasya*) is the embodiment of the very self of Veda (*vedātma-mūrti*).[353]

Veda and the Creator The Veda as undifferentiated knowledge is thus said to constitute the very nature of that supreme Brahman which is the ultimate source of the universe. The creator Brahmā is described in the Purāṇas as the manifest form that Brahman—whether identified with Viṣṇu or Śiva—assumes for the purpose of fashioning the forms of creation. Brahmā himself thus participates in the nature of Brahman and in his role as the demiurge is extolled as the embodiment of knowledge and Veda incarnate.

The Viṣṇu Purāṇa describes Brahmā as "Hiraṇyagarbha, that form of Brahman which consists of Lord Viṣṇu and which is composed of the Ṛg-, Yajur-, and Sāma-Vedas."[354] The Kūrma Purāṇa declares the *ṛcs, yajuses, sāmans,* and *atharvans* to be the inherent form (*sahaja rūpa*) of Brahmā,[355] and he in turn is said to be the embodiment of the Vedic *mantras* (*chando-mūrti*)[356] as well as their repository (*veda-nidhi*).[357]

In the Bhāgavata Purāṇa it is the creator Brahmā who is called Śabdabrahman, Brahman embodied in the Word,[358] and he is thus identified with Veda and is said to be composed of Veda (*veda-maya*)[359] and the abode of Veda (*veda-garbha*).[360] The various aspects of Brahmā's being, as Śabdabrahman, are described as constituted by the Sanskrit *varṇas* and the Vedic *mantras* and meters. The Sanskrit vowels (*svaras*) constitute his body, the sibilants (*ūṣmans*) his sense organs, the semi-vowels (*antaḥsthas*) his bodily vigor, and the consonants (*sparśas*) his life principle (*jīva*).[361] The Vedic *mantras* and meters and other primordial utterances are depicted as emerging from different parts of the body of Brahmā. The four Vedas—Ṛg, Yajur, Sāma, and Atharva—issue forth from his four mouths, together with the sacrificial apparatus associated with the priests of each Veda: the *śastras* recited by the *hotṛ* priest, the oblations (*ijyās*) offered by the *adhvaryu,* the *stutis* (praises) and *stomas* sung by the *udgātṛ,* and the expiations (*prāyaścittas*) offered by the *brahman* priest. Brahmā subsequently sends forth from his four mouths the four Upavedas, the Itihāsas and Purāṇas as the fifth Veda, and various types of sacrifices.[362] The three *vyāhṛtis*—*bhūḥ*, *bhuvaḥ*, and *svaḥ*—also come forth from Brahmā's mouths, while the syllable Om arises from the cavity of his heart.[363] The *uṣṇik* meter emerges from his bodily hair, the *gāyatrī* from his skin, the *triṣṭubh* from his flesh, the *anuṣṭubh* from his tendons, the *jagatī* from his bones, the *paṅkti* from his bone marrow, and the *bṛhatī* from his breath.[364]

Vedas as the Expressions of Divine Speech As the primordial impulses of speech that issue forth from the mouths of Brahmā, the Vedas become associated in the Purāṇas, as in earlier brahmanical texts, with Vāc, particularly as embodied in Sarasvatī/Gāyatrī/Sāvitrī. In the Purāṇas Sarasvatī and Gāyatrī/Sāvitrī become identified as a single goddess, who is depicted as emerging from the body of Brahmā as his female half, or daughter, with whom he then unites as his wife and from whom he brings forth the Vedas.[365] While Brahmā is the master of the Vedas, Sarasvatī/Gāyatrī is their mistress.[366] Like her progeny, the Vedas, Sarasvatī as the goddess of speech is at times associated in the Purāṇas with the mouths of Brahmā, which are her special abode.[367]

The association of the Vedas with the mouths of Brahmā, as the expressions of his speech, is found even in the earliest Purāṇas such as the Matsya Purāṇa. According to one passage in the Matsya Purāṇa, Brahmā is born from the cosmic egg reciting (root *paṭh*) the Vedas.[368] A second passage describes how after Brahmā performs *tapas* the Vedas manifest together with their *aṅgas* (limbs), *upāṅgas* (subordinate limbs), and methods of recitation (*pada-krama*). However, the passage then interjects a qualification by invoking the Purāṇic tradition that "of all the *śāstras* the Purāṇa was first recalled (*smṛti*) by Brahmā," and only afterward did the Vedas emerge from his mouths. While delighting in repeating (*abhyāsa*) the Vedas, Brahmā then proceeds to bring forth his mind-born sons.[369]

The emergence of the Vedic *mantras* from Brahmā's mouths is generally represented in later Purāṇic cosmogonies in the form of a standardized description of the four Vedas issuing forth, respectively, from the four mouths of Brahmā, along with certain Vedic meters, *stomas*, *sāmans*, and sacrifices. The Viṣṇu Purāṇa's account is representative.

> From his eastern mouth he [Brahmā] formed the *gāyatrī* meter, the *ṛcs*, the *trivṛt stoma*, the *rathantara sāman*, and

> the *agniṣṭoma* sacrifice. From his southern mouth he brought forth the *yajuses*, the *triṣṭubh* meter, the *pañcadaśa stoma*, the *bṛhat sāman*, and the *uktha* portion of the Sāma-Veda. From his western mouth he brought forth the *sāmans*, the *jagatī* meter, the *saptadaśa stoma*, the *vairūpa sāman*, and the *atirātra* sacrifice. From his northern mouth he brought forth the *ekaviṃśa stoma*, the *atharvan*, the *aptoryāman* sacrifice, the *anuṣṭubh* meter, and the *vairāja sāman*.[370]

This account is given in nearly identical words in the Mārkaṇḍeya, Kūrma, Liṅga, and Śiva Purāṇas.[371]

The Purāṇas also contain a number of variants of this standard account. We already noted above the account of the Bhāgavata Purāṇa, which describes the four Vedas, together with the Itihāsas and Purāṇas and various sacrifices, as emerging from the four mouths of Brahmā. However, in this account the Vedic meters come forth from various parts of Brahmā's body other than his mouths.[372] The Mārkaṇḍeya Purāṇa, in addition to the standard account, gives a second description in which the four Vedas that emerge from Brahmā's four mouths are correlated with the three *guṇas*, the three constituents of Prakṛti.[373] In a third passage the Mārkaṇḍeya Purāṇa declares itself, "this Purāṇa," to have issued forth along with the Vedas from Brahmā's mouths.[374]

In the Purāṇas the primordial utterances described in Vedic accounts—the three constituent sounds of Om, the three *vyāhṛtis*, and the three Vedas—are represented as different stages in the sequential unfoldment of the divine speech. The Purāṇic schema, which also incorporates a number of elements found in Harivaṃśa accounts, comprises six main stages: (1) the syllable Om, which as the sound-embodiment of Brahman is the fundamental, all-encompassing sound at the basis of creation; (2) the three sounds *a, u, m,* which are the constituents of Om; (3) the three *vyāhṛtis*—*bhūḥ, bhuvaḥ, svaḥ*—which are the seed syllables of the three corresponding worlds; (4) the forty-eight *varṇas*, or *akṣaras*, of Sanskrit, which are the basic structural elements of creation; (5) the three-lined *gāyatrī mantra,* or *sāvitrī*, which incorporates and expands on the three *vyāhṛtis* preceded by Om; and (6) the four Vedas—Ṛg, Yajur, Sāma, and Atharva—which are composed of various configurations of the forty-eight Sanskrit *varṇas*.

A number of variations on this pattern are found in Purāṇic cosmogonies. The Vāmana Purāṇa, for example, describes how when Brahmā breaks open the cosmic egg in the beginning of the *pratisarga* the sound Om is born, followed by *bhūḥ, bhuvaḥ,* and *svaḥ,* and subsequently *tat savitur vareṇyam,* the opening line of the *sāvitrī.*[375] No mention of the Vedas is made in this passage, however. According to an account in the Mārkaṇḍeya Purāṇa, as soon as Brahmā splits open the egg the syllable Om issues forth from his mouth, and immediately thereafter *bhūḥ, bhuvaḥ,* and *svaḥ* in sequence. Subsequently the four Vedas—Ṛg, Yajur, Sāma, and Atharva—emerge from his eastern, southern, western, and northern mouths, respectively.[376] The *sāvitrī* is not mentioned in this account.

The most elaborate account of the sequential emergence of the primordial utterances from Brahmā is found in the Bhāgavata Purāṇa.

> From the space in the supreme Brahmā's heart, when he was absorbed in meditation, came forth a sound (*nāda*), which is perceived through restraining [sensory] activity. . . . From that [sound] arose the syllable Om, composed of three parts [*a, u, m*], of unmanifest origin, self-luminous, which is the emblem of the divine Brahman, the supreme Self (Ātman). It is he who hears, when the sense of hearing is nonactive and the sense of sight inoperative, this unmanifest sound (*sphoṭa*). The manifestation of this [Om], through which speech (Vāc) is manifested, derives from the Self in the space [of the heart]. This [Om] is directly expressive of its own abode, Brahman, the supreme Self, and it is the secret essence of all the *mantra*s, the eternal seed (*bīja*) of the Vedas. This [Om], O descendant of the Bhṛgus, consists of three sounds (*varṇa*s), *a* and the rest, in which are contained three modes of being: the [three] constituents of Prakṛti (*guṇa*s), the [three] names (*nāma*s), the [three] objects (*artha*s), and the [three] states (*vṛtti*s). From these [three sounds] the unborn Lord brought forth the traditional system of *akṣara*s, distinguished as semi-vowels (*antaḥstha*s), sibilants (*ūṣman*s), vowels (*svara*s), short and long, and consonants (*sparśa*s). With this [sound system] the Lord, desiring to express the functions of the four classes of priests, [brought forth] from his four mouths the four Vedas together with the [three] *vyāhṛti*s and the syllable Om.[377]

This passage points to at least four different stages in the unfoldment of the primordial utterances. (1) The process begins with the emergence of a completely unmanifest, undifferentiated sound, Om, which can only be perceived when all sensory activity has been transcended. This unexpressed, transcendent sound contains the potentiality of all sound within it and is the sound-form of Brahman. (2) This primordial totality of sound is differentiated into three sounds—*a, u, m*—which contain various sets of three entities. With respect to these triads, the commentator Śrīdhara explains the three *guṇas* as *sattva* (purity), *rajas* (activity), and *tamas* (inertia); the three names as Ṛg, Yajur, and Sāma; the three objects as the three worlds, *bhūḥ, bhuvaḥ,* and *svaḥ;* and the three states as waking, dreaming, and deep sleep. (3) These three sounds then differentiate into the forty-eight Sanskrit *akṣaras,* or *varṇas.* (4) From the basic sound impulses contained in Sanskrit Brahmā brings forth the four Vedas as well as the three *vyāhṛtis* together with Om, which constitute the opening invocation of the *sāvitrī.*

The progression is thus from the original, all-encompassing sound Om to the three sounds *a, u, m*—which implicitly contain *bhūḥ, bhuvaḥ, svaḥ*—to the forty-eight *varṇas* of Sanskrit, to the *sāvitrī* and the four Vedas. At least three different levels of manifestation of the Veda can be discerned in this process. (1) Om as the undifferentiated totality of sound is the symbol of Brahman and is thus Śabdabrahman, Brahman embodied in the Word.[378] In this sense Om corresponds with the Veda as Śabdabrahman and is hence the "seed (*bīja*) of the Vedas," containing the potentiality of the Vedic *mantras* in yet undifferentiated form. (2) The three constituents of Om—*a, u, m*—contain in seed form (if we accept the commentator's interpretation) the three Vedas—Ṛg, Yajur, and Sāma. These three sounds are represented as the concentrated essences of the three Vedas not only in Vedic cosmogonies[379] but also in the Manu-Smṛti and certain Purāṇic texts.[380] (3) Finally, once the forty-eight Sanskrit *varṇas* have emerged from the three constituents of Om, they combine in various configurations to form the words of the four Vedas.

The process of unfoldment of the divine speech, as described in the Purāṇic passages analyzed above, can be schematized as a six-stage process. (See the figure on page 109.)

Vedas as the Blueprint of Creation There is creative power in the divine speech that issues forth from the creator Brahmā in a series of primordial utterances. Om, as described in Purāṇic cosmogonies,

Stages of Unfoldment of the Divine Speech

Om
(= Veda as Śabdabrahman)

↓

a, u, m
(most concentrated essences of three Vedas)

↓

bhūḥ, bhuvaḥ, svaḥ
(essences of three Vedas)

↓

forty-eight Sanskrit *varṇa*s

↓

sāvitrī

↓

four Vedas

contains within it the potentiality of all sound, and this potentiality is actualized when the generalized sound of Om differentiates into particularized impulses of sound, which are then precipitated to form the concrete phenomena of creation. While Om as the sound-embodiment of Brahman is the source and foundation of the entire universe, the three *vyāhṛtis*—*bhūḥ, bhuvaḥ,* and *svaḥ*—represent the seed syllables from which the three worlds—earth, midregions, and heaven—in particular are manifested. The four Vedas, as the most elaborated, differentiated expression of the sound potentiality contained in Om, are said to be composed of the basic sound impulses that structure all of the manifold forms of the cosmos, and as such they represent the detailed blueprint of creation.

The Vedic *mantras* thus assume a pivotal role in the cosmogonic process, and hence when Brahmā undertakes his role as demiurge he begins by bringing forth the four Vedas from his four mouths.

> While he was contemplating, "How shall I bring forth the aggregate worlds as before?" the Vedas issued from the four

> mouths of the creator.... From his eastern and other mouths he brought forth in succession the Vedas known as Ṛg, Yajur, Sāma, and Atharva....[381]

From Brahmā's utterance of the Vedic words, which represent the eternal, archetypal plan of creation, all beings are projected into concrete manifestation. This notion appears in the form of a standardized description that is regularly incorporated in Purāṇic accounts of creation.

> In the beginning he [Brahmā] formed from the words (*śabdas*) of the Vedas alone the names, forms, and functions of the gods and other beings. He also formed the names and appropriate offices of all the *ṛṣis* as heard (*śruta*) in the Vedas.[382]

Purāṇic accounts of the Vedas' role as the cosmic blueprint generally appear in the context of a description of the endlessly repeating cycles of creation, in which at the beginning of each new cycle the same classes of beings are brought forth by Brahmā with the same inherent natures and functions that they had assumed in a previous *kalpa*. Purāṇic cosmogonies, like the accounts of the Manu-Smṛti and Mahābhārata, point to name, form, and function as the three fundamental aspects of created beings that have their source in the Vedas. (1) The Vedas contain the *names* of all beings. These names are considered to be the natural names—rather than conventional designations—of the forms that they signify, and therefore the same names are assigned to each class of beings at the beginning of each new *kalpa*. (2) The *forms* of these various beings are brought forth through the names contained in the Vedas. The form is considered to be already inherent in its natural name and thus represents a more precipitated, consolidated expression of that name. Therefore Brahmā need only recite the words of the Vedas in order to generate the corresponding forms. (3) The Vedic words also determine the *functions* of all beings in that the special character of each type of being is held to be contained in its name. For example, when Brahmā utters the Vedic word "*gandharva,*" a special group of celestial beings spontaneously manifests whose function is to serve as heavenly musicians through "drinking speech" (*gām dhayantaḥ*). When he utters the word "*sarpa,*" a type of serpent emerges whose nature is to "creep" (root *sṛp*) on the ground.[383]

Since Brahmā's utterance of the Vedic words is held to be the means through which he manifests the manifold phenomena of creation at the beginning of each *kalpa*, it is considered vital that his utterance of every syllable be absolutely precise and free from error. The Bhāgavata Purāṇa thus describes how as Brahmā proceeds with his cosmogonic activities he beseeches Viṣṇu-Nārāyaṇa not to allow his utterance of the Vedic words to fail.[384]

The role of the Vedas in creation is expressed in another form in the Purāṇas through correlating each of the Vedas with the three *guṇas*, the three constituents of Prakṛti—*sattva* (purity), *rajas* (activity), and *tamas* (inertia)—and with the three great gods of the Hindu *trimūrti*—Brahmā, Viṣṇu, and Śiva—who preside over the three *guṇas*. The Mārkaṇḍeya Purāṇa, for example, correlates the *ṛcs* with *rajas*, the *yajus*es with *sattva*, the *sāmans* with *tamas*, and the *atharvans* with both *sattva* and *tamas*.[385] The text goes on to establish further homologies between the *ṛcs* and Brahmā, who in his role as the creator principle is characterized by *rajas*; the *yajus*es and Viṣṇu, who in his function as the maintainer of the universe is associated with *sattva*; and the *sāmans* and Śiva, who in his role as the destroyer of the universe is characterized by *tamas*.[386] The Viṣṇu Purāṇa describes a similar set of correspondences.

> Brahmā, Puruṣa [Viṣṇu], and Rudra [Śiva] constitute a triad consisting of the threefold Veda (*trayī-maya*). In the beginning of creation Brahmā is formed of the *ṛcs*; in the maintenance [of the universe] Viṣṇu is formed of the *yajus*es; and in the destruction [of the universe] Śiva is formed of the *sāmans*.[387]

The Mārkaṇḍeya Purāṇa establishes a further series of correlations between the three constituents of the syllable Om, the three

Primordial Utterances			*Cosmic Principles*		*Three Worlds*
a	*bhūḥ*	Ṛg-Veda	Brahmā (creation)	*rajas*	earth
u	*bhuvaḥ*	Yajur-Veda	Viṣṇu (maintenance)	*sattva*	midregions
m	*svaḥ*	Sāma-Veda	Śiva (destruction)	*tamas*	heaven

vyāhṛtis and the corresponding three worlds, the three Vedas, the three *guṇas*, and the *trimūrti*.[388] The fourth Veda, the Atharva-Veda, is not mentioned in this schema, which expands upon the tripartite taxonomies of Vedic texts. (See the figure on page 111.)

According to the above schema, the Vedas have a role to play not only in the creation of the universe but also in its maintenance and destruction. The role of the Vedas in the preservation of the cosmos is articulated elsewhere in the conception that periodic recitation of the Vedic *mantras* serves to enliven and maintain the universe at its most fundamental level, where the primal sounds of the cosmic blueprint eternally exist.[389]

The Eternality of the Veda In the Purāṇas the eternality of the Veda is represented in terms of the cyclical conception of time, in which throughout the never-ending cycles of creation and dissolution the Veda, and its differentiated expressions in the Vedic *mantras*, is said to remain ever the same, eternal and nonchanging. The *ṛcs*, *yajuses*, *sāmans*, and *atharvans* are described as an "eternal (*nitya*) and imperishable (*avyaya*) power"[390] that becomes latent within Nirguṇa Brahman during each period of dissolution and then becomes re-expressed at the beginning of each new *kalpa* as the power of the divine speech through which the realm of forms is projected into manifestation.

Purāṇic cosmogonies describe how when the *pratisarga* commences at the beginning of each new *kalpa*, Brahmā awakens from his night's sleep, and as he begins the work of creation the four Vedas issue forth from his four mouths. Brahmā then teaches the Vedas to his sons, the *brahmarṣis* (brahmin seers), who preserve the Vedic *mantras* through recitation and subsequently teach the *mantras* to their own sons, initiating a tradition of oral transmission through which the Vedas would be passed down to each succeeding generation.[391] As the cycle of *yugas* unfolds, the Vedas in their earthly manifestation are divided into innumerable branches (*śākhās*) in Dvāpara Yuga and eventually disappear from earth altogether in Kali Yuga. Although the mundane status of the Vedas as recited texts may change as human consciousness progressively declines through the four *yugas*, the Purāṇas insist that the Veda remains unaffected in its supramundane status as the eternal, imperishable knowledge at the basis of creation. Creations may come and go, *yugas* may begin and end, but the Veda remains forever nonchanging in its essential nature.[392]

VEDA AND CREATION IN THE DARŚANAS

The Darśanas, like the other brahmanical texts surveyed thus far, presuppose the authority of the Veda. Indeed, the primary criterion that distinguishes the six "orthodox" schools of Indian philosophy—Nyāya, Vaiśeṣika, Sāṃkhya, Yoga, Pūrva-Mīmāṃsā, and Vedānta—from heterodox systems is their acceptance of the Veda's authority. However, in contrast to the cosmogonic and cosmological speculations of Vedic and post-Vedic mythology, the Darśanas' discussions of the origin and ontology of the Veda assume the form of philosophical arguments that are aimed at establishing the authoritative status of the Vedic texts as an infallible means of correct knowledge (*pramāṇa*). Moreover, their discussion of the textual manifestation of the Veda is not limited to the Saṃhitās but also includes the Brāhmaṇas, Āraṇyakas, and Upaniṣads. The Brāhmaṇas are of particular importance to the Pūrva-Mīmāṃsā school, whose primary focus is *dharma*, while the Upaniṣads are the central texts of the Vedāntins, whose principal concern is knowledge of Brahman.

The exponents of the six Darśanas disagree about the basis of the authority of the Vedas (*veda-prāmāṇya*). Their disagreements center on two principal issues. First, do the Vedas derive from a personal agent (*pauruṣeya*), or are they uncreated and hence without an author (*apauruṣeya*)? Second, are the Vedas eternal (*nitya*) or noneternal (*anitya*)? The six systems can be grouped into three basic categories according to their responses to these two questions.

(1) Vedas as Created (Pauruṣeya) and Noneternal (Anitya)

With respect to the first question concerning the created or uncreated status of the Vedas, the exponents of the Nyāya, Vaiśeṣika, and Yoga schools maintain that the Vedas are *pauruṣeya*, for they are created by a personal god, Īśvara. The authority and infallibility of the Vedas stems from the fact that their author is not only a competent and reliable (*āpta*) person, he is also a self-dependent (*svatantra*) and omniscient (*sarva-jña*) being—Īśvara himself.[393]

With respect to the question of the eternal or noneternal status of the Vedas, the exponents of Nyāya and Vaiśeṣika argue that the Vedas cannot be eternal since they have an author. At the end of each *kalpa* the Vedas are destroyed along with the rest of creation, and at the beginning of each new *kalpa* they are re-created by Īśvara in the same form in which they existed in the previous *kalpa*. Moreover, the noneternality of the Vedas is further proved, according to the Naiyāyikas and Vaiśeṣikas, from the fact that the words (*śabdas*) and the *varṇas* that compose them are not eternal, and therefore the Vedic sentences formed by these noneternal words cannot be eternal.[394]

(2) Vedas as Uncreated (Apauruṣeya) and Noneternal (Anitya)

The exponents of Sāṃkhya also argue that *śabda* is not eternal and that the Vedas are therefore not eternal. However, the non-theistic Sāṃkhya school denies the existence of a personal god and consequently refutes the view that the Vedas are created by Īśvara. The Sāṃkhyans argue that no person, divine or human, liberated or unliberated, could have composed the Vedas. The authority of the Vedas is intrinsic and self-validating (*svataḥ-prāmāṇya*) and thus does not depend on their having been created by a reliable agent.

Vijñānabhikṣu (16th c. C.E.), in his commentary (*bhāṣya*) on the Sāṃkhya-Pravacana-Sūtras (ca. 15th c. C.E.) ascribed to Kapila,[395] maintains that while the Vedas are not composed by Īśvara or by any lesser deity, they are uttered forth by the god Brahmā at the beginning of creation. Brahmā's utterance of the Vedas does not constitute composition, for the Vedas issue forth from him effortlessly, like breathing, propelled by the unseen force of destiny (*adṛṣṭa*) and without any conscious design on Brahmā's part.[396]

(3) Vedas as Uncreated (Apauruṣeya) and Eternal (Nitya)

In opposition to the views of the other four orthodox philosophical schools, the formal schools of Vedic exegesis, Pūrva-Mīmāṃsā and Vedānta, maintain that the Vedas are *apauruṣeya*, not derived from any personal agent, human or divine, and that they are thereby eternal. Moreover, they argue that the Vedas are eternal on the basis of the Mīmāṃsā doctrines that *śabda* is eternal and that there is an eternal connection between the Vedic words and their meanings. The intrinsic validity (*svataḥ-prāmāṇya*) of the Vedas derives from their uncreated and eternal status.

In order to establish the uncreated, eternal, and authoritative status of the Vedas, the exponents of the three main schools of Vedānta—Advaita ("nondualism"), Viśiṣṭādvaita ("qualified non-dualism"), and Dvaita ("dualism")—generally adopt the essential doctrines of the Mīmāṃsā philosophy of language. In contrast to the nontheistic Mīmāṃsakas, however, who maintain that the world is beginningless, eternal, and has no creator, the Vedāntins argue that the cosmos is subject to never-ending cycles of creation and dissolution and that there is a creator who brings forth the universe in each new cycle. The nonexistence of a creator, or of any omniscient being, is one of the central arguments used by the Mīmāṃsakas to establish the *apauruṣeyatva* of the Vedas. The exponents of Vedānta, on the other hand, argue that the *apauruṣeyatva* and *nityatva* of the Vedas are not incompatible with the existence of a creator. The Advaita Vedāntins in particular maintain that the Vedas constitute the eternal blueprint that the creator employs in every *kalpa* in order to bring forth the forms and phenomena of creation in accordance with a fixed pattern.

The following analysis will focus on the arguments used by the exponents of the Pūrva-Mīmāṃsā and Advaita Vedānta schools to establish the *apauruṣeyatva, nityatva,* and *svataḥ-prāmāṇya* of the Vedas. Pūrva-Mīmāṃsā is of particular significance since the philosophy of language that it developed served as the foundation not only for the Mīmāṃsā and Vedānta arguments in support of the uncreated and eternal status of the Vedas, but also for the counter-arguments of the exponents of the other four schools. Moreover, the Mīmāṃsā philosophy of language grants an ontological status to *śabda* in general and to the Vedas in particular that is of special relevance to the present study. The Advaita Vedānta school is also germane in that it adds a number of new elements not found in the Mīmāṃsā perspective, the most important of which are its discussion of the cosmogonic role of the Vedas as the cosmic blueprint and its arguments concerning the relationship between Brahman and the Vedas. While our analysis will focus on the Pūrva-Mīmāṃsā and Advaita Vedānta schools, it is important to emphasize that even though the other four systems deny the eternal and/or uncreated status of the Vedas, they do not thereby negate their status as a cosmic principle. Thus, while the Naiyāyikas and Vaiśeṣikas maintain that the Vedas are re-created at the beginning of each new cycle of creation, they nevertheless accord the Vedas a special role as a primordial reality that is the "first-born" in creation and that forms an integral part of the very structure of the cosmos.

Pūrva-Mīmāṃsā

The central focus of the Pūrva-Mīmāṃsā system is the investigation of *dharma* as enjoined by the Vedas. In their exposition of *dharma* the Mīmāṃsakas are concerned to demonstrate the intrinsic validity (*svataḥ-prāmāṇya*) and infallibility (*avyatireka*) of the Vedas as the only true and authoritative source of knowledge of *dharma*. In this context they developed three major doctrines concerning the nature and status of the Veda: (1) *vedāpauruṣeyatva*—the Vedas are not derived from any personal agent, human or divine; (2) *vedānādi-nityatva*—the Vedas are eternal and without beginning; and (3) *veda-prāmāṇya*—the Vedas are a valid means of correct knowledge (*pramāṇa*) concerning *dharma*.

The Mīmāṃsakas, in their concern to systematize and classify the actions prescribed by the Vedas, focus only on the *mantra* and Brāhmaṇa portions of the Vedas and in particular on the injunctive (*vidhāyaka*) sections of the Brāhmaṇas. The Vedic statements (*veda-vacana*) contained in the Saṃhitās and Brāhmaṇas are composed of words, and therefore in order to prove that the Vedic statements are eternal, uncreated, and intrinsically valid sources of *dharma*-knowledge, the Mīmāṃsakas developed an elaborate philosophy of language concerning the nature of *śabda*, word. This philosophy of language encompasses a number of doctrines, all of which are ultimately aimed at establishing *vedāpauruṣeyatva, vedānādi-nityatva*, and *veda-prāmāṇya*: (1) *śabda-nityatva*—the eternality of *śabda*, word; (2) *śabdārtha-sambandha*—the relationship between word and meaning; (3) *ākṛti-vāda*—the universal as the denotation of the word; and (4) *vākyārtha*—the nature of sentence meaning.

In expounding their philosophy of language, the Mīmāṃsakas developed a number of arguments in direct refutation of the opposing theories presented by the other orthodox philosophical schools. In particular, they sought to counter the Naiyāyika and Vaiśeṣika arguments against the eternality of *śabda* and the uncreated, eternal status of the Vedas.[397] In addition, the Mīmāṃsakas refute the doctrine of *sphoṭa* developed by the grammarians, who maintain that an eternal, suprasensible, unitary "word-entity" (*sphoṭa*) exists that is totally different from the *varṇa*s and that reveals the meaning of a word all at once in a flash. The Mīmāṃsakas also refute the grammarians' doctrine of *vākya-sphoṭa*, which posits the *sphoṭa* as an indivisible, unitary whole that is totally different from the word-meanings in a sentence and that reveals the meaning of the sentence in a flash.[398]

The foundations of the Mīmāṃsā philosophy of language are established in the Tarka-Pāda, the first Pāda of the first Adhyāya of the Pūrva-Mīmāṃsā-Sūtras (ca. 200 B.C.E.). *Sūtras* 1–4 lay the groundwork for proving that the Vedas are the only valid means of knowing *dharma*; *sūtra* 5 establishes *veda-prāmāṇya* on the basis of the inherent connection between word and meaning; *sūtras* 6–23 are concerned with proving the eternality of *śabda*; *sūtras* 24–26 focus on the relationship between the Vedic sentence and its meaning; and *sūtras* 27–32 discuss the *apauruṣeyatva* of the Vedas. This philosophy of language was further explained and elaborated in the earliest known commentary on the Mīmāṃsā-Sūtras, the *Śābara*

Bhāṣya (ca. 200 C.E.). Śabara's *Bhāṣya* was in turn commented on by Prabhākara (7th c. C.E.) and Kumārila Bhaṭṭa (7th c. C.E.), from whom two divergent schools of Mīmāṃsā philosophy subsequently developed.[399]

Our discussion will briefly outline the essential constituents of the Mīmāṃsā philosophy of language and of *veda-prāmāṇya* as first elaborated in the early Mīmāṃsā represented by Śabara and later systematized by Kumārila.[400] It should be emphasized in this context that in their speculations concerning the nature of language the Mīmāṃsakas were first and foremost concerned with Vedic Sanskrit, the language of the Vedas and the language of *dharma*. They were not concerned with languages and usages different from the Vedic language, for such languages are not considered to have the eternal, uncreated status of the *veda-vacana* and therefore cannot serve as authoritative sources of knowledge of *dharma*. Kumārila declares:

> Therefore the knowledge of the inhabitants of Āryāvarta is considered authoritative with respect to words and their meanings concerning *dharma* and its branches, since they are grounded in the [Vedic] scriptures (*śāstras*).[401]

The Eternality of Śabda The Adhikaraṇa on the eternality of *śabda* (*śabda-nityatva*) is given in *sūtras* 6–23 of the Mīmāṃsā-Sūtras. The prima facie (*pūrva-pakṣa*) view is given in the form of six objections to the eternality of *śabda* (*sūtras* 6–11), followed by refutations of each of the objections (*sūtras* 12–17) and additional arguments (*sūtras* 18–23), leading to the finally established view (*siddhānta*) that *śabda* is eternal.

In commenting on this Adhikaraṇa, Śabara argues that *śabda* is eternal, indestructible, and imperishable.[402] *Śabda* is one and without parts, and therefore it is not limited to any one place[403] and it cannot be increased or decreased.[404] Śabara's main thesis is that *śabda* is not produced; it is manifested.[405] When a word is pronounced, *śabda*, which was not previously manifest, becomes manifested by sound (*nāda*) in the form of conjunctive and disjunctive air-particle waves that strike against the ether (*ākāśa*) in the ear.[406] In contradistinction to the Nyāya-Vaiśeṣika theory that *śabda* is a perishable property of ether, Śabara argues that *śabda* itself is eternal and imperishable, although its manifestation is not eternal. The manifestation ends when *nāda*, the manifesting agent, ceases to come into contact with the agent of perception, the ear.[407]

Śabara never clarifies how *śabda*, which is one and without parts, is related to the *varṇas* and to specific words (*padas*) such as *gauḥ*, "cow." He does, however, cite the view of the Vṛttikāra, an earlier commentator on the Mīmāṃsā-Sūtras, concerning the relationship between a specific *pada* and its *varṇas*, or *akṣaras*. The Vṛttikāra argues that a *pada* such as *gauḥ* is identical with the *varṇas*, *g*, *au*, and *ḥ*, that compose it, and, contrary to the *sphoṭa* doctrine, he insists that no word exists over and above these *varṇas*.[408]

Many of the questions left unanswered by Śabara are addressed by Kumārila, who provides a more systematic and differentiated analysis of the word in which he distinguishes between *śabda*, *varṇa*, *pada*, and *dhvani/nāda*. *Śabda* is described by Kumārila as an ontological category that is eternal, self-subsistent, undifferentiated, and all-pervading. This eternal, imperishable reality cannot be produced,[409] cannot increase nor decrease,[410] and cannot be destroyed.[411] Although *śabda* cannot be produced, it is manifested through human utterances.[412] The unchangeably eternal (*kūṭastha-nitya*) reality of *śabda* thus provides the foundation for the beginningless (*anādi*) process of human discourse.[413] While remaining one and without parts in its essential nature, *śabda* manifests itself at different times and in different places.[414] Not localized in one place,[415] *śabda* permeates everything and everywhere.[416] While *śabda* always exists as an omnipresent and ever-present reality, it is not always perceived,[417] for it can only be perceived when the conditions necessary for its manifestation are operative.[418]

The individual *varṇas*, as the differentiated expressions of *śabda*, are described by Kumārila as unchangeably eternal (*kūṭastha-nityatva*),[419] without parts,[420] and present everywhere.[421] The *varṇas*, while maintaining their unique and indivisible identities, manifest themselves at different times and in different places through the agency of *dhvani*, sound.

An individual word, or *pada*, such as *gauḥ*, is defined by Kumārila as a definite sequence of *varṇas* that always conveys the same integral meaning.[422] In opposition to the *pada-sphoṭa* theory, he asserts that there is no *pada* apart from the *varṇas* that constitute it.[423] Moreover, he maintains that the *padas* are eternal (*pada-nityatva*) and that the sequence of *varṇas* that constitute each *pada* is beginninglessly eternal (*anādi-nityatā*).[424]

Dhvani, or *nāda*, is described by Kumārila as the perishable sound by means of which the eternal *śabda* manifests itself in the form of *varṇa*-sounds in time and space. In the process of speaking, air from the abdomen is pushed upward to the organs of speech, which begin to vibrate, producing conjunctions and disjunctions of the air particles known as *dhvani* or *nāda*. The vibrations of the *dhvani* travel through the air until they reach the ear of the hearer, where they make an impression on the ether in the ear and thereby cause the perception of *śabda*.[425] While *śabda* and *varṇa* are without parts, *dhvani* is made up of parts, can occupy different places,[426] and can exhibit various qualities such as long or loud, fast or slow.[427]

From the above analysis we can discern three different levels of the word as described by Kumārila, two of which are beyond the range of the senses (*atīndriya*) and one of which is manifested to the sense of hearing. (1) *Śabda*, as the undifferentiated totality of the Word, one and without parts, is in its essential nature an eternal, unmanifest, all-pervading reality. (2) The *varṇa*s constitute the differentiated expressions of *śabda*, which exist on the subtle level of creation as suprasensible, eternal realities that combine in different configurations and sequences to form the eternal *pada*s. (3) *Dhvani* represents the expressed, vocalized level of sound by means of which *śabda* manifests itself to the sense of hearing in the form of articulated *varṇa*-sounds. Human speech thus represents the manifest, ephemeral expression of that imperishable *śabda* which in its essential nature is unmanifest and beyond the range of the senses.

In his discussion of *śabda-nityatva* Kumārila asserts that "the eternality [of *śabda*] is being proved for the purpose of [establishing] the authority of the Veda (*veda-pramāṇa*)."[428] *Śabda-nityatva* is necessary to establish *veda-prāmāṇya* primarily for two reasons. First, if *śabda* were not an unchanging, eternal reality, it would not be capable of expressing its meaning and the Vedic wisdom would thus have no foundation, with the consequence that *dharma*, which is based on *śruti* alone, would become baseless. Second, if *śabda* were not an unchanging, eternal reality, there would be no basis for the beginningless process of Vedic recitation and learning through which the Vedas have been transmitted to successive generations.[429] The notion that the tradition of Vedic recitation is beginningless is used elsewhere by Kumārila to prove the uncreated (*apauruṣeya*) status of the Vedas and hence to establish their authority as valid means of knowledge.

The Relationship between Word and Meaning In their reflections on the relationship between word, meaning, and object, the Mīmāṃsakas considered two types of questions. First, what is the nature of the relationship (*sambandha*) between a word (*śabda*) and its meaning (*artha*)? Is it inherent or conventional? Second, what is the object that a word denotes? Does a word denote a universal (*ākṛti*), referring to all things that belong to a class (*jāti*), or does it refer solely to a particular thing (*vyakti*)? With respect to the first question, the Mīmāṃsakas assert that the connection between word and meaning is inherent (*autpattika*), uncreated (*apauruṣeya*), and eternal (*nitya*). With respect to the second question, they maintain that a word denotes an *ākṛti*, not a *vyakti*.

The classical Mīmāṃsā statement concerning the relationship between word and meaning (*śabdārtha-sambandha*) is given in Mīmāṃsā-Sūtra I.1.5. This *sūtra* provides the cornerstone of the Mīmāṃsakas' arguments regarding the uncreated status (*apauruṣeyatva*), infallibility (*avyatireka*), and inherent validity (*svataḥ-prāmāṇya*) of the Vedas.

> The connection (*sambandha*) of the word (*śabda*) with its meaning (*artha*) is inherent (*autpattika*). Instruction (*upadeśa*) is the means of knowing it [*dharma*], and it is infallible (*avyatireka*) with regard to imperceptible things. It is a valid means of knowledge (*pramāṇa*), according to Bādarāyaṇa, as it is independent.

In his commentary on this *sūtra* Śabara understands *śabda* to refer to the words (*padas*) that form part of the eternal Vedas. The connection between these words and their meanings is *autpattika*, "inborn, inherent," which Śabara interprets as *nitya*, "constant, eternal." The *autpattika* relation between word and meaning, according to Śabara, is the means of knowing *dharma* in the form of the *agnihotra* sacrifice and other such acts that are not known by means of sense perception. This means of knowledge is infallible (*avyatireka*) in that the cognition brought about by such means is never wrong. Therefore, a cognition brought about by Vedic words is a valid means of knowledge (*pramāṇa*) in that it is independent and does not require corroboration by any other cognition or any other person.[430]

The opponents of the Mīmāṃsakas apparently attacked the authority of the Vedas by arguing that Vedic words such as *svarga* ("heaven") are not connected with any real object and hence that there is no natural relationship between word and meaning in the Vedic sentences. Kumārila emphasizes that it is in order to refute such views and thereby to prove the self-validity of the Veda that the doctrine of *autpattika sambandha* is put forward.

> A connection (*sambandha*) [between word and meaning] exists, and it is eternal (*nitya*): thus has been declared by [the words] *autpattika*, and so on, with the aim of refuting the falsity [of the Vedas]. This twofold [view] is not accepted by the adversaries.[431]

Kumārila presents a series of arguments to prove the inherent denotative power of words. He ultimately maintains that the relationship between word and meaning is *apauruṣeya*, for it does not originate from any person or from any convention, whether human or divine. This relationship was not created by human convention, nor was it established by the creator in the beginning of creation, for, according to the Mīmāṃsakas, the universe is eternal and beginningless and it therefore has no creator who brought it into being.[432]

The Universal as the Denotation of the Word Having established that the relationship between a word and its meaning is eternal and uncreated, the Mīmāṃsakas go on to examine the nature of *artha*, the denotation of a word. The term *artha* refers both to "meaning" and "thing, object," and the Mīmāṃsakas' conception of *artha* takes both senses of the term into account. On the basis of Mīmāṃsā-Sūtras I.3.30–35, they argue that a word does not refer to a particular individual thing (*vyakti*) but rather denotes a universal (*ākṛti*), encompassing all the individual members of a class (*jāti*).

Śabara defines *ākṛti* as "pure commonality (*sāmānya-mātra*) [consisting] of substance (*dravya*), qualities (*guṇas*), and actions (*karmans*)."[433] *Vyakti*, on the other hand, is defined as "that which has uncommon distinguishing characteristics (*asādhāraṇa-viśeṣa*)."[434] While the *ākṛti* cow is that combination of substance with its qualities and actions which is common to the class of cows, the *vyakti* cow is that particularized, concretized combination of properties which is unique to an individual cow. Kumārila elaborates on Śabara's definitions, discussing in detail the nature and relationship of *ākṛti* and *vyakti*.[435]

The Mīmāṃsakas' assertion that the denotation of a word (*śabdārtha*) is the *ākṛti*, not the *vyakti*, has important implications for the Mīmāṃsā philosophy of language, for the *ākṛti* alone is eternal, and only an eternal *artha* could have an eternal connection with an eternal *śabda*. If the *artha* were a *vyakti*, an individual thing, which inevitably has a limited span of existence, then the eternality of the relationship between *śabda* and *artha* could not be established.[436]

The Nature of Sentence Meaning Up to this point the Mīmāṃsakas have established that the word, its meaning (that is, the *ākṛti*), and the relation between them are eternal. However, the opponent (*pūrva-pakṣin*) in the Adhikaraṇa on sentence meaning (*vākyārtha*) (Mīmāṃsā-Sūtras I.1.24-26) maintains that this is not sufficient to prove the validity of the Vedic injunctions, since these injunctions are in the form of sentences containing a number of words, and the meaning of the sentence does not depend solely upon the meaning of the words. The opponent ultimately concludes that the Vedic sentences are mere groups of words produced by human beings and therefore, since they are not eternal, they cannot be authoritative sources of knowledge concerning *dharma*.[437]

In refutation of these arguments the Mīmāṃsakas developed a theory of sentence meaning that would uphold the eternal, uncreated, and authoritative status of the Vedas. Śabara and Kumārila both argue that the word-meanings alone give rise to the sentence meaning, and thus, in opposition to the *vākya-sphoṭa* doctrine of the grammarians, they insist that there is no need to postulate a reality (*sphoṭa*) that is different from the word-meanings.[438]

It is in the context of discussing the nature of sentence meaning that the Mīmāṃsakas clarify the distinction between Vedic language (*veda-vacana*) and ordinary human language (*laukika-vacana*). They argue that whereas in ordinary language the ordering of words in a sentence changes in accordance with the intention of the individual speaker/author, in the language of the Vedas, which have no speaker/author, the word order is eternal and nonchanging.

The Uncreated, Eternal, and Authoritative Status of the Vedas The various doctrines that form part of the Mīmāṃsā philosophy of language—the eternality of *śabda*, the eternal connection between *śabda* and *artha*, the *ākṛti* as the denotation of the word, and the nature of sentence meaning as derived from word-meanings—all contribute toward establishing that the Vedas are uncreated (*vedā-pauruṣeyatva*), eternal (*vedānādi-nityatva*), and authoritative means of knowledge (*veda-prāmāṇya*).

The last six *sūtras* (*sūtras* 27–32) of the Tarka-Pāda of the Mīmāṃsā-Sūtras are devoted specifically to *vedāpauruṣeyatva*. These *sūtras* primarily provide negative proofs in the form of refutations of the specific objections posed by the *pūrva-pakṣin* concerning the *apauruṣeyatva* of the Vedas. Kumārila, however, developed a number of independent arguments in support of the uncreated status of the Vedas. He establishes that there is no author of the Veda, human or divine, through three types of arguments.[439] First, he refutes the view that the Vedas derive from an omniscient person by arguing against the existence of an omniscient person.[440] Second, he similarly counters the thesis that the Vedas were created by the creator by establishing that no such creator exists.[441] Finally, he argues that the Vedas have no author on the basis of the fact that there is no remembrance of an agent who composed the Vedas and initiated the beginningless tradition of Vedic recitation and learning (*vedādhyayana*). If there were such an author, he would certainly have been remembered.[442]

The eternality of the Vedas (*vedānādi-nityatva*) naturally follows, in Kumārila's view, from their uncreated status, and in particular from the arguments that the connection between the Vedic words and their meanings is eternal and uncreated and that the tradition of Vedic recitation is without beginning.[443] The *apauruṣeyatva* and *anādi-nityatva* of the Vedas in turn provide the foundation for establishing *veda-prāmāṇya*. In Kumārila's system there are two types of *śabda-pramāṇa*: *pauruṣeya*, words uttered by trustworthy persons; and *apauruṣeya*, the words of the Vedas. Whereas in the case of human statements there is always the possibility of errors and defects, in the case of Vedic statements there is no possibility of defects since there is no speaker/author to whom the defects could be attributed. The intrinsic validity (*svataḥ-prāmāṇya*) and infallibility of the Vedas, according to Kumārila, is thus established beyond the shadow of any doubt as the only true and authoritative source of knowledge concerning *dharma*.[444]

Advaita Vedānta

The Mīmāṃsakas, in their concern with *dharma*, focus on the *karma-kāṇḍa*, the section of the Vedas pertaining to action, and they maintain that the purport of all the Vedic statements is either directly or indirectly connected with action, including the Upaniṣadic passages that contain existential propositions concerning existent things such as Brahman. The exponents of Advaita Vedānta, on the other hand, are primarily concerned with the *jñāna-kāṇḍa*, the portions of the Veda pertaining to knowledge, in particular knowledge of Brahman as expounded in the Upaniṣads. In refutation of the Mīmāṃsakas they argue that the Upaniṣadic passages that convey knowledge of Brahman refer exclusively to Brahman without any reference to actions. The authoritativeness of the Veda, according to the Advaitins, is thus twofold: as a source of knowledge of *dharma* (*karma-kāṇḍa*) and as a means of correct knowledge of Brahman (*jñāna-kāṇḍa*).[445] *Dharma* and Brahman are known through the Vedas alone and cannot be known through any of the other *pramāṇas*, including perception and inference.[446]

Śaṃkara (ca. 788–820 C.E.), the great exponent of Advaita Vedānta, developed the major doctrines of the Advaita system in his commentaries on the Upaniṣads, Brahma-Sūtras, and Bhagavad-Gītā, which constitute the "triple standard" (*prasthāna-traya*) on which all the Vedāntin schools of philosophy are based. Among the numerous commentators and exponents of Śaṃkara's teachings, three are of particular importance for the present study in that they offer differing interpretations of the Advaita perspective concerning the status and authority of the Veda: the Vivaraṇa school, which originated from Padmapāda, a direct disciple of Śaṃkara; the Bhāmatī school, which originated from Vācaspati Miśra (9th c. C.E.), who wrote a commentary on Śaṃkara's *Brahma-Sūtra Bhāṣya*; and Sāyaṇa (14th c. C.E.), an exponent of Advaita who is renowned for his commentaries on the Ṛg-Veda and other Saṃhitās.[447]

Despite certain differences in interpretation, the exponents of the various schools of Advaita Vedānta generally concur with the Mīmāṃsakas in asserting that the Vedas are uncreated (*apauruṣeya*), eternal (*nitya*), and intrinsically valid (*svataḥ-prāmāṇya*). Moreover, in order to establish the Vedas' status the Advaita Vedāntins make use of the essential doctrines and arguments of the Mīmāṃsaka philosophy of language. Like the Mīmāṃsakas, they maintain that (1) words (*śabdas*) are configurations of *varṇas*, with no supersensible *sphoṭa* beyond the *varṇas*, and, moreover, words are eternal since the *varṇas* that compose them are eternal; (2) the relationship between *śabda* and *artha*, words and their meanings, is intrinsic and eternal; (3) words denote universals (*ākṛtis*), which are eternal, and not individual things (*vyaktis*); and (4) the meaning of a sentence is derived from the meanings of the words that compose it.[448]

In their discussion of the uncreated, eternal status of the Vedas the Advaita Vedāntins introduce two new elements that are not found in Pūrva-Mīmāṃsā. First, in contrast to the Mīmāṃsakas, they assert that there is a creator who brings forth the universe at the beginning of each new *kalpa*, and, moreover, they emphasize the cosmogonic role of the Vedas as the eternal blueprint that the architect of creation employs. Second, while the Mīmāṃsakas do not discuss the relationship between the Vedas and Brahman, the Advaitins maintain that Brahman is the ultimate source of the eternal Vedas. Our analysis will focus primarily on these and other aspects of Śaṃkara's teachings that distinguish the Advaitin perspective from that of the Mīmāṃsakas.

The Eternality of the Vedas In his *Brahma-Sūtra Bhāṣya* Śaṃkara uses several different arguments to prove the eternality of the Vedas.

(1) Vedāpauruṣeyatva. Like the Mīmāṃsakas, Śaṃkara argues that the eternality of the Vedas is founded on their uncreated (*apauruṣeya*) status, which is established by the fact that there is no remembrance of an agent who composed them.[449]

(2) Eternality of the Vedic Words and Their Denotations. Śaṃkara also makes use of the Mīmāṃsaka argument that the authority and eternality of the Vedas derives from the fact that the Vedic words (*śabdas*) are eternal and are eternally connected to their denotations (*arthas*), which are also eternal. He cites Mīmāṃsā-Sūtra I.1.5 regarding the inherent (*autpattika*) connection between *śabda* and *artha* and, in harmony with the Mīmāṃsā perspective, goes on to assert that "it is with universals (*ākṛtis*) that words are connected, not with individual things (*vyaktis*), for as individual things are infinite [in number] it is impossible for them to assume such a connection."[450] While the Mīmāṃsakas argue that words such as "cow" denote universals, they maintain that Vedic words such as "Vasu" and "Indra" denote unique individual gods who are eternal. In refutation of this view Śaṃkara argues that the gods are not eternal and that, like other types of beings, they have limited life spans and belong to particular *ākṛtis*, which are eternal. Words such as "Indra" derive from a connection with a particular position (*sthāna*), like the words "commander of an army." Whoever occupies that particular position in a given *kalpa* is designated by the corresponding name.[451]

(3) Cosmogonic Role of the Vedas. Śaṃkara argues that the eternality of the Vedas is further established from the fact that the universe, with its fixed, eternal classes, is produced from the words of the Vedas.[452] Śaṃkara's analysis of the cosmogonic role of the Vedas will be discussed below.

(4) Scriptural Proofs. Finally, Śaṃkara cites proof texts from the Vedas themselves as well as from *smṛti* texts in support of the eternality of the Vedas.[453]

Vedas as the Blueprint of Creation Śaṃkara describes the Vedas as the subtle blueprint containing the eternal words from which the forms of creation are manifested. He begins his argument by establishing, on the basis of references from both *śruti* and *smṛti* texts, that the world is brought forth through the agency of the word (*śabda*).

> How then is it known that the world arises from the word (*śabda*)? "From direct perception (*pratyakṣa*) and inference (*anumāna*)." "Direct perception" denotes *śruti*, the authoritativeness (*prāmāṇya*) of which is due to its independence. "Inference" denotes *smṛti*, the authoritativeness of which is due to its dependence on [*śruti*]. These two prove that the creation was preceded by the word. Thus, *śruti* says, "[Saying] '*ete*' ('these') Prajāpati brought forth the gods; [saying] '*asṛgram*' ('have been poured out') he brought forth human beings; [saying] '*indavaḥ*' ('Soma drops') he brought forth the ancestors; [saying] '*tiraḥ pavitram*' ('through the filter') he brought forth the [Soma] libations; [saying] '*āśavaḥ*' ('swift') he brought forth the *stotra*; [saying] '*viśvāni*' ('all') he brought forth the *śastra*; [saying] '*abhi saubhagā*' ('for the sake of blessings') he brought forth the other beings" [PB VI.9.15; cf. JB I.94]. And, moreover, elsewhere it says, "With his mind he entered into union with Vāc" [ŚB X.6.5.4; BĀU I.2.4]. By these and other [*śruti* texts] it is declared in various places that the creation was preceded by the word. *Smṛti* also says, "In the beginning divine speech, eternal, without beginning or end, consisting of the Vedas, from which all manifestations are derived, was sent forth by Svayambhū [Brahmā]" [Mbh. XII.224.55 with n. 671*]. The "sending forth" of speech is to be understood in the sense of initiating the tradition [of Vedic recitation and learning], since any other kind of "sending forth" [of speech] that is without beginning or end is impossible. Again [*smṛti*] says, "In the beginning Maheśvara formed from the words of the Vedas alone the names, forms, and functions of beings" [cf. VP I.5.62]. And again, "In the beginning he formed from the words of the Vedas alone the particular names, activities, and conditions of all [beings]" [MS I.21].[454]

In citing the above verses Śaṃkara wishes to show, first, that the word (*śabda*) exists prior to creation and is the vehicle by means of which the creator brings forth diverse phenomena; and, second, that the particular words that the demiurge uses are the words of the Vedas. Moreover, in his interpretation of the verse from the Mahābhārata, Śaṃkara makes it clear that the creator does not create the eternal impulses of speech contained in the Vedas, for it is impossible to create that which is without beginning or end. Rather he "sends forth" the words of the Vedas in the sense that he initiates the tradition of Vedic recitation and learning in the beginning of each new *kalpa*. Śaṃkara thus emphasizes the uncreated, eternal status of the Vedas while at the same time upholding their role in creation.

Śaṃkara goes on to explain the mechanics through which the creator projects name into form.

> It is evident to us all that when undertaking something that one wishes to accomplish, one first calls to mind the word denoting it and afterward carries out one's purpose. So also we conclude that before the creation the Vedic words became manifest in the mind of the creator Prajāpati and that afterward he brought forth the objects corresponding to them. Thus, *śruti*, when it says "Uttering '*bhūḥ*' he brought forth the earth," and so on, shows that the worlds, earth and the rest, were brought forth from the words *bhūḥ*, and so on, that had become manifest in the mind [of Prajāpati].[455]

It is clear from the above statement that in Śaṃkara's perspective the Vedic words used by the creator to bring forth creation are not vocalized speech utterances but are rather unspoken thoughts or "ideas" manifested in the demiurge's mind. In this conception the creator does not even need to speak the Vedic words aloud in order to generate phenomena; he simply has to think the Vedic words and the corresponding objects spontaneously materialize. Moreover, by emphasizing that the Vedic words "become manifest" in the mind of the creator, Śaṃkara makes it clear that these words are not the creator's own thoughts, produced through his own thinking process, but are rather eternal words that manifest periodically in the demiurge's mind at the beginning of each new *kalpa*.

The Vedas, in Śaṃkara's view, constitute an archetypal plan that contains the natural names of all the forms of creation. Śaṃkara cites references from *smṛti* texts to show that the phenomenal world is brought forth according to the same fixed pattern in every *kalpa*. Although the creation is periodically created, destroyed, and re-created in a series of never-ending cycles, it is essentially the same in all *kalpas*. The various worlds, the diverse classes (*ākṛtis*) of beings such as gods, human beings, and animals, the system of social classes (*varṇas*) and stages of life (*āśramas*), the different types of religious duties, and the fruits of action are all fixed (*niyata*), in the same way that the connection between the senses and their objects is fixed. The Vedas, as *smṛti* texts confirm, contain the words that are eternally connected with these various worlds, classes of beings, and institutions, and thus they constitute the ideal blueprint that the creator employs at the beginning of each *kalpa* in order to fashion the universe anew in exact accordance with the set pattern.[456]

Brahman as the Source of the Vedas Śamkara emphasizes that the Vedas ultimately have their source in Brahman, that absolute reality which is the ground of all existence. The foundation of this Advaitin teaching is Brahma-Sūtra I.1.3, which says that Brahman is the source of the Vedas. In commenting on this verse Śaṃkara remarks that the Vedas, which possess the quality of omniscience in that they contain that all-encompassing knowledge which is the source of creation, could only have their source in an omniscient being—Brahman.

> Brahman is the source, the cause, of the great *śāstra* consisting of the Ṛg-Veda, and so on, augmented by numerous branches of knowledge, which like a lamp illuminates all things and is as if all-knowing. For the source of such a *śāstra*, distinguished as the Ṛg-Veda, and so on, and possessing the quality of omniscience, cannot be other than an omniscient being. When a treatise on any extensive subject is produced by a particular person, as the works of grammar, and so on, were by Pāṇini and others, even though its subject is only a portion of what is to be known, it is generally understood that he [the author] possesses more extensive knowledge than it [his work]. How much more can this be said of the unsurpassed omniscience and omnipotence of that great Being (*bhūta*) from whom issued as if in play, without effort, like a person breathing, that mine of all knowledge known as the Ṛg-Veda, and so on, which is divided into many different branches (*śākhās*) and which is the cause of the classes of gods, animals, and human beings

with their social divisions (*varṇas*) and stages of life (*āśramas*). According to *śruti,* "From this great Being has been breathed forth the Ṛg-Veda," and so on.[457]

Śaṃkara's argument that the Vedas ultimately derive from Brahman is not incommensurate with his assertions of their eternality. Such a perspective accords with earlier post-Vedic conceptions, which describe how at the time of dissolution the Vedas are absorbed into Brahman and remain unmanifest until the beginning of the next *kalpa,* at which time they re-emerge as the eternal expressions of that totality of knowledge which is Brahman.

The discussions of the Mīmāṃsakas and Advaitins concerning the origin and ontology of the Veda thus share certain affinities with the speculations of Vedic and post-Vedic mythology, although their discursive methods, which involve the construction of formal philosophical doctrines and arguments, of course diverge from the concrete mythological language and imagery that dominates brahmanical cosmogonic narratives. The Mīmāṃsā philosophy of language provides philosophical justification—although not explicitly constructed for that purpose—for a number of conceptions that we have encountered in Vedic and post-Vedic mythology, including the distinction between unmanifest and manifest, undifferentiated and differentiated, levels of the Word; the ontological status of the Sanskrit *varṇas,* which combine in various configurations to form the Vedic words; the intrinsic relationship between name and form; and the eternality of the Veda. Moreover, the Mīmāṃsakas' arguments concerning the inherent connection between a Vedic word and its meaning, and in particular the conception that the Vedic words are eternally connected to universal classes of objects, could be appropriated to justify the notion that the Vedas constitute the blueprint of creation—even though the Mīmāṃsakas themselves of course negate the very existence of a cosmogonic process and of a creator. Thus, we find that Śaṃkara, in constructing his Advaitin position, makes use of both Mīmāṃsaka doctrines and the mythological speculations of *śruti* and *smṛti* texts in order to substantiate his arguments concerning the creative power of speech and the cosmogonic role of the Vedas as the eternal plan containing the prototypes of all classes of phenomena.

CHAPTER 2

Torah and Creation

> "I have seen a limit to every perfection, but Thy commandment is exceedingly broad" (Ps. 119.96). Everything has a limit (*sîqô-sîm*), heaven and earth have a limit, except for one thing that has no limit. And what is that? The Torah: "The measure thereof is longer than the earth" (Job 11.9).
>
> —Genesis Rabbāh X.1

The authoritative status of the Torah as a limitlessly encompassing symbol is linked in certain rabbinic and kabbalistic traditions not only to its historical manifestation as a divinely revealed corpus of teachings, but also to its cosmological status as a suprahistorical, primordial reality that has existed from "the beginning" as an aspect of God and the immediate source of creation. Among the various representations of the Torah in rabbinic and kabbalistic texts, four main complexes can be distinguished: (1) the Torah is identified with the Word (*dābār*) of God or Name (*šēm*) of God, which participates in the reality and essence of God himself; (2) the Torah is personified—or hypostatized, in the case of kabbalistic texts—as primordial wisdom, Ḥokmāh, which serves as the architect of creation; (3) the Torah is depicted as the subtle plan or blueprint of creation, which contains the primordial elements of the divine language through which God brings forth the universe; (4) the Torah in its mundane, historical form is a concrete written text composed of words and sentences inscribed on parchment, together with an oral tradition of interpretation that seeks to clarify and elaborate the implications of its laws and teachings for subsequent generations. The following analysis will focus on the first three conceptions, which are most germane to our discussion of the cosmological status of the Torah.

The various symbolic complexes associated with the Torah are given different degrees of emphasis in different texts and periods and are continually reshaped in accordance with the exegetical, homiletical, and/or programmatic concerns of particular texts. Rabbinic speculations concerning the Torah, which have their antecedents in pre-rabbinic conceptions of primordial wisdom/Torah, emerge as early as the Mishnah (ca. 220 C.E.) and Tannaitic Midrashim (up to 400 C.E.), although these texts are predominantly concerned with halakhic issues. These conceptions are not fully crystallized and elaborated until the period of classical Amoraic Midrashim (ca. 400–640 C.E.), which is the most innovative phase, in which aggadic speculations regarding the preexistence of the Torah and its cosmogonic role proliferate. In this period a number of new modes of representing the cosmological status of the Torah emerge, perhaps at least partially fueled by the challenge posed by the political triumph of Christianity, with its doctrine of the preexistent Logos, as the official religion of the Roman empire. The Babylonian Talmud (ca. 500–600 C.E.) reiterates many of the earlier traditions, with relatively little evidence of substantive reformulation or amplification. In post-Talmudic Midrashim, particularly as represented by P^{e}sîqtā' Rabbāṯî (ca. 7th c. C.E.) and Pirqê d^{e}-R. Eliezer (ca. 8th c. C.E.), we find a new upsurge of interest in cosmological concerns, in which older aggadic traditions concerning the Torah receive new valences, becoming embedded in esoteric speculations that reflect the influence of the apocalyptic literature of the Second Temple period and Merkabah traditions.

While speculations about the Torah are not developed as part of any consistent cosmology in rabbinic sources, in the theosophical Kabbalah of thirteenth-century Spain such speculations are generally subsumed within an elaborate cosmology involving a series of divine emanations (*s^{e}p̄îrôṯ*) and a multi-tiered cosmos of upper and lower worlds. The metaphorical language used by the rabbis to describe the Torah's primordial status and cosmogonic role gives way to the language of mystical gnosis, in which the Torah is represented as participating in the hidden realm of divine spheres that is the source and basis of the created worlds.

TORAH AND CREATION IN PRE-RABBINIC TEXTS

In order to gain an understanding of the rich and complex layers of tradition that underlie rabbinic and kabbalistic speculations regarding the preexistence of the Torah and its role in creation, we will briefly survey the stages through which the concept of primordial wisdom emerged in pre-rabbinic literature and became identified with the Torah. After considering the nature of personified wisdom in Proverbs 8.22–31, our analysis will highlight the contributions of the wisdom books of the Apocrypha—the Wisdom of Ben Sira, Baruch 3.9–4.4, and the Wisdom of Solomon—to the development of the notion of preexistent wisdom, with particular attention to the identification of wisdom with Torah that is first introduced by Ben Sira and further developed by Baruch. Finally, we will consider relevant passages from the works of the Alexandrian Jewish philosophers Aristobulus and Philo, in which the Greek concept of Logos becomes identified with the Israelite concept of wisdom and ultimately, in Philo's philosophy, with the Torah.

Proverbs 8.22–31

The nature and origin of Proverbs 8.22–31, in which the figure of personified wisdom, Ḥoḵmāh, speaks of her own primordial beginnings as the first of God's works, has long been disputed by scholars. The passage is generally considered to be an independent wisdom hymn that forms part of a larger literary unit, Proverbs 1–9, which is distinguished from chapters 10–31 in structure, style, and content. Proverbs 1–9, with its cosmological speculations about wisdom and creation, is generally placed by scholars in the last stage in the development of the Israelite wisdom tradition, as characterized by theological wisdom,[1] and has been variously dated from the Persian period[2] to the early Hellenistic period (between 330 and 250 B.C.E.).[3]

In Proverbs 8.22–31 wisdom is personified as a feminine figure who declares, "The Lord made me as the beginning (*rē'šîṯ*) of His way, the first of His works of old" (v. 22). In verses 23–26 wisdom elaborates on her unique status as the primal creation of God who was brought forth before the creation of the world, when there were no depths and no springs and before the mountains and hills had been established. Wisdom goes on to proclaim in verses 27–30 that she was already present when God performed the acts of creation. "When He established the heavens I was there, . . . when He marked out the foundations of the earth, then I was beside Him as an *'āmôn*, and I was His delight day after day."[4]

The exact nature of wisdom's role in creation hinges on the interpretation of the term *'āmôn* in verse 30. This well-known *crux interpretationis* has generally been vocalized in rabbinic and kabbalistic interpretations of verse 30, as well as by many modern scholars, as *'ûmān* or *'ommān*, "artisan, craftsman"—a term that appears to have been borrowed from the Akkadian *ummânu* ("craftsman"). This vocalization is supported by the translations in the Septuagint, *harmozousa,* and in the Vulgate, *componens.*[5] According to this interpretation, wisdom is depicted in verse 30 as God's co-worker in creation. The other contending interpretation vocalizes *'āmôn* as *'āmûn* (Qal passive participle from *'āman,* "to nurse, nurture") or *'ᵉmûn* (noun), "nursling, darling." This suggestion is supported by Aquila's translation of *'āmôn* as *tithēnoumenē,* "nursling, foster-child, darling." Alternative interpretations have also been proposed.[6] It is not possible in the present study to enter into the details of the scholarly debate. However, for the purpose of our analysis the interpretation of *'āmôn* as *'ûmān,* "artisan," will be given precedence, since this is the vocalization upon which rabbinic and kabbalistic interpretations of Proverbs 8.30 are based.

A number of theories have been proposed concerning the nature of the personification of wisdom expressed in Proverbs 8.22–31. These theories can be grouped in three main categories: wisdom as a poetic personification of an attribute of God; wisdom as an objectification of the world order; and wisdom as a mythological figure. The first theory, which is espoused by R. N. Whybray, among others, maintains that wisdom in Proverbs 8.22–31 is essentially a divine attribute that has been personified to the point of hypostatization. On the basis of his analysis of certain key words in the passage, Whybray concludes that the origin of this portrayal of wisdom is primarily metaphorical, not mythological, although there may be some evidence of mythological influence.[7] The second theory, proposed by Gerhard von Rad, suggests that what is personified in Proverbs 8.22–31 is not an attribute of God but an attribute of the world, immanent in nature. The "primeval order" of the universe was objectified by the Israelites as wisdom, and this objectification, von Rad asserts, "was neither a mythological residue which unconsciously accompanied the idea, nor . . . was it a free, poetic and didactic use of imagery. . . . It was much more than simply the objective realization of such a primeval order; it was, rather, a question of crystallizing specific experiences which man had had in his encounter with it. He had experienced it not only as a static organism of order, he felt himself assailed by it, he saw it concerned about man, he experienced it as a bestower of gifts."[8] The third type of theory maintains that wisdom in Proverbs 8.22–31 derives from an originally independent mythological figure, and therefore its provenance must be sought in the mythologies of ancient Israel and/or its Near Eastern neighbors—Egypt, Mesopotamia, and

Canaan.[9] The first two theories, as espoused by Whybray and von Rad, tend to locate the source of the figure of personified wisdom in Proverbs 8.22–31 in an indigenous Israelite tradition, while the proponents of the third theory generally look for its derivation in the wisdom traditions and creation mythologies of Egypt, Mesopotamia, and Canaan.[10]

It is not within the scope of the present analysis to enter into the complex range of issues presented by these various theories of the nature and origin of the figure of personified wisdom in Proverbs 8.22–31. However, von Rad's emphasis on the experiential basis underlying Israel's formulation of personified wisdom brings to light an important dimension that is often ignored by modern scholars. It does not appear that Israelite speculations about the nature of wisdom can be reduced to mere poetic praises, nor can they be explained as simply mythological vestiges borrowed from neighboring cultures. Irrespective of the provenance of the notion of primordial wisdom, this notion was absorbed and extended by later pre-rabbinic and rabbinic texts and, through identification with the Torah, was transformed into an authoritative symbol that served to distinguish the Jewish people from all other nations as the chosen people of God.

Wisdom of Ben Sira

The portrayal of wisdom in Proverbs 1–9 is expanded and elaborated in the wisdom books of the Apocrypha, culminating in the Wisdom of Ben Sira's identification of the primordial revelation of wisdom in creation with the historical revelation of the Torah on Mount Sinai, in which preexistent wisdom descends to earth as the Book of the Torah and makes her abode with the people of Israel. The principal contribution of the Wisdom of Ben Sira (ca. 198–175 B.C.E.),[11] which is attributed to Joshua b. Eleazar b. Sira, a professional scribe and sage in Jerusalem, is its attempt to integrate wisdom teachings with the sacred history of Israel, thus bridging the gap between the wisdom tradition and the mainstream Israelite tradition that had existed in the earlier wisdom writings of the Hebrew Bible. At the very heart of Ben Sira's program of revival and integration of the ancient heritage of Israel is his identification of wisdom and Torah.

The center and climax of Ben Sira's work is the hymn to preexistent wisdom in chapter 24, in which he adds a new dimension to the speculations of Proverbs 8.22–31, describing the descent of primordial wisdom to earth to become the possession of the people of Israel. Having dwelt in the highest heavens since "the beginning,"[12] having traversed the farthest reaches of heaven and earth and acquired a possession among every people and nation, wisdom desired a resting place, a specific people among whom she might dwell.

> Then the Creator of all things gave me a commandment,
> and the one who created me assigned a place for my tent.
> And he said, "Make your dwelling in Jacob,
> and in Israel receive your inheritance."[13]

Wisdom thus "took root in an honored people" and established her seat among the people of Israel in the holy tabernacle in Jerusalem.[14] Universal wisdom, which God had originally "poured out upon all his works,"[15] assumed a particularized form and became embodied on earth in the Book of the Torah.

> All this is the book of the covenant of the Most High God,
> the law which Moses commanded us
> as an inheritance for the congregations of Jacob.[16]

Some scholars have detected echoes of certain Hellenistic texts about the goddess Isis-Astarte in this hymn.[17] Others have emphasized the parallels between Ben Sira's conception of wisdom, which is at once a cosmic ordering principle and a moral law for Jews, and the Stoic concept of Logos, which is also both a "universal law" and a moral norm for human conduct.[18] Despite any Hellenistic influences evident in Ben Sira's hymn to preexistent wisdom, there is no doubt that Ben Sira himself wished to clearly distinguish the wisdom of Israel from the alien wisdom traditions of other nations by establishing true wisdom as God's unique gift to his chosen people in the form of the Torah.

Although the Wisdom of Ben Sira is the earliest datable work that elaborates on the relationship between wisdom and Torah, the seminal expression of such an identification can be located as early as Deuteronomy 4.6 and becomes even more developed in Psalms 111 and 119.97ff. While recognizing that "the complete identification of wisdom with the Torah is an accomplished fact with ben Sirach," von Rad asserts that "this was certainly no absolute innovation, for in the light of this later age's thought this equation has to be regarded as simply a theological conclusion already latent in principle in Prov. I–IX and now come to maturity."[19] George Foot Moore points out that the manner in which Ben Sira introduces this identification "makes the impression that it was a commonplace in his time, when the study of the law and the cultivation of wisdom went hand in hand, and as in his case were united in the same person."[20] Martin Hengel has suggested that perhaps this identification originated in the circle of sages around Simeon the Righteous, the High Priest who is eulogized in the last section of Ben Sira's work along with the other great "fathers" of the Jewish tradition.[21]

Even if the identification of wisdom and Torah did not originate with Ben Sira, he is the first sage to glorify and expand on the notion in majestic hymns that served to link indissolubly cosmic, primordial wisdom with the historical phenomenon of Torah, bringing to light the suprahistorical dimensions of the "book of the covenant." The identity between wisdom and Torah is elaborated on in another book of the Apocrypha, Baruch (ca. 164–116 B.C.E.),[22] in a wisdom psalm (3.9–4.4) that draws not only on Ben Sira but also on Proverbs and Job for its language and imagery.

Wisdom of Solomon

The Wisdom of Solomon, which is generally held to have been composed in Greek by an unknown Hellenistic Jew in Alexandria in the first half of the first century C.E.,[23] carries on the tradition initiated by Ben Sira of integrating wisdom teachings with the sacred history of Israel, describing the role of wisdom in the lives of biblical heroes and in the momentous events of Israel's history, such as the Exodus from Egypt and the crossing of the Red Sea.

The second section of the Wisdom of Solomon (6.12–9.18) describes the figure of personified wisdom in more vivid and elaborate imagery than any of the other wisdom writings, canonical as well as Apocryphal. As in Proverbs 8.22–31 and Ben Sira, wisdom is portrayed as existing from "the beginning" when God brought forth the world.[24] The role of wisdom in creation, which is alluded to in Proverbs 8.30 (if *'āmôn* is understood as *'ûmān*) and Ben Sira 1.9, is a prominent concern in the Wisdom of Solomon. Wisdom is described as actively participating in creation as an associate in God's works[25] and "the fashioner of all things."[26] Once the universe is created, it is wisdom that perpetually renews and sustains it. As the "breath of the power of God" and "a pure emanation of the glory of the Almighty,"[27] wisdom streams forth and pervades the universe. While remaining one, established in herself,[28] she "reaches mightily from one end of the earth to the other," continually ordering and renewing the entire creation.[29]

Unlike Ben Sira and Baruch, the author of the Wisdom of Solomon does not explicitly identify wisdom with the Torah. He is concerned with the status of wisdom as a cosmic revelation, as a "spotless mirror" ever reflecting the eternal light of God in creation,[30] rather than with the historical revelation of wisdom as the Book of the Torah. The figure of personified wisdom in the Wisdom of Solomon thus expresses continuity with the wisdom of Proverbs 8.22–31 and Ben Sira, while at the same time emphasizing certain characteristics, such as the pervasive nature of wisdom as an ordering principle in creation, which betray the increasing influence of Stoic conceptions. The influence of Stoic as well as Platonic views concerning the nature of creation and the relationship between body and soul can be detected throughout the Wisdom of Solomon, as has long been recognized by scholars.[31] The Hellenistic Jew who composed the Wisdom of Solomon thus sought to embrace the most sublime insights of both Jewish wisdom speculation and Greek philosophy in his hymns in praise of wisdom and the sacred history of Israel.

Aristobulus

The influence of Hellenistic ideas is even more pronounced in the writings of two representatives of Alexandrian Jewish philosophy: Aristobulus (ca. 170 B.C.E.) and Philo Judaeus (ca. 20 B.C.E.–ca. 50 C.E.). The Alexandrian philosopher Aristobulus stands at the opposite end of the continuum in relation to the Palestinian sage Ben Sira, who lived at about the same time. While Ben Sira attempted to distinguish Israel's wisdom from the alien wisdom of Hellenistic thought, Aristobulus sought to harmonize the Israelite conception of wisdom with the categories of Greek philosophy. In contrast to Ben Sira's representation of wisdom as the unique possession of the Jewish people in the form of Torah, Aristobulus focuses on the universal, cosmic dimensions of wisdom, explicitly identifying it with the Logos of Stoic philosophy without any mention of Torah. Hengel describes Aristobulus's doctrine of wisdom and creation as a fusion of "the original Jewish-Palestinian conception of personified *'ḥokmā'* as the consort of God at the creation of the world with the biblical account of creation in Gen. 1–2.4a . . . with conceptions of Greek philosophical cosmology and epistemology, yet without giving up their specific features."[32] In the writings of Aristobulus the Jewish concept of wisdom is rationalized to such an extent that it is almost completely devoid of the mythological imagery used to describe wisdom in Proverbs 8.22–31, Ben Sira 24, and Wisdom of Solomon 6.12–9.18.[33]

Philo

In the works of Philo Judaeus the identification between wisdom and Torah that was established by Ben Sira is extended to include the Greek concept of Logos derived from the writings of Heraclitus, Plato, and the Stoics. Jewish conceptions of wisdom and Torah are subsumed within Philo's doctrine of the Logos, which is the governing category of his philosophy.

In developing his notion of preexistent wisdom, Philo appropriates the images of wisdom found in the wisdom books, especially in Proverbs, Ben Sira, and the Wisdom of Solomon.[34] Most of his fifteen explicit references to the wisdom books are to Proverbs,[35] and he refers in particular to Proverbs 8.22.

> Thus, in the pages of one of the inspired company, wisdom is represented as speaking of herself after this manner: "God obtained me first of all his works and founded me before the ages" [Prov. 8:22]. True, for it was necessary that all that came to the birth of creation should be younger than the mother and nurse of the All.[36]

Although Philo appears at times to distinguish wisdom, the daughter of God, from the Logos, the son of God, he for the most part fuses these concepts. The ultimate identity between Logos, wisdom, and Torah in Philo's philosophy has been emphasized by Harry Austryn Wolfson.

> Wisdom, then, is only another word for Logos, and it is used in all the senses of the term Logos. Both these terms mean, in the first place, a property of God, identical with His essence, and, like His essence, eternal. In the second place, they mean a real, incorporeal being, created by God before the creation of the world. Third, . . . Logos means also a Logos immanent in the world, and so, also wisdom . . . is used in that sense. Fourth, both Logos and wisdom are used by him in the sense of the Law of Moses. Finally, Logos is also used by Philo in the sense of one of its constituent ideas, such, for instance, as the idea of mind.[37]

Jewish conceptions of wisdom are thus reinterpreted and transformed as they are incorporated in Philo's doctrine of the Logos. Through its association with the Logos, the instrumentality of wisdom in bringing forth creation finds expression in the image of an architect who first conceives the plan of his creation in his mind before bringing it to fruition in concrete form.

> [A] trained architect . . . first sketches in his own mind wellnigh all the parts of the city that is to be wrought out, temples, gymnasia, town-halls, market-places, harbours, docks, streets, walls to be built, dwelling-houses as well as public buildings to be set up. Thus after having received in his own soul, as it were in wax, the figures of these objects severally, he carries about the image of a city which is the creation of his mind. Then by his innate power of memory, he recalls the images of the various parts of this city, and imprints their types yet more distinctly in it: and like a good craftsman he begins to build the city of stones and timber, keeping his eye upon his pattern and making the visible and tangible objects correspond in each case to the incorporeal ideas.[38]

Similarly, Philo writes, when God began to create the world, "He conceived beforehand the models of its parts, and . . . out of these He constituted and brought to completion a world discernible only by the mind, and then, with that for a pattern, the world which our senses can perceive."[39] This world of archetypal ideas is the blueprint of creation contained in the mind of the architect, who, according to Philo, is the Logos (wisdom),[40] the instrument employed by the King of all to bring forth manifest creation. The Logos is identified in other passages with the Torah, which as the ideal pattern of creation is "stamped with the seals of nature" and is "the most faithful picture of the world-polity."[41] The dual images of architect and blueprint are also used in the rabbinic tradition, as we shall see, to describe the role of the Torah in creation.

TORAH AND CREATION IN RABBINIC TEXTS

The Israelite concept of primordial wisdom underwent a number of significant transformations from its earliest expression in Proverbs 8.22–31 through the later stages of its unfoldment in the Apocryphal wisdom books, the Wisdom of Ben Sira and the Wisdom of

Solomon, and in the writings of the Alexandrian Jewish philosophers, Aristobulus and Philo. The rabbinic tradition stands at the meeting point of many streams that converge in the notion of primordial wisdom/Torah as the first of God's works, existing from "the beginning" as the instrument of creation. The currents of the Egyptian, Mesopotamian, and Canaanite wisdom traditions and creation mythologies appear to have intermingled with the stream of the indigenous Israelite wisdom tradition that gave rise to Proverbs 8.22–31. This stream gained new momentum as it flowed through Ben Sira and the Wisdom of Solomon, where it was fed by the springs of the Hellenistic tradition. As it encountered Aristobulus and Philo the stream widened to encompass even greater currents of Hellenistic influence.

It is impossible to distinguish the various currents that had become inseparably merged by the time they reached the rabbinic tradition, nor can we hope to determine definitively which streams influenced rabbinic speculations concerning the primordial Torah more than others. It should be emphasized, however, that it is unlikely that most rabbinic sages were even aware of Philo's writings, let alone directly influenced by them. On the other hand, rabbinic speculations about the preexistence of the Torah and its role in creation frequently invoke verses 22 and 30 of Proverbs 8.22–31 as proof texts. Underlying such speculations is the fundamental assumption that the Torah is identical with the figure of primordial wisdom in Proverbs 8.22–31.

Our discussions of the cosmological status of the Torah in rabbinic literature will focus on three types of texts that the rabbinic tradition itself has deemed to be the central canonical texts in which the teachings of the Oral Torah are preserved: Mishnah, Talmud, and Midrash. Within this threefold designation, we can distinguish between two types of documents: those concerned with exegesis of the Mishnah, and those concerned with exegesis of the Hebrew Bible or Written Torah.

(1) Exegesis of the Mishnah. The first type of rabbinic text is concerned with interpreting, elaborating, systematizing, and harmonizing the legal teachings of the Mishnah (ca. 220 C.E.). This category includes 'Āḇôṯ (ca. 250 C.E.), an aggadic tractate added to the Mishnah as a kind of apologia; the Tosefta (ca. end of 4th c. C.E.), a collection of halakhic supplements to the Mishnah; and the two Talmuds—the Jerusalem Talmud (ca. 400 C.E.) and the Babylonian Talmud (ca. 500–600 C.E.)—which contain sustained interpretations and amplifications of the Mishnah's teachings.

(2) Exegesis of the Hebrew Bible. The second type of rabbinic text is concerned with interpreting, extending, and applying the teachings found in the books of the Hebrew Bible or Written Torah. This category includes the various Midrashic collections, which contain exegetical expositions and homiletical discourses pertaining to specific books of the Hebrew Bible. It also includes the Midrashic interpretations of biblical passages embedded in the Jerusalem Talmud and Babylonian Talmud. We can further distinguish between three types of Midrashic collections. *Exegetical Midrashim* provide a running commentary on one of the books of the Hebrew Bible, expounding the book consecutively, chapter by chapter and verse by verse, and at times even commenting on the individual words in a verse (for example, Genesis Rabbāh). *Homiletical Midrashim* do not provide a commentary on every chapter and verse in a biblical book but instead provide homilies related to the first verse(s) of the biblical passages that are read as part of the synagogue service either on regular Sabbaths (for example, Leviticus Rabbāh and Tanḥûmā' Y^{e}lamm^{e}ḏēnû Midrashim) or on special Sabbaths and festivals (for example, P^{e}sîqtā' d^{e}-R. Kahana and P^{e}sîqtā' Rabbāṯî). *Narrative Midrashim* do not contain exegetical or homiletical expositions of biblical books but rather present a unified aggadic narrative that constitutes a kind of "rewritten Bible," retelling and expanding on the teachings and events of the biblical narrative (for example, Pirqê d^{e}-R. Eliezer and Sēḏer 'Ēliyyāhû).[42]

In determining the proper method of approaching a history of interpretations of rabbinic conceptions concerning the cosmological status of the Torah, it is necessary to take into account the distinctive nature of the rabbinic canon and of Midrashic texts in particular. The extent to which later rabbinic texts draw upon earlier documents in the canon has long been recognized by scholars. In addition, there appears to have been a common corpus of free-floating materials—sayings, aggadic traditions, stories, and scriptural exegeses—that circulated independently and that were appropriated by various documents to serve diverse redactional purposes. James Kugel has noted this point with respect to the scriptural exegeses of Midrashic texts.

> [M]idrashic explications of individual verses no doubt circulated on their own, independent of any larger exegetical context. . . . [T]hey were passed on, modified, and improved as they went, until a great many of them eventually

> entered into the common inheritance of every Jew, passed on in learning with the text of the Bible itself.[43]

In developing his theory of Midrash, Kugel gives priority to these atomistic verse-centered units and concludes that Midrashic writings "are not compositions but compilations of comments that are usually focused on isolated, individual verses. . . . The verse-centeredness of midrash is so fundamental that one hesitates even to ask why it should be so: it just *is* the way midrash proceeds."[44]

In contrast to Kugel's focus on the verse-centeredness of Midrash, other scholars have argued that not all Midrashic texts are simply random compilations that serve as a repository for independently circulating exegeses and traditions, but rather certain texts clearly constitute compositions that have shaped received materials in accordance with a distinctive redactional plan and program. The hallmark of homiletical Midrashim such as Leviticus Rabbāh is what Joseph Heinemann has termed the "literary homily," which in the case of Leviticus Rabbāh constituted a "new form—a composite of material drawn from different sermons knit together into a new literary entity—that enabled the author to shape his *midrash* as he did, to arrange the traditional material to suit his own purposes, and to deal with subjects suitable for a wider circle of readers."[45] Neusner has argued that coherence of purpose and literary structure are evident not only in homiletical Midrashim such as Leviticus Rabbāh and Pᵉsîqtā' dᵉ-R. Kahana but also in exegetical Midrashim such as Sip̄rā' and Genesis Rabbāh. Neusner distinguishes in this context between a systemic document, which is a purposeful, cogent composition that reshapes received materials in order to delineate a system of its own, and a traditional document, which is essentially an exegetical compilation that preserves and transmits received materials without recasting them in its own idiom. He maintains that the Midrashic texts of late antiquity, with the exception of the Mᵉḵîltā' dᵉ-R. Ishmael, are not traditional compilations but are rather systemic documents that exhibit their own distinctive viewpoints and polemics.[46] Such a text can be categorized as

> a composition [that] exhibits a viewpoint, a purpose of authorship distinctive to its framers or collectors and arrangers. Such a characteristic literary purpose . . . is so powerfully particular to one authorship that nearly every-

> thing at hand can be shown to have been (re)shaped for the ultimate purpose of the authorship at hand, that is, collectors and arrangers who demand the title of authors.[47]

We are thus confronted with two opposing views of Midrashic texts: as compilations of free-floating traditions and exegeses, or as cogent compositions reflecting the programmatic concerns of the redactor(s). I would concur with Steven Fraade that such dichotomies—*either* a compilation *or* a composition, *either* exegetical *or* programmatic—may not in the end be fruitful, for "documents can be located somewhere in between and still have historical significance."[48] Indeed, in excavating the symbolic and conceptual complexes associated with Torah in various rabbinic texts, I have found that the views of both Kugel and Neusner are to a certain extent validated. On the one hand, there is evidence of a number of free-floating traditions that persistently reappear in the texts. On the other hand, these traditions often receive new valences when incorporated in different documentary contexts. The way in which a particular tradition is reframed may depend upon the specific exegetical or homiletical context in which it appears, or it may reflect the broader discursive project of the text as a whole, which in turn may reflect the shifting sociohistorical conditions of the particular period.

Kugel's and Neusner's characterizations of Midrash present two alternative approaches to a history of interpretations. The tradition-centered approach would involve a topical organization that would attempt to analyze the history of specific traditions independent of their particular documentary contexts. Such an approach would apply various methods of historical-critical analysis in order to determine the different stages in the development of the tradition. One factor that would generally be taken into account in such an approach is the attribution of sayings to particular sages, which provides one possible means of dating traditions. However, such an approach is problematic in that the attributions may in some cases be pseudepigraphal, and therefore it is not possible to determine with certainty which traditions stem from which sages. Moreover, many traditions are anonymous and thus defy a method of dating based primarily on attributions. The document-centered approach to a history of interpretations, on the other hand, would give priority to documentary contexts and would be organized according to the chronological sequence of rabbinic texts based on the final date of each text's redaction. The ideal, in my view, would again be to combine aspects of both approaches, including an analysis of the development of specific traditions as well as an examination of the ways in which these traditions are transformed in various textual environments. It is not possible, however, within the scope of the present study to provide a detailed treatment either of individual traditions or of individual texts. Rather, my history of interpretations will proceed through the core strata or genres of rabbinic texts, organized roughly by chronological sequence, and will attempt to highlight the emergence and successive reformulations of certain traditions in the different strata.[49]

While the dates of the Mishnah and the two Talmuds are generally agreed upon by scholars, the dates of the various Midrashic collections are more difficult to determine. However, on the basis of a number of criteria—for example, language and terminology, style, literary forms, topical concerns, historical allusions, attributions to sages, first citations in later texts, and above all the relationship of the various Midrashim to each other and to other sources—it is possible to suggest a relative sequence of the Midrashic collections, grouped according to periods. For the purpose of the present analysis, we will distinguish among five main layers of rabbinic texts: Mishnah (ca. 220 C.E.), Tannaitic Midrashim (up to 400 C.E.), classical Amoraic Midrashim (ca. 400–640 C.E.), Babylonian Talmud (ca. 500–600 C.E.), and selected post-Talmudic Midrashim (640–1200 C.E.)—in particular, P^{e}sîqtā' Rabbāṯî (ca. 7th c. C.E.) and Tanḥûmā' Y^{e}lamm^{e}ḏēnû Midrashim (ca. 9th c. C.E.), and Pirqê d^{e}-R. Eliezer (ca. 8th c. C.E.).[50] These texts are of course themselves multilayered, containing material that may derive from substantially earlier periods than the final date of redaction. Beyond the problem of dating, it is not always possible to determine with certainty the provenance of particular documents. The lack of consensus among scholars concerning the date and place of origin of many rabbinic texts, particularly post-Talmudic Midrashim, makes it difficult to determine the exact historical-cultural and sociopolitical conditions in which they were produced.

Rabbinic speculations concerning the cosmological status of the Torah are at times embedded in a larger cosmology that generally includes a hierarchy of seven firmaments at the summit of which is God enthroned on his throne of glory.[51] The King reigns exalted on high, surrounded by hosts of different types of angels—seraphim, cherubim, ophanim, and ministering angels. The Torah is represented in certain rabbinic texts as having a special place in God's heavenly court since the beginning of creation and is variously portrayed as his daughter, his counselor, and his co-worker in creation. At the time of the revelation at Mount Sinai Moses ascended to heaven in order to bring the Torah down to earth, where it assumed the concrete form of the Book of the Torah.

Underlying rabbinic speculations concerning the Torah we find three types of associations. The Torah is at times identified with the Word (*dāḇār*) of God, an association that is particularly important in linking the Torah to the creative power of the divine language as well as in establishing its nature as both light and fire.[52] The Torah is also at times connected with the Name (*šēm*) of God, although the nature of this connection is not generally explained.[53] The Torah is most frequently identified with wisdom (*ḥoḵmāh*), and in particular with the feminine figure of personified wisdom in Proverbs 1–9, especially as she appears in the wisdom hymn in Proverbs 8.22–31. Proverbs 8.22[54] and 8.30[55] are the primary verses cited in rabbinic texts to establish the preexistence of the Torah and its role in creation. Proverbs 3.19–20 is also at times invoked in discussions of the Torah's cosmogonic role.[56]

The Torah's preexistent status as the first of God's works is represented in rabbinic texts in a number of different ways. Moreover, the concept of a primordial Torah that preceded the creation of the universe is closely linked in certain texts to the notion that the Torah itself had a central role to play in the cosmogonic process. The Torah not only existed prior to creation, but it also assumed an active role in bringing forth the works of creation. The Torah's cosmogonic role is represented in three types of formulations: (1) the Torah is the living totality of primordial wisdom, which God employed as his architect or counselor in creation; (2) the Torah is the plan or blueprint of God's creation; (3) the Torah contains the fundamental elements of the divine language through which the universe was brought forth.

In discussing rabbinic conceptions of the divine language, Hebrew, we shall see that priority is given to the written and cognitive dimensions of language as a visual phenomenon embodied in letters laden with semantic significance, and consequently less emphasis is placed on the phonic dimensions of language as an oral-aural phenomenon. This emphasis on the visual aspects of language is also evident in certain traditions in which the Torah as the Word of God is associated with images of light and fire. Although these images are often used metaphorically, they at times appear to have a cosmological significance that may be linked to a larger complex of cosmological notions in which the hierarchy of firmaments,

God's throne of glory, and the angels are portrayed in terms of both light and fire.[57]

These various representations of Torah are given different degrees of emphasis in different texts and periods. In our treatment of each stratum of texts we will briefly review the conceptions of Written Torah and Oral Torah that emerge during the period and then will turn to the major focus of our analysis: an investigation of the ways in which the texts of that period represent the pre-existence of the Torah, its role in creation, and its association with light and fire. This phase of the analysis will attempt to delineate the distinctive emphases and texture of each stratum of texts through noting the emergence of new traditions and through highlighting the ways in which earlier traditions are recontextualized and reshaped in accordance with the exegetical, homiletical, and/or programmatic concerns of particular texts.[58]

Mishnah

The Mishnah, which constitutes the foundational text of the Oral Torah, is a collection of originally oral laws (*halakhot*) that is divided into six orders (*s*ᵉ*ḏārîm*) according to subject matter, without direct reference to the Written Torah (Pentateuch). The Mishnah was compiled and redacted by R. Judah ha-Nasi in the beginning of the third century C.E. and contains the halakhic teachings of the Tannaim, the earliest rabbinic authorities, who lived in Palestine during the first two centuries of the Common Era.

The core tractates of the Mishnah are concerned primarily with halakhic matters and contain little aggadic material. With respect to cosmogonic and cosmological speculations, tractate Ḥăḡîḡāh contains a Mishnah that establishes limits to investigation and public discourse concerning *ma'ăśēh b*ᵉ*rē'šîṯ* and *ma'ăśēh merkāḇāh*.[59] Most of the aggadic speculations concerning the nature and status of the Torah are found in 'Āḇôṯ ("Fathers"), the only tractate in the Mishnah that is entirely aggadic and contains no halakhah. 'Āḇôṯ appears to have been added to the Mishnah as a kind of apologia that serves to legitimate the authority of the Mishnah by establishing an unbroken line of transmission that links the teachings of the leading Mishnaic Tannaim directly back to the original revelation at Mount Sinai. 'Āḇôṯ begins: "Moses received the Torah from Sinai and transmitted it to Joshua, and Joshua to the elders, and the elders to the prophets, and the prophets transmitted it to the men of the Great Assembly. . . . Simeon the Righteous was one of the last members of the Great Assembly.... Antigonus of Soko received [the Torah] from Simeon the Righteous." 'Āḇôṯ goes on to describe how from Antigonos of Soko the Torah was passed down to the *zûḡôṯ*, the successive pairs of leaders during the Second Temple period, culminating in Hillel and Shammai, who transmitted the Torah to the successive generations of Tannaitic leaders whose teachings are contained in the Mishnah.[60] It is by means of the chain of tradition delineated in 'Āḇôṯ that the halakhic teachings of the Mishnah, which are presented independently of the Written Torah, are implicitly ascribed a special status as forming part of the Torah that was revealed to Moses at Mount Sinai. However, a doctrine that explicitly distinguishes between two Torahs, the Written Torah and the Oral Torah, is not yet evident at this stage.

In addition to establishing a genealogy of the sages, 'Āḇôṯ attributes sayings to each authority, which together encapsulate the central ideals and values of the sages. The Torah represents one of the primary symbols to which the sayings of the sages continually point. Study and practice of Torah are celebrated throughout 'Āḇôṯ as the hallmark of the life of a sage. The sixth chapter, Qinyan Torah ("On the Acquisition of Torah"), which is added to the five Mishnah chapters of 'Āḇôṯ for liturgical reasons, consists of a collection of sayings in praise of the Torah and the sages who embody its teachings.

Among the various sayings in 'Āḇôṯ that discuss the special status of the Torah, we find the seed conceptions of certain notions that are taken up and elaborated more fully in later rabbinic texts: Torah as a preexistent entity, identified with the primordial wisdom of Proverbs 8.22–31; Torah as the instrument of creation; and the divine word as the means through which God creates.

The Preexistence of the Torah The second aphorism in 'Āḇôṯ, attributed to Simeon the Righteous (ca. 200 B.C.E.), the first sage in the chain of tradition who is mentioned by name, proclaims that the Torah is one of the three things upon which the world stands.[61] Although in the present context this appears to be simply a metaphorical way of expressing the central significance of Torah, in later rabbinic texts the notion that the Torah is the foundation of the world is construed explicitly to mean that the Torah exists prior to creation and serves as the immediate source of the universe.

Such cosmogonic notions are not entirely foreign to the sages of 'Āḇôṯ. For example, the preexistent status of the Torah, which existed prior to the revelation at Mount Sinai as one of the first of

God's works, is pointed to in an anonymous tradition that includes letters (*k*ᵉ*ṯāḇ*), writing (*miḵtāḇ*), and the tablets (*lûḥôṯ*) of the Ten Commandments as three of the ten things that were created at the end of the sixth day of creation on the eve of the first Sabbath.[62] In this passage the primordial Torah is depicted not in terms of a subtle wisdom principle but rather in terms of a concrete image of tablets engraved with letters and writing.

The association of Torah with wisdom is, however, found in a number of aphorisms that take for granted that the Torah is identified with the figure of personified wisdom in Proverbs 1–9, and in particular with the primordial wisdom of Proverbs 8.22–31.[63] The Torah, as primordial wisdom, is declared in 'Āḇôṯ VI.10 to be one of the five possessions—along with heaven and earth, Abraham, the people of Israel, and the Temple—that God took for himself. This tradition involves a word play on the verb *qānāh*, which means "to create" as well as "to acquire, possess." *Qānāh* is the verb used in Proverbs 8.22 when wisdom proclaims, "The Lord created/possessed (*qānāh*) me as the beginning of His way." As primordial wisdom the Torah thus assumes a special status as one of the five creations/possessions that God created/possessed for himself.[64]

The Torah's preexistent status is pointed to in another type of aggadic tradition that suggests that the Torah existed in the form of a book of commandments prior to the revelation at Mount Sinai and was observed by the forefathers of Israel. This tradition is found in incipient form in Qîddûšîn IV.14, which maintains that "Abraham our father observed the whole Torah before it was given, for it is written, 'Because Abraham obeyed My voice and kept My charge, My commandments (*mitzvot*), My statutes (*ḥuqqôṯ*), and My laws (*tôrōṯ*)' (Gen. 26.5)."[65]

Torah as the Instrument of Creation The notion that the Torah is one of the first, and most precious, of God's works is linked to the related notion that the Torah has a role to play in creation. R. Akiba, one of the leading Tannaim with whom are associated a number of mystical speculations, is said to have proclaimed that the Torah is the "precious instrument (*k*ᵉ*lî ḥemdāh*) by means of which the world was created."[66] The way in which the Torah served as the instrument of creation is not specified. It was left up to the later generations of sages to speculate about the nature of the Torah's cosmogonic role.

Creation through the Word 'Āḇôṯ provides the seminal expression of yet another notion that was developed further in later rabbinic speculations: God created the universe through the agency of the word. The fifth chapter of 'Āḇôṯ begins with the declaration, "By ten words (*ma'ămārôṯ*) was the world created."[67] We are not told what these ten words were, nor in what way God used them to create the world. However, as we shall see, this seed expression bore fruit in a variety of rabbinic speculations concerning the ten words.[68]

Tannaitic Midrashim

In addition to the Mishnah, in which *mishnayot* are organized topically without reference to the biblical text, the other major repositories of Tannaitic teachings are the Tannaitic Midrashim, collections of *baraitot*[69] organized in accordance with the sequence of particular pentateuchal books. Although the teachings contained in Tannaitic Midrashim are attributed almost entirely to the Tannaim of the first two centuries of the Common Era, the Midrashic collections themselves are generally held to have been compiled and edited by Amoraim in Palestine in the period between the fourth century and the beginning of the fifth century.[70]

Tannaitic Midrashim are also called Miḏrᵉšê Hălāḵāh ("Midrashim of the halakhah"), for they are predominantly halakhic expositions of the four books of the Pentateuch that contain legislation—Exodus, Leviticus, Numbers, and Deuteronomy—although a number of these Midrashim also include substantial aggadic material. Tannaitic Midrashim are all exegetical Midrashim, providing running commentaries on their respective pentateuchal books, chapter by chapter and verse by verse. Most scholars generally accept the theory proposed by D. Hoffman that distinguishes between two different types of Tannaitic Midrashim. Type A, derived from the school of R. Ishmael, includes the Mᵉḵîltā' dᵉ-R. Ishmael on Exodus, Sip̄rê on Numbers, and Mᵉḵîltā' on Deuteronomy (also called Midrash Tannaim). Type B, derived from the school of R. Akiba, includes the Mᵉḵîltā' dᵉ-R. Simeon b. Yoḥai on Exodus, Sip̄rā' on Leviticus, Sip̄rê Zûṭā' on Numbers, and Sip̄rê on Deuteronomy.[71]

Our analysis will focus on those Tannaitic Midrashim for which we have complete manuscripts: Mᵉḵîltā' dᵉ-R. Ishmael, Sip̄rā', Sip̄rê on Numbers, and Sip̄rê on Deuteronomy. To a certain extent the concerns of these exegetical Midrashim are determined by the nature of the biblical book that is being expounded. For example, the book of Leviticus deals almost exclusively with legal statutes and precepts, and consequently Sip̄rā' on Leviticus is predominantly concerned with halakhic matters and contains little aggadic material.[72] On the other hand, the book of Exodus contains major narrative portions in addition to legal material, and thus the M^{e}k̲îltā' d^{e}-R. Ishmael, although primarily focused on the halakhic sections of Exodus (Exod. 12.1–23.19; 31.12–17; 35.1–3), also includes substantial aggadic expositions on the narrative portions interspersed among these sections (Exod. 12.29–42,51; 13.17–16.27; 16.35–19.25). Similarly, almost half of the book of Deuteronomy consists of narrative, and hence the aggadic sections of Sip̄rê on Deuteronomy are nearly equal in extent to the halakhic portions. Sip̄rê on Numbers also includes a considerable amount of aggadic material. Because of the predominantly halakhic focus of the Tannaim, there is no Tannaitic Midrash on the book of Genesis, for Genesis consists entirely of narrative and does not include any legislation.

In Tannaitic Midrashim the term Torah is most often used in its narrowest sense to refer to the Pentateuch, which is the primary focus of their exegeses. However, in these texts the domain of the term is also at times extended to include the entire Hebrew Bible as well as the Mishnah, the Talmud, and the halakhah and aggadah generally. An anonymous Midrash in Sip̄rê on Deuteronomy declares that "the words of the Torah are all one, comprising the Bible (*miqrā'*), Mishnah, Talmud, *halakhot*, and *haggadot*."[73] The Sip̄rā''s conception of Torah similarly includes both laws and exegetical interpretations. According to one tradition in Sip̄rā', the Torah that was revealed to Moses at Mount Sinai included not only the written text itself but also all "its laws (*halakhot*), its subtle distinctions (*diqdûqîm*), and its interpretations (*pêrûšîm*)."[74] A second tradition, which also appears in Sip̄rê on Deuteronomy, declares that "two Torahs were given to Israel, one in writing (*bi-k̲t̲āb̲*), and the other oral (*b^{e}-'al peh*, literally, 'by mouth')."[75] This statement represents one of the earliest articulations of the rabbinic doctrine of the two Torahs, although the formal designations "Written Torah" (*tôrāh še bi-k̲t̲āb̲*) and "Oral Torah" (*tôrāh še b^{e}-'al peh*) are not yet used in this connection.

Most of the aggadic speculations concerning the Torah in Tannaitic Midrashim are concerned with elaborating on its special status as divine revelation through examining the events surrounding the giving of the Torah (*mattan tôrāh*) at Mount Sinai: where and when was the revelation of the Torah, how did it occur, to whom was the Torah given, what did the revelation include, and so on. The majority of these speculations, which will be discussed in chapter 4, are contained in the Mᵉḵîltā' dᵉ-R. Ishmael's commentary on Exodus 19–20. One of the concerns underlying these speculations, which reflects the historical conditions of the Jewish people in Palestine as a subjugated nation under Roman rule, is to establish the distinctiveness of the Jews as God's chosen people: although the Torah was offered to all nations, the people of Israel alone accepted it, and it is this divinely bestowed gift that distinguishes Israel from the gentiles. Irrespective of their apparent subordinate status in relation to other nations at the present historical moment, in the end the Jewish people, as the custodians of the Word of God, the Torah, will triumph and be exalted above all other nations.

The representations of Torah in Tannaitic Midrashim would thus appear to serve, among other purposes, a twofold function. On the one hand, by extending the meaning of the term Torah to include halakhic and aggadic interpretations of the Pentateuch, these conceptions serve to legitimate the authority of the Tannaitic expositions themselves, granting them the status of Torah. On the other hand, by emphasizing the nature of Torah as the divinely revealed Word of God that constitutes the special possession of the people of Israel, these conceptions serve the polemical concerns of the rabbis, establishing the distinctiveness of the Jews, over against all other nations, as God's chosen people.

Since there is no Tannaitic Midrash on the book of Genesis, in which the biblical account of creation is found, we do not find much speculation in these exegetical Midrashim concerning the mysteries of creation. These texts do, however, contain several relevant passages concerning the preexistent status and cosmogonic role of the Torah as well as the role of the divine word in creation. A number of the traditions found in 'Āḇôṯ are reformulated or elaborated in Tannaitic Midrashim in accordance with their distinctive concerns.

The Preexistence of the Torah Sip̄rê on Deuteronomy and the Mᵉḵîltā' contain variants of the aggadah in 'Āḇôṯ concerning the ten things that were created on the eve of the first Sabbath. The letters (*kᵉṯāḇ*), writing (*miḵtāḇ*), and tablets (*lûḥôṯ*) of the Ten Commandments are all mentioned in Sip̄rê on Deuteronomy's version of the tradition, while the Mᵉḵîltā''s enumeration includes only the letters and tablets.[76]

As in 'Āḇôṯ, in Tannaitic Midrashim the identification of the Torah with the figure of wisdom in Proverbs 1–9 is taken for granted.[77] The Meḵîltā' contains a variant of the tradition in 'Āḇôṯ VI.10 in which the Torah is identified with the primordial wisdom of Proverbs 8.22 and celebrated as one of the special creations/possessions of God. The Meḵîltā' enumerates four, rather than five, creations/possessions: the people of Israel, the land of Israel, the Temple, and the Torah.[78] Any possible cosmogonic import that might be imputed to this tradition is stripped away in the Meḵîltā''s rendering, where it is embedded in an interpretation of a verse in the Song of Moses, "Till Thy people pass over, O Lord, till the people pass over whom Thou hast possessed (*qānāh*)" (Exod. 15.16). In this exegetical context the verb *qānāh* is interpreted to mean "to possess" rather than "to create," and the tradition concerning the possessions of God becomes linked to the people of Israel's entry into the land of Israel (Canaan) that is alluded to in the Song of Moses: "Let Israel, which is called a possession (*qinyān*), come to the land, which is called a possession, and build the Temple, which is called a possession, for the sake of the Torah, which is called a possession."[79]

A parallel tradition concerning the creations/possessions of God is found in Sip̄rê on Deuteronomy. An anonymous Midrash, in commenting on a verse in the Song of Moses, "Is not He your father, who created/possessed (*qānāh*) you, who made you and established you?" (Deut. 32.6), interprets *qānāh* as "to acquire, possess" rather than "to create." It emphasizes that the people of Israel are special to God for he has acquired them as a possession and has not simply inherited them. The Midrash goes on to invoke the tradition concerning God's creations/possessions, in which it enumerates only three—the Torah, the people of Israel, and the Temple.[80]

While the notion that the Torah constitutes one of God's creations/possessions does not appear to have any cosmogonic import in the above mentioned passages in the Meḵîltā' and Sip̄rê on Deuteronomy, Sip̄rê on Deuteronomy contains another anonymous tradition in which three of the entities that are elsewhere singled out as the possessions of God—the Torah, the Temple, and the land of Israel—are each in turn ascribed a special status as the most precious of all things and the first of God's creations. In this tradition Proverbs 8.22 is invoked not to establish the Torah's role as one of God's possessions but rather to confirm its preexistent status: "The Lord made me as the beginning of His way, the first of His works of old."[81]

The existence of the Torah prior to the revelation at Mount Sinai—although not necessarily prior to creation—is pointed to in other traditions that associate the Torah with Adam, the first man, or with the patriarch Abraham. An anonymous Midrash in Sip̄rê on Deuteronomy suggests that God intended for Adam to study the Torah and observe the commandments.[82] A tradition in the Meḵîltā' ascribed to R. Nathan maintains that Abraham was shown the future revelation of the Torah. The Torah is identified with the "flaming torch" (*lappîḏ 'ēš*) in Genesis 15.17 that passed between the pieces of Abraham's sacrificial offering on the day that his covenant with God was sealed.[83]

Torah as the Instrument of Creation The aggadah that the Torah is the "instrument (*k^eli*) by means of which the world was created," which was attributed in 'Āḇôṯ to R. Akiba, is ascribed in Sip̄rê on Deuteronomy to R. Eleazar b. Zadok, an older contemporary of Akiba. The tradition is embedded in a Midrash concerning the importance of studying and practicing Torah for its own sake. The Torah is identified in the Midrash with the figure of wisdom in Proverbs 1–9, although the cosmogonic status of primordial wisdom in Proverbs 8.22–31 is not explicitly invoked. The role of the Torah as the instrument of creation remains to be explored in later Midrashim.[84]

Creation through the Word The role of the divine word in the process of creation is alluded to in a number of passages in Tannaitic Midrashim. The rabbinic epithet for God, "He who spoke (*'āmar*) and the world came into being," occurs frequently.[85] An anonymous tradition in the Meḵîltā' elaborates on the significance of the epithet, citing Psalm 33.6, "By the word (*dāḇār*) of the Lord were the heavens made," as a proof text.

> Precious is the Temple to Him who spoke (*'āmar*) and the world came into being. For when the Holy One, blessed be He, created His world, He created it with only a word (*ma'ămār*), as it is said, "By the word (*dāḇār*) of the Lord were the heavens made" (Ps. 33.6).[86]

A second tradition in the Meḵîltā' invokes Psalm 33.6 to indicate the effortlessness with which God creates.[87] However, we do not find any lengthy expositions in Tannaitic Midrashim on the role of the word in bringing forth creation. The role of the divine word in the revelation at Mount Sinai is of greater concern to the Tannaim, as will be discussed in chapter 4.

Torah as Light and Fire The Torah is associated with visual images of light and fire in a number of Midrashim. A Midrash in Sip̄rê on Numbers interprets Numbers 6.25, "The Lord make His face to shine upon you," as referring to the light of Torah, citing as a proof text Proverbs 6.23, "For the commandment (*mitzvah*) is a lamp (*nēr*) and the Torah a light (*'ôr*)."[88] The Torah is also connected with fire in several passages. An anonymous tradition in the Mᵉk̲îltā' declares, "The Torah is fire (*'ēš*), was given from fire, and is comparable to fire" and then proceeds to explain the characteristics of fire.[89] A more extensive comparison of the Torah with fire is given in an anonymous Midrash in Sip̄rê on Deuteronomy.[90] The revelation of the Torah in particular is associated with fire in Tannaitic Midrashim.[91] Several Midrashim identify the Torah with the "fiery law" in Deuteronomy 33.2: "The Lord came from Sinai, . . . at His right hand was a fiery law (*'ēš-dāt̲*) for them."[92] A Midrash in the Mᵉk̲îltā' attributed to R. Akiba maintains that words of fire (*dāb̲ār šel 'ēš*) came forth from the mouth of God at Sinai, invoking Psalm 29.7, "The voice (*qôl*) of the Lord hews out flames of fire (*lahăb̲ôt̲ 'ēš*)," as a proof text.[93] The image of the words of Torah as configurations of light or fire is of increasing significance in later rabbinic sources and assumes a cosmological import in certain kabbalistic texts, as we shall see.

Classical Amoraic Midrashim

Following the Tannaitic period the Mid̲rᵉšê Hălāk̲āh of the Tannaim give way to the Mid̲rᵉšê 'Aggād̲āh of the Amoraim. In contrast to the halakhic focus of Tannaitic Midrashim, classical Amoraic Midrashim, which are generally held to have been compiled and edited in Palestine in the fifth and sixth centuries, are almost entirely concerned with aggadic speculations and are enshrined in highly developed literary forms.

Among the literary forms that are characteristic of classical Amoraic Midrashim, mention should be made of the proem (*pᵉt̲îḥtā'*), an introductory homily that opens with an extraneous verse from another source that is then connected, through a series of aggadic interpretations, to the base verse of the pericope expounded at the beginning of the section. The proem is incorporated in the two types of Midrashim that derive from this period:

exegetical Midrashim and homiletical Midrashim. (1) *Exegetical Midrashim*. The exegetical form of Midrash, which was utilized in Tannaitic Midrashim, reached its classical expression in this period in Genesis Rabbāh (ca. 400–425 C.E.), a commentary on the book of Genesis that is the oldest and most important of the Amoraic Midrashim. The exegetical form is also utilized in Midrashim on four of the five Megillot that emerge during this period: Lamentations Rabbāh (ca. end of 5th c. C.E.), Esther Rabbāh I (sections I–VI, on Esther 1–2) (ca. 6th c. C.E.), Song of Songs Rabbāh (ca. 6th c. C.E.), and Ruth Rabbāh (ca. 6th c. C.E.). (2) *Homiletical Midrashim*. The homiletical Midrash emerges for the first time during this period and assumes two forms. One form, exemplified by Leviticus Rabbāh (ca. 5th c. C.E.), contains homilies based on the beginning verse(s) of the weekly portion (*sidrā'*) of a pentateuchal book read in regular Sabbath services in accordance with the triennial cycle of Torah reading that was current in Palestine. The second form, exemplified by P^{e}sîqtā' d^{e}-R. Kahana (ca. 5th c. C.E.), contains homiletical discourses linked to the first verse(s) of the readings from the pentateuchal and prophetic books for special Sabbaths and festivals.

In the period of classical Amoraic Midrashim aggadic concerns supersede the earlier Tannaitic focus on halakhic questions, and hence in this period attention turns to exegesis of the narrative portions of the Pentateuch contained in the book of Genesis (Genesis Rabbāh) as well as to expositions of the nonhalakhic Megillot (Lamentations Rabbāh, Esther Rabbāh I, Song of Songs Rabbāh, and Ruth Rabbāh). The Amoraim in this period are also concerned with formulating sustained homiletical discourses on theological questions, as evidenced not only in the homiletical Midrashim, Leviticus Rabbāh and P^{e}sîqtā' d^{e}-R. Kahana, but also in exegetical Midrashim such as Genesis Rabbāh and Lamentations Rabbāh.

There is substantial evidence of shared materials among the classical Amoraic Midrashim, including relatively small units—brief sayings, exegetical passages, stories, and aggadic traditions—as well as longer units of discourse. A number of sizable units of discourse are shared by both Genesis Rabbāh and Leviticus Rabbāh.[94] The relationship between Leviticus Rabbāh and P^{e}sîqtā' d^{e}-R. Kahana presents a special problem in that five complete chapters (*pārāšiyyôṯ*) of Leviticus Rabbāh are also found in P^{e}sîqtā' d^{e}-R. Kahana.[95] The exegetical Midrashim on the Megillot are all somewhat later, and all appear to have made use of both Genesis Rabbāh and Leviticus Rabbāh.

The central issues and concerns that are shared by classical Amoraic Midrashim reflect the response of rabbinic Judaism to the crisis precipitated by the Roman Empire's adoption of Christianity as the official state religion, beginning with Constantine's conversion in 312 C.E. Neusner has emphasized the profound impact that the political triumph of Christianity had in shaping rabbinic theology in the period between the end of the fourth century and the beginning of the sixth century. He distinguishes between two types of Judaisms: "Judaism without Christianity," which produced the Mishnah, 'Āḇôṯ, Tosefta, and Tannaitic Midrashim; and "Judaism despite Christianity," which produced the classical Amoraic Midrashim as well as the two Talmuds. Neusner terms the first type "Judaism without Christianity" because, although Christianity had of course already emerged as a separate religious tradition, it did not pose a sufficient challenge to provoke a major response in the documents of this period. It is only in the documents of "Judaism despite Christianity," which were produced after the political triumph of Christianity as the religion of the Roman state, that we find evidence of a sustained apologetic in response to the claims of Christianity.[96]

Four main issues were at the heart of the debate between the Jewish sages and the Christian theologians: (1) the question of who is the true Israel; (2) the meaning of history; (3) the interpretation of the Bible; and (4) the coming of the Messiah.[97] With respect to all of these issues, it was the Torah that provided the paradigmatic symbol of the Jewish people's salvation and that provided an effective challenge to Christian symbolizations of the triumphant Christ: (1) it is the Torah that distinguishes the Jewish people from all other nations, and from the Christians in particular, as the true Israel, God's chosen people; (2) it is the revelation of the Torah at Mount Sinai that constitutes the pivotal event in the salvation history of the Jewish people; (3) it is the rabbis' interpretations of the Written Torah, canonized as part of the Oral Torah revealed at Mount Sinai, that are the authoritative interpretations of the Bible; and (4) it is study of the Torah and observance of its precepts that will hasten the coming of the Messiah and the final redemption of the Jewish people in the endtimes. The rabbis do not dignify the position of their Christian adversaries by explicitly refuting their teachings. Rather, the anti-Christian polemic is implicit in the way the rabbinic writings of this period give new prominence to certain themes, such as the unique status of Israel among the nations as the custodians of Torah, the special position of the Torah in creation, the importance of study and practice of Torah, and the future redemption of Israel in the Messianic age.

In refutation of the Christians' appropriation and reinterpretation of the Jewish Bible as their "Old Testament" foreshadowing the suffering and exaltation of Christ in the "New Testament," the rabbis could claim that they alone have access to the true meaning of the Bible in the form of the Oral Torah, the oral tradition of interpretation of the Written Torah entrusted to the rabbinic sages through the chain of transmission stemming from Moses—and ultimately God himself—at Mount Sinai. By this period the rabbinic doctrine of the two Torahs was firmly established, along with the formal designations, Written Torah (*tôrāh še bi-ḵṯāḇ*) and Oral Torah (*tôrāh še bᵉ-'al peh*).[98] Moreover, the notion of Oral Torah becomes an encompassing category within which can be subsumed potentially all the teachings of subsequent generations of sages: "Bible (*miqrā'*), Mishnah, Talmud, Tosefta, Haggadah, and even that which a conscientious disciple would in the future say in front of his master—all were communicated to Moses at Sinai."[99] A Midrash in Song of Songs Rabbāh attributed to R. Joḥanan goes so far as to assert that the words of the scribes (*sôp̄ᵉrîm*) are more beloved, as well as more stringent, than the words of the Written Torah.[100] Not only are the injunctions of the sages binding, but the sages themselves are to be honored as the embodiments of Torah[101]and of the Shekhinah, the divine presence.[102] An anonymous tradition in Leviticus Rabbāh maintains that even if one has read the Written Torah and studied the Oral Torah, the inner secrets of the Torah (*siṯrê tôrāh*) will remain hidden until one has ministered to the sages.[103]

Such assertions not only serve to authorize the teachings of the rabbis in response to the external threat of Christianity, they also serve to legitimate their authority among the Jewish people themselves, who are expected to honor the sages and obey their injunctions. A homily that appears in both Pᵉsîqtā' dᵉ-R. Kahana and Lamentations Rabbāh emphasizes that it is the rabbis, as the teachers of the Bible and Mishnah, who are the true "guardians of the city" and protectors of the Jewish people. When communities fail to recompense the teachers properly, they are uprooted from the land of Israel. The homily goes on to express the standard theodicy that appears frequently in classical Amoraic Midrashim: whenever the people of Israel neglect the study and practice of Torah—both Written Torah and Oral Torah—they suffer, becoming exiled from the land and oppressed by other nations. On the other hand, when the people of Israel cherish the Torah and abide by its teachings—their synagogues and houses of study humming with voices expounding Torah—they prosper, and the nations are not able to prevail against them.[104]

The Torah is thus construed as the encompassing symbol of Jewish salvation history. After the revelation of the Torah at Mount Sinai, which represents the central turning point of that history, it is the Jewish people's adherence to Torah that is the determinative factor in the repeating cycles of sin-suffering-atonement-redemption that will culminate in the final redemption of the end-times. Moreover, the Torah not only stands at the middle and end of Jewish history, it is also the beginning point, serving as the immediate source of creation. It is perhaps at least partially in response to Christian formulations of the doctrine of the Logos, in which Christ is identified with the preexistent Word of God, that the Amoraim in this period began to expand on earlier rabbinic speculations concerning the preexistence of the Torah, its identification with primordial wisdom, and its role in creation. In refutation of Christian claims such as the one made at the beginning of the Gospel of John, "In the beginning was the Word (Logos) and the Word was with God, and the Word was God. . . . [A]ll things were made through him. . . ." (John 1.1,3), the rabbis could assert the primordial status of the Torah as the Word by means of which God brought forth creation.

The speculations found in earlier rabbinic texts concerning the preexistence of the Torah are elaborated in terms of a number of different notions in classical Amoraic Midrashim. The idea that the Torah served as the instrument of creation is also explored more fully and is represented primarily in three ways: Torah as God's architect; Torah as the blueprint of creation; and Torah as the divine language through which God brought the world into being. Most of the speculations concerning the cosmological status of the Torah are found in Genesis Rabbāh, since it is this Midrash that is concerned with understanding and interpreting the process of creation as depicted in the first two chapters of the book of Genesis. Sections I–IX, which provide a commentary on the first chapter of Genesis, are of particular relevance. The central importance of the Torah in Genesis Rabbāh's scheme of creation is evident from the outset in the fact that the text begins with a proem that celebrates the Torah, identified with the primordial wisdom of Proverbs 8.22–31, as the architect and blueprint of creation. In the course of a series of expositions the text goes on to establish that the Torah existed prior to the universe and was the first of God's works, that the world was created for the sake of the Torah, and that the mysteries of God's creation can be known only through fathoming the secrets of its blueprint, the Torah. One is not to inquire about what went before creation, about what went before the letter *bêṯ*, the first letter of the Torah, with which God created the world. Whatever God intended to be known about the mechanisms of creation he encoded in the Torah, which constitutes a cryptogram that must be deciphered through the process of interpretation in order to unlock the mysteries of creation. Genesis Rabbāh itself, in its exposition of the first book of the Torah, provides eloquent testimony to this process.

The Preexistence of the Torah As in Tannaitic conceptions, one of the foundational assumptions underlying Amoraic speculations concerning the preexistence of the Torah and its role in creation is that the Torah is identical with the figure of primordial wisdom in Proverbs 8.22–31.[105] A tradition in Genesis Rabbāh attributed to R. Abin declares that the Torah is "the incomplete form (*nôḇeleṯ*) of the wisdom (*ḥoḵmāh*) that is on high," pointing to the notion that the Written Torah that was revealed on earth within history represents only a partial manifestation of the transhistorical reality of primordial wisdom.[106] The Torah in its identification with primordial wisdom is more than an earthly book; it is personified as a living aspect of God and as a cosmic reality that has existed in heaven from the beginning.

The notion of the Torah's preexistence is articulated in classical Amoraic Midrashim in three ways: the Torah is one of several things created prior to the world; the Torah remained hidden for 974 generations before the world was created; and the Torah preceded the creation of the universe by two thousand years. With respect to the first conception, Genesis Rabbāh contains a pericope that expands upon the tradition in Sip̄rê on Deuteronomy that declared the Torah, the Temple, and the land of Israel to be the first of God's creations. The pericope begins by enumerating six preexistent things: the Torah and the throne of glory, which were actually created, and the patriarchs, the people of Israel, the Temple, and the name of the Messiah, whose creation was only contemplated. The addition of a seventh preexistent entity, repentance, is ascribed to R. Ahabah b. Ze'ira. Finally, R. Abba b. Kahana is said to have declared that of all these things the Torah was created first, preceding even the throne of glory. Proverbs 8.22 is used as the proof text to establish the priority of Torah as the first of God's works.[107] A subsequent aggadah in Genesis Rabbāh, attributed to

R. Menaḥem and R. Joshua b. Levi in the name of R. Levi, maintains that the Torah preceded the creation of the universe by six things, listing six expressions in Proverbs 8.22–31 that refer to the Torah's preexistent status.[108]

The notion that the Torah remained hidden for 974 generations before the creation of the world is alluded to in several passages in Genesis Rabbāh and Song of Songs Rabbāh. This notion is derived from interpreting Psalm 105.8 (= 1 Chron. 16.15), "The word (*dāḇār*) that He commanded after [E.V. 'for'] a thousand generations," to mean that the Torah, as the Word of God, was to have been revealed after one thousand generations. However, in actuality it was revealed after twenty-six generations (ten generations from Adam to Noah, ten from Noah to Abraham, and six from Abraham to Moses—Isaac, Jacob, Levi, Kohath, Amram, and Moses). What happened to the other 974 generations (1000 − 26 = 974)? According to a Midrash in Genesis Rabbāh, attributed to R. Huna in the name of R. Eliezer b. Jose the Galilean, they were blotted out—that is, they remained uncreated.[109]

The tradition that the Torah preceded the creation of the world by two thousand years is found in a number of Midrashim. This assertion is derived from Proverbs 8.30, "Then I [wisdom] was beside Him as an artisan (*'āmôn*), and I was His delight day after day (*yôm yôm*)"—focusing on the repetition of *yôm*, day. The sages concluded from Psalm 90.4, "For a thousand years in Thy sight are but as yesterday when it is past," that each day of the Lord is a thousand years, and thus, according to Proverbs 8.30, the Torah was with God for two divine days, or two thousand years, before the world was created. In Genesis Rabbāh this tradition, with reference to both Proverbs 8.30 and Psalm 90.4, is embedded in a short homily, attributed to R. Ḥama b. Ḥanina, that cautions against inquiring too much into the hidden mysteries of creation. The Torah alone, which existed for two thousand years prior to the world, knows what was before creation.[110] A variant of this tradition is also incorporated in Leviticus Rabbāh XIX.1–2, where it is attributed to R. Simeon b. Lakish through R. Huna b. Abin and forms part of the opening proem of a discourse on the importance of Torah study that subsequently leads to a homily on the Hebrew letters that compose the Torah.[111] Song of Songs 5.11 serves as the extraneous verse from the Ketuvim with which the proem begins.

> "His head (*rō'š*) is the finest gold, his locks (*q*ᵉ*wuṣṣôṯ*) are curls (*taltallîm*), black as a raven" (S. S. 5.11). "His head

> (*rō'š*)" refers to the Torah, as it is written, "The Lord made me *rē'šîṯ* [E.V. 'as the beginning'] of His way" (Prov. 8.22). As R. Huna said in the name of R. Simeon b. Lakish: The Torah preceded the creation of the world by two thousand [years]. "Then I was beside Him as an artisan (*'āmôn*), and I was His delight day after day (*yôm yôm*)" (Prov. 8.30), and a day of the Holy One, blessed be He, is one thousand years, as it is said, "For a thousand years in Thy sight are but as yesterday when it is past" (Ps. 90.4). "The finest gold" refers to the words of the Torah, as it is said, "More to be desired are they than gold, even much fine gold" (Ps. 19.11). The things that were created from *rē'šîṯ* [the Torah] were [thus] engraved out of the finest gold. "His locks are curls" refers to the ruled lines [used to guide the writing of a Torah scroll]. "Black as a raven" refers to the letters (*'ôṯiyyôṯ*).[112]

The proem begins by interpreting *rō'š* ("head") in Song of Songs 5.11 in light of the *rē'šîṯ* of Proverbs 8.22 as referring to the Torah. The proem then cites the tradition that the Torah existed two thousand years prior to creation, invoking Proverbs 8.30 and Psalm 90.4 as proof texts. The homily not only seeks to establish the Torah's preexistence but also alludes to its role in the cosmogonic process. In accordance with Song of Songs 5.11, "His head is the finest gold," the words of the Torah (= *rō'š*) are identified with the finest gold, and it is from this gold that things created from *rē'šîṯ*, the Torah, are said to have been engraved. The homily goes on to interpret the second half of Song of Songs 5.11 in terms of the concrete written text of the Torah scroll—its ruled lines and letters—without any attempt to clarify the relationship between the earthly Torah scroll and the primordial Torah.[113]

Another type of aggadic tradition, which is particularly emphasized in Genesis Rabbāh, associates the preexistent Torah with Adam and the patriarchs. In these conceptions the Torah is not personified as primordial wisdom that existed prior to creation but is rather depicted as the Sefer Torah that existed prior to the Sinai revelation and was at least partially revealed to Adam and to the forefathers of Israel, Abraham, Isaac, Jacob, and the sons of Jacob.

Several of the aggadot concerning Adam are incorporated in Genesis Rabbāh's exegeses of Genesis 5.1, "This is the book of the generations of Adam." One interpretation, ascribed to R. Judah b. Simon, understands the verse to mean that God showed to Adam the succession of sages—judges, scribes, and expounders (of Torah)—that would arise in subsequent generations.[114] A second interpretation of Genesis 5.1, attributed to R. Judah b. Il'ai, suggests that God considered giving the Torah to Adam but then decided against it: if he could not fulfill even six commandments, how could he be expected to observe 613 commandments? God consequently decided to give the Torah to Adam's descendants: "This is the book of the generations of Adam."[115] A third comment, ascribed to Rab, understands Genesis 5.1 to mean that Adam taught his descendants how to rule the parchment for a Torah scroll.[116] Another Midrash in Genesis Rabbāh, commenting on Genesis 3.24, identifies the Torah with the "flaming sword" (*lahaṭ ha-ḥereḇ*) that God, after expelling Adam from the Garden of Eden, put in the east of the garden in order to guard the way to the tree of life. Adam, upon seeing the flaming sword of Torah, foresaw that after twenty-six generations his descendants, the people of Israel, were destined to accept the Torah at Mount Sinai.[117]

The revelation of the Torah at Sinai was also shown to Abraham, according to a tradition in Genesis Rabbāh and P^e^sîqtā' d^e^-R. Kahana ascribed to R. Joḥanan through his student R. Simeon b. Abba. As in the parallel tradition in the M^e^ḵîltā', the Torah is identified with the "flaming torch" (*lappîḏ 'ēš*) that is depicted in Genesis 15.17 as passing between the pieces of Abraham's covenant offering.[118] Several aggadot suggest further that Abraham was not only given a vision of the future revelation of the Torah, he himself learned and practiced the Torah before it was given. According to a tradition in Genesis Rabbāh attributed to R. Simeon b. Yoḥai, Abraham did not learn the Torah from any external teacher but rather from the internal springs of wisdom gushing forth from his kidneys. Psalm 16.7 is invoked as a proof text: "I bless the Lord, who gives me counsel; in the night also my kidneys instruct me."[119] Moreover, Abraham not only studied the Torah, he also knew and practiced its laws. Like the Mishnaic tradition in Qîddûšîn IV.14, aggadot in Leviticus Rabbāh and Genesis Rabbāh interpret Genesis 26.5, "Because Abraham obeyed My voice and kept My charge, My commandments (*mitzvot*), My statutes (*ḥuqqôṯ*), and My laws (*tôrōṯ*)," to mean that Abraham observed the whole of the Torah, including even certain oral traditions that are not found in the Written Torah, such as the *'êrûḇ* concerning the preparation of food for the Sabbath on a holy day that occurs on a Friday.[120] In the course of commenting on the life histories of the patriarchs, a number of Midrashim in Genesis Rabbāh suggest that Abraham taught his sons the Torah as well and that Isaac,[121] Jacob,[122] and the sons of Jacob[123] each in turn engaged in the study of Torah.[124]

Torah as the Architect of Creation The Torah, which existed from the beginning as the first of God's creations, is also represented in classical Amoraic Midrashim as the agent through which the universe was brought forth. In the opening Midrash of Genesis Rabbāh, attributed to R. Hoshaiah, the cosmogonic role of the Torah is depicted both in terms of the active image of an architect and the more passive image of a blueprint.

> R. Hoshaiah opened: "Then I was beside Him as an *'āmôn*, and I was His delight day after day" (Prov. 8.30). . . . [*'Ā*]*môn* is an artisan (*'ûmān*). The Torah declares, "I was the working instrument (*k^elî*) of the Holy One, blessed be He." In the normal course of affairs, when a mortal king builds a palace he does not build it by his own skill but by the skill of an architect. Moreover, the architect does not build it out of his head but makes use of plans and tablets in order to know how to make the rooms and the doors. Thus, the Holy One, blessed be He, looked (*hibbîṭ*) into the Torah and created the world. And the Torah declares, "With *rē'šîṯ* [E.V. 'In the beginning'] God created" (Gen. 1.1), and *rē'šîṯ* means nothing other than the Torah, as it is said, "The Lord made me *rē'šîṯ* [E.V. 'as the beginning'] of His way" (Prov. 8.22).[125]

This proem is one of the most important Amoraic statements concerning the cosmogonic role of the Torah and thus warrants closer analysis. The proem is of the classical type common to the Amoraic Midrashim of this period, opening with the conventional introductory formula (*pāṯaḥ*) and an extraneous verse from the Ketuvim, Proverbs 8.30, and then proceeding through a series of aggadic interpretations to the base verse of the pericope: Genesis 1.1, the first verse of the Torah. The proem offers four possible interpretations of *'āmôn* in Proverbs 8.30, culminating in a fifth interpretation, in which *'āmôn* is vocalized as *'ûmān*, "artisan." The Torah's identity with the primordial wisdom of Proverbs 8.22–31 is assumed, and hence it is the Torah that is represented as the artisan or "instrument" (*k^elî*) of God—recalling the earlier sayings, attributed to R. Akiba and R. Eleazar b. Zadok, that the Torah is the "instrument (*k^elî*) by means of which the world was created."[126] The proem goes on to depict the role of God's artisan, the Torah, in terms of the dual image of the architect whom the king employs to build and the blueprint that the architect consults in building—although the interrelationship between these two images is not clarified. The culminating proclamation of the proem is put into the mouth of Torah herself: *b^{e}rē'šîṯ bārā' Elohim*. This first verse of the Torah is interpreted in light of the expression *rē'šîṯ darkô* in Proverbs 8.22, understanding *b^{e}rē'šîṯ* in Genesis 1.1 to mean *b^e-ḥoḵmāh*: "By means of wisdom/Torah God created [heaven and earth]."[127] The opening Midrash of Genesis Rabbāh thus begins and ends with the wisdom hymn in Proverbs 8.22–31, establishing the role of the Torah in creation through incorporating the two most crucial verses, 30 and 22, and linking them through a series of interpretations to the base verse of the pericope, Genesis 1.1.

Torah as the Blueprint of Creation In rabbinic texts the notion that the Torah constitutes the plan or blueprint of creation is generally depicted in three ways: as the plan that God "looked into" (*hibbîṭ*), as an architect consults his blueprint, in order to create the world; as the mental plan of creation conceived in the mind of God; or as the plan that reflects the laws and structure of the universe.

The use of the blueprint analogy in the opening proem of Genesis Rabbāh obviously conforms to the first image, although scholars have debated whether the portrayal of God "looking into" the Torah might be understood as a cognitive act of contemplation rather than as simply a perceptual act involving the faculty of sight—in which case it would also partake of the second image of a mental plan of creation. In this context a number of scholars have noted the obvious parallels between Genesis Rabbāh's use of the blueprint analogy and Philo's use of a similar image, in the passage cited earlier,[128] in which the architect is depicted as sketching the plan in his mind.[129] The similarities between the opening Midrash of Genesis Rabbāh and Plato's *Timaeus* 27f have also been noted.[130] However, scholars are not in agreement concerning the extent to which Genesis Rabbāh's portrayal of the Torah as the architect and blueprint of creation reflects the doctrine of Platonic Ideas, particularly as expressed in Philo's concept of the Logos. Ephraim Urbach has argued against such a hasty conclusion and has emphasized the essential differences in the language and imagery used by R. Hoshaiah and Philo to express the analogy of the blueprint.

> R. Hosha'ia's homily contains not the slightest reference to the world of Ideas or to the location of the Ideas. In the analogy, "the architect does not plan the building in his head, but he makes use of rolls and tablets"—a fact that Philo carefully refrained from mentioning, because it contra-

> dicted his purpose in adducing the analogy. Like the architect who looks at the rolls and tablets, so the Holy One, blessed be He, looked in the Torah, but it contains no forms and sketches of temples, gymnasia, markets and harbours, and this Torah is not a concept but the concrete Torah with its precepts and statutes, which are inscribed in letters.

Urbach goes on to assert that the analogy in R. Hoshaiah's Midrash is "only a literary embellishment."[131]

Although Urbach is correct in pointing out the differences between Philo's depiction of the blueprint as a mental plan and Genesis Rabbāh's use of the more concrete imagery of "plans and tablets," he goes too far when he attempts to limit the proem's conception of Torah to the concrete Book of the Torah. Our analysis has shown that long before the redaction of Genesis Rabbāh, a suprahistorical dimension had been superimposed on the historical phenomenon of Torah through its identification with primordial wisdom. This identification is assumed in the homily attributed to R. Hoshaiah, and thus its use of the analogy of the architect and blueprint must be viewed against the background of a conception of Torah that encompassed supramundane as well as mundane dimensions.[132]

Irrespective of whether the blueprint in Genesis Rabbāh can be interpreted as a mental plan, the notion that creation was first conceived as an idea or plan in the mind of God, which was then brought to fruition in the concrete forms and phenomena of the manifest world, was not completely foreign to the rabbinic sages—although we need not necessarily posit a Greek source for such a notion. A Midrash in Genesis Rabbāh ascribed to the rabbis suggests that God created the heaven and the earth precisely in accordance with the plan in his mind (*maḥăšāḇāh*).[133] Another Midrash in Genesis Rabbāh records a dispute between the school of Shammai and the school of Hillel concerning whether the plan (*maḥăšāḇāh*) of creation was formulated during the night and executed during the day, or whether both the planning and execution took place during the day.[134] Neither Midrash discusses the nature of the plan nor makes any mention of the Torah. However, in later Midrashim, as will be discussed below, the plan of creation conceived in the mind of God is directly linked to Torah.

The notion that the Torah constitutes a plan that reflects the laws and structure of the cosmos is pointed to in several Midrashim. An anonymous Midrash in Leviticus Rabbāh identifies the laws of Torah with the laws of nature by means of which God brought forth the universe, implying that the social and moral order laid out in the Torah reflects the cosmic order. Commenting on Leviticus 26.3, "If you walk in My statutes (*ḥuqqōṯ*)," the Midrashist connects *ḥuqqōṯ* by word analogy to a number of proof texts and thereby establishes that it was by means of the statutes of Torah that God marked out (*ḥāqaq*) the heaven and earth (Jer. 33.25), the sun and moon (Jer. 31.35), the sea (Prov. 8.29), the sand (Jer. 5.22), and the deep (Prov. 8.27).[135] The notion that there is a correspondence between the laws of Torah and the structure of the universe is expressed in a different form in a tradition in P^{e}sîqtā’ d^{e}-R. Kahana, which maintains that, of the 613 commandments (*mitzvot*) in the Torah, the 365 negative precepts correspond to the number of days in a solar year, while the 248 positive precepts correspond to the number of members in the human body.[136]

The Torah is represented in classical Amoraic Midrashim as having a role not only in bringing forth the creation but also in sustaining it. The revelation of the Torah at Mount Sinai, as will be discussed in chapter 4, is portrayed as a crucial turning point in the final establishment of creation, for if Israel had not accepted the Torah, the universe would have reverted to the original state of chaos from which it emerged.[137]

Torah as Divine Language The Torah that constitutes the plan of creation is composed of the twenty-two letters (*’ôṯiyyôṯ*) of the Hebrew alphabet that are the fundamental elements of the divine language. In classical Amoraic Midrashim the role of the Torah in creation is thus at times linked to notions of the creative power of the divine language. The Torah is connected with the divine language in a number of different ways: in its identification with the Word of God,[138] in its association with the divine Name,[139] and in its role as the repository of the Hebrew letters. The cosmogonic role of the divine language is alluded to in earlier rabbinic texts, but it is not until classical Amoraic Midrashim that the implications of this notion are elaborated and connected to the cosmogonic role of the Torah.

The rabbinic epithet for God in Tannaitic Midrashim, "He who spoke (*’āmar*) and the world came into being," also appears in classical Amoraic Midrashim.[140] "And God said, 'Let there be light,' and there was light" (Gen. 1.3)—and what he spoke, according to the sages, was Hebrew. Hebrew is the holy language (*l^{e}šôn ha-qôḏeš*), the language of God himself, which he inscribed in the Torah and which he used to create the world. "Just as the Torah was given in the holy language (*l^e^šôn qôḏeš*), so the world was created with the holy language."[141]

The cosmogonic role of the divine language is often represented in terms of the twenty-two consonants of the Hebrew alphabet that compose the Torah, which constitute the basic structural elements of creation. Speculations regarding the creative power of the Hebrew letters received their most elaborate expression in the early rabbinic period in the *Sēp̄er Y^e^ṣîrāh* ("Book of Creation") (3d–6th c. C.E.), the earliest extant Hebrew text of a speculative nature, which describes the process of creation as arising through different permutations and combinations of the twenty-two letters of the Hebrew alphabet.[142] The origins of this mystical text are obscure, and rabbinic literature does not contain anything comparable to its complex cosmology of numbers (*s^e^p̄îrôṯ*) and letters. However, rabbinic texts do contain speculations concerning the Hebrew alphabet in which the letters themselves are at times personified as configurations of divine energy, each of which has its own distinctive character and integrity.[143] Classical Amoraic Midrashim contain a number of homilies on the Hebrew letters, which focus in particular on the shape of the letters, their semantic significance, their numerical value, and their cosmic role in creation. Little attention is given to the sound value of the letters.

A homily in Genesis Rabbāh, the last portion of which is also found in P^e^sîqtā' d^e^-R. Kahana and Song of Songs Rabbāh, confronts the problem of why the world was created with *bêṯ*. *Bêṯ* is the first letter of the first word of the Torah, *b^e^rē'šîṯ*, and thus some rabbis assume that God must have created the world with *bêṯ*. The question naturally arises why God would have begun the Torah and hence creation with *bêṯ*, the second letter of the alphabet, and not with *'ālep̄*, the first letter. The *'ālep̄* itself is depicted as complaining to God about this matter during the course of the twenty-six generations prior to the revelation at Mount Sinai. A series of explanations are given, which revolve around the shape of the letter *bêṯ* (the fact that it is closed at the back and sides but open in front and has two projecting points), its numerical value (two), and its semantic significance (the fact that it is the first letter of the word *b^e^rāḵāh*, "blessing," whereas *'ālep̄* is the first letter of *'ārûr*, "cursed"). The sound value of *bêṯ* is not mentioned as an essential element in God's decision to create the world with it.[144]

According to another pericope in Genesis Rabbāh, this world was created with the letter *hē*, while the world to come was created with the letter *yōḏ*. The reasons given focus primarily on the shapes of the two letters. However, one explanation, ascribed to R. Joḥanan through his student R. Abbahu, points to the sound of the *hē*, which, unlike the other letters, does not require any effort to pronounce. Hence, as indicated in Psalm 33.6, it was through the effortless pronunciation of the *hē* that God brought forth the world: "'By the word (*dāḇār*) of the Lord' and 'the heavens were *already* made.'"[145]

The converse of the creative power of the Hebrew letters is their destructive potential. The homily in Leviticus Rabbāh XIX.1–2 discussed above, which appears with slight variations in Song of Songs Rabbāh V.11, §1–4, begins with a discussion of the preexistent status of the Torah and the importance of Torah study and then leads into a discourse on the power of the Hebrew letters of which the Torah is composed. In this context a tradition attributed to R. Ze'ira[146] interprets "His locks (*qᵉwuṣṣôṯ*) are curls (*taltallîm*)" in Song of Songs 5.11 to mean that "even those things that you regard as [merely] strokes on the letters (*qôṣîm*) in the Torah are mounds (*taltallîn*), for they have the power to destroy the entire world and make it into a mound (*tēl*)." The homily goes on to cite a variety of verses from the Written Torah in which a change in a single letter would precipitate the destruction of the world. In all cases the substitution of one consonant for another, through the slight alteration of the shape of the letter, would result in a change in semantic significance that has blasphemous connotations and therefore destructive potential.[147] The homily culminates with an emphatic assertion of its central point: not a single letter or word of the Torah can be uprooted.[148]

It is important to note in this context that it is the consonantal text of the Torah scroll that the rabbis are concerned to preserve unaltered. In the Torah scroll the consonants alone are given, without the vowels, and thus while the sequence of the consonants is fixed and cannot be changed, there is more flexibility in the method of vocalizing the words.[149] This would perhaps account for why Amoraic homilies on the letters tend to emphasize their shape as units of script more than their vocalized expression as phones.

In spite of the predominant emphasis on the written and cognitive dimensions of Hebrew—that is, on the shape and semantic significance of the letters—we do find occasional references to the phonic dimension of the divine language. When viewed from the perspective of their sound the letters become intimately linked with the creative power of the divine speech, as in the above mentioned tradition concerning the letter *hē*. That God simply spoke and the phenomenal world came into being is, according to a number of Midrashim in Genesis Rabbāh, an indication of the complete effortlessness with which he created. Psalm 33.6, "By the word (*dāḇār*) of the Lord were the heavens made," is invoked as a proof text to show that the process of creation required no labor or effort on the part of God.[150] He simply said, "Let there be light," and there was light. God speaks and it is accomplished; he commands and his will is done.

> R. Berekhiah opened in the name of R. Judah b. R. Simon: "By the word (*dāḇār*) of the Lord were the heavens made, and all their host by the breath of His mouth" (Ps. 33.6). Neither with labor nor with toil, but only with a word: "And God said, 'Let there be light'" (Gen. 1.3).[151]

God not only spoke in order to bring the world into being, he also spoke—proclaiming "Enough!" (*day*)—in order to bring the process of creation to closure and stop heaven and earth from continuing to expand.[152]

What were the words by which God called the world into being? An anonymous Midrash in Genesis Rabbāh XVII.1 invokes the earlier Mishnaic tradition, "By ten words (*ma'ămārôṯ*) was the world created,"[153] and goes on to explain what these ten words were: the first word of the Torah, *b^e^rē'šîṯ* (Gen. 1.1); the spirit/voice of God upon the waters (Gen. 1.2); and the eight commands "And God said" that appear in the account of creation in Genesis 1.3–26.[154] An alternative interpretation follows, attributed to R. Menaḥem b. Jose, in which the spirit/voice of God is not included as one of the ten words but is replaced by the ninth command "And God said" in Genesis 2.18. R. Menaḥem's interpretation is then refuted in a statement ascribed to R. Jacob b. Kirshai, who concurs with the first interpretation in including the spirit/voice of God as one of the ten words.[155]

Stages of Manifestation The relationship between the various aspects of the Torah's role in creation discussed in the previous sections—as God's architect, as the blueprint, and as divine language—is generally not discussed in classical Amoraic Midrashim. These speculations about the Torah appear rather as isolated fragments throughout the texts and are not developed in terms of a consistent cosmology. It is only on the basis of the Midrashim concerning the ten words by which the world was created that we can begin to develop an interpretive scheme in which these different aspects of the Torah's cosmogonic role, as architect, blueprint, and divine language, can be viewed as progressive manifestations of a single process. The Torah conceived as God's architect is a living, organic entity, which in its identification with primordial wisdom almost appears to take on an existence independent of God. Yet at the same time it is *God's* wisdom, which contains within itself the ideal plan of the universe. This plan conceived in the mind of God contains the "ideas" of all the forms in creation. These ideas are then spoken out by God, expressed by him in speech utterances, which are then precipitated to form the concrete phenomena of creation. From unspoken thought to vocalized speech utterances to concrete forms: this is the progressive process of creation in which the Torah participates at every stage.

The relationship between these various aspects of manifestation is represented in the first interpretation in Genesis Rabbāh XVII.1 of the ten words (*ma'ămārôṯ*) by which the world was created. *Bᵉrē'šîṯ*, the first word of the Torah, is considered to be the first word, which in this context constitutes the original unspoken Word through which the undifferentiated totality of heaven and earth were created. As discussed earlier, this primal unspoken Word, *bᵉrē'šîṯ*, is directly linked in the opening proem of Genesis Rabbāh to the creative role of the Torah as primordial wisdom. The second creative utterance was the voice, yet unexpressed, that hovered as the spirit of God over the waters (Gen. 1.2). Then the voice became vocalized and burst forth onto the expressed level of speech: "And God said, 'Let there be light'" (Gen. 1.3). This is the first of eight commands[156] that progressively unfolded the details of creation from the primordial totality. With each command, "Let there be. . . . ," it was so. The Lord spoke the name and the corresponding form appeared. In this portrayal of creation we find a progressive development from unspoken thought to spoken utterance to concrete form. The Torah as the Word of God encompasses both the cognitive and phonic dimensions of the Word, both unspoken thought and spoken utterance.

Torah as Light and Fire The Torah as the Word of God is associated in classical Amoraic Midrashim, as in Tannaitic Midrashim, not only with oral-aural images of God's speech but also with visual images of light and fire. As in Sip̄rê on Numbers, Proverbs 6.23 is invoked to establish that the Torah is light: "For the commandment (*mitzvah*) is a lamp (*nēr*) and the Torah a light (*'ôr*)."[157] The Torah is also at times identified with the light of God's Word that is celebrated in Psalm 119.105: "Thy word (*dābār*) is a lamp (*nēr*) to my feet and a light (*'ôr*) to my path."[158] The light of the divine Word illumined creation in the beginning[159] and again filled the world with its refulgent splendor when the Torah descended to earth at the time of the Sinai revelation.[160] The light of Torah is said to illumine the path of those who study and observe its commandments.[161] Moreover, several traditions emphasize that study of Torah causes the countenances of the sages to shine with its radiance,[162] just as Moses's countenance shone when he received the Torah at Sinai.[163]

The Torah as the effulgent Word of God is connected with fire as well as with light. Jeremiah 23.29, "Is not My word (*dābār*) like fire (*'ēš*)? says the Lord," is at times invoked to establish the fiery nature of the Torah.[164] The primordial Torah that existed prior to the Sinai revelation is identified, as we have seen, with the "flaming sword" (*lahaṭ ha-ḥereb*) that God placed in the Garden of Eden after Adam's fall[165] and with the "flaming torch" (*lappîd 'ēš*)[166] in the covenant with Abraham. The revelation itself is often associated with images of fire, drawing on pentateuchal allusions to the Sinai event.[167] Deuteronomy 4.11, "The mountain burned with fire (*'ēš*) to the heart of heaven," is interpreted to mean that the words of the Torah were given at Sinai in fire.[168] As in Tannaitic Midrashim, the "fiery law" in Deuteronomy 33.2, "The Lord came from Sinai, . . . at His right hand was a fiery law (*'ēš-dāt*) for them," is understood as referring to the Torah.[169] A tradition in Song of Songs Rabbāh ascribed to R. Simeon b. Lakish develops this image further, maintaining that the Torah was itself formed of fire and was written with black fire on white fire.[170] Not only the Written Torah but also the Oral Torah is characterized as fire.[171] A number of aggadot emphasize that the sages who study the Torah imbibe its fiery nature. A tradition in P^{e}sîqtā' d^{e}-R. Kahana suggests that the very being of the scholars is on fire with Torah.[172] Moreover, according to an aggadah that appears in several texts, flames of fire encircle the sages as they expound the words of Torah, recapitulating the fiery revelation at Mount Sinai.[173]

The Babylonian Talmud

In the period between the third and sixth centuries the Amoraim in Palestine compiled and edited two types of documents: the Jerusalem

Talmud, which contains exegeses of the Mishnah; and Tannaitic Midrashim and classical Amoraic Midrashim, which contain exegeses of the Hebrew Bible. During the same period the Amoraim in Babylonia compiled the Babylonian Talmud, which was brought to closure in the course of the sixth century and which included both types of material: exegeses of the Mishnah and exegeses of the Hebrew Bible. Although the Babylonian Talmud is organized in the form of a commentary on the tractates of the Mishnah, it also contains a substantial amount of Midrashic material. Large sections of aggadic Midrash are inserted in the midst of the halakhic discussions, many of which appear to have been borrowed from Palestinian Midrashim.

The doctrine of the two Torahs, the Written Torah and the Oral Torah, is reiterated in the Talmud with increased emphasis on the importance of the Oral Torah. The Mishnah and the Talmud are ascribed sacrosanct status as part of the Oral Torah that was revealed to Moses at Mount Sinai along with the Written Torah, which included the Pentateuch, Nevi'im, and Ketuvim.[174] The Oral Torah is represented as an open-ended category that encompasses not only this circumscribed corpus of teachings but ultimately all the interpretations and innovations that would be introduced by the sages in subsequent generations as part of the oral tradition.[175] A homily attributed to R. Eleazar b. Azariah invokes Ecclesiastes 12.11, "The words of the wise are as goads, and as nails firmly planted are [the words of] masters of assemblies, which are given from one Shepherd," to establish that even if the teachings of the sages at times appear to contradict one another, they were all "given from one Shepherd": "One God gave them, one leader declared them from the mouth of the Lord of all creation, blessed be He, as it is written, 'And God spoke *all* these words' (Exod. 20.1)."[176]

An aggadic tradition ascribed to Rab Judah in the name of his teacher Rab vividly illustrates the far-reaching implications of such an all-encompassing interpretation of the Oral Torah. It relates that when Moses ascended on high to receive the Torah, the Lord showed him R. Akiba, who was destined to arise as one of the greatest sages of future generations, sitting and expounding the Torah to his disciples. Moses was at first ill at ease because he could not understand their arguments. However, when they came to a certain topic and the disciples asked the master, "Whence do you know this?" R. Akiba replied, "It is a law given to Moses at Sinai," and Moses was comforted.[177] The authority vested in the rabbinic sages as the custodians of the Oral Torah is further illustrated in another aggadah, which goes so far as to assert that since the time when the Torah was given at Mount Sinai, the power to decide matters of halakhah no longer resides in heaven but rather in the consensus of the sages on earth, who even have the authority to counter the dictates of the heavenly voice (*baṯ qôl*).[178]

Several Talmudic passages establish a dichotomy between the Written Torah and the Oral Torah, suggesting that the words of the scribes (*sôp̄ᵉrîm*) must be more carefully observed than the words of the Written Torah, for whereas biblical ordinances require no reinforcement and when violated result in a variety of penalties, the enactments of the scribes require reinforcement and when transgressed incur the penalty of death.[179] Those who focus on the Mishnah and the Gemara (Talmud) are considered more meritorious than those who are concerned with the Written Torah alone.[180] One Talmudic pericope affirms the essential writtenness of the Written Torah and the essential orality of the Oral Torah, which may not be written down, culminating in a statement attributed to R. Joḥanan that gives precedence to the Oral Torah over the Written Torah: "The Holy One, blessed be He, made a covenant with Israel only for the sake of those words that were transmitted orally (*bᵉ-'al peh*), as it is said, 'For by the mouth (*'al peh*) of these words I have made a covenant with you and with Israel' (Exod. 34.27)."[181] As we shall see, the priority given to the Oral Torah is directly linked in certain post-Talmudic Midrashim to the polemic against the Christians, who had appropriated the Written Torah as their "Old Testament" but who were denied access to the teachings of the Oral Torah by virtue of their transmission through oral tradition.[182]

Most of the discussions of the Torah in the Babylonian Talmud focus on the importance of study and practice of the teachings of the Written Torah and Oral Torah. There is relatively little emphasis on cosmogonic and cosmological speculation, and thus we do not find much evidence of new modes of representing the status and role of the Torah in creation. The most extensive discussion of cosmogonic matters is found in the Gemara on Ḥăḡîḡāh II.1, the Mishnah that forbids public discourse on *ma'ăśēh bᵉrē'šîṯ*, the mysteries of creation, and *ma'ăśēh merkāḇāh*, the mysteries of the throne-chariot. In this context tractate Ḥăḡîḡāh discusses the limits of discourse concerning cosmogonic speculation and the "secrets of the Torah" (*siṯrê tôrāh*) and reiterates a number of traditions concerning the first beginnings of creation found in classical Amoraic Midrashim.[183] Additional aggadic speculations are interspersed throughout the Talmudic tractates. Most of the Talmudic discussions of the cosmological status of the Torah represent variants of traditions found in classical Amoraic Midrashim, with little evidence of substantive reinterpretation. Our analysis will briefly highlight some of the Talmudic variants of earlier traditions.

The Preexistence of the Torah In Talmudic Midrashim, as in earlier rabbinic texts, the identification of the Torah with the figure of personified wisdom in Proverbs 1–9, and in particular in her primordial status as depicted in Proverbs 8.22–31, is assumed.[184] Three types of Palestinian speculation concerning the primordial Torah are also found in the Talmud: the Torah is one of several preexistent entities; the Torah remained hidden for 974 generations before the creation of the world; and the Ten Commandments are among the ten things created on the eve of the first Sabbath.

The Talmud contains a variant of the tradition in Genesis Rabbāh that includes the Torah as one of seven preexistent things. The Talmudic version lists five of the items that are found in Genesis Rabbāh's list—the Torah, repentance, the throne of glory, the Temple, and the name of the Messiah—and invokes the same proof texts for each, including Proverbs 8.22 in the case of the Torah. However, it diverges from Genesis Rabbāh's enumeration by substituting the Garden of Eden and Gehenna for the patriarchs and the people of Israel.[185] This adaptation of the tradition may reflect the tendency evident in later rabbinic texts to shift attention away from the historical realities of this world toward transhistorical concerns such as paradise, hell, and the world to come.

The tradition that the Torah remained hidden as God's "secret treasure" (*ḥămûḏāh gᵉnûzāh*) for 974 generations before the world was created is incorporated in several aggadot.[186] The Talmud also contains a variant of the aggadah found in 'Āḇôṯ, Sip̄rê on Deuteronomy, and the Mᵉḵîltā' dᵉ-R. Ishmael concerning the ten things that were created on the eve of the first Sabbath. The letters (*kᵉṯāḇ*), writing (*miḵtāḇ*), and tablets (*lûḥôṯ*) of the Ten Commandments are included in the Talmud's enumeration, which most closely coincides with that of Sip̄rê on Deuteronomy.[187]

The Talmud includes a number of traditions that connect the preexistent Torah with Adam and the patriarchs. A Midrash attributed to R. Simeon b. Lakish provides a variant of the tradition in Genesis Rabbāh that interprets Genesis 5.1, "This is the book of the generations of Adam," to mean that God showed to Adam all future generations of sages who were destined to be expounders (of Torah).[188] All of the patriarchs are said to have fulfilled certain precepts of the Torah,[189] but Abraham in particular is singled out as the most ardent observer of the commandments.[190] A passage in Yômā' 28b ascribes to Rab the tradition that "Abraham our father fulfilled the whole Torah," invoking the standard proof text, Genesis 26.5: "Because Abraham obeyed My voice and kept My charge, My commandments (*mitzvot*), My statutes (*ḥuqqôṯ*), and My laws (*tôrōṯ*)." The implication in Genesis Rabbāh that Abraham even knew certain oral traditions is explicitly articulated in a comment attributed to Raba or R. Ashi, which interprets the plural form *tôrōṯ* to mean that Abraham observed both the Written Torah and the Oral Torah.[191]

Torah as the Instrument of Creation Speculations concerning the role of the Torah in creation are less prevalent in Talmudic Midrashim than in classical Amoraic Midrashim. Several passages do, however, maintain that God created the world with wisdom, *ḥoḵmāh,* which is identified elsewhere in the Talmud with the Torah.[192] Sanheḏrîn 38a includes a variant of a tradition found in Leviticus Rabbāh that interprets Proverbs 9.1–3 as referring to the creation of the world by means of wisdom.[193] Another tradition, ascribed to Rab through R. Zutra b. Tobiah, invokes Proverbs 3.19–20 as a proof text to establish the role of wisdom (*ḥoḵmāh*), understanding (*t^{e}ḇûnāh*), and knowledge (*da'aṯ*) in creation.[194]

The notion that the Torah constitutes the plan of creation, its laws reflecting the structure of the macrocosm and the microcosm, is pointed to in the Talmudic version of the tradition that the 365 negative commandments of the Torah correspond to the number of solar days while the 248 positive commandments correspond to the number of members in the human body.[195]

A number of aggadot suggest that the Torah is necessary not only for the creation of the universe but also for its maintenance and continuation.[196] A tradition attributed to R. Eleazar maintains that heaven and earth could not endure without the Torah, for according to Jeremiah 33.25, "If not for My covenant by day and by night, I would not have established the ordinances of heaven and earth."[197]

Torah as Divine Language As in classical Amoraic Midrashim, the relationship of the Torah to the divine language is developed in the Talmud in terms of a number of different conceptions: the Torah is identified with the Word of God;[198] it is also at times associated with the divine Name;[199] and it is celebrated as the repository of the Hebrew letters that constitute the fundamental elements of the divine language. Like their Palestinian counterparts, Talmudic speculations concerning the creative power of the divine language focus in particular on the cosmogonic role of the Hebrew letters as well as on the more generalized notion of God's speech.

Talmudic homilies on the Hebrew letters, like those in classical Amoraic Midrashim, focus primarily on the shape and semantic significance of the letters.[200] The Talmud includes a variant of the tradition that this world was created with *hē* and the world to come with *yōḏ*, incorporating a number of explanations based on the shapes of the two letters that are not found in the version in Genesis Rabbāh.[201] God created the universe with the Hebrew letters, and thus those sages who learn to decipher and to manipulate and combine the letters are described in several passages as gaining access to the mysteries of God's creative power. A tradition ascribed to Rab through his student Rab Judah suggests that Bezalel, the artisan who built the Tabernacle, tapped into this power, for he was possessed of wisdom (*ḥoḵmāh*), understanding (*tᵉḇûnāh*), and knowledge (*da'aṯ*), according to Exodus 35.31, and it is these three things that are extolled in Proverbs 3.19–20 as the means through which God brought forth the earth, the heavens, and the depths, respectively. The specialty of Bezalel's wisdom was that he "knew how to combine the letters (*'ôṯiyyôṯ*) with which heaven and earth were created."[202] Later sages are said to have mastered this science as well. For example, one tradition maintains that through studying the science of combination of the letters laid out in the *Sēp̄er Yᵉṣîrāh*, R. Ḥanina and R. Hoshaiah gained the power to create a calf that was one-third of its full size.[203]

Every jot and tittle of the letters that compose the Sefer Torah is considered holy and God-given, for even the crowns (*kᵉṯārîm*) on certain letters are held to have been affixed by God himself.[204] Given the creative power of the letters, it is considered dangerous to alter a single stroke of the letters in any way and thereby to tamper with the perfect structure of the Torah, God's blueprint. We thus find the admonition attributed to R. Ishmael when speaking to R. Meir of his work as a scribe of the Torah: "If you should perhaps omit a single letter or add a single letter, you would thereby destroy the entire world."[205]

The creative power of the Hebrew letters is linked not only to their shape but also to their sound as the fundamental elements of the divine language. As in earlier rabbinic texts, God is celebrated throughout the Talmud as "He who spoke (*'āmar*) and the world came into being."[206] Like the Mᵉkîltā' and Genesis Rabbāh, Talmudic traditions invoke Psalm 33.6, "By the word (*dāḇār*) of the Lord were the heavens made," as a proof text to show that for God speech is action.[207] "Blessed be He who says and does, who decrees and accomplishes."[208] Just as God simply spoke in order to bring the world into being, so a single command sufficed in order to bring the expansion of the world to a standstill.[209]

The Talmud includes a variant of the aggadah in Genesis Rabbāh XVII.1 concerning the ten words (*ma'ămārôṯ*) by which the world was created. The Talmudic version, which is attributed to R. Joḥanan, corresponds most closely to the interpretation of R. Menaḥem b. Jose in Genesis Rabbāh in that it does not include the spirit/voice of God that hovered over the face of the waters as one of the ten words but includes instead the ninth command "And God said." *Bᵉrē'šîṯ*, the first word of the Torah, is designated as the first of the ten words, by means of which, in accordance with Psalm 33.6, "the heavens" and "their host" (the earth) were made.[210]

Torah as Light and Fire In the Talmud, as in earlier rabbinic texts, the Torah is associated with images of light and fire. The identification of the Torah with light is established in several Midrashim by invoking the standard proof text, Proverbs 6.23, "For the commandment (*mitzvah*) is a lamp (*nēr*) and the Torah a light (*'ôr*)."[211] According to an interpretation ascribed to R. Menaḥem b. Jose, this verse means that whereas an individual commandment is like a lamp in that it only protects temporarily, the Torah is like light in that it protects permanently—in this world, in death, and in the world to come.[212] The verse is understood in another context as referring to the rabbinic sages, who, infused with the light of Torah, are the "light of the world" (*'ôrô šel 'ôlām*).[213] The light of Torah is said to enlighten (*hē'îr*) the eyes and illumine the countenance of those who study and teach it.[214] Not only are the eyes and faces of the sages said to shine, but their bodies are also at times described as radiating light.[215]

The Torah is also connected with fire in a number of passages. As in earlier rabbinic texts, the Torah is identified with the "fiery law" (*'ēš-dāṯ*) in Deuteronomy 33.2.[216] Jeremiah 23.29, "Is not My word (*dāḇār*) like fire (*'ēš*)? says the Lord," is also invoked to establish that the Torah as the Word of God partakes of the nature of fire.[217] A tradition attributed to R. Eleazar through R. Abbahu cites this verse to show that the bodies of the sages, who have imbibed the fire of God's Word/Torah, are composed of fire, and therefore the fire of Gehenna can have no power over them.[218] Moreover, the story in Ḥăḡîḡāh 14b regarding R. Joḥanan b. Zakkai and his disciples suggests that those sages who expound the mysteries of the Torah, and in particular *ma'ăśēh merkāḇāh*, have the power to cause the descent of heavenly fire and other miraculous phenomena reminiscent of the revelation at Mount Sinai.[219]

P^esîqtā' Rabbāṯî and Tanḥûmā' Y^elamm^eḏēnû Midrashim

In the post-Talmudic period from the Muslim conquest (ca. 640 C.E.) to the end of the twelfth century a range of aggadic Midrashim emerge. This period is characterized by a decline in the classical literary forms such as the proem and the development of new literary forms and themes influenced by the apocalyptic literature of the Second Temple period.

(1) Exegetical Midrashim. The exegetical form of Midrash declines in importance in this period, although we do find examples of exegetical Midrashim, among which should be mentioned Ecclesiastes Rabbāh (ca. 8th c. C.E.), Midrash on Psalms,[220] Midrash on Proverbs (ca. 10th c. C.E.), Exodus Rabbāh I (sections I–XIV, on Exodus 1–10) (ca. 10th c. C.E.), Esther Rabbāh II (sections VII–X, on Esther 3.1–8.15) (ca. 11th c. C.E.), and Numbers Rabbāh I (sections I–XIV, on Numbers 1–8, which combine exegetical and homiletical forms) (ca. 12th c. C.E.).

(2) Homiletical Midrashim. The most important Midrashic collections of this period are homiletical: P^esîqtā' Rabbāṯî (ca. 7th c. C.E.) and the closely related Tanḥûmā' Y^elamm^eḏēnû Midrashim (ca. 9th c. C.E.). P^esîqtā' Rabbāṯî imitates the liturgical program of P^esîqtā' d^e-R. Kahana, providing a sequence of homiletical discourses related to the pentateuchal and prophetic readings for festivals, fasts, and special Sabbaths. At the same time, as will be discussed below, certain *pisqā*'s are marked by a recurring literary structure that clearly links P^esîqtā' Rabbāṯî to Tanḥûmā' Y^elamm^eḏēnû Midrashim. Tanḥûmā' Y^elamm^eḏēnû Midrashim represent a distinctive new form of homiletical Midrash on the books of the Pentateuch. Like Leviticus Rabbāh, these Midrashim contain discourses based on the first verse(s) of the pentateuchal readings for regular Sabbaths, organized in accordance with the triennial cycle. Two features distinguish Tanḥûmā' Y^elamm^eḏēnû Midrashim from earlier forms of homiletical Midrash: the frequent mention of R. Tanḥuma, a Palestinian Amora of the second half of

the fourth century; and a special type of halakhic proem, beginning with the formula "*Y^{e} lamm^{e}ḏēnû rabbênû*" ("may our master teach us"), which serves as an introduction to an aggadic homily.

(3) Narrative Midrashim. The narrative form of aggadic Midrash emerges for the first time in this period. This literary form is not a collection of expositions or homilies linked to biblical verses but rather constitutes a uniform narrative that "rewrites" the Bible. Among the most important narrative Midrashim are Pirqê d^{e}-R. Eliezer (ca. 8th c. C.E), which retells certain key events described in the pentateuchal narrative, beginning with the account of creation and concluding with the journeys of the people of Israel in the wilderness; and Sēḏer 'Ēliyyāhû Rabbāh and Sēḏer 'Ēliyyāhû Zûṭā' (both before 9th c. C.E.), which reformulate the ethical and religious teachings of the Bible in accordance with the author's didactic aims.

Our analysis will focus on select Midrashim that are representative of the new types of genres that arose in the post-Talmudic period: P^{e}sîqtā' Rabbāṯî and Tanḥûmā' Y^{e}lamm^{e}ḏēnû Midrashim, and the narrative Midrash Pirqê d^{e}-R. Eliezer. Most of the earlier aggadic traditions concerning the Torah's preexistence are also found in these texts, at times assuming new valences in accordance with the contexts in which they are embedded. The role of the Torah in creation is represented through a variety of images, in which the Torah is variously depicted as God's counselor, as the artisan of creation, as the blueprint or plan of creation, and as the divine language through which God creates. The last three images are familiar from classical Amoraic Midrashim.

P^{e}sîqtā' Rabbāṯî is a composite work that provides a bridge between classical Amoraic Midrashim, in particular P^{e}sîqtā' d^{e}-R. Kahana and Leviticus Rabbāh, and Tanḥûmā' Y^{e}lamm^{e}ḏēnû Midrashim. The formal structure of the book is modeled on that of P^{e}sîqtā' d^{e}-R. Kahana and, like its predecessor, is organized in accordance with the liturgical calendar.[221] P^{e}sîqtā' Rabbāṯî contains ten *pisqā*'s that closely parallel *pisqā*'s in P^{e}sîqtā' d^{e}-R. Kahana[222] and two *pisqā*'s that resemble chapters in Leviticus Rabbāh.[223] Another major stratum of P^{e}sîqtā' Rabbāṯî is clearly linked to Tanḥûmā' Y^{e}lamm^{e}ḏēnû Midrashim: thirty of its fifty-three *pisqā*'s begin with a halakhic proem that is introduced by the formula "*Y^{e}lamm^{e}ḏēnû rabbênû*" and that generally leads into a homily introduced by the phrase "R. Tanḥuma opened [his discourse]."[224] P^{e}sîqtā' Rabbāṯî is generally held to be a Palestinian work dating from the seventh (or possibly sixth) century, although the Tanḥûmā' Y^{e}lamm^{e}ḏēnû stratum may be as late as the ninth century.[225]

Tanḥûmā' Y^{e}lamm^{e}d̲ēnû Midrashim, with the exception of the stratum in P^{e}sîqtā' Rabbāt̲î, are modeled after the Leviticus Rabbāh mode of homiletical Midrash and are thus organized in accordance with the *s^{e}d̲ārîm* of the triennial cycle of Torah reading. Although the problems posed by this literature have been vigorously debated, the general scholarly consensus is that the rubric "Tanḥûmā' Y^{e}lamm^{e}d̲ēnû" may be used to designate a corpus of aggadic Midrashim that represents a distinct literary genre characterized by halakhic proems and the frequent mention of R. Tanḥuma: the standard printed edition of the Tanḥûmā', the Buber edition of the Tanḥûmā', Exodus Rabbāh II (sections XV–LII, on Exodus 12–40), Numbers Rabbāh II (sections XV–XXIII, on Numbers 9–36), Deuteronomy Rabbāh (all versions),[226] portions of P^{e}sîqtā' Rabbāt̲î, and various other Midrashic manuscripts and fragments. All of the Tanḥûmā' Y^{e}lamm^{e}d̲ēnû Midrashim make use of Tannaitic texts, the Jerusalem Talmud, and classical Amoraic Midrashim. Although all of these works contain fragments of relatively early material, they also contain allusions to anti-Karaite polemics, which would date the final redaction of even the earliest of the extant texts as not before 800 C.E. There is no scholarly consensus concerning where the various texts that form part of the Tanḥûmā' Y^{e}lamm^{e}d̲ēnû corpus were compiled.

In their discussions of the Written Torah and Oral Torah P^{e}sîqtā' Rabbāt̲î and Tanḥûmā' Y^{e}lamm^{e}d̲ēnû Midrashim expand on a number of themes found in earlier Midrashim while occasionally adding new nuances to the older traditions. For example, the teachings of the sages contained in the Oral Torah are generally represented in earlier texts as having been received through the line of oral transmission that traces its roots back to Moses at Mount Sinai. The Tanḥûmā' and Exodus Rabbāh II contain a tradition attributed to R. Isaac that provides an alternative interpretation of how the sages received their teachings. In this view the sages as well as the prophets were themselves present at Mount Sinai, in soul if not in body, and received the teachings that they were to expound to future generations.[227]

P^{e}sîqtā' Rabbāt̲î contains a homiletical discourse, ascribed to R. Tanḥuma, on Ecclesiastes 12.11, "The words of the wise are as goads, and as nails firmly planted are [the words of] masters of assemblies, which are given from one Shepherd," which provides a more extensive commentary than the parallel homily in the Talmud attributed to R. Eleazar b. Azariah. Like its Talmudic counterpart, the homily insists that even though the sages may at times express conflicting viewpoints, all of their teachings were "given from one Shepherd."[228] In contrast to the Talmudic homily, it continues with a commentary on the subsequent verse in Ecclesiastes, "And even more than these, my son, take heed. Of making many books there is no end" (Eccles. 12.12), which it interprets to mean that one is to heed the words of the scribes even more than the words of the Written Torah—a conception that, as we have seen, is also expressed in earlier rabbinic texts.[229] Why then were not the words of the scribes written down like those of the Written Torah? Because if one were to attempt to write down all of the words of the scribes, "of making many books there would be no end" (Eccles. 12.12) and confusion would result.[230]

Several passages in P^e^sîqtā' Rabbāṯî and Tanḥûmā' Y^e^lamm^e^ḏēnû Midrashim suggest that the decision not to write down the oral traditions of the sages was based not simply on pragmatic considerations but on a divine injunction from God to Moses at Mount Sinai. A homily in P^e^sîqtā' Rabbāṯî, which appears with slight variations in the Tanḥûmā', expands upon the Talmudic tradition that the Oral Torah should not be written down, clearly linking it to an anti-Christian polemic. Moses is said to have asked that the Mishnah also be given in writing, but God foresaw that the nations would translate the Written Torah into Greek and would proclaim, "We are Israel." Therefore God decided that the Mishnah should be preserved orally as the "secret" (*misṭêrîn*) that distinguishes his true children from other nations.[231] An anonymous tradition that appears in Exodus Rabbāh II and the Tanḥûmā' depicts God as deciding to give orally not only the Mishnah but also the Talmud and Aggadah, so as to maintain a distinction between Israel and the idolatrous gentile nations that would enslave them. This tradition extends the conception of Oral Torah to include not only the Mishnah, Talmud, and Aggadah, but even the questions that future generations of scholars would ask their teachers.[232]

Most of the relevant speculations in P^e^sîqtā' Rabbāṯî concerning the role of the Torah in creation and revelation are found in those *pisqā*'s that focus on cosmological and cosmogonic concerns (*pisqā'* 46, which appears to belong to the Rosh Ha-Shanah cycle; *pisqā'* [53], which is not linked with any synagogue reading or festival; *pisqā'* 20, which forms part of the Shavuot cycle) or on the nature of the revelation at Mount Sinai (*pisqā*'s 20–21, which include homilies for Shavuot). The cosmology of P^e^sîqtā' Rabbāṯî is characteristic of the post-Talmudic period in that it gives increased emphasis to esoteric speculations concerning the mysteries of the throne-chariot (*ma'ăśēh merkāḇāh*) and the multileveled hierarchy of firmaments arrayed with hosts of various types of angels. It also contains astrological speculations concerning the signs of the Zodiac and the planets. In its cosmological discussions Pᵉsîqtā' Rabbāṯî is primarily concerned to establish correspondences between the cosmic order and the social and moral orders of human beings, in particular of the people of Israel. The Torah is central to this cosmology for it provides the link between the macrocosm and the microcosm in that it reflects God's ordering of creation and through its laws serves to bring the social and moral life of Israel into alignment with the cosmic order.

Those sections of Tanḥûmā' Yᵉlammᵉḏēnû Midrashim that are most concerned with the cosmological status of the Torah are those that focus on the account of creation in Genesis (Tanḥûmā' on the book of Genesis) or on the account of the revelation of the Torah at Mount Sinai in Exodus (Tanḥûmā' on the book of Exodus and Exodus Rabbāh II). Most of the cosmogonic speculations concerning the book of Genesis represent reiterations, elaborations, and reinterpretations of traditions found in Genesis Rabbāh and other classical Amoraic Midrashim. Speculations concerning the revelation at Mount Sinai will be discussed in chapter 4.

The Preexistence of the Torah In Pᵉsîqtā' Rabbāṯî and Tanḥûmā' Yᵉlammᵉḏēnû Midrashim, as in earlier rabbinic texts, the identification of the Torah with the primordial wisdom of Proverbs 8.22–31 is taken for granted.[233] This identification is important not only in establishing the Torah's preexistent status but also in delineating its cosmogonic role.

Pᵉsîqtā' Rabbāṯî mentions the Torah's existence prior to creation in a number of different contexts, although it does not contain any sustained discussion of the matter.[234] Proverbs 8.27 is invoked to show that the Torah, as primordial wisdom, was present when God established the heavens.[235] *Pisqā'* 46, which most likely belongs to the Rosh Ha-Shanah cycle, develops a series of correlations between the first day of creation, the first New Year's Day, and the first Sabbath. It asserts that calendar reckoning, by means of which the date of the first day of creation may be determined, begins with the creation of the Torah, and in this context the text incorporates the tradition that the Torah was created two thousand years before the creation of the world. The tradition is not elaborated nor are the standard proof texts, Proverbs 8.30 and

Psalm 90.4, cited.[236] *Pisqā'* 21, in a homily on the role of certain letters in creation that appears to be adapted largely from Genesis Rabbāh, mentions the tradition that the *'ālep̄* complained for twenty-six generations prior to the giving of the Torah and then connects this notion with Psalm 105.8, "The word (*dāb̲ār*) that He commanded after [E.V. 'for'] a thousand (*'elep̄*) generations." Although all of the ingredients are present, the text does not explicitly invoke the aggadah that the Torah was created 974 generations prior to the world (1000 – 26 = 974).[237]

In Tanḥûmā' Yelammedēnû Midrashim the Torah's primordial status is generally represented in terms of the specific role that the Torah assumed in bringing forth creation, as will be discussed below. Several passages simply state that the Torah preceded the creation of the world without speculating about the time frame or nature of its preexistence.[238]

As in earlier rabbinic texts, in Pesîqtā' Rabbāṯî and Tanḥûmā' Yelammedēnû Midrashim the existence of the Torah prior to the revelation at Mount Sinai is affirmed through linking the Torah to Adam and the patriarchs. Pesîqtā' Rabbāṯî and the Tanḥûmā' incorporate variants of the tradition that interprets Genesis 5.1, "This is the book of the generations of Adam," to mean that God showed Adam future generations. In enumerating these generations both texts include not only the sages who expound the Torah, which form part of the standard enumeration of earlier texts, but also the righteous and the wicked of each subsequent generation.[239] Elsewhere the Tanḥûmā', in commenting on Genesis 3.24, "He drove out the man, and at the east of the Garden of Eden he placed the cherubim and a flaming sword (*lahaṭ ha-ḥereb̲*) that turned every way to keep the way to the tree of life," includes the tradition that identifies the "flaming sword" with the Torah.[240] A second Midrashic comment, attributed to R. Samuel b. Naḥman, interprets "to keep the way to the tree of life" as referring to God's original intention that Adam should keep the Torah and eat from the tree of life. However, after Adam sinned God had no choice but to drive him out of the garden.[241]

Several Midrashim include the aggadah that interprets the "flaming torch" (*lappîḏ 'ēš*) in Genesis 15.17 as referring to the Torah, which God showed to Abraham.[242] The Tanḥûmā', in commenting on certain verses in Genesis concerning the patriarchs, incorporates most of the aggadot regarding the patriarchs' relationship to the Torah that are found in Genesis Rabbāh, including the notion that Abraham learned the Torah from his kidneys, that he observed all of the commandments of the Torah as indicated in

Genesis 26.5, and that his descendants Isaac, Jacob, and the sons of Jacob also studied Torah.[243] In recontextualizing these traditions, the Tanḥûmā' infuses the standard accounts with its own distinctive emphases. For example, one anonymous Midrash provides a link between the two aspects of the Torah's preexistence—prior to the revelation and prior to creation—through maintaining that God reserved the Torah for Abraham since before the world was created.[244] Another anonymous Midrash points to Abraham's case as an example for future generations: as Abraham, his son Isaac, and his grandson Jacob all learned the Torah, so should one teach the Torah to one's son and grandson.[245] The Tanḥûmā' celebrates Jacob in particular, who, as the "quiet man dwelling in tents (*yōšēḇ 'ōhālîm*)" (Gen. 25.27), went from one tent of learning or academy to another in order to perfect his knowledge of Torah.[246]

Torah as God's Counselor and Artisan A number of passages in P^{e}sîqtā' Rabbāṯî and Tanḥûmā' Y^{e}lamm^{e}ḏēnû Midrashim point to the cosmogonic role of the Torah as the instrument of creation. The foundational assumption underlying most of these discussions is once again the identification of the Torah with wisdom, particularly as celebrated in Proverbs 3.19–20 and Proverbs 8.22–31.

An anonymous Midrash in Exodus Rabbāh II declares that it was with the aid of the Torah that God created heaven and earth and then invokes Proverbs 3.19–20 as proof of the Torah's role in creation: "The Lord by wisdom (*ḥoḵmāh*) founded the earth; by understanding (*t^{e}ḇûnāh*) He established the heavens; by His knowledge (*da'aṯ*) the depths were broken up."[247] A second Midrash in Exodus Rabbāh II cites Proverbs 3.19–20 to establish that the world was created with three things—wisdom, understanding, and knowledge. Subsequently, in the context of discussing how Bezalel, the artisan who built the Tabernacle, was possessed of these three things, the Midrash links wisdom with the Torah, understanding with halakhah, and knowledge with the Talmud.[248] Proverbs 3.19–20 is also cited in the Tanḥûmā' and P^{e}sîqtā' Rabbāṯî to establish the role of wisdom in creating and ordering the cosmos, although the Torah is not explicitly mentioned in these passages.[249]

The above mentioned Midrash in Exodus Rabbāh II does not clarify in what way the Torah aided in the cosmogonic process. However, in other Tanḥûmā' Y^{e}lamm^{e}ḏēnû Midrashim the nature of the Torah's role is more specifically delineated, using a variety of images. Several passages in the Tanḥûmā' depict the Torah as a counselor with whom God consulted when he created the world.

One tradition understands the plural "Let us make man in our image" in Genesis 1.26 as referring to God and the Torah.[250] The opening Midrash of the Tanḥûmā' asserts that God took counsel (*niṯyā'ēṣ*) with the Torah when he commenced the process of creation, citing Proverbs 8.14, in which personified wisdom declares, "Counsel (*'ēṣāh*) is mine and sound wisdom."[251] The Midrash subsequently portrays the Torah's cosmogonic role in terms of the more active image of an artisan. Vocalizing the *'āmôn* of Proverbs 8.30 as *'ûmān*, "artisan," the Midrash invokes the language and imagery of Proverbs 8.22–31 to describe how through the aid of his artisan, the Torah, God established the heaven and earth, fixed the boundaries of the deep, brought forth the sun and moon, and formed all of the works of creation.[252]

Another Midrash in the Tanḥûmā' similarly invokes Proverbs 8.22–31 to affirm the Torah's role as the artisan of creation, vocalizing *'āmôn* in verse 30 as *'ûmān*.

> The Holy One, blessed be He, looked (*hibbîṭ*) into the Torah and created the world. Hence: "Then I was beside Him as an artisan (*'āmôn*)" (Prov. 8.30). This is what is written, "With *rē'šîṯ* [E.V. 'In the beginning'] God created" (Gen. 1.1). *Rē'šîṯ* means nothing other than the Torah, as it is said, "The Lord made me *rē'šîṯ* [E.V. 'as the beginning'] of His way" (Prov. 8.22). Hence: "With *rē'šîṯ* God created."[253]

This Midrash is nearly identical, verbatim, with the last portion of the opening proem of Genesis Rabbāh, discussed earlier.[254] The two Midrashim clearly stem from a common tradition, with the Tanḥûmā''s version perhaps representing the earlier of the two, since it is shorter and does not contain the more developed image of the architect and blueprint that is found in Genesis Rabbāh. Moreover, if the attribution can be trusted, the Tanḥûmā' version is ascribed to an earlier sage, the Tanna R. Judah b. Il'ai (ca. 150 C.E.), who lived nearly a century before R. Hoshaiah (ca. 225 C.E.), to whom the Genesis Rabbāh proem is attributed.

Torah as the Blueprint of Creation In the Midrash ascribed to R. Judah b. Il'ai just cited, God is said to have "looked into" (*hibbîṭ*) the Torah in order to create the world. Although this idea is not explicitly elaborated in terms of the image of a blueprint, it clearly came to be understood in that way by certain rabbis, as evidenced by the use of the blueprint analogy in the corresponding Midrash attributed to R. Hoshaiah.

In addition to the more concrete image of God "looking into" the Torah, Tanḥûmā' Y^{e}lamm^{e}ḏēnû Midrashim contain the notion that God planned the creation in his mind before he brought his plan to fruition, although this notion is not always explicitly linked to the Torah.[255] An anonymous Tanḥûmā' Y^{e}lamm^{e}ḏēnû tradition directly links the Torah, through reference to 1 Chronicles 16.15 (= Ps. 105.8), to the plan of creation that had been conceived in the mind of God for a thousand years. When the time of creation came, the plan effortlessly materialized—in one day—as the multiple phenomena of the universe.

> "My hand laid the foundation of the earth" (Isa. 48.13). The Holy One, blessed be He, said, "For My thoughts (*maḥš^{e}ḇôṯ*) are not your thoughts. . . . For as the heavens are higher than the earth, so are My ways higher than your ways and My thoughts than your thoughts" (Isa. 55.8–9). A person sits and plans (*ḥiššēḇ*), saying, "In this manner I shall build, in this manner I shall make it." He plans (*ḥāšaḇ*) in one hour what he does not produce in ten years. But the Holy One, blessed be He, is not so, for [what] He plans (*ḥāšaḇ*) in a thousand years He builds in one day, as it is said, "Remember His covenant for ever, the word (*dāḇār*) that He commanded for a thousand generations" (1 Chron. 16.15). [The heavens] were created in one day, as it is said, "By the word (*dāḇār*) of the Lord were the heavens made" (Ps. 33.6). When He created the world, the Torah, as it were, gave Him light (*hē'îr*), for the world was formless and void (*tôhû wā-ḇôhû*), as it is said, "For the commandment (*mitzvah*) is a lamp and the Torah a light (*'ôr*)" (Prov. 6.23). The Holy One, blessed be He, said, "Behold, I seek workmen (*pô'ălîn*)." The Torah said to Him, "I shall put at your disposal twenty-two workmen (*pô'ălîm*), namely, the twenty-two letters (*'ôṯiyyôṯ*) that are in the Torah."[256]

In this passage the Torah's role as the plan of creation contemplated in God's mind is connected to two other aspects of its cosmogonic role: as the light that illumined the dark chaos from which the world emerged, and as the repository of the twenty-two letters that served as God's workmen (*pô'ălîm*) in creation.

The notion that the Torah constitutes the cosmic plan is pointed to in other traditions that represent the Torah as reflecting the structure of the cosmos. For example, *pisqā'* [53] of P^{e}sîqtā'

Rabbāṯî establishes a series of correspondences between the cosmic order and the human order by showing how the sequential unfoldment of the signs of the Zodiac reflects the trajectory of human moral development, while the creation of the sun and planets mirrors the course of Israel's destiny among the nations. The *pisqā'* concludes with a celebration of the Torah, which reflects the cosmic order, while at the same time the cosmic order reflects the Torah. Psalm 19.2, "The heavens declare the glory of God," is interpreted in light of Proverbs 8.27, "When He established the heavens I [wisdom] was there," to mean that the Torah, which existed prior to the heavens and was given from the heavens, declares the glory of God's ordering of creation. The second part of Psalm 19.2, "And the firmament proclaims His handiwork," is invoked to show that the firmament itself declares the glory of the Torah.[257]

In Pesîqtā' Rabbāṯî and Tanḥûmā' Yelammedēnû Midrashim, as in earlier rabbinic texts, the Torah is associated not only with the creation of the universe but also with its maintenance. An anonymous Midrash in Exodus Rabbāh II, discussed above, maintains that just as at the time of creation heaven and earth were brought forth with the aid of the Torah, so at the time of the revelation at Mount Sinai heaven and earth would have been reduced back to their original state of chaos if Israel had not accepted the Torah. Jeremiah 33.25, "If not for My covenant by day and by night, I would not have established the ordinances of heaven and earth," is invoked as a proof text.[258]

Torah as Divine Language The Torah's role as divine language is construed in Pesîqtā' Rabbāṯî and Tanḥûmā' Yelammedēnû Midrashim, as in earlier rabbinic sources, in terms of its association with the Word of God,[259] the divine Name,[260] and the letters of the Hebrew alphabet. Several passages emphasize the cosmogonic role of the Hebrew letters that compose the Torah, as the "twenty-two workmen (*pô'ălîm*)" who assisted God in creation,[261] while other traditions are concerned more generally with the creative power of the divine word.

Pesîqtā' Rabbāṯî contains a homily on the Hebrew letters that expands on the homily in Genesis Rabbāh concerning why the world was created with the letter *bêṯ* rather than with the *'ālep̄*, focusing in particular on the shape and semantic significance of the letter without, in contrast to Genesis Rabbāh, including an explanation of its numerical value. The homily conflates the tradition concerning *bêṯ* with a second tradition, which is also found in Genesis Rabbāh as well as in the Talmud, in which this world is said to have been created with *hē* and the world to come with *yōḏ*. Pesîqtā' Rabbāṯî's version gives a somewhat different explanation from that of the other variants regarding the ways in which the shapes of the two letters are indicative of their respective roles in creation.[262] A Midrash in the Tanḥûmā' includes a variant of the tradition in Genesis Rabbāh that links the creative role of the *hē* with its sound value: the effortlessness with which the *hē* is pronounced points to the effortlessness with which God brought forth creation.[263]

The creative power of Hebrew, "the holy language (*lešôn haqôḏeš*) by means of which the world was created,"[264] is thus linked not only to the shape and semantic connotation of certain letters but also to the expressive power of speech with which the letters are pronounced. "The speech of the lips is powerful, for it is considered equivalent to the creation of the world," according to a tradition attributed to R. Ḥama b. Ḥanina in Pesîqtā' Rabbāṯî. The pericope continues with a discussion, ascribed to R. Samuel b. Naḥman, of the marvels of speech, which involves so many different positions of the tongue.[265] It is of course the creative power of the divine speech that is of special concern to the rabbinic sages. A number of Midrashim reiterate the traditional rabbinic conception that when bringing forth creation God simply spoke, simply uttered the word, and the corresponding form manifested. As indicated in Psalm 33.6, "By the word (*dāḇār*) of the Lord were the heavens made," he simply uttered the word "heavens" and immediately they "were made."[266] An aggadah in the Tanḥûmā' ascribed to R. Aḥa conflates this tradition with the notion that the heavens continued expanding until God again spoke—"Enough!"—and thereby brought the process of expansion to an end.

> R. Aḥa said: When the Holy One, blessed be He, spoke to the heavens that they should be created, they continued to expand. If He had not said to them, "Enough!" (*day*) they would have continued to expand until the dead arose.[267]

The aggadah concerning the ten words (*ma'ămārôṯ*) by which the world was created is mentioned twice in Pesîqtā' Rabbāṯî. One anonymous tradition, which appears in a discussion of the revelation at Mount Sinai, correlates the ten words (*ma'ămārôṯ*) of creation with the Ten Words (*dibberôṯ*) of revelation, the Ten Commandments. It gives an alternative enumeration to those found in Genesis Rabbāh and the Babylonian Talmud, identifying the ten words with the ten commands "And God said" in Genesis 1.3–29 and 2.18, with no mention of *b^erē'šîṯ* or the spirit/voice of God upon the waters.[268] A second tradition connects the ten words of creation with the ten days of penitence between Rosh Ha-Shanah (New Year's Day) and Yom Kippur (the Day of Atonement).[269]

Torah as Light and Fire The Torah as the divine Word is associated with both light and fire in P^esîqtā' Rabbāṯî and the Tanḥûmā' Y^elamm^eḏēnû Midrashim, as in earlier rabbinic texts. An anonymous tradition in Deuteronomy Rabbāh declares that "the words of the Torah [give] light (*'ôrāh*) to the world."[270] Another Tanḥûmā' Y^elamm^eḏēnû tradition, cited earlier,[271] emphasizes the cosmogonic import of the Torah's light, which assisted God by illumining the darkness when he commenced the process of creation. Two aggadot in Exodus Rabbāh II similarly connect the light of Torah with the light of creation: just as the process of creation commenced with light, so the process of constructing the Tabernacle began with making the Ark, which would enshrine the light of Torah that preceded even creation itself.[272]

In other Midrashim the Torah's identification with light assumes a moral connotation, as the light that illumines the soul and preserves it from the clutches of the evil inclination. Commenting on Psalm 119.105, "Thy word (*dāḇār*) is a lamp (*nēr*) to my feet and a light (*'ôr*) to my path," a discourse in P^esîqtā' Rabbāṯî ascribed to R. Tanḥuma explains that the Torah gives light, providing a lamp to guide the righteous on their path and keep them from stumbling and falling into sin.[273] A Midrash in Deuteronomy Rabbāh attributed to Bar Kappara invokes another commonly cited proof text, Proverbs 6.23, "For the commandment (*mitzvah*) is a lamp (*nēr*) and the Torah a light (*'ôr*)," and connects it with Proverbs 20.27, "The soul of a human being is the lamp (*nēr*) of the Lord," to teach that if human beings guard God's light, which is the Torah, then he will guard their light, which is the soul.[274] An anonymous pericope in Exodus Rabbāh II expands on these two traditions in P^esîqtā' Rabbāṯî and Deuteronomy Rabbāh, citing both Psalm 119.105 and Proverbs 6.23 to show that the Torah is the lamp of God that gives light to those who study and practice it, reviving the light of their souls (Prov. 20.27).[275] A tradition in P^esîqtā' Rabbāṯî interprets Psalm 36.10, "For with Thee is the fountain of life; in Thy light (*'ôr*) do we see light," to mean that through studying the Torah, which is light, Israel will see light.[276] Moreover, just as Moses, the paradigmatic sage, acquired his lustrous countenance through contact with the light of Torah,[277] so the faces of the sages who study and expound Torah are said to be illumined with its radiance.[278]

The traditional association of the Torah with fire persists in Pesîqtā' Rabbāṯî and Tanḥûmā' Yelammeḏēnû Midrashim. As in earlier rabbinic texts, the preexistent Torah is identified with the "flaming sword" (*lahaṭ ha-ḥereḇ*) in the Garden of Eden (Gen. 3.24)[279] and the "flaming torch" (*lappîḏ 'ēš*) in the covenant with Abraham (Gen. 15.17),[280] while the historical Torah revealed at Mount Sinai is identified with the "fiery law" (*'ēš-dāṯ*) at God's right hand in Deuteronomy 33.2.[281] Deuteronomy Rabbāh contains a variant of the aggadah ascribed to R. Simeon b. Lakish in Song of Songs Rabbāh in which the Torah that was given to Moses is said to have been written with black fire upon white fire. The aggadah directly links the themes of fire and light through incorporating the notion of the fiery Torah in its explanation of how Moses acquired a radiant appearance.[282] A tradition in Pesîqtā' Rabbāṯî attributed to R. Berekhiah provides a fresh interpretation that is characteristic of the text's focus on cosmological matters in that it links the Torah, as the flaming Word blazing forth at the revelation, with the mysteries of the throne of glory.[283]

Pirqê de-R. Eliezer

Pirqê de-R. Eliezer, a narrative Midrash of undetermined provenance dating from the eighth century,[284] is the most speculative of the post-Talmudic Midrashim and contains some of the most bold reformulations of earlier aggadic traditions. This narrative Midrash, which presents itself as a discourse of the Tanna R. Eliezer b. Hyrcanus, "rewrites" the pentateuchal narrative, paraphrasing and elaborating on the aggadic sections of the books of Genesis and Exodus. In attempting to present a unified, continuous narrative it nevertheless betrays its composite nature, which represents a synthesis of three types of material derived from different periods and sources: traditional rabbinic material from classical Amoraic Midrashim and the two Talmuds as well as from the Palestinian Targums; esoteric and apocalyptic material from the Apocrypha and Pseudepigrapha of the Second Temple period and from Merkabah traditions; and Arabic legends derived from Muslim sources.

In accordance with its speculative nature, most of Pirqê de-R. Eliezer's discussions of the Torah center on its status and role in creation and revelation, with relatively little emphasis on pragmatic issues such as the relationship between the Written Torah and Oral Torah or the importance of study and practice of Torah. Most of the text's speculations concerning the Torah are found in its retelling of the Genesis account of creation and of the Exodus account of the Sinai revelation. It is the cosmogonic speculations found in Pirqê d^{e}-R. Eliezer that will primarily concern us in the present section; its presentation of the revelation will be discussed in chapter 4.

The influence of certain books of the Apocryphya and Pseudepigrapha is especially evident in Pirqê d^{e}-R. Eliezer's account of creation. In expanding on the creation narrative in the first three chapters of Genesis, Pirqê d^{e}-R. Eliezer departs from the rabbinic injunction that forbids elaborate discourse on the mysteries of creation (*ma'ăśēh b^{e}rē'šîṯ*) and the mysteries of the throne-chariot (*ma'ăśēh merkāḇāh*) and incorporates a substantial amount of cosmogonic and cosmological material that echoes the language and content of the Books of Enoch, the Book of Jubilees, and the Book of Adam and Eve.[285] It also inserts into the creation narrative astronomical and astrological speculations concerning the course of the sun, moon, planets, and constellations, as well as discussions of the secrets of the calendar.

In the course of its discussion of the mysteries of the first seven days of creation and the fall of Adam and Eve (chapters 3–20), Pirqê d^{e}-R. Eliezer interweaves many of the earlier rabbinic traditions concerning the preexistence of the Torah and its role in the cosmogonic process. Although some of these traditions are simply reiterated from earlier texts with slight variations, they receive new valences by being recontextualized and integrated into a single, continuous narrative in which they are presented as different phases in the sequential unfoldment of creation.

The Preexistence of the Torah Pirqê d^{e}-R. Eliezer incorporates the tradition concerning the seven preexistent entities in the opening chapter of its account of creation. The narrative begins, "Before the world was created, the Holy One, blessed be He, and His great Name (*šēm*) alone existed. It arose in [His] mind (*maḥăšāḇāh*) to create the world."[286] The text then describes how God traced a model (*heḥĕrîṭ*) of the world, just as a king who wishes to build a palace first traces on the ground its foundations, entrances, and exits before he begins to build. However, the world thus planned was not firmly established until God created repentance.[287] The mention of repentance provides the opportunity to insert the list of seven things created prior to the world, which includes repentance. Pirqê d^{e}-R. Eliezer's enumeration coincides with the Talmudic version—the Torah, Gehinnom, the Garden of Eden, the throne of glory, the Temple, repentance, and the name of the Messiah—citing the same proof texts, including Proverbs 8.22 in the case of the Torah.[288]

The narrative goes on to describe how God took counsel with the Torah, identified with primordial wisdom, concerning the creation of the world.[289] The text continues with a discussion of the occurrences on each of the first six days of creation, devoting a separate chapter to each day.[290] Finally, after the interjection of a number of intermediary episodes centering on Adam and Eve, the text devotes a chapter to creation on the eve of the seventh day, the first Sabbath. The chapter begins with the tradition concerning the ten things created on the Sabbath eve, including the letters (*k^{e}ṯāḇ*), writing (*miḵtāḇ*), and tablets (*lûḥôṯ*) of the Ten Commandments in an enumeration that most closely coincides with 'Āḇôṯ's version.[291]

In its retelling of the biblical narratives concerning Adam and the patriarchs, Pirqê d^{e}-R. Eliezer points to their observance of the Torah prior to the revelation at Mount Sinai, reformulating and elaborating on earlier aggadic traditions. For example, Genesis 2.15, "And the Lord God took the man and put him in the Garden of Eden to till (*'āḇaḏ*) it and to keep (*šāmar*) it," is interpreted in light of Genesis 3.24, "to keep (*šāmar*) the way of the tree of life (*'ēṣ ha-ḥayyîm*)," to mean that God instructed Adam to keep the way of Torah, which as wisdom is designated as a "tree of life" (*'ēṣ ḥayyîm*) in Proverbs 3.18.[292] Later, after the creation of Eve, God is portrayed as admonishing Adam and Eve to keep (*šāmar*) his commandments (*mitzvot*).[293] Adam is represented as the first to observe the Sabbath on earth and as instituting the Havdalah ceremony at the end of the first Sabbath.[294] He is also said to have had knowledge of the tablets of the Ten Commandments that would be written by the finger of God at the future revelation at Mount Sinai.[295]

In its narrative account of the life of Abraham, Pirqê d^{e}-R. Eliezer informs us that Abraham spoke Hebrew, the holy language (*l^{e}šôn ha-qôḏeš*),[296] and invokes the standard proof text, Genesis 26.5, to establish that God expected him to observe all of the commandments (*mitzvot*) of the Torah.[297] With respect to Abraham's two grandsons, Jacob and Esau, Jacob is said to have become well versed (*bāqî*) in the Torah through his study in the "tents" (*'ōhālîm*) of learning,[298] while Esau neglected the Torah's precepts.[299]

Torah as God's Counselor In its account of creation Pirqê d^{e}-R. Eliezer, as discussed above, makes reference to the notion that God first planned his creation before bringing the plan to fruition. However, the text does not discuss the relationship of this plan to the Torah. Rather, the role of the Torah in creation is represented in Pirqê d^{e}-R. Eliezer, as in the Tanḥûmā', primarily in terms of the image of personified wisdom who served as the counselor of God.[300]

Having established that the Torah, as the primordial wisdom of Proverbs 8.22, had existed from "the beginning" as one of the first of God's works,[301] the narrative continues with a discussion of the Torah's cosmogonic role as the counselor with whom God consulted prior to bringing forth the creation.

> The Holy One, blessed be He, took counsel (*niṯyā'ēṣ*) with the Torah, whose name is wisdom (*tûšiyyāh*), in order to create the world. . . . The Torah said: The Holy One, blessed be He, took counsel (*niṯyā'ēṣ*) with me in order to create the world, as it is said, "Counsel (*'ēṣāh*) is mine and sound wisdom (*tûšiyyāh*)" (Prov. 8.14).[302]

In this passage the Torah herself speaks, assuming the voice of personified wisdom in Proverbs 8.14 in celebration of her privileged position as God's counselor. Later, in the account of the sixth day of creation, God is again described as consulting with the Torah before he created human beings. Genesis 1.26, "Let us make man in our image," is interpreted as referring to God and the Torah. The Torah forewarned God that man would come under the power of sin, but God insisted that he himself would be merciful and slow to anger. He then proceeded with his creation of the first man, Adam.[303]

Pirqê d^{e}-R. Eliezer also incorporates the Mishnaic aphorism that includes the Torah as one of the three things upon which the world stands. It supplements the 'Āḇôṯ tradition by citing as a proof text Jeremiah 33.25: "If not for My covenant by day and by night, I would not have established the ordinances of heaven and earth." This verse is also used in earlier rabbinic texts, as we have seen, to establish the Torah's role in sustaining creation.[304]

Creation through the Word The cosmogonic role of the Torah as divine language is not a major topic of speculation in Pirqê d^{e}-R. Eliezer's account of the mysteries of creation, although we do find occasional references to various aspects of the power of the Hebrew letters as well as to the role of the word in creation.

The Hebrew letters that compose the Torah share in its preexistent status. Not only are the letters included among the ten things created on the eve of the Sabbath, they also are represented as assuming a variety of roles in the lives of the forefathers since the beginning of creation. For example, the protective power of the letters is pointed to in Pirqê d^{e}-R. Eliezer's reformulation of the story of Cain and Abel, in which the sign (*'ôṯ*) that God put on Cain in order to prevent him from being slain is said to have been one of the twenty-two letters (*'ôṯiyyôṯ*) that are in the Torah.[305] The redemptive power of the letters is associated with Abraham and his descendants. As mentioned earlier, Abraham is said to have spoken Hebrew,[306] and he is also said to have been given the secret of redemption (*sôḏ ha-g^{e}'ûllāh*) associated with the five letters of the Torah, *kap̄, mēm, nûn, pēh,* and *ṣāḏēh,* that are unique in that they alone possess a second form when they appear as the final letter of a word. This secret was subsequently transmitted in turn to Isaac, Jacob, and the sons of Jacob.[307]

In Pirqê d^{e}-R. Eliezer the creative power of the divine language is represented primarily in terms of God's speech. Psalm 33.6 is invoked to establish that God simply spoke one word (*dāḇār*) and the heavens were created: "By the word (*dāḇār*) of the Lord were the heavens made."[308] Conversely, God simply spoke one word—"Enough!" (*day*)—in order to stop the heavens from expanding.[309] It was also by means of the divine utterance (*dîbbûr*) that the waters were gathered together (Gen. 1.9) and the surface of the earth was formed into mountains, hills, valleys, and seas.[310]

The aggadah concerning the ten words (*ma'ămārôṯ*) by which the world was created appears twice in Pirqê d^{e}-R. Eliezer.[311] It is incorporated at the end of the account of the first day of creation, where, like P^{e}sîqtā' Rabbāṯî, it identifies the ten words with the ten commands "And God said" in Genesis 1.3–29 and 2.18. The first word of the Torah, *b^{e}rē'šîṯ*, and the spirit/voice of God are not included in Pirqê d^{e}-R. Eliezer's enumeration.[312] In accordance with Pirqê d^{e}-R. Eliezer's synthesizing tendency, this aggadah concerning the ten words is conflated with the tradition concerning the three things enumerated in Proverbs 3.19–20—wisdom (*ḥoḵmāh*), understanding (*t^{e}ḇûnāh*), and knowledge (*da'aṯ*)—by means of which God established the earth, the heavens, and the depths, respectively.[313] The relationship between the ten words and these three attributes is not delineated.

Torah as Light and Fire Pirqê d^{e}-R. Eliezer incorporates into its account of creation an extensive description of the luminous and fiery mysteries of the Merkabah on which God is enthroned on high,[314] but it does not speculate at any length about the Torah's association with light and fire. One passage maintains that when R. Eliezer expounded the Torah his face shone like the light of the sun (*'ôr ha-ḥammāh*), sending forth rays (*qᵉrānôṯ*) like that of Moses.[315] A second passage, in discussing the revelation at Mount Sinai, interprets Deuteronomy 33.2, "At His right hand was a fiery law (*'ēš-dāṯ*) for them," to mean that the words of the Torah are like coals of fire (*gaḥălê 'ēš*).[316]

TORAH AND CREATION IN KABBALISTIC TEXTS

Rabbinic conceptions of the status and role of the Torah in creation are appropriated and reinterpreted in medieval kabbalistic texts in accordance with an elaborate cosmology involving a series of divine emanations and a hierarchy of worlds.[317] The present analysis will focus in particular on certain kabbalistic conceptions that build upon and extend rabbinic notions concerning the preexistence of the Torah, the cosmogonic role of the Torah as the architect and blueprint of creation, and the status of the Torah as divine language. In this context we will be concerned primarily with the speculations of the Zohar and the theosophical Kabbalah of thirteenth-century Spain.[318] The Zohar, the central work of theosophical Kabbalah, which derives from the late thirteenth century, is of particular significance in that it not only draws upon the *content* of earlier rabbinic traditions, but it also imitates the *form* of exegetical Midrashim, providing a commentary on the Pentateuch. The Zohar itself purports to be a rabbinic Midrash derived from the Tanna R. Simeon B. Yoḥai, an eminent disciple of R. Akiba, and thus it claims a direct line of continuity between its own esoteric teachings and the teachings of those second-century Tannaim who sought to fathom the mysteries of the Torah.[319]

Kabbalistic conceptions of Torah can only be understood with reference to the theosophical kabbalists' conceptions of divinity, in which God is represented as having both an unmanifest and a manifest dimension. The unmanifest aspect of God is generally termed 'Ên-Sôp̄ (literally, "without limit") and is described as the Godhead in itself, in its own absolute nature, as a formless, limitless, transcendent reality that is distinct from the relative phenomenal world. When the time of creation dawns, the unmanifest 'Ên-Sôp̄ emerges from its hidden abode and progressively manifests itself in ten spheres of divine emanation, termed *sᵉp̄îrôṯ*: (1) Keṯer

'Elyôn ("supreme crown"), (2) Ḥoḵmāh ("wisdom"), (3) Bînāh ("intelligence"), (4) Ḥeseḏ ("love"), (5) G^{e}ḇûrāh ("power"), (6) Tip̄'ereṯ ("beauty"), (7) Neṣaḥ ("lasting endurance"), (8) Hôḏ ("majesty"), (9) Y^{e}sôḏ ("foundation"), and (10) Malḵûṯ ("kingdom"). The ten *s^{e}p̄îrôṯ* function together as a single, unified organism, representing the manifest, dynamic, pulsating life of the Godhead in relation to creation. In their totality the *s^{e}p̄îrôṯ* are often depicted in the form of a supernal Man, each *s^{e}p̄îrāh* constituting a different part of the body of the divine anthropos.[320]

The realm of the *s^{e}p̄îrôṯ* is at times represented in kabbalistic texts as the hidden world of divine language, the ten *s^{e}p̄îrôṯ* being identified with the ten divine names as well as with the ten primordial words (*ma'ămārôṯ*) through which the world was created. Gershom Scholem writes:

> The process which the Kabbalists described as the emanation of divine energy and divine light was also characterized as the unfolding of the divine *language*. This gives rise to a deep-seated parallelism between the two most important kinds of symbolism used by the Kabbalists to communicate their ideas. They speak of attributes and of spheres of light; but in the same context they speak also of divine names and the letters of which they are composed. From the very beginnings of Kabbalistic doctrine these two manners of speaking appear side by side. The secret world of the godhead is a world of divine language, a world of divine names that unfold in accordance with a law of their own.[321]

The interrelation between divine language and light is pointed to in rabbinic texts in their use of images of light and fire to describe the Torah as the Word of God. In kabbalistic texts this notion becomes fully cosmologized through associating the Torah with the *s^{e}p̄îrôṯ*, the ten divine names/words that are spheres of divine light.[322] The Torah is at times described as encompassing the influence of all of the ten *s^{e}p̄îrôṯ* and is thus correspondingly depicted as that totality of divine unity which is the one Name containing all names, the one Word containing all words. The Torah as the Name of God or Word of God expresses that aspect of God which is revealed in and through creation. It encompasses the totality of God's manifestations in the world of emanation, the realm of the *s^{e}p̄îrôṯ*, and in the created worlds. In this context the kabbalists reinterpret the rabbinic notion of the Torah's preexistence to mean that the Torah not only precedes the creation chronologically[323] but also ontologically. The Torah is given priority not only in time but also in being, for the Torah in its primordial state participates in the reality of the *s^e^p̄îrôṯ*, the hidden realm of divine emanations that underlies and gives rise to the created worlds.

Within the realm of the *s^e^p̄îrôṯ* the Torah is at times described by the kabbalists as emerging in stages that recapitulate the process through which the *s^e^p̄îrôṯ* emanate from the unmanifest 'Ên-Sôp̄. As the Torah unfolds in progressive stages of manifestation it becomes associated in particular with those four *s^e^p̄îrôṯ* that represent key moments in the unfoldment of the divine language: Ḥoḵmāh (second *s^e^p̄îrāh*), Bînāh (third *s^e^p̄îrāh*), Tip̄'ereṯ (sixth *s^e^p̄îrāh*), and Malḵûṯ, the Shekhinah (tenth *s^e^p̄îrāh*). In its earliest and most hidden stage of manifestation as Ḥoḵmāh, the Torah is sometimes referred to by thirteenth-century kabbalists as *tôrāh q^e^ḏûmāh*, the primordial Torah.[324] The Torah as Ḥoḵmāh is not merely personified as God's co-worker in creation, it is hypostatized as the divine sphere that serves as the demiurge principle. In its association with Tip̄'ereṯ and Malḵûṯ the Torah assumes the forms of the supernal Written Torah and supernal Oral Torah, respectively. In certain kabbalistic texts, as we shall see, the various aspects of Torah are represented not only as progressive *stages* of manifestation corresponding to the divine emanations, but also as different *levels* of manifestation corresponding to the different levels of creation in the kabbalistic hierarchy of worlds.

The Zohar and Thirteenth-Century Spanish Kabbalah

Torah as the Name of God The conception that the Torah is the one great Name of God first appears among the thirteenth-century Spanish kabbalists of Gerona. Moses b. Naḥman (Naḥmanides), the eminent Talmudist who was the most authoritative representative of the circle of kabbalists in Gerona, provided the basis for this notion by maintaining, in the preface to his commentary on the Torah (Pentateuch), that the Torah can simultaneously be read on two levels: in the traditional manner, as historical narratives and commandments; or, according to a more subtle level of interpretation, as a series of divine names.

> We possess an authentic tradition showing that the entire Torah consists of the names of God and that the words we read can be divided in a very different way, so as to form [esoteric] names. . . . The statement in the Aggadah to the

> effect that the Torah was originally written with black fire on white fire obviously confirms our opinion that the writing was continuous, without division into words, which made it possible to read it either as a sequence of [esoteric] names [*'al derekh ha-shemoth*] or in the traditional way as history and commandments. Thus the Torah as given to Moses was divided into words in such a way as to be read as divine commandments. But at the same time he received the oral tradition, according to which it was to be read as a sequence of names.[325]

Naḥmanides points out that it is this subtle structure of the Torah as a sequence of divine names that accounts for the rigorous Masoretic tradition concerning the writing of a Torah scroll, in which a scroll is disqualified if even a single letter is added or omitted.

Naḥmanides's colleagues in Gerona, in particular Ezra b. Solomon and Azriel b. Menaḥem, went beyond the conception that the Torah comprises a series of divine names and asserted that the Torah is itself the one great Name of God. Ezra b. Solomon declares that "the five books of the Torah are the Name of the Holy One, blessed be He."[326] Both Ezra and his younger contemporary Azriel emphasize the organic unity of the Torah as the Name of God, which constitutes a perfect divine edifice (*binyān 'ĕlōhî*) in which there is not a single superfluous letter or point. The Torah, according to Ezra, "in its divine totality . . . is an edifice hewn from the Name of the Holy One, blessed be He."[327] Not a single letter or point can be eliminated from this organic totality without harming the entire body. Azriel writes:

> Just as in the body of a man there are limbs and joints, just as some organs of the body are more, others less, vital, so it seems to be with the Torah. To one who does not understand their hidden meaning, certain sections and verses of the Torah seem fit to be thrown into the fire; but to one who has gained insight into their true meaning they seem essential components of the Torah. Consequently, to omit so much as one letter or point from the Torah is like removing some part of a perfect edifice. Thence it also follows that in respect of its divine character no essential distinction can be drawn between the section of Genesis 36, setting forth the generations of Esau [a seemingly superfluous passage],

> and the Ten Commandments, for it is all *one* whole and *one* edifice.[328]

The Zohar, the classical text of Spanish Kabbalah, expressly assumes the identity of the Torah and the Name of God, declaring that the Torah is the one supernal Name of the Holy One.[329]

> [T]he Torah is the Name of the Holy One, blessed be He. As the Name of the Holy One is engraved in the Ten Words (creative utterances) of Creation, so is the whole Torah engraved in the Ten Words (Decalogue), and these Ten Words are the Name of the Holy One, and the whole Torah is thus one Name, the Holy Name of God Himself.[330]

In this conception the Torah as the Name of God encompasses the ten words (*ma'ămārôṯ*) of creation and the Ten Words (*dibbᵉrôṯ*) of revelation, which are identified in the Zohar with the ten *sᵉp̄îrôṯ*.[331] The Torah in its identification with the Name of God thus becomes identified with the totality of the divine emanations that constitute the manifest expression of the Godhead in relation to creation. The Zohar ultimately declares that "the Torah and the Holy One, blessed be He, are one,"[332] for God and his Name are one.[333]

The full significance of this declaration can only be understood on the basis of kabbalistic conceptions of the creative power of language, which in turn are founded on the traditional rabbinic notion that an intrinsic relationship exists between the word and what it signifies, between the name and the object that it designates. The Hebrew term *dāḇār* itself conveys the double meaning of "word" and "thing," for in ancient conceptions found throughout the Near East the name participates in the reality and essence of what is named. Understood in this context, the notion that the Torah is the Name of God leads to the conclusion that God and the Torah are one, for the Torah as God's Name represents the total manifestation of the divine essence and power, which are concentrated in his Name.

The identity of the Torah and God is asserted not only by the author of the Zohar but also, in the last third of the thirteenth century, by other theosophical kabbalists who were undoubtedly influenced by the Zohar. For example, Joseph Gikatilla, a prominent thirteenth-century Spanish kabbalist, writes:

> His Torah is in Him, and that is what the Kabbalists say, namely, that the Holy One, blessed be He, is in His Name

> and His Name is in Him, and that His Name is His Torah.[334]

Gikatilla further explains this statement with reference to a formula from the Merkabah hymns.

> It is an important principle that the ancients expressed in the words: "Thy Name is in Thee and in Thee is Thy Name." For the letters of His Name are He Himself. Even though they move away from Him, they remain firmly rooted [literally, fly away and remain with Him].[335]

The letters, according to Gikatilla, are the mystical body of God, while God is the soul of the letters.[336]

According to the most abstract level of interpretation, then, the Torah as the Name of God means that the Torah participates in the essence and power of God and that ultimately the Torah and God are one. The Torah in its most complete manifestation encompasses all of the *s^e^p̄îrôṯ*, all aspects of the Godhead; it is the one great Name of God that includes all of the divine names. How does this abstract conception of the Torah as a living manifestation of the Godhead relate to the concrete earthly form of the Book of the Torah, which is composed of words and sentences that convey specific meanings? Gikatilla provides an interpretation that links the supernal and earthly forms of the Torah. The Torah as it appears on the earthly plane, according to Gikatilla, is a living texture of names that is woven (*ne'ĕrag*) from the one true Name of God, the Tetragrammaton YHWH. All of the names in the Torah are contained in the Tetragrammaton, and the Tetragrammaton is itself woven both directly and in a secret, hidden way throughout the fabric of the Torah.[337]

> The whole Torah is a fabric of appellatives, *kinnuyim*—the generic term for the epithets of God, such as compassionate, great, merciful, venerable—and these epithets in turn are woven from the various names of God [such as *El, Elohim, Shaddai*]. But all these holy names are connected with the tetragrammaton YHWH and dependent upon it. Thus the entire Torah is ultimately woven from the tetragrammaton.[338]

Torah as Ḥoḵmāh, the Architect of Creation While the Torah as the Name of God is generally identified with the totality of the manifest Godhead, encompassing all of the ten *s^{e}p̄îrôṯ*, the Torah is also associated more specifically with the second *s^{e}p̄îrāh*, Ḥoḵmāh, which is the demiurge principle in the s^{e}p̄îrôṯic scheme. As in rabbinic texts, the Torah as Ḥoḵmāh is identified in the Zohar with the primordial wisdom of Proverbs 8.22–31 and Proverbs 3.19–20 and is celebrated as the artisan of creation.[339]

> "The Lord by wisdom founded the earth; by understanding he established the heavens" [Prov. 3.19]. When God . . . created the world, He saw that it could not exist without the Torah, as this is the only source of all laws above and below, and on it alone are the upper and lower beings established. Hence, "the Lord by wisdom founded the earth; by understanding he established the heavens", inasmuch as it is through Wisdom that all things are enabled to exist in the universe, and from it all things proceed.[340]

Whereas in rabbinic sources the Torah as wisdom is personified as a female figure, the Torah as Ḥoḵmāh is hypostatized as a male principle in the Zoharic cosmology of the *s^{e}p̄îrôṯ*. In its manifestation as Ḥoḵmāh the Torah is the Father, who unites with the Mother, Bînāh ("intelligence"), the third *s^{e}p̄îrāh*, in order to bring forth creation.[341] It is as Ḥoḵmāh that the Torah assumes its role as the architect of creation. The Zohar declares:

> When the Holy One resolved to create the world, He guided Himself by the Torah as by a plan, as has been pointed out in connection with the words "Then I was by him as [an] *amon*" [Prov. 8.30], where the word *amon* (nursling) may also be read *uman* (architect). Was the Torah, then, an architect? Yes; for if a King resolves to build him a palace, without an architect and a plan how can he proceed? Nevertheless, when the palace has been built, it is attributed to the King: "here is the palace which the King has built", because his was the thought that has thus been realized. Similarly, when the Holy One, blessed be He, resolved to create the world, He looked into His plan, and, although, in a sense, it was the plan which brought the palace into being, it is not called by its name but by that of the King. The Torah proclaims: "I was by Him [as] an architect, through me He created the world!"[342]

Torah as the Blueprint of Creation The above passage from the Zohar recalls the opening proem of Genesis Rabbāh, cited earlier,[343] in which the Torah is described as both the architect and the blueprint of creation. The passage continues with a discussion of the image of the blueprint that seeks to clarify in what way God "looked into" the Torah when creating the world. It suggests that the Torah served as the plan of creation in that it is composed of the words that God "looked into," in the sense of "contemplating through seeing" (*'istakkēl*), in order to bring forth the corresponding forms.

> When the Holy One resolved to create the world, He guided Himself by the Torah as by a plan. . . . [W]hen He resolved to create the world He looked into the Torah, into its every creative word, and fashioned the world correspondingly; for all the worlds and all the actions of all the worlds are contained in the Torah. Therefore did the Holy One, blessed be He, look into it and create the world. . . . God looked at His plan in this way. It is written in the Torah: "In the beginning God created the heavens and the earth"; He looked at this expression and created heaven and earth. In the Torah it is written: "Let there be light"; He looked at these words and created light; and in this manner was the whole world created.[344]

In another passage God is described as not only looking at the words of the Torah but also uttering them aloud in order to bring forth the phenomenal world. Commenting on Job 28.27, "Then did He see it and declare it; He established it and searched it out," the Zohar explains that God first "looked into" (*'istakkēl*) the words of the Torah; then he uttered them and thereby established the forms of creation. Seeing, declaring, establishing, and searching out correspond to the four operations through which God brought forth the universe.[345]

The Torah, as the primordial blueprint, is said to be the source of all the laws through which the various worlds and beings, above and below, were created.[346] The Zohar elaborates on the rabbinic notion that there is a correspondence between the structure of the Torah and the structure of the macrocosm and microcosm. The microcosm, the human body, is patterned after the macrocosm, and both in turn are organized in accordance with the plan of the Torah, which itself consists of different parts that combine to form a single body.

> Everyone who studies the Torah sustains the world and maintains every individual thing in its proper form. For every part that exists in man there is a corresponding element created in the world. Just as man is composed of separate parts, all of them with their own specific levels, arranged one above the other, and yet all comprising a single body, so it is with the world: all the created elements are separate parts, situated one above the other, and when they are all arranged they actually form one body. Everything is patterned on the Torah, for the Torah is all limbs and joints, and they are positioned one above the other, and when they are all arranged they become a single body.[347]

The "limbs and joints" of the body of Torah are described in the Zohar as reflecting the structure not only of the human body and of the cosmos-body but also of the body of the divine anthropos. More specifically, the commandments are described as the "limbs and joints" that join together to form the mystery of the supernal Man, encompassing both the masculine and feminine aspects of the Godhead.

> The commandments of the whole Torah are joints and limbs in the celestial mystery. And when they all are joined together they all amount to a single mystery . . . for the commandments of the Torah all reflect the mystery of man, male and female, and when they are joined together they are the single mystery of man.[348]

Unfoldment of the Divine Language In the Zohar the ten primordial words (*ma'ămārôṯ*) by which the world was created are hypostatized, becoming identified with the ten *s^e^p̄îrôṯ*. The realm of the *s^e^p̄îrôṯ* is represented as the world of divine language, in which the successive emanation of the *s^e^p̄îrôṯ* is the process through which the divine language unfolds. The stages of unfoldment of the divine language are correlated with the stages of manifestation of the Torah, as will be discussed in the following section.

The manifestation of the divine language begins with the emergence of a primordial point of divine thought—Ḥoḵmāh, wisdom, the second *s^e^p̄îrāh*. The mechanics of creation are described in a number of passages in the Zohar as the mechanics through which thought develops, for creation is viewed as simply a process of unfolding the original seed-thought of wisdom, Ḥoḵmāh, through progressive stages of development until it finds expression on the level of vocalized speech. The Zohar describes four main stages in the manifestation of the divine language—thought, inaudible voice, audible voice, and vocalized speech—which correspond to the four *s^e^p̄îrôṯ* Ḥoḵmāh, Bînāh, Tip̄'ereṯ, and Malḵûṯ, respectively.

In order to understand the role of these four *s^e^p̄îrôṯ* in the unfoldment of the divine language, we must first briefly examine the Zohar's characterizations of them as hypostatized entities that play a key role in the cosmogonic process. When the time of creation dawns, according to the Zohar, the unmanifest 'Ên-Sôp̄[349] descends into the realm of manifestation in the form of a supernal Man, Keṯer ("crown"), the first *s^e^p̄îrāh*. Keṯer is the supreme crown that shines forth as an inexhaustible fountain of light, illumining the darkness with the brightness of God's glory so that God himself, while remaining unmanifest and hidden in his essential nature, can be made known.[350] As the supernal effulgence of the Godhead known as "brightness" (*zōhar*), Keṯer contains within itself all the lights of the other *s^e^p̄îrôṯ* and the totality of creation as yet undifferentiated.[351]

Keṯer is the supreme will that sets the process of creation in motion.[352] With the "decision of the King" to create, the effulgence of Keṯer withdraws into itself and a hidden supernal point shines forth,[353] which is the *rē'šîṯ*, "beginning," of creation.[354] This primordial point is the divine thought in which God enfolds himself and the totality of the universe in potential form. From this single concentrated impulse of thought, which is identified in the Zohar with the second *s^e^p̄îrāh*, Ḥoḵmāh, the entire creation unfolds.[355] Ḥoḵmāh thus assumes the role of the Father of creation in the s^e^p̄îrôṯic scheme.

The Zohar describes how Ḥoḵmāh, the primordial point of wisdom, makes for himself a refulgent "palace" (*hêḵālā'*) or "house" (*bayiṯ*) for his honor and glory and there he sows "the holy seed in order to beget offspring for the benefit of the world."[356] This house built by wisdom, Ḥoḵmāh, is at first uninhabited and is only extended enough to make room for the seed. Then the house conceives and expands sufficiently to become habitable. Ḥoḵmāh subsequently enters the house and makes it his abode, "just as the silkworm encloses itself, as it were, in a palace of its own production which is both useful and beautiful."[357] This "inhabited house" is called Elohim and is identified with Bînāh ("intelligence"), the third *s^e^p̄îrāh*, who is the Mother in whose womb the seed of Ḥoḵmāh, the Father, is implanted.[358]

The child that is born from the impregnated "house," Bînāh, is identified in the Zohar with Tip̄'ereṯ ("beauty"), the sixth *s^e^p̄îrāh*, who as the lower Ḥoḵmāh represents the second phase of manifestation of the Father. Just as the upper Ḥoḵmāh has his counterpart in the lower Ḥoḵmāh, Tip̄'ereṯ, so the Mother above, Bînāh, has her counterpart in the Mother below, Malḵûṯ ("kingdom"), the tenth *s^e^p̄îrāh*, which is the Shekhinah. Tip̄'ereṯ and Malḵûṯ are the son and daughter who are the king and queen of the world below, mirroring the reality of the king and queen above.[359] Bînāh, the Mother above, forms a house for the upper Ḥoḵmāh, while Malḵûṯ, the Mother below, forms a house for Tip̄'ereṯ, the lower Ḥoḵmāh.[360]

Each of these four *s^e^p̄îrôṯ*—Ḥoḵmāh, Bînāh, Tip̄'ereṯ, and Malḵûṯ—is associated in the Zohar with a particular stage in the manifestation of the divine language. The process through which Ḥoḵmāh unites with Bînāh and gives birth to the son, Tip̄'ereṯ, and the daughter, Malḵûṯ, is thus sometimes described in terms of the process through which the divine thought (Ḥoḵmāh) progressively develops from an inaudible voice (Bînāh) to an audible voice (Tip̄'ereṯ) to vocalized speech (Malḵûṯ).

> When it arose in the will of the Holy One, blessed be He, to act gloriously in His own honor the desire arose from thought to extend itself, and it extended itself from the place where thought is concealed, which is unknowable, until it spread and settled in the throat, the place that gushes continuously through the mystery that is the breath of life, and then, once this thought had extended itself and settled in this place, thought was called "living God" (*Elohim ḥayyim*). . . . It wished to extend itself again, and be revealed, and thence emerged fire, wind, and water, collected together, and then Jacob emerged, a perfect man, and he was the voice that went forth and was heard. Henceforward, thought, which was concealed and silent, was heard openly. This thought extended itself yet farther in order to be revealed, and the voice struck and knocked against the lips, and then speech went forth, which perfected all, and revealed all. This means that everything is this concealed thought, which was within, and all is one.[361]

In this passage the major stages in the unfoldment of the divine language—thought, inaudible voice, audible voice, and vocalized speech—correspond to the four *s^e^p̄îrôṯ* Ḥoḵmāh, Bînāh, Tip̄'ereṯ, and Malḵûṯ, respectively. (1) From the divine will, represented by Keṯer, issues a thought, Ḥoḵmāh. (2) This concentrated impulse of thought, arising from that unknowable place where thought is concealed, expands and creates an abode for itself in the throat as Elohim Ḥayyîm, Bînāh. (3) From this silent source in the throat issues forth an audible voice, the voice of Jacob, which is Tip̄'ereṯ. (4) The voice of Jacob, striking against the lips, finds expression in vocalized speech, which is Malḵûṯ, the Shekhinah.

In another passage the Zohar clearly separates these different phases into four main stages: (1) supernal wisdom (Ḥoḵmāh), which is the thought that is not disclosed or heard; (2) the Great Voice (Bînāh), which issues forth from wisdom and discloses it a little "in a whisper which cannot be heard," flowing on without ceasing in the region of the throat and forming a house for the supernal wisdom; (3) the voice of Jacob (Tip̄'ereṯ), which is the audible voice that issues forth from the inaudible Great Voice; and (4) the outer, articulated speech (Malḵûṯ) through which the voice of Jacob emerges in the open and finds expression on the vocalized level.[362] Thought (Ḥoḵmāh) and the voice of Jacob (Tip̄'ereṯ) are male, representing the upper Ḥoḵmāh and lower Ḥoḵmāh, or Father and son, respectively, while the Great Voice (Bînāh) and vocalized speech (Malḵûṯ) are female, representing the Mother above and the Mother below, or Mother and daughter, respectively.[363] In both cases the male aspect provides the content, which is wisdom, and the female aspect discloses the content, giving it expression through speech.

The first two stages in the unfoldment of the divine language—thought (Ḥoḵmāh) and the Great Voice (Bînāh)—are said to be inaudible, taking place in silence,[364] and correspond to the expression *b^erē'šîṯ bārā' Elohim* in the first verse of the Torah, which is understood to mean "By means of Ḥoḵmāh [= *rē'šîṯ*] it ['Ên-Sôp̄] created Bînāh [= Elohim]."[365] Among the ten words (*ma'ămārôṯ*) by which the world was created, *b^erē'šîṯ* is included as the original unspoken Word, for as the Zohar explains, "even though *bereshith* is a 'saying' [*ma'ămār*], 'and He said' is not written in connection with it."[366] The last two stages in the manifestation of the divine language—the voice of Jacob (Tip̄'ereṯ) and vocalized speech (Malḵûṯ)—are said to be audible[367] and correspond to the words "And God said" in the Genesis 1 account. The words "And God said" are used for the first time in the creation narrative of Genesis 1 at the point when the child, Tip̄'ereṯ, conceived through the union of the Father and Mother, issues forth from the womb of the Mother as a voice uttering audible speech that can be heard from without.

> Hence "and God said" means that now the above-mentioned palace [Bînāh] generated from the holy seed with which it

> was pregnant. While it brought forth in silence, that which it bore was heard without. That which bore, bore in silence without making a sound, but when that issued from it which did issue, it became a voice which was heard without, to wit, "Let there be light."[368]

The four stages in the unfoldment of the divine language thus constitute a two-stage process of creation, one unmanifest and inaudible, the other manifest and audible, in which the male and female principles both participate. (1) In the first stage Ḥoḵmāh, the Father, makes a house for himself—Bînāh, the Great Voice—in which he sows his seed. The voice at this stage is still inaudible. (2) In the second stage the child, Tip̄'ereṯ, who represents the second phase of Ḥoḵmāh, issues forth from the womb of Bînāh as a voice that is heard without through the agency of Malḵûṯ, vocalized speech, who represents the second phase of the Mother. It is this audible voice that is responsible for unfolding the details of creation from the original totality by means of the series of specific commands that are introduced in the Genesis account by the words "And God said."

After having called the light into being, the voice, as described in Genesis 1, commands: "'Let there be a firmament in the midst of the waters, and let it divide the waters from the waters.' . . . and it was so."[369] The upper waters, according to the Zohar, are heaven, while the lower waters are the earth, with the firmament forming a third world between the two.[370] The voice, having established the earth, firmament, and heaven, creates all animate and inanimate beings through its successive commands, bringing forth plants, the sun, moon, and stars, animals, and human beings, each in turn.[371]

Stages of Manifestation of the Torah The four *s^e^p̄îrôṯ* Ḥoḵmāh, Bînāh, Tip̄'ereṯ, and Malḵûṯ are represented in the Zohar as participating in the divine language on two levels: they are identified, respectively, with the four letters of the ineffable Name of God, the Tetragrammaton, Yōḏ-Hē-Wāw-Hē; and they are correlated with the four principal stages in the manifestation of the divine language, thought, inaudible voice, audible voice, and vocalized speech. In its identification with the Name of God, the Torah thus includes all four *s^e^p̄îrôṯ* and the potentiality of all language. As the divine language unfolds, the Torah itself unfolds in discrete stages corresponding to Ḥoḵmāh, Bînāh, Tip̄'ereṯ, and Malḵûṯ and their linguistic counterparts.

The Zohar and other thirteenth-century kabbalistic texts generally distinguish at least three main manifestations of the Torah: (1) *tôrāh qeḏûmāh,* the primordial Torah, which is generally identified with Ḥoḵmāh, the second *sep̄îrāh,* and which is also at times associated with Bînāh, the third *sep̄îrāh;* (2) the supernal Written Torah, which is identified with Tip̄'ereṯ, the sixth *sep̄îrāh;* and (3) the supernal Oral Torah, which is identified with Malḵûṯ, the Shekhinah, the tenth *sep̄îrāh.* A set of correspondences is thus established in which four *sep̄îrôṯ* are primary.

Sep̄îrāh	*Letter of Name*	*Stage of Divine Language*	*Stage of Manifestation of Torah*
Ḥoḵmāh (Father)	Yōḏ	thought	Primordial Torah
Bînāh (Mother)	Hē	inaudible voice	
Tip̄'ereṯ (Son)	Wāw	audible voice	Written Torah
Malḵûṯ/Shekhinah (Daughter)	Hē	vocalized speech	Oral Torah

In the Zohar all three aspects of the Torah are allotted a role in creation. The primordial Torah, Ḥoḵmāh, the point of divine thought, contains the totality of creation in potential form and is said to be the source of both the Written Torah and the Oral Torah.[372] From the primordial Torah, Ḥoḵmāh, the supernal letters of the Hebrew alphabet issue forth and become crystallized as the engravings of the Written Torah, Tip̄'ereṯ.[373] The Written Torah, Tip̄'ereṯ, is said to have produced the world from the power of the writing that issues forth from Ḥoḵmāh, while the Oral Torah, the Shekhinah, is responsible for completing and preserving the world.[374] The Written Torah and Oral Torah, as the divine hypostases Tip̄'ereṯ and the Shekhinah, complement and support one another,[375] representing the unity of the male and female principles,[376] the unity of the upper and lower worlds,[377] and the unity of the Holy Name.[378] The Written Torah, which remains hidden and undisclosed in the supernal realms, is manifested through the Oral Torah.[379] The Written Torah on high rejoices in the Oral Torah below.[380]

While the different stages of manifestation of Torah are correlated with particular *sep̄îrôṯ,* the Torah is also described as encompassing all of the *sep̄îrôṯ.*[381] In its stages of unfoldment from the unmanifest 'Ên-Sôp̄ through Ḥoḵmāh and Bînāh to Tip̄'ereṯ and Malḵûṯ, the Torah encompasses all of the *sep̄îrôṯ,* all of the spheres of the Godhead, and thus, in the final analysis, the Zohar declares that God and the Torah are one.[382]

Levels of Manifestation of the Torah The various manifestations of the Torah are described by certain thirteenth-century kabbalists not only in temporal terms, as progressive stages of unfoldment corresponding to the divine emanations, but also in spatial terms, as a hierarchy of levels corresponding to the levels of creation. In this context the very form of the Torah scroll, which contains no vowels, no punctuation, and no accents, is viewed as an allusion to the fact that the Torah, while remaining nonchanging and inviolable in its essential nature, can be read in various ways, as Naḥmanides suggests, according to the manner in which one combines the letters. Gikatilla develops this notion further, concluding that the Torah is read and interpreted in a different manner in each of the manifold worlds—for example, in the world of the *s*ᵉ*p̄îrôṯ*, the world of angels, and the material world of human beings—in accordance with the nature of the world and the power of comprehension of its inhabitants.[383] Gikatilla writes:

> The scroll [i.e., the Torah] is not vocalized and has neither cantillation-notes, nor [indication where] the verse ends; since the scroll of Torah includes all the sciences, the exoteric and esoteric ones, [it] is interpreted in several ways, since man turns the verse up and down, and therefore our sages said: "Are not my words like as a fire? Saith the Lord" [Jer. 23.29][[. L]]ike the forms of the flame of fire that has neither a peculiar measure nor peculiar form, so the scroll of Torah has no peculiar form for [its] verses, but sometimes it [the verse] is interpreted so and sometimes it is interpreted otherwise, namely in the world of the angels it is read [as referring to] one issue and in the world of the spheres it is read [as referring to] another issue and in the lower world it is read [as referring to] another issue, and so in the thousands and thousands of worlds which are included in these three worlds, each one according to its capacity and comprehension, is his reading [i.e., interpretation] of the Torah.[384]

Later Kabbalistic Speculations

Levels of Manifestation of the Torah Before concluding our discussion of kabbalistic conceptions of Torah, mention should be made of several trends of speculation found in sixteenth- and seventeenth-century kabbalistic texts that further develop the notion that there are various levels of manifestation of the Torah corresponding to the levels of creation. According to these conceptions, the Torah is not only interpreted in a distinctive manner by the inhabitants of each world, it actually assumes different forms in each world. The basic structural elements of the Torah in all of its manifestations are the letters of the Hebrew alphabet, which combine in various ways to give rise to the various forms of the Torah.

Moses Cordovero, a leading sixteenth-century kabbalist of the Safed school, describes four levels of manifestation of the Torah, which are distinguished by the manner in which the letters combine and also by the degree of materialization of the letters. In its subtlest phase of manifestation, according to Cordovero, the Torah is composed of subtle letters that are different configurations of divine light. In the subsequent phase the letters progressively materialize and combine in various ways to form, first, names of God, then appellatives and predicates referring to the divine, and, finally, words formed from material letters that refer to earthly events and phenomena. Cordovero uses this progressive process of materialization to explain the state of the Torah prior to the fall, after the fall, and in the Messianic Age.[385]

Cordovero's formulation of the four forms of the Torah—subtle letters, names of God, appellatives, and material words—is developed in a somewhat different manner in writings from the school of Israel Sarug (ca. 1600 C.E.), a Lurianic kabbalist. In these texts each of the four forms of the Torah corresponds to one of the four worlds that are described by kabbalists from the sixteenth century onward as existing between the unmanifest 'Ên-Sôp̄ and the gross material world: (1) *'ăṣîlûṯ*, the world of emanation, which is the abode of the ten *s^e^p̄îrôṯ*; (2) *b^e^rî'āh*, the world of creation, which is the abode of the throne, the Merkabah (throne-chariot), and the highest angels; (3) *y^e^ṣîrāh*, the world of formation, which is the main domain of the angels; and (4) *'ăśiyyāh*, the world of making or activation, which is the spiritual archetype of the material world.

These texts describe how the unmanifest 'Ên-Sôp̄, in self-rapture, begins to move within itself, generating the movement of language and weaving a texture (*malbûš*) of the twenty-two letters of the Hebrew alphabet in the substance of 'Ên-Sôp̄ itself. This constitutes the original Torah, in which the letters, in their original sequence, contain within themselves the seeds of all possibilities for further linguistic expression. In the next phase the Torah assumes different forms corresponding to the four worlds. In the highest world, the world of *'ăṣîlûṯ*, the Torah manifests, as in the original texture, as a sequence of combinations of the Hebrew consonants. In the second world, the world of *b^erî'āh*, the Torah appears as a sequence of holy names of God, which are formed by certain further combinations of the linguistic elements found in the world of *'ăṣîlûṯ*. As it becomes increasingly more manifest, the Torah appears as a sequence of angelic names in the third world, the world of *y^eṣîrāh*. Finally, in the fourth world, the world of *'ăśiyyāh*, the Torah appears in its traditionally transmitted form.[386] The particular configuration of letters in each form of the Torah is said to reflect the laws and structure of the corresponding world. Implicit in this conception is the notion that the Torah in all its manifestations constitutes a comprehensive blueprint for all levels of existence.

All these concrete and subtle forms of the Torah are in the final analysis modifications and elaborations of the one great Name of God, for in the kabbalistic perspective it is the Name of God that is the source of all language, the source of all letters, and hence the source of all possible combinations of letters that form names, words, and sentences. In this context certain kabbalists, in particular the Lurianic school, correlate the four letters of the Tetragrammaton—Yōḏ-Hē-Wāw-Hē—with the four worlds—*'ăṣîlûṯ*, *b^erî'āh*, *y^eṣîrāh*, and *'ăśiyyāh*, respectively—and by implication with the four forms of the Torah in the four worlds. The four letters and the four worlds are in turn correlated with the four *s^ep̄îrôṯ*—Ḥoḵmāh, Bînāh, Tip̄'ereṯ, and Malḵûṯ, respectively—that correspond to the principal stages of manifestation of the Torah discussed earlier. Our previous schema can thus be expanded to incorporate a number of new elements.

S^ep̄îrāh	*World*	*Letter of Name*	*Stage of Manifestation of Torah*	*Form of Torah*
Ḥoḵmāh	*'ăṣîlûṯ*	Yōḏ	Primordial Torah	letters
Bînāh	*b^erî'āh*	Hē		names of God
Tip̄'ereṯ	*y^eṣîrāh*	Wāw	Written Torah	appellatives or angelic names
Malḵûṯ/ Shekhinah	*'ăśiyyāh*	Hē	Oral Torah	words with earthly referents

COMPARATIVE ANALYSIS 1

Veda and Torah in Creation

Structural Affinities in Symbol Systems

From our analysis of the symbol systems associated with Veda and Torah we have seen that in certain strands of the brahmanical tradition and the rabbinic and kabbalistic traditions scripture is represented as a multileveled cosmic reality that is correlated with the different levels of the Word and the different levels of creation. Four types of formulations can be distinguished, in which Veda and Torah, respectively, are variously represented as (1) the totality of the Word, which is the essence of the ultimate reality; (2) knowledge, which is an aspect of the creator principle; (3) divine language, which constitutes the archetypal blueprint of creation; and (4) a concrete corpus of oral and/or written texts.

While the seminal expressions of these conceptions are found in Vedic and rabbinic texts, the most extensive discussions are found in post-Vedic and kabbalistic texts, which reformulate and elaborate the seed speculations contained in the earlier texts, embedding them in complex cosmologies. It is in these later texts that we find the most significant parallels among representations of Veda and Torah.

(1) Scripture as the Word: The Essence of the Ultimate Reality

Veda and Torah are represented in certain strands of their respective traditions as the Word in its totality, which is the essence of the ultimate reality, particularly in its manifest form in relation to creation. The Veda is at times described in Vedic and post-Vedic mythology as the Word, *brahman,* which is the essence of Brahman and is particularly associated with the *saguṇa* dimension of Brahman that expresses itself in creation. In this context the Veda is identified in certain post-Vedic texts with Śabdabrahman, Brahman embodied in the Word. The Torah is similarly identified with the Word (*dāḇār*) of God or Name (*šēm*) of God, an identification that is generally assumed but not expanded upon in rabbinic texts. The Torah as the Word of God or Name of God is described in certain kabbalistic texts as the total manifestation of God's essence that is revealed in and through creation and is at times directly identified with God himself.

Veda and Torah are represented as participating in the ultimate reality not only as its inner essence but also as its form. The body of Brahman is described in certain Vedic and post-Vedic texts as constituted by the Vedic *mantras*, and in particular by the forty-eight *varṇa*-sounds of Sanskrit that compose the *mantras*. Similarly, certain kabbalists maintain that the mystical body of God is constituted by the letters of his Name (= Torah), while others claim that the very substance of the Godhead is woven with the twenty-two letters of the Hebrew alphabet that compose the Torah.

(2) Scripture as Knowledge: The Creator Principle

Veda and Torah are not only identified, respectively, with the essence of the ultimate reality, but are associated more specifically with that aspect of the divine which is responsible for bringing forth the phenomenal world. On this level, each is represented as the undifferentiated totality of knowledge or wisdom that serves as the immediate source of creation. The Veda is at times identified with the creator Prajāpati or Brahmā, the demiurge principle, who is extolled as the embodiment of knowledge and Veda incarnate. The Torah is personified in certain rabbinic texts as Ḥoḵmāh, primordial wisdom, which serves as God's architect or co-worker in creation. In kabbalistic texts the Torah as Ḥoḵmāh is hypostatized as the Father, who functions as the demiurge principle in the s^{e}p̄îrôṯic pleroma.

(3) Scripture as Divine Language: The Blueprint of Creation

Veda and Torah are each at times depicted as the subtle plan or blueprint of creation, its constituent sounds or letters constituting the primordial elements of the divine language from which the realm of forms is structured. On this level the Word has differentiated from its original state of unity; the one Word has given rise to words. On the most subtle level these words are the "ideas" of all the forms of creation conceived in the mind of the creator as the ideal plan of the universe. These ideas are then uttered by the creator as vocalized words, which are then precipitated to form the multiplicity of phenomena. The Vedic *mantras* are represented in certain Vedic and post-Vedic accounts as the primordial utterances through which the creator brings forth the universe. In post-Vedic texts this notion is articulated in the image of the Vedas as the archetypal plan that the creator recites in order to manifest the names, forms, and functions of all beings. In the parallel conception found in certain rabbinic and kabbalistic texts, the divine architect consults his blueprint, the Torah, "looking into," contemplating, and/or uttering its words in order to bring forth the phenomenal world.

This subtle blueprint, Veda or Torah, is at times represented as multidimensional, its various forms reflecting the laws and structure of the various levels of creation. While the Vedic *mantras* together are considered to constitute the blueprint of creation in its entirety, the Ṛg-, Yajur-, and Sāma-Vedas are each correlated more specifically with the three worlds—earth, midregions, and heaven—and with their presiding deities—Agni, Vāyu, and Sūrya/Āditya—and thus represent the plan for that particular level of creation. Similarly, the conception of Torah as the blueprint of creation is extended by certain kabbalists to include the notion that there are different forms of the Torah corresponding to each of the four worlds—*'ăṣîlûṯ, b^eri'āh, y^eṣîrāh*, and *'ăśiyyāh*—and to the four *s^ep̄îrôṯ* that are associated with each of these worlds—Ḥoḵmāh, Bînāh, Tip̄'ereṯ, and Malḵûṯ. Each of these forms of the Torah is held to constitute a plan of the corresponding world.

Another significant parallel concerns the conception of an all-encompassing sound or Name that is identified with Veda or Torah and that is the basis of all creation and the source of all language. In certain Vedic and post-Vedic texts the syllable Om is said to represent the sound embodiment of Brahman and in this sense corresponds to the Veda as Śabdabrahman. Moreover, the three constituent sounds of Om are correlated with the three Vedas and the corresponding three worlds together with their presiding deities. In certain kabbalistic schools the Tetragrammaton, YHWH, is identified with the Torah as the one great Name of God. The four letters of the Tetragrammaton are correlated with the four forms of the Torah and the four worlds together with their corresponding *s^ep̄îrôṯ*. Understood from this perspective, the Veda as Śabdabrahman and the Torah as the Name of God represent the most fundamental and encompassing level of scripture, incorporating all other levels and containing the potentiality of all linguistic expression.

(4) Scripture as Concrete Text

The primordial Word that serves as the source and blueprint of creation is represented as becoming instantiated on earth in a finite corpus of texts. Revered by their respective traditions as the concrete embodiment of the Word, these texts have been meticulously preserved and passed down from generation to generation either through oral transmission, in the case of the Vedic Saṃhitās, or in the form of a written text together with an oral tradition of interpretation, in the case of the Torah.

Levels of the Word All four of these aspects of Veda and Torah can be correlated with different levels of the Word. As we have seen, this Word cannot be delimited to either the written word or the spoken word in the sense of a circumscribed text. The conception of scripture as written text or oral text applies only to the fourth level of scripture described above, which is the mundane dimension of scripture. The Word as embodied in Veda and Torah is also represented as having a supramundane dimension, in which the two aspects of the Word—knowledge and speech—both find expression. On the subtlest level, scripture is the Word in its undifferentiated totality—Veda as *brahman*/Śabdabrahman, Torah as the Word of God or Name of God. On the second level, the knowledge dimension of the Word manifests as the immediate source of creation—Veda as Prajāpati or Brahmā, Torah as Ḥok̠māh. On the third level, the speech dimension of the Word is activated, and the totality of knowledge finds expression in the individualized impulses of divine language from which the realm of forms is manifested—Veda or Torah as the blueprint of creation.

These different levels of the Word are also at times represented as different levels of embodiment, in which the Word becomes progressively instantiated in the divine body, in the cosmos-body—including its microcosmic replica in the human body—and in a concrete "corpus" of mundane texts. Moreover, the social "body" of the communities that preserve Veda and Torah—the Aryans and the Jews—is represented as a further extension of the Word embodied in scripture. Thus, the Veda, which constitutes and reflects the body of Brahman, the body of the creator principle, and the body of the macrocosm-microcosm, is also manifested in the structure of the brahmanical social order, the *varṇa* system. Similarly, the Torah, which constitutes and reflects the body of the divine anthropos (in kabbalistic texts), the cosmos, and the human body, is also instantiated in the moral and social order of the people of Israel.[1]

Stages of Manifestation These various levels of scripture are represented in certain strands of the traditions as progressive stages of manifestation through which the Word unfolds in creation. In this context, significant structural affinities can be discerned in brahmanical and kabbalistic descriptions of the various stages of manifestation in the cosmogonic process. Creation is represented in these accounts as involving a two-stage process—one unmanifest and undifferentiated, the other manifest and differentiated—in which the male and female principles both participate.

(1) In the first stage, with the emergence of the desire to create, the male principle, who is identified with knowledge, implants his

seed in the womb of the female principle, who is generally identified with speech. That speech with which knowledge unites in this stage is still the unexpressed, transcendent level of speech. The female principle conceives and her womb expands in preparation for infusion with the life principle. Brahmanical cosmogonies describe how the male principle, the embodiment of knowledge, implants his seed in the womb of the female principle, who is at times identified with Vāc, speech. The seed is brought to fruition in a cosmic egg, which is still lifeless at this point. Similarly, the Zohar's account of creation describes how Ḥoḵmāh, wisdom, sows his seed in the "house" that he has built, Bînāh, the Great Voice. The house, which is still uninhabited, conceives and expands in preparation for habitation.

(2) In the second stage the male principle enters the womb of the impregnated female, making it his abode, and is born from it as a child, who represents the second phase of manifestation of the male principle. The child emerges from the womb of the female and speaks. This speech, which is the second phase of the female principle, is the expressed, vocalized level of speech through which the three worlds and all animate and inanimate beings are projected into concrete manifestation. In brahmanical cosmogonies the male principle enters the egg and infuses it with life, making the egg his abode. His second manifestation is then born from the egg and proclaims through speech (= second phase of Vāc) the primordial utterances from which the three worlds—earth, midregions, and heaven—and all beings are manifested. In the Zohar's account, Ḥoḵmāh encloses himself in the house that he has built, transforming it into an "inhabited house." From this inhabited house, Bînāh, is born the lower Ḥoḵmāh, Tip̄'ereṯ, who utters in vocalized speech (= Malḵûṯ, the lower Mother) a sequence of commands from which the earth, firmament, and heaven and all phenomena are brought into being.

Corresponding to this two-stage process of creation, in which the male and female principles, knowledge and speech, both participate, are two phases of scripture. (1) In the first stage scripture emerges as the undifferentiated totality of knowledge that is identified with the male principle. This stage encompasses the first two levels of scripture outlined above: scripture as the essence of the ultimate reality, and scripture as the creator principle. (2) In the second stage the wholeness of scripture/knowledge differentiates into individualized impulses of knowledge contained in the expressions of the divine language, which constitute the words that the male principle speaks when his second manifestation is born. The child speaks, and what he speaks are the words of scripture. These subtle impulses of divine language are then precipitated to form concrete phenomena. This stage corresponds to the third level of scripture as the blueprint of creation. The various stages through which the Word unfolds in creation, as described in certain brahmanical texts and in the Zohar, are schematized in the figure on page 219.

Divergences in Conceptions of Language

While we thus find significant structural affinities among the symbol systems associated with Veda and Torah, especially as expressed in the later strata of the traditions, there are also significant differences among these formulations, which are linked to three fundamental points of divergence in the traditions' conceptions of language. (1) The brahmanical tradition gives precedence to the oral channel of language, while the rabbinic and kabbalistic traditions give primary emphasis to the written register. (2) This divergence has its corollary in a corresponding divergence in modes of perception, in which brahmanical conceptions of language and text give priority to the auditory channel, while rabbinic and kabbalistic conceptions tend to emphasize the visual channel. (3) The brahmanical tradition assigns primary importance to the phonic dimension of the word, and the rabbinic and kabbalistic traditions to the cognitive dimension. These differences become apparent when we examine more closely the language and imagery that are used to represent Veda and Torah, respectively, as the blueprint of creation. We will begin by comparing the ways in which the blueprint is depicted in passages, cited earlier, from two of the latest strata of the traditions: the Bhāgavata Purāṇa and the Zohar.

The Bhāgavata Purāṇa describes how the creator Brahmā brings forth the phenomenal world through reciting the words of the Vedic *mantras*.

> While he was contemplating, "How shall I bring forth the aggregate worlds as before?" the Vedas issued from the four mouths of the creator. . . . From his eastern and other mouths he brought forth in succession the Vedas known as Ṛg, Yajur, Sāma, and Atharva. . . .[2]

From the speech utterances of the creator, from his recitation of the Vedic words, the names, forms, and functions of all beings are spontaneously manifested.

UNFOLDMENT OF THE WORD IN CREATION

VEDA	*OVERVIEW OF STAGES*	*TORAH*
	ABSOLUTE	
Nirguṇa Brahman	Absolute as the ultimate source of creation	'Ên-Sôp̄
	↓	
	WORD	
Saguṇa Brahman	The Word as the essence of the ultimate reality in relation to creation	Keṯer
Veda as *brahman*/ Śabdabrahman	Scripture as the Word	Torah as the Word or Name of God
	↓	
	KNOWLEDGE	
Creator principle	Knowledge as the immediate source of creation	Ḥoḵmāh
Veda as creator principle	Scripture as creator principle	Torah as Ḥoḵmāh
Union of creator and his consort	Union of knowledge and speech	Union of Ḥoḵmāh and Bînāh
	↓	
	SPEECH	
"Second self" of creator	Second phase of male principle is born	Lower Ḥoḵmāh (Tip̄'ereṯ)
↓	↓	↓
Vocalized speech (*vāc*)	Vocalized speech	Vocalized speech (Malḵûṯ)
↓	↓	↓
Creation	Creation	Creation
Veda differentiates into Vedic *mantras*	Differentiation of scripture	Primordial Torah differentiates into Written Torah and Oral Torah
Vedas as blueprint	Scripture as the blueprint of creation	Torah as blueprint

The Zohar describes how God brings forth heaven and earth and all phenomena through "looking into," in the sense of "contemplating through seeing," the words of the Torah.

> When the Holy One resolved to create the world, He guided Himself by the Torah as by a plan. . . . He looked into the Torah, into its every creative word, and fashioned the world correspondingly. . . . God looked at His plan in this way. It is written in the Torah: "In the beginning God created the heavens and the earth"; He looked at this expression and created heaven and earth. In the Torah it is written: "Let there be light"; He looked at these words and created light; and in this manner was the whole world created.[3]

In both the Bhāgavata Purāṇa and the Zohar the creator is described as using the words of Veda or Torah in order to bring forth the manifold forms of the universe. However, in the Bhāgavata Purāṇa the primary emphasis is on the creator speaking the words of the Vedic *mantras*, which emerge from his mouths as recited sounds. In the Zohar, on the other hand, the emphasis is on the creator contemplating, through an act of mental and visual cognition, the words of Torah, which is represented as the supernal counterpart of the written text preserved on earth.

Are these differences in emphasis systemically significant? Having abstracted out these images, we need to re-embed them in their larger textual and cultural matrices in order to interpret the meaning and significance of the differences they bring to light. What we discover is that the differences in the Bhāgavata Purāṇa's and Zohar's uses of the blueprint analogy are indeed systemically significant, in that they are consonant with the larger symbol systems reflected in their respective textual traditions as well as in the matrix of practices associated with the Vedic Saṃhitās and the Sefer Torah. With respect to the textual evidence that corroborates these findings, brief mention should be made of a few salient points.

Brahmanical Texts In the Bhāgavata Purāṇa's portrayal, the Vedic *mantras* issue forth through the speech of the creator Brahmā and manifest the realm of forms. The *oral* expression of the divine language is emphasized in this image, which carries with it an implicit emphasis on the *phonic* dimension of the Vedic words apprehended through the *auditory* channel. These emphases are consonant with representations of the Vedas found in other brahmanical texts.

(1) The image of the Vedic *mantras* as the archetypal blueprint of creation is generally associated with the speech of the creator. While the creator is at times described as seeing as well as uttering the *mantras*, he is generally depicted in Vedic and post-Vedic cosmogonies as bringing forth creation through a series of speech-acts, rather than through an act of visual or mental cognition. With the exception of Śaṃkara's conception of the creator manifesting the Vedic words in his mind,[4] there is little emphasis in brahmanical texts on the creator contemplating the words of the Vedas; he simply utters the Vedic words and the corresponding forms appear.

(2) The Vedic *mantras* as the cosmic blueprint are composed of the subtle impulses of the divine speech, which are generally identified with the forty-eight *varṇas* or *akṣaras* of Sanskrit. These *varṇas* are phones, the fundamental units of speech, and not letters, the fundamental units of script. Vedic and post-Vedic myths contain numerous speculations on the sound structure of the *varṇas* without reference to their concrete embodiment in script.

(3) The Sanskrit *varṇas/akṣaras* are represented in Vedic and post-Vedic mythology as the primordial sounds that are the structural elements of creation. The *varṇas* combine in various configurations to form the words of the Vedic *mantras* from which concrete phenomena are structured.

(4) The Vedic *mantras* are designated as *śruti*, "that which was heard" by the Vedic *ṛṣis* at the beginning of creation as primordial rhythms reverberating forth from the Transcendent. Although the phenomenology of Vedic cognition, as will be discussed in chapter 3, is described in Vedic and post-Vedic texts in terms of both hearing and seeing—hence the designation *ṛṣis*, "seers"—the *ṛṣis* are celebrated primarily for their role in preserving what they heard and saw through their speech. They "recorded" the Vedic *mantras* through their speech, thereby initiating a tradition of oral transmission through which the *mantras* would be passed down to subsequent generations.

Rabbinic and Kabbalistic Texts The Zohar's image of the Torah as the plan of creation emphasizes God contemplating through sight the words of the written text. The *written* form of the text is emphasized, in which the words of the Torah are inscribed in visible characters that God sees. The words of Torah are apprehended through the *cognitive* act of contemplation, which simultaneously involves a *visual* component. These emphases resonate with representations of the Torah found in rabbinic texts as well as in other kabbalistic texts.

(1) In rabbinic portrayals of the Torah as the plan of creation we find two different images that correspond to the Zohar's portrayal: Torah as the plan that God "looked into" in order to create the world, or Torah as the mental plan of creation contemplated in the mind of God. The written and cognitive dimensions of the words of the Torah take precedence over their phonic dimension in these images.

(2) The Torah that constitutes the blueprint of creation is composed of the twenty-two letters (*'ôṯiyyôṯ*) of the Hebrew alphabet that are the fundamental elements of the divine language. In contrast to the brahmanical emphasis on the sound units of Sanskrit, rabbinic and kabbalistic speculations tend to emphasize the script units of Hebrew, focusing in particular on the shape and semantic significance of the letters and their cosmic role in creation, with relatively little emphasis on their sound value. In certain kabbalistic texts the material letters of the Hebrew script are described as gross manifestations of the subtle letters that exist in the upper worlds. These subtle letters are generally depicted as configurations of divine light, with the emphasis again on their visible shape rather than on their sound. The mundane form of the Sefer Torah inscribed on parchment is said to mirror the supramundane form of the supernal Torah, which is inscribed in light. Such kabbalistic notions cosmologize earlier rabbinic traditions in which the Torah as the Word of God is associated with images of light and fire.

(3) The twenty-two Hebrew consonants that compose the Torah are represented in certain rabbinic and kabbalistic texts as the basic structural elements that underlie and give rise to the manifold forms of creation. The kabbalists in particular elaborate on this notion, describing how the upper and lower worlds are created through different permutations and combinations of the letters of the Torah.

(4) The primordial Torah is represented as becoming embodied on earth in the form of a concrete written text at the time of the revelation at Mount Sinai. The phenomenology of revelation, as will be discussed in chapter 4, is described in both rabbinic texts and the Zohar as a synesthetic experience that simultaneously engaged the people of Israel's faculties of sight and hearing, with more emphasis generally given to the visionary aspects of the experience. According to one rabbinic tradition, the people of Israel not only heard the voice of God proclaiming the Ten Commandments, they *saw* his voice blazing forth in words of fire.[5] The Zohar extends this notion further, describing how the people of Israel saw the voices of

God carved out upon the darkness as configurations of divine light that illumined the hidden mysteries of creation.[6] Moses is depicted as the supreme prophet, designated to be the scribe of God, who recorded what he saw and heard in the form of a written text, the Sefer Torah.

This brief survey of the textual evidence would appear to corroborate our initial observation concerning the three major points of divergence between the conceptions of language that underlie the symbol systems associated with Veda and Torah, respectively: (1) oral vs. written channels of language, (2) auditory vs. visual modes of perception, and (3) phonic vs. cognitive dimensions of the word. In Part 2 we will examine in more detail how these differences are reflected in the phenomenology of cognition of Veda and revelation of Torah. Finally, in Part 3, we will consider the extent to which these points of divergence are evident in the practices involved in the transmission, study, and appropriation of the Vedic Saṃhitās and the Sefer Torah.

Part 2

From Word to Text

CHAPTER 3

Veda and Cognition

> Formerly, in the Brahma-*kalpa*, in the assembly of exalted *brahmarṣis* uncertainty arose concerning the production of the worlds. These brahmins remained absorbed in meditation (*dhyāna*) and established in silence, immovable, having given up eating, and drinking only air, for a hundred years of the gods. Speech (*vāṇī*), consisting of *brahman* (*brahma-mayī*),[1] reached the ears of them all. The divine Sarasvatī sprang forth from the firmament.
>
> —Mbh. XII.176.6–8

In examining the status and role of Veda in creation in chapter 1, we focused primarily on four types of symbolic complexes, in which the Veda is variously represented as (1) the Word, *brahman* or Śabdabrahman, which is the essence of the ultimate reality, Brahman; (2) the totality of knowledge, which is embodied in the creator principle; (3) the blueprint containing the impulses of divine speech through which the phenomenal creation is brought forth; and (4) a concrete corpus of *mantra* collections or Saṃhitās recited as part of the Vedic sacrifices. Brahmanical texts are also concerned to delineate the process through which the primordial Word and its differentiated expressions in divine speech came to be instantiated on earth in the textual corpus of Vedic *mantras*. The *ṛṣis* are represented as the crucial link in this process, for it is they who are said to have originally "seen" and "heard" the impulses of divine speech emanating from the Transcendent and who subsequently uttered forth on the gross level of speech that which they cognized on the subtle level. In this way, *śruti*, "that which was heard" by the *ṛṣis*, was "recorded" through the vehicle of their speech and assumed a concrete form on earth as the recited texts of the *mantras*.

The *ṛṣis*, according to this traditional brahmanical conception, are the "seers" of the Vedic *mantras*, not their composers. A *ṛṣi*, according to a well-known epithet, is *satya-darśin*, "one who sees the truth," and the truth that he sees is the eternal knowledge of the Veda, which is represented as the transcendent record of the structures of reality. The title *ṛṣi* is explained with reference to his faculty of "seeing" in the Nirukta (ca. 500 B.C.E.), the commentary by Yāska on the Nighaṇṭus or lists of Vedic words: "*ṛṣi* is from seeing (*ṛṣir darśanāt*), for he saw the hymns (*stomān dadarśa*)."[2] It is on the basis of such views that Yāska maintains that the Vedas are *apauruṣeyatva*, not created by any personal agent. Elsewhere Yāska uses the expression *sākṣāt-kṛta* ("placed clearly before the eyes") to describe the nature of the *ṛṣis*' cognitions.

> The *ṛṣis* had a clear cognition (*sākṣāt-kṛta*) of *dharma*. They handed down the *mantras* by [oral] instruction to later generations, who did not have a clear cognition of *dharma*. These later generations, declining in their ability to give instruction, compiled this work, the Veda, and the Vedāṇgas to facilitate the comprehension of the details.[3]

This statement by Yāska emphasizes that the ancient *ṛṣis* had a special ability to cognize the Vedic *mantras* that was not shared by later generations. Moreover, Yāska implies that the compilation of the *mantras* into the four Saṃhitās, or collections, was not undertaken by the original *ṛṣis* but rather by later generations in order to facilitate understanding of the Vedas. A similar conception is found in the Mahābhārata and Purāṇas, which credit Veda-Vyāsa with the compilation of the Saṃhitās, as will be discussed below.[4]

The special role of the *ṛṣis* as the original seers and transmitters of the Vedic *mantras* is assumed by both Vedic and post-Vedic texts in their discussions of the origin, nature, and status of the Veda. However, the texts generally do not elaborate on the mechanisms of the *ṛṣis*' cognitions. It is only in the Ṛg-Veda Saṃhitā that we find numerous references—albeit elliptical—to the process of cognition as described by the *ṛṣis* themselves. Our analysis will thus focus primarily on the conceptions of Vedic cognition presented in the Ṛg-Veda, followed by a brief consideration of speculations in later Vedic and post-Vedic mythology concerning the nature of the *ṛṣis* and their cognitions.

VEDA AND COGNITION IN VEDIC TEXTS

Ṛg-Veda Saṃhitā

Each of the 1,028 hymns of the ten Maṇḍalas (books) of the Ṛg-Veda Saṃhitā is ascribed to a particular *ṛṣi* or group of *ṛṣis*. The names of the *ṛṣis* who cognized the hymns are given partly in the Brāhmaṇas and partly in the Ṛg-Veda Anukramaṇī, an index that lists not only the names of the *ṛṣis* but also the deities and meters of each hymn. Maṇḍalas II to VII are called the "Family Books" in that the hymns of each of these books are held to have been cognized by a particular *ṛṣi* and/or members of his family: Gṛtsamada (II), Viśvāmitra (III), Vāmadeva (IV), Atri (V), Bharadvāja (VI), and Vasiṣṭha (VII). Most of the hymns of Maṇḍala VIII are attributed to the family of Kaṇva, while the hymns of Maṇḍalas I, IX, and X are ascribed to a number of different *ṛṣis*.

The *ṛṣis* of the Ṛg-Veda frequently refer to themselves and their ancestors as the seers of the hymns. Interspersed throughout the hymns are references to the various mechanisms through which the *ṛṣis* cognized and uttered forth the hymns.[5] We will be concerned with three aspects of this process, as represented by the *ṛṣis* themselves: (1) the nature of the *ṛṣis*, who are portrayed as semidivine sages with access to transcendent knowledge; (2) the synesthetic nature of cognition, in which the *ṛṣis* are described as apprehending suprasensible phenomena through both "seeing" and "hearing"; and (3) the reciprocal dynamics of cognition, which is represented as a cyclical process in which the gods and the *ṛṣis* both assume a central role. With respect to the second point, Gonda, in his discussions of the *ṛṣis* and their cognitions, has focused in particular on the visual dimensions of the process.[6] However, as we shall see, the oral-aural dimensions of Vedic cognition are also emphasized by the *ṛṣis*.

Nature of the Ṛṣis The *ṛṣis* of the Ṛg-Veda make reference to former seers "born of old," "our ancient fathers," as well as to contemporary *ṛṣis*.[7] All brahmins, up to the present day, trace their line of descent to one of the ancient *ṛṣis* of the Ṛg-Veda, after whom the brahmanical *gotras* (exogamous clans) are named. Later texts generally speak of seven or eight primeval *gotras*, which descend from the *ṛṣis* Gautama, Bharadvāja, Viśvāmitra, Vasiṣṭha, Kaśyapa, Atri, Bhṛgu, and Agastya. Gautama, Bharadvāja, Viśvāmitra,

Vasiṣṭha, Kaśyapa, and Atri are also celebrated, along with Jamadagni, as the "seven *ṛṣis*" (*sapta ṛṣis*), who are mentioned four times in the Ṛg-Veda[8] but are not enumerated until the Śatapatha Brāhmaṇa. [9]

The *ṛṣis* of the Ṛg-Veda use a number of appellations besides *ṛṣi* to refer to the ancient seers as well as to their own contemporaries. Two frequently used designations are *vipra* and *kavi*. From his analysis of the term *vipra*, which derives from the root *vip* or *vep*, "to tremble, shake, vibrate," Gonda concludes that the term "may originally have denoted a moved, inspired, ecstatic and 'enthusiast' seer as a bearer or pronouncer of the emotional and vibrating, metrical sacred words, a seer who converted his inspirations into powerful 'carmina.'"[10] A *vipra* is thus a seer whose awareness is vibrant with the reverberations of divine speech, to which he gives vocalized expression. The related term *vipaścit*, which conveys a meaning similar to that of *vipra*, is also sometimes used. One of the most frequently occurring appellations is *kavi*, which Gonda defines as "an inspired sage who possessing esoteric wisdom sees (things hidden from others) with his mental eye."[11] The other designations for the *ṛṣis*, such as *medhāvin* and *muni*, similarly point to the inspired wisdom and transcendent knowledge of the seers.

The *ṛṣis* are represented in the Ṛg-Veda as semidivine sages who are in constant contact with the gods and who possess special knowledge and special power as the "seers of truth." A number of the ancient *ṛṣis*, including the "seven *ṛṣis*," are said to be divine,[12] immortal,[13] or descended from the gods. The Aṅgirases are celebrated as the "sons of heaven" (*divas putrāsaḥ*)[14] and the "sons of the gods" (*deva-putrāḥ*).[15] The Virūpas, sons of Aṅgiras, are said to have been born from Agni, from heaven.[16] Viśvāmitra is described as "born of the gods (*deva-jā*)" and "impelled by the gods (*deva-jūta*),"[17] while Vasiṣṭha is said to be the son of Mitra and Varuṇa.[18] The Bhṛgus are celebrated as gods because of their special abilities.[19]

The *ṛṣis* are also described throughout the Ṛg-Veda as the friends and companions of the gods, conversing with them about truths and assisting them in their creation and maintenance of the cosmic order.[20] The gods and their activities are generally the principal focus of the *ṛṣis*' hymns, which at times extol and praise particular deities while at other times invoking their aid.

The Synesthetics of Cognition The process of Vedic cognition is represented in the Ṛg-Veda as a holistic experience that involves both "seeing" and "hearing." The *ṛṣis* are characterized as seers, but what they see are the subtle reverberations of speech apprehended as inspired thoughts. A number of verbs are used in the Ṛg-Veda to denote the *ṛṣis*' "seeing," including the roots *dṛś*, *cakṣ*, and *ci*. On the basis of his analysis of these verb forms and their derivatives, Gonda concludes that such verbs are frequently used to refer to a "praeternormal and spiritual vision" of subtle phenomena and events that are beyond the range of ordinary sense perception.[21] I have adopted the term "cognition" to refer to the faculty through which the *ṛṣis* gained—on the basis of both seeing and hearing—direct experiential knowledge of certain suprasensible phenomena.[22]

The *ṛṣis* are described in the Ṛg-Veda as the masters of all knowledge, who not only know the gods intimately[23] but also the mysteries of creation.[24] Through their cognition of the Vedic hymns, which are "full of truth (*ṛta*),"[25] they have come to know everything in creation, gross and subtle, manifest and hidden, as clearly and vividly as one knows an object when one perceives it with ordinary sense perception. The *ṛṣis*, as represented in the hymns, have direct access to those subtle levels of creation where the gods abide. Having gone "in their minds" to the heavenly abodes of the gods,[26] having stationed their awareness on those celestial planes where the gods dwell, the *ṛṣis* directly "see" with their mind's eye the deities riding in their chariots, seated on their heavenly thrones, or engaged in various types of activities.[27]

> Verily, [Mitra and Varuṇa] we saw (root *dṛś*) your golden [forms] on your thrones with our visionary powers (*dhīs*), with our mind (*manas*), with our own eyes (*akṣis*), with the eyes of Soma.[28]

The seers are at times represented as cognizing with their "inner eye" or "mind's eye" not only the gods themselves but also the mechanics through which the gods bring forth creation. Ṛg-Veda X.130 describes the gods weaving the primeval sacrifice of creation, in which they use the *sāman*s as shuttles. The *ṛṣi* of the hymn says that he directly cognized this primordial sacrifice: "With mind (*manas*) as an eye (*cakṣas*) I observe (root *man*), seeing (root *dṛś*) those who first performed this sacrifice." Having cognized this divine model, this path of the ancients, the seven divine *ṛṣis*, with *stoma*s and meters, took up the reins like charioteers.[29] In the Puruṣa-Sūkta the *ṛṣis* themselves are described as performing the primeval sacrifice of creation along with the gods.[30]

The *ṛṣis* are said to have cognized not only the mechanics of creation through which the gods brought forth the universe, but also the process through which the gods themselves originated. The *ṛṣi* of Ṛg-Veda X.72, which describes the origin of the gods, introduces his hymn by declaring, "Let us now proclaim with wonder the births of the gods so that one may see (root *dṛś*) them when the hymns are recited (root *śaṅs*) in this later age."[31] Through their faculty of cognition the *ṛṣis* penetrate the deepest secrets and mysteries of creation and know the causes and origins of all things, including the connection between existence and nonexistence.[32] The origin of heaven and earth, the number of suns, dawns, and waters there are in the universe—these sages are expected to know the answers to all of the riddles of existence.[33]

The *ṛṣis* sometimes describe their cognitions—their "visions" (*dhī, dhīti*) and their "inspired thoughts" (*manīṣā, mati*)—as illumined with a supernal light.[34] Having come to the light-filled regions of the gods, the *ṛṣis* "discovered the hidden light and with true *mantras* generated the dawn."[35] In Ṛg-Veda VIII.6.8 this hidden light is directly associated with the visions of the seer.

> When the visions (*dhītis*) that are hidden glow (root *śuc* + *pra*) spontaneously, the Kaṇvas [glow] with the stream of truth (*ṛta*).[36]

A number of verses suggest that the *ṛṣi* gains access to the light of inspiration in his heart.[37]

While the language and imagery of visions and light emphasize the visual dimensions of the process of cognition, this process is at times represented as a synesthetic experience that simultaneously involves both seeing and hearing. Ṛg-Veda X.177.1–2 describes the "inspired thought" as speech that is illumined with light: the inspired sages see (root *dṛś*) with their heart (*hṛd*), with their mind (*manas*), the bird who bears speech (*vāc*), and they guard at the abode of *ṛta* this inspired thought (*manīṣā*) that is luminous and of the nature of heaven's light. The inspired thoughts of the *ṛṣis*, as the subtle reverberations of speech, are described as vibrating (root *vip*), and thus the seers themselves are deemed *vipras*. Their cognitions pulsate with both sound and light. In Ṛg-Veda III.10.5 the deity Agni is described as bringing "the lights of vibrating inspirations (*vips*)." Agni is elsewhere invoked to unseal for the eulogist "the inspired thought (*manīṣā*) with the vibration (*vepas*)."[38] The synesthetic nature of the *ṛṣi*'s experience is also suggested in

Ṛg-Veda VI.9.6, in which the light of inspiration is apprehended by both the ears and eye of the *ṛṣi*: "My ears (*karṇas*) open, my eye (*cakṣus*) opens as this light dawns that is infused in my heart (*hṛdaya*)." In Ṛg-Veda VIII.59.6 the "inspired thought (*manīṣā*), thought as realized in speech (*vāco mati*)," is described as "that which was heard (*śruta*)."

These visions and inspired thoughts take shape in the *ṛṣi*'s heart and find vocalized expression through the speech of the *ṛṣi* as recited hymns, which are described as sound-forms illumined with light: "clothed in beautiful white garments"[39] and "shining like the flame of fire,"[40] the hymns expand when recited like heaven's light.[41] The *ṛṣis*, irradiated with the light of their cognitions and "bearing light in the mouth,"[42] are themselves said to be radiant like the sun.[43]

The Dynamics of Cognition In analyzing the *ṛṣis*' descriptions of the dynamics of cognition we find that, on the one hand, the gods are represented as the inspirers of the hymns, while, on the other hand, the *ṛṣis* themselves are said to generate the hymns. However, these two portrayals are not necessarily incommensurate with one another, for the process through which the hymns emerge is represented as a cyclical process in which the gods and *ṛṣis* both have a central role:[44] the gods mediate the process of cognition through stimulating the visions and inspirations of the *ṛṣis*; these divinely inspired cognitions then take shape in the hearts of the *ṛṣis*, who give them vocalized expression in recited hymns, which in turn nourish and magnify the gods.

(1) Divine Inspiration of the Ṛṣis' Cognitions

The ultimate source of the Vedic hymns, as described by the *ṛṣis* themselves, is the Imperishable (*akṣara*), which is the abode of the gods. Ṛg-Veda I.164.39 proclaims,

> The *ṛcs* exist in the Imperishable (*akṣara*), beyond space (*vyoman*), where all the gods abide.

The *ṛcs* exist in that transcendent, imperishable realm which is beyond space, beyond the finest level of objective material existence, where the gods abide. It is in the light-filled realm of the gods that the *ṛcs* are said to be cognized, and thus the gods themselves are repeatedly represented by the *ṛṣis* as the inspirers of their cognitions.

Throughout the Ṛg-Veda the *ṛṣis* celebrate their cognitions and hymns as divine (*devī*, *daivya*) and god-given (*devatta*).[45] The hymns are said to have been "generated" (root *jan*) by the gods and hence are termed *deva-kṛta*, "made by the gods."[46] Moreover, the gods are said to have made their abode in the hymns.[47] In unfolding the hymns to the *ṛṣis*' awareness, the gods also reveal to the *ṛṣis* the knowledge of the mysteries of creation contained in the hymns.[48] Certain deities are particularly praised and invoked by the *ṛṣis* as the givers of vision (*dhī*, *dhīti*) and inspiration (*manīṣā*) and the generators of hymns. Agni,[49] Soma,[50] and Indra[51] are celebrated as the preeminent promoters of the *ṛṣis*' cognitions and are themselves called *ṛṣis* and *kavis*.[52] Agni and Soma are called *ṛṣi-kṛt*, "makers of *ṛṣis*,"[53] for as the inspirers of cognitions they enable the sages to become seers who see the true nature of things.

> O Agni, powerful in nature, when praised unseal for the eulogist the cave, the inspired thought (*manīṣā*) with the vibration (*vepas*). Give us, O resplendent one, who are very glorious, that mighty thought (*manman*) which, along with all the gods, you love.
>
> From you, O Agni, are generated the qualities of the *kavis*, from you inspired thoughts (*manīṣā*s), from you effectual recitations (*uktha*s). From you comes wealth adorned by heroic sons to the devout mortal who possesses true vision (*dhī*).[54]

Vāc, the goddess of speech, is also celebrated by the *ṛṣis* as the promoter of their cognitions, for it is Vāc who has "entered into the *ṛṣis*" and revealed her hidden nature to them, bestowing upon them the power of *brahman* and making them *ṛṣis* and sages.[55] Vāc, skilled in speech (*vaco-vid*), utters her voice aloud and approaches with hymns through which the *ṛṣis* give vocalized expression to their cognitions.[56] Sarasvatī, who is identified with Vāc in later Vedic texts, is similarly celebrated as the inspirer of the *ṛṣis*' cognitions, illuminating their visions and furthering their hymns.[57] Among the other deities who are said to be givers of vision and promoters of hymns are Varuṇa,[58] the Maruts,[59] Bṛhaspati,[60] the Aśvins,[61] Vāyu,[62] Savitṛ,[63] and Pūṣan.[64]

(2) Expression of the Hymns through the Ṛṣis' Speech

In addition to those passages in the Ṛg-Veda that describe the *ṛṣis*' cognitions as inspired by the gods, there are numerous passages that depict the *ṛṣis* themselves as "generating" (root *jan*),[65] "fashioning" (root *takṣ*),[66] or "making" (root *kṛ*)[67] the hymns. The two types of passages present two different phases in the process of cognition: in the first phase the god(s) stimulates the vision or inspiration of the *ṛṣi*, and in the second phase the *ṛṣi* gives shape to the vision through articulating it in a recited hymn. This two-phase process of cognition has been emphasized by Gonda.

> A close examination of all the Ṛgvedic texts exhibiting the term [*dhīḥ*] under discussion . . . show that the mere "revelation" of a "vision" did not suffice. The supranormal sight, the privilege of a temporary initiation into the divine secrets was necessary; it was however only the initial stage of a process. It was left to the seer to foster, develop, cultivate the *dhīḥ* which he acquired, which had been given to him or which had come to him. He had to "translate" it into audible and intelligible words. . . .[68]

The verb *takṣ* is of particular significance in this regard. *Takṣ* means "to fashion, give form to, cut" in the sense that a carpenter (*takṣaka*) fashions a form out of wood. The carpenter does not create the wood; he simply gives shape to a material that already exists. In the same way, the *ṛṣi,* in saying that he "fashions" the hymn, does not claim that he is "creating" it but rather that he is giving shape to the hymn out of the "substance" of his divinely inspired cognition. A number of passages compare the *ṛṣi*'s fashioning of a hymn to an inspired (*dhīra*) artisan's fashioning of a chariot.[69] Having fashioned the hymn out of his cognition, the *ṛṣi* sends the hymn forth through the agency of his own speech, like an artisan sending forth his newly fashioned chariot.[70]

The *ṛṣis* sometimes speak of the process of fashioning or generating the hymn as taking place in the "heart" (*hṛd, hṛdaya*), which is traditionally understood in Vedic and later Indian thought to be the seat of consciousness.[71] As Gonda has shown on the basis of his analysis of relevant verses in the Ṛg-Veda, the heart is "the place where inspiration is received and from which sacred speech originates."[72] The heart, the innermost core of consciousness, is the abode of the gods within the human microcosm; it is the meeting-place between gods and human beings. Through their practice of *tapas*[73] the *ṛṣis* transcend and establish their awareness within the heart, where they cognize the light-filled regions of the gods and penetrate into the mysteries of creation. It is within the heart that the *ṛṣis* receive their divinely inspired visions and fashion them into well-spoken words that are uttered forth in recited hymns.[74]

> To him let us proclaim (root *vac*) this hymn (*mantra*) well-fashioned from the heart (*hṛd*).[75]

The heart, as the seat of consciousness, is also the seat of *manas,* the organ of thinking, feeling, and willing.[76] Several passages describe the hymns as being fashioned with both heart and mind.

> They polish (root *mṛj*) their visions (*dhīs*) for Indra, the ancient lord, with heart (*hṛd*), mind (*manas*), and inspired thought (*manīṣā*).[77]

Other passages describe the hymns as emerging from the *ṛṣi*'s *manas,* with no explicit mention of the heart.[78]

The process of Vedic cognition, as represented by the *ṛṣis* themselves, is thus a process in which the *ṛṣi* directly cognizes the subtle reverberations of speech contained in the Vedic *mantras* as arising within his own heart, as the impulses of his own consciousness. The *ṛṣi* cognizes these reverberations as inspired thoughts (*manīṣā, mati*), to which he then gives vocalized expression through the agency of his own speech in the form of recited hymns.

> I offer to Agni, the son of power, a new and more powerful inspired hymn (*dhīti*), thought as realized in speech (*vāco mati*).[79]

The hymns are described as well-spoken words that are uttered from the heart by the *ṛṣis*, who are "skilled in speech" (*vaco-vid*).[80]

The process of Vedic cognition is thus represented as a process of following the "track of Vāc."[81] From its hidden source in the heart of the *ṛṣi*[82] speech first manifests as inspired thoughts cognized by the *ṛṣi* as impulses rising up within his own consciousness. These thoughts, which are subtle impulses of speech, then find audible expression on the gross level of creation through the voice of the *ṛṣi*, who utters them forth as articulated words. The inspired thoughts are thus brought to fruition in recited hymns through the vocalized speech of the *ṛṣis*.

> O Indra and Varuṇa, when you gave in the beginning to the *ṛṣis* inspired thought (*manīṣā*), thought as realized in speech (*vāco mati*), that which was heard (*śruta*), I saw (root *dṛś*) by means of *tapas* those places to which the

> inspired sages (*dhīras*), performing sacrifice, sent (root *sṛj*) them forth.[83]

As in the above verse, the hymns are at times described as being "sent forth" (root *sṛj*[84] or root *ṛ*[85]) through the speech of the *ṛṣis*. Several similes are used to describe this process. The *ṛṣi* sends forth his hymn like an artisan sending forth his chariot,[86] like a ship being launched on the sea,[87] like an archer discharging his arrow,[88] like the wind driving forth the clouds.[89] The hymns are ultimately sent forth to the gods, and thus a number of passages speak of the hymns as approaching the gods or being brought to them as an offering.[90]

The cycle thus completes itself. The *ṛṣi* cognizes the inspired thoughts, the subtle impulses of speech, on that subtlest level of existence which is the abode of all the gods and gives them vocalized expression through the agency of his own speech. The hymn is sent forth through the *ṛṣi*'s speech and returns to its source, where the gods reside.

> Put on your divine vision (*dhī*); send forth your speech (*vāc*) to the gods.[91]

The process of Vedic cognition is thus represented as involving a cyclical movement from the subtle to the gross and back to the subtle. The hymn emerges from the celestial regions of the gods, bestowing the blessings of cognition upon the *ṛṣi*, and then the *ṛṣi* through his speech causes the hymn to return to the gods, in turn nourishing, invigorating, and magnifying the deities.[92] The hymn flows through the agency of speech from the heart of the *ṛṣi* to the heart of the gods,[93] and the cycle is complete.

Brāhmaṇas

The Brāhmaṇas, like the Ṛg-Veda, describe the cognitions of the *ṛṣis* as involving a twofold movement: first, the act of "seeing" (root *dṛś*), by means of which the *ṛṣi* attains a praeternormal cognition; and second, the act of speaking, by means of which the *ṛṣi* gives vocalized expression to his cognition in the form of recited *mantras*. The auditory dimension of the process of cognition is implicit even in the initial act of seeing, for what the *ṛṣis* see, as represented in the Brāhmaṇas, are certain hymns (*ṛcs*) and chants (*sāmans*). The Brāhmaṇas do not elaborate on the mechanisms involved in the process but simply refer to specific *ṛṣis* who saw and uttered particular *mantras*. They give little attention to the nature and mechanics of the phenomenon of cognition in and of itself. Rather, in accordance with their sacrificial perspective, the Brāhmaṇas are primarily concerned with connecting the *ṛṣis*' cognitions to the purpose and meaning of the *mantras* in the context of the sacrificial rites.

The sacrificial concerns of the Brāhmaṇas are evident in their discussions of the archetypal *ṛṣi*, the creator Prajāpati, who is the divine prototype of the human *ṛṣis*. Prajāpati, as discussed in chapter 1, is portrayed as "seeing" (root *dṛś*) particular *ṛcs* and *sāmans*[94] as well as the sacrificial rituals in which the *mantras* are used.[95] Having seen a particular *ṛc* or *sāman*, Prajāpati then recites or praises (root *stu*) with it. The Brāhmaṇas emphasize the practical consequences of this double movement of seeing and recitation of the *mantras*, which Prajāpati uses to accomplish some specific purpose: in the initial act of creation, to bring forth beings, and in subsequent acts, to order and complete his creation through subduing his rebellious creatures and bringing forth rain and food to nourish them, and so on. Similarly, having seen a particular sacrificial ritual, he performs it in order to produce beings and accomplish other ends. The purpose for which the primordial *ṛṣi* Prajāpati originally used particular Vedic *mantras* or sacrifices is generally linked to an explanation of the purpose for which the *mantras* or sacrifices subsequently may be used by "him who knows thus"—for example, to obtain and subdue cattle, to bring rain, and so on.[96] Other gods besides Prajāpati are also at times represented as "seeing" (root *dṛś*) certain Vedic *mantras* or sacrificial rites and as subsequently reciting the *mantras* or performing the rites in order to attain particular ends.[97]

The human *ṛṣis* are represented in the Brāhmaṇas as the earthly counterparts of the primordial *ṛṣi* Prajāpati. The *ṛṣis* themselves are at times granted a divine or semidivine status. In the Śatapatha Brāhmaṇa, for example, the collective group of *ṛṣis* that are designated in the Saṃhitās as the "seven *ṛṣis*" (*sapta ṛṣis*)[98] are elevated to the status of cosmological principles that are constitutive of the creator Prajāpati himself. In the Ṛg-Veda the seven *ṛṣis* are called "our fathers,"[99] are said to be divine,[100] and are depicted as practicing *tapas*.[101] In the Atharva-Veda they are referred to as "makers of beings" (*bhūta-kṛts*)[102] and are also associated with *tapas*.[103] Building on the conceptions of the Saṃhitās, the Śatapatha Brāhmaṇa proclaims the seven *ṛṣis* to be the "first-born (*prathama-*

ja) Brahman,"[104] who exist prior to creation as the seven primordial *prāṇas* (breaths, or orifices of the sense organs)[105] that perform *tapas* and form seven *puruṣas* that join together to constitute the cosmic body of the Puruṣa Prajāpati. The body of Prajāpati is symbolically represented in the bird-shaped fire altar that is constructed in the *agnicayana* ceremony, and thus the seven *ṛṣis* are also held to be constitutive of Agni.[106] Even when the seven *ṛṣis* are designated by name for the first time—Gautama, Bharadvāja, Viśvāmitra, Jamadagni, Vasiṣṭha, Kaśyapa, and Atri—their identification with the *prāṇas* is maintained.[107] The Śatapatha Brāhmaṇa further emphasizes the cosmic nature of the seven *ṛṣis* by identifying them with the seven stars of the constellation of Ursa Major, an identification that is also developed in post-Vedic mythology.[108]

The divine or semidivine status of certain *ṛṣis* is emphasized in other Brāhmaṇas as well. The *ṛṣi* Vasiṣṭha is at times identified with Prajāpati in the Kauṣītaki Brāhmaṇa,[109] while Viśvāmitra is identified with Prajāpati's consort, Vāc.[110] Other *ṛṣis* are represented in the Brāhmaṇas as the offspring or descendants of the gods. For example, an account in the Aitareya Brāhmaṇa describes the *ṛṣi* Bhṛgu as arising from a portion of Prajāpati's spilled seed that is kindled in fire by the gods, while the Aṅgirases arise from the coals of the fire. Bhṛgu then becomes the adopted son of the god Varuṇa, a notion that is found elsewhere in the Brāhmaṇas as well as in other Vedic texts.[111] The Aṅgirases are frequently portrayed in the Brāhmaṇas as semidivine beings—and at times are explicitly designated as gods (*devas*)[112]—who contend with the divine Ādityas for the world of heaven (*svarga loka*), the "way (*ayana*) of the Aṅgirases" being distinguished from the "way (*ayana*) of the Ādityas."[113]

While the *ṛṣis* are thus at times accorded a divine or semidivine status in the Brāhmaṇas, at the same time they are represented as human sages who served as the vehicles through which the Vedic *mantras* and sacrifices were brought to earth, thereby inaugurating the recitative and sacrificial traditions that would subsequently be preserved by their descendants, the lineages of brahmin priests. Having cognized the Vedic *mantras* and various aspects of the sacrificial ritual, the *ṛṣis* established the brahmanical lineages by themselves assuming the roles of the priestly officiants—*hotṛ*, *udgātṛ*, *adhvaryu*, and *brahman*—who performed the first sacrifices on earth[114] and fulfilled other sacerdotal duties such as the anointing of kings.[115]

In giving instructions concerning the functions of the various brahmin priests in particular sacrificial rituals, the Brāhmaṇas regularly make reference to the *ṛṣis* to whom particular *mantras* are attributed. At times the name of the *ṛṣi* is simply mentioned in formulaic statements that do not explicitly refer to the process of cognition, such as "[the priest] recites a verse of Bharadvāja," or "the *praüga*-[*śāstra*] is by Medhātithi."[116] At other times the cognitions of the *ṛṣis*, like those of their divine prototype, Prajāpati, are described in terms of a twofold movement that involved first seeing (root *dṛś*) and then uttering (root *vac*) or praising (root *stu*) with certain *ṛcs* or *sāmans*. A number of passages in the Brāhmaṇas emphasize both aspects of the *ṛṣis'* role. For example, the Jaiminīya Brāhmaṇa regularly incorporates into its accounts of particular *ṛṣis* the formulaic statement that the *ṛṣi* "saw (root *dṛś*) this *sāman* and praised (root *stu*) with it."[117] The Aitareya, Kauṣītaki, and Pañcaviṃśa Brāhmaṇas focus primarily on the *ṛṣis'* role in seeing particular *ṛcs*, *sāmans*, or ritual formulae,[118] or other aspects of the sacrifice.[119] The Brāhmaṇas also occasionally mention the *ṛṣis'* utterance of the *mantras* without reference to their role in seeing them.[120]

The Brāhmaṇas at times describe the circumstances surrounding a *ṛṣi's* cognition of particular *mantras*, such as the *ṛṣi* Kavaṣa Ailūṣa's cognition of Ṛg-Veda X.30, the "child of the waters" hymn,[121] or the *ṛṣi* Śunaḥśepa's cognition of a series of *ṛcs*.[122] The gods are occasionally represented as assuming a role in granting a *ṛṣi* his cognition.[123] Like the archetypal *ṛṣi* Prajāpati, the *ṛṣis* are often portrayed as seeing and/or uttering particular *mantras* in order to attain some specific end, and this end is then identified as the purpose of the *mantras*.[124] For example, a frequently reiterated tradition maintains that the *ṛṣi* Vasiṣṭha, whose son had been slain, saw (root *dṛś*) a particular *sāman* (or *sāmans*) and thereby became rich in offspring and cattle, and thus the purpose of the *sāman*(s) is the attainment of progeny.[125] The cognition of certain *mantras* or aspects of the sacrifice by other *ṛṣis* is similarly associated with the realization of worldly ends such as food,[126] cattle,[127] rain,[128] or the discomfiture of one's enemies,[129] as well as with more abstract goals such as the attainment of a firm foundation (*pratiṣṭhā*)[130] or the world of heaven (*svarga loka*).[131]

A number of passages in the Brāhmaṇas point to the role of *tapas* in the *ṛṣi's* cognitions. Śatapatha Brāhmaṇa VI.1.1.1 explains the etymology of the term *ṛṣi* with reference to the primordial *ṛṣis* who wore themselves out (root *riṣ*) with exertion (*śram*) and *tapas*. Aitareya Brāhmaṇa II.27 refers to the *ṛṣis* as "born of *tapas*" (*tapo-ja*). A passage in the Taittirīya Brāhmaṇa depicts the *ṛṣis*, the inspired (*manīṣin*) makers of *mantras* (*mantra-kṛts*), as searching together with the gods for the goddess Vāc by means of *tapas* and exertion (*śrama*).[132] Individual *ṛṣis* are portrayed in the Brāhmaṇas as performing *tapas* or other forms of austerity (root *śram*) in order to attain their ends. Having performed *tapas*, they cognize particular *mantras* or aspects of the sacrifice and thereby obtain the means to fulfill their desires.[133]

Beyond the attainment of worldly ends and of heaven, the practice of *tapas* or meditation is at times represented in the Brāhmaṇas as the means through which the *ṛṣis* access the mysteries of creation. The Śatapatha Brāhmaṇa describes the *ṛṣis* and gods as penetrating through the process of cognition into the hidden structures of creation itself, which are reflected in the structures of the Veda and of the sacrificial order.[134] The correspondences between the structures of the sacrifice and the structures of creation are emphasized in particular in the Śatapatha Brāhmaṇa's discussion of the *agnicayana* ceremony. While the fire altar as a whole is said to represent the cosmos-body of the creator Prajāpati, the different layers of bricks of which the altar is constructed correspond to the different levels of creation: the first, third, and fifth layers represent the earth, midregions, and heaven, respectively, while the second and fourth layers represent the space between the three worlds. Śatapatha Brāhmaṇa VI.2.3.1–10 describes how certain gods gain the ability through meditation (root *cit*) to see (root *dṛś*) a particular layer of creation. Prajāpati himself sees the earth, which corresponds to the first layer of the fire altar; Indra, Agni, and Viśvakarman see the midregions, which correspond to the third layer, and so on. The *ṛṣis* are portrayed as participating with the gods in this process of cognition, in which they gain the ability to see the space between the midregions and heaven, which corresponds to the fourth layer of the fire altar.[135]

Just as the *ṛṣis* are represented in the Brāhmaṇas as the earthly counterparts of the primordial *ṛṣi* Prajāpati, seeing and uttering the *mantras* in accordance with the divine prototype, so the brahmin officiants of the sacrifice are represented as the present-day counterparts of the ancient *ṛṣis* who themselves participate in the cosmic drama by continually reenacting the primordial sacrifice and reciting the *mantras* ascribed to the *ṛṣis*. The status of the *ṛṣis* as "our fathers" assumes special significance in the Brāhmaṇas, in which descent from a *ṛṣi* is considered to be an important prerequisite for a brahmin's performance of sacrifices, for "a brahmin descended from a *ṛṣi* represents all the gods."[136] The descent of the *yajamāna*, the patron of the sacrifice, from a *ṛṣi* is also considered important, for "the gods do not eat the oblation of one who does not have descent from a *ṛṣi*."[137] In the case of a *yajamāna* who is not a brahmin, the *ṛṣi* lineage of his family priest (*purohita*) or of the *hotṛ* priest should be mentioned.[138]

Upaniṣads

The Upaniṣads take it for granted that the *ṛṣis* are the seers of the Vedic *mantras* and are not generally concerned with explaining the mechanisms of Vedic cognition. For example, the Muṇḍaka Upaniṣad mentions that "the works (*karmans*) that the *kavis* saw (root *dṛś*) in the *mantras* are variously spread forth in the three Vedas,"[139] but neither the Muṇḍaka or any of the other principal Upaniṣads elaborate on the process through which the seers cognized the *mantras*. In contrast to the Brāhmaṇas, the primary concern of the Upaniṣads is not with the seers who cognized and established the sacrificial rites but rather with the seers who cognized and transmitted the truths of Vedānta by means of which Brahman-Ātman is known.

The Muṇḍaka Upaniṣad, having mentioned the works seen by the *kavis* in the *mantras*, goes on to encourage performance of the sacrificial rituals.[140] However, it then declares the path of works to be inferior, for the sacrificial forms are "unsafe boats" that cannot free one from rebirth.[141] Knowledge of Brahman-Ātman alone is proclaimed to be the means to liberation. Those sages who attained the supreme reality of Brahman-Ātman and established the line of tradition (*vaṃśa*) through which this knowledge would be passed down to subsequent generations are celebrated in the Muṇḍaka Upaniṣad as the supreme seers (*paramarṣis*).[142] The Muṇḍaka also designates as *ṛṣis* those who follow the path of knowledge established by the ancient *ṛṣis* and, through the practice of *tapas* and meditation,[143] themselves attain realization of Brahman-Ātman.

> Having attained Him, the *ṛṣis* who are satiated with knowledge (*jñāna*), who are perfected souls (*kṛtātman*), free from passion, tranquil, having attained Him who is all-pervading in every direction, those inspired sages (*dhīras*), united in the Self (*yuktātman*), enter into the All (*sarva*) itself.[144]

A passage in the Chāndogya Upaniṣad, which also appears with slight variations in the Maitri Upaniṣad, gives a similar interpretation of the seer as one who sees and attains the All.

> The seer (*paśya*) sees (root *dṛś*) not death nor sickness nor any suffering. The seer sees only the All (*sarva*), attains the All completely.[145]

Several of the Upaniṣads pay homage to the ancient *ṛṣis* who originally saw and attained the All, Brahman-Ātman, by enumerating the lines of tradition (*vaṃśas*) that their respective Vedic schools trace back through a succession of teachers to the original *ṛṣis* and ultimately to the creator Brahmā or even Brahman itself.[146]

VEDA AND COGNITION IN POST-VEDIC MYTHOLOGY

Post-Vedic texts contain relatively few descriptions of the process of Vedic cognition. There are, however, numerous accounts in the Mahābhārata and the Purāṇas of the *ṛṣis*, who are countless in number. The *ṛṣis* are represented as a separate class of beings who are distinct from both the gods and ordinary human beings and yet participate in the nature of both. As in Vedic texts, the *ṛṣis* are often portrayed in the Mahābhārata and Purāṇas as divine or semidivine beings who are at the same time the ancestors of mortal human beings. They travel freely throughout the lower and upper worlds, accompanying the gods in their divine escapades and assisting ordinary mortals through promulgating teachings and performing sacrifices. The names and offices of the *ṛṣis*, in their special role of cognizing and transmitting the *mantras*, are recorded in the eternal blueprint of the Vedas along with the names and functions of all other types of beings.[147] In the post-Vedic accounts the conception of Vedic cognition assumes new valences through becoming embedded in cosmogonic speculations concerning the various cycles of creation, in which the *ṛṣis*' cognitions are represented not as a unique, one-time event but rather as an endlessly repeating process that occurs at the beginning of each cycle and subcycle.

In the Mahābhārata and Purāṇas the class of *ṛṣis* is further subdivided into a variety of categories. Among the most important are the *saptarṣis*, or seven seers—Gautama, Bharadvāja, Viśvāmitra, Jamadagni, Vasiṣṭha, Kaśyapa, and Atri—who, as we have seen, are also ascribed a special status in Vedic texts. In accordance with the Vedic association of the seven *ṛṣis* with the constellation of Ursa Major, these *ṛṣis* are represented as the regents of the northern quarter. Three other groups of *ṛṣis* are correspondingly assigned the role of the regents of the eastern, western, and southern quarters, respectively. Among the *brahmarṣis* or *viprarṣis*, seers of brahmanical lineage, special status is accorded to the "mind-born" sons of the creator Brahmā, who are generally enumerated as Marīci, Atri, Aṅgiras, Pulastya, Pulaha, Kratu, and Vasiṣṭha, although other sages are at times included. These sages are also designated as *prajāpatis* because of their role in producing various beings. Other categories of *ṛṣis* include *rājarṣis*, seers of royal lineage, such as Viśvāmitra,[148] and *devarṣis*, seers exalted to the status of demigods, such as Nārada. The distinctions among these categories, however, are not definitive, as some *ṛṣis* fall into more than one category. Thus, the seven *ṛṣis* are also *devarṣis*, and the renowned Vasiṣṭha in particular is celebrated as a *saptarṣi*, a *brahmarṣi*, and a *devarṣi*.

In the Mahābhārata and Purāṇas the title of *ṛṣi* is not reserved solely for the seers of the Vedic *mantras*. Building on the Upaniṣadic conception of a seer as a knower of Brahman, these texts at times use the term more generally to refer to a great sage in any age who has obtained transcendent knowledge and extraordinary powers through his practice of *tapas*. However, among the most important of the *ṛṣis* in the Mahābhārata and Purāṇas, about whom many narratives are recounted, are the seven *ṛṣis*—especially Vasiṣṭha and Viśvāmitra—the Bhṛgus, the Aṅgirases, and Agastya, all of whom are celebrated in the Ṛg-Veda as the ancient seers of the Vedic *mantras*.[149]

Mahābhārata

In the Mahābhārata the archetypal *ṛṣi*, the paradigmatic exemplar and goal of the *ṛṣis*, is—in accordance with the epic's Vaiṣṇava perspective—Viṣṇu, the supreme Godhead. Viṣṇu, who is identified with Brahman, is celebrated in the epic as the "*ṛṣi* of *ṛṣis*."

> You [Viṣṇu] are the greatest *ṛṣi* of the *ṛṣis* who burn with the heat of knowledge, who have realized the Self (Ātman) through *tapas*, who have been perfected in seeing (*darśana*) the Self, of the meritorious *rājarṣis* who never retreat in battles, endowed with all *dharmas*—of them [all] you are the goal, supreme Puruṣa.[150]

This passage recalls the Upaniṣadic conception of a seer as one who sees and realizes the supreme reality of Brahman-Ātman. It also points to the association of the *ṛṣis* with *tapas,* an association that frequently occurs in the epic's discussions of the *ṛṣis*.[151] The *ṛṣis* are represented in the epic as attaining their knowledge of Brahman and of the Vedic *mantras* not only through their own efforts in practicing *tapas* but also through the grace of Viṣṇu, the embodiment of Brahman, who is celebrated as the ultimate source from which the Vedas, as well as the *ṛṣis* themselves, emerge in the beginning of each cycle of creation.[152]

The *ṛṣis* are also portrayed in the epic as having a special relationship to the creator Brahmā, assisting him in the process of creation. Brahmā, as the primordial *ṛṣi* who first cognized the Vedic *mantras,* is described as bringing forth, in accordance with this eternal blueprint, the class of *ṛṣis* along with the other classes of beings in the beginning of each *kalpa*.[153] Certain *brahmarṣis*—in particular, Marīci, Atri, Aṅgiras, Pulastya, Pulaha, Kratu, and Vasiṣṭha—are said to have been produced from Brahmā's mind and thus are designated as his mind-born sons.[154] These seven *brahmarṣis* are ascribed a special cosmological status in the epic, together with Manu, as the eight *prakṛtis* that serve as the source and foundation of the entire universe.[155] They also assume the role of *prajāpatis* who bring forth various beings.[156] These *brahmarṣis,* who are adept in the practice of *tapas* and yoga,[157] are ordained by Viṣṇu to be the foremost knowers and teachers of the Vedas and the promulgators of the dharmic path of *pravṛtti*.[158] Other groups of *ṛṣis* are also allotted a role in the cosmogonic process. One passage enumerates seven different groups of *ṛṣis,* including the seven *ṛṣis* of the northern quarter and the three groups that serve as the regents of the other quarters, and emphasizes the role of these *ṛṣis* in manifesting the worlds and all beings.[159] Another passage mentions the seven mind-born sons of Brahmā who are *prajāpatis* and then goes on to enumerate the four groups of *ṛṣis* who govern the four quarters and are the "creators of the worlds."[160]

A number of passages in the Mahābhārata point to the role of praeternormal hearing by means of which the *ṛṣis* "heard" divine speech and attained their cognitions of the Vedic *mantras* and their knowledge of the mechanics of creation. One passage recounts how prior to the creation of the universe the *brahmarṣis,* desiring to fathom the mechanisms of cosmos production, meditated and performed various austerities.

> Formerly, in the Brahma-*kalpa,* in the assembly of exalted *brahmarṣis* uncertainty arose concerning the production of

> the worlds. These brahmins remained absorbed in meditation (*dhyāna*) and established in silence, immovable, having given up eating, and drinking only air, for a hundred years of the gods. Speech (*vāṇī*), consisting of *brahman* (*brahma-mayī*), reached the ears of them all. The divine Sarasvatī sprang forth from the firmament.[161]

The passage goes on to describe the emergence of the five gross elements (*mahābhūtas*), beginning with ether (*ākāśa*), which at first is soundless (*niḥśabda*) and motionless. The passage implies that the speech that is heard by the *ṛṣis* is the unexpressed, transcendent level of speech, for it precedes the emergence of material sound that is transmitted through ether. Moreover, this "speech consisting of *brahman* (*brahma-mayī*)" that is heard within the silence apparently refers to the Vedic *mantras*.[162] This is explicitly indicated in another passage, which speaks of the *ṛṣis* practicing *tapas* out of a desire to know the Vedas, after which "divine speech (Vāc), consisting of the Vedas (*veda-mayī*)," emerges from Brahmā, which he then employs as the blueprint of creation.[163] In both passages the *ṛṣis'* cognition of the Vedic *mantras* is described as being attained through *tapas* and involves knowledge of the mechanics of creation, for it is through the *mantras* that the phenomenal world is brought forth. A third passage, which is not directly concerned with Vedic cognition, depicts the *ṛṣis* and gods together with Brahmā as practicing *tapas* for a thousand celestial years, after which they hear (root *śru*) a voice (*vāṇī*) adorned by the Vedas and Vedāṇgas.[164]

In discussing the role of speech in the *ṛṣis'* cognitions, the Mahābhārata expands on the Ṛg-Vedic image of Vāc—identified in the epic with the goddess Sarasvatī—entering into the *ṛṣis*.[165] This image is used in an account of the process through which the *ṛṣi* Yājñavalkya, celebrated as the repository of Veda (*śruti-nidhi*), obtained his cognitions of the *yajuses* of the White Yajur-Veda from the sun god Āditya.[166] When Yājñavalkya requests of Āditya to have knowledge of the *yajuses*, the sun god commands him to open his mouth, after which the goddess Sarasvatī, consisting of speech (*vāgbhūta*), enters into his body. Later, when he thinks of Sarasvatī, she issues forth. The appearance of the goddess of speech is described in images of both light and sound: exceedingly radiant (*atiśubha*), she is adorned with the Sanskrit vowels (*svaras*) and consonants (*vyañjanas*). Inspired by Sarasvatī and by Āditya, Yājñavalkya attains the ability to cognize the *yajuses* and also to compile the Śatapatha Brāhmaṇa, the Brāhmaṇa of the White Yajur-Veda.[167] Even in contexts outside of Vedic cognition, Sarasvatī is represented as the source of the *ṛṣis'* inspiration. For example, she is described as entering into the seven *brahmarṣis* who are the mind-born sons of Brahmā in order to give them the ability to compose a special treatise on *dharma* that is in accordance with the four Vedas.[168]

The ancient *ṛṣis* who assist the creator Brahmā in the cosmogonic process are allotted the role of cognizing the Vedic *mantras* in each new cycle of creation and reestablishing the lines of tradition through which the *mantras* would be transmitted. The epic emphasizes that although the original Veda that manifests on earth through the cognitions of the *ṛṣis* is one, eternal, and nonchanging, the ability of human beings to comprehend the Veda progressively declines as the human condition itself declines, in terms of consciousness, knowledge, righteousness, and life span, through the course of the four *yugas* or ages—from Kṛta Yuga to Tretā Yuga to Dvāpara Yuga to Kali Yuga. While in Kṛta Yuga and Tretā Yuga the Veda remains one and intact, in Dvāpara Yuga the understanding of Veda diminishes to such an extent that it is necessary for a special type of *ṛṣi*, Veda-Vyāsa, to arise and to assume the role of dividing the Veda into four distinct Saṃhitās, or collections, of *mantras* in order to facilitate human understanding and preservation of this eternal knowledge.[169]

The Mahābhārata, as discussed in chapter 1, accords Kṛṣṇa Dvaipāyana Vyāsa the preeminent status of the "supreme *ṛṣi*" (*paramarṣi*)[170] and "great *ṛṣi*" (*maharṣi, mahān-ṛṣi*),[171] who not only divides the Veda in Dvāpara Yuga but also composes the epic itself as the fifth Veda. Like the ancient Vedic *ṛṣis*, Vyāsa, who is himself a descendant of the *ṛṣi* Vasiṣṭha, is represented in the epic as a semidivine being. However, even here his status surpasses that of the Vedic *ṛṣis* in that he is represented not simply as a manifestation or descendant of one of the lesser deities but as a portion (*aṃśa*) of the supreme Godhead himself, Viṣṇu-Nārāyaṇa.[172] In an extended account of Vyāsa's origins, the epic describes him as being born in a previous incarnation from the speech (Sarasvatī-Vāc) of Viṣṇu-Nārāyaṇa as the *ṛṣi* Sārasvata or Apāntaratamas. Viṣṇu-Nārāyaṇa then assigns him his role in dividing and arranging the Veda in each cycle of ages and assures him that he will be superior even to the seven *ṛṣis*.[173] The ancient Vedic *ṛṣis*, as we have seen, are described as having the ability, as a result of their *tapas*, to cognize and facilitate the process through which creation emerges in the beginning of each cycle. The speciality of the *ṛṣi* Vyāsa, who is born later in the cycle, is his ability—also gained through *tapas*—to know the past, present, and future and to see (root *dṛś*) with the "eye of knowledge" (*jñāna-cakṣus*) the events of thousands of cycles of *yugas* extending back to the beginning of the *kalpa* and extending forward into the future.[174]

Having arranged the eternal Veda into four Saṃhitās, Veda-Vyāsa then teaches the Saṃhitās, together with the Mahābhārata as the fifth Veda, to his five main disciples, who transmit them to the rest of humankind.[175] In spite of their division into four Saṃhitās, knowledge of the Vedas progressively declines from Dvāpara Yuga to Kali Yuga until, by the end of Kali Yuga, the Vedas disappear from human awareness on the earthly plane.[176] At the beginning of Kṛta Yuga, however, the Vedic *mantras* are re-cognized by the *ṛṣis* and once again are restored to their pure, pristine status as one whole and complete Veda.[177] The details of this theory of the cyclical appearance and disappearance of the Vedas on the earthly plane are still somewhat vague and sketchy in the epic and remain to be worked out more fully in Purāṇic cosmogonies.

Purāṇas

The Purāṇas, like the Mahābhārata, contain numerous accounts of the feats of the ancient Vedic *ṛṣis*, both on earth and in the celestial realms of the gods. Certain Purāṇas include extended discussions of the various functions and classes of *ṛṣis*, such as *saptarṣis*, *brahmarṣis*, *rājarṣis*, and *devarṣis*, who are generally characterized as enlightened knowers of Brahman who practice *tapas* and cognize the Vedic *mantras*.[178] In the context of Purāṇic speculations concerning the various cycles of primary and secondary creation, the *ṛṣis* are represented as semidivine beings of extraordinary knowledge and power who know the past, present, and future and who remain unaffected by the minor dissolutions that occur at the end of each secondary creation, or *pratisarga*. When the three lower worlds and all lower beings are absorbed within the body of Brahmā, the *ṛṣis* retire along with the gods to the higher worlds.[179] When the next *kalpa* begins the *ṛṣis* reappear and assist the creator Brahmā in bringing forth various types of beings in the *pratisarga*. They also cognize and reintroduce the Vedas onto earth at the beginning of each *kalpa* as well as at the beginning of each of the thousand *mahāyugas* that make up a *kalpa*.

Although the Purāṇas emphasize the role of the *ṛṣis* in periodically cognizing the Vedas, they are even less concerned than the Mahābhārata with discussing the mechanisms through which the *ṛṣis* obtained their cognitions. The Purāṇas' concern is to delineate the special cosmic *dharma* of the *ṛṣis* in periodically reviving the knowledge of Veda in the various cycles and subcycles of creation and establishing the Vedic recitative tradition through which the *mantras* would be preserved and transmitted. As discussed in chapter 1, the creator Brahmā, the "first *ṛṣi*," is described in the Purāṇas as bringing forth the four Vedas from his four mouths in the beginning of each *kalpa*. He then teaches the Vedas to the *brahmarṣis* who are his mind-born sons. These sages, who, like their father Brahmā, are skilled in reciting the Vedas, in turn teach the *mantras* to their sons, thereby inaugurating the tradition of recitative transmission.[180]

The Purāṇas, like the Mahābhārata, emphasize that the primordial Veda that issues forth from Brahmā's mouths at the beginning of each *kalpa*, and which he subsequently teaches to his sons, is a single unitary totality, which, according to Purāṇic calculations, comprises 100,000 verses. While the epic simply states that the original Veda is one and does not attempt to reconcile this notion with the conception of four types of *mantras* emerging from the creator, the Purāṇas explain that although the Veda is one, it consists of four quarters (*catuṣ-pāda*). These four quarters remain as one whole as long as human understanding is capable of grasping knowledge in its totality. However, like the epic, the Purāṇas emphasize that as the *yugas* progress from Kṛta Yuga to Tretā Yuga to Dvāpara Yuga in each cycle of four *yugas*, the strength, understanding, and morality of human beings progressively declines and their knowledge of the Veda gradually diminishes. For this reason at the beginning of each Dvāpara Yuga it becomes necessary to divide the Veda into four distinct parts in order to facilitate its preservation and understanding as well to promote the performance of the Vedic sacrifices. The Purāṇas ascribe the task of dividing the Veda to Veda-Vyāsa, who, as in the epic, is considered to be a partial incarnation of Viṣṇu. However, while in the epic Vyāsa is identified with Kṛṣṇa Dvaipāyana, the *ṛṣi* who composed the Mahābhārata, in the Purāṇas Vyāsa is not the name of a specific individual but rather the designation for a particular position—"divider of the Veda" (Veda-Vyāsa)—that is filled by different *ṛṣis* in the successive series of Dvāpara Yugas. Kṛṣṇa Dvaipāyana, the composer of the Mahābhārata, is the *ṛṣi* who fulfilled the function of Vyāsa in the most recent Dvāpara Yuga.[181]

In order to make the Veda more comprehensible, Veda-Vyāsa separates out the four types of *mantras*—*ṛcs*, *yajuses*, *sāmans*, and *atharvans*—and arranges them in sections (*vargas*), forming four Saṃhitās, or collections, of *mantras*.[182] In this conception the distinction between the terms *mantra* and Saṃhitā is vital, for although the four kinds of *mantras* emerge in the very beginning of each *kalpa*, the formal collections, Ṛg-Veda Saṃhitā, Yajur-Veda Saṃhitā, and so on, only come into existence in the third of the four *yugas* through the agency of Veda-Vyāsa.

> Then, having separated out the *ṛcs*, the sage compiled the Ṛg-Veda; having separated out the *yajuses*, he compiled the Yajur-Veda; and with the *sāmans* he compiled the Sāma-Veda. With the *atharvans* the master formed all the ceremonies suitable for kings and the function appropriate for the *brahman* priest.[183]

The Purāṇas go on to describe how Vyāsa transmitted each of the four Vedas, together with the Itihāsas and Purāṇas as the fifth Veda, to his five main disciples, respectively. His disciples subsequently divided their respective Vedas into branches (*śākhās*) and passed them down to their own disciples, who subdivided them even further, and so on.[184] In this way, the one vast tree of the Veda, having been divided by Vyāsa into four stems, soon developed into an extensive forest consisting of innumerable branches.[185] After giving a detailed description of the process through which the Veda is divided into four parts and subsequently into hundreds of *śākhās*, the Viṣṇu Purāṇa asserts that this process does not affect the eternal status of the Veda.

> Thus, the *śākhās* have been enumerated, and the subdivisions of the *śākhās*, their founders, and the reason for their division have been declared. The same divisions of the *śākhās* are established in all the *manvantaras*. The *śruti* derived from Prajāpati [Brahmā] is eternal (*nitya*). These [*śākhās*] are only its modifications (*vikalpas*).[186]

Although the division of the Veda into *śākhās* in each Dvāpara Yuga serves to facilitate its preservation and understanding, it is inevitable, according to the Purāṇas, that in the course of time as the Dvāpara Yuga passes into the final *yuga*, Kali Yuga, human intelligence and morality will continue to decline and sin and corruption will increasingly prevail, until eventually, by the end of Kali Yuga, knowledge of the Vedas is entirely lost from human consciousness. In this way at the end of each *mahāyuga* the Vedas disappear from the earth. At the beginning of the subsequent *mahāyuga* the *ṛṣis* must again reintroduce the Vedic *mantras* by giving vocalized expression through the vehicle of human speech to the subtle reverberations of the eternal Veda.

> At the end of the four *yugas* the disappearance of the Vedas occurs. The seven *ṛṣis*, having come down to earth from heaven, again introduce them.[187]

CHAPTER 4

Torah and Revelation

> When the Holy One, blessed be He, gave the Torah to Israel, the earth rejoiced but the heavens wept. . . . The Holy One, blessed be He, said to the heavens, "You who abide on high should give praise to My glory and My daughter, even more than the earth does." They said to him, "Lord of the worlds, the earth, to whom the Torah is being given, may well offer praise, but we from whom it goes forth, how can we give praise and not mourn?"
>
> —P^{e}sîqtā' Rabbāṯî 20.1

In discussing the status and role of the Torah in creation in chapter 2, we were concerned primarily with four types of formulations found in rabbinic and kabbalistic texts, in which the Torah is variously represented as (1) the Word of God or Name of God, which participates in the essence of God; (2) primordial wisdom, Ḥoḵmāh, which serves as the architect of creation; (3) the blueprint containing the elements of the divine language that structure creation; and (4) a concrete written text together with an oral tradition of interpretation. Another trend of speculation in rabbinic and kabbalistic sources concerns the mechanisms through which the primordial Torah that served as the instrument of creation came to be embodied on earth in a corpus of texts. The descent of the Torah from its supernal abode to earth is represented as occurring at a particular time and place in history: at the revelation at Mount Sinai in 1447 B.C.E., according to the traditional reckoning, which is considered the central turning point in the salvation history of the Jewish people.

Rabbinic and kabbalistic discussions of *mattan tôrāh*, the giving of the Torah, generally take as their starting point the biblical account of the Sinai revelation in the book of Exodus. The Exodus account depicts the revelation as occurring in two main phases. In the first phase God himself "came down upon Mount Sinai" (Exod. 19.20) and spoke directly to the people of Israel who stood at the foot of the mountain, declaring to them the Ten Commandments, the "Ten Words" (*'ăśereṯ ha-dibbᵉrôṯ*) of the Decalogue (Exod. 20.1–17). In the second phase of the revelation Moses assumed the role of the covenant mediator and made a series of ascents to the top of the "mountain of God" (Exod. 24.13), where God imparted to him the detailed teachings and commandments of the Torah. In his first extended sojourn on the mountain Moses remained for forty days and forty nights (Exod. 24.18), at the end of which God gave him the two tablets of the covenant "written with the finger of God" (Exod. 31.18). When Moses descended the mountain and saw the Israelites reveling in the worship of a golden calf, he cast the tablets out of his hand and broke them (Exod. 32.19). Due to Moses's intercession on behalf of the people of Israel, God conceded to renew the covenant and instructed Moses to cut two stone tablets like the first (Exod. 34.1). Moses then ascended Mount Sinai again for his second extended sojourn of forty days and forty nights (Exod. 34.4,28). When Moses descended the mountain with the second tablets of the covenant, the skin of his face shone and the Israelites were afraid to approach him (Exod. 34.29–30). Moses then assembled all of the people of Israel and imparted to them the teachings that he had received from God on the mountain (Exod. 34.32).

In addition to key verses in the Exodus account, Midrashim on the revelation of the Torah regularly invoke a number of other biblical verses that allude to the Sinai event. One of the most frequently discussed verses is Deuteronomy 33.2:

> The Lord came from Sinai,
> and dawned from Seir upon them;
> He shone forth from Mount Paran,
> He came from the ten thousands of holy ones,
> at His right hand was a fiery law (*'ēš-dāṯ*) for them.

Another biblical passage that is often invoked in Midrashim on the Sinai revelation is Psalm 68.18–19:

> The chariots (*reḵeḇ*) of God are twice ten thousand,
> thousands upon thousands;
> the Lord is among them, Sinai in holiness.
> You ascended (*'ālāh*) on high, you took a captivity captive,
> you took gifts for humanity.

As we shall see, such verses are often used to link the Sinai event with a variety of concerns that are not directly addressed in the Exodus account. For example, Deuteronomy 33.2 is sometimes cited to establish the role of the gentile nations in the giving of the Torah, while Psalm 68.18–19 serves as a means of connecting the revelation with the Merkabah vision of the prophet Ezekiel in Ezekiel 1.

TORAH AND REVELATION IN RABBINIC TEXTS

In commenting and elaborating upon biblical descriptions of the revelation at Mount Sinai, rabbinic Midrashim are concerned not only with resolving lexical problems but also with filling in the lacunae in the biblical accounts and finding answers to certain questions that are not fully addressed by the text. When was the Torah given, and on what basis were a particular month and day chosen? Why was the Torah given in the wilderness rather than in the land of Israel, and why was Mount Sinai selected among all mountains to be the site of the revelation? What is the relationship between the creation and the revelation? Why was the Torah given only to the people of Israel and not to the other nations of the world? What is the significance of Moses's ascents up the "mountain of God," and what did he do there during his sojourns of forty days and forty nights? In what manner did God transmit the Torah to him, and what did the teachings that he received include? In what sense did God "come down upon Mount Sinai" when he gave the Ten Commandments? How did the people of Israel experience the theophany? What is the significance of the Israelites' acceptance of the Torah?

Midrashim on the Sinai revelation present a variety of responses to these and other questions. Rabbinic representations of the place of the gentile nations in the giving of the Torah are of particular significance for the present analysis, for such representations provide unambiguous testimony to the Torah's role as a constitutive category that serves to circumscribe the ethnic and cultural identity of the Jewish people vis-à-vis other peoples. Our analysis will also be concerned with three trends of speculation regarding the cosmological and epistemological dimensions of the Sinai event: the role of the revelation in recapitulating and establishing the creation; the relationship between heaven and earth in the giving of the Torah; and the Israelites' reception of the theophany.

The first two forms of speculation point to the macrocosmic implications of the revelation at Mount Sinai, which is at times represented as a cosmic event that served to renovate and consolidate the creation and to overcome the boundaries separating heaven and earth. The Torah, which, according to certain Midrashim, had existed in heaven since the beginning as the instrument of creation, is depicted as coming down to earth at the revelation and entering into creation in a new way. The revelation is thus a recapitulation and renewal of creation, in which the Word of God that unfolded in the beginning of creation in order to bring forth the universe once again unfolded at the time of the revelation in order to infuse the universe with new life. A number of Midrashim emphasize that if the Israelites had not accepted the Torah at Mount Sinai, this renewal would not have been brought to fruition and the creation would have reverted to its original state of chaos.

This time of cosmic renovation is represented in a number of Midrashim as involving a transformation in the relationship between heaven and earth in which the boundaries that separate the two realms became permeable, allowing for those below to ascend to those on high and for those on high to descend to those below. Moses's ascent of Mount Sinai is often depicted in this context as an ascent to heaven, which is the abode of the preexistent Torah. Moses went up to the heavens and dwelt among God and the angels, and God and the angels in turn came down to earth and inhabited the realm of mortals. When Moses descended from heaven to earth the Torah descended with him. The descent of the Torah is at times depicted as a marriage ceremony, in which the Torah, personified as the bride, departed from the heavenly abode of her father on high and made her new home on earth with her spouse, Israel. When the Torah descended, the Shekhinah, God's presence, is said to have descended with it, and thus the marriage ceremony is also at times interpreted as taking place between God and his bride, Israel.

In overcoming the disjuncture between heaven and earth, the Sinai revelation joined together God and his chosen people in an everlasting covenant. In accordance with the pentateuchal account, the revelation of the Ten Commandments is portrayed as a theophany, in which God descended upon Mount Sinai and spoke to the Israelites face to face. This cosmic event is represented as having ramifications on the microcosmic as well as the macroscosmic level, transforming each member of the community through a personal, unmediated experience of God's glory (*kāḇôḏ*). The transformative aspects of the experience are represented graphically in accounts of hosts of angels or God himself investing the people of Israel with different types of ornaments, which are variously depicted as including crowns, girdles, a weapon engraved with the ineffable Name, and/or royal purple garments. God is also at times described as bestowing upon the Israelites the splendor (*zîw*) of his glory (*kāḇôḏ*) or of the Shekhinah. According to some accounts, the people of Israel were also granted immunity from death. However, a number of Midrashim emphasize that the gifts attained by the Israelites were conditional, tied to their promise to accept and obey the Torah, and therefore when they went astray after the golden calf their ornaments were stripped away and they lost their exalted status.

Three aspects of the Israelites' reception of the Sinai theophany are frequently emphasized in rabbinic texts. (1) The theophany is represented as a holistic, synesthetic experience, which directly engaged—and at the same time transcended—the senses, involving the faculties of both sight and hearing. The auditory dimensions of the experience are of course central: in the midst of thunder and blasting horns, the Israelites heard the voice(s) of God declaring the Ten Commandments. However, rabbinic accounts tend to give priority to the visual aspects of the experience: in the midst of blazing fire and flashing lightning, the Israelites attained a direct vision of God's glory. In addition, according to some accounts, they saw hosts of angels and supernal chariots, the seven firmaments, and the throne of glory. The people of Israel are also at times described as seeing the divine utterances coming forth from God's mouth as words of fire and subsequently witnessing their transformation from oral-aural utterances to written-visual inscriptions on the tablets. (2) A number of Midrashim emphasize the compelling power of the experience, which was so overwhelming that the Israelites pleaded with Moses to assume the role of God's mouthpiece lest they die. Several traditions insist that the Israelites did indeed die upon hearing God's voice, but they were subsequently revived. (3) Midrashic discussions of the revelation also emphasize the immediacy of the experience, in which the theophany was apprehended by each individual Israelite in accordance with his or her own particular capacity. God is at times described as manifesting multiple faces as well as multiple voices so that each individual felt as though God were looking at and addressing him or her directly. The individualized nature of the experience is often represented as a counterpart of the overwhelming power of the experience: because the Israelites were not capable of withstanding the voice of God in its full power, it became necessary for God to modulate his voice to accord with the capacity of each individual. Thus, while the Israelites' experience of the theophany was direct and immediate, it was at the same time a limited revelation.

The Sinai Revelation and Merkabah Traditions Rabbinic accounts of the Sinai revelation, as a number of scholars have noted, at times allude to Merkabah traditions associated with the prophet Ezekiel's vision in Ezekiel 1. Before turning to an analysis of specific Midrashim on the revelation, we need to consider briefly the possible significance of rabbinic allusions to the Merkabah in connection with the Sinai event. More specifically, we need to raise the issue of whether these Sinai-Merkabah traditions arise primarily out of exegetical concerns linked to Ezekiel 1, or whether they may reflect more esoteric concerns associated with heavenly ascents to the realm of the Merkabah such as those described in apocalyptic texts and Hêk̠ālôt̠ literature. The latter view would be consonant with Scholem's suggestion that there is an essential continuity among apocalyptic ascensions, the Merkabah speculations of the rabbis, and the Hêk̠ālôt̠ materials and that all represent forms of "Merkabah mysticism."[1] However, more recently David Halperin has argued that rabbinic Merkabah traditions and their association with the Sinai revelation arise not out of esoteric "mystical" concerns but rather out of exegetical and homiletical concerns rooted in the synagogue.[2]

Ezekiel 1 begins with the prophet's declaration that "the heavens were opened (*nip̄taḥ*), and I saw (*rā'āh*) visions of God" (Ezek. 1.1) and then gives an elaborate description of four "living creatures" (*ḥayyôt̠*), each with four different faces (human, lion, ox, and eagle) and accompanied by four wheels (*ophanim*). The vision culminates with a human-like manifestation of God, "the likeness of the glory (*kāḇôḏ*) of the Lord" (Ezek. 1.28) seated on his throne (*kissē'*) above the firmament (*rāqî'a*) that is over the heads of the *ḥayyôt̠*. Rabbinic discussions of both aspects of the Sinai revelation—to Moses and to the people of Israel—reflect elements of the Merkabah vision in Ezekiel 1. According to some accounts, when Moses ascended to heaven he encountered hosts of angels, including the *ḥayyôt̠*, and attained a vision of God's glory (*kāḇôḏ*) seated on his throne-chariot. In certain portrayals of the revelation to the Israelites the process is reversed: God, accompanied by hosts of angels and chariots, descended to earth and opened the heavens to the Israelites, granting them a vision of the divine glory. A number of Midrashim suggest that the Israelites' vision was not only comparable to that of Ezekiel but surpassed it. For example, according to one trend of speculation, they saw not one chariot but 22,000, and each was like the Merkabah that Ezekiel saw.

Rabbinic accounts of the revelation also exhibit parallels to the heavenly ascensions and Merkabah visions described in apocalyptic texts and in Hêḵālôṯ literature. A number of apocalyptic texts, such as the Ethiopic Book of Enoch (see especially 1 Enoch 14, which dates from the period before 175 B.C.E.) and the Apocalypse of Abraham (ca. end of 1st or beginning of 2d c. C.E.), describe how their respective heroes ascended to the heavens, where they attained visions of the Merkabah.[3] The Apocalypse of Abraham is of particular interest in that it appears to model Abraham's experience after that of Moses at Mount Sinai.[4] The most elaborate descriptions of heavenly ascents are found in the Hêḵālôṯ texts,[5] which describe the "descender to the Merkabah's"[6] journey through the heavens and through the seven palaces (*hêḵālôṯ*) of the highest heaven, where he attains a vision of the Merkabah and its attendant beings. Rabbinic descriptions of Moses's ascent are reminiscent in a number of ways of the heavenly ascents portrayed in Hêḵālôṯ texts. In particular, rabbinic discussions of Moses's struggles with hostile angels recall the frequent descriptions in Hêḵālôṯ texts of the dangers involved in the "descender to the Merkabah's" journey through the heavens, where he encounters inimical angels and other fiery celestial beings.

Ira Chernus, on the basis of his analysis of Midrashim attributed to second-century Tannaim and third-century Amoraim, has suggested that rabbinic accounts of the Israelites' collective experience at Mount Sinai also contain a number of significant parallels to descriptions of the "descent to the Merkabah" found in Hêḵālôṯ texts, "with the important exception that the Merkabah and its attendant environment had descended to the people at Sinai."[7] For example, the images of fire and lightning in rabbinic descriptions of the revelation, although building upon the imagery in Exodus 19 and 20, at the same time recall the frequent use of fire and lightning imagery in Hêḵālôṯ literature.[8] Chernus also suggests that the various ornaments with which the Israelites are said to have been invested exhibit close parallels with certain Hêḵālôṯ traditions. The crowns that the Israelites received recall the prevalent crown imagery in Hêḵālôṯ texts: the crowns of the angels, the crown of God himself, and more specifically the crowns that the "descenders to the Merkabah" receive in association with the study of Torah.[9] The royal purple garments with which the Israelites were clothed resonate with Hêk̲ālôt̲ traditions concerning the special garments associated with certain angels and the garment (*ḥālûq*) worn by God himself.[10] Chernus also suggests a possible connection between the weapon engraved with the ineffable Name that the Israelites received and the "descender to the Merkabah's" theurgic use of the names of God to protect him in his ascents from hostile angels.[11] Finally, Chernus argues that rabbinic traditions concerning the death and subsequent resurrection of the Israelites at Sinai form part of an "initiatory death schema" that represents a synthesis of exoteric traditions concerning the resurrection of the dead and esoteric traditions concerning the dangers inherent in the "descent to the Merkabah."[12]

Chernus suggests two possible explanations for the parallels between rabbinic portrayals of the Israelites' experience of the revelation and Hêk̲ālôt̲ traditions concerning the "descent to the Merkabah": rabbinic traditions concerning the Sinai theophany were consciously modeled on the ecstatic experiences of the "descenders to the Merkabah," or, conversely, the Sinai traditions originated independently and were later appropriated by the exponents of Hêk̲ālôt̲ traditions as an interpretive framework for their own experiences.[13] While Chernus concedes that the direct influence of Hêk̲ālôt̲ traditions on Tannaitic accounts is open to debate, he argues that by the late third century certain Palestinian Amoraim, in particular the school of R. Joḥanan, "knew some form of Merkabah mysticism and consciously shaped their midrashim on Sinai in its light." He concludes:

> Reviewing both the tannaitic and amoraic midrashim . . . we find a number of plausible models for reconstructing the process of historical development. It may be that Merkabah mysticism was developed within the rabbinic academies, with the midrash on Sinai being developed concurrently in those same academies; this would be the simplest explanation for the many parallels which we have found. Or it may be that Merkabah mysticism was developed outside the leading rabbinic circles in the first or early second centuries, with R. Akiba and his followers responding to it by creating new traditions about *matan Torah*. Perhaps alternatively, Merkabah mysticism was not developed until the third century, outside the academies, its imagery consciously reflecting the existing midrashic depiction of revelation; in this case the third-century amoraim would be the

ones who responded to the new creation by new midrashic creation of their own concerning Sinai.[14]

Chernus's discussion brings to light three key issues concerning the Hêḵālôṯ texts that have been a source of debate among scholars: (1) the origin and dates of the texts; (2) their relationship to rabbinic traditions concerning *ma'ăśēh merkāḇāh*; and (3) the central purpose of the Hêḵālôṯ speculations. Chernus's analysis follows the views of Scholem and Ithamar Gruenwald concerning these three issues: (1) some of the material in Hêḵālôṯ texts may derive from the Tannaitic or early Amoraic period;[15] (2) the Hêḵālôṯ material is intimately connected to the rabbinic *ma'ăśēh merkāḇāh* and serves to illuminate many otherwise obscure passages in rabbinic texts;[16] and (3) Hêḵālôṯ speculations are primarily concerned with the heavenly ascent and with delineating the ecstatic mystical practices by means of which the "descent to the Merkabah" is successfully achieved. In this context, the subgenre of Hêḵālôṯ literature termed *Śar Tôrāh*, "Prince of Torah," which contains adjurations aimed at gaining effortless mastery of the Torah, is relegated to a secondary status as a later, degenerate stage in which, in Scholem's words, "the ecstatic ascent had already lost much of its freshness and had been superseded by a greater stress on the magical elements."[17]

Since the publication of Peter Schäfer's *Synopse zur Hekhalot-Literatur* in 1981,[18] which has made some of the most important Hêḵālôṯ manuscripts accessible to scholars, a number of scholars have begun to question the basic postulates of Hêḵālôṯ research established by Scholem and his followers. In particular, the postulate that the primary focus of Hêḵālôṯ texts is the heavenly ascent has been called into question. Schäfer himself emphasizes the importance of a second category of materials in the Hêḵālôṯ texts, originally independent of the materials regarding the heavenly ascent, that is concerned with the adjuration of angels. In opposition to Scholem, he argues that theurgic adjuration, which is aimed primarily at the acquisition of knowledge of Torah, constitutes the center, and not the periphery, of Hêḵālôṯ literature: "It is not the heavenly journey which is the centre of this [Merkabah] mysticism, with adjuration on the edge, but rather the reverse. Magical adjuration is a thread woven throughout the entire Hekhalot literature."[19] Halperin has argued that these two categories of Hêḵālôṯ materials—those concerning the heavenly ascent and those concerning the adjuration of angels that predominate in the *Śar Tôrāh*—are closely intertwined both in language and content. Moreover, he maintains that the Hêḵālôṯ texts did not originate among esoteric circles of mystics but rather among the general populace, in particular the *'am hā-'āreṣ* (literally, "people of the land"). Excluded from the academies of the rabbinic elite, they sought to acquire knowledge of Torah, and the status and power that such knowledge confers, through other means: through "descending to the Merkabah" and through the magical techniques of *Śar Tôrāh*.[20]

Halperin further suggests that the authors of the Hêḵālôṯ texts took their inspirations from rabbinic traditions. While some of the Hêḵālôṯ materials may derive from late Amoraic Babylonia,[21] certain aspects of these traditions appear to be modeled after the synagogue traditions concerning the Sinai revelation that were developed in Palestine between the second and fourth centuries C.E.[22] Halperin argues, contrary to Chernus, that the links between the Sinai revelation and the Merkabah vision of Ezekiel were forged not as part of an esoteric "mystical" tradition but rather as part of an exegetical-homiletical tradition centered around Shavuot, the annual festival that celebrates the Sinai revelation.[23] The synagogue practice of reading together on Shavuot the Exodus account of revelation (Exod. 19.1ff) and Ezekiel 1, as the Torah reading and prophetic lection (*hap̄ṭārāh*), respectively, expressed and institutionalized the rabbis' perception that the Sinai event and the Merkabah vision are intimately connected.[24] Halperin suggests that the key biblical passage used by the rabbis to link Ezekiel's Merkabah vision with the Sinai revelation, as well as to establish that Moses's ascent was an ascent to heaven, is Psalm 68.18–19.[25]

> The chariots (*reḵeḇ*) of God are twice ten thousand,
> thousands upon thousands;
> the Lord is among them, Sinai in holiness.
> You ascended (*'ālāh*) on high, you took a captivity captive,
> you took gifts for humanity.

The synagogue preachers in their Shavuot homilies thus interpreted the revelation at Mount Sinai (Exod. 19.1ff) in light of the Merkabah vision of Ezekiel (Ezek. 1), with images of thousands of chariots descending to earth (Ps. 68.18) and Moses ascending to heaven (Ps. 68.19). The purpose of these homilies, Halperin suggests, was to inspire and comfort the Jewish people by recreating the immense power and grandeur of the Sinai theophany so that they could "see" with the "eyes of the heart" that which their forefathers had "seen" with the "eyes of the flesh."

> The heavens open; the hidden wonders are seen; the *merkabah* comes down, perhaps in thousands. Moses ascends on high, takes a captivity captive, brings gifts for humanity. Fire and angels are everywhere, perhaps benign, perhaps hostile. God gives Israel his Torah, and endorses it with his glory. The prophet Ezekiel sees the glory mirrored in the *merkabah.* All Israel sees it, too, at Sinai. And all Israel sees it now, in the synagogue, when the *merkabah* is read and preached. *You see it too.* This is perhaps the central message that underlies the complex and interwoven themes. *Haggadat Shema' Yiśra'el* puts it well: "You too saw, with the understanding of your heart and your mind and your soul, how [God] . . . descended in his glory on Mount Sinai. Therefore, Israel, holy nation all, you must hear and understand and know that *the Lord is our God,* by whose name we are called, in unity; *the Lord is one.*" In this, we hear the most powerful message that the synagogue *merkabah* tradition spoke to the Jewish people.[26]

Halperin elaborates on the paradigmatic power of the Shavuot homilies.

> What advantages did the expositors gain from reading Exodus 19 and Ezekiel 1 as two segments of the same context? First, Ezekiel's vivid description of the *merkabah* gave people a starting point for visualizing, "with the eyes of the heart," the full glory of the Sinai revelation. . . . This taught them the splendor and power of the authority that stood behind the Torah. Second, the stories of Moses' struggle with the angels over the Torah (which found their way into the Shabu'ot homilies through Psalm 68.19) taught them how precious the Torah was, and how precious they were to God that he chose them to receive it. All of this served to dramatize and strengthen the Jews' faith, particularly against the challenge of aggressive Christianity.[27]

Halperin further argues that it is the synagogue tradition of coupling the Merkabah and Sinai that lies behind the stories in the Tosefta and two Talmuds of R. Joḥanan b. Zakkai and his disciples expounding *ma'ăśēh merkāḇāh,* in which the miraculous events associated with their expositions replicate the wonders of the Sinai revelation.[28] Finally, Halperin maintains that it was the Shavuot homilies concerning Moses's ascent to heaven, where he struggled with the angels to obtain the Torah, that inspired certain members of the Jewish populace to develop their own methods of heavenly ascent and magical techniques in order to replicate Moses's feat and attain mastery of Torah. The development of the Hêḵālôṯ traditions was thus a direct response to, and extension of, the Sinai-Merkabah traditions expounded in the synagogue.[29]

It is significant that although the analyses of Chernus and Halperin are based on divergent assumptions concerning the origin and nature of rabbinic Merkabah speculations, their arguments converge on two main points: Merkabah traditions have a central place in rabbinic expositions of the Sinai revelation; and the Sinai event served as a legitimating paradigm for the heavenly ascents and Merkabah visions described in the Hêḵālôṯ texts. Whether we view the Hêḵālôṯ materials as reflective of a genuine quest for "mystical" experience through ecstatic practices (Scholem, Gruenwald, Chernus), or as dominated by more worldly ends such as the status and power that mastery of the Torah confers (Halperin, Schäfer), it appears that the authors of the Hêḵālôṯ texts drew their inspiration from rabbinic accounts of the giving of the Torah at Sinai. However, it also appears that the lines of influence might extend in both directions. In later rabbinic texts such as P^{e}sîqtā' Rabbāṯî and Pirqê d^{e}-R. Eliezer, as will be discussed below, we find evidence that the language and imagery of Hêḵālôṯ texts may have influenced certain descriptions of the Sinai event.

In our analysis of Sinai Midrashim in the various layers of rabbinic texts, we shall find the resonances of Merkabah traditions expressed in a variety of ways: in images of fire and celestial wonders unfolding, in accounts of Moses's ascent to the heavens and struggles with the angels over the Torah, in descriptions of hosts of angels and chariots descending with God to Sinai, in portrayals of Moses and the Israelites as visionaries whose vision of God at Sinai surpassed the experiences of Ezekiel and the other prophets. The connections between the Merkabah and Sinai may have been elaborated in the context of Shavuot homilies in Palestinian synagogues, but the affinities with the ascension traditions of apocalyptic and Hêḵālôṯ texts are also of significance in illuminating the streams of influence that flowed into and out of the synagogue traditions. In addition to the general parallels between the Sinai Midrashim and Hêḵālôṯ materials discussed above, relevant parallels to specific Hêḵālôṯ traditions will be mentioned in the notes.

Mishnah

The Mishnah contains a number of passages that recognize the central importance of the Sinai event, but it does not elaborate on the phenomenology of the revelation. As discussed in chapter 2, tractate 'Āḇôṯ begins with an enumeration of the line of transmission that stems from Mount Sinai—from Moses to Joshua to the elders to the prophets to the members of the Great Assembly to the *zûḡôṯ* to the Tannaim—and thereby implicitly grants the Tannaitic teachings contained in the Mishnah a special status as part of the Torah received by Moses at Mount Sinai.[30]

Another key passage in the Mishnah is Sanheḏrîn X.1, which includes *tôrāh min ha-šāmayim*, "the Torah is from heaven," as one of the few rabbinic dogmas that must be adhered to in order to have a share in the world to come. The meaning of this dogma is not elaborated on in this passage. In later rabbinic texts, as we shall see, the expression "the Torah is from heaven" is at times understood metaphorically to mean that the Torah derives from God, while in other contexts it is interpreted cosmologically to mean that at the time of the revelation the Torah descended from its heavenly abode onto earth.

The marriage metaphor is alluded to in Ta'ănîṯ IV.8, which interprets "the day of his wedding" in Song of Songs 3.11 as referring to the giving of the Torah, without expanding on the significance of this image. This verse is similarly interpreted in later rabbinic sources.[31]

Tannaitic Midrashim

The most extensive discussions in Tannaitic Midrashim of *mattan tôrāh* are found in those sections that provide exegeses of key passages in the Pentateuch that pertain to the Sinai revelation: the Mᵉḵîltā' dᵉ-R. Ishmael's commentary on the account of the revelation in chapters 19 and 20 of Exodus, and Sip̄rê on Deuteronomy's commentary on Deuteronomy 33.2–4.[32] Other speculations are interspersed throughout the texts.

With respect to the contents of the revelation, by the period of the Tannaitic Midrashim, as discussed in chapter 2, the concept of Torah had been extended to include not only the Hebrew Bible but also the Mishnah, Talmud, and halakhah and aggadah generally.[33] A tradition in Sip̄rā' maintains that the Torah that Moses received included all "its laws (*halakhot*), its subtle distinctions (*diqdûqîm*), and its interpretations (*pêrûšîm*)."[34] Sip̄rā' and Sip̄rê on Deuteronomy also contain seminal formulations of the rabbinic doctrine that two Torahs, one written (*bi-k̲t̲āb̲*) and the other oral (*b*ᵉ*-'al peh*), were given to Israel at Mount Sinai.[35]

Torah and the Nations Underlying many of the discussions of the Sinai revelation in Tannaitic Midrashim is a clear polemic against gentile nations. A number of Midrashim emphasize that it is the revelation of the Torah that distinguishes the people of Israel and makes them the greatest and most beautiful among nations.[36] An anonymous tradition in Sip̄rā' declares that Israel would in no way be different from other nations if it were not for the Torah.[37] Although the gentile nations covet the Torah, it is the heritage of Israel alone.[38]

Two different types of explanations are given in Tannaitic Midrashim concerning why God did not give the Torah to the gentiles. According to one explanation in Sip̄rê on Deuteronomy, before God gave the Torah he scrutinized all the nations and determined that Israel alone was worthy to receive the Torah.[39] According to a second explanation found in the Mᵉk̲îltā' as well as in Sip̄rê on Deuteronomy, God did indeed offer the Torah to all the nations of the world, but in the end none except Israel would accept it. Deuteronomy 33.2, "The Lord came from Sinai, and dawned from Seir upon them; He shone forth from Mount Paran," is interpreted to mean that God offered the Torah to the children of Esau, the Ammonites, the Moabites, and the Ishmaelites, but each in turn refused to undertake the observance of its commandments. The gentile nations' lack of acceptance of the Torah is understood as simply one more reflection of their inherent unworthiness: if they could not even uphold the seven commandments that God enjoined on all humankind in the covenant with Noah, how much less could they be expected to fulfill all the commandments of the Torah. The Israelites, on the other hand, agreed to obey the commandments even before they heard them, declaring, "All that the Lord has spoken we will do and we will hear" (Exod. 24.7). Therefore the Lord chose Israel because Israel alone chose the Lord and his Torah.[40]

An anonymous Midrash in the Mᵉk̲îltā' uses the notion that the Torah was offered to all nations to explain why the Torah was given in the wilderness and not in the land of Israel.

> The Torah was given publicly and openly, in a place owned by no one. For if the Torah had been given in the land of

> Israel, they [the Israelites] could have said to the nations of the world, "You have no portion in it." But since it was given in the wilderness, publicly and openly, in a place owned by no one, everyone desiring to accept it could come and accept it.[41]

The Mekîltā' emphasizes that because the Torah was given publicly and openly, in the wilderness and in broad daylight, the nations of the world have no excuse for not accepting it.[42] Lest certain nations should use the excuse that they could not understand the Torah because it was not given in their language, an anonymous tradition in Sip̄rê on Deuteronomy points out that God revealed the Torah in four languages: Hebrew, Roman, Arabic, and Aramaic.[43] As we shall see, this tradition is elaborated in later rabbinic texts in terms of the notion that God revealed the Torah in seventy different languages so that each nation could understand in its own vernacular.[44]

The Torah is from Heaven The revelation of the Torah is associated with heaven in a number of Midrashim. An anonymous tradition in Sip̄rê on Deuteronomy simply asserts that "the Torah was given from heaven," although the significance of this statement is not elaborated.[45] Another Midrash in Sip̄rê on Deuteronomy, attributed to the sages, understands Moses's ascent of Mount Sinai to be an ascent to heaven, where he encountered the dangers of the fiery angelic hosts: "I went among the angels, I went among the *ḥayyôṯ*, I went among the seraphim, each one of which could burn up the entire world with its inhabitants."[46]

The notion that Moses ascended to heaven represents one trend of speculation that is more fully developed in later rabbinic texts. However, it is clear that this view was not accepted by all of the rabbinic sages, as indicated in a comment in the Mekîltā' ascribed to R. Jose.

> R. Jose says: Behold, it says, "The heavens are the heavens of the Lord, and the earth He has given to human beings" (Ps. 115.16). Neither Moses or Elijah ever ascended (*'ālāh*) to heaven, nor did the glory (*kāḇôḏ*) ever descend (*yāraḏ*) below.[47]

The debate of the rabbis thus concerned not only whether or not Moses ascended to heaven at the time of revelation but also whether or not God himself descended from heaven onto earth. A passage in the M^e^k̲îltā' notes a contradiction between two verses in the book of Exodus that pertain to the revelation: Exodus 20.22, "You yourselves have seen that I have spoken with you from heaven"; and Exodus 19.20, "And the Lord came down (*yāraḏ*) upon Mount Sinai." One resolution of the problem is attributed to R. Jose's teacher, R. Akiba:

> R. Akiba says: This teaches that the Holy One, blessed be He, bent down the upper heavens onto the top of the mountain and spoke with them from heaven. And thus it says, "He bowed the heavens and came down (*yāraḏ*), and thick darkness was under His feet" (Ps. 18.10).[48]

An anonymous Midrash in the Mᵉk̲îltā' makes use of a similar image, emphasizing how when God's glory (*kāḇôḏ*) descended, he bent down the lower heavens and upper heavens onto the top of the mountain and used them as a cushion that served to separate him from direct contact with the earthly mountain.[49]

Although R. Jose, as mentioned above, is represented in the Mᵉk̲îltā' as disagreeing with his master R. Akiba by maintaining that God did not descend to earth, in another passage he is ascribed the view that God nevertheless did come forth to meet Israel, although the way in which he came forth is not explained. The passage invokes the metaphor of marriage, interpreting Deuteronomy 33.2, "The Lord came from Sinai," to mean that God came "to receive Israel as a bridegroom (*ḥāṯān*) goes forth to meet the bride (*kallāh*)."[50] While in this version of the marriage symbolism Israel is the bride who is wed to her bridegroom, God, an anonymous Midrash in Sip̄rê on Deuteronomy gives an alternative interpretation in which the Torah assumes the role of the bride who is betrothed (*mᵉ'ôrāśāh*) to her bridegroom, Israel, and thus has the status of a married woman in relation to the gentile nations. The revelation is not mentioned in this context.[51]

The Israelites' Reception of the Theophany Tannaitic Midrashim explore various dimensions of the Sinai theophany in which God appeared before all of Israel and declared the Ten Commandments. One anonymous Midrash in Sip̄rê on Deuteronomy §343 includes the Sinai event as one of the four theophanies in the sacred history of Israel in which God "shone forth" (*hôp̄î'a*).[52] Another anonymous Midrash maintains that he revealed himself (*niḡlāh*) not from just one direction but from all four directions.[53] Moreover, his voice (*qôl*) is said to have gone forth from one end of the earth to the other.[54] Several passages in the Mᵉḵîltā', commenting and expanding upon the language and imagery of the pentateuchal account, describe the theophany as accompanied by thunders upon thunders, lightnings upon lightnings, and earthquakes.[55]

(1) They Heard and Saw

The discussions of the theophany in Sip̄rê on Deuteronomy and the Mᵉḵîltā' point to the holistic, synesthetic nature of the revelation experience, which involved both auditory and visual phenomena. On the one hand, the Israelites heard God's voice proclaiming the Ten Commandments, which was accompanied by the sound of thunder and horns blasting. On the other hand, they attained a direct vision of God himself, which was accompanied by lightning flashes and blazing fire. A passage in the Mᵉḵîltā' presents the dual nature of God's manifestation as a direct response to the request of the Israelites. According to a tradition ascribed to R. Judah ha-Nasi, the Israelites said to Moses, "Our desire is to hear (*šāmaʻ*) [directly] from the mouth of our King. Hearing from the mouth of an attendant is not the same as hearing from the mouth of the King." According to another interpretation, simply hearing God speak was not sufficient for the Israelites. Thus, they said to Moses, "Our desire is to see (*rā'āh*) our King. For hearing is not comparable to seeing." God fulfilled both of their requests.[56]

Priority is given to seeing over hearing in another tradition in the Mᵉḵîltā' ascribed to R. Nathan, who emphasizes that it is the act of seeing that distinguished the Israelites' experience of the revelation from that of the gentile nations. While the gentiles were allowed to hear God's voice, they were not given the ability to see, which was granted to Israel alone.

> R. Nathan says: "You yourselves have seen (*rā'āh*) [that I have spoken with you from heaven]" (Exod. 20.22). Why is this said? Since it says, "All the kings of the earth shall praise Thee, O Lord, for they have heard (*šāmaʻ*) the words of Thy mouth" (Ps. 138.4), one might suppose that just as they heard (*šāmaʻ*), so they also saw (*rā'āh*). Therefore scripture teaches, "You yourselves have seen"—but the nations of the world have not seen.[57]

An anonymous tradition in the Mᵉḵîltā' similarly emphasizes the visionary aspects of the Israelites' experience, which surpassed that of the greatest prophets: "They saw (*rā'āh*) at that time what Isaiah and Ezekiel did not see, as it is said, 'Through the prophets I liken myself' (Hos. 12.11)." This comment implies not only that the people of Israel saw more than the Merkabah mysteries seen by Ezekiel but also that their visions were clearer and more direct, for God only "likened himself" to the prophets.[58]

A number of Midrashim focus on the phenomenology of the divine utterances, which engaged both the auditory and visual channels. An anonymous tradition in the Mᵉḵîltā' emphasizes the distinctive feature of God's speech that set it apart from ordinary human speech: God first said the Ten Commandments in one utterance, after which he said each commandment separately.[59] Several Midrashim point to the transformation of the divine utterances from an oral-aural to a written-visual medium in which the Ten Commandments became inscribed on the tablets. An anonymous Midrash in Sip̄rê on Deuteronomy, in commenting on Deuteronomy 33.2, "At His right hand was a fiery law for them," maintains that each utterance (*dibbûr*) that went forth from the mouth of God circumambulated the camp of Israel, after which it was received by the right hand of God and engraved on the tablet. The Midrash concludes: "And his voice (*qôl*) would go forth from one end of the world to the other, as it is said, 'The voice (*qôl*) of the Lord hews out flames of fire' (Ps. 29.7)."[60] The synesthetic imagery of Psalm 29.7 is interpreted in a Midrash in the Mᵉḵîltā', attributed to R. Akiba, as referring not only to the transformation of God's words from spoken (auditory) utterances to written (visual) engravings but to the very nature of the divine words, which were simultaneously heard and seen as words of fire. The Israelites not only saw that which was visible and heard that which was audible, "they saw (*rā'āh*) and heard (*šāma'*) that which was visible." Exodus 20.18, "And all the people saw (*rā'āh*) the voices (*qôlōṯ*)," is interpreted to mean that the people of Israel "saw (*rā'āh*) the word of fire (*dāḇār šel 'ēš*) coming forth from the mouth of the Dynamis (Gᵉḇûrāh) and being hewn onto the tablets, as it is said, 'The voice (*qôl*) of the Lord hews out flames of fire (*lahăḇôṯ 'ēš*)' (Ps. 29.7)."[61]

The notion that the Israelites saw the divine utterances is given a more pragmatic interpretation in an anonymous Midrash in Sip̄rê on Deuteronomy, which links the act of seeing not to esoteric words of fire but to the exoteric content of the commandments. The Israelites' apprehension of the divine utterances is described as a twofold movement in which they saw (*rā'āh*) each utterance (*dîbbēr*) and subsequently understood (*yāḏa'*) the legal ramifications of the commandment.[62] The hermeneutical dimension of the Israelites' experience is also emphasized in a comment in the Meḵîltā' attributed to R. Judah ha-Nasi, who remarks that as soon as they heard (*šāma'*) the divine utterance (*dîbbûr*) they immediately interpreted (*pêrēš*) it.[63]

The Midrash attributed to R. Akiba suggests a connection between the revelation of the Torah and fire that is frequently emphasized in Tannaitic Midrashim.[64] According to a tradition ascribed to R. Akiba's student R. Judah b. Il'ai, the people of Israel were scorched by the heat of the fire that blazed forth from the heavens.[65] Not only is the setting of the revelation described in images of fire, but the Torah itself is directly identified in one Midrash with fire.[66] Several Midrashim identify the Torah more specifically with the "fiery law" (*'ēš-dāṯ*) at God's right hand in Deuteronomy 33.2.[67]

(2) They Feared Lest They Die

A number of Midrashim point to the overpowering nature of the experience of revelation. An anonymous tradition in the Meḵîltā', which also appears in abbreviated form in Sip̄rê on Deuteronomy, emphasizes that the earth trembled so violently at the resounding forth of God's voice that the gentile nations feared that he was about to destroy the world.[68] The Israelites themselves were also terrified by the experience. Commenting on Exodus 20.18, "The people were afraid and trembled, and they stood afar off," an anonymous Midrash in the Meḵîltā' suggests that the people of Israel were so frightened that at hearing each of the Ten Commandments they moved backward twelve miles and then again moved forward twelve miles, traveling a total of 240 miles (10 × 24 = 240) on the day of the revelation. God sent the ministering angels down to lead the Israelites as they retreated and returned each time.[69] Another anonymous Midrash, commenting on Exodus 20.19, "And [the Israelites] said to Moses, 'You speak to us and we will hear, but let not God speak to us lest we die,'" interprets the Israelites' request to mean that "they did not have the strength (*kōaḥ*) to receive more than the Ten Commandments, as it is said, 'If we hear the voice of the Lord our God any more, we shall die' (Deut. 5.25)."[70] Moses responded to their request by becoming the covenant mediator for the rest of the revelation.

(3) Each According to His or Her Capacity

Despite the overpowering nature of this cosmic event that caused even the earth itself to tremble, the revelation of the Ten Commandments is also at times depicted as an immediate, intimate experience that was apprehended by each Israelite in accordance with his or her individual capacity. An anonymous Midrash in the Mekīltā' notes the plural forms in Exodus 20.18, "And all the people saw the voices (*qôlōṯ*) and the lightnings (*lappîḏim*)," which it interprets in light of Psalm 29.4, "The voice (*qôl*) of the Lord is according to power (*ba-kōaḥ*)," to mean that the divine utterances were heard by each Israelite according to his or her individual capacity (*kōaḥ*).[71]

Classical Amoraic Midrashim

There is no exegetical Midrash on the book of Exodus among the classical Amoraic Midrashim, and therefore we do not find any sustained commentary on the Exodus account of the revelation of the Torah. The most extensive discussion of the revelation is found in *pisqā'* 12 of Pesîqtā' de-R. Kahana, which is a homiletical discourse based on the first verse of the pentateuchal reading (Exod. 19.1–20.16) for Shavuot: "In the third month after the people of Israel had gone forth out of the land of Egypt, on that day they came into the wilderness of Sinai" (Exod. 19.1). In the context of interpreting the opening clause of the base verse, "in the third month," the *pisqā'* offers a variety of explanations of why there was a three-month delay between the Exodus from Egypt and the revelation at Mount Sinai. It also incorporates a number of aggadic traditions concerning the nature of the theophany at Sinai.[72] With respect to the other classical Amoraic Midrashim, Song of Songs Rabbāh evidences the most concern with the phenomenology of the revelation. It contains a substantial number of Midrashim that interpret verses from the Song of Songs as referring to the Sinai event. Aggadot concerning the revelation are interjected in various exegetical contexts in the other Midrashic collections as well.

In discussing the nature of the revelation at Mount Sinai, certain Midrashim focus on the collective experience of the Israelites, who heard directly from God's mouth the Ten Commandments—or, according to an alternative tradition, the first two of the Ten Commandments.[73] Other Midrashim are concerned primarily with the experience of Moses, who was singled out to be God's mouthpiece in mediating the rest of the Torah to the people of Israel. With respect to the Torah that Moses received, by the period of the classical Amoraic Midrashim, as discussed in chapter 2, the doctrine of the two Torahs, the Written Torah (*tôrāh še bi-ḵṯāḇ*) and the Oral Torah (*tôrāh še be-'al peh*), had become firmly established. Thus, two Torahs are said to have been given to Moses at Mount Sinai, one written and the other oral.[74] In a Midrash in Leviticus Rabbāh attributed to R. Joshua b. Levi, the Torah received by Moses is represented as an open-ended category that included the teachings of all subsequent generations of sages and their disciples: "Bible, Mishnah, Talmud, Tosefta, Haggadah, and even that which a conscientious disciple would in the future say in front of his master—all were communicated to Moses at Sinai."[75]

Torah and the Nations Many of the discussions of the Sinai revelation in classical Amoraic Midrashim reflect the vigorous polemic against gentile nations that is characteristic of this period when the persecutions of the Jews in Palestine had intensified under the Christianized Roman Empire.[76] A number of Midrashim boldly emphasize the special status of the people of Israel, who have been singled out by God among all the nations of the world as his chosen people. According to an anonymous Midrash in Song of Songs Rabbāh, Israel is the one "whom the Holy One, blessed be He, loved more than the seventy nations."[77] A Midrash in Ruth Rabbāh attributed to R. Simeon b. Yoḥai notes that it is only with the people of Israel that God has associated his name: "I am not called the God of all the nations but the God of Israel."[78]

In their enumerations of God's saving acts on behalf of his chosen people,[79] classical Amoraic Midrashim generally emphasize the pivotal role of the revelation of the Torah as the primary determinant of Israel's special status among the nations. For while other nations may have wisdom (*ḥoḵmāh*), they do not have the Torah.[80] According to a tradition attributed to R. Judah b. Simon in the name of R. Joshua b. Levi, which appears in both P^{e}sîqtā' d^{e}-R. Kahana and Ruth Rabbāh, prior to the Sinai revelation Israel had a name like that of the other nations, and it was only after they accepted the Torah that God deemed them "My people."[81] A tradition in Ruth Rabbāh goes so far as to suggest that if the people of Israel had not accepted the Torah, they would have disappeared from among the nations.[82]

A number of passages emphasize that all the nations of the world were given the opportunity to accept the Torah. As in Tannaitic Midrashim, Deuteronomy 33.2 is interpreted in a Midrash in Lamentations Rabbāh, attributed to R. Levi through his tradent R. Joshua of Siknin, to mean that God first offered the Torah to all the nations of the world, including the children of Esau (Seir) and the children of Ishmael (Paran), but each in turn refused to accept it.

Finally, when he appeared before the people of Israel with the "fiery law" in his right hand, they alone accepted it.[83] Several Midrashim maintain that God foresaw that the gentile nations would reject the Torah. Two different reasons are given for why he nevertheless went ahead and offered the Torah to them. First, according to a tradition ascribed to R. Abbahu, he did not want to give the nations cause to reproach him.[84] Second, according to a tradition attributed to R. Simon b. Pazzi, he wanted to double Israel's reward for accepting it.[85]

Classical Amoraic Midrashim enumerate a variety of rewards for the people of Israel for accepting the Torah and corresponding punishments for the gentile nations for rejecting it. A tradition ascribed to the rabbis in Leviticus Rabbāh invokes Isaiah 60.2 to establish that while the gentile nations, who rejected the Torah, are covered in "thick darkness," the people of Israel, who alone accepted the Torah, are illumined with the light of God's glory: "But upon you the Lord will shine, and His glory shall be seen upon you."[86] A homily in P^{e}sîqtā' d^{e}-R. Kahana emphasizes that the ultimate redemption of Israel and condemnation of the gentiles will come on the Day of Judgment in the time to come when God will judge all peoples according to whether or not they have occupied themselves with the Sefer Torah.[87] The only hope for the salvation of the gentiles, who did not accept the Torah at the time of revelation, is to repent, become proselytes, and follow the way of Torah.[88]

Revelation and Creation In accordance with the increased emphasis on cosmogonic themes in classical Amoraic Midrashim, we find a new trend of speculation that connects the process of revelation to that of creation, with the Torah providing the link between the two processes. In this context the people of Israel's acceptance of the Torah at Sinai is represented as necessary not only for their own preservation and salvation but also for the preservation of the entire creation.

A Midrash in Leviticus Rabbāh, attributed to R. Judah b. Simon through his tradent R. Azariah, suggests that after twenty-six generations God scrutinized his world and, finding it full of sinners, decided to destroy it. But then he noticed Israel, a single rose amidst the thorns, and when he heard them say at Sinai, "We will do and we will hear" (Exod. 24.7), he was comforted and decided to preserve the world. The world was thus saved for the sake of that for which it had been originally created: the Torah.[89] An aggadah in Song of Songs Rabbāh ascribed to R. Huna b. Abin in the name of his teacher R. Aḥa, which appears in abbreviated form in Genesis Rabbāh and Ruth Rabbāh, similarly maintains that if Israel had not accepted the Torah at Mount Sinai, God would have caused the world to revert to formlessness and emptiness (*tōhû wā-ḇōhû*).[90] Psalm 75.4, "When the earth and all its inhabitants are dissolved, it is I (*'ānōḵî*) who establish its pillars," is interpreted to mean that the world would have been dissolved, but when Israel accepted the first of the Ten Commandments, "I (*'ānōḵî*) am the Lord your God" (Exod. 20.2), on account of that "I" (*'ānōḵî*) the world was established on a firm basis.[91]

A Midrash in Song of Songs Rabbāh attributed to R. Yannai establishes an even more intimate link between the revelation and creation: as a reward for Israel's saying, "All that the Lord has spoken we will do and we will hear" (Exod. 24.7), God not only preserved the creation from destruction, he also revealed to Israel the very beginnings of the process of creation as it unfolded in the first six days.[92] A Midrash in Genesis Rabbāh, attributed to R. Berekhiah and R. Jacob b. Abina in the name of R. Abba b. Kahana, establishes a direct correlation between the process of creation and the process of revelation and suggests that each event sheds light upon the other. Thus, just as at the time of the revelation fire divided the upper and the lower realms, so it was too at the time of creation.[93] Another tradition in Genesis Rabbāh, ascribed through tradents to R. Simon b. Pazzi, emphasizes that the Torah was given in the same holy language (*lešôn ha-qôḏeš*) with which the world was created.[94] An aggadah attributed to R. Joḥanan, which appears in both Leviticus Rabbāh and Pesîqtā' de-R. Kahana, suggests that the Torah that was revealed at Mount Sinai may be even more precious than the material world that was brought forth at creation, for whereas it only took six days to create the world, it took forty days and forty nights to reveal the Torah.[95]

Ascent of Moses and Descent of the Torah In classical Amoraic Midrashim we find an increasing cosmologization of the notion that the Torah was given from heaven. Several Midrashim simply take for granted that the Torah was given from heaven, without elaborating on the notion.[96] However, a number of Midrashim depict the revelation of the Torah as a cosmic event in which the separation between heaven and earth was temporarily overcome: Moses ascended to heaven to receive the Torah, God descended from heaven to Mount Sinai to reveal the Ten Commandments, and the Torah itself descended from heaven to make its abode on earth with the people of Israel. A tradition in P^{e}sîqtā’ d^{e}-R. Kahana ascribed to R. Bebai says concerning the Sinai revelation: “The most desirable thing on high was given from heaven to Moses under heaven. And what was that? The Torah.”[97] Mount Sinai, according to a tradition in Song of Songs Rabbāh, was itself uprooted and set in the heights of heaven, becoming a representation of the cosmic mountain that stands at the juncture between heaven and earth.[98]

Moses’s ascent of Mount Sinai is portrayed in a number of Midrashim as an ascent to heaven, where God spoke with him and revealed to him the wonders of the fiery firmament.[99] A Midrash in Ruth Rabbāh attributed to R. Menaḥem b. Abin interprets Psalm 68.19, “You ascended (*‘ālāh*) on high, you took a captivity captive,” as referring to Moses, who “ascended (*‘ālāh*) on high and took the Torah captive.”[100] A tradition in Leviticus Rabbāh and P^{e}sîqtā’ d^{e}-R. Kahana, ascribed to R. Levi through his tradent R. Joshua of Siknin, suggests that because Moses did not unabashedly feast his eyes on the Shekhinah while on high but rather humbly hid his face (Exod. 3.6), his own face became infused with its radiance, as indicated in Exodus 34.29: “When Moses came down from Mount Sinai, . . . Moses did not know that the skin of his face sent forth rays (*qāran*).”[101] According to an anonymous Midrash in P^{e}sîqtā’ d^{e}-R. Kahana, when Moses descended from his sojourn on high he was like unto God, and therefore, as indicated in Exodus 34.30, the people of Israel were afraid to approach him.[102]

A pericope in Song of Songs Rabbāh VIII.11, §2 emphasizes that when Moses ascended to heaven to receive the Torah and bring it back to earth, the angels argued with God that the Torah should remain in heaven. The angels, alluding to Psalm 8.2, “O Lord our Lord, how majestic is Thy Name in all the earth; Thou who (*’ăšer*) hast set Thy glory (*hôḏ*) in the heavens,” tried to convince God that the Torah, which is his glory (*hôḏ*) and his happiness (*’ešer*), should remain in its heavenly abode and should not be given to Israel. God responded by arguing that the commandments of the Torah only apply to human beings, who are impure (Lev. 15.25) and mortal (Num. 19.14), and therefore do not concern the angels.[103] The pericope then recounts a parable ascribed to the rabbis, in which the situation is compared to a king who gave his daughter in marriage to a man in another country. When his subjects expressed concern that the king might visit her later and decide to stay with her in the other country, he reassured them that he would continue to reside with them in their town. In the same way, when God decided to give his daughter, the Torah, in marriage to Israel, the angels expressed concern that he might cause his Shekhinah to abide on the earth as well. He reassured them that although he would give the Torah to the world below, he would continue to abide with them in the upper world. This statement is then qualified by the view, attributed to R. Joshua b. Levi through his tradent R. Simon b. Pazzi, that "wherever the Holy One, blessed be He, caused His Torah to dwell, there He had His Shekhinah dwell." Psalm 148.13, "His glory (*hôḏ*) is on earth and in heaven," is invoked to establish that God's glory, the Shekhinah, is "first 'on earth' and then 'in heaven'"—that is, it is primarily on earth wherever the Torah is, but it is also in heaven in accordance with God's promise to the angels.[104]

A parable in Pᵉsîqtā' dᵉ-R. Kahana attributed to R. Abba b. Judan makes a similar use of the marriage metaphor in depicting the way in which the revelation of the Torah overcame the boundaries separating heaven and earth. A king had previously issued a decree forbidding marriage with people overseas, but then he withdrew the decree when he himself gave his own daughter in marriage to someone overseas. In the same way, before the Torah was given God had decreed the separation of heaven and earth: "The heavens are the heavens of the Lord, and the earth He has given to human beings" (Ps. 115.16). But when the Torah was given from heaven he withdrew the decree: "Moses went up (*'ālāh*) to God" (Exod. 19.3), "And the Lord came down (*yāraḏ*) upon Mount Sinai" (Exod. 19.20).[105] This aggadah implicitly counters the view attributed to R. Jose in the Mᵉḵîltā', which interprets Psalm 115.16 to mean that the lines of separation between heaven and earth are firm and that Moses did not ascend to heaven and God did not come down to earth.[106]

In both of the parables in Song of Songs Rabbāh and Pᵉsîqtā' dᵉ-R. Kahana the revelation of the Torah is depicted as a marriage ceremony in which the Torah is the bride, who is given by her father, the King on high, to an earthly bridegroom, Israel. The metaphor of marriage is frequently invoked in discussions of the revelation in classical Amoraic Midrashim, which, like the Mishnah, interpret "the day of his wedding" in Song of Songs 3.11 as referring to the giving of the Torah at Sinai.[107] While at times the Torah is portrayed as the bride who is wed to the bridegroom, Israel,[108] at other times Israel assumes the role of the bride who is wed to God himself.[109] When the Torah descended from heaven to earth, the Shekhinah, God's presence, descended with it, and thus the marriage at Mount Sinai is understood as uniting, on the one hand, Torah and Israel and, on the other hand, God and Israel. In the latter version of the wedding ceremony the Torah is sometimes depicted as the marriage contract (*k^{e}ṯûbāh*) stipulating the conditions of the union between God and Israel.[110] Another variant of the marriage metaphor portrays Moses as the spouse of God.[111]

The Israelites' Reception of the Theophany In discussing the interchange between heaven and earth that occurred at the revelation, classical Amoraic Midrashim are concerned not only with Moses's ascent to heaven and subsequent descent to earth with the Torah but also with the descent of God himself at the Sinai theophany. In addition to reiterating and amplifying traditions found in Tannaitic Midrashim, the Midrashim of this period contain several new modes of speculation that emphasize angelology and that are concerned in particular to determine the number and role of the celestial hosts that descended with God to Sinai.

(1) Descent of God and the Heavenly Hosts

In discussing the theophany, a pericope in P^{e}sîqtā' d^{e}-R. Kahana 12.22 cites a series of interpretations of Psalm 68.18, which, as discussed earlier, represents one of the key biblical verses used by the rabbis to link the Sinai event with Ezekiel's Merkabah vision: "The chariots (*reḵeḇ*) of God are twice ten thousand, thousands upon thousands; the Lord is among them, Sinai in holiness."[112] The pericope begins with an interpretation attributed to R. Abdimi of Ḥaifa, who claims a Tannaitic source for his tradition: "I learned in my mishnah that 22,000 ministering angels descended with the Holy One, blessed be He, to Sinai."[113] A tradition ascribed to R. Berekhiah then connects the number 22,000 to the number of males in the tribe of Levi, who alone among the Israelites would not go astray after the golden calf.[114] The pericope continues with an anonymous interpretation that understands the reference to chariots in Psalm 68.18 literally and compares the Israelites' experience to Ezekiel's vision of the Merkabah: "Twenty-two thousand chariots (*markāḇôṯ*) descended with the Holy One, blessed be He, and each and every chariot was [like the chariot] that Ezekiel saw."[115] This interpretation is then linked to a second tradition concerning 22,000 chariots that is cited in the name of a group from Babylonia who quote the prophet Elijah.[116] The pericope concludes with a Midrashic comment ascribed to R. Tanḥum b. Ḥanilai, who maintains that the hosts that accompanied God were innumerable.[117]

In a pair of aggadot found in P^{e}sîqtā' d^{e}-R. Kahana, variants of which also appear in Song of Songs Rabbāh and Lamentations

Rabbāh, the number of angels at Sinai is linked to their role in investing the Israelites with certain ornaments. According to one tradition ascribed to R. Joḥanan, there were 600,000 angels, each possessing a crown (*ʿăṭārāh*) with which to adorn each of the 600,000 Israelites. According to a second tradition, also attributed to R. Joḥanan through his tradent R. Abba b. Kahana, there were 1,200,000 angels, one to invest each Israelite with a crown (*ʿăṭārāh*) and the other to gird each with a weapon (*zayîn*)—or, according to a variant reading in Song of Songs Rabbāh, a girdle (*zônî*). The view that the Israelites were given girdles is ascribed more specifically to another tradent of R. Joḥanan's traditions, R. Huna b. Abin.[118]

A tradition attributed to R. Simeon b. Yoḥai, which is found in both Lamentations Rabbāh and Song of Songs Rabbāh, suggests that the Israelites were given a weapon (*zayîn*) with the ineffable Name engraved upon it, although the role of the angels is not mentioned in this context. This tradition emphasizes that the Name was removed when Israel sinned, indicating that whatever exalted status they attained through possession of the Name was temporary and contingent upon their obedience.[119] A Midrash in Pᵉsîqtā' dᵉ-R. Kahana, attributed to R. Zakkai of Shaab in the name of R. Samuel b. Naḥman, similarly emphasizes the contingent nature of the gifts bestowed upon Israel at Sinai. When the Israelites said, "All that the Lord has spoken we will do and we will hear" (Exod. 24.7), God imparted to them some of the "splendor (*zîw*) of the Shekhinah," but as soon as they turned away and worshiped the golden calf they lost their status and were condemned to die like ordinary mortals.[120]

(2) They Heard and Saw

The Sinai theophany is represented in a number of passages in classical Amoraic Midrashim as a synesthetic experience that was apprehended by the people of Israel through both hearing and seeing. The Israelites desired to hear (*šāmaʿ*) directly from God's own mouth, according to a tradition ascribed to R. Joḥanan. They also desired to see (*rā'āh*) the glory (*kāḇôḏ*) of their King, according to a tradition attributed to R. Simeon b. Yoḥai. Both of their desires were fulfilled.[121] A Midrash in Pᵉsîqtā' dᵉ-R. Kahana emphasizes that God healed the Israelites prior to giving them the Torah, and thus even the blind were granted the capacity to see and the deaf were granted the capacity to hear.[122]

A passage in Song of Songs Rabbāh I.2, §2 relates a debate concerning how many of the Ten Commandments were heard directly from the mouth of God, without Moses acting as an intermediary.

The rabbis, in accordance with the view expressed in the M^e^k̲îltā', argue that the Israelites heard all of the Ten Commandments directly from God.[123] However, this view is contended in a tradition ascribed to R. Joshua b. Levi, who argues that they only heard from God's mouth the first two commandments, "I am the Lord your God" and "You shall have no other gods before Me."[124] Song of Songs Rabbāh I.2, §2 also contains a series of aggadot concerning the method through which the commandments were transformed from speech utterances to written engravings on the tablets. The pericope includes a debate between R. Simeon b. Yoḥai and the rabbis concerning the precise manner in which each divine utterance went forth from God and circumambulated the camp of Israel before it was received by the right hand of God and inscribed on the tablet.[125] The pericope continues with a debate between R. Berekhiah and his teacher R. Ḥelbo concerning whether each utterance was inscribed of itself or by God.

Classical Amoraic Midrashim are not only concerned with the manner in which the Ten Commandments were conveyed from an oral to a written medium, they also speculate about the nature of the tablets themselves. For example, a pericope in Song of Songs Rabbāh contains a number of traditions concerning the type of material of which the tablets were made, the number of commandments (five, ten, twenty, or forty) on each tablet, and the manner in which they were written.[126] According to a tradition that is attributed to R. Ḥananyah, the nephew of R. Joshua b. Ḥananyah, between every commandment on the tablets were written the sections and minutiae of the Torah, and thus the tablets contained the seed expression of the entire Torah.[127] A tradition ascribed to R. Menaḥema in the name of R. Abun suggests that the tablets were hewn from the orb of the sun, implying that they were made of light.[128]

A number of Midrashim emphasize that, in addition to hearing God's voice, the people of Israel were granted a vision of God. P^e^sîqtā' d^e^-R. Kahana and Song of Songs Rabbāh contain variants of two traditions, one ascribed to R. Judah b. Il'ai and the other to R. Isaac, that present the experience at Mount Sinai as one of a series of theophanies in which the Israelites saw (*rā'āh*) God: they saw him in Egypt, they saw him at the Red Sea, and they saw him at Sinai.[129] One variant of the tradition attributed to R. Judah b. Il'ai emphasizes that whereas in Egypt and at the Red Sea the people of Israel saw God in the open (*b^e^-parhesyā'*), at Sinai they saw him "face to face" (*pānîm b^e^-pānîm*).[130] A tradition in P^e^sîqtā' d^e^-R.

Kahana ascribed to R. Levi asserts that because the Israelites saw the face of God, they could not die, "since anyone who has seen (*rā'āh*) the face (*pānîm*) of the King does not die, as it is said, 'In the light of a king's face (*pānîm*) there is life' (Prov. 16.15)."[131]

Another tradition in P^e^sîqtā' d^e^-R. Kahana, attributed to R. Abba b. Kahana, links the Israelites' vision of God's glory to a vision of "seven partitions of fire."

> Before Israel sinned what is written? "The appearance of the glory (*kāḇôḏ*) of the Lord was like a devouring fire (*'ēš*) on the top of the mountain before the eyes of the people of Israel" (Exod. 24.17). R. Abba b. Kahana said: There were seven partitions of fire (*m^e^ḥîṣôṯ šel 'ēš*) devouring one other, and the Israelites saw (*rā'āh*) them and were not awe-stricken nor afraid.[132]

As in Tannaitic Midrashim, the Torah itself is associated with fire in a number of passages and is identified in particular with the "fiery law" (*'ēš-dāṯ*) at God's right hand in Deuteronomy 33.2.[133] An aggadah in Song of Songs Rabbāh attributed to R. Simeon b. Lakish elaborates on this image, suggesting that the Torah was not only given in fire but was itself composed of fire, being inscribed in black fire on white fire.

> R. Simeon b. Lakish said: The Torah that the Holy One, blessed be He, gave—its parchment was of white fire and it was written with black fire. It was fire, hewn out of fire, formed of fire, and given in fire, as it is written, "At his right hand was a fiery law (*'ēš-dāṯ*) for them" (Deut. 33.2).[134]

A tradition that appears in several texts connects the fire that burns around scholars engaged in expounding Torah with the fire in which the words of Torah were originally given, suggesting that study serves as a means of replicating the fiery wonders of the Sinai theophany.[135]

(3) They Died and Were Resurrected

A number of Midrashim emphasize the overpowering impact of the revelation experience. According to a tradition in Song of Songs Rabbāh ascribed to R. Joḥanan, the Israelites shrank together in fear and trembling at every utterance that went forth from God's mouth.[136] Terrified by the life-threatening power of the divine speech, the people of Israel pleaded to Moses to serve as an intermediary between them and God. However, in succumbing to their fear of death they not only lost direct access to the full revelation, but, according to a tradition ascribed to R. Judah b. Il'ai, they also lost their ability to retain their knowledge of Torah.[137] A Midrash in Leviticus Rabbāh attributed to R. Tanḥum b. Ḥanilai emphasizes that what was too heavy for the 600,000 Israelites to bear was light for one man alone: Moses alone was capable of hearing the all-powerful voice of God and remaining alive, and thus it was he who was chosen by God to be the conduit of the divine speech.[138]

While these traditions point to the threat of death, they do not indicate that the Israelites in actuality died. However, a pericope in Song of Songs Rabbāh V.16, §3 contains a number of aggadot that suggest that the Israelites were incapable of bearing the divine voice, and thus when they heard the first of the Ten Commandments their souls departed. Contrary to the above mentioned view attributed to R. Levi, which maintains that as a result of seeing God's face the Israelites could not die, a tradition ascribed to R. Levi's teacher, R. Joḥanan, asserts that they did indeed die.

> "His speech is most sweet" (S. S. 5.16). R. Azariah and R. Aḥa in the name of R. Joḥanan said: When the Israelites heard "I" (*'ānōḵî*) at Sinai their soul fled (*pāraḥ*), as it is written, "If we hear the voice of the Lord our God any more, we shall die" (Deut. 5.25), [and] as it is written, "My soul went forth (*yāṣā'*) when he spoke" (S. S. 5.6). The Word (*dîbbûr*) returned to the Holy One, blessed be He, and said, "Lord of the world, Thou art living and enduring and Thy Torah is living and enduring, and Thou hast sent me to the dead. All of them are dead." At that moment the Holy One, blessed be He, went back and sweetened the Word for them, as it is written, "The voice (*qôl*) of the Lord is according to power (*ba-kōaḥ*), the voice of the Lord is full of majesty (*be-hāḏār*)" (Ps. 29.4).[139]

This tradition suggests that the Israelites could not bear to receive the divine Word in its full power, and thus God "sweetened" or tempered his Word so that it could serve as a source of life rather than death. The pericope continues with an interpretation of Psalm 29.4 ascribed to R. Ḥama b. Ḥanina. Like the interpretation of this verse in the Mᵉḵîltā', it suggests that this tempering of God's Word involved adapting his voice to the capacity of each individual listener: "The voice of the Lord was powerful (*ba-kōaḥ*) for the young, and the voice of the Lord was full of majesty (*be-hāḏār*) for the elderly."[140]

The tradition ascribed to R. Joḥanan implies that it was the intervention of the Word and its subsequent mitigation that allowed the Israelites to be revived and to survive the remainder of the revelation. The pericope in Song of Songs Rabbāh V.16, §3 continues with another explanation, attributed to R. Simeon b. Yoḥai, which suggests that it was the Torah itself that restored the Israelites' souls, as indicated in Psalm 19.8: "The Torah of the Lord is perfect, restoring the soul." An anonymous aggadah expands on this notion, describing how the Torah pleaded to God to be merciful and not to spoil the celebration of her wedding day by slaying his own children. The souls of the Israelites were thus restored through the intervention of the Torah.[141]

(4) Each According to His or Her Capacity

The most vivid portrayal of the way in which each individual Israelite experienced the theophany in accordance with his or her own capacity is found in P^e^sîqtā' d^e^-R. Kahana 12.25, which contains several aggadot that depict God as displaying multiple faces as well as multiple voices in order to meet each individual on his or her own level. A tradition ascribed to R. Levi, R. Joḥanan's student, suggests that each Israelite's vision of God's face was a highly personalized, intimate experience in which he or she felt that God was looking at and addressing him or her directly.

> R. Levi said: The Holy One, blessed be He, appeared to them like a statue that has faces on every side: a thousand people look at it, and it looks at all of them. So too when the Holy One, blessed be He, was speaking, each and every Israelite would say, "The Word (*dibbēr*) is speaking to me." It is not written, "I am the Lord your (plural) God," but "I am the Lord your (singular) God" (Exod. 20.2).[142]

The pericope continues with a tradition attributed to R. Jose b. Ḥanina, another student of R. Joḥanan, who compares the Israelites' experience of God's voice at Sinai to their earlier experience in the wilderness of manna, which each tasted in accordance with his or her own capacity.

> R. Jose b. Ḥanina said: The Word (*dîbbēr*) spoke to each and every individual according to his or her capacity (*kôaḥ*). And do not wonder at this matter. For when manna came down

to Israel, each and every person tasted it in accordance with his or her capacity—the infants according to their capacity, the young people according to their capacity, and the elderly according to their capacity. . . . Now if in the case of manna each and every person tasted it according to his or her capacity, so in the case of the Word each and every person heard it according to his or her capacity. David said, "The voice (*qôl*) of the Lord is according to power (*ba-kōaḥ*)" (Ps. 29.4). It is not written, "The voice of the Lord is according to *His* power," but "The voice of the Lord is according to power"—[the power] of each and every individual. The Holy One, blessed be He, said to them, "Despite the fact that you hear many voices, know that I am He [who speaks]: 'I am the Lord your God' (Exod. 20.2)."[143]

Babylonian Talmud

The Babylonian Talmud's speculation on the nature of the revelation at Mount Sinai is concentrated primarily in two extended discussions: Šabbāṯ 88a–89b, which contains a series of aggadot on the revelation, eight of which are attributed to R. Joshua b. Levi, and 'Ăḇôḏāh Zārāh 2a–3b, which incorporates a number of traditions regarding the Sinai event into its diatribe against the gentiles. The majority of other references to the revelation are interjected in Talmudic tractates at various points in the context of discussing certain halakhic issues or aggadic traditions, with the Sinai revelation itself not constituting a major focus of speculation. The Talmudic discussions include variants of a number of the traditions found in Palestinian Midrashim, with occasional evidence of new modes of construing persistent themes.

With respect to the contents of the revelation, Talmudic Midrashim generally uphold the distinction between the two phases of the revelation, in which the Ten Commandments were uttered directly by God to the people of Israel and the rest of the Torah was mediated to them through Moses. However, the contending view that the Israelites only heard the first two of the Ten Commandments directly from God, which is attributed in Song of Songs Rabbāh to R. Joshua b. Levi, is also expressed in two Talmudic Midrashim, where it is ascribed to R. Ishmael and R. Hamnuna, respectively.[144]

The Talmud, as discussed in chapter 2, reiterates the traditional doctrine that Moses received both the Written Torah and

Oral Torah on Mount Sinai. One Midrash, attributed to R. Levi b. Ḥama in the name of R. Simeon b. Lakish, maintains that the Pentateuch, Nevi'im, Ketuvim, Mishnah, and Gemara (Talmud) were given to Moses.[145] A second Midrash, ascribed to R. Ḥiyya II b. Abba in the name of R. Joḥanan, extends the notion of Oral Torah further by claiming that God showed to Moses the minutiae and the innovations that would be introduced by the scribes.[146] The teachings of the sages are at times given precedence over the Written Torah, with the sages themselves, as the embodiments of Torah, designated as "Sinai."[147] The priority of the Oral Torah is given clear expression in the assertion attributed to R. Joḥanan that God "made a covenant with Israel only for the sake of those words that were transmitted orally (*b^{e}-'al peh*)."[148] One aggadah discusses the method of transmission of the Oral Torah by means of which Moses, who learned the oral traditions directly from the mouth of God, taught what he had learned to his brother Aaron, the sons of Aaron, the elders, and the people of Israel as a whole, each in turn.[149]

Torah and the Nations A number of Talmudic Midrashim point to the involvement of the gentile nations in the revelation of the Torah, although in the end Israel alone proved worthy to be its recipients. A tradition ascribed to R. Ulla suggests that the nations of the world heard the Ten Commandments.[150] An aggadah in Šabbāṯ 88b, which is attributed to R. Joḥanan as well as to the school of R. Ishmael, maintains that every word that went forth from God's mouth divided into seventy languages, implying that each of the seventy nations of the world heard the revelation in its own vernacular.[151] A passage in Z^{e}ḇāḥîm 116a incorporates the tradition, found in both Tannaitic and classical Amoraic Midrashim, that when the Torah was given the sound reverberated from one end of the earth to the other.[152] This tradition is interwoven with another aggadah, also found in Tannaitic Midrashim, that describes how the kings of the gentiles, upon hearing the tumultuous sound, feared that God was about to destroy the world. However, when they learned that God was giving the Torah to his people, they were comforted and proclaimed, "The Lord will bless His people with peace" (Ps. 29.11).[153] Although all of the above Midrashim suggest that the gentile nations may have heard part of the revelation, there is no suggestion that they were actually offered the Torah and asked to undertake its observance. This notion is found elsewhere in the Talmud and is elaborated on in a homily in tractate 'Ăḇôḏāh Zārāh.

The homily in ʻĂḇôḏāh Zārāh 2a–3b, attributed to either R. Ḥanina b. Pappai or R. Simlai, represents one of the most carefully crafted diatribes against the gentile nations found in rabbinic texts.[154] It incorporates a number of traditions found in earlier texts and recasts them in the form of an eschatological drama in the time to come in which the nations of the world will be brought to judgment before God. The homily opens, like the corresponding homily in Pᵉsîqtā' dᵉ-R. Kahana,[155] with God holding a Sefer Torah to his bosom in the time to come and declaring that whoever has occupied himself therewith should come and receive his reward. All the nations of the world will then gather together in confusion before him, and he will ask that each nation come before him individually, one by one. The homily then gives a new inflection to an old motif: in contrast to the time of the revelation, in which God is depicted as coming to each nation one by one and offering them the Torah, in this scenario in the time to come it is the nations themselves who are portrayed as coming before God one by one and who are held accountable for not having occupied themselves with the Torah. As at the Sinai event, the kingdom of Edom or Esau—here explicitly identified with Rome—is first, followed by the kingdom of Persia. The nations who will follow Persia are not specified, and no mention is made of the other members of the cast of nations who generally appear in the revelation drama: the Ammonites, Moabites, and Ishmaelites.[156] Even though each nation will contend that all of the activities in which it has been engaged were done for the sake of the Israelites, in order that they might occupy themselves with the Torah, God will reject the gentile nations' testimonies and turn them away one by one.

The homily continues with a portrayal of the gentile nations offering a number of different arguments in their own defense. First, the nations will argue, "Is there anything that Thou hast given us [that is, the Torah] that we have not accepted?" This argument will be countered with the standard proof text, Deuteronomy 33.2, "The Lord came from Sinai, and dawned from Seir upon them; He shone forth from Mount Paran," as evidence of the fact that at the revelation God offered the Torah to every nation, but none except Israel would accept it.[157] Second, the nations will contend, "Is there anything that we accepted that we have not observed?" The counterargument to this will be, "Why did you not accept it?" Third, the nations will point out that God did not suspend the mountain over them like a vault and threaten to crush them, as he did to Israel, implying that they too would have accepted the Torah if they had been forced to do so as Israel was.[158] As a rejoinder God will remind them that they did not even uphold the seven commandments that were accepted by them as the descendants of Noah.[159] Fourth, the nations will argue, "Has Israel, who accepted the Torah, observed it?" In the end God will ask representatives of the gentile nations themselves to come and testify that Israel has observed the entire Torah. Finally, the nations will plead with God, "Offer us the Torah anew, and we shall observe it." God will relent and give them the commandment of Sukkah to carry out, and each will immediately go and make a booth on the top of his roof. However, God will cause the sun to blaze forth over them, and they will trample down their booths and run away. "Thereupon," the homily concludes, "the Holy One, blessed be He, will sit and laugh at them, as it is said, 'He who sits in heaven laughs' (Ps. 2.4)."

Revelation and Creation Like classical Amoraic Midrashim, a number of Talmudic Midrashim link the process of revelation to the process of creation and emphasize that Israel's acceptance of the Torah at Mount Sinai was necessary for the continuance of the cosmos. While the parallel tradition in Palestinian Midrashim invokes as a proof text Psalm 75.4, "When the earth and all its inhabitants are dissolved, it is I (*'ānōḵî*) who establish its pillars,"[160] Talmudic Midrashim draw upon two other biblical verses: Genesis 1.31, "And there was evening and there was morning the sixth day," and Jeremiah 33.25, "If not for My covenant by day and by night, I would not have established the ordinances of heaven and earth."

A tradition ascribed to R. Simeon b. Lakish, which appears in several different contexts in the Talmud, is based on an interpretation of Genesis 1.31. It is incorporated into an extended discussion of the revelation in Šabbāṯ 88a–89b following a reference to the tradition that God overturned the mountain above the Israelites and threatened to destroy them if they would not accept the Torah.[161] The pericope goes on to establish that the people of Israel's acceptance of the Torah was necessary not only for their own survival but also for the survival of the creation itself. A comment attributed to R. Hezekiah is interjected at this point, which interprets Psalm 76.9, "From the heavens Thou didst cause the law to be heard; the earth feared and was still," to mean that the earth feared at first, but subsequently it became still.[162] This comment is then explained with reference to the tradition ascribed to R. Simeon b. Lakish.

> Resh Lakish said: Why is it written, "And there was evening and there was morning *the* sixth day" (Gen. 1.31)? Why is there an additional "the"? This teaches that the

> Holy One, blessed be He, stipulated with the works of creation and said to them, "If Israel accepts the Torah, you shall become established, but if not, I will turn you back into formlessness and emptiness (*tôhû wā-ḇôhû*)."[163]

Genesis 1.31 is thus interpreted homiletically to mean that the continuance of morning and evening was dependent on the sixth day, that is, the sixth day of Sivan on which Israel accepted the Torah at Mount Sinai.

A variant of this tradition is also inserted into the homily in 'Ăḇôḏāh Zārāh 2a–3b concerning the judgment of the gentile nations in the time to come. In this context a reference to Jeremiah 33.25 introduces the tradition attributed to R. Simeon b. Lakish, which is then followed by the comment ascribed to R. Hezekiah.[164] Another tradition, attributed to R. Eleazar, similarly invokes Jeremiah 33.25 in order to establish the role of the Torah in sustaining creation.

> R. Eleazar said: Great is the Torah, since but for the Torah heaven and earth would not endure, as it is said, "If not for My covenant by day and by night, I would not have established the ordinances of heaven and earth" (Jer. 33.25).[165]

Ascent of Moses and Descent of the Torah Talmudic Midrashim present a variety of perspectives regarding the relationship between heaven and earth at the Sinai event. *Tôrāh min ha-šāmayim*, "the Torah is from heaven," assumes different valences in different contexts, and a range of views is expressed concerning whether Moses ascended to heaven and God descended to earth at the time of the revelation.

With respect to the Mishnaic injunction that excludes from the world to come one who denies that the Torah is from heaven, a *baraita* interprets "the Torah is from heaven" metaphorically to mean that the Torah was uttered by God. It further emphasizes that in maintaining that the whole Torah is from heaven, it is not admissible to exclude a single point, verse, or even certain hermeneutical principles such as *g^e^zērāh šāwāh*.[166] The notion of Torah in this context thus includes not only the written text but also the oral tradition of interpretation.

An aggadah attributed to R. Joshua b. Levi in Šabbāṯ 88b–89a, presents a more cosmological interpretation of the notion that "the Torah is from heaven," in which the Torah is portrayed as descending from its heavenly abode at the Sinai revelation. The Torah is depicted as the "secret treasure" that had resided with God in heaven since before the creation, and thus in order to receive the Torah Moses had to ascend to heaven, to the realm of the angels and the throne of glory, and bring it down to earth. Like the parallel tradition in Song of Songs Rabbāh VIII.11, §2, the pericope portrays the angels as arguing with God that his glory, the Torah, should not be taken from heaven and given to mortals on earth.

> When Moses ascended (*'ālāh*) on high, the ministering angels said to the Holy One, blessed be He, "Lord of the world, what is one born of woman doing among us?" He said to them, "He has come to receive the Torah." They said to him, "This secret treasure (*ḥămûḏāh g^enûzāh*), which has been hidden by Thee for 974 generations before the world was created, Thou desirest to give to flesh and blood? 'What is man that Thou art mindful of him, and the son of man that Thou dost care for him?' (Ps. 8.5). 'O Lord our Lord, how majestic is Thy Name in all the earth—so give Thy glory to the heavens.'" (Ps. 8.2).[167]

In contrast to Song of Songs Rabbāh's version of this tradition, God himself is not depicted as responding to the angels, but rather he is portrayed as giving Moses the responsibility for presenting a rebuttal.

> The Holy One, blessed be He, said to Moses, "Give them an answer." "Lord of the world," he said to Him, "I am afraid lest they burn me up with the breath of their mouths." [God] said to him, "Take hold of My throne of glory (*kissē' kāḇôḏ*) and give them an answer." As it is said, "He takes hold of the front of the throne, and [God] spreads (*paršēz*) over him His cloud" (Job 26.9). R. Naḥum said: This teaches that the Almighty spread over him some of the splendor (*zîw*) of His Shekhinah and His cloud.[168]

In reply to the angels Moses argued, with reference to the first eight of the Ten Commandments, that the Torah's commandments only concern human beings in their earthly abode and do not apply to the angels in heaven. The angels relinquished their claim to the Torah by reciting Psalm 8.10, "O Lord our Lord, how majestic is Thy Name in all the earth," but this time without adding "so give Thy glory to the heavens" (Ps. 8.2). As recompense for calling Moses a human being the angels bestowed gifts upon him, as indicated in Psalm 68.19: "You ascended on high, you took a captivity captive, you took gifts for humanity." Even the angel of death transmitted his secret to him.[169]

The pericope continues with another aggadic tradition attributed to R. Joshua b. Levi that discusses how when Moses descended to earth with the Torah, even Satan was concerned to find that the Torah was no longer in heaven.[170] The last two traditions ascribed to R. Joshua b. Levi in Šabbāṯ 89a describe other events that occurred "when Moses ascended (*'ālāh*) on high."[171] These aggadot represent one trend of speculation, evident elsewhere in the Talmud as well as in other rabbinic texts, in which it is taken for granted that Moses ascended to heaven at the time of the revelation.[172] However, we also find an opposing trend that calls into question this view as well as the view that God came down to earth.

A pericope in Sûkkāh 5a debates these two issues. It begins by citing a variant of the tradition ascribed to R. Jose in the Mᵉḵîltā', which asserts that the Shekhinah never descended to earth nor did Moses or Elijah ever ascend to heaven, invoking as a proof text Psalm 115.16, "The heavens are the heavens of the Lord, and the earth He has given to human beings."[173] Counter proof texts are then presented, including the standard ones, "And the Lord came down (*yāraḏ*) upon Mount Sinai" (Exod. 19.20) and "Moses went up (*'ālāh*) to God" (Exod. 19.3).[174] However, the prevailing view expressed in the pericope is that there was always a space of at least ten handbreadths separating heaven and earth: God remained more than ten handbreadths above the mountain, and Moses ascended to a level lower than ten handbreadths from heaven. Job 26.9, "He takes hold of the front of the throne," is interpreted as referring to Moses, implying that Moses had contact with God's throne in heaven, as the aggadah ascribed to R. Joshua b. Levi also suggests.[175] However, this notion is qualified by suggesting that the throne was itself lowered to a level more than ten handbreaths from heaven, and only then did Moses take hold of it.[176]

Irrespective of whether "the Torah is from heaven" is interpreted metaphorically or cosmologically, a famous Talmudic aggadah, which recounts a debate between R. Eliezer b. Hyrcanus and the sages, insists that the Torah has not been in heaven since the time of the revelation. Deuteronomy 30.12, "It is not in heaven," is interpreted to mean that since the Torah was given at Mount Sinai the authority for determining halakhic matters has resided in the consensus of the sages on earth, and even God himself through the agency of a heavenly voice (*bat̲ qôl*) cannot prevail over the sages' collective decisions.[177]

In classical Amoraic Midrashim, as we have seen, the descent of the Torah from heaven is at times depicted as a wedding ceremony in which the Torah is betrothed as a bride to her bridegroom, Israel. Talmudic discussions of the revelation do not generally make use of the marriage metaphor. However, several Midrashim, in the context of discussing other issues, connect the Torah with the image of a betrothed maiden through construing *môrāšāh* in Deuteronomy 33.4, "Moses commanded us a law (Torah) as an inheritance (*môrāšāh*) for the assembly of Jacob," as *me'ôrāsāh*, "betrothed."[178] The other version of the marriage ceremony, in which Israel assumes the role of the bride, is pointed to in a saying attributed to R. Ulla in which Israel is referred to as a bride who played the harlot even while under the bridal canopy, alluding to the Israelites' unfaithfulness to God when they turned away and worshiped the golden calf at Sinai.[179]

The Israelites' Reception of the Theophany In contrast to Tannaitic Midrashim and classical Amoraic Midrashim, the Talmud does not contain detailed discussions of the phenomenology of the Sinai theophany. The essential ingredients of the theophany—that God appeared before the people of Israel and spoke to them the Ten Commandments—are taken for granted without substantial speculation about the nature of God's manifestation or about the celestial hosts that accompanied him.

(1) Descent of God and the Heavenly Hosts

With respect to the descent of God, several Midrashim briefly mention that the Shekhinah made its abode on Mount Sinai during the revelation[180]—although, as we have seen, this view is qualified in the pericope in Sûkkāh 5a discussed above, which insists that the Shekhinah always remained more than ten handbreadths above the mountain.

The role of the angels in the theophany is discussed in an aggadah in Šabbāt̲ 88a attributed to R. Simai. Like the parallel tradition ascribed to R. Joḥanan in classical Amoraic Midrashim, this aggadah suggests that 600,000 angels descended with God to Sinai.

> R. Simai expounded: When the Israelites gave precedence to "we will do" over "we will hear," 600,000 ministering angels came and affixed on each and every Israelite two crowns (*ket̲ārîm*), one for "we will do" and one for "we will hear."[181]

This tradition contains two elements that are not found in the parallel tradition ascribed to R. Joḥanan. First, each angel is said to have set not merely one but two crowns upon each of the 600,000 Israelites. Second, this version of the tradition emphasizes that the crowns were not an unmerited gift but were bestowed only because the Israelites gave precedence to "we will do" over "we will hear" (Exod. 24.7)—that is, they agreed to obey the commandments even before hearing them. Hence the tradition goes on to assert that as soon as the Israelites sinned, 1,200,000 angels of destruction came down and removed the crowns, as the pentateuchal account itself indicates: "And the people of Israel stripped themselves of their ornaments from Mount Horeb onward" (Exod. 33.6).[182]

(2) They Heard and Saw

Like earlier rabbinic texts, Talmudic Midrashim represent the Sinai theophany as involving both auditory and visual phenomena. The differentiation of the divine voice is pointed to in the tradition, mentioned above, that every word split into seventy languages.[183] Another tradition, attributed to R. Joshua b. Levi, suggests that the Torah was given with five voices.[184] The pervasive power of God's voice is emphasized in several aggadot. The sound of the divine voice is represented in one passage, discussed earlier, as traveling from one end of the earth to the other so that it could be heard not only by the Israelites but by all nations.[185] A tradition ascribed to R. Joshua b. Levi emphasizes the all-pervading redolence of the divine word, maintaining that with each word that went forth from God's mouth the entire world was filled with the fragrance of spices.[186]

With respect to the visual dimensions of the revelation, Talmudic Midrashim occasionally invoke the images of fire, lightning, and light that are used in the Pentateuch itself to describe the revelation, but they do not elaborate on these images nor on the ways in which the theophany engaged in particular the sense of sight. The Torah is associated with both light and fire in Talmudic Midrashim,[187] but other than the identification of the Torah with the "fiery law" (*'ēš-dāṯ*) at the right hand of God in Deuteronomy 33.2,[188] the significance of this association is not generally explored in the context of discussing the phenomenology of the revelation. The unique visual character of the writing on the tablets of the covenant is mentioned in a tradition ascribed to R. Ḥisda, in which the letters are said to have cut through the stone so that the writing could be read from both sides.[189]

(3) They Died and Were Resurrected

The discussion of the revelation in Šabbāṯ 88a–89b includes two traditions, both ascribed to R. Joshua b. Levi, that emphasize the overpowering nature of the revelation experience. The first tradition develops further the notion found in Song of Songs Rabbāh that the souls of the Israelites departed after hearing the first of the Ten Commandments. In this tradition the "resurrection" of the dead Israelites is brought about through the dew with which God will resurrect the dead in the time to come.

> R. Joshua b. Levi said: At each and every utterance (*dîbbûr*) that issued from the mouth of the Holy One, blessed be He, the soul of Israel went forth, as it is said, "My soul went forth (*yāṣā'*) when he spoke" (S. S. 5.6). But since their soul went forth after the first commandment, how could they receive the second commandment? He brought down the dew with which He will resurrect the dead in the future and He resurrected them, as it is said, "A bounteous rain, O God, Thou didst pour down; when Thy heritage languished Thou didst restore it." (Ps. 68.10).[190]

The second tradition ascribed to R. Joshua b. Levi, which is a variant of a tradition found in Tannaitic Midrashim, maintains that upon hearing each commandment the Israelites retreated twelve miles, but then the ministering angels would lead them back.[191]

P^esîqtā' Rabbāṯî and Tanḥûmā' Y^elamm^eḏēnû Midrashim

P^esîqtā' Rabbāṯî and Tanḥûmā' Y^elamm^eḏēnû Midrashim contain a number of extended discussions of the phenomenology of the revelation at Mount Sinai. The most extensive speculations are found in *pisqā*'s 20 and 21 of P^esîqtā' Rabbāṯî, which form part of the cycle of homilies for Shavuot. *Pisqā'* 20 includes various traditions concerning the response of the inhabitants of both heaven and earth to the descent of the Torah from heaven. It culminates in an elaborate account of Moses's ascent to heaven and encounters with the imposing angels that guard the path to God's throne, followed by a description of the theophany in which God opened the seven firmaments and appeared before Israel in his glory upon his throne. *Pisqā'* 21 contains a series of discussions that pertain to the first commandment, "I am the Lord your God," and that elaborate on the nature of the theophany in which God descended upon Mount Sinai with myriads of angels and chariots and spoke with the Israelites face to face. The most extensive discussions of the Sinai event in Tanḥûmā' Yᵉlammᵉḏēnû Midrashim are found in those sections of Exodus Rabbāh II and the Tanḥûmā' that comment upon the account of the revelation in the book of Exodus.

In discussing the contents and method of transmission of the revelation, Pᵉsîqtā' Rabbāṯî and Tanḥûmā' Yᵉlammᵉḏēnû Midrashim reiterate the prevailing view that God spoke the Ten Commandments directly to the people of Israel. However, they also include the alternative view that only the first two of the Ten Commandments were declared by God and the rest were given through Moses.[192] An anonymous tradition in Numbers Rabbāh implies that the Ten Commandments inscribed on the tablets contained the entire Torah in potential form, the 613 letters from *'ānōḵî* ("I am") to *'ăšer lᵉ-rē'eḵā* ("that belongs to your neighbor") corresponding to the 613 commandments.[193]

With respect to Moses's special role as the mediator of the Torah to Israel, several aggadot depict Moses sitting at the feet of God studying Torah, like a disciple sitting at the feet of his master repeating what he had learned.[194] According to an anonymous tradition in Exodus Rabbāh II, while Moses was on high he received instruction from God during the day and then reviewed on his own at night.[195] An anonymous tradition found in Exodus Rabbāh II and the Tanḥûmā' suggests that after God communicated to Moses the Bible, Mishnah, Talmud, and Aggadah, Moses asked if he should write everything down. However, God insisted that Moses should write down only the Bible (Pentateuch, Nevi'im, and Ketuvim) and that the Mishnah, Talmud, and Aggadah should be transmitted orally in order to distinguish Israel from the idolatrous nations that would later gain dominion over them.[196] As discussed in chapter 2, a tradition in Pᵉsîqtā' Rabbāṯî and the Tanḥûmā' clearly links this notion to a polemic against the Christians. Since God foresaw that in the future the nations would appropriate the Written Torah, he determined to exclude them from the "secret" (*misṭērîn*) of the Mishnah by transmitting its teachings orally.[197]

The Tanḥûmā' and Exodus Rabbāh II contain a tradition ascribed to R. Isaac that suggests that the prophets and sages who would arise in future generations did not simply receive their teachings through a line of transmission stemming from Moses at Mount Sinai. Rather, they themselves were also present at Mount Sinai and received the teachings that they were destined to expound.

> R. Isaac said: Everything that the prophets were destined to prophesy they received from Mount Sinai, as it is written, [the covenant was made] "with him who stands here with us this day" (Deut. 29.14)—this refers to those who were already created, those who were already in existence—"and also with him who is not here with us this day" (ibid.)—this refers to those who were destined to be created. . . . This applies not only to the prophets but also to all the sages who were destined to arise. . . .[198]

Torah and the Nations The Midrashim discussed above suggest that the gentile nations were destined to be excluded from the teachings of the Oral Torah, even though they might later try to appropriate the Written Torah. A number of other Midrashim are concerned to clarify to what extent the gentile nations had a role in the original revelation at Mount Sinai and to determine why in the end the Torah was given only to Israel.

A Midrash in Pᵉsîqtā' Rabbāṯî ascribed to R. Simeon b. Yoḥai maintains that the gentile nations were disqualified from receiving the Torah because they were not worthy.[199] Another tradition in Pᵉsîqtā' Rabbāṯî similarly suggests that the gentile nations were not themselves offered the Torah, but rather they were simply passive witnesses of the theophany, terrified by the earth-shaking power of God's revelation to his people.[200] The more prevalent view, however, expressed in both Pᵉsîqtā' Rabbāṯî and Tanḥûmā' Yᵉlammᵉḏēnû Midrashim, is that the gentile nations were also given the opportunity to receive the Torah, but they refused to accept it.[201] The notion that the nations missed their opportunity at the revelation is infused with a new valence in a Midrash ascribed to R. Isaac in Deuteronomy Rabbāh, which suggests that they not only refused to accept the Torah, they also declined the lordship of God himself. For when God came down upon Mount Sinai accompanied by hosts of angels the nations chose the archangels Michael, Gabriel, and so on, as their respective patrons, while Israel alone chose God.[202] In this perspective it is not Israel's inherent worthiness that caused God to distinguish them from among all the nations but rather their willingness to accept God and his Torah.[203]

A tradition attributed to R. Joḥanan, which represents a variant of the tradition ascribed to him in the Talmud, describes the one voice of God as splitting into seven voices, which then divided into seventy languages corresponding to the seventy nations of the world.[204] One version of this tradition in the Tanḥûmā' maintains that when the nations of the world heard the voice of God in their own vernaculars they could not endure the experience and their souls departed, while the Israelites alone survived.

> R. Joḥanan said: The voice (*qôl*) went forth and split into seven voices and from seven voices into seventy languages so that all the nations would hear. Each nation heard His voice in the language of that nation and their souls departed, but Israel heard and was not harmed. How did the voice go forth? R. Tanḥuma said: It had two faces. It went forth and slew the nations, who did not accept the Torah, but it gave life to Israel, who accepted the Torah. This is what Moses said to them at the end of forty years: "For who is there of all flesh that has heard the voice of the living God speaking out of the midst of the fire as we have and has lived?" (Deut. 5.26). You heard His voice and lived, but the nations heard it and died.[205]

The first part of the statement ascribed to R. Joḥanan, regarding the one voice splitting into seven voices and seventy languages, is regularly attributed to him.[206] However, the second part of the statement, which maintains that the other nations died while Israel remained unharmed, directly contradicts the tradition ascribed to him in Song of Songs Rabbāh V.16, §3, discussed above, that the Israelites themselves died. This part of the statement most likely represents a later addition that sought to reconstrue earlier traditions concerning the life-threatening power of the divine voice in light of an anti-gentile polemic: the Word of God was a source of death to the gentile nations and a source of life to the Israelites. The tradition attributed to R. Tanḥuma emphasizes that this twofold manifestation of God's Word was in direct response to the twofold reception that the Word received: those nations who rejected the Torah were given a death sentence, while those who accepted it, the Israelites, were given life.[207]

The polemic implicit in the notion that the gentile nations rejected the Torah is further intensified in a pericope in Pᵉsîqtā' Rabbāṯî by emphasizing that they were not even worthy to be offered all of the Ten Commandments. The pericope relates a conversation between the Roman emperor Hadrian and R. Joshua b. Ḥananyah in which Hadrian is portrayed as pointing out that while God offered to Israel the first five of the Ten Commandments, which contain the Name of God, he offered to the nations only the second five of the Ten Commandments, which do not contain his Name. The implication, Hadrian suggests, is that God will not cry out against the gentile nations when they sin, since the commandments they were given do not involve his Name. R. Joshua replies that God would not want his Name mentioned with murderers, adulterers, and thieves. After the emperor departs R. Joshua recounts to his students the tradition that God offered the Torah to the nations, but each in turn refused. He offered the Torah to the children of Esau in the form of the sixth of the Ten Commandments, "You shall not kill"; to the children of Ammon and Moab in the form of the seventh commandment, "You shall not commit adultery"; and to the children of Ishmael in the form of the eighth commandment, "You shall not steal."[208]

A second Midrash in P^{e}sîqtā' Rabbāṯî reiterates the tradition found in P^{e}sîqtā' d^{e}-R. Kahana in which God is said to have foreseen that the nations would reject the Torah, but he offered it to them nevertheless in order to double Israel's reward for accepting it.[209] A Midrash in Exodus Rabbāh II presents a different perspective, which emphasizes not the rewards that the people of Israel receive for accepting the Torah but rather the punishments that they will incur if they fail to live up to the responsibility that they assumed when they agreed to obey its commandments. In this view Israel's special status among the nations involves not only a privilege but also a responsibility: fulfillment of the commandments of the Torah. God is compared to a king who wished to entrust his field to métayers. He approached four successive men in turn—corresponding presumably to the four nations of Esau, Ammon, Moab, and Ishmael—but each declined to take over the field. Finally, the fifth man that the king approached agreed to take over the field with the condition that he would till it. But as soon as he took over the field he let it lie fallow. "With whom is the king angry? With those who said, 'We cannot take it over,' or with him who took it over but after he took it over entered it and let it lie fallow? Certainly with him who took it over."[210]

Revelation and Creation The people of Israel's acceptance of the Torah is represented in a number of Midrashim as a crucial turning point not only in their own destiny as a nation but also in the destiny of the entire creation. It is through the agency of the primordial Torah that the universe emerged from chaos in the beginning of creation, and it is through the revelation of the historical Torah that the universe was renovated and consolidated. If the Israelites had not accepted the Torah, then this renewal of creation would not have been brought to completion and the world would have been reduced to its original state of chaos.[211]

A Midrash in Exodus Rabbāh II attributed to R. Tanḥuma suggests that God would not even have created the world in the beginning if he had not foreseen that Israel would accept the Torah at Mount Sinai.[212] An anonymous Midrash in this text directly connects the notion that the Torah served as the instrument of creation with the notion that Israel's acceptance of the Torah at the revelation was necessary for the continuance of creation, invoking as a proof text Jeremiah 33.25.

> If you had not accepted My Torah, I would have returned the world to formlessness and emptiness (*tōhû wā-ḇōhû*), as it is said, "If not for My covenant by day and by night, I would not have established the ordinances of heaven and earth" (Jer. 33.25). Why? Because it was by means of the Torah that I created heaven and earth, as it is said, "The Lord by wisdom (*ḥoḵmāh*) founded the earth; by understanding (*t^eḇûnāh*) He established the heavens; by His knowledge (*da'aṯ*) the depths were broken up. . . ." (Prov. 3.19–20). If you annul the covenant, you will cause Me to return the upper and lower worlds to formlessness and emptiness (*tōhû wā-ḇōhû*).[213]

A Midrash in P^esîqtā' Rabbāṯî, ascribed to R. Ḥiyya II b. Abba in the name of R. Joḥanan, interprets Psalm 76.9, "From the heavens Thou didst cause the law to be heard; the earth feared and was still," to mean that at the time of the revelation the earth feared that if Israel did not accept the Torah, it would once again be submerged in water as at the beginning of creation.[214] The pericope continues with a variant of the aggadah attributed to R. Huna b. Abin in the name of R. Aḥa, which interprets Psalm 75.4, "When the earth and all its inhabitants are dissolved, it is I (*'ānōḵî*) who establish its pillars," to mean that the world would have long ago dissolved if Israel had not accepted God's revelation of the Torah, which commenced with "I" (*'ānōḵî*): "I am the Lord your God."[215]

An anonymous Midrash in P^esîqtā' Rabbāṯî connects the *'ānōḵî* that begins the Ten Commandments with the *'ānōḵî* with which God created the worlds above and below: "I (*'ānōḵî*) am the Lord, who made all things, who stretched out the heavens alone, who spread out the earth by Myself" (Isa. 44.24).[216] The creation and revelation are correlated in another anonymous tradition in Pesîqtā' Rabbāṯî by pairing the Ten Words (*dibbᵉrôṯ*) of the revelation with the ten words (*ma'ămārôṯ*) by which the world was created.[217]

An anonymous tradition in Exodus Rabbāh XXIX.9 suggests that the Sinai revelation served not only to establish the world on a firm foundation but also to renew and revitalize the creation, infusing the entire universe with new life. The earth trembled, the mountains quaked, the pillars of heaven shook, and all of Israel trembled when they received the words of life resounding forth from the mouth of God. Exodus Rabbāh XXIX.9 concludes with two aggadot that use language and imagery to describe the revelation that recall the first beginnings of creation. Just as in the beginning the Word of God emerged from the primordial depths of silence in order to bring forth creation, so at the time of the revelation the world reverted to a state of utter silence from which the Word of God went forth in order to revitalize and consolidate the creation.

> R. Abbahu said in the name of R. Joḥanan: When the Holy One, blessed be He, gave the Torah, no bird cried out, no fowl flew, no ox lowed, the ophanim did not spread their wings, the seraphim did not say "Holy, Holy," the sea did not stir, the creatures did not speak. The world became hushed and silent, and the voice went forth: "I am the Lord your God" (Exod. 20.1).

The passage continues with a tradition attributed to R. Simeon b. Lakish, who compares the world's retreat into silence at Mount Sinai with the prophet Elijah's contest on Mount Carmel with the pagan prophets of Baal, in which the world retreated to silence and became "without form and void" as at the beginning of creation.

> [God] brought the entire world to a standstill and silenced those on high and those below, and the world became without form and void (*tōhû wā-ḇōhû*), as if there were no creature in the world. . . . How much more so was it that when the Holy One, blessed be He, spoke on Mount Sinai, the entire world became silent in order that creatures might know that there is none beside Him. Then He said, "I am the Lord your God."

Ascent of Moses and Descent of the Torah A number of traditions in Pᵉsîqtā' Rabbāṯî and Tanḥûmā' Yᵉlammᵉḏēnû Midrashim emphasize the cosmological dimensions of the revelation in which the separation between heaven and earth was overcome. Numerous Midrashim take it for granted that Moses's ascent of Mount Sinai involved an ascent to the heavens, where he sojourned with God in the realm of the angels for forty days and forty nights before descending back to earth with the Torah.[218]

The most elaborate description of Moses's ascent to the heavens is found in Pᵉsîqtā' Rabbāṯî 20.4, which bears striking affinities to Hêḵālôṯ traditions.[219] The passage recontextualizes earlier traditions concerning Moses's heavenly ascent and the opposition of the angels to the giving of the Torah, embellishing them with descriptions of the various angels who guard the fiery heaven in which God is enthroned on the Merkabah. Moses is described as being carried in a cloud to heaven, where he was accosted by a series of increasingly ferocious angels who tried to block his passage. Moses first encountered Kemuel, the angel in command of the 12,000 angels of destruction who guard the gate of the firmament. When Kemuel would not allow him to pass, Moses slew him with a single blow. His next encounter was with Hadarniel, an angel 600,000 parasangs taller than the next tallest angel, whose every word is said to be accompanied by lightning flashes. When Moses, terrified, nearly fell from his cloud, God intervened and rebuked Hadarniel and the other angels for their contentiousness, reminding them that if Israel did not receive the Torah, there would be no abiding place either for them or for God himself. With God's aid Moses succeeded in passing by the other obstructing agents: the angel Sandalphon, an angel "taller than his companions by the distance of a five-hundred-year journey . . . [who] serves behind the Merkabah and weaves crowns for his creator";[220] Rigyon, the river of fire whose coals consume angels as well as humans; and Gallizur, the angel who declares God's decrees and whose wings protect the ministering angels from the fiery breath of the *ḥayyôṯ* who bear the Merkabah. The passage continues with a description that closely resembles the Talmudic aggadah on Moses's ascension attributed to R. Joshua b. Levi.

> A troop of angels of destruction, powerful and mighty, who surround the throne of glory (*kissē' ha-kāḇôḏ*), encountered him. When Moses reached them they sought to burn him up with the breath of their mouths. What did the Holy One, blessed be He, do? He spread over him some of His splendor (*zîw*), set him before His throne, and said, "Moses, give an answer to the ministering angels." "He takes hold of the

> front of the throne, and [God] spreads over him His cloud" (Job 26.9). R. Naḥum said: This teaches that the Almighty spread over him some of the splendor (*zîw*) of the Shekhinah and His cloud. "Lord of the world," he said to Him, "I am afraid lest they burn me up with the breath of their mouths." [God] replied, "Take hold of My throne of glory and give them an answer."

Moses then proceeded to explain, with reference to four of the Ten Commandments, why the commandments of the Torah do not apply to the angels in heaven, and the angels conceded, reciting Psalm 8.10. The angel of death then conveyed the secrets of healing to him as the "gifts for humanity" mentioned in Psalm 68.19: "You ascended on high, you took a captivity captive, you took gifts for humanity."[221] The passage continues with a description of how God opened (*pāṯaḥ*) the seven firmaments (*r*ᵉ*qî'îm*) and showed to Moses the heavenly Temple.[222]

Discussions of the angels' opposition to the descent of the Torah to earth are also found in other passages in Pᵉsîqtā' Rabbāṯî and Tanḥûmā' Yᵉlammᵉḏēnû Midrashim. A passage in Pᵉsîqtā' Rabbāṯî 25.3 incorporates a tradition, which represents a variant of the aggadah in Song of Songs Rabbāh VIII.11, §2, in which God himself is portrayed as arguing directly with the angels that it would not be appropriate for the Torah to remain with them in heaven because the commandments of the Torah are applicable only to mortals, who die (Num. 19.14) and eat and drink (Lev. 11.9,4).[223] A Midrash in Deuteronomy Rabbāh gives an alternative interpretation of why the Torah was not given to the angels: it is too abstruse (*nip̄lē'ṯ*) for them, although it is not too abstruse for Israel.[224]

A number of Midrashim suggest that the angels not only tried to block Moses from taking the Torah to earth, but they actually engaged in battle with him and sought to destroy him.[225] However, the angels could not prevail over Moses, and in the end they trembled before him.[226] One of the most vivid references to Moses's struggles with the angels is found in a Midrash on the death of Moses in Deuteronomy Rabbāh, in which Moses recounts his heavenly adventures to Sammael, who had come to take away his soul.

> I ascended (*'ālāh*) and trod a path in the heavens. I engaged in a war of the angels and received a Torah of fire. I dwelt under a throne (*kissē'*) of fire and took shelter under a pillar of fire, and I spoke with [God] face to face (*pānîm b*ᵉ-

> *pānîm*). I subdued the heavenly retinue and revealed their secrets (*rāzîm*) to human beings. I received the Torah from the right hand of the Holy One, blessed be He, and taught it to Israel.[227]

Several Midrashim in Exodus Rabbāh II suggest that when Moses was on high he adapted his life-style to accord with that of the denizens of heaven. Commenting on Exodus 34.28, "And he was there with the Lord forty days and forty nights; he neither ate bread nor drank water," a Midrash cited in the name of R. Meir emphasizes that the reason Moses fasted was in order to emulate the heavenly example while on high, where there is no eating and drinking.[228] An anonymous Midrash elaborates on this notion, explaining that while in heaven Moses ate only of the bread of Torah and drank only of its waters.[229] Another anonymous tradition suggests that, like the *ḥayyôṯ* who bear the divine throne, Moses derived his nourishment from the splendor of the Shekhinah.[230] Moses is further said to have not slept during his sojourn on high,[231] where there is no distinction between day and night.[232]

When Moses descended from the heavens, he brought the Torah with him to earth. An anonymous tradition in P^{e}sîqtā' Rabbāṯî emphasizes how the heavens wept and lamented while the earth rejoiced when the Torah went forth to make its abode on earth. The parable compares the giving of the Torah to a marriage ceremony in which the Torah, as the bride of Israel, departed from the home of her father on high and went to dwell with her spouse on earth.[233] A number of other passages in P^{e}sîqtā' Rabbāṯî and Tanḥûmā' Y^{e}lamm^{e}ḏēnû Midrashim make similar use of the marriage metaphor, depicting the Torah as the bride who is wed to Israel.[234] An anonymous Midrash in Exodus Rabbāh II compares God to a king who gave his only daughter to another king in marriage and then asked if he might dwell with them, since he could not bear to leave his daughter.

> Thus, the Holy One, blessed be He, said to Israel, "I have given you the Torah. I cannot be separated from her, and yet I cannot say to you, 'Do not take her.' However, in every place to which you go, make for Me a house wherein I may dwell."[235]

When the Torah descended to earth to become the bride of Israel, God's presence thus descended with it. A tradition in Exodus

Rabbāh II ascribed to R. Berekhiah similarly emphasizes that when Israel acquired the Torah they acquired God as well, for God abides wherever the Torah is.[236] In this perspective it was not only the Torah who was wed to Israel at Mount Sinai, it was God himself. Hence we find that the marriage metaphor is used in Pᵉsîqtā' Rabbāṯî and Tanḥûmā' Yᵉlammᵉḏēnû Midrashim not only to depict the union between the Torah and Israel but also to portray the eternal covenant between the Lord and his chosen people. In this version of the wedding ceremony, Israel assumes the role of the bride,[237] and the Torah is at times portrayed as the marriage contract (*kᵉṯûbāh*) stipulating the conditions of the covenant between God and Israel.[238]

The Israelites' Reception of the Theophany In Pᵉsîqtā' Rabbāṯî and Tanḥûmā' Yᵉlammᵉḏēnû Midrashim, as in earlier rabbinic texts, the revelation at Mount Sinai is represented as involving a two-way interchange between earth and heaven, in which Moses ascended to heaven and dwelt with God and the angels, and God himself, accompanied by the angels, descended to earth and revealed his glory to the people of Israel. God is said to have come down upon Mount Sinai[239] and set his glory (*kāḇôḏ*) upon the mountain,[240] where he manifested his Godhead (*'ĕlōhûṯ*).[241] He is further described as appearing in his glory (*kāḇôḏ*),[242] revealing the Shekhinah,[243] and bestowing upon the Israelites "splendor (*zîw*) from the splendor of the Shekhinah."[244]

(1) Descent of God and the Heavenly Hosts

In discussing God's descent to Sinai, Pᵉsîqtā' Rabbāṯî and Tanḥûmā' Yᵉlammᵉḏēnû Midrashim incorporate a number of traditions concerning the role of the Merkabah in the theophany. A tradition that appears in Exodus Rabbāh II and the Tanḥûmā' points to the more sinister ramifications of the Israelite's vision of the Merkabah at Sinai, suggesting that the apostasy with the golden calf may have been a direct result of this vision. The variant in Exodus Rabbāh XLIII.8, which is attributed through tradents to R. Jose b. Ḥanina, depicts God descending to Sinai in a carriage drawn by a team of four. The passage invokes Psalm 68.18, which, as we have seen, is the key biblical verse that mentions the presence of chariots at Sinai. It also makes explicit reference to Ezekiel's vision of the four living creatures (*ḥayyôṯ*) in Ezekiel 1.10. Of the four faces of the *ḥayyôṯ*—human, lion, ox, and eagle—the passage focuses in particular on the ox, claiming that the Israelites detached the ox from the team that drew God's carriage and used it in making the golden calf.

> R. Phinehas b. Ḥama the priest said in the name of R. Abbahu, who said in the name of R. Jose b. Ḥanina: What is the meaning of "I have surely seen [the affliction of My people]" (Exod. 3.7)? The Holy One, blessed be He, said to Moses, "You see them [the people of Israel] [as they are] now, but I see how they are going to contemplate Me. I will go forth in My carriage (*qārûḵîn*) to give them the Torah, as it is said, 'The chariots (*reḵeḇ*) of God are twice ten thousand, thousands upon thousands; the Lord is among them, Sinai in holiness' (Ps. 68.18). And then they will detach one of my team of four (*ṭeṭrā'mûlîn*), as it is written, 'And the four had the face of an ox on the left side' (Ezek. 1.10)." For this reason did Moses say, "'O Lord, why does Thy wrath burn hot against Thy people?' (Exod. 32.11). Thou didst know them [of old], and now that they have made [the golden calf] Thou art angry with them?"[245]

While this tradition alludes to the darker side of the Merkabah vision, the Merkabah is generally presented in a more uplifting light as part of the glorious entourage that descended with God to Sinai. Such discussions center on several issues connected with Psalm 68.18, "The chariots (*reḵeḇ*) of God are twice ten thousand, thousands upon thousands; the Lord is among them, Sinai in holiness." Does the verse refer to chariots or to angels? How many angels/chariots were there? What role did these hosts play at the revelation? One of the most extensive discussions is found in Pᵉsîqtā' Rabbāṯî 21.7–11, which contains a series of interpretations of Psalm 68.18. The passage includes variants of a number of traditions that appear in the corresponding passage in Pᵉsîqtā' dᵉ-R. Kahana, discussed earlier, as well as in parallel pericopes in the Tanḥûmā'.[246]

The pericope in Pᵉsîqtā' Rabbāṯî begins with the interpretation ascribed to R. Abdimi, which understands Psalm 68.18 as referring to the 22,000 ministering angels that descended with God.[247] The passage then cites an aggadah attributed to R. Levi that represents a variant of the tradition ascribed to R. Berekhiah in Pᵉsîqtā' dᵉ-R. Kahana. R. Levi's aggadah links the 22,000 angels to the crown motif, maintaining that each angel bore a crown (*'ăṭārāh*) with which to adorn the 22,000 males in the tribe of Levi, who alone would remain unmoved in the frenzy associated with the golden calf.[248] The passage continues with the interpretation concerning the 22,000 chariots (*markāḇôṯ*), which in the present context is ascribed to R. Yannai the son of Simeon b. Yannai and is framed as an explicit rejoinder to the view that there were 22,000 angels.[249] The pericope then interjects the two alternative aggadot attributed to R. Joḥanan regarding the role of the angels in bestowing ornaments on the people of Israel, in which the number of angels is calculated at either 600,000, each angel bearing a crown (*'ăṭārāh*) for each Israelite, or 1,200,000, half of the angels each bearing a crown (*'ăṭārāh*) and the other half a girdle (*zônā'*).[250] The passage continues with several traditions, including the interpretation ascribed to R. Tanḥum b. Ḥanilai, that assert that the hosts accompanying God were innumerable and cannot be calculated.[251]

Several passages in the Tanḥûmā' contain a parallel but abbreviated sequence of traditions.[252] One of the most significant points of divergence is the variant reading of the Midrash attributed to R. Abdimi, which maintains that "22,000 chariots (*markāḇôṯ*) of ministering angels" descended with God.[253] This reading, which combines the motifs of chariots and angels, may represent the original reading of R. Abdimi's Midrash.[254]

A number of passages in Pᵉsîqtā' Rabbāṯî and Tanḥûmā' Yᵉlammᵉḏēnû Midrashim record debates concerning the types of ornaments with which the Israelites were adorned after they agreed to accept the Torah. A pericope in Pᵉsîqtā' Rabbāṯî 33.10[255] cites the traditions, also found in earlier texts, that the angels invested the Israelites with crowns (*'ăṭārôṯ*) and girdles (*zôniyyôṯ*) (R. Joḥanan)[256] or with a weapon (*zayîn*) on which the ineffable Name of God was engraved (R. Simeon b. Yoḥai).[257] In addition, the pericope includes a tradition, also attributed to R. Simeon b. Yoḥai, that they clothed the Israelites in royal purple garments (*'argᵉwāwnîm*).[258] A passage in Exodus Rabbāh LI.8 records a similar set of views, but it reconstrues the tradition by having God himself, rather than the angels, invest the Israelites with these ornaments. It begins with the view that "as soon as they [the Israelites] accepted the Torah the Holy One, blessed be He, clothed them with some of the splendor of His glory (*zîw hăḏārô*)."[259] It then cites the various opinions of the sages concerning the nature of this adornment: crowns (*'ăṭārôṯ*) (R. Joḥanan), a weapon (*zayin*) engraved with the ineffable Name (R. Simeon b. Yoḥai), royal purple garments (*pôrpîrāh*) (here attributed to R. Simai), or girdles (*zônā'ôṯ*) (R. Huna b. Abin).[260] The passage goes on to assert that after the Israelites sinned they were deprived of their ornaments, as indicated in Exodus 33.6: "And the people of Israel stripped themselves of their ornaments from Mount Horeb onward."[261]

Numbers Rabbāh II and the Tanḥûmā' contain variants of the tradition concerning the royal purple garments that maintain that the garments were inscribed with the ineffable Name, a notion that bears striking resemblance to Hêḵālôṯ traditions concerning the garment (*ḥālûq*) of God that is inscribed with the Tetragrammaton.[262] Moreover, the Israelites are said to have been immune from death as long as they possessed the ineffable Name,[263] a view that is similarly asserted with regard to the weapon engraved with the ineffable Name.[264]

(2) They Heard and Saw

The synesthetic nature of the revelation experience, which engaged the faculties of both hearing and sight, is emphasized in a number of Midrashim. The revelation of the Torah was not only heard by the people as the all-powerful thunderings of God's voice, it was simultaneously seen as the all-consuming brilliance of God's glory. A tradition in Exodus Rabbāh II ascribed to R. Levi emphasizes the dual nature of the theophany.

> R. Levi said: Israel asked two things of the Holy One, blessed be He—that they might see (*rā'āh*) His glory (*kāḇôḏ*) and hear (*šāma'*) His voice (*qôl*). And they did see His glory and hear His voice, as it is said, "And you said, 'Behold, the Lord our God has caused us to see (*her'āh*) His glory and His greatness, and we have heard (*šāma'*) His voice out of the midst of the fire'" (Deut. 5.24).[265]

P^esîqtā' Rabbāṯî reiterates the tradition in P^esîqtā' d^e-R. Kahana that even the blind were given the capacity to see and the deaf to hear the revelation.[266]

Several traditions point to the process of differentiation through which the one Word of God divided into many words, recalling the process of differentiation of the Word at the beginning of creation. A Midrash in the Tanḥûmā' emphasizes the original unity of God's Word, in which "the Ten Words all came forth from the mouth of the Dynamis (G^eḇûrāh) in one voice (*qôl*)."[267] A tradition in P^esîqtā' Rabbāṯî, ascribed to R. Joḥanan through his tradent R. Abbahu, similarly maintains that God first uttered all of the Ten Words together at once, and afterward he gave each commandment, fully explained, directly to the people of Israel.[268] Another tradition attributed to R. Joḥanan, discussed earlier, focuses not on the division of the one Word into Ten Words but rather on the division of the one voice into seven voices and subsequently into seventy languages.[269]

A number of Midrashim emphasize the visionary aspects of the revelation, in which the people of Israel not only heard God's voice, they also saw God face to face.[270] An aggadah in Deuteronomy Rabbāh ascribed to R. Hoshaiah, like the parallel tradition in the M^eḵîltā', asserts that even the least of the Israelites attained a vision of God that surpassed Ezekiel's Merkabah vision, implying in particular that the Israelites' vision was more direct in that they saw the Shekhinah face to face.

> R. Hoshaiah said: The lowliest person in the days of Moses saw (*rā'āh*) what Ezekiel, the greatest of the prophets, did not see—people with whom the Shekhinah spoke face to face (*pānîm b^e-p̄ānîm*), as it is said, "The Lord spoke with you face to face (*pānîm b^e-p̄ānîm*)" (Deut. 5.4).[271]

P^esîqtā' Rabbāṯî 20.4, following the account of Moses's ascent to heaven in which God opened the seven firmaments to him, describes how God also opened the seven firmaments to all of Israel and appeared to them "eye to eye" on his throne of glory. The terminology that is used to describe Israel's vision of God is reminiscent of the technical language used in Hêḵālôṯ texts.

> Thereupon the Holy One, blessed be He, opened (*pāṯaḥ*) the seven firmaments (*r^eqî'îm*) and revealed Himself (*niḡlāh*) to them eye to eye, in His beauty (*yôp̄î*), in His glory (*kāḇôḏ*), in His stature (*tô'ar*), with His crown (*keṯer*), and on His throne of glory (*kissē' kāḇôḏ*).[272]

A tradition in Deuteronomy Rabbāh, ascribed to R. Phinehas and R. Levi in the name of R. Simeon b. Lakish maintains that God split open and showed to Israel not only the seven firmaments but also the lower realms.[273] The passage provides a rationale for why God opened the seven firmaments to Israel: so that they would see that God alone reigns supreme among the heavenly hosts, and they would therefore not be tempted, as the other nations were, to choose one of the angels as their god.[274] An aggadah in P^esîqtā' Rabbāṯî, attributed to R. Phinehas in the name of R. Joshua b. Levi, suggests that this temptation was real, for when the archangels Michael and Gabriel descended on Sinai with their respective retinues the Israelites at first mistook them for God. But then God reasserted his exclusive claim on his people by declaring to them, "You are *My* children, and I am your Father."[275]

The people of Israel who stood at the foot of Mount Sinai not only saw God arrayed on his throne in the heavens, they also saw the words of Torah coming forth in fire. As in earlier rabbinic texts, the Torah is identified in a number of Midrashim with the "fiery law" (*'ēš-dāṯ*) at God's right hand in Deuteronomy 33.2.[276] A tradition in Pesîqtā' Rabbāṯî ascribed to R. Berekhiah cosmologizes this notion, linking the fiery words of Torah with the mysteries of the throne of glory. The divine Word is described as blazing forth in fire and threatening to consume everything in its path, including the angels who are themselves composed of fire. The passage emphasizes that the fire of the divine Word is more intense than that of the angels, for it alone derives from the right hand of God.

> As the Word (*dibbēr*) sought to go forth, the herald went before it and said to the battalions of fire, "Get out of the way of the Word (*dîbbûr*) so that as it goes forth it does not burn you." Immediately the angels of fire got out of the way and the *ḥayyôṯ* got out of the way, so that they would not be burned by the blast of the Word. For the fire of the Word is more fierce than the fire of the angels, since the angels come merely from the fire beneath the throne of glory (*kissē' ha-kāḇôḏ*). . . . But the fire of the Word is directly from the right hand of the Holy One, blessed be He, as it is written, "At His right hand was a fiery law (*'ēš-dāṯ*) for them" (Deut. 33.2). . . . And the Word went forth from the mouth of the Holy One, blessed be He, and came and rested over the ears [of the Israelites] and rounded itself over them. Thus: "And roundings in your ears" (Ezek. 16.12).[277]

The Torah is connected in Pesîqtā' Rabbāṯî and Tanḥûmā' Yelammeḏēnû Midrashim not only with fire but also with light.[278] The two motifs are brought together in an aggadah in Deuteronomy Rabbāh attributed to R. Simeon b. Lakish, who maintains that Moses's radiant countenance was acquired through contact with the Torah, which was written with black fire on white fire.[279] The passage continues with an alternative explanation, attributed to R. Samuel b. Naḥman, which suggests that Moses acquired his lustrous appearance from the tablets when they were passed from God's hands to his hands.[280]

(3) They Died and Were Resurrected

The overpowering impact of the theophany at Mount Sinai is pointed to in several passages in Pesîqtā' Rabbāṯî and Tanḥûmā'

Y^e^lamm^e^ḏēnû Midrashim. Even though one of the purposes of the revelation was to consolidate the creation, a number of Midrashim suggest that the initial impact was so intense that both earth and heaven quaked and the earth feared that it might be returned to chaos.[281] One Midrash in the Tanḥûmā', discussed earlier, maintains that the gentile nations were not able to endure the all-powerful voice of God and died, while the Israelites alone remained alive.[282] However, this view is countered by other Midrashim that maintain, in accordance with certain traditions found in earlier rabbinic texts, that the Israelites themselves were incapable of bearing the experience, and thus upon hearing God's voice their souls departed.[283]

With respect to the way in which the souls of the Israelites were restored, Exodus Rabbāh XXIX.4 includes a variant of the tradition in Song of Songs Rabbāh that the souls of the Israelites were restored through the intervention of the Torah.[284] The concluding pericope in P^e^sîqtā' Rabbāṯî 20.4 gives two alternative explanations. It first gives a variant of the Talmudic tradition that God revived them with the dew with which he will resurrect the souls of the righteous in the time to come.[285] It then gives an alternative explanation that, in contrast to its earlier depiction of the angels as the hostile opponents of Moses, portrays the angels as the Israelites' allies, who descended to assist in reviving them: 1,200,000 angels descended, two for each Israelite, and while one angel put his hand on the Israelite's heart, the other lifted up his or her neck so that he/she could see God face to face.

(4) Each According to His or Her Capacity

A Midrash in Exodus Rabbāh II ascribed to R. Judah ha-Nasi emphasizes that if God had come to the Israelites in the fullness of his power, they would not have been able to withstand it, and therefore he came to each individual according to his or her own capacity. Like the parallel traditions in the M^e^ḵîltā' and classical Amoraic Midrashim, this Midrash invokes Psalm 29.4, "The voice (*qôl*) of the Lord is according to power (*ba-kōaḥ*)": "It does not say, 'according to *His* power,' but 'according to power'—according to the power of each and every individual."[286] A pericope in the Tanḥûmā' elaborates on the individualized nature of the experience, in which God's voice was modulated to coincide with the capacities of people of different ages and genders.

> Come and see how the voice (*qôl*) went forth to Israel, to each and every individual according to his or her capacity

> (*kōaḥ*). The elderly heard the voice according to their capacity, and the young people according to their capacity, and the boys according to their capacity, and the small children according to their capacity, and the infants according to their capacity, and the women according to their capacity, and even Moses according to his capacity. . . . And thus it says, "The voice (*qôl*) of the Lord is according to power (*ba-kōaḥ*)" (Ps. 29.4). It does not say, "according to *His* power," but "according to [one's] power," so that each and every one of them would be able to endure it.[287]

The pericope continues with a variant of the manna analogy attributed to R. Jose b. Ḥanina.[288] In discussing how the voice of the Lord was heard "with the power of all voices," adapting itself to the needs of each individual, several traditions are careful to emphasize that although a plurality of voices was apprehended, the God who spoke is one.[289]

God not only manifested multiple voices to the Israelites, he also appeared with manifold faces. P^e^sîqtā' Rabbāṯî 21.6 gives a series of interpretations of Deuteronomy 5.4, "The Lord spoke with you face to face (*pānîm b^e^-pānîm*) at the mountain," discussing the many faces that God showed to Israel at Sinai. The pericope incorporates the statue analogy, attributed in the present context to R. Joḥanan, as well as a number of other analogies that emphasize God's ability to display many faces simultaneously so that each Israelite would experience God looking at and speaking to him or her directly.[290]

Pirqê d^e^-R. Eliezer

Pirqê d^e^-R. Eliezer gives its own account of the revelation at Mount Sinai, in which it expands upon certain key events in the biblical narrative by incorporating earlier aggadic traditions interlaced with its own distinctive mode of cosmological speculation. Chapter 41 focuses on God's descent upon Mount Sinai and the revelation of the Ten Commandments to the people of Israel. After the interjection of three chapters, which are out of place chronologically, concerning the Exodus from Egypt and the Israelites' battle with the Amalekites, the account of the revelation is resumed in chapter 45, which recounts the golden calf incident and Moses's breaking of the tablets and subsequent intercession on behalf of Israel. Chapter 46 describes Moses's second sojourn on the mountain for forty days and forty nights and subsequent descent with the Torah on Yom Kippur, the Day of Atonement.

With respect to the two phases of the revelation, chapter 41 is primarily concerned with the people of Israel's experience of the theophany at the giving of the Ten Commandments, while chapter 46 focuses on Moses's experience as the special recipient of God's revelation on the mountain. Pirqê d^e-R. Eliezer's account accords with the view that only the first two of the Ten Commandments were declared directly by God to the people of Israel, while the rest were spoken through the mouth of Moses.[291] The recipients of the commandments are said to have included not only the living members of the Israelite community but also the dead, who were revived from Sheol, and all subsequent generations who were destined to be created in the future.[292] This notion represents an expansion of the tradition ascribed to R. Isaac in the Tanḥûmā' and Exodus Rabbāh II, which maintains that the prophets and sages who would arise in future generations were present at Mount Sinai.[293]

During his sojourn on the mountain for forty days and forty nights, Moses is depicted as sitting before God like a disciple sitting before his teacher, reading (*qārā'*) the Written Law (*dāṯ miqrā'*) in the day and repeating (*šānāh*) the Oral Law (*dāṯ mišnāh*) at night.[294] He is portrayed as the first Midrashist, expounding (*dāraš*) the meaning of the words of the Written Torah and examining (*ḥāqar*) its letters.[295]

Torah and the Nations The role of the gentile nations in the giving of the Torah is not a major concern in Pirqê d^e-R. Eliezer. In the beginning of its account of the Sinai revelation the text ascribes to R. Tarphon the traditional interpretation of Deuteronomy 33.2, "The Lord came from Sinai, and dawned from Seir upon them; He shone forth from Mount Paran," as meaning that God offered the Torah to the children of Esau (Seir), the children of Ishmael (Paran), and the other nations of the world.[296] However, the gentile nations declined his offer, saying, "We do not desire the Torah, so give Thy Torah to Thy people, as it is said, 'The Lord will give strength (*'ōz*) to His people, the Lord will bless His people with peace' (Ps. 29.11)."[297]

Ascent of Moses and Descent of the Torah As in earlier rabbinic texts, the revelation of the Torah is represented in Pirqê d^e-R. Eliezer as a cosmic event in which the boundaries that separate heaven and earth became permeable. At the theophany the heavens were opened (*niptaḥ*) so that the summit of Mount Sinai extended into the heavens.[298] A tradition ascribed to R. Joshua b. Karḥa emphasizes that although Moses stood with his feet on the mountain, his body was inside (*bᵉ-tôḵ*) the heavens. From his privileged position he was able to see (*ṣāp̄āh*) and look at (*hibbîṭ*) everything in the heavens and to speak with God face to face.[299] A second tradition depicts Moses ascending (*ʿālāh*) to the heavens in order to bring the Torah down to earth.[300]

In the context of describing Moses's second sojourn on high after the breaking of the tablets, Pirqê dᵉ-R. Eliezer gives an abbreviated version of the aggadah, also found in Šabbāṯ 88b–89a and Pᵉsîqtā' Rabbāṯî 20.4, that represents the angels as attempting to dissuade Moses from taking the Torah. Moses responded by showing that the commandments of the Torah do not apply to the angels, since angels do not have fathers and mothers to honor (Exod. 20.12, fifth commandment) nor do they die (Num. 19.14). The angels conceded and bestowed gifts upon Moses, which included amulets for healing. As in the parallel traditions, Psalm 68.19 is invoked as a proof text: "You ascended on high, you took a captivity captive, you took gifts for humanity."[301]

Several passages in Pirqê dᵉ-R. Eliezer depict the giving of the Torah as a wedding ceremony, presenting both versions of the marriage metaphor. One passage portrays the revelation as a wedding between God and his bride, Israel: "The bridegroom (*ḥāṯān*) went forth to meet the bride (*kallāh*) to give to them the Torah, as it is said, 'O God, when Thou didst go forth before Thy people' (Ps. 68.8)."[302] A second passage depicts the wedding as taking place between the people of Israel and their bride, Torah. In contrast to the more usual portrayal of the Torah as the daughter who is given by God, her father, in marriage, in this parable Israel assumes the role of God's son. The parable emphasizes that God foresaw that his son, Israel, would go astray from his wife, Torah, within forty days after the wedding.[303]

The Israelites' Reception of the Theophany The revelation at Mount Sinai is presented in Pirqê dᵉ-R. Eliezer as the "sixth descent" in its schema of the "ten descents (*yᵉrîḏôṯ*)" of God from heaven to earth.[304] Chapter 41 opens with a description of the sixth of God's theophanies.

> The sixth descent was when He descended (*yāraḏ*) to Sinai, as it is said, "And the Lord came down (*yāraḏ*) upon Mount

> Sinai" (Exod. 19.20). On the sixth of Sivan the Holy One, blessed be He, revealed Himself (*niḡlāh*) to Israel on Mount Sinai. Mount Sinai was uprooted from its place, and the heavens were opened (*nip̄taḥ*), and the top of the mountain entered into the heavens. Thick darkness covered the mountain. The Holy One, blessed be He, sat on His throne (*kissē'*), and His feet stood on the thick darkness, as it is said, "He bowed the heavens and came down, and thick darkness was under His feet" (2 Sam. 22.10; Ps. 18.10).[305]

This passage vividly portrays the intermingling of heaven and earth at Sinai, in which the mountain extended into the heavens, and God, seated on his throne of glory, rested his feet on the darkness that enwrapped the mountain.

(1) Descent of God and the Heavenly Hosts

The text continues with a description of the theophany that recalls the imagery used in earlier rabbinic texts. God is portrayed, in accordance with Deuteronomy 33.2, as descending with the fiery Torah in his right hand and, in allusion to Psalm 68.18, as accompanied by "thousands upon thousands" of chariots (*reḵeḇ*) and 20,000 angels.[306] A second tradition, attributed to R. Eleazar b. Arak, depicts God as descending with 600,000 ministering angels who bore weapons (*z*ᵉ*yânôṯ*) and crowns (*'ăṭārôṯ*). In contrast to earlier traditions that suggest that each Israelite was invested with a crown[307] and/or a weapon engraved with the ineffable Name,[308] this tradition provides a fresh interpretation in which the Israelites were crowned with the "crown (*keṯer*) of the ineffable Name."[309] This notion is explicitly connected with the Merkabah mysteries in an earlier passage in Pirqê dᵉ-R. Eliezer, which portrays God as similarly adorned on his throne: "A crown (*'ăṭārāh*) is set on His head and the crown (*keṯer*) of the ineffable Name is on His forehead."[310] A tradition ascribed to R. Judah b. Il'ai describes the resplendence of the people of Israel when clothed with the Name, recalling earlier traditions concerning the special garments with which the Israelites were adorned.

> As long as a person is clothed in the garments of his splendor he is beautiful in his appearance and in his glory (*kāḇôḏ*) and in his dignity. Thus were the Israelites when they were clothed with that Name—they were as good as ministering angels before the Holy One, blessed be He.[311]

The tradition continues with a discussion of how when the Israelites went astray after the golden calf, 600,000 ministering angels again descended and stripped them of their adornments, in accordance with Exodus 33.6: "And the people of Israel stripped themselves of their ornaments."[312]

(2) They Heard and Saw

The theophany is described in Pirqê d^e-R. Eliezer, as in earlier rabbinic sources, in terms of both auditory and visual phenomena. On the one hand, the people of Israel are said to have heard (*šāma'*) the voice of God resounding forth from out of the fire and the darkness.[313] On the other hand, in a tradition ascribed to R. Judah b. Il'ai they are said to have seen (*rā'āh*) the voice of God.

> When a person speaks with his companion he is visible, but his voice is not visible. The Israelites heard (*šāma'*) the voice (*qôl*) of the Holy One, blessed be He, and saw (*rā'āh*) the voice coming forth from the mouth of the Dynamis (G^{e}ḇûrāh) with lightnings and thunderings, as it is said, "And all the people saw (*rā'āh*) the voices (*qôlôṯ*) and the lightnings" (Exod. 20.18).[314]

The Israelites not only saw God's voice, they saw God himself enthroned in the heavens that were opened before them,[315] and they saw him descending with myriads of celestial hosts, bearing the fiery Torah in his right hand.[316]

Pirqê d^e-R. Eliezer is concerned not only with the oral transmission of the Ten Commandments but also with their written form inscribed on the tablets. The tablets (*lûḥôṯ*) and the divine writing (*miḵtāḇ*) engraved upon them are both said to have been created of old (*mi-qeḏem*), on the eve of the first Sabbath.[317] They were of heavenly origin, constituting the handiwork (*ma'ăśēh yāḏ*) of God and written with the finger of God.[318] When the tablets beheld the Israelites dancing before the golden calf, the writing engraved upon them is said to have flown away (*pāraḥ*), presumably returning to its heavenly home.[319]

(3) They Died and Were Resurrected

Pirqê d^e-R. Eliezer gives a vivid portrayal of the all-encompassing power of God's voice, which caused tremors throughout creation, shaking heaven and earth and causing the dead to rise and the living to die.[320] While the voice (*qôl*) of the first commandment resurrected the dead and caused the Israelites to die, the voice of the second commandment resurrected the Israelites.[321] However, they were so terrified that they pleaded with Moses that he should speak to them rather than God, for they feared that if they heard any more of the voice of God, they would once again die. An explicit rationale is thus given for the tradition that only the first two of the commandments were spoken directly by God: the Israelites could not bear to hear any more, as evidenced by their inability to hear even one commandment without dying.[322]

TORAH AND REVELATION IN KABBALISTIC TEXTS

Rabbinic traditions concerning the revelation of the Torah at Mount Sinai are elaborated and reformulated in kabbalistic texts in accordance with their specific cosmological and epistemological concerns. As an example of this process of reformulation, our analysis will focus on the accounts of the revelation in the Zohar, which itself assumes the form of a mystical Midrash on the pentateuchal account.

Zohar

The Zohar's discussions of the Sinai revelation incorporate many of the speculations found in rabbinic texts concerning the relationship between creation and revelation, the ascent of Moses, the descent of God and the Torah, and the Israelites' reception of the theophany. While rabbinic traditions at times evidence an interest in esoteric speculation, the Zohar's appropriation of these traditions is unambiguously mystical. The theosophical system of the *s*ᵉ*p̄îrôṯ*, the ten divine emanations, provides a unifying framework in light of which the different components of the revelation narrative are recast.

The process of revelation is represented in the Zohar as a recapitulation of the process of creation, in which the *s*ᵉ*p̄îrôṯ* unfolded as they did "in the beginning." The descent of God at Sinai is understood in this context as a descent grade by grade through the various *s*ᵉ*p̄îrôṯ* until he reached the "earth," which corresponds to the lowest of the *s*ᵉ*p̄îrôṯ*, Malḵûṯ, the Shekhinah. The Torah itself unfolded in progressive stages of manifestation corresponding to the *s*ᵉ*p̄îrôṯ*. The people of Israel, as the recipients of the revelation, are described as attaining a vision of the sᵉp̄îrôṯic pleroma either directly or mediated through the Shekhinah. While God thus descended to his people, unfolding his divine emanations before their eyes, Moses alone, as the supreme prophet, is portrayed as having the ability to ascend to the Godhead and attain a clear vision of the hidden light of Torah in the upper realms of the *s^e^p̄îrôṯ*.

Torah and the Nations The cosmological and epistemological concerns of the Zohar are evident even in its discussions of Deuteronomy 33.2, "The Lord came from Sinai, and dawned from Seir upon them; he shone forth from Mount Paran," which is generally interpreted in rabbinic texts in light of the tradition that the Torah was offered to all nations. One passage in the Zohar begins with a traditional exegesis of Deuteronomy 33.2, in which Seir is interpreted as referring to the children of Esau and Paran to the children of Ishmael. However, the passage then presents a novel interpretation with cosmological import, in which Seir is understood as a name of Samael and Paran as a name of Rahab. Deuteronomy 33.2 is interpreted in this context to mean that God first offered the Torah to Samael and Rahab and the other heavenly powers who have dominion over the nations. He presented to each of them one of the prohibitive commandments of the Torah—"You shall not kill" to Samael, "You shall not commit adultery" to Rahab, and so on—knowing that they would thereby refuse the Torah and would encourage him to offer it instead to Israel. In this way, rather than coveting the Torah, the heavenly powers were eager to induce Israel to accept it by presenting them with gifts.[323]

A second passage in the Zohar gives an epistemological interpretation of Deuteronomy 33.2. The passage is concerned with a hierarchy of grades of divine revelation that were experienced by the various prophets, and in this context interprets Sinai, Seir, and Paran as referring to different grades of revelation.[324]

Revelation and Creation The Zohar elaborates on the rabbinic notion that the revelation of the Torah at Mount Sinai recapitulated the process of creation and brought it to completion. However, this notion is embedded in the Zoharic cosmology of multiple worlds and divine emanations and is thus infused with distinctively kabbalistic valences.

The Zohar emphasizes that even though the upper and lower worlds had been supported and maintained by the Torah since the beginning of creation,[325] they were not completely and unshakably established until Israel received the Torah at Mount Sinai.[326] One passage reiterates the rabbinic tradition that the earth shook and desired to return to chaos when it saw that God had offered the Torah to the nations and they had refused it, but when Israel accepted the

Torah the earth became calm again.[327] A second passage presents a different trend of speculation that suggests that the creation itself was out of alignment until the revelation restored its original integrity. All but the last two letters of the Hebrew alphabet, which are the primordial elements that structure and uphold the universe, are said to have been in inverse order since the time of Adam's transgression, and it was not until Israel accepted the Torah at Mount Sinai that the letters recovered the order they had on the day when heaven and earth were created. Through the revelation the creation was once again securely established and brought to fruition.[328]

> [The world] was not completed until Israel received the Torah at Mount Sinai, and the Tabernacle was erected. Then the worlds were completed and put on a secure foundation, and the upper and lower regions were perfumed.[329]

The Zohar suggests that the worlds were firmly established when the Torah was accepted at Mount Sinai because the revelation itself was a second creation. In the beginning of creation the Torah issued forth as the Word of God containing the ten words through which the universe was brought into being. At the time of revelation the Torah again issued forth from the heavens as the Word of God and split into the Ten Words of the Decalogue through which the universe was renovated and consolidated.[330] The correlation between the ten words (*ma'ămārôṯ*) of creation and the Ten Words (*dibbᵉrôṯ*) of revelation had already been suggested in rabbinic texts.[331] The Zohar incorporates this conception into its theosophical scheme by asserting the identity of the ten words of creation and the Ten Words of revelation with the ten *sᵉp̄îrôṯ*, the ten spheres of the Godhead.[332] The Torah as the Name of God[333] encompasses all of the *sᵉp̄îrôṯ*, which unfold as the Ten Words in creation and revelation.

> For the Torah is the Name of the Holy One, blessed be He. As the Name of the Holy One is engraved in the Ten Words (creative utterances) of Creation, so is the whole Torah engraved in the Ten Words (Decalogue), and these Ten Words are the Name of the Holy One, and the whole Torah is thus one Name, the Holy Name of God Himself.[334]

The unfoldment of the Ten Words at Mount Sinai is thus represented in the Zohar as a recapitulation of the original revelation of the divine glory at the inception of creation, in which the ten spheres of the Godhead manifested once again as they had in the beginning.

> Never before, since the Holy One created the world, had such a revelation of the Divine Glory taken place. . . . On that day the Holy One, blessed be He, rejoiced more than on any previous day since He had created the world, for Creation had no proper basis before Israel received the Torah, as is implied in the words: "But for my covenant with day and night, I had not appointed the ordinances of heaven and earth" [Jer. 33.25]. But when once Israel had received the Torah on Mount Sinai the world was duly and completely established, and heaven and earth received a proper foundation, and the glory of the Holy One was made known both above and below, and He was exalted over all.[335]

Reception of the Theophany The significance of the Sinai revelation as a theophany thus assumes new import in the Zohar, in which the descent of God and manifestation of his glory are understood with reference to the doctrine of *s^e^p̄îrôṯ*. One passage interprets "The Lord came down upon (*'al*, literally, 'above') Mount Sinai" (Exod. 19.20) in its literal sense to mean that God descended above, not onto, Sinai: God descended from grade to grade through his various emanations until he reached the "earth," the level of Malḵûṯ, the Shekhinah, which stands above Mount Sinai.[336] The Zohar emphasizes that the Israelites who stood at Mount Sinai had been purified of all earthly dross so that their bodies and souls were lucent vessels worthy to receive the light of the Godhead.[337] Moreover, the souls of all past and future generations of Israelites were also present to receive the revelation.[338]

The Zohar's accounts emphasize primarily the visionary aspects of the Israelites' experience of the theophany, for as Elliot Wolfson has argued, "gnosis for the *Zohar* is primarily visual and not auditory."[339] At Sinai the Israelites saw "face to face" and "eye to eye" the splendor of the glory of the Lord.[340] When the one Word of God divided into the Ten Words, these Words through which God's glory was manifested were simultaneously heard as audible voices and seen as configurations of divine light. In this context the Zohar goes beyond rabbinic interpretations of Exodus 20.18, "And all the people saw (*rā'āh*) the voices (*qôlōṯ*)," interpreting the voices not simply as words of fire but as the spheres of divine light, the *s^e^p̄îrôṯ* themselves, in which the mysteries of creation are inscribed.

> Said R. Abba: "It is written: 'And all the people saw the thunderings' [Exod. 20.18]. Surely it ought to be *heard* the thunderings? We have, however, been taught that the 'voices' were delineated, carved out, as it were, upon the threefold darkness, so that they could be apprehended as something visible, and they saw and heard all those wonderful things out of the darkness, cloud and cloudy darkness; and because they saw that sight they were irradiated with a supernal light, and perceived things beyond the ken of all succeeding generations, and saw face to face [Deut. 5.4]." And whence did they derive the power so to see? According to R. Jose, from the light of those voices, for there was not one of them but emitted light which made perceptible all things hidden and veiled, and even all the generations of men up to the days of King Messiah. Therefore it says: "And all the people saw the voices"; they did actually see them.[341]

The view attributed to R. Jose implies that the voices that were seen by the Israelites were the light of the *s*^{e}*p̄îrôṯ*, a view that is espoused elsewhere in the Zohar.[342] However, the passage subsequently presents another view that suggests that the Israelites' vision of the *s*^{e}*p̄îrôṯ* was mediated through the Shekhinah, the last of the divine emanations, the "voice from below, which gathered into itself all the light emanating from the other voices."[343] This view is reiterated in another passage, which maintains that whatever the people of Israel saw at Mount Sinai they saw from "one Light (the Shekhinah) in which were focused all the other lights [the upper *s*^{e}*p̄îrôṯ*]."[344]

Building on the earlier rabbinic statement that the people of Israel "saw what Isaiah and Ezekiel never saw,"[345] the Zohar is concerned to clarify in what way the Israelites' experience at Mount Sinai was qualitatively superior to the prophet Ezekiel's vision of the Merkabah, the throne-chariot. It emphasizes that while the Israelites saw God "face to face," Ezekiel saw only the "likeness" of the chariots, and even then his vision was obscured as though by many walls.[346] More specifically, the Israelites saw the upper *s*^{e}*p̄îrôṯ* as reflected in the Shekhinah, as one sees light in a crystal, whereas Ezekiel saw only the Shekhinah as revealed in her chariots, which are below the realm of the *s*^{e}*p̄îrôṯ*.[347] According to another view, the Israelites saw the five upper voices by means of which the Torah was given, whereas Ezekiel saw five corresponding lower manifestations: a stormy wind, a great cloud, flashing fire, a brightness, and the electrum.[348] Finally, at Sinai the "head" and "body" of the King were revealed, while only the "hand" or "feet" were shown to Ezekiel.[349] The prophet Isaiah's vision of the Shekhinah is said to have been comparable to that of Ezekiel,[350] and thus his experience too is relegated to a level lower than that of the Israelites, whose vision of the higher mysteries of the *s^e^p̄îrô̱t* surpassed that of all the prophets except Moses.

Moses is celebrated in the Zohar, as in rabbinic texts, as the supreme prophet, who attained a vision of the luminous reaches of the Godhead that no other prophet attained. "If the Israelites saw what no prophet ever saw, how much more true is this of Moses!"[351] The Zohar maintains, in accordance with other thirteenth-century kabbalists, that whereas all other prophets, including the patriarchs Abraham, Isaac, and Jacob, attained a vision of the Shekhinah, the lowest of the *s^e^p̄îrô̱t*, which is the "nonluminous speculum," Moses alone ascended to the level of Tip̄'ere̱t, the sixth *s^e^p̄îrāh*, which is the "luminous speculum."[352] As discussed in chapter 2, in establishing correlations between the *s^e^p̄îrô̱t* and the various manifestations of Torah, the Zohar identifies Tip̄'ere̱t with the Written Torah and Malḵû̱t, the Shekhinah, with the Oral Torah.[353] The implication is thus that while the other prophets may have had fleeting glimpses of the supernal Oral Torah, Moses is the only prophet who attained a clear vision of the hidden light of the Written Torah. The Zohar also emphasizes that whereas Moses received the divine revelation standing and gazed directly at the effulgence of the supernal glory with his faculties intact, the other prophets fell on their faces and were bereft of their faculties. Moreover, while Moses understood the divine message fully, the other prophets attained only partial understanding.[354]

In discussing the Israelites' experience of the revelation, the Zohar adapts a number of rabbinic traditions to its theosophical schema. For example, the Zohar conflates the notion that the one Word divided into Ten Words, corresponding to the ten *s^e^p̄îrô̱t*, with the rabbinic conception that the voice of God divided into seventy languages.

> We have been told that at the revelation on Mount Sinai, when the Torah was given to Israel in Ten Words, each Word became a voice, and every voice was divided into seventy voices, all of which shone and sparkled before the eyes of all Israel, so that they saw eye to eye the splendour of His

> Glory, as it is written: "And all the people *saw* the voices" [Exod. 20.18].[355]

In accordance with its cosmological concerns, the Zohar does not refer to the mundane conception of seventy languages corresponding to the seventy nations of the world, but rather it focuses instead on the phenomenology of the seventy voices as configurations of divine light. Another passage, which appropriates rabbinic images of the divine utterances encircling the Israelites and becoming inscribed on the tablets,[356] suggests that each of the Ten Words had seventy different aspects.

> [I]t [the divine Word] encircled them [the Israelites] again and impressed itself upon the tablets of stone, until the whole Ten Words were designed thereon. R. Simeon said further that every word contained all manner of legal implications and derivations, as well as all mysteries and hidden aspects; for each word was indeed like unto a treasure-house, full of all precious things. And though when one Word was uttered it sounded but as itself, yet when it was stamped upon the stone seventy different aspects were revealed in it. . . .[357]

This passage indicates that the seventy different aspects of each of the Ten Words only became apparent after the oral utterances assumed a written form on the tablets. This notion has important implications for kabbalistic hermeneutics, for it suggests that the Zohar's conception of the seventy modes of interpreting the Torah[358] is intimately connected to the fact that the text is written rather than oral.

The Zohar's concern with the visual dimensions of the revelation is evident not only in its representation of the Ten Words as visible phenomena but also in its discussions of the manner in which these Words were transcribed on the tablets of stone. The Zohar emphasizes the transmundane origins of the tablets as well as of the writing, which were both the work of God. The writing in particular is said to have had a miraculous quality in that it pierced through the tablets so that the letters were visible from both sides, a tradition that is also found in rabbinic texts.[359] With respect to the rabbinic debate concerning whether five or ten commandments were written on each tablet,[360] the Zohar reconciles the two views by insisting that although the first five Words were written on the right tablet and the second five on the left tablet, the latter were included in, and could be seen from within, the first five Words.[361]

> We have a dictum that the first five commandments include by implication the other five as well: in other words, in the first five the second five are engraved, five within five.[362]

The Zohar emphasizes that all of the Ten Words could be seen on the right tablet and were given by God's right hand (Deut. 33.2), and hence this shows that the left, the side of power/justice, corresponding to Geḇûrāh, the fifth *sep̄îrāh,* is incorporated within and tempered by the right, the side of mercy corresponding to Ḥeseḏ, the fourth *sep̄îrāh.*[363] The Zohar invokes the rabbinic tradition that the Torah was written with black fire on white fire[364] to make a similar point: the black fire represents power (Geḇûrāh) and the white fire mercy (Ḥeseḏ), and thus the left and right were united, with justice tempered by mercy.[365]

The Epistemology of Revelation The Zohar's account of the revelation emphasizes what Wolfson has termed "the hermeneutics of visionary experience." Wolfson remarks:

> As to the specific content of the visionary experience at Sinai we learn . . . that the vision had a decidedly gnostic element, i.e. through the vision the people were able to gain esoteric knowledge of the divine attributes. . . . A clear link between the visionary and epistemological is thus formed: through the vision theosophical knowledge was gained.[366]

Certain esoteric dimensions of the Israelites' visionary experience are suggested in rabbinic texts, in which the people of Israel are variously described as seeing God's glory, the throne of glory, hosts of angels and chariots, and the seven firmaments. They are also at times described as seeing the divine utterances, but what type of knowledge they gained thereby, beyond an understanding of the commandments and their implications, is not generally discussed.[367] In the Zohar's account, on the other hand, the Israelites' vision of the voices, in particular the Ten Words that are identified with the *sep̄îrôṯ,* is represented as the key epistemological experience, for it is by means of these voices/Words that the people of Israel gained access not only to legal teachings but to all the hidden mysteries of the upper and lower worlds and to the mysteries of the

Godhead itself.[368] The Ten Words that were seen by the people of Israel are said to have contained in seed form the entire knowledge of Torah, including not only its exoteric expression as laws and commandments but also its esoteric manifestation as the blueprint containing in potential form all of the phenomena of creation.

> R. Eleazar taught that in the Ten Words (Decalogue) all the other commandments were engraved, with all decrees and punishments, all laws concerning purity and impurity, all the branches and roots, all the trees and plants, heaven and earth, seas and oceans—in fact, all things.[369]

The people of Israel at Sinai are said to have comprehended the supernal wisdom, Ḥoḵmāh.[370] By means of that wisdom, which represents the highest level of manifestation of the Torah,[371] they comprehended, through both visual and mental cognition, the secrets of the Torah contained in the Ten Words.

> The Ten Words contain the essence of all the commandments, the essence of all celestial and terrestrial mysteries, the essence of the Ten Words of Creation. They were engraved on tables of stone, and all the hidden things were seen by the eyes and perceived by the minds of all Israel, everything being made clear to them. At that hour all the mysteries of the Torah, all the hidden things of heaven and earth, were unfolded before them and revealed to their eyes, for they saw eye to eye the splendour of the glory of their Lord. Never before, since the Holy One created the world, had such a revelation of the Divine Glory taken place.[372]

While the Zohar thus represents the theophany at Mount Sinai as a collective experience, in which the mysteries contained in the Ten Words were apprehended by the people of Israel as a whole, it also emphasizes, like rabbinic texts, the individualized nature of the experience, in which each person saw and understood "according to his or her grade."[373] Deuteronomy 29.10, in which Moses mentions various constituent groups among the Israelites—heads of tribes, elders, officers, men, children, women, and so on—is invoked in one passage to establish that the people of Israel who stood at the foot of Mount Sinai were divided into ten groups, five on the right and five on the left, which corresponded to the ten *s^e^pîrôṯ* and to the Ten Words. The notion that each person apprehended the Ten Words in accordance with his or her "grade" thus by implication refers in this context to the individual's inherent capacities as influenced by his or her gender, age, social status, and s^{e}p̄îrôṯic "disposition."[374]

> There, at Mount Sinai, even the embryos in their mothers' wombs had some perception of their Lord's glory, and everyone received according to his grade of perception.[375]

COMPARATIVE ANALYSIS 2

Cognition of Veda and Revelation of Torah

Traditional representations of Vedic cognition and the Sinai revelation are concerned with the mechanisms through which the unbounded Word came to be embodied on earth in a bounded corpus of texts. In the case of both Veda and Torah this process of embodiment involves not only instantiation in a concrete textual "body" but also in-corporation in the social "body" of a particular people—the Aryan community or the people of Israel—who constitute their identity in relation to the texts.

In reviewing these representations one is immediately struck by the relative paucity of brahmanical speculations in comparison with Jewish speculations. While the poets of the Ṛg-Veda speak self-referentially about the processes through which their cognitions occurred, later Vedic and post-Vedic texts take it for granted that the ancient *ṛṣis* were the seers of the Vedic *mantras* and consequently give less emphasis to the detailed mechanisms of cognition. Brahmanical texts from the period of the Brāhmaṇas onward tend to focus instead on the authoritative status of the *ṛṣis* themselves, as the primordial ancestors of the Aryan people and of the brahmanical lineages in particular, and as the initiators of the sacrificial and recitative traditions of the *karma-kāṇḍa* and the metaphysical traditions of the *jñāna-kāṇḍa*. Rabbinic and Zoharic discussions of the revelation of the Torah, on the other hand, are concerned to explicate every detail of the Sinai event: when and where the Torah was given, to whom it was given, how it was given, and so on. The clarification of such matters is considered of vital importance not only to establish the transcendent authority of the Written Torah and Oral Torah but also to establish the special destiny of Israel among all nations as God's chosen people.

Cosmogonic vs. Historical "Event"

These differences in orientation are linked to the temporal frame within which the traditions are presented—whether cosmogonic, in the case of Vedic cognition, or historical, in the case of the Sinai revelation.

The authority of the *ṛṣis'* cognitions derives from the special status of the *ṛṣis* as semidivine beings who emerged in the very beginning of creation as the progenitors of the human race and the forefathers of the Aryan people. The ancient *ṛṣis* are represented as seers of truth and knowers of *brahman*/Brahman who cognized the primordial *mantra*s and sacrifices by means of which the creation itself was brought forth. Through their cognitions the *ṛṣis* gained access to the mysteries of creation and assisted the gods in producing the phenomenal world. The process of cognition is thus presented not as an historical event occurring in a particular time and place but as a cosmogonic "event" occurring in the beginning of creation—and, according to post-Vedic texts, recurring at the onset of each new cycle. This "event" is not described in terms of historical actualities but is represented rather as a paradigmatic process occurring within the depths of the individual seer's consciousness. What is important above all is the status of the *ṛṣis* themselves as beings of highly developed consciousness capable of fathoming the deepest levels of reality where the Vedic *mantra*s abide. Once that status is established then the transcendent authority of the seers' knowledge and the lines of tradition (*vaṃśa*s) initiated by them is established. In particular, the authority of the priestly lineages is ensured, not only on the basis of their role as the custodians of the recitative and sacrificial traditions inaugurated by the *ṛṣis*, but also on the basis of the lines of descent that link each brahmanical *gotra* to a particular seer.

In contrast to the cosmogonic context in which the *ṛṣis'* cognitions are framed, the revelation of the Torah is represented as an historical event that occurred at a particular time and place to a particular people. Moreover, whereas Vedic cognition is represented as an internal process occurring within the consciousness of the individual *ṛṣi*, the Sinai revelation is portrayed as an external event that was collectively experienced by the people of Israel as a community. This communal event is regarded as the pivotal event in the salvation history of the Jewish people, in which the Israelites were singled out from among all nations to be the recipients of the Torah and to enter into an everlasting covenant with their God. In this context certain Midrashim evidence a clear polemic against the gentile nations, in which they are concerned to provide justification for why the people of Israel merited this special status.

Although the sociohistorical dimensions of the Sinai event are never lost sight of, the process of revelation is also correlated in a variety of ways with the process of creation so that it escapes the confines of its historicity while remaining grounded within it. The Torah, which is represented in certain texts as the instrument through which God brought forth the universe at the time of creation, is also represented as the instrument through which the universe was renewed and consolidated at the time of revelation. If the people of Israel had not accepted the Torah at Mount Sinai, then this renewal would not have been realized and the creation would have reverted to chaos. This historical event thus becomes infused with cosmogonic import as the crucial juncture in which the cosmos, precariously poised between renovation and dissolution, was finally established on a firm basis.

Mechanisms of Transmission: "Cognition" vs. "Revelation"

Vedic cognition and the Sinai revelation are both represented as involving a transmission of knowledge from a divine source to human participants. However, two interrelated factors distinguish the mechanisms of transmission in the two cases: first, whether the process of transmission is initiated from the side of human beings or from the side of the divine; and second, whether the divine source of the knowledge is impersonal or personal. While the term "revelation," which implies that the divine initiated the process and revealed the knowledge to human recipients, may be appropriate to describe the Sinai event, it is inappropriate to describe the *ṛṣis*' experience. A more precise term to describe the *ṛṣis*' relationship to the Veda is "cognition," for it implies an active process of acquisition of knowledge rather than a passive reception. In the expression "revelation of Torah" God is the subject, the revealer, and the Israelites are the recipients. In the expression "cognition of Veda" the *ṛṣis* are the subjects, the cognizers, without explicit reference to the role of the divine in the process.

Human vs. Divine Initiative Veda and Torah are represented in certain strands of their respective traditions as existing on subtler planes of existence beyond the gross material world. The Veda is said to be structured on the transcendent level of reality, which is the source and abode of the gods. The Torah is said to reside in heaven, which is the abode of God and the angels. In order for human beings to access the supernal knowledge of Veda or Torah, the gap between the earthly and divine realms has to be overcome. Among the possible means to accomplish this, two are of particular importance in the representations of Vedic cognition and the Sinai revelation that we have examined: human beings may ascend to the realm of the divine, or alternatively, the divine may descend to the realm of human beings. With respect to Vedic cognition, the emphasis is on the initiative of the *ṛṣis*, who "ascended" to the realm of the divine and cognized the Vedic *mantras*. With respect to the Sinai revelation, both models are evident. God descended from heaven and revealed the Ten Commandments to the people of Israel. Moses ascended to heaven—or, in the language of the Zohar, to the supernal regions of the Godhead—to receive the detailed teachings of Torah. Even in the case of Moses, however, the initiative was on the part of the divine, for Moses ascended to heaven only when called by God to do so.

This distinction between human and divine initiative, as mentioned above, is one of the factors that has led me to choose the term "cognition" rather than "revelation" to designate the *ṛṣis*' relationship to the Veda. The Veda was not revealed by the divine to the *ṛṣis*, with the *ṛṣis* assuming the role of passive recipients. Rather, the *ṛṣis* are described as actively seeking from their side to "cognize" the Veda by taking their awareness to the transcendent abode of the Veda. Even in the Ṛg-Veda, in which the process of cognition is represented as a symbiotic process involving a reciprocal exchange between the individual *ṛṣi* and the gods, the *ṛṣi* is generally described as initiating the exchange by establishing his awareness in the "heart," in the innermost depths of consciousness, which is the abode of the gods within the human microcosm. Having opened his awareness to the light-filled regions of the gods, the *ṛṣi* invoked the gods to promote his cognitions. Later Vedic and post-Vedic texts emphasize the importance of *tapas*, particularly in the form of meditation techniques, as the means through which the *ṛṣi* not only contacted the gods but also gained direct experience of that transcendent reality which is the ultimate source not only of the Veda but also of the gods: Brahman-Ātman. The process through which the *ṛṣis* attained their illumined consciousness and knowledge of Veda is thus described as primarily a product of their own efforts, involving the practice of techniques.

Whereas the process of Vedic cognition is represented as being initiated from the side of the *ṛṣis*, who "ascended" to the Transcendent and called upon the gods to aid them in their cognitions, the Sinai revelation is depicted as being initiated from the side of God, who descended to the realm of mortals and called upon the Israelite community to accept his commandments. The term "revelation" is appropriate in this context: the Torah was revealed by God to the people of Israel. The Israelites are not described as utilizing a technique to attain knowledge of Torah. Although they undertook certain purificatory measures in preparation for receiving the revelation, they did so at the instructions of God. It is God who healed them and prepared them to receive the Torah. The Torah was not acquired through their own efforts; rather, it was a gift from God, as the term used to designate the Sinai event, *mattan tôrāh*, "giving of the Torah," indicates. The language and imagery used to describe the theophany emphasize the gifts that God bestowed upon Israel. He granted the Israelites the capacity to see his glory and to hear his voice. Moreover, according to some accounts, he invested them with his splendor and adorned them, either directly or through the mediation of the angels, with various types of ornaments signifying their transformed status. Although the divine illumination and knowledge of Torah that the people of Israel received are thus represented as gifts from God, at the same time the texts emphasize that these gifts were not unconditional nor were the Israelites merely passive recipients. While the Torah might have been *offered* to all the nations of the world, it was actually *given* only to those who agreed to accept and obey its commandments: the people of Israel. The gift of Torah, as well as the other gifts that the Israelites received, was conditional upon their acceptance of the commandments and their continuing obedience. The Israelites were consequently divested of their ornaments and of their exalted status when they went astray after the golden calf.

Moses's role is more parallel to that of the *ṛṣis* in that although he is not depicted as practicing a specific technique, he is represented as acquiring the Torah at least partially through his own efforts. He is portrayed both as a warrior, who endured the dangers of the heavenly ascent and struggled with the angels over the Torah, and as an ascetic, who abstained from food and drink for forty days and nights during his heavenly sojourn. As a result of his efforts he received gifts from the angels as well as the supreme gift of Torah from God himself. He also attained an exalted status from which he did not fall: the illumination he received at Sinai was permanently reflected in the radiance of his face.

Impersonal Realization vs. Personal Relationship The distinction between acquisition of Veda through a technique and reception of the Torah as a gift is founded on a more fundamental distinction concerning the divine source of the knowledge—whether impersonal, in the case of Veda, or personal, in the case of Torah.

A number of passages in the Ṛg-Veda appear to indicate that specific gods, such as Agni, Soma, or Indra, are the source of the Vedic *mantras*. However, other passages imply that the *mantras* have an existence apart from the gods. For example, the *ṛcs* are said to exist in the Imperishable, which is itself the abode of the gods (ṚV X.164.39). Moreover, the gods themselves are at times called *ṛṣis*, although the significance of this epithet is not explained. The implications of these two notions are developed more fully in later Vedic texts. The conception that the gods are *ṛṣis* is elaborated in the Brāhmaṇas, in which the creator Prajāpati in particular is depicted as seeing and uttering the *mantras*. The ramifications of this notion, together with the notion that the *mantras* exist in the Imperishable, are delineated in the Upaniṣads and post-Vedic texts with reference to the notion of Brahman-Ātman: the creator may indeed be the primordial seer of the Vedic *mantras*, as well as the vehicle through which the *mantras* find expression in creation, but he is not thereby their source; their source lies in the Imperishable, Brahman-Ātman, from which the creator himself and all the gods arise. The *ṛṣis*, as knowers of Brahman, are thus represented as having access to a level of reality that is even higher than the gods. While the gods may at times facilitate or mediate the process of cognition, they are not the ultimate source of the Vedic *mantras*. Rather, the gods are themselves *ṛṣis* in relation to the Veda, and therefore, like their earthly counterparts, they must perform *tapas* in order to cognize the eternal *mantras*.

The transcendent reality of Brahman that is represented as the ultimate source of the Veda is impersonal; it is not a personal God with whom one enters into a personal relationship. Thus, the Veda is at times designated as *apauruṣeya*: not derived from any personal agent. If a *ṛṣi* sought to know the Veda, he practiced *tapas* and immersed his awareness in the Transcendent. He attained knowledge of Brahman by directly experiencing it and thereby attained knowledge of Veda, which is the essence of Brahman. The *ṛṣis*' attainment of Brahman and of Śabdabrahman, Veda, is thus described as the realization of an impersonal reality and not as union with a personal God. In this perspective the eternal impulses of speech that the *ṛṣis* saw and heard were not the speech of a particular deity. Rather, they were the reverberations of the Transcendent to which the *ṛṣis*, like the creator himself, gave vocalized utterance through their own speech.

The revelation at Mount Sinai, in contrast, is described in personal terms as a covenant between a personal God and his chosen people, involving gifts on the part of the divine and obligations on the part of the Israelites. The marriage metaphor that is at times used to describe the Sinai covenant emphasizes the highly personalized nature of this relationship, in which God entered into an everlasting union with Israel. According to one version of the marriage ceremony, God presented the Torah to his bride, Israel, as a marriage contract stipulating the laws and teachings to be observed by them in fulfillment of the covenant. According to the alternative version, the Torah that was given at Sinai was not merely a legal document but the bride herself, personified as a living aspect of God who entered into union with the bridegroom, Israel. This union was not abrogated in spite of the people of Israel's disobedience, for as long as they were in possession of the Torah, God's presence, the Shekhinah, would abide with them.

A number of rabbinic traditions concerning the Sinai theophany emphasize that God not only entered into a personal relationship with the community as a whole but with each and every one of the Israelites individually. He spoke to each individual in accordance with his or her own capacity. He displayed multiple faces and multiple voices so that each Israelite—young and old, male and female—felt that God was looking at and addressing him or her directly. The most intimate relationship with God is of course ascribed to Moses, who conversed with God face to face on the mountain. Moses assumed the role of God's scribe, recording the divine utterances in written form, as well as the role of God's student, to whom God explained the ramifications of each teaching orally.

The role of Moses is again comparable to that of the *ṛṣis* in that he alone among the Israelites was designated not only to receive but to transmit the revelation. And yet their roles as transmitters are strikingly different. In the case of the Torah, the divine source of the speech is personal, the speech is recorded in written form, and the role of the transmitter is to preserve not only the written record but also the oral explanations of its meaning. In the case of the Veda, the divine source of the speech is impersonal, the speech is recorded in oral form, and the primary role of the transmitters is to preserve the accuracy of the sounds without reference to their discursive meaning.

Epistemology of Cognition and Revelation

Brahmanical representations of Vedic cognition and rabbinic and Zoharic representations of the Sinai revelation emphasize the holistic, synesthetic nature of the participants' experiences, which involved both seeing and hearing. Moreover, both traditions are concerned to delineate the epistemological fruits of this seeing and hearing, which yielded esoteric knowledge of suprasensible phenomena and exoteric knowledge of injunctions and practices.

The *ṛṣis* are described as apprehending with both their eyes and ears the subtle reverberations of speech arising in the silent depths of their own consciousness as sound-forms embodied in light. Through their cognitions of the Vedic *mantras*, of the hymns (*ṛcs*) and chants (*sāmans*) that are held to be the fundamental rhythms at the basis of all creation, the *ṛṣis* attained knowledge of the hidden structures of creation and the origins of all things. They are described as seeing with their mind's eye the gods in their celestial realms, seated on their thrones or riding on their chariots, and they are also said to have experienced the transcendent reality from which the gods themselves arose. Although the visual aspects of the *ṛṣis'* experiences as "seers" are often emphasized, the oral-aural dimensions are in the end given priority, for that which the *ṛṣis* saw and heard was preserved orally through their speech and not through the visual medium of writing.

The people of Israel at Mount Sinai are similarly portrayed as apprehending the revelation through the faculties of both hearing and sight. They are described as hearing God's voice(s) proclaiming the Ten Words of the Decalogue. Although the auditory dimensions of the revelation are explored by the rabbis in the context of discussing the phenomenology of the divine utterances, the visionary aspects of the experience are generally given priority, for while the other nations are said to have heard the divine utterances, it was Israel alone that was granted the capacity to see. The Israelites are said to have seen the glory of God himself, face to face, along with other supernal mysteries, which are variously enumerated as including the throne of glory, the multileveled firmaments, and hosts of angels and chariots. The people of Israel are even at times described as seeing the divine voice(s) emerging as words of fire and as subsequently witnessing the transformation of the Ten Words from an oral-aural to a written-visual medium in which they became inscribed on the tablets of stone. Visual images predominate in discussions of the special character of the tablets and their writing as well as in representations of the flaming Torah inscribed with black fire on white fire.

While rabbinic texts at times use the language and imagery of Merkabah traditions to represent the visionary experiences of

Moses and the Israelites, the Zohar insists that their visions penetrated beyond the Merkabah to the higher regions of the Godhead in the s^e^p̄îrôṯic realm. Through their visions of the divine voices and in particular of the Ten Words, identified in the Zohar with the ten *s^e^p̄îrôṯ*, the Israelites attained mystical gnosis of the hidden mysteries of creation contained in the cosmic blueprint, the supernal Torah, and were illumined with the effulgence of the Godhead itself.

The epistemological aspects of Vedic cognition and of the Sinai revelation are described as involving not only esoteric knowledge of supernal mysteries but also exoteric knowledge of certain injunctions and practices. Thus, through their cognitions the *ṛṣis* are said to have not only gained access to the esoteric reality of the *mantras* as the blueprint revealing the subtle fabrics of creation, they also apprehended the exoteric applications of the *mantras* as hymns and chants to be recited in order to achieve specific ends. Moreover, they are said to have seen the primordial sacrifices in which the *mantras* are used and by means of which the cosmic order is perpetuated and certain worldly ends attained. The *ṛṣis* saw, heard, and uttered, preserving the *mantras* through their speech and establishing the recitative tradition. They also saw, heard, and practiced, performing the first Vedic rituals on earth and establishing the sacrificial tradition.

Through their experiences at the Sinai revelation the people of Israel are said to have not only apprehended the hidden mysteries of the Ten Words, which represent the seed expression of the entire Torah, but also to have understood the exoteric meaning of the commandments. While the *ṛṣis* are acclaimed for their role in seeing, hearing, and preserving the *form* of the divine speech, the Israelites are celebrated for their role in seeing, hearing, understanding, and accepting the *content* of the divine utterances. The act of understanding points to the hermeneutical dimensions of the experience, while the act of acceptance points to the performative obligations undertaken in fulfillment of the covenant. A Sinaitic basis is thus established for rabbinic traditions concerning the importance of interpreting and observing the commandments of Torah.

This brief comparative analysis of the phenomenology of Vedic cognition and the Sinai revelation would appear to confirm our observations at the end of Part 1 concerning the three fundamental dichotomies in the conceptions of language that underlie these symbol systems. *(1) Oral vs. Written Channels of Language.* Both Vedic cognition and the Sinai revelation are described as involving an oral component in which divine speech was apprehended. However, brahmanical traditions give priority to the oral channel as the means through which the subtle impulses of speech were recorded and transmitted, while rabbinic and Zoharic traditions give priority to the written register as the medium through which the divine utterances were transcribed and preserved. *(2) Auditory vs. Visual Modes of Perception.* The process of Vedic cognition and the Sinai revelation are both represented as synesthetic experiences involving seeing as well as hearing. Although brahmanical traditions contain ample references to the visual dimensions of the *ṛṣis*' cognitions, the auditory channel is given priority because of its linkage to the oral means by which the Vedic *mantras* were preserved. Rabbinic and Zoharic traditions also emphasize the importance of hearing, but they tend to place more emphasis on the visual dimensions, both in terms of the experiences of Moses and the Israelites and the written medium in which the Ten Commandments and Sefer Torah were preserved. *(3) Phonic vs. Cognitive Dimensions of the Word.* Brahmanical discussions of Vedic cognition give priority to the phonic over the cognitive dimension of the Vedic words, emphasizing the role of the *ṛṣis* in cognizing the Vedic *mantras* and preserving their sounds in the exact form in which they were apprehended. Although the *ṛṣis* are at times described as expounding the teachings of the Vedas, their primary role is to transmit the eternal impulses of speech, not to interpret their discursive meaning. Moses is similarly described as a transmitter of the divine speech, which he records in written form, but he also serves as an interpreter in his role as the custodian of the Oral Torah. The people of Israel are likewise represented as interpreters, who are concerned to understand the meaning and implications of the divine utterances and to implement them through observance. In this context the cognitive dimension of the words is given priority over their sound value.

Cognition and Revelation as Paradigmatic "Events"

Brahmanical representations of Vedic cognition and rabbinic and kabbalistic representations of the Sinai revelation establish a variety of paradigms that serve to authorize the sectional interests of different groups within each tradition.

Brahmanical representations of the *ṛṣis* present two basic paradigms that reflect the diverging concerns of the exponents of the *karma-kāṇḍa* and *dharma* traditions, on the one hand, and the exponents of the *jñāna-kāṇḍa* and meditation traditions, on the other. As the first human reciters of the Vedas and the first human performers of the sacrificial rites, the *ṛṣis* provide the model for the brahmin priests, who are the custodians of the recitative and sacrificial traditions. The authority of the priestly elite is ensured not only by virtue of their function, which is understood as a periodic reenactment of the primordial activities of the ancient *ṛṣis*, but also by the blood lineages of the brahmanical *gotras*, which claim a continuous line of descent from their respective *ṛṣi*-patriarchs. Moreover, this claim to *ṛṣi*-descent is ultimately a claim to divine descent, for the *ṛṣis* themselves are frequently represented as semidivine sages who are themselves descendants of the gods. The brahmin priests can thus assert their special status as human gods (*manuṣya-devas*) who, by virtue of both their function and their blood descent, alone have a legitimate claim to serve as the authoritative custodians and exponents of the Veda. They accordingly assume the prerogative not only to preserve and transmit the circumscribed corpus of Vedic *mantras* but also to expand progressively the domain of Veda to include potentially all texts, teachings, and practices of the normative tradition. Within this expanding purview of Veda, those texts and teachings that remain closest to the specialized activities of the priests themselves are those that expound the sacrificial and ritual traditions of the *karma-kāṇḍa* (Brāhmaṇas, Śrauta-Sūtras, Gṛhya-Sūtras) and the ritual and social duties of *varṇāśrama-dharma* (Dharma-Sūtras, Dharma-Śāstras, *dharma* teachings in the epics and Purāṇas, and so on). The *ṛṣis* are primarily celebrated in this context as the cocreators and maintainers of the cosmic order, who assist the gods in bringing forth the creation and who nourish and sustain the cosmos through inaugurating the recitative and sacrificial traditions and promulgating the dharmic teachings of *pravṛtti*.

While the *ṛṣis* are thus cast from one perspective as the paradigmatic exemplars of priestly traditions, from another perspective they can equally serve as paradigms for ascetic and meditation traditions. As practitioners of *tapas* and knowers of Brahman, the *ṛṣis* provide an authoritative basis for the *jñāna-kāṇḍa* and the renunciant traditions of *nivṛtti*. In the Upaniṣads the *ṛṣis* are celebrated not for their role in establishing the sacrificial rites but rather for their role in cognizing and transmitting the truths of Vedānta by means of which Brahman-Ātman is realized. The domain of the term *ṛṣi* is itself expanded in the Upaniṣads, as well as in post-Vedic texts, to include not only the ancient seers of the Vedic *mantras* but any great sage who has become a knower of Brahman through his practice of *tapas*. The term is thus freed from the bonds of blood descent that restrict the claim to legitimate knowledge to the priestly elite: while the brahmin priests may preserve the exoteric knowledge of Veda derived from the *ṛṣis*, only those sages who are knowers of Brahman can claim to be the authoritative custodians of the transcendent knowledge of Veda cognized by the ancient seers. These sages' claim to authority lies not in their blood but in their state of consciousness, through which they purportedly have direct access to the structures of reality fathomed by the first *ṛṣis*.

While the example of the *ṛṣis* can thus serve to legitimate the diverging claims of the priestly exponents of the *karman* stream and the ascetic exponents of the *jñāna* stream, it is less evident how their example might provide an authoritative basis for the *bhakti* stream. As discussed in chapter 2, one possible strategy, evident in both the Mahābhārata and the Purāṇas, is to assimilate the Veda to that deity who is upheld as the supreme Brahman—for example, Viṣṇu or Śiva. In this context the Mahābhārata asserts that Viṣṇu, whose essential nature is knowledge, Veda, is the ultimate source of the Vedic *mantras* as well as of the *ṛṣis*. Therefore, if the *ṛṣis* wished to attain knowledge of Brahman and of the Vedic *mantras*, their own efforts in practicing *tapas* had to be supplemented by the grace of Viṣṇu. The interjection of the notion of grace, along with the related notion that the roles of the *ṛṣis* are ordained by Viṣṇu, served to align the dominant model of Vedic cognition—albeit tenuously—with *bhakti*-oriented Vaiṣṇava traditions. A second strategy adopted by the Mahābhārata is to claim that the epic itself constitutes the "fifth Veda" and that the composer of the epic, Veda-Vyāsa, is the supreme *ṛṣi*, whose status surpasses that of the Vedic *ṛṣis* in that he himself constitutes a portion of the supreme Godhead, Viṣṇu-Nārāyaṇa. The Purāṇas similarly claim the status of the fifth Veda and make use of a variety of strategies to establish a transcendent source for their teachings that emulates the paradigm of Vedic cognition. On the basis of such strategies, the devotional teachings of the Mahābhārata and Purāṇas, which were intended to inspire and edify the general populace, were brought within the purview of the Veda.

In brahmanical representations of Vedic cognition there is only a single group of human participants: the *ṛṣis*, whose significance lies both in their collective status as a group of semidivine sages who are the ancestors of the Aryans and in their individual status as cognizers of particular Vedic *mantras*. Different aspects of the collective and individual activities of the *ṛṣis* are singled out by the different strands of the brahmanical tradition to legitimate their particular teachings and practices. Representations of the revelation at Mount Sinai similarly provide authoritative paradigms for the various teachings and practices of the rabbinic and kabbalistic traditions. In the Sinai event, however, there are two types of human participants, who are portrayed as the recipients of two types of revelation: the people of Israel, who received a collective revelation of the Ten Commandments; and Moses, who received a revelation of the detailed teachings of the Torah. We must accordingly consider the models presented by these two forms of revelation separately.

Moses, as the scribe of God and the first Midrashist, provides the paradigm for the rabbinic sages, who are the custodians of the scribal tradition that preserves the Written Torah and of the interpretive traditions that claim the status of Oral Torah. Just as Moses was granted a special status within the Israelite community as the recipient of the full revelation of Torah, who recorded the written text and the oral interpretations of its meaning, so the rabbis assume a special status within the Jewish community as the custodians of the Torah, dedicated to preserving every letter of the Written Torah and to codifying the authoritative interpretations that constitute the Oral Torah. The rabbis not only replicate the functions of Moses, they also claim an unbroken line of transmission that links their teachings directly back to Moses at Mount Sinai. It is by virtue of this claim to Mosaic authority that potentially any law, teaching, or practice promulgated by the rabbinic authorities can claim a place within the ever-expanding category of Oral Torah.

Moses, as the supreme prophet who saw what no other prophet ever saw, is also invoked by the kabbalists as the paradigmatic mystic to whom God revealed the esoteric teachings that their own traditions claim to preserve. As will be discussed in chapter 6, the two major types of Kabbalah, theosophical and ecstatic, developed various hermeneutical and mystical techniques in order to reproduce Moses's revelatory experience and attain a prophetic level of consciousness. Moses also provided a model for the "descenders to the Merkabah" in Hêkālôṯ texts, who evolved their own methods of heavenly ascent and magical techniques in order to replicate the supreme prophet's achievement and attain mastery of Torah.

While Moses was singled out as the only person capable of bearing the revelation in its full power, the other Israelites were not thereby excluded from the theophany. They too are represented as receiving a revelation directly from God, although it was a limited revelation, modified to accord with the capacities of each individual. The people of Israel who entered into an eternal covenant with their God at Mount Sinai are the paradigmatic representatives of the Jewish community as a whole. Moreover, according to one trend of speculation, later generations of Jews participate in the Sinai theophany not only indirectly, on the basis of their descent from the original recipients of the revelation, but also directly, for the souls of all future generations of Israelites are said to have been present at Sinai to receive the revelation.

This paradigmatic event is reenacted every year on Shavuot, the annual festival that commemorates the Sinai revelation. Some of the Sinai Midrashim may have their roots in Shavuot synagogue traditions, as we have seen, and these traditional representations of the revelation are in turn inscribed in the ongoing synagogue celebrations of Shavuot year after year. Some communities even reenact the marriage ceremony on Shavuot as a symbolic renewal of the covenant. In many Sephardic communities on the first day of Shavuot, prior to the Torah reading, a *K^{e}ṯûbāh l^{e}-Šāḇû'ôṯ* (marriage certificate of Shavuot) is read out, dated the sixth of Sivan—the date traditionally designated for the Sinai revelation—and the eternal covenant is sealed. The most widely used version of the *K^{e}ṯûbāh l^{e}-Šāḇû'ôṯ*, composed by the Safed kabbalist and poet Israel Najara (ca. 1550–1625 C.E.), celebrates the marriage between God and his bride, Israel. However, in other versions of the *K^{e}ṯûbāh* the Torah is portrayed as the bride, who is given away by her father on high to the bridegroom, Israel.

Representations of the Israelites' role in the Sinai revelation also point to what the Jewish people must do in order to fulfill the covenant. The example of the Israelites, who heard, understood, and accepted the commandments at Sinai, is replicated by their descendants in three types of activities: communal worship in the synagogue, in which the public reading of the Torah is periodically heard by the congregation; study of the Torah, in which its teachings are understood and interpreted under the guidance of the rabbis, the representatives of Mosaic authority; and practice of the Torah, in which the commandments are embodied by each individual Jew through action. With respect to study of the Torah, the notion that God's voice adapted itself at the revelation, being heard by each nation in its own vernacular and by each individual Israelite in accordance with his or her own capacity, provides a Sinaitic basis for rabbinic and kabbalistic speculations concerning the multiple interpretations of Torah, as will be discussed in chapter 6.

Traditional representations of Vedic cognition and the Sinai revelation thus provide a variety of paradigms that can be appropriated by different groups within the brahmanical Hindu and Jewish communities to authorize their sectional interests. Paradigms are established in both cases for the religious elite: the brahmin priests claim to be the direct descendants of the *ṛṣis* and replicate their activities through preserving and reciting the Vedic *mantras*; the rabbis claim a direct line of transmission from Moses and replicate his activities through preserving and interpreting the Torah. Models are also established for the more esoteric strands of the traditions: the exponents of ascetic and meditation traditions claim to access the transcendent reality of Veda by reproducing the *ṛṣis*' state of consciousness through the practice of *tapas*; the exponents of kabbalistic traditions claim to access the supernal reality of Torah by reproducing Moses's visionary experience through various hermeneutical and mystical techniques.

When we turn to paradigms for the larger religious community, we find that brahmanical representations of Vedic cognition do not provide a model of communal participation comparable to that provided by the Sinai revelation. While several strategies, discussed above, are used to establish a connection between the *ṛṣis* and popular devotional traditions, the seers' activities—cognition and recitation of the Vedic *mantras*, performance of sacrifices, practice of *tapas*, and so on—are not easily translatable into communal activities for the general populace. Recitation of the Vedas as part of the *śrauta* sacrifices does not constitute a form of congregational worship comparable to the recitation of the Torah in the synagogue. Beyond the priests who are the officiants of the sacrifice, the *yajamāna*, or patron of the sacrifice, and his wife, no human audience is required. The recitations are not intended to convey didactic teachings to a group of human worshipers; rather, they are intended to nourish the gods and to regenerate the cosmos through accurately reproducing the Vedic sounds.

Part 3

Text in Practice

CHAPTER 5

Veda in Practice

> When Prajāpati brought forth beings, he brought them forth with the *dhūrs*.[1] He poured out seed with the *retasyā* verse, he produced breath with the *gāyatrī* meter, sight with the *triṣṭubh* meter, hearing with the *jagatī* meter, and speech with the *anuṣṭubh* meter. With the *paṅkti* meter he added the body (*ātman*). Having become Prajāpati, he who, knowing thus, chants with the *dhūrs* brings forth beings.
>
> —Jaiminīya Brāhmaṇa I.99

The conceptions of Veda and Torah discussed in the previous chapters function in their respective traditions not only as pervasive and enduring textual motifs, but as paradigmatic representations that reflect and inform certain types of practices by means of which different groups within each tradition authorize their sectional interests. The following two chapters will examine the ways in which the cosmogonic and epistemological paradigms associated with Veda and Torah are reflected in practices with respect to the methods of transmission, study, and appropriation of these two scriptures.

Brahmanical representations of the Veda's role in creation and cognition are reflected primarily in (1) the modes of recitative transmission and study of the Vedic Saṃhitās, in which emphasis is placed on phonology over semantics; (2) theurgic conceptions of the role of Vedic sacrifice and recitation in maintaining the cosmic order and nourishing the gods; (3) the minimal emphasis that has been given to interpretation of the discursive meaning of the Vedic *mantras*; and (4) the modes of appropriation of the Veda, in which the priestly exponents of the *karma-kāṇḍa* appropriate the Veda through reciting and hearing the *mantras*, while the exponents of the *jñāna-kāṇḍa* seek direct realization of that transcendent reality which is the source and abode of the Veda.

Recitative Transmission of the Vedic Saṃhitās

The Vedic Saṃhitās have traditionally been preserved and passed down from generation to generation through oral transmission, by word of mouth (*āmnāya*), not through a written text. Graham, in his recent study of the oral-aural dimensions of scripture in the history of religions, suggests that "the ancient Vedic tradition represents the paradigmatic instance of scripture as spoken, recited word."[2] The fundamentally oral nature of the Vedas, as well as of other Hindu sacred texts, has been emphasized by a number of Indologists in recent years, including J. Frits Staal and Thomas Coburn.[3]

The Vedic Saṃhitās have been recited generation after generation in strictly accurate, unaltered form, syllable for syllable, accent for accent, since perhaps as early as the second millennium B.C.E. The Saṃhitās have been handed down from teacher (*guru*) to student (*śiṣya*) for over three thousand years in an unbroken chain of oral transmission known as *sampradāya*. The tradition of recitative transmission (*paṭhana*) is still alive today, especially in South India. The *sampradāya* is traditionally believed to have been initiated by the Vedic *ṛṣis*, the ancestors of the brahmanical lineages, who originally cognized the primordial impulses of speech reverberating forth from the Transcendent. The *ṛṣis* did not write down their cognitions; they recorded the *mantras* through their own speech and passed them down to their students, and in this way *śruti*, "that which was heard" by the *ṛṣis*, has been conveyed from generation to generation through oral transmission.

The tradition of preserving the Saṃhitās through oral transmission rather than through writing is thus linked by the brahmanical exponents of the Vedic recitative tradition to the transcendent status of the *mantras* as *śruti*. *Śruti* is living word, and in order for the primordial impulses of speech to remain lively and efficacious they must be transmitted by word of mouth from a qualified teacher to his students. Moreover, writing is not considered an appropriate vehicle for the sacred utterances of the *mantras* because it is regarded as an impure and ritually polluting activity. The Aitareya Āraṇyaka states that a student should not recite the Vedas after he has eaten meat, seen blood or a dead body, committed an unlawful deed, had intercourse, or engaged in writing.[4] Scribes are generally of low social standing in India,[5] and those who write down the Vedas (*vedānām lekhakas*) are particularly scorned,[6] as are reciters of the Vedas who use a written text (*likhita-pāṭhakas*).[7]

Oral transmission is traditionally held to be a more authoritative and accurate means of transmission than writing, and indeed Western scholars have found the Vedic recitative tradition to be more reliable than written manuscripts in establishing the most accurate text.[8] Every sound and syllable of the Saṃhitās has been meticulously maintained with absolute fidelity by male brahmin reciters known as *śrotriyas*, "masters of *śruti*." An entire body of literature, the Vedāṅgas, or "limbs of the Veda," was developed very early in the Vedic tradition in order to safeguard the proper preservation, recitation, and ritual use of the Saṃhitās. Among the six Vedāṅgas, *śikṣā* ("instruction") is concerned with the proper articulation and pronunciation of the Vedic sounds; *chandas* ("meter") includes texts on the various prescribed meters used in reciting the *mantras*; *vyākaraṇa* ("analysis and derivation"), in addition to grammatical works describing and analyzing the Vedic language, includes the various *prātiśākhyas*, which prescribe the methods of pronunciation that prevail in the different Vedic *śākhās* or schools; and *kalpa* ("ritual") includes the Śrauta-Sūtras and Gṛhya-Sūtras, which are concerned with the proper performance of the Vedic sacrifices and domestic rituals, in which recitation of the *mantras* assumes a central role.

In order to ensure absolute accuracy in the recitation and transmission of the Saṃhitās, a highly intricate system of mnemonic techniques is used to train each new generation of brahmin reciters. These techniques involve memorizing the text in up to eleven different modes of recitation (*pāṭhas*) that require the reciter to master the base text forward and backward and in a number of different patterns.[9] Graham writes:

> Particular Brahman caste groups still specialize in the preservation and chanting of one or another of the Vedic *saṁhitās*, and continue to learn and to transmit their texts verbatim through the most rigorous and intricate mnemonic techniques imaginable. Specifically, the same text is normally memorized in its entirety in up to eleven different modes of recitation (*pāṭhas*) that require complex grammatical and recitative manipulation of the base text. . . . In these ways, together with strict traditions of accentuation and

> melodic rendering, the base text is mastered literally forward and backward in fully acoustic fashion as a hedge against faulty transmission of any word or syllable.[10]

In the teaching and transmission of the Vedic Saṃhitās maintenance of the purity of the Vedic sounds is thus of primary importance, and in this context phonology takes precedence over semantics and the discursive meaning of the texts is all but ignored. *Śrotriyas* may be able to recite an entire Saṃhitā of the Veda by heart, but they frequently do not understand what they recite. In study of the Saṃhitās primacy is given to memorization and recitation of the texts and not to their understanding and interpretation. This emphasis is reflected in the Sanskrit term for study of the Vedas, *svādhyāya*, which means going over, repeating, or reciting to oneself.

This lack of emphasis on the discursive meaning of the Vedic *mantras* is also evident in their use in Vedic sacrifices. Staal has pointed out that even though most of the *mantras* in the Saṃhitās may have a discursive meaning, when they are recited in Vedic sacrifices they are disengaged from their original context and are employed in ways that have nothing or little to do with their meaning. What is important in Vedic rituals is not the discursive meaning of the *mantras* but rather their phonology and syntax.[11]

The brahmanical preoccupation with the phonic over the cognitive dimension of the Vedic words is further illustrated by the fact that there have been so few commentaries dedicated to interpreting the discursive meaning of the *mantras*. As will be discussed below, the hermeneutical discussions of the formal schools of Vedic exegesis, Pūrva-Mīmāṃsā and Vedānta, focus on the Brāhmaṇa and Upaniṣadic portions of the Vedas, respectively, rather than on the *mantras*.

The preoccupation in the Vedic tradition with sound over meaning, memorization over understanding, and recitation over interpretation has been noted by a number of prominent Indologists.[12] Renou remarks that "at all times, recitation constituted the principal, if not the exclusive, object of Vedic teaching . . . whilst the interpretation of the texts is treated as a poor relation."[13] In this context Staal compares the role of a *śrotriya* to that of a scribe whose primary concern is preservation of the text.

> Vedic transmission means *vedādhyāyana*. . . . [I]n this process translation or interpretation are not necessarily thought of, for the words, which are one with the meaning

> and themselves sacred, should be preserved for the world and for posterity. In this sense the *śrotriya* who recites without understanding should not be compared with a clergyman preaching from the pulpit, but rather with a medieval monk copying and illuminating manuscripts. . . .[14]

The brahmanical focus on the phonology and syntax of the Vedic Saṃhitās, with corresponding neglect of semantics, has led Staal to conclude that the Vedic *mantras* are in the final analysis meaningless and thus do not constitute linguistic utterances. He maintains that Vedic *mantras* may be more fruitfully understood in relation to the structures of music than to the structures of language.[15] Staal's comparison of the *mantras* with music resonates with the brahmanical tradition's own characterization of the *mantras* as the primordial rhythms of creation. However, in the traditional brahmanical perspective, as expressed both in mythological speculations and in the philosophical formulations of the Mīmāṃsakas and Advaitins, the fact that the discursive meaning of the *mantras* is not emphasized does not necessarily imply that they are meaningless. The preoccupation in the Vedic tradition with phonology over semantics is linked to the view of the special status of the Vedic language as a natural language in which the sound is held to constitute its own meaning. As we have seen, the Mīmāṃsakas provide philosophical justification for the mythological portrayal of the Vedas as the cosmic blueprint by establishing that in the case of Vedic words there is an inherent connection (*autpattika sambandha*) between *śabda* and *artha*, between the word and its denotation, between the name and the form that it signifies.[16] We may term this type of meaning "constitutive meaning," in contrast to discursive meaning, for in this conception the Vedic words constitute their own meaning in that they are constitutive of the forms that they signify. In this context the periodic recitation of the Vedic *mantras* is viewed as a means of periodically regenerating the cosmos by enlivening and nourishing the forms of creation at their base. As long as the purity of the sounds is preserved, the recitation of the *mantras* will be efficacious, irrespective of whether their discursive meaning is understood by human beings.

Theurgic Conceptions of Vedic Sacrifice and Recitation

The need for exactitude in recitative transmission of the Saṃhitās, as well as in performance of the Vedic sacrifices in which the *mantras* are used, is thus rooted in an awareness of the transcendent status of the *mantras*, the sounds of which are held to be the primordial rhythms that sustain the cosmos. Accurate reproduction of these primal sounds through periodic recitation and sacrificial performances is considered essential for the periodic regeneration and maintenance of the cosmic order. Conversely, any inaccuracies in either recitation or the sacrificial ritual are believed to have calamitous effects on the cosmic order and therefore require expiation (*prāyaścitta*) through various detailed procedures. The potentially destructive effect of any errors in recitation is reflected in the Pāṇinīya Śikṣā's statement that a mispronounced or wrongly used *mantra* will destroy the patron of the sacrifice (*yajamāna*), the words becoming like a thunderbolt (*vajra*).[17] In *śrauta* sacrifices the main function of the *brahman* priest is to avert such calamities through guarding against and correcting any mistakes in the *hotṛ* priest's recitation of the *ṛc*s, the *udgātṛ* priest's chanting of the *sāmans*, or the *adhvaryu* priest's performance of the sacrificial actions.

These theurgic conceptions of the role of Vedic sacrifice and recitation in maintaining the cosmos and nourishing the gods have their source in the Vedic texts themselves.[18] By the end of the Saṃhitā period, as we have seen, the sacrifice had been elevated to the status of a separate order of reality that was viewed as essential to the harmonious functioning of the other orders of reality—the human order, natural order, and divine order. In the Brāhmaṇas' discourse of sacrifice the Vedic *mantra*s are allotted a pivotal role as the primordial blueprint that contains the sound correlatives of the realm of form, reflecting and interconnecting the structures of all levels of existence.[19] Vedic texts provide a twofold paradigm for the theurgic power of Vedic sacrifice and recitation, which are elaborated in post-Vedic texts: (1) the paradigm of creation, in which the creator brings forth and orders the cosmos through sacrifice and/or through recitation of the Vedic *mantra*s that constitute the archetypal plan of creation; and (2) the paradigm of cognition, in which the ancient *ṛṣis*, in the context of assisting the gods in the process of creation, cognize the primordial *mantra*s and sacrifices and initiate the recitative and sacrificial traditions that are to be transmitted by their descendants, the brahmanical lineages, on earth.[20]

The seminal expression of this twofold paradigm is found in the oldest of the Vedic texts, the Ṛg-Veda Saṃhitā. As discussed in chapter 1, a number of Ṛg-Vedic hymns refer to the role of the sacrifice in the process of creation.[21] Ṛg-Veda X.90, the Puruṣa-Sūkta, is of particular significance in that it represents the creation as occurring through the primordial sacrifice of the cosmic body of Puruṣa. The *ṛṣis* are portrayed as assisting the gods and Sādhyas in the performance of the sacrifice, by means of which various elements of the human, natural, and divine orders are brought forth.[22] The primeval sacrifice of Puruṣa is represented as the archetypal sacrifice that provided the prototype for all future sacrifices: "With the sacrifice (*yajña*) the gods sacrificed the sacrifice. These were the first rites (*dharmas*)."[23] The Vedic *mantras* that emerge from the sacrifice of Puruṣa are not explicitly allotted a role in the cosmogonic process in the Puruṣa-Sūkta.[24] However, in Ṛg-Veda X.130 the *sāmans* and meters are represented as an integral part of the sacrifice through which the creation is "woven."[25] Moreover, the primordial sacrifice performed by the gods is depicted as a divine model that is cognized and reenacted, with *stomas* and meters, by the ancient *ṛṣis*.[26]

The sacrifice, together with the Vedic *mantras* that constitute its sound offerings, is thus represented in certain Ṛg-Vedic hymns as a paradigmatic cosmos-producing activity that is replicated by the sacrificial rituals performed by the *ṛṣis* and their descendants. The Ṛg-Veda also repeatedly celebrates the theurgic power of recitation of the hymns, which serves as a means of invigorating and magnifying the gods.[27] The *ṛṣis* are described as cognizing and sending forth the hymns through their speech in order to augment the power of the gods.[28] The following verses are representative:

> He [Indra] who grew (root *vṛdh*) through the ancient and present-day hymns (*gīrs*) of lauding *ṛṣis*.[29]
>
> Aśvins, do others than we surround you with *stomas*? The *ṛṣi* Vatsa, the son of Kaṇva, has magnified (root *vṛdh*) you with hymns (*gīrs*).[30]
>
> O Soma, we who are skilled in speech (*vaco-vid*) magnify (root *vṛdh*) you with hymns (*gīrs*).[31]

The theurgic conceptions of sacrifice and recitation found in seminal form in the Ṛg-Veda are elaborated in the sacrificial discourse of the Brāhmaṇas. The central figure in this discourse is the Puruṣa Prajāpati, who is represented as the primordial *ṛṣi* who cognized the Vedic *mantras* as well as the sacrificial rituals in which they are used. He then assumed the functions of the various priests in the primordial sacrifice, reciting the *ṛcs*, chanting the *sāmans*, and performing the sacrificial actions with the aid of the *yajus*es, in order to bring forth creation and structure an ordered cosmos.[32] The brahmin priests are represented in the Brāhmaṇas as the earthly counterparts of Prajāpati, who reproduce the cosmogonic activities of the creator every time the sacrificial rituals are performed.[33] Just as Prajāpati set the universe in motion by means of a particular sacrifice, so those who perform the sacrifice set the universe in motion.[34] Just as Prajāpati brought forth all beings by means of the sacrifice,[35] so those who reenact the primordial sacrifices are ascribed the power to produce beings.

> Prajāpati indeed is that sacrifice (*yajña*) which is being performed here and from which these beings were produced, and in the same manner are they produced thereafter even to the present day.[36]

The creative power of the sacrifice is linked not only to the priests' performance of the sacrificial actions but also to their recitation of the Vedic *mantra*s. For example, Jaiminīya Brāhmaṇa I.94 depicts Prajāpati as bringing forth the gods, human beings, ancestors, and other beings through chanting the words of a particular *sāman*.[37] The passage concludes, "Having become Prajāpati, he who, knowing thus, chants with this opening brings forth beings."[38] Prajāpati is represented as using particular Vedic *mantra*s or sacrifices not only to bring forth creation but also to establish an orderly cosmos through subduing his unruly creatures, providing them with rain and food, and so on. "He who knows thus" and replicates the activities of Prajāpati is correspondingly ascribed the power to obtain comparable ends.[39]

The theurgic efficacy of Vedic sacrifice and recitation extends to the divine realm as well, since the sacrificial order is held to have the power to influence and enliven the connections (*bandhus*) among all the orders of reality. Indeed, apart from the brahmin officiants of the sacrifice and the *yajamāna* and his wife, the primary participants in *śrauta* sacrifices are not a human group of worshipers but the gods. The sacrifice is represented in this context as a "banquet of the gods" to which the deities are invoked to come, to partake of the sacrificial offerings, and to be nourished by the recitations of the Vedic *mantra*s. The creator Prajāpati, the supreme god of the Brāhmaṇas, is described as one of the primary beneficiaries of the sacrifice, since it was he who created the sacrifice as a counterpart of himself. He himself used the sacrifice as a means not only to create and renovate the cosmos but also to revitalize his own disintegrated being after he had become exhausted from the process of creation.[40] Thus, every time the primordial sacrifices that are the counterpart of Prajāpati are reenacted, they serve as a means of reconstituting the creator. The *agnicayana* ceremony in particular is ascribed a paramount role in this process, in which the construction of the bird-shaped fire altar is understood as a theurgic activity by means of which the body of Prajāpati is reconstructed. Each time the fire altar ceremony is performed, the body of Prajāpati is reconstituted so that it can be offered up anew to regenerate and sustain the cosmos.[41]

In the Brāhmaṇas the role of Vedic sacrifice and recitation in building up the body of Prajāpati is linked to the conception that the Vedic *mantras*, meters, and various components of the sacrifice are themselves constitutive of the body or self (*ātman*) of Prajāpati.[42] This conception is elaborated in the Mahābhārata and the Purāṇas, in which the cosmic body that is constituted by the Vedic *mantras* and sacrificial elements is that of the creator Brahmā or of the supreme Godhead that is identified with Brahman, Viṣṇu or Śiva.[43] The implication of these post-Vedic conceptions is that the performance of the sacrificial rituals together with recitation of the *mantras* can serve as a means of periodically regenerating not only the body of the creator but also that of the ultimate reality, Brahman, which is the source and abode of Veda.

Interpretation of the Vedas

Brahmanical paradigms for the theurgic efficacy of Vedic sacrifice and recitation provide a cosmic rationale for the priority given to recitation over interpretation as the proper method of transmission and study of the Vedic *mantras*. The creative power of the Vedic *mantras* resides in their sounds, not in their discursive meaning, and thus the principal focus of the brahmin reciters must be to reproduce accurately the primordial sounds that are held to have been originally cognized and recited by the archetypal *ṛṣi*, the creator himself, in his cosmos-constructing activities.

While phonology takes precedence over semantics in the teaching and transmission of the Vedic Saṃhitās, we do find some evidence of interpretation of the *mantras* even in the Vedic period. The earliest evidence is found in the Brāhmaṇas, which although they are concerned primarily with delineating the purpose and application of the *mantras* within the context of the sacrificial rituals, at times attempt to explain their meaning as well. These explanations, while focused primarily on ritual matters, also include discussions of the esoteric meaning of the sacrifices and *mantras* as well as accounts of myths alluded to in the *mantras*. Soon after the Śatapatha Brāhmaṇa, however, these attempts at exegesis disappear, with the Upaniṣads only rarely citing the *mantras* and providing no substantive interpretations thereon.[44]

The major interpretive effort of the Vedic period is found in the Nirukta of Yāska (ca. 500 B.C.E.), which focuses on etymological (Adhyāyas 1–6) and mythological (Adhyāyas 7–12) data. Yāska defends the meaningfulness of the Vedic *mantras* against the attacks of his opponent Kautsa, refuting his contentions that the meaning of the *mantras* is nonsensical, contradictory, and obscure.[45] Yāska ultimately condemns those who do not understand the meaning of the Veda, while promising those who know its meaning the attainment of all good fortune and, ultimately, of heaven.[46] A number of Yāska's comments provide evidence of the threefold interpretation that was applied from an early date to the Veda as a whole as well as to particular passages: interpretation with reference to sacrificial performances (*adhiyajña*), with reference to the gods (*adhidaiva*), and with reference to the Self (*adhyātma*).[47] Yāska also makes reference to a number of different "schools" of Vedic interpretation.[48]

The importance of understanding the discursive meaning of the Vedic *mantras* is occasionally emphasized in later brahmanical texts, including the Gṛhya-Sūtras,[49] Dharma-Sūtras,[50] and Dharma-Śāstras.[51] The Dakṣa-Smṛti describes the process of study of the Vedas as involving appropriation (*svīkaraṇa*), discussion (*vicāra*), study (*abhyasana*), and recitation (*japa*).[52] The Manu-Smṛti maintains that those who know the meaning of the Vedas are more distinguished than those who merely remember the words.[53] Understanding the meaning of the Vedas, according to the Yājñavalkya-Smṛti, renders one fit to achieve immortality (*amṛta*).[54]

The threefold method of Vedic interpretation alluded to in the Nirukta is correlated in the commentaries on Manu-Smṛti VI.83 with the three principal divisions of the Vedic corpus: certain *mantras* are correlated with *adhidaiva*, the Brāhmaṇas with *adhiyajña*, and the Upaniṣads with *adhyātma*. The distinction between *adhiyajña* and *adhyātma* is of particular significance to the two schools among the six Darśanas that are concerned with Vedic exegesis: Pūrva-Mīmāṃsā, which is concerned with the interpretation (*mīmāṃsā*) of the earlier (*pūrva*), or Brāhmaṇa, portion of the

Vedas, and Vedānta, or Uttara-Mīmāṃsā, which is concerned with the interpretation of the later (*uttara*), or Upaniṣadic, portion of the Vedas. The Mīmāṃsakas focus on the *karma-kāṇḍa*, the section of the Vedas pertaining to action and *adhiyajña*, and thus they are primarily concerned with the injunctive (*vidhāyaka*) statements regarding *dharma* contained in the Brāhmaṇas. The Vedāntins, on the other hand, focus on the *jñāna-kāṇḍa*, the section of the Vedas pertaining to knowledge and *adhyātma*, and thus are concerned with the declarative (*abhidhāyaka*) statements regarding Brahman and Ātman found in the Upaniṣads. While in principle both systems maintain that the *mantra* portions of the Vedas are also authoritative, in practice the *mantras* are relegated to a secondary position within their hermeneutical discussions. In developing their respective hermeneutics the Mīmāṃsakas and the various schools of Vedānta—Advaita, Viśiṣṭādvaita, and Dvaita—had recourse to various principles and methods of interpretation as well as to the distinction between different levels of meaning.[55] At times two levels of meaning are distinguished—primary or literal (*mukhya*), and secondary or metaphorical (*gauṇa* or *jaghanya*)[56]—while at other times the traditional distinction between three senses of a word is adopted—literal (*abhidhā*), implied (*lakṣaṇā*), and allusive or suggestive (*vyañjanā*).[57]

All of the six Darśanas—including Nyāya, Vaiśeṣika, Sāṃkhya, and Yoga, which are not directly concerned with Vedic exegesis—maintain that the Vedas are completely infallible and free from any possibility of error or contradiction, forming a perfect unitary whole that is utterly consistent within itself. The Naiyāyikas and Vaiśeṣikas, for example, establish the inerrant authority of the Vedas by refuting the charges of falsehood (*anṛta*), self-contradiction (*vyāghāta*), and tautology (*punarukta*) that were brought against them.[58] The arguments developed by the six Darśanas to prove the infallible and authoritative status of the Vedas are founded on their respective conceptions of the origin and ontology of the Veda. Thus, the Naiyāyikas and Vaiśeṣikas argue that the Vedas are free of imperfections on the basis of the fact that they derive from a perfect, omniscient author—Īśvara himself. The Mīmāṃsakas and Vedāntins, on the other hand, maintain that the infallibility of the Vedas derives from their eternal, uncreated (*apauruṣeya*) status, by virtue of which there is no author, human or divine, to whom defects could be attributed.[59]

It is important to emphasize that while the Darśanas may be concerned to establish the infallible and authoritative status of the

Vedas, none of the philosophical schools, including those concerned with Vedic exegesis, the Mīmāṃsakas and Vedāntins, provide many substantive interpretations of the *mantras* that are the core *śruti* texts. It is not until the fourteenth century that we have the first comprehensive commentaries on the Ṛg-Veda and other Saṃhitās by Sāyaṇa. There were apparently commentators on the Saṃhitās prior to Sāyaṇa's time, but none of them dates to earlier than the tenth century.[60] It is remarkable that the Vedic Saṃhitās have been preserved with complete phonetic accuracy for over three thousand years, and yet so few commentaries exist that attempt to interpret their semantic content. Coburn has suggested that even the commentaries of Sāyaṇa, who flourished during the Muslim period in India, may not reflect an entirely indigenous Indian impulse but rather may have been inspired by the Islamic tradition that sacred texts are to be exegeted as well as recited.[61] In any case it is clear that Sāyaṇa's commentaries on the Saṃhitās are an exception within the long-standing tradition of Vedic learning, in which priority has been given to recitation over interpretation. This brahmanical preoccupation with phonology over semantics with respect to the Saṃhitās would appear once again to reflect an awareness of the transcendent status of the *mantras*, which as the primordial sounds at the basis of creation constitute their own meaning and therefore are not in need of any commentary.

Appropriation of the Veda

The Veda in its status as transcendent knowledge is regarded not as a corpus of books to be studied—for indeed the Vedas are preserved through spoken rather than written word—nor even as a corpus of oral texts whose discursive meaning is to be fathomed, but rather as a truth to be appropriated and realized. This perspective has been eloquently articulated by J. L. Mehta, a contemporary Indian philosopher steeped in both brahmanical and Western scholarly traditions.

> [T]he Ṛgveda . . . is a sacred text, revealed in the sense that these "formulations" are a gift of the gods (*devattam brahma*) to the Rishis who "saw" them, and therefore regarded as not man-made, with its source in the "highest region" of transcendent truth and speech. Yet it is not a Book or Scripture; like all "knowledge", its paradigmatic mode of being is to exist in the minds of men (where *esse*

> and *legere* are at one) and to be recited and chanted by them. The textuality of this text, hence, cannot be understood in terms or categories proper to "the religions of the Book" but must rather be treated as *sui generis*.[62]

Mehta further suggests that the Veda, in being preserved through oral transmission for over three thousand years by brahmins who did not understand its content, has enjoyed "the only mode of being appropriate to it and the only perpetuity possible for it—inscribed in the minds and hearts of men of faith."[63]

Exponents of the *karman* and *jñāna* streams within the brahmanical tradition have advocated alternative methods by means of which the Veda can become "inscribed in the minds and hearts of men." The priestly exponents of the *karma-kāṇḍa* and *dharma* traditions are primarily concerned with exoteric modes of appropriation, in which memorization and recitation of the Vedic *mantra*s, as well as listening to the Vedic recitations, are held to be the means through which brahmin *śrotriya*s and male members of the other twice-born *varṇa*s, *kṣatriya*s and *vaiśya*s, may inscribe the eternal sounds of *śruti* in their minds and hearts. Exponents of the *jñāna-kāṇḍa* and meditation traditions are concerned with more mystical modes of appropriation, in which they emphasize that the true reality of Veda can be realized only in the innermost depths of one's own consciousness through direct experience of that transcendent, imperishable reality which is the abode of Śabdabrahman.

The advocates of both types of appropriation invoke the paradigm of the ancient *ṛṣi*s in order to legitimate their diverging perspectives. The *karma-kāṇḍin*s emphasize the role of the *ṛṣi*s as the inaugurators of the recitative tradition. The *ṛṣi*s chose the vehicle of speech as the appropriate means through which to give expression to their primordial cognitions, and thus it is through speech that the eternal reality of *śruti* can be realized. One participates in this reality not by understanding the content of the Vedic words but by reciting or hearing the *mantra*s.[64] However, the domain of those who may participate in *śruti* in this way is circumscribed by the brahmanical authorities. The tradition of recitative transmission, as well as the role of priestly reciters at *śrauta* sacrifices, is the exclusive purview of the direct descendants of the *ṛṣi*s, the brahmins. The male members of the other twice-born *varṇa*s are also intended to learn and recite the Vedas within limited contexts. However, *śūdra*s and women are forbidden in the Dharma-Śastras from even hearing the Vedas recited, let alone reciting them.[65]

The exponents of the *jñāna-kāṇḍa*, on the other hand, emphasize that the recited texts preserved through the speech of the *ṛṣis* are only a limited manifestation of that unlimited knowledge which is Veda. In order to realize the reality of Veda it is not sufficient simply to recite or hear the *mantras*. Rather, the textuality of the recited texts must be transcended and the truth of the Veda experienced directly, on the level of one's own consciousness. In order to accomplish this goal the seeker of wisdom must follow the example of the *ṛṣis* and practice *tapas*, establishing his or her awareness on that transcendent level of reality where the eternal structures of knowledge can be directly cognized.

One of the earliest expressions of this perspective is found in Ṛg-Veda I.164.39, which declares that knowledge of the Veda is not gained through the Vedic hymns; it is gained by becoming familiar with that imperishable reality which is the abode of the hymns.

> The *ṛcs* exist in the Imperishable (*akṣara*), beyond space (*vyoman*), where all the gods abide. He who does not know that [Imperishable], what can he accomplish with the hymn? Those alone who know it sit collected.

If one has not known and experienced directly that transcendent, imperishable reality, then reciting or hearing the Vedic *mantras* will not be sufficient to realize the reality of Veda.

This perspective is elaborated in the Upaniṣads, the foundational texts of the *jñāna* stream. The Upaniṣadic sages are primarily concerned to delineate the relationship of the Veda to the ultimate reality, Brahman-Ātman, and consequently they place little emphasis on the cosmos-maintaining activities of the priestly sacrificial traditions. Their goal is rather to follow the path of knowledge established by the ancient *ṛṣis* in order to attain realization of Brahman-Ātman. In this context they are concerned not with the earthly manifestation of the *mantras* as recited texts but rather with the transcendent structure of Veda as that eternal, infinite knowledge which constitutes the very fabric of Brahman-Ātman.[66] Thus, the Muṇḍaka Upaniṣad declares that knowledge of the mundane Vedic texts is a lower form of knowledge (*aparā vidyā*) than that supreme knowledge (*parā vidyā*) by means of which the Imperishable (*akṣara*) is apprehended.[67] The Veda is assimilated to Brahman-Ātman in the Upaniṣads, and correspondingly the term *ṛṣi* is extended to include not only the ancient seers of the Vedic *mantras* but any great sage who has become a knower of Brahman-Ātman.[68] Just as the ancient *ṛṣis* performed *tapas* in order to obtain their cognitions, so those who aspire to become *ṛṣis* are urged to practice *tapas* in the form of meditation techniques in order to realize Brahman-Ātman.[69]

A number of Upaniṣads recommend using the syllable Om as a vehicle in meditation.[70] Om is identified in several Upaniṣadic passages with Brahman,[71] and in the Maitri Upaniṣad is designated more specifically as Śabdabrahman.[72] A passage in the Chāndogya Upaniṣad, recapitulating the Brāhmaṇas' system of correspondences, describes Om as the essence of the three *vyāhṛtis*, which in turn are the essences of the three Vedas.[73] Om, as the sound-form of Brahman, is thus the most concentrated essence of the Veda, and it is this seed-syllable that is to be used as a vehicle in meditation in order to attain that level of Brahman which is beyond sound.[74]

These Upaniṣadic conceptions present the beginnings of a twofold transformation in the conception of *mantra*. First, the Vedic *mantras* are reduced to root *mantras*, seed-syllables such as Om, *bhūḥ*, *bhuvaḥ*, and *svaḥ*, which are represented as the most powerful and fundamental elements of the primordial language. Second, the use of these seed-syllables, in particular Om, is transferred from a sacrificial to a meditative context. Such conceptions are further elaborated in later yoga and tantric traditions, which advocate the practice of meditation techniques that use as a vehicle specially designated *mantras* that are thought to possess sacred power. These *mantras* are frequently monosyllabic or disyllabic and are not necessarily Vedic in origin, but they are generally modeled on the prototype of Om and are upheld as potent sound-vibrations by means of which one may come to experience directly that transcendent level of reality which is the ultimate source and abode of Śabdabrahman, the Veda.[75]

CHAPTER 6

Torah in Practice

> Turn it [the Torah] and turn it, for everything is in it. Look (*ḥăzî*) into it, grow old and frail over it, and from it do not stir, for you have no better portion than it.
>
> —'Āḇôṯ V.22

Rabbinic and kabbalistic representations of the Torah's role in creation and revelation both reflect and inform practices associated with the transmission, study, and appropriation of the Sefer Torah. These representations are reflected primarily in (1) the detailed laws and highly developed scribal arts for preparing and preserving the written text of the Torah scroll; (2) the central importance given to study and interpretation of the Written Torah as a means of drawing out its manifold meanings; (3) theurgic conceptions of the role of Torah study and practice in maintaining the cosmos and strengthening God himself; and (4) the modes of appropriation of the Torah, in which the rabbinic sages seek to "own" the Torah through study and performance of the commandments, while certain kabbalists advocate mystical modes of appropriation as a means of gaining direct experience of the supernal Torah that is identical with God.

Written Transmission of the Sefer Torah

At the time of the revelation at Mount Sinai, as represented in certain rabbinic and kabbalistic texts, the primordial Torah became embodied on earth in the concrete form of a written text, the Sefer Torah or Written Torah. Moses, acting as a scribe (*sôp̄ēr*), simply recorded the words of God as they were revealed to him and, after completing the Sefer Torah, deposited it in the Ark of the Covenant. In accordance with this traditional perspective, the Jewish scribal tradition, with its detailed laws concerning the preparation of the Torah scroll, has been dedicated to copying and preserving meticulously, generation after generation, the exact text of the Sefer Torah that is believed to have been originally transmitted by God to Moses, the scribe par excellence.

The act of writing a Torah scroll is considered holy work, and therefore a scribe, when commencing to write, declares, "I hereby write this Torah scroll for the sanctity of the Torah, and all the names of God in it for the sanctity of the Name." The Talmud and later legal codes contain numerous laws regulating every aspect of the scroll's preparation, including the attitude and qualifications of the scribe; the types of parchment, writing instruments, and ink to be used and manner of their preparation; and the method of writing the letters and lines of the scroll.[1] Scrupulous attention is given to preserving accurately every "jot and tittle" of the text. Torah scrolls that are not written in accordance with these regulations or that are found to have missing or defective letters or other flaws are rendered unfit (*pāsûl*) for liturgical use in the synagogue. When viewed from the perspective of the Sefer Torah's status as the concrete embodiment of the divine Word, a single mistake in writing a Torah scroll is considered to have not only ritual but cosmic ramifications. A Talmudic aggadah ascribed to R. Meir relates an encounter he had with R. Ishmael concerning his work as a scribe of the Torah.

> When I was studying with R. Akiba, I used to put vitriol in the ink and he did not say anything to me. But when I went to R. Ishmael, he said to me, "My son, what is your occupation?" I told him, "I am a scribe [of the Torah]." He said to me, "My son, be careful in your work, for your work is the work of God (literally, 'work of heaven'). If you should perhaps omit a single letter or add a single letter, you would thereby destroy the entire world. . . ."[2]

Naḥmanides, as discussed in chapter 2, claims that the rigorous scribal tradition stipulating that a Sefer Torah is disqualified if even a single letter is added or omitted derives from the notion that the entire Torah consists of the names of God. Naḥmanides's colleagues in Gerona, Ezra b. Solomon and Azriel b. Menaḥem, cosmologized this conception even further, emphasizing the organic unity of the Torah as a perfect divine edifice hewn from the Name of God from which not a single letter or point can be eliminated without harming the entire body.[3]

The *Sēp̄er ha-Yiḥûḏ*, a late thirteenth-century kabbalistic text, suggests the even more radical view that all of the letters of the

Torah are the shapes or forms of God, and therefore a single error in the orthography disqualifies a Sefer Torah because it no longer represents the "shape of God."

> All the letters of the Torah, by their shapes, combined and separated, swaddled letters, curved ones and crooked ones, superfluous and elliptic ones, minute and large ones, and inverted, the calligraphy of the letters, the open and closed pericopes and the ordered ones, all of them are the shape of God, Blessed be He. . . . [T]he Torah, beginning with the first pericope until the last one is the shape of God, the Great and Formidable, Blessed be He, since if one letter be missing from the Scroll of Torah, or one is superfluous, or a [closed] pericope was [written] in an open fashion or an [open] pericope was [written] in a closed fashion, that Scroll of Torah is disqualified, since it has not in itself the shape of God, the Great and Formidable, because of the change [[in]] the shape caused.[4]

Since the Sefer Torah is the form of God, the act of writing a Torah scroll is tantamount to "making" God himself: "Each and every one [of the people of Israel] ought to write a scroll of Torah for himself, and the occult secret [of this matter] is that he made God himself."[5] Joseph of Hamadan, a thirteenth-century Castilian kabbalist who was a contemporary of the author of the Zohar, presents a similarly iconic view of the Torah scroll as the form of God, which is to be held up by the cantor in the synagogue so that the congregation "will see the image of the supernal form [that is, the *s^ep̄îrôṯ*]."[6]

Interpretation of the Torah

Rabbinic Hermeneutics One of the basic tenets of the rabbinic tradition is that God did not intend for the Sefer Torah to stand on its own, but rather he intended for it to be interpreted. The very manner in which the Torah scroll is written—that is, the fact that it is written only with consonants and with no vowels, no accents, and no punctuation—points to the openness of the closed text, which calls for interpretation. The text is closed in that its consonantal form is fixed and cannot be altered in any way. However, since the consonants alone are given, without the vowels, the text remains open in that it is possible to vocalize the words in a number of different ways, giving rise to a variety of possible interpretations without violating the written letter of the text. There is of course a tradition concerning the proper way to vocalize the text, but there are variations within this tradition, opening the way to multiple interpretations.[7] The text is closed in another sense, in that it is considered to be a kind of cryptogram written in the secret language of God, which conceals as much meaning as it reveals. The style of the narrative accounts of the Sefer Torah is laconic and minimalist, full of lacunae. The legal sections of the Sefer Torah are also obscure and ambiguous in places, making it difficult to determine the precise meaning and application of certain laws. Although the written text is thus closed, both in the sense that its form is fixed and its meaning at times is concealed, the very hiddenness of the written text invites interpretation.

The rabbis maintain that the tradition of interpreting the written "code" of Torah is itself God-given and derives from the original revelation at Mount Sinai. In addition to the Written Torah, God gave Moses an Oral Torah, an oral tradition of interpretation of the written text. The process of interpretation, which assumes paramount importance in the rabbinic tradition, is thus viewed as a direct continuation of the original revelation and as an extension of the text itself, not something separate from it. Through the interpretive process the closed text is opened up, the potentiality of meaning contained within it is unfolded, and the text is transformed from a bounded system into an unbounded, ongoing process mediated by the sages.[8]

The hermeneutical process is thus understood as a means of drawing out and unfolding the meaning contained in seminal form in the Sefer Torah. At the time of the revelation at Mount Sinai the vast tree of primordial wisdom, which contained the total knowledge of creation, descended onto earth and became concentrated in the seed expressions of the Book of the Torah. The sages who interpret and expound the words of the Torah thus insist that they are not generating any new knowledge. They are simply transforming potentiality into actuality; they are elaborating and making explicit different aspects of the knowledge already implicit in the Sefer Torah. It is through the Oral Torah that the tree of knowledge contained in the seed expressions of the Written Torah unfolds and bears fruit. The value of the Oral Torah in drawing out or "extracting" the meaning of the Written Torah is emphasized in a parable in Sēḏer 'Ēliyyāhû Zûṭā', which compares God to a king who gave his two servants each a measure of wheat and a bundle of flax. While the foolish servant did nothing at all with the wheat and flax, the wise servant baked bread from the wheat and spun a cloth from the flax. "When the Holy One, blessed be He, gave the Torah to Israel, He gave it to them only as wheat, to extract from it fine flour, and as flax, to extract from it a garment."[9]

The process of interpretation is viewed as serving different purposes depending on the interpreter's conception of Torah. If the Midrashist is focused on the exoteric text of the Torah, then he adopts the methods and principles of halakhic Midrash in order to clarify the meaning and application of the commandments, and he uses the methods of aggadic Midrash in order to draw out the ethical, theological, and metaphysical import of the narrative, nonlegal portions of the text. If, however, the interpreter maintains that the Torah also constitutes the blueprint revealing the structure and laws of creation, then the process of interpretation becomes a means of cracking the code of the exoteric text in order to fathom the "secrets of the Torah" (*siṯrê tôrāh, rāzê tôrāh*). Both of these hermeneutical approaches are found in the rabbinic tradition, although they are not necessarily mutually exclusive. These two approaches are exemplified, respectively, by the Tannaitic schools of R. Ishmael and R. Akiba, which, as Abraham Heschel has emphasized, developed fundamentally different approaches to the hermeneutical task. The more pragmatic school of R. Ishmael maintained that "the Torah speaks in the language of human beings,"[10] while the more mystically inclined school of R. Akiba found transcendent significance in every word and letter of the Sefer Torah.[11]

In suggesting that the Torah is customary human speech, the school of R. Ishmael was not denying the divine status of the Sefer Torah as the Word of God. On the contrary, the thirteen hermeneutical principles of R. Ishmael, like the interpretive methods of the school of R. Akiba, proceed from the fundamental assumption that the Torah in its entirety is divine and therefore constitutes a perfect and complete unity, in which there are no errors, no contradictions, and no superfluous words or letters. R. Ishmael's assertion that the Torah speaks in the language of human beings was essentially an assertion of the primacy of the exoteric text, which is rendered in a language comprehensible to human beings—albeit laconic and obscure at times—and which can be interpreted through recourse to normal modes of human reasoning and logic. The thirteen principles of R. Ishmael were thus based primarily on logical inference. His principles include, for example, *qal wā-ḥômer*, an a fortiori argument from a minor to a major premise, or vice versa; *g^e^zērāh šāwāh*, an inference based on word analogy; and the principle that the meaning of an obscure word or passage may be deduced through examining its larger context (*mē-ʿinyānô*).

The thirteen principles of R. Ishmael were developed primarily for the purpose of halakhic Midrash, which focuses on the legal portions of the Sefer Torah. These principles were evolved in direct response to a double awareness on the part of the rabbis: on the one hand, they were of course aware of the ambiguities, contradictions, redundancies, and anomalies in the text of the Torah; on the other hand, they insisted that the Torah constitutes a perfect unity and that if the interpreter probes deeply enough into the subtle nuances of each expression, he will discover that any contradictions and inconsistencies are only apparent and ultimately serve to illumine some aspect of the divine Author's intention that might otherwise go unnoticed. R. Ishmael's hermeneutical principles were thus aimed at clarifying ambiguous verses, harmonizing contradictions, and resolving other types of lexical problems in an effort to determine the precise meaning and application of the laws of the Torah.

The school of R. Akiba was also concerned with halakhic Midrash, but its hermeneutical methods were based less on logical inference than on textual scrutiny, closely examining every detail of the text for possible divine implications. R. Akiba and his disciples are portrayed in rabbinic texts as one of the more mystically oriented circles of Tannaim who sought to fathom the "secrets of the Torah,"[12] and their hermeneutical approach correspondingly appears to have been founded on a more esoteric notion of Torah than that of the school of R. Ishmael. Two of the seminal speculations in rabbinic texts concerning the Torah's cosmogonic role are attributed to R. Akiba and his student R. Judah b. Ilʿai, respectively: the notion that the Torah is the "precious instrument by means of which the world was created,"[13] and the notion that God "looked into" the Torah in order to bring forth the world.[14] Although it is not possible to determine with certainty whether such traditions indeed derive from R. Akiba and his disciples, it is clear from their interpretive methods that, contrary to the school of R. Ishmael, they proceeded from the assumption that the Torah speaks more than the language of human beings; it speaks the language of God, and therefore every single detail of the text is significant and must be examined as a possible hidden clue not only to understanding God's laws but also to fathoming the hidden mysteries. The hermeneutics of R. Akiba's school took into account every linguistic peculiarity, its interpretations extending not only to the Hebrew particles and letters but even to the apparently ornamental crowns attached to certain letters.[15] The interpretive methods of R. Akiba's school thus encompassed both exoteric and esoteric dimensions of the Torah: they were concerned with drawing out the halakhic and aggadic implications of the biblical commandments and narratives, but they were also concerned with apprehending the subtler mysteries of the Torah.[16]

In aggadic Midrashim from the classical Amoraic period onward, the school of R. Akiba's emphasis on the significance of every detail of the Torah has its counterpart in what Howard Eilberg-Schwartz has termed an "atomistic understanding of language." As part of their attempt to "recover" the divine Author's hidden intentions encoded within the Torah, the sages would break down the canonical text into its basic linguistic units—individual words—and these units into their constituent elements—the Hebrew letters—and then would manipulate the text through various hermeneutical devices, including analysis of the numerical value (*gematria*), shape, and sound of the letters, transposition of letters, splitting of words, alternative readings (*'al tiqrê*), etymologies, and other types of linguistic operations. In such hermeneutical maneuvers every word and letter of the Torah, as the fundamental components of the divine language, is ascribed manifold significations that must be "unpacked."[17] Such interpretive strategies are particularly emphasized in aggadic Midrashim, in which, free from the restraints imposed on halakhic formulations and at the same time limited by the broader parameters of rabbinic discourse, the Midrashist could exercise his limited freedom to explore the subtleties and delights of the art of interpretation and to tease out multiple meanings from a single word or verse.[18]

In contrast to the monosemantic perspective of Aristotle, who asserts that "if it be said that 'man' has an infinite number of meanings, obviously there can be no discourse; for not to have one meaning is to have no meaning," the rabbis extol the glories of polysemy and maintain, on the contrary, that if there were a singular, determinate meaning of the Torah there could be no discourse. To insist on univocality would be to end discourse with God through the interpretive process, and such an end is inconceivable.[19] A Talmudic pericope compares the words of the Torah to a fig tree with an unending supply of figs, or to a mother's breast whose flow of milk is inexhaustible, for the more one studies them the more meaning (*ṭa'am*, literally, "relish") one finds in them.[20] Another Talmudic tradition suggests that it is possible to generate "mounds upon mounds" (*tîllê tîllîm*) of expositions on every single stroke (*qôṣ*) of every letter of the Torah.[21] The multifaceted meanings ascribed to the Torah received formal articulation in two traditions concerning the number of possible modes of expounding the Torah. According to one tradition there are forty-nine ways of interpreting the Torah,[22] while according to a second tradition there are seventy modes of exposition.[23] The latter notion recalls the tradition that every utterance that issued from God's mouth at Mount Sinai was heard simultaneously in seventy languages,[24] establishing an implicit connection between the Sinai revelation and the hermeneutical process: just as in the process of revelation God's Word was heard in seventy languages, so in the process of interpretation the divine Word is expounded in seventy ways.

A number of passages in rabbinic texts suggest that interpretation of the Torah is not only a continuation of the original revelation but also serves as a means of replicating the wondrous events of the Sinai theophany. An aggadah that appears in several classical Amoraic Midrashim relates how when certain sages interconnect the verses of the Torah (Pentateuch), Nevi'im, and Ketuvim, flames of fire blaze forth around them and "the words of the Torah are joyful as on the day they were given at Sinai . . . in fire."[25] The Talmudic story in Ḥăḡîḡāh 14b of R. Joḥanan b. Zakkai and his disciples expounding *ma'ăśēh merkāḇāh* similarly invokes the language and imagery of the Sinai event to describe the miraculous phenomena that accompany their expositions: fire descends from heaven, an angel (rather than God) speaks from the fire, and hosts of angels assemble to hear the expositions, like people assembling to witness a wedding between a bridegroom and bride.[26] Several Midrashim emphasize how the faces of the sages who study and expound Torah shine with its light, suggesting an analogy with the radiant countenance that Moses received at Sinai.[27] The Israelites' experience at the Sinai theophany is also paradigmatic for the Torah scholar: just as God revealed his glory (*kāḇôḏ*) and the Shekhinah to the people of Israel, so the divine glory and the Shekhinah are said to abide with those who engage in Torah study.[28]

Kabbalistic Hermeneutics The various kabbalistic schools adopted and extended the methods of Midrashic exegesis, while at the same time introducing a number of innovative hermeneutical devices.[29] Moshe Idel has emphasized that in their quest to unfold the hidden meanings of the Torah, the schools of theosophical Kabbalah and ecstatic Kabbalah developed fundamentally different hermeneutical approaches. The exponents of theosophical Kabbalah, particularly as represented by the Zohar and the Spanish kabbalists of the late thirteenth century, generally maintained the canonical text of the Sefer Torah intact and interpreted its words and verses as symbols of the theosophical processes occurring within the *s*^e^*p̄îrôṯ*. On the other hand, the exponents of ecstatic Kabbalah, as represented by Abraham Abulafia (end of 13th c. C.E.) and his disciples, interpreted the text as allegories of psychological processes, culminating in an atomization of the canonical text into its constituent letters.[30]

In both hermeneutical approaches the process of interpretation is represented as a means to divine revelation in which the interpreter attains a level of consciousness comparable to that of the ancient prophets, which in turn enables him to discern the deepest mysteries of the text. This illumined state of consciousness is the key to penetrating to the level of the subtle blueprint: while the theosophical kabbalists decode the Torah in order to fathom the structures of the cosmos and of the Godhead, the Abulafian school "deconstructs" the text in order to disclose the structures of the human psyche. Moreover, certain kabbalists within both schools assert the ultimate identity of the Torah with God and on this basis view the hermeneutical process as a means to gaining mystical experience of the divine reality of Torah. Such conceptions constitute a departure from two basic rabbinic tenets. First, while the process of interpretation is at times connected in rabbinic sources to the Sinai revelation, it is not viewed as involving prophetic states of consciousness, for prophecy is held to have ceased with the closure of the biblical period. Second, while the Torah is represented in certain rabbinic texts as an aspect of God, it is not directly identified with God, and thus the distinctions between the interpreter, the Torah, and God are maintained in rabbinic hermeneutics.[31]

The period between 1270 and 1290 in Castile, Spain, witnessed a tremendous outburst of symbolic creation and exegesis among the theosophical kabbalists. During this period complex hermeneutical methods were elaborated in the Zohar and the works of contemporary kabbalists—in particular, Moses de Leon, the reputed author of the Zohar,[32] Joseph Gikatilla, and Joseph of Hamadan. Our analysis will focus primarily on the hermeneutical approach of the Zohar, which constituted "both the first outpouring and the climax of Kabbalistic symbolic creation."[33] The hermeneutical techniques of ecstatic Kabbalah developed by Abraham Abulafia will be considered briefly in a later section.[34]

Before turning to the Zohar, mention should be made of one trend of speculation that was current at the end of the thirteenth century among Spanish kabbalists, including Gikatilla and Joseph of Hamadan, and that extended rabbinic conceptions of the multiplicity of meanings in the Torah to an infinity of significations. These speculations, like their rabbinic antecedents, take as their starting point the very manner in which the Sefer Torah is written: the Torah scroll is written with consonants alone and no vowels in order that the limitless possibilities of meaning inherent in the consonants would not be limited by a particular method of vocalization. While the consonantal text is fixed, the vocalization remains unspecified and potentially unlimited, reflecting the infinity of meaning in the Torah. The counterpart of phonological latitude is thus semantic plenitude. Moreover, according to Gikatilla, the possibility of multiple vocalizations and multiple interpretations is not restricted to human exegetes. He maintains that the Torah is vocalized and interpreted differently in each world—the world of the *s^e^p̄îrô<u>t</u>*, the world of the angels, the lower world of human beings, and so on—in accordance with the capacity and comprehension of its inhabitants.[35]

The Zohar also emphasizes the limitless depths of the Torah and employs a variety of strategies to fathom its meanings. These strategies are founded on the assumption that the canonical text constitutes a cryptogram that needs to be deciphered in order to discern the supernal mysteries that are hidden within the text. In this context the Zohar distinguishes between the manifest and the hidden aspects of the Torah.[36] Beyond the obvious, manifest meanings of the Torah's narratives and precepts, which are intended for the general populace, the kabbalist exegete seeks to contemplate the hidden mysteries that are concealed within the exoteric text.[37] God has put all of the "hidden things" in the Torah,[38] and therefore every word contains "many secrets, many meanings, many roots, many branches."[39]

In discussing the many lights that shine in every word of Torah,[40] the Zohar thus does not evaluate all meanings on the same level. In addition to the twofold distinction between manifest and hidden, the Zohar at times makes reference to a fourfold hierarchy of meanings. These four levels of meaning, which are first referred to in the Midrash ha-Ne'ĕlām to the book of Ruth, are designated by a variety of terms in the Zohar.[41] This fourfold schema received its classical formulation in the writings of Moses de Leon (d. 1305 C.E.), who used the acronym PaRDēS ("garden" or "paradise") to refer collectively to the four levels, each consonant denoting one of the levels: (1) *p*ᵉ*šāṭ*, the literal meaning, which includes the historical and factual content of the Torah; (2) *d*ᵉ*rāšāh*, the hermeneutical meaning, which is derived through the halakhic and aggadic Midrashim of the rabbis; (3) *remez*, the allegorical meaning, which is the locus of the philosophical mode of interpretation; and (4) *sôḏ*, the mystical meaning, which is the focus of kabbalistic exegesis, in which the words of the Torah are interpreted as symbols of the recondite processes in the sᵉp̄îrôṯic realm and of the mysteries of the upper and lower worlds.[42]

The task of the kabbalist exegete, according to the Zohar, is to decode the exoteric text and contemplate the hidden secrets of the Torah,[43] the cosmic blueprint, which contains the mysteries of all levels of existence—the sᵉp̄îrôṯic world, the celestial worlds of the Merkabah and the angels, and the terrestrial world of human beings.

> In the Torah are all the celestial and sealed mysteries, which it is impossible to grasp. In the Torah are all those celestial things that are revealed and are not revealed. In the Torah are all the things of the upper world and the lower world; all the things of this world and all the things of the world to come are in the Torah.[44]

The Torah, as the blueprint that encompasses all levels of existence and reflects the structure of both the human and the divine anthropos,[45] is represented in one Zoharic passage as a multilayered organism that has garments, a body, a soul, and a "soul of souls." The passage describes how when the primordial Torah, which served as the instrument of creation, descended to earth at the Sinai revelation it assumed the garments of this world, for otherwise the world could not have endured its supernal effulgence. The narrative stories are the outer garments of the Torah, while the commandments constitute its body and the hidden mysteries its soul. The Zohar emphasizes that in order to comprehend the true reality of Torah one must penetrate beyond the garments, or narratives, and beyond the body, or commandments, to its soul, where the hidden mysteries are illumined by the light of primordial wisdom.

> Come and see. There is a garment that is seen by all. And when fools see a man in a garment that appears to them to be beautiful, they look no further. [But] the value of the gar-

> ment resides in the body, and the value of the body resides in the soul. Similarly, the Torah has a body. The commandments of the Torah are the bodies of the Torah. This body is clothed in garments, which are the narratives of this world. The fools in the world look only upon the clothes, which are the narratives of the Torah; they know no more, and do not see what is beneath the clothes. Those who know more do not look upon the clothes, but upon the body beneath the clothes. The wise, the servants of the supreme King, those who stood at Mt. Sinai, look only upon the soul, which is the foundation of all, the real Torah. And in the time to come they are destined to look upon the soul of the soul of the Torah.[46]

The kabbalists, as the "wise" whose souls were present at the Sinai revelation, have the ability to "look upon" the soul of the Torah and to penetrate its mysteries. However, the highest mysteries, which constitute the "soul of the soul" of the Torah, will be accessible to them only in the time to come. The passage goes on to correlate the various layers with the supernal realms: the heaven with their hosts are the garment, the Community of Israel (Malḵûṯ, the Shekhinah) is the body, Tip̄'ereṯ is the soul, and the Ancient Holy One (Keṯer) is the soul of souls.[47]

This passage brings to light two important points with respect to the Zoharic conception of hermeneutics. First, it suggests that there is an organic relationship between the various layers of Torah and that even though the outer garments do not constitute the essential reality of Torah, they nevertheless serve an important function in shielding the world from the overpowering brilliance of its supernal light. Although the Zohar denigrates those "fools" who focus only on the garments of the Torah and remain content with its literal meaning,[48] it does not thereby negate the outer form of the canonical text. Rather, the hermeneutical approach of the Zohar generally respects the syntax and structure of the words and verses of the Sefer Torah. The exegete uses the level of *pᵉšāṭ* as a starting point beyond which he must extend his interpretation, progressively unfolding the layers of *dᵉrāšāh* and *remez* until he discerns the hidden mysteries of *sôḏ*.[49]

Second, the passage concerning the multilayered Torah implies that the kabbalist exegete is capable of penetrating to the levels of the supernal Oral Torah, the Shekhinah (= body), and the supernal Written Torah, Tip̄'ereṯ (= soul). Moreover, it suggests that the hermeneutical process involves a visionary experience of these divine emanations and that the exegete's experience corresponds to that of the Israelites at the Sinai revelation. Understood from this perspective, the process of interpretation assumes the status of the mystical technique par excellence, in which the discernment of subtler layers of meaning serves as a means of "seeing" beneath the garment[50] and attaining a direct vision of the light of the supernal Torah in the s^e^p̄îrôṯic realm. The process of kabbalistic exegesis begins with deciphering the code of the exoteric text in order to penetrate to the hidden blueprint that itself provides the cipher by means of which the supernal mysteries are unlocked. The interpretive process culminates in a direct experience of the architect within the blueprint: a vision of the supernal Torah that is identical with God.[51]

The Zoharic paradigm for the visionary experience attained by the kabbalist exegete, as the above passage suggests, is the revelation at Mount Sinai. While rabbinic texts also at times invoke the Sinai event when discussing the fruits of Torah study, for the Zohar the revelation is not simply a past event with paradigmatic power for the scholar's present activities. As Elliot Wolfson has emphasized, the Zohar claims that through interpretation of the Torah the mystic exegete can himself attain a direct revelatory experience of the s^e^p̄îrôṯic realm comparable to that of the Israelites at Sinai.[52] The Israelites are held to have attained a vision of the five lower *s^e^p̄îrôṯ* (from Tip̄'ereṯ to the Shekhinah), either directly or mediated through the Shekhinah.[53] Like the Israelites who were granted a vision of the Shekhinah, the kabbalist is frequently represented in the Zohar as drawing down or uniting with the Shekhinah through study of the Torah.[54] One passage, commenting on Daniel 12.3, "The enlightened (*maśkilîm*) will shine like the splendor (*zōhar*) of the firmament," maintains that the "enlightened" are those with illuminated consciousness who have the ability to "contemplate through seeing" (*'istakkēl*) the Shekhinah and the hidden light of Torah that shines perpetually.[55] Another passage gives a more radical interpretation of Daniel 12.3, suggesting that the "enlightened" who comprehends on his own the hidden mysteries of the Torah can attain the level of Moses, Tip̄'ereṯ, which is "the firmament of Moses" that "stands in the middle" of the s^e^p̄îrôṯic realm.[56] And like Moses, the face of the mystic exegete shines with the light of his supernal visions.[57]

Contrary to the traditional rabbinic view, the Zohar thus suggests not only that prophecy is still possible in the post-biblical period but that the highest level of prophecy, which is generally considered the exclusive province of Moses, can be achieved by the kabbalist exegete.[58] Just as the visions of Moses surpassed that of all the prophets, so the kabbalist who engages in the study of Torah attains a level of visionary experience that is higher than that of the post-Mosaic prophets: "Those who study Torah stand above in the place called 'Torah' (i.e., *Tiferet*), [. . .] while the prophets stand lower down in the place called *'Neẓaḥ'* and *'Hod.'*"[59]

The mystical gnosis gained by the kabbalist exegete, like that attained by Moses and the people of Israel at the Sinai revelation, is primarily visual rather than auditory. In commenting on Daniel 12.3, "And the enlightened (*maśkilîm*) will shine," one passage notes that those who contemplate the divine glory and the "secret of wisdom" in Torah are called "the enlightened (*maśkilîm*)" rather than simply "the knowers (*yôḏ*^{e}*'îm*)," for they contemplate through seeing (*'istakkēl*).[60] In another passage the Zohar emphasizes that the sages, who are "full of eyes," have the capacity to see the hidden mysteries of the Torah that are concealed beneath the outer garment.[61]

The passage continues with the famous parable of the damsel in the palace, in which the layers that separate the Torah and the interpreter are progressively stripped away, culminating in a vision of the supernal Torah "face to face." The parable describes the stage-by-stage process through which the hermeneutical experience unfolds until it culminates in divine communion with the bride of Israel. The Torah is personified in the parable as a living, organic entity who wants to reveal her total reality to sincere seekers of wisdom. The Torah is compared to a damsel who is hidden in a palace while her lover constantly paces back and forth outside, watching to catch a glimpse of his beloved. In the beginning she only reveals her face to him momentarily, but then she quickly hides again, ever enflaming him with renewed passion for her. After some time, however, the lover of Torah is invited to enter the palace and explore its inner chambers.

The parable describes the hermeneutical process as involving a dynamic, symbiotic relationship between the Torah and the interpreter, in which, on the one hand, the divine reality of Torah extends herself to the interpreter and progressively reveals the deeper levels of her meaning to him, while, on the other hand, the interpreter is drawn to the Torah and seeks to fathom the increasing subtleties that she unfolds. The more the interpreter understands, the more the Torah reveals. The unfoldment of each new layer of meaning results in an increasing degree of intimacy between the Torah and her interpreter. (1) When the interpreter only understands *p*^{e}*šāṭ*,[62] the literal level of meaning, he remains outside of the palace and only catches occasional glimpses of the Torah. (2) When insight dawns he becomes capable of comprehending *d^e^rāšāh*, the hermeneutical meaning, in which the Torah speaks to him from behind a curtain. (3) When the interpreter penetrates to *haggadah* (= *remez*), the allegorical level of meaning, the Torah speaks to him through a light veil. (4) Finally, when he begins to fathom the hidden mysteries corresponding to the level of *sôḏ*, the Torah reveals herself to him "face to face," disclosing all of her secrets and concealing nothing. The interpreter then becomes a true "bridegroom of the Torah" and a "master of the house"[63] for all times. Each stage in the hermeneutical process brings the Torah and interpreter into closer and closer contact until finally they are united for all times as bridegroom and bride.[64]

The paradigm for the kabbalist exegete in this parable is once again Moses, who is himself called the "master of the house."[65] Moses is described in the passage immediately preceding the parable as donning the garments of the rainbow, a symbol of the phallus, or Y^e^sôḏ (ninth *s^e^p̄îrāh*), before entering the cloud, a symbol of the feminine Shekhinah. Having united with the Shekhinah, the supernal Oral Torah, he ascended the mountain and "saw what he saw," presumably gaining a vision of Tip̄'ereṯ, the supernal Written Torah.[66] Elsewhere in the Zohar Moses is portrayed as the husband of the Shekhinah, who through his marriage gained direct access to the bride's father, the King (Tip̄'ereṯ).[67] Emulating the example of Moses, the kabbalist exegete enters the palace and becomes the husband of the Shekhinah, the Oral Torah, and thereby gains direct access to the supernal mysteries of Tip̄'ereṯ, the Written Torah.

In the parable of the damsel in the palace the two versions of the marriage ceremony that appear in rabbinic accounts of the Sinai revelation—as a wedding between Torah and Israel, or between God and Israel—converge in the individual experience of the mystic exegete, for the supernal Torah with which he unites is represented as an aspect of God. In the mystical hermeneutics of the Zohar the distinctions among author, text, and interpreter thus ultimately collapse. The distinction between author and text dissolves because the Torah in its supernal manifestation is identified with the divine Author of the text. And in the end even the distinction between the interpreter and the author-text is overcome, for the hermeneutical process is represented as culminating in union with the divine reality embodied in the text.[68]

Theurgic Conceptions of Torah Study and Practice

Study of the Torah leads to practice. Rabbinic texts repeatedly emphasize that it is not sufficient simply to study the Torah's teachings; rather, one must actualize what one has learned through practice. "If a person has studied the Torah, he has fulfilled one commandment; if he has studied and kept [the Torah], he has fulfilled two commandments; if he has studied, kept, and performed, there is no one more meritorious than he."[69] Even the exponents of theosophical Kabbalah, who seek to discern the hidden mysteries that constitute the soul of Torah, are concerned with upholding the body of Torah through performing the commandments (*mitzvot*). In contrast to the anomian practices of ecstatic Kabbalah, the theosophical schools are strictly nomian. Indeed, as Idel has emphasized, the symbolic superstructures of theosophical Kabbalah are to a large extent aimed at providing a cosmic rationale for the commandments.[70] The dynamism of the Godhead is represented in this context as a paradigm for human activity, in which one emulates and contributes to the divine dynamics by performing the *mitzvot*. Idel remarks:

> Understanding the higher structures and dynamics, the Kabbalist is invited, even compelled, to participate in the divine mystery, not by understanding, faith, and enlightenment, but primarily by an *imitatio* of the dynamics. . . . The comprehension of the "mystery" is meaningless if not enacted in every commandment, even in every movement one performs. . . . This dynamic structure functions as a powerful instrument of ensuring the dynamism of human activity. . . .[71]

Idel maintains, in opposition to Scholem, that kabbalistic conceptions of the theurgic nature of the commandments, in which the performance of the *mitzvot* is represented as having a direct influence on the cosmos and on the Godhead, do not originate with the kabbalists but have their roots in rabbinic sources. While Scholem has emphasized that the rabbinic tradition severed the halakhah from myth by disassociating it from cosmic events,[72] Idel argues that even in extant rabbinic texts conceptions of a cosmic rationale for the commandments can be discerned.[73]

> [I]t was precisely the theurgic view of the commandments that was one of the factors that enforced the performance of the commandments, the lively interest in them, and the adherence of Jews to their rituals. . . . [L]ong before the emergence of Kabbalistic theosophy, Jews envisioned their ritual as a God-maintaining activity and . . . as universe-maintaining acts as well.[74]

In support of his view, Idel has surveyed theurgic conceptions from a range of kabbalistic texts, some of which have antecedents in rabbinic traditions.[75] Our analysis, while intersecting at points with Idel's study, will focus primarily on theurgic conceptions in rabbinic texts and in the Zohar that reflect the representations of the Torah's role in creation and revelation examined in chapters 2 and 4.[76] More specifically, we will be concerned with trends of speculation that point to the role of study and practice of Torah in maintaining the cosmos and strengthening the Godhead.

Rabbinic Texts One trend of speculation in rabbinic texts that provided the basis for later kabbalistic theurgy is the notion, discussed in chapter 2, that the Torah constitutes the plan of creation that reflects the structure of the universe. For example, an anonymous Midrash in Leviticus Rabbāh suggests that the laws of the Torah are the same laws by means of which God brought forth the cosmos.[77] Another tradition, found in P^{e}sîqtā' d^{e}-R. Kahana and the Talmud, emphasizes the correspondence between the 613 *mitzvot* of the Torah and the structure of both the macrocosm and the microcosm: the 365 negative commandments correspond to the number of days in a solar year, while the 248 positive commandments correspond to the number of members in the human body.[78] The kabbalists took these speculations one step further and concluded that if the Torah and its laws reflect the structure of the cosmos, then it is by activating the blueprint through study and practice that the cosmic order is maintained.

The seeds of such speculations are found in rabbinic texts, although their full implications are not elaborated. One of the earliest formulations of the Torah's role in sustaining creation is found in the aphorism attributed to Simeon the Righteous in 'Āḇôṯ, which includes the Torah as one of the three things upon which the world stands.[79] The other two things, the Temple service and deeds of loving-kindness, are specific modes of human activity, and thus one might infer that the Torah in this context refers to the activities associated with it: study and practice.[80] This interpretation is given in Pirqê d^{e}-R. Eliezer's rendering of the 'Āḇôṯ tradition. As a proof text for the Torah's role in sustaining the world, it cites Jeremiah 33.25, "If not for My covenant by day and by night, I would not have appointed the ordinances of heaven and earth," and then connects this verse through word analogy to Joshua 1.8, "This book of the Torah shall not depart out of your mouth, but you shall meditate on it day and night." Thus, by implication it is by meditating on the Torah day and night that heaven and earth are sustained.[81]

Another trend of speculation that points to the role of study and practice of the Torah in maintaining the cosmos is represented by the Midrashim that assert that if the people of Israel had not accepted the Torah at the Sinai revelation, God would have caused the creation to revert to chaos. By agreeing to observe the commandments, declaring "All that the Lord has spoken we will do and we will hear" (Exod. 24.7), the Israelites made it possible for the world to be established on a firm basis.[82] An anonymous Midrash in Exodus Rabbāh II extends this notion to include not only the Israelites' original acceptance of the Torah at Sinai but also their future actions in fulfillment of the covenant. It suggests that if Israel were to annul the covenant—presumably by violating the commandments of the Torah—then heaven and earth would be reduced to chaos.[83] Thus, Israel's continuing adherence to the Torah is necessary for the continuance of creation. An anonymous tradition in Deuteronomy Rabbāh frames this notion in positive terms, focusing on the contributions of study of Torah to the maintenance of the cosmos.

> The Holy One, blessed be He, said, "If you read the Torah you do a good deed (*mitzvah*) for My world, for if it were not for the Torah, the world would long ago have reverted to formlessness and emptiness (*tôhû wā-ḇôhû*)."[84]

The people of Israel, through their study and observance of Torah, are thus allotted a role in preserving the stability of the cosmos[85] and in maintaining peace in the upper and lower worlds.[86] A tradition in Esther Rabbāh II emphasizes that if Israel were to be destroyed, the world would not endure, for "it stands only through the merit of the Torah that was given to Israel, as it is said, 'If not for My covenant by day and by night, I would not have established the ordinances of heaven and earth' (Jer. 33.25)."[87]

A Talmudic tradition ascribed to R. Eleazar similarly invokes Jeremiah 33.25 as a proof text to establish the role of the Torah in sustaining the world: "Great is the Torah, since but for the Torah heaven and earth would not endure."[88] A second tradition, which immediately precedes R. Eleazar's tradition in Neḏārîm 32a, makes a similar claim for circumcision: "Great is circumcision, since but for circumcision heaven and earth would not endure."[89] These two traditions point to the cosmos-maintaining power of the two covenants, with their respective precepts, that God established with Israel: the covenant of circumcision, which was established through the patriarch Abraham, and the covenant of Torah, which was established with the entire Israelite community at Mount Sinai. A third tradition, attributed to R. Ammi, ascribes a comparable power to the activities of a particular group of Israelites, the *ma'ămāḏôṯ,* who were responsible for reciting the account of creation during the fixed times of sacrifice in the Temple: "But for the *ma'ămāḏôṯ* heaven and earth would not endure."[90]

The people of Israel, by choosing to uphold or neglect the commandments, are thus assigned a pivotal role in determining whether the cosmos is maintained or destroyed. A number of Midrashim suggest further that Israel's actions also have a direct influence on God himself and may serve either to strengthen or weaken his power.[91] For example, a passage in Pesîqtā' de-R. Kahana, after commenting on the ability of Moses to enhance the power of the Dynamis, continues with two traditions that ascribe a similar capacity to the righteous and to the Israelites generally.

> R. Azariah [said] in the name of R. Judah b. R. Simon: So long as the righteous (*tzaddikim*) perform the will of the Holy One, blessed be He, they add power (*kōaḥ*) to the Dynamis (Gebûrāh), as it says, "And now, I pray Thee, let the power (*kōaḥ*) of the Lord be great" (Num. 14.17). And if not, it is as if "you have weakened the Rock that begot you" (Deut. 32.18). R. Judah b. R. Simon [said] in the name of R. Levi b. Perata: So long as the Israelites perform the will of the Holy One, blessed be He, they add power (*kōaḥ*) to the Dynamis, as it says, "In God we shall make strength (*ḥāyil*)" (Ps. 60.14). But if not, it is as if "they are gone without strength (*kōaḥ*) before the pursuer" (Lam. 1.6).[92]

Variants of these two traditions in Lamentations Rabbāh invoke the same proof texts to establish the twofold effect of Israel's actions on God: when they act in accordance with the divine will—

presumably through observing the *mitzvot*—they augment God's power, whereas when they do not perform his will it is as if they weaken his power.[93] Another tradition ascribed to R. Judah b. Simon in the name of R. Levi b. Perata, which appears in Leviticus Rabbāh as well as in later rabbinic texts, focuses in particular on the way in which God's power is diminished through the act of adultery, a violation of one of the Ten Commandments.[94] While the above traditions suggest that Israel's observance or transgression of the commandments of the Torah has a direct impact on God, a Talmudic tradition invests the study of Torah with a similar power to influence the divine: if Israel is not engaged in the study of Torah, God becomes impoverished.[95]

Kabbalistic Texts Zoharic conceptions of the theurgic power of study and practice of Torah are directly linked to the Torah's role as the cosmic blueprint that contains the mysteries of all levels of existence. The Torah, as discussed in chapter 2, is represented in the Zohar as the primordial plan that reflects the structure of the cosmos, the human anthropos, and the divine anthropos.[96] Activation of the blueprint through study and practice is thus held to have a direct influence on every aspect of existence, serving as a means to maintain the cosmos, to strengthen and unite the masculine and feminine aspects of the Godhead, and to ensure a continuous influx from the upper to the lower realms.

A number of passages in the Zohar emphasize the role of study and/or observance of the Torah in sustaining the cosmos.[97] The Zohar, like rabbinic texts, provides a twofold paradigm for these theurgic activities: (1) the paradigm of creation, in which God himself is represented as creating and maintaining the upper and lower worlds by means of the Torah;[98] and (2) the paradigm of revelation, in which the Israelites' acceptance of the Torah at Mount Sinai is represented as the necessary condition for the firm establishment of the worlds.[99]

Several passages directly invoke the cosmogonic activity of God as a model for human activity in relation to Torah. For example, one passage describes God as "looking into" (*'istakkēl*) his blueprint, the Torah, in order to create the world.[100] The passage continues with a discussion of how the human activity of "looking into" (*'istakkēl*)—again, in the sense of "contemplating through seeing"—the mysteries of the Torah emulates the creative activity of God and serves to sustain the world.

> When He resolved to create the world He looked into the Torah, into its every creative word, and fashioned the world correspondingly. . . . When the world was all thus created, nothing was yet established properly, until He had resolved to create man, in order that he might study the Torah, and, for his sake, the world should be firmly and properly established. Thus it is that he who concentrates his mind on, and deeply penetrates into, the Torah, sustains the world; for, as the Holy One looked into the Torah and created the world, so man looks into the Torah and keeps the world alive. Hence the Torah is the cause of the world's creation and also the power that maintains its existence. Therefore blessed is he who is devoted to the Torah, for he is the preserver of the world.[101]

A second passage similarly establishes a direct connection between the role of the Torah in creating the world and the role of Torah study in maintaining the world. The passage invokes an image familiar from accounts of the Sinai revelation to establish that if human beings do not study the Torah, God will cause the cosmos to revert to chaos.

> When the Holy One, blessed be He, conceived the idea of creating the world, and sought to do so, He looked into the Torah, and then created it. . . . The Holy One, blessed be He, said to the world, when He had made it, and created man: O world, world, you and your laws can be sustained only through the Torah. That is why I created man [to live] in you, so that he might study it. But if he does not do so, I will return you to chaos. . . . Everyone who studies the Torah sustains the world and maintains every individual thing in its proper form.[102]

The passage goes on to assert that the structure of the microcosm, in which the different parts of the human being constitute a single body, corresponds to the structure of the macrocosm, in which all the elements of the cosmos are arranged to form one body. Both the microcosm and the macrocosm are in turn patterned on the Torah, which consists of "limbs and joints" that form a single body.[103] Therefore by studying the Torah, which contains "all the things of the upper world and the lower world," one "maintains every individual thing in its proper form."[104]

Several passages in the Zohar suggest that those who study the Torah not only maintain the world but also collaborate in the process of creation. The world was built and completed by means of the Torah, and therefore one who studies the Torah is celebrated as a "builder of worlds" who completes and preserves the cosmos.[105] One passage makes the even bolder claim that each new interpretation of the Torah generates a new heaven or a new earth.[106]

The Zohar emphasizes the theurgic power of study and practice not only to influence the cosmic order but also to influence the dynamics of the Godhead. It invokes the rabbinic tradition that when the people of Israel neglect the Torah they weaken the power of God, whereas when they perform righteous acts they strengthen God.[107] At the same time the Zohar extends and recasts earlier rabbinic conceptions in light of its theosophical system, in which the process of strengthening God is interpreted with reference to the s^ep̄îrôṯic pleroma. The "limbs and joints" that constitute the body of Torah are understood in this context as reflecting not only the cosmos-body and the human body but also the body of the divine anthropos.

Several Zoharic passages suggest that the "limbs and joints" of the Torah are the commandments, which join together to form the mystery of the supernal Man, encompassing both the masculine and feminine aspects of the Godhead.[108] One passage maintains that while all of the commandments of the Torah are connected with the body of the supernal King, certain commandments are connected more specifically with particular parts of his body—some with his head, some with his trunk, some with his hands, and some with his feet.[109] Having established that the commandments constitute and reflect the divine body, the Zohar emphasizes the importance of both study and practice of the *mitzvot*. First, one must understand the mystery of the commandments in order to know how the parts of the divine anthropos are arranged.[110] Second, one must diligently perform all of the commandments in order to strengthen and activate all parts of the Godhead. In transgressing a single commandment one transgresses against the body of the King[111] and diminishes the image of the s^ep̄îrôṯic pleroma.[112] Numerous passages in the Zohar emphasize the power of human deeds to generate a positive or negative influence in the supernal realm. "Any activity below stimulates a corresponding activity above."[113] Righteous actions stimulate the sources and channels within the Godhead, causing an influx from the upper to the lower *s^ep̄îrôṯ*, which in turn stream forth to nourish the lower worlds.[114] Sin, on the other hand, obstructs the channels so that the supernal streams cease to flow.[115]

The Zohar maintains further that the performance of the commandments not only has a constructive influence on the Godhead, it even has the power to "make" God. Commenting on Leviticus 26.3, "If you walk in my statutes and keep my commandments and do them," the Zohar remarks:

> "And you do them": Why is it written: "And you do them," after it is written "If you walk in my statutes, and keep my commandments"? . . . The answer is: whoever performs the commandments of the Torah and walks in its ways is regarded as if he makes the one above. The Holy one, blessed be He, says: "as if he had made me." And [the question] is raised: "And you do them"—the spelling is "And you do with them [*'itam*]." This is certainly the correct form, and when they are stirred to link to one another, so that the divine name will be in a proper state. This is certainly the meaning [of the spelling] "And you do with them."[116]

The process through which the Godhead is "made" is described in this passage as involving the unification of two divine emanations so that the Name of God will be completed. In the immediately preceding passage the two divine powers that when joined together form the holy Name are designated as the Written Torah (Tip̄'ereṯ) and the Oral Torah (the Shekhinah).[117] The implication, then, is that the performance of the commandments, which are the earthly counterpart of the supernal Written Torah and supernal Oral Torah, causes the unification of the masculine and feminine aspects of the Godhead, Tip̄'ereṯ and the Shekhinah, and thereby brings the divine Name to fruition. Conversely, transgression of the commandments impairs the divine Name and causes the exile of the Shekhinah from her supernal spouse.[118] In another passage the Zohar explicitly declares that the purpose for which the commandments are performed is "to unite the Holy One, blessed be He, with His Shekhinah throughout all the camps, above and below."[119] This power of unification is attributed in the Zohar not only to the practice of Torah but also to its study, which strengthens the Shekhinah so that she can come forth from exile to meet the supernal King, her spouse, Tip̄'ereṯ.[120]

Appropriation of the Torah

The rabbinic sages, as discussed in the previous sections, are primarily concerned with exoteric modes of appropriating the Torah, in which study and practice serve as the means through which the scholar can make the Torah his "own" Torah. The teachings of the Torah are inscribed in the sage's heart and mind through study and are activated in his limbs through the performance of the commandments. Through such methods of "embodying" the Torah—through preserving and interpreting the canonical corpus and giving corporeal expression to its teachings in actions—the sage himself becomes the embodiment of Torah.

The kabbalists, while building on rabbinic practices, at the same time reinterpret these practices as mystical modes of appropriation by means of which the mystic may go beyond the body of Torah and realize its soul, where God and Torah are one. In theosophical Kabbalah, as in the rabbinic tradition, interpretation of the Torah assumes a central place as the primary means of appropriating the Torah. However, the Zohar contains an implicit critique of those rabbis who focus solely on halakhic and aggadic interpretations and are thus concerned with only the outer garments and body of Torah. The purpose of Zoharic hermeneutics, as we have seen, is to fathom the hidden mysteries of the Torah and, by gradually penetrating to progressively subtler levels of meaning, to transcend the duality of the interpretive process altogether and enter into communion with the divine reality enshrined in the text. While the theosophical exegetes are concerned to honor and preserve the structure of the canonical text as the perfect form in which the divine is embodied, at the same time they want to penetrate through the outer form to the soul within in order to attain a visionary experience of the supernal light of Torah in the s^{e}p̄îrôṯic realm.

In contrast to the theosophical kabbalists, the exponents of ecstatic Kabbalah, as represented by Abraham Abulafia and his disciples, place less emphasis on maintaining the body of Torah. While the theosophical kabbalists emphasize the theurgic efficacy of embodying the Torah through the corporeal performance of the commandments, Abulafia allots no significant role to the commandments in his kabbalistic system and advocates instead the practice of anomian techniques that are primarily focused on the salvation of the individual mystic. Moreover, his hermeneutical techniques culminate in a "text-destroying exegesis," as Idel characterizes it, in which the canonical structure of the text is deconstructed and reduced to its primordial elements, the letters, which are then recombined in order to construct a new "text" consisting of divine names. Abulafia's "wisdom of the combination of letters" (*ḥoḵmaṯ ha-ṣêrûp̄*) involves a progressive movement from writing different permutations and combinations of the letters of the divine names, to vocalized articulation of the letter combinations, to complex mental exercises involving visualization of the letters in the "heart." Abulafia's "path of the names" culminates in a state of prophecy in which the mystic's intellect becomes united with the Active Intellect, which is identified with the supernal Torah. Union with the Active Intellect is thus tantamount to identification with the Torah, in which the mystic finds himself within the Torah and the Torah within him. While the Zohar represents the mystic's union with the Torah as a marriage involving intimate divine communion with the Torah, Abulafia describes the mystical realization of the Torah in impersonal terms as an abstract process of actualization of the human intellect's identity with the Active Intellect.[121]

COMPARATIVE ANALYSIS 3

Veda and Torah in Practice

When we turn to a comparative analysis of the regulations and practices associated with the Vedic Saṃhitās and the Sefer Torah, we find that our earlier observations regarding the three fundamental points of divergence between the two traditions—oral vs. written channels of language, auditory vs. visual modes of perception, and phonic vs. cognitive dimensions of the word—are further corroborated. The complex rules and traditions that have evolved regarding the proper methods of transmission, study, and appropriation of the Vedic Saṃhitās and the Sefer Torah are of particular interest in this regard, for it is here that we can most clearly see how differences in the conceptions of language underlying these symbol systems find expression in strikingly different practices.

Modes of Preservation: Oral vs. Written Transmission

The most obvious difference between the two scriptural traditions lies in the basic form in which the core texts have been transmitted—whether as spoken word, in the case of the Vedic Saṃhitās, or as written word, in the case of the Sefer Torah. As we have seen, the primacy of the oral or written form is traditionally held in these traditions to have been determined by the form in which these texts were originally cognized or revealed.

The traditional designation for the Vedic Saṃhitās, *śruti*, points to the fundamentally oral status of the *mantras*, which are revered as "that which was heard" by the *ṛṣis* in the beginning of creation and which perpetually maintain their orality as "that which is heard" in the ongoing recitations of brahmin *śrotriyas* in every generation. The Saṃhitās have traditionally been transmitted only through oral recitation, and there is a virtual taboo against writing down these sacred utterances because writing is regarded as a ritually polluting activity. The traditional designations for the Pentateuch—Sefer Torah, "Book of the Torah," and, *tôrāh še bi-ḵṯāḇ*, "Written Torah"—point just as emphatically to its essential status as a written text. The Sefer Torah is preserved in writing, according to the traditional rabbinic understanding, because that is the form in which God revealed it to Moses at the revelation at Mount Sinai. The act of writing a Torah scroll, far from being a ritually polluting act, is considered a holy work, undertaken for the sanctity of the Torah and for the sanctity of the divine Name.

Both traditions are equally concerned to preserve their cognized or revealed texts exactly as they are believed to have been originally received, whether in oral or written form. The absolute fidelity with which the brahmanical recitative tradition has preserved the purity of every sound and syllable of the Vedic Saṃhitās is mirrored in the scrupulous precision with which the Jewish scribal tradition has preserved every jot and tittle of the Sefer Torah. Both traditions have developed highly elaborate systems to safeguard the accurate preservation and transmission of their respective texts. The Brahman reciters of the Vedas and the scribes of the Torah assume parallel roles as copyists dedicated to reproducing verbatim the received texts of their traditions.

The highly intricate system of mnemonic techniques used to train brahmin *śrotriyas*, together with the elaborate textual apparatus evolved as part of the Vedāṅgas to ensure absolute accuracy in the preservation, recitation, and ritual use of the oral text of the Saṃhitās, reflects brahmanical conceptions of the transcendent status of the *mantras* as the primordial rhythms at the base of creation. The detailed laws and highly developed scribal arts for preparing and preserving the written text of the Sefer Torah, together with the other regulations and customs regarding the ornamentation of the Torah scroll, the public reading of the Torah, and the proper ways of reverencing the Torah scroll in synagogue worship, similarly point to conceptions of the sacred status of the Sefer Torah as a holy book that is more than a book, for as the concrete embodiment of the living Word of God it participates in the reality of God himself and must therefore be treated accordingly.

Modes of Study: Recitation vs. Interpretation

The methods of transmission of the two scriptural traditions—as oral texts, in the case of the Vedic Saṃhitās, or as a written text, in the case of the Sefer Torah—have profound implications for the proper modes of studying the two texts. With respect to the Saṃhitās, study is through memorization and recitation as a means of maintaining the phonological purity of every sound and syllable of the oral texts. With respect to the Sefer Torah, on the other hand, study is through interpretation as a means of drawing out the manifold meanings of every word and letter of the written text.

Thus, whereas the oral transmission of the Vedic Saṃhitās leads to an emphasis on phonology, memorization, and recitation, the written transmission of the Sefer Torah leads to an emphasis on semantics, understanding, and interpretation. The Vedic *mantras* do indeed have meaning, but as discussed earlier, their essential meaning is considered to be "constitutive" rather than discursive. The Vedic sounds are held to constitute their own meaning and therefore need not be understood or interpreted by the *śrotriyas* in order to be efficacious in enlivening and regenerating the cosmos. In contrast to the Vedic *mantras*, the Sefer Torah has what we might term "actuative meaning," in that its meaning is held to remain hidden unless it is actualized, drawn out, unfolded through the process of interpretation. Whereas the rabbis insist that God intended for the Sefer Torah to be interpreted, the brahmins insist that the Vedic Saṃhitās are not in need of any commentary.

We thus find a quite striking divergence of emphases in the modes of transmission and study of the Vedic Saṃhitās and the Sefer Torah. In brahmanical practices with respect to the Saṃhitās, we find an emphasis on the oral form of the texts, on highly developed recitative techniques for preserving the Vedic *mantras*, and on study of the Saṃhitās through memorization and recitation as a means of maintaining the phonological accuracy of the Vedic sounds. In traditional Jewish practices with respect to the Sefer Torah, we find an emphasis on the written form of the text, on highly developed scribal arts for preserving the written text, and on study of the text through interpretation as a means of drawing out its semantic significance.

These broad contrasts are of course an oversimplification and do not convey the full range of practices that exist within each tradition. For example, Jewish traditions also include a significant oral component, as reflected not only in the importance of the Torah reading in synagogue worship but also in the centrality in traditional Jewish life and practice of the Oral Torah. However, the differences between the traditions can be seen even in the modes of recitation adopted for the Sefer Torah and the Vedic *mantras*. The public reading of the Torah, which is the focal point of the synagogue liturgy, is a communal event in which the entire congregation participates, and therefore the Torah can be read only if a minyan of ten adult males is present. The text is read from the Torah scroll, rather than memorized, and primary importance is given to the discursive meaning of the recited words, with less emphasis on their sound value. If a word is read incorrectly in such a way that its meaning might be misunderstood, the word must be repeated. However, if there is a mistake in cantillation when reciting particular words, those words need not be repeated, since the primary focus is not on phonological precision but on communication of the content of the Torah's message to the congregation. With respect to the recitation of the Saṃhitās, on the other hand, the text is inscribed in the memories of the *śrotriyas* and not in a book. Moreover, as we have seen, the primary emphasis is on the proper pronunciation of the sounds of the *mantras*, with little regard for their discursive meaning. The purpose of Vedic recitation, especially in the context of *śrauta* sacrifices, is not to inspire or instruct a group of human worshipers but rather to maintain the cosmos through accurately reproducing the primordial sounds of the *mantras*.

If we examine more closely the modes of interpreting scripture that have been adopted by each tradition, we are once again struck by the contrasts more than the similarities. Little emphasis is placed on interpreting the discursive meaning of the Vedic Saṃhitās, in contrast to the central importance given to interpretation of the Sefer Torah. The formal schools of Vedic exegesis, Pūrva-Mīmāṃsā and Vedānta, have placed some emphasis on interpreting the Vedas, but their hermeneutical discussions center on the Brāhmaṇa and Upaniṣadic portions of the Vedas rather than on the *mantras*. Some parallels might be drawn between rabbinic hermeneutics and the hermeneutical methods of the Mīmāṃsakas, both of which are based on the assumption that their respective scriptures constitute a perfect unitary whole that is utterly devoid of errors and contradictions. However, the primary aim of Mīmāṃsaka hermeneutics is to arrive at definitive rules for the performance of *dharma*, and while this pragmatic emphasis may be comparable to that of the halakhic Midrashists, there does not appear to be any stream within the Mīmāṃsaka tradition comparable to the aggadic Midrashists, who relish the meaning of the Torah for its own sake.

Theurgic Conceptions

The designated methods of study and practice associated with Veda and Torah are represented in certain strands of their respective traditions as theurgic operations that serve the twofold function of maintaining the structures of the cosmos and of the divine realm. The exponents of the *karma-kāṇḍa* within the brahmanical tradition emphasize the theurgic efficacy of Vedic sacrifice and recitation, while certain rabbinic sages and theosophical kabbalists grant a comparable power to Torah study and practice. Moreover, each tradition invokes two types of paradigms for these theurgic practices: the paradigm of creation, in which the cosmogonic activities of the creator serve as a divine prototype for human activity; and the paradigm of cognition or revelation, in which the activities of the Vedic *ṛṣis* or of the people of Israel at Mount Sinai serve as authoritative human models.

The primary image that supports the theurgic practices associated with Veda and Torah is that of the blueprint: the Veda as the archetypal plan that reflects the structures of the human order, the natural order, and the divine order; the Torah as the blueprint that reflects the structures of the human being, the cosmos, and, according to certain kabbalists, the Godhead. Each tradition designates specific practices, modeled on the activities of the creator himself, by means of which the blueprint can be activated and the structures reflected within it nourished and sustained. In such conceptions Veda and Torah represent intermediary principles that reflect and interconnect all levels of existence, serving as the means through which human beings may not only shape their own individual and collective destinies but may directly influence the cosmos and the divine realm as well.

According to certain brahmanical conceptions, the creator brought forth and ordered the phenomenal creation through sacrifice and recitation of the Vedic *mantras*. The brahmin priests follow his example by periodically performing sacrifices and reciting the Vedic *mantras* in order to regenerate the cosmic order and to nourish and magnify the gods, including the creator himself. According to certain rabbinic conceptions, which are more fully elaborated in kabbalistic texts, God created the universe through "looking into" or contemplating his blueprint, the Torah, and using its laws to structure the cosmos. The rabbis and kabbalists emulate his example by "looking into" and interpreting the Torah and performing the commandments in order to maintain the cosmos and to strengthen and sustain God himself. The divine prototype in both cases points to the appropriate means through which the blueprint may be activated: while brahmanical practices emphasize reproduction of the sounds of the Vedic *mantras* through recitation, rabbinic and kabbalistic practices emphasize activation of the content of the Torah through interpretation and observance of the commandments.

A second model for these theurgic practices is provided by the modes of reception by means of which the original human recipients are said to have obtained and implemented the knowledge of Veda or Torah. The Vedic *ṛṣis* are represented in certain brahmanical texts as assisting the gods in the process of creation through cognizing and reciting the Vedic *mantras* and performing the first sacrifices on earth. The brahmin priests emulate the cosmos-producing activities of their ancestors by preserving the recitative and sacrificial traditions initiated by them. The Israelites' acceptance of the Torah at the Sinai revelation, in which they agreed to observe its commandments, is represented in certain rabbinic and kabbalistic texts as a crucial turning point that served to consolidate the creation and establish it on a firm basis. The Jewish people follow the example of their ancestors and ensure the preservation of creation by continuing to uphold the covenant through study and practice of Torah.

Modes of Appropriation

The theurgic practices associated with Veda and Torah are focused on conservation and maintenance—not only maintenance of the cosmic order and of the divine realm but maintenance of the social order as well. In this context the paradigmatic representations of Veda and Torah serve not only to authorize particular types of practice and modes of appropriation but also to delineate the relationship of different groups within each tradition to those practices.

The exoteric modes of appropriation promulgated by the brahmanical elite—recitation and hearing of the Vedic *mantras*—are circumscribed, limited to the male members of the three twice-born *varṇas*. Moreover, those practices to which maximal theurgic efficacy is ascribed—performance of the *śrauta* sacrifices and preservation of the Vedic recitative tradition—are reserved exclusively for those who claim direct blood descent from the *ṛṣis*, the brahmin priests. One means of justification for this hierarchy of practice is provided by the tripartite taxonomy of the Brāhmaṇas, which correlates the three higher *varṇas*, brahmins, *kṣatriyas*, and *vaiśyas*, with the three Vedas, Ṛg-Veda, Yajur-Veda, and Sāma-Veda, respectively. According to this scheme, in which the Ṛg-Veda and brahmins are ranked at the top of their respective triads, the very structure of the Veda itself, the cosmic blueprint, provides transcendent legitimation for the *varṇa* system and the hierarchy of practice perpetuated by it. No paradigm of Vedic study and practice is provided by the exponents of the *karma-kāṇḍa* and *dharma* traditions for the larger community who are excluded from the ranks of the twice-born—women, *śūdras*, and "outcastes" who are beyond the pale of the *varṇa* system. The only recourse for the exponents of popular *bhakti* traditions was to create their own texts and to assimilate them to *śruti* by deeming them the "fifth Veda" and ascribing to their verses mantric power comparable to that of the Vedic *mantras*.

The exoteric modes of appropriation promulgated by the rabbinic elite—study and practice of Torah—are, in contrast, open to all members of the Jewish community, at least in principle. Rabbinic portrayals of the Sinai revelation emphasize that all of the people of Israel—male and female, young and old—received the revelation of the Torah and agreed to accept and observe its commandments. The covenant was established with the entire Israelite community, which as a "kingdom of priests" and a "holy nation" was set apart from all other nations as the chosen people of God. Thus, all Jews are enjoined, as part of a national eschatology, to uphold the covenant by fulfilling the commandments of the Torah. Moreover, in contrast to the brahmanical prohibitions that exclude certain members of the community from hearing Vedic recitations, all members of the Jewish community are intended to participate in communal worship in the synagogue and to hear the reading of—although not necessarily to read themselves—the Sefer Torah. In principle the obligation to fulfill the commandments includes Torah study, although in practice the domain of those who are allowed to engage in sustained study of the Torah in rabbinic academies has been carefully circumscribed by the rabbis—as indicated by the existence of such categories of the "other" as the *'am hā-'āreṣ* and women. Certain practices, in particular preservation of the Written Torah and codification of the authoritative interpretations of its teachings that constitute the Oral Torah, are the exclusive province of the rabbinic elite, who as the designated heirs of Mosaic authority claim a special status within the larger Jewish community.

The theosophical kabbalists also invoke the example of Moses, emphasizing his role as the supreme prophet and mystic to whom God revealed the secrets of the Torah that their own traditions claim to preserve and unfold. The process of contemplating the hidden mysteries of the Torah through study is represented in the Zohar not only as a means of fathoming the cosmic blueprint and activating its theurgic power but also as a mystical mode of appropriation that has salvific power for the individual mystic. The goal of the kabbalist exegete is not only to emulate the interpretive activities of Moses but to attain a level of prophetic consciousness comparable to that of the supreme prophet. The purpose of Zoharic hermeneutics is to strip away the outer garments that shroud the effulgence of Torah and, like Moses, to attain a visionary experience of its supernal manifestations as the Oral Torah and Written Torah, the Shekhinah and Tip̄'eret̲. The hermeneutical process culminates in mystical union, in which one discovers the architect within the blueprint and becomes united with the divine reality of Torah, the bride of Israel, for all times.

The exponents of the *jñāna-kāṇḍa* and meditation traditions within the brahmanical tradition similarly advocate mystical modes of appropriation by means of which the seeker of wisdom may transcend the recited texts of the Vedic *mantras*, and even the level of the cosmic blueprint, in order to attain direct realization of the transcendent structure of the Veda that constitutes the very fabric of Brahman. Their goal is not to replicate the activities of the *ṛṣis* by reciting the texts preserved by them but rather to reproduce the state of consciousness by means of which the *ṛṣis* attained their cognitions. The exponents of the *jñāna-kāṇḍa* and the theosophical kabbalists thus share a concern to cultivate a state of consciousness that will allow them to experience directly that level of Veda or Torah which is identified with the ultimate reality. However, the language that is used to describe the mystical realization of Veda is radically different from that which is used in the Zohar to describe the mystical appropriation of Torah. Veda as an aspect of Brahman is an impersonal reality, and thus although the texts may speak of realizing the reality of Veda, they never speaking of communing with it. The Torah, on the other hand, is represented as a living aspect of a God who is intensely personal, and thus the Zohar at times makes use of marriage symbolism and erotic imagery to describe the intimacy of divine communion with the bride of Israel.

The methods that are advocated by the *jñāna-kāṇḍins* and the Zohar as means of attaining mystical realization of Veda or Torah also diverge sharply. While the purpose of Zoharic hermeneutics may ultimately be to overcome the distinctions between the Torah and the interpreter, interpretation of the canonical text of the Sefer Torah nevertheless serves as the primary means through which this purpose is achieved. The goal is to penetrate beyond the outer garments and body of Torah to its soul hidden within, but the garments themselves serve as the starting point. The exponents of the *jñāna-kāṇḍa* and meditation traditions, on the other hand, do not use the canonical text of the Vedic *mantras* as the starting point for their mystical techniques. They atomize the primordial language into its most fundamental units and focus on certain seed-syllables such as Om that are held to represent the most concentrated essence of the Veda. These root *mantras* are then used as vehicles in meditation to attain that level of Veda which is identical with Brahman. In Zoharic hermeneutics one penetrates increasingly subtle levels of meaning in order to transcend the interpretive process and attain a visionary experience of the light of the Godhead. In certain practices of *mantra* meditation, on the other hand, one experiences increasingly subtle levels of sound in order to transcend all sound and merge in the utter silence of Brahman.

The mystical techniques of ecstatic Kabbalah, as represented by the school of Abraham Abulafia, would appear to have more in common with brahmanical meditation practices in that Abulafia's techniques, in contrast to Zoharic hermeneutics, involve atomization of the canonical text of the Torah into its primary elements, the letters. Moreover, the goal of mystical realization of Torah is described in Abulafia's system in impersonal terms. However, the methods through which the letters of the divine names are employed in Abulafia's techniques differ in significant ways from the methods through which *mantras* are generally used in brahmanical meditation practices. Abulafia's practices involve writing and recitation of the letters as well as mental contemplation of the letters. Moreover, the internalized stage of meditation on the letters of the divine names does not focus on mental repetition of the sounds of the letters, but rather it entails complex cognitive exercises involving combinatory manipulations and visualization of the forms of the letters. Finally, the purpose of Abulafia's techniques is not to still the mind but rather to activate it in preparation for the reception of the divine influx.[1] Parallels might be drawn between Abulafia's practices and certain tantric meditation techniques that focus not only on the sounds of the *mantras* but also on visualization of the letters. However, such investigations lie beyond the scope of the present inquiry and remain to be explored in future studies.

CONCLUSION

In the course of our analysis of representations of Veda and Torah in the brahmanical tradition and the rabbinic and kabbalistic traditions, we have delineated certain structural affinities in the symbol systems of these scriptural traditions. We have also noted a number of fundamental points of divergence in the conceptions of language that underlie the symbol systems, which are reflected in textual images and conceptions as well as in practices concerning the transmission, study, and appropriation of the texts. While there are significant differences among traditional representations of Veda and Torah, they nevertheless share one important feature that is essential to our understanding of the authority and role of scripture in these traditions: Veda and Torah function in their respective traditions as symbols, and although textuality represents one facet of these multivalent symbols, they are not bound by this textual referent. Veda and Torah transcend their textual boundaries through becoming identified with the Word, which is itself represented as an encompassing category that functions on every level of reality. This Word may find its consummate expression in certain texts—the Vedic *mantra*s or the Sefer Torah—but at the same time it remains a limitless, open-ended category within which can be subsumed potentially all texts, teachings, and practices authorized by the religious elite. The legitimating authority of Veda and Torah in their respective traditions can thus be fully understood only with reference to their function as symbols.

In certain strands of these traditions the Word is represented as constitutive of the very nature of the ultimate reality, and the unfoldment of that reality in the phenomenal creation is correspondingly understood as the unfoldment of the divine language. The divine language manifested itself in the realm of forms, which are its most precipitated expressions. However, the divine language is also said to have left another record of itself in the form of a blueprint containing the primordial elements of the divine language. This blueprint is held to have been cognized by or revealed to certain privileged representatives of humanity—the Vedic *ṛṣi*s or Moses and the people of Israel—and was preserved by them in the form of earthly texts, whether oral or written. Certain texts are upheld in each tradition as the core of the cognition/revelation—the oral texts of the Vedic *mantra*s or the written text of the Sefer

Torah—and thus it is these texts that are to be preserved with scrupulous precision by the brahmin reciters and Jewish scribal tradition, respectively. The texts of these scriptures are fixed, and not a sound or syllable, word or letter may be altered. In this context Veda and Torah would appear to be bound by their textuality, their referents limited to a circumscribed body of texts. However, that textuality is itself viewed as the concrete embodiment of the divine language and thus points beyond itself to the structures of reality that are encoded within it.

Understood in this way, Veda and Torah become multidimensional symbols representing the various levels and structures of reality, with their textuality constituting only one facet of this organic network of significations. These symbols become paradigmatic for their respective traditions because they are invested with transcendent authority. Any text or teaching that wishes to legitimate its authority can do so only by assimilating itself to the authoritative symbols: Veda or Torah. If Veda and Torah were limited to their textual significations as bounded texts—the Vedic Saṃhitās and the Sefer Torah—their domain would remain closed. However, because Veda and Torah assume the status of symbols, their domain becomes open-ended and permeable, capable of absorbing a variety of texts and teachings beyond the circumscribed compass of the core texts.

The domain of the Veda as the Word (*brahman*/Śabdabrahman) and transcendent knowledge is infinite, and while brahmanical authorities might maintain that the Word found its quintessential expression in the primordial sounds of the Vedic *mantras*, it is not believed to be limited to that expression. Potentially any text or teaching can claim to be included within the purview of Veda as long as it can establish a connection between itself and the Vedic *mantras*. This may be accomplished through a variety of strategies. For example, a text might claim that its teachings derive from lost Vedic texts, or establish a genealogy that links its teachings to the Vedas. Alternatively, a text might maintain that its own teachings were part of the primordial cognitions of the *ṛṣis*, or that they derive from some comparable form of divine revelation. The Vedic *mantras*, as the core *śruti* texts, retain their authoritative status at the center of the ever-expanding domain of Veda. Whether or not their content is known or understood, their authority is acknowledged, for it is these particular texts that provide the model for all subsequent texts and teachings aspiring to the status of Veda.

The domain of the Torah as the Word of God is also potentially limitless, and while rabbinic sages might hold that the Word found its consummate expression in the Sefer Torah, it is not believed to be limited to that expression. The key to expanding the domain of Torah lies in expanding the scope of the revelation itself through claiming that the Word of God revealed to Moses at Mount Sinai included not only a written text but also the oral tradition of interpreting the written text. Thus, alongside the bounded Written Torah—which comes to include not only the Pentateuch but also the Nevi'im and Ketuvim—an open-ended category of oral teachings is established. The Oral Torah becomes a limitlessly encompassing rubric under which can be subsumed potentially all rabbinic texts and teachings. The Written Torah remains at the center as the most authoritative expression of God's Word, while the Oral Torah continually extends beyond it, occasionally paying homage to the written text of which it purports to be an interpretation.

"Embodied Communities" and Tradition-Identity

Are such representations of scripture as a multileveled cosmological principle unique to these traditions, or could we expect to find comparable conceptions in other religious traditions as part of what Wilfred Cantwell Smith has termed the "almost common human propensity to scripturalize"?[1] I would suggest that although other traditions may have developed cosmological conceptions of scripture, the specific parallels highlighted in this study between brahmanical conceptions of Veda and rabbinic and kabbalistic conceptions of Torah are not necessarily representative of a more "universal" trend to cosmologize notions of language and text, but are rather reflective of the more fundamental structural affinities shared by these particular traditions. As suggested at the outset of this study, the brahmanical and rabbinic traditions provide an alternative paradigm of "religious tradition" to the Christian-based model that has tended to dominate the academic study of religion. The brahmanical and rabbinic traditions constitute what we might term "embodied communities" in that their notions of tradition-identity, in contrast to the universalizing tendencies of missionary traditions such as "Christianities," are "embodied" in the particularities of ethnic-cultural categories defined in relation to a particular people (Aryans, Jews), a particular sacred language (Sanskrit, Hebrew), and a particular land (Āryāvarta, Israel).

The manner in which these traditions construct categories of language and canon is rooted in the "embodied" nature of these traditions. Indeed, one of the metaphors that is used to represent both Veda and Torah is that of the body. Veda as the Word is described in certain brahmanical texts as undergoing a series of successive embodiments, from subtle to gross, as the body of Brahman, the body of the creator principle, and the body of the cosmos, which in turn is reflected in the human body. The "corpus" of Vedic *mantras*, as the earthly manifestation of the cosmic blueprint, reflects and interconnects these various levels of reality. While the rabbinic tradition tends to emphasize the incorporeal nature of God, the Torah is nevertheless represented at times as an organic unity that is a living aspect of the divine and that serves as the blueprint that becomes instantiated in the structures of the cosmos and the human body. The body metaphor is extended in kabbalistic texts such as the Zohar, which correlates the "body" of Torah with the body of the divine anthropos, the cosmos-body, and the human body.

The Word embodied in texts—the Vedic *mantras* or the Sefer Torah—is further instantiated in the social "body" of the communities that preserve and transmit them. The brahmanical and rabbinic traditions constitute their communities in relation to authoritative texts and in turn become the embodiment of those texts. This process of embodiment occurs on a number of different levels: ethnic and linguistic identity, social structure, and practice.

(1) Embodiment in Ethnic and Linguistic Identity

Veda and Torah, respectively, become "incarnate" in a particular social body—the Aryan community or the people of Israel—as the constitutive category that defines its ethnic and linguistic identity over against other peoples—the non-Aryans or the gentiles. The "Aryans" and the "people of Israel" are not of course strictly delineated, closed ethnic groups, as the brahmanical tradition has absorbed various non-Aryan groups within its fold in the course of its history, just as the Jewish community has admitted gentiles through conversion and has even undertaken proselytizing efforts in certain periods.[2] Rather, these collective designations represent *idealized categories* in which tradition-identity is assigned first and foremost through birth into a community that defines itself in terms of blood descent.

The cosmological paradigms in which Veda and Torah are represented as the primordial Word that is the source and blueprint of creation would appear to present a claim to universal knowledge, and yet both traditions use a variety of strategies to circumscribe the Word and bind it linguistically, ethnically, and culturally to a specific people. The *ṛṣis* to whom cognition of the Vedic *mantras* is ascribed are at times represented as semidivine beings who assist the creator in the cosmogonic process and who are the progenitors of the entire human race. This might imply that all of humanity inherited the Veda from their ancestors, the universal progenitors. At the same time, however, brahmanical texts are careful to localize the procreative powers of the *ṛṣis* as "our fathers," the forefathers of the Aryan people, and more specifically of the brahmanical lineages that have preserved the *ṛṣis*' cognitions. The Aryans, the inhabitants of Āryāvarta, are thus designated as the heirs of the cosmic blueprint, the Veda, and of the perfected (*saṃskṛta*) language, Sanskrit, the language of the gods and the language of nature in which the Vedic *mantras* are recorded.

The Torah is also at times represented as the potential inheritance of all nations, which the people of Israel alone proved worthy to receive. Certain rabbinic traditions maintain that God considered giving the Torah to Adam and thus by implication to the descendants of Adam, the entire human race. However, in the end Adam sinned and the nations of the world, as the children of Adam and the children of Noah, were vouchsafed only seven commandments. On the other hand, the patriarch Abraham, the forefather of Israel, is held to have been so meritorious that he observed all of the commandments of the Torah even before they were given at Mount Sinai. The descendants of Abraham—Isaac, Jacob, and the sons of Jacob—followed his example, and thus even before the Sinai revelation the Torah was destined to be the inheritance of the people of Israel. At the revelation at Mount Sinai God once again extended the opportunity to all nations to receive the Torah, but Israel alone accepted God's offer. Hence the people of Israel, the descendants of Abraham, were deemed to be the custodians of the primordial blueprint, the Torah, and of the divine language, Hebrew, the language from which the world was created and in which the Torah is inscribed.

Veda and Torah thus become in-corporated in the collective identity of a particular people and are "reproduced" in the bodies of their descendants through blood lineages.

(2) Embodiment in Social Structure

The instantiation of Veda and Torah in the corporate life of the Aryans and of Israel is not limited to the biological reproduction of a particular ethnic group defined over against other ethnic groups. The process of embodiment also involves the sociocultural reproduction of a particular social structure, in which the social body is internally differentiated and legitimated with reference to the cosmic blueprint. The Word that manifests itself in the structures of the divine and of the cosmos and in a corpus of texts is also held to be embodied in the social structure of the community that constitutes itself in relation to those texts. The Aryan social order, the *varṇa* system, is represented in certain brahmanical texts as reflecting the structure of the Veda, which in turn reflects the structures of the natural and divine orders. The laws of the Torah that delineate and regulate the Israelite social order are correlated in certain rabbinic texts with the laws that generate and regulate the cosmos, a notion that is extended in certain kabbalistic texts to include the laws that constitute the Godhead as well. The social order is thus re-presented as a microcosmic reflection of the cosmic order and as divinely ordained from primordial times as the crystallized expression of the cosmic blueprint on the social plane.

In this organic model the social body, like the human body, is organized according to a hierarchical division of functions in which each part has its own separate function to perform that is vital to the efficient operation of the whole, and yet some parts inevitably perform more "exalted" tasks than others. The head naturally takes the lead, supplying the organizing principle of intelligence that directs the activities of the limbs and organs. Social status is primarily determined in the brahmanical and rabbinic traditions in relation to the authoritative symbol, and thus the "heads" of the body politic are the religious elite—the brahmin priests or the rabbis—who are themselves represented as the embodiments of Veda or Torah. They embody Veda and Torah, respectively, in their function, which is to preserve, teach, and enact the canonical texts, as well as in their lines of tradition, which are held to derive directly from the original recipients of the knowledge—the Vedic *ṛṣis* or Moses. The brahmin priests give concrete expression to the Veda through both speech and action, through recitation of the Vedic *mantras* and performance of the Vedic rituals. Moreover, they claim that it is their direct blood descent from the *ṛṣis* that gives them their privileged status as the bodily vehicles through which the Vedic recitative and sacrificial traditions are transmitted. The rabbinic sages are celebrated as Torah incarnate, who have imbibed the ocean of Torah through study and who actualize its precepts in their thoughts, words, and actions. They claim to be the representatives of Moses, the supreme prophet, in the ongoing life of their community, for it is they who have preserved the Torah that was given to Moses by God on Mount Sinai.

The locus of canonical authority thus shifts from a circumscribed corpus of texts—the Vedic Saṃhitās and the Sefer Torah—to the religious elite that preserve, transmit, and embody the texts in their teachings and actions. The brahmin priests and the rabbinic sages become the representatives of Veda and Torah, respectively, and they thus assume the authority to redefine the categories in accordance with the changing sociohistorical conditions of their communities. While preserving the boundaries of the core texts intact, they extend the domain of Veda and Torah beyond those boundaries in order to incorporate a host of other texts, teachings, and practices.

(3) Embodiment in Practice

Veda and Torah are symbols that are lived and actualized in their respective communities through practice. The sociocultural taxonomies of any community are inscribed in the bodies of its constituent members through practice, transforming the biological body into a socialized body that has internalized the symbolic schemes and values of the culture.[3] In the brahmanical and rabbinic traditions, which are religions of orthopraxy, practice assumes a paramount role as the primary vehicle through which social, cultural, and religious values are reproduced. Veda and Torah, as the encompassing symbols of their respective traditions, are inscribed through particular types of practices—primarily through recitation and sacrificial performances in the case of Veda and through study and observance of the commandments in the case of Torah. Moreover, the symbol systems associated with Veda and Torah serve to legitimate these practices as the means to activate the primordial blueprint and thereby to maintain the social, cosmic, and divine orders.

In the rabbinic tradition the core text, the Sefer Torah, is held to provide the authoritative framework for the community's practices in the form of the 613 commandments, or *mitzvot,* that regulate various aspects of religious, social, political, and economic life. The aggadic tradition that correlates the 248 positive commandments with the 248 members of the human body maintains that there is a specific part of the body that is to be activated in the performance of each *mitzvah,* and thus the Torah, as the plan reflecting the structure of the microcosm and the macrocosm, must literally be embodied by each individual Jew through action.[4] While the Sefer Torah is thus celebrated as the foundation for Jewish orthopraxy, the rabbis were nevertheless faced with the problem of establishing continuity between the ritual and sociocultural practices delineated in the biblical text and the changing religious, social, and political realities of the Jewish people in different periods and environments. It thus became necessary to adapt the category of Torah to accord with the ever-changing forms of the corporate community that it was intended to represent. Through constructing the category of Oral Torah and linking it to the original revelation at Mount Sinai as the oral tradition of interpretation of the written text, the rabbis overcame the problem of discontinuity. The integrity of the blueprint was preserved, and at the same time its content was opened up and extended through endless acts of interpretation. The rabbis were thus able to ensure the cultural continuity of the Jewish community, as well as their own authoritative position in that community, through transforming Torah from a bounded text into an open-ended symbol. Certain theosophical kabbalists, building on rabbinic traditions, exploded the symbol even further and, while reaffirming the importance of embodying the Torah through the *mitzvot*, also evolved their own practices aimed at going beyond the body of Torah in order to commune with the soul enshrined within.

In the case of the brahmanical tradition the problem of discontinuity posed by the core *śruti* texts, the Vedic Saṃhitās, was even greater than that posed by the Sefer Torah, for the Saṃhitās are primarily concerned with sacrificial rituals and do not provide a system of sociocultural practices. The *varṇa* system, for example, with the exception of a few references such as those found in the Puruṣa-Sūkta and in Taittirīya Saṃhitā VII.1.1.4–6, is not delineated in the Saṃhitās. Although the Brāhmaṇas also focus primarily on ritual concerns, the essential functions and hierarchical interrelations of the social classes are articulated in their classificatory schemas, which correlate the structure of the *varṇa* system with the *structure* of the threefold Veda—Ṛg, Yajur, and Sāma. By extending the domain of *śruti* to include the Brāhmaṇas along with the Saṃhitās, the brahmin priests invested the social system with Vedic authority on the basis of the *content* of the Veda as well.[5] In order to extend Vedic legitimation further beyond the ritual realm into the sociocultural domain, it became necessary to expand the purview of Veda to include not only *śruti* texts but also *smṛti* texts such as the Dharma-Śāstras in which the detailed duties and regulations of the *varṇāśrama-dharma* system are elaborated. The process of vedacization also served as an essential mechanism through which the brahmanical tradition accommodated and domesticated competing currents, such as certain ascetic groups and *bhakti* movements, by canonizing their teachings and practices and granting them the status of *śruti*—in the case of the ascetic teachings of the Upaniṣadic sages—or of the "fifth Veda"—in the case of the devotional teachings contained in the epics and Purāṇas.

The manner in which the categories of Veda and Torah are constructed thus reflects the more fundamental categories that interconnect the brahmanical and rabbinic traditions as two species of the same genus of "religious tradition": as ethnic-based communities that define their notions of tradition-identity in terms of ethnic, linguistic, and cultural categories; as "textual communities" that codify their symbol systems and practices in the form of scriptural canons; and as religions of orthopraxy that delineate their concern for "correct practice" in elaborate legal systems, sacrificial traditions, and purity codes. The essential feature that unites these various aspects is that of embodiment: embodiment in a particular ethnic community with a sacred language, social structure, and practices that are constituted in relation to the Word embodied in scripture.

In order to highlight further the distinctive nature of these "embodied communities," I would like to examine briefly three traditions that are missionary in orientation and that develop categories of tradition-identity that diverge from the ethnic-based model: "Christianities," "Buddhisms," and "Islams." These traditions are of course extremely diverse, and thus I will focus my analysis primarily on the early formative period of each tradition, in which the newly emerging community was in the process of evolving its own self-definition in relation to already existing religious communities.

In Christian traditions the locus of authority shifts from the Word embodied in texts to the Word incarnate as a human being. God's central revelation for Christians is in the person of Jesus Christ himself and not in the New Testament, which is a record of the revelation.[6] It is Christ who is celebrated as the preexistent Word of God, the Logos principle through whom "all things were made," and it is the person of Christ, "the Word made flesh," the incarnate God, that constitutes the central symbol of Christian traditions.[7]

The Word incarnate in Christ is also held to be embodied in the corporate community of Christians, who are represented as the "body of Christ." However, this conception contrasts sharply with the notions of embodiment associated with Veda and Torah, for the Christian community as the "body of Christ" is not constituted primarily by texts, by categories of ethnic, linguistic, and cultural identity, or by practices. Rather, the "body of Christ" represents a spiritualized, denaturalized notion of body, in which the Christian community is held to be bound together not by blood descent and not by texts and practices tied to the identity of a particular people or culture but rather by faith in Jesus Christ and the "life of the Spirit." This difference in emphasis appears to be rooted in the missionary orientation of the early Christian community, which, in opposition to the ethnic-based categories of the Jewish tradition that fostered it, established a new taxonomy that gave priority to Christ over Torah, faith over practice, and the Spirit over the physical body.

The foundations of this new taxonomy can be located in the writings of the apostle Paul, who, prior to the separation of the Christian church from the Jewish synagogue at the end of the first century C.E., embarked on an extended mission to the gentiles. Paul, as a former Pharisee who maintained that he had been specially commissioned by God to be the apostle to the gentiles,[8] was convinced that the gentiles had a legitimate place in God's plan of salvation, yet he was inevitably confronted with the question of their relationship to the Jewish people and to the Torah in particular. In opposition to the "Judaizers" among the Jewish Christians, who insisted that the gentiles had first to become Jews, bound by the covenants of circumcision and Torah, before they could be admitted to the Christian community, Paul arrived at the conviction that the gentiles could become a part of the people of God without having to pass through the law of Torah.[9]

The doctrine of justification by faith was the main argument developed by Paul in order to defend his conviction that gentiles qua gentiles, apart from the Torah of Israel, have a right to full citizenship in God's kingdom.[10] The key components of Paul's argument involve establishing that (1) for the gentiles the "law of Christ," which is associated with freedom, righteousness, and the "Spirit of life," supersedes the law of Torah, which is associated with bondage, sin, and death;[11] (2) justification is by faith in Jesus Christ apart from works of the law;[12] (3) the true children of God are not the "children of the flesh," who are bound by the covenants of circumcision and Torah "according to the flesh," but rather the "children of the promise," who are united in the covenant "according to the Spirit" that was vouchsafed to Abraham on the basis of his faith.[13] In order to establish that all those who have faith in Christ—gentiles as well as Jews—are heirs to the promise to Abraham, Paul argues that the promise was made solely on the basis of Abraham's faith in God before he was circumcised and was extended to all nations through Abraham. Moreover, Paul challenges the eternal validity of the Torah through maintaining that the law was added 430 years after the promise because of human transgressions, but now that Christ has come the original covenant with Abraham, which was based on faith alone and included all nations, is again in force and the custodianship of the law is ended.[14]

In the context of struggling with the dilemma posed by the gentile mission, Paul thus developed a conception of religious community that supplanted Jewish notions of embodiment—in Torah (text), flesh (ethnicity), and works (practice)—with a spiritualized notion of the "body of Christ," in which all members of the community, Jews and gentiles alike, are united by baptism into the "life of the Spirit" through faith in Christ.

> For just as the body is one and has many members, and all the members of the body, though many, are one body, so it is with Christ. For by one Spirit we were all baptized into one body—Jews or Greeks, slaves or free—and all were made to drink of one Spirit. . . . Now you are the body of Christ and individually members of it.[15]

Paul's theology provided the foundation for a new type of "religious tradition," which emerged as the Christian church, as distinct from the Jewish synagogue, at the end of the first century. This new religious tradition, in contrast to its parent tradition, was to become characterized as a missionary religion, proclaiming a universal gospel that was open to all peoples and all nations, and as a religion of orthodoxy, in which faith in Jesus Christ, articulated in "correct belief" and elaborated in creeds, doctrines, and theology, was given precedence over "correct practice" and works of the law.

A parallel to the manner in which the early Christian community broke away from the "embodied" categories of the Jewish tradition can be seen in the manner in which the early Buddhist community disassociated itself from the categories of the brahmanical tradition. In both cases one of the key factors in the redefinition of categories was the missionary orientation of these new communities, which sought to extend their teachings beyond the boundaries of a single constituency. Just as the missionary efforts of the early Christian community resulted in the reinterpretation of the role of the Torah and the definition of a new "Israel" in which Jews and gentiles were united through faith in Christ, so the missionizing activities of the early Buddhists were accompanied by a rejection of the authority of the Veda and the formation of a new type of community that was united through adherence to the Dhamma (Sanskrit Dharma, "doctrine, teaching"), irrespective of ethnic background, class, or sex.

The early Buddhists were one among a number of heterodox ascetic groups (*śramaṇas*) in north India in the sixth century B.C.E. that disputed orthodox brahmanical teachings. The forest-dwelling Upaniṣadic sages also posed a challenge to the priestly sacrificial tradition, but they nevertheless remained within the orthodox fold because they accepted Vedic authority, even though they reinterpreted the category of Veda to accord with their own metaphysical concerns. The Buddha Śākyamuni (ca. 560–480 B.C.E.) and his immediate disciples, on the other hand, are represented in the Suttas of the Pali canon as rejecting the authority of the Veda, along with the complex of categories in which it was embedded—textual traditions, brahmanical blood lineages, the *varṇa* system, and Vedic rituals. The early Buddhists spurned the "body"-maintaining activities of the brahmins, which were concerned with preservation of the purity of the physical body and of blood lineages, preservation of a corpus of texts in which the divine language was held to be embodied, maintenance of the social body and its hierarchical division of functions, and regeneration of the cosmos-body through periodic recitation of the Vedic *mantras* and performance of the sacrificial rituals. The Buddha's followers gave priority instead to the Dhamma, the teachings of the Buddha, which were intended to uproot attachment to all forms of embodiment—to the physical body, to sacred texts, to family, clan, or social status, and to the forms of the material world of *saṃsāra* generally—in order to realize the supreme goal of human existence, *nibbāna* (Sanskrit *nirvāṇa*, literally, "blowing out").

A new taxonomy was established by the early Buddhists in which (1) the Veda was superseded by the Dhamma as the authoritative symbol of the community;[16] (2) the authority of the brahmin priests, based on purity of descent and custodianship of the Vedic texts and rituals, was supplanted by the ideal of the *arahant* (Sanskrit *arhat*, literally, "worthy one"), whose authority rested on his or her attainment of *nibbāna* through direct experience, through "knowing" and "seeing," of the truths of the Dhamma;[17] (3) the *varṇa* system, a hierarchy of social classes based on blood descent and householder values, was replaced by the *saṃgha*, an order of monks and nuns that was open to people of all classes and ethnic backgrounds and that was united by the Dhamma, the Vinaya (rules of discipline), and the quest for *nibbāna*.[18]

In opposition to the brahmins' claim that they are the highest class, for they are the "true children of Brahmā, born from his mouth, born of Brahmā, created by Brahmā, heirs of Brahmā," the Buddha is represented as arguing that his followers, the adherents of the *saṃgha,* are supreme, for they are "born of Dhamma, created by Dhamma, heirs of Dhamma."

> [A]ll of you, though of different birth, name, clan and family, who have gone forth from the household life into homelessness, if you are asked who you are, should reply: "We are ascetics, followers of the Sakyan." He whose faith in the Tathāgatha [the Buddha] is settled, rooted, established, solid, unshakeable by any ascetic or Brahmin, any deva [god] or māra [tempter] or Brahmā or anyone in the world, can truly say: "I am a true son of Blessed Lord, born of his mouth, born of Dhamma, created by Dhamma, an heir of Dhamma." Why is that? Because . . . this designates the Tathāgata: "The Body of Dhamma" [*dhamma-kāya*], that is, "The Body of Brahmā. . . ."[19]

The divergence of the early Buddhists from the brahmanical paradigm of Veda can be seen in the way in which they developed the category of canon. The Tipiṭaka ("three baskets"), the Pali canon of the Theravāda school, which is generally held to be the earliest extant, complete canon, derives its authority from its claim to be *buddha-vacana,* the "word of the Buddha," and the repository of the Dhamma.[20] The Suttas, which form the second of the three *piṭaka*s, authenticate their claim to have been "heard" from the Buddha through the opening phrase, *evam me sutam* (Sanskrit *evam mayā śrutam*), "Thus I have heard." However, the Suttas are not thereby ascribed a status comparable to that of *śruti,* "that which was heard" by the Vedic *ṛṣi*s. The Suttas are not, like the Vedic *mantra*s, represented as the record of the cosmic blueprint that contains the expressions of the primordial language through which the creation was brought forth, but rather they are revered as the record of the Dhamma that contains the words of the Buddha through which the message of enlightenment was proclaimed. Indeed, the very notions of a cosmic blueprint and of a primordial language are rejected, for according to the Dhamma the world is in continuous flux, an ever-changing flow of processes, and there are no stable patterns and structures of reality to be mapped and encoded in language. Even if the existence of a language of the gods were conceded, the words of the Buddha would be granted a higher, "supradivine" status, for the Buddha, as an enlightened human sage, is held by the Theravādins to have achieved a level of spiritual attainment that surpasses that of the gods.

The Theravādins ascribe to the Buddha a conventional view of language, in which language is valued for its communicative power and not for any intrinsic ontological status. The didactic content of the Dhamma, as a universal teaching intended to enlighten human beings and gods alike, took precedence over a single linguistic form. The Buddha is said to have eschewed the use of Sanskrit, the sacred language of the brahmanical elite, and instead encouraged his disciples to learn and spread the Dhamma in their own dialects, in languages that would be accessible to the general populace. Moreover, in contrast to the brahmanical preoccupation with accurate preservation of the Vedic sounds with little regard for their discursive meaning, the Buddha is represented as chiding those disciples who focus solely on memorizing the Dhamma and do not understand the meaning of the texts that they recite.

> There are some foolish ones who learn the *dharma* by heart, *sūtras*, *geya*, etc., but who have learned it by heart without having examined the sense in order to (actually) understand the texts. These texts, of which they have not examined the sense in order to understand them, do not delight them at all; and the only advantage they gain from their memorization is in the area of contradicting (their adversaries) and making citations. However, they do not attain the end for which one memorizes the *dharma*. These texts badly understood will leave them miserable and unhappy for a long time. And why? Because these texts have been badly understood.[21]

The Dhamma preserved in the Pali texts is upheld as a teaching that is to be understood and above all to be lived. The texts provide a means to understanding the content of the Dhamma, but they are not regarded as an end in themselves. For in the final analysis even the texts must be dispensed with and one must become a "refuge unto oneself" in order to attain direct realization of the truths of the Dhamma.[22]

Islamic traditions present a significant test case for my contention that the brahmanical and rabbinic traditions exemplify a distinctive paradigm of "religious tradition" and that the categories of Veda and Torah are reflective of that paradigm. As in the brahmanical and rabbinic traditions, the central category that binds together the Islamic community (*ummah*) is scripture: the Qur'ān. "Islam" has been characterized as preeminently a "religion of the book,"[23] and the Qur'ān itself, as the eternal Word of God that enters into history, has been compared, both structurally and functionally, to the Torah in Jewish traditions and to the figure of Christ in Christian traditions.[24] The point that is of significance for the present study is that the "transcendent focus of Muslim faith" is a text, the Qur'ān,[25] which is characterized in a manner that resonates with certain representations of Veda and Torah that we have examined: the Qur'ān is celebrated as preexistent and uncreated; as the eternal Word of God that is an attribute of God and, like other attributes, "it is not He nor is it other than He"; and as the repository of the divine language, Arabic. Moreover, the Qur'ān, like Veda and Torah in their respective traditions, is considered the authoritative basis for Muslim orthopraxy and liturgical life, and its teachings have been elaborated in an extensive legal system that encompasses virtually every aspect of religious, social, political, and economic life.

While a number of points of comparison could be delineated between conceptions and practices associated with the Qur'ān and those associated with Veda and Torah, I would like to focus briefly on two significant differences.[26] First, the Qur'ān, although rooted in the notion of a particular sacred language, Arabic, is not thereby tied exclusively to a specific ethnic constituency but is rather represented as universal truth that is to be extended through the Arabs to all peoples. Second, the Qur'ān does not become an encompassing symbol in the way that Veda and Torah do.

The first point of divergence derives from the fact that the Islamic community from its inception has been missionary in orientation, and although the message of the Qur'ān might originally have been intended first and foremost for the Arab people, it was not to remain confined within ethnic boundaries. The foundations of this universalistic perspective can be located in the Qur'ān itself, in the manner in which the Qur'ān self-consciously constructs the category of scripture.[27] On the one hand, the Qur'ān emphasizes that the divine revelation of Allah to the prophet Muhammad (ca. 570–632 C.E.) was intended primarily for the Arab people, who had previously received no prophet or scriptural revelation.[28] Muhammad was chosen from among the "unscriptured" (*ummīyūn*) Arabs[29] to be the messenger of Allah who would convey to them an "Arabic

Recitation (*qur'ān*)" in a "clear Arabic tongue" so that they would be able to understand.[30] On the other hand, the Qur'ān makes use of a number of mechanisms to establish its own status as universal truth that is the confirmation and culmination of all previous scriptural revelations and that is thus of special relevance not only to the scriptureless Arabs but also to the "People of the Book" (*ahl al-kitāb*), the Jews and Christians.

The universalizing tendencies of the Qur'ān are evident in its conception of a heavenly Book (*kitāb*) of which the Arabic Qur'ān represents an earthly manifestation. The Qur'ānic notion of a heavenly Book, as has often been noted, reflects the influence of Jewish conceptions as well as of earlier Near Eastern conceptions of a celestial book or tablet.[31] The heavenly *kitāb* is represented in a number of Qur'ānic passages as the primordial record with Allah in which all the phenomena and events of heaven and earth are inscribed beforetime.[32] This notion recalls rabbinic conceptions of the preexistent Torah as the plan of creation, although the Qur'ān does not explicitly ascribe to Allah's Book a role in the cosmogonic process itself. In other Qur'ānic passages the *kitāb* is represented as the celestial archetype of all scripture, which is at times designated more specifically as the "Mother of the Book" (*umm al-kitāb*)[33] or the "preserved tablet" (*lauḥ maḥfūẓ*).[34] In contrast to rabbinic conceptions, in which the primordial blueprint is represented as having a single earthly manifestation in the Sefer Torah, the heavenly *Urschrift* is described in the Qur'ān as an encompassing archetype from which have been "sent down" not one but multiple scriptural revelations, including not only the Arabic Qur'ān but also the scriptures of the Jews and the Christians—in particular, the Torah (Taurāh) of Moses, the Psalms (Zabūr) of David, and the Gospel ('Injīl) of Jesus.[35] The scriptures of the People of the Book constitute only a "portion" of the archetypal Book,[36] just as that which was revealed to Muhammad is only a partial manifestation.[37]

The Qur'ānic conception of a heavenly Book is thus closely linked to the notion of successive scriptural revelations, in which "every age has a Book"[38] and "every nation has its Messenger," its prophet (*nabī*) or apostle (*rasūl*),[39] who transmits the divine revelation in the native language of his people so that its import is made clear.[40] This might at first be interpreted as an ethnic-based conception of revelation in which each people is "sent down" a scripture that represents its exclusive possession in its own language: just as the Torah is the revelation to the people of Israel in Hebrew, so the Qur'ān is the revelation to the Arab people in Arabic. However, the

Qur'ānic conception of scripture extends beyond this, for its conception of the history of revelation is cumulative. Thus, the followers of Muhammad are commanded to believe in the entire Book,[41] both that which has been "sent down" to Muhammad and that which was "sent down" to the messengers before him.[42]

> Say you: "We believe in God, and in that which has been sent down on us and sent down on Abraham, Ishmael, Isaac and Jacob, and the Tribes, and that which was given to Moses and Jesus and the Prophets, of their Lord; we make no division between any of them, and to Him we surrender."[43]

Although the above passage indicates that "no division" is made among the messages transmitted through the various prophets, in the end the Qur'ān does make a distinction, for it claims for itself the unique status of the final, culminating revelation sent through the agency of Muhammad, who as the "seal of the prophets" represents the last link in the prophetic succession.[44] The Qur'ān is celebrated as *the* Book, the quintessential scriptural revelation from the heavenly Book, that authenticates and completes all earlier revelations. The Jews and Christians, as the People of the Book, are thus invited to believe in the Book that Allah has revealed through Muhammad, which not only confirms and safeguards the teachings of their own scriptures[45] but also "makes clear" those matters that have become distorted and that have resulted in disputes and doubts.[46]

One final argument that the Qur'ān uses to establish the universal import of its message, which takes precedence over all previous revelations, is to appeal, like the apostle Paul, to the example of Abraham, whom both Jews and Christians claim as their father. Although Abraham is also revered by the Muslims as the father of the Arab people through his son Ishmael, the Qur'ānic assertion that Muhammad's followers are the true descendants of Abraham does not rest primarily on blood ties but rather on its claim to restore the pure religion of Abraham, who is celebrated as the father of faith and the first *muslim*, in the generic sense of one who has "surrendered" to God.

> People of the Book! Why do you dispute concerning Abraham? The Torah was not sent down, neither the Gospel, but after him. . . . No; Abraham in truth was not a Jew, neither a Christian; but he was a Muslim and one pure of faith; cer-

> tainly he was never of the idolaters. Surely the people standing closest to Abraham are those who followed him, and this Prophet [Muhammad], and those who believe; and God is the Protector of the believers.[47]

All those who believe in the Book revealed to the prophet Muhammad are the true children of Abraham and heirs to the promise,[48] and it is this "religion of truth," according to the Qur'ān, that Allah will cause to prevail over every other religion.[49]

The Qur'ānic conception of scripture thus reflects a different model of "religious tradition" from that reflected in brahmanical conceptions of Veda and rabbinic and kabbalistic conceptions of Torah. In the multileveled cosmologies associated with Veda and Torah the Word manifests as a cosmic blueprint with a determinate structure, which is expressed on earth in a single corpus of texts—the Vedic *mantras* or the Sefer Torah—and is further instantiated in the corporate life of a particular people. Veda and Torah become embodied in the ethnic, linguistic, and cultural identity of their respective communities, and in particular in the religious elite—the brahmin priests or rabbis—who extend the categories themselves so that Veda and Torah become encompassing symbols that are adapted to accord with the changing nature of the communities that they represent. The Qur'ānic conception of a heavenly Book, on the other hand, presents a universal archetype, which manifests on earth not in a single scriptural revelation to one people but rather in a series of revelations to different communities. The Qur'ān, as the final scripture "sent down" from the archetypal Book, is invested with the cumulative power of all previous revelations and is deemed to be the "religion of truth" that is of universal significance for all peoples. The Word embodied in the Arabic Qur'ān thus does not become embodied in a particular ethnic group. Moreover, the Qur'ān itself remains a strictly bounded category, a circumscribed text, and does not become an endlessly expanding symbol. The heavenly Book is "closed," the final revelation has been "sent down." The Word of God has manifested once and for all in the text of the Qur'ān, and neither the prophet Muhammad nor the religious elite are ascribed the authority to extend the category of revelation.

The delimited nature of the Qur'ān is illustrated by the Sunnī schools of jurisprudence (*fiqh*), which in determining the principal sources of *fiqh* establish a hierarchy that clearly distinguishes between (1) the Qur'ān, which is the authoritative Word of God; (2) the Sunnah ("custom") of Muhammad, which includes the words, deeds, and gestures of the exemplary human being who was singled out to be the prophet of Allah; and (3) *ijmāʿ*, the consensus of the community, in particular of the *ʿulamāʾ*, the legal scholars. While the Sunnah of Muhammad ranks second to the Qur'ān as the most authoritative source of Islamic law, it is not granted the status of divine revelation. Moreover, the science of jurisprudence itself, including the books of *fiqh* that classify, interpret, and apply the law, is considered the product of human intelligence. In contrast to rabbinic conceptions of the Oral Torah, the *ʿulamāʾ* are not represented as the embodiments of the Qur'ān whose own interpretations of the text are extensions of the divine revelation. The Qur'ān is a closed category, and Allah alone has the power to reopen the Book that was sealed with the last revelation to the "seal of the prophets."

The symbol systems associated with Veda and Torah thus reflect the more fundamental categories that interconnect the brahmanical and rabbinic traditions and that set these "embodied communities" apart from missionary-oriented traditions such as "Christianities," "Buddhisms," and "Islams." The significance of this comparative study, then, lies not only in its contributions to our understanding of the status, authority, and function of scripture in the brahmanical tradition and the rabbinic and kabbalistic traditions but also in its broader implications for our understanding of these traditions themselves, qua "religious traditions." While the Christian-based model of "religious tradition" emphasizes a series of hierarchical dichotomies between such categories as sacred and profane, belief and practice, doctrine and law, and universalism and particularism, the brahmanical and rabbinic traditions tend to develop other categories that bring to light a different set of relationships, such as those between religion and culture, ethnic identity and religious adherence, knowledge and practice, observance and nonobservance, and purity and impurity. The comparative study of these traditions—contrary to their stereotypical characterization as "uneasy bedfellows"—can thus provide the basis for constructing alternative paradigms of "religious tradition." While the present analysis suggests some of the directions that this research might take, this study needs to be supplemented and extended through other comparative inquiries into various aspects of brahmanical Hindu and Jewish traditions.

Beyond the Oral-Written Dichotomy

The purpose of comparative study is not only to delineate similarities but also to illuminate differences. Having proposed that two species belong to the same genus, it is also essential to ascertain the distinctive features that are unique to each species. While there are significant parallels in the manner in which the brahmanical tradition and the rabbinic and kabbalistic traditions construct categories of language and scripture, our analysis has also brought to light several dichotomies among these traditions' conceptions of language: while the brahmanical tradition gives precedence to the oral channel of language, the auditory mode of perception, and the phonic dimension of the word, the rabbinic and kabbalistic traditions tend to give priority to the written register, the visual channel, and the cognitive dimension of language. Is it possible to locate a foundational opposition that can serve to explain and interconnect these dichotomies and thus can provide an entry point into understanding the unique *Gestalt* of these traditions? One obvious explanation that might be proposed to account for these differences is that they are all founded on the basic opposition between oral and written traditions. However, even if we were to accept this hypothesis provisionally, it still remains to be established whether the dichotomy between oral and written traditions is the cause, result, or concomitant of the various factors that differentiate these scriptural traditions.

In order to test this hypothesis I would like to examine briefly some of the fundamental distinctions among oral and written traditions that have been delineated by certain anthropologists, literary historians, psychologists, and linguists, with particular attention to the work of the anthropologist Jack Goody.[50] As we shall see, while these distinctions may hold when applied to ordinary conceptions of language and to secular texts, as well as to certain types of religious texts, such distinctions become problematic when applied to traditions, such as those that are the focus of the present study, in which language and texts are ascribed the status of cosmological principles. Even those distinctions that are to a certain extent still applicable require reformulation, while other distinctions collapse entirely or may even be reversed.

(1) Auditory vs. Visual Modes of Perception

One of the most obvious distinctions between the oral and written modes of language is that while the oral mode is linked to the auditory channel and is the domain of the ear, writing adds a visual-spatial dimension to language and is thus primarily the domain of the eye. Ferdinand de Saussure defines writing as a "graphic representation of language," for it is writing that renders speech visible as graphic symbols on parchment or page. This basic dichotomy would appear to hold true in the case of the conceptions and practices associated with Veda and Torah. The brahmanical emphasis on the Vedic *mantras* as *śruti*, "that which was/is heard," is clearly linked to the oral status of the Vedas as utterances transmitted through speech. Similarly, the rabbinic and kabbalistic traditions' emphasis on the graphic form of the Hebrew letters and on the visible form of the Torah scroll is clearly connected to the written status of the text as the Book of the Torah.

However, when dealing with these traditions' conceptions of language our understanding of what constitutes "hearing" or "seeing" has to be adjusted to account for the fact that in certain strands of these traditions language is considered to have both a gross and a subtle dimension. Hence "that which was heard" by the Vedic *ṛṣis* is represented not as gross speech but as subtle impulses of sound reverberating forth from the Transcendent. These sounds were preserved on the gross level through the speech of the *ṛṣis*, but, according to the *jñāna-kāṇḍins*, the true reality of *śruti* can be apprehended only by establishing one's awareness on that transcendent level which is the source and abode of the *mantras*. Similarly, certain kabbalists maintain that the material letters inscribed on the Torah scroll are simply the gross manifestations of the subtle letters that exist in the upper worlds as configurations of divine light. In this perspective the full reality of Torah can be apprehended only through a visionary experience of the subtle realms of the Godhead where the light of the supernal Torah eternally shines.

According to such traditional formulations, then, the explanation for the differences in the conceptions and practices associated with Veda and Torah lies in the essential character of the mystical experiences through which their subtle reality can be apprehended. Even though these experiences may be described as involving both hearing and seeing, in brahmanical representations of Veda the auditory channel is emphasized, while in certain kabbalistic representations of Torah, such as those found in the Zohar, visionary experience is given priority. The implication of these conceptions is that it is this fundamental difference in the perceptual structure of mystical experience that accounts for the different modes of transmission of the earthly texts—whether oral or written—not vice versa.

The significance of such conceptions lies not in their truth claims but rather in the issues they raise concerning the epistemology of different types of perceptual orientation and their connection with modes of textual transmission in the brahmanical and Jewish traditions. The brahmanical tradition has clearly given priority to the oral-aural channel as the most appropriate means of apprehending and transmitting sacred knowledge. Even after the introduction of writing, the oral mode of transmission was preferred as the most suitable vehicle for the sacred utterances of the Vedas. This focus on the oral-aural over the written-visual has its counterpart in the essentially aniconic orientation of the Vedic tradition. The gods are invoked to take their place on the seat of sacrifice and to receive the sound-offerings of the *mantra* recitations and the oblations offered into the sacrificial fire, but they are not represented by iconic images.[51] In contrast to the imageless gods and oral *mantras* of the Vedic tradition, in the popular *bhakti* traditions of post-Vedic "Hinduism" the gods become embodied in images, and the sacred texts of devotional movements, such as the epics and Purāṇas, become embodied in written form. In accordance with the authoritative paradigm of the Vedic *mantras*, the mantric efficacy of reciting the epics and Purāṇas has been given primary emphasis even after these texts were committed to writing. However, the shift from oral to written modes of transmission also brought with it an increased emphasis on the visual channel, in which the book itself, as seen for example in Purāṇic "cults of the book," is revered as a visible icon that represents the incarnate form of the deity.[52] This emphasis on the written-visual form of sacred texts constitutes a major departure from the oral-aural Vedic model. While those aspects of post-Vedic traditions that center on image-incarnations of deities may appropriately be deemed "iconic," it is important to emphasize that such a characterization is inappropriate for the Vedic tradition itself.

The characterization of Jewish traditions as "aniconic" must also be reconsidered in this context. While rabbinic texts contain countless diatribes against the image-making practices of the gentiles, the Sefer Torah itself is at times ascribed a status comparable to that of an icon. Rabbinic representations of the Torah as a living aspect of God and the locus where the Shekhinah abides have their counterpart in laws and customs concerning the proper methods of preservation, ornamentation, and veneration of the Torah scroll as the concrete embodiment of the Word of God. For example, the methods of reverencing the Torah scroll in synagogue worship, in which the members of the congregation traditionally stand when the scroll is taken out of the Ark and bow reverently or kiss the Torah scroll as it is carried in procession around the synagogue, point to the Sefer Torah's status as an object of veneration that represents the visible presence of the divine Word. The Torah assumes an unambiguously iconic role in certain kabbalistic traditions, as we have seen, in which the Torah is ultimately identified with God and the Torah scroll is held to be the visible form of God that is to be revered accordingly.

(2) Creative Reconstruction vs. Verbatim Reproduction

A second dichotomy emphasized by Goody as well as other scholars is that while oral traditions are generally changing and fluid, written traditions are inherently more fixed and permanent. Goody draws on studies of Slavic oral poetry by Milman Parry and A. B. Lord and of certain oral cultures in West Africa to illustrate his thesis that oral traditions foster creative reconstruction, while written traditions emphasize verbatim reproduction and preservation. He maintains that in oral cultures every recitation of a text is a new creation and multiple variants proliferate, for there is no fixed "original" to reproduce. In script cultures, on the other hand, emphasis is placed on exact copying, on meticulous preservation of the written text.

While Goody's characterization of script cultures as fostering verbatim reproduction is appropriate in the case of the Jewish scribal tradition, his characterization of oral cultures as promoting creative reconstruction is problematic in the case of the Vedic recitative tradition. Goody acknowledges the fact that the case of the Vedic Saṃhitās presents a striking exception to his thesis. However, rather than revise his theory to account for the fact that these orally composed texts have been transmitted with meticulous exactitude by purely oral means for over three thousand years, he simply dismisses the findings of eminent Indologists as "incapable of proof" and asserts that "the role of writing in the composition (or possibly transcription) of the Vedas must remain a serious possibility."[53] It is not possible within the scope of the present study to provide an adequate rebuttal to Goody's assertion, which is unsubstantiated and runs counter to all the evidence.[54] Rather, what concerns us is that Goody's thesis regarding oral traditions only holds for what we might term "discursive oral traditions" and does not apply to "nondiscursive oral traditions," of which the Vedas are the paradigmatic example.

India itself does have discursive oral traditions, such as those associated with the epics and Purāṇas, that are comparable to the oral traditions Goody examines in that each oral performance allows for a creative reconstruction and retelling of the narrative.

For example, in recitative traditions associated with the *Rāmcaritmānas,* the Hindi Rāmāyaṇa, the reciter, like the bards of West African oral traditions, may adapt his or her telling of the epic to meet the needs of the specific audience for which he/she recites. What remains constant throughout these oral re-creations is the basic story line, certain essential narrative elements. While there is continuity of content, the form remains fluid and flexible. Such creative transformations are allowed because the *Mānas* is a *smṛti* text, in which discursive meaning is of central importance.[55] In the case of the Vedic Saṃhitās, however, which are granted the status of *śruti,* the discursive meaning of the texts is all but ignored in favor of accurately reproducing their sounds.

The brahmanical preoccupation with verbatim reproduction of the Vedic Saṃhitās can be fully understood only in light of the traditional understanding that the *mantra*s constitute the primordial rhythms at the base of creation. Accurate reproduction of these primal sounds through periodic recitation is considered essential to the maintenance of the cosmic order. While the oral tradition of the Vedas may be somewhat exceptional in its emphasis on recitative exactitude, any adequate theory concerning oral and written cultures must take the Vedic case into account, for it is the oldest, most well-documented example of an oral tradition in human history.

(3) Personal vs. Impersonal

The studies of Goody and other scholars suggest a third dichotomy in which oral traditions are characterized as personal and written traditions as impersonal. The personalized nature of oral transmission can be expressed in terms of three relationships. (1) The relationship between the speaker and the oral text is personal and intimate in that there is a continuum between the speaker and the words, which are internalized in the case of a memorized text. (2) The relationship between the speaker and the listeners/audience is personal in that it involves contextualized, face-to-face contact. (3) The relationship between the oral text and the listeners/audience is personal in that audience participation in an oral performance generally involves internalization of, immersion in, and engagement with the recited text.

Conversely, written traditions are characterized as impersonal. (1) The relationship between the author and the written text is impersonal in that a written text generally takes on a life of its own and is circulated independently of its author. (2) The relationship between the author and his or her readers is consequently impersonal in that a reader may interpret the author's text without his or her personal mediation. (3) The relationship between the written text and its readers is also impersonal in that the text becomes objectified as a thing, an object, that has been divorced from the consciousness that created it. As Graham remarks, "Fixing a text visually objectifies its discourse as symbols on the page and makes it possible to treat it as something abstract and impersonal, an object of analysis apart from the specific, always contextual situations of oral speech."[56]

While this dichotomy may hold for ordinary texts, it breaks down and in fact is reversed when applied to scriptures such as Veda and Torah whose textuality is represented as the mundane expression of a supramundane reality. In the case of the Vedic *mantras*, the relationship between the speaker and the audience has to be reconsidered, for the primary audience of Vedic recitations in *śrauta* rituals is held to be divine, not human. The *mantras* are recited in order to regenerate the cosmos and nourish the gods, and in this sense their focus is cosmocentric and not anthropocentric. No human audience is required other than the brahmin priests who are directly involved in the ritual performance and the *yajamāna* and his wife. Moreover, the relationship between the Vedic *mantras* and both the speaker and the audience has to be reconsidered. For even though the individual reciter or listener may be able to appropriate the *mantras* through internalizing their sounds, contrary to the usual model of oral traditions this does not involve active engagement in the semantic content of the texts, for their discursive meaning is generally not understood by the *śrotriya*, let alone the listener. The dialogic, communicative function of oral language is suspended and replaced by an impersonal process of immersion in purifying, efficacious sounds. The process of immersion in the Veda is extended even further by the exponents of the *jñāna-kāṇḍa*, who advocate transcending the recited texts and the domain of language altogether in order to merge with that impersonal, transcendent reality which is the abode of Śabdabrahman.

While the Veda thus provides a counter example to the characterization of oral traditions as personal, the Torah provides a counter example to the characterization of written traditions as impersonal. Even though the Torah is objectified as a book, it does not thereby become impersonal. On the contrary, as we have seen, the Torah is represented in certain rabbinic traditions as the living Word of God that serves as the means through which the Jewish people may continue to engage in discourse with its Author, God himself. The Author is not absent but is rather present in the text, and it is through the process of interpretation that the dialogue between the Author and the interpreter continues. Certain kabbalistic traditions extend these notions even further and represent the Book of the Torah as the outer body in which God himself is enshrined as its innermost soul. The distinction between author and text is thus overcome, for the Author resides within the text itself. Moreover, in the mystical hermeneutics of the Zohar the distinction between the interpreter and the author-text is overcome, for although the process of interpretation may begin as an intellectual exercise in which the text of the Torah is scrutinized as an object of analysis, in the end the interpretive process overcomes the duality of subject and object and culminates in intimate divine communion between the interpreter and his bride, the Torah.

We thus return to the notion of difference and, in Jonathan Z. Smith's words, to "what a difference a difference makes."[57] In order to understand and interpret the differences that distinguish Veda and Torah, it is not sufficient simply to invoke the prevailing scholarly conceptions of scripture, text, and language. Traditional representations of Veda and Torah challenge us to problematize our categories and to expand our definitions of scripture not only to include oral as well as written texts but also to account for such representations of scripture as a cosmological principle that encompasses and at the same time transcends textuality. Our conceptions of language and meaning also have to be reconsidered in this context, for we cannot fully understand the conceptions and practices associated with Veda and Torah without taking into account the ontological status ascribed to language in these traditions and the corresponding implications for notions of meaning. In the final analysis it is not only the differences that make a difference, it is the conceptions of scripture and language that underlie these differences that make a difference.

NOTES

INTRODUCTION

1. Among scholars who have critiqued the concept of a single "Hinduism" as a scholarly construct, see Heinrich von Stietencron, "Hinduism: On the Proper Use of a Deceptive Term," in *Hinduism Reconsidered*, eds. Günther D. Sontheimer and Hermann Kulke, South Asia Institute, South Asian Studies, no. 24 (New Delhi: Manohar, 1989), pp. 11–27. Von Stietencron argues that the term "Hinduism" does not refer to a single "religion" but rather denotes a civilization that includes a plurality of distinct "Hindu religions." Jacob Neusner has similarly challenged the notion of a single "Judaism" and has emphasized instead the plurality of "Judaisms" or "Judaic systems" that have developed in the course of Jewish history. See, for example, his *Death and Birth of Judaism: The Impact of Christianity, Secularism, and the Holocaust on Jewish Faith* (New York: Basic Books, 1987), esp. pp. 3–29.
2. This term derives from Brian Stock, *The Implications of Literacy: Written Language and Models of Interpretation in the Eleventh and Twelfth Centuries* (Princeton: Princeton University Press, 1983).
3. The Manu-Smṛti, for example, maintains that all traditions and philosophies that are not derived from the Veda are worthless and untrue (*anṛta*) and produce no reward after death. See MS XII.95–96; cf. MS II.10–11.
4. See Sanh. X.1, which declares that one who denies *tôrāh min ha-šāmayim*, "the Torah is from heaven," has no share in the world to come.
5. It is not within the scope of the present analysis to enter into the scholarly debate concerning the meaning of the term "symbol." In this study I use the term in accordance with Paul Ricoeur's characterization of a symbol as having a double intentionality. The first order meaning is the primary, literal signification, which points beyond itself to a second order meaning that functions as a potentially inexhaustible "surplus of signification." Veda and Torah, as we shall see, each functions as a symbol in this sense, in that each has a primary signification as a delimited corpus of texts, which opens out to a second order meaning that explodes these circumscribed limits and assimilates to itself a network of significations. For Ricoeur's analysis of the nature and function of symbols, see his *The Symbolism of Evil*, trans. Emerson Buchanan (Boston: Beacon Press, 1969), pp. 10–18, and his subsequent reflections in *Interpretation Theory: Discourse and the Surplus of Meaning* (Fort Worth: Texas Christian University Press, 1976), pp. 53–63.

6. The significance of the systematic comparison of "Hinduisms" and "Judaisms" as the basis for constructing alternative paradigms of "religious tradition" has been emphasized by Paul Morris in a series of personal communications with me. Morris has stressed in particular the heuristic value of positing two discrete models—missionary traditions ("Christianities," "Islams," "Buddhisms") and nonmissionary traditions ("Hinduisms," "Judaisms")—in order to elucidate the notion of "religious tradition." See Paul Morris, "The Discourse of Traditions: 'Judaisms' and 'Hinduisms'" (Paper delivered at the Annual Meeting of the American Academy of Religion, San Francisco, 1992).
7. For case studies of particular historical connections and cross-cultural resonances among "Judaisms" and "Hinduisms," see Hananya Goodman, ed., *Between Jerusalem and Benares: Comparative Studies in Judaism and Hinduism* (Albany: State University of New York Press, 1994). This collection of essays represents one of the first efforts by a group of scholars of Judaica and Indology to explore the affinities among these traditions. Goodman's introduction provides a brief survey of the remarkably few studies that have attempted to delineate connections among Hindu and Jewish traditions. See also the studies by Nathan Katz and Ellen S. Goldberg of the Jewish community in Cochin, India, in their *The Last Jews of Cochin: Jewish Identity in Hindu India* (Columbia, S.C.: University of South Carolina Press, 1993); idem, "The Ritual Enactments of the Cochin Jews: The Powers of Purity and Nobility," in *Ritual and Power*, ed. Barbara A. Holdrege, *Journal of Ritual Studies* 4, no. 2 (Summer 1990): 199–238.
8. For a recent discussion of problems in textual criticism by specialists in a variety of religious traditions, see the colloquium collection *The Critical Study of Sacred Texts*, ed. Wendy Doniger O'Flaherty, Berkeley Religious Studies Series (Berkeley: Graduate Theological Union, 1979). Among the numerous works on canon, see Jack N. Lightstone, "The Formation of the Biblical Canon in Judaism of Late Antiquity: Prolegomenon to a General Reassessment," *Studies in Religion/ Sciences Religieuses* 8, no. 2 (1979): 135–142; Brevard S. Childs, *Introduction to the Old Testament as Scripture* (Philadelphia: Fortress Press, 1979), chaps. 1–4; James Barr, *Holy Scripture: Canon, Authority, Criticism* (Philadelphia: Westminster Press, 1983); James A. Sanders, *From Sacred Story to Sacred Text* (Philadelphia: Fortress Press, 1987); idem, *Canon and Community: A Guide to Canonical Criticism*, Guides to Biblical Scholarship (Philadelphia: Fortress Press, 1984); idem, *Torah and Canon* (Philadelphia: Fortress Press, 1972); Sid Z. Leiman, *The Canonization of Hebrew Scripture: The Talmudic and Midrashic Evidence*, Transactions of the Connecticut Academy of Arts and Sciences, vol. 47 (Hamden, Conn.: Archon Books, 1976); idem, ed. *The Canon and Masorah of the Hebrew Bible: An Introductory Reader*, The Library of Biblical Studies (New York: Ktav, 1974); Gunnar Östborn,

Cult and Canon: A Study in the Canonization of the Old Testament, Uppsala Universitets Årsskrift, 1950, 10 (Uppsala: A.-B. Lundequistska; Leipzig: Otto Harrassowitz, 1950).

9. Among Smith's landmark studies, see in particular "The Study of Religion and the Study of the Bible," *Journal of the American Academy of Religion* 39, no. 2 (June 1971): 131–140; reprinted in *Rethinking Scripture: Essays from a Comparative Perspective*, ed. Miriam Levering (Albany: State University of New York Press, 1989), pp. 18–28; "Is the Qur'an the Word of God?" chapter 2 of his *Questions of Religious Truth* (New York: Charles Scribner's Sons, 1967), pp. 39–62; "The True Meaning of Scripture: An Empirical Historian's Nonreductionist Interpretation of the Qur'an," *International Journal of Middle Eastern Studies* 11, no. 4 (July 1980): 487–505; and "Scripture as Form and Concept: Their Emergence for the Western World," in *Rethinking Scripture*, ed. Levering, pp. 29–57. For Smith's most recent reflections on the category of scripture, see his important study *What is Scripture? A Comparative Approach* (Minneapolis: Fortress Press, 1993). Among Graham's studies, which have focused primarily on the oral-aural dimensions of scripture, see his *Beyond the Written Word: Oral Aspects of Scripture in the History of Religion* (Cambridge: Cambridge University Press, 1987), as well as his essays "*Qur'ān* as Spoken Word: An Islamic Contribution to the Understanding of Scripture," in *Approaches to Islam in Religious Studies*, ed. Richard C. Martin (Tucson: University of Arizona Press, 1985), pp. 23–40; "Scripture," *The Encyclopedia of Religion*, ed. Mircea Eliade, et al. (New York: Macmillan, 1987), s.v.; and "Scripture as Spoken Word," in *Rethinking Scripture*, ed. Levering, pp. 129–169. Levering's collection *Rethinking Scripture* was inspired by Smith's work and, in addition to his and Graham's essays, contains the contributions of a number of other scholars who have worked with Smith and who discuss their different approaches to reformulating the category of scripture as a general religious phenomenon in the comparative history of religions.

The previous lack of emphasis on scripture as a general religious phenomenon is evidenced by the absence of entries on the category of scripture in major reference works such as the *Encyclopaedia of Religion and Ethics*, ed. James Hastings (Edinburgh: T and T Clark; New York: Charles Scribner's Sons, 1908–1926). Although the recently published *The Encyclopedia of Religion*, ed. Mircea Eliade, et al. (New York: Macmillan, 1987) does contain the above mentioned article on scripture by Graham, the presence of such an entry in a major reference work is the exception rather than the rule and reflects the recent upsurge of interest in the religious category of scripture. Very few substantial cross-cultural studies of scripture have been undertaken, with the exception of *Heilige Schriften. Betrachtungen zur Religions-geschichte der antiken Mittelmeerwelt* by Johannes Leipoldt and Siegfried Morenz (Leipzig:

Otto Harrassowitz, 1953), which limits its study to the scriptural traditions of the pre-Islamic Mediterranean world—ancient Egyptian, Jewish, Greek, and Christian. Mention should also be made of the Swedish historian of religions Geo Widengren's studies of the "heavenly book" concept in pre-Islamic Near Eastern cultures, with its corresponding parallels in Islamic notions of scripture. See Geo Widengren, *The Ascension of the Apostle and the Heavenly Book*, King and Saviour, 3, Uppsala Universitets Årsskrift, 1950, 7 (Uppsala: A.-B. Lundequistska; Leipzig: Otto Harrassowitz, 1950); idem, *Muḥammad, the Apostle of God, and His Ascension*, King and Saviour, 5, Uppsala Universitets Årsskrift, 1955, 1 (Uppsala: A.-B. Lunde-quistska; Wiesbaden: Otto Harrassowitz, 1955). For a more recent treatment of a variety of scriptural traditions from a comparative perspective, see Harold Coward, *Sacred Word and Sacred Text: Scripture in World Religions* (Maryknoll, N.Y.: Orbis Books, 1988).

Most of the other works on scripture, such as the colloquium collection *Holy Book and Holy Tradition*, eds. F. F. Bruce and E. G. Rupp (Grand Rapids, Mich.: William B. Eerdmans, 1968), and the more recent collection *The Holy Book in Comparative Perspective*, eds. Frederick M. Denny and Rodney L. Taylor, Studies in Comparative Religion (Columbia, S.C.: University of South Carolina Press, 1985), treat the scriptural conceptions of each tradition separately and do not explicitly consider their possible implications in clarifying our understanding of scripture as a general religious phenomenon. See also Günter Lanczkowski, *Heilige Schriften. Inhalt, Textgestalt und Überlieferung* (Stuttgart: W. Kohlhammer, 1956).

The general category of scripture has received relatively little treatment even in the major works of phenomenology of religion. Those phenomenologists who have dealt with scripture at all, such as G. van der Leeuw, Gustav Mensching, Friedrich Heiler, and Geo Widengren, have tended to introduce a dichotomy between "holy word" and "holy writ," relegating scripture to the status of the written word, which is viewed as an ancillary development from the original spoken "word of power." See G. van der Leeuw, "The Sacred Word" and "The Written Word," chapters 58 and 64, respectively, of his *Religion in Essence and Manifestation*, vol. 2, trans. J. E. Turner, with Appendices . . . incorporating the additions of the second German edition by Hans H. Penner (1938; reprint, Gloucester, Mass.: Peter Smith, 1967), pp. 403–407, 435–446; Gustav Mensching, "Das gehörte und geschriebene Wort," chapter II.4 of his *Das Heilige Wort. Eine religionsphänomenologische Untersuchung*, Untersuchungen zur allgemeinen Religionsgeschichte, vol. 9 (Bonn: Ludwig Röhrscheid, 1937), pp. 71–88; Friedrich Heiler, "Das heilige Wort" and "Die heilige Schrift," chapters A.VII and A.VIII, respectively, of his *Erscheinungsformen und Wesen der Religion*, 2d rev. ed., Die Religionen der Menschheit, vol. 1 (Stuttgart: W.

Kohlhammer, 1979), pp. 266–364; Geo Widengren, "Heiliges Wort und Heilige Schrift," chapter 19 of his *Religionsphänomenologie* (Berlin: Walter de Gruyter, 1969), pp. 546–573.

It is striking to note that in the wide range of comparative studies by Mircea Eliade, the category of scripture has been entirely neglected in favor of myth, ritual, and other phenomena that are prevalent in "nonliterate" religious traditions.

10. Graham, *Beyond the Written Word*, p. 5.
11. The term *Wirkungsgeschichte* is used by Hans-Georg Gadamer to describe the tradition of successive interpretations in the history of a text that implicitly influences each new interpretation of a text. See Hans-Georg Gadamer, *Wahrheit und Methode. Grundzüge einer philosophischen Hermeneutik*, 4th ed. (Tübingen: J. C. B. Mohr [Paul Siebeck], 1975), esp. pp. 284–290. In the present context the term *Wirkungsgeschichte* is being used in a broader sense to include the text's role as scripture in the ongoing life of a particular religious community.
12. Graham, *Beyond the Written Word*.
13. These issues concerning alternative paradigms of "religious tradition" will be explored more fully in the conclusion.
14. Jonathan Z. Smith, "Sacred Persistence: Toward a Redescription of Canon," chapter 3 of his *Imagining Religion: From Babylon to Jonestown* (Chicago: University of Chicago Press, 1982), p. 52.
15. Ibid., p. 48.
16. The earliest references to the Veda(s) in Vedic texts generally focus on the triad *ṛc*s, *yajus*es, and *sāman*s, which are designated as the "threefold knowledge" (*trayī vidyā*) or "threefold Veda" (*traya veda*). As will be discussed in chapter 1, this emphasis on the "threefold knowledge" of the Ṛg-Veda, Yajur-Veda, and Sāma-Veda suggests that it took some time before the *atharvan*s of the Atharva-Veda were accorded an equivalent status as forming part of the "four Vedas" (*catur veda*).
17. The term *mantra* is used in the present context to refer to the *ṛc*s, *yajus*es, *sāman*s, and *atharvan*s collected in the four Saṃhitās, as distinct from the Brāhmaṇa and Upaniṣadic portions of the Veda. It should be noted, however, that although the terms *mantra* and Saṃhitā are often used interchangeably, they are not entirely synonymous, as the Taittirīya Saṃhitā (Black Yajur-Veda) contains in addition to *mantra*s some Brāhmaṇa material discussing the sacrificial ceremonies.
18. In making a distinction between "Vedic texts" and "post-Vedic texts," modern Western scholars generally adopt, on philological as well as historical grounds, this broader definition of Veda as including the Saṃhitās, Brāhmaṇas, Āraṇyakas, and Upaniṣads.
19. See Mbh. I.57.74; Mbh. XII.327.18; Rām. I.1.77; BP I.4.20; BP III.12.39; Skanda V.3.1.18; Artha Ś. I.3.1–2. The Bhāgavata Purāṇa

(I.4.20), for example, declares that "the four Vedas, known as Ṛg, Yajur, Sāma, and Atharva, were separated out [from the one Veda], and the Itihāsa-Purāṇa is called the fifth Veda (*pañcamo veda*)." As early as the Upaniṣads we find the notion that the Itihāsa and Purāṇa are "the fifth" among sacred brahmanical texts and sciences, although they are not explicitly referred to as the "fifth Veda." See CU VII.1.2,4; CU VII.2.1; CU VII.7.1, which enumerate "the Ṛg-Veda, the Yajur-Veda, the Sāma-Veda, the Atharvaṇa as the fourth (*caturtha*), Itihāsa-Purāṇa as the fifth (*pañcama*). . . ."

20. See n. 16.
21. Many of the later Upaniṣads are highly sectarian, and thus this phenomenon represents one of the strategies used by sectarian movements to legitimate their own texts through granting them the nominal status of *śruti*.
22. See Thomas Coburn's illuminating discussion of the relationship between *śruti* and *smṛti* in Hindu conceptions of scripture in "'Scripture' in India: Towards a Typology of the Word in Hindu Life," *Journal of the American Academy of Religion* 52, no. 3 (Sept. 1984): 435–459; reprinted in *Rethinking Scripture*, ed. Levering, pp. 102–128.
23. See, for example, Louis Renou and Jean Filliozat, *L'Inde classique. Manuel des études indiennes*, vol. 1 (Paris: Payot, 1947–1949), pp. 381, 270; Sarvepalli Radhakrishnan and Charles A. Moore, eds., *A Source Book in Indian Philosophy* (Princeton: Princeton University Press, 1957), p. xix; R. N. Dandekar, "Dharma, The First End of Man," in *Sources of Indian Tradition*, ed. Wm. Theodore de Bary, et al., Records of Civilization: Sources and Studies, no. 56 (New York: Columbia University Press, 1958), p. 217; Jan Gonda, *Die Religionen Indiens*, vol. 1, *Veda und älterer Hinduismus*, Die Religionen der Menschheit, vol. 11 (Stuttgart: W. Kohlhammer, 1960), p. 107; A. L. Basham, *The Wonder That Was India: A Survey of the History and Culture of the Indian Subcontinent Before the Coming of the Muslims*, 3d rev. ed. (London: Sidgwick and Jackson, 1967), pp. 112–113; Oscar Botto, "Letterature antiche dell'India," in *Storia delle Letterature d'Oriente*, ed. Oscar Botto, vol. 3 (Milan: Casa Editrice Dr. Francesco Vallardi, Società Editrice Libraria, 1969), p. 294. For a discussion and critique of such characterizations of *śruti* and *smṛti* as a distinction between "revelation" and "tradition," see Sheldon Pollock, "'Tradition' as 'Revelation': *Śruti, Smṛti*, and the Sanskrit Discourse of Power," in *Lex et Litterae: Essays on Ancient Indian Law and Literature in Honour of Oscar Botto*, eds. Siegfried Lienhard and Irma Piovano (Turin: CESMEO, forthcoming). Pollock's views will be discussed below.
24. I prefer to use the term "cognition" rather than "revelation" to refer to the process through which the *ṛṣis* apprehended the Vedic *mantras*, as will be discussed on pp. 231 with n. 22, 327–328.

25. In opposition to the view of the Mīmāṃsakas and Vedāntins that the Vedas are eternal and *apauruṣeya,* the exponents of the Nyāya, Vaiśeṣika, and Yoga schools use a variety of arguments to establish that the Vedas are noneternal (*anitya*) and *pauruṣeya,* created by the personal agency of Īśvara. The views of the philosophical schools will be discussed in chapter 1.
26. See Pollock, "'Tradition' as 'Revelation'"; idem, "From Discourse of Ritual to Discourse of Power in Sanskrit Culture," in *Ritual and Power,* ed. Holdrege, *Journal of Ritual Studies* 4, no. 2 (Summer 1990): 322–328. David Carpenter has argued that the extension of the purview of Veda beyond the ritual practices delineated in the *śruti* texts to the broader domain of sociocultural practices laid out in *smṛti* texts was accomplished primarily through shifting the locus of Vedic authority from a circumscribed set of "texts" to the brahmanical custodians who were responsible for the "ritualized reproduction of the 'divine speech' of the Vedic tradition." In the Dharma-Sūtras and Dharma-Śāstras the conduct of the brahmins became synonymous with *śiṣṭācāra,* the "practice of the learned," and was ascribed normative status alongside *śruti* and *smṛti* as an authoritative source of *dharma.* Thus, even when the teachings of the brahmins went beyond the teachings of the *śruti* texts, they were nevertheless deemed "Vedic," for they were promulgated by those who, by virtue of their privileged role as transmitters of the Vedic recitative tradition, had become "living embodiments of the Veda." See David Carpenter, "Language, Ritual, and Society: Reflections on the Authority of the Veda in India," *Journal of the American Academy of Religion* 60, no. 1 (Spring 1992): 57–77, esp. 58–63.
27. See, for example, ṚV VIII.59.6, cited on pp. 236–237. As will be discussed in chapter 3, the *ṛṣis'* cognitions are at times described in the Ṛg-Veda as synesthetic experiences that involved both hearing and seeing.
28. Maharishi Mahesh Yogi, *Maharishi's Absolute Theory of Government* (Vlodrop, Holland: Maharishi Vedic University Press, 1993), p. 14. Aurobindo Ghose, *On the Veda,* Sri Aurobindo International University Centre Collection, vol. 5 (Pondicherry: Sri Aurobindo Ashram Press, 1956), p. 11.

    Maharishi has discussed extensively the ontology of the Veda and the mechanisms through which the *ṛṣis* cognized the Vedic *mantras.* He emphasizes the transcendent status of the Veda as the infinite, eternal field of pure knowledge, which manifests in the beginning of each cycle of creation as the source and foundation of the universe. In his *On the Bhagavad-Gita: A New Translation and Commentary, Chapters 1 to 6* (Harmondsworth, Middlesex, England: Penguin Books, 1969), p. 206, Maharishi writes:

    > The first manifestation of creation is the self-illuminant effulgence of life. . . . This self-illuminant effulgence of life is called

> the Veda. . . . Just before the beginning of action, just before the beginning of the subtlest vibration, in that self-illuminant state of existence, lies the source of creation, the storehouse of limitless energy. This source of creation is the Veda, the field of almost absolute intelligence which underlies and pervades all activity responsible for the creation and evolution of life.

When this field of intelligence begins to vibrate within itself, this "vibrancy of intelligence" is *śruti*, the primordial sounds of the Vedic *mantras*. These sounds, according to Maharishi, contain all the laws of nature that are responsible for structuring the forms and phenomena of creation, and it is these sounds that were "heard" by the *ṛṣis* when they were immersed in the Transcendent. These primordial impulses of speech were simultaneously "seen" by the seers as reverberations rising up from the silent ocean of pure consciousness that contained the knowledge of all the laws of nature.

> In the beginning of creation when the entire cosmos is pure, in those pure minds which transcend and want to know something, the entire knowledge of creation . . . dawn[s]. . . . Formulas come to their vision and these become the Vedas. To visualize the laws of nature means the functioning of nature is so vivid to them, is so clear to their perception, that they know everything as one knows a thing when he visualizes it.

Maharishi Mahesh Yogi, *The Vedas* (Los Angeles: Spiritual Regeneration Movement Foundation, 1967), p. 9.

In discussing the mechanisms of Vedic cognition, Maharishi maintains that the primordial sounds of the Vedas that were heard and seen by the ancient *ṛṣis* can be accessed by anyone through following the example of the *ṛṣis* and transcending. More specifically, he emphasizes that through practice of the Transcendental Meditation technique, every human being has the potential to rise to an enlightened state of consciousness in which "the whole engineering of creation, all the secrets of Nature's silent functioning," contained in the Vedic *mantras* is available in "one's own self-referral consciousness." Maharishi Mahesh Yogi, *Maharishi's Absolute Theory of Government*, p. 14.

29. J. Muir has collected together numerous passages from Vedic and post-Vedic texts regarding the origin and cosmological status of the Veda, although apart from brief introductory statements he does not attempt to analyze and interpret the significance of, and interrelationship among, these texts. J. Muir, comp. and trans., *Original Sanskrit Texts on the Origin and History of the People of India, Their Religion and Institutions*, vol. 3, *The Vedas: Opinions of Their Authors and of Later Indian Writers on Their Origin, Inspiration, and Authority*, 2d rev. ed. (1874; reprint, Amsterdam: Oriental Press, 1967). I am partic-

ularly indebted to Muir for bringing to light a number of important passages that are pertinent to my analysis of cosmological conceptions of Veda.

30. A number of these modes of assimilation are discussed by Pollock in "From Discourse of Ritual to Discourse of Power in Sanskrit Culture," p. 332.
31. See Brian K. Smith, *Reflections on Resemblance, Ritual, and Religion* (New York: Oxford University Press, 1989), pp. 3–29, esp. 20–29; idem, "Exorcising the Transcendent: Strategies for Defining Hinduism and Religion," *History of Religions* 27, no. 1 (Aug. 1987): 32–55, esp. 45–52.
32. Smith, *Reflections on Resemblance, Ritual, and Religion*, pp. 26, 13–14; idem, "Exorcising the Transcendent," pp. 49, 40.
33. J. Gonda, *Change and Continuity in Indian Religion*, Disputationes Rheno-Trajectinae, vol. 9 (The Hague: Mouton, 1965), p. 7. For statements by other Indologists concerning the authority of the Veda as the decisive criterion of Hindu orthodoxy, see Smith, *Reflections on Resemblance, Ritual, and Religion*, p. 18, n. 45.
34. See N. Subbu Reddiar, "The Nālāyiram as Drāvida Veda," chapter 26 of his *Religion and Philosophy of Nālāyira Divya Prabandham with Special Reference to Nammāḷvār* (Tirupati: Sri Venkateswara University, 1977), pp. 680–693.
35. For a discussion of the "vedacization" of the *Rāmcaritmānas*, and of *Mānas* recitation rituals in particular, see Philip Lutgendorf, "The Power of Sacred Story: *Rāmāyaṇa* Recitation in Contemporary North India," in *Ritual and Power*, ed. Holdrege, *Journal of Ritual Studies* 4, no. 2 (Summer 1990): 115–147. See also Lutgendorf's *The Life of a Text: Performing the Rāmcaritmānas of Tulsidas* (Berkeley: University of California Press, 1991).
36. See A. K. Ramanujan, trans., *Speaking of Śiva* (Harmondsworth, Middlesex, England: Penguin Books, 1973), pp. 19–55.
37. Abhinavagupta (10th century C.E.), the most famous exponent of Kashmir Śaivism, asserts:

> [T]he wise *sādhaka* [tantric practitioner] must not choose the word of the Veda as the ultimate authority because it is full of impurities and produces meager, unstable, and limited results. Rather, the *sādhaka* should elect the Śaivite scriptures as his source. Moreover, that which according to the Veda produces sin leads, according to the left-handed doctrine, promptly to perfection. The entire Vedic teaching is in fact tightly held in the grip of *māyā* (delusional power).

Tantrāloka 37.10–12; cf. 15.595–599. Cited in Paul E. Muller-Ortega, "The Power of the Secret Ritual: Theoretical Formulations from the Tantra," in *Ritual and Power*, ed. Holdrege, *Journal of Ritual Studies* 4, no. 2 (Summer 1990): 49.

38. J. C. Heesterman, "Veda and Dharma," in *The Concept of Duty in South Asia*, eds. Wendy Doniger O'Flaherty and J. Duncan M. Derrett (New Delhi: Vikas, 1978), pp. 92–93.
39. Smith, *Reflections on Resemblance, Ritual, and Religion*, p. 20. Paul Younger has similarly noted that "in spite of the acknowledgment of its authority, the content of the *Veda* does not seem to be used very directly in guiding the later development of the Religious Tradition." Paul Younger, *Introduction to Indian Religious Thought* (Philadelphia: Westminster Press, 1972), p. 71.
40. Louis Renou, *The Destiny of the Veda in India*, trans. Dev Raj Chanana (Delhi: Motilal Banarsidass, 1965), pp. 2, 1. Renou's study provides a useful survey of the different attitudes, beliefs, and practices that the major texts, philosophical schools, and sects of the Indian tradition have adopted with respect to the Veda in the course of its history. J. L. Mehta has challenged some of Renou's perspectives on the "destiny of the Veda" and suggests that the Veda may possess an inherent potency, or *svadhā*, that has enabled it to create its own destiny in spite of the perils of history. J. L. Mehta, "The Hindu Tradition: The Vedic Root," in *The World's Religious Traditions: Current Perspectives in Religious Studies. Essays in Honour of Wilfred Cantwell Smith*, ed. Frank Whaling (Edinburgh: T. and T. Clark, 1984), pp. 33–54. See also Wilhelm Halbfass's discussion of the role and "destiny" of the Veda in traditional Hindu self-understanding in his *Tradition and Reflection: Explorations in Indian Thought* (Albany: State University of New York Press, 1991), esp. pp. 1–22.
41. Pollock, "From Discourse of Ritual to Discourse of Power in Sanskrit Culture," p. 332. See also Robert Lingat's suggestion that "in reality, it seems that when a Hindu affirms that *dharma* rests entirely upon the Veda, the word Veda does not mean in that connection the Vedic texts, but rather the totality of Knowledge, the sum of all understanding, of all religious and moral truths." Robert Lingat, *The Classical Law of India*, trans. J. Duncan M. Derrett (Berkeley: University of California Press, 1973), p. 8.
42. While Smith views the authority of the Veda as pivotal to his definition of Hinduism, he declines from including "the orthodox claim that the Veda is a body of transcendent and super- or extra-human knowledge" as part of his definition, for "from the standpoint of the academic and humanistic study of religion, the Veda, like all other canonical literatures, was entirely composed [by] human beings." Smith, *Reflections on Resemblance, Ritual, and Religion*, p. 19. I would of course agree with Smith that as scholars of religion we are not ourselves in a position to adopt the traditional brahmanical view of the Veda as transcendent knowledge. I would nevertheless argue that the authority that the Veda holds in the brahmanical tradition—if not in all Hindu traditions—is directly predicated on its status as transcendent knowl-

edge. If the Veda were stripped of that status, it would thereby lose its legitimating function as a *transcendent* source of authority.

43. J. Frits Staal's studies of Vedic recitation and ritual have provided important insights into the oral-aural character of the Vedas, in which priority is given to phonology and syntax over semantics. See particularly his *Nambudiri Veda Recitation,* Disputationes Rheno-Trajectinae, vol. 5 (The Hague: Mouton, 1961); idem, "The Concept of Scripture in the Indian Tradition," in *Sikh Studies: Comparative Perspectives on a Changing Tradition,* eds. Mark Juergensmeyer and N. Gerald Barrier, Berkeley Religious Series (Berkeley: Graduate Theological Union, 1979), pp. 121–124. For a more recent formulation of Staal's theories, see his *Rules Without Meaning: Ritual, Mantras and the Human Sciences,* Toronto Studies in Religion, vol. 4 (New York: Peter Lang, 1989), esp. pp. 191–311. See also David Carpenter, "The Mastery of Speech: Canonicity and Control in the Vedas," in *Authority, Anxiety, and Canon: Essays in Vedic Interpretation,* ed. Laurie L. Patton, SUNY Series in Hindu Studies (Albany: State University of New York Press, 1994), pp. 19–34. Carpenter argues that the canonicity of the Veda can best be defined not in terms of the delimitation of the *content* of a particular corpus of texts, as Jonathan Z. Smith's model of canon implies, but rather in terms of the delimitation of the correct *form* of speech to be employed in the sacrificial rituals.

44. It should be noted, however, that there are a variety of opinions concerning the origin and meaning of the root *yrh*. For a discussion of the scholarly debate, one may refer to Michael Fishbane's article "Torah" in *Encyclopedia Miqrā'īṯ* (Jerusalem: Mosad Bialik, 1962–1988), s.v.

45. The term "halakhah" is used to designate any normative law, practice, or custom sanctioned by rabbinic authorities, while the term "aggadah" refers to nonlegal discourse and teachings and encompasses a range of material, including moral exhortations, theological speculations, narratives, parables, and folklore.

46. For a discussion of rabbinic conceptions of Written Torah and Oral Torah, see Ephraim E. Urbach, "The Written Law and the Oral Law," chapter 12 of his *The Sages: Their Concepts and Beliefs,* vol. 1, trans. Israel Abrahams, 2d rev. ed. (Jerusalem: Magnes Press, Hebrew University, 1979), pp. 286–314. See also Martin S. Jaffee's illuminating analysis of the possible origins of the concept of Oral Torah, "How Much 'Orality' in Oral Torah? New Perspectives on the Composition and Transmission of Early Rabbinic Tradition," *Shofar* 10, no. 2 (Winter 1992): 53–72.

47. Jacob Neusner, *The Ecology of Religion: From Writing to Religion in the Study of Judaism* (Nashville: Abingdon Press, 1989), p. 240. For a brief discussion of the complex of meanings ascribed to the term Torah in various rabbinic texts, see ibid., pp. 240–249, 109–112, 120–123. For

a more extended discussion, see Neusner's *Torah: From Scroll to Symbol in Formative Judaism* (Philadelphia: Fortress Press, 1985).

48. Elliot Wolfson, in discussing the personification of the Torah as a feminine figure in rabbinic and kabbalistic texts, argues that in rabbinic sources such characterizations are generally intended metaphorically and do not imply a mythical or mystical conception of the Torah as the divine feminine.

> In [rabbinic texts] . . . it is clear that the feminine images were originally meant figuratively and are thus almost always expressed within a parabolic context as literary metaphors. I do not mean to suggest that the Torah was not personified by the rabbis; indeed, for the rabbis the Torah did assume a personality of its own, culminating in the conception of the Torah as the preexistent entity that served as the instrument with which God created the world. Nevertheless in the rabbinic writings the female images of the Torah are for the most part metaphorical in their nuance.

It is significant that Wolfson singles out the conception of the Torah as the instrument of creation as the culminating expression of the rabbis' personification of the Torah, implying that conceptions such as these might not be intended simply as a literary metaphor. Elliot Wolfson, "Female Imaging of the Torah: From Literary Metaphor to Religious Symbol," in *From Ancient Israel to Modern Judaism: Intellect in Quest of Understanding. Essays in Honor of Marvin Fox*, eds. Jacob Neusner, Ernest S. Frerichs, and Nahum M. Sarna, vol. 2, Brown Judaic Studies, no. 173 (Atlanta: Scholars Press, 1989), pp. 272–273; reprinted in his *Along the Path: Studies in Kabbalistic Myth, Symbolism, and Hermeneutics*, SUNY Series in Judaica: Hermeneutics, Mysticism, and Religion (Albany: State University of New York Press, forthcoming).

49. See Abraham Joshua Heschel, *Tôrāh min ha-Šāmayim bā-'Aspaqlaryāh šel ha-Dôrôṯ*, 2 vols. (London: Soncino Press, 1962, 1965).

50. Ḥag. II.1. Cf. the Gemara on this Mishnah, Ḥag. 11b–16a.

51. Gershom Scholem has emphasized the continuity between the speculations of these mystically oriented rabbinic circles and the Merkabah speculations of the Hêḵālôṯ texts. See, for example, his *Major Trends in Jewish Mysticism*, 3d rev. ed. (1954; reprint, New York: Schocken Books, 1961), pp. 40–43; *Jewish Gnosticism, Merkabah Mysticism, and Talmudic Tradition*, 2d ed. (New York: Jewish Theological Seminary of America, 1965). See also Ithamar Gruenwald, *Apocalyptic and Merkavah Mysticism*, Arbeiten zur Geschichte des antiken Judentums und des Urchristentums, vol. 14 (Leiden: E. J. Brill, 1980); idem, *From Apocalypticism to Gnosticism: Studies in Apocalypticism, Merkavah Mysticism and Gnosticism*, Beiträge zur Erforschung des Alten Testaments und des antiken Judentums, vol. 14 (Frankfurt: Peter Lang, 1988); Ira Chernus, *Mysticism in Rabbinic Judaism:*

Studies in the History of Midrash, Studia Judaica: Forschungen zur Wissenschaft des Judentums, vol. 11 (Berlin: Walter de Gruyter, 1982). The views of Scholem and his followers concerning the primary focus of Hêḵālôṯ speculations and their connection with rabbinic *ma'ăśēh merkāḇāh* have been challenged by Peter Schäfer and David Halperin, as will be discussed in chapter 4.

52. My own analyses of kabbalistic conceptions of Torah and language are indebted to the illuminating studies of Scholem, Moshe Idel, and Elliot Wolfson. See in particular Scholem's groundbreaking essay "The Meaning of the Torah in Jewish Mysticism," chapter 2 of his *On the Kabbalah and Its Symbolism,* trans. Ralph Manheim (New York: Schocken Books, 1965), pp. 32–86, and his article "The Name of God and the Linguistic Theory of the Kabbala," *Diogenes,* no. 79 (Fall 1972): 59–80 (Part 1); no. 80 (Winter 1972): 164–194 (Part 2). Among Idel's numerous studies, see his "T^{e}p̄îsaṯ ha-Tôrāh b^{e}-Sip̄rûṯ ha-Hêḵālôṯ w^{e}-Gilgûlẹhā ba-Qabbālāh," *Jerusalem Studies in Jewish Thought* 1 (1981): 23–84, as well as his more recent studies, "Infinities of Torah in Kabbalah," in *Midrash and Literature,* eds. Geoffrey H. Hartman and Sanford Budick (New Haven: Yale University Press, 1986), pp. 141–157; "Reification of Language in Jewish Mysticism," in *Mysticism and Language,* ed. Steven T. Katz (New York: Oxford University Press, 1992), pp. 42–79; and *Language, Torah, and Hermeneutics in Abraham Abulafia,* trans. Menahem Kallus, SUNY Series in Judaica: Hermeneutics, Mysticism, and Religion (Albany: State University of New York Press, 1989). Among Wolfson's studies, see his "Female Imaging of the Torah," cited in n. 48; "The Hermeneutics of Visionary Experience: Revelation and Interpretation in the *Zohar,*" *Religion* 18 (Oct. 1988): 311–345; "The Anthropomorphic and Symbolic Image of the Letters in the Zohar" [in Hebrew], in *Proceedings of the Third International Conference on the History of Jewish Mysticism: The Age of the Zohar,* ed. Joseph Dan, *Jerusalem Studies in Jewish Thought* 8 (1989): 147–181; "Letter Symbolism and *Merkavah* Imagery in the *Zohar,*" in *'Alei Shefer: Studies in the Literature of Jewish Thought,* ed. Moshe Ḥallamish (Ramat-Gan: Bar-Ilan University Press, 1990), pp. 195–236; and "Erasing the Erasure/Gender and the Writing of God's Body in Kabbalistic Symbolism," in his *Along the Path.*

53. Idel, in opposition to Scholem's emphasis on the Gnostic and Neoplatonic foundations of Kabbalah, has postulated "a relatively organic evolution of Jewish mysticism" in which kabbalistic conceptions are rooted in, and share deep affinities with, certain trends of rabbinic thought. He emphasizes that "far from being a total innovation, historical Kabbalah represented an ongoing effort to systematize existing elements of Jewish theurgy, myth, and mysticism into a full-fledged response to the rationalistic challenge" posed by certain Jewish philos-

ophers, in particular Maimonides. See Moshe Idel, *Kabbalah: New Perspectives* (New Haven: Yale University Press, 1988), esp. pp. 30–32, 252–253.

54. While this aspect of Veda is generally designated as "knowledge," as the etymology of the term itself suggests, the corresponding aspect of Torah is generally designated as Ḥoḵmāh, "wisdom." In the analysis that follows I will use the term "knowledge" to encompass both conceptions.
55. In discussing both brahmanical and Jewish conceptions I have used the term "creator principle" or "creator" to designate that principle which is represented as the immediate source or instrument of the cosmogonic process and the term "creation" to designate the phenomenal world that emerges through this process. However, it is important to emphasize that the Sanskrit root *sṛj*, "to emit, send forth," which is the verb that is generally used to describe the process of cosmos-production, does not refer to creation *ex nihilo* but rather to a process of emission in which the "creator" brings forth phenomena that are latent either within himself (in the case of Prajāpati in the Brāhmaṇas) or within some higher cosmic principle such as Brahman (in the case of Brahmā in most post-Vedic cosmogonies).
56. Even though the term "blueprint" is obviously a modern designation for which no literal equivalent can be found in Sanskrit or Hebrew, I have nevertheless chosen to use the term at times when discussing images of the Veda or Torah as the plan of creation in order to connote the plan's association with the architect of creation.
57. The structural similarities delineated in this study are phenomenological. By "structure" I do not wish to imply the binary structures of structuralist analysis, the archetypal structures of Jungian psychology, or the ontological structures posited by Mircea Eliade. Eliade's perspective is discussed below in n. 64.
58. The bird-shaped fire altar in the *agnicayana* ceremony, as will be discussed in chapter 3, is understood to be a representation of the body of the creator Prajāpati. However, this is an aniconic rather than an iconic representation. For a brief discussion of the distinction between aniconic and iconic images, see Diana L. Eck, *Darśan: Seeing the Divine Image in India,* 2d rev. ed. (Chambersburg, Pa.: Anima Books, 1985), pp. 32–33. Eck notes that "in the Vedic period there is virtually no evidence to indicate the use of iconic images in worship." Ibid., p. 33.
59. For a discussion of post-Vedic "Hinduism" as a "visual and visionary culture," see Eck, *Darśan.* Purāṇic "cults of the book" will be briefly discussed in chapter 1.
60. We will return to a consideration of this opposition in the conclusion.
61. Jonathan Z. Smith, "*Adde Parvum Parvo Magnus Acervus Erit,*" chapter 11 of his *Map Is Not Territory: Studies in the History of Religions,*

Studies in Judaism in Late Antiquity, vol. 23 (Leiden: E. J. Brill, 1978), pp. 240–241.

62. Jonathan Z. Smith, "In Comparison a Magic Dwells," chapter 2 of his *Imagining Religion*, pp. 19–35, esp. 35. Smith gives a more detailed critical analysis of these four modes of comparison in "*Adde Parvum Parvo Magnus Acervus Erit*." The latter essay also contains a brief bibliographic survey of recent studies on the comparative method by historians of religions and anthropologists.

63. Van der Leeuw's phenomenology of religion is concerned with the religious phenomenon qua phenomenon—that is, with "what 'appears'" to "someone"—and does not make judgments about the reality, or noumenon, that lies behind the manifest appearance, the phenomenon. His phenomenological analysis begins by classifying similar types of religious phenomena, drawn from a wide variety of religious traditions, into groups by name—sacrifice, prayer, myth, and so on. The phenomenologist, through the double movement of empathy (*Einfühlung*) and *epoche*, then seeks to grasp the "essence" (*Wesenheit*) of a particular phenomenon and the structural relations (*verständliche Zusammenhänge*) that constitute the phenomenon in order to arrive at an understanding (*das Verstehen*) of the "ideal type" (*Idealtyp*). Van der Leeuw's monumental work, *Religion in Essence and Manifestation*, is essentially a phenomenological typology that explicates the nature, structure, and meaning of the ideal types that he has arrived at through his phenomenological method. The meaning of the religious phenomena that he explicates inevitably extends beyond the meaning for any particular group of believers. For a discussion of van der Leeuw's method, see "Epilegomena," in his *Religion in Essence and Manifestation*, vol. 2, pp. 672–695; idem, "Some Recent Achievements of Psychological Research and Their Application to History, in Particular the History of Religion," "On Phenomenology and Its Relation to Theology," and "On 'Understanding,'" in *Classical Approaches to the Study of Religion: Aims, Methods and Theories of Research*, ed. Jacques Waardenburg, vol. 1, Religion and Reason, 3 (The Hague: Mouton, 1973), pp. 399–412.

64. Smith views Eliade's work as "a massive exemplar in religious studies" of the morphological approach to comparative analysis. See Smith, "In Comparison a Magic Dwells," pp. 25, 29. Although Eliade designates himself as a historian of religions rather than a phenomenologist of religion, he makes use of a structural phenomenological approach in his explorations of "patterns in comparative religion." Like van der Leeuw, in his studies of myth, symbol, and ritual Eliade draws his examples from a wide range of religious traditions—with particular emphasis on small-scale societies and Asian traditions—and seeks to grasp the universal structures that underlie and unite the particular historical manifestations of a religious phenomenon. In his analyses of

religious symbols he begins by examining and comparing, through morphological analysis and classification, a considerable number of specific manifestations of a particular religious symbol from different historical-cultural contexts. Amidst the diverse valorizations of the symbol he gradually deciphers the "structure of the symbol" and grasps the core of essential meaning that interconnects all of the particular meanings. This meaning is not limited to those meanings of which a particular group of believers were fully conscious, for in Eliade's view religious symbols have an autonomous, coherent structure that is independent of the religious person who uses them. Unlike van der Leeuw, who seeks to grasp the essence of the phenomenon but does not inquire concerning the reality that underlies the appearance, Eliade makes normative assertions concerning the ontological status and existential value of religious symbols and maintains that they are revelatory of reality, disclosing the structures of human and cosmic existence. For Eliade's delineation of his approach to the history of religions, see in particular his "Methodological Remarks on the Study of Religious Symbolism," in *The History of Religions: Essays in Methodology*, eds. Mircea Eliade and Joseph M. Kitagawa (Chicago: University of Chicago Press, 1959), pp. 86–107; *The Quest: History and Meaning in Religion* (Chicago: University of Chicago Press, 1969). For a critical analysis of Eliade's phenomenological approach, see Douglas Allen, *Structure and Creativity in Religion: Hermeneutics in Mircea Eliade's Phenomenology and New Directions*, Religion and Reason, 14 (The Hague: Mouton, 1978). For critiques of Eliade's method by anthropologists and historians of religions, see Guilford Dudley III, *Religion on Trial: Mircea Eliade and His Critics* (Philadelphia: Temple University Press, 1977), and, more recently, Jonathan Z. Smith, "In Search of Place," chapter 1 of his *To Take Place: Toward Theory in Ritual*, Chicago Studies in the History of Judaism (Chicago: University of Chicago Press, 1987), pp. 1–23. See also William E. Paden, *Religious Worlds: The Comparative Study of Religion* (Boston: Beacon Press, 1988), who addresses some of the limitations implicit in the phenomenological approaches of van der Leeuw and Eliade and proposes the concept of "religious worlds" as an alternative framework for the comparative study of religion.

65. Smith points out that the issue of difference has been ignored not only by the morphological mode of comparative analysis but by the comparative enterprise in the human sciences generally: *"[C]omparison has been chiefly an affair of the recollection of similarity. The chief explanation for the significance of comparison has been contiguity. . . .* The issue of difference has been all but forgotten." Smith attempts to counter this trend by emphasizing that questions of difference are constitutive of the very process of comparison. "[C]omparison is, at base, never identity. Comparison requires the postulation of difference as

the grounds of its being interesting (rather than tautological) and a methodical manipulation of difference, a playing across the 'gap' in the service of some useful end." Smith, "In Comparison a Magic Dwells," pp. 21, 35. Smith reiterates this point in his critique of Eliade in "In Search of Place," *To Take Place*, pp. 13–14.

66. In his critique of the various modes of comparative analysis, Smith maintains that the morphological is "the only mode to survive scrutiny" and yet is also "the one which is most offensive to us by its refusal to support a thoroughly historical method and a set of theoretical presuppositions which grant sufficient gravity to the historical encapsulation of culture." While he recognizes the importance of patterns and structures as devices for interpretation, he insists that they must be grounded in historical processes. "The responsible alternative," he suggests, is "the integration of a complex notion of pattern and system with an equally complex notion of history." Smith, "In Comparison a Magic Dwells," pp. 26, 29.

CHAPTER 1. VEDA AND CREATION

1. Relevant passages will be examined in chapter 3.
2. Regarding ṚV X.90.9, see p. 37.
3. See, for example, AV VII.54.1–2; TS VII.5.11.2; AB I.22; ŚB V.5.5.5,9–10.
4. See, for example, AB V.32; TB III.12.9.1–2; ŚB XI.5.8.3–4,6; ŚB XII.3.4.9; Ṣaḍv. B. I.5.8–10; Ṣaḍv. B. V.1.2; JB I.357; AĀ III.2.3; ŚĀ VIII.3; BĀU I.5.5; BĀU II.4.10; BĀU IV.5.11; BĀU IV.1.2; CU I.3.7; CU III.15.7; CU VII.1.2,4; CU VII.2.1; CU VII.7.1; Maitri VI.32.
5. See, for example, AB V.32–33; KB VI.10–12; TB III.10.11.5–6; ŚB I.1.4.2–3; ŚB IV.6.7.1; ŚB V.5.5.9; ŚB VI.1.1.8,10; ŚB VI.3.1.20; ŚB VII.5.2.52; ŚB X.4.2.21–22,27,30; ŚB X.5.2.1–2; ŚB XI.5.4.18; ŚB XI.5.8.4,7; JB I.357–358; JUB I.18.10; JUB I.23.5–6; JUB I.45.3; JUB I.58.2; JUB III.15.9; JUB III.19.4–6; KU II.6.
6. See, for example, ŚB V.5.5.9–10,12, where the designation *traya veda*, "threefold Veda," is juxtaposed with the expression *trayī vidyā*, "threefold knowledge." Cf. AB V.32; TB II.3.10.1; ŚB XI.5.8.3–4; JB I.358; JUB I.1.1–2; JUB I.8.1,3–4,10; JUB III.19.2.
7. *Atharvāṅgiras*es is a compound composed of "Atharvan" and "Aṅgiras," which are the names of two ancient priestly families and which also may refer to the magic formulae used by these families. The terms *atharvans* and *aṅgiras*es are sometimes used alone to denote the Atharva-Veda.
8. AV X.7.20.
9. TS VII.5.11.2: "To the *ṛc*s hail! To the *yajus*es hail! To the *sāmans* hail! To the *aṅgiras*es hail! To the Vedas hail!"

10. See, for example, TB III.12.9.1; ŚB XI.5.6.4–7; CU III.1–4; TU II.3. In ŚB XIII.4.3.3,6–8,12–14, the *atharvans* and *aṅgirases* are mentioned along with the *ṛcs*, *yajuses*, and *sāmans* as constituting the Veda. Itihāsa and Purāṇa are also deemed to be Veda in this context.
11. See, for example, CU VII.1.2,4; CU VII.2.1; CU VII.7.1, which list "the Ṛg-Veda, the Yajur-Veda, the Sāma-Veda, the Atharvaṇa as the fourth. . . ." Cf. BĀU II.4.10; BĀU IV.5.11; BĀU IV.1.2; Maitri VI.32.
12. See, for example, Śāṅkh. ŚS XVI.2.9.
13. ŚB XIII.4.3.3,6,7,14.
14. AĀ III.2.3; ŚĀ VIII.3. Cf. AV XV.3.6–8, which speaks of making a seat for a Vrātya (a member of the mendicant or vagrant class, perhaps here identified with Brahman) that is composed, among other things, of the *ṛcs*, *yajuses*, and *sāmans*. The Veda is mentioned separately as one of the constituent elements.
15. CU III.3.1–3.
16. CU III.4.
17. See, for example, ṚV II.1.2, which mentions the priests *hotṛ*, *potṛ*, *neṣṭṛ*, *agnidh*, *praśāstṛ*, *adhvaryu*, and *brahman*, and ṚV II.43.1–2, which mentions the *udgātṛ* and *sāma-ga* (*sāman* singer).
18. One of the oldest references associating the *brahman* priest with the entire *trayī vidyā* is AB V.32–34. Cf. KB VI.10–12; ŚB XI.5.8.1–7; JB I.357–358.
19. For a discussion of the origin and nature of the *ṛṣis'* cognitions, see chapter 3.
20. ṚV X.90.9, which will be discussed below.
21. See chapter 3.
22. For discussions of the cosmogonic speculations of the Ṛg-Veda and of Vedic texts generally, see W. Norman Brown, "Theories of Creation in the Rig Veda," *Journal of the American Oriental Society* 85, no. 1 (Jan.–March 1965): 23–34; idem, "The Creation Myth of the Rig Veda," *Journal of the American Oriental Society* 62, no. 2 (June 1942): 85–98; F. B. J. Kuiper, "Cosmogony and Conception: A Query," *History of Religions* 10, no. 2 (Nov. 1970): 91–138; idem, *Ancient Indian Cosmogony*, ed. John Irwin (New Delhi: Vikas, 1983); Jean Varenne, *Cosmogonies Védiques*, La Tradition: textes et études, Série française, vol. 19 (Paris: Societé d'Édition "Les Belles Lettres," 1982); B. L. Ogibenin, *Structure d'un mythe védique: Le mythe cosmogonique dans le Ṛgveda*, Approaches to Semiotics, 30 (The Hague: Mouton, 1973); Narendra Nath Bhattacharyya, *History of Indian Cosmogonical Ideas* (New Delhi: Munshiram Manoharlal, 1971), pp. 13–49. Brown's two essays are reprinted in his *India and Indology: Selected Articles*, ed. Rosane Rocher (Delhi: Motilal Banarsidass, 1978), pp. 40–52, 20–33, respectively. For surveys of Vedic mythology, see A. A. Macdonell, *Vedic Mythology*, Grundiss der indo-arischen Philologie und Altertumskunde, vol. 3, no. 1A (1897;

reprint, New York: Gordon Press, 1974); Alfred Hillebrandt, *Vedic Mythology*, trans. Sreeramula Rajeswara Sarma, 2d rev. ed., 2 vols. (Delhi: Motilal Banarsidass, 1980–1981).

23. The term *tapas* has been left untranslated throughout this study, since it is difficult to find a single word or phrase that can satisfactorily convey the complex of meanings encompassed by the term. The term literally means "heat," and in the context of the passages cited in the present study particularly refers to the internal heat generated through meditation and various types of ascetic practices, by means of which one accumulates spiritual and creative power. For an analysis of the concept of *tapas* in Vedic texts, see Walter O. Kaelber, *Tapta Mārga: Asceticism and Initiation in Vedic India* (Albany: State University of New York Press, 1989).
24. Kuiper, "Cosmogony and Conception," esp. pp. 98–107.
25. Ṛ̣V X.81.7,1,5–6.
26. ṚV X.82.1,4.
27. ṚV X.90.7. The Sādhyas are a class of demigods or celestial beings.
28. ṚV X.90.9.
29. See pp. 56–61, 69–70. Among the numerous studies of the Puruṣa-Sūkta, see W. Norman Brown, "The Sources and Nature of *puruṣa* in the Puruṣasūkta (Rigveda 10.90)," *Journal of the American Oriental Society* 51, no. 2 (June 1931): 108–118; reprinted in his *India and Indology*, pp. 5–10; Paul Mus, "Du nouveau sur Ṛgveda 10.90? Sociologie d'une grammaire," in *Indological Studies in Honor of W. Norman Brown*, ed. Ernest Bender, American Oriental Series, vol. 47 (New Haven: American Oriental Society, 1962), pp. 165–185; idem, "Où finit Puruṣa?" in *Mélanges d'Indianisme à la mémoire de Louis Renou*, Publications de l'Institut de Civilisation Indienne, no. 28 (Paris: E. de Boccard, 1968), pp. 539–563; Thomas J. Hopkins, *The Hindu Religious Tradition*, The Religious Life of Man Series (Belmont, Calif.: Wadsworth, 1971), pp. 22–25.
30. ṚV X.130.4–5, 2.
31. See, for example, TS V.1.8.3–4.
32. See, for example, TS I.6.9.1; TS III.3.7.1; TS VI.1.2.4.
33. TS V.1.8.3; TS VII.2.5.1; TS III.3.5.2; TS VI.6.10.1; TS VII.2.4.1; TS VII.3.8.1.
34. See, for example, TS VII.1.1.2,4; TS III.5.7.3; TS VII.2.5.1; cf. TS I.7.4.1; TS VII.2.4.1; TS VII.3.8.1. Prajāpati is also described as distributing the sacrifices to the gods. See TS I.7.3.2; TS VI.6.11.1.
35. Cf. JB I.68–69; PB VI.1.6–11.
36. For parallels in Vedic texts, see JB I.68–69; PB VI.1.6–11, mentioned on p. 47. JB I.68–69 gives the same *stomas*, meters, and *sāmans*, with the exception of two cases, in which the *vāmadevya sāman* is substituted for the *vairūpa* and the *yajñāyajñīya sāman* for the *vairāja*. PB VI.1.6–11 also gives the same *stomas* and meters, but it does not

include the *sāmans* in its account. The Purāṇas give a standardized account of certain *stomas*, meters, and *sāmans* emerging from the four mouths of Brahmā that replicates the Taittirīya Saṃhitā's enumeration. See VP I.5.52–55, cited on pp. 105–106. Cf. Mārk. 48.31–34; KP I.7.54–57; LP I.70.243–246; ŚP Vāyavīya. I.12.58–62.

37. See pp. 60–61.
38. TS VII.3.1.4.
39. See, for example, AV IV.1; AV X.2.25; AV X.7.32–34,36; AV X.8.1; cf. X.8.37–38. For discussions of the term *brahman*, see Paul Thieme, "Bráhman," *Zeitschrift der Deutschen Morgenländischen Gesellschaft* 102 [n.s., 27] (1952): 91–129; J. Gonda, *Notes on Brahman* (Utrecht: J. L. Beyers, 1950). On specifically Vedic usages of the term, see also Louis Renou and Liliane Silburn, "Sur la notion de *bráhman*," *Journal Asiatique* 237 (1949): 7–46.
40. AV X.7.7–8.
41. AV X.7.32–34,36; cf. X.7.17. See also the following hymn, AV X.8, which also implies an identity between Brahman and Skambha as the all-pervading reality of the universe. See especially X.8.1–2,37–38,43–44.
42. AV X.7.19. Cf. AV X.7.11, in which the term *brahman* is once again used in a more limited sense to refer to one of the phenomena (that is, the Vedic *mantras*) contained within Skambha. As we shall see, in later Vedic and post-Vedic cosmogonies the mouth is commonly associated with the Vedas as the organ of speech through which the creator utters forth the Vedic *mantras* at the beginning of creation.
43. For discussions of the role of Vāc in the Ṛg-Veda, see W. Norman Brown, "The Creative Role of the Goddess Vāc in the Rig Veda," in *Pratidānam: Indian, Iranian and Indo-European Studies Presented to Franciscus Bernardus Jacobus Kuiper on His Sixtieth Birthday*, eds. J. C. Heesterman, G. H. Schokker, and V. I. Subramoniam, Janua linguarum, Series maior, 34 (The Hague: Mouton, 1968), pp. 393–397; reprinted in his *India and Indology*, pp. 75–78; Frits Staal, "Ṛgveda 10.71 on the Origin of Language," in *Revelation in Indian Thought: A Festschrift in Honour of Professor T. R. V. Murti*, eds. Harold Coward and Krishna Sivaraman (Emeryville, Calif.: Dharma Publishing, 1977), pp. 3–14; Laurie L. Patton, "Hymn to Vāc: Myth or Philosophy?" in *Myth and Philosophy*, eds. Frank Reynolds and David Tracy, SUNY Series, Toward a Comparative Philosophy of Religions (Albany: State University of New York Press, 1990), pp. 183–213. See also Vidya Niwas Misra, "*Vāk* Legends in the *Brāhmaṇa* Literature," in *Proceedings of the Twenty-Sixth International Congress of Orientalists*, vol. 3, pt. 1 (Poona: Bhandarkar Oriental Research Institute, 1969), pp. 109–118; Carl Anders Scharbau, *Die Idee der Schöpfung in der vedischen Literatur. Eine religionsgeschichtliche Untersuchung über den frühindischen Theismus*, Veröffentlichungen des orientalischen Seminars

der Universität Tübingen, no. 5 (Stuttgart: W. Kohlhammer, 1932), pp. 123–131, 135–138; Bénard Essers, "Vāc: Het Woord als Godsgestalte en als Godgeleerdheid in de Veda, in het bijzonder in de Ṛgveda-Saṃhitā en in de Atharvaveda-Saṃhitā" (Th.D. diss., University of Groningen, Netherlands, 1952); André Padoux, "Early Speculations about the Significance and the Powers of the Word," chapter 1 of his *Vāc: The Concept of the Word in Selected Hindu Tantras,* trans. Jacques Gontier, SUNY Series in the Shaiva Traditions of Kashmir (Albany: State University of New York Press, 1990), pp. 1–29.

44. These four quarters of Vāc are later articulated in the language theories of the grammarians as four distinct levels of speech—*parā, paśyantī, madhyamā,* and *vaikharī.* The theories of the grammarian Bhartṛhari are of particular interest in this regard. For references see n. 398.
45. ṚV X.125.3,7,6,8.
46. ṚV X.125.3.
47. ṚV X.125.7.
48. ṚV X.125.5.
49. ṚV X.71.3.
50. ṚV X.71.4.
51. The mechanisms of Vedic cognition will be discussed in chapter 3.
52. The more esoteric, mystical aspects of the sacrificial ritual are explored particularly in the Āraṇyakas, "forest books" attached to the Brāhmaṇas, which were classified retroactively as the *upāsanā-kāṇḍa,* the portion of the Vedas pertaining to meditation (*upāsanā*). While this section will focus primarily on the Brāhmaṇas, occasional reference will also be made to Āraṇyakas such as the Jaiminīya Upaniṣad Brāhmaṇa that expand upon the speculations of the Brāhmaṇas.
53. For brief discussions of the problems involved in establishing a chronology of the Brāhmaṇas, see Jan Gonda, *Vedic Literature (Saṃhitās and Brāhmaṇas),* A History of Indian Literature, vol. 1, pt. 1 (Wiesbaden: Otto Harrassowitz, 1975), pp. 357–360; H. W. Bodewitz, trans., *The Jyotiṣṭoma Ritual: Jaiminīya Brāhmaṇa I, 66–364,* Orientalia Rheno-Traiectina, vol. 34 (Leiden: E. J. Brill, 1990), pp. 19–21.
54. See, for example, KB XXIII.4; TB II.2.5.3; ŚB VI.1.1.5; ŚB VI.1.1.8; ŚB VI.1.3.1; ŚB VI.2.2.9; ŚB VII.4.1.15; ŚB XI.1.6.2; JB II.47; JUB I.49.3.
55. Regarding the immanent nature of Prajāpati, Gonda remarks: "In the case of the Vedic Prajāpati creation is a process of emission and exteriorization of some being or object that formed part of, or was hidden in, the creator himself, yet does not become completely independent of him, because Prajāpati, being the Totality (*sarvam*), embraces his creatures. . . . The creator god is 'identical' with, that is immanent, inherent in, his creation. . . ." J. Gonda, "Vedic Gods and the Sacrifice," *Numen* 30, no. 1 (July 1983): 18. The all-pervading nature of Prajāpati

as the unitary principle of the cosmos is expressed in references to Prajāpati as "all" (*sarvam*) or "this all" (*idam sarvam*). See, for example, KB VI.15; KB XXV.12; ŚB I.3.5.10; ŚB IV.5.7.2; ŚB V.1.1.4; ŚB V.1.1.6; ŚB V.1.1.8–9; ŚB V.1.3.11; ŚB XIII.6.1.6; JUB I.46.2. See J. Gonda, "Reflections on *Sarva-* in Vedic Texts," *Indian Linguistics* 16 (Nov. 1955): 53–71; idem, "All, Universe and Totality in the Śatapatha-Brāhmaṇa," *Journal of the Oriental Institute* (Baroda) 32, nos. 1–2 (Sept.–Dec. 1982): 1–17.

56. See, for example, ŚB IV.6.1.4, which describes Prajāpati as the fourth over and above the three worlds of heaven, midregions, and earth. Cf. ṚV X.90.3–4, which maintains that one-quarter of Puruṣa encompasses all beings, while the other three-quarters extend beyond and are immortal.
57. ŚB VI.8.1.4; ŚB XIII.2.4.1.
58. See, for example, ŚB IV.5.7.2; ŚB X.1.3.2; ŚB X.1.4.1.
59. ŚB VI.5.3.7; ŚB VII.2.4.30; ŚB XIV.1.2.18; ŚB I.1.1.13; ŚB I.6.1.20; ŚB VI.4.1.6; ŚB XII.4.2.1; ŚB XIV.2.2.21; ŚB XIV.3.2.15; KB XXIII.2; KB XXIII.6; KB XXIX.7; PB VII.8.3; PB XVIII.6.8.
60. ŚB VI.5.3.7; ŚB VII.2.4.30; ŚB XIV.1.2.18; AB II.17; KB XI.7; JUB I.46.2.
61. See, for example, ŚB VII.3.1.42; ŚB XIII.6.2.8; cf. KB VIII.3. However, other passages clearly distinguish Prajāpati and Brahman. See, for example, TB II.8.8.10; TB III.10.11.7.
62. See, for example, AB IV.22; ŚB VII.4.2.5; ŚB VIII.2.1.10; ŚB VIII.2.3.13; ŚB IX.4.1.12.
63. See, for example, ŚB VI.2.2.5.
64. See, for example, AB II.33; ŚB II.2.4.1; ŚB II.5.1.1; ŚB VI.1.3.1; ŚB VII.5.2.6; ŚB XI.5.8.1; cf. PB XX.14.2; JB I.68; JB II.244.
65. For discussions of the figure of Prajāpati, see J. Gonda, *Prajāpati's Rise to Higher Rank* (Leiden: E. J. Brill, 1986); idem, *Prajāpati and the Year* (Amsterdam: North-Holland Publishing, 1984); idem, "In the Beginning," *Annals of the Bhandarkar Oriental Research Institute* 63 (1982): 43–62; idem, "The Creator and His Spirit (Manas and Prajāpati)," *Wiener Zeitschrift für die Kunde Südasiens* 27 (1983): 5–42; idem, "The Popular Prajāpati," *History of Religions* 22, no. 2 (Nov. 1982): 129–149; idem, "Prajāpati and *prāyaścitta*," *Journal of the Royal Asiatic Society*, no. 1 (1983): 32–54; J. R. Joshi, "Prajāpati in Vedic Mythology and Ritual," *Annals of the Bhandarkar Oriental Research Institute* 53, pts. 1–4 (1972): 101–125; Sukumari Bhattacharji, "Rise of Prajāpati in the Brāhmaṇas," *Annals of the Bhandarkar Oriental Research Institute* 64 (1983): 205–213; Santi Banerjee, "Prajāpati in the Brāhmaṇas," *Vishveshvaranand Indological Journal* 19, pts. 1–2 (June–Dec. 1981): 14–19; R. T. Vyas, "The Concept of Prajāpati in Vedic Literature," *Bhāratīya Vidyā* 38, nos. 1–4

(1978): 95–101; A. W. Macdonald, "À propos de Prajāpati," *Journal Asiatique* 240, no. 3 (1952): 323–338.

66. AB V.32; AB VII.19; KB VI.10; KB VI.15; KB XXVIII.1; TB III.2.3.1; ŚB XI.1.8.3; ŚB XIII.1.1.4; PB VIII.6.3; JB I.83; JB I.321; JB I.358; JB III.155; JB III.274.
67. AB IV.23; AB IV.25; AB V.32; KB V.3; KB XII.8; ŚB II.2.4.4–7; ŚB II.3.1.22; ŚB II.4.4.1; ŚB III.9.1.4; ŚB VI.3.1.18; ŚB VI.6.3.1; PB IV.1.4; PB VI.1.1; PB VI.3.9.
68. AB II.17; AB VI.19; KB XIII.1; KB XXVI.3; TB III.2.3.1; TB III.7.2.1; ŚB IV.2.4.16; ŚB IV.5.5.l; ŚB IV.5.6.1; ŚB IV.5.7.1; ŚB V.1.4.1; ŚB I.1.1.13; ŚB I.2.5.12; ŚB I.7.4.4; ŚB II.2.2.4; ŚB III.2.2.4; ŚB V.2.1.2; ŚB V.2.1.4; ŚB V.4.5.20–21; ŚB VI.4.1.6; ŚB XI.1.1.1; ŚB XI.1.8.3; ŚB XIV.1.2.18; ŚB XIV.2.2.21; ŚB XIV.3.2.15; PB VII.2.1; PB XIII.11.18; JB I.135.
69. ŚB XI.1.8.3.
70. Smith, *Reflections on Resemblance, Ritual, and Religion*, pp. 50–81, esp. 67.
71. PB XXV.6.2; PB XXV.17.2.
72. See, for example, AB IV.23; KB VI.15; KB V.3; ŚB II.5.1.17; ŚB II.5.2.1; ŚB II.5.2.7; ŚB II.6.3.4; PB VI.1.1–2; PB VIII.5.6; PB IV.1.4; PB XXII.9.2; JB I.67.
73. This formula is frequently repeated in the Śatapatha Brāhmaṇa. See, for example, ŚB IV.2.4.16; ŚB IV.5.5.1; ŚB IV.5.6.1; ŚB IV.5.7.1. The theurgic power ascribed to Vedic sacrifice and recitation in maintaining the cosmos will be discussed in chapter 5.
74. Smith, *Reflections on Resemblance, Ritual, and Religion*, p. 78.
75. Ibid., p. 73.
76. Ibid., p. 74.
77. The role of recitation of the Vedas in sacrificial rituals will be discussed in chapter 5.
78. See, for example, TB III.10.11.3–6. Cf. TS VII.3.1.4, cited on p. 41.
79. For the identification of the Veda with *brahman*, see in particular ŚB VI.1.1.8,10, which will be discussed below. See also JUB IV.25.3; ŚB X.2.4.6.
80. JUB I.46.1.
81. See, for example, ŚB X.4.2.26; ŚB X.3.1.1; ŚB VI.2.1.30; AB II.18; PB XIII.11.18; TB III.3.9.11; cf. ŚB XII.1.4.1–3; ŚB XII.6.1.1; KB VI.15. For the identification of the threefold Veda with Prajāpati's counterpart, the sacrifice, see ŚB I.1.4.3; ŚB V.5.5.10; ŚB III.1.1.12; JB I.358.
82. TB III.3.2.1; TB III.3.8.9.
83. See, for example, AB V.32; KB VI.10; TB II.3.10.1; ŚB VI.1.1.8–10; ŚB X.6.5.5 [= BĀU I.2.5]; ŚB XI.5.8.1–3; JB I.68–69; JB I.357; PB VII.8.8–13; Ṣaḍv. B. I.5.7; JUB III.15.4–7; JUB I.23.1–5.
84. JB I.68–69; cf. PB VI.1.6–11. See TS VII.1.1.4–6, cited on pp. 39–40, with n. 36.

85. Relevant passages will be discussed below.
86. See, for example, ŚB II.1.4.10; AB II.15; AB II.17; JB I.82; JB I.102; JB I.115; JB I.140; JB I.178; JUB II.9.6; JUB II.13.2; JUB III.39.2.
87. ŚB VI.5.3.4; ŚB X.5.1.2,5; cf. AB V.33; PB X.4.6,9.
88. See, for example, TB II.8.8.5. Cf. PB VII.8.8–13, in which Prajāpati creates the *pṛṣṭha sāmans* out of the womb (*yoni*) of the *gāyatrī* meter. In post-Vedic texts Gāyatrī is hypostatized as a feminine principle who is identified with Vāc and is the consort of the creator. Like Vāc, Gāyatrī is called in post-Vedic texts the "Mother of the Vedas." See pp. 90, 91.
89. See, for example, ŚB V.5.5.12; ŚB IV.6.7.1–3; cf. ŚB IV.5.8.4.
90. TB II.8.8.5.
91. See, for example, TB III.10.11.4.
92. See, for example, ŚB X.4.2.21.
93. ŚB XII.3.4.11.
94. For discussions of the relationship between Prajāpati and *manas*, see Gonda, "The Creator and His Spirit (Manas and Prajāpati)"; Vyas, "The Concept of Prajāpati in Vedic Literature."
95. See, for example, KB XXVI.3; TB II.2.6.2; TB III.7.1.2; JB I.68; JB II.174; JB II.195; JUB I.33.2.
96. See, for example, JB I.314.
97. See, for example, ŚB VI.1.2.6–9; ŚB X.6.5.4; cf. ŚB VI.3.1.12.
98. ŚB I.4.4.1–7. See also JUB IV.27.15–16, where mind and speech are referred to as a "couple" (*mithuna*).
99. See, for example, ŚB VII.5.1.31; ŚB XI.2.4.9; ŚB XI.2.6.3. For the identification of Sarasvatī with Vāc, see also AB II.24; AB III.1; AB III.37; AB VI.7; KB V.2; KB X.6; KB XII.8; KB XIV.4; ŚB II.5.4.6; ŚB III.1.4.9; ŚB III.9.1.9; ŚB V.2.2.13–14; ŚB V.3.4.25; ŚB V.3.5.8; ŚB V.4.5.7; ŚB XIII.1.8.5; ŚB XIV.2.1.12; ŚB XIV.2.1.15; PB VI.7.7; PB XVI.5.16; JB I.82.
100. See, for example, ŚB I.4.5.9,11; ŚB III.2.4.11; ŚB XII.9.1.13; AB II.5; JB I.19; JB I.320; JUB I.58.3–4; JUB I.40.5.
101. See, for example, ŚB I.4.5.10; ŚB IV.6.7.5; ŚB XII.9.1.13; JUB I.58.3–4; JUB I.40.5.
102. ŚB I.4.4.5–7; cf. KB XXVI.3; JUB I.47.5. While in relationship to the mind the expressed dimension of speech is emphasized, in other passages, as will be discussed below, speech is also represented as having an unexpressed dimension.
103. See, for example, ŚB I.4.5.8–11; ŚB III.2.4.11; AB II.5; JB I.19; JB I.128; JB I.320; JB I.323; JB I.329; JUB I.59.14.
104. See, for example, ŚB III.1.3.22; ŚB V.1.1.16.
105. See, for example, PB XX.14.2; JB II.244; ŚB VI.1.1.8–10; ŚB VI.1.2.6–9; ŚB VII.5.2.21; ŚB X.6.5.4–5 [= BĀU I.2.4–5]. Cf. ŚB X.5.3.1–4, which describes the mind, which was neither existent (*sat*) nor nonexistent

(*asat*), as existing alone in the beginning and desiring to become manifest, after which it produced speech.

106. PB VII.6.1–3.
107. See, for example, PB VII.6.17; JB I.128; JB I.329; AB IV.28.
108. See, for example, JB I.128; JB I.133.
109. See, for example, JB I.326; JUB I.53–54; JUB I.56–57; AB III.23; ŚB VIII.1.3.5. The *bṛhat* and *sāman* are further equated with yonder world (heaven) and the *rathantara* and *ṛc* with this world (earth). For the equation of the *bṛhat* with yonder world and the *rathantara* with this world, see AB VIII.2; PB VII.6.17; PB VII.10.6; JB I.128; JB I.146; JB I.291; JB I.293; JB I.298. The correspondences between the *sāman* and heaven and the *ṛc* and earth, as well as correlations with various human faculties, will be discussed below.
110. See, for example, JB I.102; JB I.26; Ṣaḍv. B. II.1.26, which distinguish between the expressed (*nirukta*) and unexpressed (*anirukta*) aspects of speech. See also ŚB IV.1.3.16–17, which, citing ṚV I.164.45, refers to the four quarters of Vāc, three of which are hidden while the fourth is expressed through the speech of human beings. Cf. JUB I.7.3–5.
111. For the association of Vāc with the waters, see in particular PB XX.14.2; JB II.244; ŚB VI.1.1.9, discussed below. Cf. ŚB VI.3.1.9; PB VII.7.9; PB VI.4.7; JB I.70.
112. This two-stage process of creation conforms in its essential features to the two stages delineated by Kuiper in his reconstruction of the Vedic cosmogonic myth. See pp. 35–36.
113. BĀU I.2.4–5.
114. The creator is designated in this passage as death, which is identified with Prajāpati elsewhere in the Śatapatha Brāhmaṇa. See, for example, ŚB X.4.3.1–3.
115. AB I.1; AB I.13; AB II.17; AB IV.22; AB IV.25; AB VI.19; KB VI.15; ŚB I.2.5.12; ŚB I.6.3.35; ŚB II.2.2.4; ŚB II.3.3.18; ŚB III.2.2.4; ŚB V.1.3.2; ŚB V.2.1.2; ŚB V.2.1.4; ŚB V.4.5.20–21; ŚB VI.1.2.18; ŚB VI.2.2.12; ŚB VII.4.2.31; ŚB VIII.4.3.20; ŚB X.4.2.1–2; ŚB X.4.3.3; ŚB XI.1.1.1; ŚB XI.1.6.13; PB XVI.4.12–13; JB I.135; JB I.167. For an analysis of the significance of the identification of Prajāpati with the year, see Gonda, *Prajāpati and the Year.*
116. Cf. ŚB II.1.4.11–13.
117. PB XX.14.2. This passage appears almost verbatim in JB II.244.
118. PB XX.14.3.
119. PB XX.14.5; cf. JB II.244.
120. It is not entirely clear how the verb, root *mṛś* + *abhi*, "to touch, come in contact with," is to be understood in this context.
121. Fragments of this creation account are repeated in ŚB VI.3.1.9–10, which mentions how after the waters (*ap*) went forth from Vāc, Prajāpati entered the waters with the threefold Veda (*trayī vidyā*).
122. See pp. 41–42.

123. However, see the last part of verse 10, which seems to indicate that *brahman* was created even before (*pūrva*) Prajāpati. The meaning of the verse is ambiguous.
124. See, however, PB XX.14.2 and JB II.244, discussed above, in which Prajāpati brings forth the three worlds through the sounds *a*, *ka*, and *ho*.
125. ŚB II.1.4.11–13. See also JUB I.1.3–5; Ṣaḍv. B. I.5.7. JB I.101 mentions only the creation of the earth from the utterance *bhūḥ*.
126. See, for example, AB II.16; PB VII.5.1; JB I.116; JB I.117; JB I.128; JB I.148; JB I.160.
127. See, for example, AB IV.23; KB V.3; KB XII.8; PB IV.1.4; PB VI.1.1; PB VI.3.9; PB XVIII.7.1.
128. See, for example, AB V.32; KB VI.10.
129. See, for example, AB II.15; AB II.16; AB II.33.
130. *Nivid* is the technical term used to designate eleven prose formularies, derived from the period of the Ṛg-Veda, that are composed of a series of short sentences addressed to a particular deity or group of deities. A *nivid* generally begins with an invitation to the deity to partake of the Soma libation, followed by various epithets and short invocations and concluding with a prayer for help.
131. For references identifying or relating Prajāpati and the *udgātṛ* priest, see PB VI.4.1; PB VI.5.18; PB VII.10.16; JB I.70; JB I.85; JB I.88; JB I.259; cf. ŚB IV.3.2.3.
132. PB VI.9.15; cf. JB I.94. The verse cited from the Ṛg-Veda (IX.62.1) reads:

    ete asṛgram indavas tiraḥ pavitram āśavaḥ |
    viśvāny abhi saubhagā ||

    These swift Soma drops have been poured out through
    the filter for the sake of all blessings.

    As will be discussed below, Śaṃkara cites this passage from the Pañcaviṃśa Brāhmaṇa when discussing how the world is created from the word. See p. 126.
133. Cf. JB I.117.
134. The *bahiṣpavamāna stotra* is the first *stotra* chanted at the morning pressing of the *agniṣṭoma* sacrifice. The *stotra* is composed of nine verses from the Ṛg-Veda: ṚV IX.11.1–3; ṚV IX.64.28–30; and ṚV IX.66.10–12. JB I.104 cites sections of ṚV IX.66.10–11 as the words with which Prajāpati creates beings. Cf. JB I.99, cited in chapter 5, p. 343.
135. See, for example, PB VII.10.13,15; PB VII.5.1–2; PB XIII.5.13; JB I.148; JB I.160; JB I.116; JB I.117–118; cf. PB XI.5.10.
136. See, for example, ŚB VIII.7.4.5.

137. The three *vyāhṛtis* are at times directly identified with the three Vedas. See, for example, JUB II.9.7; JUB III.18.4. However, they are more often described as their essences. See AB V.32; KB VI.10–11; ŚB XI.5.8.1–4; Ṣaḍv. B. I.5.7–10; JB I.357–358; JB I.363–364; JUB I.1.2–5; JUB I.23.6; JUB III.15.8–9.
138. See, for example, ŚB XI.1.6.3; ŚB II.1.4.11–13, discussed earlier. See also JUB I.1.3–5, cited below, and Ṣaḍv. B. I.5.7.
139. AB V.32; KB VI.10; ŚB XI.5.8.1–4; JB I.357; JUB I.1.1–7; JUB III.15.4–9; JUB I.23.1–8; cf. ŚB IV.6.7.1–2; ŚB XII.3.4.7–10; Ṣaḍv. B. I.5.7–10; Ṣaḍv. B. V.1.2; JB I.363–364.
140. JUB I.1.1–7; cf. Ṣaḍv. B. I.5.7.
141. ŚB XI.5.8.1–4. For parallel accounts, see AB V.32; KB VI.10; JB I.357; JUB III.15.4–9; JUB I.23.1–8. The account in JUB I.23.1–8 begins with Prajāpati pressing Vāc, the essence of which becomes the worlds, from which Agni, Vāyu, and Āditya are brought forth, and so on. The rest of the passage follows the standard sequence.
142. AB V.32. JUB I.23.1–8 similarly concludes with the syllable Om emerging as the essence of the three *vyāhṛtis*.
143. JB I.322; JB I.336; JUB I.18.10; JUB I.8.1–13; JUB III.19.2–7; JUB I.1.6; cf. KB VI.12. However, see JUB I.23.8–I.24.1–2, in which Prajāpati succeeds in pressing the syllable Om, and its essence (*rasa*) flows forth (root *kṣar*) and is not exhausted (root *kṣi*). Hence Om is called *akṣara* and *akṣaya*.
144. JB I.323; JUB I.10.11.
145. See pp. 106–109.
146. AB V.32–34; KB VI.10–12; JB I.357–358; ŚB XI.5.8.1–7; cf. Ṣaḍv. B. I.5.7–10; Ṣaḍv. B. V.1.2; JUB III.15–17.
147. See, for example, ŚB XII.3.4.7–10; cf. JB I.249. These correlations build upon those established earlier in the Puruṣa-Sūkta. See ṚV X.90.13.
148. See, for example, JB I.326; JUB I.53.2; JUB I.9.2; JUB III.34.1; JUB I.25.8–10; JUB I.57.7–8. The *sāman* and the *yajus* are thus associated with both mind and breath, which are intimately related in the speculations of the Brāhmaṇas. See, for example, ŚB VII.5.2.6, which describes the mind as the first of the *prāṇas* and identical with all the *prāṇas*.
149. ŚB X.4.2.21–22. Cf. JB I.332, in which the Vedic meters are identified with "all *stomas*, all animals, all gods, all worlds, all desires." With respect to the Vedic conception of the relationship between name and form (*rūpa*), see A. Coomaraswamy's definitions: "the forms, ideas, similitudes, or eternal reasons of things (*nāma*, 'name' or 'noumenon' = *forma*) and the things themselves in their accidental and contingent aspects (*rūpa*, 'phenomenon' = *figura*)." A. Coomaraswamy, "Vedic Exemplarism," *Harvard Journal of Asiatic Studies* 1, no. 1 (1936): 44. See also Maryla Falk's characterization of *nāma* as "the

inherent, unsensuous essence of the thing to which it belongs." Maryla Falk, *Nāma-Rūpa and Dharma-Rūpa: Origin and Aspects of an Ancient Indian Conception* (Calcutta: University of Calcutta, 1943), p. 16.

150. ŚB X.4.2.27.
151. ŚB IV.6.7.1–2; cf. Ṣaḍv. B. I.5.7–10; Ṣaḍv. B. V.1.2.
152. The Brāhmaṇas' representations of the brahmin priests as reproducing the cosmogonic activities of the creator will be discussed in chapter 5.
153. See, for example, ŚB II.1.4.11–12, discussed earlier.
154. Cf. TS VII.1.1.4–6, discussed on pp. 39–40.
155. For an analysis of the ways in which the *varṇas* are connected to the three Vedas and to the Vedic meters in the hierarchical taxonomy of the Brāhmaṇas, see Brian K. Smith, "Canonical Authority and Social Classification: Veda and *Varṇa* in Ancient Indian Texts," *History of Religions* 32, no. 2 (Nov. 1992): 103–125; idem, "The Veda and the Authority of Class: Reduplicating Structures of Veda and *Varṇa* in Ancient Indian Texts," in *Authority, Anxiety, and Canon*, ed. Patton, pp. 67–93. In discussing the relationship between the Vedic canon and the *varṇa* system, Smith observes:

> [T]he framework for the caste system is laid out in the Veda itself. Caste thus derives at least part of its endurance and persuasiveness from the fact that it has canonical legitimacy. Furthermore, both the Veda and the *varṇa* scheme are traced back to the dawn of time. Canon and a particular form of social classification are part of creation itself according to Vedic cosmogonies. Canon and class are not only primordial; they are also represented in the Veda as structurally reduplicative of a generalized cosmic pattern and are therefore supposedly part of the "natural order of things." Finally, because both Veda and *varṇa* are predominantly regarded as divisible into three components, canon and class are isomorphic. Thus, in addition to the legitimation the social structure receives by being part of the *content* of the Veda, the *formal authority* of the structure of the canon (which is also the structure of the universe as a whole) is lent to a vision of society also comprising three principal parts.

Smith, "Canonical Authority and Social Classification," p. 104. For an extended discussion of the role of taxonomies in legitimating the *varṇa* system, see Smith's *Classifying the Universe: The Ancient Indian Varṇa System and the Origins of Caste* (New York: Oxford University Press, 1994).

156. See, for example, ŚB II.2.2.6; ŚB IV.3.4.4; Ṣaḍv. B. I.1.29–30.
157. See, for example, ŚB II.2.2.6–7; ŚB IV.3.4.4–5.

158. See, for example, AB I.22; ŚB X.4.2.29–31; ŚB X.5.1.5; ŚB XI.2.6.13; cf. ŚB IV.3.4.5. For a discussion of the role of the Vedic sacrifice in constructing the self of the ritual participant, see Smith, *Reflections on Resemblance, Ritual, and Religion*, pp. 82–119.
159. AB I.22.
160. These dates encompass the principal Upaniṣads that were composed in the Vedic period, which ends ca. 200 B.C.E. The present analysis draws primarily from (1) the earliest prose Upaniṣads (ca. 800–500 B.C.E.), Aitareya (Ṛg-Veda), Kauṣītaki (Ṛg-Veda), Taittirīya (Black Yajur-Veda), Bṛhadāraṇyaka (White Yajur-Veda), Chāndogya (Sāma-Veda), Kena (half prose, half verse—Sāma-Veda); and (2) the later metrical Upaniṣads (ca. 500–200 B.C.E.), Kaṭha (Black Yajur-Veda), Śvetāśvatara (Black Yajur-Veda), Īśā (White Yajur-Veda), Muṇḍaka (Atharva-Veda), Praśna (half prose, half verse—Atharva-Veda). Occasional references are also given to two later Upaniṣads, which although deriving from the post-Vedic period (ca. 200 B.C.E.–200 C.E.), are generally classified as Vedic Upaniṣads: Maitri (Black Yajur-Veda) and Māṇḍūkya (Atharva-Veda).
161. The Āraṇyakas represent an intermediary position between the Brāhmaṇas and Upaniṣads in that they emphasize the more subtle, esoteric aspects of the sacrificial rituals.
162. The challenge posed by the early Buddhists, who rejected the authority of the brahmin priests and of the Veda, will be discussed in the conclusion.
163. See, for example, BĀU I.4.10–11; Maitri VI.17; BĀU I.4.1; BĀU I.4.17; AU I.1.1; CU VI.2.1; CU III.19.1; TU II.7.
164. BĀU II.3.1; cf. Maitri VI.3. Each of the Upaniṣads depicts Brahman-Ātman from its own particular perspective, in which different aspects of Brahman-Ātman's nature are emphasized. For example, the Bṛhadāraṇyaka Upaniṣad, while acknowledging the two aspects of Brahman, formed and formless, tends to emphasize the formless, transcendent aspect of Brahman-Ātman, which is *neti, neti* ("not this, not that"), completely devoid of qualities, and while dwelling in all things is at the same time other than all things. See BĀU III.6–8; BĀU III.9.26. The Chāndogya Upaniṣad, on the other hand, emphasizes the immanence of Brahman-Ātman, providing a series of definitions in which Brahman-Ātman is progressively identified with various psychical faculties (speech, mind, thought, and so on) as well as with various objective phenomena (water, heat, ether, and so on) and is ultimately proclaimed to be "this all" (*idam sarvam*). See CU VII.1–26.
165. In BĀU I.4.1, for example, Ātman is said to exist alone in the beginning in the form of a person (Puruṣa). In AU I.1–3, in contrast, Ātman and Puruṣa are distinguished: Ātman draws forth a person (Puruṣa) from the waters and shapes him.
166. See, for example, BĀU II.3.3,5; MU II.1.2; Praśna VI.5.

167. BĀU I.4.7; BĀU II.5.1–15,18; Kaṭha IV.12–13; Kaṭha VI.17; MU II.1.4,9–10; ŚU III.9,11,13–16,20–21; Maitri II.5; cf. Kaṭha VI.8–9; Praśna V.5.
168. See, for example, BĀU I.4.1–7.
169. Maitri II.5–6; cf. BĀU I.5.14–15; KU IV.16.
170. See, for example, Maitri VI.6. Cf. AU V.3; Maitri VI.8; Maitri VII.7, in which Ātman is identified with Prajāpati as well as with other gods.
171. The association of Prajāpati with time represents an extension of his identification with the year in the Brāhmaṇas. See Maitri VI.15; BĀU I.5.14–15; Praśna I.9,12–13.
172. BĀU V.5.1.
173. ŚU VI.18.
174. Maitri V.1–2; Maitri VI.5.
175. MU I.1.1–2.
176. CU III.11.4; CU VIII.15.
177. MU I.1.4–5.
178. KU I.7.
179. ŚU V.6.
180. TU I.5. This passage will be discussed on p. 70.
181. TU I.10. My translation of this obscure passage generally follows that of Robert Ernst Hume, trans., *The Thirteen Principal Upanishads*, 2d ed., rev. (Oxford: Oxford University Press, 1931), p. 281.
182. BĀU II.4.12.
183. BĀU II.4.10; BĀU IV.5.11; Maitri VI.32.
184. KU I.5. Cf. the description of the Vrātya's seat in AV XV.3.3–9 and of Indra's throne in AB VIII.12; cf. AB VIII.17.
185. MU II.1.4,6.
186. MU II.1.4,9,10.
187. CU I.7.5.
188. Praśna VI.1–6.
189. MU II.1.4.
190. BĀU II.4.11; cf. BĀU I.3.20–22; BĀU I.6.1.
191. BĀU IV.1.2; CU VII.2.1–2.
192. Maitri VI.6.
193. BĀU I.2.4–5. This passage, which also forms part of the Śatapatha Brāhmaṇa (X.6.5.4–5), was discussed earlier on p. 50.
194. BĀU III.8.9.
195. Cf. BĀU I.4.7, in which the world is said to become differentiated by name and form.
196. See, for example, CU IV.17.1–3; CU II.23.2–3; CU I.3.7; CU III.15.5–7; BĀU I.5.4–5; Maitri VI.5. TU I.5 provides one of the rare variants of this set of correspondences, in which the *sāmans*, rather than the *yajus*es, are associated with the utterance *bhuvaḥ*, the midregions, and Vāyu. The correlations with the faculties of speech, breath, and the eye are not mentioned in these Upaniṣadic passages.

197. See, for example, CU IV.17.1–3; CU II.23.2–3; cf. BĀU I.5.1–13.
198. Maitri VI.5.
199. TU I.5. This "3 + 1" structure is evident elsewhere in the Upaniṣads. See, for example, the Māṇḍūkya Upaniṣad's discussion of the three states of consciousness—waking, dreaming, and deep sleep—to which a fourth (*caturtha*), transcendent state of consciousness is added, which is designated in the Bṛhadāraṇyaka Upaniṣad (V.14.3–4,6–7) as *turīya* and in the Maitri Upaniṣad (VI.19; VII.11) as *turya*. One of the most well known examples of this "3 + 1" structure is the addition of *mokṣa* to the *trivarga*—*kāma*, *artha*, and *dharma*—as the fourth end of human life (*puruṣārtha*). See Troy Organ, "Three into Four in Hinduism," *Ohio Journal of Religious Studies* 1, no. 2 (July 1973): 7–13.
200. In CU II.23.2–3, which is a variant of AB V.32, discussed earlier on p. 57, Om is represented as the essence of the three *vyāhṛtis*, which in turn represent the essences of the three Vedas. CU I.1.1–2 provides a different interpretation, in which Om, identified with the *udgītha*, constitutes the essence of the *sāman*, which in turn constitutes the essence of the *ṛc*. See also Praśna V.2–7.
201. TU I.8; Kaṭha II.16; Praśna V.2; Maitri VI.5; Maitri VI.22–23. Cf. Māṇḍ. 12, in which Om is identified with Ātman.
202. Maitri VI.22–23.
203. Nirmal Kumar Bose, "Caste in India," *Man in India* 31, nos. 3–4 (July–Dec. 1951): 113.
204. Gerald James Larson and Ram Shankar Bhattacharya, eds., *Sāṃkhya: A Dualist Tradition in Indian Philosophy*, Encyclopedia of Indian Philosophies, vol. 4 (Princeton: Princeton University Press, 1987), p. 121.
205. Ibid., p. 5. See pp. 4–9 for Larson's discussion of the Proto-Sāṃkhya phase in the development of the term *sāṃkhya*.
206. For an extended analysis of the figure of Brahmā, and of his Vedic antecedents in the creator Prajāpati as well as in the divine priest Bṛhaspati, see Greg Bailey, *The Mythology of Brahmā* (Delhi: Oxford University Press, 1983), esp. pp. 63–82.
207. The enumeration of the twenty-five *tattvas* given here, together with the translation of the Sanskrit terms, follows Larson, *Sāṃkhya*, p. 49.
208. See pp. 48, 67.
209. MS II.6–7,10–13.
210. MS II.7.
211. MS I.102; I.33–35.
212. MS XI.244; I.58; cf. IX.46.
213. MS XII.95–96.
214. The emergence of the "*mahābhūtas* and the rest" was previously mentioned in MS I.6, cited above. See also I.14–15,18,75–78.
215. MS I.22,24,34–41.
216. MS I.31; cf. I.87–105,109.

217. MS I.50–57,64–74,79–80. Although the Manu-Smṛti delineates the post-Vedic understanding of *kalpas, manvantaras,* and *yugas,* it does not distinguish between cycles of primary creation (*sarga*) and secondary creation (*pratisarga*).
218. See pp. 49–53.
219. See, for example, MS II.76–77; V.28.
220. MS I.23.
221. The *gāyatrī mantra,* or *sāvitrī,* will be discussed on pp. 91–93, 106–108.
222. MS II.76–77,81.
223. MS I.23; XII.94,99.
224. MS XII.94.
225. MS XII.94–96.
226. MS I.28–30.
227. MS I.21.
228. MS XII.97–99. The verb *prasidhyati* in v. 97 means "to result from" when used with the ablative. The verb in v. 98 is *prasūyante,* "to be born, produced," although the commentators construe the verb as *prasidhyanti.* The last part of v. 98, *prasūtir guṇa-karmataḥ,* has a number of variant readings and its meaning has been variously interpreted.
229. The Rāmāyaṇa is not included in the discussion, since it does not evidence the same concern for cosmogonic speculation.
230. No extant recension of the text has this number of verses.
231. V. S. Sukthankar, "Epic Studies VI: The Bhṛgus and the Bhārata. A Text-Historical Study," *Annals of the Bhandarkar Oriental Research Institute* 18, pt. 1 (1936): 68.
232. For discussions of issues involved in the study and interpretation of the Mahābhārata, see J. A. B. van Buitenen, trans. and ed., *The Mahābhārata,* vol. 1 (Chicago: University of Chicago Press, 1973), pp. xiii–xxxv; Barend A. van Nooten, *The Mahābhārata,* Twayne's World Authors Series, 131 (New York: Twayne Publishers, 1971); Alf Hiltebeitel, *The Ritual of Battle: Krishna in the Mahābhārata,* Symbol, Myth, and Ritual Series (Ithaca: Cornell University Press, 1976), pp. 27–76; Ruth Cecily Katz, *Arjuna in the Mahabharata: Where Krishna Is, There Is Victory,* Studies in Comparative Religion (Columbia, S.C.: University of South Carolina Press, 1989), pp. 1–26. For a survey of the mythology of the Mahābhārata, see E. Washburn Hopkins, *Epic Mythology,* Grundiss der indo-arischen Philologie und Altertumskunde, vol. 3, no. 1B (1915; reprint, Delhi: Motilal Banarsidass, 1974).
233. Although the influence of these three streams is evident throughout the eighteen books of the Mahābhārata, its most fully articulated expression is found in the two didactic books, Śānti-Parvan (Book XII) and Anuśāsana-Parvan (Book XIII), and in the Bhagavad-Gītā

(VI.23–40). The synthetic "philosophy" of the Bhagavad-Gītā gives a place to each of these streams as alternative paths to liberation—*karma-yoga*, the path of action; *jñāna-yoga*, the path of knowledge; and *bhakti-yoga*, the path of devotion—although in the final analysis devotion is proclaimed to be the supreme yoga in which all paths converge.

234. Mbh. I.57.74; XII.327.18. See James L. Fitzgerald, "India's Fifth Veda: The *Mahābhārata*'s Presentation of Itself," *Journal of South Asian Literature* 20, no. 1 (Winter–Spring 1985): 125–140.
235. Mbh. I.1.205; I.56.17; XVIII.5.52 with n. 57*.
236. See Mbh. XII.334.9; XII.337, esp. 4–5,37–38,55.
237. See, for example, Mbh. XII.337.3,4; XV.36.3; I.1.56; I.99.13; XII.327.15.
238. See, for example, Mbh. I.2.95; cf. III.46.2. See also XII.337.52, in which Vyāsa is said to be superior to the seven *ṛṣis*.
239. Mbh. I.2.95–96; cf. I.1.47–48. For additional references to Vyāsa as a seer, see, for example, I.1.53,60,62; I.2.215; I.54.1,5; I.99.14; VI.2.1; XII.1.3–4; cf. I.2.168,211,219,231. The epic's portrayal of Vyāsa's role as a *ṛṣi* will be discussed further in chapter 3.
240. Mbh. XII.337.4–5.
241. Mbh. I.54.3–5; VI.2.1.
242. See, for example, Mbh. XII.327.15.
243. Mbh. I.1.52; I.54.5; I.99.14; I.57.72–75; XII.314.23–24; XII.327.15–18; XII.337.39–44,11–15. Vyāsa's role in dividing the Veda will be discussed in chapter 3. For an analysis of how the Mahābhārata's depiction of Vyāsa serves to legitimate its claim to be the fifth Veda, see Bruce M. Sullivan, *Kṛṣṇa Dvaipāyana Vyāsa and the Mahābhārata: A New Interpretation* (Leiden: E. J. Brill, 1990), esp. pp. 29–31, 81–101, 112–117. Sullivan argues that Vyāsa represents the earthly counterpart of the creator Brahmā in the Mahābhārata in that both figures represent the brahmanical ideals of *pravṛtti* and *dharma* and assume a pivotal role in disseminating the Vedas.
244. Mbh. I.1.191.
245. Mbh. I.56.15; cf. I.1.19.
246. See, for example, Mbh. XII.314.45, in which Vyāsa instructs his disciples to teach the members of all four *varṇas*.
247. The modes of preservation and transmission of the Saṃhitās will be discussed in chapter 5.
248. This passage is generally regarded as late and is not included in the constituted text of the critical edition because it occurs in a relatively small portion of the manuscript tradition. It is given in the critical edition in Mbh. I, App. I, no. 1. For a translation of the passage, see Sullivan, *Kṛṣṇa Dvaipāyana Vyāsa and the Mahābhārata*, pp. 118–119.
249. Sullivan, *Kṛṣṇa Dvaipāyana Vyāsa and the Mahābhārata*, p. 12.

250. C. Mackenzie Brown, "Purāṇa as Scripture: From Sound to Image of the Holy Word in the Hindu Tradition," *History of Religions* 26, no. 1 (Aug. 1986): 76.
251. Mbh. I.2.235.
252. Mbh. I.1.204. This *śloka* and the *śloka* cited immediately above (I.2.235) appear together in Vāyu 1.200–201, cited on p. 96, with the Purāṇa being substituted for the epic in the first *śloka*.
253. Mbh. I.1.208–209.
254. Among its accounts of creation the Harivaṃśa contains a passage, I.23–27, that closely resembles the account in the Manu-Smṛti, I.8–13.
255. In this scenario Viṣṇu is described as progressively unfolding his four-fold form: from Vāsudeva (Paramātman, the supreme Self) to Saṃkarṣaṇa (*jīvātman,* the embodied Self) to Pradyumna (*manas,* mind) to Aniruddha (*ahaṃkāra,* ego).
256. The twenty-three evolutes of Prakṛti are intellect, ego, mind, five sense capacities, five action capacities, five objects of the senses (in classical Sāṃkhya termed "subtle elements"), and five gross elements. For the Sanskrit designations of the twenty-five *tattvas* in normative Kārikā-Sāṃkhya, see p. 74.
257. In the descriptions of the emergence of the *tattvas* Brahmā is at times identified with the *mahat-tattva* as the principle of cosmic intellect. However, his relationship to the process through which the *tattvas* emerge is not clearly articulated in the epic—a point that will await clarification until the Purāṇic period when a distinction is made between *sarga* or primary creation, in which the *prākṛta* creations or *tattvas* derived from Prakṛti are evolved, and *pratisarga* or secondary creation, in which the *vaikṛta* creations of Brahmā are brought forth.
258. Viṣṇu is also at times identified in the epic with Hiraṇyagarbha.
259. In the Pāñcarātra scheme the lotus from which Brahmā is born emerges from the navel of Aniruddha.
260. Brahmā is similarly associated with both the cosmic egg and the lotus in the Purāṇas, as will be discussed later in this chapter.
261. Mbh. XII.262.1; XII.224.60.
262. See also Mbh. XII.335.29, in which the creator Brahmā refers to the Vedas as his "highest (*uttama*) *brahman*."
263. Mbh. XII.326.67; XII.335.17; cf. XII.330.30.
264. See, for example, Mbh. XII.330.32–34; XII.271.27; XIII.135.27; XIII.143.34; XIV.53.8. See also VI.31.17 [Bhagavad-Gītā].
265. Mbh. XII.330.32–34.
266. See, for example, Mbh. XII.326.50.
267. Mbh. XII.271.25.
268. Mbh. III, App. I, no. 27, 44–52, esp. 47,51. See also Hariv. 31.21–30, esp. 22–23,30; Hariv. App. I, no. 42, 154–195, esp. 156,165,167–168,179,187. The notion that Viṣṇu's boar form is Veda incarnate is

further developed in the Purāṇas, as will be discussed later in this chapter.

269. Mbh. XII.335.44,54,74.
270. Mbh. III.187.14; III.192.11; XII.203.14; VI.63.5. See also XII.203.8, where Viṣṇu is referred to as the "source of Veda" (*brahmaṇo mukha*).
271. See, for example, Mbh. XII.330.35–38; cf. XII.335.71.
272. See, for example, Mbh. XIII.15.30,34; XII, App. I, no. 28, 262–265,291; cf. XIII.17.88–89.
273. Mbh. XIII.17.88–89; cf. XIII.85.4–6; XII, App. I, no. 28, 262–265.
274. Mbh. III.186.6; III.194.11; XII.327.46; I.1.30.
275. Mbh. XII.175.15.
276. Mbh. III.194.12.
277. See pp. 105–107.
278. Mbh. XII.203.8,14,18, for example, describes Viṣṇu as the ultimate source of the Vedas, which Brahmā then acquires. See also XII.200.33 with n. 545*; XII.181.2; XII.314.46; XII.327.30; XII.335.25; XII.160.21.
279. Mbh. XII.335.29–30.
280. Mbh. XII.335.44; cf. XII.335.54,74.
281. Mbh. XII.335.18–67.
282. Sarasvatī is celebrated as the Mother of the Vedas in Mbh. XII.326.52. Gāyatrī/Sāvitrī is designated in a similar manner in Mbh. VI, App. I, no. 1, 24; Hariv. App. I, no. 41, 487–488. In Mbh. VI, App. I, no. 1, 23–24, which forms part of a hymn to the goddess Durgā, Durgā is celebrated "as Sarasvatī, as Sāvitrī, the Mother of the Vedas," indicating perhaps a direct correlation between Sarasvatī and Sāvitrī, although in the epic the two goddesses are generally depicted as distinct goddesses.
283. For the identification of Sarasvatī with Vāc, speech, see, for example, Mbh. XII.231.8; XII.306.6; IX.41.31; cf. XII.176.8.
284. Mbh. XII.306.6,14.
285. Mbh. XII.231.8.
286. See, for example, Mbh. XII.327.94.
287. Mbh. VI.63.5.
288. See, for example, Mbh. XII.326.7–8; XII.327.81; cf. XII.335.50.
289. Mbh. XII.8533 (Calcutta ed.). Sanskrit text cited in Muir, *Original Sanskrit Texts,* vol. 3, p. 16. Cf. the critical edition, XII.224.55 with n. 671*, which reads *nityā* in place of *vidyā.*
290. The latter part of this passage is cited below on p. 93.
291. See, for example, Mbh. XII.176.6–8; XII.306.1–25; cf. XII.322.32–33. These passages will be discussed in more detail in chapter 3.
292. Mbh. XIV.44.6; Hariv. App. I, no. 42, 317.
293. The *gāyatrī mantra* may be translated as follows: "Let us attain that desirable radiance of the divine Savitṛ, who shall stimulate our visions."

294. See, for example, Mbh. VI, App. I, no. 1, 24; Hariv. App. I, no. 41, 487–488. In the former verse Gāyatrī/Sāvitrī as the Mother of the Vedas is identified with the goddess Durgā, while in the latter verse it is in her form as the three-lined *gāyatrī mantra* that she is thus designated.
295. Hariv. 11,665ff (Calcutta ed.). Sanskrit text cited in Muir, *Original Sanskrit Texts*, vol. 3, p. 13. Cf. the critical edition, App. I, no. 41, 780–792, which reads *brahma-saṃsthita* rather than *varṇa-saṃsthita* in line 786.
296. AĀ III.2.3; ŚĀ VIII.3.
297. Hariv. App. I, no. 42, 309–320. *Vaṣaṭ* is the formula uttered by the *hotṛ* priest at the conclusion of a sacrificial verse.
298. See pp. 106–109.
299. See, for example, Mbh. XII.224.55 with n. 671*–XII.224.56 with n. 672*; XII.335.30,66.
300. Mbh. XII.335.30.
301. Mbh. XII.335.66.
302. See, for example, Mbh. XII.327.84; XII.326.57–58; XII.224.56 with n. 672*.
303. Mbh. XII.224.56 with n. 672*.
304. The terms used are generally *sanātana* or *śāśvata*. See, for example, Mbh. I.1.52; XII.59.24; XII.181.2; XII.262.15,26; XII.293.18; XII.304.26; XII.335.27; XII.337.68.
305. See Mbh. XII.8533 (Calcutta ed.), cited on p. 90, with n. 289.
306. These conceptions will be discussed further in chapter 3.
307. In the late Purāṇic period *pūjā* gradually replaced *yajña*, the Vedic fire sacrifice, as the principal form of worship for the majority of Hindus, including brahmins.
308. Rajendra Chandra Hazra, "The Purāṇas," in *The Cultural Heritage of India*, vol. 2, 2d rev. ed. (Calcutta: Ramakrishna Mission Institute of Culture, 1962), pp. 246–247.
309. One of the earliest formulations of this definition is found in the *Amarakośa* (ca. 5th c. C.E.), which defines "Purāṇa" as "that which has five characteristics (*pañca-lakṣaṇa*)" (Śabdādivarga 5). A number of the extant Purāṇas use this term to define themselves, giving an enumeration of the five characteristics. For a collation of relevant Purāṇic passages, see Pandurang Vaman Kane, *History of Dharmaśāstra (Ancient and Mediaeval Religious and Civil Law in India)*, vol. 5, pt. 2, Government Oriental Series (Poona: Bhandarkar Oriental Research Institute, 1962), p. 839 with n. 1365.
310. For a discussion of some of the issues in the scholarly debate concerning the nature and origin of the genre of texts known as "Purāṇas," including the fact that the contents of the extant Purāṇas do not conform to the *pañca-lakṣaṇa* definition, see Thomas B. Coburn, "The Study of the Purāṇas and the Study of Religion," *Religious Studies* 16, no. 3 (Sept. 1980): 341–352. For a discussion of the problems involved

in attempting to delimit a Purāṇic "canon," see Giorgio Bonazzoli, "The Dynamic Canon of the Purāṇa-s," *Purāṇa* 21, no. 2 (July 1979): 116–166.

311. See, for example, BP I.4.20; BP III.12.39; Skanda V.3.1.18. Cf. CU VII.1.2,4; CU VII.2.1; CU VII.7.1, which list "Itihāsa-Purāṇa" as the "fifth" after the Ṛg-Veda, Yajur-Veda, Sāma-Veda, and Atharvaṇa. A number of other references in Vedic texts associate the term Purāṇa (singular) with the Veda(s). For example, AV XI.7.24, in discussing the remnant of the sacrificial offering, speaks of the "*ṛcs*, *sāmans*, meters, Purāṇa, together with the *yajus*." ŚB XIII.4.3.13, in describing the procedures for a particular sacrifice, specifies that the *adhvaryu* should say, "The Purāṇa is the Veda; this it is," and then should "relate some Purāṇa." A passage that occurs in BĀU II.4.10; BĀU IV.5.11; and Maitri VI.32 describes the Itihāsa and Purāṇa as being breathed forth from the great Being along with the Ṛg-Veda, Yajur-Veda, Sāma-Veda, and *atharvāṅgiras*es.
312. MP 289.9; Vāyu 1.18.
313. See, for example, Vāyu 1.11; BP I.3.40–42; BP II.8.28.
314. Vāyu 1.200–201. Variants of these two *śloka*s appear in separate places in the Mahābhārata, in I.2.235 and I.1.204, cited earlier on p. 83.
315. BP III.12.37,39. See also Mārk. 45.20.
316. MP 3.3–4. Variants of this account are given in MP 53.3–4; Vāyu 1.60–61; Brahm. I.1.1.40–41; Padma Sṛṣṭi. 1.45; Nār. I.92.22–23.
317. Purāṇic accounts of the process through which Vyāsa divides the one Veda into four will be discussed in chapter 3.
318. MP 53.3–11.
319. See, for example, Padma Sṛṣṭi. 1.45–52; Nār. I.92.22–26; LP I.1.1–3.
320. Brahm. I.2.34.21; Vāyu 60.21; VP III.6.16.
321. Bṛahm. I.2.34.12–16; Brahm. I.2.35.63–69; Vāyu 60.12–16,55–61; VP III.4.7–10; VP III.6.17–20; cf. Agni 271.10–12. See also BP XII.7.5–7, which gives a somewhat different account.
322. It should be noted, however, that certain Purāṇas forbid *śūdra*s and women from reading or reciting the texts themselves. See, for example, Devī XII.14.24.
323. Coburn, "'Scripture' in India," esp. pp. 445–455. The emphasis on sound over discursive meaning in the Vedic recitative tradition will be discussed in chapter 5.
324. Brown, "Purāṇa as Scripture," pp. 75–76.
325. For a discussion of relevant references, see ibid., pp. 77–78. For an analysis of the role and interrelationship of oral and written transmission in the Purāṇas, see Giorgio Bonazzoli, "Composition, Transmission and Recitation of the Purāṇa-s," *Purāṇa* 25, no. 2 (July 1983): 254–280.
326. Brown, "Purāṇa as Scripture," p. 78.

327. See Brown's discussion of the Purāṇic cult of the book, in which he emphasizes certain parallel developments in the Mahāyāna Buddhist tradition. Brown also notes a late passage, which appears at the end of the Mahābhārata, that recommends worshiping the physical text of the epic through offerings. Ibid., pp. 78–83.
328. The standardized list of twenty-five *tattvas* conforms to the enumeration in the normative Kārikā-Sāṃkhya system, given earlier on p. 74.
329. For discussions of the problems involved in the study and dating of the Purāṇas, as well as descriptions of the character and contents of individual Purāṇas, see Ludo Rocher, *The Purāṇas,* A History of Indian Literature, vol. 2, pt. 3 (Wiesbaden: Otto Harrassowitz, 1986); R. C. Hazra, *Studies in the Purāṇic Records on Hindu Rites and Customs,* 2d ed. (Delhi: Motilal Banarsidass, 1975).
330. For an extended analysis of Purāṇic conceptions of creation, see Madeleine Biardeau, *Études de Mythologie Hindoue,* vol. 1, *Cosmogonies purāṇiques,* Publications de l'École Française d'Extrême Orient, vol. 128 (Paris: École Française d'Extrême Orient, 1981).
331. See, for example, VP I.2.28–29; Mārk. 46.3–9; KP I.4.5–13; KP II.6.1–8.
332. See, for example, BP III.5.23–26,49; BP III.26.19. In the Bhāgavata Purāṇa Prakṛti is at times designated as *māyā,* in accordance with the text's Advaita Vedānta perspective. See also MP 2.25–32, which represents a variant of Manu-Smṛti I.5–13, cited on pp. 77–78, in which Nārāyaṇa is described as implanting his seed in the waters. For a discussion of the role of the female principle in Purāṇic cosmogonies, see Tracy Pintchman, *The Rise of the Goddess in the Hindu Tradition* (Albany: State University of New York Press, 1994), chap. 3.
333. See p. 78. See also pp. 49–53, in which the Brāhmaṇas' descriptions of the two-stage process of creation are discussed.
334. See pp. 49–57.
335. Compare the figure on p. 53, which schematizes the two stages of creation as represented in the Brāhmaṇas.
336. VP VI.4.42.
337. VP III.3.22; VP I.22.81.
338. VP III.3.29–30.
339. The division of the four Vedas into *śākhās* will be discussed in chapter 3.
340. VP I.22.81–83.
341. See VP II.11.7–11. Cf. Mārk. 102.15–16,20–22; Mārk. 103.6; Mārk. 104.28, which identify the supreme Puruṣa with the sun, whose Self is the Veda (*vedātman*), whose body is the Veda (*veda-mūrti*), and who abides in the Veda (*veda-saṃsthita*).
342. MP 164.20.
343. MP 167.12.
344. KP I.6.15.

345. VP I.4.21,39.
346. MP 248.67–73; VP I.4.9,22–23,32–34; BP III.13.34–44, esp. 34,41,44.
347. VP I.4.25,34.
348. KP I.6.8; LP I.70.126.
349. Mārk. 47.3–9, esp. 8. In the Viṣṇu Purāṇa (I.4.3–5) Viṣṇu-Nārāyaṇa is said to assume the form of Brahmā in order to rescue the earth, although it is clearly Viṣṇu-Nārāyaṇa and not Brahmā who is eulogized as the boar.
350. See, for example, ŚP Rudra. II.15.46,52,64.
351. ŚP Rudra. I.8.1–53. Cf. BP III.12.34–35,37–40,44–47, discussed below, which describes the creator Brahmā in a similar way as Śabdabrahman, whose form is composed of the Sanskrit *varṇas* and the Vedic *mantras* and meters.
352. KP II.3.6,20; KP I.10.46,68.
353. KP I.10.47; cf. KP I.50.24.
354. VP IV.1.4.
355. KP I.2.26.
356. KP I.4.39.
357. KP I.9.19.
358. BP III.11.34; BP III.12.48.
359. BP III.8.15; BP III.9.43; cf. BP II.6.34.
360. BP III.12.1; BP III.13.6.
361. BP III.12.46–47. Cf. ŚP Rudra. I.8.1–53, mentioned above, which describes Śiva as Śabdabrahman, whose body is composed of the Sanskrit *varṇas*.
362. BP III.12.34–35,37–40; cf. BP XII.6.44.
363. BP III.12.44; cf. BP XII.6.37–39,44.
364. BP III.12.45–46.
365. See, for example, MP 3.30–44; MP 171.21–24.
366. MP 4.7,10.
367. See, for example, BP III.12.26.
368. MP 2.31.
369. MP 3.2–5. Verses 3–4 of this passage were cited earlier on p. 96.
370. VP I.5.52–55. Compare the Taittirīya Saṃhitā's account (VII.1.1.4–6), cited on pp. 39–40, which gives the same four clusters of *stomas*, meters, and *sāmans*, although only the first cluster is described as emerging from the creator's mouth, while the other three clusters issue forth from other parts of his body. See also JB I.68–69; PB VI.1.6–11.
371. See, for example, Mārk. 48.31–34; KP I.7.54–57; LP I.70.243–246; ŚP Vāyavīya. I.12.58–62.
372. See BP III.12.34–35,37–40,44–47, discussed above. Cf. BP XII.6.44.
373. Mārk. 102.1–7. The correlation of the Vedas with the three *guṇas* will be discussed on pp. 111–112.
374. Mārk. 45.20.

375. Vām. Sāromāhātmya 22.30–32.
376. Mārk. 101.21–102.6.
377. BP XII.6.37–44.
378. As mentioned earlier, the term Śabdabrahman is first introduced in Maitri VI.22–23, where it is identified with Om. Om is commonly identified with Brahman in the Purāṇas. See, for example, VP III.3.21, which declares that "Om is the eternal Brahman consisting of one syllable *(ekākṣara)*." Cf. Mārk. 42.14; Mārk. 101.27; ŚP Rudra. I.8.13–15.
379. See pp. 57, 70.
380. See MS II.76, cited on p. 79. Mārk. 42.8–9 explicitly identifies the three constituents of Om with the three Vedas.
381. BP III.12.34,37.
382. VP I.5.62–63. This passage appears with slight variations in Mārk. 48.42–43; KP I.7.64–65; LP I.70.257–259; ŚP Vāyavīya. I.12.67–69.
383. See, for example, VP I.5.44–45,42–43.
384. BP III.9.24; cf. BP III.12.34.
385. Mārk. 102.1–7.
386. Mārk. 102.19.
387. VP II.11.12–13. Cf. Mārk. 102.19, which expresses this idea in nearly identical words.
388. Mārk. 42.4,8–11.
389. This conception will be discussed in chapter 5.
390. KP I.2.26.
391. See, for example, BP XII.6.44–46. Cf. Mārk. 45.20–23. The *brahmarṣis* will be discussed in chapter 3.
392. See, for example, VP III.6.31–32, cited in chapter 3, p. 250. Cf. Vāyu 61.75. See chapter 3 for a discussion of Purāṇic conceptions of the process through which the Vedas are divided into branches and are progressively lost to human consciousness in the four *yugas*.
393. Vātsyāyana (ca. 5th c. C.E.), in his commentary *(bhāṣya)* on the Nyāya-Sūtras of Gautama, and Uddyotakara (ca. 7th c. C.E.), in his *Vārttika* on Vātsyāyana's *Bhāṣya,* maintain that the Vedas are the work of a reliable person, although they do not explicitly mention that Īśvara is that reliable person who is the author of the Vedas. However, the later exponents of Nyāya, such as Jayanta (9th c. C.E.) and Udayana (11th c. C.E.), expressly assert that the Vedas are the work of Īśvara.
394. For the Sanskrit text and translation of some of the arguments given by the exponents of Nyāya and Vaiśeṣika in support of the *pauruṣeya* and noneternal status of the Vedas, see Muir, *Original Sanskrit Texts,* vol. 3, pp. 108–133. For a brief summary of these arguments, see K. Satchidananda Murty, *Revelation and Reason in Advaita Vedānta* (Waltair: Andhra University; New York: Columbia University Press, 1959), pp. 222–237. For an extended discussion of the authority and role of the Veda in Nyāya and Vaiśeṣika, see George Chemparathy,

L'autorité du Veda selon les Nyāya-Vaiśeṣikas (Louvain-la-Neuve: Centre d'Histoire des Religions, 1983).

395. Although the Sāṃkhya-Pravacana-Sūtras are attributed to Kapila, they appear to have been written by an unknown author some time around the fifteenth century C.E.

396. See especially SPS V.45–51, with the *Bhāṣya* of Vijñānabhikṣu. These and other relevant passages are cited in Muir, *Original Sanskrit Texts,* vol. 3, pp. 133–138.

397. For a discussion of the doctrines and interrelationship of the Mīmāṃsā and Nyāya theories of language, see Madeleine Biardeau, *Théorie de la connaissance et philosophie de la parole dans le brahmanisme classique,* Le monde d'outre-mer passé et présent, ser. 1, Études 23 (Paris: Mouton, 1964), pp. 65–247. For analyses of the contrasting roles that the Veda has assumed in Nyāya and Vaiśeṣika apologetics and in Mīmāṃsā hermeneutics, see Chemparathy, *L'autorité du Veda selon les Nyāya-Vaiśeṣikas*; Halbfass, "The Presence of the Veda in Indian Philosophical Reflection," chapter 2 of his *Tradition and Reflection,* pp. 23–49.

398. For discussions of the doctrine of *sphoṭa* and other aspects of the theories of language developed by the grammarians, see Bruno Liebich, "Über den Sphoṭa (Ein Kapitel über die Sprachphilosophie der Inder)," *Zeitschrift der Deutschen Morgenländischen Gesellschaft* 77 [n.s., 2] (1923): 208–219; John Brough, "Theories of General Linguistics in the Sanskrit Grammarians," *Transactions of the Philological Society* (1951): 27–46; Otto Strauss, "Altindische Spekulationen über die Sprache und ihre Probleme," *Zeitschrift der Deutschen Morgenländischen Gesellschaft* 81 [n.s., 6] (1927): 125–136; Prabhat Chandra Chakravarti, *The Philosophy of Sanskrit Grammar* (Calcutta: University of Calcutta, 1930), esp. chap. 4, "Theory of *Sphoṭa*"; idem, *The Linguistic Speculations of the Hindus* (Calcutta: University of Calcutta, 1933); Biardeau, *Théorie de la connaissance et philosophie de la parole dans le brahmanisme classique,* pp. 31–63, 251–442; Gaurinath Sastri, *A Study in the Dialectics of Sphoṭa,* rev. ed. (Delhi: Motilal Banarsidass, 1980); idem, *The Philosophy of Word and Meaning: Some Indian Approaches with Special Reference to the Philosophy of Bhartṛhari,* Calcutta Sanskrit College Research Series, no. 5 (Calcutta: Sanskrit College, 1959); K. Kunjunni Raja, *Indian Theories of Meaning,* The Adyar Library Series, vol. 91 (Adyar, Madras: Adyar Library and Research Centre, 1963), esp. chap. 3, "*Sphoṭa*: The Theory of Linguistic Symbols"; Harold G. Coward, *Bhartṛhari,* Twayne's World Authors Series, 403 (Boston: Twayne Publishers, 1976); idem, *The Sphoṭa Theory of Language: A Philosophical Analysis* (Delhi: Motilal Banarsidass, 1980); David Seyfort Ruegg, *Contributions à l'histoire de la philosophie linguistique indienne,* Publications de l'Institut de Civilisation Indienne, no. 7 (Paris: E. de Boccard, 1959), pp. 5–14, 31–99;

David Carpenter, "Bhartṛhari and the Veda," in *Texts in Context: Traditional Hermeneutics in South Asia*, ed. Jeffrey R. Timm (Albany: State University of New York Press, 1992), pp. 17–32.

399. Prabhākara's commentary on the *Śābara Bhāṣya* is known as the *Bṛhatī*. Kumārila's commentary is in three parts: *Ślokavārttika* (Adhyāya I, Pāda l); *Tantravārttika* (Adhyāya I, Pādas 2–4; Adhyāya II; Adhyāya III); *Ṭupṭīkā* (Adhyāyas IV-XII).

400. For detailed analyses of the Mīmāṃsā philosophy of language and of *veda-prāmāṇya* as expounded by Śabara, Prabhākara, and Kumārila, see Francis X. D'Sa, *Śabdaprāmāṇyam in Śabara and Kumārila: Towards a Study of the Mīmāṃsā Experience of Language*, Publications of the De Nobili Research Library, vol. 7 (Vienna: Institut für Indologie der Universität Wien, 1980); idem, "Offenbarung ohne einen Gott: Kumārilas Theorie der Worterkenntnis," in *Offenbarung, Geistige Realität des Menschen. Arbeitsdokumentation eines Symposiums zum Offenbarungsbegriff in Indien*, ed. Gerhard Oberhammer, Publications of the De Nobili Research Library, vol. 2 (Vienna: Indologisches Institut der Universität Wien, 1974), pp. 93–105; Ganganatha Jha, *Pūrva-Mīmāṁsā in Its Sources*, 2d ed. (Varanasi: Banaras Hindu University, 1964), esp. pp. 97–135, 147–186. For an alternative interpretation, see Puruṣottama Bilimoria, *Śabdapramāṇa: Word and Knowledge. A Doctrine in Mīmāṃsā-Nyāya Philosophy (with reference to Advaita Vedānta-paribhāṣā 'Agama')—Towards a Framework for Śruti-prāmāṇya*, Studies of Classical India, vol. 10 (Dordrecht: Kluwer Academic Publishers, 1988); idem, "On the Idea of Authorless Revelation (Apauruṣeya)," in *Indian Philosophy of Religion*, ed. Roy W. Perrett (Dordrecht: Kluwer Academic Publishers, 1989), pp. 143–166. My own analysis is particularly indebted to D'Sa's lucid exposition of *śabda-prāmāṇya*.

401. TV p. 220.3–4. References to the *Tantravārttika* are to the page and line number of the Sanskrit edition in *Mīmāṃsādarśana*, vol. 1, Ānandāśrama Sanskrit Series, no. 97 (Poona: Ānandāśrama, 1929).

402. See ŚBh. I.1.6.6–I.1.6.23, pp. 73.1–91.8. References to the *Śābara Bhāṣya* are to the page and line number of the Sanskrit edition in *Mīmāṃsādarśana*, vol. 1, Ānandāśrama Sanskrit Series, no. 97 (Poona: Ānandāśrama, 1929).

403. See ŚBh. I.1.6.15, pp. 80.9–82.5.

404. ŚBh. I.1.6.17, pp. 83.6–8, 84.3–4.

405. ŚBh. I.1.6.12, p. 76.3–4.

406. ŚBh. I.1.6.17, p. 84.2–3.

407. ŚBh. I.1.6.13, pp. 76.7–80.3.

408. ŚBh. I.1.5.5, pp. 45.7–9, 48.7–10.

409. ŚV Śabdanityatā. 36–37.

410. ŚV Śabdanityatā. 210–219.

411. ŚV Śabdanityatā. 156.

412. ŚV Śabdanityatā. 37.
413. ŚV Śabdanityatā. 5–6.
414. ŚV Śabdanityatā. 198–200; 171.
415. ŚV Śabdanityatā. 79.
416. ŚV Śabdanityatā. 170–171.
417. ŚV Śabdanityatā. 39–40.
418. ŚV Śabdanityatā. 40.
419. ŚV Śabdanityatā. 290–291.
420. ŚV Sphoṭa. 11–14.
421. ŚV Sphoṭa. 65.
422. ŚV Śabdanityatā. 284–287.
423. ŚV Sphoṭa. 117–121.
424. ŚV Śabdanityatā. 287–290.
425. ŚV Śabdanityatā. 121–124; 130.
426. ŚV Śabdanityatā. 79.
427. ŚV Śabdanityatā. 214–215; 221; 301–302; Sphoṭa. 54.
428. ŚV Śabdanityatā. 7.
429. ŚV Śabdanityatā. 3–7.
430. ŚBh. I.1.5.5, pp. 23.3–25.2.
431. ŚV Sambandhākṣepavāda 4–5; cf. 1–3.
432. See ŚV Sambandhākṣepaparihāra 12–117 for Kumārila's refutations of the notion that human or divine convention is the source of the relationship between word and meaning. The arguments in Sambandhākṣepaparihāra 42–117 establish the *apauruṣeyatva* of the Vedas through refuting the existence of a creator of the universe.
433. ŚBh. I.3.9.30, p. 294.2–3.
434. ŚBh. I.3.9.30, p. 296.1.
435. For a detailed analysis of Kumārila's conceptions of *ākṛti* and *vyakti*, see D'Sa, *Śabdaprāmāṇyam in Śabara and Kumārila*, pp. 151–165.
436. ŚV Ākṛti. l.
437. ŚBh. I.1.7.24, pp. 91.10–95.6.
438. For a discussion of the theory of sentence meaning, and in particular the theory of *bhāvanā*, formulated by Śabara and Kumārila, see D'Sa, *Śabdaprāmāṇyam in Śabara and Kumārila*, pp. 98–104, 166–179.
439. For a discussion of these arguments, see ibid., pp. 192–197.
440. See ŚV Codanā. 116–136.
441. See ŚV Sambandhākṣepaparihāra 42–117, esp. 114–116.
442. See ŚV Vākya. 366–369; Vedanityatā. 1–14.
443. See ŚV Vākya. 365–366.
444. In the very last *kārikā* of the *Ślokavārttika* Kumarila declares that "thus the authoritativeness (*pramāṇatva*) of the [Vedic] injunctions with respect to *dharma* has been established by means of arguments." ŚV Vedanityatā 15.
445. See BSB I.1.3–I.1.4.
446. See BSB I.1.4; III.1.25.

447. For a brief enumeration of the members of each of these schools and of other important exponents of Advaita Vedānta, see Murty, *Revelation and Reason in Advaita Vedānta,* pp. xvii–xix.
448. For a discussion of the arguments developed by the various exponents and schools of Advaita Vedānta in support of each of these doctrines, see Murty, *Revelation and Reason in Advaita Vedānta,* esp. pp. 3–52.
449. BSB I.3.29.
450. BSB I.3.28.
451. BSB I.3.28.
452. BSB I.3.29; cf. I.3.28.
453. BSB I.3.29; cf. I.3.28.
454. BSB I.3.28. For discussions of the passages cited from the Brāhmaṇas, Mahābhārata, Viṣṇu Purāṇa, and Manu-Smṛti, see pp. 55, 50, 90 with n. 289, 110, 80.
455. BSB I.3.28.
456. BSB I.3.30; cf. I.3.28–I.3.29. For a discussion of relevant *smṛti* texts, see pp. 79–80, 93, 109–110.
457. BSB I.1.3. Śaṃkara's citation from *śruti* is from BĀU II.4.10; BĀU IV.5.11; Maitri VI.32, discussed on p. 67.

CHAPTER 2. TORAH AND CREATION

1. For discussions of the different stages in the development of the Israelite wisdom tradition, and of the contribution of Proverbs 1–9 to that development, see Gerhard von Rad, *Old Testament Theology,* vol. 1, trans. D. M. G. Stalker (New York: Harper and Row, 1962), pp. 418–453, esp. 441–453; Walther Eichrodt, *Theology of the Old Testament,* vol. 2, trans. J. A. Baker, The Old Testament Library (Philadelphia: Westminster Press, 1967), pp. 80–92; James L. Crenshaw, *Old Testament Wisdom: An Introduction* (Atlanta: John Knox Press, 1981), pp. 91–99.
2. R. N. Whybray, *Wisdom in Proverbs: The Concept of Wisdom in Proverbs 1–9,* Studies in Biblical Theology, no. 45 (London: SCM Press, 1965), p. 106.
3. Martin Hengel, *Judaism and Hellenism: Studies in Their Encounter in Palestine during the Early Hellenistic Period,* vol. 1, trans. John Bowden (Philadelphia: Fortress Press, 1974), p. 153 with n. 289.
4. The term *'āmôn* has generally been interpreted by scholars as meaning either "artisan, craftsman" or "nursling," as will be discussed immediately below.
5. The meaning "artisan, craftsman" is almost certain for *'ommān* in S.S. 7.2 and also makes reasonable sense for *'āmôn* in Jer. 52.15.
6. For the details of the scholarly debate, see Gerhard von Rad, *Wisdom in Israel,* trans. James D. Martin (London: SCM Press, 1972), p. 152; Whybray, *Wisdom in Proverbs,* pp. 101–102; Hengel, *Judaism and*

Hellenism, vol. 1, p. 153 with n. 291; R. B. Y. Scott, "Wisdom in Creation: The *'āmôn* of Proverbs VIII 30," *Vetus Testamentum* 10 (1960): 213–223.

7. See Whybray, *Wisdom in Proverbs*, pp. 72–104, esp. 98–104.
8. Von Rad, *Wisdom in Israel*, p. 174. See also pp. 144–176.
9. For references see n. 10 below. Some scholars have proposed theories that combine elements from these three types of interpretation. For example, Helmer Ringgren has suggested that wisdom is fundamentally the hypostatization of a divine attribute to which mythological characteristics taken from other traditions have been added in order to enhance the vividness of wisdom's portrayal. See Helmer Ringgren, *Word and Wisdom: Studies in the Hypostatization of Divine Qualities and Functions in the Ancient Near East* (Lund: Håkan Ohlssons, 1947), pp. 128–149.
10. Some scholars have sought the provenance of personified wisdom in the Egyptian concept of Maat. For analyses of the possible influence of Egyptian sources on the Israelite figure of wisdom, see Christa Bauer-Kayatz, *Studien zu Proverbien 1–9. Eine form- und motivgeschichtliche Untersuchung unter Einbeziehung ägyptischen Vergleichsmaterials*, Wissenschaftliche Monographien zum Alten und Neuen Testament, vol. 22 (Neukirchen-Vluyn: Neukirchener, 1966); idem, *Einführung in die alttestamentliche Weisheit*, Biblische Studien, vol. 55 (Neukirchen-Vluyn: Neukirchener, 1969). See also von Rad, *Wisdom in Israel*, p. 153; cf. Ernst Würthwein, "Egyptian Wisdom and the Old Testament," in *Studies in Ancient Israelite Wisdom*, ed. James L. Crenshaw, The Library of Biblical Studies (New York: Ktav, 1976), pp. 117–118; Georg Fohrer, "Sophia," in *Studies in Ancient Israelite Wisdom*, ed. Crenshaw, pp. 65–67. Other scholars, such as Berend Gemser and Ringgren, have attempted to locate a prototype for Proverbs 8.22–31 in Egyptian and Mesopotamian creation hymns. See Berend Gemser, *Sprüche Salomos*, 2d rev. ed., Handbuch zum Alten Testament, Series 1, 16 (Tübingen: J. C. B. Mohr [Paul Siebeck], 1963), pp. 47–49; Ringgren, *Word and Wisdom*, p. 102. For a summary and critique of these theories, see R. N. Whybray, "Proverbs VIII 22–31 and Its Supposed Prototypes," in *Studies in Ancient Israelite Wisdom*, ed. Crenshaw, pp. 390–400. For a discussion of possible Canaanite-Phoenician sources of the Israelite figure of wisdom, see W. F. Albright, "Some Canaanite-Phoenician Sources of Hebrew Wisdom," in *Wisdom in Israel and in the Ancient Near East*, eds. M. Noth and D. Winton Thomas, *Supplements to Vetus Testamentum* 3 (1969): 1–15, esp. 7–8. Gustav Boström argues that the figure of Astarte-Ištar, the goddess of love, lies behind the personification of wisdom in Proverbs. However, according to this theory, Astarte-Ištar did not serve the positive function of a prototype but rather posed as an antithetical figure over against which the Israelite figure of wisdom was established as a rival. See Gustav Boström, *Pro-*

verbiastudien. Die Weisheit und das fremde Weib in Spr. 1–9, Lunds Universitets Årsskrift, n.s., pt. 1, vol. 30, no. 3 (Lund: C. W. K. Gleerup, 1935), pp. 156–174.

In addition to the above theories, which look for the origins of the figure of personified wisdom in Proverbs in Ancient Near Eastern cultures, some scholars have sought to establish Greek influence as the background for such a concept. See, for example, Eichrodt, *Theology of the Old Testament,* vol. 2, p. 85. However, Hengel has cautioned against such theories of Hellenistic influence on Israelite wisdom speculation, since the Greek *sophia* was personified as a divine entity relatively late. See Hengel, *Judaism and Hellenism,* vol. 1, p. 154 with n. 298.

For refutations of the various theories that attempt to derive the personified wisdom of Proverbs from Egyptian, Mesopotamian, or Canaanite sources, see Whybray, *Wisdom in Proverbs,* pp. 82–92; idem, "Proverbs VIII 22–31 and Its Supposed Prototypes." For other theories concerning the origin and function of the figure of wisdom in Proverbs, see Burton L. Mack, *Logos und Sophia: Untersuchungen zur Weisheitstheologie im hellenistischen Judentum,* Studien zur Umwelt des Neuen Testaments, vol. 10 (Göttingen: Vandenhoeck and Ruprecht, 1973), pp. 13–62; Bernhard Lang, *Wisdom and the Book of Proverbs: A Hebrew Goddess Redefined* (New York: Pilgrim Press, 1986); Claudia V. Camp, *Wisdom and the Feminine in the Book of Proverbs,* Bible and Literature Series, 11 (Sheffield, England: Almond, JSOT Press, 1985).

11. These dates follow George W. E. Nickelsburg, *Jewish Literature Between the Bible and the Mishnah: A Historical and Literary Introduction* (Philadelphia: Fortress Press, 1981), p. 64. Crenshaw narrows the dates to between 190 and 180 B.C.E. Crenshaw, *Old Testament Wisdom,* p. 57.
12. BS 2.4,9; cf. 1.4.
13. BS 24.8. Translations of the Wisdom of Ben Sira and the Wisdom of Solomon are from Herbert G. May and Bruce M. Metzger, eds., *The New Oxford Annotated Bible with the Apocrypha. Revised Standard Version* (New York: Oxford University Press, 1977).
14. BS 24.10–12.
15. BS 1.9.
16. BS 24.24.
17. See Hengel, *Judaism and Hellenism,* vol. 1, pp. 158–159.
18. Ibid., pp. 159–160.
19. Von Rad, *Old Testament Theology,* vol. 1, p. 445.
20. George Foot Moore, *Judaism in the First Centuries of the Christian Era, the Age of the Tannaim,* vol. 1 (Cambridge: Harvard University Press, 1927), p. 265.

21. Hengel, *Judaism and Hellenism*, vol. 1, pp. 161, 132. See p. 148 regarding the aphorism about the Torah attributed to Simeon the Righteous. See also n. 61 concerning the probable identification of Simeon the Righteous with Simeon II (ca. 200 B.C.E.).
22. For the dating of Baruch, see Nickelsburg, *Jewish Literature Between the Bible and the Mishnah*, pp. 113–114.
23. Nickelsburg suggests that the Wisdom of Solomon may have been written during the reign of Caligula (37–41 C.E.). See Nickelsburg, *Jewish Literature Between the Bible and the Mishnah*, p. 184.
24. Wis. 6.22; 9.9.
25. Wis. 8.4.
26. Wis. 7.22; 8.6; cf. 9.2.
27. Wis. 7.25.
28. Wis. 7.27.
29. Wis. 8.1; 7.27.
30. Wis. 7.25.
31. See, for example, Crenshaw, *Old Testament Wisdom*, pp. 179–180.
32. Hengel, *Judaism and Hellenism*, vol. 1, p. 167.
33. See ibid., pp. 165–169.
34. Philo's reliance on the wisdom books has been emphasized by Jean Laporte in his essay "Philo in the Tradition of Biblical Wisdom Literature," in *Aspects of Wisdom in Judaism and Early Christianity*, ed. Robert L. Wilken (Notre Dame: University of Notre Dame Press, 1975), pp. 103–141.
35. Ibid., pp. 104–106.
36. Ebr. 31. Philo's use of the term "nurse" (*tithēnē*) to describe wisdom appears to reflect in the active mode the Hebrew *'āmôn* of Proverbs 8.30, which, as discussed on p. 134, was translated by Aquila in the passive sense of *tithēnoumenē*, "nursling." See Laporte, "Philo in the Tradition of Biblical Wisdom Literature," p. 115; Harry Austryn Wolfson, *Philo: Foundations of Religious Philosophy in Judaism, Christianity, and Islam*, vol. 1, 4th printing, rev. (Cambridge: Harvard University Press, 1968), pp. 266–269. Translations of Philo are from F. H. Colson and G. H. Whitaker, trans., *Philo*, 12 vols., The Loeb Classical Library (London: William Heinemann; Cambridge: Harvard University Press, 1929–1962).
37. Wolfson, *Philo*, vol. 1, p. 258. See also pp. 253–261.
38. Op. 17–18.
39. Op. 19.
40. Op. 20, 24–25.
41. II Mos. 14, 51; cf. Op. 3.
42. Because such texts do not generally link their narratives explicitly to biblical verses, some scholars would prefer not to term them Midrash at all. Nevertheless, they do represent interpretations—or rather reinterpretations—of the biblical narrative, and thus in this sense they

qualify as Midrash even if they do not explicitly cite the biblical verses that are being reformulated.

The role of Midrash in the rabbinic tradition will be briefly discussed in chapter 6. For discussions of the various categories of Midrashic literature, see Moshe David Herr, "Midrash," *Encyclopaedia Judaica* (New York: Macmillan, 1971), s.v.; H. L. Strack and G. Stemberger, *Introduction to the Talmud and Midrash*, trans. Markus Bockmuehl, [7th rev. ed.] (Edinburgh: T and T Clark, 1991); John Bowker, *The Targums and Rabbinic Literature: An Introduction to Jewish Interpretations of Scripture* (Cambridge: Cambridge University Press, 1969); Leopold Zunz, *Ha-D^{e}rāšôṯ b^e-Yiśrā'ēl*, trans. M. E. Zack, notes by Chanoch Albeck (Jerusalem: Mosad Bialik, 1947). For relevant secondary works on the principles and characteristics of Midrash, see chapter 6, n. 16.

43. James Kugel, "Two Introductions to Midrash," *Prooftexts* 3, no. 2 (May 1983): 147; reprinted in *Midrash and Literature*, eds. Hartman and Budick, p. 95.
44. Ibid., p. 146.
45. Joseph Heinemann, "Profile of a Midrash: The Art of Composition in Leviticus Rabba," *Journal of the American Academy of Religion* 39, no. 2 (June 1971): 144.
46. Among Neusner's more recent works that discuss his methodological approach to rabbinic texts, see in particular Jacob Neusner with William Scott Green, *Writing with Scripture: The Authority and Uses of the Hebrew Bible in the Torah of Formative Judaism* (Minneapolis: Fortress Press, 1989); Neusner, *The Ecology of Religion*; idem, *Ancient Judaism and Modern Category-Formation: "Judaism," "Midrash," "Messianism," and Canon in the Past Quarter-Century*, Studies in Judaism (Lanham, Md.: University Press of America, 1986). Richard Sarason has similarly noted the role of "redactional-editorial activity in shaping, recasting, or restyling materials to fit their literary context in a particular document" and, like Neusner, has emphasized the need for more sustained studies of the distinctive redactional and stylistic characteristics of the various Midrashic texts. Richard S. Sarason, "Toward a New Agendum for the Study of Rabbinic Midrashic Literature," in *Studies in Aggadah, Targum and Jewish Liturgy in Memory of Joseph Heinemann*, eds. Ezra Fleischer and Jakob J. Petuchowski (Jerusalem: Magnes Press, Hebrew University, 1981), pp. 55–73, esp. 58.
47. Neusner, *Ancient Judaism and Modern Category-Formation*, p. 44.
48. Steven D. Fraade, "Interpreting Midrash 1: Midrash and the History of Judaism," *Prooftexts* 7, no. 2 (May 1987): 179–194, esp. 185–186.
49. One aspect of an extended study would involve testing the consistency with which specific traditions are attributed to specific rabbis in the various texts, in order to determine whether a more general pattern

emerges in which certain types of speculation are regularly associated with certain rabbinic circles or schools (for example, the school of R. Akiba, or R. Joḥanan's circle of students and colleagues). Such an investigation will have to be postponed until a future study. In the present study I have, however, generally indicated the attributions where possible, although in some cases—such as traditions in which there is no consistency of attribution among the multiple variants, or pericopes that include a series of traditions with separate attributions—I have chosen to leave out the attributions in order not to burden the discussion unduly.

50. The Jerusalem Talmud has not been included in the present study primarily for practical reasons, given the already ambitious scope of my project and the sheer volume of material contained in the texts on which I have chosen to focus.
51. See, for example, Ḥag. 12b; Lev. R. XXIX.11 = Pes. K. 23.10; Deut. R. II.32.
52. See, for example, Sip̄rê Num. §112; Gen. R. XXVIII.4; Gen. R. I.10; Song R. V.11, §4; Pes. K. Suppl. 3.2; Sanh. 99a; Šeb. 13a; Ber. 22a; Taan. 4a; Taan. 7a; Šab. 88b; Sanh. 34a; Pes. R. 8.5; Pes. R. 33.10; Pes. R. 21.21; Exod. R. XXXVI.3.
53. See, for example, Lev. R. III.7; Song R. I.3, §1; Song R. VIII.11, §2; Ber. 6a; Ber. 21a; Ber. 11b; Šab. 88b–89a; Šab. 115b–116a; Mak. 11a; Deut. R. VII.3; Deut. R. VIII.2; Pes. R. 25.3.
54. See, for example, Sip̄rê Deut. §37; Gen. R. I.1; Gen. R. I.4; Gen. R. I.8; Lev. R. XIX.1; Song R. V.11, §1; Ned. 39b; Pes. 54a; Tanḥ., ed. Buber, Bᵉrē'šîṯ §5; PRE §3, f. 6a.
55. See, for example, Gen. R. I.1; Gen. R. VIII.2; Lev. R. XIX.1; Song R. V.11, §1; Tanḥ., ed. Buber, Bᵉrē'šîṯ §5; Tanḥ. Bᵉrē'šîṯ §1; Exod. R. XXX.9.
56. See, for example, Gen. R. I.4; Song R. V.11, §4; Exod. R. XLVII.4; Tanḥ. Bᵉrē'šîṯ §1. Regarding the role of wisdom in creation, with no explicit mention of the Torah, see Lev. R. XI.1; Ḥag. 12a; Ber. 55a; Tanḥ., ed. Buber, Bᵉrē'šîṯ §15; Exod. R. XLVIII.4; PRE §3, f. 8b.
57. The association of images of fire with Merkabah traditions will be discussed in chapter 4. The tendency of rabbinic texts, as well as certain kabbalistic sources, to give priority to the written-visual aspects of the divine language over the oral-aural aspects has been emphasized by Elliot Wolfson in his recent study "Erasing the Erasure."
58. In the case of traditions that reappear in the various strata, each time a particular text's treatment of the tradition is discussed, references to variants of the tradition in other rabbinic texts will be given in the notes.
59. Ḥag. II.1. Cf. the Gemara on this Mishnah, Ḥag. 11b–16a, which will be discussed below.
60. 'Ab. I–IV.

61. 'Ab. I.2. The other two things are the Temple service and deeds of loving-kindness. Cf. Pes. R. 5.3; PRE §16, f. 36b. Strack and Hengel take Simeon the Righteous to be Simeon II, who, according to Josephus, lived at the beginning of the second century B.C.E. See Strack and Stemberger, *Introduction to the Talmud and Midrash*, p. 70; Hengel, *Judaism and Hellenism*, vol. 1, p. 131.
62. 'Ab. V.6. *Miktāḇ*, "writing," might also be vocalized *makteḇ*, "writing instrument." This notion apparently derives from Exod. 32.15–16, which describes the tablets as the work of God and the writing with which they were engraved as the writing of God. The other seven items are the mouth of the earth, the mouth of the well, the mouth of the she-ass, the rainbow, the manna, the rod, and the Shamir. Variants of this tradition are found in Sip̄rê Deut. §355; Mek., ed. Lauterbach, Wayassa' §6, vol. 2, pp. 124–125; Pes. 54a; PRE §19, f. 44a.
63. See, for example, 'Ab. VI.10 (Qinyan Torah); 'Ab. VI.7 (Qinyan Torah).
64. 'Ab. VI.10 (Qinyan Torah). Cf. Mek., ed. Lauterbach, Šîrāṯā' §9, vol. 2, pp. 75–76; Sip̄rê Deut. §309; Pes. 87b. Cf. also Gen. R. I.4, which includes the Torah along with the people of Israel and the Temple as three of the six or seven things that precede the creation of the world.
65. The notion that Abraham observed the Torah is found as early as the Pseudepigrapha and Apocrypha. See, for example, 2 Baruch 57.1–2; cf. Jubilees 23.10. For parallel rabbinic traditions that cite Genesis 26.5 as a proof text, see Lev. R. II.10; Gen. R. XCV.3; Gen. R. LXIV.4; Yoma 28b; Tanḥ., ed. Buber, Lek̲ Lᵉk̲ā §1; Tanḥ., ed. Buber, Lek̲ Lᵉk̲ā §14; Tanḥ., ed. Buber, Tôlᵉḏôṯ §1; Tanḥ., ed. Buber, Wa-yiggaš §12; PRE §31, f. 69a–69b.
66. 'Ab. III.14. A similar statement is attributed to R. Eleazar b. Zadok in Sip̄rê Deut. §48. Cf. also Šab. 88b and Zeb. 116a, in which the Torah is described, respectively, as the "secret treasure" (*ḥămûḏāh gᵉnûzāh*) or "precious treasure" (*ḥemdāh ṭôḇāh*) that was hidden for 974 generations prior to the creation of the world.
67. 'Ab. V.1.
68. See, for example, Gen. R. XVII.1; RH 32a; Meg. 21b; Pes. R. 21.19; Pes. R. 40.5; PRE §3, f. 8b; PRE §32, f. 74a.
69. *Baraitot* (singular *baraita*) are "external" teachings attributed to the Tannaim that do not form part of the Mishnah redacted by Judah ha-Nasi.
70. The Tannaim, the earliest rabbinic authorities in Palestine whose teachings are preserved in the Mishnah and in Tannaitic Midrashim, are distinguished from the later rabbinic authorities, the Amoraim, who lived in Palestine and Babylonia between the third and sixth centuries and who were responsible for the interpretations and elaborations of Mishnaic teachings that crystallized in the Jerusalem Talmud and Babylonian Talmud, respectively. The Amoraim in Palestine were

also apparently responsible for compiling the Tannaitic Midrashim as well as the later classical Amoraic Midrashim.

71. See D. Hoffmann, *Zur Einleitung in die halachischen Midraschim* (Berlin: M. Driesner, 1886–1887). Chanoch Albeck, while accepting the division between the two types of Tannaitic Midrashim, disputes their connection with the schools of R. Ishmael and R. Akiba. See Chanoch Albeck, *Untersuchungen über die halakischen Midraschim,* Veröffentlichungen der Akademie für die Wissenschaft des Judentums (Berlin: Akademie-Verlag, 1927). For a summary of the scholarly debate, including the more recent arguments of Louis Finkelstein and Gary Porton, see Strack and Stemberger, *Introduction to the Talmud and Midrash,* pp. 270–272.
72. Indeed, the halakhic nature of Leviticus posed a problem for later Amoraic interpreters, who were primarily concerned with aggadic questions. Perhaps in order to circumvent this problem the editor(s) of Leviticus Rabbāh, the Amoraic Midrash on Leviticus, chose to abandon the exegetical form of Midrash in favor of a homiletical form that allowed for more freedom in departing from the biblical text and reinterpreting its halakhic concerns in terms of the more pressing theological issues of the period.
73. Sip̄rê Deut. §306; cf. Sip̄rê Deut. §317.
74. Sip̄rā', B^e-ḥûqqôṯay, Pereq 8.
75. Sip̄rā', B^e-ḥûqqôṯay, Pereq 8. In Sip̄rê Deut. §351 this tradition is attributed to R. Gamaliel.
76. Sip̄rê Deut. §355; Mek., ed. Lauterbach, Wa-yassa' §6, vol. 2, pp. 124–125. Cf. 'Ab. V.6. Both accounts agree with 'Āḇôṯ on six of the ten items: the letters, the tablets, the rainbow, the manna, the mouth of the earth, and the mouth of the she-ass. With respect to the four additional items in 'Āḇôṯ's enumeration—the writing, the mouth of the well, the rod, and the Shamir—Sip̄rê on Deuteronomy includes the writing and the well in its initial enumeration of the ten things, while the M^ek̲îltā' includes the rod and the Shamir. The sepulcher of Moses and the cave in which Moses and Elijah stood are also included in the initial enumerations of Sip̄rê on Deuteronomy and the M^ek̲îltā'. All three versions include a subsidiary list of items following the initial list of ten things. Cf. also Pes. 54a; PRE §19, f. 44a.
77. The Torah is identified with the primordial wisdom of Prov. 8.22 in Mek., ed. Lauterbach, Šîrāṯā' §9, vol. 2, p. 76; Sip̄rê Deut. §37; Sip̄rê Deut. §309; Sip̄rê Deut. §317. It is identified more generally with wisdom in Proverbs 1–9 in Mek., ed. Lauterbach, Wa-yassa' §1, vol. 2, p. 92; Mek., ed. Lauterbach, Ba-ḥōḏeš §10, vol. 2, p. 279; Sip̄rê Deut. §47; Sip̄rê Deut. §48; Sip̄rê Deut. §87.
78. Mek., ed. Lauterbach, Šîrāṯā' §9, vol. 2, pp. 75–76. Cf. 'Ab. VI.10 (Qinyan Torah). Both texts include the Torah, the people of Israel, and the Temple in their enumerations. The M^ek̲îltā' gives the land of Israel as

the fourth, whereas 'Āḇôṯ includes the heaven and earth and Abraham. Cf. also Sip̄rê Deut. §309, discussed immediately below, and Pes. 87b.

79. Mek., ed. Lauterbach, Šîrāṯā' §9, vol. 2, p. 76. This tradition is linked to a parallel tradition in the Mᵉḵîltā', which includes the people of Israel, the land of Israel, the Temple, and the Torah as the four inheritances. See Mek., ed. Lauterbach, Šîrāṯā' §10, vol. 2, pp. 77–78.

80. Sip̄rê Deut. §309. As in the other variants of this tradition, Prov. 8.22 is cited as a proof text to establish that the Torah is one of God's possessions. Cf. 'Ab. VI.10 (Qinyan Torah); Mek., ed. Lauterbach, Šîrāṯā' §9, vol. 2, pp. 75–76; Pes. 87b.

81. Sip̄rê Deut. §37. In later rabbinic texts the Torah is included among six or seven things that were created prior to the world. See, for example, Gen. R. I.4; Ned. 39b; Pes. 54a; PRE §3, f. 6a–6b.

82. Sip̄rê Deut. §41. Commenting on Gen. 2.15, "And the Lord God took the man and put him in the Garden of Eden to till (*'āḇaḏ*) it and to keep (*šāmar*) it," the Midrash interprets "to till it" to mean study of the Torah and "to keep it" to mean observance of the commandments. Cf. the interpretations of Gen. 2.15 in Gen. R. XVI.5; PRE §12, f. 29b. Targum Neofiti 1 renders Gen. 2.15, "And the Lord God took the man and caused him to dwell in the garden of Eden so that he do service according to the Law and keep its commandments." Cf. Fragment Targums P and V and Targum Pseudo-Jonathan to Gen. 2.15. See also 2 Enoch 31.1, "And I created a garden in Eden in the east, that he should observe the testament and keep the command."

83. Mek., ed. Lauterbach, Ba-ḥôḏeš §9, vol. 2, p. 268. The "flaming torch" (*lappîḏ 'ēš*) is interpreted in light of the parallel expression that is used in Exod. 20.18 to describe the revelation of the Torah at Mount Sinai: "And all the people saw the thunderings (*qôlōṯ*, literally, "voices") and the lightnings (*lappîḏim*)." Cf. Gen. R. XLIV.21; Pes. K. 5.2 = Pes. R. 15.2; Tanḥ. Pᵉqûḏê §8; Exod. R. LI.7.

84. Sip̄rê Deut. §48. Cf. 'Ab. III.14.

85. *Mî še-'āmar wᵉ-hāyāh hā-'ôlām*. See, for example, Mek., ed. Lauterbach, Bᵉ-šallaḥ §7, vol. 1, p. 248; Mek., ed. Lauterbach, Šîrāṯā' §3, vol. 2, p. 26; Mek., ed. Lauterbach, Šîrāṯā' §4, vol. 2, p. 32; Mek., ed. Lauterbach, Šîrāṯā' §8, vol. 2, pp. 62, 63; Mek., ed. Lauterbach, Šîrāṯā' §10, vol. 2, pp. 78–79; Mek., ed. Lauterbach, Wa-yassa' §1, vol. 2, p. 92; Mek., ed. Lauterbach, Ba-ḥôḏeš §8, vol. 2, p. 263; Mek., ed. Lauterbach, Ba-ḥôḏeš §9, vol. 2, p. 275; Sip̄rê Deut. §49; Sip̄rê Deut. §307; Sip̄rê Deut. §343; Sip̄rê Num. §102; Sip̄rê Num. §103. Cf. Gen. R. IV.4; Gen. R. XXIV.2; Lev. R. III.7; Pes. K. Suppl. 1.15; Esth. R. I.12; Song R. IV.5, §1; 'Erub. 13b; Meg. 13b; Soṭ. 10b; Qid. 30b; Qid. 31a; Sanh. 19a; Pes. R. 21.7.

86. Mek., ed. Lauterbach, Šîrāṯā' §10, vol. 2, pp. 78–79.

87. Mek., ed. Lauterbach, Ba-ḥôḏeš §7, vol. 2, p. 255. Cf. Gen. R. III.2; Gen. R. IV.6; Gen. R. XII.10; Gen. R. XXVII.1; Šab. 119b; Pes. R. 49.10; Pes. R. 27.4; Pes. R. 23.5; Tanḥ., ed. Buber, Bᵉrēʾšîṯ §11; Deut. R. V.13; PRE §7, f. 15b.
88. Sip̄rê Num. §41. Prov. 6.23 is a standard proof text that is regularly invoked in later rabbinic texts to establish that the Torah is light. See, for example, Lam. R. Proem XXIII; Soṭ. 21a; Taan. 7b; Meg. 16b; Pes. R. 46.3; Deut. R. IV.4; Exod. R. XXXIV.2; Exod. R. XXXVI.3.
89. Mek., ed. Lauterbach, Ba-ḥôḏeš §4, vol. 2, pp. 220–221; cf. Mek., ed. Lauterbach, Ba-ḥôḏeš §5, vol. 2, p. 237.
90. Sip̄rê Deut. §343.
91. See, for example, Mek., ed. Lauterbach, Ba-ḥôḏeš §4, vol. 2, pp. 220–221; Mek., ed. Lauterbach, Ba-ḥôḏeš §9, vol. 2, pp. 266, 268, 270; Mek., ed. Lauterbach, Ba-ḥôḏeš §5, vol. 2, p. 235; Mek., ed. Lauterbach, Bᵉ-šallaḥ §7, vol. 1, p. 247; Sip̄rê Deut. §343; Sip̄rāʾ, Wa-yiqrāʾ, Nᵉḏāḇāh, Pārāšāh 1. The use of images of fire in accounts of the Sinai revelation, and the parallel use of fire imagery in the Merkabah traditions of Hêḵālôṯ texts, will be discussed in chapter 4.
92. See, for example, Mek., ed. Lauterbach, Ba-ḥôḏeš §5, vol. 2, p. 235; Mek., ed. Lauterbach, Bᵉ-šallaḥ §7, vol. 1, p. 247; Sip̄rê Deut. §343. The form *ʾēš-dāṯ* in Deut. 33.2 is corrupt, and a number of emendations have been suggested. My translation follows the traditional rendering in rabbinic texts, which interprets the expression as referring to the "fiery law" of Torah. Deut. 33.2 is a frequently cited proof text in later rabbinic sources. Cf. Song R. V.11, §6; Pes. K. Suppl. 1.17; Pes. K. Suppl. 1.20; Lev. R. IV.1; Lam. R. III.1, §1; Song R. I.9, §4; Beṣ. 25b; Ber. 6a; Ber. 62a; Soṭ. 4b; Pes. R. 33.10; Tanḥ., ed. Buber, Bᵉrēʾšîṯ §4; Exod. R. XLI.4; Num. R. XXII.9; Deut. R. V.4; PRE §41, f. 96a.
93. Mek., ed. Lauterbach, Ba-ḥôḏeš §9, vol. 2, p. 266.
94. For an analysis of some of these shared units, see Jacob Neusner, *The Integrity of Leviticus Rabbah: The Problem of the Autonomy of a Rabbinic Document*, Brown Judaic Studies, no. 93 (Chico, Calif.: Scholars Press, 1985), pp. 157–182.
95. Chapter 20 of Leviticus Rabbāh parallels *pisqāʾ* 26 of Pᵉsîqtāʾ dᵉ-R. Kahana; chapters 27–30 parallel *pisqāʾ*s 9, 8, 23, and 27, respectively. The question concerning which collection borrowed from the other has been a topic of scholarly debate, although the present consensus appears to be that both works were compiled at about the same time in the fifth century and that later editors or copyists transferred sections of one collection to the other. For a discussion of the problem, see William G. Braude and Israel J. Kapstein, trans., *Pěsiḳta dě-Raḇ Kahăna: R. Kahana's Compilation of Discourses for Sabbaths and Festal Days* (Philadelphia: Jewish Publication Society, 1975), pp. xlix–li. See also Neusner's analysis of one of the chapters shared by

both Leviticus Rabbāh and P^{e}sîqtā' d^{e}-R. Kahana in his *The Integrity of Leviticus Rabbah*, pp. 182–215.

96. Neusner, *The Ecology of Religion*, pp. 280–281, 289–290.
97. See Neusner, *Death and Birth of Judaism*, pp. 33–48; idem, *The Ecology of Religion*, pp. 289–290.
98. See, for example, Song R. I.3, §2; Song R. I.2, §5; Song R. I.10, §1; Song R. II.5, §1; Pes. K. 12.5; Pes. K. 15.5; Lam. R. Proem II; cf. Lev. R. III.7.
99. This statement is attributed to R. Joshua b. Levi in Lev. R. XXII.1. See also Lev. R. XV.2. Cf. Exod. R. XLVII.1; Tanḥ., ed. Buber, Kî Ṯiśśā' §17.
100. Song R. I.2, §2. Cf. 'Erub. 21b; RH 19a; Taan. 17b; Pes. R. 3.2.
101. See, for example, Song R. I.3, §1, in which R. Akiba is referred to as "the halakhah" and "the Torah," and R. Eliezer is compared to the Ark of the Covenant, his stone seat representing Mount Sinai.
102. See Song R. II.5, §3.
103. Lev. R. III.7.
104. Pes. K. 15.5; Lam. R. Proem II.
105. Prov. 8.22 is used as a proof text in Gen. R. I.1; Gen. R. I.4; Gen. R. I.8; Lev. R. XI.3; Lev. R. XIX.1; Song R. V.11, §1. Prov. 8.30 is invoked in Gen. R. I.1; Gen. R. VIII.2; Gen. R. LXXXV.9; Lev. R. XIX.1; Song R. V.11, §1. Lev. R. XXXV.4 cites Prov. 8.27 and 8.29. Prov. 3.19 is invoked in Gen. R. I.4 and Song R. V.11, §4. Cf. Lev. R. XI.1; Gen. R. XXVII.1; Pes. K. 4.4 [= Pes. R. 14.10], which allude to the role of wisdom in creation without explicit mention of the Torah. The Torah is also at times identified with the personified wisdom of Proverbs 1–9 generally, without necessarily implying any cosmological import. See, for example, Gen. R. XLIII.6; Gen. R. LIX.2; Gen. R. LXX.5; Lev. R. XI.3; Lev. R. XXV.1; Lev. R. XXIX.5 = Pes. K. 23.5; Lev. R. XXX.1 = Pes. K. 27.1 [= Pes. R. 51.1]; Lev. R. XXXV.6; Pes. K. 12.13; Song R. I.1, §3; Song R. VIII.5, §1.
106. Gen. R. XVII.5; Gen. R. XLIV.17.
107. Gen. R. I.4. Cf. Sip̄rê Deut. §37; Ned. 39b; Pes. 54a; PRE §3, f. 6a–6b.
108. Gen. R. I.8.
109. Gen. R. XXVIII.4. Cf. Gen. R. I.10 and its variant in Song R. V.11, §4. A tradition in Song R. IV.4, §9 ascribed to R. Berekhiah declares that God foreshortened the thousand generations in order to bring the people of Israel the Torah. A Midrash in Song R. IV.4, §1 designates Moses as he "who came for a thousand generations." See also Gen. R. I.4; Gen. R. XXI.9; Lev. R. IX.3; Lev. R. XXIII.3; Pes. K. 12.24, which mention the tradition that the Torah was revealed after twenty-six generations. The tradition that the Torah remained hidden for 974 generations before the world was created is expressed more directly in the Babylonian Talmud, in Šab. 88b and Zeb. 116a; cf. Ḥag. 13b–14a; Pes. 118a. Cf. also Pes. R. 21.21; Pes. R. 5.3.
110. Gen. R. VIII.2.

111. This homily, including the tradition concerning the Torah's preexistent status, is also found with slight variations in Song R. V.11, §1–4. The homily in Song of Songs Rabbāh culminates with an allusion to the tradition that the Torah, which was to have been commanded after one thousand generations, was in fact revealed after twenty-six generations.
112. Lev. R. XIX.1.
113. This homily appears almost verbatim in Song R. V.11, §1. Song of Songs Rabbāh omits the reference to the primordial Torah being engraved in gold, although it does interpret "the finest gold" as referring to the words of Torah. The tradition that the Torah existed two thousand years prior to the universe is also briefly mentioned, without explicit reference to Prov. 8.30 and Ps. 90.4, in Pes. K. 12.24, where it is conflated with the tradition that the Torah was revealed after twenty-six generations. Cf. Pes. R. 46.1.

    Closely related to the notions discussed above regarding the preexistence of the Torah is the frequently repeated assertion that the world was created for the sake of the Torah, a concept that assumes that the Torah was at least contemplated, if not actually created, by God prior to creation. See, for example, Gen. R. I.4; Gen. R. I.10; Gen. R. XII.2; Lev. R. XXIII.3; Song R. V.11, §4. Cf. Pes. R. 21.21, et al.
114. Gen. R. XXIV.2. Cf. Sanh. 38b; ʻAZ 5a; Pes. R. 23.1; Tanḥ., ed. Buber, B^{e}rē'šîṯ §28.
115. Gen. R. XXIV.5. See also Gen. R. XVI.5, which interprets Gen. 2.15, "And the Lord God took the man and put him in the Garden of Eden to till (*ʻāḇaḏ*) it and to keep (*šāmar*) it," to mean that God intended for Adam to observe the Sabbath or, according to an alternative interpretation, to offer sacrifices. Cf. Sip̄rê Deut. §41; PRE §12, f. 29b.
116. Gen. R. XXIV.7.
117. Gen. R. XXI.9. Cf. Tanḥ., ed. Buber, B^{e}rē'šîṯ §25.
118. Gen. R. XLIV.21; Pes. K. 5.2 [= Pes. R. 15.2]; cf. Gen. R. XLIX.2. The parallel tradition in Mek., ed. Lauterbach, Ba-ḥôḏeš §9, vol. 2, p. 268, is attributed to R. Nathan. Cf. Tanḥ. P^{e}qûḏê §8; Exod. R. LI.7. The images of both the "flaming sword" and the "flaming torch" point to the association of the Torah, and of the revelation in particular, with fire—an association that is also found in Tannaitic Midrashim, as we have seen, and that will be discussed further below.
119. Gen. R. LXI.1; Gen. R. XCV.3. The kidneys were traditionally viewed as a source of wisdom and counsel. Cf. Tanḥ., ed. Buber, Wa-yiggaš §12. See also Gen. R. XLIII.6, which interprets Gen. 14.18, "And Melchizedek king of Salem brought out bread and wine," to mean that he revealed the Torah to Abraham. "Bread" and "wine" are understood in light of Prov. 9.5, "Come, eat of my bread and drink of the wine I [wisdom] have mixed," as referring to the Torah.

120. Lev. R. II.10; Gen. R. XCV.3; cf. Gen. R. XLIX.2; Gen. R. LXIV.4. Cf. Qid. IV.14; Yoma 28b; Tanḥ., ed. Buber, Lek̲ Lᵉk̲ā §1; Tanḥ., ed. Buber, Lek̲ Lᵉk̲ā §14; Tanḥ., ed. Buber, Tôlᵉd̲ôt̲ §1; Tanḥ., ed. Buber, Wa-yiggaš §12; PRE §31, f. 69a–69b.
121. Gen. R. LVI.11; cf. Lev. R. II.10.
122. Gen. R. LXVI.1; Gen. R. LXIII.10; Gen. R. XCV.3; cf. Lev. R. II.10. Gen. R. LXIII.10 understands Gen. 25.27, "Jacob was a quiet man, dwelling in tents (*yōšēb̲ 'ōhālîm*)," to mean that Jacob studied in two tents or houses of study. Targum Onkelos, Targum Neofiti 1, and Targum Pseudo-Jonathan, in their respective renderings of Gen. 25.27, similarly interpret "tents" as referring to the house(s) of study in which Jacob served. Cf. Pes. R. 5.7; Tanḥ., ed. Buber, Tôlᵉd̲ôt̲ §1; Tanḥ., ed. Buber, Tôlᵉd̲ôt̲ §2; Tanḥ., ed. Buber, Wa-yišlaḥ §9; Tanḥ., ed. Buber, Wa-yiggaš §12; Tanḥ. Šᵉmôt̲ §1; PRE §32, f. 73a, 73b.

    In contrast to Jacob, who studied and observed the Torah, his brother Esau is said to have been estranged from the commandments of the Torah. See, for example, Ruth R. Proem III.
123. Gen. R. XCV.3; Gen. R. XCIV.3; cf. Lev. R. II.10. Cf. Tanḥ., ed. Buber, Wa-yiggaš §12.
124. But cf. Song R. I.2, §5 and Song R. I.3, §1, which suggest that while the patriarchs observed select precepts, they did not observe all of the 613 *mitzvot* that Israel later received at Mount Sinai. Cf. Exod. R. XXX.9.
125. Gen. R. I.1.
126. See 'Ab. III.14; Sip̄rê Deut. §48.
127. The last portion of this pericope is replicated almost verbatim in Tanḥ., ed. Buber, Bᵉrē'šît̲ §5, where it is attributed to R. Judah b. Il'ai. A similar conjunction of Gen. 1.1 and Prov. 8.22 is found in Targum Neofiti 1 to Gen. 1.1, in which *bᵉrē'šît̲ bārā' Elohim* is interpreted as *bᵉ-ḥok̲māh bārā'*. Cf. Fragment Targums P and V to Gen. 1.1.
128. See p. 140.
129. See, for example, Moore, *Judaism*, vol. 1, pp. 267–268; Hengel, *Judaism and Hellenism*, vol. 1, p. 171; Urbach, *The Sages*, vol. 1, pp. 198–200; Henry Slonimsky, "The Philosophy Implicit in the Midrash," *Hebrew Union College Annual* 27 (1956): 244–246.
130. See, for example, Henry A. Fischel, "The Transformation of Wisdom in the World of Midrash," in *Aspects of Wisdom in Judaism and Early Christianity*, ed. Wilken, p. 80. Urbach notes that Maimonides, in discussing the expression *histakkēl* ("to look at, contemplate"), which corresponds to *hibbîṭ* in the Midrash attributed to R. Hoshaiah, remarks that "Plato uses this very expression when he states that God contemplates the world of Ideas and thus produces the existing beings." Moses Maimonides, *Guide for the Perplexed*, pt. 2, chap. 6. Cited in Urbach, *The Sages*, vol. 1, p. 199 with n. 69.
131. Urbach, *The Sages*, vol. 1, p. 200.

132. This does not mean to suggest that the author of the Genesis Rabbāh proem necessarily appropriated all of the Hellenistic elements that were incorporated into the Jewish conception of Torah/wisdom by the writers of the wisdom books of the Apocrypha and by the Alexandrian Jewish philosophers Aristobulus and Philo. In particular, it is highly unlikely that the proem's author borrowed directly from Philo in the analogy of the blueprint. Indeed, he was probably not even aware of Philo's writings. The similarities between their uses of the analogy can better be explained by their access to a common tradition, which intermingled traditional Jewish wisdom speculation with Greek philosophical categories.
133. Gen. R. I.13.
134. Gen. R. XII.14. Cf. Tanḥ., ed. Buber, B^{e}rē'šîṯ §17.
135. Lev. R. XXXV.4.
136. Pes. K. 12.1; cf. Lev. R. XII.3. Cf. Mak. 23b. "Members" (*'ēḇārîm*) refers to the joints, bones, or organs that are covered with flesh and sinews, not including the teeth. The 248 members of the body are listed in the Mishnah in 'Ohol. I.8.
137. See, for example, Lev. R. XXIII.3; Song R. VII.1, §1; Song R. I.9, §6; Gen. R. LXVI.2; Ruth R. Proem I, discussed in chapter 4, pp. 274–275.
138. See, for example, Gen. R. XXVIII.4; Gen. R. I.10; Song R. V.11, §4; Pes. K. Suppl. 3.2.
139. See, for example, Lev. R. III.7; Song R. I.3, §1; Song R. VIII.11, §2.
140. See, for example, Gen. R. IV.4; Gen. R. XXIV.2; Lev. R. III.7; Pes. K. Suppl. 1.15; Esth. R. I.12; Song R. IV.5, §1. Cf. Mek., ed. Lauterbach, B^{e}-šallaḥ §7, vol. 1, p. 248; Mek., ed. Lauterbach, Šîrāṯā' §3, vol. 2, p. 26; Mek., ed. Lauterbach, Šîrāṯā' §4, vol. 2, p. 32; Mek., ed. Lauterbach, Šîrāṯā' §8, vol. 2, pp. 62, 63; Mek., ed. Lauterbach, Šîrāṯā' §10, vol. 2, pp. 78, 79; Mek., ed. Lauterbach, Wa-yassa' §1, vol. 2, p. 92; Mek., ed. Lauterbach, Ba-ḥōḏeš §8, vol. 2, p. 263; Mek., ed. Lauterbach, Ba-ḥôḏeš §9, vol. 2, p. 275; Sip̄rê Deut. §49; Sip̄rê Deut. §307; Sip̄rê Deut. §343; Sip̄rê Num. §102; Sip̄rê Num. §103; 'Erub. 13b; Meg. 13b; Soṭ. 10b; Qid. 30b; Qid. 31a; Sanh. 19a; Pes. R. 21.7.
141. This tradition appears in Gen. R. XXXI.8 and Gen. R. XVIII.4, where it is attributed to R. Phinehas and R. Hezekiah (or R. Ḥilkiah) in the name of R. Simon b. Pazzi. Cf. Tanḥ., ed. Buber, Nōaḥ §28.
142. See, for example, *Sēp̄er Y^{e}ṣîrāh* 2.2: "Twenty-two letters are the foundation: He engraved them, He hewed them out, He combined them, He weighed them, and He set them at opposites, and He formed through them everything that is formed and everything that is destined to be formed." For discussions of the *Sēp̄er Y^{e}ṣîrāh,* see Gershom Scholem, "The Sefer Yeẓirah," in his *Kabbalah,* Library of Jewish Knowledge (Jerusalem: Keter, 1974), pp. 23–30; idem, "The Name of God and the Linguistic Theory of the Kabbala," pt. 1, pp. 72–76; Elias Lipiner, *The Metaphysics of the Hebrew Alphabet* [in Hebrew] (Jerusalem: Magnes

Press, Hebrew University, 1989), pp. 112–166. For a translation and commentary on the text, see David R. Blumenthal, "*Sefer Yetsira*: Text and Commentary," chapter 3 of his *Understanding Jewish Mysticism: A Source Reader*, [vol. 1], *The Merkabah Tradition and the Zoharic Tradition*, The Library of Judaic Learning, vol. 2 (New York: Ktav, 1978), pp. 15–44.

143. The Hebrew letters are personified in several homilies in classical Amoraic Midrashim. For example, in Lam. R. Proem XXIV the personified letters come before God one by one to testify that Israel had transgressed the Torah. In Lev. R. XIX.2 and Song R. V.11, §4 the *yōḏ* prostrates itself before God and laments that it has been removed from the name of Sarai, the righteous wife of Abraham. In Gen. R. I. 10, Pes. K. 12.24, and Song R. V.11, §4 the *'ālep̄*, the first letter of the Hebrew alphabet, is depicted as complaining to God that the world should have been created with it and not with *bêṯ*, the second letter. This latter tradition found vivid expression in a later mystically oriented text, *2 Alphabet of R. Akiba* (ca. 7th–9th c. C.E.), in a pericope that portrays a competition among the twenty-two letters in which each letter comes before God one by one to present its case concerning why he should create the world with it. See *2 Alphabet of R. Akiba*, in *Bêṯ ha-Miḏrāš*, ed. Adolph Jellinek, vol. 3, 3d ed. (Jerusalem: Wahrmann Books, 1967), pp. 50–55.

144. Gen. R. I.10; cf. Pes. K. 12.24; Song R. V.11, §4. Cf. Pes. R. 21.21.

145. Gen. R. XII.10. Cf. Men. 29b; Pes. R. 21.21; Tanḥ., ed. Buber, Beˈrē'šîṯ §16.

146. In Song R. V.11, §2 this tradition is ascribed to R. Levi.

147. Lev. R. XIX.2; cf. Song R. V.11, §2. For example, in Exod. 34.14, "For you shall bow down to no other (*'aḥēr*) god," if the *rēš* of *'aḥēr* is changed to a *dāleṯ* the text would read, "For you shall not bow down to the one (*'eḥāḏ*) God." Cf. 'Erub. 13a.

148. Song R. V.11, §1–4 replicates most of the homily in Lev. R. XIX.1–2, appending at the end, in §4, the tradition found in Gen. R. I.10 in which the *'ālep̄* complains to God about his creation of the world with *bêṯ* rather than with it.

149. There is of course a traditional method of vocalization, but there are variations within this tradition.

150. Gen. R. III.2; Gen. R. IV.6; Gen. R. XII.10; Gen. R. XXVII.1. Cf. Mek., ed. Lauterbach, Šîrāṯā' §10, vol. 2, pp. 78–79; Mek., ed. Lauterbach, Ba-ḥôḏeš §7, vol. 2, p. 255; Šab. 119b; Pes. R. 49.10; Pes. R. 27.4; Pes. R. 23.5; Tanḥ., ed. Buber, Beˈrē'šîṯ §11; Deut. R. V.13; PRE §7, f. 15b.

151. Gen. R. III.2; cf. Gen. R. XII.10; Gen. R. XXVII.1. Variants of this tradition, which emphasize that God created the world "neither with labor nor with toil," are also found in Gen. R. X.9 and Gen. R. XII.2, although no mention is made in these passages of creation through the word.

152. Gen. R. XLVI.3. This interpretation is derived by reading the divine name El Shaddai in Gen. 17.1 as *še-day*, "who [said] 'enough.'" Cf. Ḥag. 12a; Tanḥ., ed. Buber, Bᵉrēʾšîṯ §11; Tanḥ., ed. Buber, Leḵ Lᵉḵā §25; Tanḥ., ed. Buber, Mi-qēṣ §12; Tanḥ., ed. Buber, Mi-qēṣ §16; PRE §3, f. 7b.
153. ʾAb. V.1.
154. Gen. 1.3, 6, 9, 11, 14–15, 20, 24, 26. The spirit (*rûaḥ*) of God moving upon the face of the waters in Gen. 1.2 is understood in light of Ps. 29.3, "The voice (*qôl*) of the Lord is upon the waters," to mean the voice of God.
155. Cf. RH 32a; Meg. 21b; Pes. R. 21.19; Pes. R. 40.5; PRE §3, f. 8b; PRE §32, f. 74a.
156. Gen. 1.3, 6, 9, 11, 14–15, 20, 24, 26.
157. See, for example, Lam. R. Proem XXIII. Cf. Sip̄rê Num. §41; Soṭ. 21a; Taan. 7b; Meg. 16b; Pes. R. 46.3; Deut. R. IV.4; Exod. R. XXXIV.2; Exod. R. XXXVI.3.
158. See, for example, Song R. I.2, §3, which identifies the Torah with the word in Ps. 119.105, although it is not concerned in this context with discussing the Torah's nature as light. This verse is, however, cited in this connection in later rabbinic texts. See, for example, Exod. R. XXXVI.3, which cites both Ps. 119.105 and Prov. 6.23 in its discussion of how the words of Torah give forth light. Cf. also Pes. R. 8.5.
159. Gen. R. III.1 interprets Ps. 119.130, "The opening of Thy words (*dᵉḇārîm*) gives light (*hēʾîr*)," to mean that the opening of God's mouth in speech at the beginning of creation brought forth light: "And God said, 'Let there be light.'" No explicit mention is made of the Torah in this Midrash. The variant of this tradition in Exod. R. L.1 uses Ps. 119.130 to establish a connection between the light of creation and the light of Torah.
160. For the association of the revelation of the Torah with light, see, for example, Gen. R. XXVI.7.
161. See, for example, Lam. R. Proem II.
162. See, for example, Pes. K. 4.4 [= Pes. R. 14.10]; Lev. R. XIX.1; Lev. R. XXX.2 = Pes. K. 27.2 [= Pes. R. 51.4]. Cf. Ber. 17a; Ber. 5b; PRE §2, f. 4a.
163. See, for example, Lev. R. XX.10 = Pes. K. 26.9; Song R. III.7, §5. The lustrous appearance of Moses's countenance is of particular interest in later rabbinic texts. Cf. Deut. R. III.12; Exod. R. XLVII.6; Exod R. XXXIII.1; Pes. R. 10.6; Pes. R. 21.6; Deut. R. XI.3; PRE §2, f. 4a.
164. See, for example, Pes. K. Suppl. 3.2. Cf. Ber. 22a; Taan. 7a; Taan. 4a.
165. Gen. R. XXI.9. Cf. Tanḥ., ed. Buber, Bᵉrēʾšîṯ §25.
166. Gen. R. XLIV.21; Pes. K. 5.2 [= Pes. R. 15.2]. Cf. Mek., ed. Lauterbach, Ba-ḥôḏeš §9, vol. 2, p. 268; Tanḥ. Pᵉqûḏê §8; Exod. R. LI.7.
167. For additional references concerning the use of images of fire in accounts of the Sinai event, see chapter 4.

168. Lev. R. XVI.4; Song R. I.10, §2; Ruth R. VI.4; cf. Song R. I.12, §1.
169. See, for example, Song R. V.11, §6; Pes. K. Suppl. 1.17; Pes. K. Suppl. 1.20; Lev. R. IV.1; Lam. R. III.1, §1; Song R. I.9, §4. Cf. Mek., ed. Lauterbach, Ba-ḥôdeš §5, vol. 2, p. 235; Mek., ed. Lauterbach, Be-šallaḥ §7, vol. 1, p. 247; Sip̄rê Deut. §343; Beṣ. 25b; Ber. 6a; Ber. 62a; Soṭ. 4b; Pes. R. 33.10; Tanḥ., ed. Buber, Berē'šîṯ §4; Exod. R. XLI.4; Num. R. XXII.9; Deut. R. V.4; PRE §41, f. 96a.
170. See Song R. V.11, §6, cited in chapter 4, p. 281. Cf. Deut. R. III.12.
171. An anonymous Midrash in Song R. II.5, §1 reads *'ăšîšôṯ* in S. S. 2.5, "Sustain me with raisins (*'ăšîšôṯ*)," as *'iššôṯ*, "fires"—the two fires of Written Torah and Oral Torah. Cf. Pes. K. 12.3.
172. Pes. K. Suppl. 3.2. Cf. 'Ab. VI.10; Ḥag. 27a.
173. Lev. R. XVI.4; Song R. I.10, §2; Ruth R. VI.4; cf. Pes. K. Suppl. 1.17. In the version of this tradition in Lev. R. XVI.4 and Song R. I.10, §2, Ben Azzai is asked whether he has been exploring the "chambers of the Merkabah," since the study of *ma'ăśēh merkāḇāh* was associated with the appearance of fire. He replies no, that he has been interconnecting verses from the Torah (Pentateuch), Nevi'im, and Ketuvim. The association of Merkabah traditions with fire imagery will be discussed in chapter 4. Cf. Ḥag. 14b; Suk. 28a.
174. See, for example, Šab. 31a; Ber. 5a; 'Erub. 54b.
175. See, for example, Meg. 19b.
176. Ḥag. 3b. See Heinemann's discussion of this homily in Joseph Heinemann with Jakob J. Petuchowski, eds., *Literature of the Synagogue* (New York: Behrman House, 1975), pp. 113–117. Cf. Pes. R. 3.2; Num. R. XV.22.
177. Men. 29b.
178. BM 59b.
179. 'Erub. 21b; RH 19a; Taan. 17b. Cf. Song R. I.2, §2; Pes. R. 3.2.
180. BM 33a.
181. Giṭ. 60b.
182. See Pes. R. 5.1; Tanḥ., ed. Buber, Wa-yērā' §6; Tanḥ., ed. Buber, Kî Ṯiśśā' §17; Exod. R. XLVII.1,3, which will be discussed on p. 182.
183. Ḥag. 11b–16a.
184. See, for example, Ned. 39b; Pes. 54a; Pes. 87b, in which Prov. 8.22 is invoked as a proof text. For the identification of the Torah with wisdom in Proverbs 1–9 generally, see, for example, Ber. 32b; Šab. 88b; Taan. 7a; MQ 9a; MQ 16b. Cf. MQ 25b–26a.
185. Ned. 39b; Pes. 54a. Both passages include the same proof texts for the seven preexistent items, with the exception that Pes. 54a does not cite Ps. 93.2 to substantiate the preexistence of the Temple. Cf. Gen. R. I.4; PRE §3, f. 6a–6b.

The Talmud, in Pes. 87b, also contains a variant of the tradition found in 'Āḇôṯ and Tannaitic Midrashim in which the Torah is celebrated as one of the creations/possessions of God, with Prov. 8.22 as a proof text. The Talmud's enumeration, which most closely resembles that of 'Āḇôṯ, includes heaven and earth, the Temple, and the people of Israel as the other creations/possessions. Cf. 'Ab. VI.10 (Qinyan Torah); Mek., ed. Lauterbach, Šîrāṯā' §9, vol. 2, pp. 75–76; Sip̄rê Deut. §309.

See also the tradition in Sanh. 91b, ascribed to Rab Judah in the name of Rab, in which the Torah is said to be an inheritance destined for Israel since the six days of creation.

186. This tradition is incorporated in an aggadah ascribed to R. Joshua b. Levi in Šab. 88b and to R. Eleazar of Modi'im in Zeb. 116a. The expressions "secret treasure" (*ḥămûḏāh g^enûzāh*) (Šab. 88b) and "precious treasure" (*ḥemdāh ṭôḇāh*) (Zeb. 116a) recall the designation of the Torah as the "precious instrument" (*k^elî ḥemdāh*) with which the world was created in 'Ab. III.14. Ḥag. 13b–14a mentions the 974 generations that remained uncreated, and Pes. 118a refers to the twenty-six generations prior to the revelation of the Torah. Cf. Gen. R. XXVIII.4; Gen. R. I.10; Song R. V.11, §4; and other relevant references from classical Amoraic Midrashim cited earlier in n. 109. Cf. also Pes. R. 21.21; Pes. R. 5.3.

187. This tradition appears twice in Pes. 54a, with variations only in the subsidiary items appended to the initial list of ten items. Cf. 'Ab. V.6; Sip̄rê Deut. §355; Mek., ed. Lauterbach, Wa-yassa' §6, vol. 2, pp. 124–125. The Talmudic version agrees with Sip̄rê Deut. §355 in its initial enumeration of the ten items: the well, the manna, the rainbow, the letters, the writing, the tablets, the sepulcher of Moses, the cave in which Moses and Elijah stood, the mouth of the she-ass, and the mouth of the earth. The subsidiary items are also found in Sip̄rê on Deuteronomy's version. Cf. also PRE §19, f. 44a.

188. Sanh. 38b; 'AZ 5a. The parallel tradition in Gen. R. XXIV.2 is ascribed to R. Judah b. Simon. Cf. Pes. R. 23.1; Tanḥ., ed. Buber, B^erē'šîṯ §28.

189. See, for example, 'AZ 3a.

190. Ned. 32a. Cf. 'AZ 9a, which cites the tradition that the duration of the world is divided into three two-thousand year periods: the pre-Torah period, the period of the Torah, and the period of the Messiah. The period of the Torah is calculated as beginning with Abraham, when he was fifty-two years old and had "gotten souls" in Haran (Gen. 12.5)—that is, when he and Sarah had begun to convert nonbelievers to worship of the one God.

191. Cf. Qid. IV.14; Lev. R. II.10; Gen. R. XCV.3; Gen. R. LXIV.4; Gen. R. XLIX.2; Tanḥ., ed. Buber, Leḵ L^eḵā §1; Tanḥ., ed. Buber, Leḵ L^eḵā §14; Tanḥ., ed. Buber, Tôl^eḏôṯ §1; Tanḥ., ed. Buber, Wa-yiggaš §12; PRE §31, f. 69a–69b.

192. For references see n. 184.

193. Cf. Lev. R. XI.1.

194. Ḥag. 12a; cf. Ber. 55a. Cf. Exod. R. XLVIII.4.

195. In Mak. 23b this tradition is attributed to R. Simlai. Cf. Pes. K. 12.1; Lev. R. XII.3.
196. As will be discussed in chapter 4, this conception is linked in several traditions to the notion that if Israel had not accepted the Torah at Mount Sinai, the creation would have reverted to chaos. See, for example, Šab. 88a; ʿAZ 3a; ʿAZ 5a, discussed on pp. 287–288.
197. See Ned. 32a, cited in chapter 4, p. 288, and chapter 6, pp. 376–377. Cf. Pes. 68b.
198. See, for example, Sanh. 99a; Šeb. 13a; Ber. 22a; Taan. 4a; Taan. 7a; Šab. 88b; Sanh. 34a. All of these passages, with the exception of Sanh. 99a and Šeb. 13a, assume that the Torah is identical with the divine Word in Jer. 23.29, "Is not My word (*dāḇār*) like fire (*'ēš*), says the Lord, and like a hammer that breaks the rock in pieces?" The association of the Torah with fire will be discussed below.
199. See, for example, Ber. 6a; Ber. 21a; Ber. 11b; Šab. 88b–89a; Šab. 115b–116a; Mak. 11a.
200. See, for example, Šab. 104a.
201. Men. 29b. Cf. Gen. R. XII.10; Pes. R. 21.21; Tanḥ., ed. Buber, B^{e}rē'šîṯ §16.
202. Ber. 55a.
203. Sanh. 65b; Sanh. 67b.
204. Šab. 89a; Men. 29b. See also the story in ʿAZ 18a regarding the martyrdom of R. Ḥanina (Ḥananyah) b. Teradion, which suggests that when a Torah scroll is destroyed (in this case through burning) the letters ascend to their supernal source. A tradition ascribed to R. Alexandri in Pes. 87b similarly maintains that when the tablets of the covenant were broken by Moses at Mount Sinai, the letters flew up and returned to their source. Cf. PRE §45, f. 107b–108a.
205. ʿErub. 13a. Cf. Lev. R. XIX.2; Song R. V.11, §2.
206. See, for example, ʿErub. 13b; Meg. 13b; Soṭ. 10b; Qid. 30b; Qid. 31a; Sanh. 19a. Cf. Mek., ed. Lauterbach, B^{e}-šallaḥ §7, vol. 1, p. 248; Mek., ed. Lauterbach, Šîrāṯā' §3, vol. 2, p. 26; Mek., ed. Lauterbach, Šîrāṯā' §4, vol. 2, p. 32; Mek., ed. Lauterbach, Šîrāṯā' §8, vol. 2, pp. 62, 63; Mek., ed. Lauterbach, Šîrāṯā' §10, vol. 2, pp. 78, 79; Mek., ed. Lauterbach, Wa-yassaʿ §1, vol. 2, p. 92; Mek., ed. Lauterbach, Ba-ḥôḏeš §8, vol. 2, p. 263; Mek., ed. Lauterbach, Ba-ḥôḏeš §9, vol. 2, p. 275; Sip̄rê Deut. §49; Sip̄rê Deut. §307; Sip̄rê Deut. §343; Sip̄rê Num. §102; Sip̄rê Num. §103; Gen. R. IV.4; Gen. R. XXIV.2; Lev. R. III.7; Pes. K. Suppl. 1.15; Esth. R. I.12; Song R. IV.5, §1; Pes. R. 21.7.
207. See, for example, the statement attributed to R. Eleazar in Šab. 119b. A tradition in Ḥag. 14a, ascribed to R. Jonathan through R. Samuel b. Naḥman, interprets the second half of Ps. 33.6, "By the word (*dāḇār*) of the Lord were the heavens made, and all their host by the breath of His mouth," to mean that an angel is created from every utterance that goes forth from God's mouth. Cf. Mek., ed. Lauterbach, Šîrāṯā' §10, vol.

2, pp. 78–79; Mek., ed. Lauterbach, Ba-ḥôḏeš §7, vol. 2, p. 255; Gen. R. III.2; Gen. R. IV.6; Gen. R. XII.10; Gen. R. XXVII.1; Pes. R. 49.10; Pes. R. 27.4; Pes. R. 23.5; Tanḥ., ed. Buber, Bᵉrē'šîṯ §11; Deut. R. V.13; PRE §7, f. 15b.

208. Ber. 57b.

209. See Ḥag. 12a, which contains a variant of the tradition in Gen. R. XLVI.3 that God proclaimed "Enough!" (reading El Shaddai in Gen. 17.1 as *še-day*, "who [said] 'enough'") in order to stop the world from expanding. Cf. Tanḥ., ed. Buber, Bᵉrē'šîṯ §11; Tanḥ., ed. Buber, Leḵ Lᵉḵā §25; Tanḥ., ed. Buber, Mi-qēṣ §12; Tanḥ., ed. Buber, Mi-qēṣ §16; PRE §3, f. 7b.

210. Meg. 21b; RH 32a. In Meg. 21b all nine commands "And God said" are designated as occurring in the first chapter of Genesis, which means that the ninth command would be Gen. 1.29 and not Gen. 2.18, as R. Menaḥem b. Jose is said to have proposed. Cf. Gen. R. XVII.1; 'Ab. V.1; Pes. R. 21.19; Pes. R. 40.5; PRE §3, f. 8b; PRE §32, f. 74a.

211. See, for example, Soṭ. 21a; Taan. 7b; Meg. 16b; cf. BB 4a. Cf. Sip̄rê Num. §41; Lam. R. Proem XXIII; Pes. R. 46.3; Deut. R. IV.4; Exod. R. XXXIV.2; Exod. R. XXXVI.3.

212. Soṭ. 21a. Cf. the tradition attributed to R. Eleazar in Ket. 111b, which maintains that he who makes use of the light of Torah will be revived by the light of Torah at the time of the resurrection.

213. BB 4a. This interpretation, ascribed to Baba b. Buta, appears in the context of an account of how Herod slew all of the rabbis and thereby extinguished the light of the world.

214. Ber. 17a; Tem. 16a; 'Erub. 13b.

215. See, for example, Ber. 5b; BM 84a. Cf. Pes. K. 4.4 = Pes. R. 14.10; Lev. R. XIX.1; Lev. R. XXX.2 = Pes. K. 27.2 = Pes. R. 51.4; PRE §2, f. 4a.

216. Beṣ. 25b; Ber. 6a; Ber. 62a; Soṭ. 4b. Cf. Mek., ed. Lauterbach, Ba-ḥôḏeš §5, vol. 2, p. 235; Mek., ed. Lauterbach, Bᵉ-šallaḥ §7, vol. 1, p. 247; Sip̄rê Deut. §343; Song R. V.11, §6; Pes. K. Suppl. 1.17; Pes. K. Suppl. 1.20; Lev. R. IV.1; Lam. R. III.1, §1; Song R. I.9, §4; Pes. R. 33.10; Tanḥ., ed. Buber, Bᵉrē'šîṯ §4; Exod. R. XLI.4; Num. R. XXII.9; Deut. R. V.4; PRE §41, f. 96a.

217. See, for example, Ber. 22a; Taan. 7a; Taan. 4a; cf. Ḥag. 27a. Cf. also Pes. K. Suppl. 3.2.

218. Ḥag. 27a. Conversely, BB 79a suggests that those who depart from the fiery words of Torah are themselves consumed by fire and fall into Gehenna. Cf. 'Ab. II.10; Pes. K. Suppl. 3.2.

219. See also Suk. 28a. Cf. Lev. R. XVI.4; Song R. I.10, §2; Ruth R. VI.4; Pes. K. Suppl. 1.17. For a discussion of Ḥag. 14b, and its parallels in T Ḥag. II.1 and JT Ḥag. II.1, 77a, see David J. Halperin, *The Faces of the Chariot: Early Jewish Responses to Ezekiel's Vision* (Tübingen: J. C. B. Mohr [Paul Siebeck], 1988), pp. 13–19; idem, *The Merkabah in Rabbinic Literature*, American Oriental Series, vol. 62 (New Haven:

American Oriental Society, 1980), pp. 107–140. See also Ephraim E. Urbach, "The Traditions about Merkabah Mysticism in the Tannaitic Period" [in Hebrew], in *Studies in Mysticism and Religion Presented to Gershom G. Scholem on His Seventieth Birthday,* eds. E. E. Urbach, R. J. Zwi Werblowsky, and Ch. Wirszubski (Jerusalem: Magnes Press, Hebrew University, 1967), pp. 2–11 [Hebrew section]. The origin and nature of rabbinic Merkabah speculations will be discussed in chapter 4.

220. The final compilation of the earlier part of the Midrash, on Psalms 1–118, has been variously dated from the seventh century to the ninth century or later. For a summary of the scholarly debate, see William G. Braude, trans., *The Midrash on Psalms,* vol. 1, Yale Judaica Series, vol. 13 (New Haven: Yale University Press, 1959), pp. xxv–xxxii.

221. The numbering of *pisqā*'s and sections in subsequent references follows that of William G. Braude, trans., *Pesikta Rabbati: Discourses for Feasts, Fasts, and Special Sabbaths,* 2 vols., Yale Judaica Series, vol. 18 (New Haven: Yale University Press, 1968). Braude's numbering of *pisqā*'s is based primarily on the critical edition of M. Friedmann (Vienna, 1880), which is the Hebrew edition upon which my own translations are based. See ibid., vol. 1, p. 28 with n. 41.

222. The two P^{e}sîqtā's share five entire chapters that are nearly identical, with *pisqā*'s 15–18 and 32 of P^{e}sîqtā' Rabbāṯî paralleling *pisqā*'s 5–8 and 18, respectively, of P^{e}sîqtā' d^{e}-R. Kahana. In addition, there is a substantial amount of parallel material in Pes. R. §14 and Pes. K. §4; Pes. R. §29/30A and §29/30B and Pes. K §16; Pes. R. §[51] and Pes. K. §27; Pes. R. §[52] and Pes. K. §28. For a comparative analysis of the literary structures and topical programs of P^{e}sîqtā' d^{e}-R. Kahana and P^{e}sîqtā' Rabbāṯî, see Jacob Neusner, *From Tradition to Imitation: The Plan and Program of Pesiqta Rabbati and Pesiqta deRab Kahana,* Brown Judaic Studies, no. 80 (Atlanta: Scholars Press, 1987).

223. *Pisqā*'s 18 and [51] of P^{e}sîqtā' Rabbāṯî closely resemble chapters 28 and 30, respectively, of Leviticus Rabbāh.

224. *Pisqā*'s 1–14, 19, 25, 29, 31, 33, 38–45, 47–[49] follow this pattern, with the exception that *pisqā*'s 38 and 45 do not include the formulaic "R. Tanḥuma opened (*pāṯaḥ*)."

225. For a summary of the scholarly debate concerning the date and provenance of P^{e}sîqtā' Rabbāṯî, see Braude, trans., *Pesikta Rabbati,* vol. 1, pp. 20–26.

226. The halakhic proems in Deuteronomy Rabbāh begin with the formula, "*Hălāḵāh 'āḏām mi-Yiśrā'ēl mahû*" ("What is the halakhah for an Israelite?"), instead of the more usual "*Y^{e}lamm^{e}ḏēnû rabbênû*" with which the halakhic proems of other Tanḥûmā' Y^{e}lamm^{e}ḏēnû Midrashim begin.

227. See Tanḥ. Yiṯrô §11, cited in chapter 4, p. 295. Cf. Exod. R. XXVIII.6.

228. Pes. R. 3.2. Cf. Ḥag. 3b. See also Num. R. XV.22, which gives a brief commentary on Eccles. 12.11.
229. Cf. Song R. I.2, §2; 'Erub. 21b; RH 19a; Taan. 17b.
230. Pes. R. 3.2. Cf. 'Erub. 21b.
231. Pes. R. 5.1; Tanḥ., ed. Buber, Wa-yērā' §6. Cf. Giṭ. 60b. See Heinemann's discussion of the Tanḥûmā"s version of this homily in *Literature of the Synagogue*, pp. 153–155.
232. Exod. R. XLVII.1; Tanḥ., ed. Buber, Kî Ṯiśśā' §17; cf. Exod. R. XLVII.3; Exod. R. XLVII.7. Cf. Lev. R. XXII.1. See also Pes. R. 21.6 and Num. R. XVIII.21, which contain the standard enumeration of the contents of the revelation: Bible, Mishnah, Talmud, and Aggadah.
233. See, for example, Pes. R. 53.2; Tanḥ., ed. Buber, B^{e}rē'šîṯ §5; Tanḥ. B^{e}rē'šîṯ §1; Exod. R. XXX.9. The creative role of wisdom in Prov. 3.19–20 is linked to the Torah in Exod. R. XLVII.4; Tanḥ. B^{e}rē'šîṯ §1; cf. Exod. R. XLVIII.4. With respect to the identification of the Torah with the personified wisdom of Proverbs 1–9 generally, see, for example, Pes. R. 51.1 [= Pes. K. 27.1; Lev. R. XXX.1]; Tanḥ. B^{e}rē'šîṯ §1; Tanḥ., ed. Buber, Nōaḥ §2; Tanḥ., ed. Buber, Wa-yišlaḥ §9; Exod. R. XLVII.7; Deut. R. I.1; Deut. R. VII.3; cf. Exod. R. XXX.5; Exod. R. XLI.3.
234. See, for example, Pes. R. 46.1; Pes. R. 42.3; Pes. R. 53.2.
235. Pes. R. 53.2.
236. Pes. R. 46.1. Cf. Gen. R. VIII.2; Lev. R. XIX.1; Song R. V.11, §1; Pes. K. 12.24.
237. Pes. R. 21.21. The twenty-six generations between the time of creation and the Sinai revelation are also mentioned in Pes. R. 5.3. Cf. Gen. R. I.10; Song R. V.11, §4. For additional parallels from classical Amoraic Midrashim and the Babylonian Talmud, see nn. 109, 186.

    The pericope in Pes. R. 21.21 also includes the notion that the world was created for the sake of the Torah. Cf. Gen. R. I.4; Gen. R. I.10; Gen. R. XII.2; Lev. R. XXIII.3; Song R. V.11, §4.
238. See, for example, Exod. R. XXX.9; Exod. R. XXXIV.2.
239. Pes. R. 23.1; Tanḥ., ed. Buber, B^{e}rē'šîṯ §28. Cf. Gen. R. XXIV.2; Sanh. 38b; 'AZ 5a.
240. Tanḥ., ed. Buber, B^{e}rē'šîṯ §25. Cf. Gen. R. XXI.9.
241. Tanḥ., ed. Buber, B^{e}rē'šîṯ §25. Cf. PRE §12, f. 29b.
242. Pes. R. 15.2 [= Pes. K. 5.2]; Tanḥ. P^{e}qûḏê §8; Exod. R. LI.7. Cf. Mek., ed. Lauterbach, Ba-ḥōḏeš §9, vol. 2, p. 268; Gen. R. XLIV.21.
243. Tanḥ., ed. Buber, Wa-yiggaš §12; Tanḥ., ed. Buber, Leḵ L^{e}ḵā §1; Tanḥ., ed. Buber, Leḵ L^{e}ḵā §14; Tanḥ., ed. Buber, Tôl^{e}ḏôṯ §1; Tanḥ., ed. Buber, Tôl^{e}ḏôṯ §2; Tanḥ., ed. Buber, Wa-yišlaḥ §9; Tanḥ. Š^{e}môṯ §1. Tanḥ., ed. Buber, Wa-yiggaš §12 reiterates almost verbatim Gen. R. XCV.3. Cf. Gen. R. LXI.1; Gen. R. LXIV.4; Gen. R. XLIX.2; Gen. R. LXIII.10; Gen. R. LXVI.1; Gen. R. XCIV.3. Cf. also Qid. IV.14; Lev. R. II.10; Yoma 28b; Ned. 32a; PRE §31, f. 69a–69b; PRE §32, f. 73a, 73b.

For an alternative perspective, see the tradition in Exod. R. XXX.9 that maintains that Abraham and Jacob were only given a limited number of commandments (eight and nine, respectively) and that it was only to the people of Israel at Mount Sinai that all of the commandments of the Torah were given. Cf. Song R. I.2, §5; Song R. I.3, §1.

244. Tanḥ., ed. Buber, Lek̲ L^e^k̲ā §14.
245. Tanḥ., ed. Buber, Tôl^e^d̲ôt̲ §1.
246. Tanḥ., ed. Buber, Wa-yišlaḥ §9; Tanḥ., ed. Buber, Tôl^e^d̲ôt̲ §1; Tanḥ., ed. Buber, Tôl^e^d̲ôt̲ §2; Tanḥ. Š^e^môt̲ §1; cf. Tanḥ., ed. Buber, Wa-yiggaš §12. See also Pes. R. 5.7, which similarly invokes Gen. 25.27 to establish that Jacob set up tents for studying Torah. Cf. Gen. R. LXIII.10; PRE §32, f. 73a, 73b.
247. Exod. R. XLVII.4.
248. Exod. R. XLVIII.4. Cf. Exod. R. XLI.3, which links wisdom, understanding, and knowledge, as expressed in Prov. 2.6, to the Torah. Cf. also Ḥag. 12a; Ber. 55a; PRE §3, f. 8b.
249. Tanḥ., ed. Buber, B^e^rē'šît̲ §15; Pes. R. 46.3; cf. Pes. R. 49.10; Tanḥ., ed. Buber, B^e^rē'šît̲ §34; Pes. R. 14.10 [= Pes. K. 4.4]. Cf. Gen. R. XXVII.1.
250. Tanḥ. P^e^qûd̲ê §3. Cf. PRE §11, f. 27b. An alternative interpretation is given in earlier rabbinic texts, which often understand "Let us make man" to mean that God took counsel with the ministering angels prior to creating the first human being. See, for example, Gen. R. VIII.4; Gen. R. VIII.8; Gen. R. XVII.4; Pes. K. 4.3 [= Pes. R. 14.9]. This interpretation is also found in Pes. R. 14.9 [= Pes. K. 4.3]; Num. R. XIX.3.
251. Tanḥ. B^e^rē'šît̲ §1. Cf. PRE §3, f. 6b.
252. Tanḥ. B^e^rē'šît̲ §1.
253. Tanḥ., ed. Buber, B^e^rē'šît̲ §5.
254. See Gen. R. I.1, discussed on pp. 164–166.
255. See, for example, Tanḥ., ed. Buber, B^e^rē'šît̲ §17, which includes a variant of the tradition in Gen. R. XII.14 concerning the debate between the school of Shammai and the school of Hillel over whether God conceived the plan (*maḥăšāb̲āh*) of creation during the night or the day.
256. Hebrew text cited in Ephraim E. Urbach, ed., "Ś^e^rîd̲ê Tanḥûmā' Y^e^lamm^e^d̲ēnû," *Qōb̲eṣ 'al Yād̲* 6 (16), pt. 1 (1966): 20. Urbach briefly discusses this passage in *The Sages*, vol. 1, pp. 200–201.
257. Pes. R. 53.2; cf. Pes. R. 20.2. "Handiwork" (*ma'ăśēh yād̲*) in Ps. 19.2 is understood with reference to Exod. 32.16, "And the tablets were the work of God (*ma'ăśēh Elohim*)," as meaning the tablets of the Ten Commandments.
258. Exod. R. XLVII.4. Cf. Exod. R. XL.1; Exod. R. XXIX.9; Pes. R. 21.4; Pes. R. 21.21, which will be discussed in chapter 4.
259. See, for example, Pes. R. 8.5; Exod. R. XXXVI.3; Pes. R. 33.10; Pes. R. 21.21.
260. See, for example, Deut. R. VII.3; Deut. R. VIII.2; Pes. R. 25.3.
261. See the Tanḥûmā' Y^e^lamm^e^d̲ēnû tradition cited on p. 187.

262. Pes. R. 21.21. Concerning *bêṯ* cf. Gen. R. I.10; Pes. K. 12.24; Song R. V.11, §4. Concerning *yōḏ* and *hē* cf. Gen. R. XII.10; Men. 29b.
263. Tanḥ., ed. Buber, B^{e}rē'šîṯ §16. As in Gen. R. XII.10, this tradition is attributed to R. Joḥanan through his student R. Abbahu.
264. Tanḥ., ed. Buber, Nōaḥ §28. Cf. Gen. R. XXXI.8; Gen. R. XVIII.4.
265. Pes. R. 33.8.
266. Pes. R. 49.10; Pes. R. 27.4; Tanḥ., ed. Buber, B^{e}rē'šîṯ §11; Deut. R. V.13; cf. Pes. R. 23.5. Cf. Mek., ed. Lauterbach, Šîrāṯā' §10, vol. 2, pp. 78–79; Mek., ed. Lauterbach, Ba-ḥôḏeš §7, vol. 2, p. 255; Gen. R. III.2; Gen. R. IV.6; Gen. R. XII.10; Gen. R. XXVII.1; Šab. 119b; PRE §7, f. 15b.
267. Tanḥ., ed. Buber, B^{e}rē'šîṯ §11; cf. Tanḥ., ed. Buber, Leḵ L^{e}ḵā §25; Tanḥ., ed. Buber, Mi-qēṣ §12; Tanḥ., ed. Buber, Mi-qēṣ §16. Cf. Gen. R. XLVI.3; Ḥag. 12a; PRE §3, f. 7b.
268. Pes. R. 21.19. Cf. 'Ab. V.1; Gen. R. XVII.1; RH 32a; Meg. 21b; PRE §3, f. 8b; PRE §32, f. 74a.
269. Pes. R. 40.5.
270. Deut. R. VII.3.
271. See p. 187.
272. See Exod. R. XXXIV.2, which invokes Prov. 6.23, "For the commandment (*mitzvah*) is a lamp (*nēr*) and the Torah a light (*'ôr*)," and Exod. R. L.1, which cites Ps. 119.130, "The opening of Thy words (*d^{e}ḇārîm*) gives light (*hē'îr*)." Cf. Gen. R. III.1. Parallel Midrashim that invoke Prov. 6.23 will be discussed below.
273. Pes. R. 8.5. Cf. Exod. R. XXXVI.3, discussed below, which similarly cites Ps. 119.105. Cf. also Pes. R. 46.3, which maintains that the Torah (Pentateuch), Nevi'im, and Ketuvim are the light that illuminates Israel's darkness and makes atonement possible.
274. Deut. R. IV.4. Cf. Pes. R. 46.3; Exod. R. XXXIV.2; Exod. R. XXXVI.3, which similarly invoke Prov. 6.23 to establish that the Torah is light. Cf. also Sip̄rê Num. §41; Lam. R. Proem XXIII; Soṭ. 21a; Taan. 7b; Meg. 16b.
275. Exod. R. XXXVI.3.
276. Pes. R. 53.2; cf. Pes. R. 53.1. See also Pes. R. 36.1, which understands Ps. 36.10 to mean that through the Torah, the "fountain of life," one will enjoy God's light in the time to come.
277. Deut. R. III.12; Exod. R. XLVII.6; Exod. R. XXXIII.1; cf. Pes. R. 10.6; Pes. R. 21.6; Deut. R. XI.3. Cf. Lev. R. XX.10 = Pes. K. 26.9; Song R. III.7, §5; PRE §2, f. 4a.
278. Pes. R. 14.10 [= Pes. K. 4.4]; cf. Pes. R. 51.4 [= Pes. K. 27; Lev. R. XXX.2]. Cf. Lev. R. XIX.1; Ber. 17a; Ber. 5b; PRE §2, f. 4a.
279. Tanḥ., ed. Buber, B^{e}rē'šîṯ §25. Cf. Gen. R. XXI.9.
280. Pes. R. 15.2 [= Pes. K. 5.2]; Tanḥ. P^{e}qûḏê §8; Exod. R. LI.7. Cf. Mek., ed. Lauterbach, Ba-ḥôḏeš §9, vol. 2, p. 268; Gen. R. XLIV.21.

281. Pes. R. 33.10; Tanḥ., ed. Buber, B[e]rē'šîṯ §4; Exod. R. XLI.4; Num. R. XXII.9; Deut. R. V.4. Cf. Mek., ed. Lauterbach, Ba-ḥôḏeš §5, vol. 2, p. 235; Mek., ed. Lauterbach, B[e]-šallaḥ §7, vol. 1, p. 247; Sip̄rê Deut. §343; Song R. V.11, §6; Pes. K. Suppl. 1.17; Pes. K. Suppl. 1.20; Lev. R. IV.1; Lam. R. III.1, §1; Song R. I.9, §4; Beṣ. 25b; Ber. 6a; Ber. 62a; Soṭ. 4b; PRE §41, f. 96a.
282. Deut. R. III.12. Cf. Song R. V.11, §6.
283. See Pes. R. 33.10, cited in chapter 4, p. 308.
284. The provenance of Pirqê d[e]-R. Eliezer has been debated by scholars, who have suggested theories assigning the text to a variety of locations, including Palestinian, Babylonian, Byzantine, and Muslim milieus. For a brief summary of the debate, see Gerald Friedlander, trans., *Pirḳê de Rabbi Eliezer (The Chapters of Rabbi Eliezer the Great)*, 4th ed. (New York: Sepher-Hermon Press, 1981), pp. liv–lv.
285. For a discussion of some of the parallels between the text of Pirqê d[e]-R. Eliezer and these and other works of the Apocrypha and Pseudepigrapha, see Friedlander, trans., *Pirḳê de Rabbi Eliezer*, pp. xxi–liii. The relationship of rabbinic Merkabah traditions to the speculations of Hêḵālôṯ texts will be discussed in chapter 4.
286. PRE §3, f. 5b.
287. PRE §3, f. 5b–6a. The mention of entrances and exits recalls the discussion of the plan of the Temple with "its exits and its entrances" in Ezek. 43.10–11.
288. PRE §3, f. 6a–6b. Cf. Ned. 39b; Pes. 54a; Gen. R. I.4.
289. PRE §3, f. 6b. The role of the Torah as God's counselor will be discussed below.
290. PRE §3, §4, §5, §6, §9, §11.
291. PRE §19, f. 44a. Cf. 'Ab. V.6; Sip̄rê Deut. §355; Mek., ed. Lauterbach, Wa-yassa' §6, vol. 2, pp. 124–125; Pes. 54a. Pirqê d[e]-R. Eliezer's initial list of ten items agrees with that of 'Āḇôṯ, except that it substitutes the ram of Abraham for the rod. Cf. PRE §3, f. 7a–7b, in which the Warsaw edition (1852) appears to confuse the tradition concerning the ten things created on the eve of the first Sabbath with an alternative tradition concerning the things created on the second day of creation. Six of the ten items given in 'Āḇôṯ's initial list, including the letters and writing, are incorporated in an enumeration of the eight things that were created on the second day. The second set of tablets is included in a list of the ten things that arose in the thought (*maḥăšāḇāh*) of God. See Friedlander, trans., *Pirḳê de Rabbi Eliezer*, p. 14, n. 1.
292. PRE §12, f. 29b. See nn. 82 and 115 regarding the interpretations of Gen. 2.15 found in Sip̄rê Deut. §41, Gen. R. XVI.5, and other sources. Cf. also Tanḥ., ed. Buber, B[e]rē'šîṯ §25, which renders Gen. 3.24 "to keep the way *to* the tree of life," in which keeping the way = Torah is understood to be the means to eating from the tree of life.
293. PRE §12, f. 30b.

294. PRE §19, f. 44a; §20, f. 46a–46b. Cf. Gen. R. XVI.5.
295. PRE §20, f. 47b.
296. PRE §26, f. 60b.
297. PRE §31, f. 69a–69b. Cf. Qid. IV.14; Lev. R. II.10; Gen. R. XCV.3; Gen. R. LXIV.4; Yoma 28b; Tanḥ., ed. Buber, Lek̲ L^{e}k̲ā §1; Tanḥ., ed. Buber, Lek̲ L^{e}k̲ā §14; Tanḥ., ed. Buber, Tôl^{e}d̲ôt̲ §1; Tanḥ., ed. Buber, Wa-yiggaš §12.
298. PRE §32, f. 73a, 73b. Cf. Gen. R. LXIII.10; Gen. R. LXVI.1; Gen. R. XCV.3; Lev. R. II.10; Pes. R. 5.7; Tanḥ., ed. Buber, Tôl^{e}d̲ôt̲ §1; Tanḥ., ed. Buber, Tôl^{e}d̲ôt̲ §2; Tanḥ., ed. Buber, Wa-yišlaḥ §9; Tanḥ., ed. Buber, Wa-yiggaš §12; Tanḥ. Š^{e}môt̲ §1.
299. See PRE §39, trans. Friedlander, pp. 310–311. This passage is not included in the Warsaw edition (1852). Cf. Ruth R. Proem III.
300. As in earlier rabbinic texts, the identification of the Torah with the personified wisdom of Proverbs 1–9 is assumed. See, for example, PRE §3, f. 6a, 6b; §12, f. 29b.
301. PRE §3, f. 6a.
302. PRE §3, f. 6b. Cf. Tanḥ. B^{e}rē'šît̲ §1.
303. PRE §11, f. 27b. Cf. Tanḥ. P^{e}qûd̲ê §3.
304. PRE §16, f. 36b. Cf. 'Ab. I.2; Pes. R. 5.3. Cf. also Esth. R. VII.13; Pes. 68b; Ned. 32a; Exod. R. XLVII.4.
305. PRE §21, f. 49b. See Gen. 4.15.
306. PRE §26, f. 60b.
307. PRE §48, f. 116a.
308. PRE §7, f. 15b. Cf. Mek., ed. Lauterbach, Šîrāt̲ā' §10, vol. 2, pp. 78–79; Mek., ed. Lauterbach, Ba-ḥôd̲eš §7, vol. 2, p. 255; Gen. R. III.2; Gen. R. IV.6; Gen. R. XII.10; Gen. R. XXVII.1; Šab. 119b; Pes. R. 49.10; Pes. R. 27.4; Pes. R. 23.5; Tanḥ., ed. Buber, B^{e}rē'šît̲ §11; Deut. R. V.13.
309. PRE §3, f. 7b. Cf. Gen. R. XLVI.3; Ḥag. 12a; Tanḥ., ed. Buber, B^{e}rē'šît̲ §11; Tanḥ., ed. Buber, Lek̲ L^{e}k̲ā §25; Tanḥ., ed. Buber, Mi-qēṣ §12; Tanḥ., ed. Buber, Mi-qēṣ §16.
310. PRE §5, f. 11b–12a.
311. PRE §3, f. 8b; §32, f. 74a.
312. PRE §3, f. 8b. Cf. Pes. R. 21.19. Cf. also 'Ab. V.1.; Gen. R. XVII.1; RH 32a; Meg. 21b; Pes. R. 40.5.
313. PRE §3, f. 8b. Cf. Exod. R. XLVIII.4; Ḥag. 12a; Ber. 55a.
314. See PRE §4.
315. PRE §2, f. 4a. Cf. Pes. K. 4.4 = Pes. R. 14.10; Lev. R. XIX.1; Lev. R. XXX.2 = Pes. K. 27.2 = Pes. R. 51.4; Ber. 17a; Ber. 5b. For parallel traditions concerning the radiance of Moses's countenance, see Lev. R. XX.10 = Pes. K. 26.9; Song R. III.7, §5; Deut. R. III.12; Exod. R. XLVII.6; Exod. R. XXXIII.1; Pes. R. 10.6; Pes. R. 21.6; Deut. R. XI.3.
316. PRE §41, f. 96a. Cf. 'Ab. II.10, which compares the words of the sages to coals of fire. Cf. also Mek., ed. Lauterbach, Ba-ḥôd̲eš §5, vol. 2, p. 235; Mek., ed. Lauterbach, B^{e}-šallaḥ §7, vol. 1, p. 247; Sip̄rê Deut.

§343; Song R. V.11, §6; Pes. K. Suppl. 1.17; Pes. K. Suppl. 1.20; Lev. R. IV.1; Lam. R. III.1, §1; Song R. I.9, §4; Beṣ. 25b; Ber. 6a; Ber. 62a; Soṭ. 4b; Pes. R. 33.10; Tanḥ., ed. Buber, B^{e}rē'šîṯ §4; Exod. R. XLI.4; Num. R. XXII.9; Deut. R. V.4.

317. Kabbalistic conceptions of language and Torah have been discussed from a variety of perspectives by Scholem, Idel, and Wolfson. See in particular Scholem, "The Meaning of the Torah in Jewish Mysticism"; idem, "The Name of God and the Linguistic Theory of the Kabbala"; Idel, "T^{e}p̄îsaṯ ha-Tôrāh b^{e}-Sip̄rûṯ ha-Hêḵālôṯ w^{e}-Gilgûlệhā ba-Qabbālāh"; idem, "Infinities of Torah in Kabbalah"; idem, "Reification of Language in Jewish Mysticism"; idem, *Language, Torah, and Hermeneutics in Abraham Abulafia*; Wolfson, "Female Imaging of the Torah"; idem, "The Hermeneutics of Visionary Experience"; idem, "The Anthropomorphic and Symbolic Image of the Letters in the Zohar"; idem, "Letter Symbolism and *Merkavah* Imagery in the *Zohar*"; idem, "Erasing the Erasure." See also Isaiah Tishby's discussion of Zoharic conceptions of the Torah in his *The Wisdom of the Zohar: An Anthology of Texts,* vol. 3, trans. David Goldstein, The Littman Library of Jewish Civilization (Oxford: Oxford University Press, 1989), pp. 1077–1154. For an extended analysis of the role of language in Jewish mystical traditions, see Lipiner, *The Metaphysics of the Hebrew Alphabet.*

318. The exponents of ecstatic Kabbalah, particularly as represented by the school of Abraham Abulafia, developed conceptions of Torah and language that are distinctly different from those elaborated by the theosophical kabbalists. The views of Abulafia, which have been discussed at length by Idel, will be discussed briefly in chapter 6. For a more detailed exposition, see Idel, *Language, Torah, and Hermeneutics in Abraham Abulafia.*

319. For discussions of the nature, structure, and significance of the Zohar, see Scholem, *Major Trends in Jewish Mysticism,* pp. 156–243; Tishby, *The Wisdom of the Zohar,* vol. 1, pp. 1–126; Daniel Chanan Matt, trans., *Zohar: The Book of Enlightenment,* The Classics of Western Spirituality (New York: Paulist Press, 1983), pp. 3–39. Scholem, Tishby, and Matt concur in attributing the Zohar to the thirteenth-century Spanish kabbalist Moses de Leon. However, this view has been challenged by Yehuda Liebes, who argues that the Zohar does not derive from a single person but rather from the circle of kabbalists that emerged in the mid-thirteenth century in Castile, Spain. See "How the Zohar Was Written," chapter 2 of his *Studies in the Zohar,* trans. Arnold Schwartz, Stephanie Nakache, and Penina Peli, SUNY Series in Judaica: Hermeneutics, Mysticism, and Religion (Albany: State University of New York Press, 1993), pp. 85–138. See also Idel, *Kabbalah,* p. 380, n. 66.

320. For a detailed analysis of the various ways in which the s^{e}p̄îrôṯ have been interpreted in kabbalistic texts, see Idel, *Kabbalah*, pp. 136–153.
321. Scholem, "The Meaning of the Torah in Jewish Mysticism," pp. 35–36.
322. The role of mystical exegesis of the Torah as a means of attaining a visionary experience of the supernal light of Torah will be discussed in chapter 6.
323. The Zohar reiterates the rabbinic notion that the Torah preceded the creation of the world by two thousand years. See, for example, Zohar II.84b; II.161a; III.91b; III.159a. Zohar III.34b provides a variant of the tradition that includes the Torah as one of seven preexistent things. However, in its enumeration, which coincides with the Talmudic version, it represents the seven entities as seven lights that were created before the world.
324. See, for example, the letter of Ezra b. Solomon published by Gershom Scholem in *Sēp̄er Bialik* (1934), p. 159; Azriel b. Menaḥem of Gerona, *Pêrûš hā-'Aggāḏôṯ*, ed. Isaiah Tishby (Jerusalem: Mekize Nirdamim, Mosad ha-Rav Kook, 1945), p. 77 with n. 5. Noted in Scholem, "The Meaning of the Torah in Jewish Mysticism," p. 41. The Zohar's portrayal of the Torah as Ḥoḵmāh will be discussed below.
325. Moses b. Naḥman (Naḥmanides), *Pêrûšê ha-Tôrāh*, ed. Ḥayyim Dov (Charles B.) Chavel, vol. 1 (Jerusalem: Mosad ha-Rav Kook, 1959), pp. 6–7. Cited in Scholem, "The Meaning of the Torah in Jewish Mysticism," p. 38.
326. Ezra b. Solomon, Commentary on the Talmudic 'Aggāḏôṯ, Vatican MS Cod. Hebr. 294, f. 34a. Cited in Scholem, "The Meaning of the Torah in Jewish Mysticism," p. 39. Cf. Azriel, *Pêrûš hā-'Aggāḏôṯ*, pp. 37, 76; Jacob b. Sheshet, *Sēp̄er hā-'Ĕmûnāh w^{e}-ha-Biṭṭāḥôn*, in *Kiṯḇê Rabbênû Mosheh b. Naḥman*, ed. Ḥayyim Dov (Charles B.) Chavel, vol. 2 (Jerusalem: Mosad ha-Rav Kook, 1963), pp. 353–448, esp. chap. 19 [ascribed erroneously to Naḥmanides]. A similar thesis is found in *Sēp̄er ha-Ḥayyîm*, a text that emerged independently of the Gerona kabbalists and was printed in the first three decades of the thirteenth century in France. *Sēp̄er ha-Ḥayyîm*, MS Parma de Rossi (1390), f. 135a. Noted in Scholem, "The Name of God and the Linguistic Theory of the Kabbala," pt. 1, p. 78.
327. MS Leiden, Warner 32, f. 23a. Cited in Scholem, "The Meaning of the Torah in Jewish Mysticism," p. 44.
328. Azriel, *Pêrûš hā-'Aggāḏôṯ*, pp. 37–38. Cited in Scholem, "The Meaning of the Torah in Jewish Mysticism," p. 45. See also Tishby's discussion of the views of Ezra b. Solomon and Azriel in *The Wisdom of the Zohar*, vol. 3, pp. 1079–1080.
329. Zohar II.90b; II.124a; II.87a; II.161b; III.13b; III.35b,36a; III.73a; III.80b; III.113a; III.298b.
330. Zohar II.90b.

331. The Zohar's identification of the ten words of creation with the Ten Words of revelation will be discussed in chapter 4.
332. Zohar II.60b; cf. II.60a.
333. Zohar II.86a.
334. MS Jerusalem, 8° 597, f. 21b. Cited in Scholem, "The Meaning of the Torah in Jewish Mysticism," p. 44. Gikatilla's work is contained in this manuscript under the name of Isaac b. Farḥi or Peraḥia. Menaḥem Recanati (ca. 1300 C.E.) similarly ascribes to the kabbalists the notion that God and the Torah are one: "The Torah is not outside Him, and He is not something outside the Torah. Therefore the kabbalists say that the Holy One, blessed be He, *is* the Torah." Menaḥem Recanati, *Ṭa'ămê ha-Miṣwôṯ*, ed. S. Lieberman (London: Makhon Otzar ha-Ḥokhmah, 1962), f. 2a. For discussions of passages in other kabbalistic texts that emphasize the identity of the Torah with the Name of God, and ultimately with God himself, see Idel, "T^{e}p̄îsaṯ ha-Tôrāh b^{e}-Sip̄rûṯ ha-Hêḵālôṯ w^{e}-Gilgûlêḥā ba-Qabbālāh," pp. 49–84; idem, *Kabbalah*, pp. 244–247.
335. MS Jerusalem, 8° 597, f. 228b. Cited in Scholem, "The Meaning of the Torah in Jewish Mysticism," p. 44.
336. Cf. the passage from the *Sēp̄er ha-Yiḥûḏ*, cited in chapter 6, pp. 360–361, which maintains that the letters of the Torah are the shapes or forms of God. For a discussion of the ways in which linguistic symbolism concerning the divine Name and the twenty-two Hebrew letters is connected with Merkabah imagery in the writings of Gikatilla and in the Zohar, see Wolfson, "Letter Symbolism and *Merkavah* Imagery in the *Zohar*." For other studies exploring various aspects of letter symbolism in the Zohar, see Wolfson, "The Anthropomorphic and Symbolic Image of the Letters in the Zohar"; idem, "Erasing the Erasure"; M. Oron, "The Narrative of the Letters and Its Source: A Study of a Zoharic Midrash on the Letters of the Alphabet" [in Hebrew], in *Studies in Jewish Mysticism Presented to Isaiah Tishby on His Seventy-Fifth Birthday*, eds. Joseph Dan and Joseph Hacker, *Jerusalem Studies in Jewish Thought* 3, nos. 1–2 (1983–1984): 97–109; Lipiner, *The Metaphysics of the Hebrew Alphabet*, pp. 85–111. See also Stephen G. Wald, *The Doctrine of the Divine Name: An Introduction to Classical Kabbalistic Theology*, Brown Judaic Studies, no. 149 (Atlanta: Scholars Press, 1988), which contains a critical edition, annotated translation, and analysis of *Siṯrê 'Ôṯiyyôṯ* ("Secrets of the Letters"), a discourse on the letters of the divine names that is printed in Zohar Ḥāḏāš (1b–7b).
337. Joseph Gikatilla, *Ša'ăr[ê] 'Ôrāh* (Offenbach: Zeligman Raiz, 1715), f. 2b, 4b; cf. 51a. See Scholem's discussions in "The Name of God and the Linguistic Theory of the Kabbala," pt. 2, pp. 178–179; "The Meaning of the Torah in Jewish Mysticism," pp. 42–43.

338. Gikatilla, *Ša'ăr[ê] 'Ôrāh*, f. 2b. Cited in Scholem, "The Meaning of the Torah in Jewish Mysticism," p. 42.
339. Zohar I.5a; I.47a; I.134a–134b; II.161a; III.35b; I.207a.
340. Zohar I.207a. While the Torah is generally identified with Ḥoḵmāh in the Zohar, it is also at times described as having its source in the supernal wisdom. See, for example, Zohar III.81a: "There is no Torah without wisdom and no wisdom without Torah, both being in the same grade, the root of the Torah being in the supernal Wisdom by which it is sustained." Cf. Zohar II.121a.
341. It should be noted, however, that the primordial Torah is at times associated with Bînāh as well as with Ḥoḵmāh. See, for example, Zohar II.85a, which suggests that the Torah is an emanation of both Ḥoḵmāh, the Father, and Bînāh, the Mother. Moreover, as will be discussed below, the Torah in its later stages of manifestation as the Written Torah and Oral Torah becomes identified, respectively, with Tip̄'ereṯ, the son (the sixth *s*ᵉ*p̄îrāh*), and Malḵûṯ, the daughter (the tenth *s*ᵉ*p̄îrāh*, which is the Shekhinah). The gender of the Torah in its various manifestations thus encompasses both male and female.
342. Zohar II.161a.
343. See Gen. R. I.1, discussed on pp. 164–166.
344. Zohar II.161a. God is similarly described elsewhere in the Zohar as "contemplating through seeing" (*'istakkēl*) the Torah in order to create the world. See, for example, Zohar I.5a, discussed below, and I.134a. Cf. I.90a (Siṯrê Tôrāh).
345. Zohar I.5a.
346. Zohar I.207a. For the Torah's role in bringing forth creation, see also I.24b (Tîqqûnîm); II.200a; III.152a; and the references cited above in n. 339.
347. Zohar I.134b; cf. I.186b; II.25a (Rā'ăyā' Mᵉhêmnā').
348. Zohar II.162b; cf. II.165b. The Zohar's conception of the commandments will be discussed more fully in chapter 6.
349. In the Zohar 'Ên-Sôp̄ is described as an unmanifest, limitless, transcendent reality that is "hidden and removed far beyond all ken." See, for example, Zohar I.103a–103b; II.42b (Rā'ăyā' Mᵉhêmnā'); II.239a. According to Zohar II.42b (Rā'ăyā' Mᵉhêmnā'), "In the beginning, before shape and form had been created, He was without form and similitude." As the source of the divine emanations from which creation is brought forth, 'Ên-Sôp̄ is called the "cause above all causes." Zohar I.22b (Tîqqûnîm); II.42b (Rā'ăyā' Mᵉhêmnā').
350. See Zohar II.42b (Rā'ăyā' Mᵉhêmnā'), which declares: "Had the brightness of the glory of the Holy One, blessed be His Name, not been shed over the whole of His creation, how could He have been perceived even by the wise? He would have remained unapprehendable, and the words 'The whole earth is full of His glory' [Isa. 6.3] could never be spoken with truth."

351. Zohar I.15a.
352. Zohar II.239a.
353. Zohar I.2a; I.3b; I.15a; I.18a.
354. As will be discussed below, this primordial point is identified in the Zohar with Ḥoḵmāh, the second *s*[e]*p̄îrāh*, who is designated as *rē'šîṯ*. See Zohar I.3b; I.15a–15b; I.29b; I.30b; I.31b; cf. I.24b (Tîqqûnîm); I.145a.
355. See, for example, Zohar II.20a (Midrash ha-Ne'ĕlām): "When it arose in thought before the Holy One, blessed be He, to create His world, all the worlds arose in one thought and with this thought they were all created. This is the meaning of 'With wisdom have You made them all' [Ps. 104.24]. And with this thought, which is wisdom, this world and the world above were created." See also I.29a; I.3b; I.21a; III.5b; cf. III.42b–43a.
356. Zohar I.15a.
357. Zohar I.15a–15b.
358. Zohar I.15a–15b.
359. See, for example, Zohar I.22a (Tîqqûnîm); III.290a ('Iḏrā' Zûṭā').
360. Zohar I.50b; I.29a; cf. I.39b; II.85b.
361. Zohar I.74a.
362. Zohar I.50b. See also I.246b, which emphasizes that the four stages in the unfoldment of the divine language are ultimately one.
363. Zohar I.50b.
364. Zohar I.50b; cf. 141b.
365. See, for example, Zohar I.15a; I.31b. 'Ên-Sôp̄ is understood to be the unmanifest subject of the sentence.
366. Zohar I.16b.
367. Zohar I.50b; cf. I.141b.
368. Zohar I.16b.
369. Gen. 1.3,6–7.
370. Zohar III.32b; I.17b; I.29b; I.46a–46b.
371. Gen. 1.11–27.
372. Zohar III.5b; III.261a.
373. See, for example, Zohar I.15b; I.16b.
374. Zohar I.47b.
375. Zohar I.17b; I.47b; cf. I.71b–72a.
376. Zohar II.238b; II.205b–206a.
377. Zohar II.161b; II.205b.
378. Zohar III.113a; II.161b.
379. Zohar II.200a.
380. Zohar II.205b.
381. See, for example, Zohar II.85a.
382. Zohar II.60a,60b.
383. See the concluding section of Gikatilla's *Ša'ărê Ṣeḏeq* published in Efraim Gottlieb, *Studies in the Kabbala Literature* [in Hebrew], ed.

Joseph Hacker (Tel Aviv: Tel Aviv University, 1976), pp. 154–155. See also Scholem's discussion in "The Name of God and the Linguistic Theory of the Kabbala," pt. 2, pp. 179–180.

384. Gikatilla, *Šaʿărê Ṣeḏeq* [concluding section], in Gottlieb, *Studies in the Kabbala Literature,* pp. 154–155. Cited in Idel, "Infinities of Torah in Kabbalah," p. 150.

385. Moses Cordovero, *Šîʿûr Qômāh* (Warsaw, 1883; reprint, Jerusalem: Aḥuzat Yisrael, 1966), f. 63b. A number of kabbalists speculated about the nature and structure of the Torah in different ages—in particular before the fall and in the Messianic Age. For a discussion of these various speculations, see Scholem, "The Meaning of the Torah in Jewish Mysticism," pp. 66–86. For a survey of pre-rabbinic and rabbinic traditions concerning the nature of the Torah in the Messianic Age, see W. D. Davies, *Torah in the Messianic Age and/or the Age to Come,* Journal of Biblical Literature Monograph Series, vol. 7 (Philadelphia: Society of Biblical Literature, 1952). See also Urbach, *The Sages,* vol. 1, pp. 308–314; Gershom Scholem, *The Messianic Idea in Judaism and Other Essays on Jewish Spirituality* (New York: Schocken Books, 1971), pp. 19–24, 52–58.

386. This doctrine is first developed in *Lîmmûḏê ʾĂṣîlûṯ* (Munkács: Samuel Kahn, 1897), f. 3a, 15a–15b, 21d–22a, which is printed under the name of Ḥayyim Vital but in Scholem's view was undoubtedly written by Israel Sarug. Cf. Menaḥem Azariah of Fano, *Šiḇʿîm û-Štayim Yᵉḏîʿôṯ* (Lvov, 1867); Naphtali b. Jacob Elḥanan Bacharach, *ʿĒmeq ha-Meleḵ* (Amsterdam, 1648; reprint, Bene Berak: Yahadut, 1973), chap. 1, esp. end of §4. See Scholem's discussions in "The Name of God and the Linguistic Theory of the Kabbala," pt. 2, pp. 181–182; "The Meaning of the Torah in Jewish Mysticism," pp. 73–74.

COMPARATIVE ANALYSIS 1. VEDA AND TORAH IN CREATION

1. We will return to this notion of embodiment in the conclusion.
2. BP III.12.34,37.
3. Zohar II.161a.
4. See BSB I.3.28, cited in chapter 1, p. 127.
5. Mek., ed. Lauterbach, Ba-ḥōḏeš §9, vol. 2, p. 266; cf. Pes. R. 33.10; PRE §41, f. 98a.
6. Zohar II.81a–81b; III.146a; cf. II.93b–94a. The Zohar's treatment of the Sinai theophany as a visionary experience will be discussed in chapter 4.

CHAPTER 3. VEDA AND COGNITION

1. See n. 161.
2. Yāska cites the definition of Aupamanyava in Nir. II.11; cf. VII.3.
3. Nir. I.20.
4. See pp. 247–248, 249–250.
5. Many of the *ṛṣis*' statements concerning the nature and mechanics of Vedic cognition have been collected by Muir in *Original Sanskrit Texts,* vol. 3, pp. 217–286, although he does not attempt to analyze and interpret the statements apart from giving short introductions to each section.
6. Gonda's analyses focus particularly on *dhī, dhīti,* and related terms used to denote the "visions" of the *ṛṣis*. For a brief summary of Gonda's views, see "Poetry, Poet, Poem," chapter 2 of his *Vedic Literature,* pp. 65–91. For a more extended discussion, see his *The Vision of the Vedic Poets,* Disputationes Rheno-Trajectinae, vol. 8 (The Hague: Mouton, 1963).
7. ṚV I.1.2; I.45.3; I.48.14; I.80.16; I.118.3; I.131.6; I.139.9; I.175.6; IV.20.5; IV.50.1; V.42.6; VI.19.4; VI.21.5; VI.21.8; VI.22.2; VI.50.15; VII.18.1; VII.29.4; VII.53.1; VII.76.4; VII.91.1; VIII.36.7; VIII.43.13; IX.96.11; IX.110.7; X.14.15; X.54.3; X.66.14; X.67.1; X.96.5; X.98.9. See Muir, *Original Sanskrit Texts,* vol. 3, pp. 218–224. The *ṛṣis* also distinguish between ancient hymns and new hymns. For references see ibid., pp. 224–232. Among the ancient *ṛṣis* that are mentioned are Atri, Kaṇva, Bhṛgu, Aṅgiras, and Atharvan. See, for example, ṚV I.45.3; I.80.16; I.139.9; VIII.43.13; X.14.6. For a brief discussion of these and other important *ṛṣis* mentioned in the Ṛg-Veda, see Macdonell, *Vedic Mythology,* pp. 140–147.
8. ṚV IV.42.8; X.82.2; X.109.4; X.130.7.
9. ŚB XIV.5.2.5–6 [= BĀU II.2.3–4].
10. Gonda, *The Vision of the Vedic Poets,* p. 39. See pp. 36–40 for Gonda's analysis of the various occurrences of the term in the Ṛg-Veda.
11. Gonda, "Poetry, Poet, Poem," *Vedic Literature,* p. 71. See also Gonda's *The Vision of the Vedic Poets,* pp. 42–50, for his analysis of the occurrences of the term *kavi* in the Ṛg-Veda.
12. ṚV X.130.7.
13. See, for example, ṚV X.62.1; VIII.48.3; cf. X.20.10.
14. ṚV III.53.7; X.67.2; cf. IV.2.15.
15. ṚV X.62.4.
16. ṚV X.62.5–6.
17. ṚV III.53.9.
18. ṚV VII.33.11.
19. ṚV X.92.10.

20. See, for example, ṚV VII.76.4; X.62.1; I.179.2; X.90.7. For a discussion of the roles of the various *ṛṣis* in helping to carry out the activities of specific gods, see Macdonell, *Vedic Mythology*, pp. 140–147.
21. See Gonda, *The Vision of the Vedic Poets*, pp. 27–34, 56–57.
22. See pp. 327–328 for a discussion of why I have adopted the term "cognition" rather than "revelation" to describe the *ṛṣis*' relationship to the Veda.
23. See, for example, ṚV VIII.48.3.
24. See, for example, ṚV III.29.15; I.164.6,18; VII.33.7,9,12; IX.87.3; X.5.2; X.114.2; X.129.4.
25. ṚV VIII.95.5; cf. VIII.76.12.
26. ṚV III.38.5–6; cf. I.22.20; V.30.2.
27. See, for example, ṚV I.18.9; I.88.5; I.139.2; I.22.19–20; I.164.31 [= X.177.3]; III.38.5–6; X.55.5; X.124.9.
28. ṚV I.139.2. It is not entirely clear to what the adjective *hiraṇyaya* ("golden") refers, since the term appears in the singular. A number of other verses describe the seer as seeing with his "inner eye" or "mind's eye." See, for example, ṚV X.130.6, discussed below, in which the *ṛṣi* says, "With mind (*manas*) as an eye (*cakṣas*) I observe (root *man*), seeing (root *dṛś*) those who first performed this sacrifice." The role of the mind in the process of cognition will be discussed later.
29. ṚV X.130.2,6,7. For a brief discussion of this hymn, see chapter 1, pp. 38–39.
30. ṚV X.90.7.
31. ṚV X.72.1.
32. See, for example, ṚV X.129.4; I.164.6,18; III.29.15; VII.33.7,9,12; IX.87.3; X.5.2; X.114.2.
33. See, for example, ṚV I.185.1; X.88.18.
34. For an analysis of the terms *dhī*, *dhīti*, *manīṣā*, and related terms used in the Ṛg-Veda to refer to the cognitions of the *ṛṣis*, see Gonda, *The Vision of the Vedic Poets*, pp. 51–56, 68–225. For a discussion of the role of light in the Ṛg-Veda and later texts, see ibid., pp. 266–275, esp. 271–275.
35. ṚV VII.76.4; cf. VIII.48.3.
36. See also the immediately preceding verse, ṚV VIII.6.7.
37. See, for example, ṚV VI.9.6; X.177.1–2. See also III.26.8. The role of the heart in the *ṛṣis*' cognitions will be discussed below.
38. ṚV IV.11.2.
39. ṚV III.39.2.
40. ṚV VIII.6.7.
41. ṚV I.173.1; cf. VII.34.1; X.4.6; IX.9.8.
42. ṚV X.67.10.
43. See, for example, ṚV VII.33.8; VIII.6.10; VIII.3.3. See also VIII.6.8, cited earlier.

44. For Gonda's discussion of this cyclical process, see *The Vision of the Vedic Poets,* esp. pp. 64–66; "Poetry, Poet, Poem," *Vedic Literature,* pp. 66–67. I noted this cyclical process during my own research prior to reading Gonda's work, and thus my own interpretation, while in basic agreement with Gonda, differs somewhat from his formulation.
45. See, for example, ṚV I.37.4; III.18.3; IV.43.1; VII.34.1,9; VII.97.3; VIII.27.13; X.176.2.
46. See, for example, ṚV X.61.7; X.88.8; VII.97.3.
47. ṚV I.40.5.
48. See, for example, ṚV IV.5.3; VII.87.4; IX.95.2; I.179.2.
49. See, for example, ṚV I.18.6–7; II.9.4; III.10.5; IV.5.3,6; IV.6.1; IV.11.2–3; X.45.5; cf. VI.9. For references to Agni as a *ṛṣi,* see I.31.1; III.21.3; VI.14.2; I.66.4; as a *kavi,* see I.12.6; I.71.10; I.128.8; III.19.1; IV.2.12; IV.3.16; V.4.3; X.91.3, et al.
50. See, for example, ṚV VI.47.3; IX.25.5–6; IX.47.4; IX.76.4; IX.95.5; IX.96.5–7,17–18; IX.107.7,18; cf. IX.99.6. For references to Soma as a *ṛṣi,* see IX.35.4; IX.54.1; IX.66.20; IX.87.3; IX.96.6; IX.107.7; as a *kavi,* see VI.39.1; IX.25.6; IX.47.4; IX.50.4; IX.68.5; IX.86.20; IX.96.17; IX.107.7,18, et al.
51. See, for example, ṚV III.34.5; VI.18.15; VI.34.1; VI.35.5; VI.69.2; VIII.13.7; VIII.59.6; VIII.63.4. For references to Indra as a *ṛṣi,* see V.29.1; VIII.6.41; VIII.16.7; as a *kavi,* see I.11.4; I.130.9; I.175.4; III.42.6; III.52.6; VI.20.4; VI.32.3; VII.18.2; VIII.45.14; IX.86.13; cf. X.112.9.
52. For a discussion of the role of these and other gods as the promoters of the *ṛṣis'* inspirations, see Gonda, *The Vision of the Vedic Poets,* esp. pp. 17–18, 28–57.
53. ṚV I.31.16; IX.96.18.
54. ṚV IV.11.2–3.
55. ṚV X.71.3,4; X.125.5.
56. ṚV VIII.101.16.
57. ṚV I.3.11–12; II.3.8; VI.49.7.
58. See, for example, ṚV I.105.15; VII.88.4; VIII.59.6; cf. VIII.41.5–6.
59. The Maruts are called *kavis* (ṚV V.57.8; V.52.13; VI.49.6; VII.59.11), who are possessed of *manīṣā* (V.57.2), the promoters of *dhī* (VII.36.7), and the makers of hymns (*brahma-kṛt*) III.32.2; cf. VIII.89.1,3).
60. See, for example, ṚV II.23.1–2; I.40.5; X.36.5; cf. X.98.2–3,7.
61. See, for example, ṚV I.34.5; I.112.2; I.117.23.
62. See, for example, ṚV VIII.26.25; cf. I.23.3.
63. See, for example, ṚV III.62.10, which is the *sāvitrī,* or *gāyatrī mantra,* discussed in chapter 1.
64. See, for example, ṚV X.26.4; III.62.8.
65. ṚV I.109.2; III.2.1; VII.15.4; VII.22.9; VII.26.1; VII.31.11; VII.94.1; VIII.43.2; VIII.88.4; VIII.95.5; IX.73.2; X.7.2; X.23.6; X.67.1; X.91.14.

66. Ṛ̣V I.62.13; I.67.4; I.109.1; I.130.6; I.171.2; II.19.8; II.35.2; III.39.1; V.2.11; V.29.15; V.73.10; VI.16.47; VI.32.1; VII.7.6; VII.64.4; VIII.6.33; X.39.14.
67. ṚV I.20.1; I.31.18; I.47.2; I.61.16; I.117.25; I.184.5; II.39.8; IV.6.11; IV.16.20–21; VI.52.2; VII.35.14; VII.37.4; VII.97.9; VIII.62.4; VIII.90.3; X.54.6; X.101.2.
68. Gonda, *The Vision of the Vedic Poets,* p. 106.
69. ṚV I.130.6; V.2.11; V.29.15; V.73.10; VII.64.4; X.39.14.
70. ṚV I.61.4; I.94.1; VII.34.1.
71. See, for example, ṚV I.67.4; I.171.2; II.35.2; III.39.1; VI.16.47; X.91.14; I.60.3; I.61.2; cf. X.71.8; X.119.5. For a discussion of the nature and function of the heart in the Ṛg-Veda and later Indian texts, see Gonda, *The Vision of the Vedic Poets,* pp. 276–288.
72. Gonda, *The Vision of the Vedic Poets,* p. 281.
73. See, for example, ṚV VIII.59.6; X.109.4; X.154.5.
74. For a discussion of relevant verses, see Gonda, *The Vision of the Vedic Poets,* pp. 276–283.
75. ṚV II.35.2; cf. I.67.4; III.39.1.
76. See ṚV X.71.8, in which the impulses of *manas* (*manaso javas*) are said to have been fashioned with the heart.
77. ṚV I.61.2; cf. I.171.2.
78. See, for example, ṚV VII.64.4; VIII.95.5.
79. ṚV I.143.1.
80. See, for example, ṚV I.67.4; I.78.5; I.91.11; II.35.2; III.39.1; IV.3.16; V.45.4; V.73.10; VI.32.1; X.54.6; X.116.9.
81. ṚV X.71.3.
82. ṚV X.71.3; cf. I.164.45.
83. ṚV VIII.59.6. My translation is indebted to that of Gonda, *The Vision of the Vedic Poets,* p. 211.
84. See, for example, ṚV II.35.1; VI.16.37.
85. See, for example, ṚV I.116.1; VII.61.2; VIII.12.31; VIII.13.26; X.4.1; X.116.9.
86. ṚV I.61.4; I.94.1; VII.34.1.
87. ṚV X.116.9; cf. X.101.2; II.42.1.
88. ṚV X.42.1.
89. ṚV I.116.1.
90. See, for example, ṚV VIII.5.18; I.64.1; I.102.1; IV.32.12; VII.4.1; VIII.12.10; X.20.10.
91. ṚV VII.34.9.
92. ṚV I.10.5; I.91.11; II.11.2; II.12.14; II.39.8; III.32.13; III.34.1–2; IV.32.12; V.11.5; V.22.4; V.31.4,10; VI.44.13; VII.19.11; VIII.6.1,11–12,21,31,35; VIII.8.8; VIII.13.16; VIII.14.5,11; VIII.44.2,12,22; VIII.62.4; VIII.74.1,8–9; VIII.93.27; VIII.95.6–7; VIII.98.8; IX.73.2; X.4.7; X.63.17, et al.

93. See, for example, ṚV I.16.7; IV.41.1; IV.43.1; VII.86.8; VII.101.5; X.47.7; X.91.13.
94. See, for example, AB II.16; PB VII.5.1; JB I.116; JB I.117; JB I.128; JB I.148; JB I.160.
95. See, for example, AB IV.23; KB V.3; KB XII.8; PB IV.1.4; PB VI.1.1; PB VI.3.9; PB XVIII.7.1.
96. With respect to Prajāpati seeing and then reciting certain *ṛc*s or *sāmans* for specific purposes, see, for example, PB VII.10.13–17; PB VII.5.1–3; PB XIII.5.13; JB I.148; JB I.160; JB I.116; JB I.117–118. With respect to his seeing and performance of certain sacrifices to accomplish particular ends, see AB IV.23; KB V.3; KB XII.8; PB IV.1.4–5; PB VI.1.1–3; PB VI.3.9–10; PB XVIII.7.1.
97. See, for example, PB VIII.1.4–12; PB IX.1.1–2; JB I.155; JB I.157–158; KB XXI.1.
98. The seven *ṛṣis* are mentioned four times in the Ṛg-Veda, in ṚV IV.42.8; ṚV X.82.2; ṚV X.109.4; ṚV X.130.7. For references to the seven *ṛṣis* in the later Saṃhitās, see AV VI.40.1; AV X.8.9; AV XI.1.1,24; AV XI.3.2; AV XII.1.39; VS XIV.28; VS XVII.26 [= ṚV X.82.2].
99. ṚV IV.42.8.
100. ṚV X.130.7.
101. ṚV X.109.4.
102. AV XI.1.1,24; AV XII.1.39.
103. AV XII.1.39.
104. ŚB VIII.6.1.5; cf. ŚB IX.4.4.4; ŚB IX.5.1.45. These passages comment on verses from the Vājasaneyi Saṃhitā (XV.10; XVIII.52,58) that refer to the "first-born *ṛṣis*." Cf. AV X.7.14.
105. The term *prāṇa*, generally translated "breath" or "vital air," is at times used in the Brāhmaṇas and other Vedic texts to refer to the seven orifices of the sense organs in the head: two eyes, two ears, two nostrils, and mouth. This latter meaning is supported by ŚB VIII.4.3.6, which associates the seven *ṛṣis* with the seven *prāṇas* in the head. For other references to the seven *prāṇas* in the head, see ŚB III.1.3.21; ŚB VI.4.2.5; ŚB XIII.1.7.2. See also AB I.17; AB III.3; JUB II.5.8–10; JUB II.6.7–9.
106. The account of the seven primordial *ṛṣis* combining to form Prajāpati-Agni is given in ŚB VI.1.1.1–7, at the beginning of the section in the Śatapatha Brāhmaṇa that focuses on the *agnicayana* ceremony (Kāṇḍas VI-X). This primordial event, in which the seven *ṛṣis*, or simply "the *ṛṣis*," are identified with the *prāṇas*, is alluded to in later passages: ŚB VII.2.3.5; ŚB IX.1.2.21; ŚB IX.2.1.13; ŚB IX.2.3.44. The identification of the (seven) *ṛṣis* with the *prāṇas* is also mentioned in ŚB XIV.5.2.5–6 [= BĀU II.2.3–4]; ŚB VIII.4.1.5; ŚB VIII.6.1.5; cf. ŚB VIII.4.3.6. See also AB II.27, which says that "the *ṛṣis*, divine, guardians of the body, born of *tapas* (*tapo-ja*), are the *prāṇas*." The antecedent of this notion is found in the Atharva-Veda (XI.3.2), which identifies the seven *ṛṣis* with the *prāṇas* and *apānas*.

107. ŚB XIV.5.2.5–6 [= BĀU II.2.3–4]. Elsewhere in the Śatapatha Brāhmaṇa several of these *ṛṣis* are identified with specific faculties: Vasiṣṭha with the breath (*prāṇa*) (ŚB VIII.1.1.6), Bharadvāja with the mind (ŚB VIII.1.1.9), Jamadagni with the eye (ŚB VIII.1.2.3), and Viśvāmitra with the ear (ŚB VIII.1.2.6). See n. 105.
108. ŚB II.1.2.4; ŚB XIII.8.1.9. Cf. Nir. X.26.
109. See, for example, KB XXV.2; KB XXVI.15. Cf. ŚB II.4.2.2.
110. See, for example, KB X.5; KB XV.1; KB XXIX.3.
111. AB III.33–34. Fragments of this story appear in ŚB I.7.4.4; ŚB IV.5.1.8. See also ŚB XI.6.1.1–13; JB I.42–44, which recount the story of Bhṛgu and the lesson that he learns from his father Varuṇa. PB XVIII.9.1 and JB II.201 describe Bhṛgu as arising from a portion of the luster (*bharga*) of Varuṇa. Cf. TU III.1, in which Bhṛgu asks his father Varuṇa to teach him about Brahman.
112. AB VIII.12; AB VIII.17.
113. AB IV.17; AB VI.34–35; AB I.16; KB XXX.6; KB XVIII.10; ŚB IV.4.5.19–20. See also PB XX.11.3, in which two of the Aṅgirases are represented as having been left behind by the other Aṅgirases, who went to the world of heaven. The two *ṛṣis* practice *tapas* and see *sāmans* and, after performing a two-day rite, attain heaven. Cf. PB VIII.2.6 regarding the Atharvans attaining heaven through seeing *sāmans*.
114. See, for example, AB VII.15–17; AB II.19; AB VI.34–35; AB I.16; KB XXVIII.1; KB IV.8; KB XXVI.15; KB XXX.6; ŚB XI.2.3.7; ŚB I.6.2.7; ŚB IV.3.4.21; PB XXI.9.2; PB XX.11.3; JB II.235.
115. AB VIII.21–23.
116. These types of formulaic statements are particularly common in the Kauṣītaki Brāhmaṇa. See KB X.5; KB XV.1; KB XXI.2; KB XXII.3; KB XXIV.5; KB XXV.2; KB XXVI.15; KB XXIX.2–5; KB XXX.1. Cf. AB VIII.3; AB I.21.
117. JB I.149–152; JB I.155; JB I.160; JB I.163; JB I.165; JB I.215–217; JB III.82. Cf. JB I.147; AB II.25; AB III.49.
118. AB II.19; AB II.20; AB VI.18; KB XXVIII.1; KB XXVIII.2; KB XXVIII.8; PB IV.7.3; PB VIII.2.2,4,6; PB VIII.5.9,12; PB XI.5.14; PB XII.12.6; PB XIX.3.8; PB XX.11.3.
119. AB VII.17; AB VI.34; KB IV.8; KB XXX.3; KB XXX.9; PB XXI.9.2; JB II.235.
120. See, for example, AB VII.13–18, which recounts the story of the *ṛṣi* Śunaḥśepa and the circumstances under which he came to recite certain *ṛcs*. The account does mention that he saw (root *dṛś*) a certain aspect of the sacrificial ritual, but it does not describe him seeing the *ṛcs*. See also AB VIII.26; ŚB I.7.4.4; ŚB II.5.1.4, which cite *ṛcs* that have been "uttered (root *vac*) by the *ṛṣi*."
121. AB II.19.
122. AB VII.13–18.
123. See, for example, PB VII.10.10; JB I.147.

124. PB IV.7.3; PB VIII.2.2,4,6; PB VIII.5.9,12; PB XIX.3.8; JB I.147; JB I.149–152; JB I.155; JB I.160; JB I.163; JB I.165; JB I.215–217; KB XXVIII.8.
125. PB IV.7.3; PB VIII.2.4; PB XIX.3.8; JB I.150. Cf. KB IV.8, in which Vasiṣṭha is depicted as seeing a particular sacrificial rite and sacrificing with it in order to obtain offspring and cattle.
126. JB I.165; JB I.215.
127. PB VIII.5.12; JB I.160; JB I.217.
128. PB VIII.5.9.
129. JB I.152; JB I.163.
130. PB VIII.2.2; JB I.147; JB I.216.
131. PB VIII.2.6; PB XX.11.3; JB I.163; JB II.235; cf. PB VIII.5.9.
132. TB II.8.8.5. Cf. JUB IV.14.5–6. For other references to the *ṛṣis* as *mantra-kṛts*, see JB I.147; JB I.151; JUB I.45.2.
133. KB XXVIII.1; PB XX.11.3; JB I.160; JB I.215; JB I.217; JB II.235.
134. For a discussion of the Brāhmaṇas' conceptions of the correspondences between the Veda, the sacrificial order, and the cosmic order, see chapter 1.
135. See esp. ŚB VI.2.3.7–8,10; cf. ŚB VIII.4.1.5.
136. ŚB XII.4.4.6.
137. KB III.2.
138. See, for example, AB VII.26.
139. MU I.2.1.
140. MU I.2.1–6.
141. MU I.2.7–10.
142. MU I.1.1–2; MU III.2.11.
143. MU I.2.11; MU III.1.5; MU II.2.3–4,6.
144. MU III.2.5.
145. CU VII.26.2; Maitri VII.11.
146. Extensive *vaṃśas* are given in BĀU II.6.1–3; BĀU IV.6.1–3; BĀU VI.5.1–4; cf. BĀU VI.3.6–12. A brief enumeration of key teachers is given in CU III.11.4; CU VIII.15; MU I.1.1–2. Such *vaṃśas* are also found in the Brāhmaṇas and Āraṇyakas. See, for example, ŚB X.6.5.9 [cf. BĀU VI.5.4]; ŚB XIV.9.4.30–33 [cf. BĀU VI.5.1–3]; JUB III.40–42; JUB IV.16–17.
147. See Mbh. XII.224.56 with n. 672*; VP I.5.62–63, cited in chapter 1, pp. 93, 110. Cf. Mārk. 48.42–43; KP I.7.64–65; LP I.70.257–259; ŚP Vāyavīya. I.12.67–69.
148. The Vedic antecedents of the post-Vedic *rājarṣis* are found in the *rājanyarṣis*, who are occasionally mentioned in the Brāhmaṇas. See, for example, PB XII.12.6.
149. For a discussion of some of the myths associated with these and other *ṛṣis* in the Mahābhārata as well as the Rāmāyaṇa, see Hopkins, *Epic Mythology*, pp. 176–189.
150. Mbh. III.13.48–49; cf. XII.337.69.

151. See, for example, Mbh. XII.181.19; XII.203.17; XII.224.55; XII.322.31, 33,52; XII.327.39–42; XIV.50.14; XIII, App. I, no. 18, 92–94. See also XII.176.6–8, cited below, which describes the *ṛṣis* as obtaining their cognitions through meditation (*dhyāna*) and various austerities. Cf. MS XI.244.
152. See, for example, Mbh. XII.203.12–22. Cf. VI.63.5–6; XIII.143.32,40, which describe Viṣṇu or Kṛṣṇa as the ultimate source of all beings, including the *ṛṣis*.
153. See Mbh. XII.224.56 with n. 672*, cited in chapter 1, p. 93. See also I.1.30–34, esp. 33–34.
154. See, for example, Mbh. XII.160.15–16; XII.327.61; XII.200.17.
155. Mbh. XII.322.27–29,38; XII.327.29–30; cf. XIV.50.12.
156. See, for example, Mbh. XII.160.15–20; XII.201.2–4. The term *prajāpati* is also used at times to refer to *ṛṣis* other than the mind-born sons of Brahmā. XIII.85.34–35, for example, describes the *ṛṣis* Bhṛgu and Kavi along with Aṅgiras (one of Brahmā's mind-born sons) as *prajāpatis* who are the progenitors of many peoples.
157. See, for example, Mbh. XII.322.29,31,33,52; XII.327.39–42.
158. Mbh. XII.327.61–62.
159. Mbh. XIII, App. I, no. 18, 62–95, esp. 66,84,91.
160. Mbh. XII.201.2–4,25–34, esp. 33,26. See also XII.181.19; XIII.32.24.
161. The critical edition, Mbh. XII.176.6–8, reads *dharma-mayī* rather than *brahma-mayī*. However, *brahma-mayī* is attested by both the Bombay edition (XII.183.6–8) and the Calcutta edition (XII.6809–6811) as well as by certain manuscript traditions. One commentator interprets *dharma-mayī* as *veda-mayī*.
162. See n. 161.
163. See Mbh. XII.224.55 with n. 671*–XII.224.56 with n. 672*, cited in chapter 1, pp. 90, 93.
164. Mbh. XII.327.39–42. The voice in this passage is that of Viṣṇu.
165. See in particular ṚV X.71.3.
166. See BĀU VI.5.3 [= ŚB XIV.9.4.33], which maintains that "these white *yajus*es that derive from Āditya are declared by Yājñavalkya of the Vājasaneyi school."
167. Mbh. XII.306.1–25.
168. Mbh. XII.322.26–52, esp. 32–33.
169. Regarding the progressive decline in knowledge of the Vedas in the successive *yugas*, see, for example, Mbh. III.148.10–37; XII.224.22–27,62–69; XII.230.7–18; XII.59.13–21. For references concerning Vyāsa's division of the Veda, see n. 175.
170. See, for example, Mbh. I.2.95; cf. III.46.2. See also XII.337.52, mentioned below, in which Viṣṇu-Nārāyaṇa tells Vyāsa that he will be superior even to the seven *ṛṣis*.
171. See, for example, Mbh. XII.337.3,4; XV.36.3; I.1.56; I.99.13; XII.327.15. For additional references to Vyāsa as a seer, see, for example, I.1.53,

60,62; I.2.215; I.54.1,5; I.99.14; VI.2.1; XII.1.3–4; cf. I.2.168,211,219, 231.

172. See Mbh. XII.337, esp. 4–5,37–38,55; XII.334.9.
173. Mbh. XII.337.37–57.
174. Mbh. XII.327.21–23; XII.337.49–50. See also Sullivan's discussion of the epic's portrayal of Vyāsa's role as a *ṛṣi* in his *Kṛṣṇa Dvaipāyana Vyāsa and the Mahābhārata*, pp. 29–31.
175. Mbh. I.1.52; I.54.5; I.99.14; I.57.72–75; XII.314.23–24; XII.327.15–18; XII.337.39–44,11–15.
176. Mbh. III.148.26–29,33; XII.224.25,66; XII.230.14–15,17; XII.59.21; XII.203.17.
177. See, for example, Mbh. XII.203.17. In the following verses, 18–20, individual *ṛṣis* are credited with acquiring certain teachings that supplement the Vedas. For example, the Vedāṅgas are acquired by the *ṛṣi* Bṛhaspati; Gāndharva-Veda, the Upaveda pertaining to music, by Nārada; and Dhanur-Veda, the Upaveda pertaining to archery, by Bharadvāja.
178. See, for example, Vāyu 59.79–106; Vāyu 61.80–103.
179. See, for example, VP VI.4.1–7.
180. See, for example, BP XII.6.44–46. Cf. Mārk. 45.20–23.
181. See, for example, VP III.3.9–20; VP III.4.1–5; Vāyu 23.119–218; KP I.49.47–I.50.10; LP I.7.11–18; LP I.24.12–140. The seeds of this conception are found in the Mahābhārata's account of the origins of Vyāsa (XII.337.37–57), discussed earlier. The sage Apāntaratamas, a previous incarnation of Kṛṣṇa Dvaipāyana, is described as being produced from the speech of Nārāyaṇa, who ordains that he will divide the Veda in every *manvantara*.
182. See, for example, VP III.2.56; VP III.3.1–III.4.14; Vāyu 60.11–23; KP I.50.10–20; BP I.4.14–20,24; BP XII.6.46–50.
183. VP III.4.13–14.
184. See, for example, VP III.4.7–III.6.20; Vāyu 60.12–16,24–31,63–66; Vāyu 61.1–77; KP I.50.12–14; BP I.4.21–23; BP XII.6.51–XII.7.7.
185. VP III.4.15.
186. VP III.6.31–32; cf. Vāyu 61.75.
187. VP III.2.44; cf. Vāyu 61.121–122.

CHAPTER 4. TORAH AND REVELATION

1. Scholem, *Major Trends in Jewish Mysticism*, pp. 40–43; idem, *Jewish Gnosticism, Merkabah Mysticism, and Talmudic Tradition*. Scholem's arguments will be discussed further below.
2. A number of Halperin's arguments, as discussed in his *The Faces of the Chariot*, will be discussed below. Certain aspects of his argument are developed in his earlier work, *The Merkabah in Rabbinic Literature*.

3. For a discussion of the role of the Merkabah in apocalyptic texts, see Halperin, *The Faces of the Chariot*, pp. 63–114. For a general introduction to apocalyptic literature, see D. S. Russell, *The Method and Message of Jewish Apocalyptic, 200 BC–AD 100*, The Old Testament Library (Philadelphia: Westminster Press, 1964).
4. See Halperin, *The Faces of the Chariot*, pp. 103–113, esp. 109–110.
5. For a brief discussion of the major works of Hêḵālôṯ literature, see Halperin, *The Faces of the Chariot*, pp. 363–366; Peter Schäfer, ed., *Synopse zur Hekhalot-Literatur*, Texte und Studien zum Antiken Judentum, vol. 2 (Tübingen: J. C. B. Mohr [Paul Siebeck], 1981), pp. vi–viii; Scholem, *Jewish Gnosticism, Merkabah Mysticism, and Talmudic Tradition*, pp. 5–7. For more detailed discussions of the major texts, see Gruenwald, *Apocalyptic and Merkavah Mysticism*. See also Peter Schäfer's critique of Gruenwald's delineation of the "works" of Hêḵālôṯ literature in "Tradition and Redaction in Hekhalot Literature," *Journal for the Study of Judaism* 14, no. 2 (Dec. 1983): 172–181; reprinted in his *Hekhalot-Studien*, Texte und Studien zum Antiken Judentum, vol. 19 (Tübingen: J. C. B. Mohr [Paul Siebeck], 1988), pp. 8–16. In contrast to the conventionally accepted view espoused by Scholem and Gruenwald, Halperin does not consider the *Visions of Ezekiel* (*R*[e]*'ûyyôṯ Y*[e]*ḥezqē'l*) to be part of the Hêḵālôṯ literature. See Halperin, *The Faces of the Chariot*, pp. 287–288; cf. Schäfer, "Tradition and Redaction in Hekhalot Literature," p. 173.
6. See Scholem's discussion of the paradoxical use of the verb *yāraḏ*, "to descend," to refer to the "ascent" to the Merkabah in his *Major Trends in Jewish Mysticism*, pp. 46–47; idem, *Jewish Gnosticism, Merkabah Mysticism, and Talmudic Tradition*, p. 20 with n. 1.
7. Chernus, *Mysticism in Rabbinic Judaism*, p. 11. For Chernus's arguments, see ibid., pp. 1–73, esp. 1–32. Chernus points out that in discussing the theophany the sages at times invoke verses from the Song of Songs, and in particular the descriptions of the body of the beloved in chapter 5, especially verses 10–16, which, according to Scholem and Saul Lieberman, represents the biblical *locus classicus* of the *šî'ûr qômāh* speculations concerning the measurements of the body of God. Ibid., pp. 4, 18, 22–23, 37, 60. See Scholem, *Jewish Gnosticism, Merkabah Mysticism, and Talmudic Tradition*, p. 37; idem, *On the Mystical Shape of the Godhead: Basic Concepts in the Kabbalah*, trans. Joachim Neugroschel, ed. Jonathan Chipman (New York: Schocken Books, 1991), pp. 22–23, 30–32; idem, *Major Trends in Jewish Mysticism*, p. 63; Saul Lieberman, "Mišnaṯ Šîr ha-Šîrîm," in Scholem, *Jewish Gnosticism, Merkabah Mysticism, and Talmudic Tradition*, Appendix D, pp. 118–126, esp. 123.
8. For sample citations, see Chernus, *Mysticism in Rabbinic Judaism*, pp. 6–7.
9. Ibid., pp. 9–10.

10. Ibid., pp. 8–9, 10. For a discussion of the garment of God, see Scholem, *Jewish Gnosticism, Merkabah Mysticism, and Talmudic Tradition*, pp. 56–64.
11. Chernus, *Mysticism in Rabbinic Judaism*, pp. 5–6. Scholem has suggested that the seals on which the names were inscribed served a "twin function as a protective armour and as a magical weapon." Scholem, *Major Trends in Jewish Mysticism*, p. 50.
12. Chernus, *Mysticism in Rabbinic Judaism*, pp. 33–73.
13. Ibid., pp. 11–16.
14. Ibid., p. 32.
15. In *Jewish Gnosticism, Merkabah Mysticism, and Talmudic Tradition*, p. 40, Scholem assigns at least three parts of the Hêḵālôṯ literature to the Tannaitic or early Amoraic period: (1) descriptions of the ascent and its dangers; (2) the celestial hymns preserved in *Hêḵālôṯ Rabbāṯî*; and (3) *šî'ûr qômāh* speculations. He later reaffirms his conclusions in his *Origins of the Kabbalah*, ed. R. J. Zwi Werblowsky, trans. Allan Arkush (Philadelphia: Jewish Publication Society; Princeton: Princeton University Press, 1987), pp. 18–23. Gruenwald is more cautious: "Some of the literary remains of the Merkavah Mysticism may well go back to the second century C.E., yet the material as it lies before us today reveals clear traces of the work of later editors, who not only added new material to the old, but also interfered with the old texts before them. This is true of the two main aspects of Merkavah Mysticism: the material found in rabbinical literature and the *Hekhalot* literature." Gruenwald, *From Apocalypticism to Gnosticism*, p. 101.
16. Scholem, in *Major Trends in Jewish Mysticism*, p. 43, asserts that there is an "essential continuity of thought concerning the Merkabah in all its three stages: the anonymous conventicles of the old apocalyptics; the Merkabah speculation of the Mishnaic teachers who are known to us by name; and the Merkabah mysticism of late and post-Talmudic times, as reflected in the [Hêḵālôṯ] literature which has come down to us." In *Jewish Gnosticism, Merkabah Mysticism, and Talmudic Tradition* Scholem discusses a number of examples of "the way in which the material found in these [Hêḵālôṯ] texts amplifies and often explains the exoteric passages in the Talmud and the Midrash related to them" (p. 56). Gruenwald, while recognizing the continuity between certain rabbinic speculations and Hêḵālôṯ traditions, also emphasizes an important point of distinction: "There is . . . one major difference between the rabbinical Merkavah speculations and the Hekhalot literature: the rabbinical speculations are mainly concerned with the study of the doctrine of the Merkavah [*ma'ăśēh merkāḇāh*], while the *Hekhalot* literature records mystical experiences, the most important of which naturally are the heavenly ascensions. But it would be absolutely wrong to say that the rabbinical Merkavah mate-

rial is devoid of any ecstatic experiences. On the contrary, most of this material contains descriptions of visions of fire, which by all standards are a common mystical experience." Gruenwald, *From Apocalypticism to Gnosticism*, p. 101.

17. Scholem, *Jewish Gnosticism, Merkabah Mysticism, and Talmudic Tradition*, p. 12. Gruenwald concurs with Scholem on this point. See Gruenwald, *Apocalyptic and Merkavah Mysticism*, pp. 143, 171. Chernus, in *Mysticism in Rabbinic Judaism*, p. 10, similarly accepts Scholem's conclusions regarding the relatively late date of the *Śar Tôrāh* material.
18. See also Peter Schäfer, ed., *Geniza-Fragmente zur Hekhalot-Literatur*, Texte und Studien zum Antiken Judentum, vol. 6 (Tübingen: J. C. B. Mohr [Paul Siebeck], 1984); idem, ed., *Konkordanz zur Hekhalot-Literatur*, 2 vols., Texte und Studien zum Antiken Judentum, vols. 12–13 (Tübingen: J. C. B. Mohr [Paul Siebeck], 1986, 1988).
19. Peter Schäfer, *Gershom Scholem Reconsidered: The Aim and Purpose of Early Jewish Mysticism*, The Twelfth Sacks Lecture (Oxford: Oxford Centre for Postgraduate Hebrew Studies, 1986), p. 8. See also Peter Schäfer, "Engel und Menschen in der Hekhalot-Literatur," *Kairos*, n. s., 22, nos. 3–4 (1980): 201–225. Both essays are reprinted in his *Hekhalot-Studien*, pp. 277–295, 250–276. Among Schäfer's other critiques of Scholem's views, he argues that the heavenly "ascent does not culminate in a vision, but rather in the Merkavah mystic's participation in the heavenly liturgy," which is itself a reflection of the earthly liturgy of the synagogue. The "descender to the Merkabah" thus serves as an "emissary of the earthly congregation" who represents Israel before God in the heavenly liturgy and at the same time conveys God's assurance to Israel that their earthly liturgy is joyously received. See *Gershom Scholem Reconsidered*, pp. 9–12. For an extended study of the Hêk̲ālôt̲ literature, see Schäfer's *The Hidden and Manifest God: Some Major Themes in Early Jewish Mysticism*, trans. Aubrey Pomerance, SUNY Series in Judaica: Hermeneutics, Mysticism, and Religion (Albany: State University of New York Press, 1992).
20. Halperin, *The Faces of the Chariot*, pp. 359–446. Halperin admits his indebtedness to Urbach's observation that the dialogues in the *Śar Tôrāh* myth represent the perspective of the social underdog over against the rabbinic elite. See Urbach, "The Traditions about Merkabah Mysticism in the Tannaitic Period," pp. 23–25 [Hebrew section]. For alternative perspectives on the role and significance of *Śar Tôrāh* traditions, see Joseph Dan, *Three Types of Ancient Jewish Mysticism*, The Seventh Annual Rabbi Louis Feinberg Memorial Lecture in Judaic Studies (Cincinnati: Judaic Studies Program, University of Cincinnati, 1984), pp. 24–31; Idel, "T^{e}p̄îsat̲ ha-Tôrāh b^{e}-Sip̄rût̲ ha-Hêk̲ālôt̲ w^{e}-Gilgûlẹhā ba-Qabbālāh." Dan similarly suggests that the

Śar Tôrāh myth may derive from a writer who "felt that he and his group were unjustly placed in a secondary position in the Jewish world, without mastery of the Torah and the halakha, disregarded by Jews and non-Jews, having an inferior social and political status" (p. 27).

21. Among the Hêkālôṯ materials that may derive from Babylonia, in Halperin's view, are the myth of *Śar Tôrāh, Hêkālôṯ Rabbāṯî,* and the Genizah fragment published by Gruenwald that Halperin terms the "Ozhayah text." Halperin, *The Faces of the Chariot,* pp. 362, 384 with n. 28, 434–437, 368–370.
22. Ibid., pp. 362, 385, 443. Schäfer, in *Gershom Scholem Reconsidered,* p. 18, similarly posits a connection between the Hêkālôṯ materials and synagogue traditions, as mentioned in n. 19, suggesting in particular that "the context in which this ritual of adjuration and the heavenly journey took place was the synagogue liturgy." Moreover, both Schäfer and Halperin maintain that the authors of the Hêkālôṯ texts were not rabbis. However, in contrast to Halperin's suggestion that these texts derive from nonelite circles within the general populace during the rabbinic period, Schäfer conjectures that they may have originated in an elite group of scholar-mystics in the post-rabbinic period. See ibid., pp. 13–19.
23. See in particular Halperin's discussions of Pes. K. 12.22, Šab. 88b–89a, and Pes. R. 20.4 and their parallels, which he maintains form the core of the synagogue traditions that interpret the Sinai revelation and the Merkabah in light of each other. Halperin, *The Faces of the Chariot,* pp. 141–149, 262–358. These passages will be discussed in the course of our analysis of Sinai Midrashim. Halperin suggests that Sinai and the Merkabah may have been linked as early as pre-Christian Alexandria, as indicated in the Septuagint's translation of Ezekiel 43.2. Ibid., pp. 57–59.
24. Ibid., pp. 18, 120 with note a, 447–448.
25. Ibid., pp. 18, 142–149, 301–305, 316–317, 355, 448.
26. Ibid., p. 355.
27. Ibid., p. 448.
28. For Halperin's discussion of T Ḥag. II.1; JT Ḥag. II.1, 77a; and BT Ḥag. 14b, see *The Faces of the Chariot,* pp. 13–19. For a more detailed exposition, see his *The Merkabah in Rabbinic Literature,* esp. pp. 107–140. See also Urbach, "The Traditions about Merkabah Mysticism in the Tannaitic Period," pp. 2–11 [Hebrew section].
29. Halperin, *The Faces of the Chariot,* pp. 385, 443.
30. 'Ab. II–IV.
31. See Lev. R. XX.10 = Pes. K. 26.9; Song R. III.11, §2; Lam. R. Proem XXXIII; cf. Pes. K. 1.3. For an analysis of the use of marriage symbolism to depict the Sinai theophany in rabbinic and other sources, see Wolfson, "Female Imaging of the Torah," esp. pp. 274–285.

32. For an exposition of Sip̄rê on Deuteronomy's commentary on Deut. 33.2–4 in §343–§345, see Steven D. Fraade, *From Tradition to Commentary: Torah and Its Interpretation in the Midrash Sifre to Deuteronomy*, SUNY Series in Judaica: Hermeneutics, Mysticism, and Religion (Albany: State University of New York Press, 1991), pp. 25–68.
33. See, for example, Sip̄rê Deut. §306, cited in chapter 2, p. 151. Cf. Sip̄rê Deut. §317.
34. Sip̄rā', B^{e}-ḥûqqôṯay, Pereq 8.
35. Sip̄rā', B^{e}-ḥûqqôṯay, Pereq 8; Sip̄rê Deut. §351.
36. See, for example, Sip̄rā', B^{e}-ḥûqqôṯay, Pereq 8; Mek., ed. Lauterbach, Ba-ḥōḏeš §9, vol. 2, pp. 270, 272.
37. Sip̄rā', B^{e}-ḥûqqôṯay, Pereq 8.
38. Mek., ed. Lauterbach, Ba-ḥôḏeš §10, vol. 2, p. 279; Sip̄rê Deut. §345.
39. Sip̄rê Deut. §311. Cf. Pes. R. 50.2.
40. Mek., ed. Lauterbach, Ba-ḥôḏeš §5, vol. 2, pp. 234–237; Sip̄rê Deut. §343; cf. Mek., ed. Lauterbach, Ba-ḥôḏeš §1, vol. 2, pp. 198–200. For a discussion of the subtle differences between the variants of this tradition in Sip̄rê on Deuteronomy and the M^{e}ḵîltā', see Fraade, *From Tradition to Commentary*, pp. 32–36. Deut. 33.2 is similarly interpreted in later rabbinic texts to mean that God offered the Torah to the children of Esau and other nations. See Lam. R. III.1, §1; Pes. K. Suppl. 1.15; 'AZ 2a–2b; Pes. R. 21.2/3; PRE §41, f. 95b.
41. Mek., ed. Lauterbach, Ba-ḥôḏeš §1, vol. 2, p. 198.
42. Mek., ed. Lauterbach, Ba-ḥôḏeš §1, vol. 2, pp. 198–200; Mek., ed. Lauterbach, Ba-ḥôḏeš §5, vol. 2, pp. 232, 236–237.
43. Sip̄rê Deut. §343. This tradition is derived from an interpretation of Deut. 33.2.
44. See Šab. 88b; Tanḥ. Š^{e}môṯ §25; Tanḥ., ed. Buber, Š^{e}môṯ §22; Tanḥ. Yiṯrô §11; Exod. R. XXVIII.6.
45. Sip̄rê Deut. §306; cf. Sip̄rê Deut. §343.
46. Sip̄rê Deut. §306. See also Sip̄rā', Wa-yiqrā', N^{e}ḏāḇāh, Pereq 2, which alludes to Moses entering the realm of the angels. Moses's struggles with the angels are explicitly discussed in later rabbinic texts. See, for example, Šab. 88b–89a; Pes. R. 20.4; Tanḥ., ed. Buber, Kî Ṯiśśā' §13; Tanḥ. Ha'ăzînû §3; Tanḥ., ed. Buber, Ha'ăzînû §3; Exod. R. XXVIII.1; Exod. R. XLI.7; Exod. R. XLII.4; Deut. R. III.11; Deut. R. XI.10; Deut. R. XI.3; Deut. R. IX.2; Pes. R. 10.6.
47. Mek., ed. Lauterbach, Ba-ḥôḏeš §4, vol. 2, p. 224. A variant of this tradition is also found in the Talmud, in Suk. 5a.
48. Mek., ed. Lauterbach, Ba-ḥôḏeš §9, vol. 2, pp. 275–276.
49. Mek., ed. Lauterbach, Ba-ḥôḏeš §4, vol. 2, p. 224.
50. Mek., ed. Lauterbach, Ba-ḥôḏeš §3, vol. 2, pp. 218–219. Cf. PRE §41, f. 96b.
51. Sip̄rê Deut. §345. This interpretation is obtained through construing *môrāšāh* in Deut. 33.4, "Moses commanded us a law (Torah) as an

inheritance (*môrāšāh*) for the assembly of Jacob," as *me'ôrāśāh*, "betrothed." Cf. Pes. 49b; Sanh. 59a; Ber. 57a; Exod. R. XXXIII.7.

52. Two of the theophanies point to past events in Israel's history—the Exodus from Egypt and the revelation at Mount Sinai—while the third and fourth are expected to occur in the endtimes—in the days of Gog and Magog and in the days of the Messiah. The proof text given for the Sinai event is Deut. 33.2, "He shone forth (*hôpî'a*) from Mount Paran."
53. Sip̄rê Deut. §343.
54. Sip̄rê Deut. §343.
55. Mek., ed. Lauterbach, Ba-ḥōḏeš §3, vol. 2, pp. 218–219; Mek., ed. Lauterbach, Ba-ḥôḏeš §9, vol. 2, pp. 266–267.
56. Mek., ed. Lauterbach, Ba-ḥôḏeš §2, vol. 2, p. 209. Cf. Song R. I.2, §3; Exod. R. XXIX.4; Exod. R. XLI.3.
57. Mek., ed. Lauterbach, Ba-ḥōḏeš §9, vol. 2, p. 275.
58. Mek., ed. Lauterbach, Ba-ḥōḏeš §3, vol. 2, p. 212. Cf. Mek., ed. Lauterbach, Šîrāṯā' §3, vol. 2, p. 24, where a variant of this tradition, attributed to R. Eliezer, is given in the context of describing the Israelites' experience at the Red Sea. R. Eliezer's version invokes not only Hos. 12.11 but also Ezek. 1.1, "The heavens were opened, and I saw visions of God." A parallel tradition in Deut. R. VII.8, cited below on p. 307, is attributed to R. Hoshaiah and limits its comparison to Ezekiel, without mention of Isaiah. See Halperin's analysis of these passages in *The Faces of the Chariot*, pp. 211–216. For his discussion of the relationship of the Merkabah to the theophany at the Red Sea and to the waters motif generally, see pp. 176–187, 194–249.
59. Mek., ed. Lauterbach, Ba-ḥôḏeš §4, vol. 2, pp. 228–229; Mek., ed. Lauterbach, Šîrāṯā' §8, vol. 2, p. 62. Cf. Pes. R. 21.5; Tanḥ. Yiṯrô §11.
60. Sip̄rê Deut. §343.
61. Mek., ed. Lauterbach, Ba-ḥôḏeš §9, vol. 2, p. 266. Cf. Sip̄rā', Wa-yiqrā', Neḏāḇāh, Pārāšāh 1, which includes the revelation of the Torah as one of the occasions at which an utterance accompanied by fire came forth from the mouth of God and was addressed to Moses. Philo gives an interpretation of Exod. 20.18 similar to that of R. Akiba in which he emphasizes that the people of Israel saw the voice of God, which was visible to their eyes. For references, see Wolfson, "The Hermeneutics of Visionary Experience," p. 327, n. 11. See also PRE §41, f. 98a, cited below on p. 314.

The image of words of fire coming forth from God's mouth is also found in Hêḵālôṯ texts. See, for example, *Hêḵālôṯ Rabbāṯî* 24.3: "And His words shall drop as perfume, flowing forth in flames of fire. . . . You are He who revealed Your secret to Moses, and You did not hide any of Your power from him. When the word went out of Your mouth, all the high mountains would shake and stand in great terror, and all of them were burned in flames of fire." Cited in Chernus, *Mysticism in Rabbinic Judaism*, p. 3.

62. Sip̄rê Deut. §313.
63. Mek., ed. Lauterbach, Ba-ḥôḏeš §9, vol. 2, p. 267.
64. See, for example, Mek., ed. Lauterbach, Ba-ḥôḏeš §4, vol. 2, pp. 220–221; Mek., ed. Lauterbach, Ba-ḥôḏeš §9, vol. 2, pp. 266, 268, 270; Mek., ed. Lauterbach, Ba-ḥôḏeš §5, vol. 2, p. 235; Mek., ed. Lauterbach, B^e-šallaḥ §7, vol. 1, p. 247; Sip̄rê Deut. §343; Sip̄rā', Wa-yiqrā', N^eḏāḇāh, Pārāšāh 1.
65. Mek., ed. Lauterbach, Ba-ḥôḏeš §9, vol. 2, p. 270; cf. Mek., ed. Lauterbach, Ba-ḥôḏeš §4, vol. 2, p. 221. For parallel Hêḵālôṯ traditions concerning the "descender to the Merkabah" being burned by heavenly fire, see Chernus, *Mysticism in Rabbinic Judaism*, pp. 6–7.
66. Mek., ed. Lauterbach, Ba-ḥôḏeš §4, vol. 2, pp. 220–221; cf. Sip̄rê Deut. §343.
67. Sip̄rê Deut. §343; Mek., ed. Lauterbach, Ba-ḥôḏeš §5, vol. 2, p. 235; Mek., ed. Lauterbach, B^e-šallaḥ §7, vol. 1, p. 247.
68. Mek., ed. Lauterbach, Ba-ḥôḏeš §5, vol. 2, pp. 233–234; Mek., ed. Lauterbach, 'Ămālēq §3, vol. 2, pp. 162–163; Sip̄rê Deut. §343. Cf. Zeb. 116a; Pes. R. 20.1.
69. Mek., ed. Lauterbach, Ba-ḥôḏeš §9, vol. 2, p. 269. This tradition also appears in Ba-ḥôḏeš §2, vol. 2, p. 202, where it is attributed to R. Akiba. See also Sip̄rê Deut. §313. Cf. Šab. 88b.
70. Mek., ed. Lauterbach, Ba-ḥôḏeš §9, vol. 2, pp. 270–271. For an alternative interpretation, in which God is said to have spoken only the first two commandments directly to the people, while the rest were spoken through the mouth of Moses, see Song R. I.2, §2; Hor. 8a; Mak. 23b–24a; Pes. R. 22.3; Exod. R. XXXIII.7; Exod. R. XLII.8; PRE §41, f. 97b, 98a.
71. Mek., ed. Lauterbach, Ba-ḥôḏeš §9, vol. 2, pp. 266–267. Cf. Song R. V.16, §3; Pes. K. 12.25; Tanḥ. Š^emôṯ §25; Tanḥ., ed. Buber, Š^emôṯ §22; Tanḥ., ed. Buber, Yiṯrô §17; Exod. R. XXXIV.1; Exod. R. XXIX.1; Tanḥ. Yiṯrô §11; Exod. R. XXVIII.6.
72. Halperin has suggested that a substantial portion of P^esîqtā' d^e-R. Kahana's exposition, in particular 12.12–25, was not a part of the original text but represents an extract from a lost recension of the Tanḥûmā' that was later interpolated into several manuscripts of the P^esîqtā'. He points out that only two of the five manuscripts used in Mandelbaum's critical edition of the P^esîqtā' contain most (though not all) of the material in Pes. K. 12.12–25. He also notes the close correspondence between this material and Tanḥ., ed. Buber, Yiṯrô §7–17. Halperin, *The Faces of the Chariot*, pp. 142–143.
73. See Song R. I.2, §2, which will be discussed further below.
74. See, for example, Song R. I.2, §5. For general references to the two Torahs, see Song R. I.3, §2; Song R. I.10, §1; Song R. II.5, §1; Pes. K. 12.5; Pes. K. 15.5; Lam. R. Proem II; cf. Lev. R. III.7. See chapter 2, p. 158.

75. Lev. R. XXII.1; cf. Lev. R. XV.2. Cf. Exod. R. XLVII.1; Tanḥ., ed. Buber, Kî Ṯiśśā' §17. See also the Midrash ascribed to R. Ḥanina b. Pappai in Pes. K. 12.25, which suggests that God appeared to Israel with multiple faces—stern, neutral, friendly, and joyous—corresponding to the revelation of the Bible, Mishnah, Talmud, and Aggadah, respectively. Cf. Pes. R. 21.6.
76. See chapter 2, pp. 157–159.
77. Song R. II.1, §1; cf. Song R. I.2, §3.
78. Ruth R. Proem I.
79. See, for example, Pes. K. 16.3; Lam. R. II.13, §17. Cf. Pes. R. 29/30A.3.
80. Lam. R. II.9, §13.
81. Pes. K. 12.23; Ruth R. Proem I. In Ruth Rabbāh this tradition is attributed to R. Judah b. Simon, with no mention of R. Joshua b. Levi. Cf. Exod. R. XLVII.3.
82. Ruth R. Proem I.
83. Lam. R. III.1, §1; cf. Pes. K. Suppl. 1.15. While the pericope in Lam. R. III.1, §1 is attributed to R. Joshua of Siknin in the name of R. Levi in the Vilna edition (1887), it is ascribed to R. Joshua b. Levi in Buber's edition (1899), which gives a slightly more elaborate account of God's offering of the Torah to all nations. Cf. Mek., ed. Lauterbach, Ba-ḥôḏeš §5, vol. 2, pp. 234–237; Sip̄rê Deut. §343; 'AZ 2a–2b; Pes. R. 21.2/3; PRE §41, f. 95b. The tradition that the gentile nations refused to accept the Torah is also mentioned, without reference to Deut. 33.2, in Gen. R. LIII.9; Lev. R. VI.6; Pes. K. 5.2 [= Pes. R. 15.2]; Pes. K. Suppl. 2.1; Lam. R. Proem XXIV; Esth. R. Proem III; cf. Song R. II.3, §1; Pes. K. 12.10.
84. Pes. K. Suppl. 1.15.
85. Pes. K. 5.2 [= Pes. R. 15.2]; cf. Lam. R. III.1, §1. In Pes. R. 15.2 this tradition is attributed to R. Ḥanina b. Pappai.
86. Lev. R. VI.6.
87. Pes. K. Suppl. 2.1. The first part of this homily, which is attributed to either R. Ḥinena (Ḥanina) b. Pappai or R. Simlai, is also found in 'AZ 2a–2b, which will be discussed below. Cf. Lev. R. XXVII.7 = Pes. K. 9.6; Lev. R. XIII.2; Lev. R. XXIII.6; Song R. II.2, §6.
88. Pes. K. 12.20; Lev. R. II.9.
89. Lev. R. XXIII.3.
90. The expression *tōhû wā-ḇōhû* derives from Gen. 1.2, "The earth was formless and void (*tōhû wā-ḇōhû*), and darkness was upon the face of the deep," and is generally understood in rabbinic texts as referring to the state of primordial chaos from which the world emerged.
91. Song R. VII.1, §1; Song R. I.9, §6; Gen. R. LXVI.2; Ruth R. Proem I. Cf. Pes. R. 21.4; Pes. R. 21.21. In Song R. I.9, §6 this tradition is attributed to R. Ḥanina, rather than R. Huna, in the name of R. Aḥa. For an alternative perspective, see Pes. K. 19.6, which suggests that even after the

revelation of the Torah the world was still somewhat unstable and was not established on a firm foundation until the Temple was built.

92. Song R. I.4, §2.
93. Gen. R. IV.2.
94. Gen. R. XVIII.4; Gen. R. XXXI.8. While the first tradent is R. Phinehas in both variants, the second tradent is given as either R. Ḥilkiah (Gen. R. XVIII.4) or R. Hezekiah (Gen. R. XXXI.8).
95. Lev. R. XXX.1 = Pes. K. 27.1 [= Pes. R. 51.1]. Cf. Exod. R. XLVII.5; Pes. R. 21.21.
96. See, for example, Lev. R. XXXV.6; Lev. R. XV.2.
97. Pes. K. 12.7.
98. Song R. VIII.5, §1. This tradition is derived from Deut. 4.11, "And you came near and stood under the mountain." Later in the passage God is said to have threatened to crush the Israelites under the mountain if they would not accept the Torah. For other traditions concerning the uprooted mountain, see Mek., ed Lauterbach, Ba-ḥôḏeš §3, vol. 2, p. 219; 'AZ 2b; Šab. 88a. For a study of Mount Sinai traditions in the Hebrew Bible and their parallels in Canaanite traditions concerning the cosmic mountain, see Richard J. Clifford, *The Cosmic Mountain in Canaan and the Old Testament,* Harvard Semitic Monographs, vol. 4 (Cambridge: Harvard University Press, 1972), esp. pp. 107–123.
99. See, for example, Song R. I.12, §1; Song R. III.11, §2; Pes. K. 1.3; Pes. K. 4.7 [= Pes. R. 14.13]; Pes. K. Suppl. 1.9; Deut. R. XI.4; Lev. R. XXXI.5; Ruth R. II.3; cf. Pes. K. 6.1 [= Pes. R. 16.2].
100. Ruth R. II.3.
101. Lev. R. XX.10 = Pes. K. 26.9.
102. Pes. K. Suppl. 1.9. Cf. Deut. R. XI.4.
103. Variants of this tradition, in which God himself argues with the angels, appear in Pes. R. 25.3; Tanḥ., ed. Buber, Bᵉ-ḥuqqōṯay §6; Tanḥ. Bᵉ-ḥuqqōṯay §4. An alternative version of the debate, in which Moses rather than God argues with the angels, is found in Šab. 88b–89a; Pes. R. 20.4; PRE §46, f. 110b. The commandments that are invoked to convince the angels differ among the variants. See Peter Schäfer, *Rivalität zwischen Engeln und Menschen. Untersuchungen zur rabbinischen Engelvorstellung,* Studia Judaica: Forschungen zur Wissenchaft des Judentums, vol. 8 (Berlin: Walter de Gruyter, 1975), pp. 119–139. See also Joseph P. Schultz, "Angelic Opposition to the Ascension of Moses and the Revelation of the Law," *The Jewish Quarterly Review* 61, no. 4 (Apr. 1971): 282–307.

    See also Lev. R. XXXI.5, which gives a series of interpretations of Prov. 21.22, "A wise man scales (*'ālāh*) the city of the mighty and brings down the stronghold (*'ōz*) of trust." The "wise man scales (*'ālāh*) the city of the mighty" is understood as referring to Moses, who "went up (*'ālāh*) to God" (Exod. 19.3). He brought down the Torah, which, according to an interpretation attributed to R. Judah b. Il'ai, is the "stronghold" (*'ōz*) that was the "trust" of the angels, who thought that the Torah was given to them until God informed them otherwise. Cf. PRE §46, f. 110b.

104. Once the Tabernacle, and later the Temple, was built, the Shekhinah is said to have made its abode in particular on the Ark of the Covenant in which the Sefer Torah was kept. See, for example, Song R. III.10, §2; Lev. R. XX.4 = Pes. K. 26.4; cf. Pes. K. 1.1.
105. Pes. K. 12.11.
106. Cf. Mek., ed. Lauterbach, Ba-ḥōḏeš §4, vol. 2, p. 224; Suk. 5a.
107. See, for example, Lev. R. XX.10 = Pes. K. 26.9; Song R. III.11, §2; Lam. R. Proem XXXIII; cf. Pes. K. 1.3. Cf. Taan. IV.8.
108. In addition to Song R. VIII.11, §2 and Pes. K. 12.11, discussed above, see Lev. R. XX.10 = Pes. K. 26.9; Lev. R. XXV.1; Song R. III.11, §2; cf. Song R. V.16, §3; Pes. K. 12.19.
109. See, for example, Pes. K. 22.4; Pes. K. 22.5; Pes. K. 12.11; Pes. K. 19.4; Song R. I.2, §3; Song R. VIII.5, §1; Lam. R. III.21, §7; cf. Pes. K. 12.17.
110. See, for example, Pes. K. 19.4 and Lam. R. III.21, §7, which present two versions of a parable attributed to R. Joḥanan through his tradent R. Abba b. Kahana. Another variant of the parable appears in Pes. R. 21.15. The parable's use of the marriage contract metaphor emphasizes the Torah's role as a symbol of God's promise of redemption, rather than its role as a set of obligations to be fulfilled by Israel. For other uses of the metaphor, cf. Exod. R. XLVI.1; Exod. R. XLVII.2; Deut. R. III.12; Deut. R. III.17.
111. See the tradition attributed to R. Jonathan in Pes. K. Suppl. 1.9.
112. Halperin, in *The Faces of the Chariot*, pp. 141–149, suggests that the pericope in Pes. K. 12.22, along with its parallels in Pesîqtā' Rabbāṯî and Tanḥûmā' Yelammeḏēnû Midrashim, which will be discussed in a later section, may be portions of lost Shavuot sermons. This pericope might thus represent one of the earliest remnants of synagogue traditions that utilized Ps. 68.18 to interpret the Sinai revelation in light of Ezekiel's Merkabah vision. As Halperin notes, two recensions of this material can be distinguished: (1) Pes. K. 12.22 and Tanḥ., ed. Buber, Yiṯrô §14; and (2) Tanḥ. Ṣaw §12 and Tanḥ., ed. Buber, Ṣaw §16. Pes. R. 21.7 combines elements of both recensions. Variants of particular traditions will be given in nn. 113–117.
113. As will be discussed in a later section, Pes. R. 21.7 follows Peśîqtā' de-R. Kahana's reading of "22,000 ministering angels," as does Deut. R., ed. Lieberman, p. 68 (the attribution is misconstrued as "R. Ammi of Jaffa"). This reading is also presupposed in Exod. R. XXIX.2. However, an alternative reading, "22,000 chariots (*markāḇôṯ*) of ministering angels," appears in the parallel pericope in Tanḥ., ed. Buber, Yiṯrô §14, as well as in Tanḥ. Wa-yišlaḥ §2; Tanḥ. Be-miḏbar §14 (without attribution); Tanḥ., ed. Buber, Be-miḏbar §15 (without attribution). The recension in Tanḥ. Ṣaw §12 and Tanḥ., ed. Buber, Ṣaw §16 reads

"22,000 chariots (*markāḇôṯ*)." Halperin argues that "22,000 chariots of ministering angels" is the original reading. That *markāḇôṯ* may have dropped out of the version preserved in Pes. K. 12.22, Pes. R. 21.7, and Deut. R., ed. Lieberman, p. 68, is suggested by the *šel* ("of") that awkwardly appears immediately after the numeral in these texts—hence reading, literally, "22,000 of ministering angels." See Halperin, *The Faces of the Chariot*, pp. 143–148, esp. 143 with note n. Cf. PRE §41, f. 95b–96a.

114. The tradition regarding the 22,000 males in the tribe of Levi derives from Num. 3.39. Cf. Pes. R. 21.7; Tanḥ., ed. Buber, Yiṯrô §14; Tanḥ. Ṣaw §12; Tanḥ., ed. Buber, Ṣaw §16. As will be discussed below, Pes. R. 21.7 ascribes this tradition to R. Levi.

115. In the parallel pericope in Tanḥ., ed. Buber, Yiṯrô §14, as in P^{e}sîqtā' d^{e}-R. Kahana, the tradition is anonymous. In Tanḥ. Ṣaw §12 and Tanḥ., ed. Buber, Ṣaw §16 this tradition is ascribed to R. Yannai, while Pes. R. 21.7 attributes it to R. Yannai the son of R. Simeon b. Yannai.

116. See Chernus, *Mysticism in Rabbinic Judaism*, pp. 27–30, for a discussion of the possibility that there were two separate traditions concerning the presence of chariots at Sinai, one originating in Palestine and the other brought from Babylonia.

117. Cf. Pes. R. 21.8.

118. Pes. K. 16.3; Song R. IV.4, §1; Lam. R. II.13, §17. Cf. Pes. R. 21.7; Pes. R. 33.10; Pes. R. 29/30A.3; Pes. R. 10.6; Tanḥ., ed. Buber, T^{e}ṣawweh §7; Tanḥ., ed. Buber, add. to Š^{e}laḥ §1; Tanḥ., ed. Buber, Wā-'ērā' §9; Tanḥ. Š^{e}laḥ §13; Exod. R. LI.8; Num. R. XVI.24. See also Šab. 88a, which contains a different tradition, ascribed to R. Simai, concerning 600,000 angels bearing crowns. PRE §47, f. 112a, gives yet another version of this tradition, attributed to R. Eleazar b. Arak, regarding 600,000 angels bearing crowns and weapons. For a brief discussion of the parallel use of crown imagery in Hêḵālôṯ texts, see Chernus, *Mysticism in Rabbinic Judaism*, pp. 9–10.

119. Lam. R. Proem XXIV; Song R. I.4, §2; Song R. IV.12, §2; Song R. V.7, §1; Song R. VIII.5, §1. Cf. Pes. R. 33.10; Exod. R. XLV.3; Exod. R. LI.8; Tanḥ., ed. Buber, Wā-'ērā' §9; Tanḥ., ed. Buber, T^{e}ṣawweh §7; Tanḥ., ed. Buber, add. to Š^{e}laḥ §1. Chernus, in *Mysticism in Rabbinic Judaism*, pp. 5–6, suggests that the Sinai traditions concerning the weapon engraved with the ineffable Name may be connected to Hêḵālôṯ traditions concerning the "descender to the Merkabah's" use of seals inscribed with theurgic names, which functioned as "weapons" that protected him from hostile angels in his heavenly journeys. See n. 11.

120. Pes. K. 4.4 [= Pes. R. 14.10]. Cf. Pes. R. 21.6. See also Exod. R. LI.8, in which God is said to have clothed the Israelites with the "splendor of His glory" (*zîw hăḏārô*). See p. 305 with n. 259.

121. Song R. I.2, §3; cf. Song R. II.14, §4. Cf. Mek., ed. Lauterbach, Ba-ḥôḏeš §2, vol. 2, p. 209; Exod. R. XXIX.4; Exod. R. XLI.3.
122. Pes. K. 12.19; cf. Pes. K. 5.16 [= Pes. R. 15.22]; Lev. R. XVIII.4; Song R. IV.7, §1. Cf. Pes. R. 7.7.
123. Cf. Mek., ed. Lauterbach, Ba-ḥôḏeš §9, vol. 2, pp. 270–271.
124. As Chernus notes, in *Mysticism in Rabbinic Judaism*, pp. 34–35, this view may be linked to another tradition ascribed to R. Joshua b. Levi in the Babylonian Talmud (Šab. 88b), cited below on p. 293, which maintains that the souls of the Israelites departed after hearing the first commandment but were subsequently revived so that they could receive the second commandment. The implication is that they could not bear to hear more than two commandments directly from God. This conclusion is explicitly drawn in PRE §41, f. 97b, 98a, as will be discussed in a later section. The view that the Israelites only heard the first two commandments from God's mouth is similarly ascribed to R. Joshua b. Levi in Pes. R. 22.3 and Exod. R. XLII.8. However, it is also at times attributed to other sages: R. Ishmael (Hor. 8a), R. Hamnuna (Mak. 23b–24a), or the sages (Exod R. XXXIII.7).
125. The view ascribed to R. Simeon b. Yoḥai represents a variant of the tradition in Sip̄rê Deut. §343. The debate between R. Simeon and the rabbis concerns whether God's left hand, representing the attribute of justice, was involved in the process.
126. Song R. V.14, §1–2.
127. Song R. V.14, §2. Cf. Num. R. XVIII.21; Exod. R. XLVI.1.
128. Song R. V.14, §1.
129. The tradition ascribed to R. Judah b. Il'ai appears in Pes. K. 1.2 and Song R. III.9, §1. The tradition attributed to R. Isaac appears in Pes. K. 5.8 [= Pes. R. 15.8] and Song R. II.9, §1.
130. See Song R. III.9, §1, which invokes Deut. 33.2, "The Lord came from Sinai," as the proof text for the Israelites' vision of God at Sinai. The other version of R. Judah's tradition in Pes. K. 1.2 invokes instead Deut. 5.4, "The Lord spoke with you face to face (*pānîm b^{e}-pānîm*)." The variant of R. Isaac's tradition in Pes. K. 5.8 [= Pes. R. 15.8] cites Deut. 33.2, while the other version of this tradition in Song R. II.9, §1 cites both Deut. 5.4 and Deut. 33.2.
131. Pes. K. 12.22. Cf. Tanḥ., ed. Buber, Yiṯrô §14. See also the tradition in Lev. R. XVIII.3 and Song R. VIII.6, §1, which maintains that as soon as the people of Israel said, "All that the Lord has spoken we will do and we will hear" (Exod. 24.7), the angel of death lost his power over them. Other traditions concerning the immunity from death gained by the Israelites will be discussed below on p. 306.
132. Pes. K. 5.3 [= Pes. R. 15.3]. A variant of this tradition appears in Song R. III.7, §5, where it is attributed to R. Levi. See also Gen. R. IV.2, mentioned earlier, which suggests that at the revelation fire divided the upper realms and the lower realms.

133. Song R. V.11, §6; Song R. I.9, §4; Pes. K. Suppl. 1.17; Pes. K. Suppl. 1.20; Lam. R. III.1, §1; Lev. R. IV.1.
134. Song R. V.11, §6. Cf. Deut. R. III.12.
135. Lev. R. XVI.4; Song R. I.10, §2; Ruth R. VI.4; cf. Pes. K. Suppl. 1.17. In Lev. R. XVI.4 and Song R. I.10, §2 Ben Azzai is asked whether he was dealing with the "chambers of the Merkabah," since the study of *ma'ăśēh merkāḇāh* was associated with manifestations of fire. Cf. Ḥag. 14b and its parallels in T Ḥag. II.1 and JT Ḥag. II.1, 77a, mentioned on p. 263 with n. 28. Cf. also Suk. 28a.
136. Song R. IV.4, §1.
137. Song R. I.2, §4.
138. Lev. R. I.1; Lev. R. I.4.
139. Cf. Song R. V.6, §1. The tradition that the Israelites died at Mount Sinai is ascribed to a variety of rabbis in later texts. See in particular Šab. 88b; Exod. R. XXIX.4; Exod. R. XXIX.9; PRE §41, f. 97b, in which S. S. 5.6, "My soul went forth when he spoke," is similarly interpreted as referring to the death of the Israelites upon hearing God's voice. See also Pes. R. 20.4. As mentioned earlier, Chernus suggests that these traditions concerning the death and resurrection of the Israelites form part of an "initiatory death schema" that combines elements of Hêḵālôṯ traditions concerning the dangers of the heavenly ascent and rabbinic traditions concerning the resurrection of the dead. See Chernus, *Mysticism in Rabbinic Judaism*, pp. 33–73.
140. Song R. V.16, §3. See also the interpretation of Ps. 29.4 in Pes. K. 12.25, discussed below. Cf. Mek., ed. Lauterbach, Ba-ḥôḏeš §9, pp. 266–267; Tanḥ. Š^{e}môṯ §25; Tanḥ., ed. Buber, Š^{e}môṯ §22; Tanḥ., ed. Buber, Yiṯrô §17; Exod. R. XXXIV.1; Exod. R. XXIX.1; Tanḥ. Yiṯrô §11; Exod. R. XXVIII.6. The individualized nature of the revelation experience is emphasized in another tradition in Song R. I.2, §2, ascribed to the rabbis, which suggests that each of the commandments went in turn to each of the Israelites and asked if he or she would undertake to observe it.
141. A variant of this tradition concerning the intervention of the Torah appears in Exod. R. XXIX.4. For other explanations of the manner in which the Israelites were revived, see Šab. 88b; Pes. R. 20.4; PRE §41, f. 97b.
142. Cf. Tanḥ., ed. Buber, Yiṯrô §17. See also Pes. R. 21.6, in which the analogy of the statue is attributed to R. Joḥanan and is subsequently elaborated by R. Levi in a series of traditions concerning the many faces with which God appeared at Sinai.
143. Cf. Tanḥ., ed. Buber, Yiṯrô §17; Tanḥ. Š^{e}môṯ §25; Tanḥ., ed. Buber, Š^{e}môṯ §22.
144. Hor. 8a; Mak. 23b–24a. Cf. Song R. I.2, §2; Pes. R. 22.3; Exod. R. XXXIII.7; Exod. R. XLII.8; PRE §41, f. 97b, 98a. See n. 124.
145. Ber. 5a.

146. Meg. 19b.
147. See, for example, Ber. 64a; Hor. 14a.
148. Giṭ. 60b. Cf. Pes. R. 5.1; Tanḥ., ed. Buber, Wa-yērā' §6. For a discussion of other references concerning the relationship between the Written Torah and Oral Torah in the Talmud, see chapter 2, pp. 173–174.
149. 'Erub. 54b.
150. Qid. 31a.
151. This represents an extension of the earlier view in Sip̄rê Deut. §343 that God spoke four languages at the revelation. Cf. Tanḥ. Š^{e}môṯ §25; Tanḥ., ed. Buber, Š^{e}môṯ §22; Tanḥ. Yiṯrô §11; Exod. R. XXVIII.6, in which this tradition is attributed to R. Joḥanan.
152. Cf. Sip̄rê Deut. §343; Song R. I.2, §2.
153. Cf. Mek., ed. Lauterbach, Ba-ḥôḏeš §5, vol. 2, pp. 233–234; Mek., ed. Lauterbach, 'Ămālēq §3, vol. 2, pp. 162–163; Sip̄rê Deut. §343; Pes. R. 20.1.
154. See Heinemann's discussion of this homily in *Literature of the Synagogue*, pp. 161–166.
155. Cf. Pes. K. Suppl. 2.1, which includes the first part of the homily in 'AZ 2a–2b.
156. Cf. Mek., ed. Lauterbach, Ba-ḥôḏeš §5, vol. 2, pp. 234–237; Sip̄rê Deut. §343; Lam. R. III.1, §1; Pes. R. 21.2/3; PRE §41, f. 95b.
157. The tradition that God offered the Torah to all nations is attributed to R. Joḥanan in the present context. Cf. Mek., ed. Lauterbach, Ba-ḥôḏeš §5, vol. 2, pp. 234–237; Sip̄rê Deut. §343; Lam. R. III.1, §1; Pes. K. Suppl. 1.15; Pes. R. 21.2/3; PRE §41, f. 95b.
158. The aggadah that God threatened Israel by suspending the mountain over them is also found in Šab. 88a, where, as will be discussed below, it is linked to the notion that if Israel had not accepted the Torah, God would have returned the creation to chaos. In both cases the tradition is attributed to R. Abdimi. This aggadah has antecedents in several traditions in Palestinian Midrashim. An anonymous tradition in the M^{e}ḵîltā' d^{e}-R. Ishmael interprets Exod. 19.17, "And they stood under the mountain," to mean that the mountain was uprooted and the people of Israel came and stood under it. See Mek., ed Lauterbach, Ba-ḥôḏeš §3, vol. 2, p. 219. A passage in Song R. VIII.5, §1, invoking Deut. 4.11, "And you came near and stood under the mountain," conveys two additional points: first, the uprooted mountain stood in the heights of heaven; and, second, God threatened to crush the Israelites under the mountain if they did not accept the Torah.
159. See also BK 38a. Cf. Mek., ed. Lauterbach, Ba-ḥôḏeš §5, vol. 2, pp. 235–236; Sip̄rê Deut. §343.
160. See Song R. VII.1, §1; Song R. I.9, §6; Gen. R. LXVI.2; Ruth R. Proem I. Cf. Pes. R. 21.4; Pes. R. 21.21.
161. Šab. 88a; cf. 'AZ 2b, discussed above. As mentioned in n. 158, both variants of the tradition are ascribed to R. Abdimi.

162. Šab. 88a. Cf. the series of interpretations of Ps. 76.9 ascribed to R. Joḥanan through tradents in Pes. R. 21.4.
163. Šab. 88a. Variants of this tradition appear in 'AZ 3a, discussed below, and 'AZ 5a.
164. 'AZ 3a.
165. Ned. 32a; cf. Pes. 68b; Šab. 33a. R. Eleazar's comment in Ned. 32a is preceded by an alternative interpretation that understands "covenant" in Jer. 33.25 as referring to the covenant of circumcision. This second interpretation, which is also found in Šab. 137b, represents a variant of the Mishnaic tradition in Ned. III.11, which construes Jer. 33.25 to mean that if it were not for circumcision, God would not have created the world.
166. Sanh. 99a; cf. 'AZ 18a. Cf. Sanh. X.1. *G*^{e}*zērāh šāwāh* is an inference based on word analogy.
167. Šab. 88b. My translation of Ps. 8.2 follows Halperin's suggestion that *t*^{e}*nāh* is understood by the Midrashist as the imperative of *nāṯan*, "to give." Halperin, *The Faces of the Chariot*, p. 298, n. 56. For variants of the tradition that the Torah was created 974 generations before the creation of the world, see chapter 2.
168. Šab. 88b. The Midrash of Job 26.9 attributed to R. Naḥum understands *paršēz* as an acronym for *PêRēś SHaddai Zîw*, "The Almighty spread the splendor." This Midrash also appears in the parallel tradition in Pes. R. 20.4. In Suk. 5a, discussed below, this Midrash is attributed to R. Tanḥum. See also n. 226 regarding the variants of this Midrash in Tanḥûmā' Y^{e}lamm^{e}ḏēnû Midrashim.
169. Šab. 88b–89a. Cf. Pes. R. 20.4, which incorporates a variant of the latter portion of R. Joshua b. Levi's aggadah. See also PRE §46, f. 110b, which includes an abbreviated version of this tradition. The alternative form of the debate, in which God rather than Moses argues with the angels, is found not only in Song R. VIII.11, §2 but also in Pes. R. 25.3; Tanḥ., ed. Buber, B^{e}-ḥuqqōṯay §6; Tanḥ. B^{e}-ḥuqqōṯay §4. See Schäfer, *Rivalität zwischen Engeln und Menschen*, pp. 119–139; Schultz, "Angelic Opposition to the Ascension of Moses and the Revelation of the Law."
170. Šab. 89a.
171. Three other traditions ascribed to R. Joshua b. Levi in Šab. 88b will be discussed below. Abraham Weiss has suggested, in his *Studies in the Literature of the Amoraim* [in Hebrew] (New York: Yeshiva University, 1962), pp. 260–261, that the aggadot attributed to R. Joshua b. Levi in Šab. 88b–89a may originally have constituted an independent collection. Building on this suggestion, Halperin, in *The Faces of the Chariot*, pp. 310–313, argues that these aggadot, together with the expositions of Ps. 68.19 ascribed to R. Joshua b. Levi in Tanḥ. Ha'ăzînû §3; Tanḥ., ed. Buber, Ha'ăzînû §3; and JT Šab. XVI.1, 15c, may derive from a cycle of Shavuot sermons. He speculates that

> Joshua b. Levi delivered, over a more or less extended period of time, a number of sermons on the theme of Moses' heavenly ascension, within the context of the Sinai revelation. The details changed from time to time, but the essential point stayed the same. Moses braved the terror of the angels in order to take Torah from heaven with his own hands. The angels, violently hostile at first, became supporters and benefactors of Moses and the whole Israelite people. The most likely occasion for these sermons, we may well suppose, was Shabu'ot. (p. 311)

Halperin further suggests that the Sinai ascension traditions found in Pes. R. 20.4 and its parallels, which will be discussed below on pp. 300–301 with n. 222, may represent late reconstructions of R. Joshua b. Levi's third-century sermons.

172. See, for example, Men. 29b.
173. Cf. Mek., ed. Lauterbach, Ba-ḥôḏeš §4, vol. 2, p. 224.
174. Cf. Pes. K. 12.11, which cites these two proof texts to establish that at the time of the revelation the separation between heaven and earth was overcome.
175. Like R. Joshua b. Levi's aggadah, this passage incorporates the Midrash that interprets Job 26.9 to mean that "the Almighty spread over him some of the splendor (*zîw*) of His Shekhinah and His cloud." However, whereas in Šab. 88b and Pes. R. 20.4 the Midrash is attributed to R. Naḥum, in this context it is ascribed to R. Tanḥum. See n. 168. See also n. 226 regarding the variants of this Midrash in Tanḥûmā' Y^e^lamm^e^ḏēnû Midrashim.
176. This pericope appears in the context of a discussion of the Mishnaic injunction in Suk. I.1 that a Sukkah, the booth that is to be constructed for the festival of Sukkot, must be at least ten handbreadths high. This leads to a discussion of the Ark of the Covenant, which is said to be a total of ten handbreadths high including the Ark cover. In accordance with Exod. 25.22, which indicates that God spoke to Moses from above the Ark cover, it is concluded that the Shekhinah always remains at least ten handbreadths above the earth. Hence the ensuing discussion concerning whether Moses ascended to heaven and God descended to earth insists on maintaining a space of at least ten handbreadths between heaven and earth.
177. BM 59b. Cf. Deut. R. VIII.6.
178. Pes. 49b; Sanh. 59a; Ber. 57a. Cf. Sip̄rê Deut. §345; Exod. R. XXXIII.7.
179. Šab. 88b; Giṭ. 36b. Cf. Song R. VIII.5, §1.
180. See, for example, Soṭ. 5a; Taan. 21b; Šab. 87a; Yeb. 62a.
181. See also Šab. 88b, which maintains that with every word that went forth from the mouth of God two crowns were set, although the angels are not mentioned in this context. Cf. Pes. K. 16.3; Song R. IV.4, §1; Lam. R. II.13, §17; Pes. R. 21.7; Pes. R. 33.10; Pes. R. 29/30A.3; Pes. R. 10.6; Tanḥ., ed. Buber, T^e^ṣawweh §7; Tanḥ., ed. Buber, add. to

Š^elaḥ §1; Tanḥ., ed. Buber, Wā-'ērā' §9; Tanḥ. Š^elaḥ §13; Exod. R. LI.8; Num. R. XVI.24; PRE §47, f. 112a. In discussing the parallel Hêḵālôṯ traditions concerning crowns, Chernus notes that *Hêḵālôṯ Rabbāṯî* 11.1, in *Bêṯ ha-Miḏrāš*, ed. Jellinek, vol. 3, p. 91, speaks of the crowns that are "affixed" (*qāšar*) to the heads of the angels, employing the same term that is used in the tradition ascribed to R. Simai. Chernus, *Mysticism in Rabbinic Judaism*, p. 10.

182. Cf. Pes. R. 10.6; Exod. R. LI.8; Exod. R. XLV.2; PRE §47, f. 112b.
183. Šab. 88b. Cf. Tanḥ. Š^emôṯ §25; Tanḥ., ed. Buber, Š^emôṯ §22; Tanḥ. Yiṯrô §11; Exod. R. XXVIII.6.
184. Ber. 6b.
185. Zeb. 116a. Cf. Sip̄rê Deut. §343; Song R. I.2, §2.
186. Šab. 88b.
187. For a discussion of relevant references, see chapter 2, pp. 178–179.
188. Beṣ. 25b; Ber. 6a; Ber. 62a; Soṭ. 4b.
189. Šab. 104a; cf. Meg. 2b–3a. This tradition is based on Exod. 32.15, which says that the tablets "were written on both sides; on the one side and on the other were they written."
190. Šab. 88b. Cf. Song R. V.16, §3; Song R. V.6, §1; Pes. R. 20.4; Exod. R. XXIX.4; Exod. R. XXIX.9; PRE §41, f. 97b. See n. 124 regarding the possible connection between this tradition and the tradition ascribed to R. Joshua b. Levi in Song R. I.2, §2 that the Israelites only heard two commandments directly from God. See also Chernus's discussion of R. Joshua b. Levi's aggadah and its parallels in Hêḵālôṯ texts in *Mysticism in Rabbinic Judaism*, pp. 34–41.
191. Šab. 88b. Cf. Mek., ed. Lauterbach, Ba-ḥôḏeš §9, vol. 2, p. 269; Mek., ed. Lauterbach, Ba-ḥôḏeš §2, vol. 2, p. 202; Sip̄rê Deut. §313.
192. In Pes. R. 22.3 and Exod. R. XLII.8 this view is attributed to R. Joshua b. Levi, while in Exod. R. XXXIII.7 it is ascribed to the sages. Cf. Song R. I.2, §2; Hor. 8a; Mak. 23b–24a; PRE §41, f. 97b, 98a.
193. Num. R. XVIII.21; cf. Exod. R. XLVI.1. Cf. Song R. V.14, §2.
194. See, for example, Exod. R. XLI.5; Exod. R. XLVII.5; Exod. R. XLVII.8; Exod. R. L.2; Pes. R. 14.10 [= Pes. K. 4.4].
195. Exod. R. XLVII.5; Exod. R. XLVII.8.
196. Exod. R. XLVII.1; Tanḥ., ed. Buber, Kî Ṯiśśā' §17; cf. Exod. R. XLVII.3; Exod. R. XLVII.7.
197. Pes. R. 5.1; Tanḥ., ed. Buber, Wa-yērā' §6. Cf. Giṭ. 60b. For a discussion of other relevant references concerning the Written Torah and Oral Torah, see chapter 2, pp. 181–182.
198. Tanḥ. Yiṯrô §11; cf. Exod. R. XXVIII.6. See also the tradition ascribed to R. Joshua b. Levi in Exod. R. XLII.8, which maintains that Moses delivered the prophecies of all the other prophets along with his own. Cf. PRE §41, f. 97a–97b.

199. Pes. R. 50.2. Cf. Sip̄rê Deut. §311. See also Pes. R. 29/30A.3, which contains a variant of the tradition in Pes. K. 16.3 and Lam. R. II.13, §17 concerning God's saving acts on behalf of his chosen people.
200. Pes. R. 20.1. Cf. Mek., ed. Lauterbach, Ba-ḥôḏeš §5, vol. 2, pp. 233–234; Mek., ed. Lauterbach, ʿĂmālēq §3, vol. 2, pp. 162–163; Sip̄rê Deut. §343; Zeb. 116a.
201. See, for example, Pes. R. 21.2/3; Pes. R. 30.4; Pes. R. 15.2 [= Pes. K. 5.2]; Pes. R. 40.5; Exod. R. XXVII.9.
202. Deut. R. II.34. Cf. Deut. R., ed. Lieberman, pp. 65–66, discussed below, which similarly suggests that the gentile nations chose the angels to be their gods.
203. See, for example, Exod. R. XLVII.3; cf. Deut. R. VII.9. Cf. Pes. K. 12.23; Ruth R. Proem I.
204. Tanḥ. Š^{e}môṯ §25; Tanḥ., ed. Buber, Š^{e}môṯ §22; Tanḥ. Yiṯrô §11; Exod. R. XXVIII.6. The notion of seven voices appears to be based on Psalm 29, which mentions the voice of the Lord seven times. Cf. Šab. 88b.
205. Tanḥ. Š^{e}môṯ §25; cf. Tanḥ., ed. Buber, Š^{e}môṯ §22.
206. For references, see n. 204.
207. For the antecedents of the tradition attributed to R. Tanḥuma, see Lev. R. I.11 and Song R. II.3, §5, in which a tradition ascribed to R. Simon b. Pazzi similarly describes the twofold manifestation of the divine utterance. However, this tradition refers to a post-Sinaitic context.
208. Pes. R. 21.2/3. Cf. Mek., ed. Lauterbach, Ba-ḥôḏeš §5, vol. 2, pp. 234–237; Sip̄rê Deut. §343; Lam. R. III.1, §1; Pes. K. Suppl. 1.15; ʿAZ 2a–2b; PRE §41, f. 95b.
209. Pes. R. 15.2 [= Pes. K. 5.2]. While this tradition is attributed to R. Simon b. Pazzi in P^{e}sîqtā' d^{e}-R. Kahana, it is ascribed to R. Ḥanina b. Pappai in P^{e}sîqtā' Rabbāṯî.
210. Exod. R. XXVII.9; cf. Pes. R. 21.16.
211. It should be noted that in addition to the traditions discussed below, there are other traditions that view the final step in the establishment of creation as not the revelation of the Torah but the setting up of the Tabernacle or the building of the Temple of Solomon. For example, a pericope in Pes. R. 5.3 cites the Mishnaic aphorism ('Ab. I.2) that celebrates the Torah, the Tabernacle/Temple service, and deeds of loving-kindness as the three foundations upon which the world stands. It then goes on to assert that until the Tabernacle was set up the universe was like a chair standing on only two legs—deeds of loving-kindness and Torah—but once the Tabernacle was built the universe became firmly established. See also Pes. R. 7.4, which links the setting up of the Tabernacle to the first day of creation, and Pes. R. 6.6, which claims that the work of creation was not complete until the Temple of Solomon was finished. The Tabernacle and Temple are

of course linked to the Torah as the sacred abodes in which the Ark of the Covenant was enshrined.

212. Exod. R. XL.1.
213. Exod. R. XLVII.4; cf. Deut. R. VIII.5.
214. Pes. R. 21.4. Cf. the interpretation of this verse ascribed to R. Hezekiah in Šab. 88a; ʿAZ 3a.
215. Pes. R. 21.4; cf. Pes. R. 21.21. Cf. Song R. VII.1, §1; Song R. I.9, §6; Gen. R. LXVI.2; Ruth R. Proem I.
216. Pes. R. 33.8. This Midrash cites numerous proof texts to establish the role of *'ānōḵî* not only in creation and revelation but also in other key events in the salvation history of Israel.
217. Pes. R. 21.19. Cf. Pes. R. 40.5, which correlates the ten days of penitence with both the ten words by which the world was created and the Ten Commandments. For a discussion of the ten words of creation, see chapter 2.
218. See, for example, Pes. R. 20.4; Pes. R. 14.13 [= Pes. K. 4.7]; Pes. R. 10.6; Pes. R. 5.3; Pes. R. 47.4; Tanḥ., ed. Buber, Kî Ṯiśśā' §13; Tanḥ. Ha'ăzînû §3; Tanḥ., ed. Buber, Ha'ăzînû §3; Exod. R. XXVIII.1; Exod. R. XLVII.5; Exod. R. XLI.5; Exod. R. XLI.7; Exod. R. XLII.4; Num. R. XIX.7; Deut. R. XI.3; Deut. R. XI.4; Deut. R. XI.10; Deut. R. III.11; Deut. R. IX.2; cf. Pes. R. 16.2 [= Pes. K. 6.1]; Pes. R. 48.3; Num. R. XXI.16.
219. See n. 222 below.
220. Cf. the description of Sandalphon in Ḥag. 13b.
221. Cf. Šab. 88b–89a. See also PRE §46, f. 110b. While in these passages "gifts" in Ps. 68.19 is interpreted as referring to the gifts that the angels bestowed upon Moses, in other passages it is understood to mean the "great gift" of Torah itself. See, for example, Tanḥ. Ha'ăzînû §3; Tanḥ., ed. Buber, Ha'ăzînû §3; Exod. R. XXVIII.1; Exod. R. XXXIII.2.
222. Cf. Song R. III.11, §2; Pes. K. 1.3. The conclusion of Pes. R. 20.4, which describes God opening the seven firmaments and revealing himself to the entire Israelite community, will be discussed below. For an exposition of Pes. R. 20.4 and its parallels, see Karl-Erich Grözinger, *Ich bin der Herr, dein Gott! Eine rabbinische Homilie zum Ersten Gebot (PesR 20)*, Frankfurter Judaistische Studien, vol. 2 (Bern: Herbert Lang; Frankfurt: Peter Lang, 1976). Grözinger argues that the account of Moses's ascent and struggles with the angels conflates two independent sources. (1) The opening words of Pes. R. 20.4, "when Moses ascended on high," and the account of Moses seizing God's throne and debating with the angels over the Torah derive from the Midrash of R. Joshua b. Levi preserved in Šab. 88b–89a. (2) The details of Moses's heavenly ascent derive from an "apocalypse of Moses," which described his ascent through seven (or three) heavens, culminating in a vision of God seated on his throne. See ibid., esp. pp.

130–141. See also Halperin's discussion of Pes. R. 20.4 and its parallels and his critique of Grözinger's theory in *The Faces of the Chariot*, pp. 289–322. While acknowledging the dependence of Pes. R. 20.4 on Šab. 88b–89a, he argues against the existence of an "apocalypse of Moses" as an independent source. As discussed earlier in n. 171, Halperin speculates that Pes. R. 20.4 and its parallels may represent late reconstructions of a cycle of third-century Shavuot sermons on Moses's heavenly ascent delivered by R. Joshua b. Levi, portions of which are preserved in Šab. 88b–89a. Ibid., pp. 307–313.

A number of scholars have noted the links between Hêḵālôṯ traditions and the account of Moses's heavenly ascent in Pes. R. 20.4 and its parallels. See, for example, Zunz, *Ha-D^{e}rāšôṯ b^{e}-Yiśrā'ēl*, p. 379, n. 16; Schäfer, *Rivalität zwischen Engeln und Menschen*, pp. 128–135; Grözinger, *Ich bin der Herr, dein Gott!*, pp. 130–214 passim; Halperin, *The Faces of the Chariot*, pp. 355–356, 407–427. Halperin notes in particular that "the ascension story of *Pesiqta* and its parallels shares the *Hekhalot* literature's portrayal of heaven as a terrifying place, filled with monstrous angels bearing fantastic names. It also shares a concern with the details of the heavenly liturgy, as we see from *Pesiqta*'s account of the progress of Sandalphon's wreaths toward God's head" (pp. 355–356). He argues that certain Hêḵālôṯ materials may have been inspired by the Shavuot sermon cycle concerning Moses's ascension, while at the same time these materials have left the traces of their reciprocal influence on the texts—Pes. R. 20.4 and its parallels—that reflect the Shavuot cycle.

223. Cf. Tanḥ., ed. Buber, B^{e}-ḥuqqōṯay §6; Tanḥ. B^{e}-ḥuqqōṯay §4. This tradition is ascribed to R. Aḥa in Pes. R. 25.3, while the variant in Song R. VIII.11, §2 is attributed to R. Judan. See also Deut. R. VII.9.

224. Deut. R. VIII.2.

225. In addition to Pes. R. 20.4, discussed above, see also Tanḥ., ed. Buber, Kî Ṯiśśā' §13; Tanḥ. Ha'ăzînû §3; Tanḥ., ed. Buber, Ha'ăzînû §3; Exod. R. XXVIII.1; Exod. R. XLI.7; Exod. R. XLII.4; Deut. R. III.11; Deut. R. XI.10; Deut. R. XI.3; Deut. R. IX.2; Pes. R. 10.6. See Schäfer, *Rivalität zwischen Engeln und Menschen*, pp. 135–147.

226. See Exod. R. XXVIII.1; Deut. R. XI.10; Deut. R. III.11; Deut. R. XI.3; Deut. R. IX.2. See also Exod. R. XLI.7; Exod. R. XLII.4; Tanḥ., ed. Buber, Kî Ṯiśśā' §13, which, like Pes. R. 20.4, include variants of the Midrash that interprets Job 26.9 to mean that Moses took hold of God's throne and God spread the splendor of his Shekhinah and/or his cloud over him to protect him from the hostile angels. The attributions of this Midrash vary in the different versions: R. Naḥum (Šab. 88b; Pes. R. 20.4); R. Tanḥum (Suk. 5a); R. Azariah in the name of R. Judah b. Simon in the name of R. Judah b. Il'ai (Exod. R. XLII.4); anonymous (Exod. R. XLI.7; Tanḥ., ed. Buber, Kî Ṯiśśā' §13).

227. Deut. R. XI.10.

228. Exod. R. XLVII.5; cf. Deut. R. XI.4; Pes. R. 16.2 [= Pes. K. 6.1]; Pes. R. 48.3; Num. R. XXI.16. The full attribution in Exod. R. XLVII.5 is R. Tanḥuma in the name of R. Eleazar and R. Abin, in the name of R. Meir.
229. Exod. R. XLVII.5; cf. Exod. R. XLVII.7.
230. Exod. R. XLVII.5; cf. Exod. R. XLVII.7.
231. Exod. R. XLVII.7.
232. Exod. R. XLVII.8.
233. Pes. R. 20.1. Portions of this passage are cited on p. 253.
234. See, for example, Pes. R. 20.1; Pes. R. 20.2; Exod. R. XXXIII.1; Exod. R. XXXIII.7; Exod. R. XLI.5; Deut. R. VII.9; cf. Exod. R. XXIX.4.
235. Exod. R. XXXIII.1; cf. Exod. R. XXXIII.7.
236. Exod. R. XXXIII.6; cf. Exod. R. XXXIII.7.
237. Pes. R. 21.15; Exod. R. XXIX.3; Exod. R. XLII.8; Exod. R. XLVI.1; Exod. R. XLVII.2; Deut. R. III.10; Deut. R. III.12; Deut. R. III.17. Cf. Pes. R. 5.10, in which God is portrayed not as the spouse of Israel but as the father who gives his daughter, Israel, in marriage.
238. Pes. R. 21.15; Exod. R. XLVI.1; Exod. R. XLVII.2; Deut. R. III.12; Deut. R. III.17. Cf. Pes. K. 19.4; Lam. R. III.21, §7.
239. See, for example, Pes. R. 7.3; Pes. R. 21.6; Pes. R. 5.3.
240. Pes. R. 7.3.
241. Exod. R. LI.8. See also Num. R. XIX.16, which associates Mount Sinai with the Shekhinah.
242. See Pes. R. 20.4, cited below.
243. Deut. R. VII.9.
244. Pes. R. 21.6; cf. Pes. R. 14.10 [= Pes. K. 4.4]. As in the variant of this tradition in Pes. K. 4.4, this tradition is ascribed to R. Zakkai of Shaab in the name of R. Samuel b. Naḥman. Cf. Exod. R. LI.8, cited below, in which God is said to have clothed the Israelites with the "splendor of His glory" (*zîw hăḏārô*). See n. 259.
245. *Qārûḵîn* and *ṭeṭrā'mûlîn* are loan words from the Greek *karoucha* and the postulated form *tetramoulon*, respectively. For a detailed analysis of this passage and its parallels in Exod. R. XLII.5 and Tanḥ. Kî Ṯiśśā' §21, see Halperin, *The Faces of the Chariot*, pp. 169–176. For his discussion of other relevant rabbinic passages that point to a connection between the Merkabah and the golden calf incident, see pp. 157–193. Halperin suggests that its association with Israel's apostasy represents one aspect of the "dark side of the *merkabah*" that may account for certain rabbis' efforts to restrict the expounding of *ma'ăśēh merkāḇāh*.
246. Cf. Pes. K. 12.22, discussed on p. 278. The Tanḥumā' pericopes will be discussed briefly below. See Halperin's analysis of these passages in *The Faces of the Chariot*, pp. 141–149.
247. Pes. R. 21.7. Pᵉsîqtā' Rabbāṯî, as well as Deut. R., ed. Lieberman, p. 68 (the attribution is misconstrued as "R. Ammi of Jaffa") and Exod. R.

XXIX.2, follows P^{e}sîqtā' d^{e}-R. Kahana's reading of "22,000 ministering angels." Variants of this tradition in the Tanḥûmā' will be discussed below. Cf. PRE §41, f. 95b–96a.

248. Pes. R. 21.7. Cf. Tanḥ., ed. Buber, Yiṯrô §14; Tanḥ. Ṣaw §12; Tanḥ., ed. Buber, Ṣaw §16, which, like Pes. K. 12.22, attribute the tradition regarding the Levites to R. Berekhiah and make no mention of the crown motif.
249. Pes. R. 21.7. This tradition is ascribed to R. Yannai in Tanḥ. Ṣaw §12 and Tanḥ., ed. Buber, Ṣaw §16. However, in Pes. K. 12.22 and Tanḥ., ed. Buber, Yiṯrô §14 the tradition is anonymous.
250. Pes. R. 21.7; cf. Pes. R. 33.10; Pes. R. 29/30A.3; Pes. R. 10.6; Tanḥ., ed. Buber, T^{e}ṣawweh §7; Tanḥ., ed. Buber, add. to Š^{e}laḥ §1; Tanḥ., ed. Buber, Wā-'ērā' §9; Tanḥ. Š^{e}laḥ §13; Exod. R. LI.8; Num. R. XVI.24. Cf. Pes. K. 16.3; Song R. IV.4, §1; Lam. R. II.13, §17; Šab. 88a; PRE §47, f. 112a.
251. Pes. R. 21.8; cf. Exod. R. XXIX.8. Cf. Pes. K. 12.22.
252. Tanḥ., ed. Buber, Yiṯrô §14 parallels the pericope in Pes. K. 12.22 discussed earlier. A second recension of this material is given in Tanḥ. Ṣaw §12 and Tanḥ., ed. Buber, Ṣaw §16. All of these passages begin with a version of the interpretation ascribed to R. Abdimi, followed by variants of the tradition concerning the 22,000 Levites and the tradition concerning the 22,000 chariots. See nn. 247–249 for specific parallels to these and other passages in the Tanḥûmā'.
253. Tanḥ., ed. Buber, Yiṯrô §14; Tanḥ. Wa-yišlaḥ §2; Tanḥ. B^{e}-miḏbar §14 (without attribution); Tanḥ., ed. Buber, B^{e}-miḏbar §15 (without attribution). The recension in Tanḥ. Ṣaw §12 and Tanḥ., ed. Buber, Ṣaw §16 reads "22,000 chariots (*markāḇôṯ*)."
254. See n. 113.
255. For parallel pericopes in the Tanḥûmā', see Tanḥ., ed. Buber, T^{e}ṣawweh §7; Tanḥ., ed. Buber, add. to Š^{e}laḥ §1; Tanḥ., ed. Buber, Wā-'ērā' §9.
256. Cf. Pes. R. 21.7; Pes. R. 29/30A.3; Pes. R. 10.6; Tanḥ., ed. Buber, T^{e}ṣawweh §7; Tanḥ., ed. Buber, add. to Š^{e}laḥ §1; Tanḥ., ed. Buber, Wā-'ērā' §9; Tanḥ. Š^{e}laḥ §13; Exod. R. LI.8; Num. R. XVI.24. Cf. also Pes. K. 16.3; Song R. IV.4, §1; Lam. R. II.13, §17; Šab. 88a; PRE §47, f. 112a.
257. Cf. Exod. R. XLV.3; Exod. R. LI.8; Tanḥ., ed. Buber, Wā-'ērā' §9; Tanḥ., ed. Buber, T^{e}ṣawweh §7; Tanḥ., ed. Buber, add. to Š^{e}laḥ §1. Cf. also Lam. R. Proem XXIV; Song R. I.4, §2; Song R. IV.12, §2; Song R. V.7, §1; Song R. VIII.5, §1.
258. The tradition regarding the royal purple garments is generally attributed to R. Simai, as in Exod. R. LI.8 discussed below. See also Exod. R. XLV.2; Num. R. XVI.24; Tanḥ., ed. Buber, Wā-'ērā' §9; Tanḥ., ed. Buber, T^{e}ṣawweh §7; Tanḥ., ed. Buber, add. to Š^{e}laḥ §1. In Tanḥ. Š^{e}laḥ §13 this tradition is attributed to R. Huna. See also Deut. R.

VII.11 regarding the special nature of the heavenly garments with which the angels invested the Israelites at Mount Sinai.

259. Scholem connects the expression "splendor of His glory" (*zîw hădārô*) in this passage to Hêkālôt traditions concerning the garment (*ḥālûq*) of God. He points out that this same phrase is used in a hymn in chapter 3 of *Hêkālôt Rabbātî* that describes the "Garment of Zohararíel JHWH, God of Israel." The phrase also occurs in an aggadic tradition attributed to R. Samuel b. Naḥman that discusses how God created light: "The Holy One, blessed be He, wrapped Himself in it [light] as in a garment, and the splendor of His glory (*zîw hădārô*) shone forth from one end of the world to the other" (Gen. R. III.4). R. Samuel b. Naḥman's involvement in esoteric speculations is well attested. Scholem, *Jewish Gnosticism, Merkabah Mysticism, and Talmudic Tradition*, pp. 131–132, 58–61. It is important to note in this context that another tradition, cited earlier, that speaks of the "splendor (*zîw*) from the splendor of the Shekhinah" that was bestowed on the Israelites at Sinai is similarly attributed to R. Samuel b. Naḥman through his tradent R. Zakkai of Shaab. Pes. R. 21.6; cf. Pes. R. 14.10 [= Pes. K. 4.4].

260. For references to variants of specific traditions, see nn. 256–258.

261. Exod. R. LI.8; cf. Exod. R. XLV.2; Pes. R. 10.6. Cf. Šab. 88a; PRE §47, f. 112b.

262. This tradition is attributed to R. Simai in Num. R. XVI.24 and to R. Huna in Tanḥ. Šᵉlaḥ §13. Scholem, citing Ben Zion Luria, *Bêṯ Miqrā'* 7, no. 4 (March 1963): 108, suggests that the version of the aggadah concerning Israel's purple garment that mentions that the ineffable Name was inscribed on it may have been the original version. He connects this tradition with a description of the garment of God in *Hêkālôt Rabbātî* 3.4: "the Garment of Zohararíel JHWH, God of Israel . . . is every part engraved from within and from without JHWH JHWH." Scholem, *Jewish Gnosticism, Merkabah Mysticism, and Talmudic Tradition*, pp. 131–132, 59–60. As Chernus points out, Scholem erroneously conflates the tradition concerning the purple garment with the tradition regarding "the splendor of His glory" with which the Israelites are clothed in Exod. R. LI.8. See Chernus, *Mysticism in Rabbinic Judaism*, pp. 8–9. Cf. PRE §47, f. 112b.

263. Num. R. XVI.24; Tanḥ. Šᵉlaḥ §13.

264. Exod. R. LI.8; Tanḥ., ed. Buber, Wā-'ērā' §9; Tanḥ., ed. Buber, add. to Šᵉlaḥ §1. For other traditions concerning the immunity from death that was conferred on the Israelites at Sinai and subsequently lost, see Exod. R. XXXII.1; Exod. R. XLI.7. Cf. Lev. R. XVIII.3; Song R. VIII.6, §1.

265. Exod. R. XXIX.4. A variant of this tradition appears in Exod. R. XLI.3, where it is ascribed to R. Phinehas, who is frequently a tradent of R.

Levi's traditions. See also Mek., ed. Lauterbach, Ba-ḥôdeš §2, vol. 2, p. 209; Song R. I.2, §3.

266. Pes. R. 15.22 [= Pes. K. 5.16]; cf. Pes. R. 7.7. Cf. Pes. K. 12.19; Lev. R. XVIII.4; Song R. IV.7, §1.
267. Tanḥ. Yitrô §11.
268. Pes. R. 21.5. Cf. Mek., ed. Lauterbach, Ba-ḥôdeš §4, vol. 2, pp. 228–229; Mek., ed. Lauterbach, Šîrāṯā' §8, vol. 2, p. 62.
269. Tanḥ. Š^{e}môṯ §25; Tanḥ., ed. Buber, Š^{e}môṯ §22; Tanḥ. Yitrô §11; Exod. R. XXVIII.6. Cf. Šab. 88b.
270. See, for example, Pes. R. 20.4; Pes. R. 21.6; Tanḥ., ed. Buber, Yitrô §14; Deut. R. VII.8; Pes. R. 47.2; Pes. R. 15.8 [= Pes. K. 5.8]; Exod. R. XXIX.4; Exod. R. XLI.3.
271. Deut. R. VII.8. Cf. Mek., ed. Lauterbach, Ba-ḥôdeš §3, vol. 2, p. 212.
272. Cf. PRE §41, f. 95b. See Scholem's discussion of the parallels between Pes. R. 20.4 and *Hêḵālôṯ Rabbāṯî* 24.3:

> King of Kings, God of Gods and Lord of Lords . . .
> Who covers the Heavens with the wing of His magnificence,
> And in His majesty [*hāḏār*] appeared from the heights,
> From His beauty [*yôp̄î*] the deeps were enkindled,
> And from His stature [*tō'ar*] the Heavens are sparkling
> His stature sends out the lofty,
> And His crown [*keṯer*] blazes out the mighty,
> And His garment [*ḥālûq*] flows with the precious. . . .
> And His words shall drop as perfumes,
> Flowing forth in flames of fire. . . .

Cited in Scholem, *Jewish Gnosticism, Merkabah Mysticism, and Talmudic Tradition*, pp. 61–62. Scholem remarks that "it is obvious that the term *To'ar* (stature) here has the same meaning as *Komah* in *Shiur Komah.*" Ibid., p. 62. He emphasizes that such passages "do not employ mere poetic figures of speech, but a consistent technical language developed by the Merkabah mystics." Ibid, p. 68 with n. 12. See also Chernus, *Mysticism in Rabbinic Judaism*, pp. 58–59.

Scholem also notes the parallel between Pes. R. 20.4 and a line in the *Visions of Ezekiel* (*R^{e}'ûyyôṯ Y^{e}ḥezqē'l*): "While Ezekiel was gazing the Holy One opened (*pāṯaḥ*) to him the seven firmaments (*r^{e}qî'îm*), and he saw the Dynamis (G^{e}ḇûrāh)." *R^{e}'ûyyôṯ Y^{e}ḥezqē'l*, ed. Ithamar Gruenwald, in *Temirin: Texts and Studies in Kabbala and Hasidism*, ed. Israel Weinstock, vol. 1 (Jerusalem: Mosad ha-Rav Kook, 1972), p. 111. Scholem, *Jewish Gnosticism, Merkabah Mysticism, and Talmudic Tradition*, pp. 67–68. Halperin also notes this parallel, but, contrary to Scholem, asserts that the *Visions of Ezekiel* is not a Hêḵālôṯ text. He suggests rather that the *Visions* may preserve remnants of Shavuot sermons that pertain to the Merkabah vision described in

Ezekiel 1, the *hap̄ṭārāh* reading for Shavuot. Pes. R. 20.4 and its parallels, on the other hand, preserve portions of the other half of the Shavuot sermon cycle that pertains to the Sinai event recounted in Exodus 19.1ff, the Torah reading for Shavuot. See Halperin, *The Faces of the Chariot*, pp. 288–289, 313–317.

273. Deut. R., ed. Lieberman, p. 65; cf. Deut. R. II.32. For other traditions concerning the splitting of the seven firmaments, see Deut. R., ed. Lieberman, p. 65, n. 13; p. 66, n. 1. For a discussion of the parallels between this passage in Deuteronomy Rabbāh, Pes. R. 20.4, and the *Visions of Ezekiel*, see Halperin, *The Faces of the Chariot*, pp. 313–317. R. Simeon b. Lakish's association with Merkabah speculations is pointed to in an abstruse comment attributed to him in Genesis Rabbāh: "The patriarchs—they are the Merkabah." Gen. R. XLVII.6; LXIX.3; LXXXII.6. See Chernus, *Mysticism in Rabbinic Judaism*, pp. 19–21; Scholem, *Major Trends in Jewish Mysticism*, p. 79.

274. Deut. R., ed. Lieberman, pp. 65–66. Cf. Deut. R. II.34, discussed earlier, which similarly suggests that when God came down on Sinai accompanied by hosts of angels, the gentile nations chose Michael, Gabriel, and so on, to be their respective patrons, while Israel alone chose God. See also the conclusion of Pes. R. 20.4, which maintains that God revealed himself to the Israelites face to face so that they would not be led astray and worship other gods.

275. Pes. R. 21.11; cf. Exod. R. XXIX.2.

276. See, for example, Pes. R. 33.10; Pes. R. 21.2/3; Tanḥ., ed. Buber, B^{e}rē'šîṯ §4; Exod. R. XLI.4; Num. R. XXII.9; Deut. R. V.4; cf. Deut. R. XI.10.

277. Pes. R. 33.10.

278. For a discussion of relevant references, see chapter 2, pp. 190–191.

279. Deut. R. III.12. A variant of this tradition appears in Exod. R. XLVII.6, without reference to the Torah being written with black fire on white fire. Cf. Song R. V.11, §6.

280. Deut. R. III.12; cf. Exod. R. XLVII.6. For other references to the radiant countenance that Moses acquired at the revelation, see Exod. R. XXXIII.1; Deut. R. XI.3; Pes. R. 10.6; Pes. R. 21.6.

281. Exod. R. XXIX.9; Pes. R. 21.5; Pes. R. 21.4.

282. Tanḥ. Š^{e}môṯ §25; Tanḥ., ed. Buber, Š^{e}môṯ §22.

283. In Pes. R. 20.4 this notion appears as part of an anonymous tradition. In Exod. R. XXIX.9 the tradition that the Israelites died upon hearing God's voice is attributed to R. Simon b. Pazzi, a student of R. Joshua b. Levi to whom a variant of this tradition is ascribed in Šab. 88b. In Exod. R. XXIX.4 this notion appears immediately following the tradition ascribed to R. Levi regarding Israel's request to see God's glory and hear God's voice. See Chernus, *Mysticism in Rabbinic Judaism*, pp. 44–48, for a discussion of the problems involved in determining which of the traditions in Exod. XXIX.4 might derive from R. Levi. The

variant of this tradition in Song R. V.16, §3 is ascribed to R. Levi's teacher, R. Joḥanan. See also PRE §41, f. 97b.

284. Cf. Song R. V.16, §3.

285. Cf. Šab. 88b. Friedmann's edition does not include the reference to the dew of resurrection. However, the dew is mentioned in the Parma MS 1240, Casanata MS 3324, and the Prague edition that contains marginal notations based on the Parma MS. Braude, trans., *Pesikta Rabbati*, vol. 1, p. 411, n. 55.

286. Exod. R. XXXIV.1. Cf. Mek., ed. Lauterbach, Ba-ḥōḏeš §9, pp. 266–267; Song R. V.16, §3; Pes. K. 12.25. See also Tanḥ. Šemôṯ §25, discussed immediately below, and Tanḥ., ed. Buber, Šemôṯ §22; Tanḥ., ed. Buber, Yiṯrô §17; Exod. R. XXIX.1; Tanḥ. Yiṯrô §11; Exod. R. XXVIII.6.

287. Tanḥ. Šemôṯ §25; cf. Tanḥ., ed. Buber, Šemôṯ §22. An abbreviated version of this tradition in Exod. R. XXIX.1 is ascribed to R. Levi. See also Tanḥ. Yiṯrô §11, which interprets Ps. 29.4 to mean that God spoke to Moses with a voice that he could endure.

288. Tanḥ. Šemôṯ §25; cf. Tanḥ., ed. Buber, Šemôṯ §22; Tanḥ., ed. Buber, Yiṯrô §17. Cf. Pes. K. 12.25. This tradition appears in the same pericope as the traditions ascribed to R. Joḥanan and R. Tanḥuma, discussed earlier, that maintain that when the nations heard God's voice they died, while Israel alone survived. The manna analogy is adapted to the anti-gentile polemic that pervades the pericope by adding that, just as the manna tasted differently to each of the Israelites, so it tasted differently to the nations: it was bitter as coriander. Cf. Song R. II.3, §3.

289. Exod. R. XXVIII.6; Exod. R. XXIX.1; Tanḥ., ed. Buber, Yiṯrô §17. Cf. Pes. K. 12.25.

290. In Pes. K. 12.25 and Tanḥ., ed. Buber, Yiṯrô §17 the statue analogy is attributed to R. Joḥanan's student, R. Levi. A number of traditions in Pes. R. 21.6 concerning God's multiple faces are ascribed to R. Levi. See also Pes. R. 21.15, which suggests that God addressed the Ten Commandments at Sinai to individuals in the hope that he could thereby restrain each from individual violations of the commandments in the future.

291. See PRE §41, f. 97b, 98a, discussed below.

292. PRE §41, f. 97a–97b.

293. Cf. Tanḥ. Yiṯrô §11; Exod. R. XXVIII.6.

294. PRE §46, f. 110b, 109b.

295. PRE §46, f. 110b.

296. Cf. Mek., ed. Lauterbach, Ba-ḥōḏeš §5, vol. 2, pp. 234–237; Sip̄rê Deut. §343; Lam. R. III.1, §1; Pes. K. Suppl. 1.15; Pes. R. 21.2/3.

297. PRE §41, f. 95b. "Strength" (*ʿōz*) in Ps. 29.11 is understood in this passage, as in other rabbinic sources, as a reference to the Torah. Cf. Sip̄rê Deut. §343; Mek., ed. Lauterbach, Ba-ḥōḏeš §5, vol. 2., p. 234; Mek., ed. Lauterbach, Ba-ḥōḏeš §1, vol. 2, p. 198; Mek., ed. Lauterbach,

'Ămālēq §3, vol. 2, p. 163; Zeb. 116a. *'Ōz* in Prov. 21.22, "A wise man scales the city of the mighty and brings down the stronghold (*'ōz*) of trust," is similarly interpreted in PRE §46, f. 110b, as a designation for the Torah. Cf. Lev. R. XXXI.5.

298. See PRE §41, f. 95b, cited below on pp. 312–313.
299. PRE §41, f. 96b.
300. PRE §46, f. 110b. Prov. 21.22, "A wise man scales (*'ālāh*) the city of the mighty and brings down the stronghold (*'ōz*) of trust," is invoked as a proof text. Cf. Lev. R. XXXI.5.
301. PRE §46, f. 110b. Cf. Šab. 88b–89a; Pes. R. 20.4. See also the alternative version of this tradition, in which God himself argues with the angels, in Song R. VIII.11, §2; Pes. R. 25.3; Tanḥ., ed. Buber, B[e]-ḥuqqōṯay §6; Tanḥ. B[e]-ḥuqqōṯay §4.
302. PRE §41, f. 96b. Cf. Mek., ed. Lauterbach, Ba-ḥôḏeš §3, vol. 2, pp. 218–219.
303. PRE §41, f. 97b–98a.
304. PRE §14, f. 32b; §41, f. 95b. In some editions of Pirqê d[e]-R. Eliezer the ten descents are enumerated in §14 as (1) the Garden of Eden, (2) the dispersion at the Tower of Babel, (3) Sodom, (4) the thorn bush, (5) Egypt, (6) Sinai, (7) the cleft of the rock, (8) and (9) the Tent of Meeting, and (10) a future descent. Other editions, including the Warsaw edition (1852), list a second descent at the cleft of the rock in place of Egypt, which Friedlander considers to be an incorrect reading. See Friedlander, trans., *Pirḳê de Rabbi Eliezer,* p. 97 with nn. 5, 7. As Friedlander points out in his introduction, the "ten descents" may constitute one of three originally distinct sections that are interwoven in this composite work. Only eight of the ten descents are recounted in the extant versions of the text, which is one among a number of factors that has led scholars to conclude that a portion of the text is missing. See ibid., pp. xv–xviii. Cf. Sip̄rê Num. §93; Mek., ed. Lauterbach, Ba-ḥôḏeš §3, vol. 2, p. 212, which mention that ten descents of God are referred to in the Torah, although the descents are not enumerated.
305. PRE §41, f. 95b. For references to God opening the heavens in other rabbinic texts, see Pes. R. 20.4; Deut. R., ed. Lieberman, p. 65 with n. 13; p. 66, n. 1; Deut. R. II.32; and n. 273.
306. PRE §41, f. 95b–96a. This appears to be another variant of the tradition ascribed to R. Abdimi in earlier rabbinic texts. As discussed earlier, one version of R. Abdimi's tradition mentions 22,000 (rather than 20,000) angels. See Pes. K. 12.22; Pes. R. 21.7; Exod. R. XXIX.2. Alternative readings mention 22,000 chariots (*markāḇôṯ*) of angels, or simply 22,000 chariots. See Tanḥ. Wa-yišlaḥ §2; Tanḥ. Ṣaw §12; Tanḥ., ed. Buber, Yiṯrô §14; Tanḥ., ed. Buber, Ṣaw §16. See n. 113.
307. Cf. Pes. K. 16.3; Song R. IV.4, §1; Lam. R. II.13, §17; Šab. 88a; Pes. R. 21.7; Pes. R. 29/30A.3; Pes. R. 33.10; Pes. R. 10.6; Tanḥ., ed. Buber,

T^{e}ṣawweh §7; Tanḥ., ed. Buber, add. to Š^{e}laḥ §1; Tanḥ., ed. Buber, Wā-'ērā' §9; Tanḥ. Š^{e}laḥ §13; Exod. R. LI.8; Num. R. XVI.24.

308. Cf. Lam. R. Proem XXIV; Song R. I.4, §2; Song R. IV.12, §2; Song R. V.7, §1; Song R. VIII.5, §1; Pes. R. 33.10; Exod. R. XLV.3; Exod. R. LI.8; Tanḥ., ed. Buber, Wā-'ērā' §9; Tanḥ., ed. Buber, T^{e}ṣawweh §7; Tanḥ., ed. Buber, add. to Š^{e}laḥ §1.

309. PRE §47, f. 112a. By attributing this tradition to R. Eleazar b. Arak, who is described in T Ḥag. II.1; JT Ḥag. II.1, 77a; and BT Ḥag. 14b as expounding *ma'ăśēh merkāḇāh* before his teacher, Joḥanan b. Zakkai, Pirqê d^{e}-R. Eliezer may wish to imply a link between the notion that the Israelites were crowned with the "crown of the ineffable Name" and Merkabah speculations. This link is explicitly established in an earlier passage in the text, as will be discussed immediately below.

310. PRE §4, f. 9b–10a. *Hêḵālôṯ Zûṭartî*, in *Synopse zur Hekhalot-Literatur*, ed. Schäfer, §372, gives a parallel description of God on his throne: "On his forehead is the crown (*keṯer*) of the ineffable Name, woven of fire. On his head is a crown (*'ăṭārāh*) of majesty." Halperin argues that the similarities between the two passages are not a result of direct borrowing but rather stem from a common tradition of synagogue Merkabah exegesis upon which both sources drew. See Halperin, *The Faces of the Chariot*, Appendix 6, pp. 511–517, esp. 511–513.

311. PRE §47, f. 112b. Cf. Exod. R. LI.8 and n. 259 regarding the tradition that God clothed the Israelites with "the splendor of His glory (*zîw hăḏārô*)." See also Num. R. XVI.24, Tanḥ. Š^{e}laḥ §13, and n. 262 concerning the tradition that God clothed them with a garment inscribed with the ineffable Name.

312. PRE §47, f. 112b. Cf. Šab. 88a; Pes. R. 10.6; Exod. R. LI.8; Exod. R. XLV.2.

313. PRE §41, f. 97a–98a; §46, f. 109a.

314. PRE §41, f. 98a. The parallel is noteworthy between this tradition and the tradition ascribed to R. Judah b. Il'ai's teacher, R. Akiba, in Mek., ed. Lauterbach, Ba-ḥōḏeš §9, vol. 2, p. 266, cited on p. 270. However, since the tradition appears only in Pirqê d^{e}-R. Eliezer, which is a late text that generally emphasizes esoteric speculations, the authenticity of the attribution cannot be accepted with any certainty.

315. See PRE §41, f. 95b, cited on pp. 312–313.

316. PRE §41, f. 95b–96a.

317. PRE §46, f. 110a; §19, f. 44a. The notion that the letters, writing, and tablets of the Ten Commandments were created on the eve of the first Sabbath first appears in the Mishnah and is reiterated in later rabbinic texts. See chapter 2 for a discussion of relevant references.

318. PRE §46, f. 110a; §20, f. 47b; §48, f. 116a; §52, f. 127a. See Exod. 32.16; Exod. 31.18.

319. PRE §45, f. 107b–108a. Cf. the Talmudic tradition attributed to R. Alexandri in Pes. 87b, which maintains that when Moses broke the

tablets of the covenant, the letters flew up and returned to their supernal source.

320. PRE §41, f. 97a–97b.
321. PRE §41, f. 97a–97b. Cf. Song R. V.16, §3; Song R. V.6, §1; Šab. 88b; Pes. R. 20.4; Exod. R. XXIX.4; Exod. R. XXIX.9.
322. PRE §41, f. 97b, 98a. Cf. Song R. I.2, §2; Hor. 8a; Mak. 23b–24a; Pes. R. 22.3; Exod. R. XXXIII.7; Exod. R. XLII.8.
323. Zohar III.192a–193a.
324. Zohar II.130b–131a.
325. Zohar I.24b (Tîqqûnîm); I.47a–47b; I.134a–134b; I.185a; I.207a; II.161a–161b; II.200a; III.152a.
326. Zohar III.117a; I.89a; II.94a; III.298b. I.89a and II.94a invoke the proof text often cited by rabbinic texts, Jer. 33.25, "If not for My covenant by day and by night, I would not have established the ordinances of heaven and earth." The role of Torah study and practice in sustaining the world will be discussed in chapter 6.
327. Zohar III.193a. Cf. III.91b, in which the earth's quaking is attributed not to the nations' refusal of the Torah but to the fact that God offered this precious preexistent treasure to the uncircumcised nations in the first place. When God revealed the Torah to Israel at Mount Sinai the earth's fears were allayed.
328. Zohar I.55b–56a.
329. Zohar III.117a.
330. See Zohar II.83a–83b.
331. See, for example, Pes. R. 21.19.
332. Zohar II.43a (Rā'ăyā' M^{e}hêmnā'); II.93b; II.90b; II.82a; II.200a.
333. Zohar II.90b; II.124a; II.87a; II.161b; III.13b; III.35b,36a; III.73a; III.80b; III.113a; III.298b. For a discussion of the Zohar's identification of the Torah with the Name of God, see chapter 2, p. 200.
334. Zohar II.90b. For the identification of the *s^{e}p̄îrôṯ* with the Name of God, see, for example, II.86a.
335. Zohar II.94a.
336. Zohar II.86a.
337. See, for example, Zohar II.94a; I.52b.
338. Zohar II.83b; I.91a; II.94a. Cf. PRE §41, f. 97a–97b, mentioned on p. 311.
339. Wolfson, "The Hermeneutics of Visionary Experience," p. 324. Wolfson argues that visionary experience is central not only to the Zohar's accounts of the Sinai revelation but also to its conceptions of the process of interpretation, as will be discussed in chapter 6. My own analysis of the role of visionary experience in the Zohar is indebted to Wolfson's insightful exposition. For an extended discussion of the central importance of visionary experience in medieval Jewish mysticism, see Wolfson's forthcoming book, *Through a Speculum That Shines: Vision*

and Imagination in Medieval Jewish Mysticism (Princeton: Princeton University Press, forthcoming).

340. Zohar II.82b; II.93b–94a; II.146a; II.83b; I.91a; II.82a. Cf. Pes. R. 20.4, cited on p. 307. See also Exod. R. LI.8, which describes God as clothing the Israelites with the "splendor of His glory" (*zîw hăḏārô*). See p. 305 with n. 259.
341. Zohar II.81a–81b. Cf. Mek., ed. Lauterbach, Ba-ḥôḏeš §9, vol. 2, p. 266; PRE §41, f. 98a, cited on pp. 270, 314.
342. Zohar II.194a. See also III.261a.
343. Zohar II.81b. Cf. I.91a, which maintains that the Israelites gazed upon the "other mirror (*ḥêzû*)" (= the Shekhinah) and the upper *s^e^p̄îrôṯ*. For a discussion of these and other relevant passages from the Zohar concerning the visionary nature of the Sinai theophany, see Wolfson, "The Hermeneutics of Visionary Experience," esp. pp. 313–317. Wolfson's analysis includes a discussion of parallel passages from other kabbalistic texts, such as the *Sēp̄er ha-Bāhîr* and the writings of the thirteenth-century Spanish kabbalists of Gerona, Naḥmanides and Ezra b. Solomon. He also notes interpretations of Exod. 20.18 by a variety of medieval Jewish philosophers and scholars.
344. Zohar II.146a. Cf. II.82a, in which the upper voices are said to have been revealed in one.
345. Mek., ed. Lauterbach, Ba-ḥôḏeš §3, vol. 2, p. 212; cf. Deut. R. VII.8.
346. Zohar II.82a,82b. Cf. Ezek. 1.5.
347. Zohar II.82a. Both Ezekiel and Isaiah are said to have had comparable visions of the Shekhinah.
348. Zohar II.82a. Cf. Ezek. 1.4. The five voices by means of which the Torah was given are also mentioned in II.90b. Cf. Ber. 6b. For an alternative view, see II.206a, which says that the Torah was given with seven voices.
349. Zohar II.82a. Cf Ezek. 1.3.
350. Zohar II.82a.
351. Zohar II.82a.
352. See, for example, Zohar I.170b–171a; II.23a–23b; II.82b; III.268b. The expressions "luminous speculum" and "nonluminous speculum" derive from rabbinic texts. See, for example, Yeb. 49b; cf. Lev. R. I.14. See Wolfson, "The Hermeneutics of Visionary Experience," pp. 331–332, nn. 26–27, for additional references from the Zohar as well as from other kabbalistic texts. As Wolfson notes, in addition to the view that the visions of all prophets except Moses were mediated through the Shekhinah, the Zohar occasionally makes reference to the alternative kabbalistic view that Neṣaḥ and Hôḏ, the seventh and eighth *s^e^p̄îrôṯ*, are the sources of prophetic inspiration. See, for example, III.35a. For an analysis of the complex symbolism used in II.23a–23b to distinguish the level of prophecy attained by Moses from that of the

patriarchs, see Blumenthal, *Understanding Jewish Mysticism*, [vol. 1], pp. 133–139.
353. See chapter 2, p. 209.
354. Zohar I.170b–171a; III.268b–269a.
355. Zohar II.146a. Cf. Šab. 88b; Tanḥ. Šᵉmôṯ §25; Tanḥ., ed. Buber, Šᵉmôṯ §22; Tanḥ. Yiṯrô §11; Exod. R. XXVIII.6.
356. Cf. Sip̄rê Deut. §343; Song R. I.2, §2, discussed on pp. 270, 280.
357. Zohar II.83b.
358. Zohar I.54a; I.47b. See chapter 6 for a discussion of Zoharic hermeneutics.
359. Zohar II.84a–84b. Cf. Šab. 104a; Meg. 2b–3a, discussed on p. 292. As mentioned in n. 189, this tradition is based on Exod. 32.15.
360. Cf. Mek., ed. Lauterbach, Ba-ḥôḏeš §8, pp. 262–264; Song R. V.14, §1; Exod. R. XLVII.6.
361. Zohar II.84a–84b.
362. Zohar II.90a.
363. Zohar II.84a–84b; II.90a–90b.
364. See Song R. V.11, §6; Deut. R. III.12, discussed on pp. 281, 308.
365. Zohar II.84a; cf. III.154b.
366. Wolfson, "The Hermeneutics of Visionary Experience," p. 316.
367. See, for example, Sip̄rê Deut. §313, which maintains that the Israelites saw and understood each divine utterance that went forth from the mouth of God. However, the knowledge that they gained is described in terms of the legal ramifications of the commandments, with no mention of any esoteric knowledge. The tradition ascribed to R. Akiba that describes the Israelites as seeing words of fire coming forth from God's mouth may have some esoteric connotation, but the significance of this statement is not expanded upon. See Mek., ed. Lauterbach, Ba-ḥôḏeš §9, vol. 2, p. 266, cited on p. 270, with n. 61. See also PRE §41, f. 98a, cited on p. 314.
368. Zohar II.93b; II.81a–81b; II.83b; II.90b; II.146a; cf. II.156b.
369. Zohar II.90b.
370. Zohar II.82a.
371. See chapter 2, pp. 202, 208–209, for a discussion of the Zohar's identification of the Torah with Ḥoḵmāh.
372. Zohar II.93b–94a.
373. Zohar II.82a; II.83b; II.94a.
374. Zohar II.82a.
375. Zohar II.94a.

CHAPTER 5. VEDA IN PRACTICE

1. Bodewitz explains *dhūr*s as "particular modifications applied in the singing of the first six (Gāyatrī) verses of the Out-of-doors laud [*bahiṣpavamāna stotra*]. The first verse is the Retasyā. The second and fol-

lowing verses are so modified as to become Gāyatrī, Triṣṭubh, Jagatī, etc." Bodewitz, trans., *The Jyotiṣṭoma Ritual,* p. 231, n. 19. Regarding the *bahiṣpavamāna stotra,* the first *stotra* chanted at the morning pressing of the *agniṣṭoma* sacrifice, see chapter 1, p. 55 with n. 134.

2. Graham, *Beyond the Written Word,* p. 68.
3. Staal, *Nambudiri Veda Recitation,* pp. 11–17; idem, "The Concept of Scripture in the Indian Tradition"; idem, *Rules Without Meaning,* esp. pp. 191–311; Coburn, "'Scripture' in India." See also Walther Eidlitz, *Der Glaube und die heiligen Schriften der Inder* (Olten: Walter-Verlag, 1957), pp. 11–29; Renou, *The Destiny of the Veda in India,* pp. 23–26; Gonda, *Vedic Literature,* pp. 43–45.
4. AĀ V.3.3.
5. See Lewis Lancaster, "Buddhist Literature: Its Canons, Scribes, and Editors," in *The Critical Study of Sacred Texts,* ed. O'Flaherty, pp. 224–225.
6. Mbh. XIII.24.70.
7. Pāṇ. Śi. 32; Yājñ. Śi. 198; Nār. Śi. II.8.19.
8. Graham, *Beyond the Written Word,* p. 72.
9. For a brief summary of these modes of recitation, see ibid., p. 72. For a more detailed description of the *pāṭhas* and other recitative techniques, one may refer to K. V. Abhyankar and G. V. Devasthali, *Vedavikṛtilakṣaṇa-Saṁgraha: A Collection of Twelve Tracts on Vedavikṛtis and Allied Topics,* Research Unit Publications, no. 5 (Poona: Bhandarkar Oriental Research Institute, 1978), esp. pp. xvii–xlix; Staal, *Nambudiri Veda Recitation,* esp. pp. 21–30, 40–52; N. A. Jairazbhoy, "Le chant védique," in *Encyclopédie des musiques sacrées,* ed. Jacques Porte, vol. 1 (Paris: Labergerie, 1968), pp. 144–161. For a survey of the status of the Vedic recitative tradition in various parts of contemporary India, see V. Raghavan, *The Present Position of Vedic Recitation and Vedic Sakhas* (Kumbhakonam: Veda Dharma Paripalana Sabha, 1962); Staal, *Nambudiri Veda Recitation,* pp. 18–20.
10. Graham, *Beyond the Written Word,* p. 72. Graham's description is based on the sources cited in n. 9.
11. See Staal, *Rules Without Meaning,* pp. 191–311.
12. Renou, *The Destiny of the Veda in India,* pp. 23–26; Staal, *Nambudiri Veda Recitation,* pp. 16–17; idem, "The Concept of Scripture in the Indian Tradition," p. 122; Coburn, "'Scripture' in India," pp. 445–447; Gonda, *Vedic Literature,* pp. 43–44. P. V. Kane remarks that "it appears that from very ancient times the Veda was only committed to memory and most men learned in the Veda never cared to know its meaning." Kane, *History of Dharmaśāstra,* vol. 2, p. 358. The brahmanical emphasis on recitation over interpretation was noted by the Arab scholar al-Bīrūnī (11th c. C.E.), who observes that "the Brahmins recite the Veda without understanding it, and learn it from one another" and that "few among them learn the explanations and fewer

still is the number of those who master its content and interpretation to the point of being able to hold out in a controversy (*brahmodya*)." Cited in Renou, *The Destiny of the Veda in India*, pp. 29–30.

13. Renou, *The Destiny of the Veda in India*, p. 23.
14. Staal, *Nambudiri Veda Recitation*, p. 17.
15. See Staal, *Rules Without Meaning*, pp. 191–311.
16. See chapter 1, pp. 119–121.
17. Pāṇ. Śi. 52; cf. Nār. Śi. I.1.5.
18. The term "theurgy" is used in the present context to refer to practices intended to influence the structures of the cosmos and/or divine realm.
19. See chapter 1, pp. 56–60.
20. These paradigms have been discussed in chapters 1 and 3, respectively.
21. See ṚV X.90; X.130; X.81.1,5–6; X.82.1, discussed in chapter 1, pp. 36–39.
22. ṚV X.90.7; cf. X.82.4.
23. ṚV X.90.16.
24. ṚV X.90.9.
25. See ṚV X.130.2,4–5, discussed in chapter 1, pp. 38–39.
26. ṚV X.130.6–7.
27. ṚV I.10.5; I.91.11; II.11.2; II.12.14; II.39.8; III.32.13; III.34.1–2; IV.32.12; V.11.5; V.22.4; V.31.4,10; VI.44.13; VII.19.11; VIII.6.1,11–12,21,31,35; VIII.8.8; VIII.13.16; VIII.14.5,11; VIII.44.2,12,22; VIII.62.4; VIII.74.1,8–9; VIII.93.27; VIII.95.6–7; VIII.98.8; IX.73.2; X.4.7; X.63.17, et al.
28. For a discussion of the Ṛg-Veda's treatment of the mechanics of cognition as represented by the *ṛṣis* themselves, see chapter 3, pp. 229–237.
29. ṚV VI.44.13.
30. ṚV VIII.8.8.
31. ṚV I.91.11.
32. For a discussion of relevant passages, see chapter 1, pp. 54–55.
33. The Aitareya Brāhmaṇa identifies Prajāpati with the *hotṛ* priest, while the Pañcaviṃśa and Jaiminīya Brāhmaṇas associate the creator with the *udgātṛ*. See, for example, AB II.15; AB II.16; PB VI.4.1; PB VI.5.18; PB VII.10.16; JB I.70; JB I.85; JB I.88; JB I.259; cf. ŚB IV.3.2.3.
34. PB XXV.6.2; PB XXV.17.2.
35. See, for example, AB IV.23; KB VI.15; KB V.3; ŚB II.5.1.17; ŚB II.5.2.1; ŚB II.5.2.7; ŚB II.6.3.4; PB VI.1.1–2; PB VIII.5.6; PB IV.1.4; PB XXII.9.2; JB I.67.
36. As noted in chapter 1, this formula is frequently repeated in the Śatapatha Brāhmaṇa. See, for example, ŚB IV.2.4.16; ŚB IV.5.5.l; ŚB IV.5.6.1; ŚB IV.5.7.1. Cf. ŚB II.5.1.17; AB II.33; AB IV.23.
37. See the variant of this passage, PB VI.9.15, cited in chapter 1, p. 55.

38. See also JB I.99, cited on p. 343. Cf. JB I.104; PB VII.5.1,4.
39. With respect to the recitation of certain *ṛcs* or *sāmans* for specific purposes, see, for example, PB VII.10.13–17; PB VII.5.1–3; PB XIII.5.13; JB I.148; JB I.160; JB I.116; JB I.117–118. With respect to the performance of certain sacrifices to obtain particular ends, see KB V.3; KB XII.8; PB IV.1.4–5; PB VI.1.1–3; PB VI.3.9–10; PB XXII.9.2–3.
40. See chapter 1, p. 45.
41. The *agnicayana* ceremony is described in Kāṇḍas VI–X of the Śatapatha Brāhmaṇa. For an analysis of various aspects of the *agnicayana*, see Frits Staal, *Agni: The Vedic Ritual of the Fire Altar*, 2 vols. (Berkeley: Asian Humanities Press, 1983).
42. See, for example, ŚB X.4.2.26; ŚB X.3.1.1; ŚB VI.2.1.30; AB II.18; PB XIII.11.18; TB III.3.9.11; cf. ŚB XII.1.4.1–3; ŚB XII.6.1.1; KB VI.15.
43. See chapter 1, pp. 87–88, 102–105.
44. For Upaniṣadic references to the *mantras*, see Renou, *The Destiny of the Veda in India*, pp. 19–20.
45. Nir. I.15–I.16.
46. Nir. I.18. Even the *śikṣā* texts, which are concerned with correct pronunciation of the Vedic *mantras*, at times denounce those reciters who do not know the meaning (*anartha-jña*) of the *mantras* they recite. See, for example, Pāṇ. Śi. 32; Yājñ. Śi. 198.
47. Nir. X.26; XI.4.
48. The Nirukta mentions the interpretations of a number of different groups: *yājñikas* (V.11; VII.4; VII.23; XI.29; XI.31; XIII.9); *aitihāsikas* (II.16; XII.1); *nairuktas* (I.12; II.8; II.14; II.16; III.8; III.14; V.11; VII.4; XI.29; XI.31; XIII.9, et al.); *parivrājakas* (II.8); *naidānas* (VI.9; VII.12); and *vaiyākaraṇas* (IX.5; XIII.9). For a discussion of Yāska and the "schools" of Vedic interpretation mentioned by him, see Ram Gopal, *The History and Principles of Vedic Interpretation* (New Delhi: Concept Publishing, 1983), pp. 7–93; S. K. Gupta, "Ancient Schools of Vedic Interpretation," *Journal of the Ganganatha Jha Research Institute* 16 (Nov. 1958–Feb. 1959): 143–153.
49. See, for example, Mān. GS I.2.8; Kāṭh. GS III.1; Vār. GS IX.7.
50. See, for example, Vaikh. DS VIII.3.
51. See, for example, Dakṣa II.27; MS XII.103; Yājñ. III.156,159; Uśanas III.81–82,86. For a discussion of these references, as well as the references from the Gṛhya-Sūtras and Dharma-Sūtras mentioned in the two previous notes, see Renou, *The Destiny of the Veda in India*, p. 25.
52. Dakṣa II.27.
53. MS XII.103.
54. Yājñ. III.156,159; cf. MS XII.102.
55. For a brief discussion of these hermeneutical principles and methods, particularly as developed and applied by the Mīmāṃsakas and Śaṃkara, see Renou, *The Destiny of the Veda in India*, pp. 35–53. Among more recent studies, see Francis X. Clooney, "Why the Veda

Has No Author: Language as Ritual in Early Mīmāṃsā and Post-Modern Theology," *Journal of the American Academy of Religion* 55, no. 4 (Winter 1987): 659–684; idem, "Vedānta, Commentary, and the Theological Component of Cross-Cultural Study," in *Myth and Philosophy,* eds. Reynolds and Tracy, pp. 287–314; idem, "Binding the Text: Vedānta as Philosophy and Commentary," in *Texts in Context,* ed. Timm, pp. 47–68; Anantanand Rambachan, "Where Words Can Set Free: The Liberating Potency of Vedic Words in the Hermeneutics of Śaṅkara," in *Texts in Context,* ed. Timm, pp. 33–46. Timm's *Texts in Context* also contains essays on the role of hermeneutics in a variety of other Hindu traditions as well as in other South Asian religions.

56. See Renou, *The Destiny of the Veda in India,* pp. 37–38, 44.
57. Gonda, *Vedic Literature,* p. 46.
58. See especially the commentaries on NS II.1.57–68; Vaiś. I.1.2–3; Vaiś. X.2.8–9. For the Sanskrit text and translation of these *sūtras,* along with selected commentaries, see Muir, *Original Sanskrit Texts,* vol. 3, pp. 111–120, 122–124.
59. See chapter 1, pp. 113–129.
60. For a discussion of the commentaries of Sāyaṇa as well as of earlier and later commentators, see Gopal, *The History and Principles of Vedic Interpretation,* pp. 94–140.
61. Coburn, "'Scripture' in India," pp. 454–455.
62. Mehta, "The Hindu Tradition: The Vedic Root," p. 50.
63. Ibid., p. 37.
64. See Coburn's suggestion that "*śruti* must be seen as an ongoing and experientially based feature of the Hindu religious tradition" and that recitation and hearing of the Vedic *mantras,* as cognized and preserved by the *ṛṣis,* constitute "sacramental activities" by means of which this ongoing participation in *śruti* may be realized. Coburn, "'Scripture' in India," pp. 442–447.
65. For the prohibitions against *śūdras* learning, reciting, or hearing the Vedas, see, for example, MS III.156; MS X.127; MS IV.99. For the restrictions against women studying the Vedas or performing sacrificial rituals, see MS IX.18; MS IV.205–206; MS XI.36–37. However, the presence of the *yajamāna*'s wife is required at *śrauta* sacrifices.
66. For a discussion of relevant passages, see chapter 1, pp. 66–67.
67. MU I.1.4–5.
68. See chapter 3, pp. 242–243.
69. For a discussion of the role of "meditative *tapas*" in the Upaniṣads, see Kaelber, *Tapta Mārga,* esp. pp. 83–100.
70. See, for example, MU II.2.4,6; Praśna V.1–7; ŚU I.13–14; Maitri VI.22–26,28.
71. TU I.8; Kaṭha II.16; Praśna V.2; Maitri VI.5; Maitri VI.22–23. Cf. Māṇḍ. 12, in which Om is identified with Ātman.
72. Maitri VI.22–23.

73. CU II.23.2–3, which is a variant of AB V.32. For a discussion of the antecedents of this conception in the Brāhmaṇas, see chapter 1, p. 57.
74. See Maitri VI.22–23.
75. For a discussion of the role of *mantras* in various aspects of Indian thought and practice, see the recent collection *Understanding Mantras*, ed. Harvey P. Alper, SUNY Series in Religious Studies (Albany: State University of New York Press, 1989), which contains an extensive bibliographic essay by Alper. See also J. Gonda, "The Indian Mantra," *Oriens* 16 (1963): 244–297; Shashi Bhusan Dasgupta, "The Role of Mantra in Indian Religion," in his *Aspects of Indian Religious Thought* (Calcutta: A. Mukherjee, 1957), pp. 22–41; Alex Wayman, "The Significance of Mantra-s, from the Veda Down to Buddhist Tantric Practice," *The Adyar Library Bulletin* 39 (1975): 65–89; Padoux, "The Mantra," chapter 7 of his *Vāc*, pp. 372–426; idem, ed., *Mantras et diagrammes rituels dans l'Hindouisme*, Centre National de la Recherche Scientifique, Équipe de recherche, no. 249, L'Hindouisme: textes, doctrines, pratiques (Paris: Éditions du Centre National de la Recherche Scientifique, 1986).

CHAPTER 6. TORAH IN PRACTICE

1. For a brief description of the laws and traditions concerning the writing of the Torah scroll, see Louis Isaac Rabinowitz, "Sefer Torah," *Encyclopaedia Judaica* (New York: Macmillan, 1971), s.v. See also the works cited in the article's bibliography.
2. 'Erub. 13a.
3. See chapter 2, pp. 198–200.
4. MS Milano-Ambrosiana 62, f. 113b. Cited in Idel, "Infinities of Torah in Kabbalah," p. 145. See Idel's discussion of this passage in his "T^{e}p̄îsaṯ ha-Tôrāh b^{e}-Sip̄rûṯ ha-Hêḵālôṯ ẇ^{e}-Gilgûlệhā ba-Qabbālāh," pp. 62–64.
5. MS Milano-Ambrosiana 62, f. 113b. Cited in Idel, *Kabbalah*, p. 188.
6. The full text and reference for this passage are given below in n. 51.
7. Howard Eilberg-Schwartz remarks, "The very idea of vowel notation is incompatible with the sages' assumption that God created language out of consonants. Since the links among words are based on their consonantal (i.e., molecular) structure, the addition of vowels to the scriptural text would have intimated that a word has only one interpretation. The divine Author, however, intended scriptural words to evoke all the links that had been encoded in language and, consequently, did not include vowel notation." Howard Eilberg-Schwartz, "Who's Kidding Whom? A Serious Reading of Rabbinic Word Plays," *Journal of the American Academy of Religion* 55, no. 4 (Winter 1987): 778. Eilberg-Schwartz's suggestion that certain hermeneutical methods employed by the rabbis

were based on an "atomistic understanding of language" will be discussed below.

8. See Susan A. Handelman, *The Slayers of Moses: The Emergence of Rabbinic Interpretation in Modern Literary Theory*, SUNY Series on Modern Jewish Literature and Culture (Albany: State University of New York Press, 1982), esp. pp. 39, 49.
9. Sēḏer 'Ēliyyāhû Zûṭā' §2.
10. See, for example, Sip̄rê Num. §112; Ber. 31b.
11. See Heschel, *Tôrāh min ha-Šāmayim bā-'Aspaqlaryāh šel ha-Dôrôṯ*.
12. Scholem remarks that "R. Akiva, a central figure in the world of rabbinic Judaism, is also the legitimate representative of a mysticism within its boundaries." Scholem, *Kabbalah*, p. 14. Scholem's assessment of R. Akiba's mystical orientation is in part based on the story in Ḥag. 14b–15b (cf. T Ḥag. II.3–4; JT Ḥag. II.1, 77b; Song R. I.4, §1) of the four sages who entered *pardēs* ("garden," understood by Scholem as "paradise"). While the other sages either died (Ben Azzai), went mad (Ben Zoma), or became an apostate (Elisha b. Abuya), R. Akiba alone "ascended unharmed and descended unharmed" (Ḥag. 15b). Scholem interprets the passage in light of parallel passages in Hêḵālôṯ texts as referring to a mystical ascent to the Merkabah. See Scholem, *Major Trends in Jewish Mysticism*, pp. 52–53; idem, *Jewish Gnosticism, Merkabah Mysticism, and Talmudic Tradition*, pp. 14–19. See also Halperin's discussion of the various versions of the *pardēs* episode, in which he refutes some of Scholem's conclusions, in *The Faces of the Chariot*, pp. 29–37, 194–210.
13. 'Ab. III.14.
14. See Tanḥ., ed. Buber, Beˢrē'šîṯ §5, cited in chapter 2, p. 186.
15. See the aggadah in Men. 29b, ascribed to Rab Judah in the name of Rab, which relates how when Moses ascended on high and found God affixing crowns to certain letters, he inquired of him why he was doing so. God replied that in the future a man named Akiba would arise who would "expound upon each tittle (*qôṣ*) mounds upon mounds (*tîllîn tîllîn*) of laws."
16. For a brief discussion of the thirteen principles of R. Ishmael and the hermeneutical methods of R. Akiba, see Louis Jacobs, "Hermeneutics," *Encyclopaedia Judaica* (New York: Macmillan, 1971), s.v. For discussions of the principles and characteristics of Midrash, as well as of the interrelationship between Midrash, halakhah, and aggadah, see Judah Goldin, "From Text to Interpretation and from Experience to the Interpreted Text," *Prooftexts* 3, no. 2 (May 1983): 157–168; idem, "The Freedom and Restraint of Haggadah," in *Midrash and Literature*, eds. Hartman and Budick, pp. 57–76; William Scott Green, "Romancing the Tome: Rabbinic Hermeneutics and the Theory of Literature," in *Text and Textuality*, ed. Charles E. Winquist, *Semeia* 40 (1987): 147–168; Handelman, *The Slayers of Moses*, pp. 27–82; Joseph

Heinemann, "The Nature of the Aggadah," in *Midrash and Literature,* eds. Hartman and Budick, pp. 41–55; Barry W. Holtz, "Midrash," in *Back to the Sources: Reading the Classic Jewish Texts,* ed. Barry W. Holtz (New York: Summit Books, 1984), pp. 177–211; Kugel, "Two Introductions to Midrash"; Roger Le Déaut, "A propos d'une définition du midrash," *Biblica* 50, no. 3 (1969): 395–413; Gary G. Porton, "Defining Midrash," in *The Study of Ancient Judaism,* ed. Jacob Neusner, vol. 1 (New York: Ktav, 1981), pp. 55–92; Slonimsky, "The Philosophy Implicit in the Midrash." In addition to the essays noted above by Goldin, Heinemann, and Kugel, Hartman and Budick's collection, *Midrash and Literature,* contains a number of essays that examine the relationship of Midrash to a variety of literary genres. The various forms of "midrashic imagination" are further explored in the more recent collection edited by Michael Fishbane, *The Midrashic Imagination: Jewish Exegesis, Thought, and History* (Albany: State University of New York Press, 1993). For extended treatments of Midrash and aggadah, see Daniel Boyarin, *Intertextuality and the Reading of Midrash,* Indiana Studies in Biblical Literature (Bloomington: Indiana University Press, 1990); David Weiss Halivni, *Midrash, Mishnah, and Gemara: The Jewish Predilection for Justified Law* (Cambridge: Harvard University Press, 1986); idem, *Peshat and Derash: Plain and Applied Meaning in Rabbinic Exegesis* (New York: Oxford University Press, 1991); Isaak Heinemann, *Darkê hā-'Aggādāh,* 3d ed. (Jerusalem: Magnes Press, Hebrew University, 1970); Joseph Heinemann, *Aggadah and Its Development* [in Hebrew] (Jerusalem: Keter, 1974); Max Kadushin, *Organic Thinking: A Study in Rabbinic Thought* (New York: Jewish Theological Seminary of America, 1938); idem, *The Rabbinic Mind,* 3d ed. (New York: Bloch Publishing, 1972); Jacob Neusner, *Midrash in Context: Exegesis in Formative Judaism* (Philadelphia: Fortress Press, 1983); idem, *Midrash as Literature: The Primacy of Documentary Discourse,* Studies in Judaism (New York: Lanham, 1987); Neusner with Green, *Writing with Scripture*; David Stern, *Parables in Midrash: Narrative and Exegesis in Rabbinic Literature* (Cambridge: Harvard University Press, 1991); I. Wartski, *Lᵉšôn ha-Midrāšîm* (Jerusalem: Mosad ha-Rav Kook, 1970); Addison G. Wright, *The Literary Genre Midrash* (Staten Island, N.Y.: Alba House, 1967). For discussions of the antecedents of Midrash in the Bible and pre-rabbinic literature, see Renée Bloch, "Écriture et tradition dans le judaïsme: Aperçus sur l'origine du Midrash," *Cahiers Sioniens* 8, no. 1 (Mar. 1954): 9–34; idem, "Note méthodologique pour l'étude de la littérature rabbinique," *Recherches de Science Religieuse* 43 (1955): 194–227; idem, "Midrash," *Dictionnaire de la Bible, Supplément,* ed. L. Pirot, et al. (Paris: Librairie Letouzey et Ané, 1957), s. v.; Michael Fishbane, *Biblical Interpretation in Ancient Israel* (Oxford: Clarendon Press, 1985); idem, "Inner

Biblical Exegesis: Types and Strategies of Interpretation in Ancient Israel," in *Midrash and Literature,* eds. Hartman and Budick (New Haven: Yale University Press, 1986), pp. 19–37; idem, *The Garments of Torah: Essays in Biblical Hermeneutics,* Indiana Studies in Biblical Literature (Bloomington: Indiana University Press, 1989); James L. Kugel, *In Potiphar's House: The Interpretive Life of Biblical Texts* (San Francisco: Harper, 1990); idem, "Early Interpretation: The Common Background of Later Forms of Biblical Exegesis," in James L. Kugel and Rowan A. Greer, *Early Biblical Interpretation,* Library of Early Christianity (Philadelphia: Westminster Press, 1986), pp. 9–106; Geza Vermes, "Bible and Midrash: Early Old Testament Exegesis," in *The Cambridge History of the Bible,* vol. 1, eds. P. R. Ackroyd and C. F. Evans (Cambridge: Cambridge University Press, 1970), pp. 199–231; idem, *Scripture and Tradition in Judaism: Haggadic Studies,* 2d rev. ed., Studia Post-Biblica, vol. 4 (Leiden: E. J. Brill, 1973); idem, *Post-Biblical Jewish Studies,* Studies in Judaism in Late Antiquity, vol. 8 (Leiden: E. J. Brill, 1975). For additional references, please refer to the bibliography.

17. See Eilberg-Schwartz's provocative analysis in "Who's Kidding Whom?"
18. See Goldin, "The Freedom and Restraint of Haggadah," esp. p. 63.
19. See Aristotle, *Metaphysica,* Gamma 4, 1006b, 6–10. Cited in Handelman, *The Slayers of Moses,* p. 13. Handelman remarks that "the infinity of meaning and plurality of interpretation are as much the cardinal virtues, even divine imperatives, for Rabbinic thought as they are the cardinal sins for Greek thought." Ibid., p. 21. While Handelman is correct in emphasizing the primacy of "plurality of interpretation" in rabbinic thought, the expression "infinity of meaning" requires qualification. As Idel has noted, the rabbinic notion of a multiplicity of meanings is significantly different from the kabbalistic conception of an *infinity* of significations in the Torah. See Idel, "Infinities of Torah in Kabbalah," p. 148 with n. 31. See also Green, "Romancing the Tome," pp. 161–165, in which Green critiques Handelman's use of the expression "endless multiple meanings" to describe rabbinic hermeneutics and emphasizes instead the limitations imposed on the interpretive process by the rabbinic arbiters of discourse.
20. ʿErub. 54a–54b. The analogy of the fig tree is ascribed to R. Ḥiyya II b. Abba in the name of R. Joḥanan, while the analogy of the breast is attributed to R. Samuel b. Naḥman.
21. ʿErub. 21b. This tradition, ascribed to R. Ḥisda in the name of Mar Ukba, is presented as a Midrashic comment on S. S. 5.11, "His locks (*qᵉwuṣṣôṯ*) are curls (*taltallîm*)." Cf. the parallel interpretation attributed to R. Azariah in Song R. V.11, §1. See also the aggadah in Men. 29b, discussed in n. 15, concerning R. Akiba's propensity to pile up "mounds upon mounds" (*tîllîn tîllîn*) of interpretations on every tittle.

22. See, for example, Pes. K. 4.4 = Pes. R. 14.10; Lev. R. XXVI.2; Pes. K. 4.2; Pes. R. 14.6; Pes. R. 21.6. This tradition is understood more specifically to mean that the Torah can be interpreted in forty-nine ways in order to determine what is unclean and in forty-nine ways in order to determine what is clean.
23. See, for example, Num. R. XIII.15, which mentions the seventy "faces" (*pānîm*) of the Torah.
24. See Šab. 88b; Tanḥ. Š^{e}môṯ §25; Tanḥ., ed. Buber, Š^{e}môṯ §22; Tanḥ. Yiṯrô §11; Exod. R. XXVIII.6, discussed in chapter 4, pp. 285, 292, 295–296, 306.
25. Lev. R. XVI.4; cf. Song R. I.10, §2; Ruth R. VI.4. See also Pes. K. Suppl. 1.17. See chapter 2, n. 173.
26. Cf. Suk. 28a. See chapter 4, p. 263 with n. 28. For other passages that associate the sages with fire, see 'Ab. VI.10; Pes. K. Suppl. 3.2; Ḥag. 27a.
27. This analogy is explicitly drawn in PRE §2, f. 4a, discussed in chapter 2, p. 196. See also Pes. K. 4.4 = Pes. R. 14.10; Lev. R. XIX.1; Lev. R. XXX.2 = Pes. K. 27.2 = Pes. R. 51.4; cf. Ber. 17a; Ber. 5b. These passages were discussed briefly in chapter 2.
28. See, for example, 'Ab. III.2; 'Ab. III.6; Pes. K. 5.8 = Pes. R. 15.9; Song R. II.9, §2; Ber. 6a; Deut. R. VII.2. See also Song R. II.5, §3, which suggests that entertaining scholars is like entertaining the Shekhinah.
29. Joseph Dan emphasizes the continuities between early kabbalistic hermeneutics and traditional Midrashic methods in "Midrash and the Dawn of Kabbalah," in *Midrash and Literature*, eds. Hartman and Budick, pp. 127–139. Idel focuses on the more innovative dimensions of kabbalistic interpretation in his essay "Infinities of Torah in Kabbalah," which follows Dan's essay, pp. 141–157. See also Betty Roitman, "Sacred Language and Open Text," in the same volume, pp. 159–175.
30. See Idel, *Kabbalah*, pp. 200–249.
31. See Idel, "Infinities of Torah in Kabbalah," pp. 143–144.
32. As discussed in chapter 2, n. 319, the view that the Zohar is the exclusive composition of Moses de Leon has been disputed by Liebes in his essay "How the Zohar Was Written." See also Idel, *Kabbalah*, p. 380, n. 66.
33. See Idel, *Kabbalah*, pp. 210–218, esp. 215.
34. See pp. 382–383.
35. See chapter 2, p. 210. For Gikatilla's views, see Gottlieb, *Studies in the Kabbala Literature*, pp. 112, 129–130, 154–155. See also Scholem's discussion in "The Name of God and the Linguistic Theory of the Kabbala," pt. 2, pp. 179–180. As Idel notes, the notion of multiple vocalizations is first discussed by Jacob b. Sheshet (middle of the 13th c. C.E.) and is further developed by the Castilian kabbalists Gikatilla and Joseph of Hamadan, whose views in turn influenced kabbalists such

as Baḥya b. Asher and Menaḥem Recanati. For a discussion of relevant passages, see Idel, *Kabbalah*, pp. 213–215; idem, "Infinities of Torah in Kabbalah," pp. 146–147, 150.

36. See, for example, Zohar II.230b; III.71b; III.73a; III.159a.
37. See, for example, Zohar III.73a.
38. Zohar II.98b.
39. Zohar II.55b; cf. I.134b–135a; I.145b; I.234b; II.12a; II.59b; III.149a–149b; III.202a; Zohar Ḥāḏāš 6d (Midrash ha-Ne'ĕlām).
40. Zohar III.202a.
41. Zohar Ḥāḏāš 83a. The passage uses the image of a nut to depict the layers of meaning in the Torah: *ma'ăśeh*, the outer, literal meaning; *midrash*, the hermeneutical meaning derived through rabbinic exegesis; *haggadah*, which appears to refer to some allegorical method of interpretation; and *sôḏ*, the mysteries discerned through kabbalistic exegesis. Zohar III.202a uses the image of a tree to describe the manifold meanings of the Torah. The four levels are mentioned, although there is a shift in terminology: *p^ešāṭā'* (literal), *d^erāšā'* (hermeneutical), *remez* (allegorical), and *rāzîn* (mystical). In addition, reference is made to other methods of interpretation, including *gematria*, interpretation on the basis of the numerical value of the letters. See also Zohar II.99a–99b, discussed below, which makes reference to the fourfold system of interpretation in recounting the parable of the damsel in the palace. See Scholem, "The Meaning of the Torah in Jewish Mysticism," pp. 54–57; Tishby, *The Wisdom of the Zohar*, vol. 3, pp. 1083–1085.
42. The later Zoharic strata, the Rā'āyā' M^ehêmnā' and the Tiqqûnê Zohar, make use of the term *pardēs* to denote the four levels of meaning, although the terms used to designate the levels diverge at times from Moses de Leon's formulation. See Zohar Ḥāḏāš 102d (Tîqqûnîm); 107c (Tîqqûnîm); Zohar III.110a (Rā'āyā' M^ehêmnā'); I.26b (Tîqqûnîm). For a discussion of these passages, see Scholem, "The Meaning of the Torah in Jewish Mysticism," pp. 57–59; Tishby, *The Wisdom of the Zohar*, vol. 3, p. 1090. For an analysis of the historical development of the kabbalistic conception of the fourfold meaning of the Torah, as well as of the historical antecedents of this notion in Philo, Christian and Islamic hermeneutics, and medieval Jewish philosophy, see Scholem, "The Meaning of the Torah in Jewish Mysticism," pp. 50–62. See also A. van der Heide, "PARDES: Methodological Reflections on the Theory of the Four Senses," *Journal of Jewish Studies* 34, no. 2 (Autumn 1983): 147–159. For an illuminating discussion of the interrelationship in Zoharic hermeneutics between the exoteric or literal meaning (*p^ešāṭ*) and the esoteric or mystical meaning (*sôḏ*), see Elliot R. Wolfson, "Beautiful Maiden without Eyes: *Peshat* and *Sod* in Zoharic Hermeneutics," in *The Midrashic Imagination*, ed. Fishbane, pp. 155–203.

43. See, for example, Zohar Ḥāḏāš 70d (Šîr ha-Šîrîm); 105a (Tîqqûnîm); 105c (Tîqqûnîm); 106b (Tîqqûnîm); Zohar II.2a.
44. Zohar I.134b.
45. For references, see chapter 2, pp. 203–204.
46. Zohar III.152a.
47. Zohar III.152a. For a discussion of the various ways in which the Zohar makes use of the image of garments, see Dorit Cohen-Alloro, *The Secret of the Garment in the Zohar* [in Hebrew], Research Projects of the Institute of Jewish Studies, Monograph Series, 13 (Jerusalem: Hebrew University, 1987).
48. In addition to Zohar III.152a, cited above, see III.149b; I.163a. Tishby argues that the Zohar's polemic is aimed not at the rabbis but rather at "the extremist philosophizers, the Averroist heretics, who did not share the basic belief in the twofold, revealed and hidden, significance of Torah, but saw it only in its literal sense, and made fun of it." Tishby, *The Wisdom of the Zohar,* vol. 3, p. 1082.
49. See, for example, Zohar II.99a–99b, which will be discussed below. Cf. III.149a–149b.
50. See Zohar II.98b, which will be discussed below.
51. For a discussion of the identification of the Torah with God in the Zohar and other texts of thirteenth-century Spanish Kabbalah, see chapter 2, pp. 200–201 with n. 334. Cf. the view of Joseph of Hamadan: "Since the Torah is his form, blessed be he, we were ordered to study the Torah, in order to know that archetype of the supernal form, as some Kabbalists have said: 'Cursed be he that does [not] hold up all the words of this Torah' [Deut. 27.26]—to the congregation—so that they will see the image of the supernal form: moreover, the person who studies the Torah . . . sees the supernal secrets and he sees the glory of God, literally." *Ṭa'ămê ha-Miṣwôṯ,* MS Jerusalem, 8° 3925, f. 110b. Cited in Idel, *Kabbalah,* p. 190. The "archetype/image of the supernal form" (*dûḡmā' šel ṣûrāh hā-'elyônāh*), as Idel notes, refers to the ten *s*ᵉ*p̄îrôṯ*. See also Idel's discussion in "Tᵉp̄îsaṯ ha-Tôrāh bᵉ-Sip̄rûṯ ha-Hêḵālôṯ wᵉ-Gilgûlệhā ba-Qabbālāh," pp. 64–65.
52. For a detailed analysis of the mechanisms through which the Zohar correlates the processes of interpretation and revelation, see Wolfson, "The Hermeneutics of Visionary Experience," pp. 317–325.
53. See chapter 4, pp. 318–320.
54. See, for example, Zohar I.72a; I.92b; I.115b; I.135b; I.164a; I.245a; II.94b; II.134b (Rā'ăyā' Mᵉhêmnā'); II.155b; II.163b; II.188b; II.200a; III.22a; III.35a; III.36a; III.61a; III.268a–268b; III.298a; Zohar Ḥāḏāš 29a (Siṯrê Tôrāh). Mystical exegesis is also described as a means of cleaving to God. See, for example, Zohar II.213b; II.217a; III.36a; Zohar Ḥāḏāš 27d. For a discussion of relevant passages, see Wolfson, "The Hermeneutics of Visionary Experience," pp. 317–318, 313 with n. 8.

55. Zohar I.15b–16a. A number of passages in the Zohar suggest that the faces of the mystics become illumined with the light of the Shekhinah. See, for example, I.9a; II.163b, in which the companions of R. Simeon b. Yoḥai are themselves deemed the "face of the Shekhinah." See also II.209a.
56. Zohar II.23a. See also the interpretations of Dan. 12.3 in Zohar II.2a; Zohar Ḥāḏāš 105a (Tîqqûnîm); 105c (Tîqqûnîm); 106b (Tîqqûnîm).
57. R. Simeon b. Yoḥai, who is celebrated in the Zohar as the preeminent master who revealed the hidden light of Torah (Zohar II.193b), is credited in III.132b ('Iḏrā' Rabbā') with seeing what no one had seen since Moses's ascent of Mount Sinai. Moreover, the passage suggests that he attained a status even higher than Moses in that he knew that his face shone, while Moses did not (Exod. 34.29). See also Zohar III.144a–144b ('Iḏrā' Rabbā'); I.15b–16a; II.2a; I.190a; Zohar Ḥāḏāš 105a (Tîqqûnîm). See also n. 55. For a discussion of other passages that correlate the experience of the mystic exegete with that of Moses, see Wolfson, "The Hermeneutics of Visionary Experience," pp. 319–325.
58. Commenting on Zohar II.23a, mentioned above, Blumenthal remarks concerning the radicalness of its claims:

> We have, then, two very important points being made: (1) that the mystics can perceive the sefirot; and (2) that they can "reach" even to Tiferet, which is higher than the Patriarchs, and which is equal to the level of Moses. These two points, especially the latter, are very radical, for they imply that man still has direct revelatory contact with God, and that this exists even on the level of Moses. Both implications contradict the teachings of Rabbinic Judaism, which had asserted, as a matter of dogma, that "prophecy" (i.e., direct revelatory contact) had ceased with the Biblical period, and that Moses' prophecy was so superior that no one, not even another Biblical prophet, could attain that level. Both of these dogmas are here called into question.

Blumenthal, *Understanding Jewish Mysticism,* [vol. 1], p. 135.
59. Zohar III.35a. As noted in chapter 4, p. 320 with n. 352, the Zohar generally maintains that the visions of the prophets other than Moses were mediated through the Shekhinah, the tenth *s*[e]*p̄îrāh,* although Neṣaḥ and Hôḏ, the seventh and eighth *s*[e]*p̄îrôṯ,* are also at times said to be the source of prophetic inspiration, as in the present passage.
60. Zohar Ḥāḏāš 105a (Tîqqûnîm); cf. 105c (Tîqqûnîm); 106b (Tîqqûnîm); Zohar II.2a. See also Zohar Ḥāḏāš 70d (Šîr ha-Šîrîm). The term *'istakkēl,* as discussed in chapter 2, is also the term used to describe God's activity of "looking into" the Torah, his blueprint, in order to bring forth creation. The Zohar establishes a direct connection between the kabbalist's activity of "looking into" the Torah and God's cosmogonic activity in several passages, as will be discussed below on pp. 378–379 with n. 101. As Wolf-

son notes, although the Zohar gives priority to the visual over the auditory mode, other kabbalists emphasize the supremacy of the auditory mode. See Wolfson, "The Hermeneutics of Visionary Experience," p. 321 with n. 86. Idel, in "Reification of Language in Jewish Mysticism," suggests that while the exponents of theosophical Kabbalah tend to give precedence to the written-visual dimensions of language, the exponents of ecstatic Kabbalah shift the emphasis to the oral-aural.

61. Zohar II.98b.
62. The term *pᵉšāṭ* does not appear until the very end of the passage. See Matt, trans., *Zohar*, p. 253, for a discussion of this passage's use of the term.
63. Cf. Zohar II.134b, where this appellation is applied to the righteous (*tzaddik*). It is also used with reference to Moses, as will be discussed below.
64. Zohar II.99a–99b. Cf. III.35b–36a, which similarly suggests that the Torah is open to receive those who seek to unite with her.
65. Zohar I.236b; I.239a; II.22b; II.238b.
66. Zohar II.99a. See Idel, *Kabbalah*, pp. 227–229; Wolfson, "The Hermeneutics of Visionary Experience," pp. 322–324. Cf. Tishby, *The Wisdom of the Zohar*, vol. 1, p. 196, and Matt, trans., *Zohar*, p. 251, who interpret the rainbow as a symbol of the Shekhinah, which is garbed in a cloud.
67. Zohar II.22b; cf. I.239a; II.235a; II.238a; III.4b. See Tishby, *The Wisdom of the Zohar*, vol. 3, pp. 874–875.
68. For a discussion of passages in other kabbalistic texts that similarly view the study of Torah as a means to mystical union with the divine reality of Torah, see Idel, *Kabbalah*, pp. 243–247.
69. Sip̄rê Deut. §48.
70. See Idel, *Kabbalah*, pp. xiii–xv, 156–157.
71. Ibid., p. 232.
72. Scholem, *On the Kabbalah and Its Symbolism*, pp. 94–95. Tishby reiterates Scholem's position in *The Wisdom of the Zohar*, vol. 3, p. 1161.
73. Idel, *Kabbalah*, pp. 156–157, 170–171.
74. Ibid., p. 171.
75. See ibid., pp. 156–199.
76. Idel's study, while citing a few references from the Zohar, does not give an extended analysis of Zoharic theurgy. Moreover, most of the rabbinic passages discussed below, with the exception of those concerning the augmentation of God's power, are not analyzed by Idel.
77. See Lev. R. XXXV.4, discussed in chapter 2, pp. 166–167.
78. See Pes. K. 12.1; Mak. 23b, discussed in chapter 2, pp. 167, 176.
79. 'Ab. I.2.
80. This inference was made by a number of commentators. See, for example, Judah Goldin, trans., *The Living Talmud: The Wisdom of the*

Fathers and Its Classical Commentaries (New York: New American Library, 1957), pp. 46–47.

81. PRE §16, f. 36b.
82. See Lev. R. XXIII.3; Gen. R. LXVI.2; Song R. VII.1, §1; Song R. I.9, §6; Ruth R. Proem I; Šab. 88a; ʻAZ 3a; ʻAZ 5a; Pes. R. 21.4; Pes. R. 21.21; Exod. R. XLVII.4; cf. Exod. R. XL.1; Deut. R. VIII.5. For a discussion of these passages, see chapter 4, pp. 274–275, 287–288, 297–298.
83. See Exod. R. XLVII.4, cited in chapter 4, p. 298.
84. Deut. R. VIII.5.
85. See Gen. R. LXVI.2; Song R. VII.1, §1. This tradition appears in both texts in pericopes that include the aggadah that if Israel had not accepted the Torah, the world would have been dissolved. See also the traditions that celebrate the righteous, the *tzaddikim*, for their role in maintaining the cosmos. See, for example, ʼAb. V.1, which asserts that the righteous sustain the world while the wicked destroy it. Cf. Tanḥ., ed. Buber, Tôlᵉḏôṯ §11, which suggests that the righteous collaborate with God in creation.
86. See, for example, the tradition ascribed to R. Alexandri in Sanh. 99b: "Whoever is engaged in Torah for its own sake makes peace in the family above and the family below." See also the tradition ascribed to R. Joshua of Siknin in the name of R. Levi in Song R. I.2, §5, which suggests that when the people of Israel abide in purity they have the power to influence the beings of the upper and lower worlds.
87. Esth. R. VII.13; cf. Esth. R. VII.11.
88. Ned. 32a. This tradition is cited in full in chapter 4, p. 288. Cf. Pes. 68b.
89. Ned. 32a; cf. Šab. 137b. This tradition represents a variant of the Mishnaic tradition in Ned. III.11, which invokes Jer. 33.25 to establish that if it were not for circumcision, God would not have created the world.
90. Meg. 31b. In Taan. 27b this tradition is ascribed to R. Jacob b. Aḥa in the name of R. Assi.
91. For a detailed exposition of relevant passages, see Idel, *Kabbalah*, pp. 157–166.
92. Pes. K. 25.1. My translation of Ps. 60.14 follows that of Idel, *Kabbalah*, p. 158 with n. 23.
93. Lam. R. I.6, §33. See also Pes. R. 33.11.
94. Lev. R. XXIII.12; cf. Pes. R. 24.2. A variant of this tradition in Numbers Rabbāh I (IX.1) is ascribed to R. Isaac.
95. Meg. 11a; cf. Taan. 7b.
96. See chapter 2, pp. 203–204.
97. See, for example, Zohar II.161a–161b; I.134b; I.47a; I.77a; II.155b; III.35a.

98. See, for example, Zohar I.5a; I.24b (Tîqqûnîm); I.47a–47b; I.134a–134b; I.185a; I.207a; II.161a–161b; II.200a; III.35b; III.152a. See chapter 2, pp. 202–204.
99. See, for example, Zohar III.117a; I.89a; II.94a; III.298b; III.193a, discussed in chapter 4, pp. 316–318.
100. See Zohar II.161a, cited in chapter 2, p. 203.
101. Zohar II.161a–161b. See also I.5a, which suggests that the modes of operation by means of which God created the world through the Torah—"looking into" (*'istakkēl*) and uttering its words, and so on—provides a model for the proper method of Torah study.
102. Zohar I.134a–134b.
103. As will be discussed below, the "limbs and joints" of the body of Torah are identified in other passages with the commandments.
104. See Zohar I.134b, portions of which are cited in chapter 2, p. 204, and above on p. 379. See also I.77a, which maintains that since everything stands upon the Torah, "when Israel study the Torah the world is sustained and they are sustained, and the pillars stand in their place with complete security."
105. Zohar I.47a.
106. Zohar I.4b–5a; cf. III.35a.
107. See, for example, Zohar II.155b.
108. See Zohar II.162b, cited in chapter 2, p. 204. Cf. II.165b.
109. Zohar II.85b.
110. Zohar II.165b.
111. Zohar II.85b.
112. Zohar II.162b.
113. Zohar III.31b; cf. III.38b; III.92a–92b; III.110b; III.113b; I.77b; I.86b; II.47b; III.112b.
114. See, for example, Zohar I.58a; I.67a.
115. Zohar I.58a; I.67a; III.297a–297b.
116. Zohar III.113a. The translation is from Idel, *Kabbalah*, p. 187. See ibid., pp. 185–189, for Idel's discussion of the possible sources of the formula "as if he had made me" and its use in other kabbalistic texts. Cf. III.113b; III.110b.
117. Zohar III.113a.
118. Zohar III.113a; III.4b.
119. Zohar II.119a (Rā'ăyā' M^{e}hêmnā'). As Tishby notes, such Zoharic conceptions may be the source of the formula that is recited before performing a commandment in later kabbalistic liturgy: "For the purpose of uniting the Holy One, blessed be He, with His Shekhinah." Tishby, *The Wisdom of the Zohar*, vol. 3, p. 1160.
120. See Zohar III.22a; III.36a; III.268a; I.191b; cf. II.163b.
121. For a detailed exposition of Abulafia's hermeneutical methods and ecstatic techniques and their historical antecedents in philosophical and mystical sources, see Idel, *Language, Torah, and Hermeneutics in*

Abraham Abulafia; idem, *The Mystical Experience in Abraham Abulafia*, trans. Jonathan Chipman, SUNY Series in Judaica: Hermeneutics, Mysticism, and Religion (Albany: State University of New York Press, 1988); idem, "Abraham Abulafia and *Unio Mystica*," chapter 1 of his *Studies in Ecstatic Kabbalah*, SUNY Series in Judaica: Hermeneutics, Mysticism, and Religion (Albany: State University of New York, 1988), pp. 1–31; idem, *Kabbalah*, pp. 97–103. For a discussion of the relationship between the hermeneutical approaches of the theosophical kabbalists and Abulafia, see ibid., pp. 200–249. See also Scholem's discussions of Abulafia in "The Name of God and the Linguistic Theory of the Kabbala," pt. 2, pp. 184–193; "Abraham Abulafia and the Doctrine of Prophetic Kabbalism," chapter 4 of his *Major Trends in Jewish Mysticism*, pp. 119–155.

COMPARATIVE ANALYSIS 3. VEDA AND TORAH IN PRACTICE

1. Idel has emphasized that although there may be superficial similarities between Abulafia's techniques and yogic practices, there are significant points of divergence. See Idel, *The Mystical Experience in Abraham Abulafia*, pp. 39–40; idem, *Kabbalah*, p. 97.

CONCLUSION

1. Smith, "Scripture as Form and Concept," p. 45.
2. Even though the brahmanical and Jewish traditions are not generally characterized as missionary religions, there is nevertheless some evidence of proselytizing tendencies in these traditions. See, for example, Arvind Sharma, "Ancient Hinduism as a Missionary Religion," *Numen* 39, no. 2 (Nov. 1992): 175–192; Bernard J. Bamberger, *Proselytism in the Talmudic Period*, rev. ed. (New York: Ktav, 1968); William G. Braude, *Jewish Proselyting in the First Five Centuries of the Common Era, the Age of the Tannaim and Amoraim*, Brown University Studies, vol. 6 (Providence: Brown University, 1940).
3. See Catherine Bell, "The Ritual Body and the Dynamics of Ritual Power," in *Ritual and Power*, ed. Holdrege, *Journal of Ritual Studies* 4, no. 2 (Summer 1990): 299–313. Bell's essay draws on the insights of Pierre Bourdieu, *Outline of a Theory of Practice*, trans. Richard Nice, Cambridge Studies in Social Anthropology, 16 (Cambridge: Cambridge University Press, 1977), and Michel Foucault, *Discipline and Punish: The Birth of the Prison*, trans. Alan Sheridan (New York: Random House, Vintage Books, 1979). For an extended discussion, see

Bell's *Ritual Theory, Ritual Practice* (New York: Oxford University Press, 1992).

4. See Pes. K. 12.1; cf. Mak. 23b. For a discussion of this tradition, as well as of other traditions that illustrate the intimate relationship between the body and Torah in Jewish thought, see Paul Morris, "The Embodied Text: Covenant and Torah," *Religion* 20 (Jan. 1990): 77–87. For recent works that have contributed significantly to our understanding of the discourse of the body in Jewish traditions, particularly in relation to issues of gender and sexuality, see the collection of essays *People of the Body: Jews and Judaism from an Embodied Perspective*, ed. Howard Eilberg-Schwartz, SUNY Series, the Body in Culture, History, and Religion (Albany: State University of New York Press, 1992), and Daniel Boyarin, *Carnal Israel: Reading Sex in Talmudic Culture*, The New Historicism: Studies in Cultural Poetics (Berkeley: University of California Press, 1993). I regret that these two books were not available until after this manuscript was in the final stages of production, and I was thus not able to incorporate their insights into my own reflections on the "embodied" nature of the rabbinic tradition.
5. See Smith, "Canonical Authority and Social Classification"; idem, "The Veda and the Authority of Class"; idem, *Classifying the Universe*, esp. chaps. 2 and 9.
6. This point is emphasized by Wilfred Cantwell Smith in "Scripture as Form and Concept," p. 30; "Some Similarities and Some Differences Between Christianity and Islām," chapter 13 of his *On Understanding Islam: Selected Studies*, Religion and Reason, 19 (The Hague: Mouton, 1981), p. 239.
7. See John 1.1–3,14; cf. Col. 1.15–17.
8. Gal. 1.13–16; Gal. 2.7–9; Rom. 11.13; Rom. 15.15–16.
9. Krister Stendahl has emphasized that Paul's attitude toward the Torah can only be properly understood in the wider context of his mission to the gentiles. Stendahl remarks:

> Paul had not arrived at his view of the Law by testing and pondering its effect upon his conscience; it was his grappling with the question about the place of the Gentiles in the Church and in the plan of God, with the problem Jews/Gentiles or Jewish Christians/Gentile Christians, which had driven him to that interpretation of the Law which was to become his in a unique way.

Krister Stendahl, *Paul Among Jews and Gentiles and Other Essays* (Philadelphia: Fortress Press, 1976), p. 84. A similar view is expressed by Lloyd Gaston in "Paul and the Torah," in *Antisemitism and the Foundations of Christianity*, ed. Alan Davies (New York: Paulist Press, 1979), pp. 48–71; reprinted in his *Paul and the Torah* (Vancouver: University of British Columbia Press, 1987), pp. 15–34.

10. Most of the passages in Paul's letters regarding justification by faith appear in the context of his concern with the larger issue of the relation between Jews and gentiles. Thus, in Rom. 3.28–30 he writes, "For we hold that a man is justified by faith apart from works of law. Or is God the God of Jews only? Is he not the God of Gentiles also? Yes, of Gentiles also, since God is one; and he will justify the circumcised on the ground of their faith and the uncircumcised through their faith." Cf. Gal. 2.14–16; Rom. 1.16–17. Translations of New Testament writings are from May and Metzger, eds., *The New Oxford Annotated Bible with the Apocrypha.*
11. Paul's letters were written to congregations that were predominantly made up of gentiles. See, for example, 1 Thess. 1.9; Gal. 4.8; Gal. 5.2; 1 Cor. 12.2; Phil. 3.2–3; Rom. 1.5–6,13; Rom. 11.13,28; Rom. 15.15–16. His new theology of the law was thus addressed to a gentile audience in order to reassure them that they need not be burdened by the law but would attain salvation directly through Christ. In Rom. 10.4 Paul declares, "For Christ is the end of the law, that every one who has faith may be justified." Through the advent of Christ humankind is liberated from the yoke of the law (Gal. 5.1; Rom. 7.6) and enters into the "new life of the Spirit" under the "law of Christ" (Rom. 7.6; Rom. 8.2; Gal. 6.2; 1 Cor. 9.21). For Paul's extended arguments concerning the relationship of the gentiles to the Jewish people and the Torah, see Galatians 2–5 and Romans 2–11. As discussed in n. 14 below, it is important to emphasize that although Paul did not expect gentile Christians to be bound by the law, there is no indication that he intended Jewish Christians to abandon the Torah. See Gaston, "Paul and the Torah," pp. 55, 65–66.
12. Gal. 2.16; Rom. 3.28.
13. See Rom. 9.6–8; Gal. 4.21–31.
14. Regarding the promise to Abraham, see Galatians 3–4 and Romans 4, 9. In Gal. 3.23–29 Paul writes:

> Now before faith came, we were confined under the law, kept under restraint until faith should be revealed. So that the law was our custodian until Christ came, that we might be justified by faith. But now that faith has come, we are no longer under a custodian; for in Christ Jesus you are all sons of God, through faith. For as many of you as were baptized into Christ have put on Christ. There is neither Jew nor Greek, there is neither slave nor free, there is neither male nor female; for you are all one in Christ Jesus. And if you are Christ's, then you are Abraham's offspring, heirs according to promise.

Paul argues that for gentiles Christ is the fulfillment of the promise given to Abraham concerning all nations, while for Jews Christ is the fulfillment of the Torah given at Mount Sinai. At the same time Paul indicates that the new life in Christ does not mean that the Torah has ceased to have significance for the people of Israel (see Rom. 3.31). Even though Jews and Gentiles become one in Christ (Gal. 3.28; 1 Cor. 12.13), this unity does not obliterate the uniqueness of the Jewish people. Paul asserts in 1 Cor. 7.18,20:

> Was any one at the time of his call already circumcised? Let him not seek to remove the marks of circumcision. Was any one at the time of his call uncircumcised? Let him not seek circumcision. . . . Every one should remain in the state in which he was called.

Jews remain Jews and gentiles remain gentiles, and yet both are transformed and united through their new life in Christ. In Romans 9–11 Paul insists on the continuing significance of the Jewish people even apart from faith in Christ. See W. D. Davies's discussion of Paul's treatment of Israel in Romans in "Paul and the People of Israel," *New Testament Studies* 24, no. 1 (Oct. 1977): 12–39. For recent analyses of Paul's perspectives on the Torah/*nomos*, see Gaston, *Paul and the Torah*; E. P. Sanders, *Paul, the Law, and the Jewish People* (Philadelphia: Fortress Press, 1983); Heikki Räisänen, *Paul and the Law* (Philadelphia: Fortress Press, 1986). See also Peter J. Tomson, *Paul and the Jewish Law: Halakha in the Letters of the Apostle to the Gentiles*, Compendia Rerum Iudaicarum ad Novum Testamentum, Section 3, Jewish Traditions in Early Christian Literature, vol. 1 (Assen, Netherlands: Van Gorcum; Minneapolis: Fortress Press, 1990), who emphasizes the practical—not simply theological—significance of the law in Paul's teaching.

15. 1 Cor. 12.12–13,27; cf. Rom. 12.4–5. In *Carnal Israel* Boyarin argues that the "disembodied universalism" advocated by Paul is contiguous with Hellenistic Jewish conceptions in which the essence of the human being is the soul, which is housed in a body. In rabbinic Judaism, on the other hand, the essence of the human being is the body. While in rabbinic representations the body is the "very site of human significance," in early Christian appropriations of dualist Hellenistic notions the body is devalued along with the counterparts of corporeality that are central to rabbinic traditions: sexuality and procreation, ethnicity, historical memory, and historical interpretations of scripture. Differences in discourses of the body thus became a "key area of cultural contention" between rabbinic Judaism and early Christian traditions, which "manifested itself in several seemingly disparate areas of sociocultural practice, indeed in arenas as seemingly unconnected as gender and marriage practices, methods of interpretation of scripture, and ideologies of ethnicity and history." See *Carnal Israel*, pp. 1–10, 230–235, esp. 6–7.

16. In the Mahāparinibbāna Sutta (D 16.2.24–26), which describes the events surrounding the Buddha's death, Ānanda, his closest disciple, is said to have asked the Buddha to clarify how the *saṃgha* will carry on without his leadership, implying that perhaps he should establish some person or institution as his successor. The Buddha replies:

> [Y]ou should live as islands unto yourselves, being your own refuge, with no one else as your refuge, with the Dhamma as an island, with the Dhamma as your refuge, with no other refuge.

Elsewhere in the same Sutta (D 16.6.1) the Buddha elaborates on this point:

> Ānanda, it may be that you will think: "The Teacher's instruction has ceased, now we have no teacher!" It should not be seen like this, Ānanda, for what I have taught and explained to you as Dhamma and discipline [*vinaya*] will, at my passing, be your teacher.

Translations of the Dīgha-Nikāya are from Maurice Walshe, trans., *Thus Have I Heard: The Long Discourses of the Buddha, Dīgha-Nikāya* (London: Wisdom Publications, 1987).

17. See, for example, Dīgha-Nikāya 13, in which the Buddha is portrayed as deriding the brahmin priests, along with their ancestors, the Vedic *ṛṣis*, "the makers of the mantras, the expounders of the mantras, whose ancient verses are chanted, pronounced and collected by the Brahmins of today" (13.13), for teaching "a path that they do not know or see," like a line of blind men (13.15). "[T]heir threefold knowledge [the Veda] is called the threefold desert, the threefold wilderness, the threefold destruction" (13.36). The brahmins, who are characterized as learned in the three Vedas, bound by the fetters of ignorance, encumbered by wives and wealth, impure, and undisciplined, are contrasted with an *arahant*, a fully enlightened Buddha, who is "endowed with wisdom and conduct," has realized directly the truths of the Dhamma, and "displays the fully-perfected and purified holy life" (13.27–40). See also D 4.

18. In certain passages of the Suttas the Buddha is represented as acknowledging the fourfold division of functions of the *varṇa* system, although he insists that the *khattiyas* (Sanskrit *kṣatriyas*) are superior to the brahmins. At the same time, however, he argues that the nature and destiny of the members of the four classes are determined not by birth but by their actions. Hence a person from any of the four classes can abandon the householder duties and class distinctions of the *varṇa* system, join the *saṃgha*, and become an *arahant*, who has realized the supreme goal of human existence. See, for example, D 27; M 2.147–154; Sn 136. In D 27.31 the Buddha declares:

> [W]hoever of these four castes, as a monk, becomes an Arahant who has destroyed the corruptions, done what had to be done, laid down the burden, attained to the highest goal, completely destroyed the fetter of becoming, and become liberated by the highest insight, he is declared to be chief among them in accordance with Dhamma. . . .

19. D 27.3,9.
20. The Theravāda tradition maintains that the first two sections of the Pali canon, the Vinaya-Piṭaka and the Sutta-Piṭaka, were compiled at the First Council held at Rājagṛha immediately following the Buddha's death. It is clear, however, that the codification of the oral form of the canon was a gradual process that occurred over a period of nearly three hundred years. For a discussion of the formation of the Tipiṭaka, see Étienne Lamotte, *History of Indian Buddhism: From the Origins to the Śaka Era,* trans. Sara Webb-Boin under the supervision of Jean Dantinne (Louvain-la-Neuve: Université Catholique de Louvain, Institut Orientaliste, 1988), pp. 140–191. See also Lamotte's "La critique d'authenticité dans le bouddhisme," in *India Antiqua* (Leiden: E. J. Brill, 1947), pp. 213–222. Among more recent studies, see Steven Collins's illuminating essay on the social context in which the Pali canon emerged, "On the Very Idea of the Pali Canon," *Journal of the Pali Text Society* 15 (1990): 89–126.
21. M 1.133. Cited in Reginald A. Ray, "Buddhism: Sacred Text Written and Realized," in *The Holy Book in Comparative Perspective,* eds. Denny and Taylor, p. 165. For a discussion of early Buddhist perspectives on the relationship between the "letter" of the text (*vyañjana*) and its "meaning" (*artha*), see Étienne Lamotte, "La critique d'interprétation dans le bouddhisme," *Annuaire de l'institut de philologie et d'histoire orientales et slaves* 9 (1949): 344–348.
22. See D 16.2.26, cited in n. 16.
23. Van der Leeuw, *Religion in Essence and Manifestation,* vol. 2, p. 438.
24. The analogy between the Qur'ān and Christ has been emphasized in particular by Wilfred Cantwell Smith, who asserts that "Qur'ān is to Muslims what Christ is to Christians." See Smith, "Scripture as Form and Concept," p. 30; idem, "Some Similarities and Some Differences Between Christianity and Islām," pp. 238–239, 244–245. See also Graham, *Beyond the Written Word,* pp. 87, 121 with n. 3; Frederick M. Denny, "Islam: Qur'an and Hadith," in *The Holy Book in Comparative Perspective,* eds. Denny and Taylor, p. 97.
25. Graham, *Beyond the Written Word,* p. 87. See also Smith, "Scripture as Form and Concept," p. 30: "It is difficult to exaggerate the centrality, and the transcendence, of the Muslim scripture for Muslim faith."
26. For a brief comparison of Muslim conceptions of the Qur'ān with other traditions' notions of scripture, see Graham, *Beyond the Written Word,* pp. 84–88.

27. Arthur Jeffery, in *The Qur'ān as Scripture* (New York: Russell F. Moore, 1952), emphasizes the extent to which Qur'ānic notions of scripture draw upon Jewish and Christian conceptions. He argues that Muhammad took over from his Jewish and Christian contemporaries certain conceptions concerning the nature of scripture, the prophetic office, and the mechanisms of revelation and used them as the basis for his own interpretation of the role of the Qur'ān as scripture. Among the unique elements in the Qur'ānic conception of scripture, Graham has emphasized its "generic idea of scripture," which was "present from the beginning in Islam as part and parcel of the history of prophecy and revelation." See Graham, *Beyond the Written Word*, pp. 81–84, esp. 83. For a general discussion of the nature and role of the Qur'ān, see Denny, "Islam: Qur'an and Hadith."
28. S 32.3; 28.46; 34.44; 35.40; 68.37.
29. S 62.2; cf. 2.151; 3.164; 7.157. For a discussion of the term *ummīyūn* in 62.2 and the title *al-nabī al-ummī* ("the prophet of the unscriptured") in 7.157, see Denny, "Islam: Qur'an and Hadith," pp. 90–91.
30. S 12.2; 43.3; 20.113; 39.28; 41.3; 42.7; 26.195; 16.103; 46.12; 13.37.
31. See Jeffery, *The Qur'ān as Scripture*, pp. 9–17; Geo Widengren, "Holy Book and Holy Tradition in Islam," in *Holy Book and Holy Tradition*, eds. Bruce and Rupp, pp. 210–220; idem, *The Ascension of the Apostle and the Heavenly Book*; idem, *Muḥammad, the Apostle of God, and His Ascension*. For a brief summary of the conceptions of the heavenly book in Near Eastern traditions, see Graham, *Beyond the Written Word*, pp. 50–51, 83–84.
32. See, for example, S 6.59; 10.61; 11.6; 22.70; 27.75; 34.3; 35.11; 57.22; 6.38; 9.36; 50.4.
33. For references that imply that the Qur'ān itself is derived from the archetypal Book (*kitāb*), see S 10.37; 12.1–2; 43.2–3; 56.77–80; 44.2–3. Regarding the *umm al-kitāb* see 43.2–4: "By the Clear Book, behold, We have made it an Arabic Koran; haply you will understand; and behold, it is in the Essence of the Book [*umm al-kitāb*], with Us; sublime indeed, wise." See also 13.39. Translations of Qur'ānic verses are from Arthur J. Arberry, trans., *The Koran Interpreted*, 2 vols. in 1 (New York: Macmillan, 1955).
34. S 85.21–22.
35. For a discussion of passages in the Qur'ān concerning the Torah, Psalms, and Gospel, see Jeffery, *The Qur'ān as Scripture*, pp. 64–67. With the later expansion of Islam into Iran and India, the Avesta of the Zoroastrians and the Veda of the brahmanical Hindus were also recognized as legitimate scriptural revelations.
36. S 3.23; 4.44,51.
37. A number of passages imply that even that which was "sent down" to Muhammad himself was only part of the archetypal Book. See, for

example, S 18.27: "Recite what has been revealed to thee of the Book of thy Lord." See also 29.45; 35.31; cf. 2.231; 17.39.

38. S 13.38.
39. S 10.47. See also 16.36; 35.24; cf. 23.44.
40. S 14.4.
41. S 3.119.
42. S 2.4; 2.136; 3.84; 4.136; 4.162; 5.59; 29.46; 42.15; 2.285.
43. S 2.136. This verse is repeated in 3.84.
44. S 33.40. See also 2.253, which indicates that Allah has preferred some of the apostles over others.
45. See, for example, S 4.47: "You who have been given the Book, believe in what We have sent down, confirming what is with you." See also 2.41,89,91,97; 3.3; 3.81; 5.48; 6.92; 10.37; 35.31; 37.37; 46.12,30; cf. 26.192–197.
46. S 5.19 emphasizes Muhammad's role as the apostle sent by Allah to the People of the Book: "People of the Book, now there has come to you Our Messenger, making things clear to you. . . . Indeed, there has come to you a bearer of good tidings and a warner." A number of passages suggest that Muhammad's role is more specifically to "make clear" to the Jews and Christians those teachings of their scriptures that have been obscured or about which they are in dispute. See, for example, 5.15; 16.44,64; 27.76; 3.23; 74.31.
47. S 3.65–68. See Jeffery, *The Qur'ān as Scripture*, pp. 75–78, for a discussion of the arguments used by the Qur'ān to establish that the Qur'ānic revelation restores the religion of Abraham.
48. In S 2.129 Abraham is represented as praying to Allah to send among the Arabs "a Messenger, one of them, who shall recite to them Thy signs, and teach them the Book and the Wisdom, and purify them." The advent of the Arab prophet Muhammad, to whom "the Book and the Wisdom" are revealed, is interpreted as a direct fulfillment of Abraham's prayer. See, for example, 62.2; 2.151; 3.164; 4.113. The coming of Muhammad is also said to have been foretold in the Torah and in the Gospel (7.157; 61.6).
49. S 9.33; cf. 58.22.
50. My remarks are based primarily on Goody's analysis of written and oral cultures in his *The Interface Between the Written and the Oral*, Studies in Literacy, Family, Culture and the State (Cambridge: Cambridge University Press, 1987).
51. See n. 58 of the introduction.
52. See chapter 1, pp. 97–98.
53. Goody, *The Interface Between the Written and the Oral*, pp. 110–122, esp. 113. See also Walter J. Ong, *Orality and Literacy: The Technologizing of the Word*, New Accents (London: Methuen, 1982), pp. 65–66, who similarly questions whether the Vedas originated from an "absolutely verbatim oral tradition" totally independent of written texts.

54. For a critique of Goody's remarks on the Vedic tradition, see Frits Staal, "The Independence of Rationality from Literacy," *European Journal of Sociology* 30 (1989): 301–310.
55. See the recent collection of essays *Many Rāmāyaṇas: The Diversity of a Narrative Tradition in South Asia,* ed. Paula Richman (Berkeley: University of California Press, 1991).
56. Graham, *Beyond the Written Word,* p. 15. See also Paul Ricoeur, "Speaking and Writing," chapter 2 of his *Interpretation Theory,* pp. 25–44; idem, *Hermeneutics and the Human Sciences: Essays on Language, Action and Interpretation,* ed. and trans. John B. Thompson (Cambridge: Cambridge University Press; Paris: Editions de la Maison des Sciences de l'Homme, 1981), pp. 139–140, 145–149.
57. Jonathan Z. Smith, "What a Difference a Difference Makes," in *"To See Ourselves as Others See Us": Christians, Jews, "Others" in Late Antiquity,* eds. Jacob Neusner and Ernest S. Frerichs (Chico, Calif.: Scholars Press, 1985), pp. 3–48.

ABBREVIATIONS

I. INDOLOGICAL SOURCES

AĀ	Aitareya Āraṇyaka
AB	Aitareya Brāhmaṇa
Agni	Agni Purāṇa
Artha Ś.	Kauṭilīya Artha-Śāstra
AU	Aitareya Upaniṣad
AV	Atharva-Veda Saṃhitā
BĀU	Bṛhadāraṇyaka Upaniṣad
BP	Bhāgavata Purāṇa
Brahm.	Brahmāṇḍa Purāṇa
BSB	Brahma-Sūtra Bhāṣya
CU	Chāndogya Upaniṣad
Dakṣa	Dakṣa-Smṛti
Devī	Devī-Bhāgavata Purāṇa
Hariv.	Harivaṃśa
JB	Jaiminīya Brāhmaṇa
JUB	Jaiminīya Upaniṣad Brāhmaṇa
Kaṭha	Kaṭha Upaniṣad
Kāṭh. GS	Kāṭhaka Gṛhya-Sūtra
KB	Kauṣītaki Brāhmaṇa
KP	Kūrma Purāṇa
KU	Kauṣītaki Upaniṣad
LP	Liṅga Purāṇa
Maitri	Maitri Upaniṣad
Māṇḍ.	Māṇḍūkya Upaniṣad
Mān. GS	Mānava Gṛhya-Sūtra
Mārk.	Mārkaṇḍeya Purāṇa
Mbh.	Mahābhārata
MP	Matsya Purāṇa
MS	Manu-Smṛti
MU	Muṇḍaka Upaniṣad
Nār.	Nārada Purāṇa
Nār. Śi.	Nāradīya Śikṣā
Nir.	Nirukta
NS	Nyāya-Sūtras
Padma	Padma Purāṇa

Pāṇ. Śi.	Pāṇinīya Śikṣā
PB	Pañcaviṃśa Brāhmaṇa
PMS	Pūrva-Mīmāṃsā-Sūtras
Praśna	Praśna Upaniṣad
Rām.	Rāmāyaṇa
ṚV	Ṛg-Veda Saṃhitā
ŚĀ	Śāṅkhāyana Āraṇyaka
Ṣaḍv. B.	Ṣaḍviṃśa Brāhmaṇa
Śāṅkh. ŚS	Śāṅkhāyana Śrauta-Sūtra
ŚB	Śatapatha Brāhmaṇa
ŚBh.	Śābara Bhāṣya
Skanda	Skanda Purāṇa
ŚP	Śiva Purāṇa
SPS	Sāṃkhya-Pravacana-Sūtras
ŚU	Śvetāśvatara Upaniṣad
ŚV	Ślokavārttika
TB	Taittirīya Brāhmaṇa
TS	Taittirīya Saṃhitā
TU	Taittirīya Upaniṣad
TV	Tantravārttika
Uśanas	Uśanas-Smṛti
Vaikh. DS	Vaikhānasa Dharma-Sūtra
Vaiś.	Vaiśeṣika-Sūtras
Vām.	Vāmana Purāṇa
Vār. GS	Vāraha Gṛhya-Sūtra
Vāyu	Vāyu Purāṇa
VP	Viṣṇu Purāṇa
VS	Vājasaneyi Saṃhitā
Yājñ.	Yājñavalkya-Smṛti
Yājñ. Śi.	Yājñavalkya Śikṣā

II. BIBLICAL AND JUDAIC SOURCES

Hebrew Bible

References to the Hebrew Bible generally follow the standard abbreviations.

Tractates of the Mishnah, Jerusalem Talmud, or Babylonian Talmud

'Ab.	'Āḇôṯ
ʿAZ	ʿĂḇôḏāh Zārāh
BB	Bāḇā' Baṯrā'
Ber.	Bᵉrāḵôṯ
Beṣ.	Bêṣāh
BM	Bāḇā' Mᵉṣîʿā'
ʿErub.	ʿÊrûḇîn
Giṭ.	Gîṭṭîn
Ḥag.	Ḥăḡîḡāh
Hor.	Hôrāyôṯ
Ket.	Kᵉṯûbôṯ
Mak.	Makkôṯ
Meg.	Mᵉḡillāh
Men.	Mᵉnāḥôṯ
MQ	Môʿēḏ Qāṭān
Ned.	Nᵉḏārîm
'Ohol.	'Ohŏlôṯ
Pes.	Pᵉsāḥîm
Qid.	Qîddûšîn
RH	Rō'š ha-Šānāh
Šab.	Šabbāṯ
Sanh.	Sanhedrîn
Šeb.	Šᵉḇûʿôṯ
Šeq.	Šᵉqālîm
Soṭ.	Sôṭāh
Suk.	Sûkkāh
Taan.	Taʿănîṯ
Tem.	Tᵉmûrāh
Yeb.	Yᵉḇāmôṯ
Yoma	Yômā'
Zeb.	Zᵉḇāḥîm

References to the Tosefta and Jerusalem Talmud are prefixed by T and JT, respectively.

Midrashic Collections

Deut. R.	Deuteronomy Rabbāh
Esth. R.	Esther Rabbāh
Exod. R.	Exodus Rabbāh
Gen. R.	Genesis Rabbāh
Lam. R.	Lamentations Rabbāh
Lev. R.	Leviticus Rabbāh
Mek.	Mᵉk̲îltā' dᵉ-R. Ishmael
Num. R.	Numbers Rabbāh
Pes. K.	Pᵉsîqtā' dᵉ-R. Kahana
Pes. R.	Pᵉsîqtā' Rabbāṯî
PRE	Pirqê dᵉ-R. Eliezer
Ruth R.	Ruth Rabbāh
Sip̄rê Deut.	Sip̄rê on Deuteronomy
Sip̄rê Num.	Sip̄rê on Numbers
Song R.	Song of Songs Rabbāh
Tanḥ.	Tanḥûmā'

Other

BS	Ben Sira
Ebr.	De Ebrietate (Philo)
Mos.	De Vita Mosis (Philo)
Op.	De Opificio Mundi (Philo)
Wis.	Wisdom of Solomon

III. OTHER SOURCES

New Testament

All references to the New Testament follow the standard abbreviations.

Pali Canon

D	Dīgha-Nikāya
M	Majjhima-Nikāya
Sn	Sutta-Nipāta

Qur'ān

S	Sūrah

NOTE ON TRANSLATION AND TRANSLITERATION

The translations of all Sanskrit passages are my own. For editions of Sanskrit texts cited, please refer to the bibliography. The transliteration of Sanskrit terms generally follows the scientific system adopted by the *Journal of the American Oriental Society*.

The translations of passages from rabbinic texts are my own. With respect to biblical verses, my translations generally follow the standard translation, Herbert G. May and Bruce M. Metzger, eds., *The New Oxford Annotated Bible with the Apocrypha. Revised Standard Version* (New York: Oxford University Press, 1977). However, I have at times rendered the verse to accord with the Midrashist's interpretation. The translations of passages from the Zohar, unless otherwise indicated, are cited either from Isaiah Tishby and Fischel Lachower, eds., *The Wisdom of the Zohar: An Anthology of Texts*, trans. David Goldstein, 3 vols. (Oxford: Oxford University Press, 1989), or from Harry Sperling, Maurice Simon, and Paul P. Levertoff, trans., *The Zohar*, 2d ed., 5 vols. (London: Soncino Press, 1984). In the case of the Zohar and other medieval kabbalistic texts in which I have cited the translations of other scholars, I have consulted the original text myself, with the exception of several manuscripts that were not available to me. For editions of Hebrew and Aramaic texts, please refer to the bibliography.

The transliteration of Hebrew terms generally follows the scientific system adopted by the *Journal of Biblical Literature*, with two exceptions: (1) spirantized *b^eḡaḏk^ep̄aṯ* letters have been marked; and (2) a hyphen has been inserted after the definite article *ha-* (with consequent loss of doubling), the prepositions *b^e-*, *l^e-*, and *k^e-*, and the conjunction *w^e-*, in order to facilitate reading by the nonspecialist. In the case of well-known Hebrew terms (for example, Shekhinah, Kabbalah) and texts (for example, Torah, Mishnah, Talmud), the common conventional spelling has been retained. The rendering of names of rabbis (for example, Akiba, Joḥanan) and kabbalistic scholars (for example, Azriel b. Menaḥem, Moses Cordovero) also follows conventional usage wherever possible, although it is sometimes difficult to determine what constitutes the most common convention with respect to proper names.

I have used male pronouns deliberately throughout most of the sections of this study, since the textual communities that are the primary focus of the study—the Brahmanical custodians of the Veda and the rabbinic custodians of the Torah—were exclusively male traditions in the periods with which I am concerned.

SELECTED BIBLIOGRAPHY

I. INDOLOGICAL SOURCES

A. Editions and Translations of Sanskrit and Pali Sources

Saṃhitās

Atharva-Veda Saṃhitā.

Bandhu, Vishva, et al., eds. 5 vols. Vishveshvaranand Indological Series, 13–17. Hoshiarpur: Vishveshvaranand Vedic Research Institute, 1960–1964.

Translations:

Whitney, William Dwight, trans. *Atharva-Veda Saṁhitā.* Revised and edited by Charles Rockwell Lanman. 2 vols. Harvard Oriental Series, vols. 7–8. Cambridge: Harvard University Press, 1905.

Bloomfield, Maurice, trans. *Hymns of the Atharva-Veda, Together with Extracts from the Ritual Books and the Commentaries.* Sacred Books of the East, vol. 42. Oxford: Clarendon Press, 1897.

Ṛg-Veda Saṃhitā.

Müller, F. Max, ed. 2d ed. 4 vols. London: Oxford University Press, 1890–1892.

Translations:

Geldner, Karl Friedrich, trans. *Der Rig-Veda.* 4 vols. Harvard Oriental Series, vols. 33–36. Cambridge: Harvard University Press, 1951–1957.

Griffith, Ralph T. H., trans. *The Hymns of the Rigveda*. 2d ed. 2 vols. Benares: E. J. Lazarus, 1896–1897.

O'Flaherty, Wendy Doniger, trans. *The Rig Veda: An Anthology*. Harmondsworth, Middlesex, England: Penguin Books, 1981. [Anthology]

Taittirīya Saṃhitā.

Röer, E. (vol. 1), E. B. Cowell (vols. 1–2), Maheśachandra Nyāyaratna (vols. 3–5), and Satyavrata Sāmaśramī (vol. 6), eds. 6 vols. Bibliotheca Indica, no. 26. Calcutta: Asiatic Society of Bengal, 1860–1899.

Translation:

Keith, Arthur Berriedale, trans. *The Veda of the Black Yajus School Entitled Taittiriya Sanhita*. 2 vols. Harvard Oriental Series, vols. 18–19. Cambridge: Harvard University Press, 1914.

Vājasaneyi Saṃhitā.

Weber, Albrecht, ed. Berlin: Ferd. Dümmler; London: Williams and Norgate, 1852.

Translation:

Griffith, Ralph T. H., trans. *The Texts of the White Yajur-Veda*. Benares: E. J. Lazarus, 1899.

Brāhmaṇas, Āraṇyakas, Upaniṣads, and Vedāṅgas

Aitareya Āraṇyaka.

Keith, Arthur Berriedale, ed. Anecdota Oxoniensia, Aryan Series, pt. 9. Oxford: Clarendon Press, 1909.

Translation:

Keith, Arthur Berriedale, ed. and trans. *Aitareya Āraṇyaka*. Anecdota Oxoniensia, Aryan Series, pt. 9. Oxford: Clarendon Press, 1909.

Aitareya Brāhmaṇa.

Sāmaśramī, Satyavrata, ed. 4 vols. Bibliotheca Indica, no. 134. Calcutta: Asiatic Society of Bengal, 1895–1906.

Translation:

Keith, Arthur Berriedale, trans. *Rigveda Brāhmaṇas: The Aitareya and Kauṣītaki Brāhmaṇas of the Rigveda*. Harvard Oriental Series, vol. 25. Cambridge: Harvard University Press, 1920.

Jaiminīya Brāhmaṇa.

Vira, Raghu, and Lokesh Chandra, eds. Sarasvati-Vihara Series, vol. 31. Nagpur: International Academy of Indian Culture, 1954.

Translations:

Bodewitz, H. W., trans. *Jaiminīya Brāhmaṇa I, 1–65*. Orientalia Rheno-Traiectina, vol. 17. Leiden: E. J. Brill, 1973.

______, trans. *The Jyotiṣṭoma Ritual: Jaiminīya Brāhmaṇa I, 66–364*. Orientalia Rheno-Traiectina, vol. 34. Leiden: E. J. Brill, 1990.

Jaiminīya Upaniṣad Brāhmaṇa.

Oertel, Hanns, ed. *Journal of the American Oriental Society* 16, no. 1 (1894): 79–260.

Translation:

Oertal, Hanns, ed. and trans. *The Jāiminīya or Talavakāra Upaniṣad Brāhmaṇa. Journal of the American Oriental Society* 16, no. 1 (1894): 79–260.

Kauṣītaki Brāhmaṇa (Śāṅkhāyana Brāhmaṇa).

Bhattacharya, Harinarayan, ed. Calcutta Sanskrit College Research Series, no. 73. Calcutta: Sanskrit College, 1970.

Translation:

Keith, Arthur Berriedale, trans. *Rigveda Brāhmaṇas: The Aitareya and Kauṣītaki Brāhmaṇas of the Rigveda.* Harvard Oriental Series, vol. 25. Cambridge: Harvard University Press, 1920.

Nāradīya Śikṣā.

Bhise, Usha R., ed. Bhandarkar Oriental Research Institute, Research Unit Series, no. 8. Poona: Bhandarkar Oriental Research Institute, 1986.

Translation:

Bhise, Usha R., ed. and trans. *Nāradīya Śikṣā, with the Commentary of Bhaṭṭa Śobhākara.* Bhandarkar Oriental Research Institute, Research Unit Series, no. 8. Poona: Bhandarkar Oriental Research Institute, 1986.

Nirukta of Yāska.

Sarup, Lakshman, ed. 1920–1927. Reprint. Delhi: Motilal Banarsidass, 1967.

Translation:

Sarup, Lakshman, ed. and trans. *The Nighaṇṭu and the Nirukta: The Oldest Indian Treatise on Etymology, Philology, and Semantics.* 1920–1927. Reprint. Delhi: Motilal Banarsidass, 1967.

Pañcaviṃśa Brāhmaṇa (Tāṇḍya Brāhmaṇa).

Vedāntavāgīśa, Ānandachandra, ed. 2 vols. Bibliotheca Indica, no. 62. Calcutta: Asiatic Society of Bengal, 1870–1874.

Translation:

Caland, W., trans. *Pañcaviṃśa-Brāhmaṇa: The Brāhmaṇa of Twenty Five Chapters*. Bibliotheca India, no. 255. Calcutta: Asiatic Society of Bengal, 1931.

Pāṇinīya Śikṣā.

Ghosh, Manmohan, ed. 2d ed. Delhi: Asian Humanities Press, 1986.

Translation:

Ghosh, Manmohan, ed. and trans. *Pāṇinīya Śikṣā, or the Śikṣā Vedāṅga Ascribed to Pāṇini*. 2d ed. Delhi: Asian Humanities Press, 1986.

Ṣaḍviṃśa Brāhmaṇa.

Sharma, Bellikoth Ramachandra, ed. Kendriya Sanskrit Vidyapeetha Series, 9. Tirupati: Kendriya Sanskrit Vidyapeetha, 1967.

Translation:

Bollée, W. B., trans. *Ṣaḍviṃśa Brāhmaṇa*. Utrecht: Drukkerij A. Storm, 1956.

Śāṅkhāyana Āraṇyaka.

Pāṭhaka, Śrīdhara Śāstrī, ed. Ānandāśrama Sanskrit Series, no. 90. Poona: Ānandāśrama Press, 1922.

Translation:

Keith, Arthur Berriedale, trans. *The Śāṅkhāyana Āraṇyaka, with an Appendix on the Mahāvrata*. Oriental Translation Fund, n.s., vol. 18. London: Royal Asiatic Society, 1908.

Śatapatha Brāhmaṇa.

Weber, Albrecht, ed. 1855. 2d ed. (reprint). Chowkhamba Sanskrit Series, no. 96. Varanasi: Chowkhamba Sanskrit Series Office, 1964.

Translation:

Eggeling, Julius, trans. *The Śatapatha-Brâhmaṇa according to the Text of the Mâdhyandina School*. 5 vols. Sacred Books of the East, vols. 12, 26, 41, 43, 44. Oxford: Clarendon Press, 1882–1900.

Taittirīya Brāhmaṇa.

Goḍabole, Nārāyaṇa Śāstrī, ed. 3 vols. Ānandāśrama Sanskrit Series, no. 37. 1898. Reprint. Poona: Ānandāśrama Press, 1979.

Translation:

Dumont, Paul-Emile, trans. In *Proceedings of the American Philosophical Society* 92, no. 6 (Dec. 1948): 447–503; 95, no. 6 (Dec. 1951): 628–675; 98, no. 3 (June 1954): 204–223; 101, no. 2 (Apr. 1957): 216–243; 106, no. 3 (June 1962): 246–263; 107, no. 2 (Apr. 1963): 177–182; 107, no. 5 (Oct. 1963): 446–460; 108, no. 4 (Aug. 1964): 337–353; 109, no. 6 (Dec. 1965): 309–341; 113, no. 1 (Feb. 1969): 34–66. [Partial Translation]

Upaniṣads.

Limaye, V. P., and R. D. Vadekar, eds. *Eighteen Principal Upaniṣads*, vol. 1. Poona: Vaidika Saṁśodhana Maṇḍala, 1958.

Translation:

Hume, Robert Ernest, trans. *The Thirteen Principal Upanishads*. 2d ed., rev. Oxford: Oxford University Press, 1931.

Dharma-Śāstras, Epics, and Purāṇas

Agni Purāṇa.

Ānandāśrama Sanskrit Series, no. 41. Poona: Ānandāśrama Press, 1900.

Translation:

Gangadharan, N., trans. *The Agni Purāṇa*. 4 vols. Ancient Indian Tradition and Mythology, vols. 27–30. Delhi: Motilal Banarsidass, 1984–1987.

Bhāgavata Purāṇa.

Shastri, J. L., ed. Delhi: Motilal Banarsidass, 1983.

Translations:

Tagare, Ganesh Vasudeo, trans. *The Bhāgavata Purāṇa*. 5 vols. Ancient Indian Tradition and Mythology, vols. 7–11. Delhi: Motilal Banarsidass, 1976–1978.

Goswami, C. L., trans. *Srīmad Bhāgavata Mahāpurāṇa*. 2 vols. Gorakhpur: Gita Press, 1971.

Brahmāṇḍa Purāṇa.

Shastri, J. L, ed. Delhi: Motilal Banarsidass, 1973.

Translation:

Tagare, Ganesh Vasudeo, trans. *The Brahmāṇḍa Purāṇa.* 5 vols. Ancient Indian Tradition and Mythology, vols. 22–26. Delhi: Motilal Banarsidass, 1983–1984.

Devī-Bhāgavata Purāṇa.

Bombay: Veṅkaṭeśvara Press, 1919.

Translation:

Vijnanananda, Swami, alias Hari Prasanna Chatterji, trans. *The Sri Mad Devi Bhagavatam.* Sacred Books of the Hindus, vol. 26, pts. 1–4. 1921–1923. Reprint. New York: AMS Press, 1974.

Harivaṃśa.

Vaidya, P. L., ed. 2 vols. Poona: Bhandarkar Oriental Institute, 1969–1971. [critical edition]

Calcutta: Asiatic Society of Bengal, 1839. [Calcutta edition]

Translation:

Langlois, M. A., trans. *Harivansa, ou histoire de la famille de Hari.* 2 vols. Paris: Oriental Translation Fund of Great Britain and Ireland, 1834–1835.

Kūrma Purāṇa.

Gupta, Anand Swarup, ed. Varanasi: All-India Kashi Raj Trust, 1972.

Translations:

Bhattacharya, Ahibhushan, and Satkari Mukherji, et al., trans. *The Kūrma Purāṇa.* Edited by Anand Swarup Gupta. Varanasi: All-India Kashi Raj Trust, 1972.

Tagare, Ganesh Vasudeo, trans. *The Kūrma-Purāṇa*. 2 vols. Ancient Indian Tradition and Mythology, vols. 20–21. Delhi: Motilal Banarsidass, 1981–1982.

Liṅga Purāṇa.

Shastri, J. L., ed. 1980. Reprint. Delhi: Motilal Banarsidass, 1985.

Translation:

A Board of Scholars, trans. *The Liṅga-Purāṇa*. 2 vols. Ancient Indian Tradition and Mythology, vols. 5–6. Delhi: Motilal Banarsidass, 1973.

Mahābhārata.

Sukthankar, Vishnu S., S. K. Belvalkar, and P. L. Vaidya, eds. 19 vols. and 6 vols. of indexes. Poona: Bhandarkar Oriental Research Institute, 1933–1972. [critical edition]

5 vols. Calcutta: Education Committee's Press (vol. 1); Asiatic Society of Bengal (vols. 2–5), 1834–1839. [Calcutta edition]

Translations:

Buitenen, J. A. B. van, trans. and ed. *The Mahābhārata*. 3 vols. Chicago: University of Chicago Press, 1973–1978. [Books I–V]

[Ganguli, Kisari Mohan, trans.] *The Mahabharata of Krishna-Dwaipayana Vyasa*. Published and distributed by Pratap Chandra Roy. 2d ed. 12 vols. Calcutta: Oriental Publishing, [n.d.].

Manu-Smṛti.

Dave, Jayantakrishna Harikrishna, ed. 6 vols. Bhāratīya Vidyā Series, vols. 29, 33, 37–40. Bombay: Bharatiya Vidya Bhavan, 1972–1985.

Translations:

Bühler, Georg, trans. *The Laws of Manu.* Sacred Books of the East, vol. 25. 1886. Reprint. New York: Dover, 1969.

Doniger, Wendy, with Brian K. Smith, trans. *The Laws of Manu.* New York: Penguin Books, 1991.

Mārkaṇḍeya Purāṇa.

Banerjea, K. M., ed. Bibliotheca Indica, no. 29. Calcutta: Asiatic Society of Bengal, 1862.

Translation:

Pargiter, F. Eden, trans. *The Mārkaṇḍeya Purāṇa.* Bibliotheca Indica, no. 125. Calcutta: Asiatic Society of Bengal, 1904.

Matsya Purāṇa.

Ānandāśrama Sanskrit Series, no. 54. Poona: Ānandāśrama Press, 1907.

Translation:

A Taluqdar of Oudh, trans. *The Matsya Puranam.* 2 vols. Sacred Books of the Hindus, vol. 17, pts. 1–2. Allahabad: Pâṇini Office, 1916–1917.

Nārada Purāṇa.

Bombay: Veṅkaṭeśvara Press, 1923. Reprint. Delhi: Nag Publishers, 1984.

Translation:

Tagare, Ganesh Vasudeo, and Hemendra Nath Chakravorty, trans. *The Nārada-Purāṇa.* 5 vols. Ancient Indian Tradition and

Mythology, vols. 15–19. Delhi: Motilal Banarsidass, 1980–1982.

Padma Purāṇa.

Maṇḍalīka, Viśvanātha Nārāyaṇa, ed. 4 vols. in 3. Ānandāśrama Sanskrit Series, suppl. no. 1. Poona: Ānandāśrama Press, 1893–1894.

Translation:

Deshpande, N. A., trans. *The Padma-Purāṇa.* 5 vols. Ancient Indian Tradition and Mythology, vols. 39–43. Delhi: Motilal Banarsidass, 1988–1990. [in progress]

Rāmāyaṇa of Vālmīki.

Bhatt, G. H., and U. P. Shah, eds. 7 vols. Baroda: Oriental Institute, 1960–1975.

Translations:

Robert P. Goldman, ed. *The Rāmāyaṇa of Vālmīki: An Epic of Ancient India.* Princeton Library of Asian Translations. Princeton: Princeton University Press, 1984–. [in progress]

Shastri, Hari Prasad, trans. *The Ramayana of Valmiki.* 3d ed. 3 vols. London: Shanti Sadan, 1976. [condensation of central narrative]

Śiva Purāṇa.

2 vols. Bombay: Veṅkaṭeśvara Press, 1906.

Translation:

A Board of Scholars, trans. *The Śiva-Purāṇa.* 4 vols. Ancient Indian Tradition and Mythology, vols. 1–4. Delhi: Motilal Banarsidass, 1969–1970.

Skanda Purāṇa.

7 vols. Bombay: Veṅkaṭeśvara Press, 1908–1910.

Vāmana Purāṇa.

Gupta, Anand Swarup, ed. Varanasi: All India Kashiraj Trust, 1968.

Translation:

Mukhopadhyaya, Satyamsu Mohan, and Ahibhushan Bhattacharya, et al., trans. *The Vāmana Purāṇa.* Edited by Anand Swarup Gupta. Varanasi: All India Kashiraj Trust, 1968.

Vāyu Purāṇa.

Ānandāśrama Sanskrit Series, no. 49. 1905. Reprint. Poona: Ānandāśrama Press, 1983.

Translation:

Tagare, G. V., trans. *The Vāyu Purāṇa.* 2 vols. Ancient Indian Tradition and Mythology, vols. 37–38. Delhi: Motilal Banarsidass, 1987–1988.

Viṣṇu Purāṇa.

Vidyasagara, Jibananda, ed. Calcutta: Saraswati Press, 1882.

Translation:

Wilson, H. H., trans. *The Vishńu Puráńa: A System of Hindu Mythology and Tradition.* 3d ed. Calcutta: Punthi Pustak, 1961.

Darśanas

Brahma-Sūtra Bhāṣya of Śaṃkara.

Āchārya, Nārāyan Rām, ed. 3d ed. Bombay: Nirṇaya Sāgar Press, 1948.

Translation:

Thibaut, George, trans. *The Vedânta-Sûtras with the Commentary by Śaṅkarâcârya*. 2 vols. Sacred Books of the East, vols. 34, 38. Oxford: Clarendon Press, 1890–1896.

Śābara-Bhāṣya of Śabara.

In *Mīmāṃsādarśana*. 6 vols. Ānandāśrama Sanskrit Series, no. 97. Poona: Ānandāśrama Press, 1929–1934.

Translation:

Jha, Ganganatha, trans. *Śābara-Bhāṣya*. 1933–1936. 2d ed. (reprint). 3 vols. Gaekwad's Oriental Series, nos. 66, 70, 73. Baroda: Oriental Institute, 1973–1974.

Ślokavārttika of Kumārila Bhaṭṭa.

Śāstrī, Dvārikādāsa, ed. Prācyabhārati Series, 10. Varanasi: Tara Publications, 1978.

Translation:

Jhā, Gaṅgānātha, trans. *Çlokavārttika*. Bibliotheca Indica, no. 146. Calcutta: Asiatic Society of Bengal, 1907.

Tantravārttika of Kumārila Bhaṭṭa.

In *Mīmāṃsādarśana*, vols. 1–3. Ānandāśrama Sanskrit Series, no. 97. Poona: Ānandāśrama Press, 1929–1931.

Translation:

Jhā, Gaṅgānātha, trans. *Tantravārttika*. 2 vols. Bibliotheca Indica, no. 161. Calcutta: Asiatic Society of Bengal, 1924.

Pali Canon

Dīgha-Nikāya.

Walshe, Maurice, trans. *Thus Have I Heard: The Long Discourses of the Buddha, Dīgha-Nikāya.* London: Wisdom Publications, 1987.

Majjhima-Nikāya.

Horner, I. B., trans. *The Collection of the Middle Length Sayings (Majjhima-Nikāya).* 3 vols. Pali Text Society, Translation Series, nos. 29–31. London: Pali Text Society, 1954–1959.

Sutta-Nipāta.

Norman, K. R., trans., with alternative translations by I. B. Horner and Walpola Rahula. *The Group of Discourses (Sutta-Nipāta).* Pali Text Society, Translation Series, no. 44. London: Pali Text Society, 1984.

B. Secondary Sources

Abegg, Emil. "Die Lehre von der Ewigkeit des Wortes bei Kumārila." In *ANTIDWPON. Festschrift Jacob Wackernagel.* Göttingen: Vandenhoeck and Ruprecht, 1923, pp. 255–264.

Abhyankar, K. V., and G. V. Devasthali, comp. and ed. *Veda-vikṛtilakṣaṇa-Saṁgraha: A Collection of Twelve Tracts on Vedavikṛtis and Allied Topics.* Research Unit Publications, no. 5. Poona: Bhandarkar Oriental Research Institute, 1978.

Allen, W. Sidney. *Phonetics in Ancient India.* London Oriental Series, vol. 1. 1953. Reprint. London: Oxford University Press, 1965.

Alper, Harvey P., ed. *Understanding Mantras.* SUNY Series in Religious Studies. Albany: State University of New York Press, 1989.

Apte, V. M. "The 'Spoken Word' in Sanskrit Literature." *Bulletin of the Deccan College Research Institute* 4, no. 4 (June 1943): 269–280.

Bailey, Greg. *The Mythology of Brahmā.* Delhi: Oxford University Press, 1983.

Ballantyne, Dr. "The Eternity of Sound: A Dogma of the Mímánsá." *The Pandit* (Benares) 1, no. 5 (1866): 68–71, 86–88.

Banerjee, Santi. "Prajāpati in the Brāhmaṇas." *Vishveshvaranand Indological Journal* 19, pts. 1–2 (June–Dec. 1981): 14–19.

Basham, A. L. *The Wonder That Was India: A Survey of the History and Culture of the Indian Sub-continent before the Coming of the Muslims.* 3d. rev. ed. London: Sidgwick and Jackson, 1967.

Bhandarkar, Ramkrishna Gopal. "The Veda in India." *The Indian Antiquary* 3 (May 1874): 132–135.

Bhattacharji, Sukumari. "Rise of Prajāpati in the Brāhmaṇas." *Annals of the Bhandarkar Oriental Research Institute* 64 (1983): 205–213.

Bhattacharya, Dipak. "Cosmogony and Rituo-Philosophical Integrity in the *Atharvaveda.*" *Vishveshvaranand Indological Journal* 15, pt. 1 (March 1977): 1–12.

Bhattacharya, Gopika Mohan. "A Study on the Eternity of Sound." *Calcutta Review* 142, no. 1 (Jan. 1957): 61–71.

Bhattacharyya, Narendra Nath. *History of Indian Cosmogonical Ideas.* New Delhi: Munshiram Manoharlal, 1971.

Biardeau, Madeleine. *Études de Mythologie Hindoue.* Vol. 1, *Cosmogonies purāṇiques.* Publications de l'École Française d'Extrême Orient, vol. 128. Paris: École Française d'Extrême Orient, 1981.

———. *Théorie de la connaissance et philosophie de la parole dans le brahmanisme classique.* Le monde d'outre-mer passé et présent, ser. 1, Études 23. Paris: Mouton, 1964.

Bilimoria, Puruṣottama. "On the Idea of Authorless Revelation (Apauruṣeya)." In *Indian Philosophy of Religion,* edited by Roy W. Perrett. Dordrecht: Kluwer Academic Publishers, 1989, pp. 143–166.

———. *Śabdapramāṇa: Word and Knowledge. A Doctrine in Mīmāṃsā-Nyāya Philosophy (with reference to Advaita Vedānta-paribhāṣā 'Agama')—Towards a Framework for Śruti-prāmāṇya.* Studies of Classical India, vol. 10. Dordrecht: Kluwer Academic Publishers, 1988.

———. "Sruti and Apauruseya: An Approach to Religious Scriptures and Revelation." *Journal of Dharma* 7, no. 3 (July–Sept. 1982): 275–291.

Bloomfield, Maurice. *The Religion of the Veda: The Ancient Religion of India.* American Lectures on the History of Religions, 7th Series. New York: G. P. Putnam's Sons, 1908.

Bonazzoli, Giorgio. "Composition, Transmission and Recitation of the Purāṇa-s." *Purāṇa* 25, no. 2 (July 1983): 254–280.

———. "The Dynamic Canon of the Purāṇa-s." *Purāṇa* 21, no. 2 (July 1979): 116–166.

Bose, Nirmal Kumar. "Caste in India." *Man in India* 31, nos. 3–4 (July–Dec. 1951): 107–123.

Botto, Oscar. "Letterature antiche dell'India." In *Storia delle Letterature d'Oriente,* edited by Oscar Botto, vol. 3. Milan: Casa Editrice Dr. Francesco Vallardi, Società Editrice Libraria, 1969, pp. 5–350.

Brough, John. "Some Indian Theories of Meaning." *Transactions of the Philological Society* (1953): 161–176.

———. "Theories of General Linguistics in the Sanskrit Grammarians." *Transactions of the Philological Society* (1951): 27–46.

Brown, Cheever Mackenzie. *God as Mother: A Feminine Theology in India. An Historical and Theological Study of the Brahmavaivarta Purāṇa*. Hartford, Vt.: Claude Stark, 1974.

———. "Purāṇa as Scripture: From Sound to Image of the Holy Word in the Hindu Tradition." *History of Religions* 26, no. 1 (Aug. 1986): 68–86.

———. *The Triumph of the Goddess: The Canonical Models and Theological Visions of the Devī-Bhāgavata Purāṇa*. SUNY Series in Hindu Studies. Albany: State University of New York Press, 1990.

Brown, W. Norman. "The Creation Myth of the Rig Veda." *Journal of the American Oriental Society* 62, no. 2 (June 1942): 85–98. Reprinted in his *India and Indology: Selected Articles*, pp. 20–33.

———. "The Creative Role of the Goddess Vāc in the Rig Veda." In *Pratidānam: Indian, Iranian and Indo-European Studies Presented to Franciscus Bernardus Jaccobus Kuiper on His Sixtieth Birthday*, edited by J. C. Heesterman, G. H. Schokker, and V. I. Subramoniam. Janua linguarum, Series maior, 34. The Hague: Mouton, 1968, pp. 393–397. Reprinted in his *India and Indology: Selected Articles*, pp. 75–78.

———. *India and Indology: Selected Articles*, edited by Rosane Rocher. Delhi: Motilal Banarsidass, 1978.

———. "The Sources and Nature of *puruṣa* in the Puruṣasūkta (Rigveda 10.90)." *Journal of the American Oriental Society* 51, no. 2 (June 1931): 108–118. Reprinted in his *India and Indology: Selected Articles*, pp. 5–10.

———. "Theories of Creation in the Rig Veda." *Journal of the American Oriental Society* 85, no. 1 (Jan.–March 1965): 23–34. Reprinted in his *India and Indology: Selected Articles*, pp. 40–52.

Buitenen, J. A. B. van. "Hindu Sacred Literature." *The New Encyclopedia Britannica: Macropaedia*. 15th ed. Chicago: Helen Hemingway Benton, 1974. S.v.

Caland, W. "De Ontdekkingsgeschiedenis van den Veda." *Verslagen en Mededeelingen der Koninklijke Akademie van Wetenschappen.* Afdeeling Letterkunde. Ser. 5, vol. 3 (1918): 261–334.

Carpenter, David. "Bhartṛhari and the Veda." In *Texts in Context: Traditional Hermeneutics in South Asia,* edited by Jeffrey R. Timm. Albany: State University of New York Press, 1992, pp. 17–32.

———. "Language, Ritual, and Society: Reflections on the Authority of the Veda in India." *Journal of the American Academy of Religion* 60, no. 1 (Spring 1992): 57–77.

———. "The Mastery of Speech: Canonicity and Control in the Vedas." In *Authority, Anxiety, and Canon: Essays in Vedic Interpretation,* edited by Laurie L. Patton. SUNY Series in Hindu Studies. Albany: State University of New York Press, 1994, pp. 19–34.

Chakravarti, Prabhat Chandra. *The Linguistic Speculations of the Hindus.* Calcutta: University of Calcutta, 1933.

———. *The Philosophy of Sanskrit Grammar.* Calcutta: University of Calcutta, 1930.

Chemparathy, George. *L'autorité du Veda selon les Nyāya-Vaiśeṣikas.* Louvain-la-Neuve: Centre d'Histoire des Religions, 1983.

———. "The Veda as Revelation." *Journal of Dharma* 7, no. 3 (July–Sept. 1982): 253–274.

Clooney, Francis X. "Binding the Text: Vedānta as Philosophy and Commentary." In *Texts in Context: Traditional Hermeneutics in South Asia,* edited by Jeffrey R. Timm. Albany: State University of New York Press, 1992, pp. 47–68.

———. *Thinking Ritually: Rediscovering the Pūrva Mīmāṃsā of Jaimini.* Publications of the De Nobili Research Library, vol. 17. Vienna: Institut für Indologie der Universität Wien, 1990.

———. "Vedānta, Commentary, and the Theological Component of Cross-Cultural Study." In *Myth and Philosophy,* edited by

Frank Reynolds and David Tracy. SUNY Series, Toward a Comparative Philosophy of Religions. Albany: State University of New York Press, 1990, pp. 287–314.

———. "Why the Veda Has No Author: Language as Ritual in Early Mīmāṃsā and Post-Modern Theology." *Journal of the American Academy of Religion* 55, no. 4 (Winter 1987): 659–684.

Coburn, Thomas B. *Devī-Māhātmya: The Crystallization of the Goddess Tradition.* Delhi: Motilal Banarsidass, 1984.

———. *Encountering the Goddess: A Translation of the Devī-Māhātmya and a Study of Its Interpretation.* SUNY Series in Hindu Studies. Albany: State University of New York Press, 1991.

———. "'Scripture' in India: Towards a Typology of the Word in Hindu Life." *Journal of the American Academy of Religion* 52, no. 3 (Sept. 1984): 435–459. Reprinted in *Rethinking Scripture: Essays from a Comparative Perspective,* edited by Miriam Levering. Albany: State University of New York Press, 1989, pp. 102–128.

———. "The Study of the Purāṇas and the Study of Religion." *Religious Studies* 16, no. 3 (Sept. 1980): 341–352.

Collins, Steven. "Notes on Some Oral Aspects of Pali Literature." *Indo-Iranian Journal* 35 (1992): 121–135.

———. "On the Very Idea of the Pali Canon." *Journal of the Pali Text Society* 15 (1990): 89–126.

Coomaraswamy, A. "Vedic Exemplarism." *Harvard Journal of Asiatic Studies* 1, no. 1 (1936): 44–64.

Coward, Harold G. *Bhartṛhari.* Twayne's World Authors Series, 403. Boston: Twayne Publishers, 1976.

———. "The Meaning and Power of Mantras in Bhartṛhari's *Vākyapadīya.* In *Understanding Mantras,* edited by Harvey P. Alper. SUNY Series in Religious Studies. Albany: State University of New York Press, 1989, pp. 165–176.

———. "The Role of Scripture in the Self-Definition of Hinduism and Buddhism in India." *Studies in Religion/Sciences Religieuses* 21, no. 2 (1992): 129–144.

———. *The Sphoṭa Theory of Language: A Philosophical Analysis.* Delhi: Motilal Banarsidass, 1980.

_______, ed. *"Language" in Indian Philosophy and Religion.* SR Supplements, 5. Waterloo, Ontario: Wilfred Laurier University Press, 1978.

Coward, Harold, and Krishna Sivaraman, eds. *Revelation in Indian Thought: A Festschrift in Honour of Professor T. R. V. Murti.* Emeryville, Calif.: Dharma Publishing, 1977.

Dandekar, R. N. "Dharma, The First End of Man." In *Sources of Indian Tradition,* edited by Wm. Theodore de Bary, et al. Records of Civilization: Sources and Studies, no. 56. New York: Columbia University Press, 1958, pp. 216–235.

Dasgupta, Shashi Bhusan. "The Role of Mantra in Indian Religion." In his *Aspects of Indian Religious Thought.* Calcutta: A. Mukherjee, 1957, pp. 22–41.

Dasgupta, Surendranath. *A History of Indian Philosophy.* 5 vols. Cambridge: Cambridge University Press, 1922–1955.

De Smet, Richard V. "Language and Philosophy in India." In *Proceedings of the XIIth International Congress of Philosophy.* Vol. 10, *Eastern Philosophies and Western Thought.* Florence: Sansoni, 1960, pp. 47–54.

Devasthali, G. V. *Religion and Mythology of the Brāhmaṇas, with Particular Reference to the Śatapatha-Brāhmaṇa.* The Bhau Vishnu Ashtekar Vedic Research Series, vol. 1. Poona: University of Poona, 1965.

D'Sa, Francis X. "Offenbarung ohne einen Gott: Kumārilas Theorie der Worterkenntnis." In *Offenbarung, Geistige Realität des Menschen. Arbeitsdokumentation eines Symposiums zum Offenbarungsbegriff in Indien.* Edited by Gerhard Oberhammer. Publications of the De Nobili Research Library, vol. 2. Vienna: Indologisches Institut der Universität Wien, 1974, pp. 93–105.

———. *Śabdaprāmāṇyam in Śabara and Kumārila: Towards a Study of the Mīmāṃsā Experience of Language.* Publications of the De Nobili Research Library, vol. 7. Vienna: Institut für Indologie der Universität Wien, 1980.

Eck, Diana L. *Darśan: Seeing the Divine Image in India.* 2d rev. ed. Chambersburg, Pa.: Anima Books, 1985.

Edgerton, Franklin. *The Beginnings of Indian Philosophy.* Cambridge: Harvard University Press, 1965.

Eidlitz, Walther. *Der Glaube und die heiligen Schriften der Inder.* Olten: Walter-Verlag, 1957.

Essers, Bénard. "Vāc: Het Woord als Godsgestalte en als Godgeleerdheid in de Veda, in het bijzonder in de Ṛgveda-Saṃhitā en in de Atharvaveda-Saṃhitā." Th.D. diss., University of Groningen, Netherlands, 1952.

Falk, Maryla. *Nāma-Rūpa and Dharma-Rūpa: Origin and Aspects of an Ancient Indian Conception.* Calcutta: University of Calcutta, 1943.

Findly, Ellison Banks. "*Mántra kaviśastá*: Speech as Performative in the Ṛgveda." In *Understanding Mantras*, edited by Harvey P. Alper. SUNY Series in Religious Studies. Albany: State University of New York Press, 1989, pp. 15–47.

Fitzgerald, James L. "India's Fifth Veda: The *Mahābhārata*'s Presentation of Itself." *Journal of South Asian Literature* 20, no. 1 (Winter–Spring 1985): 125–140.

Frauwallner, Erich. *Geschichte der indischen Philosophie.* 2 vols. Salzburg: Otto Müller, 1953, 1956. Eng. trans. V. M. Bedekar. *History of Indian Philosophy.* 2 vols. Delhi: Motilal Banarsidass, 1973.

———. "Mīmāṃsāsūtram I,1,6–23." *Wiener Zeitschrift für die Kunde Süd- und Ostasiens* 5 (1961): 113–124.

Ghose, Aurobindo. *On the Veda.* Sri Aurobindo International University Centre Collection, vol. 5. Pondicherry: Sri Aurobindo Ashram Press, 1956.

Ghosh, Manomohan. "Prātiśākhyas and Vedic Śākhās." *Indian Historical Quarterly* 11, no. 4 (Dec. 1935): 761–768.

Gonda, Jan. "All, Universe and Totality in the Śatapatha-Brāhmaṇa." *Journal of the Oriental Institute* (Baroda) 32, nos. 1–2 (Sept.–Dec. 1982): 1–17.

———. *Change and Continuity in Indian Religion.* Disputationes Rheno-Trajectinae, vol. 9. The Hague: Mouton, 1965.

———. "The Creator and His Spirit (Manas and Prajāpati)." *Wiener Zeitschrift für die Kunde Südasiens* 27 (1983): 5–42.

———. "In the Beginning." *Annals of the Bhandarkar Oriental Research Institute* 63 (1982): 43–62.

———. "The Indian Mantra." *Oriens* 16 (1963): 244–297.

———. *Notes on Brahman.* Utrecht: J. L. Beyers, 1950.

———. *Notes on Names and the Name of God in Ancient India.* Verhandelingen der Koninklijke Nederlandse Akademie van Wetenschappen, Afd. Letterkunde, n.s., vol. 75, no. 4. Amsterdam: North-Holland Publishing, 1970.

———. "The Popular Prajāpati," *History of Religions* 22, no. 2 (Nov. 1982): 129–149.

———. "Prajāpati and *prāyaścitta*." *Journal of the Royal Asiatic Society,* no. 1 (1983): 32–54.

———. *Prajāpati and the Year.* Amsterdam: North-Holland Publishing, 1984.

———. *Prajāpati's Rise to Higher Rank.* Leiden: E. J. Brill, 1986.

———. *Pūṣan and Sarasvatī.* Amsterdam: North-Holland Publishing, 1985.

———. "Reflections on *Sarva-* in Vedic Texts." *Indian Linguistics* 16 (Nov. 1955): 53–71.

———. *Die Religionen Indiens.* Vol. 1, *Veda und älterer Hinduismus.* Die Religionen der Menschheit, vol. 11. Stuttgart: W. Kohlhammer, 1960.

———. "Vedic Gods and the Sacrifice." *Numen* 30, no. 1 (July 1983): 1–34.

———. *Vedic Literature (Saṃhitās and Brāhmaṇas).* A History of Indian Literature, vol. 1, pt. 1. Wiesbaden: Otto Harrassowitz, 1975.

———. *Vedic Ritual: The Non-Solemn Rites.* Handbuch der Orientalistik. Division 2: Indien, vol. 4, pt. 1. Leiden: E. J. Brill, 1980.

———. *The Vision of the Vedic Poets.* Disputationes Rheno-Trajectinae, vol. 8. The Hague: Mouton, 1963.

Gopal, Ram. *The History and Principles of Vedic Interpretation.* New Delhi: Concept Publishing, 1983.

Gupta, S. K. "Ancient Schools of Vedic Interpretation." *Journal of the Ganganatha Jha Research Institute* 16, pts. 1–2 (Nov. 1958–Feb. 1959): 143–153.

Halbfass, Wilhelm. *Tradition and Reflection: Explorations in Indian Thought.* Albany: State University of New York Press, 1991.

Hazra, Rajendra Chandra. "The Purāṇas." In *The Cultural Heritage of India,* vol. 2. 2d rev. ed. Calcutta: Ramakrishna Mission Institute of Culture, 1962, pp. 240–270.

______. *Studies in the Purāṇic Records on Hindu Rites and Customs.* 2d ed. Delhi: Motilal Banarsidass, 1975.

Heesterman, Jan C. "Die Autorität des Veda." In *Offenbarung, Geistige Realität des Menschen. Arbeitsdokumentation eines Symposiums zum Offenbarungsbegriff in Indien*, edited by Gerhard Oberhammer. Publications of the De Nobili Research Library, vol. 2. Vienna: Indologisches Institut der Universität Wien, 1974, pp. 29–40.

———. "Power and Authority in Indian Tradition." In *Tradition and Politics in South Asia*, edited by R. J. Moore. New Delhi: Vikas, 1979, pp. 60–85.

———. "Veda and Dharma." In *The Concept of Duty in South Asia*, edited by Wendy Doniger O'Flaherty and J. Duncan M. Derrett. New Delhi: Vikas, 1978, pp. 80–95.

Hillebrandt, Alfred. *Vedic Mythology*. Translated by Sreeramula Rajeswara Sarma. 2d rev. ed. 2 vols. Delhi: Motilal Banarsidass, 1980–1981.

Hiltebeitel, Alf. *The Ritual of Battle: Krishna in the Mahābhārata*. Symbol, Myth, and Ritual Series. Ithaca: Cornell University Press, 1976.

Holdrege, Barbara A. "Veda and Torah: The Word Embodied in Scripture." In *Between Jerusalem and Benares: Comparative Studies in Judaism and Hinduism*, edited by Hananya Goodman. Albany: State University of New York Press, 1994, pp. 103–179.

———. "Veda in the Brāhmaṇas: Cosmogonic Paradigms and the Delimitation of Canon." In *Authority, Anxiety, and Canon: Essays in Vedic Interpretation*, edited by Laurie L. Patton. SUNY Series in Hindu Studies. Albany: State University of New York Press, 1994, pp. 35–66.

Hopkins, E. Washburn. *Epic Mythology*. Grundiss der indo-arischen Philologie und Altertumskunde, vol. 3, no. 1B. 1915. Reprint. Delhi: Motilal Banarsidass, 1974.

Hopkins, Thomas J. *The Hindu Religious Tradition*. The Religious Life of Man Series. Belmont, Calif.: Wadsworth, 1971.

Howard, Wayne. *Sāmavedic Chant*. New Haven: Yale University Press, 1977.

Inden, Ronald. *Imagining India*. Oxford: Basil Blackwell, 1990.

Jairazbhoy, N. A. "Le chant védique." In *Encyclopédie des musiques sacrées*, edited by Jacques Porte, vol. 1. Paris: Labergerie, 1968, pp. 135–161.

Jha, Ganganatha. *Pūrva-Mīmāṁsā in Its Sources*. 2d ed. Varanasi: Banaras Hindu University, 1964.

Johnson, Willard. *Poetry and Speculation of the Ṛg Veda*. Hermeneutics: Studies in the History of Religions. Berkeley: University of California Press, 1980.

Joshi, J. R. "Prajāpati in Vedic Mythology and Ritual." *Annals of the Bhandarkar Oriental Research Institute* 53, pts. 1–4 (1972): 101–125.

Kaelber, Walter O. *Tapta Mārga: Asceticism and Initiation in Vedic India*. Albany: State University of New York Press, 1989.

Kane, Pandurang Vaman. *History of Dharmaśāstra (Ancient and Mediaeval Religious and Civil Law in India)*. 2d ed. 5 vols. in 8. Government Oriental Series. Poona: Bhandarkar Oriental Research Institute, 1968–1975.

Katz, Ruth Cecily. *Arjuna in the Mahabharata: Where Krishna Is, There Is Victory*. Studies in Comparative Religion. Columbia, S.C.: University of South Carolina Press, 1989.

Keith, Arthur Berriedale. *The Religion and Philosophy of the Veda and Upaniṣads*. 2 vols. Harvard Oriental Series, vols. 31–32. Cambridge: Harvard University Press, 1925.

Kennedy, Vans. *Researches into the Nature and Affinity of Ancient and Hindu Mythology*. London: Longman, Rees, Orme, Brown, and Green, 1831.

Klostermaier, Klaus. "The Creative Function of the Word." In *"Language" in Indian Philosophy and Religion*, edited by Harold G.

Coward. SR Supplements, 5. Waterloo, Ontario: Wilfred Laurier University Press, 1978.

Kuiper, F. B. J. *Ancient Indian Cosmogony*. Edited by John Irwin. New Delhi: Vikas, 1983.

———. "The Basic Concept of Vedic Religion." *History of Religions* 15, no. 2 (Nov. 1975): 107–120. Reprinted in his *Ancient Indian Cosmogony*, pp. 9–22.

———. "Cosmogony and Conception: A Query." *History of Religions* 10, no. 2 (Nov. 1970): 91–138. Reprinted in his *Ancient Indian Cosmogony*, pp. 90–137.

Laine, J. "The Notion of 'Scripture' in Modern Indian Thought." *Annals of the Bhandarkar Oriental Research Institute* 64 (1983): 165–179.

Lamotte, Étienne. "La critique d'authenticité dans le bouddhisme." In *India Antiqua*. Leiden: E. J. Brill, 1947, pp. 213–222.

———. "La critique d'interprétation dans le bouddhisme." *Annuaire de l'institut de philologie et d'histoire orientales et slaves* 9 (1949): 341–361.

———. *Histoire du Bouddhisme Indien, des origines à l'ère Śaka*. Bibliothèque du *Muséon*, vol. 43. Louvain: Institut Orientaliste, 1958. Eng. trans. Sara Webb-Boin under the supervision of Jean Dantinne. *History of Indian Buddhism: From the Origins to the Śaka Era*. Louvain-la-Neuve: Université Catholique de Louvain, Institut Orientaliste, 1988.

Lancaster, Lewis. "Buddhist Literature: Its Canons, Scribes, and Editors." In *The Critical Study of Sacred Texts*, edited by Wendy Doniger O'Flaherty. Berkeley Religious Studies Series. Berkeley: Graduate Theological Union, 1979, pp. 215–229.

Larson, Gerald James, and Ram Shankar Bhattacharya, eds. *Sāṃkhya: A Dualist Tradition in Indian Philosophy*. Encyclopedia of Indian Philosophies, vol. 4. Princeton: Princeton University Press, 1987.

Lester, Robert C. "Hinduism: Veda and Sacred Texts." In *The Holy Book in Comparative Perspective,* edited by Frederick M. Denny and Rodney L. Taylor. Studies in Comparative Religion. Columbia, S.C.: University of South Carolina Press, 1985, pp. 126–147.

Liebich, Bruno. "Über den Sphoṭa (Ein Kapitel über die Sprachphilosophie der Inder)," *Zeitschrift der Deutschen Morgenländischen Gesellschaft* 77 [n.s., 2] (1923): 208–219.

Lingat, Robert. *The Classical Law of India.* Translated by J. Duncan M. Derrett. Berkeley: University of California Press, 1973.

Lutgendorf, Philip. *The Life of a Text: Performing the Rāmcaritmānas of Tulsidas.* Berkeley: University of California Press, 1991.

———. "The Power of Sacred Story: *Rāmāyaṇa* Recitation in Contemporary North India." In *Ritual and Power,* edited by Barbara A. Holdrege. *Journal of Ritual Studies* 4, no. 2 (Summer 1990): 115–147.

Macdonald, A. W. "À propos de Prajāpati." *Journal Asiatique* 240, no. 3 (1952): 323–338.

Macdonell, A. A. *Vedic Mythology.* Grundiss der indo-arischen Philologie und Altertumskunde, vol. 3, no. 1A. 1897. Reprint. New York: Gordon Press, 1974.

Macdonell, A. A., and Arthur Berriedale Keith. *Vedic Index of Names and Subjects.* 2 vols. Indian Texts Series. London: John Murray, 1912.

Mahārāj, B. H. Bon. "The Uniqueness of Vedic Reading." *Śāradā Piṭha Pradīpa: A Bi-Annual Journal of Indological Research Institute, Dwarka* 7, no. 1 (Feb. 1967): 1–13.

Maharishi Mahesh Yogi. *Maharishi's Absolute Theory of Government.* Vlodrop, Holland: Maharishi Vedic University Press, 1993.

———. *On the Bhagavad-Gita: A New Translation and Commentary, Chapters 1 to 6.* Harmondsworth, Middlesex, England: Penguin Books, 1969.

———. *The Vedas*. Los Angeles: Spiritual Regeneration Movement Foundation, 1967.

Malamoud, Charles. *Le svādhyāya: Récitation personnelle du Veda. Taittirīya Āraṇyaka, Livre II*. Publications de l'Institut de Civilisation Indienne, no. 42. Paris: Institut de Civilisation Indienne, 1977.

Mehta, J. L. "The Hindu Tradition: The Vedic Root." In *The World's Religious Traditions: Current Perspectives in Religious Studies. Essays in Honour of Wilfred Cantwell Smith*, edited by Frank Whaling. Edinburgh: T. and T. Clark, 1984, pp. 33–54.

Miller, Jeanine. *The Vedas: Harmony, Meditation and Fulfilment*. London: Rider, 1974.

Misra, Vidya Niwas. "*Vāk* Legends in the *Brāhmaṇa* Literature." In *Proceedings of the Twenty-Sixth International Congress of Orientalists*, vol. 3, pt. 1. Poona: Bhandarkar Oriental Research Institute, 1969, pp. 109–118.

Muir, J., comp. and trans. *Original Sanskrit Texts on the Origin and History of the People of India, Their Religion and Institutions*. Vol. 3, *The Vedas: Opinions of Their Authors and of Later Indian Writers on Their Origin, Inspiration, and Authority*. Vol. 4, *Comparison of the Vedic with the Later Representations of the Principal Indian Deities*. 2d rev. ed. 1874. Reprint. Amsterdam: Oriental Press, 1967.

Muller-Ortega, Paul E. "The Power of the Secret Ritual: Theoretical Formulations from the Tantra." In *Ritual and Power*, edited by Barbara A. Holdrege. *Journal of Ritual Studies* 4, no. 2 (Summer 1990): 41–59.

Murti, T. R. V. "The Philosophy of Language in the Indian Context." In *Studies in Indian Thought: Collected Papers of Prof. T. R. V. Murti*, edited by Harold G. Coward. Delhi: Motilal Banarsidass, 1983, pp. 357–376.

Murty, K. Satchidananda. *Revelation and Reason in Advaita Vedānta*. Waltair: Andhra University; New York: Columbia University Press, 1959.

Mus, Paul. "Du nouveau sur Ṛgveda 10.90? Sociologie d'une grammaire." In *Indological Studies in Honor of W. Norman Brown*, edited by Ernest Bender. American Oriental Series, vol. 47. New Haven: American Oriental Society, 1962, pp. 165–185.

———. "Où finit Puruṣa?" In *Mélanges d'Indianisme à la mémoire de Louis Renou*. Publications de l'Institut de Civilisation Indienne, no. 28. Paris: E. de Boccard, 1968, pp. 539–563.

Nagaswamy, R. "Vedic Scholars in the Ancient Tamil Country as Gleaned from the Saṅgam Classics and South Indian Inscriptions." *Vishveshvaranand Indological Journal* 3, pt. 2 (Sept. 1965): 192–204.

Nooten, Barend A. van. *The Mahābhārata*. Twayne's World Authors Series, 131. New York: Twayne Publishers, 1971.

Oberhammer, Gerhard. "Die Überlieferungsautorität im Hinduismus." In *Offenbarung, Geistige Realität des Menschen. Arbeitsdokumentation eines Symposiums zum Offenbarungsbegriff in Indien*, edited by Gerhard Oberhammer. Publications of the De Nobili Research Library, vol. 2. Vienna: Indologisches Institut der Universität Wien, 1974, pp. 41–92.

Oberhammer, Gerhard, and Hans Waldenfels. *Überlieferungsstruktur und Offenbarung. Aufriss einer Reflexion des Phänomens im Hinduismus mit theologischen Anmerkungen*. Publications of the De Nobili Research Library, Occasional Papers, 1. Vienna: Institut für Indologie der Universität Wien, 1980. Eng. trans. Anand Amaladass. "The Structure of Tradition and Revelation: Reflection on 'the Phenomenon' in Hinduism." In Gerhard Oberhammer, *Philosophy of Religion in Hindu Thought*, translated and edited by Anand Amaladass. Sri Garib Dass Oriental Series, no. 93. Delhi: Sri Satguru Publications, 1989, pp. 1–23.

O'Flaherty, Wendy Doniger. "The Origins of Heresy in Hindu Mythology." *History of Religions* 10, no. 4 (May 1971): 271–333.

O'Flaherty, Wendy Doniger, and J. Duncan M. Derrett, eds. *The Concept of Duty in South Asia*. New Delhi: Vikas, 1978.

Ogibenin, B. L. *Structure d'un mythe védique: Le mythe cosmogonique dans le Ṛgveda*. Approaches to Semiotics, 30. The Hague: Mouton, 1973.

Oldenberg, H. *Ancient India: Its Language and Religions*. 2d ed. Calcutta: Punthi Pustak, 1962.

Organ, Troy. "Three into Four in Hinduism." *Ohio Journal of Religious Studies* 1, no. 2 (July 1973): 7–13.

Padoux, André. "Mantras—What Are They?" In *Understanding Mantras,* edited by Harvey P. Alper. SUNY Series in Religious Studies. Albany: State University of New York Press, 1989, pp. 295–318.

———. *Vāc: The Concept of the Word in Selected Hindu Tantras.* Translated by Jacques Gontier. SUNY Series in the Shaiva Traditions of Kashmir. Albany: State University of New York Press, 1990.

______, ed., *Mantras et diagrammes rituels dans l'Hindouisme.* Centre National de la Recherche Scientifique, Équipe de recherche, no. 249. L'Hindouisme: textes, doctrines, pratiques. Paris: Éditions du Centre National de la Recherche Scientifique, 1986.

Panikkar, Raimundo, ed. and trans. *The Vedic Experience: Mantramañjarī. An Anthology of the Vedas for Modern Man and Contemporary Celebration.* Berkeley: University of California Press, 1977.

Parpola, Asko. "On the Symbol Concept of the Vedic Ritualists." In *Religious Symbols and Their Functions,* edited by Haralds Biezais. Stockholm: Almquist and Wiksell, 1979, pp. 139–153.

Patton, Laurie L. "Hymn to Vāc: Myth or Philosophy?" In *Myth and Philosophy,* edited by Frank Reynolds and David Tracy. SUNY Series, Toward a Comparative Philosophy of Religions. Albany: State University of New York Press, 1990, pp. 183–213.

______, ed. *Authority, Anxiety, and Canon: Essays in Vedic Interpretation.* SUNY Series in Hindu Studies. Albany: State University of New York Press, 1994.

Pintchman, Tracy. *The Rise of the Goddess in the Hindu Tradition.* Albany: State University of New York Press, 1994.

Pollock, Sheldon. "From Discourse of Ritual to Discourse of Power in Sanskrit Culture." In *Ritual and Power,* edited by Barbara A. Holdrege. *Journal of Ritual Studies* 4, no. 2 (Summer 1990): 315–345.

———. "'Tradition' as 'Revelation': *Śruti, Smṛti,* and the Sanskrit Discourse of Power." In *Lex et Litterae: Essays on Ancient Indian Law and Literature in Honour of Oscar Botto,* edited by Siegfried Lienhard and Irma Piovano. Turin: CESMEO, forthcoming.

Potter, Karl H., ed. *Advaita Vedānta up to Śaṃkara and His Pupils.* Encyclopedia of Indian Philosophies, vol. 3. Princeton: Princeton University Press, 1981.

_______, ed. *Indian Metaphysics and Epistemology: The Tradition of Nyāya-Vaiśeṣika up to Gaṅgeśa.* Encyclopedia of Indian Philosophies, vol. 2. Delhi: Motilal Banarsidass, 1977.

Radhakrishnan, Sarvepalli, and Charles A. Moore, eds. *A Source Book in Indian Philosophy.* Princeton: Princeton University Press, 1957.

Raghavan, V. *The Present Position of Vedic Recitation and Vedic Sakhas.* Kumbhakonam: Veda Dharma Paripalana Sabha, 1962.

———. "Vedic Chanting; Music, Dance and Drama." In *International Seminar on Traditional Cultures in South-East Asia.* Bombay: Orient Longmans, 1960, pp. 168–178.

Raja, K. Kunjunni. *Indian Theories of Meaning.* The Adyar Library Series, vol. 91. Adyar, Madras: Adyar Library and Research Centre, 1963.

Ramanujan, A. K., trans., *Speaking of Śiva.* Harmondsworth, Middlesex, England: Penguin Books, 1973.

Rambachan, Anantanand. "Where Words Can Set Free: The Liberating Potency of Vedic Words in the Hermeneutics of Śaṅkara."

In *Texts in Context: Traditional Hermeneutics in South Asia,* edited by Jeffrey R. Timm. Albany: State University of New York Press, 1992, pp. 33–46.

Raster, Peter. "Die verborgenen drei Viertel: Aspekte de sprachlichen Tiefendimension in der indischen und europäischen Sprachtheorie." In *Allgemeine Sprachwissenschaft, Sprachtypologie und Textlinguistik: Festschrift für Peter Hartmann,* edited by Manfred Faust. Tübingen: Gunter Narr, 1983, pp. 211–220.

Ray, Reginald. "Buddhism: Sacred Text Written and Realized." In *The Holy Book in Comparative Perspective,* edited by Frederick M. Denny and Rodney L. Taylor. Studies in Comparative Religion. Columbia, S.C.: University of South Carolina Press, 1985, pp. 148–180.

Renou, Louis. *Le destin du Véda dans l'Inde. Études védiques et pāṇinéennes,* vol. 6. Publications de l'Institut de Civilisation Indienne, no. 10. Paris: E. de Boccard, 1960. Eng. ed. and trans. Dev Raj Chanana. *The Destiny of the Veda in India.* Delhi: Motilal Banarsidass, 1965.

———. *Les écoles védiques et la formation du Veda.* Cahiers de la Société Asiatique, 9. Paris: Imprimerie Nationale, 1947.

———. "Les pouvoirs de la parole dans le Ṛgveda." In his *Études védiques et pāṇinéennes,* vol. 1. Publications de l'Institut de Civilisation Indienne, no. 1. Paris: E. de Boccard, 1955, pp. 1–27.

———. *Religions of Ancient India.* Jordan Lectures 1951. London: Athlone Press, 1953.

———. *Sanskrit et culture. L'apport de l'Inde à la civilisation humaine.* Paris: Payot, 1950.

———. *Vedic India.* Translated by Philip Spratt. Classical India, vol. 3. Delhi: Indological Book House, 1971.

______, trans. *Hymnes spéculatifs du Véda.* Connaissance de l'Orient. Collection UNESCO d'oeuvres représentatives, Série indienne. Paris: Gallimard, 1956.

Renou, Louis, and Jean Filliozat. *L'Inde classique. Manuel des études indiennes.* 2 vols. Paris: Payot, 1947–1949 (vol.1); Paris: Imprimerie Nationale, 1953 (vol. 2).

Renou, Louis, and Liliane Silburn. "Sur la notion de *bráhman.*" *Journal Asiatique* 237 (1949): 7–46.

Richman, Paula, ed. *Many Rāmāyaṇas: The Diversity of a Narrative Tradition in South Asia.* Berkeley: University of California Press, 1991.

Rocher, Ludo. "Mantras in the *Śivapurāṇa.*" In *Understanding Mantras,* edited by Harvey P. Alper. SUNY Series in Religious Studies. Albany: State University of New York Press, 1989, pp. 177–203.

———. "Max Müller and the Veda." In *Mélanges Armand Abel,* vol. 3, edited by A. Destrée. Leiden: E. J. Brill, 1978, pp. 221–235.

———. *The Purāṇas.* A History of Indian Literature, vol. 2, pt. 3. Wiesbaden: Otto Harrassowitz, 1986.

Ruegg, David Seyfort. *Contributions à l'histoire de la philosophie linguistique indienne.* Publications de l'Institut de Civilisation Indienne, no. 7. Paris: E. de Boccard, 1959.

Santucci, James A. *An Outline of Vedic Literature.* The American Academy of Religion Aids to the Study of Religion Series, no. 5. Missoula, Mont.: Scholars Press, 1976.

Sastri, Gaurinath. *The Philosophy of Word and Meaning: Some Indian Approaches with Special Reference to the Philosophy of Bhartṛhari.* Calcutta Sanskrit College Research Series, no. 5. Calcutta: Sanskrit College, 1959.

———. *A Study in the Dialectics of Sphoṭa.* Rev. ed. Delhi: Motilal Banarsidass, 1980.

Scharbau, Carl Anders. *Die Idee der Schöpfung in der vedischen Literatur. Eine religionsgeschichtliche Untersuchung über den frühindischen Theismus.* Veröffentlichungen des orientalischen Seminars der Universität Tübingen, no. 5. Stuttgart: W. Kohlhammer, 1932.

Scharfe, Hartmut. *Grammatical Literature*. A History of Indian Literature, vol. 5, pt. 2. Wiesbaden: Otto Harrassowitz, 1977.

Sharma, Arvind. "Ancient Hinduism as a Missionary Religion." *Numen* 39, no. 2 (Nov. 1992): 175–192.

Sivaraman, Krishna. "The Word as a Category of Revelation." In *Revelation in Indian Thought: A Festschrift in Honour of Professor T. R. V. Murti*, edited by Harold Coward and Krishna Sivaraman. Emeryville, Calif.: Dharma Publishing, 1977, pp. 45–64.

Smith, Brian K. "Canonical Authority and Social Classification: Veda and *Varṇa* in Ancient Indian Texts." *History of Religions* 32, no. 2 (Nov. 1992): 103–125.

———. *Classifying the Universe: The Ancient Indian Varṇa System and the Origins of Caste*. New York: Oxford University Press, 1994.

———. "Exorcising the Transcendent: Strategies for Defining Hinduism and Religion." *History of Religions* 27, no. 1 (Aug. 1987): 32–55.

———. *Reflections on Resemblance, Ritual, and Religion*. New York: Oxford University Press, 1989.

———. "The Veda and the Authority of Class: Reduplicating Structures of Veda and *Varṇa* in Ancient Indian Texts." In *Authority, Anxiety, and Canon: Essays in Vedic Interpretation*, edited by Laurie L. Patton. SUNY Series in Hindu Studies. Albany: State University of New York Press, 1994, pp. 67–93.

Sontheimer, Günther D., and Hermann Kulke, eds. *Hinduism Reconsidered*. South Asia Institute, South Asian Studies, no. 24. New Delhi: Manohar, 1989.

Staal, J. Frits. *Agni: The Vedic Ritual of the Fire Altar*. 2 vols. Berkeley: Asian Humanities Press, 1983.

———. "The Concept of Scripture in the Indian Tradition." In *Sikh Studies: Comparative Perspectives on a Changing Tradition,* edited by Mark Juergensmeyer and N. Gerald Barrier. Berkeley Religious Studies Series. Berkeley: Graduate Theological Union, 1979, pp. 121–124.

———. "The Independence of Rationality from Literacy." *European Journal of Sociology* 30 (1989): 301–310.

———. "The Meaninglessness of Ritual." *Numen* 26, no. 1 (1979): 2–22.

———. *Nambudiri Veda Recitation.* Disputationes Rheno-Trajectinae, vol. 5. The Hague: Mouton, 1961.

———. "Ṛgveda 10.71 on the Origin of Language." In *Revelation in Indian Thought: A Festschrift in Honour of Professor T. R. V. Murti,* edited by Harold Coward and Krishna Sivaraman. Emeryville, Calif.: Dharma Publishing, 1977, pp. 3–14.

———. *Rules Without Meaning: Ritual, Mantras and the Human Sciences.* Toronto Studies in Religion, vol. 4. New York: Peter Lang, 1989.

———. "Vedic Mantras." In *Understanding Mantras,* edited by Harvey P. Alper. SUNY Series in Religious Studies. Albany: State University of New York Press, 1989, pp. 48–95.

Stietencron, Heinrich von. "Hinduism: On the Proper Use of a Deceptive Term." In *Hinduism Reconsidered,* edited by Günther D. Sontheimer and Hermann Kulke. South Asia Institute, South Asian Studies, no. 24. New Delhi: Manohar, 1989, pp. 11–27.

Strauss, Otto. "Altindische Spekulationen über die Sprache und ihre Probleme." *Zeitschrift der Deutschen Morgenländischen Gesellschaft* 81 [n.s., 6] (1927): 99–151.

Subbu Reddiar, N. "The Nālāyiram as Drāvida Veda." Chapter 26 of his *Religion and Philosophy of Nālāyira Divya Prabandham with Special Reference to Nammāḷvār.* Tirupati: Sri Venkateswara University, 1977, pp. 680–693.

Sukthankar, V. S. "Epic Studies VI: The Bhṛgus and the Bhārata. A Text-Historical Study." *Annals of the Bhandarkar Oriental Research Institute* 18, pt. 1 (1936): 1–76.

Sullivan, Bruce M. *Kṛṣṇa Dvaipāyana Vyāsa and the Mahābhārata: A New Interpretation.* Leiden: E. J. Brill, 1990.

Taber, John. "Are Mantras Speech Acts? The Mīmāṃsā Point of View." In *Understanding Mantras,* edited by Harvey P. Alper. SUNY Series in Religious Studies. Albany: State University of New York Press, 1989, pp. 144–164.

Thieme, Paul. "Bráhman." *Zeitschrift der Deutschen Morgenländischen Gesellschaft* 102 [n.s., 27] (1952): 91–129.

Timm, Jeffrey R., ed. *Texts in Context: Traditional Hermeneutics in South Asia.* Albany: State University of New York Press, 1992.

Varenne, Jean. *Cosmogonies Védiques.* La Tradition: textes et études, Série française, vol. 19. Paris: Societé d'Édition "Les Belles Lettres," 1982.

Vyas, R. T. "The Concept of Prajāpati in Vedic Literature." *Bhāratīya Vidyā* 38, nos. 1–4 (1978): 95–101.

Wayman, Alex. "The Significance of Mantra-s, from the Veda Down to Buddhist Tantric Practice." *The Adyar Library Bulletin* 39 (1975): 65–89.

Weber, Albrecht. "Die Hoheit der vâc." *Indische Studien* (Leipzig) 18 (1898): 117–125.

———. "Vâc und λογοσ." *Indische Studien* (Leipzig) 9 (1865): 473–480.

Wheelock, Wade T. "The Mantra in Vedic and Tantric Ritual." In *Understanding Mantras,* edited by Harvey P. Alper. SUNY Series in Religious Studies. Albany: State University of New York Press, 1989, pp. 96–122.

Winternitz, M. *Geschichte der indischen Litteratur.* 2d ed. 3 vols. Leipzig: C. F. Amelangs, 1909–1920. Eng. trans. S. Ketkar and

H. Kohn, revised by the author. *A History of Indian Literature.* 2 vols. 1927–1933. 2d ed. New Delhi: Oriental Books Reprint Corporation, 1972.

Younger, Paul. *Introduction to Indian Religious Thought.* Philadelphia: Westminster Press, 1972.

Zachariae, Theodor. Review of *De Ontdekkingsgeschiedenis van den Veda,* by W. Caland. *Göttingische gelehrte Anzeigen* 183, nos. 7–9 (July–Sept. 1921): 148–165. Eng. trans. H. Hosten. *Journal of Indian History* 2, pt. 2 (May 1923): 129–157.

II. BIBLICAL AND JUDAIC SOURCES

A. Editions and Translations of Hebrew, Aramaic, and Other Primary Sources

Bible, Apocrypha, and Pseudepigrapha

Hebrew Bible.

Elliger, K., and W. Rudolph, eds. Stuttgart: Deutsche Bibelstiftung, 1977.

Translation:

May, Herbert G., and Bruce M. Metzger, eds. *The New Oxford Annotated Bible with the Apocrypha. Revised Standard Version.* New York: Oxford University Press, 1977.

Apocrypha and Pseudepigrapha.

May, Herbert G., and Bruce M. Metzger, eds. *The New Oxford Annotated Bible with the Apocrypha. Revised Standard Version.* New York: Oxford University Press, 1977.

Charles, R. H., ed. *The Apocrypha and Pseudepigrapha of the Old Testament.* 2 vols. Oxford: Clarendon Press, 1913.

Charlesworth, James H., ed. *The Old Testament Pseudepigrapha.* 2 vols. Garden City, N. Y.: Doubleday, 1983–1985.

Philo

Colson, F. H., and G. H. Whitaker, trans. *Philo.* 12 vols. The Loeb Classical Library. London: William Heinemann; Cambridge: Harvard University Press, 1929–1962.

Targums

Fragment Targums

Klein, Michael L., ed. *The Fragment-Targums of the Pentateuch According to Their Extant Sources,* vol. 1. Analecta Biblica: Investigationes Scientificae in Res Biblicas, 76. Rome: Biblical Institute Press, 1980.

Translation:

Klein, Michael L., trans. *The Fragment-Targums of the Pentateuch According to Their Extant Sources,* vol. 2. Analecta Biblica: Investigationes Scientificae in Res Biblicas, 76. Rome: Biblical Institute Press, 1980.

Targum Neofiti 1

Díez Macho, Alejandro, ed. 6 vols. Textos y Estudios, 7–11, 20. Madrid: Consejo Superior de Investigaciones Científicas, 1968–1979.

Translations:

Díez Macho, Alejandro, et al., trans. *Neophyti 1: Targum Palestinense MS de la Biblioteca Vaticana.* 6 vols. Textos y Estudios,

7–11, 20. Madrid: Consejo Superior de Investigaciones Científicas, 1968–1979.

McNamara, Martin, trans. *Targum Neofiti 1: Genesis*. The Aramaic Bible: The Targums, vol. 1A. Collegeville, Minn.: Liturgical Press, 1992.

Targum Onkelos

Sperber, Alexander, ed. In *The Bible in Aramaic, Based on Old Manuscripts and Printed Texts*. Vol. 1, *The Pentateuch According to Targum Onkelos*. Leiden: E. J. Brill, 1959.

Translation:

Aberbach, Moses, and Bernard Grossfield, trans. *Targum Onkelos to Genesis*. New York: Ktav; Denver: Center for Judaic Studies, University of Denver, 1982.

Targum Pseudo-Jonathan

Clarke, E. G., ed. Hoboken, N. J.: Ktav, 1984.

Translations:

Le Déaut, Roger, trans. *Targum du Pentateuque*. 5 vols. Sources chrétiennes, nos. 245, 256, 261, 271, 282. Paris: Éditions du Cerf, 1978–1981.

Maher, Michael, trans. *Targum Pseudo-Jonathan: Genesis*. The Aramaic Bible: The Targums, vol. 1B. Collegeville, Minn.: Liturgical Press, 1992.

Rabbinic Texts

Babylonian Talmud.

I. Epstein, ed. London: Soncino Press, 1960–.

Translation:

Epstein, I., ed. *The Babylonian Talmud.* 1935–1952. Reprint. 18 vols. London: Soncino Press, 1961.

Deuteronomy Rabbāh.

In *Midrash Rabbāh,* vol. 2. Vilna: Romm, 1887.

Hallevy, E. E., ed. In *Midrash Rabbāh,* vol. 8. Tel Aviv: Machbaroth Lesifrut, 1963.

Lieberman, Saul, ed. 1940. 3d ed. Jerusalem: Wahrmann Books, 1974.

Translation:

Rabinowitz, J., trans. In *The Midrash Rabbah,* edited by H. Freedman and Maurice Simon, vol. 3. London: Soncino Press, 1977.

Ecclesiastes Rabbāh.

In *Midrash Rabbāh,* vol. 2. Vilna: Romm, 1887.

Translation:

Cohen, A., trans. In *The Midrash Rabbah,* edited by H. Freedman and Maurice Simon, vol. 4. London: Soncino Press, 1977.

Esther Rabbāh.

In *Midrash Rabbāh,* vol. 2. Vilna: Romm, 1887.

Translations:

Simon, Maurice, trans. In *The Midrash Rabbah,* edited by H. Freedman and Maurice Simon, vol. 4. London: Soncino Press, 1977.

Neusner, Jacob, trans. *Esther Rabbah I: An Analytical Translation.* Brown Judaic Studies, no. 182. Atlanta: Scholars Press, 1989.

Exodus Rabbāh.

In *Midrash Rabbāh,* vol. 1. Vilna: Romm, 1887.

Hallevy, E. E., ed. In *Midrash Rabbāh,* vols. 3–4. Tel Aviv: Machbaroth Lesifrut, 1963.

Shinan, Avigdor, ed. Jerusalem: Dvir, 1984. [Exodus Rabbāh I]

Translation:

Lehrman, S. M., trans. In *The Midrash Rabbah,* edited by H. Freedman and Maurice Simon, vol. 2. London: Soncino Press, 1977.

Genesis Rabbāh.

Theodor, J., and Chanoch Albeck, eds. 1903–1936. 2d ed. 3 vols. Jerusalem: Wahrmann Books, 1965.

Translations:

Freedman, H., trans. In *The Midrash Rabbah,* edited by H. Freedman and Maurice Simon, vol. 1. London: Soncino Press, 1977.

Neusner, Jacob, trans. *Genesis Rabbah: The Judaic Commentary to the Book of Genesis—A New American Translation.* 3 vols. Brown Judaic Studies, nos. 104–106. Atlanta: Scholars Press, 1985.

Jerusalem Talmud.

Krotoshin, 1866.

Translation:

Neusner, Jacob, et al., trans. *The Talmud of the Land of Israel: A Preliminary Translation and Explanation.* 35 vols. Chicago Studies in the History of Judaism. Chicago: University of Chicago Press, 1982–1993.

Lamentations Rabbāh.

In *Midrash Rabbāh,* vol. 2. Vilna: Romm, 1887.

Buber, Solomon, ed. Vilna: Romm, 1899.

Translation:

Cohen, A., trans. In *The Midrash Rabbah,* edited by H. Freedman and Maurice Simon, vol. 4. London: Soncino Press, 1977.

Leviticus Rabbāh.

Margulies, Mordecai, ed. 5 vols. Jerusalem: American Academy for Jewish Research, 1953–1960.

Translations:

Israelstam, J., and Judah J. Slotki, trans. In *The Midrash Rabbah,* edited by H. Freedman and Maurice Simon, vol. 2. London: Soncino Press, 1977.

Neusner, Jacob, trans. *Judaism and Scripture: The Evidence of Leviticus Rabbah.* Chicago Studies in the History of Judaism. Chicago: University of Chicago Press, 1986.

M^{e}ḵîltā' d^{e}-R. Ishmael.

Jacob Z. Lauterbach, ed. 3 vols. Philadelphia: Jewish Publication Society, 1933–1935.

Horovitz, H. S., and I. A. Rabin, eds. 1931. 2d ed. Jerusalem: Bamberger and Wahrmann, 1960.

Translations:

Lauterbach, Jacob Z., trans. *Mekilta de-Rabbi Ishmael.* 3 vols. Philadelphia: Jewish Publication Society, 1933–1935.

Neusner, Jacob, trans. *Mekhilta According to Rabbi Ishmael: An*

Analytical Translation. 2 vols. Brown Judaic Studies, nos. 148, 154. Atlanta: Scholars Press, 1988.

Midrash T^{e}hillîm.

Buber, Solomon, ed. Vilna: Romm, 1891.

Translation:

Braude, William G., trans. *The Midrash on Psalms.* 2 vols. Yale Judaica Series, vol. 13. New Haven: Yale University Press, 1959.

Mishnah.

Albeck, Chanoch, ed. 6 vols. Jerusalem: Mosad Bialik; Tel Aviv: Dvir, 1952–1958.

Blackman, Philip, ed. 2d rev. ed. 7 vols. New York: Judaica Press, 1963–1964.

Translations:

Danby, Herbert, trans. *The Mishnah.* Oxford: Oxford University Press, 1933.

Blackman, Philip, trans. *Mishnayoth.* 2d rev. ed. 7 vols. New York: Judaica Press, 1963–1964.

Neusner, Jacob, trans. *The Mishnah: A New Translation.* New Haven: Yale University Press, 1988.

Goldin, Judah, trans. *The Living Talmud: The Wisdom of the Fathers and Its Classical Commentaries.* New York: New American Library, 1957.

Numbers Rabbāh.

In *Midrash Rabbāh,* vol. 2. Vilna: Romm, 1887.

Hallevy, E. E., ed. In *Midrash Rabbāh*, vols. 6–7. Tel Aviv: Machbaroth Lesifrut, 1963.

Translation:

Slotki, Judah J., trans. In *The Midrash Rabbah*, edited by H. Freedman and Maurice Simon, vol. 3. London: Soncino Press, 1977.

P^{e}sîqtā' d^e-R. Kahana.

Mandelbaum, Bernard, ed. 2 vols. New York: Jewish Theological Seminary of America, 1962.

Translations:

Braude, William G., and Israel J. Kapstein, trans. *Pĕsiḳta dĕ-Rab̲ Kahăna: R. Kahana's Compilation of Discourses for Sabbaths and Festal Days*. Philadelphia: Jewish Publication Society, 1975.

Neusner, Jacob, trans. *Pesiqta deRab Kahana: An Analytical Translation.* 2 vols. Brown Judaic Studies, nos. 122–123. Atlanta: Scholars Press, 1987.

P^{e}sîqtā' Rabbāṯî.

Friedmann, M. ed. Vienna: [privately published], 1880.

Translation:

Braude, William G., trans. *Pĕsiḳta Rabbati: Discourses for Feasts, Fasts, and Special Sabbaths*. 2 vols. Yale Judaica Series, vol. 18. New Haven: Yale University Press, 1968.

Pirqê d^e-R. Eliezer.

Warsaw: Bomberg, 1852.

Translation:

Friedlander, Gerald, trans. *Pirḳê de Rabbi Eliezer (The Chapters of Rabbi Eliezer the Great)*. 4th ed. New York: Sepher-Hermon Press, 1981.

Ruth Rabbāh.

In *Midrash Rabbāh,* vol. 2. Vilna: Romm, 1887.

Lerner, Myron Bialik, ed. In "The Book of Ruth in Aggadic Literature and Midrash Ruth Rabba" [in Hebrew], vol. 2. Ph.D. diss., Hebrew University, 1971.

Translations:

Rabinowitz, L., trans. In *The Midrash Rabbah,* edited by H. Freedman and Maurice Simon, vol. 4. London: Soncino Press, 1977.

Neusner, Jacob, trans. *Ruth Rabbah: An Analytical Translation.* Brown Judaic Studies, no. 183. Atlanta: Scholars Press, 1989.

Sēḏer 'Ēliyyāhû Rabbāh.

Friedmann, M., ed. 1902. 2d ed. Jerusalem: Bamberger and Wahrmann, 1960.

Translation:

Braude, William G., and Israel J. Kapstein, trans. *Tanna dĕḇe Eliyyahu: The Lore of the School of Elijah.* Philadelphia: Jewish Publication Society, 1981, pp. 41–396.

Sēḏer 'Ēliyyāhû Zûṭā'.

Friedmann, M., ed. 1902. 2d ed. Jerusalem: Bamberger and Wahrmann, 1960.

Translation:

Braude, William G., and Israel J. Kapstein, trans. *Tanna dĕḇe Eliyyahu: The Lore of the School of Elijah*. Philadelphia: Jewish Publication Society, 1981, pp. 399–464.

Sip̄rā'.

Weiss, I. H., ed. Vienna: Jacob Schlossberg, 1862.

Finkelstein, Louis, ed. 4 vols. New York: Jewish Theological Seminary of America, 1983–1990.

Translation:

Neusner, Jacob, trans. *Sifra: An Analytical Translation*. 3 vols. Brown Judaic Studies, nos. 138–140. Atlanta: Scholars Press, 1988.

Sip̄rê on Deuteronomy.

Finkelstein, Louis, ed. Notes by H. S. Horovitz. 1939. Reprint. New York: Jewish Theological Seminary of America, 1969.

Translations:

Hammer, Reuven, trans. *Sifre: A Tannaitic Commentary on the Book of Deuteronomy*. Yale Judaica Series, vol. 24. New Haven: Yale University Press, 1986.

Neusner, Jacob, trans. *Sifre to Deuteronomy: An Analytical Translation*. 2 vols. Brown Judaic Studies, nos. 98, 101. Atlanta: Scholars Press, 1987.

Sip̄rê on Numbers.

Horovitz, H. S., ed. 1917. 2d ed. Jerusalem: Wahrmann Books, 1966.

Translation:

Neusner, Jacob, trans. *Sifré to Numbers: An American Translation and Explanation.* 2 vols. Brown Judaic Studies, nos. 118–119. Atlanta: Scholars Press, 1986. [in progress]

Song of Songs Rabbāh.

In *Midrash Rabbāh,* vol. 2. Vilna: Romm, 1887.

Dunsky, Samson, ed. Jerusalem: Dvir, 1980.

Translations:

Simon, Maurice, trans. In *The Midrash Rabbah,* edited by H. Freedman and Maurice Simon, vol. 4. London: Soncino Press, 1977.

Neusner, Jacob, trans. *Song of Songs Rabbah: An Analytical Translation.* 2 vols. Brown Judaic Studies, nos. 197–198. Atlanta: Scholars Press, 1989.

Tanḥûmā'.

Jerusalem: Lewin-Epstein, 1965.

Buber, Solomon, ed. 1885. Reprint. 5 vols. in 2. Jerusalem: Ortsel, 1964.

Urbach, Ephraim E., ed. "Śᵉrîḏê Tanḥumā' Yᵉlammᵉḏēnû." *Qōḇeṣ 'al Yāḏ* 6 (16), pt. 1 (1966): 1–54.

Translation:

Townsend, John T., trans. *Midrash Tanḥuma (S. Buber Recension).* Vol. 1, *Genesis.* Hoboken, N.J.: Ktav, 1989.

Hêḵālôṯ Texts

Hêḵālôṯ Rabbāṯî. In *Bāttê Miḏrāšôṯ,* edited by Solomon Aaron Wertheimer, vol. 1. 5th ed. Jerusalem: Ktab Yad Wasepher, 1989, pp. 63–136.

Hêkālôṯ Rabbāṯî. In *Bêṯ ha-Miḏrāš*, edited by Adolph Jellinek, vol. 3. 3d ed. Jerusalem: Wahrmann Books, 1967, pp. 83–108.

R^e*'ûyyôṯ Y*^e*ḥezqē'l* [Visions of Ezekiel]. Edited by Ithamar Gruenwald. In *Temirin: Texts and Studies in Kabbala and Hasidism*, edited by Israel Weinstock, vol. 1. Jerusalem: Mosad ha-Rav Kook, 1972, pp. 101–139.

Schäfer, Peter, ed. *Geniza-Fragmente zur Hekhalot-Literatur*. Texte und Studien zum Antiken Judentum, vol. 6. Tübingen: J. C. B. Mohr (Paul Siebeck), 1984.

______, ed. *Konkordanz zur Hekhalot-Literatur*. 2 vols. Texte und Studien zum Antiken Judentum, vols. 12–13. Tübingen: J. C. B. Mohr (Paul Siebeck), 1986–1988.

______, ed. *Synopse zur Hekhalot-Literatur*. Texte und Studien zum Antiken Judentum, vol. 2. Tübingen: J. C. B. Mohr (Paul Siebeck), 1981.

Kabbalistic Texts and Other Mystical Writings

1 Alphabet of R. Akiba. In *Bêṯ ha-Miḏrāš*, edited by Adolph Jellinek, vol. 3. 3d ed. Jerusalem: Wahrmann Books, 1967, pp. 12–49.

2 Alphabet of R. Akiba. In *Bêṯ ha-Miḏrāš*, edited by Adolph Jellinek, vol. 3. 3d ed. Jerusalem: Wahrmann Books, 1967, pp. 50–64.

Azriel b. Menaḥem of Gerona. *Pêrûš hā-'Aggāḏôṯ*. Edited by Isaiah Tishby. Jerusalem: Mekize Nirdamim, Mosad ha-Rav Kook, 1945.

Bacharach, Naphtali b. Jacob Elḥanan. *'Ēmeq ha-Meleḵ*. Amsterdam, 1648. Reprint. Bene Berak: Yahadut, 1973.

Cordovero, Moses. *D*^e*rîšôṯ b*^e*-'Inyānê Mal'āḵîm*. Edited by Reuben Margaliot. Jerusalem: Mosad ha-Rav Kook, 1945.

———. *Šî'ûr Qômāh*. Warsaw, 1883. Reprint. Jerusalem: Aḥuzat Yisrael, 1966.

Gikatilla, Joseph. *Ša'ăr[ê] 'Ôrāh*. Offenbach: Zeligman Raiz, 1715.

———. *Ša'ărê Ṣeḏeq* [concluding section]. In Efraim Gottlieb, *Studies in the Kabbala Literature* [in Hebrew], edited by Joseph Hacker. Tel Aviv: Tel Aviv University, 1976, pp. 132–162.

Jacob b. Sheshet. *Sēp̄er hā-'Ĕmûnāh w^{e}-ha-Biṭṭāḥôn*. In *Kiṯḇê Rabbênû Mosheh b. Naḥman*, edited by Ḥayyim Dov (Charles B.) Chavel, vol. 2. Jerusalem: Mosad ha-Rav Kook, 1963, pp. 353–448. [ascribed erroneously to Naḥmanides]

Menaḥem Azariah of Fano. *Šiḇ'îm û-Štayim Y^{e}ḏî'ôṯ*. Lvov, 1867.

Moses b. Naḥman (Naḥmanides). *Pêrûšê ha-Tôrāh*. Edited by Ḥayyim Dov (Charles B.) Chavel. 2 vols. Jerusalem: Mosad ha-Rav Kook, 1959–1960.

Translation:

Chavel, Charles B., trans. *Rambam (Nachmanides), Commentary on the Torah*. 5 vols. New York: Shilo, 1971–1976.

Recanati, Menaḥem. *Ṭa'ămê ha-Miṣwôṯ*. Edited by S. Lieberman. London: Makhon Otzar ha-Ḥokhmah, 1962.

Sarug, Israel. *Lîmmûḏê 'Ăṣîlûṯ*. Munkács: Samuel Kahn, 1897. [ascribed erroneously to Ḥayyim Vital]

Sēp̄er Y^{e}ṣîrāh. Jerusalem: Lewin-Epstein, 1965.

Translations:

Stenring, Knut, trans. *The Book of Formation (Sepher Yetzirah)*. 1923. Reprint. New York: Ktav, 1970.

Blumenthal, David R., trans. "*Sefer Yetsira*: Text and Commentary." Chapter 3 of his *Understanding Jewish Mysticism: A Source Reader*. [Vol. 1], *The Merkabah Tradition and the Zoharic Tra-*

dition. The Library of Judaic Learning, vol. 2. New York: Ktav, 1978, pp. 15–44.

Zohar. Edited by Reuben Margaliot. 4th ed. 3 vols. Jerusalem: Mosad ha-Rav Kook, 1964.

Zohar Ḥāḏāš. Edited by Reuben Margaliot. 1953. Reprint. Jerusalem: Mosad ha-Rav Kook, 1978.

Tiqqûnê ha-Zohar. Edited by Reuben Margaliot. 1948. Reprint. Jerusalem: Mosad ha-Rav Kook, 1978.

Translations:

Tishby, Isaiah, and Fischel Lachower, trans. and eds. *Mišnaṯ ha-Zohar*. 2 vols. Jerusalem: Mosad Bialik, 1971, 1961. Eng. trans. David Goldstein. *The Wisdom of the Zohar: An Anthology of Texts*. 3 vols. The Littman Library of Jewish Civilization. Oxford: Oxford University Press, 1989. [Anthology]

Sperling, Harry, Maurice Simon, and Paul P. Levertoff, trans. *The Zohar*. 2d ed. 5 vols. London: Soncino Press, 1984.

Matt, Daniel Chanan, trans. *Zohar: The Book of Enlightenment*. The Classics of Western Spirituality. New York: Paulist Press, 1983. [Anthology]

B. Secondary Sources

Albeck, Chanoch. *Untersuchungen über die halakischen Midraschim*. Veröffentlichungen der Akademie für die Wissenschaft des Judentums. Berlin: Akademie-Verlag, 1927.

Albright, W. F. "Some Canaanite-Phoenician Sources of Hebrew Wisdom." In *Wisdom in Israel and in the Ancient Near East*, edited by M. Noth and D. Winton Thomas. *Supplements to Vetus Testamentum* 3 (1969): 1–15.

Altmann, Alexander. *Studies in Religious Philosophy and Mysticism*. Ithaca: Cornell University Press, 1969.

Avi-Yonah, M. *The Jews under Roman and Byzantine Rule: A Political History of Palestine from the Bar Kokhba War to the Arab Conquest*. 1976. Reprint. New York: Schocken Books; Jerusalem: Magnes Press, Hebrew University, 1984.

Bacher, Wilhelm. *Die Agada der babylonischen Amoräer*. 2d ed. 1913. Reprint. Hildesheim: Georg Olms, 1967.

———. *Die Agada der palästinensischen Amoräer*. 3 vols. 1892–1899. Reprint. Hildesheim: Georg Olms, 1965.

———. *Die Agada der Tannaiten*. 2d rev. ed. Strassburg: Karl J. Trübner, 1903.

———. *Die exegetische Terminologie der jüdischen Traditionsliteratur*. 1899–1905. Reprint. 2 vols. in 1. Darmstadt: Wissenschaftliche Buchgesellschaft, 1965.

Bamberger, Bernard J. *Proselytism in the Talmudic Period*. Rev. ed. New York: Ktav, 1968.

Barr, James. *Holy Scripture: Canon, Authority, Criticism*. Philadelphia: Westminster Press, 1983.

Bauer-Kayatz, Christa. *Einführung in die alttestamentliche Weisheit*. Biblische Studien, vol. 55. Neukirchen-Vluyn: Neukirchener, 1969.

———. *Studien zu Proverbien 1–9. Eine form- und motivgeschichtliche Untersuchung unter Einbeziehung ägyptischen Vergleichsmaterials*. Wissenschaftliche Monographien zum Alten und Neuen Testament, vol. 22. Neukirchen-Vluyn: Neukirchener, 1966.

Bloch, Renée. "Écriture et tradition dans le judaïsme: Aperçus sur l'origine du Midrash." *Cahiers Sioniens* 8, no. 1 (Mar. 1954): 9–34.

———. "Midrash." *Dictionnaire de la Bible, Supplément,* edited by L. Pirot, et al. Paris: Librairie Letouzey et Ané, 1928–. S.v. Eng. trans. Mary Howard Callaway. "Midrash." In *Approaches to Ancient Judaism: Theory and Practice,* edited by William Scott Green. Brown Judaic Studies, no. 1. Missoula, Mont.: Scholars Press, 1978, pp. 29–50.

———. "Note méthodologique pour l'étude de la littérature rabbinique." *Recherches de Science Religieuse* 43 (1955): 194–227. Eng. trans. William Scott Green with William J. Sullivan. "Methodological Note for the Study of Rabbinic Literature." In *Approaches to Ancient Judaism: Theory and Practice,* edited by William Scott Green. Brown Judaic Studies, no. 1. Missoula, Mont.: Scholars Press, 1978, pp. 51–75.

Blumenthal, David R. *Understanding Jewish Mysticism: A Source Reader.* [Vol. 1], *The Merkabah Tradition and the Zoharic Tradition.* Vol. 2, *The Philosophic-Mystical Tradition and the Hasidic Tradition.* The Library of Judaic Learning, vols. 2, 4. New York: Ktav, 1978, 1982.

Bokser, Ben Zion. *The Jewish Mystical Tradition.* New York: Pilgrim Press, 1981.

Boström, Gustav. *Proverbiastudien. Die Weisheit und das fremde Weib in Spr. 1–9.* Lunds Universitets Årsskrift, n.s., pt. 1, vol. 30, no. 3. Lund: C. W. K. Gleerup, 1935.

Bowker, John. *The Targums and Rabbinic Literature: An Introduction to Jewish Interpretations of Scripture.* Cambridge: Cambridge University Press, 1969.

Boyarin, Daniel. *Carnal Israel: Reading Sex in Talmudic Culture.* The New Historicism: Studies in Cultural Poetics. Berkeley: University of California Press, 1993.

———. *Intertextuality and the Reading of Midrash.* Indiana Studies in Biblical Literature. Bloomington: Indiana University Press, 1990.

Braude, William G. *Jewish Proselyting in the First Five Centuries of the Common Era, the Age of the Tannaim and Amoraim.* Brown University Studies, vol. 6. Providence: Brown University, 1940.

———. "Open Thou Mine Eyes." In *Understanding the Talmud,* edited by Alan Corré. New York: Ktav, 1975, pp. 55–61.

Bregman, Marc. "The Triennial Haftarot and the Perorations of the Midrashic Homilies." *Journal of Jewish Studies* 32, no. 1 (Spring 1981): 74–84.

Brown, Ronald. "Midrashim as Oral Traditions." *Hebrew Union College Annual* 47 (1976): 181–189.

The Cambridge History of the Bible. Vol. 1, *From the Beginnings to Jerome,* edited by P. R. Ackroyd and C. F. Evans. Vol. 2, *The West from the Fathers to the Reformation,* edited by G. W. H. Lampe. Cambridge: Cambridge University Press, 1970, 1969.

Camp, Claudia V. *Wisdom and the Feminine in the Book of Proverbs.* Bible and Literature Series, 11. Sheffield, England: Almond, JSOT Press, 1985.

Chernus, Ira. *Mysticism in Rabbinic Judaism: Studies in the History of Midrash.* Studia Judaica: Forschungen zur Wissenschaft des Judentums, vol. 11. Berlin: Walter de Gruyter, 1982.

Childs, Brevard S. *Introduction to the Old Testament as Scripture.* Philadelphia: Fortress Press, 1979.

Clifford, Richard J. *The Cosmic Mountain in Canaan and the Old Testament.* Harvard Semitic Monographs, vol. 4. Cambridge: Harvard University Press, 1972.

Cohen, Abraham. "Gemara and Midrash." In *Understanding the Talmud,* edited by Alan Corré. New York: Ktav, 1975, pp. 21–26.

Cohen, Shaye J. D. *From the Maccabees to the Mishnah.* Library of Early Christianity. Philadelphia: Westminster Press, 1987.

Cohen-Alloro, Dorit. *The Secret of the Garment in the Zohar* [in

Hebrew]. Research Projects of the Institute of Jewish Studies, Monograph Series, 13. Jerusalem: Hebrew University, 1987.

Conzelmann, Hans. "The Mother of Wisdom." In *The Future of Our Religious Past: Essays in Honour of Rudolf Bultmann,* edited by James M. Robinson. Translated by Charles E. Carlston and Robert P. Scharlemann. New York: Harper and Row, 1971, pp. 230–243.

Crenshaw, James L. *Old Testament Wisdom: An Introduction.* Atlanta: John Knox Press, 1981.

_______, ed. *Studies in Ancient Israelite Wisdom.* The Library of Biblical Studies. New York: Ktav, 1976.

Dan, Joseph. "Midrash and the Dawn of Kabbalah." In *Midrash and Literature,* edited by Geoffrey H. Hartman and Sanford Budick. New Haven: Yale University Press, 1986, pp. 127–139.

———. *Three Types of Ancient Jewish Mysticism.* The Seventh Annual Rabbi Louis Feinberg Memorial Lecture in Judaic Studies. Cincinnati: Judaic Studies Program, University of Cincinnati, 1984.

_______, ed. *The Early Kabbalah.* Translated by Ronald C. Kiener. The Classics of Western Spirituality. New York: Paulist Press, 1986.

_______, ed. *Proceedings of the First International Conference on the History of Jewish Mysticism: Early Jewish Mysticism. Jerusalem Studies in Jewish Thought* 6, nos. 1–2 (1987).

_______, ed. *Proceedings of the Second International Conference on the History of Jewish Mysticism: The Beginnings of Jewish Mysticism in Medieval Europe. Jerusalem Studies in Jewish Thought* 6, nos. 3–4 (1987).

_______, ed. *Proceedings of the Third International Conference on the History of Jewish Mysticism: The Age of the Zohar. Jerusalem Studies in Jewish Thought* 8 (1989).

Dan, Joseph, and Frank Talmage, eds. *Studies in Jewish Mysticism: Proceedings of Regional Conferences Held at the University of*

California, Los Angeles and Mcgill University in April, 1978. Cambridge, Mass.: Association for Jewish Studies, 1982.

Davies, W. D. "Paul and the People of Israel." *New Testament Studies* 24, no. 1 (Oct. 1977): 4–39.

———. *Paul and Rabbinic Judaism: Some Rabbinic Elements in Pauline Theology*. Philadelphia: Fortress Press, 1980.

———. *Torah in the Messianic Age and/or the Age to Come.* Journal of Biblical Literature Monograph Series, vol. 7. Philadelphia: Society of Biblical Literature, 1952.

Eichrodt, Walther. *Theology of the Old Testament.* Translated by J. A. Baker. 2 vols. The Old Testament Library. Philadelphia: Westminster Press, 1961–1967.

Eilberg-Schwartz, Howard. "Who's Kidding Whom? A Serious Reading of Rabbinic Word Plays." *Journal of the American Academy of Religion* 55, no. 4 (Winter 1987): 765–788.

_______, ed. *People of the Body: Jews and Judaism from an Embodied Perspective.* SUNY Series, The Body in Culture, History, and Religion. Albany: State University of New York Press, 1992.

Fine, Lawrence. "Kabbalistic Texts." In *Back to the Sources: Reading the Classic Jewish Texts,* edited by Barry W. Holtz. New York: Summit Books, 1984, pp. 305–359.

_______, trans. *Safed Spirituality: Rules of Mystical Piety, The Beginning of Wisdom.* The Classics of Western Spirituality. New York: Paulist Press, 1984.

Fischel, Henry A. "The Transformation of Wisdom in the World of Midrash." In *Aspects of Wisdom in Judaism and Early Christianity,* edited by Robert L. Wilken. Notre Dame: University of Notre Dame Press, 1975, pp. 67–101.

Fishbane, Michael. *Biblical Interpretation in Ancient Israel.* Oxford: Clarendon Press, 1985.

———. *The Garments of Torah: Essays in Biblical Hermeneutics.* Indiana Studies in Biblical Literature. Bloomington: Indiana University Press, 1989.

———. "Inner Biblical Exegesis: Types and Strategies of Interpretation in Ancient Israel." In *Midrash and Literature,* edited by Geoffrey H. Hartman and Sanford Budick. New Haven: Yale University Press, 1986, pp. 19–37.

———. "Torah." *Encyclopedia Miqrā'îṯ.* Jerusalem: Mosad Bialik, 1962–1988. S.v.

———. "Torah and Tradition." In *Tradition and Theology in the Old Testament,* edited by Douglas A. Knight. Philadelphia: Fortress Press, 1977, pp. 275–300.

_______, ed. *The Midrashic Imagination: Jewish Exegesis, Thought, and History.* Albany: State University of New York Press, 1993.

Fleischer, Ezra, and Jakob J. Petuchowski, eds. *Studies in Aggadah, Targum and Jewish Liturgy in Memory of Joseph Heinemann* [in English and Hebrew]. Jerusalem: Magnes Press, Hebrew University, 1981.

Fohrer, Georg. "Sophia." In *Studies in Ancient Israelite Wisdom,* edited by James L. Crenshaw. The Library of Biblical Studies. New York: Ktav, 1976, pp. 63–83.

Fraade, Steven D. *From Tradition to Commentary: Torah and Its Interpretation in the Midrash Sife to Deuteronomy.* SUNY Series in Judaica: Hermeneutics, Mysticism, and Religion. Albany: State University of New York Press, 1991.

———. "Interpreting Midrash 1: Midrash and the History of Judaism." *Prooftexts* 7, no. 2 (May 1987): 179–194.

———. "Interpreting Midrash 2: Midrash and Its Literary Contexts." *Prooftexts* 7, no. 3 (Sept. 1987): 284–300.

Gammie, John G., et al., eds. *Israelite Wisdom: Theological and Literary Essays in Honor of Samuel Terrien.* Missoula, Mont.: Scholars Press, 1978.

Gaston, Lloyd. "Paul and the Torah." In *Antisemitism and the Foundations of Christianity,* edited by Alan Davies. New York: Paulist Press, 1979, pp. 48–71. Reprinted in his *Paul and the Torah,* pp. 15–34.

———. *Paul and the Torah.* Vancouver: University of British Columbia Press, 1987.

Gemser, Berend. *Sprüche Salomos.* 2d rev. ed. Handbuch zum Alten Testament, Series 1, 16. Tübingen: J. C. B. Mohr (Paul Siebeck), 1963.

Gerhardsson, Birger. *Memory and Manuscript: Oral Tradition and Written Transmission in Rabbinic Judaism and Early Christianity.* Translated by Eric J. Sharpe. Acta seminarii neotestamentici upsaliensis, 22. Lund: C. W. K. Gleerup; Copenhagen: Ejnar Munksgaard, 1961.

Ginzberg, Louis. *Genizah Studies in Memory of Doctor Solomon Schechter.* Vol. 1, *Midrash and Haggadah* [in Hebrew]. Texts and Studies of the Jewish Theological Seminary of America, vol. 7. 1928. Reprint. New York: Hermon Press, 1969.

———. *The Legends of the Jews.* 7 vols. Philadelphia: Jewish Publication Society, 1909–1938.

———. *On Jewish Law and Lore.* Philadelphia: Jewish Publication Society, 1955.

Goldin, Judah. "The Freedom and Restraint of Haggadah." In *Midrash and Literature,* edited by Geoffrey H. Hartman and Sanford Budick. New Haven: Yale University Press, 1986, pp. 57–76. Reprinted in his *Studies in Midrash and Related Literature,* pp. 253–269.

———. "From Text to Interpretation and from Experience to the Interpreted Text." *Prooftexts* 3, no. 2 (May 1983): 157–168. Reprinted in his *Studies in Midrash and Related Literature,* pp. 271–281.

———. "Midrash and Aggadah." *The Encyclopedia of Religion,* edited by Mircea Eliade, et al. New York: Macmillan, 1987. S.v.

———. "Of Change and Adaptation in Judaism." *History of Religions* 4, no. 2 (Winter 1965): 269–294. Reprinted in his *Studies in Midrash and Related Literature,* pp. 215–237.

———. *Studies in Midrash and Related Literature.* Edited by Barry L. Eichler and Jeffrey H. Tigay. Philadelphia: Jewish Publication Society, 1988.

Gottlieb, Efraim. *Studies in the Kabbala Literature* [in Hebrew]. Edited by Joseph Hacker. Tel Aviv: Tel Aviv University, 1976.

Grant, Robert M., with David Tracy. *A Short History of the Interpretation of the Bible.* 1963. 2d rev. ed. Philadelphia: Fortress Press, 1984.

Green, William Scott. "Romancing the Tome: Rabbinic Hermeneutics and the Theory of Literature." In *Text and Textuality,* edited by Charles E. Winquist. *Semeia* 40 (1987): 147–168. Partially reprinted as "Writing with Scripture: The Rabbinic Uses of the Hebrew Bible." Chapter 2 of Jacob Neusner with William Scott Green, *Writing with Scripture: The Authority and Uses of the Hebrew Bible in the Torah of Formative Judaism.* Minneapolis: Fortress Press, 1989, pp. 7–23.

Grözinger, Karl-Erich. *Ich bin der Herr, dein Gott! Eine rabbinische Homilie zum Ersten Gebot (PesR 20).* Frankfurter Judaistische Studien, vol. 2. Bern: Herbert Lang; Frankfurt: Peter Lang, 1976.

Gruenwald, Ithamar. *Apocalyptic and Merkavah Mysticism.* Arbeiten zur Geschichte des antiken Judentums und des Urchristentums, vol. 14. Leiden: E. J. Brill, 1980.

———. *From Apocalypticism to Gnosticism: Studies in Apocalypticism, Merkavah Mysticism and Gnosticism.* Beiträge zur Erforschung des Alten Testaments und des antiken Judentums, vol. 14. Frankfurt: Peter Lang, 1988.

———. "Knowledge and Vision: Towards a Clarification of Two 'Gnostic' Concepts in the Light of their Alleged Origins." *Israel Oriental Studies* 3 (1973): 63–107. Reprinted in his *From Apoc-*

alypticism to Gnosticism: Studies in Apocalypticism, Merkavah Mysticism and Gnosticism, pp. 65–123.

Halivni, David Weiss. *Midrash, Mishnah, and Gemara: The Jewish Predilection for Justified Law*. Cambridge: Harvard University Press, 1986.

———. *Peshat and Derash: Plain and Applied Meaning in Rabbinic Exegesis*. New York: Oxford University Press, 1991.

Halperin, David J. *The Faces of the Chariot: Early Jewish Responses to Ezekiel's Vision*. Tübingen: J. C. B. Mohr (Paul Siebeck), 1988.

———. *The Merkabah in Rabbinic Literature*. American Oriental Series, vol. 62. New Haven: American Oriental Society, 1980.

Handelman, Susan A. *The Slayers of Moses: The Emergence of Rabbinic Interpretation in Modern Literary Theory*. SUNY Series on Modern Jewish Literature and Culture. Albany: State University of New York Press, 1982.

Hartman, Geoffrey H., and Sanford Budick. *Midrash and Literature*. New Haven: Yale University Press, 1986.

Heide, A. van der, "PARDES: Methodological Reflections on the Theory of the Four Senses." *Journal of Jewish Studies* 34, no. 2 (Autumn 1983): 147–159.

Heinemann, Isaak. *Darḵê hā-'Aggāḏāh*. 3d ed. Jerusalem: Magnes Press, Hebrew University, 1970.

Heinemann, Joseph. *Aggadah and Its Development* [in Hebrew]. Jerusalem: Keter, 1974.

———. "The Nature of the Aggadah." In *Midrash and Literature*, edited by Geoffrey H. Hartman and Sanford Budick. New Haven: Yale University Press, 1986, pp. 41–55.

———. "The Proem in the Aggadic Midrashim—A Form-Critical Study." In *Studies in Aggadah and Folk-Literature*, edited by

Joseph Heinemann and Dov Noy. *Scripta Hierosolymitana* 22 (1971): 100–122.

———. "Profile of a Midrash: The Art of Composition in Leviticus Rabba." *Journal of the American Academy of Religion* 39, no. 2 (June 1971): 141–150.

Heinemann, Joseph, with Jakob J. Petuchowski, eds. *Literature of the Synagogue.* New York: Behrman House, 1975.

Hengel, Martin. *Judaism and Hellenism: Studies in Their Encounter in Palestine during the Early Hellenistic Period.* Translated by John Bowden. 2 vols. Philadelphia: Fortress Press, 1974.

Herr, Moshe David. "Midrash." *Encyclopaedia Judaica.* New York: Macmillan, 1971. S.v.

Heschel, Abraham Joshua. *Tôrāh min ha-Šāmayim bā-'Aspaqlaryāh šel ha-Dôrôṯ.* 2 vols. London: Soncino Press, 1962–1965.

Hoffmann, D. *Zur Einleitung in die halachischen Midraschim.* Berlin: M. Driesner, 1886–1887.

Holdrege, Barbara A. "The Bride of Israel: The Ontological Status of Scripture in the Rabbinic and Kabbalistic Traditions." In *Rethinking Scripture: Essays from a Comparative Perspective,* edited by Miriam Levering. Albany: State University of New York Press, 1989, pp. 180–261.

———. "Veda and Torah: The Word Embodied in Scripture." In *Between Jerusalem and Benares: Comparative Studies in Judaism and Hinduism,* edited by Hananya Goodman. Albany: State University of New York Press, 1994, pp. 103–179.

Holtz, Barry W. "Midrash." In *Back to the Sources: Reading the Classic Jewish Texts,* edited by Barry W. Holtz. New York: Summit Books, 1984, pp. 177–211.

Idel, Moshe. "Infinities of Torah in Kabbalah." In *Midrash and Literature,* edited by Geoffrey H. Hartman and Sanford Budick. New Haven: Yale University Press, 1986, pp. 141–157.

———. *Kabbalah: New Perspectives*. New Haven: Yale University Press, 1988.

———. *Language, Torah, and Hermeneutics in Abraham Abulafia*. Translated by Menahem Kallus. SUNY Series in Judaica: Hermeneutics, Mysticism, and Religion. Albany: State University of New York Press, 1989.

———. *The Mystical Experience in Abraham Abulafia*. Translated by Jonathan Chipman. SUNY Series in Judaica: Hermeneutics, Mysticism, and Religion. Albany: State University of New York Press, 1988.

———. "Reification of Language in Jewish Mysticism." In *Mysticism and Language*, edited by Steven T. Katz. New York: Oxford University Press, 1992, pp. 42–79.

———. *Studies in Ecstatic Kabbalah*. SUNY Series in Judaica: Hermeneutics, Mysticism, and Religion. Albany: State University of New York Press, 1988.

———. "T^{e}p̄îsaṯ ha-Tôrāh b^{e}-Sip̄rûṯ ha-Hêḵālôṯ w^{e}-Gilgûlệhā ba-Qabbālāh." *Jerusalem Studies in Jewish Thought* 1 (1981): 23–84.

Jacobs, Louis. "Hermeneutics." *Encyclopaedia Judaica*. New York: Macmillan, 1971. S.v.

———. *Jewish Biblical Exegesis*. The Chain of Tradition Series, vol. 4. New York: Behrman House, 1973.

———. *Jewish Mystical Testimonies*. Jerusalem: Keter, 1976.

———. *Structure and Form in the Babylonian Talmud*. Cambridge: Cambridge University Press, 1991.

———. *The Talmudic Argument: A Study in Talmudic Reasoning and Methodology*. Cambridge: Cambridge University Press, 1984.

———. *A Tree of Life: Diversity, Flexibility, and Creativity in Jewish Law*. The Littman Library of Jewish Civilization. Oxford: Oxford University Press, 1984.

Jaffee, Martin S. "How Much 'Orality' in Oral Torah? New Perspectives on the Composition and Transmission of Early Rabbinic Tradition." *Shofar* 10, no. 2 (Winter 1992): 53–72.

Kadushin, Max. *Organic Thinking: A Study in Rabbinic Thought.* New York: Jewish Theological Seminary of America, 1938.

———. *The Rabbinic Mind.* 3d ed. New York: Bloch Publishing, 1972.

Kagin, Zipporah. "Divergent Tendencies and Their Literary Moulding in the Aggadah." In *Studies in Aggadah and Folk-Literature,* edited by Joseph Heinemann and Dov Noy. *Scripta Hierosolymitana* 22 (1971): 151–170.

Kasher, Menaḥem M. *Tôrāh Šᵉlēmāh.* 43 vols. Jerusalem and New York, 1927–. Eng. trans. under the editorship of Harry Freedman. *Encyclopedia of Biblical Interpretation.* 9 vols. New York: American Biblical Encyclopedia Society, 1953–1979.

Katz, Nathan, and Ellen S. Goldberg. *The Last Jews of Cochin: Jewish Identity in Hindu India.* Columbia, S.C.: University of South Carolina Press, 1993.

———. "The Ritual Enactments of the Cochin Jews: The Powers of Purity and Nobility." In *Ritual and Power,* edited by Barbara A. Holdrege. *Journal of Ritual Studies* 4, no. 2 (Summer 1990): 199–238.

Kugel, James L. *In Potiphar's House: The Interpretive Life of Biblical Texts.* San Francisco: Harper, 1990.

———. "Two Introductions to Midrash." *Prooftexts* 3, no. 2 (May 1983): 131–155. Reprinted in *Midrash and Literature,* edited by Geoffrey H. Hartman and Sanford Budick. New Haven: Yale University Press, 1986, pp. 77–103.

Kugel, James L., and Rowan A. Greer. *Early Biblical Interpretation.* Library of Early Christianity. Philadelphia: Westminster Press, 1986.

Lang, Bernhard. *Wisdom and the Book of Proverbs: A Hebrew Goddess Redefined.* New York: Pilgrim Press, 1986.

Laporte, Jean. "Philo in the Tradition of Biblical Wisdom Literature." In *Aspects of Wisdom in Judaism and Early Christianity,* edited by Robert L. Wilken. Notre Dame: University of Notre Dame Press, 1975, pp. 103–141.

Le Déaut, Roger. "A propos d'une définition du midrash." *Biblica* 50, no. 3 (1969): 395–413. Eng. trans. "Apropos a Definition of Midrash." *Interpretation* 25, no. 3 (July 1971): 259–282.

Lehrman, S. M. *The World of the Midrash.* Popular Jewish Library. London: Thomas Yoseloff, 1961.

Leiman, Sid Z. *The Canonization of Hebrew Scripture: The Talmudic and Midrashic Evidence.* Transactions of the Connecticut Academy of Arts and Sciences, vol. 47. Hamden, Conn.: Archon Books, 1976.

_______, ed. *The Canon and Masorah of the Hebrew Bible: An Introductory Reader.* The Library of Biblical Studies. New York: Ktav, 1974.

Levine, Lee I. *The Rabbinic Class of Roman Palestine in Late Antiquity.* Jerusalem: Yad Izhak Ben-Zvi; New York: Jewish Theological Seminary of America, 1989.

Lieberman, Saul. "Mišnaṯ Šîr ha-Šîrîm." In Gershom G. Scholem, *Jewish Gnosticism, Merkabah Mysticism, and Talmudic Tradition,* Appendix D. 2d ed. New York: Jewish Theological Seminary of America, 1965, pp. 118–126.

Liebes, Yehuda. "How the Zohar Was Written." Chapter 2 of his *Studies in the Zohar,* pp. 85–138.

———. *Studies in Jewish Myth and Jewish Messianism.* Translated by Batya Stein. SUNY Series in Judaica: Hermeneutics, Mysticism, and Religion. Albany: State University of New York Press, 1993.

———. *Studies in the Zohar.* Translated by Arnold Schwartz, Stephanie Nakache, and Penina Peli. SUNY Series in Judaica: Hermeneutics, Mysticism, and Religion. Albany: State University of New York Press, 1993.

Lightstone, Jack N. "The Formation of the Biblical Canon in Judaism of Late Antiquity: Prolegomenon to a General Reassessment." *Studies in Religion/Sciences Religieuses* 8, no. 2 (1979): 135–142.

Lipiner, Elias. *The Metaphysics of the Hebrew Alphabet* [in Hebrew]. Jerusalem: Magnes Press, Hebrew University, 1989.

Mack, Burton L. *Logos und Sophia: Untersuchungen zur Weisheitstheologie im hellenistischen Judentum.* Studien zur Umwelt des Neuen Testaments, vol. 10. Göttingen: Vandenhoeck and Ruprecht, 1973.

Mann, Jacob, and Isaiah Sonne. *The Bible as Read and Preached in the Old Synagogue: A Study in the Cycles of the Readings from Torah and Prophets, as well as from the Psalms, and in the Structure of the Midrashic Homilies.* 2 vols. The Library of Biblical Studies. 1940. Reprint. New York: Ktav, 1971 (vol. 1); Cincinnati: Hebrew Union College, 1966 (vol. 2).

Mirsky, S. K. "The Schools of Hillel, R. Ishmael and R. Akiba in Pentateuchal Interpretation." In *Essays Presented to Chief Rabbi Israel Brodie on the Occasion of His Seventieth Birthday,* edited by H. J. Zimmels, J. Rabbinowitz, and I. Finestein, vol. 1. Jews' College Publications, n.s., no. 3. London: Soncino Press, 1967, pp. 291–299.

Montefiore, C. G., and H. Loewe, eds. *A Rabbinic Anthology.* 1938. Reprint. New York: Schocken Books, 1974.

Moore, George Foot. "The Idea of Torah in Judaism." In *Understanding the Talmud,* edited by Alan Corré. New York: Ktav, 1975, pp. 160–175.

———. *Judaism in the First Centuries of the Christian Era, the Age of the Tannaim.* 3 vols. Cambridge: Harvard University Press, 1927–1930.

Morris, Paul. "The Embodied Text: Covenant and Torah." *Religion* 20 (Jan. 1990): 77–87.

Murphy, Roland E. *Wisdom Literature: Job, Proverbs, Ruth, Canticles, Ecclesiastes, and Esther.* The Forms of the Old Testament Literature, vol. 13. Grand Rapids, Mich.: William B. Eerdmans, 1981.

Neusner, Jacob. *Ancient Judaism and Modern Category-Formation: "Judaism," "Midrash," "Messianism," and Canon in the Past Quarter-Century.* Studies in Judaism. Lanham, Md.: University Press of America, 1986.

———. *Death and Birth of Judaism: The Impact of Christianity, Secularism, and the Holocaust on Jewish Faith.* New York: Basic Books, 1987.

———. *The Ecology of Religion: From Writing to Religion in the Study of Judaism.* Nashville: Abingdon Press, 1989.

———. *From Tradition to Imitation: The Plan and Program of Pesiqta Rabbati and Pesiqta deRab Kahana.* Brown Judaic Studies, no. 80. Atlanta: Scholars Press, 1987.

———. *The Integrity of Leviticus Rabbah: The Problem of the Autonomy of a Rabbinic Document.* Brown Judaic Studies, no. 93. Chico, Calif.: Scholars Press, 1985.

———. *Midrash as Literature: The Primacy of Documentary Discourse.* Studies in Judaism. New York: Lanham, 1987.

———. *Midrash in Context: Exegesis in Formative Judaism.* Philadelphia: Fortress Press, 1983.

———. *Torah: From Scroll to Symbol in Formative Judaism.* Philadelphia: Fortress Press, 1985.

______, ed. *The Study of Ancient Judaism.* 2 vols. New York: Ktav, 1981.

Neusner, Jacob, with William Scott Green. *Writing with Scripture: The Authority and Uses of the Hebrew Bible in the Torah of Formative Judaism.* Minneapolis: Fortress Press, 1989.

Nickelsburg, George W. E. *Jewish Literature Between the Bible and the Mishnah: A Historical and Literary Introduction.* Philadelphia: Fortress Press, 1981.

Noth, M., and D. Winton Thomas, eds. *Wisdom in Israel and in the Ancient Near East. Supplements to Vetus Testamentum* 3 (1969).

Oron, M. "The Narrative of the Letters and Its Source: A Study of a Zoharic Midrash on the Letters of the Alphabet" [in Hebrew]. In *Studies in Jewish Mysticism Presented to Isaiah Tishby on His Seventy-Fifth Birthday,* edited by Joseph Dan and Joseph Hacker. *Jerusalem Studies in Jewish Thought* 3, nos. 1–2 (1983–1984): 97–109.

Östborn, Gunnar. *Cult and Canon: A Study in the Canonization of the Old Testament.* Uppsala Universitets Årsskrift, 1950, 10. Uppsala: A.-B. Lundequistska; Leipzig: Otto Harrassowitz, 1950.

Petuchowski, Jakob J. *Ever Since Sinai: A Modern View of Torah.* Rev. 3d ed. Milwaukee: B. Arbit Books, 1979.

Porton, Gary G. "Defining Midrash." In *The Study of Ancient Judaism,* edited by Jacob Neusner, vol. 1. New York: Ktav, 1981, pp. 55–92.

———. *Understanding Rabbinic Midrash: Texts and Commentary.* The Library of Judaic Learning, vol. 5. Hoboken, N.J.: Ktav, 1985.

Rabinowitz, Louis Isaac. "Sefer Torah." *Encyclopaedia Judaica.* New York: Macmillan, 1971. S.v.

Rabinowitz, Louis Isaac, and Warren Harvey. "Torah." *Encyclopaedia Judaica.* New York: Macmillan, 1971. S.v.

Rad, Gerhard von. *Old Testament Theology.* Translated by D. M. G. Stalker. 2 vols. New York: Harper and Row, 1962–1965.

———. *Wisdom in Israel.* Translated by James D. Martin. London: SCM Press, 1972.

Räisänen, Heikki. *Paul and the Law*. Philadelphia: Fortress Press, 1986.

Rathaus, Ariel. "Reading the Bible in the Midrashic Tradition." *Service International de Documentation Judéo-Chrétienne* 9, no. 2 (1976): 12–18.

Rawidowicz, Simon. "On Interpretation." Chapter 2 of his *Studies in Jewish Thought*, edited by Nahum N. Glatzer. Philadelphia: Jewish Publication Society, 1974, pp. 45–80.

Ringgren, Helmer. *Word and Wisdom: Studies in the Hypostatization of Divine Qualities and Functions in the Ancient Near East*. Lund: Håkan Ohlssons, 1947.

Roitman, Betty, "Sacred Language and Open Text." In *Midrash and Literature*, edited by Geoffrey H. Hartman and Sanford Budick. New Haven: Yale University Press, 1986, pp. 159–175.

Rosenbaum, Jonathan. "Judaism: Torah and Tradition." In *The Holy Book in Comparative Perspective*, edited by Frederick M. Denny and Rodney L. Taylor. Studies in Comparative Religion. Columbia, S. C.: University of South Carolina Press, 1985, pp. 10–35.

Rosenthal, Erwin I. J. "The Study of the Bible in Medieval Judaism." In *The Cambridge History of the Bible*, vol. 2, edited by G. W. H. Lampe. Cambridge: Cambridge University Press, 1969, pp. 252–279.

Russell, D. S. *The Method and Message of Jewish Apocalyptic, 200 BC–AD 100*. The Old Testament Libary. Philadelphia: Westminster Press, 1964.

Sanders, E. P. *Paul and Palestinian Judaism: A Comparison of Patterns of Religion*. London: SCM Press, 1977.

———. *Paul, the Law, and the Jewish People*. Philadelphia: Fortress Press, 1983.

———. "Paul's Attitude Toward the Jewish People." In *Interpreting Saint Paul. Union Seminary Quarterly Review* 33, nos. 3–4 (Spring–Summer 1978): 175–187.

Sanders, James A. *Canon and Community: A Guide to Canonical Criticism.* Guides to Biblical Scholarship. Philadelphia: Fortress Press, 1984.

———. *From Sacred Story to Sacred Text.* Philadelphia: Fortress Press, 1987.

———. *Torah and Canon.* Philadelphia: Fortress Press, 1972.

Sarason, Richard S. "Toward a New Agendum for the Study of Rabbinic Midrashic Literature." In *Studies in Aggadah, Targum and Jewish Liturgy in Memory of Joseph Heinemann,* edited by Ezra Fleischer and Jakob J. Petuchowski. Jerusalem: Magnes Press, Hebrew University, 1981, pp. 55–73.

Schäfer, Peter. "Engel und Menschen in der Hekhalot-Literatur," *Kairos,* n.s., 22, nos. 3–4 (1980): 201–225. Reprinted in his *Hekhalot-Studien,* pp. 250–276.

———. *Gershom Scholem Reconsidered: The Aim and Purpose of Early Jewish Mysticism.* The Twelfth Sacks Lecture. Oxford: Oxford Centre for Postgraduate Hebrew Studies, 1986. Reprinted in his *Hekhalot-Studien,* pp. 277–295.

———. *Hekhalot-Studien.* Texte und Studien zum Antiken Judentum, vol. 19. Tübingen: J. C. B. Mohr (Paul Siebeck), 1988.

———. *The Hidden and Manifest God: Some Major Themes in Early Jewish Mysticism.* Translated by Aubrey Pomerance. SUNY Series in Judaica: Hermeneutics, Mysticism, and Religion. Albany: State University of New York Press, 1992.

———. *Rivalität zwischen Engeln und Menschen. Untersuchungen zur rabbinischen Engelvorstellung.* Studia Judaica: Forschungen zur Wissenchaft des Judentums, vol. 8. Berlin: Walter de Gruyter, 1975.

———. "Tradition and Redaction in Hekhalot Literature." *Journal for the Study of Judaism* 14, no. 2 (Dec. 1983): 172–181. Reprinted in his *Hekhalot-Studien,* pp. 8–16.

Schechter, Solomon. *Aspects of Rabbinic Theology*. New York: Schocken Books, 1961.

Scholem, Gershom G. *Jewish Gnosticism, Merkabah Mysticism, and Talmudic Tradition*. 2d ed. New York: Jewish Theological Seminary of America, 1965.

———. *Kabbalah*. Library of Jewish Knowledge. Jerusalem: Keter, 1974.

———. *Major Trends in Jewish Mysticism*. 3d rev. ed. 1954. Reprint. New York: Schocken Books, 1961.

———. "The Meaning of the Torah in Jewish Mysticism." Chapter 2 of his *On the Kabbalah and Its Symbolism*, pp. 32–86.

———. *The Messianic Idea in Judaism and Other Essays on Jewish Spirituality*. New York: Schocken Books, 1971.

———. "The Name of God and the Linguistic Theory of the Kabbala." *Diogenes*, no. 79 (Fall 1972): 59–80 (Part 1); no. 80 (Winter 1972): 164–194 (Part 2).

———. *On the Kabbalah and Its Symbolism*. Translated by Ralph Manheim. New York: Schocken Books, 1965.

———. *Origins of the Kabbalah*. Edited by R. J. Zwi Werblowsky. Translated by Allan Arkush. Philadelphia: Jewish Publication Society; Princeton: Princeton University Press, 1987.

———. *Von der mystischen Gestalt der Gottheit: Studien zu Grundbegriffen der Kabbala*. Zürich: Rhein-Verlag, 1962. Eng. trans. Joachim Neugroschel. *On the Mystical Shape of the Godhead: Basic Concepts in the Kabbalah*. Edited and revised by Jonathan Chipman. New York: Schocken Books, 1991.

Schultz, Joseph P. "Angelic Opposition to the Ascension of Moses and the Revelation of the Law." *The Jewish Quarterly Review* 61, no. 4 (Apr. 1971): 282–307.

Scott, R. B. Y. "Wisdom in Creation: The *'āmôn* of Proverbs VIII 30." *Vetus Testamentum* 10 (1960): 213–223.

Silver, Daniel Jeremy. *The Story of Scripture: From Oral Tradition to the Written Word.* New York: Basic Books, 1990.

Slonimsky, Henry. "The Philosophy Implicit in the Midrash." *Hebrew Union College Annual* 27 (1956): 235–290.

Steiner, George. "Our Homeland, the Text." *Salmagundi* 66 (Winter–Spring 1985): 4–25.

Stendahl, Krister. *Paul Among Jews and Gentiles and Other Essays.* Philadelphia: Fortress Press, 1976.

Stern, David. *Parables in Midrash: Narrative and Exegesis in Rabbinic Literature.* Cambridge: Harvard University Press, 1991.

Strack, Hermann L., and Günter Stemberger. *Einleitung in Talmud und Midrasch.* 7th rev. ed. Münich: C. H. Beck, 1982. Eng. trans. Markus Bockmuehl. *Introduction to the Talmud and Midrash.* Edinburgh: T and T Clark, 1991.

Tomson, Peter J. *Paul and the Jewish Law: Halakha in the Letters of the Apostle to the Gentiles.* Compendia Rerum Iudaicarum ad Novum Testamentum. Section 3, Jewish Traditions in Early Christian Literature, vol. 1. Assen, Netherlands: Van Gorcum; Minneapolis: Fortress Press, 1990.

Urbach, Ephraim E. *The Sages: Their Concepts and Beliefs.* Translated by Israel Abrahams. 2d rev. ed. 2 vols. Jerusalem: Magnes Press, Hebrew University, 1979.

———. "Torah." *The Encyclopedia of Religion,* edited by Mircea Eliade, et al. New York: Macmillan, 1987. S.v.

———. "The Traditions about Merkabah Mysticism in the Tannaitic Period" [in Hebrew]. In *Studies in Mysticism and Religion Presented to Gershom G. Scholem on His Seventieth Birthday,* edited by E. E. Urbach, R. J. Zwi Werblowsky, and Ch. Wirszubski. Jerusalem: Magnes Press, Hebrew University, 1967, pp. 1–28 [Hebrew section].

Vermes, Geza. "Bible and Midrash: Early Old Testament Exegesis." In *The Cambridge History of the Bible,* vol. 1, edited by P. R.

Ackroyd and C. F. Evans. Cambridge: Cambridge University Press, 1970, pp. 199–231.

———. *Post-Biblical Jewish Studies*. Studies in Judaism in Late Antiquity, vol. 8. Leiden: E. J. Brill, 1975.

———. *Scripture and Tradition in Judaism: Haggadic Studies*. 2d rev. ed. Studia Post-Biblica, vol. 4. Leiden: E. J. Brill, 1973.

Wald, Stephen G. *The Doctrine of the Divine Name: An Introduction to Classical Kabbalistic Theology*. Brown Judaic Studies, no. 149. Atlanta: Scholars Press, 1988.

Wartski, I. *Lešôn ha-Midrāšîm*. Jerusalem: Mosad ha-Rav Kook, 1970.

Weingreen, J. "Exposition in the Old Testament and in Rabbinic Literature." In *Promise and Fulfillment: Essays Presented to Professor S. H. Hooke in Celebration of His Ninetieth Birthday*, edited by F. F. Bruce. Edinburgh: T and T Clark, 1963, pp. 187–201.

———. "Oral Torah and Written Records." In *Holy Book and Holy Tradition*, edited by F. F. Bruce and E. G. Rupp. Grand Rapids, Mich.: William B. Eerdmans, 1968, pp. 54–67.

———. "The Torah Speaks in the Language of Human Beings" [title in Hebrew]. In *Interpreting the Hebrew Bible: Essays in Honour of E. I. J. Rosenthal*. Edited by J. A. Emerton and Stefan C. Reif. Cambridge: Cambridge University Press, 1982, pp. 267–275.

Weiss, Abraham. *Studies in the Literature of the Amoraim* [in Hebrew]. New York: Yeshiva University, 1962.

Whybray, R. N. "Proverbs VIII 22–31 and Its Supposed Prototypes." In *Studies in Ancient Israelite Wisdom*, edited by James L. Crenshaw. The Library of Biblical Studies. New York: Ktav, 1976, pp. 390–400.

———. *Wisdom in Proverbs: The Concept of Wisdom in Proverbs 1–9*. Studies in Biblical Theology, no. 45. London: SCM Press, 1965.

Wilckens, Ulrich. *Weisheit und Torheit: Eine exegetisch-religionsgeschichtliche Untersuchung zu 1. Kor. 1 und 2.* Beiträge zur historischen Theologie, 26. Tübingen: J. C. B. Mohr (Paul Siebeck), 1959.

Wilken, Robert L., ed. *Aspects of Wisdom in Judaism and Early Christianity.* Notre Dame: University of Notre Dame Press, 1975.

Wolfson, Elliot R. *Along the Path: Studies in Kabbalistic Myth, Symbolism, and Hermeneutics.* SUNY Series in Judaica: Hermeneutics, Mysticism, and Religion. Albany: State University of New York Press, forthcoming.

———. "The Anthropomorphic and Symbolic Image of the Letters in the Zohar" [in Hebrew]. In *Proceedings of the Third International Conference on the History of Jewish Mysticism: The Age of the Zohar,* edited by Joseph Dan. *Jerusalem Studies in Jewish Thought* 8 (1989): 147–181.

———. "Beautiful Maiden without Eyes: *Peshat* and *Sod* in Zoharic Hermeneutics." In *The Midrashic Imagination: Jewish Exegesis, Thought, and History,* edited by Michael Fishbane. Albany: State University of New York Press, 1993, pp. 155–203.

———. "Circumcision, Vision of God, and Textual Interpretation: From Midrashic Trope to Mystical Symbol." *History of Religions* 27, no. 2 (1987): 189–215.

———. "Erasing the Erasure/ Gender and the Writing of God's Body in Kabbalistic Symbolism." In his *Along the Path: Studies in Kabbalistic Myth, Symbolism, and Hermeneutics.*

———. "Female Imaging of the Torah: From Literary Metaphor to Religious Symbol." In *From Ancient Israel to Modern Judaism: Intellect in Quest of Understanding. Essays in Honor of Marvin Fox,* edited by Jacob Neusner, Ernest S. Frerichs, and Nahum M. Sarna, vol. 2. Brown Judaica Studies, no. 173. Atlanta: Scholars Press, 1989, pp. 271–307. Reprinted in his *Along the Path: Studies in Kabbalistic Myth, Symbolism, and Hermeneutics.*

———. "The Hermeneutics of Visionary Experience: Revelation and Interpretation in the *Zohar.*" *Religion* 18 (Oct. 1988): 311–345.

———. "Letter Symbolism and *Merkavah* Imagery in the *Zohar.*" In *'Alei Shefer: Studies in the Literature of Jewish Thought,* edited by Moshe Ḥallamish. Ramat-Gan: Bar-Ilan University Press, 1990, pp. 195–236.

Wolfson, Harry Austryn. *Philo: Foundations of Religious Philosophy in Judaism, Christianity, and Islam.* 4th printing, rev. 2 vols. Cambridge: Harvard University Press, 1968.

———. "The Pre-existent Koran and the Pre-existent Law." Chapter 4 of his *Repercussions of the Kalam in Jewish Philosophy.* Cambridge: Harvard University Press, 1979, pp. 85–113.

Wright, Addison G. *The Literary Genre Midrash.* Staten Island, N.Y.: Alba House, 1967.

Würthwein, Ernst. "Egyptian Wisdom and the Old Testament." In *Studies in Ancient Israelite Wisdom,* edited by James L. Crenshaw. The Library of Biblical Studies. New York: Ktav, 1976, pp. 113–133.

Zunz, Leopold. *Die gottesdienstlichen Vorträge der Juden, historisch entwickelt.* 2d rev. ed. Frankfurt: J. Kauffmann, 1892. Heb. trans. M. E. Zack. *Ha-D^{e}rāšôṯ b^{e}-Yiśrā'ēl.* Notes by Chanoch Albeck. Jerusalem: Mosad Bialik, 1947.

III. GENERAL

Allen, Douglas. *Structure and Creativity in Religion: Hermeneutics in Mircea Eliade's Phenomenology and New Directions.* Religion and Reason, 14. The Hague: Mouton, 1978.

Bell, Catherine. "The Ritual Body and the Dynamics of Ritual Power." In *Ritual and Power,* edited by Barbara A. Holdrege. *Journal of Ritual Studies* 4, no. 2 (Summer 1990): 299–313.

———. *Ritual Theory, Ritual Practice.* New York: Oxford University Press, 1992.

Berger, Peter L. "Between Jerusalem and Benares: The Coming Contestation of Religions." Chapter 6 of his *The Heretical Imperative: Contemporary Possibilities of Religious Affirmation.* Garden City, N. Y.: Anchor Press, Doubleday, 1979, pp. 157–189.

Bertholet, Alfred. "Die Macht der Schrift in Glauben und Aberglauben." *Abhandlungen der Deutschen Akademie der Wissenschaften zu Berlin.* Philosophisch-historische Klasse. 1948, no. 1.

Bourdieu, Pierre. *Outline of a Theory of Practice.* Translated by Richard Nice. Cambridge Studies in Social Anthropology, 16. Cambridge: Cambridge University Press, 1977.

Bruce, F. F., and E. G. Rupp, eds. *Holy Book and Holy Tradition.* Grand Rapids, Mich.: William B. Eerdmans, 1968.

Buck, Harry M. "Saving Story and Sacred Book: Some Aspects of the Phenomenon of Religious Literature." In *Search the Scriptures: New Testament Studies in Honor of Raymond T. Stamm,* edited by J. M. Myers, O. Reimherr, and H. N. Bream. Gettysburg Theological Studies, no. 3. Leiden: E. J. Brill, 1969, pp. 79–94.

Coward, Harold. *Sacred Word and Sacred Text: Scripture in World Religions.* Maryknoll, N.Y.: Orbis Books, 1988.

Denny, Frederick M. "Islam: Qur'an and Hadith." In *The Holy Book in Comparative Perspective,* edited by Frederick M. Denny and Rodney L. Taylor. Studies in Comparative Religion. Columbia, S.C.: University of South Carolina Press, 1985, pp. 84–108.

Denny, Frederick M., and Rodney L. Taylor, eds. *The Holy Book in Comparative Perspective.* Studies in Comparative Religion. Columbia, S.C.: University of South Carolina Press, 1985.

Douglas, Mary. *Purity and Danger: An Analysis of Concepts of Pollution and Taboo.* London: Routledge and Kegan Paul, 1966.

Dudley, Guilford, III. *Religion on Trial: Mircea Eliade and His Critics*. Philadelphia: Temple University Press, 1977.

Eliade, Mircea. "Methodological Remarks on the Study of Religious Symbolism." In *The History of Religions: Essays in Methodology*, edited by Mircea Eliade and Joseph M. Kitagawa. Chicago: University of Chicago Press, 1959, pp. 86–107.

———. *The Quest: History and Meaning in Religion*. Chicago: University of Chicago Press, 1969.

Foucault, Michel. *The Archaeology of Knowledge and the Discourse on Language*. Translated by A. M. Sheridan Smith. New York: Random House, Pantheon Books, 1972.

———. *Discipline and Punish: The Birth of the Prison*. Translated by Alan Sheridan. New York: Random House, Vintage Books, 1979.

———. *The Order of Things: An Archaeology of the Human Sciences*. New York: Random House, Pantheon Books, 1970.

Frick, Heinrich. "Ideogramm, Mythologie und das Wort." In *Rudolf Otto Festgruss*, edited by Heinrich Frick. Marburger Theologische Studien, no. 3. Gotha: Leopold Klotz, 1931, pp. 1–20.

Gadamer, Hans-Georg. *Wahrheit und Methode. Grundzüge einer philosophischen Hermeneutik*. 4th ed. Tübingen: J. C. B. Mohr (Paul Siebeck), 1975. Eng. trans. *Truth and Method*. Edited by Garrett Barden and John Cumming. New York: Crossroad, 1982.

Gill, Sam D. "Nonliterate Traditions and Holy Books: Toward a New Model." In *The Holy Book in Comparative Perspective*, edited by Frederick M. Denny and Rodney L. Taylor. Studies in Comparative Religion. Columbia: University of South Carolina Press, 1985, pp. 224–239.

Goodman, Hananya, ed. *Between Jerusalem and Benares: Comparative Studies in Judaism and Hinduism*. Albany: State University of New York Press, 1994.

Goody, Jack. *The Interface Between the Written and the Oral.* Studies in Literacy, Family, Culture and the State. Cambridge: Cambridge University Press, 1987.

Graham, William A. *Beyond the Written Word: Oral Aspects of Scripture in the History of Religion.* Cambridge: Cambridge University Press, 1987.

———. "The Earliest Meaning of 'Qur'ān'." *Die Welt des Islams,* n.s., 23–24 (1984): 361–377.

———. "*Qur'ān* as Spoken Word: An Islamic Contribution to the Understanding of Scripture." In *Approaches to Islam in Religious Studies,* edited by Richard C. Martin. Tucson: University of Arizona Press, 1985, pp. 23–40.

———. "Scripture." *The Encyclopedia of Religion,* edited by Mircea Eliade, et al. New York: Macmillan, 1987. S.v.

———. "Scripture as Spoken Word." In *Rethinking Scripture: Essays from a Comparative Perspective,* edited by Miriam Levering. Albany: State University of New York Press, 1989, pp. 129–169.

———. "Those who Study and Teach the Qur'an." In *International Congress for the Study of the Qur'an.* Series 1. Canberra: Australian National University, 1980, pp. 9–28.

Heiler, Friedrich. "Das heilige Wort" and "Die heilige Schrift." Chapters A.VII and A.VIII, respectively, of his *Erscheinungsformen und Wesen der Religion.* 2d rev. ed. Die Religionen der Menschheit, vol. 1. Stuttgart: W. Kohlhammer, 1979, pp. 266–364.

Holdrege, Barbara A. "Comparative Religion with a Difference." In *The Notion of "Religion" in Comparative Research: Selected Proceedings of the XVIth Congress of the International Association for the History of Religions, Rome, 3rd–8th September, 1990,* edited by Ugo Bianchi. Storia delle Religioni, 8. Rome: "L'Erma" di Bretschneider, 1994, pp. 803–812.

______, ed. *Ritual and Power. Journal of Ritual Studies* 4, no. 2 (Summer 1990).

Izutsu, Toshihiko. *Language and Magic: Studies in the Magical Function of Speech.* Studies in the Humanities and Social Relations. Tokyo: Keio Institute of Philological Studies, 1956.

Jeffery, Arthur. *The Qur'ān as Scripture.* New York: Russell F. Moore, 1952.

Katz, Steven T, ed. *Mysticism and Language.* New York: Oxford University Press, 1992.

Lanczkowski, Günter. *Heilige Schriften. Inhalt, Textgestalt und Überlieferung.* Stuttgart: W. Kohlhammer, 1956.

Leeuw, G. van der. *Religion in Essence and Manifestation.* Translated by J. E. Turner, with Appendices . . . incorporating the additions of the second German edition by Hans H. Penner. 1938. Reprint. 2 vols. Gloucester, Mass.: Peter Smith, 1967.

Leipoldt, Johannes. "Zur Geschichte der Auslegung." *Theologische Literaturzeitung* 75, nos. 4–5 (Apr.–May 1950): 229–234.

Leipoldt, Johannes, and Siegfried Morenz. *Heilige Schriften. Betrachtungen zur Religionsgeschichte der antiken Mittelmeerwelt.* Leipzig: Otto Harrassowitz, 1953.

Levering, Miriam, ed. *Rethinking Scripture: Essays from a Comparative Perspective.* Albany: State University of New York Press, 1989.

Lincoln, Bruce. *Discourse and the Construction of Society: Comparative Studies of Myth, Ritual, and Classification.* New York: Oxford University Press, 1989.

———. *Myth, Cosmos, and Society: Indo-European Themes of Creation and Destruction.* Cambridge: Harvard University Press, 1986.

———. "The Tyranny of Taxonomy." *Occasional Papers of the University of Minnesota Center for Humanistic Studies* 1 (1985).

Long, Charles H. *Significations: Signs, Symbols, and Images in the Interpretation of Religion.* Philadelphia: Fortress Press, 1986.

Mensching, Gustav. *Das heilige Wort. Eine religionsphänomenologische Untersuchung.* Untersuchungen zur allgemeinen Religionsgeschichte, vol. 9. Bonn: Ludwig Röhrscheid, 1937.

Morenz, Siegfried. "Entstehung und Wesen der Buchreligion." *Theologische Literaturzeitung* 75, no. 12 (Dec. 1950): 709–716.

Morris, Paul. "The Discourse of Traditions: 'Judaisms' and 'Hinduisms.'" Paper delivered at the Annual Meeting of the American Academy of Religion, San Francisco, 1992.

O'Flaherty, Wendy Doniger. *Other Peoples' Myths: The Cave of Echoes.* New York: Macmillan, 1988.

———, ed. *The Critical Study of Sacred Texts.* Berkeley Religious Studies Series. Berkeley: Graduate Theological Union, 1979.

Ong, Walter J. *Interfaces of the Word: Studies in the Evolution of Consciousness and Culture.* Ithaca: Cornell University Press, 1977.

———. *Orality and Literacy: The Technologizing of the Word.* New Accents. London: Methuen, 1982.

———. *The Presence of the Word: Some Prolegomena for Cultural and Religious History.* 2d ed. Minneapolis: University of Minnesota, 1981.

Paden, William E. *Religious Worlds: The Comparative Study of Religion.* Boston: Beacon Press, 1988.

[Qur'ān]. *The Koran Interpreted.* Translated by Arthur J. Arberry. 2 vols. in 1. New York: Macmillan, 1955.

Ricoeur, Paul. *Hermeneutics and the Human Sciences: Essays on Language, Action and Interpretation.* Edited and translated by John B. Thompson. Cambridge: Cambridge University Press; Paris: Editions de la Maison des Sciences de l'Homme, 1981.

———. *Interpretation Theory: Discourse and the Surplus of Meaning.* Fort Worth: Texas Christian University Press, 1976.

———. *The Symbolism of Evil.* Translated by Emerson Buchanan. Boston: Beacon Press, 1969.

Roest Crollius, Ary A. *Thus Were They Hearing: The Word in the Experience of Revelation in Qur'ān and Hindu Scriptures.* Documenta missionalia, 8. Rome: Università Gregoriana Editrice, 1974.

Saussure, Ferdinand de. *Cours de linguistique générale.* Edited by Charles Bally and Albert Sechehaye, in collaboration with Albert Riedlinger. 3d ed. Paris: Payot, 1969. Eng. trans. Wade Baskin. *Course in General Linguistics.* 1959. Reprint. New York: McGraw-Hill, 1966.

Sharpe, Eric J. *Comparative Religion: A History.* New York: Charles Scribner's Sons, 1975.

Smith, Jonathan Z. "*Adde Parvum Parvo Magnus Acervus Erit.*" Chapter 11 of his *Map Is Not Territory,* pp. 240–264.

———. *Imagining Religion: From Babylon to Jonestown.* Chicago: University of Chicago Press, 1982.

———. "In Comparison a Magic Dwells." Chapter 2 of his *Imagining Religion,* pp. 19–35.

———. *Map Is Not Territory: Studies in the History of Religions.* Studies in Judaism in Late Antiquity, vol. 23. Leiden: E. J. Brill, 1978.

———. "Sacred Persistence: Toward a Redescription of Canon." Chapter 3 of his *Imagining Religion,* pp. 36–52.

———. *To Take Place: Toward Theory in Ritual.* Chicago Studies in the History of Judaism. Chicago: University of Chicago Press, 1987.

———. "What a Difference a Difference Makes." In *"To See Ourselves as Others See Us": Christians, Jews, "Others" in Late Antiquity,* edited by Jacob Neusner and Ernest S. Frerichs. Chico, Calif.: Scholars Press, 1985, pp. 3–48.

Smith, Wilfred Cantwell. "Is the Qur'an the Word of God?" Chapter 2 of his *Questions of Religious Truth*. New York: Charles Scribner's Sons, 1967, pp. 39–62.

———. "Scripture as Form and Concept: Their Emergence for the Western World." In *Rethinking Scripture: Essays from a Comparative Perspective*, edited by Miriam Levering. Albany: State University of New York Press, 1989, pp. 29–57.

———. "Some Similarities and Some Differences Between Christianity and Islām." Chapter 13 of his *On Understanding Islam: Selected Studies*. Religion and Reason, 19. The Hague: Mouton, 1981, pp. 233–246.

———. "The Study of Religion and the Study of the Bible." *Journal of the American Academy of Religion* 39, no. 2 (June 1971): 131–140. Reprinted in *Rethinking Scripture: Essays from a Comparative Perspective*, edited by Miriam Levering. Albany: State University of New York Press, 1989, pp. 18–28.

———. "The True Meaning of Scripture: An Empirical Historian's Nonreductionist Interpretation of the Qur'an." *International Journal of Middle Eastern Studies* 11, no. 4 (July 1980): 487–505.

———. *What is Scripture? A Comparative Approach*. Minneapolis: Fortress Press, 1993.

Steiner, George. *After Babel: Aspects of Language and Translation*. London: Oxford University Press, 1975.

Stock, Brian. *The Implications of Literacy: Written Language and Models of Interpretation in the Eleventh and Twelfth Centuries*. Princeton: Princeton University Press, 1983.

Vansina, Jan. *Oral Tradition: A Study in Historical Methodology*. Translated by H. M. Wright. Chicago: Aldine, 1965.

———. *Oral Tradition as History*. Madison: University of Wisconsin Press, 1985.

Waardenburg, Jacques, ed. *Classical Approaches to the Study of Religion: Aims, Methods and Theories of Research.* Religion and Reason, 3. The Hague: Mouton, 1973.

Widengren, Geo. *The Ascension of the Apostle and the Heavenly Book.* King and Saviour, 3. Uppsala Universitets Årsskrift, 1950, 7. Uppsala: A.-B. Lundequistska; Leipzig: Otto Harrassowitz, 1950.

———. "Heiliges Wort und Heilige Schrift." Chapter 19 of his *Religionsphänomenologie.* Berlin: Walter de Gruyter, 1969, pp. 546–573.

———. "Holy Book and Holy Tradition in Islam." In *Holy Book and Holy Tradition,* edited by F. F. Bruce and E. G. Rupp. Grand Rapids, Mich.: William B. Eerdmans, 1968, pp. 210–236.

———. *Muḥammad, the Apostle of God, and His Ascension.* King and Saviour, 5. Uppsala Universitets Årsskrift, 1955, 1. Uppsala: A.-B. Lundequistska; Wiesbaden: Otto Harrassowitz, 1955.

INDEX

Aaron, 285
R. Abba, 319
R. Abba b. Judan, 277
R. Abba b. Kahana, 160, 275, 279, 281, 514n.110
R. Abbahu, 169, 178–179, 274, 299, 304, 306, 487n.263
R. Abdimi of Ḥaifa, 278, 304, 305, 518nn.158, 161, 526n.252, 531n.306
Abel, 195
Abhinavagupta, 429n.37
Abhyankar, K. V., 536n.9
R. Abin or Abun, 160, 280, 525n.228
'Ăḇôḏāh Zārāh, 284, 285–287, 288
'Āḇôṯ, 141, 147–150, 152, 153, 154, 157, 175, 193, 194, 265, 359, 375–376
Abraham, 161, 488n.291
  and Arabs, 411, 558n.48
  ascent to heaven, 259
  and circumcision, 377, 404
  and commandments/*mitzvot*, 149, 163, 175–176, 184–185, 193, 399, 486n.243
  and covenant with God, 154, 163, 172, 191, 377, 404–405
  faith of, 404–405, 411–412
  as first Muslim, 411–412
  and gentile nations, 404–405, 553n.14
  and Hebrew letters, 195
  and Malḵûṯ/Shekhinah or Oral Torah, 320
  and Merkabah, 259
  as one of God's special creations/possessions, 149, 471–472 n.78
  and Qur'ān, 411–412, 558nn.47, 48
  and revelation of Torah, 154, 163
  and Sarah, 478n.143, 481n.190
  and secret of redemption, 195
  spoke Hebrew, 193, 195
  and Torah, 149, 154, 162, 163, 172, 175–176, 184–185, 191, 193, 399, 470n.65, 475n.119, 486n.243
Abraham, Apocalypse of, 259
Abulafia, Abraham, 367, 382–383, 393, 490n.318, 550–551n.121, 551n.1
R. Abun. *See* R. Abin
Adam, 161
  and commandments/*mitzvot*, 154, 163, 193, 472n.82
  creation of, 194
  and Eve, 192, 193
  fall of, 192
  and Garden of Eden, 163, 172, 184, 193, 472n.82, 475n.115
  and Hebrew letters, 317
  and revelation of Torah, 163
  and Sabbath, 193, 475n.115
  and tablets of Ten Commandments, 193
  and Torah, 154, 162–163, 172, 175, 184, 193, 399, 472n.82
  and tree of life, 163, 184, 193
Adam and Eve, Book of, 192
adhibhūta (relating to the material world; the natural order), 34, 46. *See also* correspondences
adhidaiva (relating to the gods; the divine order), 34, 46, 352. *See also* correspondences
adhiyajña (relating to the sacrifice; the sacrificial order), 34, 46, 352–353. *See also* correspondences
adhvaryu (type of priest), 438n.17, 457n.311

adhvaryu (continued)
and Brahmā, 104
and *brahman* priest, 348
and Prajāpati, 54, 58, 60
and seers/*ṛṣis*, 239
and Yajur-Veda, 33, 44
and *yajus*es, 33, 54, 60
adhyātma (relating to the self; the human order), 34, 46, 352–353. *See also* correspondences
Āditya (sun; sun god). *See* Sūrya
Ādityas (group of deities), 239
Advaita Vedānta, 23, 99, 114, 115, 123–129, 347, 458n.332. *See also* Vedānta
focus on *jñāna-kāṇḍa*, 123–124, 353
focus on knowledge of Brahman/ Brahman-Ātman, 123–124, 353
focus on Upaniṣads, 123–124, 352–353
schools of, 124, 464nn.447, 448
Agastya (Vedic seer), 229, 244
aggadah/Aggadah or Haggadah (nonlegal discourse; homiletical teachings)
definition and use of term, 431n.45
as Oral Torah, 12, 158, 182, 273, 294, 485n.232, 512n.75
as Torah, 151, 152, 265
Agni (fire; god of fire), 447n.141. *See also* fire
and *a*, first constituent of Om, 57–58, 70
and brahmins, 38, 39, 40
and earth, 38, 56–58, 70, 215
and *gāyatrī* meter, 39, 40
as inspirer of cognitions and hymns, 232, 234, 330
and primordial utterance *bhūḥ*, 56–58
and Ṛg-Veda, 38, 56–58, 70, 79, 215
and seers/*ṛṣis*, 230, 232, 234, 236, 239, 241, 330, 498n.49, 500n.106
and speech, 38, 58
agnicayana (type of Vedic sacrifice), 239, 241, 351, 434n.58, 500n.106, 538n.41
āgnīdhrīya or *dakṣiṇa* (type of sacrificial fire), 33, 58
agniṣṭoma (type of Vedic sacrifice), 106, 446n.134, 536n.1
R. Aḥa, 189, 274–275, 282, 298, 512n.91, 524n.223
R. Ahabah b. Ze'ira, 160
āhavanīya (type of sacrificial fire), 33, 58
Aitareya Āraṇyaka, 32, 344
Aitareya Brāhmaṇa, 44, 54–55, 57, 239, 240
R. Akiba, 149, 154, 155, 164, 173, 196, 260, 268, 270, 271, 360, 364, 474n.101, 510n.61, 511n.69, 532n.314, 535n.367, 541nn.12, 15, 543n.21
R. Akiba, school of, 15, 150, 260, 363, 364–365, 469n.49, 471n.71
ākṛti (universal class), 463n.435. *See also śabda* and *artha*
as the denotation of the word/ *śabda*, 116, 120, 121–122, 124, 125, 128, 129
as eternal, 121–122, 124, 125
and gods, 125
and individual thing/*vyakti*, 120, 121–122, 124, 125
akṣaras (Sanskrit phones). *See varṇas*
Albeck, Chanoch, 471n.71
Albright, W. F., 465n.10
'ālep̄ (Hebrew letter)
complained for twenty-six generations, 168, 184, 478nn.143, 148
semantic significance of, 168
R. Alexandri, 482n.204, 532–533n.319, 549n.86

Allah, 409–413, 558nn.44, 46, 48
Allen, Douglas, 436n.64
Alper, Harvey P., 540n.75
2 Alphabet of R. Akiba, 478n.143
'al tiqrê (interpretation based on an alternative reading), 365
Āḷvārs, 10
āmahīyava (type of *sāman*), 55
'am hā-'āreṣ ("people of the land"; uneducated common people)
  excluded from study of Torah, 391
  and Hêḵālôṯ traditions, 262
  and mastery of Torah, 262
  and rabbinic sages, 262, 391
R. Ammi, 377
Ammonites, 266, 286, 297
'āmôn (artisan; nursling), 133–134, 137, 161, 162, 164, 186, 202, 464nn.4, 5, 464–465n.6, 467n.36. *See also 'ûmān*
Amram, 161
angels, 369, 482n.207
  adjuration of, 261–262
  categories of, 145, 182–183
  commandments/*mitzvot* do not apply to, 276, 289, 301, 312
  crowns of, 259, 521n.181
  and "descender to the Merkabah," 259, 260, 515n.119
  descent from heaven, 256, 258, 264, 278–279, 291–292, 293–294, 303–305, 309, 313–314, 529n.274
  and fire, 146–147, 259, 267, 289, 300, 308, 366
  garments of, 259–260
  and gentile nations, 295, 307, 522n.202, 529n.274
  God took counsel with, 486n.250
  and Hêḵālôṯ traditions, 259, 260, 261–262, 515n.119, 521n.181, 524n.222
  and interpretation of Torah, 210, 366, 368
  and light, 146–147
  and lightning, 300
  and Merkabah, 258, 300
  and Moses, 258, 259, 263–264, 267, 276, 288–290, 293, 300–302, 303, 309, 312, 329, 509n.46, 513–514n.103, 519n.169, 520n.171, 523nn.221, 222, 524n.226
  names of, and Torah, 212
  names of, and world of formation/*y^{e}ṣîrāh*, 212
  and people of Israel, 256–257, 271, 278–279, 291–292, 293, 304–305, 307, 309, 313–314, 322, 329, 332, 520n.171, 526–527n.258
  and revelation of Torah, 256–257, 258, 259, 263–264, 267, 271, 276–277, 278–279, 288–290, 291–292, 293–294, 295, 300–302, 303–305, 307, 308, 309, 312, 313–314, 322, 329, 332, 509n.46, 513–514n.103, 514–515n.113, 515n.118, 519n.169, 520n.171, 523n.221, 523–524n.222, 524n.226, 525–526n.247, 526–527n.258, 529n.274, 531nn.301, 306
  and world of creation/*b^{e}rî'āh*, 211
  and world of formation/*y^{e}ṣîrāh*, 211, 212
Aṅgiras (Vedic seer), 230, 244, 245, 496n.7, 503n.156
Aṅgirases (descendants of Aṅgiras; Vedic seers; ancient priestly family), 230, 239, 244, 437n.7, 501n.113
'ānōḵî ("I"; first word of Ten Commandments), 275, 282, 287, 294, 298, 523n.216
Antigonus of Soko, 148
anuṣṭubh (type of Vedic meter), 40, 106, 343
apocalyptic traditions, 132, 179, 191, 505n.3

apocalyptic traditions *(continued)*
  and ascent to heaven, 258, 259, 264
  and Hêkālôt traditions, 258, 259, 264, 506n.16
  and Merkabah, 258, 259, 264, 505n.3, 506n.16
  and rabbinic Merkabah traditions, 258, 259, 264, 506n.16
  and revelation of Torah, 258, 259, 264
Apocrypha, 191, 192, 470n.65, 488n.285. *See also* Baruch; Wisdom of Ben Sira; Wisdom of Solomon
  wisdom books of, 23, 133, 135–138, 140–141, 477n.132
appropriation of Torah, 5, 24, 26, 223, 382–383, 385, 390–393, 395
  through direct experience of supernal Torah, 359, 382–383, 391–393, 415
  divine communion vs. impersonal realization, 383, 392, 393
  exoteric modes of, in rabbinic tradition, 359, 382, 391
  mystical modes of, in kabbalistic traditions, 359, 382–383, 391–393, 415
  through study and practice of Torah, 359, 382, 391–393
appropriation of Veda(s), 5, 24, 26, 223, 354–357, 385, 390–393, 395
  through direct realization of transcendent Veda, 343, 355–357, 392–393, 415, 419
  exoteric modes of, in *karma-kāṇḍa* and *dharma* traditions, 343, 355, 390–391
  as impersonal realization, 392, 419
  mystical modes of, in *jñāna-kāṇḍa* and meditation traditions, 343, 355–357, 392–393, 415, 419
  through reciting and hearing Vedic *mantras*, 343, 355, 390–391, 419, 539n.64
aptoryāman (type of Vedic sacrifice), 106
Arabic
  and Arabs, 409–410
  as divine language, 409
  and Qur'ān, 409–410, 412, 557n.33
  and revelation of Torah, 267
  as sacred language, 409
Arabs
  and Abraham, 411, 558n.48
  and Arabic, 409–410
  and Muhammad, 409–410, 558n.48
  and Qur'ān, 409–410, 558n.48
arahant ("worthy one" who has attained *nibbāna*), 406, 555n.17, 555–556n.18
Āraṇyakas, 23, 29, 31, 35, 113. *See also specific Āraṇyakas*
  definition and use of term, 7, 441n.52, 449n.161
  and sacrifice, 441n.52, 449n.161
  as *śruti*, 7–8, 10
  as Veda, 7, 425n.18
Arberry, Arthur J., 557n.33
Aristobulus, 23, 133, 138–139, 140–141, 477n.132
Aristotle, 365, 543n.19
Ark of the Covenant, 474n.101, 520n.176
  and light, 190
  and Sefer Torah/Torah, 190, 359, 416, 514n.104, 522–523n.211
  and Shekhinah, 514n.104
  and Tabernacle, 190, 514n.104, 522–523n.211
  and Temple, 514n.104, 522–523n.211
artha (meaning; thing, object). *See śabda* and *artha*

Aryans
and Āryāvarta, 117, 397, 399
as custodians of Veda(s), 3, 216, 398–399
ethnic-cultural identity of, and Veda(s), 3, 216, 325, 398–399, 412
linguistic identity of, and Veda(s), 3, 398–399, 412
and non-Aryans, 398–399
Sanskrit as language of, 3, 117, 397, 399
seers/*ṛṣis* as forefathers of, 325, 326, 336, 399
Āryāvarta (land of the Aryans)
and Aryans, 117, 397, 399
asat (nonexistence), 63, 444–445n.105
ascetic traditions
and *jñāna-kāṇḍa* or *jñāna* stream, 30, 62–63, 71, 335–336
and meditation traditions, 71, 335–336, 339
seers/*ṛṣis* as paradigm for, 335–336, 339
and *tapas*, 335, 339, 439n.23
and Upaniṣads, 30, 63, 71, 335–336, 402, 406
and Veda(s), 63, 402, 406
'ăśeret ha-dibb^erôt (Ten Words; Ten Commandments). *See* Ten Commandments
R. Ashi, 176
'ăṣîlût (world of emanation)
as abode of *s^epîrôt*, 211
and Hebrew letters, 212
and Ḥokmāh, 212, 215
and primordial Torah, 212
and Yōd, first letter of Tetragrammaton, 212
'ăśiyyāh (world of making)
and Hē, fourth letter of Tetragrammaton, 212
and Malkût/Shekhinah, 212, 215
and Oral Torah, 212
as spiritual archetype of material world, 211
āśramas (stages of life), 71, 76, 80, 128–129. *See also dharma: varṇāśrama-dharma*
R. Assi, 549n.90
astrology, 183, 188, 192
Aśvins (twin deities), 234, 349
Atharvan (Vedic seer), 496n.7
Atharvans (descendants of Atharvan; Vedic seers; ancient priestly family), 437n.7, 501n.113
atharvans, *aṅgiras*es, or *atharvāṅgiras*es (incantations and imprecations that constitute the Atharva-Veda), 34, 437n.9, 438n.10. *See also* Atharva-Veda
and Atharva-Veda, 7
and Ātman, 66
and Being, 67, 457n.311
and Brahmā, 40, 104, 106
and Brahman, 112
and *brahman* priest, 250
definition and use of term, 31–32, 437n.7
as fourth Veda, 31, 425n.16, 426n.19, 438n.11
and Itihāsa-Purāṇa, 32
and Puruṣa, 66
and *sattva*, 111
and Skambha, 41–42
and Śiva, 88
and speech, 106
as *śruti*, 7
and *tamas*, 111
and Viṣṇu, 87
and Vyāsa, 249–250
Atharva-Veda, 29, 34, 39, 40, 41–42, 53, 72–73, 238, 437n.7. *See also atharvans*
and *atharvans* or *atharvāṅgiras*es, 7

Atharva-Veda *(continued)*
and Brahmā, 104, 107, 110, 218
and *brahman* priest, 33
and creator principle, 92
definition and use of term, 7, 31, 33
as fourth Veda, 31, 33, 73, 425n.16, 426n.19, 438n.11
and Puruṣa, 91
and speech, 106–107, 110, 218
and Viṣṇu, 87
atirātra (type of Vedic sacrifice), 106
Ātman (Self). *See also brahman/* Brahman
and Brahman, 63, 107
cosmic body of, 66, 68
and mind, 66, 68
and Om, 69–70, 107, 451n.201, 539n.71
and Prajāpati, 65, 68, 450n.170
and Puruṣa, 65, 66, 68, 449n.165
as universal ground of existence, 63
and Veda(s), 66, 68
Viṣṇu as, 85, 102, 454n.255
Atri (Vedic seer), 229, 230, 239, 243, 244, 245, 496n.7
Avesta, 557n.35
R. Azariah, 274, 282, 377, 524n.226, 543n.21
Azriel b. Menaḥem of Gerona, 199–200, 360, 491nn.324, 326, 328

Baba b. Buta, 483n.213
Babylonian Talmud, 23, 132, 141, 142, 145, 157, 172–179, 181, 188–190, 191, 193, 263, 284–293, 295, 300, 309, 360, 365–366, 470n.70. *See also* Talmud
as commentary on Mishnah, 173
includes Midrashic material, 173
and Palestinian Midrashim, 173
Bacharach, Naphtali b. Jacob Elḥanan, 495n.386
Bādarāyaṇa, 120
bahiṣpavamāna (type of *stotra*), 55, 446n.134, 535–536n.1
Baḥya b. Asher, 544–545n.35
Bailey, Greg, 451n.206
Bamberger, Bernard J., 551n.2
bandhus (connections), 44, 46, 58, 69, 350. *See also* correspondences
Banerjee, Santi, 442n.65
Bar Kappara, 190
Barr, James, 422n.8
Baruch, 133, 137, 138–139, 467n.22
2 Baruch, 470n.65
Basham, A. L., 426n.23
Bauer-Kayatz, Christa, 465n.10
R. Bebai, 276
Bell, Catherine, 551–552n.3
Ben Azzai, 480n.173, 517n.135, 541n.12
Ben Zoma, 541n.12
R. Berekhiah, 170, 191, 275, 278, 280, 302–303, 304, 308, 474n.109, 526n.248
b^e^rē'šîṯ ("in the beginning"; first word of Torah), 189–190
as *b^e^-ḥoḵmāh*, 165, 207, 476n.127
as first word of Torah, 168, 170, 171, 178, 195
as one of ten words of creation/ *ma'ămārôṯ*, 170, 171, 178, 207
as original unspoken Word, 171, 207
b^e^rî'āh (world of creation)
as abode of highest angels, 211
as abode of Merkabah, 211
as abode of throne, 211
and Bînāh, 212, 215
and Hē, second letter of Tetragrammaton, 212
and names of God, 212
bêṯ (Hebrew letter), 487n.262
as first letter of Torah, 160, 168
numerical value of, 168, 188
semantic significance of, 168, 188

shape of, 168, 188
sound of, 168
world created with, 160, 168, 188, 478nn.143, 148
Bezalel, 177, 185
Bhagavad-Gītā, 72, 81, 124, 452–453n.233
Bhāgavata Purāṇa, 73, 96, 99, 100–101, 103, 104–105, 107, 111, 218, 220
bhakti (devotional) traditions or *bhakti* stream. *See also bhakti-yoga*
bhakti texts, and mantric efficacy, 391
bhakti texts, and *śruti*, 10, 391
and epics/Itihāsas, 72, 402, 416
iconic aspects of, 19, 416
and Mahābhārata, 30, 72, 81–82
and post-Vedic brahmanical synthesis, 71–72
and Purāṇas, 30, 72, 94, 402, 416
and seers/*ṛṣis*, 336, 339
and Śiva, 72, 81, 94
and *śūdras*, 94
and Veda(s), 10–11, 19, 336, 391, 402, 416
and Viṣṇu, 72, 81, 94
and women, 94
bhakti-yoga (yoga of devotion), 453n.233
Bhāmatī school, 124
Bharadvāja (Vedic seer), 229, 239, 240, 243, 501n.107, 504n.177
Bhartṛhari, 441n.44
Bhattacharji, Sukumari, 442n.65
Bhattacharya, Ram Shankar, 451n.204
Bhattacharyya, Narendra Nath, 438n.22
Bhṛgu (Vedic seer), 229, 239, 496n.7, 501n.111, 503n.156
Bhṛgus (descendants of Bhṛgu; Vedic seers), 230, 244
bhūḥ (sacred utterance; sound correlative of earth), 68
and *a*, first constituent of Om, 57–58, 79, 106, 108, 109, 111
and Brahmā, 111
and brahmins, 54, 61
and earth, 51, 54, 56–58, 59, 61, 92, 109, 111, 127, 446n.125
and fire/Agni, 56–58
and Om, 57–58, 79, 92–93, 106–109, 111, 357
and *rajas*, 111
and Ṛg-Veda, 51, 56–58, 61, 79, 111
as root *mantra*, 357
and speech, 51, 54, 58, 59, 106–109
bhuvaḥ (sacred utterance; sound correlative of midregions), 68
and breath, 58
and *kṣatriyas*, 54, 61
and midregions, 51, 54, 56–58, 61, 92, 109, 111, 450n.196
and Om, 57–58, 79, 92–93, 106–109, 111, 357
as root *mantra*, 357
and *sattva*, 111
and speech, 51, 54, 59, 106–109
and *u*, second constituent of Om, 57–58, 79, 106, 108, 109, 111
and Viṣṇu, 111
and wind/Vāyu, 56–58, 450n.196
and Yajur-Veda, 51, 56–58, 61, 79, 111
Biardeau, Madeleine, 458n.330, 461nn.397, 398
Bible. *See* Hebrew Bible; New Testament
Bilimoria, Puruṣottama, 462n.400
Bînāh (intelligence, understanding; third *s^{e}pîrāh*), 197
as Elohim, 205, 206–207
as female principle, 207, 217
as the Great Voice, 207–208, 217
and Hē, second letter of Tetragrammaton, 208, 209, 212

Bînāh *(continued)*
and Ḥoḵmāh, 202, 205, 206, 207, 208, 217, 219
as house for Ḥoḵmāh, 205, 206, 207, 208, 217
as inaudible voice, 205, 206–208, 209
as Mother above, 202, 205, 206, 207, 209, 493n.341
as palace, 205, 207–208
as queen of world above, 206
and Torah, 202, 209, 493n.341
and unfoldment of divine language, 198, 205, 206–209
and world of creation/*b^erî'āh*, 212, 215
Bīrūnī, Abū al-Rayḥān al-Khwārizmī al-, 536–537n.12
Black Yajur-Veda. *See* Taittirīya Saṃhitā
Bloch, Renée, 542n.16
blueprint or plan of creation, 194. *See also* *maḥăšāḇāh*
and divine language, 16, 17, 24, 131, 167, 213, 214, 216, 217–218, 222, 253, 395, 407
and Hebrew letters, 17, 167, 212, 214, 222
and Logos, 140
as mental plan, 127, 140, 165–166, 171, 187, 214, 220, 221–222, 389, 486n.255
as model of world, 192
scripture as, 17, 213, 214–215, 218, 219
and speech, 24, 29, 47, 73, 102, 216, 217–218, 221, 227
Torah as, 16, 17, 24, 26, 131, 140, 146, 159–160, 164–167, 170, 171, 176, 177, 180, 186–188, 196, 202–204, 212, 213, 214–215, 216, 218–220, 221–222, 253, 323, 333, 363, 367, 369, 371, 375, 378–379, 389, 391, 392, 395, 398, 399–400, 401, 402, 410, 412, 434n.56, 477n.132, 547n.60
use of term, 434n.56
Veda(s) as, 9, 16, 17, 24, 26, 29, 30, 47, 59, 62, 73, 75–76, 77, 79–80, 93, 95, 99, 101, 102, 108–112, 115, 124–125, 126–128, 129, 213, 214–215, 216, 218–221, 227, 243, 245, 246, 333, 347, 348, 389, 390, 392, 395, 398, 399–400, 401, 407, 412, 434n.56
as world of archetypal ideas, 140
Blumenthal, David R., 478n.142, 534–535n.352, 547n.58
boar. *See* sacrificial boar
Bodewitz, H. W., 441n.53, 535–536n.1
body. *See also* body, cosmic; body, human; body, of cosmos; body, social
of Christ, 403–404, 405
of Dhamma, 407
of Torah, 15, 199, 203–204, 325, 360, 369–370, 374, 379, 380, 382, 392, 398, 402, 420, 550n.103
of Veda, 325, 398
body, cosmic
of Ātman, 66, 68
of Brahmā, 101, 104–105, 106, 248, 351, 407, 459n.351
of Brahman/Brahman-Ātman, 41, 42, 66, 102, 214, 216, 351, 398
and commandments/*mitzvot*, 204, 380
of creator principle, 34, 216, 398
of divine anthropos, 197, 204, 216, 320, 380, 398
of God, 201, 214, 505n.7
and Hebrew letters, 201, 214
of Prajāpati, 39–40, 47, 60, 66, 238–239, 241, 351, 434n.58, 459n.370

of Puruṣa, 35, 37–38, 41, 66, 68, 91–92, 349, 458n.341
of sacrificial boar, 87, 103
and Sanskrit *varṇas*, 91–92, 104, 214, 459nn.351, 361
and *s^e^pîrôt*, 197, 380
of Śiva, 88, 104, 351, 459n.361
of Skambha, 41–42, 53, 66
and Torah, 204, 214, 216, 380, 398
and Veda(s), 34, 37–38, 39–40, 41–42, 47, 53, 60, 66, 68, 87, 88, 91–92, 102, 103, 104–105, 106, 214, 216, 351, 398, 458n.341, 459nn.351, 370
of Viṣṇu, 85, 87, 90, 102, 103, 351
body, human
and commandments/*mitzvot*, 167, 176, 375, 401, 477n.136
and soul, 138, 554n.15
and Spirit, 403–405
and Torah, 167, 176, 203–204, 216, 369, 375, 378, 379, 380, 389, 398, 401, 477n.136, 552n.4
and Veda(s), 38, 56, 58, 216, 398
body, of cosmos
and Prajāpati, 59, 241
and Torah, 203–204, 216, 379, 380, 398
and Veda(s), 59, 216, 398, 406
and Viṣṇu, 85
body, social
and Torah, 216, 325, 398–402
and Veda(s), 216, 325, 398–402, 406
Bonazzoli, Giorgio, 456–457n.310, 457n.325
Book of the Torah. *See* Sefer Torah
Bose, Nirmal Kumar, 451n.203
Boström, Gustav, 465–466n.10
Botto, Oscar, 426n.23
Bourdieu, Pierre, 551n.3
Bowker, John, 468n.42
Boyarin, Daniel, 542n.16, 552n.4, 554n.15
Brahmā (creator god), 94
and *a*, first constituent of Om, 111
and Brahman/Brahman-Ātman, 65–66, 67, 73, 99, 104, 434n.55
and brahmins, 104, 107, 407
and Bṛhaspati, 451n.206
and categories of priests, 104, 107
cosmic body of, 101, 104–105, 106, 248, 351, 407, 459n.351
and cosmic egg, 77–78, 86, 100, 101–102, 105, 107, 454n.260
and *dharma*, 453n.243
and earth, 111
and epics/Itihāsas, 104–105, 106
four mouths of, 40, 88, 96, 104, 105–106, 107, 109–110, 112, 218, 220, 249, 440n.36
and *gāyatrī*/Gāyatrī or *sāvitrī*/Sāvitrī, 79, 89–90, 91, 105, 107
and gods, 79, 86, 88, 96, 246
as guru of gods, 88
and heart, 105, 107
as Hiraṇyagarbha, 86, 104
as instrumental cause, 86, 101
and knowledge, 88, 104, 214, 216
and lines of tradition/*vaṃśas*, 243
and lotus, 86, 101, 454nn.259, 260
and Mahābhārata, 82
as *mahat-tattva*, 454n.257
and meditation, 78, 91, 107
and meters, 104, 105–106, 440n.36, 459n.351
mind-born sons of, 105, 244, 245, 247, 249, 503n.156
and Nārāyaṇa, 77–78, 101–102, 103
and Om, 79, 102, 105, 107, 111
and orders of reality, 79, 111
and Prajāpati, 65, 73, 78, 86, 89, 451n.206
as primordial seer/*ṛṣi*, 245, 249
and primordial utterance *bhūḥ*, 111

Brahmā *(continued)*
  and Purāṇas, 96, 97, 104–105, 106
  and Puruṣa, 73, 78, 91, 100, 101–102
  and *rajas*, 111
  and *ṛcs*, 111
  and Ṛg-Veda, 111
  as Śabdabrahman, 104, 459n.351
  and sacrifice, 103, 104–106, 351
  as sacrificial boar, 103
  and *sāmans*, 105–106, 440n.36
  and Sanskrit *varṇas*, 104, 107, 459n.351
  and Sarasvatī, 89–90, 105
  and *śastras*, 104
  and *śāstras*, 96, 97, 105
  and seers/*ṛṣis*, 86, 96, 112, 244, 245, 246, 247, 248, 249, 503n.156
  and Śiva, 86, 104, 111
  and speech/Vāc, 89–90, 101–102, 105–111, 114, 126, 127, 218, 220
  and *śruti*, 250
  and *stomas*, 104, 105–106, 440n.36
  and *tapas*, 105, 246
  and three *vyāhṛtis*, 79, 102, 105, 107
  and three worlds, 78, 84, 85–86, 88, 101, 248
  and *vaikṛta* creations, 99, 100–101, 454n.257
  and Veda(s), 40, 65–66, 67, 73, 79–80, 82, 88–89, 90, 91, 93, 96, 99, 102, 103, 104–112, 114, 126, 127, 214, 216, 218, 220, 245, 246, 249, 250, 351, 440n.36, 453n.243, 454n.262, 459n.351
  and Viṣṇu, 82, 86, 88–89, 93, 101–102, 104, 111, 455n.278, 459n.349
  and Vyāsa, 82, 453n.243
  as Word/Śabdabrahman, 104
brahman (type of priest), 438n.17
  and *adhvaryu* priest, 348
  and *atharvans*, 250
  and Atharva-Veda, 33
  and Brahmā, 104
  and expiatory formulas/*prāyaścittas*, 33, 348
  and *hotṛ* priest, 348
  and Prajāpati, 60
  and seers/*ṛṣis*, 239
  and three Vedas, 33, 438n.18
  and *udgātṛ* priest, 348
brahman/Brahman or Brahman-Ātman (Word; universal ground of existence), 84. *See also* Ātman; Śabdabrahman
  and Ātman, 63, 107
  and Brahmā, 65–66, 67, 73, 99, 104, 434n.55
  cosmic body of, 41, 42, 66, 102, 214, 216, 351, 398
  as cosmic principle, 34, 40, 41, 66, 70, 72–73
  and creator principle, 30, 40, 63, 64, 73, 330
  definition and use of term, 40–41, 440n.39
  Devī as, 99
  as formed and formless, 63–64, 449n.164
  and gods, 328, 330
  as immanent and transcendent, 63–64, 449n.164
  as imperishable, 66, 67, 75, 330
  as impersonal, 87, 330, 392
  and Īśvara, 100, 101
  and knowledge, 66–67, 75, 87, 102–104, 128–129, 356
  knowledge of, as focus of Vedānta/Advaita Vedānta, 113, 123–124, 353
  and lines of tradition/*vaṃśas*, 243
  as manifest and unmanifest, 63–64, 78, 85, 100, 101

Nirguṇa Brahman, 64, 78, 85, 87, 94, 100, 101, 112, 219
and Om, 70, 106–109, 215, 357, 460n.378
and orders of reality, 69–70
and Prajāpati, 44, 52–53, 64, 65–66, 67, 442n.61, 446n.123
and Prakṛti, 99, 100
and primordial utterance *mahaḥ*, 70
and Puruṣa, 64–66, 67, 68, 91–92, 99, 100
realization of, and meditation, 242, 328, 357, 393
realization of, and *tapas*, 242, 244–245, 328, 330, 335, 336, 357
and sacrifice, 103, 351
sacrificial boar as, 103
Saguṇa Brahman, 64, 78, 85, 100, 101, 104, 213, 219
and Sanskrit *varṇas*, 91–92, 104, 214
and seers/*ṛṣis*, 42, 66, 234, 238–239, 242–243, 244–245, 248, 326, 328, 330, 335–336, 356–357
Śiva as, 30, 73, 86, 87, 88, 100, 102, 103–104, 336, 351
Skambha as, 41, 53, 66, 440n.41
and speech/Vāc, 42, 47, 65–66, 68, 103, 227, 234, 246
as transcendent, 63–64, 85, 328, 330, 449n.164
two forms of, 70, 87
as ultimate source of creation, 30, 40, 63, 76, 86, 99–100, 104, 219
as universal ground of existence, 63, 69, 128
and Veda(s), 24, 29, 30, 34, 40–42, 47, 50, 52–53, 59, 60, 65, 66–67, 70, 72–73, 75, 79, 81, 82, 87, 88, 89, 91–92, 99, 101, 102–104, 112, 115, 123–124, 125, 128–129, 213, 214, 216, 219, 227, 246, 328, 330, 336, 351, 356, 392, 393, 396, 398, 440n.42, 443n.79, 454n.262
Viṣṇu as, 30, 73, 81, 82, 85, 86, 87, 94, 100, 102–103, 104, 244, 245, 336, 351
as Word, 24, 29, 34, 40–41, 47, 50, 52, 53, 60, 66, 67, 70, 91–92, 213, 216, 219, 227, 396
Brāhmaṇas, 23, 29, 31, 35, 36, 43–62, 66, 68, 70, 71, 75, 78, 229, 237–242, 325, 330, 349–352, 357, 441nn.52, 53, 449n.161. *See also specific Brāhmaṇas*
and *adhiyajña*, 352–353
and categories of priests, 44
definition and use of term, 7, 43
as discourse of sacrifice, 22, 43–44, 62, 63, 348, 349
as focus of Pūrva-Mīmāṃsā, 113, 116, 346, 352–353, 388
as part of *karma-kāṇḍa*, 30, 43, 62, 71, 335, 353
as *śruti*, 7–8, 10, 402
as Veda, 7, 402, 425n.18
Brahmāṇḍa Purāṇa, 97
brahmanical texts. *See also* brahmanical tradition; and *specific brahmanical texts*
problems with delimiting historical-cultural contexts of, 22
brahmanical tradition. *See also* brahmins; brahmanical texts; brahmanical tradition and rabbinic tradition
aniconic aspects of, 19, 416, 434n.58
and Āryāvarta, 397
and canonical authority, ix, 2, 21–22, 400–401, 448n.155
canon of, ix, 2, 21–22, 448n.155
and early Buddhist tradition, 405–408, 449n.162, 555n.17
as "embodied community," 397–403, 406, 412, 413

brahmanical tradition *(continued)*
emphasis on auditory mode of perception, 17–19, 218–221, 223, 334, 385, 414–417
emphasis on oral channel of language, 17–19, 218–221, 223, 334, 344–345, 385–387, 414–420
emphasis on phonic dimension of words, 18, 218–221, 223, 334, 346–347, 385, 386–388, 414
as ethnocultural system, ix, 3, 397–403, 406, 412, 413
iconic aspects of, 19, 416, 434n.58
and levels of embodiment, 398–403
as religion of orthopraxy, ix, 3, 401–403
and Sanskrit, 3, 397
as textual community, ix, 2, 21, 403
and three streams of post-Vedic brahmanical synthesis, 70–72
Veda as constitutive category of, ix–x, 2–3, 398–403
brahmanical tradition and rabbinic tradition. *See also* brahmanical tradition; "Hinduisms" and "Judaisms"; rabbinic tradition
and canonical authority, ix, 2, 21–22
cognition of Veda(s) and revelation of Torah, 325–339
divergences in conceptions of language, 17–19, 218–223, 333–334, 385–388, 395, 414–420
as "embodied communities," 397–403, 412, 413
as ethnocultural systems, ix, 3, 397–403, 412, 413
and levels of embodiment, 398–403
as religions of orthopraxy, ix, 3, 401–403
represent distinctive paradigm of "religious tradition," ix, 2–3, 6, 397–403, 408–409, 412, 413, 422n.6
scripture/canon as constitutive category of, ix–x, 2–3, 21, 398–403
structural affinities between traditions, ix–x, 2–3, 6, 25, 397–403, 408–409, 412, 413
structural affinities in symbol systems, 16–17, 24, 213–219, 395, 434n.57
as textual communities, ix, 2, 21, 403
Veda and Torah in practice, 385–393
Brahma-Sūtras, 124, 128
brahmins (priests). *See also* *adhvaryu*; *brahman*; brahmanical tradition; *hotṛ*; *udgātṛ*
authority of, 2, 60–61, 326, 335–336, 390, 400–401, 406, 427n.26
and Brahmā, 104, 107, 407
brahmin reciters/*śrotriyas*, 83, 345–347, 355, 385–388, 395–396, 419
categories of priests, 33, 44, 54–55, 58, 60, 104, 107, 239, 348, 438n.17
as custodians of sacrificial tradition, 326, 334–335, 390, 400, 406
as custodians of Vedic recitative tradition, 12, 60, 83, 98, 326, 334–335, 339, 345–347, 355, 385–388, 390, 395–396, 400, 406, 427n.26, 555n.17
and descent from seers/*ṛṣis*, 229, 239, 241–242, 325, 326, 335–336, 339, 344, 348, 355, 390, 399, 400, 555n.17
and earth, 38, 61
as embodiments of Veda, 400–401, 412, 427n.26
and fire/Agni, 38, 39, 40

and *gāyatrī* meter, 39, 40, 61
as human gods, 61, 241, 335
lineages of, and seers/*ṛṣis*, 229, 239, 325, 326, 335–336, 344, 348, 399, 400, 555n.17
as officiants of sacrifice, 33, 60, 241, 339, 348, 350, 406, 419
priestly functions of, and Prajāpati, 39, 54–55, 58, 60, 62, 349–350, 446n.131, 448n.152, 537n.33
and primordial utterance *bhūḥ*, 54, 61
and Ṛg-Veda, 38, 61, 390
seers/*ṛṣis* as paradigm for, 239, 241, 334–336, 339, 348, 355, 390
Braude, William G., 473n.95, 484nn.220, 221, 225, 551n.2
breath, 343, 501n.107. *See also* *prāṇa*(s)
and midregions, 38, 58
and mind, 447n.148
and primordial utterance *bhuvaḥ*, 58
and *sāmans*, 447n.148
and Sāma-Veda, 58
and wind/Vāyu, 38, 58
and Yajur-Veda, 38, 58
and *yajus*es, 447n.148
Bṛhadāraṇyaka Upaniṣad, 50, 65, 67, 68–69, 126
Bṛhaspati (deity), 234, 451n.206
bṛhat (type of *sāman*), 39, 106
and heaven, 445n.109
and mind, 49
and Prajāpati, 49
and *rathantara sāman*, 49
and *sāmans*, 49, 445n.109
Brough, John, 461n.398
Brown, Cheever Mackenzie, 83, 98, 454n.250, 457nn.324–326, 458n.327
Brown, W. Norman, 438n.22, 439n.29, 440n.43
Bruce, F. F., 424n.9
Buddha Śākyamuni, 406–408, 555nn.16, 17, 555–556n.18, 556n.20
Buddhist tradition, early, 63. *See also* Mahāyāna Buddhist tradition
and break from embodied categories of brahmanical tradition, 405–408
and conventional view of language, 408
and Dhamma, 405–408, 555nn.16, 17, 555–556n.18
and ideal of *arahant*, 406, 555n.17, 555–556n.18
meditation traditions, 71
missionary orientation of, 403, 405, 408, 413, 422n.6
and Pali canon, 6, 407–408, 556n.20
and paradigms of "religious tradition," 6, 403, 405–408, 413, 422n.6
and quest for liberation/*nibbāna*, 406–408, 555–556n.18
and *saṃgha*, 406–407, 555n.16, 555–556n.18
and social classes/*varṇa*s, 406–407, 555–556n.18
and Veda(s), 405–406, 407–408, 449n.162, 555n.17
Budick, Sanford, 542n.16
Buitenen, J. A. B. van, 452n.232

Cain, 195
Camp, Claudia V., 466n.10
Canaanite traditions, 134–135, 141, 465–466n.10, 513n.98
canon. *See also* scripture
authority of, ix, x, 2, 21–22, 400–401, 448n.155
brahmanical canon, ix, 2, 21–22, 448n.155

canon *(continued)*
as constitutive category of brahmanical and rabbinic traditions, ix–x, 2–3, 21, 398–403
and form of scripture, 4
model of, 6, 431n.43
Pali canon, 6, 407–408, 556n.20
rabbinic canon, ix, 2, 21–22, 141–142
studies of, 4, 422–423n.8
and tradition-identity, 3, 397–398
Carpenter, David, 427n.26, 431n.43, 462n.398
Chakravarti, Prabhat Chandra, 461n.398
chandas (meter). *See* meters
Chāndogya Upaniṣad, 32, 68, 71, 242–243, 357
chariots. *See also ma'ăśēh merkāḇāh*; Merkabah; *reḵeḇ*
descent from heaven, 258, 262, 264, 278, 293–294, 304–305, 313
of gods, 231, 332
and people of Israel, 257, 258–259, 278, 322, 332
and revelation of Torah, 254, 257, 258, 262, 264, 278, 293–294, 303–305, 313, 322, 332, 514–515n.113, 515n.116, 526nn.252, 253, 531n.306
Chemparathy, George, 460–461n.394, 461n.397
Chernus, Ira, 259–261, 262, 264, 432–433n.51, 505nn.7–9, 506nn.11–14, 507n.17, 510n.61, 511n.65, 515nn.116, 118, 119, 516n.124, 517n.139, 521nn.181, 190, 527n.262, 529nn.273, 283
Childs, Brevard S., 422n.8
Christ. *See also* Jesus of Nazareth
body of, as spiritualized notion, 403–404, 405
body of, Christian community as, 403–404, 405
as God's central revelation, 403
as instrument of creation, 159, 403
as preexistent, 159, 403
and Qur'ān, 409, 556n.24
as symbol, 157, 403
and Torah, 404–405, 553n.11, 553–554n.14
as Word/Logos, 159, 403
Christian traditions
and appropriation of Hebrew Bible/Written Torah, 158, 174, 182, 294, 295
and break from embodied categories of Jewish tradition, 403–405, 554n.15
Christ as God's central revelation, 403
Christian community as body of Christ, 403–404, 405
claim to be true Israel, 157, 182, 405
discourse of body in, 554n.15
doctrine of Logos, 132, 159, 403
emphasis on faith and belief over practice, 3, 403–405, 413, 553nn.10, 11, 553–554n.14
emphasis on Spirit over body, 403–405, 553n.11, 554n.15
excluded from Oral Torah, 158, 174, 182, 294, 295
hermeneutics, 545n.42
missionary orientation of, 3, 403–405, 413, 422n.6
and New Testament, 6, 158, 403
and paradigms of "religious tradition," ix, 2–3, 6, 397, 403–405, 413, 422n.6
and Paul's doctrine of justification by faith, 404–405, 553nn.10, 11, 553–554n.14
and Paul's mission to gentiles, 404–405, 552n.9, 553nn.10, 11, 553–554n.14

and people of Israel/Jews, 157–158, 263, 273, 404–405, 552n.9, 553nn.10, 11, 553–554n.14
polemic against, 157–158, 174, 182, 294
political triumph of, 132, 157
and rabbinic tradition, 132, 157–158, 159, 554n.15
as religion of orthodoxy, 405
and Torah, 158, 174, 182, 294, 295, 404–405, 552n.9, 553nn.10, 11, 553–554n.14
and two types of Judaisms, 157
as universal gospel, open to all, 405
1 Chronicles, 161, 187
circumcision, 553n.10, 554n.14
and Abraham, 377, 404
covenant of, 377, 404, 519n.165
role in creating and maintaining cosmos, 377, 519n.165, 549n.89
classical Amoraic Midrashim, 23, 132, 145, 155–173, 174–175, 176, 177, 180, 181, 183, 191, 272–284, 285, 287, 291, 309, 366, 470–471n.70. *See also specific Midrashim*
exegetical Midrashim, 155–156
homiletical Midrashim, 155–156
and "Judaism despite Christianity," 157
as Mid̲r^ešê 'Aggād̲āh, 155
and polemic against Christians, 157–158
and proem, 155
shared materials among, 156, 473–474n.95
and theodicy, 158–159
Clifford, Richard J., 513n.98
Clooney, Francis X., 538–539n.55
Coburn, Thomas B., 97–98, 344, 354, 426n.22, 456n.310, 457n.323, 536nn.3, 12, 539nn.61, 64
cognition of Veda(s), 25, 227–251, 325–339. *See also ṛṣi*(s); *śruti*
and cognition of mechanics and mysteries of creation, 34, 231–232, 234, 235, 241, 245–246, 247, 326, 332, 333, 428n.28
and cognition of suprasensible phenomena, 229, 231, 332
as cosmogonic "event," 326
definition and use of term "cognition," 231, 327, 328, 426n.24, 497n.22
embodiment of Word in texts, 24, 26, 227, 325
emphasis on auditory aspects of experience, 18, 221, 332, 334
epistemology of, 230–232, 331–333
and gods, 34, 229, 230, 231–232, 233–235, 236–237, 238, 240–241, 246, 328, 330, 332, 354, 498nn.52, 59
human vs. divine initiative, 327–328
and light, 232–233, 235, 328, 332, 497n.34
as means to attain specific ends, 238, 240, 241
mechanisms of, 228, 229–237, 238, 242, 243, 245–246, 248–249, 325, 327–334, 427–428n.28, 438n.19, 441n.51, 496n.5, 498n.44, 537n.28
and meditation, 227, 245–246, 328, 357, 428n.28, 503n.151
as paradigmatic, 334–337, 339, 348, 355, 356–357, 389–390
as realization of an impersonal reality, 330
reciprocal dynamics of, 229, 233–237, 328
role of heart in, 232, 233, 235–236, 237, 328, 497n.37, 499nn.71, 76
role of mind in, 230, 231, 236,

cognition of Veda(s) *(continued)* 332, 497n.28, 499n.76
and *ṛta*, 231, 232
and Sarasvatī, 90–91, 227, 234, 246–247
and seers/*ṛṣis*, 8–10, 12, 18, 34, 43, 76, 82, 94, 221, 227–251, 325–339, 344, 348, 354, 355, 356–357, 385, 389–390, 395–396, 398–399, 407, 415, 426n.24, 427n.27, 427–428n.28, 438n.19, 496n.5, 497nn.22, 28, 34, 37, 501n.113, 502n.132, 503n.151, 537n.28, 539n.64
and *śruti*, 8–10, 18, 221, 227, 344, 385, 407, 415, 426n.24, 428n.28
as synesthetic experience involving both sight and hearing, 8–9, 18, 221, 227, 229, 230–233, 237, 330, 331–333, 334, 427n.27, 428n.28
and *tapas*, 76, 235, 236–237, 240–241, 246, 248, 328, 330, 336, 339, 356, 357, 501n.113
twofold movement of seeing and recitation, 54, 221, 237–238, 240, 241, 330, 333, 500n.96, 501n.120
as two-phased cyclical process, 233, 235, 237, 498n.44
Cohen-Alloro, Dorit, 546n.47
Collins, Steven, 556n.20
Colson, F. H., 467n.36
commandments, 493n.348. *See also mitzvah/mitzvot*; practice of Torah
and Abraham, 149, 163, 175–176, 184–185, 193, 399, 486n.243
and Adam, 154, 163, 193, 472n.82
apply to human beings, not angels, 276, 289, 301, 312
and body, human, 167, 176, 375, 401, 477n.136
and body, of divine anthropos, 204, 380
as body of Torah, 204, 369–370, 374, 380, 550n.103
correlated with microcosm and macrocosm, 167, 176, 183, 375, 401
cosmic rationale for, 374–375
and light, 155, 171–172, 178, 187, 190, 487n.272
and Malkût/Shekhinah or Oral Torah, 381, 550n.119
and mystery of supernal Man, 204, 380
and Name of God, 381
observance of, as means of augmenting God's power, 374–375, 377–378, 380–381, 389, 401
observance of, as means of maintaining cosmos, 374–377, 378, 380, 389–390, 401
observance of, as means of stimulating influx from *s^e^p̄îrôṯ*, 380–381
observance of, as means of uniting male and female aspects of Godhead, 378, 381, 550n.119
observance of, as method of embodying Torah, 338, 382, 401, 402
and patriarchs, 175–176, 476n.124, 486n.243
and power to "make" God, 381
and *s^e^p̄îrôṯ*, 380–381
seven commandments, and gentile nations, 266, 286–287, 399
613 commandments, 163, 167, 176, 294, 375, 401, 476n.124
theurgic efficacy of, 374–381, 382, 389–390
and Tip̄'ereṯ or Written Torah, 381
comparative study of religion, x
comparative historical analysis, overview of method of, 21–25

as critical to scholarly enterprise, 19–20
critiques of, ix, 19–21, 435n.62, 436n.64, 436–437n.65, 437n.66
four modes of comparison, 20, 435n.62
morphological approach, 20–21, 435n.63, 435–436n.64, 436–437n.65, 437n.66
morphological approach, critiques of, 20–21, 436n.64, 436–437n.65, 437n.66
Constantine, 157
Coomaraswamy, A., 447n.149
Cordovero, Moses, 211, 495n.385
correspondences, 49, 241, 445n.109. *See also bandhus*
horizontal and vertical, 46
quadripartite taxonomies, 39–40, 70, 73, 209, 212, 215
Torah and social and moral orders, 166–167, 183, 188, 216, 400
Torah correlated with microcosm and macrocosm, 167, 176, 183, 203–204, 216, 369, 375, 378, 379, 380, 389, 398, 401
tripartite taxonomies, 38, 40, 56–58, 60–61, 69–70, 73, 79, 111–112, 215, 357, 390, 402, 448n.155, 450n.196
Veda(s) and orders of reality, 33–34, 37–38, 39–40, 44, 46, 56–58, 60–61, 62, 67–68, 69–70, 79, 111–112, 215, 216, 348, 349, 350, 389, 398, 400, 450n.196, 502n.134
cosmic egg, 35, 60, 84. *See also* Hiraṇyagarbha
and Brahmā, 77–78, 86, 100, 101–102, 105, 107, 454n.260
and creator principle, 217
and Nārāyaṇa, 77–78, 101–102
and Prajāpati, 45, 50, 52
and Puruṣa, 78, 100, 101–102
and *tattvas*, 85, 100
and three worlds, 53, 78, 101–102
and Viṣṇu, 100, 101–102
and the waters, 36, 50, 52, 53, 77–78, 101
cosmogony and cosmology. *See also* blueprint; correspondences; *ma'ăśēh b^erē'šîṯ*
cycles of creation, 74–76, 78, 79–80, 85, 88, 93, 94, 95, 96, 99, 100–102, 110, 112, 113, 114–115, 124–125, 127–128, 129, 243, 245, 247–251, 326, 427n.28, 452n.217, 460n.392, 503n.169, 504n.181
in kabbalistic texts, 16, 132, 196–212, 216–219
levels of creation/reality, 17, 132, 198, 210–212, 213, 214–215, 241, 326, 395, 396
mysteries of creation, 15, 34, 152, 159–160, 161, 174, 192, 194, 222–223, 231–232, 234, 235, 241, 318–319, 321, 322–323, 326, 332, 333, 368, 369, 371, 378, 546n.51
in post-Vedic mythology, 72–76, 77–80, 81, 84–94, 95, 99–112, 216–219, 458nn.330, 332
in rabbinic texts, 15–16, 132, 145–147, 148–150, 152–155, 159–172, 174–179, 182–196
revelation and creation, 167, 188, 255–256, 274–275, 287–288, 297–299, 309, 315, 316–318, 323, 326–327, 376, 378, 390, 482n.196, 518n.158, 549n.85
seers/*ṛṣis* and creation, 34, 36, 37, 227, 230, 231–232, 234, 235, 238, 241, 244, 245–246, 247, 248, 326, 332, 333, 335, 348, 349, 390, 398–399, 428n.28
two stages of creation, 35–36, 49–53, 55, 78, 79, 84–86, 101–102,

cosmogony and cosmology (cont.)
208, 216–219, 445n.112, 458nn.333, 335
in Vedic texts, 34–43, 44–62, 63–70, 216–219, 438–439n.22, 445n.112, 458nn.333, 335
cosmology. *See* cosmogony and cosmology
covenant
of circumcision, 377, 404, 519n.165
between God and Abraham, 154, 163, 172, 191, 377, 404–405
between God and people of Israel, 174, 256, 278, 285, 295, 298, 303, 326, 330–331, 333, 338, 376–377, 390, 391, 404
Coward, Harold G., 424n.9, 461n.398
creation. *See* cosmogony and cosmology
creator principle. *See also* Brahmā; Prajāpati; Puruṣa; Viśvakarman
as archetypal seer/*ṛṣi*, 351
arguments regarding existence vs. nonexistence of, 114–115, 121, 123, 124–125, 463n.432
and Brahman/Brahman-Ātman, 30, 40, 63, 64, 73, 330
cosmic body of, 34, 216, 398
and cosmic egg, 217
and *gāyatrī*/Gāyatrī or *sāvitrī*/Sāvitrī, 92, 444n.88
Hiraṇyagarbha as, 36
and knowledge, 17, 24, 29, 213, 214, 216–217, 219
and Manu-Smṛti, 76–77
and Om, 92
and sacrifice, 389
and scripture, 17, 213, 214, 217, 219
and *smṛti* teachings, 76–77
and speech, 68–69, 73, 214, 217–218, 219, 221, 330, 440n.42
and *tapas*, 76–77
and three *vyāhṛtis*, 92
and three worlds, 35, 36
use of term, 434n.55
and Veda(s), 17, 24, 29, 30, 34, 67–69, 73, 77, 81, 92, 115, 124–125, 213, 214, 216, 219, 221, 227, 330, 348, 351, 389, 398, 440n.42
and word/*śabda*, 126–127
Crenshaw, James L., 464n.1, 466n.11, 467n.31
crown(s)
of angels, 259, 521n.181
of "descenders to the Merkabah," 259
and fire, 532n.310
of God, 259, 300, 307, 313, 528n.272, 532n.310
and Hêḵālôṯ traditions, 259, 515n.118, 521n.181, 528n.272, 532n.310
of ineffable Name, 313, 532nn.309, 310
and Merkabah, 313, 532nn.309, 310
people of Israel invested with, 256–257, 259, 279, 291–292, 304–305, 313, 515n.118, 520n.181, 532n.309
and revelation of Torah, 256–257, 259, 279, 291–292, 304–305, 313, 515n.118, 520n.181, 532n.309

da'aṯ (knowledge), 176, 177, 185, 195, 298. *See also* knowledge
dāḇār (word; Word), 24, 131, 146, 154, 155, 161, 169, 170, 172, 178, 184, 187, 189, 190, 195, 200, 213, 270, 479n.159, 482nn.198, 207, 487n.272. *See also* word/Word
Dakṣa-Smṛti, 352

dakṣiṇa (type of sacrificial fire). *See* *āgnīdhrīya*
Dan, Joseph, 507–508n.20, 544n.29
Dandekar, R. N., 426n.23
Daniel, book of, 371, 372
Darśanas, 23, 29, 113–129, 352–354. *See also specific Darśanas*
 acceptance of Vedic authority, 113
 debates regarding created vs. uncreated status of Veda(s), 113–115
 debates regarding eternal vs. noneternal status of Veda(s), 113–115
 as six orthodox schools of Indian philosophy, 113
Dasgupta, Shashi Bhusan, 540n.75
David, 410
Davies, W. D., 495n.385, 554n.14
Day of Judgment, 274, 286, 288. *See also* redemption, final
deities. *See* gods
Denny, Frederick M., 424n.9, 556n.24, 557nn.27, 29
d^erāšāh (hermeneutical meaning), 369, 370, 373, 545n.41
Deuteronomy, 136, 150, 151, 153, 155, 172, 178, 191, 196, 254, 255, 265, 266, 270, 271, 273–274, 281, 282, 286, 290, 291, 292, 295, 296, 306, 307, 308, 310, 311, 313, 316, 319, 322, 323, 377
Deuteronomy Rabbāh, 181, 190, 191, 295, 301–302, 307, 308, 376, 484n.226
Devasthali, G. V., 536n.9
Devī (the Goddess)
 as Brahman, 99
 and Veda(s), 99
devotional traditions. *See bhakti* traditions
Dhamma (doctrine, teaching)
 authority of, 406
 body of, 407
 and early Buddhist tradition, 405–408, 555nn.16, 17, 555–556n.18
 and gods, 408
 and Pali canon, 407–408
 and quest for liberation/*nibbāna*, 406, 555–556n.18
 and *saṃgha*, 406–407, 555n.16, 555–556n.18
 as symbol, 406
 as truths to be understood and realized, 406, 408, 555n.17
 as universal teaching, open to all, 405–408, 555–556n.18
dharma (cosmic ordering principle; system of ritual and social duties). *See also dharma* traditions
 and Brahmā, 453n.243
 in Dharma-Śāstras, 71, 76, 335, 402
 discourse of, in Manu-Smṛti, 76
 and ends of human life/ *puruṣārthas*, 451n.199
 in epics/Itihāsas, 71, 335
 as focus of Pūrva-Mīmāṃsā, 113, 115, 123, 353, 388
 in Mahābhārata, 81
 in Purāṇas, 71, 94, 335
 Sanskrit as language of, 117
 and seers/*ṛṣis*, 228, 245, 247, 249, 335
 and *smṛti*, 8, 402, 427n.26
 and *śruti*, 119, 427n.26
 threefold science of, 76
 varṇāśrama-dharma, 71, 76, 80, 81, 94, 128–129, 335, 402
 and Veda(s), 76, 79, 115–117, 119, 120, 122, 123, 124, 247, 430n.41, 463n.444
 and Vyāsa, 453n.243
Dharma-Śāstras, ix, 2, 80, 352, 355. *See also specific Dharma-Śāstras*

Dharma-Śāstras *(continued)*
and *karman* stream, 71, 72
as products of post-Vedic brahmanical synthesis, 71–72
and science of *dharma*, 71, 76, 335, 402
as *smṛti*, 8, 402
and Viṣṇu, 103
Dharma-Sūtras, 2, 71, 76, 335, 352
dharma traditions. *See also dharma*
and appropriation of Veda(s) through reciting and hearing *mantras*, 355, 390–391
and *karma-kāṇḍa* or *karman* stream, 71, 81, 334–335, 355, 390–391
and seers/*ṛṣis*, 334–335, 355
dhī or *dhīti* (vision), 231, 232, 234, 235, 236, 237, 496n.6, 497n.34, 498n.59
dhvani or *nāda* (sound), 117–119
dhyāna (meditation). *See* meditation
dîbbēr (utterance; Word), 270, 283, 308. *See also* word/Word
dîbbûr (utterance; Word), 195, 270, 271, 282, 293, 308. *See also* word/Word
divine anthropos
body of, 197, 204, 216, 320, 380, 398
and commandments/*mitzvot*, 204, 380
and *s*ᵉ*p̄îrôṯ*, 197, 380
and Torah, 204, 216, 369, 378, 380, 398
divine language. *See* language, divine
divine name(s). *See* Name of God; names of God
divine speech. *See* speech
divine word. *See* word/Word
Doniger, Wendy. *See* O'Flaherty, Wendy Doniger
D'Sa, Francis X., 462n.400, 463nn.435, 438
Dudley, Guilford, III, 436n.64
Durgā (goddess), 455n.282, 456n.294
Dvaita Vedānta, 114, 353. *See also* Vedānta

earth, 241
and *a*, first constituent of Om, 57–58, 70, 111
and Brahmā, 111
and brahmins, 38, 61
and fire/Agni, 38, 56–58, 70, 215
and heaven, as one of God's special creations/possessions, 149, 471–472n.78, 481n.185
and heaven, at revelation of Torah, 253, 255–256, 267–268, 275–278, 288–291, 299–305, 311–313, 327–328, 520nn.174, 176
as lower waters, 208
and Malḵûṯ/Shekhinah, 315, 318
and primordial utterance *bhūḥ*, 51, 54, 56–58, 59, 61, 92, 109, 111, 127, 446n.125
and *rajas*, 111
and *rathantara sāman*, 445n.109
and *ṛcs*, 59, 445n.109
and Ṛg-Veda, 38, 51, 56–58, 60, 61, 70, 111, 215
and sacrificial boar, 87, 103, 459n.349
and speech, 38, 58
Ecclesiastes, 173, 181–182
Ecclesiastes Rabbāh, 179
Eck, Diana L., 434nn.58, 59
egg. *See* cosmic egg
Egyptian traditions, 134–135, 141, 465–466n.10
Eichrodt, Walther, 464n.1, 466n.10
Eidlitz, Walther, 536n.3
Eilberg-Schwartz, Howard, 365, 540–541n.7, 543n.17, 552n.4
ekaviṃśa (twenty-one-versed *stoma*), 40, 106

R. Eleazar, 176, 178–179, 288, 376–377, 482n.207, 483n.212, 519n.165, 525n.228
R. Eleazar b. Arak, 313, 515n.118, 532n.309
R. Eleazar b. Azariah, 173, 181
R. Eleazar b. Zadok, 154, 164, 470n.66
R. Eleazar of Modi'im, 481n.186
Eliade, Mircea, 20, 423n.9, 425n.9, 434n.57, 435–436n.64, 437n.65
R. Eliezer b. Hyrcanus, 191, 196, 290, 474n.101, 510n.58
R. Eliezer b. Jose the Galilean, 161
Elijah, 267, 278, 290, 299, 471n.76, 481n.187
Elisha b. Abuya, 541n.12
Enoch, 259
Enoch, Books of, 192, 259, 472n.82
'Ên-Sôp̄ (infinite, endless; unmanifest aspect of God), 494n.365
  and divine language, 211
  and four worlds, 211
  and Hebrew letters, 211
  and *s^e^p̄îrôṯ*, 196–197, 198, 205, 207, 209–210
  and Torah, 209–210, 211
  as transcendent, 196, 493n.349
  as ultimate source of creation, 219, 493n.349
  as unmanifest Godhead, 196, 198, 205, 209, 211, 493n.349
epics or Itihāsas, 35, 80, 83. *See also* Harivaṃśa; Mahābhārata; Rāmāyaṇa
  and Being, 67, 457n.311
  and *bhakti* traditions or stream, 72, 402, 416
  and Brahmā, 104–105, 106
  and *dharma*, 71, 335
  didactic function of, 97–98, 99
  and discursive oral traditions, 417–418
  emphasis on both sound and meaning, 97–98
  as fifth Veda or as Veda, 7, 8, 10, 95–96, 104–105, 250, 402, 425–426n.19, 438n.10, 457n.311
  iconic veneration of, 19, 416
  and mantric efficacy, 416
  open to general populace, 99
  as products of post-Vedic brahmanical synthesis, 71–72
  as *smṛti*, 8
  and Vedic paradigm, 10, 19, 416
  and Viṣṇu, 103
  and Vyāsa, 250
  as written texts, 19, 416
'ēš (fire), 154, 155, 163, 172, 178, 184, 191, 196, 270, 271, 281, 292, 308, 472n.83, 473n.92, 482n.198. *See also* fire
Esau, 199–200
  and Torah, 193, 476n.122
Esau, children of, 266, 273–274, 286, 297, 311, 316, 509n.40
Essers, Bénard, 441n.43
Esther, book of, 156, 179
Esther Rabbāh, 156, 179, 376
eternal
  Logos as, 139
  Purāṇas as, 96
  Qur'ān as, 409
  relationship between word/*śabda* and meaning/*artha* as, 114, 120–122, 123, 124, 125, 128, 129
  Sanskrit *varṇas* as, 118–119, 124
  speech as, 126, 127, 330, 334
  śruti as, 250
  Veda(s) as, 8, 9, 29, 32, 65, 67, 75–76, 77, 79–80, 82, 84, 93–94, 95, 99, 110, 112, 113, 114, 115–117, 122–123, 124–125, 126, 127, 128, 129, 228, 243, 245, 247, 248, 250, 251, 330, 334, 353, 355, 356, 427nn.25, 28
  wisdom as, 139

eternal *(continued)*
word/*śabda* as, 114, 116, 117–119, 122, 124, 125
Eve, 192, 193
Exodus, 150, 151, 152, 153, 173, 177, 179, 181, 183, 191, 192, 253–254, 255, 259, 262, 263, 265, 266, 267–268, 269, 270, 271, 272, 274, 275, 276, 277, 279, 281, 283, 284, 290, 292, 294, 299, 302, 304, 305, 312–313, 314, 318–319, 320–321, 376
Exodus Rabbāh, 179, 181, 182, 183, 185, 188, 190, 294–295, 297, 298, 299, 302–304, 305, 306, 309, 311, 376
eye, 501n.107
and heaven, 38, 58
and primordial utterance *svaḥ*, 58
and Sāma-Veda, 38, 58
and sun/Sūrya/Āditya, 38, 58
Ezekiel
and fire, 319–320
firmaments or heavens opened to, 258, 528n.272
and glory of God, 258, 263
and *ḥayyôṯ*, 258, 303
and Isaiah, 320, 534n.347
and Malḵûṯ/Shekhinah or Oral Torah, 319–320, 534n.347
and Merkabah, 255, 258–259, 262, 263, 270, 278, 303, 307, 319, 514n.112, 528–529n.272
and Moses, 264, 320
and people of Israel, 258–259, 264, 269–270, 278, 307, 319–320, 510n.58
and revelation of Torah, 255, 258–259, 262, 278, 514n.112, 528–529n.272
Ezekiel, book of, 15, 255, 258, 262, 263, 303, 304, 308
Ezra b. Solomon, 199, 360, 491nn.324, 326–328, 534n.343
Falk, Maryla, 447–448n.149
Filliozat, Jean, 426n.23
Finkelstein, Louis, 471n.71
fiqh (jurisprudence)
as product of human intelligence, 413
sources of, 412–413
fire. *See also* Agni; *'ēš*
and angels, 146–147, 259, 267, 289, 300, 308, 366
and creation, 275
and crown of God, 532n.310
and Ezekiel, 319–320
and firmaments, 146–147, 276
of Gehenna, 178–179, 483n.218
and *ḥayyôṯ*, 267, 300, 308
and heaven, 172, 179, 271, 300, 366, 511n.65
and Hêḵālôṯ traditions, 259, 473n.91, 510n.61, 511n.65, 528n.272
and interpretation of Torah, 172, 179, 281, 366, 480n.173, 517n.135
and light, 191, 308
and Merkabah, 179, 195–196, 259, 264, 366, 469n.57, 473n.91, 480n.173, 507n.16, 511n.65, 517n.135
and mouth of God, 155, 257, 270, 510n.61, 535n.367
and Oral Torah, 172, 480n.171
and people of Israel, 222, 257, 270, 271, 281, 296, 306, 308, 314, 318, 332, 535n.367
and rabbinic sages, 172, 178–179, 281, 366, 489n.316, 544n.26
and revelation of Torah, 155, 172, 179, 191, 196, 222, 254, 257, 259, 263, 264, 269, 270, 271, 275, 281, 292, 301, 306, 308, 314, 318, 322, 332, 366, 473n.91, 475n.118, 479n.167, 510n.61, 516n.132, 535n.367
and study of Torah, 172, 179, 281,

366, 480n.173, 517n.135
and throne of glory, 146–147, 191, 301, 308
and Torah, 18, 146, 147, 154, 155, 163, 171–172, 178–179, 184, 190, 191, 195–196, 197, 198–199, 210, 222, 254, 271, 273–274, 281, 292, 301, 308, 313, 314, 322, 332, 366, 472n.83, 473n.92, 475n.118, 480n.171, 482n.198, 483n.218
Torah written with black fire on white fire, 172, 191, 198–199, 281, 308, 322, 332
and Veda(s), 233
and voice(s) of God, 155, 222, 270, 296, 306, 314, 318, 332
and word/Word of God/*dāḇār/dîbbēr/dîbbûr*, 18, 146, 155, 171, 172, 178–179, 190, 191, 197, 210, 222, 257, 270, 308, 318, 332, 482n.198, 483n.218, 510n.61, 535n.367
and Written Torah, 172, 480n.171
firmaments. *See also* heaven
and fire, 146–147, 276
hierarchy of, 145, 146–147, 182–183, 332
and light, 146–147
opened to Ezekiel, 528n.272
opened to Moses, 276, 301, 307
opened to people of Israel, 257, 293, 307, 322, 332, 523n.222, 529n.273
and revelation of Torah, 257, 276, 293, 301, 307, 322, 332, 523n.222, 529n.273
seven firmaments, 145, 257, 293, 301, 307, 322, 523n.222, 528n.272, 529n.273
as third world between heaven and earth, 208
Fischel, Henry A., 476n.130
Fishbane, Michael, 431n.44, 542–543n.16
Fitzgerald, James L., 453n.234
Fohrer, Georg, 465n.10
Foucault, Michel, 551n.3
four forms of Torah. *See also* Torah
and 'Ên-Sôp̄, 211
and four letters of Tetragrammaton, 212, 215
and four worlds, 211–212, 215
and Hebrew letters, 211–212
and *s^e^p̄îrôṯ*, 212, 215
and stages of manifestation of Torah, 212
four worlds. *See also 'ăṣîlûṯ; 'ăśiyyāh; b^e^rî'āh; y^e^ṣîrāh*
and 'Ên-Sôp̄, 211
and four forms of Torah, 211–212, 215
and four letters of Tetragrammaton, 212, 215
and Hebrew letters, 211–212
and *s^e^p̄îrôṯ*, 212, 215
and stages of manifestation of Torah, 212
Fraade, Steven D., 144, 468n.48, 509nn.32, 40
Fragment Targums, 472n.82, 476n.127
Friedlander, Gerald, 488nn.284, 285, 291
Friedmann, M., 484n.221

Gadamer, Hans-Georg, 425n.11
R. Gamaliel, 471n.75
Gaṇeśa (deity), 82–83
Garden of Eden, 531n.304
and Adam, 163, 172, 184, 193, 472n.82, 475n.115
as one of six or seven things created prior to the world, 175, 193
and Torah, 163, 172, 184, 191, 193, 472n.82
gārhapatya (type of sacrificial fire), 33, 58

garment(s). *See also ḥālûq*
of angels, 259–260
of God, 259–260, 306, 506n.10, 527nn.259, 262, 528n.272
and Hêḵālôṯ traditions, 259–260, 306, 506n.10, 527nn.259, 262, 528n.272
inscribed with Name of God, 306, 527n.262, 532n.311
people of Israel invested with, 256–257, 259–260, 305–306, 313, 526–527n.258, 527n.262, 532n.311
and revelation of Torah, 256–257, 259–260, 305–306, 313, 526–527n.258, 527n.262, 532n.311
of Torah, 369–370, 371, 372, 382, 392
in Zohar, 546n.47
Gaston, Lloyd, 552n.9, 553n.11, 554n.14
Gautama (Vedic seer), 229, 239, 243
gāyatrī/Gāyatrī or *sāvitrī*/Sāvitrī (type of Vedic meter; three-lined *mantra*; goddess)
and Brahmā, 79, 89–90, 91, 105, 107
and brahmins, 39, 40, 61
and creator principle, 92, 444n.88
and fire/Agni, 39, 40
as *gāyatrī mantra*, 79, 91, 92–93, 106–109, 452n.221, 455n.293, 456n.294, 498n.63
as goddess of speech, 89–90, 91, 105
as meter, 39, 61, 91, 92, 105, 343, 444n.88, 535–536n.1
as Mother of Vedas, 90, 91, 444n.88, 455n.282, 456n.294
and Om, 79, 92–93, 106–109
and Prajāpati, 39, 79, 343, 444n.88
and Puruṣa, 91–92
and Sanskrit *varṇas*, 92–93, 106–109
and Sarasvatī, 89–90, 91, 105, 455n.282
and speech/Vāc, 89–90, 91, 105, 106–109, 444n.88
and three *vyāhṛtis*, 79, 92–93, 106–109
and Veda(s), 79, 90, 91–93, 105, 106–109, 444n.88, 455n.282, 456n.294
G^e^ḇûrāh (power; fifth *s^e^p̄îrāh*), 197, 270, 306, 314, 322, 377, 528n.272
Gehenna or Gehinnom (hell)
fire of, 178–179, 483n.218
as one of six or seven things created prior to the world, 175, 193
gematria (interpretation based on numerical value of Hebrew letters), 365. *See also* letters, Hebrew: numerical value of
Gemser, Berend, 465n.10
Genesis, 15, 138, 149, 151, 152, 154, 156, 159, 162–163, 164, 167, 170, 171, 175, 176, 183, 184–185, 189–190, 191, 192, 193, 194, 195, 199–200, 207, 208, 287–288
Genesis Rabbāh, 131, 142, 143, 156, 159, 160–161, 162–163, 164–166, 168–169, 170, 171, 175, 176, 177, 178, 183, 184–185, 186, 188–190, 203, 274–275
gentile nations
and Abraham, 404–405, 553n.14
and angels, 295, 307, 522n.202, 529n.274
excluded from Oral Torah, 182, 294, 295
and final redemption, 274, 286–287, 288
heard divine utterances, 285, 332
heard voice(s) of God, 269, 292, 295–296, 309, 338, 530n.288
and heavenly powers, 316

image-making practices of, 416
and Name of God, 296–297
and Paul's doctrine of justification by faith, 404–405, 553nn.10, 11, 553–554n.14
Paul's mission to, 404–405, 552n.9, 553nn.10, 11, 553–554n.14
and people of Israel/Jews, 135, 136, 138, 152, 157, 158–159, 182, 188, 255, 266–267, 268, 269, 273–274, 285–287, 292, 294, 295–297, 307, 309, 311, 316, 325, 326, 329, 332, 338, 391, 398–399, 404–405, 529n.274, 530n.288, 533n.327, 552n.9, 553nn.10, 11, 553–554n.14
and revelation of Torah, 152, 182, 255, 266–267, 269, 271, 273–274, 284, 285–287, 292, 294, 295–297, 307, 309, 311, 316, 325, 326, 329, 332, 338, 391, 399, 509n.40, 512n.83, 518n.157, 529n.274, 530n.288, 533n.327
and seven commandments, 266, 286–287, 399
and Ten Words of revelation/Ten Commandments, 285, 296–297
and wisdom/*ḥoḵmāh*, 273
and Word of God, 296

g^ezērāh šāwāh (inference based on word analogy), 288, 363–364, 519n.166

Ghose, Aurobindo, 9, 427n.28

Gikatilla, Joseph, 200–201, 210, 367, 368, 492nn.334–337, 493n.338, 494n.383, 495n.384, 544–545n.35

girdles
people of Israel invested with, 256–257, 279, 305
and revelation of Torah, 256–257, 279, 305

glory of God. *See also kāḇôḏ*
and Ezekiel, 258, 263
and interpretation of Torah, 366, 372, 546n.51
and light, 274, 493n.350
and Moses, 258, 320
and people of Israel, 256, 257, 258, 263, 274, 279, 281, 293, 303, 305, 306, 307, 318, 320–321, 322, 323, 324, 329, 332, 366, 515n.120, 525n.244, 527n.262, 529n.283, 532n.311, 534n.340
and revelation of Torah, 256, 257, 258, 263, 267, 268, 274, 279, 281, 293, 303, 305, 306, 307, 317–318, 320–321, 322, 323, 324, 329, 332, 366, 515n.120, 525n.244, 527nn.259, 262, 529n.283, 532n.311, 534n.340
role in cosmogonic process, 317–318, 323
and *s^epîrôṯ*, 317–318, 320–321
and study of Torah, 366, 372, 546n.51
and Ten Words of revelation/Ten Commandments, 317–318, 320–321, 323
and Torah, 253, 276, 289, 546n.51

God. *See also* divine anthropos; 'Ên-Sôp̄; glory of God; Name of God; *s^ep̄îrôṯ*; Shekhinah; voice(s) of God; word/Word
augmenting power of, through practice of Torah, 359, 374–375, 377–378, 380–381, 388–389, 401
augmenting power of, through study of Torah, 359, 375, 378, 380, 388–389, 401
body of, 201, 214, 505n.7
as bridegroom of Israel, 256, 268, 277–278, 291, 303, 312, 331, 338, 373

God *(continued)*
and covenant with Abraham, 154, 163, 172, 191, 377, 404–405
and covenant with people of Israel, 174, 256, 278, 285, 295, 298, 303, 326, 330–331, 333, 338, 376–377, 390, 391, 404
crown(s) of, 259, 300, 307, 313, 528n.272, 532n.310
descent from heaven, 254, 255, 256, 258, 264, 267–268, 275–278, 288, 290, 291, 293–294, 303–305, 310, 312–313, 314, 315, 327–328, 520n.176, 529n.274, 531n.304
descent of, and *s^e^pîrôṯ*, 315–316, 318
'Ên-Sôp̄ as unmanifest Godhead, 196, 198, 205, 209, 211, 493n.349
essence and power of, contained in Name, 131, 200, 201, 213, 253
face(s) of, 155, 256, 257, 280–281, 283, 293–294, 301–302, 307, 309, 310, 312, 318, 319, 331, 332, 512n.75, 516n.130, 517n.142, 529n.274, 530n.290
face(s) of, and light, 155, 280–281
as father of Torah, 145–146, 253, 256, 276–277, 302, 312, 338
four theophanies of, 268, 510n.52
garment of, 259–260, 306, 506n.10, 527nn.259, 262, 528n.272
and Hebrew letters, 201, 214, 360–361, 492n.336
as "He who spoke and the world came into being," 154, 167, 170, 177–178, 472n.85
and light, 138, 155, 268, 274, 280–281, 318, 333, 393, 487n.276, 510n.52, 527n.259
and Logos, 159
as manifest and unmanifest, 196, 205
Moses as like unto, 276
mouth of, and fire, 155, 257, 270, 510n.61, 535n.367
as one with his Name, 200–201
people of Israel/Jews as chosen people of, 135, 136, 152, 157, 256, 263, 266, 273, 285, 295, 311, 325, 330–331, 391, 522n.199
as personal God, 330–331, 392
s^e^pîrôṯ as manifest Godhead in relation to creation, 196–197, 200, 202, 317–318
and Sinai theophany, 255, 256–259, 262–263, 264, 268–272, 278–284, 291–294, 295, 303–310, 311–316, 317–324, 329, 331, 332–333, 337–338, 495n.6, 510n.52, 512n.75, 516n.130, 517n.142, 523n.222, 529nn.274, 283, 534n.343
ten descents of, 312, 531n.304
Torah as counselor of, 145–146, 180, 185–186, 193, 194, 488n.289
Torah as co-worker of, 145–146, 198, 214
Torah as daughter of, 145–146, 253, 256, 276–277, 302, 312, 338
Torah as essence of, 131, 200, 201, 213, 214, 253
Torah as form of, 214, 361, 417, 546n.51
Torah as living aspect of, 15, 16, 131, 160, 201, 331, 367, 386, 392, 398, 416
Torah as one with, 200–201, 209–210, 213, 359, 367, 371, 373, 382, 417, 492n.334, 546n.51
wisdom/Ḥoḵmāh as co-worker of, 134, 137, 138, 198, 214
wisdom/Ḥoḵmāh as personifica-

tion of attribute of, 134–135, 465n.9
gods. *See also specific deities*
and Brahmā, 79, 86, 88, 96, 246
and Brahman/Brahman-Ātman, 328, 330
brahmins as human gods, 61, 241, 335
and Buddha, 408
chariots of, 231, 332
and cycles of creation, 100, 101, 125, 128, 248
and Dhamma, 408
and heart, 235, 328
and human faculties, 38, 56, 58
images of, 19, 94, 95, 416, 434n.58
and the Imperishable, 233, 330, 356
as inspirers of cognitions and hymns, 34, 229, 232, 233–235, 236–237, 240, 328, 330, 354, 498nn.52, 59
and light, 232, 233, 235, 328
and meditation, 241
and meters, 38–39, 40, 447n.149
names of, as denoting universal classes/*ākṛtis*, 125
and Prajāpati, 39–40, 55, 56–58, 126, 350, 447n.141
and Puruṣa, 37–38, 67–68, 349
realms of, 34, 231, 232, 233, 235, 237, 248, 327, 328, 330, 332, 356
and sacrifice, 19, 37, 38–39, 231, 238, 343, 348, 349, 350, 389, 401, 416, 439n.34
and seers/*ṛṣis*, 34, 37, 66–67, 229, 230, 231–232, 233–235, 236–237, 238, 239, 240–241, 243, 246, 248, 326, 328, 330, 332, 335, 348, 349, 354, 390, 497n.20, 498nn.49–52, 59, 500n.106, 501n.111
and Skambha, 41
and social classes/*varṇas*, 38, 39–40
and *tapas*, 240–241, 246, 330
and three constituents of Om, 57–58, 69–70, 111, 215
and three *guṇas*, 111
and three *vyāhṛtis*, 56–58, 111
and three worlds, 38, 56–58, 70, 111, 215
thrones of, 231, 332
and Veda(s), 34, 38, 39, 56–58, 59, 66–67, 70, 79, 96, 110, 111, 128–129, 215, 229, 231, 232, 233–235, 236–237, 238, 240, 246, 327, 328, 330, 339, 343, 348, 349, 350–351, 354, 388–389, 401, 416, 419, 498nn.52, 59
Goldberg, Ellen S., 422n.7
golden calf, 254, 257, 278, 279, 291, 303–304, 310, 314, 329, 525n.245
Goldin, Judah, 541n.16, 543n.18, 548–549n.80
Gonda, Jan, 229, 230, 231, 235, 426n.23, 429n.33, 440n.39, 441nn.53, 55, 442nn.55, 65, 444n.94, 445n.115, 496nn.6, 10, 11, 497nn.21, 34, 498nn.44, 52, 499nn.68, 71, 72, 74, 83, 536nn.3, 12, 539n.57, 540n.75
Goodman, Hananya, 422n.7
Goody, Jack, 414, 417, 418, 558nn.50, 53, 559n.54
Gopal, Ram, 538n.48, 539n.60
Gottlieb, Efraim, 494–495n.383, 495n.384, 544n.35
Graham, William A., 4, 5, 344, 345–346, 419, 423n.9, 425nn.10, 12, 536nn.2, 8, 10, 556nn.24–26, 557nn.27, 31, 559n.56
grammarians, Indian, 116, 122, 441n.44, 461n.398
Greek or Hellenistic traditions, 136, 137–140, 141, 466n.10,

Greek or Hellenistic traditions *(continued)*
477n.132, 554n.15. *See also* Aristotle; Platonic traditions; Stoic traditions
Green, William Scott, 468n.46, 541n.16, 542n.16, 543n.19
Gṛhya-Sūtras, 71, 335, 345, 352
Grözinger, Karl-Erich, 523–524n.222
Gṛtsamada (Vedic seer), 229
Gruenwald, Ithamar, 261, 264, 432n.51, 505n.5, 506n.15, 506–507n.16, 507n.17, 508n.21
guṇas (constituents of Prakṛti). *See also* Prakṛti; *rajas*; *sattva*; *tamas*
  and Prakṛti, 100, 106, 107, 111
  and three constituents of Om, 107, 108, 111–112
  and three *vyāhṛtis*, 111–112
  and three worlds, 111–112
  and *trimūrti*, 111–112
  and Veda(s), 106, 108, 111–112, 459n.373
Gupta, S. K., 538n.48

Hadrian, 296–297
Haggadah. *See* aggadah/Aggadah
Ḥăğîğāh, 147, 174, 179, 366
halakhah (law; normative legal teachings), ix, 185
  and consensus of the rabbinic sages, 174, 290–291
  definition and use of term, 431n.45
  and myth, 374
  as Oral Torah, 12
  as Torah, 151, 152, 265–266
Halbfass, Wilhelm, 430n.40, 461n.397
Halivni, David Weiss, 542n.16
Halperin, David J., 258, 261–264, 433n.51, 483–484n.219, 504n.2, 505nn.3–5, 507n.20, 508nn.21–29, 510n.58, 511n.72, 514n.112, 515n.113, 519n.167, 519–520n.171, 524n.222, 525nn.245, 246, 528–529n.272, 529n.273, 532n.310, 541n.12
ḥālûq (garment), 259–260, 306, 527n.259, 528n.272. *See also* garment(s)
R. Ḥama b. Ḥanina, 161, 189, 282–283
R. Hamnuna, 284, 516n.124
R. Ḥananyah, nephew of R. Joshua b. Ḥananyah, 280
R. Ḥananyah b. Teradion, 482n.204
Handelman, Susan A., 541nn.8, 16, 543n.19
R. Ḥanina, 177, 512n.91
R. Ḥanina b. Pappai, 286, 512nn.75, 85, 87, 522n.209
Harivaṃśa, 23, 80, 84, 89–90, 91–93, 94, 106
Hartman, Geoffrey H., 542n.16
Hastings, James, 423n.9
ḥayyôṯ (living creatures), 258, 267, 300, 302, 303, 308
Hazra, Rajendra Chandra, 94–95, 456n.308, 458n.329
hē/Hē (Hebrew letter; letter of Tetragrammaton), 487n.262
  and Bînāh, 208, 209, 212
  and Malḵûṯ/Shekhinah, 208, 209, 212
  and Oral Torah, 209, 212
  shape of, 169, 177, 189
  sound of, 169–170, 189
  this world created with, 168–169, 177, 188–189
  and world of creation/*b^erî'āh*, 212
  and world of making/*'ăśiyyāh*, 212
heart
  as abode of gods, 235, 328

and Brahmā, 105, 107
and mind, 236, 499n.76
and Om, 105, 107
and Puruṣa, 65
role in Vedic cognition, 232, 233, 235–236, 237, 328, 497n.37, 499nn.71, 76
as seat of consciousness, 235, 328
heaven, 241. *See also* firmaments
ascent of Abraham to, 259
ascent of "descender to the Merkabah" to, 259, 260, 261–262, 337, 507n.19, 515n.119
ascent of Elijah to, 267, 290
ascent of Enoch to, 259
ascent of Moses to, 146, 173, 256, 258, 259, 262, 263–264, 267, 275–277, 278, 288–290, 293, 299–302, 303, 307, 311–312, 328, 329, 513n.103, 520nn.171, 176, 523–524n.222, 541n.15
ascent to, and Merkabah, 258, 259, 260, 261–262, 264, 300, 337, 506nn.15, 16, 507n.19, 508n.22, 515n.119, 517n.139, 524n.222, 541n.12
attainment of world of, 43, 61, 240, 241, 352
and *bṛhat sāman*, 445n.109
descent of angels from, 256, 258, 264, 278–279, 291–292, 293–294, 303–305, 309, 313–314, 529n.274
descent of chariots from, 258, 262, 264, 278, 293–294, 304–305, 313
descent of God from, 254, 255, 256, 258, 264, 267–268, 275–278, 288, 290, 291, 293–294, 303–305, 310, 312–313, 314, 315, 327–328, 520n.176, 529n.274, 531n.304
descent of primordial wisdom from, 15, 135–136, 362
descent of Shekhinah from, 256, 276–278, 290
descent of Torah from, 15, 146, 172, 253, 256, 265, 275–278, 288–291, 293, 299–300, 301, 302, 311–312, 315, 317, 327–328, 369, 513n.103
and earth, as one of God's special creations/possessions, 149, 471–472n.78, 481n.185
and earth, at revelation of Torah, 253, 255–256, 267–268, 275–278, 288–291, 299–305, 311–313, 327–328, 520nn.174, 176
and eye, 38, 58
and fire, 172, 179, 271, 300, 366, 511n.65
heavenly Temple, 301
and *m*, third constituent of Om, 57–58, 70, 111
and Mount Sinai, 276, 311–312, 313, 518n.158
opened to Ezekiel, 258
opened to people of Israel, 258, 263, 311–312, 313, 314, 531n.305
and patron of sacrifice/*yajamāna*, 43, 61
and primordial utterance *svaḥ*, 51, 54, 56–58, 61, 92, 109, 111
and revelation of Torah, 15, 135–136, 146, 172, 173, 253, 255–256, 258, 259, 262, 263–264, 265, 267–268, 275–278, 288–291, 293–294, 299–305, 307, 309, 310, 311–314, 315, 317, 327–328, 329, 362, 369, 513n.103, 518n.158, 520nn.171, 174, 176, 523–524n.222, 529n.274, 531nn.304, 305, 541n.15
and *sāmans*, 59, 445n.109
and Sāma-Veda, 38, 51, 56–58, 60, 61, 70, 111, 215
and seers/*ṛṣis*, 230, 239, 501n.113

heaven *(continued)*
and Śiva, 111
and sun/Sūrya/Āditya, 38, 56–58, 70, 215
and *tamas*, 111
as upper waters, 208
and *vaiśyas*, 38, 61
Hebrew. *See also* letters, Hebrew
as alphabet composed of letters/ *'ôṯiyyôṯ*, 18
creative power of, 167–168, 189, 275, 399
as divine language, 18, 167–168, 399
as language of people of Israel/ Jews, 3, 397, 399
as language with which the world was created, 167–168, 189, 275, 399
relationship between name and form, 171, 189, 200, 203
and revelation of Torah, 267, 275
as sacred/holy language, 3, 18, 167–168, 189, 193, 275, 397
spoken by Abraham, 193, 195
and Torah, 167–168, 275, 399, 410
Hebrew Bible. *See also* Ketuvim; Nevi'im; Pentateuch; Sefer Torah; Torah; Written Torah; and *specific biblical books*
exegesis of, 141–142, 172–173
as Tanakh, 12
as Torah, 12, 151, 265
wisdom literature of, 23, 135
as Written Torah, 12–13, 141–142, 158, 273, 294, 485n.232, 512n.75
Heesterman, Jan C., 11, 430n.38
Heide, A. van der, 545n.42
Heiler, Friedrich, 424–425n.9
Heinemann, Isaak, 542n.16
Heinemann, Joseph, 143, 468n.45, 480n.176, 485n.231, 518n.154, 541–542n.16
Hêḵālôṯ Rabbāṯî, 506n.15, 508n.21, 510n.61, 521n.181, 527nn.259, 262, 528n.272
Hêḵālôṯ traditions, 505n.5. *See also* Merkabah; Merkabah traditions, rabbinic
and adjuration of angels, 261–262
and *'am hā-'āreṣ*, 262
and angels, 259, 260, 261–262, 515n.119, 521n.181, 524n.222
and apocalyptic traditions, 258, 259, 264, 506n.16
and ascent to heaven, 258, 259, 260, 261–262, 264, 300, 337, 506nn.15, 16, 507n.19, 508n.22, 515n.119, 517n.139, 524n.222, 541n.12
and ascent to heaven, dangers of, 259, 260, 506n.15, 515n.119, 517n.139, 524n.222
and crown(s), 259, 515n.118, 521n.181, 528n.272, 532n.310
and "descender to the Merkabah," 259–260, 261–262, 337, 505n.6, 507n.19, 511n.65, 515n.119
and ecstatic mystical practices, 261, 264, 506n.16
and fire, 259, 473n.91, 510n.61, 511n.65, 528n.272
and four sages who entered *pardēs*, 541n.12
and garment(s), 259–260, 306, 506n.10, 527nn.259, 262, 528n.272
and general populace, 262–264, 507–508n.20, 508n.22
and lightning, 259
and *ma'ăśēh merkāḇāh*, 261
and mastery of Torah, 261–262, 263–264, 337, 507–508n.20
and Merkabah, 201, 258–264, 432–433n.51, 506nn.15, 16,

507n.19, 515n.119, 532n.310, 541n.12
Moses as paradigm for, 259, 263–264, 337, 524n.222
and names of God, 260, 506n.11, 515n.119
origin and dates of texts, 261–262, 506n.15
and rabbinic Merkabah traditions, 258–264, 432–433n.51, 488n.285, 506–507n.16, 524n.222, 532n.310
and revelation of Torah, 258–264, 300, 306, 307, 337, 505n.7, 510n.61, 511n.65, 515nn.118, 119, 517n.139, 521nn.181, 190, 524n.222, 527n.259, 528n.272, 532n.310
and *Śar Tôrāh*, 261–262, 507n.17, 507–508n.20, 508n.21
and seven palaces/*hêkālôt*, 259
and *šî'ûr qômāh*, 505n.7, 506n.15, 528n.272
and study of Torah, 259
and synagogue traditions, 262–264, 507n.19, 508n.22, 524n.222, 532n.310
two categories of material, 261–262
R. Ḥelbo, 280
Hellenistic traditions. *See* Greek or Hellenistic traditions
Hengel, Martin, 137, 138, 464n.3, 464–465n.6, 466nn.10, 17, 18, 467nn.21, 32, 33, 470n.61, 476n.129
hermeneutics. *See* interpretation of Torah; interpretation of Veda(s)
Herr, Moshe David, 468n.42
Heschel, Abraham Joshua, 15, 363, 432n.49, 541n.11
Ḥesed (love, mercy; fourth *s^e^pîrāh*), 197, 322
R. Hezekiah, 287, 288, 477n.141, 513n.94
R. Ḥilkiah, 477n.141, 513n.94
Hillebrandt, Alfred, 439n.22
Hillel, 148
Hillel, school of, 166, 486n.255
Hiltebeitel, Alf, 452n.232
"Hinduisms." *See also* ascetic traditions; *bhakti* traditions; brahmanical tradition; "Hinduisms" and "Judaisms"; tantric traditions
as federation of cultures, 70
and three streams of post-Vedic brahmanical synthesis, 70–72
variety of, 1, 421n.1
Vedic authority as constitutive of, 10, 429n.33, 430n.42
"Hinduisms" and "Judaisms." *See also* brahmanical tradition and rabbinic tradition; "Hinduisms"; "Judaisms"
characterizations of differences between, ix, 1, 2, 19, 413
comparative study of, ix–x, 1, 413, 422nn.6, 7
and paradigms of "religious tradition," ix, 2–3, 413, 422n.6
Hiraṇyagarbha (golden egg or embryo). *See also* cosmic egg
Brahmā as, 86, 104
as creator principle, 36
Prajāpati as, 44
Viṣṇu as, 454n.258
R. Ḥisda, 292, 543n.21
R. Ḥiyya II b. Abba, 285, 298, 543n.20
hôd/Hôd (glory, majesty; eighth *s^e^pîrāh*), 197, 276, 277, 372, 534n.352, 547n.59
Hoffmann, D., 150, 471n.71
ḥokmāh/Ḥokmāh (wisdom; second *s^e^pîrāh*), 197. *See also* wisdom
as artisan/*'āmôn* or architect of creation, 24, 131, 133–134, 202, 214, 253

ḥoḵmāh/Ḥoḵmāh *(continued)*
associated with understanding/ *tᵉḇûnāh* and knowledge/*da'aṯ*, 176, 177, 185, 195, 298
bᵉrē'šîṯ as *bᵉ-ḥoḵmāh*, 165, 207, 476n.127
and Bînāh, 202, 205, 206, 207, 208, 217, 219
as demiurge principle, 198, 202, 214, 219
as Father, 202, 205, 207, 208, 209, 214, 493n.341
as female figure, 133, 146
as first of God's works, 133
and gentile nations, 273
as God's co-worker in creation, 134, 138, 198, 214
and Hebrew letters, 209, 212
as instrument of creation, 165, 176, 177, 185, 195, 298
as king of world above, 206
as male principle, 202, 207, 217
and Malḵûṯ/Shekhinah or Oral Torah, 209
and people of Israel, 323
as primordial or preexistent, 24, 131, 133, 198, 202, 205, 209, 212, 214, 253, 493n.341, 494n.354
as primordial point, 205, 209, 494n.354
as primordial Torah/*tôrāh qᵉḏûmāh*, 198, 209, 212, 493n.341
as *rē'šîṯ*, 133, 205, 207, 494n.354
and revelation of Torah, 323
termed *'āmôn*, 133–134, 202, 464nn.4, 5, 464–465n.6
as thought, 204–205, 206–208, 209, 494n.355
and Tip̄'ereṯ or Written Torah, 209
Torah as, 24, 131, 146, 160, 165, 176, 185, 198, 202, 209, 212, 214, 216–217, 219, 253, 298, 323, 434n.54, 491n.324, 493nn.340, 341, 535n.371
and unfoldment of divine language, 198, 204–205, 206–209
and world of emanation/*'ăṣîlûṯ*, 212, 215
and Yōḏ, first letter of Tetragrammaton, 208, 209, 212
Holtz, Barry W., 542n.16
Hopkins, E. Washburn, 452n.232, 502n.149
Hopkins, Thomas J., 439n.29
Hosea, 269–270
R. Hoshaiah, 164–166, 177, 186, 307, 476n.130, 510n.58
hotṛ (type of priest), 438n.17, 456n.297
and Brahmā, 104
and *brahman* priest, 348
and patron of sacrifice/ *yajamāna*, 242
and Prajāpati, 54, 58, 60, 537n.33
and *ṛcs*, 33, 54, 60, 348
and Ṛg-Veda, 33, 44
and seers/*ṛṣis*, 239
Viśvakarman as, 36
hṛd or *hṛdaya* (heart). *See* heart
Hume, Robert Ernst, 450n.181
R. Huna b. Abin, 161–162, 274–275, 279, 298, 305, 512n.91, 526n.258, 527n.262

Idel, Moshe, 366–367, 374–375, 382–383, 433n.52, 433–434n.53, 490nn.317–319, 491n.320, 492n.334, 495n.384, 507n.20, 540nn.4, 5, 543n.19, 544nn.29–33, 544–545n.35, 546n.51, 548nn.60, 66, 68, 70, 71, 73–76, 549nn.91, 92, 550n.116, 550–551n.121, 551n.1
immortal
seers/*ṛṣis* as, 230

Vāc as, 48
Veda(s) as, 48, 67, 75
imperishable
Brahman as, 66, 67, 75, 330
gods and the Imperishable, 233, 330, 356
Vāc as, 48
Veda(s) and the Imperishable, 66, 67, 233, 330, 356
Veda(s) as, 48, 67, 75, 94, 112, 355
word/*śabda* as, 117–119
Indra (deity), 349
as inspirer of cognitions and hymns, 234, 236–237, 330
and *kṣatriyas*, 39, 40
and seers/*ṛṣis*, 234, 236–237, 241, 330, 498n.51
and *triṣṭubh* meter, 39, 40
interpretation of Torah, 361–373, 386–388. *See also* Midrash; Oral Torah; study of Torah
and Abulafia's "path of the names," 382–383, 393, 550–551n.121
and Abulafia's "wisdom of the combination of letters," 383, 393
antecedents of Midrash, 542–543n.16
actuative meaning, 387
and angels, 210, 366, 368
and atomization of canonical text into constituent letters, 365, 367, 382–383, 393
and "contemplating through seeing"/*'istakkēl*, 371, 372, 378–379, 389, 547n.60, 550n.101
as continuation of Sinai revelation, 362, 366
and distinctions among author, text, and interpreter, 367, 373, 392, 419
emphasis on cognitive over phonic dimension of words, 18, 361–373, 386–388
and fire, 172, 179, 281, 366, 480n.173, 517n.135
focus on every word and letter, 15, 311, 363, 364–366, 541n.15, 543n.21
forty-nine modes of interpretation, 366, 544n.22
four levels of meaning, 368–369, 370, 372–373, 545nn.41, 42
and glory of God, 366, 372, 546n.51
God intended for Sefer Torah to be interpreted, 361–362, 387
hermeneutical process as visionary experience, 370–372, 382, 392, 393, 533n.339
importance of, 333, 359, 362
and infinity of meaning in Torah, 368, 543n.19
kabbalist exegete and Malḵûṯ/Shekhinah or Oral Torah, 370–371, 373, 392, 547n.55
kabbalist exegete and Moses, 337, 339, 371–372, 373, 391–392, 547nn.57, 58
kabbalist exegete and patriarchs, 547n.58
kabbalist exegete and prophets, 337, 367, 371–372, 383, 391–392, 547n.58
kabbalist exegete and *s^e^p̄îrôṯ*, 370–372, 373, 382, 392, 546n.51, 547n.58
kabbalist exegete and Tip̄'ereṯ or Written Torah, 370–372, 373, 392, 547n.58
kabbalist exegete as bridegroom of Torah, 373
kabbalist exegete as radiant with light, 371, 547nn.55, 57
kabbalistic hermeneutics, 321, 366–373, 382–383, 391–393, 535n.358, 544n.29, 550–551n.121
and light, 172, 178, 190–191, 196,

interpretation of Torah *(continued)*
366, 371, 382, 393, 491n.322, 547nn.55, 57
limited freedom of aggadic Midrashist, 365, 543n.19
as means of clarifying meaning and application of laws, 363–364
as means of cleaving to God, 546n.54
as means of deciphering or decoding the cryptogram, 160, 362, 363, 367, 368, 369, 371
as means of drawing out multiplicity of meanings, 18, 338, 359, 362–363, 365–366, 368, 386–387, 388, 541n.15, 543nn.19, 21, 545n.41
as means of fathoming hidden mysteries of Torah, 364–365, 366–367, 368, 369–371, 372–373, 374, 378, 382, 391, 546n.51
as means of fathoming mysteries of creation and of Godhead, 367, 368, 369, 371, 378, 546n.51
as means of fathoming structures of human psyche, 367
as means of opening up closed text, 361–362, 387
as means of penetrating beyond garments and body of Torah to its soul, 369–371, 374, 382, 392, 402
as means of recovering divine Author's hidden intentions, 364–365
as means of replicating Sinai revelation, 172, 179, 263, 281, 337, 338, 366, 367, 370–372, 373, 391–392, 546n.52
as means of resolving lexical problems, 364
as means to direct experience of supernal Torah, 339, 367, 371, 372–373, 382–383, 392–393, 491n.322
as means to divine communion with Torah, 372–373, 382, 383, 392, 420, 548n.68
as means to prophetic state of consciousness, 337, 367, 371–372, 383, 391–392, 547n.58
methods and principles of aggadic Midrash, 363, 365–366, 541–542n.16
methods and principles of halakhic Midrash, 288, 363–365, 541–542n.16
Moses as first Midrashist, 311, 337
Moses as interpreter of Torah, 294, 311, 331, 334, 337, 339, 391–392
multiple vocalizations of consonantal text, 210, 361–362, 368, 478n.149, 540n.7, 544–545n.35
and preservation of canonical text, 367, 370, 382, 392
rabbinic hermeneutics, 361–366, 388, 541–542n.16
rabbinic interpretations as authoritative, 157, 158, 337, 391, 554n.15
rabbinic sages as mediators of, 337, 338, 339, 362, 391, 543n.19
school of R. Akiba vs. school of R. Ishmael, 15, 363–365
and s^e*pîrôṯ*, 210, 368, 370–372, 373, 382, 392, 546n.51, 547n.58
seventy modes of interpretation, 321, 366, 544n.23
and Shekhinah, 366, 370–371, 373, 392, 547n.55
as strategy for extending canon, 6–7, 397, 402

thirteen principles of R. Ishmael, 363–364, 541n.16
Torah interpreted differently in different worlds, 210–211, 368
interpretation of Veda(s), 351–354, 388
commentaries by Sāyaṇa, 124, 354, 539n.60
constitutive meaning of Vedic words, 347, 354, 387
discursive meaning of Vedic *mantras* secondary, 12, 97–98, 343, 346–347, 351, 387, 388, 408, 418, 419, 457n.323, 536–537n.12
importance of understanding discursive meaning of Vedic *mantras*, 352, 538n.46
interpretation of Vedic *mantras*, in Brāhmaṇas, 351–352
interpretation of Vedic *mantras*, in Nirukta, 352
levels of meaning, 353
principles and methods of interpretation, 353, 388, 538–539n.55
schools of Vedic exegesis focus on Brāhmaṇas and Upaniṣads, 346, 352–354, 388
"schools" of Vedic interpretation, 352, 538n.48
threefold method of interpretation, 352–353
Isaac, 161, 411
and Hebrew letters, 195
and Malḵûṯ/Shekhinah or Oral Torah, 320
and secret of redemption, 195
and Torah, 162, 163, 184–185, 399
R. Isaac, 181, 280, 294–295, 311, 516nn.129, 130, 549n.94
Isaiah
and Ezekiel, 320, 534n.347
and Malḵûṯ/Shekhinah or Oral Torah, 320, 534n.347
and people of Israel, 269–270, 319–320
Isaiah, book of, 187, 274, 298
Ishmael, 411
R. Ishmael, 177, 284, 360, 363–364, 516n.124, 541n.16
Ishmael, children of, 266, 273–274, 286, 297, 311, 316
R. Ishmael, school of, 15, 150, 285, 363–364, 471n.71
Islamic traditions, 191, 354
and Abraham, 411–412, 558nn.47, 48
and generic idea of scripture, 557n.27
hermeneutics, 545n.42
missionary orientation of, 403, 409–412, 413, 422n.6
and Muhammad, 409–413, 557–558n.37, 558nn.46, 48
and paradigms of "religious tradition," 6, 403, 408–413, 422n.6
and "People of the Book," 410–411, 558nn.45, 46
and Qur'ān, 6, 409–413, 556nn.24–26, 557nn.27, 33, 35, 557–558n.37, 558nn.45–48
Qur'ān as constitutive category of, 409
as religion of orthopraxy, 409
as "religion of the book," 409
and sources of *fiqh*, 412–413
and successive scriptural revelations, 410–411, 412, 557n.35
Israel, land of
not site of revelation of Torah, 255, 266–267
as one of four inheritances, 472n.79
as one of God's special creations/possessions, 153, 471–472n.78
and people of Israel/Jews, 153, 397

Israel, people of
and acceptance of Torah, 152, 163, 167, 188, 255, 256, 266, 273–275, 279, 286–288, 292, 295–298, 305, 316–318, 327, 329, 333, 338, 376, 378, 390, 391, 399, 482n.196, 513n.98, 516n.131, 518n.158, 549n.85
and acceptance of Torah, necessary for continuance of creation, 167, 188, 256, 274–275, 287–288, 297–298, 316–318, 327, 376, 378, 390, 482n.196, 518n.158, 549n.85
all past and future generations were present at revelation of Torah, 311, 318, 338
and angels, 256–257, 271, 278–279, 291–292, 293, 304–305, 307, 309, 313–314, 322, 329, 332, 520n.171, 526–527n.258
attained access to mysteries of creation, 222–223, 275, 318–319, 321, 322–323, 332, 333
attained vision of *s^{e}pîrôṯ*, 315, 318–320, 332–333, 370–371, 534n.343
as bridegroom of Torah, 256, 268, 276–278, 291, 302–303, 312, 331, 338, 372, 373, 392
as bride of God, 256, 268, 277–278, 291, 303, 312, 331, 338, 373
and chariots, 257, 258–259, 278, 322, 332
as chosen people of God, 135, 136, 152, 157, 256, 263, 266, 273, 285, 295, 311, 325, 330–331, 391, 522n.199
and Christians, 157–158, 263, 273, 404–405, 552n.9, 553nn.10, 11, 553–554n.14
and covenant with God, 174, 256, 278, 285, 295, 298, 303, 326, 330–331, 333, 338, 376–377, 390, 391, 404
as custodians of Torah, 3, 152, 157, 216, 398–399
died and were resurrected, 257, 260, 282–283, 293, 296, 309, 314–315, 516n.124, 517nn.139, 141, 529n.283
ethnic-cultural identity of, and Torah, 3, 135, 136, 138, 152, 157, 182, 216, 255, 266, 273–274, 285–287, 294, 295–297, 311, 316, 325, 326, 329, 391, 398–399, 412, 481n.185
experienced Sinai theophany according to each individual's capacity, 257–258, 271–272, 282–284, 309–310, 331, 337–338
experienced Sinai theophany according to each individual's "grade," 323–324
experienced Sinai theophany as overpowering, 257, 271, 281–283, 293, 308–309, 314–315
and Ezekiel, 258–259, 264, 269–270, 278, 307, 319–320, 510n.58
and face(s) of God, 256, 257, 280–281, 283, 293–294, 307, 309, 310, 318, 319, 331, 332, 512n.75, 516n.130, 529n.274
feared lest they die, 257, 271, 281–282, 314–315
and final redemption, 157–158, 274, 286–287, 514n.110
and fire, 222, 257, 270, 271, 281, 296, 306, 308, 314, 318, 332, 535n.367
firmaments or heavens opened to, 257, 258, 263, 293, 307, 311–312, 313, 314, 322, 332, 523n.222, 529n.273, 531n.305
and gentile nations, 135, 136, 138, 152, 157, 158–159, 182, 188, 255, 266–267, 268, 269, 273–274, 285–287, 292, 294,

295–297, 307, 309, 311, 316, 325, 326, 329, 332, 338, 391, 398–399, 404–405, 529n.274, 530n.288, 533n.327, 552n.9, 553nn.10, 11, 553–554n.14
and glory of God, 256, 257, 258, 263, 274, 279, 281, 293, 303, 305, 306, 307, 318, 320–321, 322, 323, 324, 329, 332, 366, 515n.120, 525n.244, 527n.262, 529n.283, 532n.311, 534n.340
and golden calf, 254, 257, 278, 279, 291, 303–304, 310, 314, 329, 525n.245
granted immunity from death, 257, 281, 282, 306, 516n.131, 527n.264
heard and saw, 222, 257, 269–271, 279–281, 292, 306–308, 314, 318–324, 329, 332, 333, 334, 529n.283
heard divine utterances, 270–271, 272, 280, 293, 332, 333
heard voice(s) of God, 222, 257, 269, 271, 280, 282–284, 292, 295–296, 306–307, 309–310, 314–315, 318, 329, 331, 332, 338, 517n.139, 529n.283, 530n.288
Hebrew as language of, 3, 397, 399
and Hebrew letters, 317, 478n.143
interpreted divine utterances, 271, 334
invested with crowns, 256–257, 259, 279, 291–292, 304–305, 313, 515n.118, 520n.181, 532n.309
invested with garments, 256–257, 259–260, 305–306, 313, 526–527n.258, 527n.262, 532n.311
invested with girdles, 256–257, 279, 305
invested with ornaments, 256–257, 259–260, 278–279, 291–292, 304–306, 313, 329, 515nn.118, 119, 520n.181, 526–527n.258, 527n.262, 532nn.309, 311
invested with weapon(s), 256–257, 260, 279, 305–306, 313, 515nn.118, 119
and Isaiah, 269–270, 319–320
Israelite wisdom tradition, 133, 135, 136, 137, 138, 141, 464n.1, 477n.132
as kingdom of priests and holy nation, 391
and land of Israel, 153, 397
and light, 190, 222–223, 274, 318–319, 320–321, 333, 487n.273
linguistic identity of, and Torah, 3, 398–399, 412
and Malḵûṯ/Shekhinah, 315, 319, 371, 534n.343
and Merkabah, 258–259, 263, 270, 278, 303–304, 307, 332–333, 525n.245
Mount Sinai suspended over, 286, 287, 513n.98, 518n.158
and Name of God, 256–257, 260, 279, 296–297, 305–306, 313, 527n.262, 532n.309, 532nn.309–311
as one of four inheritances, 472n.79
as one of God's special creations/possessions, 149, 153, 471n.78, 481n.185
as one of six or seven things created prior to the world, 160, 470n.64
as paradigmatic representatives of Jewish community, 338, 378, 389–390
and prophets, 264, 269–270, 319–320
purification of, 318, 329

Israel, people of *(continued)*
and reception of Sinai theophany, 255, 256–259, 262–263, 264, 268–272, 278–284, 291–294, 303–310, 311, 312–315, 318–324, 329, 331, 332–333, 337–338, 512n.75, 516n.130, 523n.222, 529nn.274, 283, 534n.343
as recipients of revelation of Torah, 151, 152, 163, 167, 188, 222–223, 253, 254, 255, 256–260, 262–263, 264, 266–267, 268–272, 273–275, 276–284, 285–288, 291–294, 295–299, 300, 302–310, 311, 312–315, 316–324, 325–334, 337–339, 366, 370–372, 376, 378, 389–390, 391, 395–396, 399, 410, 476n.124, 482n.196, 486n.243, 510n.61, 511n.70, 512n.75, 513n.98, 516nn.124, 130, 131, 517nn.139, 140, 518n.158, 521n.190, 523n.222, 529nn.274, 283, 530nn.288, 290, 533n.327, 534n.343, 549n.85
saw and understood, 270–271, 322–324, 333, 535n.367
saw configurations of divine light, 222–223, 318–319, 320–321
saw divine utterances, 257, 270–271, 308, 322–323, 333, 535n.367
saw God, 264, 269, 280–281, 283, 307, 309, 318, 319, 332, 516n.130, 529n.274
saw hidden wonders, 262–263
saw or spoke with God face to face, 256, 280–281, 283, 293–294, 307, 309, 310, 318, 319, 332, 516n.130, 529n.274
saw voice(s) of God, 222–223, 270, 272, 314, 318–321, 322–323, 332, 333, 472n.83, 510n.61
and Shekhinah, 257, 279, 303, 307, 315, 319, 331, 366, 371, 527n.259, 534n.343
social and moral order of, and Torah, 166–167, 183, 216, 400
social hierarchy of, and *s^{e}pîrôṯ*, 323–324
social hierarchy of, and Torah, 3, 262, 323–324, 337, 339, 390, 391, 398, 399–402, 507–508n.20
stripped of ornaments, 257, 292, 305, 314, 329
and Ten Words of revelation/Ten Commandments, 222, 254, 255, 256, 257, 268, 269, 270–272, 275–276, 279–280, 282, 284, 291, 293, 294, 296–297, 306, 310, 311, 314–315, 317–318, 320–324, 328, 332, 333, 337, 511n.70, 516n.124, 517n.140, 521n.190, 530n.290
and throne of glory, 257, 293, 307, 308, 313, 314, 322, 332
as true Israel, 157, 182
understood meaning of commandments, 270–271, 322–323, 333, 334, 338, 535n.367
and wisdom/Ḥoḵmāh, 135–136, 323
and word/Word of God/*dāḇār*/*dîbbēr*/*dîbbûr*, 222, 257, 270, 282–284, 296, 299, 308, 318, 332, 535n.367
Israelites. *See* Israel, people of
Īśvara (Lord)
and Prakṛti, 100, 101
and Puruṣa, 100
as Saguṇa Brahman, 100, 101
and Veda(s), 113, 114, 353, 427n.25, 460n.393
Īśvarakṛṣṇa, 74
Itihāsas. *See* epics

Jacob, 161, 411

and Hebrew letters, 195
and Malḵûṯ/Shekhinah or Oral Torah, 320
and secret of redemption, 195
and tents of learning, 185, 193, 476n.122, 486n.246
Tip̄'ereṯ as voice of, 206–207
and Torah, 162, 163, 184–185, 193, 399, 476n.122, 486nn.243, 246
Jacob, sons of
and Hebrew letters, 195
and secret of redemption, 195
and Torah, 162, 163, 184–185, 399
R. Jacob b. Abina, 275
R. Jacob b. Aḥa, 549n.90
R. Jacob b. Kirshai, 170
Jacob b. Sheshet, 491n.326, 544–545n.35
Jacobs, Louis, 541n.16
Jaffee, Martin S., 431n.46
jagatī (type of Vedic meter), 106, 343, 535–536n.1
and *vaiśyas*, 39, 40, 61
and Viśvadevas, 39, 40
Jaiminīya Brāhmaṇa, 44, 47, 51, 55, 126, 240, 350
Jaiminīya Upaniṣad Brāhmaṇa, 56–57, 441n.52
Jain traditions, 63, 71
Jairazbhoy, N. A., 536n.9
Jamadagni (Vedic seer), 230, 239, 243, 501n.107
Jayanta, 460n.393
Jeffery, Arthur, 557nn.27, 31, 35, 558n.47
Jellinek, Adolph, 478n.143, 521n.181
Jeremiah, book of, 172, 176, 178, 188, 194, 210, 287, 288, 298, 318, 376–377
Jerusalem Talmud or Palestinian Talmud, 141, 142, 145, 157, 172–173, 181, 191, 263, 469n.50, 470n.70. *See also* Talmud
Jesus of Nazareth, 410, 411. *See also* Christ
Jews. *See* Israel, people of
Jha, Ganganatha, 462n.400
jñāna-kāṇḍa (section of the Veda[s] pertaining to knowledge). *See also jñāna* traditions
and *adhyātma*, 353
and appropriation of Veda(s) through direct realization, 343, 355–357, 392–393, 415, 419
and ascetic traditions, 30, 62–63, 71, 335–336
as focus of Vedānta/Advaita Vedānta, 123–124, 353
and *jñāna* stream, 71, 334, 335–336, 355–357, 392–393
and meditation traditions, 71, 334, 335–336, 355–357, 392–393
and seers/*ṛṣis*, 325, 334, 335–336, 355, 356–357, 392
and Upaniṣads, 30, 62, 71, 123, 353
jñāna (knowledge) traditions or *jñāna* stream. *See also jñāna-kāṇḍa*; *jñāna-yoga*; knowledge
and appropriation of Veda(s) through direct realization, 343, 355–357, 392–393, 415, 419
and ascetic traditions, 71, 335–336
and *jñāna-kāṇḍa*, 71, 334, 335–336, 355–357, 392–393
and Mahābhārata, 72, 81
and meditation traditions, 71, 334, 335–336, 355–357, 392–393
and post-Vedic brahmanical synthesis, 70–72
and Proto-Sāṃkhya speculations, 71–72, 81

jñāna traditions *(continued)*
and Purāṇas, 72
and seers/*ṛṣis*, 334, 335–336, 355, 356–357, 392
jñāna-yoga (yoga of knowledge), 453n.233
Job, book of, 131, 137, 203, 289, 290, 300–301
R. Joḥanan, 158, 163, 169, 174, 178, 275, 279, 281, 282, 283, 285, 291, 292, 295–296, 298, 299, 305, 306, 310, 469n.49, 487n.263, 514n.110, 517n.142, 518nn.151, 157, 519n.162, 529–530n.283, 530nn.288, 290, 543n.20
R. Joḥanan, school of, 260, 469n.49
R. Joḥanan b. Zakkai, 179, 263, 366, 532n.309
John, Gospel of, 159
R. Jonathan, 482n.207, 514n.111
R. Jose b. Ḥalafta, 267, 268, 277, 290, 319
R. Jose b. Ḥanina, 283–284, 303–304, 310
Joseph of Hamadan, 361, 367, 368, 544–545n.35, 546n.51
Joshi, J. R., 442n.65
Joshua, 147, 265
Joshua, book of, 376
Joshua b. Eleazar b. Sira, 135
R. Joshua b. Ḥananyah, 296–297
R. Joshua b. Karḥa, 312
R. Joshua b. Levi, 160–161, 273, 277, 280, 284, 288–290, 292, 293, 300, 307, 474n.99, 481n.186, 512nn.81, 83, 516n.124, 519n.169, 519–520n.171, 520n.175, 521nn.190, 192, 198, 523n.222, 524n.222, 529n.283
R. Joshua of Siknin, 273–274, 276, 512n.83, 549n.86
Jubilees, Book of, 192, 470n.65
R. Judah b. Ezekiel, 173, 177, 481n.185, 541n.15
R. Judah b. Il'ai, 163, 186, 271, 280, 282, 313, 314, 364, 476n.127, 513–514n.103, 516nn.129, 130, 524n.226, 532n.314
R. Judah b. Simon, 162–163, 170, 273, 274, 377, 378, 481n.188, 512n.81, 524n.226
R. Judah ha-Nasi, 147, 269, 271, 309, 470n.69
"Judaisms." *See also* apocalyptic traditions; Hêkālôṯ traditions; "Hinduisms" and "Judaisms"; kabbalistic traditions; Merkabah traditions, rabbinic; rabbinic tradition
and Christian traditions, 132, 157–158, 159, 263, 273, 403–405, 552n.9, 553nn.10, 11, 553–554n.14, 554n.15
discourse of body in, 552n.4, 554n.15
two types of, in relation to Christian traditions, 157
variety of, 1–2, 421n.1
R. Judan, 524n.223
Jungian psychology, 434n.57

Kabbalah, ecstatic, 337, 366–367, 374, 382–383, 393, 490n.318, 548n.60, 550–551n.121. *See also* Abulafia, Abraham
Kabbalah, theosophical, 23, 132, 196–212, 315–324, 337, 360–361, 366–373, 374–375, 378–381, 382, 389–390, 391–393, 402, 490n.318, 548n.60, 551n.121. *See also* Zohar
kabbalistic traditions. *See also* Kabbalah, ecstatic; Kabbalah, theosophical; kabbalists; and *specific kabbalists and kabbalistic texts*
continuity with rabbinic traditions, 16, 433–434n.53

emphasis on cognitive dimension of words, 18, 218–220, 221–223, 334, 366–373, 385, 386–388, 414
emphasis on visual mode of perception, 17–19, 218–220, 221–223, 334, 385, 414–417, 469n.57, 533–534n.339, 547–548n.60
emphasis on written channel of language, 17–18, 218–220, 221–223, 334, 359–361, 385–387, 414–420, 469n.57, 548n.60
iconic aspects of, 19, 361, 417, 546n.51
kabbalists. *See also* Kabbalah, ecstatic; Kabbalah, theosophical; kabbalistic traditions; and *specific kabbalists*
kabbalist exegete and Malḵûṯ/ Shekhinah or Oral Torah, 370–371, 373, 392, 547n.55
kabbalist exegete and Moses, 337, 339, 371–372, 373, 391–392, 547nn.57, 58
kabbalist exegete and patriarchs, 547n.58
kabbalist exegete and prophets, 337, 367, 371–372, 383, 391–392, 547n.58
kabbalist exegete and *s*ᵉ*p̄îrôṯ*, 370–372, 373, 382, 392, 546n.51, 547n.58
kabbalist exegete and Tip̄'ereṯ or Written Torah, 370–372, 373, 392, 547n.58
kabbalist exegete as bridegroom of Torah, 373
kabbalist exegete as radiant with light, 371, 547nn.55, 57
Moses as paradigm for, 337, 339, 371–372, 373, 391–392, 547nn.57, 58
present at revelation of Torah, 370
kāḇôḏ (glory), 256, 257, 258, 267, 268, 279, 281, 303, 306, 307, 313, 366. *See also* glory of God
Kadushin, Max, 542n.16
Kaelber, Walter O., 439n.23, 539n.69
kalpa (day of Brahmā), 74–75, 97, 101, 110, 111, 112, 113, 115, 124, 125, 127–128, 129, 227, 245, 248, 249, 250, 452n.217
Kalpa-Sūtras, 71. *See also* Dharma-Sutras; Gṛhya-Sūtras; Śrauta-Sūtras
Kane, Pandurang Vaman, 456n.309, 536n.12
Kaṇva (Vedic seer), 229, 349, 496n.7
Kaṇvas (descendants of Kaṇva; Vedic seers), 232
Kapila, 114, 461n.395
Kapstein, Israel J., 473n.95
karma-kāṇḍa (section of the Veda[s] pertaining to action). *See also* *karman* traditions
and *adhiyajña*, 353
and appropriation of Veda(s) through reciting and hearing *mantras*, 343, 355, 390–391
and Brāhmaṇas, 30, 43, 62, 71, 335, 353
and *dharma* traditions, 71, 334–335, 355, 390–391
as focus of Pūrva-Mīmāṃsā, 123, 353
and *karman* stream, 71, 334–336, 355, 390–391
and seers/*ṛṣis*, 325, 334–336, 355, 389
karman (action) traditions or *karman* stream. *See also* *karma-kāṇḍa*; *karma-yoga*
and appropriation of Veda(s) through reciting and hearing *mantras*, 343, 355, 390–391
and Dharma-Śāstras, 71, 72
and *dharma* traditions, 71, 81,

karman traditions *(continued)*
334–335, 355, 390–391
and *karma-kāṇḍa*, 71, 334–336, 355, 390–391
and Mahābhārata, 72, 81
and post-Vedic brahmanical synthesis, 70–71
and Purāṇas, 72
and sacrificial traditions, 71
and seers/*ṛṣis*, 334–336, 355
karma-yoga (yoga of action), 453n.233
Kashmir Śaiva tradition, 11, 429n.37
Kaśyapa (Vedic seer), 229, 230, 239, 243
Kaṭha Upaniṣad, 71
Katz, Nathan, 422n.7
Katz, Ruth Cecily, 452n.232
Kauṣītaki Brāhmaṇa, 44, 239, 240
Kauṣītaki Upaniṣad, 66, 67
Kautsa, 352
Kavaṣa Ailūṣa (Vedic seer), 240
Kavi (seer), 503n.156
k^elî (instrument), 149, 154, 164, 481n.186
k^eṯāḇ (letters), 148–149, 152, 175, 193. *See also* letters, Hebrew
Keṯer (crown; first *s^ep̄îrāh*), 196–197, 219, 370
as divine will, 205, 206
and light, 205
as supernal Man, 205
Ketuvim (Writings)
as Written Torah, 12–13, 173, 285, 294, 397
kissē' ha-kāḇôḏ (throne of glory). *See* throne of glory
knowledge. *See also da'aṯ; jñāna* traditions; wisdom
as aspect of word/Word, 16–17, 216
associated with wisdom/*ḥoḵmāh* and understanding/*t^eḇûnāh*, 176, 177, 185, 195, 298, 486n.248
and Brahmā, 88, 104, 214, 216
and Brahman/Brahman-Ātman, 66–67, 75, 87, 102–104, 128–129, 356
of Brahman/Brahman-Ātman, as focus of Vedānta/Advaita Vedānta, 113, 123–124, 353
of Brahman/Brahman-Ātman, and seers/*ṛṣis*, 242–243, 244–245, 248, 326, 328, 330, 335–336, 356–357
and creator principle, 17, 24, 29, 213, 214, 216–217, 219, 227
discourse of, in Upaniṣads, 22, 62–63
as instrument of creation, 176, 177, 185, 195, 298
lower and higher forms of, 65, 356
as male principle, 48, 216–217
as means to liberation/*mokṣa*, 62–63, 72, 81, 242, 453n.233
and Prajāpati, 48, 214, 216
scripture as, 17, 213, 214, 217, 219
and seers/*ṛṣis*, 229, 230, 231, 244, 248, 326, 336
and Śiva, 102, 103–104
as source of creation, 17, 29, 214, 219
and speech, 16–17, 216–219
Veda(s) as, 7, 9, 11–12, 17, 24, 29, 30, 31, 32, 43, 60, 65, 66, 67, 70, 75, 76, 77, 87, 90, 93, 94, 99, 102–103, 104, 112, 128–129, 213, 214, 216–217, 219, 227, 228, 247, 336, 354, 356, 396, 427n.28, 430n.41, 430–431n.42, 434n.54
and Viṣṇu, 87, 102–103, 336
Kohath, 161
Kratu (seer), 244, 245
Kṛṣṇa, 85, 503n.152
Kṛṣṇa Dvaipāyana Vyāsa. *See* Vyāsa

kṣatriyas (rulers and warriors), 555n.18
and Indra, 39, 40
and midregions, 38, 61
and Prajāpati, 39, 54
and primordial utterance *bhuvaḥ*, 54, 61
and recitation and hearing of Veda(s), 355
and *triṣṭubh* meter, 39, 40, 61
and wind/Vāyu, 38
and Yajur-Veda, 38, 61, 390
Kugel, James L., 142–143, 144, 468nn.43, 44, 542n.16, 543n.16
Kuiper, F. B. J., 35–36, 438n.22, 439n.24, 445n.112
Kumārila Bhaṭṭa, 117, 118–119, 120–121, 122, 123, 462nn.399, 400, 463nn.432, 435, 438, 444
Kūrma Purāṇa, 100, 103, 104, 106

Lamentations, 377
Lamentations Rabbāh, 156, 158, 273–274, 278–279, 377–378
Lamotte, Étienne, 556nn.20, 21
Lancaster, Lewis, 536n.5
Lanczkowski, Günter, 424n.9
land of Israel. *See* Israel, land of
Lang, Bernhard, 466n.10
language, 433n.52, 490n.317. *See also* Hebrew; language, divine; letters, Hebrew; Sanskrit; speech; *varṇas*; word/Word
actuative meaning, 387
atomistic understanding of, 365, 540–541n.7
and auditory vs. visual modes of perception, 17–19, 146, 218–223, 334, 385, 414–417, 469n.57, 547–548n.60
characteristics of word/*śabda*, 117–119
cognitive and phonic dimensions of word, 16–17, 18, 146, 169, 171, 218–223, 334, 346–347, 385, 386–388, 414
constitutive vs. discursive meaning, 347, 354, 387
conventional view of, in early Buddhist tradition, 408
divergences in conceptions of, 17–19, 218–223, 333–334, 385–388, 395, 414–420
Mīmāṃsā philosophy of, 114–123, 129, 347, 461n.397, 462n.400
ontological status of, 420
oral vs. written channels, 17–19, 146, 169, 218–223, 333–334, 344–345, 359–361, 385–387, 414–420, 424n.9, 469n.57, 548n.60, 558n.50
relationship between name and form, 59, 69, 110, 127, 129, 171, 189, 200, 203, 221, 347, 447–448n.149
relationship between Vedic sentence and meaning, 116, 122, 124, 125, 463n.438
relationship between word and meaning, 114, 116, 119–122, 123, 124, 125, 128, 129, 346–347, 463n.432
structural affinities in conceptions of, 16–17, 215–216
and tradition-identity, 3, 397–398
Vedic language contrasted with ordinary human language, 117, 122
language, divine. *See also* Hebrew; language; letters, Hebrew; Sanskrit; speech; *varṇas*; word/Word
Arabic as, 409
and blueprint or plan of creation, 16, 17, 24, 131, 167, 213, 214, 216, 217–218, 222, 253, 395, 407

language, divine *(continued)*
creative power of, 16, 17, 131, 146, 159, 167–170, 177, 180, 195, 200, 214, 216, 217–218, 253, 395, 399, 407
and 'Ên-Sôp̄, 211
Hebrew as, 18, 167–168, 399
and Hebrew letters, 17, 18, 167, 176–177, 214, 222
and Name of God, 212, 215
and Qur'ān, 409
Sanskrit as, 399
scripture as, 17, 213, 214, 217–218
*s*ᵉ*p̄îrôṯ* as world of, 197, 204
stages of unfoldment of, and Torah, 198, 204, 208–209
stages of unfoldment of, correlated with *s*ᵉ*p̄îrôṯ*, 198, 204–209, 494n.362
and Torah, 16, 17, 24, 131, 146, 159, 167–170, 176–178, 180, 188–190, 194–195, 196, 198, 204, 208–209, 211–212, 213, 214, 216, 253, 364, 395, 396, 399
and Veda(s), 16, 17, 213, 214, 216, 395, 396, 399, 406, 407
Laporte, Jean, 467nn.34–36
Larson, Gerald James, 71–72, 451nn.204, 205, 207
law. *See* commandments; halakhah; *mitzvah*/ *mitzvot*
Le Déaut, Roger, 542n.16
Leeuw, G. van der, 20, 424n.9, 435nn.63, 64, 436n.64, 556n.23
Leiman, Sid Z., 422n.8
Leipoldt, Johannes, 423–424n.9
*l*ᵉ*šôn ha-qôḏeš* (holy language; Hebrew), 167–168, 189, 193, 275. *See also* Hebrew; language, divine
letters, Hebrew. *See also* Hebrew; *k*ᵉ*ṯāḇ*; *'ôṯiyyôṯ*; and *specific letters*
and Abraham, 195
Abulafia's "wisdom of the combination of letters," 383, 393
and Adam, 317
'ālep̄ complained for twenty-six generations, 168, 184, 478nn.143, 148
ascend to supernal source, 314, 482n.204
and Bezalel, 177
and blueprint or plan of creation, 17, 167, 212, 214, 222
and body, of God, 201, 214
and Cain, 195
as configurations of divine energy, 168
as configurations of divine light, 211, 222, 415
creative power of, 160, 168–169, 177, 184, 187, 188–189, 222, 317, 477n.142, 478nn.143, 148
crowns on letters, 177, 364–365, 541n.15
destructive potential of, 169, 177, 360
as elements of the divine language, 17, 18, 167, 176–177, 214, 222
and 'Ên-Sôp̄, 211
and four forms of Torah, 211–212
and four worlds, 211–212
as God's workmen in creation, 187, 188
and Ḥoḵmāh, 209, 212
and interpretation of Torah, 15, 311, 363, 364–366, 367, 382–383, 393, 541n.15, 543n.21
and Isaac, 195
and Jacob, 195
materialization of, 211
and Merkabah, 492n.336
and Name of God, 212
of Name of God, as body of God, 201, 214

of names of God, 383, 393, 492n.336
of names of God, as vehicles in meditation, 383, 393
of names of God, contemplation of, 383, 393
of names of God, visualization of, 383, 393
of names of God, writing and recitation of, 383, 393
numerical value of, 168, 188, 365
as one of ten things created on eve of first Sabbath, 148–149, 152, 175, 193, 195, 471n.76, 481n.187, 488n.291, 532n.317
and people of Israel, 317, 478n.143
personification of, 168, 478n.143
and primordial Torah/*tôrāh qᵉḏûmāh*, 209, 212
protective power of, 195
and revelation of Torah, 317
science of combination of, 177
and secret of redemption, 195
semantic significance of, 146, 168, 169, 177, 188, 189, 222, 364–366, 478n.147
shapes of, 18, 168, 169, 177, 188, 189, 222, 360–361, 365, 415
as shapes or forms of God, 360–361, 492n.336
and sons of Jacob, 195
sound of, 168, 169–170, 177, 189, 222, 365
strokes of letters or tittles, 169, 177, 365–366, 541n.15, 543n.21
as structural elements of creation, 168, 222, 317, 477n.142
this world created with *hē*, 168–169, 177, 188–189
and Tip̄'ereṯ or Written Torah, 209
and Torah, 17, 161, 162, 166, 167, 168–169, 176–177, 187, 188–189, 195, 209, 211–212, 214, 222, 360–361, 365, 367, 382–383, 393, 492n.336
transcendent significance of, 15, 363
as units of script, 169, 222
world created with *bêṯ*, 160, 168, 188, 478nn.143, 148
and world of emanation/*'ăṣîlûṯ*, 212
world to come created with *yōḏ*, 168–169, 177, 188–189
Levering, Miriam, 423n.9
Levi, 161
R. Levi, 160–161, 273–274, 276, 280–281, 282, 283, 304, 306, 307, 478n.146, 512n.83, 515n.114, 516n.132, 517n.142, 527–528n.265, 529–530n.283, 530nn.287, 290, 549n.86
Levi, tribe of, 278, 304, 515n.114, 526nn.248, 252
R. Levi b. Ḥama, 285
R. Levi b. Perata, 377, 378
Leviticus, 150, 151, 167, 276, 301, 381, 471n.72
Leviticus Rabbāh, 142, 143, 156, 158, 161–162, 163, 166–167, 169, 176, 179, 180, 273, 274, 275, 276, 282, 375, 378, 471n.72, 473–474n.95, 484n.223
liberation, 62–63, 72, 81, 242, 453n.233, 556n.18. *See also mokṣa*
Lieberman, Saul, 505n.7
Liebes, Yehuda, 490n.319, 544n.32
Liebich, Bruno, 461n.398
light. *See also 'ôr*
and angels, 146–147
and Ark of the Covenant, 190
and commandments/*mitzvot*, 155, 171–172, 178, 187, 190, 487n.272

light *(continued)*
  and creation, 172, 190, 479n.159
  and face of God, 155, 280–281
  and fire, 191, 308
  and firmaments, 146–147
  and glory of God, 274, 493n.350
  and God, 138, 155, 268, 274, 280–281, 318, 333, 393, 415, 487n.276, 510n.52, 527n.259
  and gods, 232, 233, 235, 328
  and Hebrew letters, 211, 222, 415
  and interpretation of Torah, 172, 178, 190–191, 196, 366, 371, 382, 393, 491n.322, 547nn.55, 57
  and kabbalist exegete, 371, 547nn.55, 57
  and Keṯer, 205
  and Malḵûṯ/Shekhinah, 319, 547n.55
  and Moses, 172, 190–191, 196, 254, 276, 308, 315–316, 320, 329, 366, 371, 479n.163, 489n.315, 529n.280, 547n.57
  and people of Israel, 190, 222–223, 274, 318–319, 320–321, 333, 487n.273
  and practice of Torah, 190
  and rabbinic sages, 172, 178, 190–191, 196, 366, 483n.213
  and revelation of Torah, 172, 222–223, 254, 276, 292, 308, 315–316, 318–319, 320–321, 329, 333, 366, 371, 479n.160, 529n.280, 547n.57
  and Sarasvatī, 246
  and seers/*ṛṣis*, 232–233, 235, 328, 332, 497n.34
  and *s*^e^*p̄îrôṯ*, 197, 205, 318–319, 320, 371, 382
  and Shekhinah, 276, 319, 547n.55
  and soul, 190
  and study of Torah, 172, 178, 190–191, 196, 366, 371, 382, 393, 491n.322, 547nn.55, 57
  and tablets of Ten Commandments, 280, 308
  and throne of glory, 146–147
  and Torah, 18, 146, 147, 155, 171–172, 178, 187, 190–191, 195–196, 197, 222, 292, 308, 315–316, 320, 366, 368, 369, 370, 371, 382, 392, 415, 473n.88, 479nn.158, 159, 483n.212, 487nn.272–274, 276, 491nn.322, 323, 547n.57
  and Veda(s), 232–233, 332, 427–428n.28, 497n.34
  and Vedic cognition, 232–233, 235, 328, 332, 497n.34
  and voice(s) of God, 222–223, 318–319, 320–321
  and wisdom, 369
  and word/Word of God/*dāḇār*, 18, 146, 171–172, 190, 197, 222, 368, 479nn.158, 159, 487n.272
Lightstone, Jack N., 422n.8
Liṅga Purāṇa, 73, 97, 100, 103, 106
Lingat, Robert, 430n.41
Lipiner, Elias, 477–478n.142, 490n.317, 492n.336
Logos
  as artisan or architect of creation, 140
  and blueprint or plan of creation, 140
  Christ as, 159, 403
  Christian doctrine of, 132, 159, 403
  as eternal, 139
  and God, 159
  as instrument of creation, 140, 159, 403
  as preexistent, 132, 159, 403
  as son of God, 139
  and Torah, 133, 139–140, 165
  and wisdom, 133, 136, 138, 139–140
Lomaharṣaṇa, 97

Lord, A. B., 417
lûḥôṯ (tablets), 148–149, 152, 175, 193, 314. *See also* tablets of Ten Commandments
Luria, Ben Zion, 527n.262
Lurianic school, 211–212
Lutgendorf, Philip, 429n.35

ma'ămārôṯ (ten words by which the world was created), 150, 170–171, 178, 189–190, 195, 197, 200, 204, 207, 298–299, 317. *See also* ten words of creation
ma'ăśēh bᵉrē'šîṯ (mysteries of creation), 15, 147, 174, 192. *See also* cosmogony and cosmology
ma'ăśēh merkāḇāh (mysteries of the throne-chariot), 15, 147, 174, 179, 182–183, 192, 261, 263, 366, 433n.51, 480n.173, 506n.16, 517n.135, 525n.245, 532n.309. *See also* chariots; Hêḵālôṯ traditions; Merkabah; Merkabah traditions, rabbinic
Macdonald, A. W., 443n.65
Macdonell, A. A., 438–439n.22, 496n.7, 497n.20
Mack, Burton L., 466n.10
macrocosm and microcosm. *See* correspondences
madhyamā (level of speech), 441n.44
Mahābhārata, 23, 72–73, 74–76, 80–94, 95–96, 99, 103, 110, 126, 127, 228, 243–248, 249, 351, 452n.232
  authority of, 82
  and *bhakti* traditions or stream, 30, 72, 81–82
  and Brahmā, 82
  and *dharma,* 81
  as encyclopedia of Hindu teachings, 72, 81
  as fifth Veda, 7, 82–84, 247, 248, 336, 453n.243
  Gaṇeśa as scribe of, 82–83
  iconic veneration of, 458n.327
  as Kārṣṇa Veda, 82
  as *kṣatriya* narrative, 81
  open to general populace, including *śūdras* and women, 82, 83, 336, 453n.246
  as oral text, 82–83, 98
  as product of post-Vedic brahmanical synthesis, 71–72, 80–81
  and seers/*ṛṣis*, 83
  as *smṛti,* 72
  and *śruti,* 72
  as superior to Veda(s), 83–84
  as synthesis of *karman, jñāna,* and *bhakti* streams, 72, 81, 452–453n.233
  as Vaiṣṇava text, 81–82
  and Vedic paradigm, 72, 82–84, 336
  and Vyāsa, 82–83, 247–248, 336
  as written text, 82–83, 98
Maharishi Mahesh Yogi, 9, 427–428n.28
maḥăšāḇāh (plan; thought), 166, 192, 486n.255, 488n.291. *See also* blueprint
Mahāyāna Buddhist tradition, 458n.327. *See also* Buddhist tradition, early
Maimonides, Moses, 433–434n.53, 476n.130
Maitri Upaniṣad, 67, 68, 69–70, 242–243, 357
Malḵûṯ or Shekhinah (kingdom; tenth *sᵉp̄îrāh*), 197. *See also* Shekhinah
  and Abraham, 320
  as body of Torah, 370
  and commandments/*mitzvot,* 381, 550n.119
  as daughter, 206, 207, 209, 493n.341

Malk̲ût̲ *(continued)*
and earth, 315, 318
exile of, 381
and Ezekiel, 319–320, 534n.347
as female principle, 207, 209, 217, 381
and Hē, fourth letter of Tetragrammaton, 208, 209, 212
and Ḥok̲māh, 209
as house for Tip̄'eret̲, 206
and interpretation of Torah, 370–371, 373, 392, 547n.55
and Isaac, 320
and Isaiah, 320, 534n.347
and Jacob, 320
and kabbalist exegete, 370–371, 373, 392, 547n.55
and light, 319, 547n.55
and Moses, 373, 392
as Mother below, 206, 207, 208, 217
and Name of God, 209, 381
as nonluminous speculum, 320, 534n.352
as Oral Torah, 198, 209, 212, 320, 370, 373, 381, 392, 493n.341
and patriarchs, 320
and people of Israel, 315, 319, 371, 534n.343
and practice of Torah, 381
and prophets, 319–320, 534n.352, 547n.59
as queen of world below, 206
and revelation of Torah, 315, 318, 319, 371, 373, 534n.343
role in cosmogonic process, 209
and study of Torah, 370–371, 373, 381, 392, 547n.55
and Tip̄'eret̲, 206, 207, 208, 209, 217, 219, 373, 381, 392
and unfoldment of divine language, 198, 205, 206–209
as vocalized speech, 205, 206–208, 209, 217, 219
and world of making/*'ăśiyyāh*, 212, 215
manas (mind). *See* mind
Mandelbaum, Bernard, 511n.72
manīṣā (inspired thought), 232, 233, 234, 236, 497n.34, 498n.59
manna, 283–284, 310, 470n.62, 471n.76, 481n.187, 530n.288
mantras (designated sounds held to possess sacred power), 540n.75. *See also mantras*, Vedic
efficacy of, in *bhakti* texts, 391
efficacy of, in epics/Itihāsas, 416
efficacy of, in Purāṇas, 97–98, 416
Om as root *mantra*, 357, 393
in tantric traditions, 357, 393
three *vyāhṛtis* as root *mantras*, 357
in Upaniṣads, 357
as vehicles in meditation, 357, 393
in yoga traditions, 357
mantras, Vedic (versified portions of Saṃhitās). *See also atharvans*; *ṛcs*; *sāmans*; Saṃhitās; Veda(s); *yajuses*
and *adhidaiva*, 352
as center of canon, 62, 396
as consummate expression of Word, 62, 395, 396
as core *śruti* texts, 7, 9, 354, 395–396
definition and use of term, 425n.17
discursive meaning/content secondary, 343, 346–347, 351, 387, 388, 396, 408, 419, 431n.43, 457n.323, 536–537n.12
as fixed texts, 62, 395–396
and Saṃhitās, 7, 249–250, 425n.17
as sound offerings of sacrifice, 34, 37, 47, 349, 416

Manu
as omniscient, 76
as progenitor of human race, 76
as seer/*ṛṣi*, 76
and seers/*ṛṣis*, 76–77
and *smṛti* teachings, 76–77
and Veda(s), 76
Manu-Smṛti or Mānava Dharma-Śāstra, 23, 35, 74–80, 84, 86, 93, 101, 108, 110, 126, 352
authority of, 76–77
and creator principle, 76–77
as discourse of *dharma*, 76
as divine revelation, 10, 76–77
and Manu, 76–77
as product of post-Vedic brahmanical synthesis, 72
as *smṛti*, 72, 76–77
and *śruti*, 72, 76
and Vedic paradigm, 10, 72, 76–77
manvantara (interval of Manu), 74–75, 95, 250, 452n.217, 504n.181
Marīci (Vedic seer), 244, 245
Mārkaṇḍeya Purāṇa, 100, 103, 106, 107, 111–112
marriage symbolism
God as bridegroom of Israel, 256, 268, 277–278, 291, 303, 312, 331, 338, 373
God as father of bride, Torah, 256, 276–277, 302, 312, 338
and interpretation of Torah, 372–373, 392, 420
Israel as bridegroom of Torah, 256, 268, 276–278, 291, 302–303, 312, 331, 338, 372, 373, 392
Israel as bride of God, 256, 268, 277–278, 291, 303, 312, 331, 338, 373
kabbalist exegete as bridegroom of Torah, 373
Moses as husband of Shekhinah, 373
Moses as spouse of God, 278
and revelation of Torah, 256, 265, 268, 276–278, 283, 291, 302–303, 312, 331, 338, 373, 508n.31, 514n.110, 525n.237
Torah as bride of Israel, 256, 268, 276–278, 291, 302–303, 312, 331, 338, 372–373, 392, 420
Torah as marriage contract, 278, 303, 331, 338, 514n.110
Mar Ukba, 543n.21
Maruts (group of deities), 234, 498n.59
Matsya Purāṇa, 96–97, 100, 103, 105
Matt, Daniel Chanan, 490n.319, 548nn.62, 66
mattan tôrāh (giving of the Torah at Mount Sinai). *See* revelation of Torah
May, Herbert G., 466n.13, 553n.10
Medhātithi (Vedic seer), 240
meditation. *See also* meditation traditions; *tapas*
and atomization of Vedic language into constituent sounds, 393
and Brahmā, 78, 91, 107
in ecstatic Kabbalah, 383, 393
and gods, 241
letters of names of God as vehicles in, 383, 393
mantras as vehicles in, 357, 393
as means to access mysteries of creation, 227, 241, 245–246, 428n.28
as means to direct experience of supernal Torah, 383, 393
as means to prophetic state of consciousness, 383
as means to realize Brahman/Brahman-Ātman, 242, 328, 357, 393
as means to realize transcendent

meditation *(continued)*
Veda, 328, 357, 393, 428n.28
as means to Vedic cognition, 227, 245–246, 328, 357, 428n.28, 503n.151
and Nārāyaṇa, 77–78
Om as vehicle in, 357, 393
and Prajāpati, 49
and seers/*ṛṣis*, 227, 241, 242, 245–246, 328, 357, 428n.28, 503n.151
in tantric traditions, 357, 393
and *tapas*, 241, 242, 328, 357, 439n.23, 539n.69
on Torah, as means of maintaining cosmos, 376
in Upaniṣads, 357, 539n.69
and *upāsanā-kāṇḍa*, 441n.52
in yoga traditions, 357
meditation traditions. *See also* meditation
and appropriation of Veda(s) through direct realization, 355–357, 392–393
and ascetic traditions, 71, 335–336, 339
Buddhist meditation traditions, 71
Jain meditation traditions, 71
and *jñāna-kāṇḍa* or *jñāna* stream, 71, 334, 335–336, 355–357, 392–393
seers/*ṛṣis* as paradigm for, 334, 335–336, 339, 355, 356–357, 392
and *tapas*, 335, 339, 356, 357
Mehta, J. L., 354–355, 430n.40, 539nn.62, 63
R. Meir, 177, 302, 360, 525n.228
M^e^ḵîltā' d^e^-R. Ishmael, 143, 150, 151, 152, 153, 154, 155, 163, 175, 178, 265, 266–268, 269–270, 271, 272, 277, 280, 282, 290, 307, 309
M^e^ḵîltā' d^e^-R. Simeon b. Yoḥai, 150
M^e^ḵîltā' on Deuteronomy. *See* Midrash Tannaim
R. Menaḥem, 160–161
R. Menaḥema, 280
Menaḥem Azariah of Fano, 495n.386
R. Menaḥem b. Abin, 276
R. Menaḥem b. Jose, 170, 178, 483n.210
Mensching, Gustav, 424n.9
Merkabah (throne-chariot), 369, 483–484n.219. *See also* apocalyptic traditions; chariots; Hêḵālôṯ traditions; Merkabah traditions, rabbinic
and Abraham, 259
and angels, 258, 300
and apocalyptic traditions, 258, 259, 264, 505n.3, 506n.16
and ascent to heaven, 258, 259, 260, 261–262, 264, 300, 337, 506nn.15, 16, 507n.19, 515n.119, 541n.12
and crown, 313, 532nn.309, 310
and "descender to the Merkabah," 259–260, 261–262, 337, 505n.6, 507n.19, 511n.65, 515n.119
and Enoch, 259
and Ezekiel, 255, 258–259, 262, 263, 270, 278, 303, 307, 319, 514n.112, 528–529n.272
and fire, 179, 195–196, 259, 264, 366, 469n.57, 473n.91, 480n.173, 507n.16, 511n.65, 517n.135
and golden calf, 303–304, 525n.245
and *ḥayyôṯ*, 258, 300, 302, 303
and Hebrew letters, 492n.336
and Hêḵālôṯ traditions, 258–264, 432–433n.51, 506nn.15, 16, 507n.19, 515n.119, 532n.310, 541n.12
ma'ăśēh merkāḇāh, 15, 147, 174,

179, 182–183, 192, 261, 263, 366, 433n.51, 480n.173, 506n.16, 517n.135, 525n.245, 532n.309
and Moses, 258, 300, 332–333
and Name of God, 492n.336
and patriarchs, 529n.273
and people of Israel, 258–259, 263, 270, 278, 303–304, 307, 332–333, 525n.245
and rabbinic Merkabah traditions, 258–264, 432–433n.51, 506n.15, 506–507n.16, 508n.23, 514n.112, 528–529n.272, 532nn.309, 310
and revelation of Torah, 179, 255, 258–264, 270, 278, 300, 303–304, 307, 313, 332–333, 366, 508n.23, 514n.112, 514–515n.113, 525n.245, 526n.253, 528–529n.272, 531n.306, 532nn.309, 310
and the waters, 510n.58
and world of creation/*b^e rî'āh*, 211
Merkabah traditions, rabbinic, 132, 191, 483–484n.219. *See also* Hêḵālôṯ traditions; Merkabah
and apocalyptic traditions, 258, 259, 264, 506n.16
and Hêḵālôṯ traditions, 258–264, 432–433n.51, 488n.285, 506–507n.16, 524n.222, 532n.310
and Merkabah, 258–264, 432–433n.51, 506n.15, 506–507n.16, 508n.23, 514n.112, 528–529n.272, 532nn.309, 310
and revelation of Torah, 258–264, 508n.23, 514n.112, 519–520n.171, 524n.222, 528–529n.272, 532nn.309, 310
and Shavuot homilies, 262–264, 514n.112, 519–520n.171, 524n.222, 528–529n.272
and synagogue traditions, 258, 262–264, 508n.23, 514n.112, 519–520n.171, 524n.222, 528–529n.272, 532n.310
Mesopotamian traditions, 134–135, 141, 465–466n.10
Messiah, name of
as one of six or seven things created prior to the world, 160, 175, 193
Messianic Age, 157–158, 319, 481n.190, 510n.52. *See also* redemption, final
and Torah, 211, 495n.385
meters, 345, 439–440n.36. *See also* *specific meters*
and Brahmā, 104, 105–106, 440n.36, 459n.351
and gods, 38–39, 40, 447n.149
and Prajāpati, 39–40, 47, 50, 59, 343, 351, 459n.370
and Puruṣa, 37
and sacrifice, 37, 38–39, 349, 457n.311
and seers/*ṛṣis*, 231, 349
and social classes/*varṇas*, 40, 61, 448n.155
and Viṣṇu, 87
method. *See* comparative study of religion
Metzger, Bruce M, 466n.13, 553n.10
microcosm and macrocosm. *See* correspondences
Midrash. *See also* interpretation of Torah; and *specific Midrashim*
antecedents of, 542–543n.16
categories of, 142, 468n.42
as compilations vs. compositions, 142–144, 468n.46
exegetical Midrashim, 142, 143, 150, 152, 155–156, 179, 196
free-floating traditions, 142–143, 144
homiletical Midrashim, 142, 143, 155–156, 179–181, 471n.72
methods and principles of agga-

Midrash *(continued)*
dic Midrash, 363, 365–366, 541–542n.16
methods and principles of halakhic Midrash, 288, 363–365, 541–542n.16
narrative Midrashim, 142, 180, 191, 467–468n.42
as Oral Torah, 12–13, 141
problems with attributions, 144, 468–469n.49
problems with delimiting historical-cultural contexts of, 145
problems with determining dates and provenance of, 145
scholarly debates concerning nature of, 142–144, 468n.46
tradition-centered approach vs. document-centered approach, 144–145
as verse-centered, 142–143
Midrash on Proverbs, 179
Midrash on Psalms, 179, 484n.220
Midrash Tannaim, 150
midregions, 241
and breath, 38, 58
and *kṣatriyas*, 38, 61
and primordial utterance *bhuvaḥ*, 51, 54, 56–58, 61, 92, 109, 111, 450n.196
and *sattva*, 111
and *u*, second constituent of Om, 57–58, 70, 111
and Viṣṇu, 111
and wind/Vāyu, 38, 56–58, 70, 215, 450n.196
and Yajur-Veda, 38, 51, 56–58, 60, 61, 70, 111, 215
and *yajus*es, 59
miktāb (writing), 148–149, 152, 175, 193, 314, 470n.62. *See also* writing
Mīmāṃsā. *See* Pūrva-Mīmāṃsā
Mīmāṃsā-Sūtras. *See* Pūrva-Mīmāṃsā-Sūtras
mind, 454nn.255, 256, 501n.107
and Ātman, 66, 68
and breath/*prāṇas*, 447n.148
and *bṛhat sāman*, 49
and heart, 236, 499n.76
and Prajāpati, 48–49, 50, 126, 127, 444n.94
role in Vedic cognition, 230, 231, 236, 332, 497n.28, 499n.76
and *sāmans*, 49, 447n.148
and Sāma-Veda, 58
and speech/Vāc, 48–49, 50, 126, 444nn.98, 102, 444–445n.105
and Veda(s), 48–49, 236
and Yajur-Veda, 58
and *yajus*es, 447n.148
Mishnah, 2, 15, 23, 132, 145, 147–150, 157, 170, 265, 277, 288, 470nn.69, 70
authority of, 147
and chain of tradition from Sinai revelation, 147–148, 265
distinguishes people of Israel/Jews from gentile nations, 182, 294
exegesis of, 141, 172–173
as Oral Torah, 12–13, 141, 147, 158, 173, 182, 273, 285, 294, 485n.232, 512n.75
as secret, 182, 294
as Torah, 148, 151, 265
and Written Torah, 147–148, 174
Misra, Vidya Niwas, 440n.43
Mitra (deity), 230, 231
mitzvah/*mitzvot* (commandments), 149, 155, 163, 167, 171–172, 176, 178, 187, 190, 193, 374, 375, 376, 377–378, 380, 401, 402, 476n.124, 487n.272. *See also* commandments
Moabites, 266, 286, 297
mokṣa (liberation from cycle of rebirth), 62–63, 81, 451n.199. *See also* liberation
Mokṣadharma (section of Mahābhārata), 72, 81

Moore, Charles A., 426n.23
Moore, George Foot, 136–137, 466n.20, 476n.129
Morenz, Siegfried, 423–424n.9
Morris, Paul, 422n.6, 552n.4
Moses, 136, 161, 410, 411, 474n.109
abstained from food and drink, 302, 329
and angels, 258, 259, 263–264, 267, 276, 288–290, 293, 300–302, 303, 309, 312, 329, 509n.46, 513–514n.103, 519n.169, 520n.171, 523nn.221, 222, 524n.226
and angels, struggles with, 259, 263–264, 289, 300–302, 309, 329, 509n.46, 513n.103, 519n.169, 520n.171, 523n.222, 524n.226
ascent of "mountain of God," 254, 255
ascent to Godhead, 315–316, 328
ascent to heaven, 146, 173, 256, 258, 259, 262, 263–264, 267, 275–277, 278, 288–290, 293, 299–302, 303, 307, 311–312, 328, 329, 513n.103, 520nn.171, 176, 523–524n.222, 541n.15
attained vision of light of Torah, 315–316, 320
attained vision of *s^e^pîrôṯ*, 315–316, 320, 332–333, 371, 373, 392
authority of, 337, 338, 391
and chain of tradition from Sinai revelation, 147–148, 158, 181, 265, 294, 337, 339, 400
as covenant mediator, 254, 257, 271, 272, 279, 281–282, 284, 294, 311, 314–315, 331, 337, 511n.70
death of, 301
as disciple of God, 294, 311, 331
and Ezekiel, 264, 320
firmaments opened to, 276, 301, 307
as first Midrashist, 311, 337
and glory of God, 258, 320
heard voice(s) of God, 282, 310, 530n.287
as husband of Shekhinah, 373
as interpreter of Torah, 294, 311, 331, 334, 337, 339, 391–392
and kabbalist exegete, 337, 339, 371–372, 373, 391–392, 547nn.57, 58
as like unto God, 276
and Malḵûṯ/Shekhinah or Oral Torah, 373, 392
and Merkabah, 258, 300, 332–333
and other prophets, 264, 320, 372, 521n.198, 534n.352, 547n.59
as paradigmatic, 190–191, 259, 263–264, 337, 338, 339, 366, 371–372, 373, 391–392, 400, 524n.222, 547nn.57, 58
as paradigm for Hêḵālôṯ traditions, 259, 263–264, 337, 524n.222
as paradigm for kabbalists, 337, 339, 371–372, 373, 391–392, 547nn.57, 58
as paradigm for rabbinic sages, 190–191, 337, 338, 339, 366, 391, 400
and patriarchs, 320, 534–535n.352
as radiant with light, 172, 190–191, 196, 254, 276, 308, 329, 366, 371, 479n.163, 489n.315, 529n.280, 547n.57
as recipient of revelation of Torah, 146, 147–148, 151, 158, 173, 181, 182, 191, 199, 223, 254, 255, 256, 258, 259, 263–264, 265–266, 267, 271, 272–273, 275–277, 278, 279, 281–

Moses *(continued)*
282, 284–285, 288–290, 293, 294, 299–302, 308, 310–312, 315–316, 320, 328, 329, 331, 332–333, 334, 337, 339, 359–360, 362, 366, 385–386, 391–392, 395–396, 397, 400, 510n.61, 513–514n.103, 520n.171, 523n.221, 523–524n.222, 530n.287
role in augmenting God's power, 377
saw God, 264, 523n.222
as scribe of God, 13, 223, 331, 334, 337, 359–360
sepulcher of, 471n.76, 481n.187
and Shekhinah, 276, 289, 301, 302, 373, 392, 520n.175, 524n.226
shown heavenly Temple, 301
and sojourns of forty days and forty nights, 254, 255, 300, 302, 310–311, 329
spoke with God, 276, 301–302, 312, 331
spoke with God face to face, 301–302, 312, 331
as spouse of God, 278
as supreme prophet, 223, 315–316, 320, 337, 371–372, 391–392, 400, 547n.58
and tablets of Ten Commandments, 254, 308, 310, 312, 482n.204, 532–533n.319
and throne of glory, 288–289, 290, 293, 300–302, 523n.222, 524n.226
and Tip̄'ereṯ or Written Torah, 320, 371, 373, 392
Moses b. Naḥman. *See* Naḥmanides
Moses de Leon, 367, 368–369, 490n.319, 544n.32, 545n.42
Mount Sinai. *See* revelation of Torah
Muhammad, 557n.27
and Arabs, 409–410, 558n.48
as prophet of Allah, 409–413, 558nn.46, 48
as recipient of revelation of Qur'ān, 409–413, 557–558n.37, 558n.48
as "seal of the prophets," 411, 413
Sunnah of, 412–413
Muir, J., 428–429n.29, 455n.289, 456n.295, 460n.394, 461n.396, 496nn.5, 7, 539n.58
Muller-Ortega, Paul E., 429n.37
Muṇḍaka Upaniṣad, 67–68, 242, 356
Murty, K. Satchidananda, 460n.394, 464nn.447, 448
Mus, Paul, 439n.29

nāda (sound). *See dhvani*
Naḥmanides, 198–199, 210, 360, 491n.325, 534n.343
R. Naḥum, 301, 519n.168, 520n.175, 524n.226
Najara, Israel, 338
name and form, 59, 69, 110, 127, 129, 171, 189, 200, 203, 221, 347, 447–448n.149, 450n.195
Name of God, 192, 276, 289. *See also* names of God; *šēm*; Tetragrammaton
and commandments/*mitzvot,* 381
contains essence and power of God, 131, 200, 201, 213, 253
crown of, 313, 532nn.309, 310
engraved on weapon, 256–257, 260, 279, 305–306, 313, 515n.119
and four forms of Torah, 212, 215
and four worlds, 212, 215
and gentile nations, 296–297
and Hebrew letters, 212
inscribed on garment(s), 306, 527n.262, 532n.311
letters of, as body of God, 201, 214
and Malkûṯ/Shekhinah or Oral Torah, 209, 381

and Merkabah, 492n.336
as one with God, 200–201
and people of Israel, 256–257, 260, 279, 296–297, 305–306, 313, 527n.262, 532nn.309, 311
and practice of Torah, 381
and revelation of Torah, 256–257, 260, 279, 296–297, 305–306, 313, 317, 515n.119, 527n.262, 532nn.309, 311
and *s*^e^*p̄îrôṯ*, 197, 200, 208–209, 212, 215, 317, 533n.334
as source of all language, 212, 215
and stages of manifestation of Torah, 209, 212
and ten words of creation/ *ma'ămārôṯ*, 200, 317
and Ten Words of revelation/Ten Commandments, 200, 296–297, 317
and Tip̄'ereṯ or Written Torah, 209, 381
and Torah, 24, 131, 146, 167, 176, 188, 197, 198–201, 202, 208–209, 212, 213, 214, 215, 216, 219, 253, 317, 360, 386, 492n.334, 533n.333
names of God. *See also* Name of God
Abulafia's "path of the names," 382–383, 393
and "descender to the Merkabah," 260, 515n.119
and Hêḵālôṯ traditions, 260, 506n.11, 515n.119
letters of, 383, 393, 492n.336
letters of, as vehicles in meditation, 383, 393
letters of, contemplation of, 383, 393
letters of, visualization of, 383, 393
letters of, writing and recitation of, 383, 393
s^e^*p̄îrôṯ* as, 197, 201
and Tetragrammaton, 201
theurgic use of, 260, 506n.11, 515n.119
and Torah, 197, 198–199, 201, 211, 212, 360, 382–383
and world of creation/*b*^e^*rî'āh*, 212
Nammāḻvār, 10
Nārada (seer), 244, 504n.177
Nārada Purāṇa, 97
Nārāyaṇa, 86. *See also* Viṣṇu
and Brahmā, 77–78, 101–102, 103
and cosmic egg, 77–78, 101–102
and meditation, 77–78
and Puruṣa, 101–102
as sacrificial boar, 103
and the waters, 77–78, 101, 458n.332
Nāsadīya hymn (Ṛg-Veda X.129), 36
R. Nathan, 154, 269, 475n.118
N^e^ḏārîm, 377
Neṣaḥ (lasting endurance; seventh *s*^e^*p̄îrāh*), 197, 372, 534n.352, 547n.59
Neusner, Jacob, 13–14, 143–144, 157, 421n.1, 431–432n.47, 468nn.46, 47, 473n.94, 473–474n.95, 474nn.96, 97, 484n.222, 542n.16
Nevi'im (Prophets)
as Written Torah, 12–13, 173, 285, 294, 397
New Testament
Christian conceptions of, 6, 158, 403
as record of revelation, 403
Nickelsburg, George W. E., 466n.11, 467nn.22, 23
Nighaṇṭus, 228
Nirguṇa Brahman. *See* Brahman
Nirukta, 228, 352
Noah, 161, 266, 286–287, 399
Nooten, Barend A. van, 452n.232
Numbers, 150, 155, 179, 181, 276, 301, 312, 377

Numbers Rabbāh, 179, 181, 294, 306
Nyāya, 8, 96, 113–114, 115, 117, 353, 427n.25, 460n.393, 460–461n.394, 461n.397
Nyāya-Sūtras, 460n.393

O'Flaherty, Wendy Doniger, 422n.8
Ogibenin, B. L., 438n.22
Om (sacred sound or utterance; sound correlative of Brahman)
  and Ātman, 69–70, 107, 451n.201, 539n.71
  and Brahmā, 79, 102, 105, 107, 111
  and Brahman, 70, 106–109, 215, 357, 460n.378
  and creator principle, 92
  as essence of Veda(s), 57, 70, 107–109, 357, 393, 451n.200
  and *gāyatrī*/Gāyatrī or *sāvitrī*/Sāvitrī, 79, 92–93, 106–109
  and gods, 57–58, 69–70, 111, 215
  and heart, 105, 107
  and Prajāpati, 57–58, 79, 447n.143
  as root *mantra*, 357, 393
  as Śabdabrahman, 70, 108, 215, 357, 460n.378
  and Sanskrit *varṇas*, 92–93, 106–109
  and Śiva, 111
  as source and basis of creation, 106, 109, 215
  as source of all language, 215
  and speech, 58, 106–109
  and three *guṇas*, 107, 108, 111–112
  and three *vyāhṛtis*, 57–58, 69, 70, 79, 92–93, 106–109, 111–112, 357, 447n.142, 451n.200
  and three worlds, 57–58, 69–70, 111–112, 215
  and *trimūrti*, 111–112
  as truth, 57
  and Veda(s), 57–58, 69–70, 79, 92–93, 106–109, 111–112, 215, 357, 393, 451n.200, 460n.380
  as vehicle in meditation, 357, 393
  and Viṣṇu, 111
  as Word/Śabdabrahman, 70, 108
Ong, Walter J., 558n.53
'ôr (light), 155, 172, 178, 187, 190, 196, 487n.272. *See also* light
oral and written traditions, x. *See also* language: oral vs. written channels
  and auditory vs. visual modes of perception, 17–19, 146, 218–223, 334, 385, 414–417, 469n.57, 547–548n.60
  brahmanical emphasis on oral channel, 17–19, 218–221, 223, 334, 344–345, 385–387, 414–420
  and creative reconstruction vs. verbatim reproduction, 417–418
  dichotomy between, 25, 414–420
  discursive vs. nondiscursive oral traditions, 417–418
  and epistemology of perceptual orientation, 415–416
  kabbalistic emphasis on written channel, 17–18, 218–220, 221–223, 334, 359–361, 385–387, 414–420, 469n.57, 548n.60
  and personal vs. impersonal modes of transmission, 418–420
  rabbinic emphasis on written channel, 17–18, 146, 169, 218–220, 221–223, 334, 359–360, 385–387, 414–420, 469n.57
Oral Torah, 413. *See also* Written Torah; Torah
  aggadah/Aggadah/Haggadah as, 12, 158, 182, 273, 294, 485n.232, 512n.75
  centrality of, 387

Christians excluded from, 158, 174, 182, 294, 295
and commandments/*mitzvot*, 381
definition and use of term, 12–13, 431n.46
distinguishes people of Israel/ Jews from gentile nations, 182, 294, 295
as encompassing category, 158, 397
and fire, 172, 480n.171
gentile nations excluded from, 182, 294, 295
and Hē, fourth letter of Tetragrammaton, 209, 212
and Ḥok̲māh, 209
and kabbalist exegete, 370, 373, 392
Malk̲ût̲/Shekhinah as, 198, 209, 212, 320, 370, 373, 381, 392, 493n.341
method of transmission of, 285
Midrash as, 12–13, 141
Mishnah as, 12–13, 141, 147, 158, 173, 182, 273, 285, 294, 485n.232, 512n.75
and Moses, 373, 392
and Name of God, 209, 381
not to be written down, 174, 182, 294
as open-ended category, 13, 173, 337, 397
and patriarchs, 320
and primordial Torah/*tôrāh q^{e}d̲ûmāh*, 209, 219
and prophets, 320
rabbinic sages as custodians of, 173–174, 337, 391
and revelation of Torah, 13, 157, 158, 173–174, 182, 272–273, 284–285, 294, 311, 325, 331, 362, 397, 402
role in cosmogonic process, 209
Talmud as, 12–13, 141, 158, 173, 182, 273, 285, 294, 485n.232, 512n.75
teachings of rabbinic sages as, 13, 158, 173–174, 181–182, 273, 285, 337, 397
Tosefta as, 158, 273
and world of making/*'ăśiyyāh*, 212
and Written Torah, 12–13, 22, 147, 148, 151, 157, 158, 173–174, 176, 181–182, 191–192, 209, 219, 272–273, 284–285, 311, 337, 362, 373, 381, 392, 397, 431n.46, 518n.148, 521n.197
orders of reality. *See* correspondences
Organ, Troy, 451n.199
Oron, M., 492n.336
Östborn, Gunnar, 422–423n.8
'ôt̲iyyôt̲ (letters), 18, 162, 167, 177, 187, 195, 222. *See also* letters, Hebrew

pada (word), 118–119
Paden, William E., 436n.64
Padmapāda, 124
Padma Purāṇa, 97
Padoux, André, 441n.43, 540n.75
Palestinian Talmud. *See* Jerusalem Talmud
Pali canon
discursive meaning primary, 408
early Buddhist conceptions of, 6, 407–408, 556n.20
formation of, 556n.20
relationship between "letter"/ *vyañjana* and meaning/*artha*, 556n.21
as repository of Dhamma, 407–408
and Veda(s), 407–408
as "word of the Buddha"/*buddhavacana*, 407–408
pañcadaśa (fifteen-versed *stoma*), 39, 106

Pāñcarātra, 84, 85, 454nn.255, 259
Pañcaviṃśa or Tāṇḍya Brāhmaṇa, 44, 49, 51, 55, 126, 240
Pāṇini, 128
Pāṇinīya Śikṣā, 348
paṅkti (type of Vedic meter), 343
parā (level of speech), 441n.44
paradigms of "religious tradition," x, 425n.13
  and brahmanical and rabbinic traditions, ix, 2–3, 6, 397–403, 408–409, 412, 413, 422n.6
  and Buddhist traditions, 6, 403, 405–408, 413, 422n.6
  and Christian traditions, ix, 2–3, 6, 397, 403–405, 413, 422n.6
  and "Hinduisms" and "Judaisms," ix, 2–3, 413, 422n.6
  and Islamic traditions, 6, 403, 408–413, 422n.6
Paran, Mount, 254, 266, 273–274, 286, 311, 316, 510n.52
pardēs (garden; paradise)
  as acronym, 368–369, 545n.42
  four sages who entered, 541n.12
  and Hêḵālôṯ traditions, 541n.12
Parry, Milman, 417
paśyantī (level of speech), 441n.44
pāṭhas (modes of Vedic recitation), 345–346, 536n.9
patriarchs. *See also* Abraham; Isaac; Jacob
  and commandments/*mitzvot*, 175–176, 476n.124, 486n.243
  and kabbalist exegete, 547n.58
  and Malḵûṯ/Shekhinah or Oral Torah, 320
  and Merkabah, 529n.273
  and Moses, 320, 534–535n.352
  as one of six or seven things created prior to the world, 160
  and Torah, 149, 162, 163, 175–176, 184–185, 193, 399, 476n.124
Patton, Laurie L., 440n.43
Paul, the apostle
  and break from embodied categories of Jewish tradition, 404–405, 554n.15
  and doctrine of justification by faith, 404–405, 553nn.10, 11, 553–554n.14
  and mission to gentiles, 404–405, 552n.9, 553nn.10, 11, 553–554n.14
  and Torah, 404–405, 552n.9, 553nn.10, 11, 553–554n.14
Pentateuch. *See also* Sefer Torah; Torah; Written Torah
  as Sefer Torah, 12, 385
  as Torah, 12, 151
  as Written Torah, 12–13, 147, 173, 285, 294, 385, 397
people of Israel. *See* Israel, people of
p^{e}šāṭ (literal meaning), 369, 370, 372–373, 545nn.41, 42, 548n.62
P^{e}sîqtā' d^{e}-R. Kahana, 142, 143, 156, 158, 163, 167, 168, 172, 179, 180, 272, 273, 274, 275, 276, 277, 278–279, 280–281, 283–284, 286, 297, 304, 306, 375, 377, 473–474n.95, 484n.222
P^{e}sîqtā' Rabbāṯî, 132, 142, 145, 179–191, 195, 253, 264, 293–310, 312, 484nn.221–225
p^{e}ṯîḥtā' (proem). *See* proem
Petuchowski, Jakob J., 480n.176
phenomenology of religion, 20–21, 424–425n.9, 435n.63, 435–436n.64
Philo Judaeus, 23, 133, 138, 139–141, 165, 467nn.34, 36, 477n.132, 510n.61, 545n.42
philosophy, Greek. *See* Aristotle; Greek or Hellenistic traditions; Platonic traditions; Stoic traditions
philosophy, Indian. *See* Darśanas
philosophy, medieval Jewish, 433–

434n.53, 534n.343, 545n.42, 550–551n.121. *See also* Maimonides, Moses
R. Phinehas b. Ḥama, 304, 307, 477n.141, 513n.94, 527–528n.265
Pintchman, Tracy, 458n.332
Pirqê d^{e}-R. Eliezer, 132, 142, 145, 180, 191–196, 264, 310–315, 376, 488nn.284, 285
  narrative Midrash, 191
  rewrites pentateuchal narrative, 191
  synthesis of three types of material, 191
plan of creation. *See* blueprint
Platonic traditions, 138, 139, 165, 476n.130
Pollock, Sheldon, 8–9, 11–12, 426n.23, 427n.26, 429n.30, 430n.41
Porton, Gary G., 471n.71, 542n.16
post-Talmudic Midrashim, 23, 132, 145, 179–196, 293–315. *See also specific Midrashim*
  exegetical Midrashim, 179
  homiletical Midrashim, 179–181
  narrative Midrashim, 180
  and polemic against Christians, 174
Prabhākara, 117, 462nn.399, 400
practice of Torah, 374–381, 388–390. *See also* commandments
  and final redemption, 157, 159, 274, 286–287
  as hallmark of life of a sage, 148
  importance of, 154, 157–158, 174, 191–192, 333, 380
  for its own sake, 154
  and light, 190
  and Malkût/Shekhinah or Oral Torah, 381, 550n.119
  as means of augmenting God's power, 359, 374–375, 377–378, 380–381, 388–389, 401
  as means of maintaining cosmos, 359, 374–377, 378, 380, 388–390, 401, 533n.326, 549n.86
  as means of stimulating influx from *s^{e}p̄îrôṯ*, 380–381
  as means of uniting male and female aspects of Godhead, 378, 381, 550n.119
  as method of embodying Torah, 338, 382, 401, 402
  and Name of God, 381
  open to all members of Jewish community, 391
  and power to "make" God, 381
  and theodicy, 158–159
  theurgic efficacy of, 359, 374–381, 382, 388–390
  and Tip̄'ereṯ or Written Torah, 381
Prajāpati (creator god), 434n.55, 442–443n.65
  and *adhvaryu* priest, 54, 58, 60
  and *agnicayana*, 239, 241, 351, 434n.58, 500n.106
  and Ātman, 65, 68, 450n.170
  and body, of cosmos, 59, 241
  and Brahmā, 65, 73, 78, 86, 89, 451n.206
  and *brahman*/Brahman/Brahman-Ātman, 44, 52–53, 64, 65–66, 67, 442n.61, 446n.123
  and *brahman* priest, 60
  and *bṛhat sāman*, 49
  cosmic body of, 39–40, 47, 60, 66, 238–239, 241, 351, 434n.58, 459n.370
  and cosmic egg, 45, 50, 52
  and death, 445n.114
  and *gāyatrī*/Gāyatrī or *sāvitrī*/Sāvitrī, 39, 79, 343, 444n.88
  and gods, 39–40, 55, 56–58, 126, 350, 447n.141
  as Hiraṇyagarbha, 44
  and *hotṛ* priest, 54, 58, 60, 537n.33

Prajāpati *(continued)*
as immanent and transcendent, 44, 441–442n.55, 442n.56
and knowledge, 48, 214, 216
as lord of speech, 48
and meditation, 49
and meters, 39–40, 47, 50, 59, 343, 351, 459n.370
and mind, 48–49, 50, 126, 127, 444n.94
and Om, 57–58, 79, 447n.143
and orders of reality, 56–58, 69, 79
and priestly functions, 39, 54–55, 58, 60, 62, 349–350, 446n.131, 448n.152, 537n.33
as primordial seer/*ṛṣi*, 39, 54, 238, 240, 241, 330, 349, 500n.96
and Puruṣa, 39, 44, 50, 52, 64, 65, 66, 238–239, 349
and sacrifice, 30, 39, 44–47, 50, 54, 55, 58, 60, 61, 63, 126, 238, 349–351, 439n.34, 443n.81, 500n.96
and sacrificial fires, 58
and *sāmans*, 39–40, 47, 49, 444n.88, 459n.370
and *śastras*, 55, 126
saw and recited, 54, 221, 238, 240, 241, 330, 500n.96
and seers/*ṛṣis*, 238–239, 240, 241, 500n.106
and Skambha, 41, 53
and social classes/*varṇas*, 39–40, 54
as soul of cosmos-body, 59
and speech/Vāc, 30, 45, 47–53, 54–56, 60, 62, 68, 89, 126, 127, 239, 445n.121, 446n.134, 447n.141
and *śruti*, 250
and *stomas*, 39–40, 47, 59, 459n.370
and *stotras*, 55, 126
as supreme god, 30, 44, 64, 350
and *tapas*, 45, 52, 54, 57, 68
and three *vyāhṛtis*, 51, 54, 56–58, 68, 79
and three worlds, 35, 36, 50–51, 54, 56–58, 442n.56, 446n.124
and *udgātṛ* priest, 54, 55, 58, 60, 446n.131, 537n.33
and Veda(s), 30, 39–40, 46, 47–53, 54–62, 65, 66, 67, 79, 89, 126, 127, 214, 216, 238, 250, 330, 349–351, 444n.88, 445n.121, 446n.134, 459n.370, 500n.96
as Viśvakarman, 44
and the waters, 45, 50, 52–53, 445n.121
and word/*śabda*, 126
and year, 50, 445n.115, 450n.171
Prakṛti (primordial matter; nature), 74. *See also gunas*
and Brahman, 99, 100
eight *prakṛtis*, 245
as female principle, 100, 101
and Īśvara, 100, 101
as material cause, 100
as matrix of creation, 100
as *māyā*, 458n.332
and *prākṛta* creations, 99, 100, 454n.257
and Puruṣa, 99, 100
and *tattvas*, 85, 100, 454nn.256, 257
and three *guṇas*, 100, 106, 107, 111
and Viṣṇu, 85–86
and the waters, 101
pramāṇa (valid means of knowledge), 96, 113, 116, 120, 124. *See also śabda*: *śabda-pramāṇa*; *veda-prāmāṇya*
prāṇa(s) (breaths; orifices of the sense organs), 58, 501n.107. *See also* breath
and mind, 447n.148

and seven seers/*saptarṣis*, 238–239, 500nn.105, 106
Praśna Upaniṣad, 68
pratisarga or *visarga* (secondary creation), 75, 95, 99, 100, 101, 107, 112, 248, 452n.217, 454n.257
prāyaścitta (expiation; penance), 33, 76, 104, 348
preexistent or primordial
Christ as, 159, 403
Logos as, 132, 159, 403
Qur'ān as, 409, 410
seers/*ṛṣis* as, 238–239, 500nn.104, 106
six or seven things created prior to the world, 160, 175, 192–193, 470n.64, 472n.81, 480n.185, 491n.323
ten things created on eve of first Sabbath, 148–149, 152, 175, 193, 195, 314, 470n.62, 471n.76, 481n.187, 488n.291, 532n.317
Torah as, 14–15, 24, 131, 132–133, 135–137, 139, 141, 145–146, 147, 148–149, 152, 153, 154, 159, 160–164, 166, 169, 171, 172, 175–176, 180, 183–185, 188, 190, 191, 192–193, 194, 195, 196, 197–198, 202, 209, 212, 214, 219, 222, 253, 256, 288–289, 297, 359, 362, 369, 398, 399, 401, 410, 432n.48, 470nn.64, 66, 471n.77, 472n.81, 474n.109, 475nn.111, 113, 480–481n.185, 481n.186, 491n.323, 493n.341, 519n.167, 533n.327
wisdom/Ḥoḵmāh as, 15, 24, 131, 132–133, 135–137, 139, 141, 146, 148, 149, 153, 154, 159, 160, 162, 164, 166, 171, 175, 183, 188, 193, 194, 198, 202, 205, 209, 212, 214, 253, 362, 369, 471n.77, 493n.341, 494n.354
Word as, ix, 24, 43, 62, 159, 215, 398, 403
word/*śabda* as, 126–127
pre-rabbinic texts, 132–140
priests. *See adhvaryu; brahman;* brahmins; *hotṛ; udgātṛ*
primordial Torah, 132, 162. *See also* Torah; *tôrāh qᵉḏûmāh*
descent from heaven, 15, 253, 369
embodied in Book of the Torah/Sefer Torah, 15, 222, 253, 359
and fire, 172
as first of God's works, 141, 146
and Hebrew letters, 209, 212
Ḥoḵmāh as, 198, 209, 212, 493n.341
as instrument of creation, 141, 253, 297, 369
and Oral Torah, 209, 219
and revelation of Torah, 15, 253, 369
and world of emanation/*'ăṣîlûṯ*, 212
and Written Torah, 209, 219
and Yōḏ, first letter of Tetragrammaton, 209, 212
proem, 155, 161–162, 164–165, 179–180
prophets, 557n.27. *See also* Ezekiel; Isaiah; Moses; Muhammad
and chain of tradition from Sinai revelation, 147–148, 265, 294
and grades of divine revelation, 316
and Hôḏ, 372, 534n.352, 547n.59
and kabbalist exegete, 337, 367, 371–372, 383, 391–392, 547n.58
and Malḵûṯ/Shekhinah or Oral Torah, 319–320, 534n.352, 547n.59
and Moses, 264, 320, 372, 521n.198, 534n.352, 547n.59

prophets *(continued)*
Moses as supreme prophet, 223, 315–316, 320, 337, 371–372, 391–392, 400, 547n.58
Muhammad as "seal of the prophets," 411, 413
and Neṣaḥ, 372, 534n.352, 547n.59
and people of Israel, 264, 269–270, 319–320
present at revelation of Torah, 181, 294–295, 311
succession of, in Islamic traditions, 410–411, 558n.44
Proverbs, 133–135, 136, 137, 138–139, 140–141, 146, 148, 149, 153, 154, 155, 159, 160, 161, 162, 164–165, 171–172, 175, 176, 177, 178, 183–184, 185, 186, 187, 188, 190, 193, 194, 195, 202, 280–281, 298
Proverbs 8.22–31, 133–135, 137, 138–139, 140–141, 146, 148, 149, 153, 154, 159, 160, 161, 162, 164–165, 175, 183–184, 185, 186, 193, 194, 202
Psalms, 136, 154, 155, 161, 162, 163, 169, 170, 172, 178, 183–184, 187, 188, 189, 190, 195, 254, 255, 262, 263, 267, 268, 269, 270, 272, 275, 276, 277, 278, 282, 283, 284, 285, 287, 289–290, 293, 298, 301, 303, 304, 309, 310, 311, 312, 313, 377, 410, 557n.35
Pseudepigrapha, 191, 192, 470n.65, 488n.285
pūjā (worship; ritual offerings), 19, 94, 456n.307
Pulaha (seer), 244, 245
Pulastya (seer), 244, 245
Purāṇas, 23, 35, 40, 72–73, 74–76, 80, 83, 84, 85, 86, 88, 90, 94–112, 228, 243–244, 248–251, 335, 351, 458n.329. *See also specific Purāṇas*
and Being, 67, 457n.311
and *bhakti* traditions or stream, 30, 72, 94, 402, 416
and Brahmā, 96, 97, 104–105, 106
"canon" of, 456–457n.310
and *dharma*, 71, 94, 335
didactic function of, 97–98, 99
and discursive oral traditions, 417
emphasis on both sound and meaning, 97–98
as encyclopedias of Hindu teachings, 72, 94
as eternal, 96
as fifth Veda or as Veda, 7, 8, 10, 95–97, 104–105, 250, 336, 402, 425–426n.19, 438n.10, 457n.311
as first of all *śāstras*, 96, 97, 99, 105
five characteristics of/*pañca-lakṣaṇa*, 95, 456nn.309, 310
iconic veneration of, 19, 98, 416, 458n.327
and mantric efficacy, 97–98, 416
open to general populace, including *śūdras* and women, 97, 98–99, 336, 457n.322
as oral texts, 98, 457n.325
primordial Purāṇa and eighteen Purāṇas, 96–97
as products of post-Vedic brahmanical synthesis, 71–72, 94
Purāṇa Saṃhitās and eighteen Purāṇas, 97
Purāṇa-Veda, 95, 99
Purāṇic "cults of the book," 98, 416, 434n.59, 458n.327
recitation of, 97, 98, 457n.322
recitation of, fruits of hearing, 97, 98
as *smṛti*, 8, 72
and *śruti*, 72
as synthesis of *dharma*, *bhakti*,

and tantric traditions, 94
and Vedic paradigm, 10, 19, 72, 95–99, 336, 416
and Viṣṇu, 96
and Vyāsa, 96–97, 250
as Word/*śabda*, 96
writing or copying of, fruits of, 98
as written texts, 19, 98, 416, 457n.325
Puruṣa (cosmic Man; pure consciousness), 74
and Ātman, 65, 66, 68, 449n.165
and Brahmā, 73, 78, 91, 100, 101–102
and *brahman*/Brahman/Brahman-Ātman, 64–66, 67, 68, 91–92, 99, 100
cosmic body of, 35, 37–38, 41, 66, 68, 91–92, 349, 458n.341
and cosmic egg, 78, 100, 101–102
as creator principle, 65, 67
and *gāyatrī*/Gāyatrī or *sāvitrī*/Sāvitrī, 91–92
and gods, 37–38, 67–68, 349
and heart, 65
as immanent and transcendent, 37, 64–65, 442n.56
as immortal, 442n.56
and Īśvara, 100
and meters, 37
and Nārāyaṇa, 101–102
and orders of reality, 37–38, 67–68, 349
and Prajāpati, 39, 44, 50, 52, 64, 65, 66, 238–239, 349
and Prakṛti, 99, 100
and sacrifice, 37–38, 40, 41, 349
and Sanskrit *varṇas*, 91–92
and seers/*ṛṣis*, 238–239
and social classes/*varṇas*, 38
and speech, 68
as sun, 458n.341
and three worlds, 38
and Veda(s), 37, 41, 65, 66, 67–68, 91–92, 349, 458n.341
and Viṣṇu, 85, 100, 101–102, 244
as Word/*brahman*, 91–92
Puruṣa-Sūkta (Ṛg-Veda X.90), 36–38, 39, 40, 44, 56, 64, 68, 85, 231, 348, 402, 439n.29, 447n.147
Pūrva-Mīmāṃsā, 8, 23, 96, 114–123, 124, 125, 352–354, 427n.25, 538n.55
focus on Brāhmaṇas, 113, 116, 346, 352–353, 388
focus on *dharma*, 113, 115, 123, 353, 388
focus on *karma-kāṇḍa*, 123, 353
philosophy of language, 114–123, 129, 347, 461n.397, 462n.400
as school of Vedic exegesis, 114, 346, 352–354, 388
schools of, 117
Pūrva-Mīmāṃsā-Sūtras, 116–117, 118, 120, 121, 122–123, 125
Pūṣan (deity), 234

qal wā-ḥômer (argument from a minor to a major premise), 363–364
Qîddûšîn, 149, 163
Qinyan Torah, 148
qôl/*qôlōṯ* (voices), 155, 269, 270, 272, 282, 284, 296, 306, 309, 310, 314, 318, 472n.83. *See also* voice(s) of God
Qur'ān
and Abraham, 411–412, 558nn.47, 48
and Arabic, 409–410, 412, 557n.33
and Arabs, 409–410, 558n.48
authority of, 409, 412
as bounded category, 412–413
and Christ, 409, 556n.24
as constitutive category of Islamic traditions, 409
and divine language, 409

Qur'ān *(continued)*
as divine revelation, 409–413, 557n.27, 557–558n.37, 558nn.45, 47, 48
as eternal, 409
and generic idea of scripture, 557n.27
and Gospel of Jesus, 410, 557n.35, 558n.48
and heavenly Book/*kitāb*, 410–411, 412, 424n.9, 557nn.31, 33, 557–558n.37
Islamic conceptions of, 6, 409–413, 556nn.24–26, 557nn.27, 33, 35, 557–558n.37, 558nn.45–48
and Muhammad, 409–413, 557–558n.37, 558n.48
not an encompassing symbol, 409, 412
and "People of the Book," 410–411, 558nn.45, 46
as preexistent, 409, 410
as quintessential, culminating revelation, 411, 412
and sources of *fiqh*, 412–413
and successive scriptural revelations, 410–411, 412, 557n.35
and Torah, 409, 410, 557n.35, 558n.48
as transcendent, 409, 556n.25
as uncreated, 409
as universal truth, open to all, 409–412
and Veda(s), 557n.35
as Word of God, 409, 412

Rab, 163, 173, 176, 177, 481n.185, 541n.15
Raba, 176
rabbinic sages. *See also* rabbinic tradition; and *specific rabbis*
and *'am hā-'āreṣ*, 262, 391
as authoritative interpreters of Torah, 157, 158, 337, 391, 554n.15
authority of, 2, 158, 173–174, 182, 290–291, 337, 338, 391, 400–401, 402
and chain of tradition from Sinai revelation, 147–148, 158, 181, 265, 294, 337, 339, 400
circumscribe study of Torah in rabbinic academies, 391
consensus of, and halakhah, 174, 290–291
as custodians of Oral Torah, 173–174, 337, 391
as custodians of scribal tradition, 337
as custodians of Written Torah, 337, 391
designated as "Sinai," 285
as embodiments of Shekhinah, 158, 544n.28
as embodiments of Torah, 148, 158, 285, 382, 400–401, 412, 474n.101
and fire, 172, 178–179, 281, 366, 489n.316, 544n.26
honoring of, 158
as mediators of interpretation of Torah, 337, 338, 339, 362, 391, 543n.19
Moses as paradigm for, 190–191, 337, 338, 339, 366, 391, 400
present at revelation of Torah, 181, 294–295, 311
as radiant with light, 172, 178, 190–191, 196, 366, 483n.213
teachings of, as Oral Torah, 13, 158, 173–174, 181–182, 273, 285, 337, 397
words of scribes and words of Written Torah, 158, 174, 182
rabbinic texts. *See also* Midrash; rabbinic tradition; and *specific rabbinic texts*
problems with delimiting

historical-cultural contexts of, 22, 145
problems with determining dates and provenance of, 145
two types of documents, 141–142, 172–173
rabbinic tradition. *See also* brahmanical tradition and rabbinic tradition; rabbinic sages; rabbinic texts
aniconic aspects of, 19, 416
and canonical authority, ix, 2, 21–22, 400–401
canon of, ix, 2, 21–22, 141–142
and Christian traditions, 132, 157–158, 159, 554n.15
continuity with kabbalistic traditions, 16, 433–434n.53
discourse of body in, 552n.4, 554n.15
as "embodied community," 397–403, 412, 413, 552n.4, 554n.15
emphasis on cognitive dimension of words, 18, 146, 169, 218–220, 221–223, 334, 361–366, 385, 386–388, 414
emphasis on visual mode of perception, 17–19, 146, 218–220, 221–223, 334, 385, 414–417, 469n.57
emphasis on written channel of language, 17–18, 146, 169, 218–220, 221–223, 334, 359–360, 385–387, 414–420, 469n.57
as ethnocultural system, ix, 3, 397–403, 412, 413, 554n.15
and Hebrew, 3, 397
iconic aspects of, 19, 386, 416–417
and land of Israel, 397
and levels of embodiment, 398–403
multiplicity of voices in, 15
mystical circles, 15, 196, 260–261, 364, 432n.51, 541n.12
as religion of orthopraxy, ix, 3, 401–403
as textual community, ix, 2, 21, 403
Torah as constitutive category of, ix–x, 2–3, 255, 398–403
two types of Judaisms, in relation to Christian traditions, 157
Rabinowitz, Louis Isaac, 540n.1
Rad, Gerhard von, 134–135, 136, 464nn.1, 6, 465nn.8, 10, 466n.19
Radhakrishnan, Sarvepalli, 426n.23
Raghavan, V., 536n.9
Räisänen, Heikki, 554n.14
Raja, K. Kunjunni, 461n.398
rajas (activity; one of the three *guṇas*)
and *a*, first constituent of Om, 111
and Brahmā, 111
and earth, 111
and Om, 108, 111
and primordial utterance *bhūḥ*, 111
and *ṛcs*, 111
and Ṛg-Veda, 111
Ramanujan, A. K., 429n.36
Rāmāyaṇa of Vālmīki, 452n.229
as fifth Veda, 7
as product of post-Vedic brahmanical synthesis, 71–72, 80
Rambachan, Anantanand, 539n.55
Rāmcaritmānas
discursive meaning primary, 418
as fifth Veda, 10
as Hindi Veda, 10
multiple retellings of, 418
recitation of, 418, 429n.35
as *smṛti*, 418
vedacization of, 429n.35
rathantara (type of *sāman*), 39
and *bṛhat sāman*, 49
and earth, 445n.109

rathantara (continued)
and *ṛcs*, 49, 105, 445n.109
and speech/Vāc, 49
Ravi (sun; sun god). *See* Sūrya
Ray, Reginald, 556n.21
rāzê tôrāh (secrets of the Torah), 15, 363. *See also siṯrê tôrāh*; Torah: secrets or mysteries of
ṛcs (verses that constitute the Ṛg-Veda), 62, 70, 437n.9, 438nn.10, 14. *See also* Ṛg-Veda
and Brahmā, 40, 104, 105, 111
and Brahman/Brahman-Ātman, 42, 66, 102, 112
definition and use of term, 31–32, 33
and earth, 59, 445n.109
and *hotṛ* priest, 33, 54, 60, 348
and the Imperishable, 233, 330, 356
as limited, 29, 41
as part of threefold Veda, 31, 34, 425n.16
and patron of sacrifice/ *yajamāna*, 61
and Prajāpati, 39, 50, 54, 60, 238, 349–350, 500n.96
and Puruṣa, 37, 67–68
and *rajas*, 111
and *rathantara sāman*, 49, 105, 445n.109
and Ṛg-Veda, 7, 32, 250
and sacrifice, 33, 37, 39, 43, 54, 60, 238, 240, 348, 349–350, 457n.311
and *sāmans*, 49
and seers/*ṛṣis*, 237, 240, 501n.120
and Śiva, 88
and Skambha, 41–42
as source of form, 59
and speech/Vāc, 47, 49, 50, 54, 60, 105
as *śruti*, 7
and Viṣṇu, 87, 102, 103
and Vyāsa, 249–250
Recanati, Menaḥem, 492n.334, 544–545n.35
recitation of Sefer Torah, 387–388
as communal event, 339, 387–388, 391
discursive meaning primary, 387–388
emphasis on cognitive over phonic dimensions of words, 387–388
emphasis on meaning over sound, 387–388
emphasis on semantics over phonology, 387–388
hearing of, open to all Jews, 391
intended to convey didactic teachings, 388
methods of recitation, 387–388
public reading of Torah in synagogue, 338, 339, 386, 387–388, 391
recitation of Vedic Saṃhitās, 9, 29, 44, 58, 65, 344–351, 385–390, 415–419, 443n.77. *See also* study of Veda(s); transmission of Vedic Saṃhitās
by Brahmā, 105, 110, 218, 220, 249
by brahmin reciters/*śrotriyas*, 83, 345–347, 355, 385–388, 395–396, 419
constitutive meaning of Vedic words, 347, 354, 387
by creator principle, 214, 221, 348, 351, 389
discursive meaning secondary, 12, 97–98, 343, 346–347, 351, 387, 388, 408, 418, 419, 457n.323, 536–537n.12
emphasis on phonic over cognitive dimension of words, 18, 346–347, 386–388
emphasis on phonology over semantics, 343, 346–347, 351, 354, 386–388, 431n.43

emphasis on sound over meaning, 97–98, 346–347, 351, 386–388, 408, 418, 419, 457n.323
by gods, 238
hearing of, as sacramental activity, 539n.64
hearing of, restricted to male members of three higher social classes/*varṇas*, 82, 97, 355, 390–391
as means of creation, 54–55, 60, 73, 238, 343, 348–350, 389, 390
as means of maintaining purity of Vedic sounds, 12, 18, 346–347, 386–387
as means of nourishing and magnifying gods, 237, 339, 343, 348, 349, 350–351, 388–389, 401, 419
as means of regeneration and rectification of cosmic order, 46–47, 55, 60, 112, 238, 335, 339, 343, 347–351, 387, 388–390, 401, 406, 418, 419, 443n.73
as means to attain specific ends, 55, 238, 240, 333, 350, 500n.96, 538n.39
methods of pronunciation, 88, 89, 345
methods of recitation, 88, 105, 387
modes of recitation/*pāṭhas*, 345–346, 536n.9
as nondiscursive oral tradition, 417
not communal event, 339, 388, 419
not intended to convey didactic teachings, 339, 388
not sufficient to realize transcendent Veda, 356
by Prajāpati, 54–55, 238, 240, 241, 330, 349–350, 500n.96
restricted to male members of three higher social classes/*varṇas*, 82, 97, 355, 390–391
as sacramental activity, 539n.64
by seers/*ṛṣis*, 34, 94, 112, 227, 233, 235–238, 240, 241, 249, 333, 334–335, 339, 356, 390, 501n.120
śūdras excluded from, 82, 97, 355, 390–391, 539n.65
theurgic efficacy of, 343, 347–351, 388–390, 443n.73
tradition of recitative transmission, 249, 344–347, 355, 385–387
and Vedāṅgas, 345, 386
Vedic recitative tradition, beginningless, 119, 123
Vedic recitative tradition, brahmanical custodians of, 12, 60, 83, 98, 326, 334–335, 339, 345–347, 355, 385–388, 390, 395–396, 400, 406, 427n.26, 555n.17
Vedic recitative tradition, initiated by Brahmā, 112, 126, 127, 249
Vedic recitative tradition, initiated by seers/*ṛṣis*, 112, 239, 249, 325, 326, 333, 334–335, 339, 344, 348, 355, 390
and verbatim reproduction of Vedic sounds, 97–98, 339, 345–347, 348, 351, 386–387, 388, 389, 395–396, 408, 417–418, 427n.26
by Viṣṇu, 89, 90
women excluded from, 82, 97, 355, 390–391, 539n.65
redemption, final. *See also* Day of Judgment; Messianic Age; resurrection of the dead
and gentile nations, 274, 286–287, 288
and people of Israel, 157–158, 274, 286–287, 514n.110

redemption, final *(continued)*
and practice of Torah, 157, 159, 274, 286–287
and study of Torah, 157
rekeḇ (chariots), 254, 262, 278, 304, 313. *See also* chariots
remez (allegorical meaning), 369, 370, 373, 545n.41
Renou, Louis, 11, 346, 426n.23, 430n.40, 440n.39, 536nn.3, 12, 537nn.12, 13, 538nn.44, 51, 55, 539n.56
repentance
as one of six or seven things created prior to the world, 160, 175, 192–193
rᵉqîʻîm (firmaments). *See* firmaments
rē'šîṯ (beginning), 133, 162, 164, 186, 205, 207, 494n.354
resurrection of the dead, 260, 293, 309, 311, 314, 483n.212, 517n.139, 530n.285. *See also* redemption, final
people of Israel died and were resurrected, 257, 260, 282–283, 293, 309, 314–315, 516n.124, 517nn.139, 141
Rᵉ'ûyyôṯ Yᵉḥezqē'l (Visions of Ezekiel), 505n.5, 528n.272, 529n.273
revelation of Torah at Mount Sinai, 25, 253–324, 325–339. *See also* Israel, people of; Moses
and Abraham, 154, 163
and Adam, 163
all past and future generations were present, 311, 318, 338
and angels, 256–257, 258, 259, 263–264, 267, 271, 276–277, 278–279, 288–290, 291–292, 293–294, 295, 300–302, 303–305, 307, 308, 309, 312, 313–314, 322, 329, 332, 509n.46, 513–514n.103, 514–515n.113, 515n.118, 519n.169, 520n.171, 523n.221, 523–524n.222, 524n.226, 525–526n.247, 526–527n.258, 529n.274, 531nn.301, 306
and apocalyptic traditions, 258, 259, 264
ascent of Moses of "mountain of God," 254, 255
ascent of Moses to Godhead, 315–316, 328
ascent of Moses to heaven, 146, 173, 256, 258, 259, 262, 263–264, 267, 275–277, 278, 288–290, 293, 299–302, 303, 307, 311–312, 328, 329, 513n.103, 520nn.171, 176, 523–524n.222, 541n.15
biblical account of, 183, 253–255, 262, 265, 292, 294
chain of tradition from, 147–148, 158, 181, 265, 294, 337, 339, 400
and chariots, 254, 257, 258, 262, 264, 278, 293–294, 303–305, 313, 322, 332, 514–515n.113, 515n.116, 526nn.252, 253, 531n.306
as cosmic event, 255–256, 271–272, 275, 311
and covenant between God and people of Israel, 174, 256, 278, 285, 295, 298, 303, 326, 330–331, 333, 338, 376–377, 390, 391
definition and use of term "revelation," 327, 328–329
descent of angels from heaven, 256, 258, 264, 278–279, 291–292, 293–294, 303–305, 309, 313–314, 529n.274
descent of chariots from heaven, 258, 262, 264, 278, 293–294, 304–305, 313
descent of God, and *sᵉp̄îrôṯ*, 315–316, 318

descent of God from heaven, 254, 255, 256, 258, 264, 267–268, 275–278, 288, 290, 291, 293–294, 303–305, 310, 312–313, 314, 315, 327–328, 520n.176, 529n.274, 531n.304
descent of primordial wisdom from heaven, 15, 135–136, 362
descent of Shekhinah from heaven, 256, 276–278, 290
descent of Torah from heaven, 15, 146, 172, 253, 256, 265, 275–278, 288–291, 293, 299–300, 301, 302, 311–312, 315, 317, 327–328, 369, 513n.103
and divine utterances, 257, 270–271, 272, 280, 293, 321, 322, 332, 333, 334, 510n.61, 535n.367
divine vs. human initiative, 327–329
embodiment of Word in texts, 24, 26, 325
emphasis on visual aspects of experience, 18, 222–223, 257, 269–271, 307–308, 318–324, 332, 334, 495n.6, 533n.339, 534n.343
epistemology of, 255, 322–324, 331–333
experienced according to each individual's capacity, 257–258, 271–272, 282–284, 309–310, 331, 337–338
experienced according to each individual's "grade," 323–324
and Ezekiel, 255, 258–259, 262, 278, 514n.112, 528–529n.272
and face(s) of God, 256, 257, 280–281, 283, 293–294, 301–302, 307, 309, 310, 312, 318, 319, 331, 332, 512n.75, 516n.130, 517n.142, 529n.274, 530n.290
and fire, 155, 172, 179, 191, 196, 222, 254, 257, 259, 263, 264, 269, 270, 271, 275, 281, 292, 301, 306, 308, 314, 318, 322, 332, 366, 473n.91, 475n.118, 479n.167, 510n.61, 516n.132, 535n.367
and gentile nations, 152, 182, 255, 266–267, 269, 271, 273–274, 284, 285–287, 292, 294, 295–297, 307, 309, 311, 316, 325, 326, 329, 332, 338, 391, 399, 509n.40, 512n.83, 518n.157, 529n.274, 530n.288, 533n.327
and glory of God, 256, 257, 258, 263, 267, 268, 274, 279, 281, 293, 303, 305, 306, 307, 317–318, 320–321, 322, 323, 324, 329, 332, 366, 515n.120, 525n.244, 527nn.259, 262, 529n.283, 532n.311, 534n.340
and golden calf, 254, 257, 278, 279, 291, 303–304, 310, 314, 329, 525n.245
heard in seventy languages, 267, 285, 292, 295–296, 306, 320–321, 366
and Hebrew, 267, 275
and Hebrew letters, 317
and Hêḵālôṯ traditions, 258–264, 300, 306, 307, 337, 505n.7, 510n.61, 511n.65, 515nn.118, 119, 517n.139, 521nn.181, 190, 524n.222, 527n.259, 528n.272, 532n.310
as historical event, 131, 160, 253, 297, 325, 326–327
as immediate, individualized experience, 257–258, 271–272, 282–284, 309–310, 323–324, 331, 337–338, 517n.140, 530n.290
and interpretation of Torah, 172, 179, 263, 281, 321, 337, 338, 362, 366, 367, 370–372, 373, 391–392, 546n.52

revelation of Torah *(continued)*
- and intervention of Torah, 283, 309, 517n.141
- justice/G^e^ḇûrāh was tempered by mercy/Ḥeseḏ, 322
- kabbalists were present, 370
- and light, 172, 222–223, 254, 276, 292, 308, 315–316, 318–319, 320–321, 329, 333, 366, 371, 479n.160, 529n.280, 547n.57
- and lightning, 257, 259, 269, 272, 292, 314, 472n.83
- and Malḵûṯ/Shekhinah, 315, 318, 319, 371, 373, 534n.343
- as marriage ceremony, 256, 265, 268, 276–278, 283, 291, 302–303, 312, 331, 338, 373, 508n.31, 514n.110, 525n.237
- and Merkabah, 179, 255, 258–264, 270, 278, 300, 303–304, 307, 313, 332–333, 366, 508n.23, 514n.112, 514–515n.113, 525n.245, 526n.253, 528–529n.272, 531n.306, 532nn.309, 310
- Moses as covenant mediator, 254, 257, 271, 272, 279, 281–282, 284, 294, 311, 314–315, 331, 337, 511n.70
- Moses as recipient of revelation, 146, 147–148, 151, 158, 173, 181, 182, 191, 199, 223, 254, 255, 256, 258, 259, 263–264, 265–266, 267, 271, 272–273, 275–277, 278, 279, 281–282, 284–285, 288–290, 293, 294, 299–302, 308, 310–312, 315–316, 320, 328, 329, 331, 332–333, 334, 337, 339, 359–360, 362, 366, 385–386, 391–392, 395–396, 397, 400, 510n.61, 513–514n.103, 520n.171, 523n.221, 523–524n.222, 530n.287
- Moses as scribe of God, 13, 223, 331, 334, 337, 359–360
- Moses's sojourns of forty days and forty nights, 254, 255, 300, 302, 310–311, 329
- Mount Sinai in heaven, 276, 311–312, 313, 518n.158
- Mount Sinai suspended over people of Israel, 286, 287, 513n.98, 518n.158
- Mount Sinai uprooted, 276, 313, 513n.98, 518n.158
- and Name of God, 256–257, 260, 279, 296–297, 305–306, 313, 317, 515n.119, 527n.262, 532nn.309, 311
- and opening of firmaments or heavens, 257, 258, 263, 276, 293, 301, 307, 311–312, 313, 314, 322, 332, 523n.222, 529n.273, 531n.305
- and Oral Torah, 13, 157, 158, 173–174, 182, 272–273, 284–285, 294, 311, 325, 331, 362, 397, 402
- as overpowering experience, 257, 271, 281–283, 293, 308–309, 314–315
- as paradigmatic, 259–261, 262–264, 334, 337–339, 366, 371–372, 378, 389–390
- people of Israel as recipients of revelation, 151, 152, 163, 167, 188, 222–223, 253, 254, 255, 256–260, 262–263, 264, 266–267, 268–272, 273–275, 276–284, 285–288, 291–294, 295–299, 300, 302–310, 311, 312–315, 316–324, 325–334, 337–339, 366, 370–372, 376, 378, 389–390, 391, 395–396, 399, 410, 476n.124, 482n.196, 486n.243, 510n.61, 511n.70, 512n.75, 513n.98, 516nn.124, 130, 131, 517nn.139, 140, 518n.158, 521n.190,

523n.222, 529nn.274, 283, 530nn.288, 290, 533n.327, 534n.343, 549n.85
people of Israel died and were resurrected, 257, 260, 282–283, 293, 296, 309, 314–315, 516n.124, 517nn.139, 141, 529n.283
people of Israel granted immunity from death, 257, 281, 282, 306, 516n.131, 527n.264
people of Israel invested with crowns, 256–257, 259, 279, 291–292, 304–305, 313, 515n.118, 520n.181, 532n.309
people of Israel invested with garments, 256–257, 259–260, 305–306, 313, 526–527n.258, 527n.262, 532n.311
people of Israel invested with girdles, 256–257, 279, 305
people of Israel invested with ornaments, 256–257, 259–260, 278–279, 291–292, 304–306, 313, 329, 515nn.118, 119, 520n.181, 526–527n.258, 527n.262, 532nn.309, 311
people of Israel invested with weapon(s), 256–257, 260, 279, 305–306, 313, 515nn.118, 119
people of Israel's acceptance of Torah, 152, 163, 167, 188, 255, 256, 266, 273–275, 279, 286–288, 292, 295–298, 305, 316–318, 327, 329, 333, 338, 376, 378, 390, 391, 399, 482n.196, 513n.98, 516n.131, 518n.158, 549n.85
people of Israel stripped of ornaments, 257, 292, 305, 314, 329
as pivotal event in Jewish salvation history, 157, 159, 253, 326
prophets and sages were present, 181, 294–295, 311
and rabbinic Merkabah traditions, 258–264, 508n.23, 514n.112, 519–520n.171, 524n.222, 528–529n.272, 532nn.309, 310
as recapitulation and consolidation of creation, 167, 188, 255–256, 274–275, 287–288, 297–299, 309, 315, 316–318, 323, 326–327, 376, 378, 390, 482n.196, 518n.158, 549n.85
Sefer Torah as core revelation, 13, 14, 395–396
and *s^{e}pîrôṯ*, 315–324, 332–333, 370–371, 373, 392, 534n.343
and Shavuot, 182, 262, 272, 293, 338, 514n.112, 519–520n.171, 524n.222, 528–529n.272
and Shekhinah, 256, 257, 276–278, 279, 289, 290, 291, 301, 302, 303, 307, 315, 318, 319, 366, 371, 373, 520nn.175, 176, 524n.226, 525n.241, 527n.259, 534n.343
sixth of Sivan as date of, 288, 313, 338
as synesthetic experience involving both sight and hearing, 18, 222, 257, 269–271, 279–281, 292, 306–308, 314, 318–324, 329, 331–333, 334, 529n.283
and tablets of Ten Commandments, 193, 254, 257, 270, 280, 292, 308, 310, 312, 314, 321–322, 323, 332, 482n.204, 532–533n.319
and ten words of creation/ *ma'ămārôṯ*, 317, 323
and Ten Words of revelation/Ten Commandments, 222, 254, 255, 256, 257, 268, 269, 270–272, 275–276, 279–280, 282, 284, 285, 289, 291, 293, 294, 296–297, 298–299, 306, 310, 311, 314–315, 317–318, 320–324, 328, 332, 333, 334, 337,

revelation of Torah *(continued)*
511n.70, 516n.124, 517n.140, 521n.190, 530n.290
as theophany, 255, 256–259, 262–263, 264, 268–272, 278–284, 291–294, 295, 303–310, 311–316, 317–324, 329, 331, 332–333, 337–338, 495n.6, 510n.52, 512n.75, 516n.130, 517n.142, 523n.222, 529nn.274, 283, 534n.343
and throne of glory, 257, 288–289, 290, 293, 300–302, 307, 308, 313, 314, 322, 332, 523n.222, 524n.226
and thunder, 257, 269, 314, 472n.83
and Tip̄'ereṯ, 320, 371, 373
Torah as bride of Israel, 256, 268, 276–278, 291, 302–303, 312, 331, 338, 373
Torah as marriage contract, 278, 303, 331, 338, 514n.110
Torah revealed after twenty-six generations, 161, 163, 168, 184, 274, 474n.109, 475nn.111, 113, 481n.186, 485n.237
Torah written with black fire on white fire, 172, 191, 198–199, 281, 308, 322, 332
two phases of, 253–254, 284, 311
two Torahs were given, 13, 151, 158, 173, 266, 272–273
and unfoldment of mysteries of creation, 222–223, 275, 318–319, 321, 322–323, 332, 333
as union with a personal God, 330–331
and voice(s) of God, 155, 222–223, 257, 269, 270, 271, 272, 280, 282–284, 292, 295–296, 299, 306–307, 309–310, 314–315, 318–321, 322–323, 329, 331, 332, 333, 338, 472n.83, 510n.61, 517n.139, 522n.204, 529n.283, 530nn.287, 288, 534nn.344, 348
wilderness as site of, 255, 266–267
and wisdom/Ḥoḵmāh, 15, 135–136, 323, 362
words of God recorded verbatim, 13, 331, 334, 359
and word/Word of God/*dāḇār/ dîbbēr/dîbbûr*, 14, 154–155, 191, 222, 256, 257, 270, 282–284, 292, 296, 299, 306, 308, 317, 318, 320, 332, 366, 510n.61, 535n.367
and Written Torah, 13, 158, 173–174, 182, 272–273, 284–285, 294, 311, 325, 331, 362, 385–386, 397

Ṛg-Veda, 29, 33–39, 40, 42–43, 55, 64, 73, 85, 91, 228, 229–237, 238, 240, 325, 328, 330, 348–349, 354, 356, 426n.19, 438n.11. *See also ṛcs*
and *a*, first constituent of Om, 57–58, 70, 79, 108, 111
Anukramaṇī, 229
and Ātman, 66
and Being, 67, 128, 129, 457n.311
and Brahmā, 79, 104, 107, 110, 111, 218
and brahmins, 38, 61, 390
commentary by Sāyaṇa, 124, 354
and creator principle, 92
definition and use of term, 7, 31–32, 33
and earth, 38, 51, 56–58, 60, 61, 70, 111, 215
Family Books, 229
and fire/Agni, 38, 56–58, 70, 79, 215
and *hotṛ* priest, 33, 44
as part of threefold Veda, 31, 425n.16
and Prajāpati, 56–58, 62
and primordial utterance *bhūḥ*, 51, 56–58, 61, 79, 111

and Puruṣa, 66, 91
and *rajas*, 111
and *ṛcs*, 7, 32, 250
and Śiva, 104
and speech, 38, 58, 62, 106–108, 110, 218
and Viṣṇu, 87
and Vyāsa, 250
Richman, Paula, 559n.55
Ricoeur, Paul, 421n.5, 559n.56
Ringgren, Helmer, 465nn.9, 10
Rocher, Ludo, 458n.329
Roitman, Betty, 544n.29
Romaharṣaṇa. *See* Lomaharṣaṇa
Rosh Ha-Shanah (New Year's Day), 182, 183, 190
ṛṣi(s) (seers), 31, 227–251, 325–339, 496n.7, 502n.149, 504n.177. *See also* cognition of Veda(s); *śruti*; and *specific ṛṣis*
and Agni, 230, 232, 234, 236, 239, 241, 330, 498n.49, 500n.106
attained transcendent knowledge, 229, 230, 244, 326, 336
authority of, 325, 326, 336
and *bhakti* traditions or stream, 336, 339
and Brahmā, 86, 96, 112, 244, 245, 246, 247, 248, 249, 503n.156
Brahmā as primordial seer/*ṛṣi*, 245, 249
and *brahman*/Brahman/Brahman-Ātman, 42, 66, 234, 238–239, 242–243, 244–245, 248, 326, 328, 330, 335–336, 356–357
and brahmanical lineages, 229, 239, 325, 326, 335–336, 344, 348, 399, 400, 555n.17
brahmin seers/*brahmarṣis*/*viprarṣis*, 112, 227, 244, 245–246, 247, 248, 249, 460n.391
categories of, 243–244, 248
and cognition of Veda(s), 8–10, 12, 18, 34, 43, 76, 82, 94, 221, 227–251, 325–339, 344, 348, 354, 355, 356–357, 385, 389–390, 395–396, 398–399, 407, 415, 426n.24, 427n.27, 427–428n.28, 438n.19, 496n.5, 497nn.22, 28, 34, 37, 501n.113, 502n.132, 503n.151, 537n.28, 539n.64
cognized mechanics and mysteries of creation, 34, 231–232, 234, 235, 241, 245–246, 247, 326, 332, 333, 428n.28
cognized suprasensible phenomena, 229, 231, 332
as cosmological principles, 238, 245
creator principle as archetypal seer/*ṛṣi*, 351
and cycles of creation, 100, 101, 243, 245, 247, 248–249, 251, 326
definition and use of term "cognition," 231, 327, 328, 426n.24, 497n.22
descent from, 229, 239, 241–242, 325, 326, 335–336, 339, 344, 348, 355, 390, 399, 400, 555n.17
and *dharma*, 228, 245, 247, 249, 335
and *dharma* traditions, 334–335, 355
divine seers/*devarṣis*, 244, 248
as eight *prakṛtis*, 245
etymology of term, 240
as fashioners of hymns, 234–235, 240–241, 555n.17
as forefathers of Aryans, 325, 326, 336, 399
gave vocalized expression to Vedic *mantras*, 34, 42–43, 230, 233, 234–238, 240, 241, 251, 330, 333, 349, 355, 501n.120
and gods, 34, 37, 66–67, 229, 230,

ṛṣi(s) *(continued)*
231–232, 233–235, 236–237, 238, 239, 240–241, 243, 246, 248, 326, 328, 330, 332, 335, 348, 349, 354, 390, 497n.20, 498nn.49–52, 59, 500n.106, 501n.111
heard impulses of speech, 227, 232–233, 236, 245–246, 330, 332, 344, 415, 428n.28
and heaven, 230, 239, 501n.113
as immortal, 230
and Indra, 234, 236–237, 241, 330, 498n.51
initiated metaphysical traditions, 325
initiated sacrificial tradition, 239, 325, 326, 333, 334–335, 348, 390
initiated tradition of oral transmission, 43, 83, 94, 112, 221, 228, 247, 249, 344
initiated Vedic recitative tradition, 112, 239, 249, 325, 326, 333, 334–335, 339, 344, 348, 355, 390
inspired thoughts of, 230–231, 232–233, 234, 235–237
and *jñāna-kāṇḍa* or *jñāna* stream, 325, 334, 335–336, 355, 356–357, 392
and *karma-kāṇḍa* or *karman* stream, 325, 334–336, 355, 389
knew past, present, and future, 248
as knowers of Brahman/Brahman-Ātman, 242–243, 244–245, 248, 326, 328, 330, 335–336, 356–357
and knowledge, 229, 230, 231, 244, 248, 326, 336
and light, 232–233, 235, 328, 332, 497n.34
and lines of tradition/*vaṃśa*s, 242, 243, 247, 326, 502n.146
as lords of created beings/*prajāpati*s, 76, 244, 245, 503n.156
and Mahābhārata, 83
and Manu, 76–77
and meditation, 227, 241, 242, 245–246, 328, 357, 428n.28, 503n.151
and meters, 231, 349
as mind-born sons of Brahmā, 244, 245, 247, 249, 503n.156
names of, in Veda(s), 93, 110, 243
not focused on discursive meaning of Vedic *mantra*s, 331, 334
as "our fathers," 229, 238, 241, 399
as paradigmatic, 241, 334–337, 339, 348, 355, 356–357, 389–390, 392, 428n.28
as paradigm for ascetic and meditation traditions, 334, 335–336, 339, 355, 356–357, 392
as paradigm for brahmin priests, 239, 241, 334–336, 339, 348, 355, 390
possessed special power, 230, 244, 248
and Prajāpati, 238–239, 240, 241, 500n.106
Prajāpati as primordial seer/*ṛṣi*, 39, 54, 238, 240, 241, 300, 349, 500n.96
preserved Vedic *mantra*s through their speech, 9, 43, 94, 112, 221, 227, 331, 332, 333, 334, 344, 356, 415
as primordial or preexistent, 238–239, 500nn.104, 106
as primordial *prāṇa*s, 238–239, 500nn.105, 106
and Puruṣa, 238–239
as regents of four quarters, 243–244, 245
role in cosmogonic process, 36, 37, 227, 230, 231, 238, 244, 245–246, 247, 248, 326, 335, 348,

349, 390, 398–399
role of heart in Vedic cognition, 232, 233, 235–236, 237, 328, 497n.37, 499nn.71, 76
role of mind in Vedic cognition, 230, 231, 236, 332, 497n.28, 499n.76
royal seers/*rājarṣis*, 244, 248, 502n.148
and sacrifice, 37, 231, 236–237, 238, 239–242, 243, 325, 326, 333, 334–335, 339, 348, 349, 390, 497n.28, 501n.120, 502n.125
and Sarasvatī, 90–91, 227, 234, 246–247
saw and heard, 8–9, 18, 221, 227, 229, 230–233, 237, 330, 332, 333, 334, 427n.27, 428n.28
saw and uttered, 237–238, 240, 241, 333, 501n.120
saw with mind's eye, 230, 231, 332, 497n.28
as seers of truth, 9, 228, 230, 231, 326
as seers of Vedic *mantras*, 43, 82, 228, 229, 237–238, 240, 241, 242, 244, 325, 335, 354, 356, 501n.113
as semidivine or divine, 229, 230, 231, 238–239, 243, 248, 326, 335, 336, 398–399, 500n.106, 501n.111
as separate class of beings, 243, 245
seven seers/*saptarṣis*, 229–230, 231, 238–239, 243–244, 247, 248, 251, 453n.238, 500nn.98, 105, 106, 501n.107, 503n.170
and Soma, 231, 234, 330, 498n.50
and speech/Vāc, 9, 34, 42–43, 94, 221, 227, 230–231, 232–233, 234–237, 239, 240–241, 245–246, 251, 330, 331, 332, 333, 334, 344, 349, 355, 356, 415, 428n.28
and *śruti*, 8–10, 18, 221, 227, 344, 385, 407, 415, 426n.24
and *stomas*, 231, 349
and *tapas*, 76, 235, 236–237, 238–239, 240–241, 242, 244–245, 246, 247–248, 328, 330, 335, 336, 339, 356, 357, 500n.106, 501n.113
termed *kavis*, 230, 234, 242, 496n.11
termed *medhāvins*, 230
termed *munis*, 230
termed *vipras*, 230, 232
terms for "seeing," 231
and Ursa Major, 239, 243
visions of, 231, 232–233, 234, 235–237, 496n.6
and Viṣṇu, 87, 244–245, 336, 503n.152
Viṣṇu as archetypal seer/*ṛṣi*, 244
Viśvakarman as, 36, 241
Vyāsa as, 82, 83, 247–248, 336, 453nn.238, 239, 503n.170, 503–504n.171, 504n.174
and yoga, 245
ṛta (cosmic ordering principle; truth)
and sacrifice, 33
and Vedic cognition, 231, 232
Rudra (deity). *See* Śiva
Ruegg, David Seyfort, 461n.398
Rupp, E. G., 424n.9
Russell, D. S., 505n.3
Ruth Rabbāh, 156, 273, 274–275, 276

Śabara, 116–118, 120, 121, 122, 462n.400, 463n.438
Šabbāṯ, 284, 285, 287, 288–290, 291–292, 293, 312
Sabbath, 163, 183
and Adam, 193, 475n.115
biblical readings on, 142, 156, 179
ten things created on eve of first

Sabbath *(continued)*
Sabbath, 148–149, 152, 175, 193, 195, 314, 470n.62, 471n.76, 481n.187, 488n.291, 532n.317
śabda (word). *See also śabda* and *artha*; word/Word
characteristics of, 117–119
and creator principle, 126–127
and *dhvani* or *nāda*, 117–119
encompasses unspoken thought and vocalized speech, 127
as eternal, 114, 116, 117–119, 122, 124, 125
as imperishable, 117–119
and individual words/*padas*, 118–119
as instrument of creation, 126–127
as noneternal, 113–114
as ontological category, 115, 118
and Prajāpati, 126
as preexistent, 126–127
Purāṇas as, 96
śabda-pramāṇa, 123, 462n.400
and Sanskrit *varṇas*, 118–119, 124
Vedic words/*śabdas* as blueprint or plan of creation, 80, 93, 110
śabda and *artha* (word and meaning). *See also ākṛti*; *śabda*
constitutive meaning of Vedic words, 347, 354, 387
relationship between, as eternal, 114, 120–122, 123, 124, 125, 128, 129
relationship between, as inherent/*autpattika*, 116, 119–121, 124, 125, 129, 347
relationship between, as uncreated/*apauruṣeya*, 120–121, 123, 463n.432
words as denoting universal classes/*ākṛtis*, 116, 120, 121–122, 124, 125, 128, 129
Śabdabrahman (Brahman embodied in the Word). *See also brahman*/Brahman; word/Word
Brahmā as, 104, 459n.351
Om as, 70, 108, 215, 357, 460n.378
as one of two forms of Brahman, 70, 87
and Sanskrit *varṇas*, 104, 459nn.351, 361
Śiva as, 104, 459n.361
Veda(s) as, 24, 29, 73, 103, 108–109, 213, 215, 216, 219, 227, 330, 355, 357, 396, 419
sacrifice, 77, 347–351, 389–390. *See also specific sacrifices*
as aniconic, 19, 416, 434n.58
in Āraṇyakas, 441n.52, 449n.161
and Brahmā, 103, 104–106, 351
and Brahman, 103, 351
brahmins as officiants of, 33, 60, 241, 339, 348, 350, 406, 419
and categories of priests, 33, 44, 54–55, 58, 60, 104, 239, 348
and creator principle, 389
discourse of, in Brāhmaṇas, 22, 43–44, 62, 63, 348, 349
fruits of, for patron of sacrifice/*yajamāna*, 43, 61, 449n.158
and gods, 19, 37, 38–39, 231, 238, 343, 348, 349, 350, 389, 401, 416, 439n.34
as means of creation, 33, 35, 36–39, 45–46, 55, 60, 63, 238, 326, 348–350, 389
as means of nourishing and magnifying gods, 343, 348, 350, 389, 401
as means of reconstituting Prajāpati, 45, 350–351
as means of regeneration and rectification of cosmic order, 30, 43, 44, 45–47, 55, 58, 60, 62, 333, 335, 343, 347–351, 356, 389–390, 401, 406, 443n.73

as means to attain specific ends, 43, 238, 240, 241, 333, 350, 500n.96, 502n.125, 538n.39
and meters, 37, 38–39, 349, 457n.311
and orders of reality, 33–34, 37–38, 44, 46, 58, 67–68, 241, 348, 349, 350, 502n.134
and Prajāpati, 30, 39, 44–47, 50, 54, 55, 58, 60, 61, 63, 126, 238, 349–351, 439n.34, 443n.81, 500n.96
and *pūjā*, 19, 456n.307
and Puruṣa, 37–38, 40, 41, 349
and *ṛta*, 33
and sacrificial boar, 87, 103
and sacrificial fires, 33, 58
sacrificial tradition, brahmanical custodians of, 326, 334–335, 390, 400, 406
sacrificial tradition, initiated by seers/*ṛṣis*, 239, 325, 326, 333, 334–335, 348, 390
in Saṃhitā period, 32–34
and seers/*ṛṣis*, 37, 231, 236–237, 238, 239–242, 243, 325, 326, 333, 334–335, 339, 348, 349, 390, 497n.28, 501n.120, 502n.125
and Śiva, 351
in Temple, 377
theurgic efficacy of, 343, 347–351, 389–390, 443n.73
and Veda(s), 11, 19, 29, 33, 34, 37–39, 41, 43, 44, 46–47, 50, 54, 55, 56, 58, 60, 61, 65, 73, 87, 103, 104–106, 126, 227, 231, 238, 240, 241, 249, 333, 339, 345, 346, 347–351, 352, 355, 401, 402, 406, 416, 427n.26, 431n.43, 443nn.77, 81, 446n.134, 457n.311, 502n.134
and Viṣṇu, 87, 103, 351
and Viśvakarman, 36
sacrificial boar
Brahmā as, 103
as Brahman, 103
cosmic body of, 87, 103
and earth, 87, 103, 459n.349
Nārāyaṇa as, 103
and sacrifice, 87, 103
and speech, 87, 103
and Veda(s), 87, 103, 454–455n.268
Viṣṇu as, 87, 103, 454–455n.268, 459n.349
and the waters, 87, 103
Ṣaḍviṃśa Brāhmaṇa, 44
sages. *See* rabbinic sages
Saguṇa Brahman. *See* Brahman
śākhās (Vedic branches or schools), 87, 88, 102, 103, 112, 128, 250, 345, 458n.339
sāmans (chants that constitute the Sāma-Veda), 62, 70, 437n.9, 438nn.10, 14, 439–440n.36. *See also* Sāma-Veda; and *specific sāmans*
and Brahmā, 40, 104, 105–106, 440n.36
and Brahman/Brahman-Ātman, 42, 66, 102, 112
and breath, 447n.148
and *bṛhat sāman*, 49, 445n.109
definition and use of term, 31–32, 33
and heaven, 59, 445n.109
as instrument of creation, 39, 231, 349
as limited, 29, 41
and mind, 49, 447n.148
as part of threefold Veda, 31, 34, 425n.16
and patron of sacrifice/*yajamāna*, 61
and Prajāpati, 39–40, 47, 49, 50, 54, 55, 60, 238, 349, 350, 444n.88, 459n.370, 500n.96
and Puruṣa, 37, 67–68

sāmans (continued)
and *ṛcs*, 49
and sacrifice, 33, 37, 39, 43, 54, 55, 60, 231, 238, 240, 348, 349–350, 457n.311
and Sāma-Veda, 7, 32, 250
and seers/*ṛṣis*, 237, 240, 501n.113
and Śiva, 88, 111
as Skambha, 41–42
as source of light, 59
and speech/Vāc, 47, 50, 54, 55, 60, 105–106
as *śruti*, 7
and *tamas*, 111
and *udgātṛ* priest, 33, 54, 60, 348
and Viṣṇu, 87, 102, 103
and Vyāsa, 249–250
Sāma-Veda, 29, 55, 73, 426n.19, 438n.11. *See also sāmans*
and Ātman, 66
and Being, 67, 457n.311
and Brahmā, 79, 104, 107, 110, 218
and breath, 58
and creator principle, 92
definition and use of term, 7, 31–32, 33
and eye, 38, 58
and heaven, 38, 51, 56–58, 60, 61, 70, 111, 215
and *m*, third constituent of Om, 57–58, 70, 79, 108, 111
and mind, 58
as part of threefold Veda, 31, 425n.16
and Prajāpati, 56–58, 62
and primordial utterance *svaḥ*, 51, 56–58, 61, 79, 111
and Puruṣa, 66, 91
and sacrificial boar, 103
and *sāmans*, 7, 32, 250
and Śiva, 104, 111
and speech, 62, 106–108, 110, 218
and sun/Sūrya/Āditya/Ravi, 38, 56–58, 70, 79, 215
and *tamas*, 111
and *udgātṛ* priest, 33, 44
and *vaiśyas*, 38, 61, 390
and Viṣṇu, 87
and Vyāsa, 250
šāmayim (heaven). *See* heaven
saṃgha (monastic community)
and Dhamma, 406–407, 555n.16, 555–556n.18
open to people of all social classes, 406–407, 555–556n.18
and quest for liberation/*nibbāna*, 406, 555–556n.18
Saṃhitās, 17, 23, 24, 25, 26, 29, 30, 31, 32–43, 66, 70, 71, 113, 116, 227, 229–237, 238, 348, 396, 453n.247. *See also* Atharva-Veda; *mantras*, Vedic; Ṛg-Veda; Sāma-Veda; Veda(s); Yajur-Veda
as center of canon, 6, 400–401
commentaries by Sāyaṇa, 124, 354, 539n.60
as core *śruti* texts, 7–8, 402
definition and use of term, 7, 33
discursive meaning/content secondary, 7, 11, 12, 97–98, 346–347, 388, 408, 418, 430n.39, 431n.43, 457n.323, 536–537n.12
division of one Veda into four Saṃhitās, 82, 96, 228, 247–248, 249–250, 453n.243, 457n.317, 503n.169, 504n.181
as fixed texts, 6, 97–98, 344, 345–346, 386, 417
interpretation of, 351–354, 388
and *mantras*, 7, 249–250, 425n.17
oral transmission of, 18, 82, 215, 223, 344–347, 385–387, 417–418
recitation of, 343, 344–351, 385–390
and *Tiruvāymoḻi*, 10
as Veda, 7, 425n.18

Śaṃkara, 124, 125–129, 221, 446n.132, 464n.457, 538n.55
Sāṃkhya, 99, 113, 114, 353
  Kārikā-Sāṃkhya, 74, 454n.256, 458n.328
  Proto-Sāṃkhya, 71–72, 74, 75, 81, 84, 85, 451n.205
Sāṃkhya-Kārikā, 74
Sāṃkhya-Pravacana-Sūtras, 114, 461n.395
2 Samuel, 313
R. Samuel b. Naḥman, 184, 189, 279, 308, 482n.207, 525n.244, 527n.259, 543n.20
Sanders, E. P., 554n.14
Sanders, James A., 422n.8
Sanhedrin, 176, 265
Śāṅkhāyana Āraṇyaka, 32
Sanskrit. *See also śabda*; *śabda* and *artha*; *varṇas*
  constitutive meaning of Vedic words, 347, 354, 387
  characteristics of word/*śabda*, 117–119
  as language of Aryans, 3, 117, 397, 399
  as language of *dharma*, 117
  as language of the gods, 399
  relationship between name/*nāma* and form/*rūpa*, 59, 69, 110, 127, 129, 221, 347, 447–448n.149
  relationship between Vedic sentence/*vākya* and meaning/*artha*, 116, 122, 124, 125, 463n.438
  relationship between word/*śabda* and meaning/*artha*, 114, 116, 119–122, 123, 124, 125, 128, 129, 346–347, 463n.432
  as sacred language, 3, 18, 397, 408
  as sound system composed of phones/*varṇas*, 18
  Vedic language as natural language, 347
  Vedic language contrasted with ordinary human language, 117, 122
  Vedic word order as eternal, 122
saptadaśa (seventeen-versed *stoma*), 39, 106
Sarason, Richard S., 468n.46
Sarasvatī (goddess)
  and Brahmā, 89–90, 105
  and *gāyatrī*/Gāyatrī or *sāvitrī*/Sāvitrī, 89–90, 91, 105, 455n.282
  as goddess of speech, 89–90, 105, 246
  as inspirer of cognitions and hymns, 90–91, 227, 234, 246–247
  and light, 246
  as Mother of Vedas, 90, 455n.282
  and Sanskrit *varṇas*, 90, 246
  and Sarasvat, 48
  and seers/*ṛṣis*, 90–91, 227, 234, 246–247
  and speech/Vāc, 48, 89–90, 105, 234, 246, 247, 444n.99, 455n.283
  and Veda(s), 90–91, 105, 227, 234, 246–247, 455n.282
  and Viṣṇu, 90, 247
  and Vyāsa, 247
  and the waters, 90
  and Yājñavalkya, 246
sarga (primary creation), 75, 95, 99, 100, 101, 452n.217, 454n.257
Śar Tôrāh
  and adjuration of angels, 261–262
  and Hêḵālôṯ traditions, 261–262, 507n.17, 507–508n.20, 508n.21
  and mastery of Torah, 261–262, 507–508n.20
Sarug, Israel, 211, 495n.386
śastras (hymns of praise), 54

śastras (continued)
and Brahmā, 104
and Prajāpati, 55, 126
śāstras (normative teachings or treatises)
and Brahmā, 96, 97, 105
and Purāṇas, 96, 97, 99, 105
and Veda(s), 8–9
and Viṣṇu, 96
Sastri, Gaurinath, 461n.398
sat (existence), 63, 444–445n.105
Śatapatha Brāhmaṇa, 44, 45, 48–49, 50–53, 54, 57, 59, 126, 230, 238–239, 240, 241, 246, 352
sattva (purity; one of the three *guṇas*)
and *atharvans*, 111
and midregions, 111
and Om, 108, 111
and primordial utterance *bhuvaḥ*, 111
and *u*, second constituent of Om, 111
and Viṣṇu, 111
and Yajur-Veda, 111
and *yajus*es, 111
Saussure, Ferdinand de, 414
Savitṛ (deity), 234, 455n.293
sāvitrī/Sāvitrī (three-lined *gāyatrī mantra*; goddess). *See gāyatrī*/Gāyatrī
Sāyaṇa, 124, 354, 539n.60
Schäfer, Peter, 261, 264, 433n.51, 505n.5, 507nn.18, 19, 508n.22, 513n.103, 519n.169, 524nn.222, 225, 532n.310
Scharbau, Carl Anders, 440–441n.43
Scholem, Gershom G., 197, 258, 261, 264, 374, 432n.51, 433nn.51–53, 477n.142, 490nn.317, 319, 491nn.321, 324–328, 492nn.334, 335, 337, 493n.338, 495nn.383, 385, 386, 504n.1, 505nn.5–7, 506nn.10, 11, 15, 16, 507nn.17, 19, 527nn.259, 262, 528n.272, 541n.12, 544n.35, 545nn.41, 42, 548n.72, 551n.121
Schultz, Joseph P., 513n.103
Scott, R. B. Y., 465n.6
scribal tradition. *See also* scribes; transmission of Sefer Torah
laws for preparing and preserving Torah scroll, 359–360, 386, 540n.1
Moses as scribe of God, 13, 223, 331, 334, 337, 359–360
not a single letter may be added or omitted, 169, 177, 199, 360–361
and preservation of consonantal text, 169, 361
rabbinic sages as custodians of, 337
and verbatim reproduction of written text, 177, 199, 337, 359–361, 386, 387, 395–396, 417
writing of Torah scroll, as holy work, 360, 386
writing of Torah scroll, cosmic ramifications of, 177, 199, 360–361
writing of Torah scroll, ritual ramifications of, 199, 360–361
writing of Torah scroll, tantamount to "making" God, 361
scribes. *See also* scribal tradition
attitude and qualifications of, 360
authority of, 158, 174, 182
of low social standing in India, 344
Moses as scribe of God, 13, 223, 331, 334, 337, 359–360
words of, and words of Written Torah, 158, 174, 182
words of, not to be written down, 182

scripture. *See also* canon; Torah; Veda(s)
authority of, ix, x, 4, 5, 395, 413
in biblical and orientalist scholarship, 3–4
as blueprint or plan of creation, 17, 213, 214–215, 218, 219
comparative studies of, 423–424n.9
as concrete text, ix–x, 17, 213, 215
as constitutive category of brahmanical and rabbinic traditions, ix–x, 2–3, 21, 398–403
as constitutive category of Islamic traditions, 409
as cosmological principle or cosmic reality, ix–x, 5–6, 16–17, 213, 397, 420
cosmological status of, 5
and creator principle, 17, 213, 214, 217, 219
as divine language, 17, 213, 214, 217–218
as essence of ultimate reality, 17, 213, 217, 219
form of, in studies of canon, 4
four levels of, 17, 213–216, 217–219
function of, ix, 5, 395, 413, 425n.11
as general religious category, 4, 5, 423n.9, 424n.9
generic idea of, 557n.27
heavenly book/*kitāb* as archetype of all scripture, 410, 412, 557n.33, 557–558n.37
as knowledge/wisdom, 17, 213, 214, 216, 217, 219, 434n.54
and levels of creation, 17, 213
as multileveled, ix–x, 5, 17, 213, 397
oral dimensions of, 5, 16, 344, 420, 423n.9
as relational category, x, 4, 5
sacred status of, 4
as "sacred writing" or "holy writ," 5, 16, 424n.9
as source of creation, 17, 214, 216, 219
and speech, 214, 216, 217–218, 219
and stages of creation, 17, 216–219
successive scriptural revelations, 410–411, 412, 557n.35
as supratextual category, ix–x, 5, 16, 215–216, 395, 396, 420
as Word, ix–x, 16–17, 213, 215–216, 219, 395, 403
Sēḏer 'Ēliyyāhû Rabbāh, 142, 180
Sēḏer 'Ēliyyāhû Zûṭā', 180, 362–363
Sefer Torah (Book of the Torah; Torah scroll), 24, 25, 26, 162. *See also* Pentateuch; Torah; Written Torah
and Ark of the Covenant, 359, 416, 514n.104, 522–523n.211
book as outer body of Torah, 15, 420
as center of canon, 6, 400–401
as closed and open, 361–362
consonants alone given, without vowels or punctuation, 169, 210, 361, 368, 540n.7
as consummate expression of Word of God, 14, 395, 396–397
as core revelation, 13, 14, 395–396
definition and use of term, 12
as fixed text, 6, 169, 177, 210, 360–362, 368, 386, 395–396
as form of God, 361, 417, 546n.51
as gross manifestation of supernal Torah, 222, 415
iconic veneration of, 19, 361, 386, 416–417, 546n.51
interpretation of, 359, 361–373, 386–388
multiple vocalizations of consonantal text, 210, 361–362, 368,

Sefer Torah *(continued)*
478n.149, 540n.7, 544–545n.35
ornamentation of, 386, 416
Pentateuch as, 12, 385
primordial wisdom/Torah embodied in, 15, 136, 146, 359, 362
procession of, 416–417
public reading of, 338, 339, 386, 387–388, 391
and *s*ᵉ*p̄îrôṯ*, 361, 546n.51
as verbatim record of words of God, 13, 359
as visible form or embodiment of Word of God, 18, 19, 360, 363, 386, 416–417
written transmission of, 18, 223, 334, 359–361, 385–387, 395–396, 416, 540n.1
Seir, 254, 266, 273–274, 286, 311, 316
šēm (name; Name of God), 24, 131, 146, 192, 213. *See also* Name of God
sentence meaning. *See vākyartha*
Sēp̄er ha-Bāhîr, 534n.343
Sēp̄er ha-Ḥayyîm, 491n.326
Sēp̄er ha-Yiḥûḏ, 360–361, 492n.336, 540nn.4, 5
*Sēp̄er Y*ᵉ*ṣîrāh*, 168, 177, 477–478n.142
*s*ᵉ*p̄îrôṯ* (divine emanations), 214, 491n.320. *See also specific s*ᵉ*p̄îrôṯ*
activation of, through practice of Torah, 380–381
and body of divine anthropos, 197, 380
and commandments/*mitzvot*, 380–381
and descent of God, 315–316, 318
as divine hypostases, 205–206
and 'Ên-Sôp̄, 196–197, 198, 205, 207, 209–210
enumeration of, 196–197
and four forms of Torah, 212, 215
and four letters of Tetragrammaton, 208–209, 212, 215
and four worlds, 212, 215
and glory of God, 317–318, 320–321
and interpretation of Torah, 210, 368, 370–372, 373, 382, 392, 546n.51, 547n.58
and light, 197, 205, 318–319, 320, 371, 382
as manifest Godhead in relation to creation, 196–197, 200, 202, 317–318
and mysteries of creation, 318–319
and Name of God, 197, 200, 208–209, 212, 215, 317, 533n.334
as names of God, 197, 201
and revelation of Torah, 315–324, 332–333, 370–371, 373, 392, 534n.343
role in cosmogonic process, 205–206, 209, 216–219, 315, 317–318
and social hierarchy of Israelites, 323–324
and stages of manifestation of Torah, 198, 204, 208–210, 212, 315, 320
and stages of unfoldment of divine language, 198, 204–209, 494n.362
and study of Torah, 370–372, 373, 380, 381, 382, 392, 546n.51, 547n.58
as supernal Man, 197, 380
and ten words of creation/ *ma'ămārôṯ*, 197, 200, 204, 317
and Ten Words of revelation/Ten Commandments, 200, 317, 320, 322–323, 333
and Torah, 132, 197–198, 200, 201, 202, 204, 208–210, 212, 215, 315, 317, 320, 361, 367,

369, 370–372, 373, 380–381, 382, 392, 493n.341, 546n.51
vision of, attained by kabbalist exegete, 370–372, 373, 382, 392, 546n.51, 547n.58
vision of, attained by Moses, 315–316, 320, 332–333, 371, 373, 392
vision of, attained by people of Israel, 315, 318–320, 332–333, 370–371, 534n.343
and voices of God, 318–319
as world of divine language, 197, 204
and world of emanation/*'ăṣîlûṯ*, 211
Shammai, 148
Shammai, school of, 166, 486n.255
Sharma, Arvind, 551n.2
Shavuot, 182, 262–264, 272, 293, 338, 514n.112, 519–520n.171, 524n.222, 528–529n.272
Shekhinah (divine presence). *See also* Malkûṯ
and Abraham, 320
and Ark of the Covenant, 514n.104
and commandments/*mitzvot*, 381, 550n.119
descent from heaven, 256, 276–278, 290
and Ezekiel, 319–320, 534n.347
and interpretation of Torah, 366, 370–371, 373, 392, 547n.55
and Isaac, 320
and Isaiah, 320, 534n.347
and Jacob, 320
and kabbalist exegete, 370–371, 373, 392, 547n.55
and light, 276, 319, 547n.55
as Malkûṯ, 198, 206, 207, 209, 212, 217, 315, 318, 319–320, 370–371, 373, 381, 392, 493n.341, 534nn.343, 347, 352, 547n.55, 547n.59, 550n.119
and Moses, 276, 289, 301, 302, 373, 392, 520n.175, 524n.226
and patriarchs, 320
and people of Israel, 257, 279, 303, 307, 315, 319, 331, 366, 371, 527n.259, 534n.343
and practice of Torah, 381, 550n.119
and prophets, 319–320, 534n.352, 547n.59
rabbinic sages as embodiment of, 158, 544n.28
and revelation of Torah, 256, 257, 276–278, 279, 289, 290, 291, 301, 302, 303, 307, 315, 318, 319, 366, 371, 373, 520nn.175, 176, 524n.226, 525n.241, 527n.259, 534n.343
and study of Torah, 366, 370–371, 373, 381, 392, 547n.55
and Torah, 198, 209, 212, 256, 276–278, 320, 331, 370, 373, 381, 392, 416, 493n.341, 514n.104
śikṣā (science of pronunciation of Vedic *mantras*), 88, 89, 345, 538n.46
Silburn, Liliane, 440n.39
R. Simai, 291–292, 305, 515n.118, 521n.181, 526n.258, 527n.262
R. Simeon b. Abba, 163
R. Simeon b. Lakish, 161–162, 172, 175, 191, 281, 285, 287–288, 299, 307, 308, 529n.273
R. Simeon b. Yoḥai, 163, 196, 273, 279, 280, 283, 295, 305, 321, 516n.125, 547nn.55, 57
Simeon the Righteous, 137, 147–148, 375–376, 467n.21, 470n.61
R. Simlai, 286, 482n.195, 512n.87
R. Simon b. Pazzi, 274, 275, 277, 477n.141, 522nn.207, 209, 529n.283

Sinai, Mount. *See* revelation of Torah
Sip̄rā', 143, 150, 151, 265–266
Sip̄rê on Deuteronomy, 150, 151, 152, 153, 154, 155, 160, 175, 265, 266, 267, 268–269, 270–271
Sip̄rê on Numbers, 150, 151, 155, 171
Sip̄rê Zûṭā', 150
sit̲rê tôrāh (secrets of the Torah), 15, 158, 174, 363. *See also rāzê tôrāh*; Torah: secrets or mysteries of
šî'ûr qômāh (measurement of the body of God), 505n.7, 506n.15, 528n.272
Śiva (deity)
  and *bhakti* traditions or stream, 72, 81, 94
  and Brahmā, 86, 104, 111
  as Brahman/Brahman-Ātman, 30, 73, 86, 87, 88, 100, 102, 103–104, 336, 351
  cosmic body of, 88, 104, 351, 459n.361
  as destroyer, 86, 111
  and heaven, 111
  and knowledge, 102, 103–104
  and *m*, third constituent of Om, 111
  as Nirguṇa Brahman, 100
  and orders of reality, 111
  and primordial utterance *svaḥ*, 111
  as Śabdabrahman, 104, 459n.361
  and sacrifice, 351
  as Saguṇa Brahman, 104
  and *sāmans*, 111
  and Sāma-Veda, 111
  and Sanskrit *varṇas*, 104, 459n.361
  and *tamas*, 111
  as ultimate source of creation, 100
  and Veda(s), 30, 73, 87, 88, 99, 102, 103–104, 111, 336, 351
  and Viṣṇu, 86, 100, 111
  as Word/Śabdabrahman, 104
Śiva Purāṇa, 73, 100, 103–104, 106
six or seven things created prior to the world, 160, 175, 192–193, 470n.64, 472n.81, 480n.185, 491n.323
Skambha (support; primordial foundation of the cosmos)
  as Brahman, 41, 53, 66, 440n.41
  cosmic body of, 41–42, 53, 66
  and gods, 41
  and Prajāpati, 41, 53
  and three worlds, 41
  and Veda(s), 41–42, 53, 66, 440n.42
Slonimsky, Henry, 476n.129, 542n.16
Smith, Brian K., 10, 11, 45, 46, 429nn.31–33, 430nn.39, 42, 443nn.70, 74–76, 448n.155, 449n.158, 552n.5
Smith, Jonathan Z., 6, 19–20, 420, 425nn.14, 15, 431n.43, 434–435n.61, 435nn.62, 64, 436n.64, 436–437n.65, 437n.66, 559n.57
Smith, Wilfred Cantwell, 4, 397, 423n.9, 551n.1, 552n.6, 556nn.24, 25
smṛti ("that which was remembered"; designation for certain authoritative post-Vedic texts)
  authority of, 126
  as composed by personal authors, 8
  and creator principle, 76–77
  definition and use of term, 7–8, 426n.23
  and *dharma*, 8, 402, 427n.26
  Dharma-Śāstras as, 8, 402
  didactic function of, 97
  epics/Itihāsas as, 8

included within purview of Veda, 8–9, 402, 427n.26
Mahābhārata as, 72
and Manu, 76–77
Manu-Smṛti as, 72, 76–77
as open-ended category, 8
Purāṇas as, 8, 72
Rāmcaritmānas as, 418
as source of proof texts, 125–126, 127–128, 129, 464n.456
and *śruti*, 7–9, 22, 72, 76, 97, 126, 402, 426nn.22, 23, 427n.26
as teachings "remembered" from lost Vedic texts, 8, 10
as "that which was remembered," 7, 8

sôḏ (mystical meaning), 369, 370, 373, 545nn.41, 42

Soma (deity), 349
as inspirer of cognitions and hymns, 234, 330
and seers/*ṛṣi*s, 231, 234, 330, 498n.50

Song of Songs, 161–162, 169, 265, 272, 277, 282, 293, 505n.7

Song of Songs Rabbāh, 156, 158, 161, 168, 169, 172, 191, 272, 273, 274–275, 276–277, 278–280, 281, 282–283, 284, 289, 293, 296, 301, 309

sôp̄ᵉrîm (scribes). *See* scribal tradition; scribes

soul
and body, 138, 554n.15
and light, 190
souls of gentiles departed, 296
souls of people of Israel departed, 282–282, 293, 309, 516n.124, 517n.139
of Torah, 15, 369–370, 374, 382, 392, 402, 420

speech, 343. *See also dāḇār*; *dîbbēr*; *dîbbûr*; language; language, divine; *ma'ămārôṯ*; Vāc; word/Word
as aspect of word/Word, 16–17, 216
and blueprint or plan of creation, 24, 29, 47, 73, 102, 216, 217–218, 221, 227
and Brahmā, 89–90, 101–102, 105–111, 114, 126, 127, 218, 220
and *brahman*/Brahman, 103, 227, 246
creative power of, 29, 32, 35, 42, 43, 47–55, 59, 60, 62, 68–69, 73, 81, 90, 102, 108–111, 112, 126–127, 129, 154, 167, 169–170, 171, 177–178, 189, 195, 203, 208, 214, 216, 217–218, 219, 220, 221, 227, 446n.134, 479n.159, 482n.207, 550n.101
and creator principle, 68–69, 73, 214, 217–218, 219, 221, 330, 440n.42
and earth, 38, 58
as eternal, 126, 127, 330, 334
as expressed and unexpressed, 47, 49, 50, 52–53, 55, 171, 217, 444n.102, 445n.110
as female principle, 34, 48, 207, 216–217
and fire/Agni, 38, 58
and *gāyatrī*/Gāyatrī or *sāvitrī*/Sāvitrī, 89–90, 91, 105, 106–109
God as "He who spoke and the world came into being," 154, 167, 170, 177–178, 472n.85
"And God said," 170, 171, 178, 189–190, 195, 207, 208, 479n.159, 483n.210
and knowledge/wisdom, 16–17, 207, 216–219
levels of, 49–53, 441n.44
as means to stop expansion of world, 170, 178, 189, 195, 483n.209
and mind, 48–49, 444nn.98, 102, 444–445n.105

speech *(continued)*
and Om, 58, 106–109
and Prajāpati, 30, 47–53, 54–56, 60, 62, 68, 89, 126, 127, 446n.134
and primordial utterance *bhūḥ*, 58
and Puruṣa, 68
and *rathantara sāman*, 49
and *ṛcs*, 49
and Ṛg-Veda, 38, 58
and sacrificial boar, 87, 103
and Sanskrit *varṇas*, 90, 106–109, 221, 246
and Sarasvatī, 48, 89–90, 105, 234, 246, 247, 455n.283
and scripture, 214, 216, 217–218, 219
and seers/*ṛṣis*, 9, 34, 42–43, 94, 221, 227, 230–231, 232–233, 234–237, 245–246, 251, 330, 331, 332, 333, 334, 344, 349, 355, 356, 415, 428n.28
stages of unfoldment of, 106–109
and thought, 16–17, 171, 204–207, 232–233, 236, 237
and three *vyāhṛtis*, 51, 54, 58, 59, 62, 106–109
and three worlds, 50–51, 54, 217
and Torah, 171, 203, 214, 216–218, 219, 331, 334, 550n.101
as transcendent, 50, 52, 217, 246
and Veda(s), 9, 24, 29, 30, 32, 34, 35, 42–43, 47–56, 58, 59, 60, 62, 68–69, 73, 81, 89, 90, 94, 101, 102, 105–111, 112, 114, 126–127, 129, 214, 216–218, 219, 220, 221, 227, 230–231, 232, 233, 234–237, 245, 246, 251, 330, 331, 332, 333, 334, 344, 349, 354, 355, 356, 415, 427n.26, 428n.28, 431n.43, 440n.42, 446n.134
and Viṣṇu, 90, 247, 503n.164, 504n.181
and Viśvakarman, 36
and Vyāsa, 247, 504n.181
sphoṭa (unitary word-entity distinct from the *varṇas*), 116, 118, 122, 124, 461n.398
Śrauta-Sūtras, 71, 335, 345
Śrīdhara, 108
śrotriyas (brahmin reciters of the Veda[s]), 345–347, 355, 385–388, 419
śruti ("that which was heard"; designation for Veda[s]). *See also* cognition of Veda(s); *ṛṣi*(s)
Āraṇyakas as, 7–8, 10
and *bhakti* texts, 10, 391
and Brahmā, 250
Brāhmaṇas as, 7–8, 10, 402
as closed, 7–8
as cognition of seers/*ṛṣis*, 8–10, 18, 221, 227, 344, 385, 407, 415, 426n.24, 428n.28
definition and use of term, 7–9, 426nn.23, 24
and *dharma*, 119, 427n.26
as eternal, 250
extension of domain of term, 7–8, 10, 402, 426n.21
as living word, 344
and Prajāpati, 250
sacramental function of, 97, 539n.64
and *smṛti*, 7–9, 22, 72, 76, 97, 126, 402, 426nn.22, 23, 427n.26
as source of proof texts, 126, 127, 129, 464n.457
as "that which was heard," 7, 9, 18, 221, 227, 233, 236, 344, 385, 407, 415, 428n.28
Upaniṣads as, 7–8, 10, 402, 426n.21
Veda(s) as, 7–9, 18, 72, 76, 93, 119, 126, 221, 227, 250, 344, 355, 385, 391, 396, 402, 407, 415, 418, 426nn.21, 24, 427n.26, 428n.28, 539n.64

Vedic *mantras* or Saṃhitās as core *śruti* texts, 7–8, 9, 354, 395–396, 402
as Vedic texts "heard" in recitation, 8–9, 385
Staal, J. Frits, 344, 346–347, 431n.43, 440n.43, 536nn.3, 9, 11, 12, 537nn.14, 15, 538n.41, 559n.54
Stemberger, Günter, 468n.42, 470n.61, 471n.71
Stendahl, Krister, 552n.9
Stern, David, 542n.16
Stietencron, Heinrich von, 421n.1
Stock, Brian, 421n.2
Stoic traditions, 136, 138
stomas (lauds), 439–440n.36, 447n.149
and Brahmā, 104, 105–106, 440n.36
and Prajāpati, 39–40, 47, 59, 459n.370
and seers/*ṛṣis*, 231, 349
stotras (lauds)
and Prajāpati, 55, 126
Strack, Hermann L., 468n.42, 470n.61, 471n.71
Strauss, Otto, 461n.398
structuralism, 434n.57
study of Torah, 5, 24, 26, 223, 374–381, 385, 388–390, 395. *See also* interpretation of Torah
'am hā-'āreṣ excluded from, 391
circumscribed by rabbinic sages, 391
and "contemplating through seeing"/*'istakkēl*, 371, 372, 378–379, 389, 547n.60, 550n.101
and "descender to the Merkabah," 259
emphasis on cognitive over phonic dimension of words, 18, 361–373, 386–388
and final redemption, 157
and fire, 172, 179, 281, 366, 480n.173, 517n.135
and glory of God, 366, 372, 546n.51
as hallmark of life of a sage, 148
importance of, 154, 157–158, 161, 169, 174, 191–192, 359, 380
through interpretation, 18, 338, 359, 386–388
for its own sake, 154, 549n.86
and light, 172, 178, 190–191, 196, 366, 371, 382, 393, 491n.322, 547nn.55, 57
and Malḵûṯ/Shekhinah or Oral Torah, 370–371, 373, 381, 392, 547n.55
as means of augmenting God's power, 359, 375, 378, 380, 388–389, 401
as means of creation, 380
as means of maintaining cosmos, 204, 359, 375–376, 378–380, 388–390, 401, 533n.326, 549n.86, 550n.104
as means of uniting male and female aspects of Godhead, 378, 381
and *s*[e]*p̄îrôṯ*, 370–372, 373, 380, 381, 382, 392, 546n.51, 547n.58
and Shekhinah, 366, 370–371, 373, 381, 392, 547n.55
and theodicy, 158–159
theurgic efficacy of, 359, 374–381, 388–390, 391
and Tip̄'ereṯ or Written Torah, 370–372, 373, 381, 392, 547n.58
women excluded from, 391
study of Veda(s), 5, 24, 26, 223, 352, 385, 395. *See also* recitation of Vedic Saṃhitās
discursive meaning of Vedic *mantras* secondary, 12, 97–98, 343, 346–347, 351, 387, 388, 408, 418, 419, 457n.323, 536–537n.12

study of Veda(s) *(continued)*
emphasis on memorization and recitation, 18, 346, 351, 354, 386–388, 536–537n.12
emphasis on phonic over cognitive dimension of words, 18, 346–347, 386–388
emphasis on phonology over semantics, 343, 346–347, 351, 354, 386–388, 431n.43
emphasis on sound over meaning, 97–98, 346–347, 351, 386–388, 408, 418, 419, 457n.323
termed *svādhyāya*, 346
understanding and interpretation secondary, 346–347, 351, 354, 355, 387, 536–537n.12
Subbu Reddiar, N., 429n.34
śūdras (servants and manual laborers)
and access to Mahābhārata, 82
and access to Purāṇas, 97, 98, 457n.322
and *bhakti* practices, 94
excluded from reciting or hearing Veda(s), 82, 97, 355, 390–391, 539n.65
and Prajāpati, 40
Sûkkāh, 290, 291
Sukthankar, V. S., 452n.231
Sullivan, Bruce M., 82–83, 453nn.243, 248, 249, 504n.174
sun. *See* Sūrya
Śunaḥśepa (Vedic seer), 240, 501n.120
Sūrya or Āditya or Ravi (sun; sun god), 447n.141
and eye, 38, 58
and heaven, 38, 56–58, 70, 215
and *m*, third constituent of Om, 57–58, 70
and primordial utterance *svaḥ*, 56–58
and Sāma-Veda, 38, 56–58, 70, 79, 215
and *vaiśyas*, 38
and Yājñavalkya, 246, 503n.166
and *yajus*es, 246, 503n.166
svaḥ (sacred utterance; sound correlative of heaven), 68
and eye, 58
and heaven, 51, 54, 56–58, 61, 92, 109, 111
and *m*, third constituent of Om, 57–58, 79, 106, 108, 109, 111
and Om, 57–58, 79, 92–93, 106–109, 111, 357
as root *mantra*, 357
and Sāma-Veda, 51, 56–58, 61, 79, 111
and Śiva, 111
and speech, 51, 54, 59, 106–109
and sun/Sūrya/Āditya, 56–58
and *tamas*, 111
and *vaiśyas*, 54, 61
Svayambhū (the Self-existent), 76, 90, 126
Śvetāśvatara Upaniṣad, 66–67, 71
symbol
Christ as, 157, 403
definition and use of term, 421n.5
Dhamma as, 406
ontological status of, 436n.64
Torah as, ix–x, 2, 5, 6, 12–14, 15, 131, 135, 157, 159, 395, 396, 400, 401, 402, 412, 421n.5
Veda as, ix–x, 2, 5, 6, 7–8, 11–12, 395, 396, 400, 401, 412, 421n.5
synagogue traditions
biblical readings, 142, 156, 179, 181, 262, 263, 272
and Hêḵālôṯ traditions, 262–264, 507n.19, 508n.22, 524n.222, 532n.310
and iconic veneration of Torah scroll, 361, 386, 416–417, 546n.51
and procession of Torah, 416–417
and public reading of Torah, 338, 339, 386, 387–388, 391

and rabbinic Merkabah traditions, 258, 262–264, 508n.23, 514n.112, 519–520n.171, 524n.222, 528–529n.272, 532n.310
and Shavuot, 182, 262–264, 272, 293, 338, 514n.112, 519–520n.171, 524n.222, 528–529n.272

Ta'ănît, 265
Tabernacle
and Ark of the Covenant, 190, 514n.104, 522–523n.211
and Bezalel, 177, 185
and establishment of creation, 317, 522n.211
tablets of Ten Commandments, 488n.291. *See also lûḥôṯ*; Ten Commandments
and Adam, 193
contained entire Torah, 280
left and right tablets, 321–322
and light, 280, 308
manner in which written, 280, 292, 321, 521n.189
material of, 280
and Moses, 254, 308, 310, 312, 482n.204, 532–533n.319
number of commandments on each tablet, 280, 321–322
as one of ten things created on eve of first Sabbath, 148–149, 152, 175, 193, 314, 470n.62, 471n.76, 481n.187, 532n.317
and revelation of Torah, 193, 254, 257, 270, 280, 292, 308, 310, 312, 314, 321–322, 323, 332, 482n.204, 532–533n.319
of transmundane origin, 314, 321
as work of God, 314, 321, 470n.62, 486n.257
writing flew away, 314, 482n.204, 532–533n.319
written by God, 193, 254, 280, 314, 321, 470n.62
Tad Ekam (That One), 35, 36, 40
Taittirīya Brāhmaṇa, 44, 47–48, 59, 240–241
Taittirīya Saṃhitā or Black Yajur-Veda, 29, 31, 39–40, 41, 44, 45, 47, 54, 402, 425n.17. *See also* Yajur-Veda
Taittirīya Upaniṣad, 66, 67, 68
Talmud, 185. *See also* Babylonian Talmud; Jerusalem Talmud
as Oral Torah, 12–13, 141, 158, 173, 182, 273, 285, 294, 485n.232, 512n.75
as Torah, 151, 265
and Written Torah, 174
tamas (inertia; one of the three *guṇas*)
and *atharvans*, 111
and heaven, 111
and *m*, third constituent of Om, 111
and Om, 108, 111
and primordial utterance *svaḥ*, 111
and *sāmans*, 111
and Sāma-Veda, 111
and Śiva, 111
Tanakh. *See* Hebrew Bible
R. Tanḥum, 519n.168, 520n.175, 524n.226
Tanḥûmā', 181, 182, 183, 184–186, 189, 194, 294–296, 303, 304, 305, 306, 309–310, 311
R. Tanḥuma b. Abba, 179–180, 181–182, 190, 296, 298, 484n.224, 522n.207, 525n.228, 530n.288
Tanḥûmā' Yᵉlammᵉḏēnû Midrashim, 142, 145, 179–191, 293–310, 484n.226. *See also specific Midrashim*
distinguishing features of, 179–181
homiletical Midrashim, 179–181

R. Tanḥum b. Ḥanilai, 278, 282, 305
Tannaitic Midrashim, 23, 132, 145, 150–155, 156, 157, 167, 172–173, 181, 265–272, 273–274, 278, 281, 285, 291, 293, 470–471n.70. *See also specific Midrashim*
  authority of, 152
  as collections of *baraitot*, 150
  exegetical Midrashim, 150, 152
  granted status of Torah, 152
  as Mid̠r^e^šê Hălāk̠āh, 150, 155
  Type A, from school of R. Ishmael, 150, 471n.71
  Type B, from school of R. Akiba, 150, 471n.71
tantric traditions
  and *mantras*, 357, 393
  and meditation, 357, 393
  and Purāṇas, 94
  and Veda(s), 10–11, 429n.37
tapas (meditation; austerity). *See also* meditation
  and ascetic traditions, 335, 339, 439n.23
  and Brahmā, 105, 246
  creative power of, 35, 45, 52, 57, 68, 247
  and creator principle, 76–77
  definition and use of term, 439n.23
  and gods, 240–241, 246, 330
  as means to access mysteries of creation, 235, 241, 246, 247–248
  as means to attain specific ends, 241
  as means to realize Brahman/Brahman-Ātman, 242, 244–245, 328, 330, 335, 336, 357
  as means to realize transcendent Veda, 328, 330, 339, 356, 357
  as means to Vedic cognition, 76, 235, 236–237, 240–241, 246, 248, 328, 330, 336, 339, 356, 357, 501n.113
  and meditation, 241, 242, 328, 357, 439n.23, 539n.69
  and meditation traditions, 335, 339, 356, 357
  and Prajāpati, 45, 52, 54, 57, 68
  and seers/*ṛṣis*, 76, 235, 236–237, 238–239, 240–241, 242, 244–245, 246, 247–248, 328, 330, 335, 336, 339, 356, 357, 500n.106, 501n.113
  and Vyāsa, 247–248
Targum Neofiti 1, 472n.82, 476nn.122, 127
Targum Onkelos, 476n.122
Targum Pseudo-Jonathan, 472n.82, 476n.122
Targums, 191, 472n.82, 476nn.122, 127. *See also specific Targums*
R. Tarphon, 311
tattvas (elementary principles), 74, 75, 78, 81, 84, 85, 99, 100, 101, 451nn.207, 214, 454nn.256, 257, 458n.328
Taylor, Rodney L., 424n.9
taxonomies. *See* correspondences
t^e^b̠ûnāh (understanding), 176, 177, 185, 195, 298
Temple, 154, 488n.287
  and Ark of the Covenant, 514n.104, 522–523n.211
  and establishment of creation, 512–513n.91, 522n.211
  heavenly Temple, 301
  as one of four inheritances, 472n.79
  as one of God's special creations/possessions, 149, 153, 471n.78, 481n.185
  as one of six or seven things created prior to the world, 160, 175, 193, 470n.64, 480n.185
  sacrifice in, 377
  Temple service as one of three

things upon which the world stands, 375–376, 470n.61, 522n.211
and wisdom, 136
Ten Commandments or Ten Words of revelation, 378. *See also* tablets of Ten Commandments
and gentile nations, 285, 296–297
and glory of God, 317–318, 320–321, 323
and mysteries of creation, 321, 322–323, 333
and Name of God, 200, 296–297, 317
only first two commandments spoken directly by God, 272, 280, 284, 294, 311, 315, 511n.70, 516n.124, 521n.190
and people of Israel, 222, 254, 255, 256, 257, 268, 269, 270–272, 275–276, 279–280, 282, 284, 291, 293, 294, 296–297, 306, 310, 311, 314–315, 317–318, 320–324, 328, 332, 333, 337, 511n.70, 516n.124, 517n.140, 521n.190, 530n.290
and revelation of Torah, 222, 254, 255, 256, 257, 268, 269, 270–272, 275–276, 279–280, 282, 284, 285, 289, 291, 293, 294, 296–297, 298–299, 306, 310, 311, 314–315, 317–318, 320–324, 328, 332, 333, 334, 337, 511n.70, 516n.124, 517n.140, 521n.190, 530n.290
and *s^e^pîrôṯ*, 200, 317, 320, 322–323, 333
seventy aspects of each Word, 321
and ten days of penitence, 523n.217
and ten words of creation/ *ma'ămārôṯ*, 189, 200, 298–299, 317, 323, 492n.331
and Torah, 200, 294, 317, 323, 333
transformation from oral-aural to written-visual medium, 257, 270, 280, 321, 332
ten things created on eve of first Sabbath, 148–149, 152, 175, 193, 195, 314, 470n.62, 471n.76, 481n.187, 488n.291, 532n.317
ten words of creation, 150, 170–171, 178, 189–190, 195, 207. *See also ma'ămārôṯ*
and Name of God, 200, 317
and revelation of Torah, 317, 323
and *s^e^pîrôṯ*, 197, 200, 204, 317
and ten days of penitence, 190, 523n.217
and Ten Words of revelation/Ten Commandments, 189, 200, 298–299, 317, 323, 492n.331
and Torah, 171, 200, 317, 323
Ten Words of revelation. *See* Ten Commandments
Tetragrammaton. *See also* Name of God
and four forms of Torah, 212, 215
and four worlds, 212, 215
inscribed on garment(s), 306, 527n.262
and names of God, 201
and *s^e^pîrôṯ*, 208–209, 212, 215
and stages of manifestation of Torah, 209, 212
and Torah, 201, 209, 212, 215
Theravāda Buddhist tradition. *See* Buddhist tradition, early
Thieme, Paul, 440n.39
three Vedas, 31, 34, 73, 242, 425n.16, 437n.6, 443n.81, 555n.17. *See also* Ṛg-Veda; Sāma-Veda; *traya veda*; *trayī vidyā*; Veda(s); Yajur-Veda
and Brahmā, 79
and *brahman* priest, 33, 438n.18
and *gāyatrī*/Gāyatrī or *sāvitrī*/ Sāvitrī, 79

three Vedas *(continued)*
and gods, 38, 56–58, 70, 79, 111, 215
and human faculties, 38, 56, 58
and Om, 57–58, 69–70, 79, 106, 108–109, 111–112, 215, 357, 451n.200, 460n.380
and Prajāpati, 50, 52–53, 54, 56–59, 60, 62, 79, 349–350, 445n.121
and Śiva, 103–104
and social classes/*varṇas*, 38, 61, 390, 402, 448n.155
and speech/Vāc, 47, 48–49, 50, 52–53, 60, 62
and three constituents of Om, 57–58, 69–70, 79, 106, 108–109, 111–112, 215, 460n.380
and three *guṇas*, 108, 111–112
and three priests, 58
and three sacrificial fires, 58
and three *vyāhṛtis*, 51, 54, 56–58, 59, 61, 62, 68, 69, 79, 106, 109, 111–112, 357, 447n.137, 451n.200
and three worlds, 38, 51, 54, 56–58, 59, 60, 61, 70, 111–112, 215
and *trimūrti*, 111–112
and Viṣṇu, 102–103
three worlds, 241. *See also* earth; heaven; midregions
and Brahmā, 78, 84, 85–86, 88, 101, 248
and cosmic egg, 53, 78, 101–102
and creator principle, 35, 36
and gods, 38, 56–58, 70, 111, 215
and human faculties, 38, 56, 58
and Prajāpati, 50–51, 54, 56–58, 442n.56, 446n.124
and Puruṣa, 38
and Skambha, 41
and social classes/*varṇas*, 38, 61
and speech, 50–51, 54, 217
and three constituents of Om, 57–58, 69–70, 111–112, 215
and three *guṇas*, 111–112
and three *vyāhṛtis*, 51, 54, 56–58, 61, 92, 106, 108, 109, 111–112
and *trimūrti*, 111–112
and Veda(s), 38, 51, 54, 56–58, 59, 60, 61, 70, 111–112, 215
throne-chariot. *See ma'ăśēh merkāḇāh*; Merkabah
throne of glory, 145, 532n.310
and fire, 146–147, 191, 301, 308
and light, 146–147
and Moses, 288–289, 290, 293, 300–302, 523n.222, 524n.226
as one of six or seven things created prior to the world, 160, 175, 193
and people of Israel, 257, 293, 307, 308, 313, 314, 322, 332
and revelation of Torah, 257, 288–289, 290, 293, 300–302, 307, 308, 313, 314, 322, 332, 523n.222, 524n.226
and Word of God/*dîbbēr/dîbbûr*, 191, 308
and world of creation/*b^{e}rî'āh*, 211
time, cycles of. *See* cosmogony and cosmology: cycles of creation; *kalpa; manvantara; yugas*
Timm, Jeffrey R., 539n.55
Tip̄'ereṯ (beauty; sixth *s^{e}p̄îrāh*), 197
as audible voice, 205, 206–208, 209
and commandments/*mitzvot*, 381
and Hebrew letters, 209
and Ḥoḵmāh, 209
and interpretation of Torah, 370–372, 373, 392, 547n.58
and kabbalist exegete, 370–372, 373, 392, 547n.58
as king of world below, 206
as lower Ḥoḵmāh, 205–206, 207, 208, 217, 219
as luminous speculum, 320, 534n.352
as male principle, 207, 209, 217, 381

and Malkût/Shekhinah, 206, 207, 208, 209, 217, 219, 373, 381, 392
and Moses, 320, 371, 373, 392
and Name of God, 209, 381
and practice of Torah, 381
and revelation of Torah, 320, 371, 373
role in cosmogonic process, 209
as son, 206, 207, 209, 493n.341
as soul of Torah, 370
and study of Torah, 370–372, 373, 381, 392, 547n.58
and unfoldment of divine language, 198, 205, 206–209
as voice of Jacob, 206–207
and Wāw, third letter of Tetragrammaton, 208, 209, 212
and world of formation/*y^e ṣîrāh*, 212, 215
as Written Torah, 198, 209, 212, 320, 370, 373, 381, 392, 493n.341
Tipiṭaka, 407, 556n.20
Tiruvāymoḷi
as Dravidian Veda or Tamil Veda, 10
Tishby, Isaiah, 490nn.317, 319, 491n.328, 545nn.41, 42, 546n.48, 548nn.66, 67, 72, 550n.119
tōhû wā-bōhû (formlessness and emptiness), 187, 274–275, 288, 298, 299, 376, 512n.90
Tomson, Peter J., 554n.14
Torah. *See also* appropriation of Torah; commandments; four forms of Torah; Hebrew Bible; interpretation of Torah; Oral Torah; Pentateuch; practice of Torah; primordial Torah; recitation of Sefer Torah; revelation of Torah; Sefer Torah; study of Torah; *tôrāh min ha-šāmayim*; *tôrāh q^e dûmāh*; transmission of Sefer Torah; Veda and Torah; Written Torah
and Abraham, 149, 154, 162, 163, 172, 175–176, 184–185, 191, 193, 399, 470n.65, 475n.119, 486n.243
and Adam, 154, 162–163, 172, 175, 184, 193, 399, 472n.82
and Ark of the Covenant, 190, 359, 416, 514n.104, 522–523n.211
as artisan/*'āmôn* or architect of creation, 24, 131, 140, 146, 159, 161, 162, 164–165, 166, 170, 171, 180, 186, 196, 202, 203, 214, 253, 371, 392
authority of, ix–x, 2, 13–14, 131, 135, 262–264, 325, 395, 396, 398, 400–401, 413
and Bînāh, 202, 209, 493n.341
as blueprint or plan of creation, 16, 17, 24, 26, 131, 140, 146, 159–160, 164–167, 170, 171, 176, 177, 180, 186–188, 196, 202–204, 212, 213, 214–215, 216, 218–220, 221–222, 253, 323, 333, 363, 367, 369, 371, 375, 378–379, 389, 391, 392, 395, 398, 399–400, 401, 402, 410, 412, 434n.56, 477n.132, 547n.60
and body, human, 167, 176, 203–204, 216, 369, 375, 378, 379, 380, 389, 398, 401, 477n.136, 552n.4
and body, of cosmos, 203–204, 216, 379, 380, 398
and body, of divine anthropos, 204, 216, 369, 378, 380, 398
and body, of God, 214
and body, social, 216, 325, 398–402
body of, 15, 199, 203–204, 325, 360, 369–370, 374, 379, 380,

Torah *(continued)*
382, 392, 398, 402, 420, 550n.103
bread of, 302, 475n.119
as bride of Israel, 256, 268, 276–278, 291, 302–303, 312, 331, 338, 372–373, 392, 420
and Christ, 404–405, 553n.11, 553–554n.14
and Christian traditions, 158, 174, 182, 294, 295, 404–405, 552n.9, 553nn.10, 11, 553–554n.14
as constitutive category of rabbinic tradition, ix–x, 2–3, 255, 398–403
correlated with microcosm and macrocosm, 167, 176, 183, 203–204, 216, 369, 375, 378, 379, 380, 389, 398, 401
as cosmological principle or cosmic reality, ix–x, 5, 16–17, 25, 160, 213, 397, 420
cosmological status of, 16, 131, 132, 141, 142, 145, 159
as cryptogram to be deciphered or decoded, 160, 362, 363, 367, 368, 369, 371
as daughter of God, 145–146, 253, 256, 276–277, 302, 312, 338
definition and use of term, 12–14, 431n.44, 431–432n.47
descent from heaven, 15, 146, 172, 253, 256, 265, 275–278, 288–291, 293, 299–300, 301, 302, 311–312, 315, 317, 327–328, 369, 513n.103
distinguishes people of Israel/Jews from gentile nations, 135, 136, 138, 152, 157, 182, 255, 266, 268, 273–274, 285–287, 294, 295–297, 311, 316, 325, 326, 329, 391, 398–399
and divine language, 16, 17, 24, 131, 146, 159, 167–170, 171, 176–178, 180, 188–190, 194–195, 196, 198, 204, 208–209, 211–212, 213, 214, 216, 253, 364, 395, 396, 399
embodied in Book of the Torah/Sefer Torah, 15, 146, 222, 253, 359
emphasis on cognitive over phonic dimension of words, 18, 146, 169, 218–220, 221–223, 334, 361–373, 385, 386–388, 414
emphasis on visual mode of perception, 17–19, 146, 155, 165, 171, 218–220, 221–223, 334, 385, 414–417, 469n.57, 533–534n.339, 547–548n.60
emphasis on written over oral channel of language, 17–18, 146, 169, 218–220, 221–223, 334, 359–361, 385–387, 414–420, 469n.57, 548n.60
encompasses male and female aspects of Godhead, 204, 209, 380, 381, 493n.341
as encompassing symbol/category, x, 2, 6, 12–14, 131, 158, 159, 395, 397, 401, 412
and 'Ên-Sôp̄, 209–210, 211
and Esau, 193, 476n.122
as essence of God, 131, 200, 201, 213, 214, 253
and ethnic-cultural identity of people of Israel/Jews, 3, 135, 136, 138, 152, 157, 182, 216, 255, 266, 273–274, 285–287, 294, 295–297, 311, 316, 325, 326, 329, 391, 398–399, 412, 481n.185
and the fall, 211, 495n.385
as female figure, 146, 202, 209, 381, 432n.48, 493n.341
and fire, 18, 146, 147, 154, 155, 163, 171–172, 178–179, 184, 190, 191, 195–196, 197, 198–

199, 210, 222, 254, 271, 273–274, 281, 292, 301, 308, 313, 314, 322, 332, 366, 472n.83, 473n.92, 475n.118, 480n.171, 482n.198, 483n.218
as first of God's works, 141, 146, 148–149, 159, 160, 164, 194
as form of God, 214, 361, 417, 546n.51
and four levels of scripture/Word, 17, 213–216, 217–219
four types of representations of, 17, 24, 131, 213–216, 253
and four worlds, 211–212, 215
and Garden of Eden, 163, 172, 184, 191, 193, 472n.82
garments of, 369–370, 371, 372, 382, 392
and glory of God, 253, 276, 289, 546n.51
God "looked into"/*hibbîṭ*/*'istakkēl*, 164, 165, 166, 186–187, 202, 203, 214, 220, 222, 364, 378–379, 389, 476n.130, 493n.344, 547n.60, 550n.101
as God's counselor in creation, 145–146, 180, 185–186, 193, 194, 488n.289
as God's co-worker in creation, 145–146, 198, 214
and gold, 162, 475n.113
and Hebrew, 167–168, 275, 399, 410
and Hebrew letters, 17, 161, 162, 166, 167, 168–169, 176–177, 187, 188–189, 195, 209, 211–212, 214, 222, 360–361, 365, 367, 382–383, 393, 492n.336
hidden for 974 generations before the world was created, 160, 161, 175, 184, 289, 470n.66, 474n.109, 481n.186, 519n.167
as historical and transhistorical, 131, 137, 160, 166, 297
infallibility of, 363, 364, 388
as instrument of creation, 14, 141, 148, 149, 154, 159, 164, 165, 176, 185, 188, 253, 256, 297, 298, 327, 364, 369, 378–379, 380, 432n.48, 481n.186
and Isaac, 162, 163, 184–185, 399
and Jacob, 162, 163, 184–185, 193, 399, 476n.122, 486nn.243, 246
and levels of creation/reality, 17, 198, 210–212, 213, 214–215, 395, 396
and levels of embodiment, 216, 398–403
levels of manifestation of, 198, 210–212
and light, 18, 146, 147, 155, 171–172, 178, 187, 190–191, 195–196, 197, 222, 292, 308, 315–316, 320, 366, 368, 369, 370, 371, 382, 392, 415, 473n.88, 479nn.158, 159, 483n.212, 487nn.272–274, 276, 491nn.322, 323, 547n.57
as limited/bounded and unlimited/boundless, 2, 6, 13, 14, 131, 362, 368, 395, 396–397, 400–401
and linguistic identity of people of Israel/Jews, 3, 398–399, 412
as living aspect of God, 15, 16, 131, 160, 201, 331, 367, 386, 392, 398, 416
and Logos, 133, 139–140, 165
as male principle, 202, 209, 381, 493n.341
and Malḵûṯ/Shekhinah, 198, 209, 212, 320, 370, 373, 381, 392, 493n.341
as marriage contract, 278, 303, 331, 338, 514n.110
mastery of, and Hêḵālôṯ traditions, 261–262, 263–264, 337, 507–508n.20
as mental plan, 165–166, 171,

Torah *(continued)*
187, 214, 220, 221–222, 389
and Messianic Age, 211, 495n.385
and model of canon, 6–7
as multilayered organism, 369–370, 382
as multileveled, ix–x, 5, 17, 25, 213, 214–215, 397, 412
and mystery of supernal Man, 204, 380
and Name of God/*šēm*, 24, 131, 146, 167, 176, 188, 197, 198–201, 202, 208–209, 212, 213, 214, 215, 216, 219, 253, 317, 360, 386, 492n.334, 533n.333
and names of angels, 212
and names of God, 197, 198–199, 201, 211, 212, 360, 382–383
as nonchanging, 210
as one of four inheritances, 472n.79
as one of God's special creations/possessions, 149, 153, 471n.78, 472n.80, 480–481n.185
as one of six or seven things created prior to the world, 160, 175, 193, 470n.64, 472n.81, 480n.185, 491n.323
as one of three things upon which the world stands, 148, 194, 375–376, 522n.211
as one with God, 200–201, 209–210, 213, 359, 367, 371, 373, 382, 417, 492n.334, 546n.51
as open-ended category, x, 6, 13, 173, 273, 337, 395, 396–397, 402
as organic unity, 199–200, 360, 398
as paradigmatic, x, 2, 6, 13, 157, 343, 390, 396
and patriarchs, 149, 162, 163, 175–176, 184–185, 193, 399, 476n.124
and Paul, the apostle, 404–405, 552n.9, 553nn.10, 11, 553–554n.14
people of Israel/Jews as custodians of, 3, 152, 157, 216, 398–399
as perfect divine edifice, 199, 360
as perfect unity, 363, 364, 388
and Platonic Ideas, 165, 476n.130
preceded creation of the world by two thousand years, 160, 161–162, 183–184, 475n.113, 491n.323
as primordial or preexistent, 14–15, 24, 131, 132–133, 135–137, 139, 141, 145–146, 147, 148–149, 152, 153, 154, 159, 160–164, 166, 169, 171, 172, 175–176, 180, 183–185, 188, 190, 191, 192–193, 194, 195, 196, 197–198, 202, 209, 212, 214, 219, 222, 253, 256, 288–289, 297, 359, 362, 369, 398, 399, 401, 410, 432n.48, 470nn.64, 66, 471n.77, 472n.81, 474n.109, 475nn.111, 113, 480–481n.185, 481n.186, 491n.323, 493n.341, 519n.167, 533n.327
as primordial wisdom, 15, 24, 131, 132–133, 135–137, 139, 141, 146, 148, 149, 153, 159, 160, 162, 164, 166, 171, 175, 183, 193, 194, 202, 214, 253, 362, 369, 471n.77
and Qur'ān, 409, 410, 557n.35, 558n.48
rabbinic sages as embodiments of, 148, 158, 285, 382, 400–401, 412, 474n.101
reflects laws and structures of cosmos, 165, 166–167, 176, 183, 187–188, 203–204, 212, 214–215, 216, 363, 367, 369,

375, 378, 379, 380, 389, 398, 400, 401
reflects structures and processes of Godhead, 204, 216, 367, 369, 378, 380, 389, 398, 400
as *rē'šîṯ*, 162, 164, 186
role in cosmogonic process, 132–133, 146, 147, 149, 152, 159, 162, 164, 165, 167, 170, 171, 174, 176, 180, 182, 183, 184, 185–186, 191–192, 194, 196, 359, 364, 375, 379, 493n.346, 550n.101
role in maintaining cosmos, 148, 167, 176, 188, 194, 204, 255–256, 274–275, 287–288, 297–299, 316–318, 327, 359, 374–377, 378–380, 388–390, 401, 482n.196, 518n.158, 522n.211, 533n.326, 549n.85, 550n.104
secrets or mysteries of, 15, 158, 174, 179, 196, 321, 323, 333, 363, 364, 365, 366, 367, 368, 369, 370, 371, 372, 373, 374, 378, 382, 391, 546n.51
and *s^{e}pîrôṯ*, 132, 197–198, 200, 201, 202, 204, 208–210, 212, 215, 315, 317, 320, 361, 367, 369, 370–372, 373, 380–381, 382, 392, 493n.341, 546n.51
and Shekhinah, 198, 209, 212, 256, 276–278, 331, 320, 370, 373, 381, 392, 416, 493n.341, 514n.104
and social and moral orders, 166–167, 183, 187–188, 216, 400
and social hierarchy, 3, 216, 262, 323–324, 325, 337, 339, 343, 390, 391, 398, 399–402, 507–508n.20
and sons of Jacob, 162, 163, 184–185, 399
soul of, 15, 369–370, 374, 382, 392, 402, 420
as source of all laws above and below, 202, 203
as source of creation, 15, 17, 26, 131, 148, 159, 214, 215, 216, 219, 398
as source of legitimation, x, 3, 13–14, 147–148, 152, 158, 264, 334, 337–339, 343, 390, 391, 395, 396–397, 399–402
speaks in language of human beings, 15, 363
and speech, 171, 203, 214, 216–218, 219, 331, 334, 550n.101
and stages of creation, 17, 208, 216–219
stages of manifestation of, 170–171, 198, 204, 208–210, 212, 315, 320
and stages of unfoldment of divine language, 198, 204, 208–209
strategies for extending domain of term, 6–7, 12–14, 147–148, 151, 152, 265–266, 396–397, 401–402, 412
as supratextual category, ix–x, 5, 15, 16, 160, 166, 215–216, 395, 396, 420
as symbol, ix–x, 2, 5, 6, 12–14, 15, 131, 135, 157, 159, 395, 396, 400, 401, 402, 412, 421n.5
and tablets of Ten Commandments, 280
and ten things created on eve of first Sabbath, 148–149, 152, 175, 193, 195, 314, 470n.62, 471n.76, 481n.187, 488n.291, 532n.317
and ten words of creation/ *ma'ămārôṯ*, 171, 200, 317, 323
and Ten Words of revelation/Ten Commandments, 200, 294, 317, 323, 333
and Tetragrammaton, 201, 209, 212, 215

Torah *(continued)*
and Tip̄'ereṯ, 198, 209, 212, 320, 370, 373, 381, 392, 493n.341
as transcendent, x, 15, 325, 396
and tree of life, 163, 184, 193, 488n.292
two Torahs, 13, 148, 151, 158, 173, 266, 272–273, 511n.74
waters of, 302
as wisdom/Ḥokmāh, 15, 24, 131, 132–133, 135–137, 139–140, 141, 146, 148, 149, 153, 154, 159, 160, 162, 164, 165, 166, 171, 175, 176, 183, 185, 186, 188, 193, 194, 198, 202, 209, 212, 214, 216–217, 219, 253, 298, 323, 362, 369, 434n.54, 471n.77, 474n.105, 480n.184, 485n.233, 486n.248, 489n.300, 491n.324, 493nn.340, 341, 535n.371
as Word of God/*dāḇār*, ix–x, 14, 16–17, 18, 19, 24, 25, 26, 131, 146, 152, 159, 161, 167, 171–172, 176, 178–179, 184, 187, 188, 190, 191, 197, 213, 215–216, 219, 222, 253, 317, 360, 363, 386, 395, 396–397, 398, 400, 403, 412, 416–417, 419, 479n.158, 482n.198
world created for sake of, 159–160, 274, 475n.113, 485n.237
as written text, 6, 13, 17–18, 24, 131, 146, 162, 169, 213, 215, 218, 220, 221, 222, 223, 253, 288, 331, 334, 337, 359–362, 385–387, 395–396, 397, 402, 414–420, 540n.1
as written text together with oral tradition of interpretation, 13, 17, 24, 131, 215, 253, 288, 331, 337, 361–362, 397, 402
written with black fire on white fire, 172, 191, 198–199, 281, 308, 322, 332
tôrāh min ha-šāmayim (Torah is from heaven), 265, 288, 421n.4
tôrāh q^{e}ḏûmāh (primordial Torah), 198, 209. *See also* primordial Torah
Torah scroll. *See* Sefer Torah
tôrāh še b^{e}-'al peh (Oral Torah). *See* Oral Torah
tôrāh še bi-ḵṯāḇ (Written Torah). *See* Written Torah
Tosefta, 141, 157, 263
as Oral Torah, 158, 273
transcendent
Brahman/Brahman-Ātman as, 63–64, 85, 328, 330, 449n.164
'Ên-Sôp̄ as, 196, 493n.349
Prajāpati as, 44
Puruṣa as, 37, 64–65
Qur'ān as, 409, 556n.25
speech/Vāc as, 42, 50, 52, 217, 246
Torah as, x, 15, 325, 396
Veda(s) and the Transcendent, 9, 43, 221, 227, 330, 344, 415, 428n.28
Veda(s) as, x, 7, 9, 10, 12, 62, 72, 76, 228, 233, 327, 328, 336, 339, 343, 344, 347–348, 354, 355, 357, 386, 390, 392, 396, 419, 427n.28, 430–431n.42
transmission of Sefer Torah, 5, 24, 26, 223, 359–361, 385–387. *See also* scribal tradition; Torah: as written text
and epistemology of perceptual orientation, 415–416
laws for preparing and preserving Torah scroll, 359–360, 540n.1
not a single letter may be added or omitted, 169, 177, 199, 360–361
and preservation of consonantal text, 169, 361

and scribal tradition, 177, 199, 359–360, 395–396
and verbatim reproduction of written text, 177, 199, 337, 359–361, 386, 387, 395–396, 417
writing of Torah scroll, as holy work, 360, 386
through written channel, 17–18, 169, 218, 223, 331, 334, 337, 359–361, 385–387, 395–396, 414–420, 540n.1

transmission of Vedic Saṃhitās, 5, 24, 26, 223, 343, 344–347, 385–387, 453n.247. *See also* recitation of Vedic Saṃhitās; Veda(s): as oral texts
by Brahmā, 96, 112, 249
by brahmin reciters/*śrotriyas*, 83, 345–347, 355, 385–388, 395–396, 419
and epistemology of perceptual orientation, 415–416
through nondiscursive oral tradition, 417
not through written channel, 82, 344–345, 354, 385
through oral channel, 17–18, 19, 43, 82, 83, 94, 98, 112, 215, 218, 221, 223, 228, 331, 334, 344–347, 354, 355, 385–387, 395–396, 414–420, 558n.53
oral transmission more reliable than written manuscripts, 345
tradition of oral transmission, 43, 83, 94, 112, 221, 228, 344–347, 385–387
tradition of oral transmission, initiated by seers/*ṛṣis*, 43, 83, 94, 112, 221, 228, 247, 249, 344
tradition of recitative transmission, 249, 344–347, 355, 385–387
and Vedāṅgas, 345, 386
and verbatim reproduction of Vedic sounds, 97–98, 339, 345–347, 348, 351, 386–387, 388, 389, 395–396, 408, 417–418, 427n.26
by Viṣṇu, 96
writing as ritually polluting, 344, 385

traya veda (threefold Veda), 31, 56, 425n.16, 437n.6. *See also* three Veda(s); *trayī vidyā*; Veda(s)

trayī vidyā (threefold knowledge; designation for three Veda[s]), 31, 33, 49, 52, 59, 66, 425n.16, 437n.6, 438n.18, 445n.121. *See also* three Vedas; *traya veda*; Veda(s)

tree of life
and Adam, 163, 184, 193
and Torah, 163, 184, 193, 488n.292
wisdom as, 193

trimūrti ("having three forms"; Brahmā, Viṣṇu, and Śiva). *See also* Brahmā; Śiva; Viṣṇu
and three constituents of Om, 111–112
and three *guṇas*, 111–112
and three *vyāhṛtis*, 111–112
and three worlds, 111–112
and Veda(s), 111–112

triṣṭubh (type of Vedic meter), 106, 343, 535–536n.1
and Indra, 39, 40
and *kṣatriyas*, 39, 40, 61

trivṛt (nine-versed *stoma*), 39, 105

Tulsīdās, 10

tzaddikim (the righteous), 548n.63
role in augmenting God's power, 377
role in creating and maintaining cosmos, 549n.85

Udayana, 460n.393

Uddyotakara, 460n.393

udgātṛ (type of priest), 438n.17
and Brahmā, 104
and *brahman* priest, 348
and Prajāpati, 54, 55, 58, 60, 446n.131, 537n.33
and *sāmans*, 33, 54, 60, 348
and Sāma-Veda, 33, 44
and seers/*ṛṣis*, 239
uktha (verse), 106
R. Ulla, 285, 291
'ûmān (artisan), 133–134, 137, 164, 186. *See also 'āmôn*
umm al-kitāb (Mother of the Book), 410, 557n.33
Upaniṣads, 23, 29, 31, 62–70, 72–73, 75, 78, 83, 84, 86, 96, 99, 124, 242–243, 330, 335–336, 356–357, 449n.161. *See also specific Upaniṣads*
and *adhyātma*, 352–353
and ascetic traditions, 30, 63, 71, 335–336, 402, 406
and Being, 67
categories of, 449n.160
definition and use of term, 7, 62–63
as discourse of knowledge, 22, 62–63
as focus of Vedānta/Advaita Vedānta, 113, 123–124, 346, 352–353, 388
and *mantras*, 357
and meditation, 357, 539n.69
as part of *jñāna-kāṇḍa*, 30, 62, 71, 123, 353
as permeable category, 7
as *śruti*, 7–8, 10, 402, 426n.21
as Veda, 7, 402, 425n.18
Upavedas, 103, 104
Urbach, Ephraim E., 165–166, 431n.46, 476nn.129–131, 484n.219, 486n.256, 495n.385, 507n.20, 508n.28
Uttara-Mīmāṃsā. *See* Vedānta
Vāc (speech; goddess of speech), 440–441n.43. *See also* speech
and Brahmā, 89, 105
and *brahman*/Brahman/Brahman-Ātman, 42, 47, 65–66, 68, 234
creative power of, 42, 43, 47–53, 217
as differentiated and undifferentiated, 47, 51, 53
as expressed and unexpressed, 47, 49, 50, 52–53, 55, 217, 445n.110
as female principle, 34, 48, 217
four quarters of, 42, 441n.44, 445n.110
and *gāyatrī*/Gāyatrī or *sāvitrī*/Sāvitrī, 89–90, 91, 105, 444n.88
as goddess of speech, 35, 42, 89, 90, 234
as hidden and revealed, 42–43, 445n.110
as immanent and transcendent, 42
as immortal, 48
as imperishable, 48
as infinite, 48
as inspirer of cognitions and hymns, 42–43, 234, 246
levels of, 49–53, 441n.44
and mind, 48–49, 50, 126
as Mother of Vedas, 47–48, 90, 444n.88
and Prajāpati, 30, 45, 47–53, 62, 89, 126, 239, 445n.121, 447n.141
and *rathantara sāman*, 49
and *ṛcs*, 49
and Sarasvatī, 48, 89–90, 105, 234, 246, 247, 444n.99, 455n.283
and seers/*ṛṣis*, 34, 42–43, 234, 236, 239, 240–241, 246
as transcendent, 42, 50, 52, 217, 246

and Veda(s), 30, 34, 35, 42–43, 47–53, 62, 65–66, 68, 89, 90, 105, 219, 234, 236, 240–241, 246, 444n.88
and Viṣṇu, 247
and Vyāsa, 247
and the waters, 35, 42, 50, 51, 52–53, 445nn.111, 121
as Word/*brahman*, 47
Vācaspati Miśra, 124
vaikharī (level of speech), 441n.44
vairāja (type of *sāman*), 40, 106, 439n.36
vairūpa (type of *sāman*), 39, 106, 439n.36
Vaiśeṣika, 8, 113–114, 115, 117, 353, 427n.25, 460–461n.394, 461n.397
vaiśyas (merchants, agriculturalists, and artisans)
and heaven, 38, 61
and *jagatī* meter, 39, 40, 61
and Prajāpati, 39, 54
and primordial utterance *svaḥ*, 54, 61
and recitation and hearing of Veda(s), 355
and Sāma-Veda, 38, 61, 390
and sun/Sūrya, 38
and Viśvadevas, 39, 40
Vājasaneyi Saṃhitā or White Yajur-Veda, 39, 44, 246, 503n.166. *See also* Yajur-Veda
vākyārtha (sentence meaning), 116, 122, 124
Vālmīki, 7, 71, 80
Vāmadeva (Vedic seer), 229
vāmadevya (type of *sāman*), 439n.36
Vāmana Purāṇa, 106–107
vaṃśas (lines of tradition), 242, 243, 326, 502n.146
Varenne, Jean, 438n.22
varṇas (social classes), 71, 78. *See also* brahmins; *dharma*: *varṇāśrama-dharma*; *kṣatriyas*; *śūdras*; *vaiśyas*
and early Buddhist tradition, 406–407, 555–556n.18
and gods, 38, 39–40
and meters, 40, 61, 448n.155
and orders of reality, 60–61
and Prajāpati, 39–40, 54
and Puruṣa, 38
and three *vyāhṛtis*, 54, 61
and three worlds, 38, 61
and Veda(s), 38, 40, 61, 80, 82, 97, 128–129, 216, 355, 390–391, 400, 402, 406, 448n.155
varṇas or *akṣaras* (Sanskrit phones). *See also* Sanskrit
and body, cosmic, 91–92, 104, 214, 459nn.351, 361
and Brahmā, 104, 107, 459n.351
and *brahman*/Brahman, 91–92, 104, 214
and *dhvani* or *nāda*, 118–119
as eternal, 118–119, 124
and *gāyatrī*/Gāyatrī or *sāvitrī*/Sāvitrī, 92–93, 106–109
and individual words/*padas*, 118–119
as noneternal, 113–114
and Om, 92–93, 106–109
ontological status of, 129
as phones, not letters, 18, 221
and Puruṣa, 91–92
and Śabdabrahman, 104, 459nn.351, 361
and Sarasvatī, 90, 246
and Śiva, 104, 459n.361
sound of, 221
and speech, 90, 106–109, 221, 246
as structural elements of creation, 106, 221
and three *vyāhṛtis*, 92–93, 106–109
and Veda(s), 92–93, 106–109, 214, 221
and Word/*brahman*, 91–92
and word/*śabda*, 118–119, 124

varṇāśrama-dharma (duties of the four social classes and stages of life). *See dharma: varṇāśrama-dharma*
Varuṇa (deity), 230, 231, 234, 236, 239, 501n.111
Vasiṣṭha (Vedic seer), 229, 230, 239, 240, 243, 244, 245, 501n.107, 502n.125
Vatsa (Vedic seer), 349
Vātsyāyana, 460n.393
Vāyu (wind; god of wind), 447n.141
  and breath, 38, 58
  as inspirer of cognitions and hymns, 234
  and *kṣatriyas*, 38
  and midregions, 38, 56–58, 70, 215, 450n.196
  and primordial utterance *bhuvaḥ*, 56–58, 450n.196
  and seers/*ṛṣis*, 234
  and *u*, second constituent of Om, 57–58, 70
  and Yajur-Veda, 38, 56–58, 70, 79, 215
Vāyu Purāṇa, 95–96, 97
Veda(s). *See also* appropriation of Veda(s); *atharvans*; Atharva-Veda; cognition of Veda(s); interpretation of Veda(s); *mantras*, Vedic; *ṛcs*; recitation of Vedic Saṃhitās; Ṛg-Veda; *sāmans*; Sāma-Veda; Saṃhitās; *śruti*; study of Veda(s); three Vedas; transmission of Vedic Saṃhitās; *traya veda*; *trayī vidyā*; Veda and Torah; *vedānādi-nityatva*; *vedāpauruṣeyatva*; *veda-prāmāṇya*; Yajur-Veda; *yajuses*
  Aryans as custodians of, 3, 216, 398–399
  and ascetic traditions, 63, 402, 406
  and Ātman, 66, 68
  authority of, ix–x, 2, 5, 9–12, 29, 62, 72, 76–77, 79, 87, 94, 113, 114, 115–117, 119, 120, 122–123, 124, 125, 126, 353–354, 395, 396, 398, 400–401, 402, 405–406, 413, 416, 421n.3, 427n.26, 429n.33, 430n.39, 430–431n.42, 448n.155, 449n.162, 460–461n.39, 463n.444
  authority of, as constitutive of "Hinduism," 10, 429n.33, 430n.42
  as basis or foundation of creation, 52, 53, 54, 60, 69, 81, 94, 112, 354, 427n.28
  and Being, 67, 128
  and *bhakti* traditions or stream, 10–11, 19, 336, 391, 402, 416
  as blueprint or plan of creation, 9, 16, 17, 24, 26, 29, 30, 47, 59, 62, 73, 75–76, 77, 79–80, 93, 95, 99, 101, 102, 108–112, 115, 124–125, 126–128, 129, 213, 214–215, 216, 218–221, 227, 243, 245, 246, 333, 347, 348, 389, 390, 392, 395, 398, 399–400, 401, 407, 412, 434n.56
  and body, cosmic, 34, 37–38, 39–40, 41–42, 47, 53, 60, 66, 68, 87, 88, 91–92, 102, 103, 104–105, 106, 214, 216, 351, 398, 458n.341, 459nn.351, 370
  and body, human, 38, 56, 58, 216, 398
  and body, of cosmos, 59, 216, 398, 406
  and body, social, 216, 325, 398–402, 406
  body of, 325, 398
  and Brahmā, 40, 65–66, 67, 73, 79–80, 82, 88–89, 90, 91, 93, 96, 99, 102, 103, 104–112, 114, 126, 127, 214, 216, 218, 220, 245, 246, 249, 250, 351,

440n.36, 453n.243, 454n.262, 459n.351
and *brahman*/Brahman/ Brahman-Ātman, 24, 29, 30, 34, 40–42, 47, 50, 52–53, 59, 60, 65, 66–67, 70, 72–73, 75, 79, 81, 82, 87, 88, 89, 91–92, 99, 101, 102–104, 112, 115, 123–124, 125, 128–129, 213, 214, 216, 219, 227, 246, 328, 330, 336, 351, 356, 392, 393, 396, 398, 440n.42, 443n.79, 454n.262
brahmins as embodiments of, 400–401, 412, 427n.26
branches/*śākhās* of, 87, 88, 102, 103, 112, 128, 250, 345, 458n.339, 460n.392
and categories of priests, 33, 44, 54–55, 58, 60, 104, 107, 348
as constitutive category of brahmanical tradition, ix–x, 2–3, 398–403
as cosmological principle or cosmic reality, ix–x, 5, 16–17, 25, 44, 47, 84, 115, 213, 397, 420
cosmological status of, 16, 29, 76, 80, 428–429n.29
as created/*pauruṣeya*, 8, 113, 427n.25, 460n.394
and creator principle, 17, 24, 29, 30, 34, 67–69, 73, 77, 81, 92, 115, 124–125, 213, 214, 216, 219, 221, 227, 330, 348, 351, 398, 440n.42
and cycles of creation, 75–76, 79–80, 88, 93, 94, 95, 96, 101–102, 110, 112, 113, 115, 124–125, 127–128, 129, 243, 245, 247–251, 326, 427n.28, 460n.392, 503n.169, 504n.181
definition and use of term, 7–9, 31–32, 425n.18, 438n.10
destiny of, 430n.40
and destruction of cosmos, 111–112
and Devī, 99
and *dharma*, 76, 79, 115–117, 119, 120, 122, 123, 124, 247, 430n.41, 463n.444
as differentiated and undifferentiated, 47, 50, 52–53, 60, 62, 66, 67, 75, 102–103
distinguishes Aryans from non-Aryans, 398–399
and divine language, 16, 17, 213, 214, 216, 395, 396, 399, 406, 407
division of one Veda into four Saṃhitās, 82, 96, 228, 247–248, 249–250, 453n.243, 457n.317, 503n.169, 504n.181
Dravidian Veda or Tamil Veda, 10
and early Buddhist tradition, 405–406, 407–408, 449n.162, 555n.17
emphasis on auditory mode of perception, 17–19, 218–221, 223, 334, 385, 414–417
emphasis on oral over written channel of language, 17–19, 218–221, 223, 334, 344–345, 385–387, 414–420
emphasis on phonic over cognitive dimension of words, 18, 218–221, 223, 334, 346–347, 385, 386–388, 414
emphasis on sound over meaning, 97–98, 346–347, 351, 386–388, 408, 418, 419, 457n.323
as encompassing symbol/category, x, 2, 6, 7–9, 395, 401, 412
as energy/*śakti* of Viṣṇu, 103
as eternal, 8, 9, 29, 32, 65, 67, 75–76, 77, 79–80, 82, 84, 93–94, 95, 99, 110, 112, 113, 114, 115–117, 122–123, 124–125, 126, 127, 128, 129, 228, 243, 245, 247, 248, 250, 251, 330, 334, 353, 355, 356, 427nn.25, 28

Veda(s) *(continued)*
and ethnic-cultural identity of Aryans, 3, 216, 325, 398–399, 412
extension of term to include *smṛti*, 8–9, 402, 427n.26
fifth Veda, 7, 8, 10, 82–84, 95–97, 104–105, 247, 248, 250, 336, 391, 402, 425–426n.19, 453n.243, 457n.311
and fire, 233
and four levels of scripture/Word, 17, 213–216, 217–219
four quarters of, 249
four types of representation of, 17, 24, 29, 213–216, 227
and *gāyatrī*/Gāyatrī or *sāvitrī*/Sāvitrī, 79, 90, 91–93, 105, 106–109, 444n.88, 455n.282, 456n.294
and gods, 34, 38, 39, 56–58, 59, 66–67, 70, 79, 96, 110, 111, 128–129, 215, 229, 231, 232, 233–235, 236–237, 238, 240, 246, 327, 328, 330, 339, 343, 348, 349, 350–351, 354, 388–389, 401, 416, 419, 498nn.52, 59
Hindi Veda, 10
as immortal, 48, 67, 75
as imperishable, 48, 67, 75, 94, 112, 355
and the Imperishable, 66, 67, 233, 330, 356
infallibility of, 113, 115, 120, 123, 353–354, 388
as infinite, 8, 12, 32, 47, 48, 62, 65, 84, 356, 396, 427n.28
as instrument of creation, 38–39, 89, 91, 93, 349
and Īśvara, 113, 114, 353, 427n.25, 460n.393
intrinsic validity of, 114, 115–116, 119, 120, 123, 124
Kārṣṇa Veda, 82
as knowledge, 7, 9, 11–12, 17, 24, 29, 30, 31, 32, 43, 60, 65, 66, 67, 70, 75, 76, 77, 87, 90, 93, 94, 99, 102–103, 104, 112, 128–129, 213, 214, 216–217, 219, 227, 228, 247, 336, 354, 356, 396, 427n.28, 430n.41, 430–431n.42, 434n.54
levels of, 32, 51–53, 66, 102–103, 108
and levels of creation/reality, 17, 213, 214–215, 326, 395, 396
and levels of embodiment, 216, 398–403
and light, 232–233, 332, 427–428n.28, 497n.34
as limited/bounded and unlimited/boundless, 2, 6, 12, 29, 30, 41, 43, 47, 62, 84, 356, 395, 396, 400–401
and linguistic identity of Aryans, 3, 398–399, 412
and maintenance of cosmos, 111–112
and Manu, 76
as mental plan, 127, 221
and mind, 48–49, 236
and model of canon, 6–7, 431n.43
and mouth(s), 40, 41, 52–53, 79, 88, 96, 104, 105–106, 107, 109–110, 112, 218, 220, 249, 440nn.36, 42
as multileveled, ix–x, 5, 17, 25, 213, 214–215, 397, 412
as nonchanging, 94, 112, 247
as noneternal, 113–114, 427n.25, 460n.394
and Om, 57–58, 69–70, 79, 92–93, 106–109, 111–112, 215, 357, 393, 451n.200, 460n.380
ontology of, 29, 113, 129, 353, 427n.28
as open-ended category, x, 6, 62, 395, 396
as oral texts, 6, 12, 17–18, 19, 24,

43, 60, 73, 82, 83, 94, 98, 112, 213, 215, 218, 220, 221, 223, 228, 331, 334, 344–347, 354, 355, 385–387, 395–396, 414–420, 431n.43, 558n.53
and orders of reality, 33–34, 37–38, 39–40, 44, 46, 56–58, 60–61, 62, 67–68, 69–70, 79, 111–112, 215, 216, 348, 349, 350, 389, 398, 400, 450n.196, 502n.134
and Pali canon, 407–408
as paradigmatic, x, 2, 6, 9–10, 19, 76–77, 82–84, 95–99, 336, 343, 390, 396, 407, 416
as paradigm for epics/Itihāsas, 10, 19, 416
as paradigm for Mahābhārata, 82–84, 336
as paradigm for Manu-Smṛti, 10, 76–77
as paradigm for Purāṇas, 10, 19, 95–99, 336, 416
and patron of sacrifice/ *yajamāna*, 61
and Prajāpati, 30, 39–40, 46, 47–53, 54–62, 65, 66, 67, 79, 89, 126, 127, 214, 216, 238, 250, 330, 349–351, 445n.121, 446n.134, 459n.370, 500n.96
Purāṇa-Veda, 95, 99
and Puruṣa, 37, 41, 65, 66, 67–68, 91–92, 349, 458n.341
and Qur'ān, 557n.35
reflects structures of cosmos, 56, 61, 62, 214–215, 216, 241, 348, 389, 398, 400, 448n.155
rejection of, 10–11, 405–406, 429n.37, 449n.162, 555n.17
restricted to male members of three higher social classes/ *varṇas*, 82, 97, 355, 390–391
as rhythms of creation, 9, 221, 332, 347–348, 386, 418
as Śabdabrahman, 24, 29, 73, 103, 108–109, 213, 215, 216, 219, 227, 330, 355, 357, 396, 419
sacramental function of, 97, 539n.64
and sacrifice, 11, 19, 29, 33, 34, 37–39, 41, 43, 44, 46–47, 50, 54, 55, 56, 58, 60, 61, 65, 73, 87, 103, 104–106, 126, 227, 231, 238, 240, 241, 249, 333, 339, 345, 346, 347–351, 352, 355, 401, 402, 406, 416, 427n.26, 431n.43, 443nn.77, 81, 446n.134, 457n.311, 502n.134
and sacrificial boar, 87, 103, 454–455n.268
and Sanskrit *varṇas*, 92–93, 106–109, 214, 221
and Sarasvatī, 90–91, 105, 227, 234, 246–247, 455n.282
and seers/*ṛṣis*, 8–10, 12, 18, 34, 42–43, 66–67, 76, 82, 83, 93, 94, 96, 110, 112, 221, 227–251, 325–339, 344, 348, 349, 354, 355, 356–357, 385, 389–390, 395–396, 398–399, 407, 415, 426n.24, 427n.27, 427–428n.28, 496n.5, 497n.22, 501nn.113, 120, 502n.132, 539n.64, 555n.17
and Śiva, 30, 73, 87, 88, 99, 102, 103–104, 111, 336, 351
and Skambha, 41–42, 53, 66, 440n.42
and social classes/*varṇas*, 38, 40, 61, 80, 82, 97, 128–129, 216, 355, 390–391, 400, 402, 406, 448n.155
and social hierarchy, 3, 40, 61, 82, 97, 216, 325, 334–337, 339, 343, 355, 390–391, 398, 399–402, 406, 448n.155
as source of creation, 9, 12, 17, 26, 29, 54–56, 59, 60, 75–76, 80, 90, 94, 126, 128–129, 214,

Veda(s) *(continued)*
215, 216, 219, 349–350, 398, 427–428n.28, 446n.134
as source of legitimation, x, 3, 9–12, 40, 61, 76–77, 82, 334–337, 339, 343, 355, 390–391, 395, 396, 399–402, 426n.21, 431n.42, 448n.155, 453n.243
and speech/Vāc, 9, 24, 29, 30, 32, 34, 35, 42–43, 47–56, 58, 59, 60, 62, 65–66, 68–69, 73, 81, 89, 90, 94, 101, 102, 104, 105–111, 112, 114, 126–127, 129, 214, 216–218, 219, 220, 221, 227, 230–231, 232, 233, 234–237, 240–241, 245, 246, 251, 330, 331, 332, 333, 334, 344, 349, 354, 355, 356, 415, 427n.26, 428n.28, 431n.43, 440n.42, 444n.88, 446n.134
as *śruti*, 7–9, 18, 72, 76, 93, 119, 126, 221, 227, 250, 344, 355, 385, 391, 396, 402, 407, 415, 418, 426nn.21, 24, 427n.26, 428n.28, 539n.64
and stages of creation, 17, 49–53, 55, 79, 101–102, 216–219
strategies for extending domain of term, 6–10, 43, 62, 63, 335, 396, 401, 402, 412, 427n.26
strategies of assimilation to, 7, 9–10, 72, 76–77, 82–84, 95–99, 336, 391, 396, 402, 426n.21, 429n.30, 453n.243
subversion of, 11, 429n.37
as supratextual category, ix–x, 5, 11, 16, 32, 84, 215–216, 354, 356, 395, 396, 419, 420
as symbol, ix–x, 2, 5, 6, 7–8, 11–12, 395, 396, 400, 401, 412, 421n.5
and tantric traditions, 10–11, 429n.37
and three *guṇas*, 106, 108, 111–112, 459n.373
and three *vyāhṛtis*, 51, 54, 56–58, 59, 61, 62, 68, 69, 70, 79, 92–93, 106–109, 111–112, 357, 447n.137, 451n.200
and three worlds, 38, 51, 54, 56–58, 59, 60, 61, 70, 111–112, 215
as transcendent, x, 7, 9, 10, 12, 62, 72, 76, 228, 233, 327, 328, 336, 339, 343, 344, 347–348, 354, 355, 357, 386, 390, 392, 396, 419, 427n.28, 430–431n.42
and the Transcendent, 9, 43, 221, 227, 330, 344, 415, 428n.28
and *trimūrti*, 111–112
as uncreated/*apauruṣeya*, 8, 113, 114–117, 119, 120, 122–123, 124, 125, 127, 228, 330, 353, 427n.25, 463n.432
and *varṇāśrama-dharma*, 80, 128–129
veda-puruṣa, 32, 92
and Viṣṇu, 30, 73, 82, 87–89, 90, 94, 96, 99, 102–103, 111, 245, 336, 351, 454–455n.268, 455nn.270, 278
and Vyāsa, 82–83, 96, 97, 228, 247–248, 249–250, 453n.243, 457n.317, 503n.169, 504n.181
as without beginning, 90, 93, 115–116, 123, 126, 127
as Word/*brahman*/Śabdabrahman, ix–x, 12, 16–17, 18, 24, 25, 26, 29, 30, 31, 32, 34, 41, 42, 43, 47, 50, 52–53, 60, 62, 66–67, 70, 73, 84, 87, 103, 213, 215–216, 219, 227, 395, 396, 398, 400, 403, 412
and *yugas*, 96, 112, 247–248, 249–251, 460n.392, 503n.169
Veda and Torah. *See also* Torah; Veda(s)
and affinities between brahmanical and rabbinic traditions, ix–x, 2–3, 6, 25, 397–403, 408–409, 412, 413

cognition of Veda(s) and revelation of Torah, 325–339
divergences in conceptions of language, 17–19, 218–223, 333–334, 385–388, 395, 414–420
structural affinities in symbol systems, 16–17, 24, 213–219, 395, 434n.57
Veda and Torah in practice, 385–393
vedānādi-nityatva (Veda[s] as eternal and without beginning), 115–116, 122–123. *See also* Veda(s): as eternal; Veda(s): as without beginning
Vedāṅgas, 71, 103, 228, 246, 345, 386, 504n.177
Vedānta or Uttara-Mīmāṃsā, 8, 114–115, 352–354, 427n.25. *See also* Advaita Vedānta; Dvaita Vedānta; Viśiṣṭādvaita Vedānta
focus on *jñāna-kāṇḍa*, 353
focus on knowledge of Brahman/ Brahman-Ātman, 113, 353
focus on Upaniṣads, 113, 346, 352–353, 388
as school of Vedic exegesis, 114, 346, 352–354, 388
schools of, 114, 353
vedāpauruṣeyatva (Veda[s] as uncreated, not derived from any personal agent), 114–116, 119, 120, 122–123, 124, 125, 463n.432. *See also* Veda(s): as uncreated/*apauruṣeya*
veda-prāmāṇya (Veda[s] as valid means of knowledge), 113, 114, 115–117, 119, 120, 122–123, 124, 126, 462n.400, 463n.444. *See also* Veda(s): authority of; Veda(s): intrinsic validity of
Vedic *mantras*. *See mantras*, Vedic
Vermes, Geza, 543n.16
Vijñānabhikṣu, 114, 461n.396
Vīraśaiva tradition, 10–11
Virūpas (descendants of Aṅgiras; Vedic seers), 230
visarga (secondary creation). *See pratisarga*
Visions of Ezekiel. *See Rᵉʾûyyôṯ Yᵉḥezqēʾl*
Viśiṣṭādvaita Vedānta, 114, 353. *See also* Vedānta
Viṣṇu or Viṣṇu-Nārāyaṇa (deity)
as archetypal seer/*ṛṣi*, 244
as Ātman/Paramātman, 85, 102, 454n.255
and *bhakti* traditions or stream, 72, 81, 94
and body, of cosmos, 85
and Brahmā, 82, 86, 88–89, 93, 101–102, 104, 111, 455n.278, 459n.349
as Brahman/Brahman-Ātman, 30, 73, 81, 82, 85, 86, 87, 94, 100, 102–103, 104, 244, 245, 336, 351
cosmic body of, 85, 87, 90, 102, 103, 351
and cosmic egg, 100, 101–102
and Dharma-Śāstras, 103
emanations/*vyūhas* of, 84, 85, 454n.255
and epics/Itihāsas, 103
as formed and formless, 85
grace of, 245, 336
as Hari, 85
as Hiraṇyagarbha, 454n.258
and knowledge, 87, 102–103, 336
as Kṛṣṇa, 85
as lord of speech, 90
and lotus, 86, 101
as maintainer, 86, 111
as manifest and unmanifest, 85
and meters, 87
and midregions, 111
as Nirguṇa Brahman, 85, 87, 94, 100

Viṣṇu *(continued)*
and orders of reality, 111
and Prakṛti, 85–86
and primordial utterance *bhuvaḥ*, 111
and Purāṇas, 96
and Puruṣa, 85, 100, 101–102, 244
and sacrifice, 87, 103, 351
as sacrificial boar, 87, 103, 454–455n.268, 459n.349
as Saguṇa Brahman, 85
and Sarasvatī, 90, 247
and *śāstras*, 96
and *sattva*, 111
and seers/*ṛṣis*, 87, 244–245, 336, 503n.152
and Śiva, 86, 100, 111
as soul of cosmos-body, 85
and speech/Vāc, 90, 247, 503n.164, 504n.181
and sun, 103
and *u*, second constituent of Om, 111
as ultimate source of creation, 84, 85–86, 89, 100, 503n.152
as Vāsudeva, 85, 454n.255
and Veda(s), 30, 73, 82, 87–89, 90, 94, 96, 99, 102–103, 111, 245, 336, 351, 454–455n.268, 455nn.270, 278
and Vyāsa, 82, 96, 247, 249, 336, 503n.170, 504n.181
and the waters, 86, 101
as Word/*śabda*, 103
and Yajur-Veda, 111
and *yajus*es, 111
Viṣṇu-Nārāyaṇa (deity). *See* Viṣṇu
Viṣṇu Purāṇa, 73, 97, 100, 102–103, 104, 105–106, 126, 250
Viśvadevas (group of deities)
and *jagatī* meter, 39, 40
and *vaiśyas*, 39, 40
Viśvakarman (deity)
as creator principle, 35, 36
as *hotṛ* priest, 36
as lord of speech, 36
Prajāpati as, 44
and sacrifice, 36
as seer/*ṛṣi*, 36, 241
Viśvāmitra (Vedic seer), 229, 230, 239, 243, 244, 501n.107
Vivaraṇa school, 124
voice(s) of God, 195. *See also qôl/qôlōṯ*
"according to power," 272, 282–284, 309–310
and fire, 155, 222, 270, 296, 306, 314, 318, 332
and gentile nations, 269, 292, 295–296, 309, 338, 530n.288
and light, 222–223, 318–319, 320–321
and Moses, 282, 310, 530n.287
and mysteries of creation, 222–223, 318–319, 322–323, 333
as one of ten words of creation/*ma'ămārôṯ*, 170, 171
and people of Israel, 222–223, 257, 269, 270, 271, 272, 280, 282–284, 292, 295–296, 306–307, 309–310, 314–315, 318–321, 322–323, 329, 331, 332, 333, 338, 472n.83, 510n.61, 517n.139, 529n.283, 530n.288
and revelation of Torah, 155, 222–223, 257, 269, 270, 271, 272, 280, 282–284, 292, 295–296, 299, 306–307, 309–310, 314–315, 318–321, 322–323, 329, 331, 332, 333, 338, 472n.83, 510n.61, 517n.139, 522n.204, 529n.283, 530nn.287, 288, 534nn.344, 348
and *s^{e}p̄îrôṯ*, 318–319
as source of death and source of life, 296, 309, 530n.288
and the waters, 170, 171, 178, 189–190, 479n.154

vyāhṛtis (sacred utterances; sound correlatives of three worlds). *See also bhūḥ; bhuvaḥ; svaḥ*
  and Brahmā, 79, 102, 105, 107
  and creator principle, 92
  and *gāyatrī*/Gāyatrī or *sāvitrī*/Sāvitrī, 79, 92–93, 106–109
  and gods, 56–58, 111
  and human faculties, 56, 58
  and Om, 57–58, 69, 70, 79, 92–93, 106–109, 111–112, 357, 447n.142, 451n.200
  and Prajāpati, 51, 54, 56–58, 68, 79
  and primordial utterance *mahaḥ*, 70
  as root *mantras*, 357
  and Sanskrit *varṇas*, 92–93, 106–109
  and social classes/*varṇas*, 54, 61
  and speech, 51, 54, 58, 59, 62, 106–109
  and three constituents of Om, 57–58, 69, 79, 106, 108, 109, 111–112
  and three *guṇas*, 111–112
  and three priests, 58
  and three sacrificial fires, 58
  and three worlds, 51, 54, 56–58, 61, 92, 106, 108, 109, 111–112
  and *trimūrti*, 111–112
  and Veda(s), 51, 54, 56–58, 59, 61, 62, 68, 69, 70, 79, 92–93, 106–109, 111–112, 357, 447n.137, 451n.200
vyakti (individual thing), 120, 121–122, 124, 125, 463n.435
Vyas, R. T., 442–443n.65, 444n.94
Vyāsa
  as author and transmitter of Mahābhārata, 82–83, 247–248, 336
  and Brahmā, 82, 453n.243
  and *dharma*, 453n.243
  and epics/Itihāsas, 250
  Gaṇeśa as scribe of, 82–83
  knew past, present, and future, 247–248
  as portion of Viṣṇu, 82, 96, 247, 249, 336
  and Purāṇas, 96–97, 250
  and Sarasvatī, 247
  as seer/*ṛṣi*, 82, 83, 247–248, 336, 453nn.238, 239, 503n.170, 503–504n.171, 504n.174
  as semidivine, 247
  and speech/Vāc, 247, 504n.181
  as superior to Vedic seers/*ṛṣis*, 247, 336, 453n.238, 503n.170
  and *tapas*, 247–248
  and Veda(s), 82–83, 96, 97, 228, 247–248, 249–250, 453n.243, 457n.317, 503n.169, 504n.181
  and Viṣṇu, 82, 96, 247, 249, 336, 503n.170, 504n.181
  and *yugas*, 96, 247–248, 249–250

Wald, Stephen G., 492n.336
Walshe, Maurice, 555n.16
Wartski, I., 542n.16
waters, 84
  and cosmic egg, 36, 50, 52, 53, 77–78, 101
  earth as lower waters, 208
  as female principle, 35, 101
  heaven as upper waters, 208
  as matrix of creation, 35
  and Merkabah, 510n.58
  and Nārāyaṇa, 77–78, 101, 458n.332
  and Prajāpati, 45, 50, 52–53, 445n.121
  and Prakṛti, 101
  and sacrificial boar, 87, 103
  and Sarasvatī, 90
  and speech/Vāc, 35, 42, 50, 51, 52–53, 445nn.111, 121
  and spirit of God, 170, 171, 178, 189–190, 479n.154

waters *(continued)*
of Torah, 302
and Viṣṇu-Nārāyaṇa, 86, 101
and voice of God, 170, 171, 178, 189–190, 479n.154
wāw/Wāw (Hebrew letter; letter of Tetragrammaton)
and Tip̄'ereṯ, 208, 209, 212
and world of formation/*y^eṣîrāh*, 212
and Written Torah, 209, 212
Wayman, Alex, 540n.75
weapon(s)
engraved with Name of God, 256–257, 260, 279, 305–306, 313, 515n.119
people of Israel invested with, 256–257, 260, 279, 305–306, 313, 515nn.118, 119
and revelation of Torah, 256–257, 260, 279, 305–306, 313, 515nn.118, 119
Weiss, Abraham, 519n.171
Whitaker, G. H., 467n.36
White Yajur-Veda. *See* Vājasaneyi Saṃhitā
Whybray, R. N., 134–135, 464n.2, 465nn.7, 10, 466n.10
Widengren, Geo, 424–425n.9, 557n.31
wind. *See* Vāyu
wisdom. *See also* *ḥoḵmāh*/Ḥoḵmāh; knowledge
as artisan/*'āmôn* or architect of creation, 24, 131, 133–134, 137, 140, 161, 162, 164, 186, 202, 214, 253
as aspect of word/Word, 16–17, 216
associated with understanding/*t^eḇûnāh* and knowledge/*da'aṯ*, 176, 177, 185, 195, 298, 486n.248
and Astarte-Ištar, 465n.10
and Canaanite traditions, 134–135, 141, 465–466n.10
as cosmic ordering principle, 136, 137–138, 185
as daughter of God, 139
descent from heaven, 15, 135–136, 362
and Egyptian traditions, 134–135, 141, 465–466n.10
embodied in Book of the Torah/Sefer Torah, 136, 362
as eternal, 139
as female figure, 133, 146, 202
as first of God's works, 133, 139, 141, 194
and gentile nations, 273
as God's co-worker in creation, 134, 137, 138, 198, 214
and Hellenistic traditions, 136, 137–140, 141, 466n.10, 477n.132
as innermost soul of Torah, 15, 369
as instrument of creation, 140, 141, 165, 176, 177, 185, 195, 298
and Isis-Astarte, 136
Israelite wisdom tradition, 133, 135, 136, 137, 138, 141, 464n.1, 477n.132
and light, 369
and Logos, 133, 136, 138, 139–140
and Maat, 465n.10
as male principle, 207
and Mesopotamian traditions, 134–135, 141, 465–466n.10
as moral law, 136
as Mother, 139
as mythological figure, 134–135, 465n.9, 465–466n.10
as an objectification of the world order, 134–135
and people of Israel, 135–136, 323
as personification of attribute of God, 134–135, 465n.9
as primordial or preexistent, 15,

24, 131, 132–133, 135–137, 139, 141, 146, 148, 149, 153, 154, 159, 160, 162, 164, 166, 171, 175, 183, 188, 193, 194, 202, 214, 253, 362, 369, 471n.77
as *rē'šîṯ*, 133, 162, 164, 186
and revelation of Torah, 15, 135–136, 323, 362
role in cosmogonic process, 137, 154, 469n.56, 474n.105, 485n.233
and *sophia*, 466n.10
and speech, 16–17, 207
and Temple, 136
termed *'āmôn*, 133–134, 137, 161, 162, 164, 186, 202, 464nn.4, 5, 464–465n.6, 467n.36
Torah as, 15, 24, 131, 132–133, 135–137, 139–140, 141, 146, 148, 149, 153, 154, 159, 160, 162, 164, 165, 166, 171, 175, 176, 183, 185, 186, 188, 193, 194, 202, 214, 216–217, 253, 298, 323, 362, 369, 434n.54, 471n.77, 474n.105, 480n.184, 485n.233, 486n.248, 489n.300
as tree of life, 193
as unique possession of people of Israel/Jews, 135–136, 138
Wisdom of Ben Sira, 133, 135–137, 138–139, 140–141
Wisdom of Solomon, 133, 137–139, 140–141, 467n.23
Wolfson, Elliot R., 318, 322, 371, 432n.48, 433n.52, 469n.57, 490n.317, 492n.336, 508n.31, 510n.61, 533–534n.339, 534nn.343, 352, 535n.366, 545n.42, 546nn.52, 54, 547n.57, 547–548n.60, 548n.66
Wolfson, Harry Austryn, 139, 467nn.36, 37
women
and access to Mahābhārata, 82
and access to Purāṇas, 97, 98, 457n.322
and *bhakti* practices, 94
excluded from reciting or hearing Veda(s), 82, 97, 355, 390–391, 539n.65
excluded from study of Torah, 391
and revelation of Torah, 310, 323–324, 331, 391
role of wife of patron of sacrifice/*yajamāna*, 339, 350, 419, 539n.65
word/Word. *See also brahman*/Brahman; *dāḇār*; *dîbbēr*; *dîbbûr*; language; language, divine; *ma'ămārôṯ*; *śabda*; Śabdabrahman; speech; Ten Commandments; ten words of creation
Brahmā as, 104
brahman as, 24, 29, 34, 40–41, 47, 50, 52, 53, 60, 66, 67, 70, 91–92, 213, 216, 219, 227, 396
Christ as, 159, 403
cognitive and phonic dimensions of, 16–17, 18, 146, 169, 171, 218–223, 334, 346–347, 385, 386–388, 414
as cosmological principle or cosmic reality, ix–x, 16–17, 25, 213, 395
embodied in scripture/texts, 16, 24, 26, 215–216, 227, 325, 398, 400, 403, 412
encompasses unspoken thought and vocalized speech, 16–17, 171
as essence of ultimate reality, 17, 213, 219, 395
and fire, 18, 146, 155, 171, 172, 178–179, 190, 191, 197, 210, 222, 257, 270, 308, 318, 332, 482n.198, 483n.218, 510n.61, 535n.367

word/Word *(continued)*
and gentile nations, 296
as infinite, 32, 84
knowledge/wisdom and speech as two aspects of, 16–17, 216
levels of, 17, 25, 129, 213–216
and light, 18, 146, 171–172, 190, 197, 222, 368, 479nn.158, 159, 487n.272
as means of creation, 14, 148, 126–127, 150, 152, 154, 159, 169, 170–171, 178, 187, 188, 189–190, 194, 195, 197, 200, 204, 207, 215, 216, 256, 298, 299, 306, 317, 403, 478n.151, 482n.207
as multileveled, ix–x, 17, 25, 213, 412
Om as, 70, 108
and people of Israel, 222, 257, 270, 282–284, 296, 299, 308, 318, 332, 535n.367
as primordial or preexistent, ix, 24, 43, 62, 159, 215, 398, 403
Purāṇas as, 96
Puruṣa as, 91–92
Qur'ān as, 409, 412
and revelation of Torah, 14, 154–155, 191, 222, 256, 257, 270, 282–284, 292, 296, 299, 306, 308, 317, 318, 320, 332, 366, 510n.61, 535n.367
and Sanskrit *varṇas*, 91–92
scripture as, ix–x, 16–17, 213, 215–216, 219, 395, 403
Sefer Torah as consummate expression of, 14, 395, 396–397
Sefer Torah as verbatim record of words of God, 13, 359
Sefer Torah as visible form or embodiment of, 18, 19, 360, 363, 386, 416–417
Śiva as, 104
as source of death and source of life, 296
and stages of creation, 216–219
and throne of glory, 191, 308
Torah as, ix–x, 14, 16–17, 18, 19, 24, 25, 26, 131, 146, 152, 159, 161, 167, 171–172, 176, 178–179, 184, 187, 188, 190, 191, 197, 213, 215–216, 219, 222, 253, 317, 360, 363, 386, 395, 396–397, 398, 400, 403, 412, 416–417, 419, 479n.158, 482n.198
as unlimited, 12, 29, 30, 41, 43, 54, 62, 395
Vāc as, 47
Veda(s) as, ix–x, 12, 16–17, 18, 24, 25, 26, 29, 30, 31, 32, 34, 41, 42, 43, 47, 50, 52–53, 60, 62, 66–67, 70, 73, 84, 87, 103, 213, 215–216, 219, 227, 395, 396, 398, 400, 403, 412
Vedic *mantras* as consummate expression of, 62, 395, 396
Viṣṇu as, 103
worlds. *See* four worlds; three worlds
Wright, Addison G., 542n.16
writing. *See also* language: oral vs. written channels; *miktāb*; oral and written traditions; scribal tradition; scribes
as graphic representation of language, 414
as one of ten things created on eve of first Sabbath, 148–149, 152, 175, 193, 314, 470n.62, 471n.76, 481n.187, 488n.291, 532n.317
as ritually polluting, 344, 385
role in cosmogonic process, 209
of Torah scroll, as holy work, 360, 386
Written Torah, 17, 163. *See also* Hebrew Bible; Oral Torah; Pentateuch; Sefer Torah; Torah
Christian appropriation of, 158, 174, 182, 294, 295

and commandments/*mitzvot*, 381
definition and use of term, 12–13, 431n.46
and fire, 172, 480n.171
Hebrew Bible as, 12–13, 141–142, 158, 273, 294, 485n.232, 512n.75
and Hebrew letters, 209
and Ḥokmāh, 209
interpretation of, 359, 361–373, 386–388
and kabbalist exegete, 370, 373, 392
Ketuvim as, 12–13, 173, 285, 294, 397
and Mishnah, 147–148, 174
and Moses, 320, 373, 392
and Name of God, 209, 381
Nevi'im as, 12–13, 173, 285, 294, 397
and Oral Torah, 12–13, 22, 147, 148, 151, 157, 158, 173–174, 176, 181–182, 191–192, 209, 219, 272–273, 284–285, 311, 337, 362, 373, 381, 392, 397, 431n.46, 518n.148, 521n.197
Pentateuch as, 12–13, 147, 173, 285, 294, 385, 397
and primordial Torah/*tôrāh qᵉdūmāh*, 209, 219
rabbinic sages as custodians of, 337, 391
and revelation of Torah, 13, 158, 173–174, 182, 272–273, 284–285, 294, 311, 325, 331, 362, 385–386, 397
role in cosmogonic process, 209
and Talmud, 174
Tip̄'ereṯ as, 198, 209, 212, 320, 370, 373, 381, 392, 493n.341
and Wāw, third letter of Tetragrammaton, 209, 212
and words of scribes, 158, 174, 182
and world of formation/*yᵉṣîrāh*, 212

Würthwein, Ernst, 465n.10

yajamāna (patron of sacrifice), 339, 348, 350, 419
and construction of divine self, 43, 61, 449n.158
conveyed to world of heaven, 43, 61
and descent from a seer/*ṛṣi*, 241–242
and *hotṛ* priest, 242
self of, constituted by Veda(s), 61
wife of, 339, 350, 419, 539n.65
yajña (Vedic sacrifice). *See* sacrifice
Yājñavalkya (Vedic seer), 246, 503n.166
Yājñavalkya-Smṛti, 352
yajñāyajñīya (type of *sāman*), 439n.36
Yajur-Veda, 29, 39, 73, 426n.19, 438n.11. *See also* Taittirīya Saṃhitā; Vājasaneyi Saṃhitā; *yajus*es
and *adhvaryu* priest, 33, 44
and Ātman, 66
and Being, 67, 457n.311
and Brahmā, 79, 104, 107, 110, 218
and breath, 38, 58
and creator principle, 92
definition and use of term, 7, 31–32, 33
and *kṣatriyas*, 38, 61, 390
and midregions, 38, 51, 56–58, 60, 61, 70, 111, 215
and mind, 58
as part of threefold Veda, 31, 425n.16
and Prajāpati, 56–58, 62
and primordial utterance *bhuvaḥ*, 51, 56–58, 61, 79, 111
and Puruṣa, 66, 91
and *sattva*, 111
and Śiva, 104

Yajur-Veda *(continued)*
and speech, 62, 106–108, 110, 218
and *u*, second constituent of Om, 57–58, 70, 79, 108, 111
and Viṣṇu, 87, 111
and Vyāsa, 250
and wind/Vāyu, 38, 56–58, 70, 79, 215
and *yajus*es, 7, 32, 250
*yajus*es (sacrificial formulae that constitute the Yajur-Veda), 62, 70, 437n.9, 438nn.10, 14. *See also* Yajur-Veda
and *adhvaryu* priest, 33, 54, 60
and Brahmā, 40, 104, 106
and Brahman/Brahman-Ātman, 42, 66, 102, 112
and breath, 447n.148
definition and use of term, 31–32, 33
as limited, 29, 41
and midregions, 59
and mind, 447n.148
as part of threefold Veda, 31, 34, 425n.16
and patron of sacrifice/*yajamāna*, 61
and Prajāpati, 50, 54, 60, 349–350
and Puruṣa, 37, 67–68
and sacrifice, 33, 37, 43, 54, 60, 348, 349–350, 457n.311
and *sattva*, 111
and Śiva, 88
as Skambha, 41–42
as source of motion, 59
and speech/Vāc, 47, 50, 54, 106
as *śruti*, 7
and sun/Āditya, 246, 503n.166
and Viṣṇu, 87, 102, 103, 111
and Vyāsa, 249–250
and Yājñavalkya, 246, 503n.166
and Yajur-Veda, 7, 32, 250
R. Yannai, 275, 515n.115, 526n.249
R. Yannai b. Simeon b. Yannai, 304–305, 515n.115
Yāska, 228, 352, 496n.2, 538n.48
year, 49, 55, 78
and Prajāpati, 50, 445n.115, 450n.171
y^{e}*ṣîrāh* (world of formation)
as abode of angels, 211
and names of angels, 212
and Tip̄'eret̲, 212, 215
and Wāw, third letter of Tetragrammaton, 212
and Written Torah, 212
Y^{e}sôd̲ (foundation; ninth *s*^{e}*p̄îrāh*), 197, 373
yôd̲/Yôd̲ (Hebrew letter; letter of Tetragrammaton), 478n.143, 487n.262
and Ḥok̲māh, 208, 209, 212
and primordial Torah/*tôrāh q*^{e}*d̲ûmāh*, 209, 212
shape of, 169, 177, 189
and world of emanation/*'ăṣîlût̲*, 212
world to come created with, 168–169, 177, 188–189
Yoga (school of Indian philosophy), 8, 113, 353, 427n.25
yoga, 71, 453n.233, 551n.1
and *mantras*, 357
and meditation, 357
and seers/*ṛṣi*s, 245
Yômā', 176
Yom Kippur (Day of Atonement), 190, 310–311
Younger, Paul, 430n.39
*yuga*s (ages), 74–75, 95, 96, 112, 247–248, 249–251, 452n.217, 460n.392, 503n.169

R. Zakkai of Shaab, 279, 525n.244, 527n.259
Z^{e}b̲āḥîm, 285
R. Ze'ira, 169
zîw (splendor), 257, 279, 289, 300, 301, 303, 305, 515n.120,

525n.244, 527n.259, 532n.311, 534n.340
zîw hăḏārô (splendor of his glory), 305, 515n.120, 525n.244, 527n.259, 532n.311, 534n.340
Zohar, 23, 196, 200, 202–210, 217–219, 220, 221–223, 315–324, 325, 328, 331–333, 334, 361, 367–373, 375, 378–381, 382, 383, 391–393, 398, 415, 420, 490nn.317, 319
  author(s) of, 367, 490n.319, 544n.32
  as central work of theosophical Kabbalah, 196
  and exegetical Midrashim, 196, 315
  and second-century Tannaim, 196
Zunz, Leopold, 468n.42, 524n.222
R. Zutra b. Tobiah, 176